COMPOSING PROCESSES

You will learn how to:

- maintain engagement with your intellectual and rhetorical problem (Chapters 1, 2, 3, 18)
- use a variety of exploratory techniques such as freewriting, idea-mapping, playing the believing/doubting game, and reading with and against the grain (Chapters 2, 3, 6)
- reduce writer's block by lowering your expectations for early drafts (Chapter 18, writing projects chapters)
- use multiple drafts to achieve your desired result (Chapter 2, 3, 18, writing projects chapters)
- give and receive constructive feedback through peer reviews of drafts (Chapter 18, writing projects chapters)
- follow the revision practices of experts (Chapter 18)
- draft and revise closed form prose by using readers' expectations for unity, coherence, and old-before-new (Chapter 19)
- draft and revise open form prose by following the principles of narration, precise detail, artistic style, and strategic violation of closed-form "rules" (Chapter 20)
- edit for gracefulness, clarity, and correctness (Chapters 18, 19, handbook chapters, writing projects chapters)

THE CONVENTIONS OF WRITING

You will learn how to:

- follow the conventions and formats of different genres (Chapters 1, 4, 19)
- adapt the tone, structure, content, and style of your writing to different writing situations (Chapters 3, 4, 19, 20, 25, 26, writing projects chapters)
- cite and document your sources using conventions appropriate to your audience and genre (Chapter 23)
- edit your prose for correct grammar, punctuation, and spelling (Chapters 18, 19, handbook chapters)

Note to instructors:

These learning goals are keyed to the Council of Writing Program Administration's "Outcomes Statements for First-Year Composition" (WPA: Writing Program Administration 23.1/2 (Fall/Winter 1999): 59-63. The WPA statement places outcomes under four categories: Rhetorical Knowledge; Critical Thinking, Reading, and Writing; Processes; and Knowledge of Conventions.

The
Allyn & Bacon
Guide to Writing

The Allyn & Bacon Guide to Writing

THIRD EDITION

John D. Ramage
Arizona State University

John C. Bean
Seattle University

June Johnson
Seattle University

Longman

New York San Francisco Boston
London Toronto Sydney Tokyo Singapore Madrid
Mexico City Munich Paris Cape Town Hong Kong Montreal

Senior Vice President and Publisher: Joseph Opiela
Vice President and Publisher: Eben W. Ludlow
Development Manager: Janet Lanphier
Development Editor: Marion B. Castellucci
Executive Marketing Manager: Ann Stypuloski
Supplements Editor: Teresa Ward
Media Supplements Editor: Nancy Garcia
Production Manager: Donna DeBenedictis
Project Coordination, Text Design, and Electronic Page Makeup: Elm Street
    Publishing Services, Inc.
Cover Designer/Manager: Wendy Ann Fredericks
Cover Art: © Jim Ward Morris/Artville, LLC
Photo Researcher: Shaie Dively/PhotoSearch, Inc.
Manufacturing Buyer: Al Dorsey
Printer and Binder: RR Donnelley & Sons Company, Crawfordsville
Cover Printer: Phoenix Color Corporation

For permission to use copyrighted material, grateful acknowledgment is made to the copyright holders on pages 814 to 817, which are hereby made part of this copyright page.

Library of Congress Cataloging-in-Publication Data
Ramage, John D.
    The Allyn and Bacon guide to writing/John D. Ramage, John C. Bean, June Johnson—3rd ed.
        p.   cm.
    Includes index.
    ISBN 0-321-10622-9
    1. English language—Rhetoric—Handbooks, manuals, etc. 2. English language—Grammar—Handbooks, manuals, etc. 3. Report writing—Handbooks, manuals, etc. 4. College readers. I. Title: Guide to writing. II. Bean, John C. III. Johnson, June. IV. Title.

    PE1408.R18 2003
    808´.0427—dc21   2002067146

Please visit our website at http://www.ablongman.com/ramage

ISBN 0-321-10622-9 (Complete Edition)
ISBN 0-321-10621-0 (Brief Edition)
ISBN 0-321-09326-7 (Concise Edition)

1 2 3 4 5 6 7 8 9 10—DOC—05 04 03 02

Brief Contents

PART FIVE
A Guide to Special Writing and Speaking Occasions 683

PART SIX
A Guide to Editing 731

Detailed Contents

PART TWO
Writing Projects 85

PART FOUR

A Rhetorical Guide to Research 573

CHAPTER 21 An Introduction to Research 575

CHAPTER 22 Finding and Evaluating Sources 581

PART FIVE

A Guide to Special Writing and Speaking Occasions 683

PART SIX

A Guide to Editing 731

HANDBOOK 1   Improving Your Editing Skills 733

HANDBOOK 2 Understanding Sentence Structure 739

Writing Projects

Thematic Contents

The Allyn and Bacon Guide to Writing, third edition, contains 55 essays—34 by professional writers and 21 by students. In addition, the text contains a number of visual texts (advertisements, political photographs, posters, and Web sites) that can lead to productive thematic discussions. These essays and visual texts can be clustered thematically in the following ways:

GENDER ISSUES

POPULAR CULTURE, MEDIA, AND ADVERTISING

IDENTITY AND VALUES

SOCIAL PROBLEMS AND PUBLIC CHOICES

PARENTS, CHILDREN, AND FAMILY

VIOLENCE, PUBLIC SAFETY, AND INDIVIDUAL RIGHTS

Preface

We are grateful for the enthusiastic reviews of *The Allyn and Bacon Guide to Writing*, which has been hailed as the most successful college rhetoric published in over a decade. In this third edition we have made substantive improvements while retaining the signature strengths of the second edition. Users of the second edition have praised the book's lively and engaged instruction, effective writing assignments, and practical classroom activities, all solidly grounded in current theory and research. In either the regular or brief edition, the book has been adopted at a wide range of two- and four-year institutions. From all quarters, instructors have praised the book's theoretical coherence and explanatory power, which help students produce interesting, idea-rich essays and help composition teachers create pedagogically effective, challenging, and intellectually stimulating courses.

As in the second edition, in the third edition we offer comprehensive instruction in rhetoric and composition, a flexible sequence of writing assignments (focusing on academic/professional writing balanced with personal and narrative forms), numerous examples of student and professional writing, and thorough guides to research and editing. We have also maintained our distinctive emphasis on writing and reading as rhetorical acts and on problem posing, critical thinking, and inquiry.

The third edition is particularly strengthened by the presence of our new coauthor, June Johnson, a colleague of John Bean's at Seattle University. June contributed significantly to the second edition of *The Allyn and Bacon Guide to Writing* and then became coauthor of our other textbook, *Writing Arguments: A Rhetoric with Readings*, Fifth Edition. We now welcome her as coauthor of *The Allyn and Bacon Guide to Writing*, Third Edition. Her many years' experience as a writing teacher, plus her grounding in pedagogy, rhetorical theory, and composition studies, gives us a greatly expanded range and depth of expertise.

WHAT'S NEW IN THE THIRD EDITION

Building on the text's well-established strengths, we have revised the book significantly to increase its flexibility, depth, clarity, and usefulness. Here is what's new:

- An attractive four-color design that enhances the book's visual appeal and presents examples of visual rhetoric and document design in full color.
- An expanded emphasis throughout on the social/rhetorical context of academic, workplace, and civic prose including visual literacy and document design. To introduce these emphases, we have substantially revised

Chapters 3, 4, and 5 to focus more clearly on the rhetorical dimensions of problem posing and thesis seeking, to explain the rhetorical power of images and document design, and to show how words and images work together for rhetorical effect. For example, in Chapter 5, we use the political debate over the Arctic National Wildlife Refuge (ANWR) to illustrate the impact of images on verbal arguments.

■ The full-page images at the beginning of each of the book's major parts. These images invite student analysis of the visual rhetoric of posters, flyers, Web pages, and ads. (A detailed note on these part openers is provided in "Using the Part Opener Images" on p. xlvi.)

■ A new writing assignment chapter on "Analyzing and Synthesizing Ideas" (Chapter 13). Designed as a next stage beyond Chapter 6, "Reading Rhetorically," in which students summarize and respond to one reading, this chapter teaches students how to respond to multiple readings by analyzing the ideas of others and synthesizing them into their own arguments. This chapter gives instructors an additional pedagogical strategy for helping students integrate reading and writing in order to meet the demands of synthesis assignments across the disciplines.

■ A complete rewriting of Part Four on research (Chapters 21–24). Now called "A Rhetorical Guide to Research," Part Four is based on an improved pedagogical strategy for teaching research writing—a strategy derived from our recent classroom research, our increased attention to rhetorical reading, and our experience with students' difficulties in negotiating print and cyberspace sources. These chapters, which teach seven essential skills for effective research writing, comprise a powerful new approach for accelerating students' growth as thinkers, readers, and researchers.

■ An expanded discussion of the rhetoric of Web sites (in Chapter 22). Focusing on both the visual and verbal dimensions of Web sites, this chapter helps students analyze and evaluate Web sources and become savvy users of the World Wide Web.

■ Improved explanation of MLA and APA styles, with special attention given to the latest MLA and APA guidelines for citing electronic sources (Chapter 23).

■ A new extended example of a student researcher investigating a problem—in this case, whether metal detectors in schools are effective in combating school violence. By showing this student's work in various stages— journal entry, an exploratory essay, and a researched argument (Chapters 1, 8, 22, and 23)—we illustrate how a student writer reads and uses sources rhetorically.

■ A new chapter on oral communication, which combines earlier material on working in groups with a new section on giving speeches and PowerPoint presentations (Chapter 25).

■ Substantial revision of Chapter 10, "Analyzing Images," to help students better understand visual rhetoric. Using many new examples of advertisements and referring frequently to images throughout the text—for example, photographs, news illustrations, Web site images, flyers, and corporate advertisements—we explain how images exert persuasive effects on audiences.

■ Substantial revision of Chapter 11, "Analyzing Numerical Data," focusing on the rhetorical power of tables, graphs, and charts and providing a new microtheme assignment that helps students learn how to construct and use graphics in their own writing.

■ A new extended example in Chapter 16, "Making an Evaluation," focusing on student disagreements about the value of the Experience Music Project, an interactive rock 'n' roll museum.

■ A new student example of a practical proposal (that a campus store should carry "cruelty-free" personal and household products not tested on animals) in Chapter 17, "Proposing a Solution." This chapter also includes a new writing assignment option to create a public affairs advocacy advertisement integrating words and images in a flyer, brochure, Web page, or poster.

■ A new section on making document design serve rhetorical purposes in Chapter 19, "Composing and Revising Closed-Form Prose." Also the material in this chapter has been reorganized and substantially revised for greater clarity and usefulness.

■ Substantial revision of Chapter 20, "Composing and Revising Open-Form Prose," to make it parallel in structure with Chapter 19. By organizing our advice into discrete lessons that can be taught independently, we have made this chapter's advice easier for students to grasp and apply to their own drafts.

■ Expanded treatment of self-reflective writing to include more instruction on assembling portfolios (Chapter 27).

■ Cross-references placed in margins—a new design feature that highlights the connections among parts of the text and makes it easy to find related material elsewhere in the book.

■ Nine new student essays and seventeen new contemporary professional essays, chosen for their student appeal, liveliness, and intellectual engagement.

■ Updated and new examples and illustrations throughout the text.

DISTINCTIVE FEATURES OF THE TEXT

With these changes, the third edition of *The Allyn and Bacon Guide to Writing* has the following distinctive features:

■ Emphasis on writing and reading as processes of inquiry, problem posing, and critical thinking.

■ Classroom-tested writing assignments that guide students through all phases of the reading and writing processes and make frequent use of collaboration and peer review. Assignments are designed to promote intellectual growth and to stimulate the kind of critical thinking valued in college courses.

- Balanced coverage of academic writing and personal and narrative forms, placing nonfiction writing on a continuum from thesis-driven "closed-form" writing to narrative-based "open-form" writing.

- Focus on closed-form writing as an entry into an academic or civic conversation; equivalent focus on reading as the ability to summarize a text and speak back to it in a variety of ways.

- Emphasis on teaching students to read rhetorically; to understand the differences between print and cyberspace sources; to analyze the rhetorical occasion, genre, context, and intended audience of sources; to evaluate sources according to appropriate criteria; and to negotiate the World Wide Web with confidence.

- Coverage of visual rhetoric and document design with particular emphasis on Web sites and other texts where words and images work together for rhetorical effect.

- A sequenced skill-based approach to research that teaches students expert strategies for conducting academic research in a rhetorical environment.

- Instructional emphases that meet Writing Program Administrators (WPA) guidelines for outcome goals in first-year composition courses. (The third edition of the *Instructor's Resource Manual* by Susanmarie Harrington of Indiana University Purdue University Indianapolis discusses the correlation of The WPA Outcomes Statement and the third edition of *The Allyn and Bacon Guide to Writing*.)

- A friendly, encouraging tone that respects students and treats them as serious learners.

- Accessible readings on current and enduring questions that illustrate rhetorical principles and represent a balance between professional and student writers.

- Clear and flexible organization that allows instructors to create a coherent course design while using only the chapters they need, based on course emphases, instructor's interests, length of the term, and the preparation level of students.

STRUCTURE OF
THE ALLYN AND BACON GUIDE TO WRITING

Part One, "A Rhetoric for College Writers," provides a conceptual framework for *The Allyn and Bacon Guide to Writing* by showing how inquiring writers pose problems, pursue them through discussion and exploratory writing, and solve them within a rhetorical context shaped by the writer's purpose, audience, and genre. Chapter 1 shows how writers grapple with both subject matter and rhetorical problems, introducing the concept of a continuum from closed to open forms of prose. Chapter 2 presents an array of techniques for exploring ideas and deepening inquiry, including strategies for making exploratory writing and discussion a regular habit. Chapter 3 explains how academic writers use rhetorical awareness of audience to pose good questions, formulate a surprising thesis, and support that thesis through a hierarchical structure of points and particulars. It also introduces visual rhetoric by showing how arguments can be made with images as well as words. Chapter 4 extends the discussion of rhetoric by showing how a writer's decisions about content, structure, style, and document design are informed by the writer's purpose, intended audience, and genre.

Part Two, "Writing Projects," contains thirteen self-contained assignment chapters arranged according to the purposes for writing: to learn, to express, to explore, to inform, to analyze and synthesize, and to persuade. Each chapter guides students through the process of generating and exploring ideas, composing and drafting, and revising and editing. Concluding each chapter are "Guidelines for Peer Reviews," which sum up the important features in the assignments and facilitate detailed, helpful peer reviews. The heart of each chapter is a writing project designed to teach students new ways of seeing and thinking. The exploratory exercises in each assignment chapter help students generate ideas for their essays, while developing their skills at posing problems, delaying closure, speaking back to texts, valuing alternative points of view, and thinking dialectically.

Part Three, "A Guide to Composing and Revising," comprises three self-contained chapters of nuts-and-bolts strategies for composing and revising along the continuum from closed to open forms. Chapter 18 explains how experienced writers use multiple drafts to manage the complexities of writing and suggests ways that students can improve their own writing processes. It also includes instruction on how to conduct peer reviews. Chapter 19 presents ten self-contained lessons—derived from reader expectation theory—on composing and revising closed-form prose. Chapter 20 shifts from closed to open forms. Now organized into self-contained lessons parallel to those in Chapter 19, this chapter teaches principles for composing and revising open-form prose.

Part Four, "A Rhetorical Guide to Research," presents pedagogically sequenced instruction for helping students learn how to conduct searches, evaluate sources, and incorporate sources into their own writing. Research skills are taught within a rhetorical context with special attention given to the rhetoric of Web sites. Chapter 21 introduces students to the demands of college-level research and previews seven essential skills they will learn in the next chapters. Chapter 22 covers the first five of these skills: arguing one's own thesis; understanding different kinds of sources; using purposeful search strategies; using rhetorical knowledge to read and evaluate sources; and understanding the rhetoric of Web sites. Chapter 23 explains the last two skills: how to incorporate sources into one's own writing and how to cite and document them effectively using MLA or APA formats. Finally, Chapter 24 teaches additional research skills such as using specialized reference materials, exploring ideas in electronic forums, and conducting field research.

Part Five, "A Guide to Special Writing and Speaking Occasions," advises students in a number of special areas. Chapter 25 focuses on oral communication including working in groups and giving speeches and PowerPoint presentations. Chapter 26, drawing on research on timed writing, shows students how to plan and draft an exam essay by applying the principles of rhetorical assessment discussed throughout the text. Chapter 27 draws on research in reflective writing to teach students how to think metacognitively about their own composing processes, produce self-reflective evaluations of their own work, and assemble end-of-term portfolios.

Finally, Part Six, "A Guide to Editing," is a concise handbook of grammar, usage, mechanics, punctuation, style, and editing. The first chapter develops self-assessment skills and includes a series of brief write-to-learn microthemes aimed at helping students learn important grammatical and stylistic concepts. The second chapter reviews basic concepts of grammar and sentence structure. The third chapter explains fragments, comma splices, and run-ons within the context of the main punctuation rules for signaling phrases and clauses to readers. The fourth and fifth chapters address usage and style concerns, and the final chapter is devoted to punctuation and mechanics.

STRATEGIES FOR USING *THE ALLYN AND BACON GUIDE TO WRITING*

The text's logical organization makes it easy to design a new syllabus or adapt the text to your current syllabus. Key rhetorical concepts that students should know early in the course are developed in Part One, while explanations of compositional strategies and skills—which students will practice recursively throughout the course—are placed in Part Three. Students can work their way through assigned material in Part Three while engaged with writing assignments from Part Two. Additional instructional material related to research and to special writing occasions is included in Parts Four and Five.

Although there are many ways to use *The Allyn and Bacon Guide to Writing*, the most typical course design has students read material from Chapters 1–4 (Part One) during the opening weeks. The brief, informal write-to-learn projects in these chapters can be used either for overnight homework assignments or for in-class discussion.

For the rest of the course, instructors typically assign writing project chapters from the array of options available in Part Two, Chapters 5–17. While students are engaged with the writing projects in these chapters, instructors can assign material from the compositional chapters in Part Three, or from the additional instructional materials in Parts Four and Five and the Handbook, selected and sequenced according to their own needs. Each of the lessons on composing and revising closed-form prose (Chapter 19) or open-form prose (Chapter 20) is designed for coverage in a half hour or less of class time. (For suggestions on how to select and sequence materials from Parts Three, Four, and Five, see the sample syllabi in the *Instructor's Resource Manual*.) While students are working on a writing project, classroom discussion can alternate between issues related directly to the assignment (invention exercises, group brainstorming, peer review workshops) and those focusing on instructional matter from the rest of the text.

USING THE WRITING PROJECTS IN PART TWO

Because each of the thirteen assignment chapters in Part Two is self-contained, instructors can select and organize the writing projects in the way that best fits their course goals and their students' needs. The projects in Chapters 5 and 6 introduce students to the rhetorical ways of observing and reading that underpin mature academic thinking, showing students how to analyze a text, pose questions about it, and understand and resist the text's rhetorical strategies.

Chapter 7, on autobiographical narrative, is the text's primary "open-form" assignment. Introducing students to strategies of plot, character, and dramatic tension, the project often produces surprisingly sophisticated narratives. Some teachers like to give this assignment early in the course—on the grounds that personal writing should precede more academic forms. Others like to give it last—on the grounds that open-form writing is more complex and subtle than closed-form prose. We have found that either choice can work well. Teachers often pair Chapter 7 with Chapter 20, on composing and revising open-form prose.

Chapter 8's assignment, an exploratory essay, asks students to narrate their engagement with a problem and their attempts to resolve it. Teachers may want to pair this chapter with Part Four on research writing, using the exploratory essay as the first stage of a major research project. The two student essays in this chapter are, in fact, early explorations for finished projects that appear later in the text.

Chapter 9, on informative writing, urges students to reach beyond straightforward reporting by employing a "surprising-reversal" strategy aimed at altering the reader's initial assumptions about the topic. Surprising reversal is a powerful rhetorical move that can be used to enliven almost any kind of informative, analytical, or persuasive prose.

The five writing projects in the analysis/synthesis section (Chapters 10–14) allow instructors to select among different kinds of phenomena for analysis. Chapter 10 focuses on images—photographs and advertisements. Chapter 11 focuses on numerical data, teaching students how to analyze numbers used in argument and how to design and incorporate quantitative graphics into their own prose (see the microtheme assignment option within the chapter). Chapter 12 focuses on analyzing a short story. Chapter 13—new to this edition—teaches students how to analyze and synthesize ideas from two or more readings. Finally, Chapter 14 focuses on the analysis of causes and consequences of a phenomenon. All these chapters teach the generic skills of close observation, close reading, and close attention to detail while offering specific guidance in the skills unique to each category of analysis.

The persuasion chapters (Chapters 15–17) teach key concepts of argumentation. Providing a strong introduction to both academic and civic argument, they combine accessible Toulmin and stasis approaches while emphasizing argument as truth seeking and consensus seeking rather than as a win/lose debate. Chapter 15 teaches the generic structure and procedures of classical argument. Chapter 16 focuses on evaluation arguments and Chapter 17 on proposal arguments. A new feature in Chapter 17 is an assignment option to create a public affairs advocacy advertisement.

FLEXIBILITY OF
THE ALLYN AND BACON GUIDE TO WRITING

Although *The Allyn and Bacon Guide to Writing* is a comprehensive rhetoric, it is designed to be highly teachable in a wide variety of courses and settings. Through all editions, our goal has been to offer instructors multiple possibilities for course design. To that end, *The Allyn and Bacon Guide to Writing* allows numerous options for selecting and sequencing chapters to suit courses with different writing emphases and student needs. Instructors may teach some chapters thoroughly, while assigning others largely for students' preparation outside of class.

Consider, for example, one's options for teaching Chapter 19, on composing and revising closed-form prose. The chapter consists of ten self-contained mini-lessons that can be assigned all at once for several class days of discussion or assigned one lesson at a time at appropriate moments throughout the course. The lessons can be assigned primarily as background reading, or they can be used in class as short instructional modules. (Each lesson is designed to be covered in a half hour or less of class time.) Moreover, some of the lessons can be omitted or mixed and matched in different order.

The same kind of flexibility is offered by the design of the whole text. Our intent has been to give instructors appealing choices and to equip them with pedagogical material that has both depth and breadth.

SUPPLEMENTS FOR
THE ALLYN AND BACON GUIDE TO WRITING

The Allyn and Bacon Guide to Writing is supported by a variety of helpful supplements for instructors and students.

For Instructors

- The third edition of the *Instructor's Resource Manual* has been revised by Susanmarie Harrington of Indiana University Purdue University, Indianapolis. This edition of the *Instructor's Resource Manual* integrates emphases for meeting the Writing Program Administrators guidelines for outcome goals in first-year composition courses. It continues to offer detailed teaching suggestions to help both experienced and new instructors; practical teaching strategies for composition instructors in a question-and-answer format; suggested syllabi for courses of various lengths and emphases; chapter-by-chapter teaching suggestions; answers to handbook exercises; suggestions for using the text with non-native speakers; suggestions for using the text in an electronic classroom; transparency masters for class use; and annotated bibliographies.
- *The Allyn and Bacon Guide to Writing Companion Website* by Tim McGee of The College of New Jersey enables instructors to access online writing exercises, Web links keyed to specific chapters, and teaching tips; post and

make changes to their syllabi; hold chat sessions with individual students or groups of students; and receive e-mail and essay assignments directly from students. (*http://www.ablongman.com/ramage*)

■ *An Introduction to Teaching Composition in an Electronic Environment*, developed by Eric Hoffman and Carol Scheidenhelm, both of Northern Illinois University, offers a wealth of computer-related classroom activities. It also provides detailed guidance for both experienced and inexperienced instructors who wish to make creative use of technology in a composition environment.

■ *The Allyn and Bacon Sourcebook for College Writing Teachers*, Second Edition, compiled by James C. McDonald of the University of Louisiana at Lafayette, provides instructors with a varied selection of readings written by composition and rhetoric scholars on both theoretical and practical subjects.

■ *Teaching College Writing*, an invaluable instructor's resource guide developed by Maggy Smith of the University of Texas at El Paso, is available to adopters who wish to explore additional teaching tips and resources.

■ "Longman Resources for Instructors" also includes these other helpful texts: *Using Portfolios*, by Kathleen McClelland of Auburn University; *Comp Tales*, a collection of writing teachers' accounts of their teaching experiences, edited by Richard Haswell and Min-Zhan Lu; and the videos *Writing, Teaching, and Learning*, by David Jolliffe, and *Writing Across the Curriculum: Making It Work*, produced by Robert Morris College and the Public Broadcasting System.

■ Coursecompass is a nationally hosted, interactive online course management system powered by BlackBoard. This easy-to-use and customizable program enables professors to tailor content and functionality to meet individual course needs. For more information, or to see a demo, visit www.coursecompass.com

For Students

■ *The Allyn and Bacon Guide to Writing Companion Website* presents chapter summaries; writing exercises; the course syllabus; Web links keyed to specific text sections; Peer Review checklists, student writing samples, and the ability to chat with and e-mail classmates and the instructor. (*http://www.ablongman.com/ramage*)

■ The Literacy Library Series (*Public Literacy*, by Elizabeth Ervin of the University of North Carolina at Wilmington; *Workplace Literacy*, by Rachel Spilka of the University of Wisconsin, Milwaukee; and *Academic Literacy*, by Stacia Neeley of Texas Christian University) offers additional models and instruction for writing in each of these three different contexts.

■ *Visual Communication: A Writer's Guide*, Second Edition, by Susan Hilligoss and Sharon Howard, both of Clemson University, examines the rhetoric and principles of visual design, with an emphasis throughout on audience and genre. Practical guidelines for incorporating graphics and visuals are featured along with sample planning worksheets and design samples and exercises.

▦ *Analyzing Literature: A Guide for Students*, Second Edition, by Sharon James McGee of Southern Illinois University at Edwardsville, provides advice and sample student papers to help students interpret and discuss works from a variety of literary genres.

▦ *Researching Online*, Fifth Edition, by David Munger and Shireen Campbell of Davidson College, gives students detailed, step-by-step instructions for performing electronic searches; for using e-mail, listservs, Usenet newsgroups, IRC, and MUDs and MOOs to do research; and for assessing the validity of electronic sources.

▦ *The Longman Writer's Journal*, by Mimi Markus of Broward Community College, provides students with their own personal space for writing. It contains journal writing strategies, sample journal entries by other students, and many writing prompts and topics to help get students writing.

▦ *The Allyn and Bacon Guide to Writing* may also be packaged with other books at a discount. Two dictionaries are available: *Merriam-Webster's Collegiate Dictionary*, Tenth Edition, a hardcover desk dictionary, and *The New American Webster Handy College Dictionary*, Third Edition, a briefer paperback dictionary. Also, in conjunction with Penguin Putnam, Longman is proud to offer a variety of Penguin titles, such as Mike Rose's *Lives on the Boundary* and Julia Alvarez's *How the Garcia Girls Lost Their Accents*.

▦ *The Mercury Reader* offers a database of nearly 500 classic and contemporary reading selections, with accompanying pedagogical elements, from which instructors can create a customized book tailored to course-specific needs. An optional genre-based Table of Contents is available from *The Mercury Reader*, thus allowing instructors to create a custom reader that complements the approach of *The Allyn and Bacon Guide to Writing*. For more information, please visit *http://www.pearsoncustom.com/database/merc.html*.

▦ *Take Note!* is a complete research information-management tool for students working on projects that require the use of outside sources. This cross-platform CD-ROM integrates note taking, outlining, and bibliography management into one easy-to-use package.

ACKNOWLEDGMENTS

We wish to give special thanks to several composition scholars who wrote commissioned sections of the book for this edition. Thanks to Tim McGee of The College of New Jersey, who wrote our new section on giving speeches and PowerPoint presentations (Chapter 25). Thanks also to Alice Gillam of the University of Wisconsin–Milwaukee, who revised the chapter on self-reflective writing to place greater emphasis on preparing course portfolios (Chapter 27), and to Virginia Chappell of Marquette University, who revised Chapter 12 on analyzing a short story. Finally we wish to thank again Christy Friend of the

University of South Carolina, Columbia, who wrote Chapter 26 on essay examinations for the first edition, and Daniel Anderson of the University of North
Carolina at Chapel Hill, who wrote the first- and second-edition material on electronic writing and research, some of which is retained in Chapter 24.

Our deep thanks and appreciation again go to Eben Ludlow, our editor, with
whom we have worked productively for more than sixteen years. Now vice president of Longman Publishers, Eben is one of the most experienced and insightful
editors in college publishing and the best editor any textbook writer could wish
for. For this edition we are also particularly grateful to development editor Marion
Castellucci, who provided extensive and invaluable editorial assistance as we
negotiated the demands of a four-color text with images and a complex design.

We would also like to thank the many scholars and teachers who reviewed *The
Allyn and Bacon Guide to Writing* in its various stages. Several scholars gave us
chapter-by-chapter advice at each stage of the manuscript, and to them we owe
our deepest appreciation: Susanmarie Harrington of Indiana University Purdue
University, Indianapolis; Larry Beason of the University of South Alabama; Peggy
Jolly of the University of Alabama at Birmingham; Bonnie Lenore Kyburz of Utah
Valley State College; and Allison Fernley of Salt Lake Community College. In
addition, Joe Law of Wright State University provided an expert critique of the
research chapters in Part Four.

Many others gave us initial advice on how to proceed with the third edition:
Lisa Bickmore of Salt Lake Community College; Virginia Chappell of Marquette
University; Gregory R. Glau of Arizona State University; Loretta S. Gray of Central
Washington University; Karen P. Ryan of Gannon University; Rebecca Todd of
Xavier University; and Barbara Wenner of the University of Cincinnati.

Most of all we are indebted to our students, who have made the teaching of
composition such a joy. We thank them for their insights and for their willingness to engage with problems, discuss ideas, and, as they compose and revise,
share with us their frustrations and their triumphs. They have sustained our love
of teaching and inspired us to write this book.

Finally, John Bean thanks his wife, Kit, also a professional composition
teacher, whose dedication to her students as writers and individuals manifests
the sustaining values of our unique profession. John also thanks his children,
Matthew, Andrew, Stephen, and Sarah, who have grown to adulthood since he
began writing textbooks, and offers a special welcome to Matt's wife Katey and
our new grandchildren. June Johnson thanks her friends Ellen and John Caster,
who contributed valuable ideas about visual design from their knowledge as
artists and art educators. She is especially appreciative of her husband, Kenneth
Bube, for his loving support, his interest in teaching, and his expert understanding of the importance of writing in mathematics and the sciences. Finally, she
thanks her daughter, Jane Ellen, who has offered encouragement and support in
countless ways.

John D. Ramage
John C. Bean
June Johnson

Using the Part Opener Images

A s part of our pedagogical approach to the use of color in the third edition, we have chosen a functional rather than decorative use for the part openers to the six major parts of this textbook. Each part opener image combines verbal and visual elements, each grows out of a lively rhetorical context, and each is rhetorically complex and potent in its appeal to its audience. In addition, these part openers represent a range of genres and purposes: a 1924 advertisement for Hoover vacuum cleaners (p. 2); a contemporary Adbusters anti-ad for "Malboro Country" (p. 84); a contemporary public affairs advocacy advertisement for World Vision's campaign to feed children in Afghanistan (p. 476); the home page of an advocacy Web site, Women Against Gun Control (p. 572); a 1930s classic poster, "Years of Dust," for the Resettlement Administration's effort to help farmers during the Dust Bowl (p. 682); and a flyer given to tourists at Yellowstone National Park (p. 730).

We have selected these verbal-visual texts with a number of pedagogical goals in mind:

- To enhance this edition's emphasis on rhetorical context by offering for discussion engaging, rhetorically rich, real-world images
- To help students develop their visual literacy skills through the examination of intriguing visual texts
- To expand students' understanding of genres
- To illustrate how highly visual texts contribute to public conversations and controversies (cross-references in the chapters point out thematic connections among the text's readings and the part openers)
- To inspire students and instructors to find and incorporate other visual-verbal texts in class activities and assignments

These part openers can serve as the basis for class discussions and writing activities. The caption for each part opener briefly explains the image's rhetorical context, historical moment, and genre, and highlights important features. "The Guidelines for Exploring the Rhetorical Power of Visual Design" below offer questions to encourage critical thinking and writing.

GUIDELINES FOR EXPLORING THE RHETORICAL POWER OF VISUAL DESIGN

1. What strategies of visual design (use of type, layout, color, and images) does this visual-verbal text employ? What is the ratio of verbal text to visual text?

2. What is the relationship between words and images? For example: Are the words slogans? Do the words comment on the image? Does the image illustrate the ideas in the verbal text?

3. What social conversation or controversy is this visual-verbal text part of? Who do you think is the targeted audience of this text? What knowledge, values, and assumptions does this audience have?

4. How would you describe the purpose of this text? What is its angle of vision?

5. How effective is this text for its intended audience? How do the verbal and visual elements collaborate to achieve the text's rhetorical effect?

6. Do you think this visual-verbal text is a memorable, thought-provoking, or compelling contribution to its public conversation? Why or why not?

The
Allyn and Bacon
Guide to Writing

you darling!

"Give her a Hoover and you give her the Best"

The HOOVER
It BEATS ··· as it Sweeps   as it Cleans

ANOTHER year has slipped by since you last thought of giving her a Hoover.

But *she* has thought of it many times.

As cleaning days come and go she struggles resolutely with the only "tools" she has in her "workshop," your home.

And they are woefully inadequate, wasteful of time and strength.

As she wields her broom foot by foot across the dusty, dirty rugs her arms rebel and her back seems near to breaking.

Yet she tries to greet you with a smile when you come home at night.

In your heart you pay her tribute. "She's a brave little woman," you say.

But why put her courage to such an unfair test?

Why ask her to bear her burdens patiently when they can so easily be lifted?

The Hoover will save her strength.

The Hoover will speed her work.

The Hoover will safeguard her pride in a clean home.

You cannot afford to deny her these things for the small monthly payments which The Hoover costs.

Don't disappoint her again this Christmas!

Show her that you really *do* care, and throughout her lifetime your thoughtfulness will be ever in her mind.

PART ONE

A Rhetoric for College Writers

This 1924 ad for "The Hoover" appeared fifteen years after the invention of the Hoover Suction Sweeper, the earliest portable electric vacuum cleaner. Such inventions were important to the middle class in the 1920s when domestic help became almost nonexistent. This ad spends little time explaining how this well-known invention works. Instead, it focuses on all it will do for its buyers and users, and thus why it is worth the investment.

To discuss and analyze this appliance ad, see the questions in the section entitled "Using the Part Opener Images" that follows the Preface.

CHAPTER 1

Posing Problems
The Demands of College Writing

It seems to me, then, that the way to help people become better writers is not to tell them that they must first learn the rules of grammar, that they must develop a four-part outline, that they must consult the experts and collect all the useful information. These things may have their place. But none of them is as crucial as having a good, interesting question.

—Rodney Kilcup, *Historian*

Our purpose in this introductory chapter is to help you see writers as questioners and problem posers—a view of writing that we believe will lead to your greatest growth as a college-level thinker and writer. In particular, we want you to think of writers as people who pose interesting questions or problems and struggle to work out answers or responses to them. As we show in this chapter, writers pose two sorts of problems: *subject-matter problems* (for example, Should the homeless mentally ill be placed involuntarily in mental hospitals?) and *rhetorical problems* (for example, How much background about the homeless population does my audience need? What is their current attitude about mental institutions? What form and style should I use?).

We don't mean to make this focus on problems sound scary. Indeed, humans pose and solve problems all the time and often take great pleasure in doing so. Psychologists who study critical and creative thinking see problem solving as a productive and positive activity. According to one psychologist, "Critical thinkers are actively engaged with life. [. . .] They appreciate creativity, they are innovators, and they exude a sense that life is full of possibilities."* By focusing first on the kinds of problems that writers pose and struggle with, we hope to increase your own engagement and pleasure in becoming a writer.

In this chapter we introduce you to the following concepts and principles:

- Why a writing course is valuable, with special emphasis on the connection between writing and thinking
- How writers pose subject-matter problems, in which they wrestle with the complexities of their topics

---

* Academic writers regularly document their sources. The standard method for documenting sources in student papers and in many professional scholarly articles is the MLA or the APA citation system explained in Chapter 23. By convention, textbook authors usually cite their sources under an "Acknowledgments" section. To find our source for this quotation (or for the quotation from Kilcup above), see the acknowledgments at the end of the text.

- How writers pose rhetorical problems, in which they must make decisions about content, organization, and style based on their purpose, audience, and genre
- How the rules of writing vary along a continuum from closed to open prose
- How to ask good subject-matter questions and show how they are problematic and significant

The chapter concludes with a brief writing assignment in which you can try your own hand at proposing a subject-matter question.

WHY TAKE A WRITING COURSE?

Before turning directly to the notion of writers as questioners and problem posers, let's ask why a writing course can be valuable for you.

For some people, being a writer is part of their identity, so much so that when asked, "What do you do?" they are apt to respond, "I'm a writer." Poets, novelists, scriptwriters, journalists, technical writers, grant writers, self-help book authors, and so on see themselves as writers the way other people see themselves as chefs, realtors, bankers, or musicians. But many people who don't think of themselves primarily as writers nevertheless *use* writing—often frequently—throughout their careers. They are engineers writing proposals or project reports; attorneys writing legal briefs; nurses writing patient assessments; business executives writing financial analyses or management reports; concerned citizens writing letters to the editor about public affairs; college professors writing articles for scholarly journals.

In our view, all these kinds of writing are valuable and qualify their authors as writers. If you already identify yourself as a writer, then you won't need much external motivation for improving your writing. But if you have little interest in writing for its own sake and aspire instead to become a nurse, an engineer, a business executive, a social worker, or a marine biologist, then you might question the benefits of taking a writing course.

What are these benefits? First of all, the skills you learn in this course will be directly transferable to your other college courses, where you will have to write papers in a wide variety of styles. Lower-division (general education or core) courses often focus on general academic writing, while upper-division courses in your major introduce you to the specialized writing and thinking of your chosen field. What college professors value are the kinds of questioning, analyzing, and arguing skills that this course will help you develop. You will emerge from this course as a better reader and thinker and a clearer and more persuasive writer, able to meet the demands of different academic writing situations.

Effective writing skills are also essential for most professional careers. To measure the importance of writing to career success, researchers Andrea Lunsford and Lisa Ede recently surveyed randomly selected members of such professional organizations as the American Consulting Engineers Counsel, the American Institute of Chemists, the American Psychological Association, and the International City Management Association. They discovered that members of these organizations spend, on average, forty-four percent of their professional time writing, including (most commonly) letters, memos, short reports, instructional materials, and professional articles and essays.

Besides the pragmatic benefits of college and career success, learning to write well can bring you the personal pleasure of a richer mental life. As we show throughout this text, writing is closely allied to thinking and to the innate satisfaction you take in exercising your curiosity, creativity, and problem-solving ability. Writing connects you to others and helps you discover and express ideas that you would otherwise never think or say. Unlike speaking, writing gives you time to think deep and long about an idea. Because you can revise writing, it lets you pursue a problem in stages, with each new draft reflecting a deeper, clearer, or more complex level of thought. In other words, writing isn't just a way to express thought; it is a way to do the thinking itself. The act of writing stimulates, challenges, and stretches your mental powers and, when you do it well, is profoundly satisfying.

SUBJECT-MATTER PROBLEMS: THE STARTING POINT OF WRITING

Having made a connection between writing and thinking, we now move to the spirit of inquiry that drives the writing process. Thus far in your writing career, you may have imagined writing primarily as gathering and assembling information. Someone handed you a broad topic area (for example, contemporary urban America) or a narrower topic area (homelessness), and you collected and wrote information about that topic. In the process of writing your paper, you may have learned some interesting things about your subject matter. But if you approached your writing in this way, you weren't approximating the thinking processes of most experienced writers. Experienced writers usually see their subject matter in terms of questions or problems rather than broad or narrow topic areas. They typically enjoy posing questions and pursuing answers. They write to share their discoveries and insights with readers interested in the same problems.

Shared Problems Unite Writers and Readers

Everywhere we turn, we see writers and readers forming communities based on questions or problems of mutual interest. Perhaps nowhere are such communities more evident than in academe. Many college professors are engaged in research projects stimulated and driven by questions or problems. At a recent workshop for new faculty members, we asked participants to write a brief description of a question or problem that motivated them to write a seminar paper or article. Here is a sampling of their responses.

> **A Biochemistry Professor** During periods of starvation, the human body makes physiological adaptations to preserve essential protein mass. Unfortunately, these adaptations don't work well during long-term starvation. After the body depletes its carbohydrate storage, it must shift to depleting protein in order to produce glucose. Eventually, this loss of functional protein leads to metabolic dysfunction and death. Interestingly, several animal species are capable of surviving for extensive periods without food and water while conserving protein and maintaining glucose levels.

How do the bodies of these animals accomplish this feat? I wanted to investigate the metabolic functioning of these animals, which might lead to insights into the human situation.

A Nursing Professor Being a nurse who had worked with terminally ill or permanently unconscious patients, I saw doctors and nurses struggle with the question of when to withdraw life-supporting systems. I wondered how philosophers and ethicists went about deciding these issues and how they thought physicians and other clinicians should make the decision to withdraw life support. I wanted to answer this question: What is the relationship between the way "experts" say we should solve complex ethical problems and the way it actually happens in a clinical context? So I chose to look at this problem by reading what philosophers said about this topic and then by interviewing physicians and nurses in long-term care facilities (nursing homes) in the United States and the Netherlands—asking them how they made decisions to withdraw life support from patients with no hope of recovery.

A Journalism Professor Several years ago, I knocked on the wooden front door of the home of an elderly woman in Tucson, Arizona. Tears of grief rolled down her cheeks as she opened the door. The tears turned to anger when I explained that I was a reporter and wished to talk with her about her son's death in jail. Her face hardened. "What right do you have coming here?" I recall her saying. "Why are you bothering me?" Those questions have haunted me throughout my journalism career. Do journalists have the right to intrude on a person's grief? Can they exercise it any time they want? What values do journalists use to decide when to intrude and violate someone's privacy?

Of course these are not new college students speaking about problems they posed; they are college professors recalling problems that fueled a piece of professional writing. We share these problems with you to persuade you that most college professors value question asking and want you to be caught up, as they are, in the spirit of inquiry.

As you progress through your college career, you will find yourself increasingly engaged with questions. All around college campuses you'll find clusters of professors and students asking questions about all manner of curious things—the reproductive cycles of worms and bugs, the surface structure of metals, the social significance of obscure poets, gender roles among the Kalahari Bushmen, the meaning of Balinese cockfighting, the effect of tax structure on economies, the rise of labor unions in agriculture, the role of prostitutes in medieval India, the properties of concrete, and almost anything else a human being might wonder about. A quick review of the magazine rack at any large grocery store reveals that similar communities have formed around everything from hot rods to model railroads, from computers to kayaks to cooking.

At the heart of all these communities of writers and readers is an interest in common questions and the hope for better or different answers. Writers write because they have something new or surprising or challenging to say in response to a question. Readers read because they share the writer's interest in the problem and want to deepen their understanding.

The Writer as Problematizer

Few writers discover their "answers" in a blinding flash. And even fewer writers produce a full-blown essay in a moment of inspiration. Professionals may require weeks, months, or years of thinking to produce a single piece of writing.

A new insight may start out as a vague sense of uncertainty, an awareness that you are beginning to see your subject (the metabolism of a starving animal, the decision to let a patient die, a grieving mother's anger at a journalist) differently from how others see it. You feel a gap between your view of a topic and your audience's view of the same topic and write to fill these gaps, to articulate your different view. Rarely, however, do writers know at the outset what they will write in the end. Instead, they clarify and refine their thoughts in the act of writing.

One of the common causes of weak writing is the writer's tendency to reach closure too quickly. It's difficult, of course, to keep wrestling with a question. It's easier simply to ignore alternative views and material that doesn't fit and to grab hold of the first solution that comes to mind. What characterizes a successful writer is the ability to live with uncertainty and to acknowledge the insufficiency of an answer.

One term that describes serious writers is *problematizers*; that is, serious writers are not merely problem solvers but problem posers, people who problematize their lives. We learned the term *problematize* from South American educator Paulo Freire, who discovered that adult literacy was best taught as a problem-solving activity tied to essential themes in his students' daily lives. Freire's method contrasts starkly with the traditional mode of teaching literacy, which Freire called "the banking method." The goal of the banking method is to deposit knowledge in students' memory banks, rather than teach students to discover or question or act.

The banking method encourages a passive attitude, not only toward learning, but also toward reality. Freire characterized students indoctrinated in such methods as "submerged in reality," unable to distinguish between the way things are and the way things might or should be. When people are taught to read and write by the banking method, they are likely to learn the word *water* by constantly repeating an irrelevant, self-evident sentence such as, "The water is in the well." Using Freire's method of teaching literacy, students might learn the word *water* by asking, "Is the water in our village dirty or clean?" and if the water is dirty, asking, "Why is the water dirty? Who is responsible?" The power of reading and writing lies in making discriminations, in unveiling alternative ways of seeing the world in which we live. By using language to problematize reality, Freire's students learned the meaning of written words because they recognized the power of those words.

Skilled writers, thus, are seekers after alternatives who look deliberately for questions, problems, puzzles, and contradictions. They realize that they can't write anything significant if they don't bring something new or challenging to the reader, something risky enough to spark disagreement or complex enough to be misunderstood. The surest way to improve your writing is to ground your essay in a question or problem that will motivate your thinking and help you establish a purposeful relationship with your audience. In the process, you'll have to live for a while with the sense of incompleteness, ambiguity, and uncertainty—the effects of engagement with any real problem.

Posing a Problem:
A Case Study of a Beginning College Writer

So far we have talked about how professional writers pose problems. In this section we show you how student writer Christopher Leigh posed a problem for an argumentative paper requiring research.

At the start of his process, Christopher was interested in the issue of school violence. Like many of his classmates, Christopher had been disturbed by the massacre at Columbine High School in Littleton, Colorado, in April 1999. When he discussed Columbine with his small group in his first-year composition course, he explained that these killings were especially unsettling for him because Columbine seemed like a safe, middle-class school with no previous record of violence. He wondered what would cause a normal-seeming group of kids to open fire on their classmates.

When he started doing research, he had formulated only a broad question: What can be done to prevent school violence? On his first trip to the library, however, he came across an article on psychological profiling. Here is what he wrote in his journal on that day:

> Today I came across an article in the *New York Times* that disturbed me. It was about psychological profiling, which means that they figure out psychological traits that are apt to indicate a person may become violent. Then they look for kids in the schools that fit those traits. After reading this article, I began to think about whether or not the use of profiles to identify potentially violent students is effective, and if it is somehow a violation of students' rights or privacy. Profiles that use signs such as "antisocial behavior" and "mood swings" may be problematic because almost any student would fit the profiles at some point. Think of all the bad, depressing days that teenagers have. And singling out a student because he or she fits the profile is never going to be able to predict for sure if that student will become violent. I know someone who was suspended for making a joke about a bomb, and even though it was a careless remark, she had no intention of doing harm. So profiling may victimize students who are not violent. Right now my feeling is that profiling in any form is wrong, but I need to learn more about how they are used and if they are effective. Also if they violate students' rights, and how other students feel about them.

After writing this journal entry, Christopher wrote out his new research question as follows: Is psychological profiling an effective way to help reduce school violence? When he discussed this question with his small group, his friends thought it was an interesting question worth researching. The group was divided about profiling. Some thought that schools should do everything they can to identify disturbed classmates and intervene with psychological counseling. Others thought profiling is a total violation of privacy. This division of opinion convinced Christopher that the question was a good one.

We will return to Christopher's story occasionally throughout this text. You can read his final paper in Chapter 23, pages 647–658, where Christopher argues against metal detectors in schools—a moderately changed focus from his initial interest in psychological profiling. You can also read his earlier exploratory paper (Ch. 8, pp. 180–184), which narrates the evolution of his thinking as he researched ways of preventing school violence.

Types of Subject-Matter Questions

Academic researchers often conduct two kinds of research: applied research, in which they try to solve a practical problem in the real world, and pure research, in which they pursue knowledge for its own sake. We call these two types of research questions *practical-application questions* and *pure-knowledge questions,* both of which examine what is true about the world. Frequently, writers also explore *values questions,* which focus not on what is true about the world but on how we should act in it. A famous illustration of these kinds of questions involves the development of atomic power:

- ▪ **Pure-knowledge question:** Is it possible to split the atom?
- ▪ **Practical-application question:** How can we use our knowledge of splitting the atom to build an atomic bomb?
- ▪ **Values question:** Should scientists build an atomic bomb? Should the United States drop it on Hiroshima and Nagasaki?

For Writing and Discussion

Almost any topic area gives rise to pure-knowledge questions, practical-application questions, and values questions. In this exercise we invite you to generate questions about a topic area such as "animals" or "music" or some other area chosen by your instructor. For illustration, we have chosen "animals" and "music" because these areas are widely studied by university researchers across many disciplines—for example, a biochemist studying animal metabolism or a social psychologist studying the effect of music videos on teenage sexual values. Additionally, almost everyone has some personal experience with animals or music, from owning a pet or watching birds on a power line, to observing the effects of a lullaby on a baby or noting the evolution and significance of one's own musical tastes.

1. Working in small groups, brainstorm a dozen or so good questions about animals or music (or a topic area chosen by your instructor). These should be questions that puzzle at least one person in your group and that cannot be answered by simple facts. What you seek are questions that require research and critical thinking and that lead to tentative answers in the form of extended verbal explanations, analyses, or arguments. Try generating questions in each of our three categories, but don't worry if some questions don't fit neatly into a category. Here are some examples of questions about animals and music.

(continued)

Pure-Knowledge Questions

Animals

- Why did dinosaurs become extinct?
- Why does my dog always bark at people who wear hats and not at anyone else?
- When salmon return from the sea to spawn, how do they know to return to the same river or stream where they were spawned?

Music

- Does rap music promote violence?
- How can our ears hear the difference between a trumpet and a violin playing the same note?
- What do ancient musical instruments tell us about the cultures that produced them?
- Why are there so few successful female hard-rock bands?

Practical-Application Questions

Animals

- Can zoos be used to preserve endangered species?
- Is there an effective, humane way to train a dog not to bark?
- Can international whaling laws allow some commercial whaling without endangering whale species?

Music

- How can lovers of hip-hop keep corporations from controlling the development of the music?
- Does music therapy help people who have suffered brain injuries?
- Has the use of synthesizers in rock music decreased the need for musical talent and knowledge of music?

Values Questions

Animals

- Is saving the spotted owl worth the economic costs?
- Is it ethical to eat meat?
- Is it cruel to keep animals in a zoo?
- Should the Makah Indians be allowed to hunt gray whales for cultural reasons?

Music

- Should music appreciation be taught in public schools?
- Whose music is likely to have a more negative effect on children, Eminem's or Britney Spears's?
- Should people be able to share music freely on the Internet without being subject to copyright violation?

2. After each group has generated a dozen or more questions, try to reach consensus on your group's three best questions to share with the whole class. Be ready to explain why some questions are better than others.

RHETORICAL PROBLEMS: REACHING READERS EFFECTIVELY

As we suggested in the introduction, writers wrestle with two categories of problems: subject-matter problems and rhetorical problems. The previous section introduced you to subject-matter problems; we turn now to rhetorical problems.

In their final products, writers need to say something significant about their subjects to an audience, for a purpose, in an appropriate form and style. This network of questions related to audience, purpose, form, and style constitute rhetorical problems, and these problems often loom as large for writers as do the subject-matter problems that drive their writing in the first place. Indeed, rhetorical problems and subject-matter problems are so closely linked that writers can't address one without addressing the other. For example, the very questions you ask about your subject matter are influenced by your audience and purpose. Before you can decide what to say about content, you need to ask: Who am I writing for and why? What does my audience already know (and not know) about my topic? Will the question I pose already interest them, or do I have to hook their interest? What effect do I want my writing to have on that audience? How should I structure my essay, and what tone and voice should I adopt?

In Chapters 3 and 4, we discuss extensively the rhetorical problems that writers must pose and solve. In this chapter we simply introduce you to one extended example of a rhetorical problem. From a student's point of view, we might call this "the problem of varying rules." From our perspective, we call it "the problem of choosing closed versus open forms."

AN EXAMPLE OF A RHETORICAL PROBLEM: WHEN TO CHOOSE CLOSED VERSUS OPEN FORMS

In our experience, beginning college writers are often bothered by the ambiguity and slipperiness of rules governing writing. Many beginning writers wish that good writing followed consistent rules such as "Never use 'I' in a formal paper" or "Start every paragraph with a topic sentence." The problem is that different kinds of writing follow different rules, leaving the writer with rhetorical choices rather than with hard-and-fast formulas for success. To develop this point, we begin by asking you to consider a problem about how writing might be classified.

Read the following short pieces of nonfiction prose. The first is a letter to the editor written by a professional civil engineer in response to a newspaper editorial arguing for the development of wind-generated electricity. The second short piece is entitled "Rain and the Rhinoceros." It was written by the American poet and religious writer Thomas Merton, a Trappist monk. After reading the two samples carefully, proceed to the discussion questions that follow.

R e a d i n g s

■ DAVID ROCKWOOD ■
A LETTER TO THE EDITOR

1   Your editorial on November 16, "Get Bullish on Wind Power," is based on fantasy rather than fact. There are several basic reasons why wind-generated power can in no way serve as a reasonable major alternative to other electrical energy supply alternatives for the Pacific Northwest power system.

First and foremost, wind power is unreliable. Electric power generation is 2
evaluated not only on the amount of energy provided, but also on its ability
to meet system peak load requirements on an hourly, daily, and weekly
basis. In other words, an effective power system would have to provide
enough electricity to meet peak demands in a situation when the wind energy would be unavailable—either in no wind situations or in severe blizzard
conditions, which would shut down the wind generators. Because wind
power cannot be relied on at times of peak needs, it would have to be
backed up by other power generation resources at great expense and dupli-
cation of facilities.

Secondly, there are major unsolved problems involved in the design of 3
wind generation facilities, particularly for those located in rugged mountain
areas. Ice storms, in particular, can cause sudden dynamic problems for the
rotating blades and mechanisms which could well result in breakdown or
failure of the generators. Furthermore, the design of the facilities to meet
the stresses imposed by high winds in these remote mountain regions, in
the order of 125 miles per hour, would indeed escalate the costs.

Thirdly, the environmental impact of constructing wind generation facil- 4
ities amounting to 28 percent of the region's electrical supply system (as
proposed in your editorial) would be tremendous. The Northwest Electrical
Power system presently has a capacity of about 37,000 megawatts of hydro
power and 10,300 megawatts of thermal, for a total of about 48,000
megawatts. Meeting 28 percent of this capacity by wind power generators
would, most optimistically, require about 13,400 wind towers, each with
about 1,000 kilowatt (one megawatt) generating capacity. These towers,
some 100 to 200 feet high, would have to be located in the mountains of
Oregon and Washington. These would encompass hundreds of square miles
of pristine mountain area, which, together with interconnecting transmis-
sion facilities, control works, and roads, would indeed have major adverse
environmental impacts on the region.

There are many other lesser problems of control and maintenance of 5
such a system. Let it be said that, from my experience and knowledge as a
professional engineer, the use of wind power as a major resource in the
Pacific Northwest power system is strictly a pipe dream.

▪ THOMAS MERTON ▪
"RAIN AND THE RHINOCEROS"
(From *Raids on the Unspeakable*)

Let me say this before rain becomes a utility that they can plan and dis- 1
tribute for money. By "they" I mean the people who cannot understand that
rain is a festival, who do not appreciate its gratuity, who think that what has
no price has no value, that what cannot be sold is not real, so that the only

way to make something *actual* is to place it on the market. The time will come when they will sell you even your rain. At the moment it is still free, and I am in it. I celebrate its gratuity and its meaninglessness.

2   The rain I am in is not like the rain of cities. It fills the woods with an immense and confused sound. It covers the flat roof of the cabin and its porch with insistent and controlled rhythms. And I listen, because it reminds me again and again that the whole world runs by rhythms I have not yet learned to recognize, rhythms that are not those of the engineer.

3   I came up here from the monastery last night, sloshing through the corn fields, said Vespers, and put some oatmeal on the Coleman stove for supper. . . . The night became very dark. The rain surrounded the whole cabin with its enormous virginal myth, a whole world of meaning, of secrecy, of silence, of rumor. Think of it: all that speech pouring down, selling nothing, judging nobody, drenching the thick mulch of dead leaves, soaking the trees, filling the gullies and crannies of the wood with water, washing out the places where men have stripped the hillside! What a thing it is to sit absolutely alone, in a forest, at night, cherished by this wonderful, unintelligible, perfectly innocent speech, the most comforting speech in the world, the talk that rain makes by itself all over the ridges, and the talk of the watercourses everywhere in the hollows!

4   Nobody started it, nobody is going to stop it. It will talk as long as it wants, this rain. As long as it talks I am going to listen.

5   But I am also going to sleep, because here in this wilderness I have learned how to sleep again. Here I am not alien. The trees I know, the night I know, the rain I know. I close my eyes and instantly sink into the whole rainy world of which I am a part, and the world goes on with me in it, for I am not alien to it.

For Writing and Discussion

Working in small groups or as a whole class, try to reach consensus on the following specific tasks:

1. What are the main differences between the two types of writing? If you are working in groups, help your recorder prepare a presentation describing the differences between Rockwood's writing and Merton's writing.

2. Create a metaphor, simile, or analogy that best sums up your feelings about the most important differences between Rockwood's and Merton's writing: "Rockwood's writing is like . . . , but Merton's writing is like. . . ."

3. Explain why your metaphors are apt. How do your metaphors help clarify or illuminate the differences between the two pieces of writing?

Now that you have done some thinking on your own about the differences between these two examples, turn to our brief analysis.

Distinctions between Closed and Open Forms of Writing

David Rockwood's letter and Thomas Merton's mini-essay are both examples of nonfiction prose. But as these examples illustrate, nonfiction prose can vary enormously in form and style. From the perspective of structure, we can place nonfiction prose along a continuum that goes from closed to open forms of writing (see Figure 1.1).

Of our two pieces of prose, Rockwood's letter illustrates tightly closed writing and falls at the far left end of the continuum. The elements that make this writing closed are the presence of an explicit thesis in the introduction (i.e., wind-generated power isn't a reasonable alternative energy source in the Pacific Northwest) and the writer's consistent development of that thesis throughout the body (i.e., "First and foremost, wind power is unreliable. . . . Secondly, there are major unsolved [design] problems. . . . Thirdly, . . ."). Once the thesis is stated, the reader knows the point of the essay and can predict its structure. The reader also knows that the writer's point won't change as the essay progresses. Because its structure is transparent and predictable, the success of closed-form prose rests entirely on its ideas, which must "surprise" readers by asserting something new, challenging, doubtful, or controversial. It aims to change readers' view of the subject through the power of reason, logic, and evidence. Closed-form prose is what most college professors write when doing their own scholarly research, and it is what they most often expect of their students. It is also the most common kind of writing in professional and business contexts.

Closed Forms ─┬──────────────┬──────────────┬─ Open Forms

Top-down thesis-based prose
- thesis explicitly stated in introduction
- all parts of essay linked clearly to thesis
- body paragraphs develop thesis
- structure forecast

Thesis-seeking prose
- essay organized around a question rather than a thesis
- essay explores the problem or question
- many ways of looking at problem are expressed
- writer often tells stories to reveal problem's complexity
- writer may or may not arrive at thesis

Thesis as implicit theme
- narrative based
- uses literary techniques
- often called "literary nonfiction" (belletristic)
- often used to heighten or deepen a problem, show its human significance

Delayed-thesis prose
- thesis appears near end
- text reads as mystery
- reader held in suspense

Thesis as speculation, often highly personalized
- speculative points often emerge out of narrative
- often characterized by digressions and musings
- thesis may be only implied

FIGURE 1.1 ■ A Continuum of Essay Types: Closed to Open Forms

Merton's "Rain and the Rhinoceros" falls toward the right end of the closed-to-open continuum. It resists reduction to a single, summarizable thesis. Although Merton praises rain, and clearly opposes the consumer culture that will try to "sell" you the rain, it is hard to pin down exactly what he means by "festival" or by rain's "gratuity and its meaninglessness." The main organizing principle of Merton's piece, like that of most open-form prose, is a story or narrative—in this case the story of Merton's leaving the monastery to sleep in the rain-drenched cabin. Rather than announce a thesis and support it with reasons and evidence, Merton lets his point emerge suggestively from his story and his language. Open-form essays still have a focus, but the focus is more like a theme in fiction than like a thesis in argument. Readers may argue over its meaning in the same way that they argue over the meaning of a film or poem or novel.

As you can see from the continuum in Figure 1.1, essays can fall anywhere along the scale. Not all thesis-with-support writing has to be top down, stating its thesis explicitly in the introduction. In some cases writers choose to delay the thesis, creating a more exploratory, open-ended, "let's think through this together" feeling before finally stating the main point late in the essay. In some cases writers explore a problem without *ever* finding a satisfactory thesis, creating an essay that is thesis seeking rather than thesis supporting, an essay aimed at deepening the question, refusing to accept an easy answer. Such essays may replicate their author's process of exploring a problem and include digressions, speculations, conjectures, multiple perspectives, and occasional invitations to the reader to help solve the problem. When writers reach the far right-hand position on the continuum, they no longer state an explicit thesis. Instead, like novelists or short story writers, they embed their points in plot, imagery, dialogue, and so forth, leaving their readers to *infer* a theme from the text.

Where to Place Your Writing along the Continuum

Clearly, essays at opposite ends of this continuum operate in different ways and obey different rules. Because each position on the continuum has its appropriate uses, the writer's challenge is to determine which sort of writing is most appropriate for a given situation.

As you will see in later chapters, the kind of writing you choose depends on your purpose, your intended audience, and your genre (a *genre* is a recurring type of writing with established conventions, such as an academic article, a newspaper feature story, a grant proposal, an article for *Seventeen* or *Rolling Stone,* a Web page, and so forth). Thus, if you were writing an analytical paper for an academic audience, you would typically choose a closed-form structure, and your finished product would include elements such as the following:

■ An explicit thesis in the introduction
■ Forecasting of structure
■ Cohesive and unified paragraphs with topic sentences

- ▪ Clear transitions between sentences and between parts
- ▪ No digressions

But if you were writing an autobiographical narrative about, say, what family means to you, you would probably move toward the open end of the continuum and violate one or more of these conventions (note how extensively Merton violates them). It's not that open-form prose doesn't have rules; it's that the rules are different, just as the rules for jazz are different from the rules for a classical sonata.

For another perspective on how rules vary, consider two frequently encountered high school writing assignments: the five-paragraph theme and the personal-experience narrative (for example, the infamous "What I Did Last Summer" essay). The five-paragraph theme is a by-the-numbers way to teach closed-form, thesis-with-support writing. It emphasizes logical development, unity, and coherence. The five-paragraph structure may emerge naturally if you are writing an argument based on three supporting reasons—an introductory paragraph, three body paragraphs (one for each reason), and a concluding paragraph. Rockwood's letter is a real-world example of a five-paragraph theme even though Rockwood certainly didn't have that format in mind when writing.

In contrast, the "What I Did Last Summer" assignment calls for a different sort of writing, probably an open-form, narrative structure closer to Merton's piece about the night in the rain. Whether the writer chooses a closed-form or an open-form approach depends on the intended audience of the piece and the writer's purpose.

For Writing and Discussion

Do you and your classmates most enjoy writing prose at the closed or more open end of the continuum? Prior to class discussion, work individually by recalling a favorite piece of writing that you have done in the past. Jot down a brief description of the kind of writing this was (a poem, a personal-experience essay, a research paper, a newspaper story, a persuasive argument). Then, working in small groups or as a whole class, report one at a time on your favorite piece of writing and speculate where it falls on the continuum from closed to open forms. Are you at your best in closed-form writing that calls for an explicit thesis statement and logical support? Or are you at your best in more open and personal forms?

Is there a wide range of preferences in your class? If so, how do you account for this variance? If not, how do you account for the narrow range?

CHAPTER SUMMARY

This chapter introduced you to the notion of writers as questioners and problem posers who wrestle with both subject-matter and rhetorical problems. We have shown how writers start with questions or problems about their subject matter rather than with topic areas, and how they take their time resolving the uncertainties raised by such questions. We saw that writers must ask questions about their rhetorical situation and make decisions about content, form, and style based on their understanding of their purpose, their audience, and their genre. We described how the rules governing writing vary as the writer moves along the continuum from closed to open forms.

The next chapter looks closely at how writers pose problems and pursue them in depth through behind-the-scenes exploratory writing and talking.

BRIEF WRITING PROJECT

We close out this chapter with a brief writing project aimed at helping you appreciate historian Rodney Kilcup's advice to writers: Begin with "a good, interesting question." (See the epigraph to this chapter, p. 5.) As you will see later in this text, your brief essay will be similar in structure to the question-posing part of a typical academic introduction.

> Write a one-page (double-spaced) essay that poses a question about animals or music (or about some other topic provided by your instructor). Besides explaining your question clearly and providing needed background, you will need to help readers understand two things about it: (1) why the question is problematic—that is, what makes it a genuine question or problem; and (2) why the question is significant or worth pursuing—that is, what benefit will come from solving it. Your essay should not answer the question; your purpose is only to ask it.

This assignment builds on the For Writing and Discussion exercise on pages 11 and 12, which asked you to brainstorm questions about animals or music. For this assignment, choose a puzzling question about animals or music that interests you. Aim your essay at readers who are not familiar with your question. Your task is to make your question interesting to those readers. To hook their interest, you have to explain what your question is (often providing needed background) and then elaborate on the question by showing two things about it: why the question is problematic and why it is significant. To illustrate what we mean by these terms, we provide the following student essay as an example.

R e a d i n g

■ AMANDA HIGGINS (STUDENT) ■
COUNTRY MUSIC COOL?

For a long, long time I detested country music. My father was an avid country fan when I was younger, forcing my brother and me to listen to the twangs of such country artists as Johnny Cash and Merle Haggard. On long car trips we would whine and complain until finally our mother would change the music only to "soothe her nerve endings." Recently, though,

Statement of question

One hypothesis

Second hypothesis

Third hypothesis

Shows significance of question

and for no apparent reason, I have begun to listen to country music. Instead of pop and hip-hop, the tunes of Kenny Chesney, JoDee Messina, Tim McGraw, and Phil Vasser now fill my car. Only recently have I begun to question why this change came about. I have also noticed that I am not the only one with this sudden interest in the country music scene. Why is country music gaining popularity?

One theory is that at a certain age, people change or broaden their musical tastes. Maybe now that I am in college I feel like exploring other kinds of music and can now appreciate the music my father exposed me to as a child. Maybe other young adults are experiencing a similar growth in tolerance and interest.

Another possibility is that country music itself has become more upbeat and updated. The music has gone from the "my dog died and my wife threw me out" twang to a more upbeat mood. Even the more melancholy country music of such artists as Reba has a new cutting edge twist. Maybe country music has also deliberately updated its sound in order to compete with the pop and rap industry and to entice listeners who like these other genres.

Perhaps country music has not just redesigned its sound but also given itself a facelift. The trendy outfits of the Dixie Chicks and SheDasie along with the more masculine looks of Rascal Flats or Tim McGraw have recently become popular. For example, at a recent Tim McGraw/Kenny Chesney concert, I noticed the two artists' tight fitting pants and stylish shirts. I am not sure if this look is in because the music is more trendy or if the music is more trendy because of the new look, but this concert was certainly selling CDs, posters, and T-shirts.

I would like to understand if my new interest in country music was influenced by my family, by my need for something new, or by changes in the country music industry itself. Being able to explain the new popularity of country music would help us understand what causes the musical tastes of individuals and groups to change and also to understand more about the contemporary popular music scene and about how music is marketed.

With this illustration as a starting point, let's look more closely at what we mean by a problematic and significant question.

Showing Why Your Question Is Problematic

To understand what we mean by a problematic question, you need to understand how a closed-form essay's question is related to its thesis statement. As we will explain in more detail later (in Chapters 2 and 3), a thesis statement is the writer's new, interesting, surprising, or challenging answer to a question or problem that intrigues the reader. Often at the beginning of the writing process, the question is problematic to the writer as well. The writer's thesis grows out of a process of engaged inquiry, critical thinking, and, in many cases, research. The strategy of most academic introductions is to engage the reader's interest in the problem or question that the thesis will address. The Brief Writing Project for this chapter gives you practice in posing a problem—a writing "move" that you will use frequently when you write academic introductions. Remember that your goal in this assignment is simply to pose an interesting question and show why it is problematic, not to answer it.

A question is said to be problematic if it has no apparent answers or if the answers that first come to a reader's mind can be shown to be unsatisfactory. A question whose answer can be looked up in an encyclopedia or completely answered by an expert is not problematic. Problematic questions imply either that the answer is not known or that it is not agreed upon by experts. In other words, problematic questions imply answers that have to be argued for, that have to be justified with reasons and evidence. Some strategies writers can use to show that a question is problematic are given in the following chart.

We explain how to write academic introductions on pp. 29–30 and 512–517.

Strategies for Showing that a Question Is Problematic

POSSIBLE STRATEGY	EXAMPLE
Show how your own (or previous researchers') attempts to solve the problem have failed.	If your problem were "How can I train my dog not to dig holes in the yard?" you could show how your various attempts to solve the problem all failed.
Show different ways that people have attempted to answer the question (different theories or competing explanations) and indicate how no one answer is fully adequate.	If you were puzzled by the way male rock bands greatly outnumber female rock bands, you could briefly summarize several theories and show why each one isn't fully convincing.
Show the alternative points of view on a values issue.	If your problem were whether it is ethical to burn your own CDs using Napster.com, you could summarize the arguments of the music industry versus the arguments of Napster.com and show why neither argument is fully satisfactory.
Show why an expected or "easy" answer isn't satisfactory.	Suppose you asked, "What is the social function of mosh pits at concerts?" You would need to show why the conservative adult answer of "Mosh pits are a glorified brawl" isn't satisfactory.
Narrate your own attempts to think through the problem, revealing how none of your possible answers fully satisfied you.	You might use the strategy "Part of me thinks this . . . ; but another part of me thinks this. . . ." or "I used to think . . . , but now I think . . . ." For example, if you ask, "Is it ethical to eat meat?" you might describe your shifting positions on this issue and show why no single position satisfies you.

Showing Why Your Question Is Significant

Often a question can be problematic without seeming significant to an audience. A reader might not know why Anne's little sister hated piano lessons while her brother loved them and yet not care about the question. Thus writers often need to show why a problem is worth pursuing in order to keep readers from saying, "So what?" or "Who cares?" It is easy to show the significance of practical-application questions because their solutions will help solve real-world problems such as reducing school violence, getting rid of acid rain, or finding a cure for AIDS. But when you pose a pure-knowledge question, the significance of finding an answer is harder to see. What professional scholars do is show how solving one knowledge question will help them understand another, larger knowledge question. For example, if we understand why Rogers and Hammerstein musicals lost their popularity in the 1960s, we will have a better idea of how cultural change occurs. Here are two typical ways that writers can show the significance of a problem.

Strategies for Showing that a Problem Is Significant	
POSSIBLE STRATEGY	EXAMPLE
Show how solving the problem will lead to practical, real-world benefits.	If we find out what odors trigger the mating of certain insects, we might discover an environmentally safe method of controlling their populations.
Show how solving a pure-knowledge problem will help us solve a larger, more important knowledge problem.	If we understand why middle-class white teenagers are attracted to hip-hop, we might better understand how ethnic and class differences get socially constructed.

Planning Your Essay

A premise throughout this book is that a good finished product grows out of a rich exploratory process. We suggest that you talk through your proposed essay with a classmate, explaining your question and showing why it is problematic and significant. Make an informal outline or flowchart for the essay in which you plan out each of the required parts. Here are some examples of student plans that led to successful question-posing essays.

Example 1

I would like to question the ethics of interspecies transplants and show why it is not an easy question to answer.

Illustrate question with case of a man who had a transplant of a baboon heart.

View One: Interspecies transplants are unethical. It is unethical to "play God" by taking the organs of one species and placing them into another.

View Two: Interspecies transplants may save lives. Medical research done with the intention of improving human life is ethical.

This is a significant problem because it causes us to question the limits of medical research and to ask what it means to be human.

Example 2

I am wondering whether Eminem's music ought to be censored in some way or at least kept out of the hands of children or unknowledgeable listeners.

Show how I am conflicted by all the different points of view:

- I agree that his lyrics are vile, misogynistic, homophobic, and obscene. Children should not be allowed to listen to his music.

- Yet I believe in free speech.

- Also rap is more complex than the general public realizes. Eminem's irony and complexity are often misunderstood. Therefore, serious listeners should have access to his music.

- Additionally, there may be some value just in expressing politically incorrect thoughts, but not if doing so just leads to more hatred.

Explain how I am left with a dilemma about whether or not to censor Eminem and if so, how.

This is an important question because it involves the larger question of individual freedom versus public good.

CHAPTER 2

Pursuing Problems
Exploratory Writing and Talking

When Ofelya Bagdasaryan completed her first university exam in the United States, she was confident that she would earn a high grade. "I had studied hard, memorized the material and written it perfectly in the examination book," she recalled.

But Ofelya, 26, a recent immigrant from Armenia in the former Soviet Union, was in for a rude shock. When the exams were returned the following week, she discovered that the professor had given her a D. "But I repeated exactly what the textbook said," she told her teaching assistant. "Yes," he replied, "but you didn't tell us your [judgment of what the book said]."

—DAVID WALLECHINSKY, *JOURNALIST*

My professor said that I received a low grade on this essay because I just gave my opinion. Then she said that she didn't care *what my* opinion *was; she wanted an argument.*

—STUDENT OVERHEARD IN HALLWAY

"In management, people don't merely 'write papers,' they solve problems," said [business professor Kimbrough Sherman]. . . . He explained that he wanted to construct situations where students would have to "wallow in complexity" and work their way out, as managers must.

—A. KIMBROUGH SHERMAN, *MANAGEMENT PROFESSOR*

In the previous chapter, we introduced you to the role of the writer as questioner and problem poser. In this chapter and the next, we narrow our focus primarily to academic writing, which most frequently means closed-form, thesis-based essays and articles. Mastering this kind of writing is necessary to your success in college and requires a behind-the-scenes ability to think deeply and rigorously about problems, pursuing them at length. In this chapter we show you how to use exploratory writing and talking to do this behind-the-scenes work. In particular, you will learn the following:

- The kind of thinking that college professors value—what one professor calls "wallow[ing] in complexity"
- How each academic discipline is a field of inquiry and argument, not just a repository of facts and concepts to be learned

- ▓ How the thinking process of posing questions and proposing answers is reflected in the introductions of academic articles
- ▓ How to do exploratory writing and talking through freewriting, idea mapping, dialectic discussion, active reading and research, and other strategies
- ▓ How to deepen and complicate your thinking through the "believing and doubting game"

WHAT DOES A PROFESSOR WANT?

It is important for you to understand the kind of thinking that most college professors look for in student writing. As the first two chapter-opening quotations indicate, many first-year college students are baffled by their professors' responses to their writing. Ofelya Bagdasaryan mistakenly thought her teacher wanted her to rehash her textbook. The second student thought her teacher wanted her to describe how she felt about a subject (opinion), not explain why someone else ought to feel the same way (argument). But as management professor A. Kimbrough Sherman explains in the third quotation, college instructors expect students to wrestle with problems by applying the concepts, data, and thought processes they learn in a course to new situations. As Sherman puts it, students must learn to "wallow in complexity and work their way out."

Learning to Wallow in Complexity

Wallowing in complexity is not what most first-year college students aspire to do. (Certainly that wasn't what we, the authors of this text, had uppermost in our minds when we sailed off to college!) New college students tend to shut down their creative thinking processes too quickly and head straight for closure to a problem. Harvard psychologist William Perry, who has studied the intellectual development of college students, found that few of them become skilled wallowers in complexity until late in their college careers. According to Perry, most students come to college as "dualists," believing that all questions have right or wrong answers, that professors know the right answers, and that the student's job is to learn them. Of course, these beliefs are partially correct. First-year students who hope to become second-year students must indeed understand and memorize mounds of facts, data, definitions, and basic concepts.

But true intellectual growth requires the kind of problematizing we discussed in Chapter 1. It requires students to *do* something with their new knowledge, to apply it to new situations, to conduct the kinds of inquiry, research, analysis, and argument pursued by experts in each discipline. Instead of confronting only questions that have right answers, students need to confront what cognitive psychologists call "ill-structured problems."

An ill-structured problem is one that may not have a single, correct answer. Often these problems require the thinker to operate in the absence of full and complete data. People face ill-structured problems every day in their personal lives: What should I major in? Should I continue to date person X? Should I take this job or keep looking? Likewise, many decisions in professional and public life are excruciatingly difficult precisely because they concern ill-structured problems that are unsolvable in any clear-cut and certain way: What should be done about homelessness? What public policies will best solve the problem of global warming or the lack of affordable health care for our citizens or of world-wide terrorism?

Similarly, college professors pursue ill-structured problems in their professional writing. The kinds of problems vary from discipline to discipline, but they all require the writer to use reasons and evidence to support a tentative solution. Because your instructors want you to learn how to do the same kind of thinking, they often phrase essay exam questions or writing assignments as ill-structured problems. They are looking not for one right answer, but for well-supported arguments that acknowledge alternative views. A C paper and an A paper may have the same "answer" (identical thesis statements), but the C writer may have waded only ankle deep into the mud of complexity, whereas the A writer wallowed in it and worked a way out.

What skills are required for successful wallowing? Specialists in critical thinking have identified the following:

1. The ability to pose problematic questions
2. The ability to analyze a problem in all its dimensions—to define its key terms, determine its causes, understand its history, appreciate its human dimension and its connection to one's own personal experience, and appreciate what makes it problematic or complex
3. The ability (and doggedness) to find, gather, and interpret facts, data, and other information relevant to the problem (often involving library, Internet, or field research)
4. The ability to imagine alternative solutions to the problem, to see different ways in which the question might be answered and different perspectives for viewing it
5. The ability to analyze competing approaches and answers, to construct arguments for and against alternatives, and to choose the best solution in light of values, objectives, and other criteria that you determine and articulate
6. The ability to write an effective argument justifying your choice while acknowledging counterarguments

We discuss and develop these skills throughout this text.

In addition to these generic thinking abilities, critical thinking requires what psychologists call "domain-specific" skills. Each academic discipline has its own characteristic ways of approaching knowledge and its own specialized habits of mind. The questions asked by psychologists differ from those asked by historians or anthropologists; the evidence and assumptions used to support arguments in literary analysis differ from those in philosophy or sociology.

What all disciplines value, however, is the ability to manage complexity, and this skill marks the final stage of William Perry's developmental scheme. At an intermediate stage of development, after they have moved beyond dualism, students become what Perry calls "multiplists." At this stage students believe that since the experts disagree on many questions, all answers are equally valid. Professors want students merely to have an opinion and to state it strongly. A multiplist believes that a low grade on an essay indicates no more than that the teacher didn't like his or her opinion. Multiplists are often cynical about professors and grades; to them, college is a game of guessing what the teacher wants to hear. Students emerge into Perry's final stages—what he calls "relativism" and "commitment in relativism"—when they are able to take a position in the face of complexity and to justify that decision through reasons and evidence while weighing and acknowledging contrary reasons and counterevidence. The three quotations that open this chapter exemplify Perry's scheme: Whereas the first student sees her task as recalling right answers, the second sees it as forcefully expressing an opinion, and Professor Sherman articulates what is expected at Perry's last stages—wading into the messiness of complexity and working your way back to solid ground.

Seeing Each Academic Discipline as a Field of Inquiry and Argument

When you study a new discipline, you must learn not only the knowledge that scholars in that discipline have acquired over the years, but also the processes they used to discover that knowledge. It is useful to think of each academic discipline as a network of conversations in which participants exchange information, respond to each other's questions, and express agreements and disagreements. The scholarly articles and books that many of your instructors write (or would write if they could find the time) are formal, permanent contributions to an ongoing discussion carried on in print. By extension, your college's or university's library is a huge collection of conversations frozen in time. Each book or article represents a contribution to a conversation; each writer agreed with some of his or her predecessors and disagreed with others.

As each discipline evolves and changes, its central questions evolve also, creating a fascinating, dynamic conversation that defines the discipline. At any given moment, scholars are pursuing hundreds of cutting-edge questions in each discipline. Table 2.1 provides examples of questions that scholars have debated over the years as well as questions they are addressing today.

Of course, students can't immediately address the current, cutting-edge questions of most disciplines, particularly the sciences. But even novice science students can examine historical controversies. Beginning physics students, for example, can wrestle with Archimedes' problem of how to measure the volume of a crown, or with other early problems concerning the mechanics of levers, pulleys, and inclined planes. In the humanities and social sciences, beginning students are often asked to study, explore, and debate some of the enduring questions that have puzzled generations of scholars:

- ▪ Is there a rational basis for belief in God?
- ▪ Why does Hamlet delay?
- ▪ Should Truman have dropped the atomic bomb on Hiroshima? On Nagasaki?
- ▪ What is the most just economic system?
- ▪ Do humans have free will?

TABLE 2.1 ◾ Scholarly Questions in Different Disciplines

Field	Examples of Current Cutting-Edge Questions	Examples of Historical Controversies
Anatomy	What is the effect of a pregnant rat's alcohol ingestion on the development of fetal eye tissue?	In 1628, William Harvey produced a treatise arguing that the heart, through repeated contractions, caused blood to circulate through the body. His views were attacked by followers of the Greek physician Galen.
Literature	To what extent does the structure of a work of literature, for example Conrad's *Heart of Darkness,* reflect the class and gender bias of the author?	In the 1920s, a group of New Critics argued that the interpretation of a work of literature should be based on close examination of the work's imagery and form and that the intentions of the writer and the biases of the reader were not important. These views held sway in U.S. universities until the late 1960s, when they came increasingly under attack by deconstructionists and other postmoderns, who claimed that author intentions and reader's bias were important parts of the work's meaning.
Rhetoric/ Composition	How does hypertext structure and increased attention to visual images in Web-based writing affect the composing processes of writers?	Prior to the 1970s, college writing courses in the United States were typically organized around the rhetorical modes (description, narration, exemplification, comparison and contrast, and so forth). This approach was criticized by the expressivist school associated with the British composition researcher James Britton. Since the 1980s, composition scholars have proposed various alternative strategies for designing and sequencing assignments.
Psychology	What are the underlying causes of gender identification? To what extent are differences between male and female behavior explainable by nature (genetics, body chemistry) versus nurture (social learning)?	In the early 1900s under the influence of Sigmund Freud, psychoanalytic psychologists began explaining human behavior in terms of unconscious drives and mental processes that stemmed from repressed childhood experiences. Later, psychoanalysts were opposed by behaviorists, who rejected the notion of the unconscious and explained behavior as responses to environmental stimuli.

As you study a discipline, you are learning how to enter its network of conversations. To do so, you have to build up a base of knowledge about the discipline, learn its terminology, observe its conversations, read its major works, see how it asks questions, and learn its methods. To help you get a clearer sense of how written "conversation" works within a discipline—that is, how a writer poses a question and proposes an answer—the next section examines a typical introduction to an academic article.

How a Prototypical Introduction Poses a Question and Proposes an Answer

To illustrate the typical structure of an academic introduction, we will use as our prototype a widely cited article by theoretical physicist Evelyn Fox Keller originally published in 1974 in *Harvard Magazine*. (A *prototype* is the most typical or generic instance of a class. Thus a prototype dog might be a medium-sized mutt but not a Great Dane or a toy poodle; a prototype bird might be a robin or a blackbird or a crow, but not a hummingbird, a pelican, or an ostrich.) Because *Harvard Magazine* is an alumni publication rather than a specialized science journal, Keller's influential article is free of heavy academic jargon, making it easy to see the question/solution structure of a typical closed-form introduction.

Women in Science: An Analysis of a Social Problem

Are women's minds different from men's minds? In spite of the women's movement, the age-old debate centering around this question continues. We are surrounded by evidence of *de facto* differences between men's and women's intellects—in problems that interest them, in the ways they try to solve those problems, and in the professions they choose. Even though it has become fashionable to view such differences as environmental in origin, the temptation to seek an explanation in terms of innate differences remains a powerful one.   *Presentation of question*

Perhaps the area in which this temptation is strongest is in science. Even those of us who would like to argue for intellectual equality are hard pressed to explain the extraordinarily meager representation of women in science, particularly in the upper echelons. Some would argue that the near absence of great women scientists demonstrates that women don't have the minds for true scientific creativity. While most of us would recognize the patent fallacies of this argument, it nevertheless causes us considerable discomfort. After all, the doors of the scientific establishment appear to have been open to women for some time now—shouldn't we begin to see more women excelling?   *Shows why the question is problematic and significant*

In the last fifty years the institutional barriers against women in science have been falling. During most of that time, the percentage of women scientists has declined, although recent years have begun to show an upswing. Of those women who do become scientists, few are represented in the higher academic ranks. In order to have a proper understanding of these data [the original article includes several tables showing the data], it is necessary to review the many influences that operate. I would like to argue that the convenient explanation that men's minds are intrinsically different from women's is not only unwarranted by the evidence, but in fact reflects a mythology that is in itself a major contribution to the phenomenon observed.   *Presentation of thesis*

This introduction, like most introductions to academic articles, includes the following prototypical features:

- *Focus on a clear question or problem to be investigated.* In this case the question is stated explicitly: "Are women's minds different from men's minds?" In many introductions, the question is implied rather than stated directly.

- *Elaboration on the question, showing why it is both problematic and significant.* In this case, Keller highlights competing explanations for the low number of famous women scientists: innate differences versus environment. The social significance of the problem is implied throughout.

- *The writer's tentative "answer" to this question (the essay's* thesis), *which must bring something new, surprising, or challenging to the audience.* In closed-form articles, the thesis is stated explicitly, usually at the end of the introduction, following the expected sequence of question first and then the answer. Here Keller takes a strong stand in favor of environment over innate differences.

- *[optional] A forecasting statement previewing the content and shape of the rest of the article ("First I will discuss X, then Y, and finally Z").* Keller's introduction doesn't forecast the structure of her article, but it clearly announces her two purposes: (1) to show that evidence does not support the intrinsic difference theory; and (2) to show that the intrinsic difference myth itself helps explain the paucity of women scientists.

Of course, the body of Keller's article has to present strong arguments to support her controversial thesis. What she presents is a shocking account of the social forces that hindered her professional development as a theoretical physicist: sexual favor seeking and harassment; "isolation, mockery, and suspicion"; "incessant prophecies of failure"; and the pressure to conform to conventional views about women. She concludes that preconceptions about gender roles "serve as strait jackets for men and women alike." Her article is often cited, favorably or unfavorably, by those on all sides of this debate, for the controversy between innate differences and environment in the formation of gender roles still rages today.

We have used Keller's article to show how academic writers—in posing a problem and proposing an answer—join an ongoing conversation. Many of the papers you will be asked to write in college will require you, in some way, to exhibit the same kind of thinking—to pose a problem; to assert a tentative, risky answer (your thesis); and to support it with reasons and evidence. One of the major aims of this book is to teach you how to do this kind of thinking and writing.

In the rest of this chapter we explain the behind-the-scenes role of exploratory writing and talking. The neatness of Keller's introduction—its statement of a focused problem and its confidently asserted thesis—masks the messiness of the exploratory process that precedes the actual writing of an academic essay. Underneath the surface of finished academic papers is a long process of exploratory writing and talking—periods of intense thinking, reflecting, studying, researching, notebook or journal writing, and sharing. Through this process, the writer defines the question or problem and eventually works out an answer or response. Some of your professors may build opportunities for exploratory writing and talking directly into the course in the form of journals, in-class freewriting, collaborative group work, e-mail exchanges, class discussions and debates, and so forth. Other teachers will spend most of the class time lecturing, leaving you on your own to explore ideas. The rest of this chapter presents strategies and techniques that many writers have found useful for exploring ideas.

TECHNIQUES FOR EXPLORATORY WRITING AND TALKING

To use language for exploration, you need to imagine a friendly, nonjudgmental audience with whom you can share ideas in a risk-free environment. Exploratory writing and talking jogs your memory, helps you connect disparate ideas, lets you put difficult concepts into your own words, and invites you to see the relevance of your studies to your own life. When you write down your thoughts, you'll have a record of your thinking that you can draw on later. Moreover, as you will discover, the very act of recording your thoughts stimulates more ideas. Here are some of the ways you can develop the regular habit of exploratory writing and talking:

- *Keep a journal or learning log.* Many teachers assign journals in their courses. These are modeled after the journals or research logs used by professional scholars and writers to record daily observations, reflect on questions, and develop ideas in progress. You can keep a journal or learning log for any of your courses by posing questions about course material and exploring your answers, thus interacting with course material in a powerful way.

  An example of Christopher Leigh's journal entry is shown on p. 10.

- *Join electronic discussion forums.* At many institutions, teachers set up listservs, electronic bulletin boards, or chat rooms that connect students with each other. The great advantage of exploring ideas electronically is that you can formulate your own ideas and also get responses from others. You and classmates can share questions and insights, rehearse your understanding of course material, and try out new ideas. Also, if you are researching a particular problem, you can sometimes find people interested in the same topic through an Internet listserv, newsgroup, or chat room.

  For instructions on finding and using newsgroups and chat rooms, see pp. 673–675.

- *Participate effectively in class discussions.* The key to effective class discussion, whether as a whole class or in small groups, is learning to listen to classmates' ideas and to build your own contributions on what others have said. This is the skill of dialectic discussion that we explain shortly. Sometimes students are so intent on rehearsing what they want to say that they don't hear or acknowledge other voices in the room. Think of class discussions as a mutual search for the best solutions to a problem rather than an arena for one-upmanship.

In the rest of this section, we describe five useful techniques for exploratory writing and talking: freewriting, focused freewriting, idea mapping, dialectic discussions, and active reading and research.

Freewriting

Freewriting, also sometimes called *nonstop writing* or *silent, sustained writing,* asks you to record your thinking directly. To freewrite, put pen to paper (or sit at your computer screen, perhaps turning *off* the monitor so that you can't see what you are writing) and write rapidly, *nonstop,* for ten to fifteen minutes at a stretch. Don't worry about grammar, spelling, organization, transitions, or other features of edited writing. The object is to think of as many ideas as possible. Some freewriting looks like stream of consciousness. Some is more organized and focused, although it lacks the logical connections and development that would make it suitable for an audience of strangers.

Many freewriters find that their initial reservoir of ideas runs out in three to five minutes. If this happens, force yourself to keep your fingers moving. If you can't think of anything to say, write, "Relax" over and over (or "This is stupid" or "I'm stuck") until new ideas emerge.

What do you write about? The answer varies according to your situation. Often you will freewrite in response to a question or problem posed by your instructor. Sometimes you will pose your own questions and use freewriting to explore possible answers or simply generate ideas. Here is an example of a student's freewrite in response to the prompt "What puzzles you about homelessness?"

> Let's see, what puzzles me about homelessness? Homeless homeless. Today on my way to work I passed a homeless guy who smiled at me and I smiled back though he smelled bad. What are the reasons he was out on the street? Perhaps an extraordinary string of bad luck. Perhaps he was pushed out onto the street. Not a background of work ethic, no place to go, no way to get someplace to live that could be afforded, alcoholism. To what extent do government assistance, social spending, etc, keep people off the street? What benefits could a person get that stops "the cycle"? How does welfare affect homelessness, drug abuse programs, family planning? To what extent does the individual have control over homelessness? This question of course goes to the depth of the question of how community affects the individual. Relax, relax. What about the signs that I see on the way to work posted on the windows of businesses that read, "please don't give to panhandlers it only promotes drug abuse etc" a cheap way of getting homeless out of the way of business? Are homeless the natural end of unrestricted capitalism? What about the homeless people who are mentally ill? How can you maintain a living when haunted by paranoia? How do you decide if someone is mentally ill or just laughs at society? If one can't function obviously. How many mentally ill are out on the street? If you are mentally ill and have lost the connections to others who might take care of you I can see how you might end up on the street. What would it take to get treatment? To what extent can mentally ill be treated? When I see a homeless person I want to ask, How do you feel about the rest of society? When you see "us" walk by how do you think of us? Do you possibly care how we avoid you?

Note how this freewrite rambles, moving associatively from one topic or question to the next. Freewrites often have this kind of loose, associative structure. The value of such freewrites is that they help writers discover areas of interest or rudimentary beginnings of ideas. When you read back over one of your freewrites, try to find places that seem worth pursuing. Freewriters call these places "hot spots," "centers of interest," "centers of gravity," or simply "nuggets" or "seeds." The student who wrote the preceding freewrite discovered that he was particularly interested in the cluster of questions beginning "What about the homeless people who are mentally ill?" and he eventually wrote a research paper proposing a public policy for helping the mentally ill homeless. Because we believe this technique is of great value to writers, we suggest that you use it to generate ideas for class discussions and essays.

Focused Freewriting

Freewriting, as we have just described it, can be quick and associational, like brainstorming aloud on paper. Focused freewriting, in contrast, is less associational and aimed more at developing a line of thought. You wrestle with a specific problem or question, trying to think and write your way into its complexity and multiple points of view. Because the writing is still informal, with the emphasis on your ideas and not on making your writing grammatically or stylistically polished, you don't have to worry about spelling, punctuation, grammar, or organizational structure. Your purpose is to deepen and extend your thinking on the problem. Some instructors will create prompts or give you specific questions to ponder, and they may call this kind of exploratory writing "focused freewriting," "learning log responses," "writer's notebook entries," or "thinking pieces." You can see examples of focused freewriting in students' responses to the learning log tasks in Chapter 13.

Examples of these learning log entries are found on pp. 313–320.

Idea Mapping

Another good technique for exploring ideas is *idea mapping,* a more visual method than freewriting. To make an idea map, draw a circle in the center of a page and write down your broad topic area (or a triggering question or your thesis) inside the circle. Then record your ideas on branches and subbranches that extend out from the center circle. As long as you pursue one train of thought, keep recording your ideas on subbranches off the main branch. But as soon as that chain of ideas runs dry, go back and start a new branch.

Often your thoughts will jump back and forth between one branch and another. This technique will help you see them as part of an emerging design rather than as strings of unrelated ideas. Additionally, idea mapping establishes at an early stage a sense of hierarchy in your ideas. If you enter an idea on a subbranch, you can see that you are more fully developing a previous idea. If you return to the hub and start a new branch, you can see that you are beginning a new train of thought.

An idea map usually records more ideas than a freewrite, but the ideas are not as fully developed. Writers who practice both techniques report that they can vary the kinds of ideas they generate depending on which technique they choose. Figure 2.1 shows a student's idea map made while he was exploring issues related to the grading system.

FIGURE 2.1 ▪ Idea Map on Problems with the Grading System

Dialectic Discussion

Another effective way to explore the complexity of a topic is through face-to-face discussions with others, whether in class, over coffee in the student union, or late at night in bull sessions. Not all discussions are productive; some are too superficial and scattered, others too heated. Good ones are *dialectic*—participants with differing views on a topic try to understand each other and resolve their differences by examining contradictions in each person's position. The key to dialectic conversation is careful listening, made possible by an openness to each other's views. A dialectic discussion differs from a talk show shouting match or a pro/con debate in which proponents of opposing positions, their views set in stone, attempt to win the argument. In a dialectic discussion, participants assume that each position has strengths and weaknesses and that even the strongest position contains inconsistencies, which should be exposed and examined. When dialectic conversation works well, participants scrutinize their own positions more critically and deeply, and often alter their views. True dialectic conversation implies growth and change, not a hardening of positions.

For more discussion on how to work cooperatively with others through dialectic discussion, see Chapter 25 on oral communication.

Active Reading and Research

If dialectic discussion engages you in live, face-to-face conversation with others, active reading and research engage you in conversation with others through reading. The key is to become an *active* reader who both listens to a piece of writing and speaks back to it through imaginative interaction with its author.

When you pursue a question through active reading and research, you join the conversation of others who have contemplated and written about your problem. Not all college writing assignments require library or field research, but many do, and most of the rest can benefit by the process. The writing assignments in Part Two of this text involve varying degrees of research, depending on the assignments selected by your instructor and the problems you choose to pursue.

Chapters 6 and 13 offer instruction on how to become an active reader, reading both with and against the grain. Chapter 22 describes how to find sources, read them rhetorically, and use them effectively in your own writing.

For Writing and Discussion

The following exercise is a simulation game that asks you to try some of the exploratory writing and talking techniques we have discussed.

The Situation. The city attorney of a large U.S. city* has proposed a "get-tough" policy on "vagrants and panhandlers" in the city's downtown shopping areas. It is time, says the city attorney, to stand up for the rights of ordinary citizens to enjoy their city. Supported by the mayor, the city attorney is ready to present his proposal to the city council, which will vote to pass or reject the proposal. The details of the proposal are outlined in the following newspaper article:

Proposed Law Calls for Fines, Arrests

Proposed public-conduct ordinances before the Seattle City Council focus on repeated drinking in public, urinating in public, sitting or lying on public streets, aggressive panhandling, and public drug trafficking. Among their provisions:

- The second and any subsequent drinking-in-public offense becomes a criminal misdemeanor punishable by up to 90 days in jail, a $1,000 fine, and up to one year of probation.

- The second and any subsequent offense of urinating or defecating in public becomes a criminal misdemeanor punishable by up to 90 days in jail, a $1,000 fine, and up to one year of probation.

- The purchase, possession, or consumption of alcohol by those between ages 18 and 21 becomes a criminal misdemeanor punishable by jail, fine, and probation.

- Between 7 A.M. and 9 P.M., it would be unlawful to sit or lie on sidewalks in commercial areas, including Broadway, the University District, other neighborhoods, and downtown.

(continued)

---

* The actual city is Seattle, Washington, but this proposal is similar to those being debated in many cities across the United States. For the purposes of this simulation game, assume that the city in question is any city close to your college or university where homelessness is a serious problem.

▨ A tighter definition of "intimidation" would be created to make the present law against aggressive panhandling more effective in prosecution.

▨ Alleys where drug trafficking occurs could be closed for specific periods of the day or night, except for authorized use. Those who enter without permission could be arrested.

The Task. In class, hold a simulated public hearing on this issue. Assign classmates to play the following roles: (1) a homeless person; (2) a downtown store owner; (3) a middle-class suburban home owner who used to shop downtown but hasn't done so for years because of all the "bums" lying on the streets; (4) an attorney from the American Civil Liberties Union who advocates for the civil rights of the homeless; (5) a college student who volunteers in a homeless shelter and knows many of the homeless by name; (6) a city council member supporting the proposal; (7) a city council member opposing it. Every class member should be assigned to one of these roles; later, all students assigned to a role will meet as a group to select the person to participate in the actual simulation.

The Procedure. (1) Begin with five minutes of freewriting. Class members should explore their own personal reactions to this ordinance. (2) Class members should freewrite again, this time from the perspective of the character they have been assigned to play in the simulation. (3) Classmates should meet in groups according to assigned roles in the simulation, share freewrites, and make a group idea map exploring all the arguments that the group's assigned character might make. Group members can choose a person to play the role; those not chosen can play members of the city council. (4) Allow time for people playing the roles to develop their arguments fully and to exchange views. (5) After each participant has spoken, the remaining members of the class, acting as city council members, should sit in a circle and hold a dialectic discussion (listening carefully to each other rather than conducting a shouting match), trying to decide whether to accept or reject the city attorney's proposal. (6) Finally, the class should hold a vote to see whether the proposal is accepted or rejected.

CHAPTER SUMMARY

In this chapter we looked at the kind of wallowing in complexity that professors expect from students and introduced techniques for exploratory writing and talking that will help you become fully engaged in an academic problem. We saw how an academic essay contributes to a conversation by posing a question and then offering a tentative and risky answer. We also saw how an academic essay is preceded by a process of thinking, reflecting, studying, researching, and talking. The starting point for such an essay is exploratory writing and talking. We explained five strategies for exploring ideas—freewriting, focused freewriting, idea mapping, dialectic conversation, and active reading and research—and offered suggestions for making exploratory writing and talking a regular habit throughout your academic career.

BRIEF WRITING PROJECT

One of the best ways to deal with a problem is to play what writing theorist Peter Elbow calls the "believing and doubting game." This game helps you appreciate the power of alternative arguments and points of view by urging you to formulate and explore alternative positions. To play the game, you imagine a possible answer to a problematic question and then systematically try first to believe that answer and then to doubt it.

Playing the Believing and Doubting Game

Play the believing and doubting game with one of the following assertions (or another assertion provided by your instructor) by freewriting your believing and doubting responses following the example on pages 38–39. Spend fifteen minutes believing and then fifteen minutes doubting for a total of thirty minutes.

1. State and federal governments should legalize hard drugs.
2. Grades are an effective means of motivating students to do their best work.
3. If I catch someone cheating on an exam or plagiarizing a paper, I should report that person to the instructor.
4. The city should pass a get-tough policy on vagrants (see For Writing and Discussion exercise on pp. 35–36).
5. In recent years advertising has made enormous gains in portraying women as strong, independent, and intelligent.
6. For grades 1 through 12, the school year should be extended to eleven months.
7. It is a good idea to make children take music lessons.
8. States should legalize marriage for gays and lesbians.
9. To help fight terrorism, airport security should use racial or ethnic profiling.
10. Hate speech should be forbidden on college campuses.

When you play the believing side of this game, you try to become sympathetic to an idea or point of view. You listen carefully to it, opening yourself to the possibility that it is true. You try to appreciate why the idea has force for so many people; you try to accept it by discovering as many reasons as you can for believing it. It is easy to play the believing game with ideas you already believe in, but the game becomes more difficult, sometimes even frightening and dangerous, when you try believing ideas that seem untrue or disturbing.

The doubting game is the opposite of the believing game. It calls for you to be judgmental and critical, to find fault with an idea rather than to accept it. When you doubt a new idea, you try your best to falsify it, to find counterexamples that disprove it, to find flaws in its logic. Again, it is easy to play the doubting game with ideas you don't like, but it, too, can be threatening when you try to doubt ideas that are dear to your heart or central to your own worldview.

Student Example

Here is how one student played the believing and doubting game with the following assertion from professional writer Paul Theroux that emphasizing sports is harmful to boys.

> Just as high school basketball teaches you how to be a poor loser, the manly attitude towards sports seems to be little more than a recipe for creating bad marriages, social misfits, moral degenerates, sadists, latent rapists and just plain louts. I regard high school sports as a drug far worse than marijuana.

Believe

Although I am a woman I have a hard time believing this because I was a high school basketball player and believe high school sports are *very* important. But here goes. I will try to believe this statement even though I hate it. Let's see. It would seem that I wouldn't have much first-hand experience with how society turns boys into men. I do see though that Theroux is right about some major problems. Through my observations, I've seen many young boys go through humiliating experiences with sports that have left them scarred. For example, a 7-year-old boy, Matt, isn't very athletic and when kids in our neighborhood choose teams, they usually choose girls before they choose Matt. I wonder if he sees himself as a sissy and what this does to him? I have also experienced some first-hand adverse affects of society's methods of turning boys into men. In our family, my dad spent much of his time playing football, basketball, and baseball with my brother. I've loved sports since I was very young so I was eager to play. In order to play with them, I had to play like a boy. Being told you threw or played like a girl was the worst possible insult you could receive. The phrase, "be tough" was something I heard repeatedly while I was growing up. Whenever I got hurt, my dad would say, "Be tough." It didn't matter how badly I was hurt, I always heard the same message. Today, I think, I have a very, very difficult time opening up and letting people get to know me, because for so long I was taught to keep everything inside. Maybe sports does have some bad effects.

Doubt

I am glad I get to doubt this too because I have been really mad at all the sports bashing that has been going on in class. I think much of what Theroux says is just a crock. I know that the statement "sports builds character" is a cliché, but I really believe it. It seems to me that the people who lash out at sports clichés are those who never experienced these aspects of athletics and therefore don't understand them. No one can tell me that sports didn't contribute to some of my best and most meaningful friendships and growing experiences. I am convinced that I am a better person because through sports I have had to deal with failure, defeat, frustration, sacrificing individual desires for the benefit of the team, and so on. After my last high school basketball game when after many years of mind games, of hating my coach one minute and the next having deep respect for him, of big games lost on my mistakes, of hours spent alone in the gym, of wondering if the end justifies the means, my coach put his arm around me and told me he was proud. Everything, all the pain, frustration, anxiety, fear, and sacrifice of the past years seemed so worthwhile. You might try to tell me that this story is hackneyed and trite, but I won't listen because it is a part of me, and something you will never be able to damage or take away. I think athletes share a special bond. They know what it is like to go through the physical pain of practice time and again. They understand the wide variety of emotions felt (but rarely expressed). They also know what a big role the friendships of teammates and coaches play in an athlete's life.

We admire this writer a great deal—both for the passion with which she defends sports in her doubting section and for the courage of walking in a sports basher's shoes in the believing section. This exercise clearly engaged and stretched her thinking.

This brief writing assignment asks you to stretch your own thinking by using the same strategies to believe and doubt your own chosen or assigned assertion.

CHAPTER 3

Thinking Rhetorically about Question, Thesis, and Support

The commonsense, conventional understanding of writing is as follows. Writing is a two-step process. First you figure out your meaning, then you put it into language. . . . This idea of writing is backwards. . . . Meaning is not what you start out with but what you end up with.

—Peter Elbow, *Writing Teacher and Theorist*

Chapter 2 explained how to use exploratory writing and talking to discover and develop ideas. This chapter and the next describe the kinds of problems that experienced writers try to solve as they move beyond exploratory writing and talking to produce a formal finished product. In this chapter we explain how to think rhetorically about the subject matter of an essay: its question, its thesis, and its support. The next chapter continues our discussion of rhetoric by focusing more fully on the writer's context: purpose, audience, and genre.

By "thinking rhetorically" about subject matter, we mean being aware that writers always write about their subjects to an audience for a purpose. In this chapter we show you how writers of thesis-based prose seek a final product that poses a good question, has an engaging thesis, and supports that thesis with strong arguments and convincing details. The resulting essay will seldom be the "whole truth" on the writer's question or the final answer that ends all further discussion. Rather, the essay reveals the writer's perspective on the issue, a certain stance or angle of vision. When you think rhetorically about your subject matter, therefore, you realize that you are entering a conversation of differing views, often with consequences at stake. As an ethical writer, you are obligated to consider other voices in the conversation, to seek the best solution to the question, and to take responsibility for your own stance.

In Part Three of this text, "A Guide to Composing and Revising," we give you compositional advice on the actual drafting and revising of an essay. Our goal here is to stand back from the nuts and bolts of writing to give you some big-picture advice based on a few easy-to-learn rhetorical principles. Specifically, we want to show you how thinking rhetorically about your subject matter can make a stunning improvement in your writing. Your payoff for reading this chapter will be a marked increase in your ability to write engaging and meaningful prose for the audience you are targeting—for example, your classmates in this composition course, the readers of a niche magazine that covers one of your favorite interests, or the community of sociologists for a sociology term paper. The rhetorical advice in this chapter will also help you as a reader because it will make you more aware of how authors try to entice you into the worldview of their texts.

In this chapter you will learn the following principles:

■ How to use rhetorical thinking to deepen your inquiry into your subject

■ How to ask a question that engages your audience's interest

■ How to create a surprising thesis statement aimed at changing your reader's view of your topic

■ How to support your thesis with a network of points and particulars

■ How to appreciate that any essay (yours or someone else's) reflects the writer's "angle of vision," for which the writer must take responsibility

■ How to change your reader's view of a topic with images as well as words

THINKING RHETORICALLY TO DEEPEN INQUIRY

Beginning writers often don't appreciate the extent to which experienced writers struggle with ideas. Unlike beginning writers, who often think of revision as cleaning up errors in a rough draft, experienced writers use the writing process to "wallow in complexity." The more experienced the writer, the more likely that he or she will make large-scale, global revisions in a draft rather than local sentence-level changes.

See Chapter 18 for a full description of a writer's processes.

Why do experienced writers struggle so much with ideas? They do so because they are thinking rhetorically about their subject matter. That is, they are thinking not only about their subject matter but also about how readers with different perspectives will respond to their views—a process that drives them to rethink their ideas and push deeper. Because they are confident in their ability to rewrite and revise, they don't worry about having their final ideas set in stone when they begin to write. Early in the writing process they may be unsure of what they want to say or where their ideas are headed. As Peter Elbow puts it (in the epigraph for this chapter), "Meaning is not what you start out with but what you end up with." To appreciate Elbow's point, consider the following partial transcript of a writing center conference in which the student writer is responding to a political science assignment: Is U.S. involvement in Central America a case of imperialism?

TUTOR: If I said, tell me whether or not this is imperialism, what's your first gut reaction? . . .

WRITER: There's very strong arguments for both. It's just all in how you define it.

TUTOR: Okay, who's doing the defining?

WRITER: Anybody. That's just it, there's no real clear definition. Over time it's been distorted. I mean, before, imperialism used to be like the British who go in and take Hong Kong, set up their own little thing that's their own British government. That's true imperialism. But the definition's been expanded to include indirect control by other means, and what exactly that is, I guess you have to decide. So I don't know. I don't think we really have control in Central America, so that part of me says no that's not imperialism. But other parts of me say we really do control a lot of what is going on in Central America by the amount of dollars and where we put them. So in that essence, we do have imperialism. . . .

> TUTOR: So you're having a hard time making up your mind whether it is or isn't imperialism?
>
> WRITER: Yes! The reason why I'm undecided is because I couldn't create a strong enough argument for either side. There's too many holes in each side. If I were to pick one side, somebody could blow me out of the water. . . .

This student writer is blocked because she thinks she has to make up her mind about her issue before she starts writing. The assigned problem requires her both to define imperialism and to argue whether U.S. activity in Central America meets the definition. What we admire about this student is that she is "wallowing in complexity," fully aware of the problem's difficulty and actively confronting alternative views. The best way for her to think through these complexities, we would argue, is to start doing exploratory writing—freewriting, idea mapping, or another of the strategies described in Chapter 2. This exploratory writing can then evolve into a first draft. Our point here is that the act of writing generates thought. The more she writes, the more she will clarify her own ideas. Her first drafts may have to be dismantled once she finally commits herself to a position. But the discarded drafts won't have been wasted; they will have helped her to manage the complexity of the assignment.

This writer needs to realize that her difficulty is a sign of strength. A good thesis statement is risky. Knowing that a skeptical reader might "blow [you] out of the water" motivates you to provide the best support possible for your thesis while acknowledging the power of opposing views. Perhaps this writer hopes that a miraculous insight will give her the "correct" solution that will make the paper easy to write. "In your dreams," we reply. To think rhetorically means to understand that no final and correct solution exists, just weaker solutions and stronger ones. But by thinking rhetorically, and by trusting in the power of multiple drafts, she can take a more enlightened and ethically responsible stance than she would have taken by just writing the paper off the top of her head.

POSING A QUESTION THAT ENGAGES YOUR AUDIENCE

Chapter 1, pp. 20–22, shows you how to pose questions that are problematic and significant.

In the previous example about imperialism, the instructor assigned a question to address—one that deeply engaged the instructor, who served as the primary audience for this paper. In many of your writing situations, however, you will need to pose your own question. To think rhetorically, you need to make this question interesting, problematic, and significant for your intended audience.

As we explained in Chapters 1 and 2, different academic fields pose questions in different ways. Similarly, readers of different kinds of magazines are engaged by different kinds of questions. To engage a targeted audience, you have to pose a question that connects to your readers' interests and ways of thinking. Let's suppose, for example, that you are interested in rap music. If you want to write about rap music, you have to pose an engaging question about it. The kinds of questions you might pose would vary from audience to audience. Here are some examples:

- *Psychology course*: Does rap music increase misogynistic or homophobic attitudes in listeners?
- *Sociology course*: Based on a random sampling of students interviewed, how does the level of appreciation for rap music vary by ethnicity, class, age, and gender?
- *Rhetoric/composition course*: What images of rap artists, urban life, and women do the lyrics of rap songs portray?
- *Readers of a local newspaper*: Should Eminem have been nominated for a Grammy award?
- *Readers of* Rolling Stone: Why are West Coast rappers like Ice Cube currently dissing New York?

In each of these cases, the writer understands how readers in a particular community pose questions. Your best strategy for engaging readers is to pose a question using the characteristic ways of thinking in the discipline (as in the preceding examples from literature, psychology, sociology, and rhetoric/composition) or a question that hooks into your readers' range of interests. For example, the Eminem question would interest newspaper readers who followed the "cultural wars" debate about Eminem after he was nominated for four Grammys in the spring of 2001; the Ice Cube question would interest *Rolling Stone* readers who were puzzled by the East Coast–West Coast controversy in hip-hop. Any time you pose questions about subjects already interesting to your readers or connected in some way to their values, beliefs, or characteristic ways of thinking, you are off to a good start.

Sometimes, however, you will want to pose a question that may not already interest your intended audience. In such cases, your introduction must explain in more detail why your question is interesting, problematic, and worth solving. The length of your introduction is a function of how much your audience already knows and cares about your question and how much background they need.

For the nuts and bolts of composing an introduction, see Chapter 19, pp. 512–515.

SEEKING A SURPRISING THESIS

As we have seen, most academic writing has a closed, thesis-based form. By *thesis based* we mean that the writer aims to support a main point or thesis statement, which is the writer's one-sentence summary answer to the problem or question that the paper addresses. The writer supports the thesis with reasons and evidence because he or she assumes that the audience will regard it skeptically and will test it against other possible answers. As the quotation from Peter Elbow implies, many writers do not formulate their final arguments until quite late in the writing process because they are constantly testing their ideas as they draft. The underlying motivation for multiple drafting is the search for a strong argument headed by a strong thesis.

But what makes a thesis strong? For one thing, a strong thesis usually contains an element of uncertainty, risk, or challenge. A strong thesis implies a counter-thesis. According to Elbow, a thesis has "got to stick its neck out, not just hedge or wander. [It is] something that can be quarreled with." Elbow's sticking-its-neck-out metaphor is a good one, but we prefer to say that a strong thesis *surprises* the reader with a new, unexpected, different, or challenging view of the writer's topic. By surprise, we intend to connote, first of all, freshness or newness for the reader. Many kinds of closed-form prose don't have a sharply contestable thesis of the sticking-its-neck-out kind highlighted by Elbow. A geology report, for example, may provide readers with desired information about rock strata in an exposed cliff, or a Web page for diabetics may explain how to coordinate meals and insulin injections during a plane trip across time zones. In these cases, the information is surprising because it satisfies the intended readers' needs.

In other kinds of closed-form prose, especially academic or civic prose addressing a problematic question or a disputed issue, surprise requires an argumentative, risky, or contestable thesis. In these cases also, surprise is not inherent in the material but in the intended readers' reception; it comes from the writer's providing an adequate or appropriate response to the readers' presumed question or problem.

In this section, we present two ways of creating a surprising thesis: (1) trying to change your reader's view of your subject; and (2) giving your thesis tension.

Try to Change Your Reader's View of Your Subject

To change your reader's view of your subject, you must first imagine how the reader would view the subject *before* reading your essay. Then you can articulate how you aim to change that view. A useful exercise is to write out the "before" and "after" views of your imagined readers:

Before reading my essay, my readers think this way about my topic:

_____ .

After reading my essay, my readers will think this different way about my

topic: _____ .

You can change your reader's view of a subject in several ways.* First, you can enlarge it. Writing that enlarges a view is primarily informational; it provides new ideas and data to add to a reader's store of knowledge about the subject. For example, a research paper on wind-generated electricity might have the following thesis: "The technology for producing wind-generated electricity has improved remarkably in recent years." (Before reading my essay, the reader has only limited, out-of-date knowledge of wind-power technology; after reading my essay, the reader will have up-to-date knowledge.)

Second, you can clarify your reader's view of something that was previously fuzzy, tentative, or uncertain. Writing of this kind often explains, analyzes, or interprets. Engineers, for example, in comparing the environmental impact of

---

* Our discussion of how writing changes a reader's view of the world is indebted to Richard Young, Alton Becker, and Kenneth Pike, *Rhetoric: Discovery and Change* (New York: Harcourt Brace & Company, 1971).

dams versus wind towers might be uncertain how to calculate the environmental impact of dams when their costs (loss of fish runs, destruction of streams and natural habitats) are weighed against their benefits (flood control, irrigation, power generation). An economist might write an article that would clarify this problem. (Before reading my article, engineers and politicians will be uncertain how to measure the environmental costs of dams. After reading my article, these people will have a clearer understanding of how to calculate these costs.)

Still another kind of change occurs when an essay actually restructures a reader's whole view of a subject. Such essays persuade readers to change their minds or make decisions. These essays can threaten a reader's identity because they shake up closely held beliefs and values. For example, in Chapter 1 we printed a letter to the editor written by a civil engineer who argued that "wind-generated power can in no way serve as a reasonable major alternative [to hydro, coal-fired, or nuclear power]." (Before reading my letter, the reader believes that wind-generated power is a solution to our energy crisis; after reading my letter, the reader will believe that wind-generated power is a pipe dream.) One person we know—a committed environmentalist with high hopes for wind energy—said that this letter persuaded him that large-scale harnessing of wind energy wouldn't work. He was visibly dismayed; the engineer's argument had knocked his view of wind energy off its props. (We aren't saying, of course, that the engineer is *correct*. We are saying only that his letter persuaded at least one of our acquaintances to change his mind about wind energy.)

Surprise, then, is the measure of change an essay brings about in a reader. Of course, to bring about such change requires more than just a surprising thesis; the essay itself must persuade the reader that the thesis is sound as well as novel. Later in this chapter, we talk about how writers support a thesis through a network of points and particulars.

Give Your Thesis Tension

Another element of a surprising thesis is tension. By *tension* we mean the reader's sensation of being stretched from a familiar, unsurprising idea to a new, surprising one or of being pulled in two or more directions at once by opposing ideas.

Theses that induce stretching are compelling because they continually give the reader something new to consider. Often the purpose of these essays is to inform, explain, or analyze. They are satisfying because they fill gaps in knowledge as they take the reader on a journey from old, familiar ground into new territory—stretching the reader, as it were, into a new place. Stretching theses teach readers something they didn't already know about a subject.

A surprising thesis also may set up tension between alternative ways of looking at an issue such as the tension between the writer's claim and various counter-claims. The writer's thesis pulls the reader in one direction while counter-theses pull in another. Both kinds of tension are good. A tensionless thesis—one that is not new, surprising, or contestable—makes for boring reading, like being trapped in an elevator with piped-in Barry Manilow music.

One of the best ways to create tension in a thesis statement is to begin the statement with an *although* or *whereas* clause: "Whereas most people believe X, this essay asserts Y." The *whereas* or *although* clause summarizes the reader's "before" view of your topic or the counterclaim that your essay opposes; the main clause states the surprising view or position that your essay will support. You may choose to omit the *although* clause from your actual essay, but formulating it first will help you achieve focus and surprise in your thesis. The examples that follow illustrate the kinds of tension we have been discussing and show why tension is a key requirement for a good thesis.

Question	What effect has the telephone had on our culture?
Thesis without Tension	The invention of the telephone has brought many advantages to our culture.
Thesis with Tension	Although the telephone has brought many advantages to our culture, it may also have contributed to the increase of violence in our society.
Question	Do reservations serve a useful role in contemporary Native American culture?
Thesis without Tension	Reservations have good points and bad points.
Thesis with Tension	Although my friend Wilson Real Bird believes that reservations are necessary for Native Americans to preserve their heritage, the continuation of reservations actually degrades Native American culture.

In the first example, the thesis without tension (telephones have brought advantages to our culture) is a truism with which everyone would agree and hence lacks surprise. The thesis with tension places this truism (the reader's "before" view) in an *although* clause and goes on to make a risky or contestable assertion. The surprising idea that the telephone contributes to violence shakes up our old, complacent view of the telephone as a beneficent instrument and gives us a new way to regard telephones.

In the second example, the thesis without tension may not at first seem tensionless because the writer sets up an opposition between good and bad points. But *almost anything* has good and bad points, so the opposition is not meaningful, and the thesis offers no element of surprise. Substitute virtually any other social institution (marriage, the postal service, the military, prisons), and the statement that it has good and bad points would be equally true. The thesis with tension, in contrast, is risky. It commits the reader to argue that reservations have degraded Native American culture and to oppose the counterthesis that reservations are needed to *preserve* Native American culture. The reader now feels genuine tension between two opposing views.

Tension, then, is a component of surprise. The writer's goal is to surprise the reader in some way, thereby bringing about some kind of change in the reader's view. Here are some specific strategies you can use to surprise a reader:

■ Give the reader new information or clarify a confusing concept.

■ Make problematic something that seems nonproblematic by showing paradoxes or contradictions within it, by juxtaposing two or more conflicting points of view about it, or by looking at it more deeply or complexly than expected.

- Identify an unexpected effect, implication, or significance of something.
- Show underlying differences between two concepts normally thought to be similar or underlying similarities between two concepts normally thought to be different.
- Show that a commonly accepted answer to a question isn't satisfactory or that a commonly rejected answer may be satisfactory.
- Oppose a commonly accepted viewpoint, support an unpopular viewpoint, or in some other way take an argumentative stance on an issue.
- Propose a new solution to a problem.

For Writing and Discussion

It is difficult to create thesis statements on the spot because a writer's thesis grows out of an exploratory struggle with a problem. However, through brief exploratory writing and talking, it is sometimes possible to arrive at a thesis that is both surprising and arguable. Working individually, spend ten minutes freewriting on one of the following topics chosen by your class or the instructor:

competitive sports	mathematics education
commuting by automobile	television talk shows
homelessness	sex-education classes
gangs	zoos

Then, working in small groups or as a whole class, share your freewrites, looking for elements in each person's freewrite that surprise other members of the class. From the ensuing discussion, develop questions or problems that lead to one or more surprising thesis statements. Each thesis should be supportable through personal experiences, previous reading and research, or critical thinking. For example:

Topic	Competitive sports
Question	Is it psychologically beneficial to participate in competitive sports?
Surprising Thesis	Although we normally think that playing competitive sports is good for us psychologically, the psychological traits that coaches try to develop in athletes are like anorectic dieting.

SUPPORTING YOUR THESIS WITH POINTS AND PARTICULARS

Of course, a surprising thesis is only one aspect of an effective essay. An essay must also persuade the reader that the thesis is believable as well as surprising. Although tabloid newspapers have shocking headlines ("Britney Spears Videos

Contain FBI Spy Secrets!") skepticism quickly replaces surprise when you look inside and find the article's claims unsupported. A strong thesis, then, must both surprise the reader and be supported with convincing particulars.

In fact, the particulars are the flesh and muscle of writing and comprise most of the sentences. In closed-form prose, these particulars are connected clearly to points, and the points precede the particulars. In this section, we explain this principle more fully.

How Points Convert Information to Meaning

When particulars are clearly related to a point, the point gives meaning to the particulars, and the particulars give force and validity to the point. Particulars constitute the evidence, data, details, examples, and subarguments that develop a point and make it convincing. By themselves, particulars are simply information—mere data without meaning.

In the following example, you can see for yourself the difference between information and meaning. Here is a list of information:*

- In almost all species on earth, males are more aggressive than females.
- Male chimpanzees win dominance by brawling.
- To terrorize rival troops, they kill females and infants.
- The level of aggression among monkeys can be manipulated by adjusting their testosterone levels.
- Among humans, preliminary research suggests that male fetuses are more active in the uterus than female fetuses.
- Little boys play more aggressively than little girls despite parental efforts to teach gentleness to boys and aggression to girls.

To make meaning out of this list of information, the writer needs to state a point—the idea, generalization, or claim—that this information supports. Once the point is stated, a meaningful unit (point with particulars) springs into being:

Point

Aggression in human males may be a function of biology rather than culture. In almost all species on earth, males are more aggressive than females. Male chimpanzees win dominance by brawling; to terrorize rival troops, they kill females and infants. Researchers have shown that the level of aggression among monkeys can be manipulated by adjusting their testosterone levels. Among humans, preliminary research suggests that male fetuses are more active in the uterus than female fetuses. Also, little boys play more aggressively than little girls despite parental efforts to teach gentleness to boys and aggression to girls.

Particulars

Once the writer states this point, readers familiar with the biology/culture debate about gender differences immediately feel its surprise and tension. The writer now uses the particulars as evidence to support a point.

To appreciate the reader's need for a logical connection between points and particulars, note how readers would get lost if, in the preceding example, the

*The data in this exercise are adapted from Deborah Blum, "The Gender Blur," *Utne Reader* Sept. 1998: 45–48.

writer included a particular that seemed unrelated to the point ("Males also tend to be taller and heavier than women"—a factual statement, but what does it have to do with aggression?) or if, without explanation, the writer added a particular that seemed to contradict the point ("Fathers play more roughly with baby boys than with baby girls"—another fact, but one that points to culture rather than biology as a determiner of aggression).

Obviously, reasonable people seek some kind of coordination between points and particulars, some sort of weaving back and forth between them. Writing teachers use a number of nearly synonymous terms for expressing this paired relationship: points/particulars, generalizations/specifics, claims/evidence, ideas/details, interpretations/data, meaning/support.

How Removing Particulars Creates a Summary

What we have shown, then, is that skilled writers weave back and forth between generalizations and specifics. The generalizations form a network of higher-level and lower-level points that develop the thesis; the particulars (specifics) support each of the points and subpoints in turn. In closed-form prose, the network of points is easily discernible because points are clearly highlighted with transitions, and main points are placed prominently at the heads of paragraphs. (In open-form prose, generalizations are often left unstated, creating gaps where the reader must actively fill in meaning.)

If you remove most of the particulars from a closed-form essay, leaving only the network of points, you will have written a summary or abstract of the essay. As an example, reread the civil engineer's letter to the editor arguing against the feasibility of wind-generated power (pp. 13–14). The writer's argument can be summarized in a single sentence:

> Wind-generated power is not a reasonable alternative to other forms of power in the Pacific Northwest because wind power is unreliable, because there are major unsolved problems involved in the design of wind-generation facilities, and because the environmental impact of building thousands of wind towers would be enormous.

What we have done in this summary is remove the particulars, leaving only the high-level points that form the skeleton of the argument. The writer's thesis remains surprising and contains tension, but without the particulars the reader has no idea whether to believe the generalizations or not. The presence of the particulars is thus essential to the success of the argument.

For Writing and Discussion

Compare the civil engineer's original letter with the one-sentence summary just given and then note how the engineer uses specific details to support each point. How do these particulars differ from paragraph to paragraph? How are they chosen to support each point?

How to Use Your Knowledge about Points and Particulars When You Revise

The lesson to learn here is that in closed-form prose, writers regularly place a point sentence in front of detail sentences. When a writer begins with a point, readers interpret the ensuing particulars not as random data but rather as *evidence* in support of that point. The writer depends on the particulars to make the point credible and persuasive.

This insight may help you clarify two of the most common kinds of marginal comments that readers (or teachers) place on writers' early drafts. If your draft has a string of sentences giving data or information unconnected to any stated point, your reader is apt to write in the margin, "What's your point here?" or "Why are you telling me this information?" or "How does this information relate to your thesis?" Conversely, if your draft tries to make a point that isn't developed with particulars, your reader is apt to write marginal comments such as "Evidence?" or "Development?" or "Could you give an example?" or "More details needed."

For more about the importance of points, see pp.518–521, which discuss topic sentences in paragraphs.

Don't be put off by these requests; they are a gift. It is common in first drafts for main points to be unstated, buried, or otherwise disconnected from their details and for supporting information to be scattered confusingly throughout the draft or missing entirely. Having to write point sentences obliges you to wrestle with your intended meaning: Just what am I trying to say here? How can I nutshell that in a point? Likewise, having to support your points with particulars causes you to wrestle with the content and shape of your argument: What particulars will make this point convincing? What further research do I need to do to find these particulars? In Part Three of this text, which is devoted to advice about composing and revising, we show how the construction and location of point sentences are essential for reader clarity. Part Three also explains various composing and revising strategies that will help you create effective networks of points and particulars.

How Particulars Can Be Arranged on a Scale of Abstraction

We have said that writers weave back and forth between points and particulars. But the distinction between points and particulars is a matter of context. A point in one context might be a particular in another. For example, the sentence "Male fetuses are more active than female fetuses" served as a particular to support the point that gender differences are more biological than cultural. But suppose that experts disagreed about the activity level of fetuses. In this case, the sentence "Male fetuses are more active than female fetuses" would be a point. A particular in support of this point might be "Over a two-hour period, male fetuses kicked the uterine wall an average of twenty-five percent more frequently than did female fetuses."* What matters is the relative position of sentences along a scale of abstraction.

As an illustration of such a scale, consider the following list of words descending from the abstract to the specific:

Clothing ⟶ footwear ⟶ shoes ⟶ sandals ⟶ Birkenstocks ⟶ my old hippie Birkenstocks with the salt stains

*This is a hypothetical example only.

In descriptive and narrative prose, writers often use sensory details that are very low on the scale of abstraction. Note how shifting down the scale improves the vividness of the following passage:

Mid-scale	The awkward, badly dressed professor stood at the front of the room.
Low on the scale	At the front of the room stood the professor, a tall, gawky man with inch-thick glasses, an enormous Adam's apple, wearing a manure brown jacket, burgundy and gray plaid pants, a silky vest with what appeared to be "scenes from an aquarium" printed on it, and a polka dot blue tie.

The details in the more specific passage help you experience the writer's world. They don't just tell you that the professor was dressed weirdly; they *show* you.

Academic or professional prose also often uses particulars that are low on the scale of abstraction—statistics, facts, quotations, or specific examples. Civil engineer David Rockwood uses low-on-the-scale numerical data about the size and number of wind towers to convince readers that wind generation of electricity entails environmental damage. But particulars don't always have to be concrete sensory details (such as the colors of the professor's tie and jacket) or highly specific factual or numerical data (such as those used in Rockwood's letter). Some kinds of writing remain at fairly high levels of abstraction, especially in academic prose on theoretical or philosophical topics. Yet even the most theoretical kind of prose will include several layers on the scale. Each of the assignment chapters in Part Two of this text gives advice on finding the right kinds and levels of particulars to support each essay.

For Writing and Discussion

Working as individuals, what kinds of particulars could you use to support each of the provided points? Share your results as a whole class or in small groups.

1. The weather was beautiful yesterday.
2. I was shocked by the messiness of Bill's dorm room.
3. Advertising in women's fashion magazines creates a distorted and unhealthy view of beauty.
4. Although freewriting looks easy, it is actually quite difficult.
5. At the introductory level, chemistry is much more abstract than physics.

RECOGNIZING A WRITER'S "ANGLE OF VISION"

Another important rhetorical concept is "angle of vision," which refers to the way that a thesis statement commits a writer to a particular view of a subject that emphasizes some particulars and de-emphasizes others. By saying that the writer writes from an "angle of vision," we mean that the writer cannot take a godlike stance that allows a universal, all-seeing, completely true, and whole way of knowing. Rather, the writer looks at the subject from a certain location, or, to use another metaphor, the writer wears a lens that colors or filters the topic in a certain way. The angle of vision, lens, or filter determines what part of a topic gets "seen" and what remains "unseen," what gets included or excluded from the writer's essay, what gets emphasized or de-emphasized, and so forth. It even determines what words get chosen out of an array of options—for example, whether you say "affirmative action" or "reverse discrimination," "terrorist" or "freedom fighter," "public servant" or "politician."

A good illustration of angle of vision is the political cartoon on stem cell research shown in Figure 3.1, which appeared in national newspapers in early summer 2001 when President Bush was contemplating his stance on federal funding for stem cell research. As the cartoon shows, nobody sees stem cells from a universal position. Each stakeholder has an angle of vision that emphasizes some aspects of stem cell research and de-emphasizes or censors other aspects. In the chart on page 53, we try to suggest how each of these angles of vision produces a different "picture" of the field.

In this cartoon, President Bush is cast as an inquirer trying to negotiate multiple perspectives. The cartoon treats Bush satirically—as if he were concerned only

FIGURE 3.1 ■ Political Cartoon Illustrating Angle of Vision

Angle of Vision on Stem Cell Research

ANGLE OF VISION	WORDS OR PHRASES USED TO REFER TO STEM CELLS	PARTICULARS THAT GET "SEEN" OR EMPHASIZED
Disease sufferer	Cluster of tiny cells that may help repair damaged tissues or grow new ones	The diseases that may be cured by stem cell research; the suffering of those afflicted; scientists as heroes; shelves of frozen stem cells; cells as objects that would just be thrown out if not used for research; emphasis on cures
Priest	Embryo as potential human life formed by union of sperm and egg	Moral consequences of treating human life as means rather than ends; scientists as Dr. Frankensteins; single embryo as potential baby
Scientist	Blastocysts, which are better suited for research than adult stem cells	Scientific questions that research would help solve; opportunities for grants and scholarly publication; emphasis on gradual progress rather than cures
Businessperson	New area for profitable investments	Potential wealth for company that develops new treatments for diseases or injuries
President Bush (at time of cartoon, Bush was uncertain of his stance)	Afraid to say "cluster of cells," "embryo," or "blastocyst" because each term has political consequences	Political consequences of each possible way to resolve the stem cell controversy; need to appease supporters from the Right without appearing callous to sufferers of diseases; need to woo Catholic vote

with the political implications of his decision. But if we think of him as seeking an ethically responsible stance, then his dilemma stands for all of us as writers confronting a problematic question. In such cases, we all have to forge our own individual stance and be ethically responsible for our decision, while acknowledging other stances and recognizing the limitations of our own.

Where do our stances come from? The stance we take on questions is partly influenced by our life experiences and knowledge, by our class and gender, by our ethnicity and sexual orientation, by our personal beliefs and values, and by our ongoing intentions and desires. But our stance can also be influenced by our rational and empathic capacity to escape from our own limitations and see the world from different perspectives, to imagine the world more fully. We have the power to take stances that are broader and more imaginative than our original limited vision, but we also never escape our own roots and situations in life.

The brief writing project at the end of this chapter will help you understand the concept of "angle of vision" more fully. Your instructor might also assign Chapter 5, which explores angle of vision in more depth.

See pp. 87–107 for further discussion of angle of vision.

For Writing and Discussion

Background: The following letters to the editor appeared in the *New York Times* on July 21, 2001. The letters respond to a column entitled "The Thought Police" by Bob Herbert, a columnist who attacked an Ohio court decision that sent a man to prison for writing pornographic stories about children in his own private journal. The man had previously served a prison sentence for child molestation. Herbert claimed that the court violated the man's freedom of speech, convicting him for what he thought rather than for what he did. The *New York Times* identified the occupations of three of the letter writers—a lawyer, a psychologist, and a criminal justice professor. The fourth is identified by name only.

  Task: Working in small groups or as a whole class, show how the angle of vision of each writer produces a somewhat different picture of the case.

1. What is each writer's thesis statement? (Because these are short letters to the editor, the thesis may be implied. You can reconstruct it by summarizing each writer's answer to the question "Was the Ohio court correct in sentencing this person to prison?")
2. What seems to be the center of interest for each writer? What element of the issue is most emphasized in each case?
3. What elements of the issue are de-emphasized or omitted from each perspective?
4. For each writer, what underlying values, assumptions, or beliefs give rise to that writer's angle of vision?

1. To the Editor:
     In "The Thought Police" (column, July 19) Bob Herbert appropriately raises the alarm regarding the Orwellian assault on fundamental freedoms reflected by the prison term given an Ohio man for entries (albeit reprehensible) made in his private journal.

     The offending Ohio statute and broad interpretation thereof by relevant authorities are a natural extension of hate-crime laws, which take an activity clearly identified as criminal (for example, murder or assault and battery) and make it a separate crime if the already criminal act was committed while thinking a certain (unacceptable) way.

     These laws have been effected with the best intentions but are frightening to all who are concerned with basic liberties. Viewpoints, however unpopular, and whether thought, spoken or written, should never be the subject of criminal sanction in this country.

Peter M. Hoskinski
Stamford, Conn., July 19, 2001
The writer is a lawyer.

2. To the Editor:
     It's not just First Amendment lawyers who should be alarmed by the conviction and sentencing of an Ohio man for writing down descriptions of torture and molestation of children for his own use (news article, July 14).

     Mental health professionals should be equally concerned, as should anyone else who would be discomfited if his or her innermost thoughts and mental images—expressed privately—were put on public display.

The opportunity to express oneself without censoring the mind's content is a requisite of psychotherapeutic endeavors. More than that, it may be therapeutic in its own right in that free expression of what is unsavory or hostile may prevent what is suppressed from finding an outlet in overt behavior, which is the appropriate arena for the attention of public guardians.

Marcus J. Wiesner
Montclair, N.J., July 16, 2001
The writer is a psychologist.

3. To the Editor:

In his July 19 column, Bob Herbert describes the case of Brian Dalton, an Ohio man who was convicted of child pornography for writings in a private journal.

The criminal justice question in this case is about dangerousness as a basis for criminal conviction. Mr. Herbert's analogy of Philip Roth's "Portnoy's Complaint" doesn't work, because Mr. Roth himself never raised an issue of dangerousness.

Mr. Dalton does raise such an issue because he has already been convicted of child pornography. His track record suggests he might present a clear and present danger to children.

The chief purpose of American criminal justice is to prevent crime, not react to it after it happens. Criminal justice agencies will therefore often be charged with trampling First Amendment liberties, as for example in the New Jersey profiling issue. But the problem with profiling in New Jersey was that there was never an issue of dangerousness. In the Dalton case, there unfortunately is.

Robert R. Sullivan
New York, July 19, 2001
The writer is professor emeritus at John Jay College of Criminal Justice.

4. To the Editor:

Bob Herbert (column, July 19) defends an Ohio man's right to his private salacious thoughts about imagined children and his civil right to be able to write them in a journal. But isn't it possible that this man, who was on probation from a conviction involving pornographic photographs of children, might not be able to contain his thoughts on paper and might eventually practice them in reality?

Isn't it also possible that the reason his parole officer felt he had to reveal the existence of this journal was that he felt this man had the propensity to put into practice his private written thoughts? Part of the parole officer's duties was to get to know the person assigned to him, and perhaps he felt the responsibility to try to avert potential danger to children.

Carol Belford
New York, July 19, 2001

CHANGING YOUR READERS' VIEW WITH IMAGES AS WELL AS WORDS

So far we have focused on language as the medium of communication between writer and reader. But photographs, paintings, drawings, graphs, pie charts, and other visual images can be used rhetorically to change an audience's view of a subject. With the advent of the World Wide Web and desktop publishing, facilitated by word-processing programs that easily integrate images into text, writers are increasingly using visual images to help create and support their arguments. Analysts of the 2000 Bush/Gore presidential campaign often mention the powerful effect of two images that hurt Al Gore. Figure 3.2 shows the cover of the

The rhetoric of visual images and of mathematical tables and graphs is discussed in detail in Chapters 10 and 11.

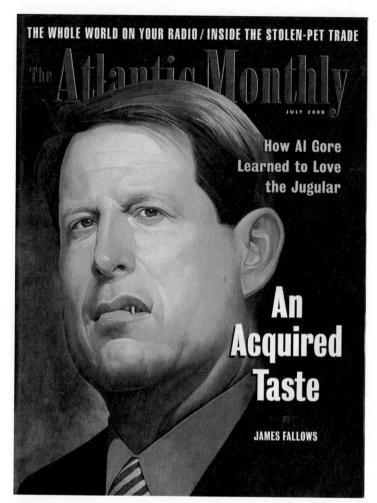

FIGURE 3.2 ■ Drawing of Al Gore on *Atlantic Monthly* Cover

Cover Art by Roberto Parada. © Roberto Parada 2002.

Atlantic Monthly for July 2000. Because *Atlantic Monthly* readers tend to be liberal, the majority of them could be expected to be Gore supporters. The effect of this drawing was to raise doubts in readers' minds about their image of a nurturing, caring Al Gore. Another influential image working against Al Gore is shown in Figure 3.3, which depicts a bug-eyed Florida ballot counter looking through a magnifying glass at a contested ballot.*

* Bush's election was made certain when the U.S. Supreme Court upheld a declaration by Florida's election commission that Bush defeated Gore in the extremely close Florida race. Gore asked for a recount of ballots in four Florida counties, resulting in highly contested disputes about what constituted a legal vote. At issue were "hanging chads" and "dimples." A "chad" is the little confetti-sized piece of paper punched out of a ballot by the voter's stylus. A chad is said to "hang" if it is not pushed out all the way but remains attached by a corner. A "dimple" occurs if the chad has been distended but not pushed out.

FIGURE 3.3 ■ Florida Ballot Counter

For Writing and Discussion

Working in small groups or as a whole class, share your answers to the following questions:

1. Consider the *Atlantic Monthly* cover and the ballot photograph to be visual arguments with implied thesis statements. What is the implied thesis of each image? What point does each one implicitly make in an argument?

2. It is fairly easy to see how the *Atlantic Monthly* cover tries to change its readers' views of Al Gore. However, the ballot photograph is more complex.

   a. How does its effect work against Al Gore's demand for a manual recount of votes during the contested Florida election?

   b. How does the visual composition of the ballot photograph—the angle from which it is shot, the way it is cropped and framed—contribute to its rhetorical effect?

   c. Imagine a photograph of ballot counters or ballot counting that would have worked in Gore's favor. How would it differ from this photograph?

3. At the beginning of each part of this text, we have included classic examples of visual arguments or presentations that use words and text together to change viewers' understanding of a topic. Your instructor may choose one or more examples of these visual arguments for discussion.

CHAPTER SUMMARY

In this chapter we have looked at the subject matter of a closed-form essay—its question, thesis, and support—from a rhetorical perspective. We have shown how thinking rhetorically causes writers to struggle with multiple perspectives. We have also shown how successful writers pose questions that interest their audiences, create surprising thesis statements aimed at changing their readers' views, and support the thesis with a network of points and particulars. We then turned to the concept of "angle of vision," showing how writers choose words and select and arrange evidence based on their particular way of seeing a subject. Finally, we have shown how a writer can change a reader's view of a topic with images as well as words.

BRIEF WRITING PROJECT

The brief writing project for this chapter will give you practice at using particulars to support a contestable thesis. At the same time, it will show you how your thesis commits you to an angle of vision that emphasizes some details and de-emphasizes others. You will see that details are not simply inert data that you can plug randomly into a paragraph to support a point. Rather, you must select and arrange data purposively and choose your words carefully for best effect.

Background: You are an assistant professor of business at Snodgrass College. One day you receive a letter from a local bank requesting a confidential evaluation of a former student, one Uriah Randolph Riddle (U. R. Riddle), who has applied for a job as a management trainee. The bank wants your assessment of Riddle's intelligence, aptitude, dependability, and ability to work with people. You haven't seen U. R. for several years, but you remember him well. Here are some facts and impressions you recall about Mr. Riddle:

- Very temperamental student, seemed moody, something of a loner
- Long hair and very sloppy dress—seemed like a misplaced street person; often twitchy and hyperactive
- Absolutely brilliant mind; took lots of liberal arts courses and applied them to business
- Wrote a term paper relating different management styles to modern theories of psychology—the best undergraduate paper you ever received. You gave it an A+ and remember learning a lot from it yourself.
- Had a strong command of language—the paper was very well written
- Good at mathematics; could easily handle all the statistical aspects of the course
- Frequently missed class and once told you that your class was boring
- Didn't show up for the midterm. When he returned to class later, he said only that he had been out of town. You let him make up the midterm, and he got an A.
- Didn't participate in a group project required for your course. He said the other students in his group were idiots.

- You thought at the time that Riddle didn't have a chance of making it in the business world because he had no talent for getting along with people.
- Other professors held similar views of Riddle—brilliant, but rather strange and hard to like; an odd duck.

You are in a dilemma because you want to give Riddle a chance (he's still young and may have had a personality transformation of some sort), but you also don't want to damage your own professional reputation by falsifying your true impressions.

> *Your task:* Using details from the preceding list, write two different letters of evaluation as follows:
>
> - In your first letter, adopt an angle of vision supportive of Riddle. Role-play that you have decided to take a gamble with Riddle and give him a chance at this career. Your thesis (worded however you want to put it) will be, in effect, "Riddle will be a good bank manager." Write as strong a recommendation as possible while remaining honest.
> - In your second letter, adopt an angle of vision that does not support Riddle. Role-play that you don't want to jeopardize your credibility with the bank when you recommend other students. Your thesis will be, in effect, "Riddle doesn't have the personality for this job." You want to warn the bank against hiring Mr. Riddle, but you don't want to hide Riddle's strengths or good points. Try to be fair but to convey an overall negative impression.

Your goal here is to write two different versions of an honest letter to the bank. You know that letters of this sort are not effective unless points are supported with specific examples and details. Which details you choose, how you word them, and how you arrange them are all part of your challenge.

Write your two letters as homework. In class, your instructor might ask you to work in groups or as a whole class to share your letters and discuss how different letters achieve different rhetorical effects. In version 1, to what extent does honesty compel you to mention all your negative memories? Is it possible to mention negative items without emphasizing them? How? In version 2, how can you mention Riddle's positive traits without undercutting your negative thesis?

CHAPTER 4

Thinking Rhetorically about Purpose, Audience, and Genre

It is amazing how much so-called writing problems clear up when the student really cares, when he is realistically put into the drama of somebody with something to say to somebody else.

—JAMES MOFFETT, *WRITING TEACHER AND THEORIST*

In Chapter 3, we showed you how to think rhetorically about your subject matter. Because writers write to an audience for a purpose, the question you pose, the thesis you assert, and the support you provide are all influenced by your intended audience and purpose. We showed you how writers seek a surprising thesis supported with convincing details and how their choice of what to include and exclude is partly determined by their audience and their angle of vision.

In this chapter, we extend our discussion of rhetorical thinking by probing three key variables in a writer's rhetorical context: purpose, audience, and genre. While thinking about subject matter, writers also think about their rhetorical context, posing questions about their purpose (What am I trying to accomplish in this paper?), their audience (What are my readers' values and assumptions? What do they already know and believe about my subject?), and genre (What kind of document am I writing? What are its requirements for structure, style, and document design?). We show how your answers to these questions influence many of the decisions you make as a writer. We end by explaining the generic rhetorical context assumed by most teachers for college papers across the disciplines.

In this chapter you will learn the following principles:

- How to think productively about your purpose, audience, and genre
- How to make decisions about structure and style based on your analysis of these elements
- How to recognize and employ document design features appropriate for different genres
- How to understand the generic rhetorical context for most college papers

HOW WRITERS THINK ABOUT PURPOSE

We said in Chapter 1 that people naturally enjoy posing and pursuing subject-matter problems. It is less clear that people naturally enjoy writing about these problems. If asked, "Why do you write?" many of you might well answer, "Because teachers like you tell me to." If given your own choice in junior or senior high, perhaps many of you might have avoided school writing as diligently as you avoided canned spinach or bad hair days.

In this section, we want to help you think productively about your purpose for writing, which can be examined from several different perspectives: the motivating occasion that gets you going, your desire to change your reader's view of your topic, and your rhetorical aim. All three perspectives will help you think productively about purpose and increase your savvy as a writer. Let's look at each in turn.

Purpose as a Response to a Motivating Occasion

If you are compelled to write because your teacher has assigned a paper, your situation is roughly parallel to that of a businessperson having to place the marketing report on her boss's desk by Friday afternoon or a team of engineers working round-the-clock to get a proposal in the mail by the fifteenth.

Almost all writing is compelled by some sort of motivating occasion or exigency.* This exigency can be external (someone giving you a task and setting a deadline) or internal (your awareness of a problem stimulating your desire to bring about some change in people's views). Thus, when engineer David Rockwood read a newspaper editorial supporting wind-power projects, his own belief in the impracticality of wind power motivated him to write a letter to the editor in rebuttal (see pp. 13–14). But he also knew that he had to write the letter within one or two days or else it stood no chance of being published. His exigency thus included both internal and external factors.

Although you might think that school is the only place where people are compelled to write, some element of external compulsion is present in nearly every writing situation. But you should understand that this external compulsion is almost never the sole motivation for writing. Consider a middle manager requested by the company vice president to write a report explaining why his division's profits are down. The manager is motivated by several factors: He wants to provide a sound analysis of why profits have declined; he wants to propose possible solutions that will remedy the situation; he wants to avoid looking personally responsible for the dip in profits; he wants to impress the vice president in the hope that she will promote him to upper management; and so on.

College students' motivations for writing can be equally complex: In part, you write to meet a deadline; in part, you write to please the teacher and get a good grade. But ideally you also write because you have become engaged with an intellectual problem and want to say something significant about it. Our point here is

---

* An *exigency* is an urgent or pressing situation requiring immediate attention. Rhetoricians use the term to describe the event or occasion that causes a writer to begin writing.

that your purposes for writing are always more complex than the simple desire to meet an assignment deadline.

Purpose as a Desire to Change Your Reader's View

See Chapter 3, pp. 43–47, for an explanation of surprise in thesis statements.

Another productive way to think about purpose is to focus on the change you want to bring about in your audience's view of the subject. When you are given a college writing assignment, this view of purpose engages you directly with the intellectual problem specified in the assignment. This view of purpose has already been introduced in Chapter 3, where we explained the importance of surprise as a measure of what is new or challenging in your essay. For most essays, you can write a one-sentence, nutshell statement about your purpose.

> My purpose is to give my readers a vivid picture of my difficult struggle with Graves' disease.
> My purpose is to raise serious doubts about the value of the traditional grading system.
> My purpose is to inform my readers about the surprising growth of the marijuana industry in the Midwestern farm states.
> My purpose is to explain how Thoreau's view of nature differs in important ways from that of contemporary environmentalists.
> My purpose is to persuade the general public that wind-generated electricity is not a practical energy alternative in the Pacific Northwest.

Chapter 19, pp. 515–516, shows you how purpose statements can be included in closed-form introductions.

In closed-form academic articles, technical reports, and other business and professional pieces, writers often place explicit purpose statements in their introductions along with the thesis. In most other forms of writing, the writer uses a behind-the-scenes purpose statement to achieve focus and direction but seldom states the purpose explicitly. Writing an explicit purpose statement for a paper is a powerful way to nutshell the kind of change you want to bring about in your reader's view of the subject.

Purpose as Rhetorical Aim

Another powerful way to think about purpose is through the general concept of "rhetorical aim." Rhetoricians have shown how specific purpose statements of the kind just discussed can be classified into broad categories based on similarities in their intended effects on readers. Situating your writing project within one or more of these broad categories can help you understand typical ways that your essay can be structured and developed. In this section, we identify six different rhetorical aims of writing: to express, to explore, to inform, to analyze and synthesize, to persuade, and to give aesthetic pleasure. The writing assignments in Part Two of this text are based on these rhetorical aims.*

* An additional aim, not quite parallel to these others, is sometimes called "writing-to-learn." When your purpose is writing-to-learn, your writing is aimed at helping you understand an important concept or learn a skill necessary for expert performance in a discipline. Teachers often design writing-to-learn assignments focusing on specific course learning goals. In Part Two of this text, the first two assignments (for Chapters 5 and 6) are writing-to-learn pieces.

Writing to Express or Share (Expressive Purpose)

When you adopt this general purpose, you place your own life—your personal experiences and reflections—at the center of your readers' attention, showing what it is like to see or feel the world your way. Writing expressively in a diary or journal has therapeutic value by allowing you to vent your feelings and explore your thoughts. Often, however, you may choose to write expressively to move or touch other readers, to make public certain moments of your own life, to invite readers to see connections between your life and theirs.

The essays in Chapter 7 illustrate writing with an expressive aim.

Expressive writing usually follows the impulse to share rather than to argue or disagree. It says, in effect, "While you read my story, you can momentarily see the world through my eyes and appreciate the uniqueness, yet commonness, of my experience." Instead of creating surprise through an argumentative thesis, expressive writing achieves surprise by offering the reader access to the private experiences of another human being.

Expressive writing usually falls near the open end of our closed-to-open continuum. When an expressive purpose is joined to a literary one (which we describe shortly), the writer produces autobiographical pieces that function in a literary way, using image, plot, character, and symbol.

Writing to Inquire or Explore (Exploratory Purpose)

Although exploratory writing is closely linked to expressive writing, it usually focuses more on subject-matter problems than on the writer's life. You use exploratory writing to wade into complexity via freewriting, idea mapping, journal keeping, note taking, e-mail exchanges, letter writing, drafting, and any other writing that probes a subject and deepens your thinking. Its goal is to help you ask questions, explore possible answers, consider alternative views, pursue conflicting trains of thought, expand and clarify your thinking, and generally delay closure on a question in order to work your way through the complexity of your subject.

The essays in Chapter 8 illustrate writing with an exploratory aim.

Exploratory writing is usually unfinished, behind-the-scenes work not intended to be read by others, but it sometimes results in a formal, finished product. In these cases, the writing aims to *pose* or *deepen* a problem, to muddy waters that the reader thought were clear. It doesn't *support* a thesis: it *seeks* a thesis. It perplexes the reader by revealing new questions about a topic, by showing how various approaches to that topic are unsatisfactory or how certain aspects of a topic are more problematic than previously supposed. Because exploratory writing often takes a narrative shape, dramatizing the process of the writer's thinking about a subject, it usually falls toward the open end of the closed-to-open continuum.

Writing to Inform or Explain (Informative Purpose)

When your purpose is informative, you see yourself as more knowledgeable than your reader about your topic. You create surprise by enlarging the reader's view of a topic, providing new ideas and information based on your own experiences or research. When you write to inform, you adopt the role of teacher in relation to your reader. You imagine that the reader will trust your authority and not dispute what you say. Although informative writing usually has a closed-form structure, it may fall anywhere along the continuum from closed to open.

The essays in Chapter 9 illustrate writing with an informative aim.

Writing to Analyze, Synthesize, or Interpret (Analysis/Synthesis Purpose)

When your purpose is to analyze and synthesize, you examine problematic aspects of a subject and, through your own critical thinking and research, offer tentative ways to resolve these problems. When you analyze a subject, you break it down into its parts to see the relationships among them and to understand the whole better. For instance, you might examine the parts of an article on public transportation published in a public affairs magazine to see what kinds of evidence it uses to support its main claim and how the article appeals to its target audience. When you synthesize, you put together ideas you have gathered from your various analyses into a new whole that represents your enlarged and enriched understanding of a subject or issue. In a synthesis, you present your new informed independent view. For example, after reading several articles on proposed public transportation plans for your city, you might write a synthesis essay that explains what you consider the most feasible and most publicly supported solution to the local traffic problem. When you analyze and synthesize, your goal is to challenge your readers with a new or more illuminating way of seeing, thinking about, or understanding your subject, often unsettling your readers' old familiar ways of regarding the text, data, or phenomenon.

Analytic writing, combined with synthesis, constitutes the most common kind of academic prose. It typically takes a closed-form structure. The introduction poses a question about the text, data set, or phenomenon being examined. The body presents the writer's attempt to answer or resolve the question. Because the readers generally regard the solution as *tentative*, the writer must support it with good arguments and particulars. Analytic writing presupposes a more skeptical audience than does informative prose. The writer might not expect readers to argue back, but will certainly expect them to test his or her ideas against their own experiences and hypotheses.

Writing to Persuade (Persuasive Purpose)

When your purpose is persuasive, you enter a conversation in which people are in disagreement over a controversial issue. You think of your audience as jurors who must be convinced that your position on the issue is sounder than other positions. When you write to persuade, you surprise your readers with reasons and evidence that you hope will sway them to your view of the issue and thereby change their beliefs or actions.

Persuasive writing can fall anywhere along the closed-to-open continuum. It often takes the form of a tightly structured, closed-form argument consisting of reasons and evidence set out in a logical, point-by-point format. But it may also have a very open structure; for example, a powerful story or a collage of emotionally charged scenes might be extremely persuasive in influencing readers' views on an issue.

When writing persuasively, writers usually imagine skeptical readers vigorously questioning their claims. Writers must therefore anticipate and respond to objections, actively appreciating and role-playing alternative points of view. This emphasis on accommodating alternative views and on appealing to the values and beliefs of the readers distinguishes persuasive writing from most analytic writing.

Chapter 13 offers further explanation of analysis and synthesis.

The essays in Chapters 10–14 illustrate different kinds of analysis and synthesis.

We call a closed-form persuasive piece a "classical argument," which we treat in detail in Chapter 15.

The essays in Chapters 15–17 illustrate various kinds of persuasive writing.

Writing to Entertain or Give Aesthetic Pleasure (Literary Purpose)
Sometimes writers focus not on themselves (expressive prose), nor on the subject matter (exploratory, informative, and analytic prose), nor on the reader (persuasive prose), but on the artistic shaping of language. When you adopt a literary purpose, you treat language as a medium like paint or clay. You explore its properties and its sounds and rhythms. We typically think of literary writing as fiction or poetry, but nonfiction prose can also use literary techniques. Such prose is often called "literary nonfiction" or "belletristic prose." Literary nonfiction usually combines a literary purpose with one or more other purposes—for example, an expressive purpose (an autobiographical essay about a turning point in your life) or an exploratory purpose (your contemplation of a spiderweb).

The essays in Chapter 20 on open-form writing illustrate nonfiction writing with a literary purpose.

For Writing and Discussion

As a class, choose one of the following topic areas or another provided by your instructor. Then imagine six different writing situations in which a hypothetical writer would compose an essay about the selected topic. Let each situation call for a different purpose. How might a person write about the selected topic with an expressive purpose? An exploratory purpose? An informative purpose? An analytic purpose? A persuasive purpose? A literary purpose? How would each essay surprise its readers?

baseball	animals	hospices or nursing homes*
homelessness	music	dating or marriage
advertising	elections	school violence

Working on your own or in small groups, create six realistic scenarios, each of which calls for prose in a different category of purpose. Then share your results as a whole class. Here are two examples based on the topic "hospices."

Expressive Purpose	Working one summer as a volunteer in a hospice for dying cancer patients, you befriend a woman whose attitude toward death changes your life. You write an autobiographical essay about your experiences with this remarkable woman.
Analytic Purpose	You are a hospice nurse working in a home care setting. You and your colleagues note that sometimes family members cannot adjust psychologically to the burden of living with a dying person. You decide to investigate this phenomenon. You interview "reluctant" family members in an attempt to understand the causes of their psychological discomfort so that you can provide better counseling services as a possible solution. You write a paper for a professional audience analyzing the results of your interviews.

---

* If this topic interests you, see how student writer Sheridan Botts wrote about hospices, first with an exploratory purpose (Ch. 8, pp. 185–188) and later with a persuasive purpose (Ch. 17, pp. 456–459).

HOW WRITERS THINK ABOUT AUDIENCE

In our discussion of purpose, we already had a lot to say about audience. What you know about your readers—their familiarity with your subject matter, their reasons for reading, their closeness to you, their values and beliefs—affects most of the choices you make as a writer.

The value of moving from old information to new information is explained in Chapter 19, pp. 499–500 and 512–514.

In assessing your audience, you must first consider what, to them, is old information and what is new information. You'll ask questions like these: What in my essay will be familiar and what will be new, challenging, and surprising? How much background will my readers need? What can I assume they know and don't know? What is their current view of my topic that I am trying to change?

As you think about your readers' current views on your topic, you also need to think about their methods and reasons for reading. Imagine that you want to persuade your boss to reconfigure your office's computer network. You've discussed your ideas with her briefly, and she's asked you to write a formal proposal for the next technology meeting. Knowing of her harried environment—people waiting to see her, meetings to attend, e-mails piling up, memos and reports filling her in-box—you use a tightly closed structure for your proposal. Your document must be clear, concise, summarizable, and immediately comprehensible. The same reader in a different mood and setting may turn to a more leisurely kind of prose, say an article in her favorite magazine or a new book on her favorite subject, where she might enjoy the subtlety and stylistic pleasures of open-form prose.

Now consider how a change in audience can affect the content of a piece. Suppose you want voters in your city to approve a bond issue to build a new baseball stadium. If most members of your audience are baseball fans, you can appeal to their love of the game, the pleasure of a new facility, and so forth. But nonbaseball fans won't be moved by these arguments. To reach them, you must tie the new baseball stadium to their values. You can argue that a new stadium will bring new tax revenues to the city, clean up a run-down area, revitalize local businesses, or stimulate the tourist industry. Your purpose remains the same—to persuade taxpayers to fund the stadium—but the content of your argument changes if your audience changes.

In college, you often seem to be writing for an audience of one—your instructor. However, most instructors try to read as a representative of a broader audience. To help college writers imagine these readers, many instructors try to design writing assignments that provide a fuller sense of audience. They may ask you to write for the readers of a particular magazine or journal, or they may create case assignments with built-in audiences (for example, "You are an accountant in the firm of Numbers and Fudge; one day you receive a letter from . . ."). If your instructor does not specify an audience, you can generally assume the audience to be what we like to call "the generic academic audience"— student peers who have approximately the same level of knowledge and expertise in the field as you do, who are engaged by the question you address, and who want to read your writing and be surprised in some way.

Assessing Your Audience

In any writing situation, you can use the following questions to help you make decisions about content, form, and style:

1. Who is going to read what I write? A specific individual? A specific group with special interests? Or a general readership with wide-ranging interests and backgrounds?

2. What relationship do I have to these readers? Do I and my readers have an informal, friendly relationship or a polite, formal one? Is my readers' expertise in my general subject area greater, less, or equal to mine?

3. How much do my readers already know about the specific problem I address? How much background will I have to provide?

4. How much interest do my readers bring to my topic? Do I need to hook readers with a vivid opening and use special techniques to maintain their interest throughout? Or are they interested enough in the problem I am examining that the subject matter itself will drive their reading? (In persuasive writing, particularly in writing that proposes a solution to a problem, you may need to shock your readers into awareness that the problem exists.)

How to hook your readers' interest through an effective introduction is covered in Chapter 19, pp. 512–515.

5. What are my audience's values, beliefs, and assumptions in relation to my topic? If I am writing on a controversial issue, will my readers oppose my position, be neutral to it, or support it? To which of their values, beliefs, or assumptions can I appeal? Will my position unsettle or threaten my audience or stimulate a strong emotional response? (Because a concern for audience is particularly relevant to persuasive writing, we treat these questions in more depth in Chapters 15 through 17.)

Posing these questions will not lead to any formulaic solutions to your writing problems, but it can help you develop strategies that will appeal to your audience and enable you to achieve your purpose.

For Writing and Discussion

Working on your own, imagine that you enjoyed a fun party last weekend. (a) Describe that party in a letter to a close friend, inventing the details needed to show your friend how great the party was. (b) Describe the same party in a letter to a parent (or some other person whose differences from your friend would lead to a different description.) Note: You may substitute any other event or phenomenon that you could describe in different ways to different audiences.

Then, in small groups or as a class, share excerpts from your two letters. What changes did you make in your description as a result of changes in your audience?

HOW WRITERS THINK ABOUT GENRE

The term *genre* refers to broad categories of writing that follow certain conventions of style, structure, approach to subject matter, and document design. Literary genres include the short story, the novel, the epic poem, the limerick, the sonnet, and so forth. Nonfiction prose has its own genres: the business memo, the technical manual, the scholarly article, the scientific report, the popular magazine article (each magazine, actually, has its own particular conventions), the Web page, the five-paragraph theme (a school genre), the newspaper editorial, the cover letter for a job application, the legal contract, the advertising brochure, and so forth.

The concept of genre creates strong reader expectations and places specific demands on writers. How you write any given letter, report, or article is influenced by the structure and style of hundreds of previous letters, reports, or articles written in the same genre. If you wanted to write for *Reader's Digest,* for example, you would have to use the conventions that appeal to its older, conservative readers: simple language, subjects with strong human interest, heavy reliance on anecdotal evidence in arguments, an upbeat and optimistic perspective, and an approach that reinforces the conservative ethos of individualism, self-discipline, and family. If you wanted to write for *Seventeen* or *Rolling Stone,* however, you would need to use quite different conventions.

To illustrate the relationship of a writer to a genre, we sometimes draw an analogy with clothing. Although most people have a variety of different types of clothing in their wardrobes, the genre of activity for which they are dressing (Saturday night movie date, job interview, wedding) severely constrains their choice and expression of individuality. A man dressing for a job interview might express his personality through choice of tie or quality and style of business suit; he probably wouldn't express it by wearing a Hawaiian shirt and sandals. Even when people deviate from a convention, they tend to do so in a conventional way. For example, teenagers who do not want to follow the genre of "teenager admired by adults" form their own genre of purple hair and pierced body parts. The concept of genre raises intriguing and sometimes unsettling questions about the relationship of the unique self to a social convention or tradition.

These same kinds of questions and constraints perplex writers. For example, academic writers usually follow the genre of the closed-form scholarly article. This highly functional form achieves maximum clarity for readers by orienting them quickly to the article's purpose, content, and structure. Readers expect this format, and writers have the greatest chance of being published if they meet these expectations. In some disciplines, however, scholars are beginning to publish more experimental, open-form articles. They may slowly alter the conventions of the scholarly article, just as fashion designers alter styles of dress.

For an example of a scientific research report, see "Women and Smoking in Hollywood Movies: A Content Analysis," pp. 138–144.

The genre of the scholarly article varies enormously from discipline to discipline, both in the kinds of questions that specialists pose about their subject matter and in the style and structure of articles. As a specific example of a genre that many college students regularly encounter, we have placed a description of the *scientific research report* on the next page. This genre is commonly used in fields that conduct empirical research, such as the physical or social sciences, nursing, medicine, business, engineering, education, and other fields.

For Writing and Discussion

1. On this page we offered you a brief description of the conventions governing *Reader's Digest* articles, which appeal mainly to older, conservative readers. For this exercise, prepare similar descriptions of the conventions that govern articles in several other magazines such as *Rolling Stone, Sports Illustrated,*

The Scientific Research Report

A scientific research report, sometimes called an "experimental" or "technical" report, is a formal paper addressed primarily to professionals who are interested in the results of an investigation. Its readers want to know why the investigation was undertaken, how it was conducted, what was learned, and whether the findings are significant and useful. Experimental reports usually follow a standard five-part format:

1. *Introduction.* This section explains the purpose of the investigation, what problem was addressed, and what makes the problem both problematic and significant. The introduction often includes a review of the literature that summarizes previous research addressing the same or a related problem. In many scientific disciplines, it is conventional to conclude the introduction with a hypothesis, a tentative answer to the question, which the investigation confirms or disconfirms.
2. *Methods.* Sometimes called *methodology* or *procedures,* the methods section details in cookbook fashion how the investigators conducted the research. It provides enough details so that other researchers can replicate the investigation. This section usually includes the following subsections: (a) research design; (b) apparatus and materials; and (c) procedures followed.
3. *Findings (results).* This section presents the empirical results of the investigation, the data discovered in the experiment. The findings may be displayed in figures, tables, graphs, or charts. Usually, the findings are not interpreted in this section.
4. *Discussion.* This section is the main part of the scientific report. It explains the significance of the findings by relating what was discovered to the problem set out in the introduction and by detailing how the investigation did or did not accomplish its original purpose—that is, whether it answered the questions outlined in the introduction. (Did it confirm/disconfirm the writer's hypothesis?) This section also discusses the usefulness and significance of the findings and explores new questions raised by the experiment.
5. *Conclusions and recommendations.* This last section focuses on the main points learned from the investigation and, in some cases, on the practical applications of the investigation. If the investigation was a pure research project, this section often summarizes the most important findings and recommends areas for further research. If the investigation was aimed at making a practical decision (for example, an engineering design decision), this section recommends appropriate actions.

Cosmopolitan, Details, The New Yorker, or *Psychology Today.* Each person should bring to class a copy of a magazine that he or she enjoys reading. The class should then divide into small groups according to similar interests. Your instructor may supply a few scholarly journals from different disciplines. In preparing a brief profile of your magazine, consider the following:

- Scan the table of contents. What kinds of subjects or topics does the magazine cover?
- Look at the average length of articles. How much depth and analysis are provided?
- Consider the magazine's readership. Does the magazine appeal to particular political or social groups (liberal/conservative, male/female, young/old, white-collar/blue-collar, in-group/general readership)?

(continued)

- ■ Look at the advertisements. What kinds of products are most heavily advertised in the magazine? Who is being targeted by these advertisements? What percentage of the magazine consists of advertisements?

- ■ Read representative pages, including the introductions, of some articles. Would you characterize the prose as difficult or easy? Intellectual or popular? Does the prose use the jargon, slang, or other language particular to a group? Are the paragraphs long or short? How are headings, inserts, visuals, and other page-formatting features used? Is the writing formal or informal?

- ■ Think about what advice you would give a person who wanted to write a freelance article for this magazine.

2. Imagine that someone interested in hospices (see the example in the For Writing and Discussion exercise on p. 65) wanted to write an article about hospices for your chosen magazine. What approach would the writer have to take to have a hospice-related article published in your magazine? There may be no chance of this happening, but be creative. Here is an example:

> Ordinarily *Sports Illustrated* would be an unlikely place for an article on hospices. However, *SI* might publish a piece about a dying athlete in a hospice setting. It might also publish a piece about sports memories of dying patients or about watching sports as therapy.

RHETORICAL CONTEXT AND YOUR CHOICES ABOUT STRUCTURE

So far in this chapter, we have examined purpose, audience, and genre as components of a writer's rhetorical context. In this section and the next, our goal is to help you appreciate how these variables influence a writer's choices regarding structure and style. Although there is no formula that allows you to determine an appropriate structure and style based on particular purposes, audiences, and genres, there are some rules of thumb that can help you make decisions. Let's look first at structure.

Because most academic, business, and professional writing uses a closed-form structure, we spend a significant portion of this text advising you how to write such prose. But open-form prose is equally valuable and is often more subtle, complex, and beautiful, so it is good to practice writing at different positions on the continuum. The following advice will help you decide when closed or open forms are more appropriate:

When is closed-form prose most appropriate?

- ■ When your focus is on the subject matter itself and your goal is to communicate efficiently to maximize clarity. In these cases, your purpose is usually to inform, analyze, or persuade.

- ■ When you imagine your audience as a busy or harried reader who needs to be able to read quickly and process ideas rapidly. Closed-form prose is easy to summarize; moreover, a reader can speed-read closed-form prose by scanning the introduction and then glancing at headings and the openings of paragraphs, where writers place key points.

- When the conventional genre for your context is closed-form writing and you choose to meet, rather than break, readers' expectations.
- When you encounter any rhetorical situation that asks you to assert and support a thesis in response to a problem or question.

When is a more open form desirable?

- When you want to delay your thesis rather than announce it in the introduction (for example, to create suspense). A delayed thesis structure is less combative and more friendly; it conveys an unfolding "let's think through this together" feeling.
- When your purpose is expressive, exploratory, or literary. These purposes tend to be served better through narrative rather than through thesis-with-support writing.
- When you imagine your audience reading primarily for enjoyment and pleasure. In this context you can often wed a literary purpose to another purpose.
- When the conventional genre calls for open-form writing—for example, autobiographical narratives, character sketches, or personal reflective pieces. Popular magazine articles often have a looser, more open structure than do scholarly articles or business reports.
- When you are writing about something that is too complex or messy to be captured in a fixed thesis statement, or when you feel constrained by the genre of thesis with support.

RHETORICAL CONTEXT AND YOUR CHOICES ABOUT STYLE

Writers need to make choices not only about structure but also about style. By *style,* we mean the choices you make about how to say something. Writers can say essentially the same thing in a multitude of ways, each placing the material in a slightly different light, subtly altering meaning, and slightly changing the effect on readers. In this section we illustrate more concretely the many stylistic options open to you and explain how you might go about making stylistic choices.

Factors That Affect Style

As we shall see, style is a complex composite of many factors. We can classify the hundreds of variables that affect style into four broad categories:

1. *Ways of shaping sentences:* long/short, simple/complex, many modifiers/few modifiers, normal word order/frequent inversions or interruptions, mostly main clauses/many embedded phrases and subordinate clauses
2. *Types of words:* abstract/concrete, formal/colloquial, unusual/ordinary, specialized/general, metaphoric/literal, scientific/literary
3. *The implied personality projected by the writer (often called* voice *or* personal*):* expert/layperson, scholar/student, outsider/insider, political liberal/conservative, neutral observer/active participant

4. *The writer's implied relationship to the reader and the subject matter (often called* tone*):* intimate/distant, personal/impersonal, angry/calm, browbeating/sharing, informative/entertaining, humorous/serious, ironic/literal, passionately involved/aloof

Recognizing Different Styles and Voices

When discussing style, rhetoricians often use related terms such as *voice* and *persona*. We can distinguish these terms by thinking of style as analyzable textual features on a page (length and complexity of sentences, level of abstraction, and so forth) and of voice or persona as the reader's impression of the writer projected from the page. Through your stylistic choices, you create an image of yourself in your readers' minds. This image can be cold or warm, insider or outsider, humorous or serious, detached or passionate, scholarly or hip, antagonistic or friendly, and so forth.

What style you adopt depends on your purpose, audience, and genre. Consider, for example, the following thought exercise: Suppose you are interested in the subject of flirting. (Perhaps you have asked a research question such as the following: How has concern about sexual harassment affected views on flirting in the workplace? Or, When is flirting psychologically and emotionally healthy?) You decide to do library research on flirting and are surprised by the different styles and genres you encounter. Here are the opening paragraphs of three different articles that discuss flirting—from a scholarly journal, from a fairly intellectual special interest magazine, and from a popular magazine devoted to women's dating and fashion. At the moment, we are considering only differences in the verbal styles of these articles. Later in this chapter, we reproduce the actual opening pages of two of these articles as they originally appeared in order to discuss document design.

Scholarly Journal

[From the *Journal of Sex Research*]
Sexual Messages: Comparing Findings from Three Studies

Sexual socialization is influenced by a wide range of sources, including parents, peers, and the mass media (Hyde & DeLameter, 1997). In trying to understand the process by which young people acquire their sexual beliefs, attitudes, and behaviors, the study of media provides information about potential socializing messages that are an important part of everyday life for children and adolescents (Greenberg, Brown, & Buerkel-Rothfuss, 1993). The significance of media content in this realm stems from a number of unique aspects surrounding its role in the lives of youth, including its early accessibility and its almost universal reach across the population.

Electronic media, and television in particular, provide a window to many parts of the world, such as sexually related behavior, that would otherwise be shielded from young audiences. Long before many parents begin to discuss sex with their children, answers to such questions as "When is it OK to have sex?" and "With whom does one have sexual relations?" are provided by messages delivered on television. These messages are hardly didactic, most often coming in the form of scripts and plots in fictional entertainment programs. Yet the fact that such programs do not intend to teach sexual socialization lessons hardly mitigates the potential influence of their portrayals.

—Dale Kunkel, Kirstie M. Cope, and Erica Biely

Special Interest Magazine

[From *Psychology Today*]
The New Flirting Game

"It may be an ages-old, biologically-driven activity, but today it's also played with artful self-awareness and even conscious calculation" [opening lead in large, all-caps text].

To hear the evolutionary determinists tell it, we human beings flirt to propagate our genes and to display our genetic worth. Men are constitutionally predisposed to flirt with the healthiest, most fertile women, recognizable by their biologically correct waist-hip ratios. Women favor the guys with dominant demeanors, throbbing muscles and the most resources to invest in their offspring.

Looked at up close, human psychology is more diverse and perverse than the evolutionary determinists would have it. We flirt as thinking individuals in a particular culture at a particular time. Yes, we may express a repertoire of hardwired nonverbal expressions and behaviors—staring eyes, flashing brows, opened palms—that resemble those of other animals, but unlike other animals, we also flirt with conscious calculation. We have been known to practice our techniques in front of the mirror. In other words, flirting among human beings is culturally modulated as well as biologically driven, as much art as instinct.

—Deborah A. Lott

Women's Dating and Fashion Magazine

[From *Cosmopolitan*]
Flirting with Disaster

"I'd never be unfaithful, but . . ." [opening lead in very large type].

"You're in love and totally committed—or are you? You dirty danced with a cute guy at the office party, and make an effort to look sexy for the man in the coffee shop. Are you cheating without knowing it?" [second lead in large type]

I think I've been cheating on my partner. Let me explain. I went out clubbing recently with a really good friend, a guy I've known for years. We both love to dance. [. . .] [W]henever we get together, there comes a moment, late in the evening, when I look at him and feel myself beginning to melt. [. . .] This is not the way people who are "just friends" touch each other.

[. . .] So I suppose the question is, at what point does flirting stop being harmless fun and become an actual betrayal of your relationship?

—Lisa Sussman and Tracey Cox

For Writing and Discussion

Working in small groups or as a whole class, analyze the differences in the styles of these three samples.

1. How would you describe differences in the length and complexity of sentences, in the level of vocabulary, and in the degree of formality?

2. How do the differences in styles create different voices, personas, and tones?

(continued)

3. Based on clues from style and genre, who is the intended audience of each piece? What is the writer's purpose? How does each writer hope to surprise the intended audience with something new, challenging, or valuable?

4. How are the differences in content and style influenced by differences in purpose, audience, and genre?

RHETORICAL CONTEXT AND YOUR CHOICES ABOUT DOCUMENT DESIGN

When thinking about structure and style, writers also need to consider document design. Document design refers to the visual features of a text. The "look" of a document is closely bound to the rhetorical context, to the way writers seek to communicate with particular audiences for particular purposes, and to the audience's expectations for that genre of writing. In this section, we explain the main components of document design that you will encounter as a reader. In Chapter 19, Lesson 8, we explain some principles of document design that you can use as a writer for producing different kinds of texts.

Historically, the use of images to convey information is more important than we may realize. Alphabets, for example, derived from picture drawings, and in earlier centuries, when only a small portion of the population could read, images—such as on signs—were an important means of communication. Now in the twenty-first century, some cultural critics theorize that we are moving from a text-based culture to an image-based culture. These critics speculate that visual communication has become more important, partly because of the increased pace of life, the huge volume of information that bombards us daily, and the constantly improving technology for creating better and more varied electronic images. We rely more heavily on information transmitted visually, and we depend on receiving that information more quickly. Visual details become a shorthand code for conveying this information concisely, quickly, and vividly. The visual details of document design are part of a code for recognizing genres and part of audience expectations that writers must meet.

As a writer, you are often expected to produce manuscript (typed pages of text) rather than a publication-ready document.* When your task is to produce manuscript, your concerns for document design usually focus on margins, font style and size, location of page numbers, and line spacing. As an academic writer, you generally produce manuscripts following the style guidelines of the Modern Language Association (MLA), the American Psychological Association (APA), or some other scholarly organization. In business and professional settings, you employ different kinds of manuscript conventions for writing letters, memoranda, or reports.

Chapter 23, pp. 617–667, explains MLA and APA conventions.

In contrast to manuscript, today's writers are sometimes asked to use desktop publishing software to produce camera-ready or Web-ready documents that have a professional visual appeal (such as a pamphlet or brochure, a Web page, a

---

* The word *manuscript* literally means "hand writing" and refers to the days when writers submitted pen-and-ink copies to a printer. Today we should probably call what writers produce from their computers a "typescript" or "computer printout," but the old word "manuscript" is still the most common.

poster, a marketing proposal that incorporates visuals and graphics, or some oth-er piece with a "professionally published" look). Occasionally in your manuscript documents, you may want to display ideas or information visually—for example, with graphs, tables, or images.

See Chapter 11 for suggestions about when and how to use graphics and tables.

Key Components of Document Design

The main components of document design are use of type, use of space and lay-out, use of color, and use of graphics or images.

Use of Type

Type comes in different typeface styles, or fonts, that are commonly grouped in three font families: serif fonts that have tiny extensions on the letters, which make them easier to read for long documents; sans serif fonts that lack these extensions on the letters and are good for labels, headings, and Web documents; and specialty fonts, often used for decorative effect, that include script fonts and special symbols. Common word processing programs usually give you a huge array of fonts. Some examples of different fonts are shown in the box below.

Fonts also come in different sizes, measured in points (one point = 1/72 of an inch). Much type in printed texts is set in ten or twelve points. In addition, fonts can be formatted in different ways: boldface, italics, underlining, or shading.

Font style and size contribute to the readability and overall impression of a text. Scholarly publications use few, plain, and regular font styles that don't draw atten-tion to the type. Their use of fonts seeks to keep the readers' focus on the content of the document, to convey a serious tone, and to maximize the readers' conven-ience in grappling with the ideas of the text. (Teachers regularly expect a conserva-tive font such as CG Times, Times New Roman, or Courier New for academic papers. Were you to submit an academic paper in a specialty or scripted font, you'd make a "notice me" statement, analogous to wearing a lime green jumpsuit to a college reception.) In academic papers, boldface can be used for headings and italics for occasional emphasis, but otherwise design flourishes are seldom used.

Popular magazines, on the other hand, tend to use fonts playfully and artisti-cally, using a variety of fonts and sizes to attract readers' attention initially and to make a document look pleasingly decorative on the page. Although the body text

Examples of Font Styles		
FONT STYLE	FONT NAME	EXAMPLE
Serif fonts	Times New Roman	Have a good day!
	Courier New	Have a good day!
Sans serif fonts	Arial	**Have a good day!**
	Century Gothic	Have a good day!
Specialty fonts	Monotype Corsiva	*Have a good day!*
	Symbol	Ηαϖε α γοοδ δαψ!

of articles is usually the same font throughout, the opening page often uses a variety of fonts and sizes, and font variations may occur throughout the text to highlight key ideas for readers who are reading casually or rapidly.

Use of Space and Layout of Documents

Layout refers to how the text is formatted on the page. Layout includes the following elements:

- The size of the page itself
- The proportion of text to white space
- The arrangement of text on the page (single or multiple columns, long or short paragraphs, spaces between paragraphs)
- The size of the margins
- The use of justification (alignment of text with the left margin or both margins)
- The placement of titles
- The use of headings and subheadings to signal main and subordinate ideas and main parts of the document
- The spacing before and after headings
- The use of numbered or bulleted lists
- The use of boxes to highlight ideas or break text into visual units

Academic and scholarly writing calls for simple, highly functional document layouts. Most scholarly journals use single or double columns of text that are justified at both margins to create a regular, even look. (In preparing an academic manuscript, however, justify only the left-hand margin, leaving the right margin ragged.) Layout—particularly the presentation of titles and headings and the formatting of notes and bibliographic data—is determined by the style of the individual journal, which treats all articles identically. The layout of scholarly documents strikes a balance between maximizing the amount of text that fits on a page and ensuring readability by using headings and providing adequate white space in the margins.

In contrast, popular magazines place text in multiple columns that are often varied and broken up by text in boxes or by text wrapped around photos or drawings. Readability is important, but so is visual appeal and entertainment: readers must enjoy looking at the pages. Many popular magazines try to blur the distinction between content and advertising so that ads become part of the visual appeal. This is why, in fashion magazines, the table of contents is often buried a dozen or more pages into the magazine. The publisher wants to coax readers to look at the ads as they look for the contents. (In contrast, the table of contents for most academic journals is on the cover.)

Use of Color

Colors convey powerful messages and appeals, even affecting moods. While manuscripts are printed entirely in black, published documents often use color to identify and set off main ideas or important information. Color-tinted boxes can indicate special features or allow magazines to print different but related articles on the same page.

Academic and scholarly articles and books use color minimally, if at all, relying instead on different font styles and sizes to make distinctions in content. Popular magazines, on the other hand, use colors playfully, artistically, decoratively, and strategically to enhance their appeal and, thus, their sales. Different colors of type may be used for different articles within one magazine or within articles themselves. Some articles may be printed on colored paper to give variety to the whole magazine.

Use of Graphics or Images

Graphics include visual displays of information such as tables, line graphs, bar graphs, pie charts, maps, cartoons, illustrations, and photos.

As with the use of type, space, and color, the use of graphics indicates the focus, seriousness, function, and complexity of the writing. In scientific articles and books, many of the important findings of the articles may be displayed in complex, technical graphs and tables. Sources of information for these graphics are usually prominently stated, with key variables clearly labeled. In the humanities and social sciences, content-rich photos and drawings also tend to be vital parts of an article, even the subject of the analysis.

How visuals convey an argument is discussed in Chapter 3, pp. 55–57. More detailed discussion of drawings and photographs is found in Chapter 10 and of numeric visuals in Chapter 11.

Popular magazines typically use simple numeric visuals (for example, a colorful pie chart or a dramatic graph) combined with decorative use of images, especially photos. If photos appear, it is worthwhile to consider how they are used. For example, do photos aim to look realistic and spontaneous like documentary photos of disaster scenes, sports moments, or people at work, or are they highly constructed, aesthetic photos? (Note that many political photos are meant to look spontaneous but are actually highly scripted—for example, a photograph of the president mending a fence with a horse nearby). Are they concept (thematic) photos meant to illustrate an idea in an article (for example, a picture of a woman surrounded by images of pills, doctors, expensive medical equipment, and wrangling employers and insurance agents, to illustrate an article on health care costs)? The use of photos and illustrations can provide important clues about a publication's angle of vision, philosophy, or political leaning. For example, the *Utne Reader* tends to use many colored drawings rather than photos to illustrate its articles. These funky drawings with muted colors suit the magazine's liberal, socially progressive, and activist angle of vision.

Understanding the political slant of magazines, newspapers, and Web sites is essential for researchers. See Chapter 22, pp. 603–604.

Examples of Different Document Designs

In our earlier discussion of style, we reprinted the opening paragraphs of three articles on flirting. Figures 4.1 and 4.2 show the opening pages of two of these articles as they appeared in *The Journal of Sex Research* and *Psychology Today* (*Cosmopolitan* would not permit these images in its opening two-page spread to be reproduced for this textbook. However, we describe the opening pages in some detail in the For Writing and Discussion exercise on page 80, discussion question 4).

Sexual Messages on Television: Comparing Findings From Three Studies

Dale Kunkel, Kirstie M. Cope, and Erica Biely
University of California Santa Barbara

Television portrayals may contribute to the sexual socialization of children and adolescents, and therefore it is important to examine the patterns of sexual content presented on television. This report presents a summary view across three related studies of sexual messages on television. The content examined ranges from programs most popular with adolescents to a comprehensive, composite week sample of shows aired across the full range of broadcast and cable channels. The results across the three studies identify a number of consistent patterns in television's treatment of sexual content. Talk about sex and sexual behaviors are both found frequently across the television landscape, although talk about sex is more common. Most sexual behaviors tend to be precursory in nature (such as physical flirting and kissing), although intercourse is depicted or strongly implied in roughly one of every eight shows on television. Perhaps most importantly, the studies find that TV rarely presents messages about the risks or responsibilities associated with sexual behavior.

Sexual socialization is influenced by a wide range of sources, including parents, peers, and the mass media (Hyde & DeLameter, 1997). In trying to understand the process by which young people acquire their sexual beliefs, attitudes, and behaviors, the study of media provides information about potential socializing messages that are an important part of everyday life for children and adolescents (Greenberg, Brown, & Buerkel-Rothfuss, 1993). The significance of media content in this realm stems from a number of unique aspects surrounding its role in the lives of youth, including its early accessibility and its almost universal reach across the population.

Electronic media, and television in particular, provide a window to many parts of the world, such as sexually-related behavior, that would otherwise be shielded from young audiences. Long before many parents begin to discuss sex with their children, answers to such questions as "When is it OK to have sex?" and "With whom does one have sexual relations?" are provided by messages delivered on television. These messages are hardly didactic, most often coming in the form of scripts and plots in fictional entertainment programs. Yet the fact that such programs do not intend to teach sexual socialization lessons hardly mitigates the potential influence of their portrayals.

While television is certainly not the only influence on sexual socialization, adolescents often report that they use portrayals in the media to learn sexual and romantic scripts and norms for sexual behavior (Brown, Childers, & Waszak, 1990). Indeed, four out of ten (40%) teens say they have gained ideas for how to talk to their boyfriend or girlfriend about sexual issues directly from media portrayals (Kaiser Family Foundation, 1998).

Just as it is well established that media exposure influences social behaviors such as aggression and social stereotyping, there is a growing body of evidence documenting the possible effects of sexual content on television (Huston, Wartella, & Donnerstein, 1998). For example, two studies have reported correlations between watching television programs high in sexual content and the early initiation of sexual intercourse by adolescents (Brown & Newcomer, 1991; Peterson, Moore, & Furstenberg, 1991), while another found heavy television viewing to be predictive of negative attitudes toward remaining a virgin (Courtright & Baran, 1980). An experiment by Bryant and Rockwell (1994) showed that teens who had just viewed television dramas laden with sexual content rated descriptions of casual sexual encounters less negatively than teens who had not viewed any sexual material.

Another important aspect of sexual socialization involves the development of knowledge about appropriate preventative behaviors to reduce the risk of infection from AIDS or other sexually-transmitted diseases. When teenagers begin to engage in sexual activity, they assume the risk of disease as well as the risk of unwanted pregnancy, and it appears that many lack adequate preparation to avoid such negative consequences.

Two Americans under the age of 20 become infected with HIV every hour (Office of National AIDS Policy, 1996). Almost one million teenagers become pregnant every year in the United States (Kirby, 1997). In the face of these sobering statistics, it is important to consider the extent to which media portrayals engage in or overlook concerns such as these, which are very serious issues in the lives of young people today.

In summary, media effects research clearly suggests that television portrayals contribute to sexual socialization.

The Family Hour Study was supported by the Henry J. Kaiser Family Foundation (Menlo Park, CA) and Children Now (Oakland, CA). The Teen Study was the Master's Thesis for Kirstie M. Cope. The V-Chip Study was supported by the Henry J. Kaiser Family Foundation. The authors wish to thank Carolyn Colvin, Ed Donnerstein, Wendy Jo Farinola, Ulla Foehr, Jim Potter, Vicky Rideout, and Emma Rollin, each of whom made significant contributions to one or more of the studies summarized here.

Address correspondence to Dr. Dale Kunkel, Department of Communication, University of California Santa Barbara, Santa Barbara, CA 93106: e-mail: kunkel@ahshaw.ucsb.edu.

The Journal of Sex Research   Volume 36, Number 3, August 1999: pp. 230–236

FIGURE 4.1 ▪ Opening Page from Article in the *Journal of Sex Research*

THE NEW
Flirting Game

IT MAY BE AN AGES-OLD, BIOLOGICALLY-DRIVEN ACTIVITY, BUT TODAY IT'S ALSO PLAYED WITH ARTFUL SELF-AWARENESS AND EVEN CONSCIOUS CALCULATION.

By Deborah A. Lott

To hear the evolutionary determinists tell it, we human beings flirt to propagate our genes and to display our genetic worth. Men are constitutionally predisposed to flirt with the healthiest, most fertile women, recognizable by their biologically correct waist-hip ratios. Women favor the guys with dominant demeanors, throbbing muscles and the most resources to invest in them and their offspring.

Looked at up close, human psychology is more diverse and perverse than the evolutionary determinists would have it. We flirt as thinking individuals in a particular culture at a particular time. Yes, we may express a repertoire of hardwired non-verbal expressions and behaviors—staring eyes, flashing brows, opened palms—that resemble those of other animals, but unlike other animals, we also flirt with conscious calculation. We have been known to practice our techniques in front of the mirror. In other words, flirting among human beings is culturally modulated as well as biologically driven, as much art as instinct.

In our culture today, it's clear that we do not always choose as the object of our desire those people the evolutionists might deem the most biologically desirable. After all, many young women today find the pale, androgynous, scantily muscled yet emotionally expressive Leonardo DiCaprio more appealing than the burly Tarzans (Arnold Schwartzenegger, Bruce Willis, etc.) of action movies. Woody Allen may look nerdy but he's had no trouble winning women—and that's not just because he has material resources, but because humor is also a precious cultural commodity. Though she has no breasts or hips so to speak of, Ally McBeal still attracts because there's ample evidence of a quick and quirky mind.

In short, we flirt with the intent of assessing potential lifetime partners, we flirt to have easy, no-strings-attached sex, and we flirt when we are not looking for either. We flirt because, most simply, flirtation can be a liberating form of play, a game with suspense and ambiguities that brings joys of its own. As Philadelphia-based social psychologist Tim Perper says, "Some flirters appear to want to prolong the interaction because its pleasurable and erotic in its own right, regardless of where it might lead."

Here are some of the ways the game is currently being played.

TAKING The Lead

When it comes to flirting today, women aren't waiting around for men to make the advances. They're taking the lead. Psychologist Monica Moore, Ph.D. of Webster University in St. Louis, Missouri, has spent more than 2000 hours observing women's flirting maneuvers in restaurants, singles bars and at parties. According to her findings, women give non-verbal cues that get a flirtation rolling fully two-thirds of the time. A man may think he's making the first move because he is the one to literally move from wherever he is to the woman's side, but usually he has been summoned.

By the standards set out by evolutionary psychologists, the women who attract the most

PHOTOGRAPHY BY FRANK VERONSKY

42

FOR WRITING AND DISCUSSION

Working individually or in small groups, analyze how content, style, genre, and document design are interrelated in these articles.

1. How does the document design of each article—its use of fonts, layout, color, and graphics—identify each piece as a scholarly article or an article in a popular magazine? From your own observation, what are typical differences in the document design features of an academic article and a popular magazine article? For example, how are fonts and color typically used in articles in women's and men's fashion magazines?

2. What makes the style and document design of each article appropriate for its intended audience and purpose?

3. What is the function of the abstract (article summary) at the beginning of the academic journal article? What is the function of the large-font "leads" at the beginning of popular articles?

4. Consider the photographs that accompany popular magazine articles. To illustrate the concept of flirting as potential cheating, the opening page (not shown) of the *Cosmopolitan* article, quoted on page 73, features a two-page spread showing a beautiful, young, mysterious woman in a low-cut dress that shows her glistening tan skin. She is looking seriously but coyly at the reader, and behind her are shadowy images of handsome men in loosely buttoned white shirts and sports coats. Think about the photograph in the *Psychology Today* article shown in Figure 4.2. Is it a realistic, candid "documentary" photo? Is it a scripted photo? Is it a concept photo aimed at illustrating the article's thesis or question? What aspects of the *Psychology Today* photo appeal to psychological themes and interests and make it appropriate for the content, audience, and genre of the article? How do you think photos accompanying *Cosmopolitan* articles differ from photos accompanying articles in *Psychology Today*?

5. If you downloaded these articles from an electronic database, they would usually have the same textual appearance—single column typescript with no visuals. How do the visual cues in the original print version of the articles provide important contextual clues for reading the articles and using them in your own research? Why do experienced researchers prefer the original print version of articles rather than downloaded articles whenever possible?

A GENERIC RHETORICAL CONTEXT FOR COLLEGE WRITING

How can you transfer this chapter's discussion of rhetorical context, style, and document design to the writing assignments you typically receive in college? Our general advice is to pay attention to cues about purpose, audience, and genre in your instructors' assignments and, when in doubt, to ask your instructors questions about their expectations. Our specific advice is that you should assume a "default" or "generic" rhetorical context unless the assignment suggests something different.

What Do We Mean by a "Default" or "Generic" Rhetorical Context?

We have spent years studying the assignments of professors across the curriculum and have found that, unless they specify otherwise, instructors generally assume the following context:

- *Purpose.* Generally, instructors want you to write a closed-form, thesis-governed essay in response to a problem the instructor provides or to a problem that you must pose yourself. The most common rhetorical aims are informative, analysis/synthesis, or persuasion.
- *Audience.* Generally, instructors ask you to write to fellow classmates who share approximately the same level of expertise in a discipline as you do. Your goal is to say something new and challenging to this audience (but not necessarily to the instructor, who has a much higher level of expertise).
- *Genre.* Generally, instructors expect you to follow the manuscript requirements of the discipline, often MLA or APA style. Instructors vary considerably, however, in how much they care about exact formats.

Given this generic context, what is an appropriate writer's voice for college papers? For most college assignments, we recommend that students approximate their natural speaking voices to give their writing a conversational academic style. By "natural," we mean a voice that strives to be plain and clear while retaining the engaging quality of a person who is enthusiastic about the subject.

Of course, as you become an expert in a discipline, you often need to move toward a more scholarly voice. For example, the prose in an academic journal article can be extremely dense in its use of technical terms and complex sentence structure, but expert readers in that field understand and expect this voice. Students sometimes try to imitate a dense academic style before they have achieved the disciplinary expertise to make the style sound natural. The result can seem pretentiously stilted and phony. Writing with clarity and directness within your natural range will usually create a more effective and powerful voice.

Besides striving for a natural voice, you need to be aware of subtle features of your prose that project your image to readers. For example, in an academic article, the overt function of documentation and a bibliography is to enable other scholars to track down your cited sources. But a covert function is to create an air of authority for you, the writer, to assure readers that you have done your professional work and are fully knowledgeable and informed. Judicious use of the discipline's specialized language and formatting can have a similar effect. Your image is also reflected in your manuscript's form, appearance, and editorial correctness. Sloppy or inappropriately formatted manuscripts, grammatical errors, misspelled words, and other problems send a signal to the reader that you are unprofessional.

See Chapter 23, pp. 631–667, for lessons on how to cite and document sources professionally.

Assignments That Specify Different Rhetorical Contexts

Although the majority of college writing assignments assume the generic rhetorical context we have just described, many ask students to write in different genres and styles. At our own universities, for example, some professors ask students to link their writing to service-learning projects by creating Web sites, pamphlets, brochures, proposals, or news stories related to the organizations they are serving. Others ask students to role-play characters in a case study—writing as a marketing manager to a corporate policy board or as a lobbyist to a legislator. Still others ask students to write short stories using course ideas and themes or to create imaginary dialogues between characters with different points of view on a course issue. When you get such assignments, enter into their spirit. You'll usually be rewarded for your creative ability to imagine different voices, genres, and styles.

SUMMARY OF CHAPTER 4 AND PART ONE

In this chapter we have looked at how experienced writers think rhetorically about purpose, audience, and genre. We began by examining how writers think productively about each of these elements in their rhetorical context, and then we considered how variations in purpose, audience, and genre influence a writer's choices about structure, style, and document design. We concluded with a brief discussion of the generic rhetorical context assumed in most college writing assignments.

This chapter concludes Part One, "A Rhetoric for College Writers." Together, the chapters in Part One give you a background on how writers pose problems, how they pursue them through exploratory writing and talking, and how they try to solve them during the processes of composing and revising. Writers think rhetorically about their subject matter by asking questions that interest particular audiences and by responding to these questions with surprising theses supported by compelling particulars. They understand also how a writer's particular angle of vision on a subject influences the writer's tone, word choice, and decisions about what to include and exclude. Simultaneously, they think rhetorically about their purpose, audience, and genre as a means of making choices about content, structure, style, and document design. This background knowledge should prepare you to tackle the writing assignments in Part Two. Further help for your Part Two assignments is provided in Part Three, which gives nuts-and-bolts instruction on composing and revising, and in Part Four, which treats research writing in detail.

BRIEF WRITING PROJECT

This assignment asks you to try your hand at translating a piece of writing from one rhetorical context to another. As background, you need to know that each month's *Reader's Digest* includes a section called "News from the World of Medicine," which contains one or more mini-articles reporting on recent medical research. The writers of these pieces scan articles in medical journals, select items of potential interest to the general public, and translate them from a formal, scientific style into a popular style. Here is a typical example of a *Reader's Digest* mini-article:

For Teeth, Say Cheese

Cheese could be one secret of a healthy, cavity-free smile, according to a recent study by a professor of dentistry at the University of Alberta in Edmonton, Canada.

In the study, John Hargreaves found that eating a piece of hard cheese the size of a sugar cube at the end of a meal can retard tooth decay. The calcium and phosphate present in the cheese mix with saliva and linger on the surface of the teeth for up to two hours, providing protection against acid attacks from sweet food or drink.

—Penny Parker

Now compare this style with the formal scientific style in the following excerpts, the introduction and conclusion of an article published in the *New England Journal of Medicine.*

From "Aspirin as an Antiplatelet Drug"

Introduction: The past 10 years have witnessed major changes in our understanding of the pathophysiologic mechanisms underlying vascular occlusion and considerable progress in the clinical assessment of aspirin and other antiplatelet agents. The purpose of this review is to describe a rational basis for antithrombotic prophylaxis and treatment with aspirin. Basic information on the molecular mechanism of action of aspirin in inhibiting platelet function will be integrated with the appropriate clinical pharmacologic data and the results of randomized clinical trials. . . .

Conclusions: Aspirin reduces the incidence of occlusive cardiovascular events in patients at variable risk for these events. Progress in our understanding of the molecular mechanism of the action of aspirin, clarification of the clinical pharmacology of its effects on platelets, and clinical testing of its efficacy at low doses have contributed to a downward trend in its recommended daily dose. The present recommendation of a single loading dose of 200–300 mg followed by a daily dose of 75–100 mg is based on findings that this dose is as clinically efficacious as higher doses and is safer than higher doses. The satisfactory safety profile of low-dose aspirin has led to ongoing trials of the efficacy of a combination of aspirin and low-intensity oral anti-coagulants in high-risk patients. Finally, the efficacy of a cheap drug such as aspirin in preventing one fifth to one third of all important cardiovascular events should not discourage the pharmaceutical industry from attempting to develop more effective antithrombotic drugs, since a sizeable proportion of these events continue to occur despite currently available therapy.

—Carlo Patrono

Assume that you are a writer of mini-articles for the medical news section of *Reader's Digest.* Translate the findings reported in the article on aspirin into a *Reader's Digest* mini-article.

Although the style of the medical article may seem daunting at first, a little work with a good dictionary will help you decipher the whole passage. The original article by Dr. Patrono followed the experimental report format described on page 69 and included sections entitled "Introduction," "Methods," "Findings," "Discussion," and "Conclusions." We have reprinted here most of the introduction and the complete conclusions section. Because Patrono's conclusion summarizes the important findings reported and analyzed in the body of the report, these two sections provide all the information you need for your mini-article.

Welcome to **Malboro Country.**

NO SMOKING
IN THIS BUILDING

SURGEON GENERAL'S WARNING:
Smoking causes hypothermia
as well as premature death.

This ad, "Malboro Country," appears on the Web site for Adbusters.org. Adbusters is a media foundation with a global network that sponsors a Web site and a magazine dedicated to this purpose: "We want folks to get mad about corporate disinformation, injustices in the global economy, and any industry that pollutes our physical and mental commons" (http://adbusters.org/information/guidelines/). Nonpartisan in its politics, this media foundation claims a diverse audience of artists, activitists, writers, pranksters, parents, students, educators, and entrepreneurs.

To discuss and analyze this antismoking campaign ad, see the questions in the section entitled "Using the Part Opener Images" that follows the Preface.

PART TWO

Writing Projects

CHAPTER 5

Seeing Rhetorically
The Writer as Observer

ABOUT SEEING RHETORICALLY

Earlier in your school career, you may have been asked in an English class to write a description of a scene as if you were painting a picture of it in words. As you observed your scene carefully, trying to use sensory details to appeal to sight, sound, touch, smell, and even taste, you might have imagined that you were creating a true and objective description of your scene. But consider what happens to a description assignment if we give it a rhetorical twist. Suppose we asked you to write *two* descriptions of the same scene from two different perspectives or angles of vision (caused, say, by different moods or intentions) and then to analyze how the two descriptions differed. We could then ask you to reflect on the extent to which any description of a scene is objective as opposed to being shaped by the observer's intentions, experiences, beliefs, or moods.

Our goal in this chapter is to help you understand more fully the rhetorical concept of perspective, which we introduced in Chapter 3 using the metaphors "angle of vision," "interpretive lens," or "filter." Learning to ask *why* a text includes certain details and not others and to ponder *how* a text creates its dominant impression will help you analyze any text more critically and understand the complex factors that shape what a writer sees.

Angle of vision is explained on pp. 51–53. See also the U. R. Riddle Brief Writing Project on pp. 58–59.

Your writing assignment for this chapter belongs to a category that we call "writing to learn." Many instructors from across the disciplines use writing-to-learn assignments intended to help students understand important disciplinary concepts. The assignment in this chapter, while teaching you about angle of vision, also shows you some of the subtle ways that language and perception are interconnected.

EXPLORING RHETORICAL OBSERVATION

One of the intense national debates early in George W. Bush's presidency was whether the federal government should permit oil exploration in the Coastal Plain of the Arctic National Wildlife Refuge (ANWR). Arguments for and against drilling in the ANWR regularly appeared in newspapers and magazines, and numerous advocacy groups created Web sites to argue their cases. Nearly every argument contained descriptions of the ANWR, either in words or images, that operated rhetorically to advance the writer's position. In the following exercise, we ask you to analyze how depictions of the ANWR (either verbal descriptions or photographs) differed depending on whether the writer or photographer (or person selecting the photographs) opposed or supported oil exploration.

In the following three sets of exhibits, we provide a selection of photographs of the ANWR, two verbal descriptions of the ANWR, and two descriptions of the ANWR by political figures. Peruse these exhibits and then proceed to the questions that follow.

Exhibit 1: Photographs of the ANWR

In this exhibit are four photographs of the ANWR, two creating an anti-exploration rhetorical effect and two creating a pro-exploration effect.

FIGURE 5.1 ■ Polar Bear with Cubs

FIGURE 5.2 ■ Caribou and Truck

Anti-Exploration Photographs

The first anti-exploration photograph is Figure 5.1, Polar Bear with Cubs. This photograph accompanied a newspaper op-ed column entitled "Arctic Wildlife Refuge: Protect This Sacred Place."

The second anti-exploration photograph is Figure 5.2, Caribou and Truck. This photograph, showing caribou crossing a road in front of a semi, typifies Alaskan scenes intended to show the potential conflict between human purposes and nature.

Pro-Exploration Photographs

The first pro-exploration photograph is Figure 5.3, Bears on Pipelines. This photograph, labeled "Wildlife grow accustomed to oil explorations at Prudhoe Bay," is part of a pamphlet produced by Arctic Power, an advocacy group in favor of drilling. We accessed the pamphlet through the organization's Web site. In Figure 5.3, the text accompanying the photograph is included.

Wildlife grow accustomed to oil operations at Prudhoe Bay.

ANWR has the nation's best potential for major additions to U.S. oil supplies

Most geologists think the Coastal Plain of the Artic National Wildlife Refuge has the best prospects for major additions to U.S. domestic oil supply. This is the part of ANWR set aside by Congress in 1980 for further study of its petroleum potential. There is a good chance that very large oil and gas fields, equal to the amount found at Prudhoe Bay further west, could be discovered in ANWR's coastal plain.

The Coastal Plain has very attractive geology and lies between areas of the Alaska North Slope and the Canadian Beaufort Sea where there have been major oil and gas discoveries. Oil and gas deposits have been discovered near ANWR's western border, and a recent oil discovery may result in the first pipeline built to the western boundary of the Coastal Plain.

Although the Coastal Plain was reserved for study of its oil potential, Congress must act to open it for oil and gas exploration. Alaskans and residents of the North Slope, including the Inupiat community of Kaktovik, within ANWR, widely support exploring the Coastal Plain.

FIGURE 5.3 ■ Bears on Pipelines

FIGURE 5.4 ▪ ANWR Coastal Plain

The second pro-exploration photograph is Figure 5.4, ANWR Coastal Plain. This photograph of the ANWR appeared in a different section of the Arctic Power Web site.

Exhibit 2: Two Verbal Descriptions of the ANWR

Anti-Exploration Description

The following quotation is the opening of a newspaper feature article in which freelance writer Randall Rubini describes his bicycle tour through the Prudhoe Bay area of Alaska.

> The temperature is 39 degrees. The going is slow but finally I am in motion. The bike churns through big rocks and thick gravel that occasionally suck the wheels to a dead halt.
>
> Sixty miles to the east lies the Arctic National Wildlife Refuge, a place ARCO [a major oil-refining company] describes as "a bleak and forbidding land where temperatures plunge to more than 40 degrees below zero and the sun is not seen for nearly two months each year." To me the refuge is 19.5 million acres of unspoiled wilderness believed to contain crude oil and natural gas fields.
>
> Prudhoe Bay production is on the decline, and oil corporations are salivating over the prospect of drilling on the 125-mile-long stretch of coastal plain within the refuge.
>
> The area is a principal calving ground for the 180,000-member porcupine caribou herd that annually migrates to the windswept plain, seeking relief from insects.
>
> The refuge also provides habitat for grizzlies, wolves, musk oxen, wolverines, and arctic foxes. Polar bears hunt over the ice and come ashore. Millions of waterfowl, seabirds, and shorebirds nest here.

Pro-Exploration Description

The following passage appeared in the Web site for Arctic Power, a pro-exploration advocacy group. It accompanied the photograph shown in Figure 5.4.

These facts [about ANWR] are not as pretty or as emotionally appealing [as the descriptions of ANWR by anti-exploration writers]. But they are important for anyone involved in the ANWR debate. On the coastal plain, the Arctic winter lasts for 9 months. It is dark continuously for 56 days in midwinter. Temperatures with the wind chill can reach –110 degrees F. It's not pristine. There are villages, roads, houses, schools, and military installations. It's not a unique Arctic ecosystem. The coastal plain is only a small fraction of the 88,000 square miles that make up the North Slope. The same tundra environment and wildlife can be found throughout the circumpolar Arctic regions. The 1002 Area [the legal term for the plot of coastal plain being contested] is flat. That's why they call it a plain. [. . .]

Some groups want to make the 1002 Area a wilderness. But a vote for wilderness is a vote against American jobs.

Exhibit 3: Descriptions of the ANWR by Political Figures

Jimmy Carter's Description of the ANWR

The following is the opening passage of an op-ed column by former president Jimmy Carter entitled "Make This Natural Treasure a National Monument."

Rosalynn [Carter's wife] and I always look for opportunities to visit parks and wildlife areas in our travels. But nothing matches the spectacle of wildlife we found on the coastal plain of America's Arctic National Wildlife Refuge in Alaska. To the north lay the Arctic Ocean; to the south rolling foothills rose toward the glaciated peaks of the Brooks Range. At our feet was a mat of low tundra plant life, bursting with new growth, perched atop the permafrost.

As we watched, 80,000 caribou surged across the vast expanse around us. Called by instinct older than history, this Porcupine (River) caribou herd was in the midst of its annual migration. To witness this vast sea of caribou in an uncorrupted wilderness home, and the wolves, ptarmigan, grizzlies, polar bears, musk oxen and millions of migratory birds, was a profoundly humbling experience. We were reminded of our human dependence on the natural world.

Sadly, we were also forced to imagine what we might see if the caribou were replaced by smoke-belching oil rigs, highways and a pipeline that would destroy forever the plain's delicate and precious ecosystem.

The Governor of Alaska's Description of the ANWR

The following passage is from Governor [of Alaska] Tony Knowles's angry and direct response to Carter's call for national monument status for ANWR.

You [Jimmy Carter] are wrong in ignoring the pressing needs of Alaska's Native families, especially those living on the Arctic Slope, whose lives depend on the delicate care of a fragile environment for sustenance, and whose hopes are nourished by the jobs, education, and decent quality of life that oil and gas development has and will bring to their children.

Analyzing the Exhibits

Working in small groups or as a whole class, try to reach consensus answers to the following questions:

1. How do each of the photographs in Exhibit 1 create visual arguments opposing or supporting oil exploration in the ANWR? What is the verbal argument underlying each of the photos?

2. As we explained in Chapter 3, angle of vision focuses readers' attention on some details of a scene rather than others; it accounts for what is "seen" and "not seen" by a given writer. In all three exhibits, what do the opponents of oil exploration tend to "see" and "not see" when they describe the ANWR? What do the proponents of oil exploration tend to "see" and "not see"?

3. When opponents of oil exploration mention oil companies or oil wells, they often try to plant a quick negative picture in the reader's mind. What rhetorical strategies do the anti-exploration writers use in Exhibits 2 and 3 to give a negative impression of oil companies?

4. In the same exhibits, how do supporters of oil exploration try to create positive feelings about drilling in the ANWR?

WRITING PROJECT

Your writing project for this chapter is to write two descriptions and an analysis. The assignment has two parts.*

Part A: Find an indoor or outdoor place where you can sit and observe for fifteen or twenty minutes in preparation for writing a focused description of the scene that will enable your readers to see what you see. Here is the catch: You are to write *two* descriptions of the scene. Your first description must convey a favorable impression of the scene, making it appear pleasing or attractive. The second description must convey a negative, or unfavorable, impression, making the scene appear unpleasant or unattractive. Both descriptions must contain only factual details and must describe exactly the same scene from the same location at the same time. It's not fair, in other words, to describe the scene in sunny weather and then in the rain or otherwise to alter factual details. Each description should be one paragraph long (approximately 125–175 words).

Part B—Self-reflection on What You Learned (300–400 words): Attach to your two descriptions a self-reflective analysis of what you learned by reading this chapter and by writing your contrasting descriptions. Take your reader behind the scenes to show how you created your two descriptions. Then reflect on what you have learned about the concept "angle of vision" and about the strategies writers use to shape their readers' view of a subject.

* For this assignment, we are indebted to two sources: (1) Richard Braddock, *A Little Casebook in the Rhetoric of Writing* (Englewood Cliffs, NJ: Prentice-Hall, 1971); and (2) Kenneth Dowst, "Kenneth Dowst's Assignment," *What Makes Writing Good?* eds. William E. Coles, Jr., and James Vopat (Lexington, MA: D.C. Heath, 1985), pp. 52–57.

Part A of the assignment asks you to describe the same scene in two different ways, giving your first description a positive tone and the second description a negative one. You can choose from any number of scenes: the lobby of a dormitory or apartment building, a view from a park bench or a window, a favorite (or unfavorite) room, a scene at your workplace, a busy street, a local eating or drinking spot, or whatever interests you. Part B of the assignment asks you to explain how you created your contrasting scenes and to reflect on what you learned from this exercise about seeing rhetorically.

More discussion of this assignment, as well as a student example of two contrasting descriptions, occurs later in this chapter. As we noted earlier, this assignment results in a thought exercise rather than in a self-contained essay that requires an introduction, transitions between parts, and so forth. You can label your sections simply "Descriptions" and "Analysis and Reflection."

UNDERSTANDING OBSERVATIONAL WRITING

In this section, we elaborate on the concept of angle of vision. We explore what factors influence angle of vision and show how a writer's angle of vision shapes the language he or she chooses, or, to put it inversely, how the chosen language both conveys and creates the angle of vision. We also examine the complex relationship between perception and belief by explaining how previous knowledge, cultural background, interests, and values influence perceptions.

Considering the Factors That Shape Perception

On the face of it, terms such as *observation, perception,* and *seeing* seem nonproblematic. Objects are objects, and the process of perceiving an object is immediate and automatic. However, perception is never a simple matter. Consider what we call "the expert-novice phenomenon": Experts on any given subject notice details about that subject that the novice overlooks. An experienced bird-watcher can distinguish dozens of kinds of swallows by subtle differences in size, markings, and behaviors, whereas a non–bird-watcher sees only a group of birds of similar size and shape. Similarly, people observing an unfamiliar game (for example, an American watching cricket or a Nigerian watching baseball) don't know what actions or events have meaning and, hence, don't know what to look for. Psychologists have found that after observing an inning of baseball, avid baseball fans remember numerous details about the play on the field, none of which are noticed by people unfamiliar with the game, who may, however, have vivid recollections of people in the stands or of a player's peculiar mannerisms. In short, prior knowledge or the absence of it causes people to see different things.

In addition to prior knowledge, cultural differences affect perception. An American watching two Japanese business executives greet each other might not know that they are participating in an elaborate cultural code of bowing, eye contact, speech patterns, and timing of movements that convey meanings about social status. An Ethiopian newly arrived in the United States and an American sitting in a doctor's office will see different things when the nurse points to one of them to come into the examination room: The American notices nothing remarkable about the scene; he or she may remember what the nurse was wearing or something about the wallpaper. The Ethiopian, on the other hand, is likely to remember the nurse's act of pointing, a gesture of rudeness used in Ethiopia only to beckon children or discipline dogs. Again, observers of the same scene see different things.

Your beliefs and values can also shape your perceptions, often creating blind spots. You might not notice data that conflict with your beliefs and values. Or you might perceive contradictory data at some level, but if they don't register in your mind as significant, you disregard them. Consider, for example, how advocates of gun control focus on a child's being accidentally killed because the child found a loaded firearm in Dad's sock drawer, while opponents of gun control focus on burglaries or rapes being averted because the home owner had a pistol by the bedside. The lesson here is that people note and remember whatever is consistent with their worldview much more readily than they note and remember inconsistencies. What you believe is what you see.

Another factor determining what you see is mood. We know that when people are upbeat they tend to see things through "rose-colored glasses"—a cliché with a built-in reference to angle of vision. When you are in a good mood, you see the flowers in a meadow. When you are depressed, you see the discarded wrappers from someone's pack of gum. The late nineteenth-century Impressionist painters were so interested in the relationship between a phenomenon being observed and the observer's interior life that they created a new style of painting that tried to reflect both landscape and mood simultaneously.

More direct and overt is the influence of rhetorical purpose. Consider again the case of the Arctic National Wildlife Refuge mentioned earlier in this chapter. In the passage by Randall Rubini (p. 90), the author juxtaposes his own view of the ANWR as an "unspoiled wilderness" against ARCO's view of the ANWR as a "'bleak and forbidding land.'" Note how each way of seeing the ANWR serves the political purposes of the author. Opponents of oil exploration focus on the unspoiled beauty of the land, listing fondly the names of different kinds of animals that live there. What remains "unseen" in their descriptions are the native villages and military installations on the Coastal Plain and any references to economic issues, the U.S. need for domestic oil, or jobs. In contrast, supporters of oil exploration shift the focus from the caribou herds (their descriptions don't "see" the animals), to the bleak and frigid landscape and the native communities that would benefit from jobs.

This example suggests the ethical dimension of description. Rhetorical purpose entails responsibility. All observers must accept responsibility for what they see and for what they make others see because their descriptions can have real-world consequences—for example, no jobs for a group of people or potential harm to an animal species and an ecosystem. We should reiterate, however, that neither perspective on the ANWR is necessarily dishonest; each is true in a limited way. In any description, writers necessarily—whether consciously or unconsciously—include some details and exclude others. But the writer's intent is nevertheless to influence the reader's way of thinking about the described phenomenon, and ethical readers must be aware of what is happening. By noting what is *not there,* readers can identify a piece's angle of vision and analyze it. The reader can see the piece of writing not as the whole truth but as one person's perspective that can seem like the whole truth if one simply succumbs to the text's rhetorical power.

Finally, let's look at one more important factor that determines angle of vision—what we might call a writer's "guiding ideology" or "belief system." We touched on this point earlier when we showed how one's belief system can create blind spots. Let's examine this phenomenon in more depth by seeing how different beliefs about the role of women in primitive societies cause two anthropologists to describe a scene in different ways. What follows are excerpts from the works of two female anthropologists studying the role of women in the !Kung tribe* of the African Kalahari Desert (sometimes called the "Bushmen"). Anthropologists have long been interested in the !Kung because they still hunt and forage for food in the manner of their prehistoric ancestors.

Here is how anthropologist Lorna Marshal describes !Kung women's work:

Marshal's Description

Women bring most of the daily food that sustains the life of the people, but the roots and berries that are the principal plant foods of the Nyae Nyae !Kung are apt to be tasteless, harsh and not very satisfying. People crave meat. Furthermore, there is only drudgery in digging roots, picking berries, and trudging back to the encampment with heavy loads and babies sagging in the pouches of the karosses: there is no splendid excitement and triumph in returning with vegetables.

—Lorna Marshal, *The !Kung of Nyae Nyae*

And here is how a second anthropologist describes women's work:

Draper's Description

A common sight in the late afternoon is clusters of children standing on the edge of camp, scanning the bush with shaded eyes to see if the returning women are visible. When the slow-moving file of women is finally discerned in the distance, the children leap and exclaim. As the women draw closer, the children speculate as to which figure is whose mother and what the women are carrying in the karosses. [. . .]

!Kung women impress one as a self-contained people with a high sense of self-esteem. There are exceptions—women who seem forlorn and weary—but for the most part, !Kung women are vivacious and self-confident. Small groups of women forage in the Kalahari at distances of eight to ten miles from home with no thought that they need the protection of the men or of the men's weapons should they encounter any of the several large predators that also inhabit the Kalahari.

—P. Draper, "!Kung Women: Contrasts in Sexual Egalitarianism
in Foraging and Sedentary Contexts"

As you can see, these two anthropologists "read" the !Kung society in remarkably different ways. Marshal's thesis is that !Kung women are a subservient class

* The word *!Kung* is preceded by an exclamation point in scholarly work to indicate the unique clicking sound of the language.

relegated to the heavy, dull, and largely thankless task of gathering vegetables. In contrast, Draper believes that women's work is more interesting and requires more skill than other anthropologists have realized. Her thesis is that there is an egalitarian relationship between men and women in the !Kung society.

The source of data for both anthropologists is careful observation of !Kung women's daily lives. But the anthropologists are clearly not seeing the same thing. When the !Kung women return from the bush at the end of the day, Marshal sees their heavy loads and babies sagging in their pouches, whereas Draper sees the excited children awaiting the women's return.

So which view is correct? That's a little like asking whether the ANWR is an "unspoiled wilderness" or a "'bleak and forbidding land.'" If you believe that women play an important role in !Kung society, you "see" the children eagerly awaiting the women's return at the end of the day, and you note the women's courage in foraging for vegetables "eight to ten miles from home." If you believe that women are basically drudges in this culture, then you "see" the heavy loads and babies sagging in the pouches of the karosses. The details of the scene, in other words, are filtered through the observer's interpretive screen.

Conducting a Simple Rhetorical Analysis

Our discussion of two different views of the ANWR and two different views of the role of women in !Kung society shows how a seemingly objective description of a scene reflects a specific angle of vision that can be revealed through analysis. Rhetorically, a description subtly persuades the reader toward the author's angle of vision. This angle of vision isn't necessarily the author's "true self" speaking, for authors *create* an angle of vision through rhetorical choices they make while composing. We hope you will discover this insight for yourself while doing the assignment for this chapter.

In this section we describe five textual strategies writers often use (consciously or unconsciously) to create the persuasive effect of their texts. Each strategy creates textual differences that you can discuss in your rhetorical analysis.

Strategy 1: Writers Can State Their Meaning or Intended Effect Directly

Often writers state their point or angle of vision openly, so readers do not need to infer the writer's meaning or intentions. For example, the first anthropologist says that "there is only drudgery in digging roots" while the second anthropologist says, "!Kung women impress one as a self-contained people with a high sense of self-esteem." The first writer announces her meaning directly—women's work is drudgery; in contrast, the second writer announces a more positive meaning.

Strategy 2: Writers Can Select Details That Convey Their Intended Effect and Omit Those That Don't

Another strategy for creating an angle of vision (and therefore influencing a reader's view) is to select details that further the writer's purpose and omit those that do not. For example, the details selected by Marshal, the first anthropologist, focus on the tastelessness of the vegetables and the heaviness of the women's loads, creating an overall impression of women's work as thankless and exhausting. The details chosen by Draper, the second anthropologist, focus on the excitement of the children awaiting their mothers' return and the fearlessness of the women as they forage "eight to ten miles from home," creating an impression of self-reliant women performing an essential task. As a specific example, Marshal includes the detail "babies sagging in the pouches of the karosses" while Draper includes "clusters of children standing on the edge of camp." The different details create different rhetorical effects.

Strategy 3: Writers Can Choose Words with Connotations That Convey Their Intended Effect

Writers can also influence readers through their choice of words. Because words carry emotional connotations as well as denotative meanings, any given word is a kind of lens that filters its subject in a certain way. Marshal chooses words connoting listlessness and fatigue such as *drudgery, trudging, heavy,* and *sagging.* In contrast, Draper chooses words connoting energy: the children *scan* the bush, *leap and exclaim,* and *speculate,* while the women *forage.*

Strategy 4: Writers Can Use Figurative Language That Conveys Their Intended Effect

Figurative language—metaphors, similes, and analogies that compare or equate their subjects to something else—can profoundly affect perception of a subject. When Rubini writes that oil companies are "salivating" for new oil-drilling opportunities, the reader's negative image of drooling dogs is transferred subconsciously to the oil companies. If those same companies were said to be "exploring new paths toward American independence from foreign oil," the reader might see them in a quite different light.

Strategy 5: Writers Can Create Sentence Structures That Convey Their Intended Effect

Another subtle way to control the rhetorical effect of a passage is through sentence structure. By placing key words and phrases in emphatic positions (for example, at the end of a long sentence, in a short sentence surrounded by long sentences, or in a main clause rather than a subordinate clause), writers can emphasize some parts of the passage while de-emphasizing others. Consider the difference in emphasis of these two possible sentences for a letter of recommendation for U. R. Riddle (from the Brief Writing Project in Chapter 3, pp. 58–59):

> Although U. R. Riddle was often moody and brusque in my classes, he is surely a genius.
> Although U. R. Riddle is surely a genius, he was often moody and brusque in my classes.

Most readers will agree that the first version emphasizes Riddle's brilliance and the second version emphasizes his less-than-peachy personality. The passages are equally factual—they both contain the same information—but they subtly convey different impressions.

Next consider how the first anthropologist, Marshal, uses sentence structure to create a negative feeling about !Kung women's plant-gathering role:

> Women bring most of the daily food that sustains the life of the people, but the roots and berries that are the principal plant foods of the Nyae Nyae !Kung are apt to be tasteless, harsh and not very satisfying. People crave meat.

Here the writer's emphasis is on meat as highly desirable (the short sentence "People crave meat" in an environment of long sentences is especially emphatic) and on vegetables as "tasteless, harsh and not very satisfying" (these words occur in the stressed position at the end of a long sentence). We could rewrite this passage, keeping the same facts, but creating a quite different rhetorical effect:

> Although the !Kung people crave meat and consider the plant food of the Kalahari tasteless, harsh, and not very satisfying, the women nevertheless provide most of the daily food that sustains the life of the people.

In this version, the emphasis is on how the women sustain the life of the people—a point presented in a nonstressed position in the original passage.

For Writing and Discussion

What follows is a student example of two contrasting descriptions written for the assignment in this chapter. Read the descriptions carefully. Working individually, analyze the descriptions rhetorically to explain how the writer has created contrasting impressions through overt statements of meaning, selection and omission of details, word choice, figurative language, and sentence structure. (You will do the same thing for your own two descriptions in Part B of the assignment.) Spend approximately ten minutes doing your own analysis of this example and taking notes. Then, working in small groups or as a whole class, share your analyses, trying to reach agreement on examples of how the writer has created different rhetorical effects by using the five strategies just explained.

Description 1: Positive Effect

The high ceiling and plainness of this classroom on the second floor of the Administration Building make it airy, spacious, and functional. This classroom, which is neither dusty and old nor sterile and modern, has a well-used, comfortable feel like the jeans and favorite sweater you put on to go out for pizza with friends. Students around me, who are focused on the assignment, read the instructor's notes on the chalkboard, thumb through their texts, and jot down ideas in their notebooks spread out on the spacious two-person tables. In the back of the room, five students cluster around a table and talk softly and intently about the presentation they are getting ready to make to the class. Splashes of spring sunshine filtering through the blinds on the tall windows brighten the room with natural light, and a breeze pungent with the scent of newly mown grass wafts through the open ones, sweeps over the students writing at their desks, and passes out through the door to the hall. As I glance out the window, I see a view that contributes to the quiet harmony of the environment: bright pink and red rhododendron bushes and manicured beds of spring flowers ring the huge lawn where a few students are studying under the white-blossomed cherry trees.

Description 2: Negative Effect

The high ceiling of this classroom on the second floor of the Administration Building cannot relieve the cramped, uncomfortable feeling of this space, which is filled with too many two-person tables, some of them crammed together at awkward angles. A third of the chalkboard is blocked from my view by the bulky television, VCR, and overhead projector that are stacked on cumbersome carts and wreathed in electrical cords. Students around me, working on the assignment, scrape their chairs on the bare linoleum floor as they try to see the chalkboard where some of the instructor's notes are blotted out by the shafts of sunlight piercing through a few bent slats in the blinds. In the back of the room, five students cluster around a table, trying to talk softly about their presentation, but their voices bounce off the bare floors. Baked by the sun, the classroom is so warm that the instructor has allowed us to open the windows, but the wailing sirens of ambulances racing to the various hospitals surrounding the campus distract us. The breeze, full of the smell of mown lawn, brings warm air from outside into this stuffy room. Several students besides me gaze longingly out the window at the bright pink and red rhododendrons in the garden and at the students reading comfortably in the shade under the white-blossomed cherry trees.

Readings

The readings for this chapter consist of two eyewitness accounts of an event that occurred on the Congo River in Africa in 1877.* The first account is by the famous British explorer Henry Morton Stanley, who leads an exploration party of Europeans into the African interior. The second account is by the African tribal chief Mojimba, as told orally to a Belgian missionary, Fr. Frassle, who recorded the story. The conflicting accounts suggest the complexity of what happens when different cultures meet for the first time.

HENRY MORTON STANLEY'S ACCOUNT

We see a sight that sends the blood tingling through every nerve and fibre of the body . . . a flotilla of gigantic canoes bearing down upon us. A monster canoe leads the way . . . forty men on a side, their bodies bending and swaying in unison as with a swelling barbarous chorus they drive her down towards us . . . the warriors above the manned prow let fly their spears. . . . But every sound is soon lost in the ripping crackling musketry. . . . Our blood is up now. It is a murderous world, and we feel for the first time that we hate the filthy vulturous ghouls who inhabit it. . . . We pursue them . . . and continue the fight in the village streets with those who have landed, hunt them out into the woods, and there only sound the retreat, having returned the daring cannibals the compliment of a visit.

* These readings are taken from Donald C. Holsinger, "A Classroom Laboratory for Writing History," *Social Studies Review* 31.1 (1991): 59–64. The role-playing exercise following the readings is also adapted from this article.

MOJIMBA'S ACCOUNT

When we heard that the man with the white flesh was journeying down the [Congo] we were open-mouthed with astonishment. . . . He will be one of our brothers who were drowned in the river. . . . We will prepare a feast, I ordered, we will go to meet our brother and escort him into the village with rejoicing! We donned our ceremonial garb. We assembled the great canoes. . . . We swept forward, my canoe leading, the others following, with songs of joy and with dancing, to meet the first white man our eyes had beheld, and to do him honor. But as we drew near his canoes there were loud reports, bang! bang! And fire-staves spat bits of iron at us. We were paralyzed with fright . . . they were the work of evil spirits! "War! That is war!" I yelled. . . . We fled into our village—they came after us. We fled into the forest and flung ourselves on the ground. When we returned that evening our eyes beheld fearful things: our brothers, dead, dying, bleeding, our village plundered and burned, and the water full of dead bodies. The robbers and murderers had disappeared.

Thinking Critically about the Two Accounts

Our purpose in presenting these two accounts is to raise the central problem examined in this chapter: the rhetorical nature of observation—that is, how observation is shaped by values, beliefs, knowledge, and purpose and therefore represents an angle of vision or one perspective.

1. How do the two accounts differ?
2. What is common to both accounts? Focusing on common elements, try to establish as many facts as you can about the encounter.
3. How does each observer create a persuasive effect by using one or more of the five strategies described on pages 96–98 (overt statement of meaning, selection/omission of details, connotations of words, figurative language, ordering and shaping of sentences)?
4. What differences in assumptions, values, and knowledge shape these two interpretations of events?
5. As a class, try the following role-playing exercise:

    Background: You are a newspaper reporter who has a global reputation for objectivity, accuracy, and lack of bias. You write for a newspaper that has gained a similar reputation and prides itself on printing only the truth. Your editor has just handed you two eyewitness accounts of an incident that has recently occurred in central Africa. You are to transform the two accounts into a brief front-page article (between sixty and ninety words) informing your readers what happened. You face an immediate deadline and have no time to seek additional information.

    Task: Each class member should write a sixty to ninety word newspaper account of the event, striving for objectivity and lack of bias. Then share your accounts.

6. As a class, play the believing and doubting game with this assertion: "It is possible to create an objective and unbiased account of the Congo phenomenon."

COMPOSING YOUR ESSAY

Since the assignment for this chapter has two parts—Part A, calling for two contrasting descriptions, and Part B, calling for rhetorical analysis and reflection—we address each part separately.

Exploring Rationales and Details for Your Two Descriptions

To get into the spirit of this unusual assignment, you need to create a personal rationale for why you are writing two opposing descriptions. Our students have been successful imagining any one of the following three rationales:

Rationales for Writing Opposing Descriptions

- *Different moods:* One approach is to imagine observing your scene in different moods. How could I reflect a "happy" view of this scene? How could I reflect a "sad" view of this scene? Be sure, however, to focus entirely on a description of the scene, not on your mood itself. Let the mood determine your decisions about details and wording, but don't put yourself into the scene. The reader should infer the mood from the description.

- *Verbal game:* Here you see yourself as a word wizard trying consciously to create two different rhetorical effects for readers. In this scenario, you don't worry how you feel about the scene but how you want your reader to feel. Your focus is on crafting the language to influence your audience in different ways.

- *Different rhetorical purposes:* In this scenario, you imagine your description in service of some desired action. You might want authorities to improve an ugly, poorly designed, or nonfunctional space (for example, a poorly designed library reading room or a dilapidated apartment house next to a littered vacant lot). Or you might want to give public recognition to someone for a beautiful, well-designed, or particularly functional space (for example, a new campus entrance arch or a well-designed computer lab). In this scenario, you begin with a strongly held personal view of your chosen scene—something you want to commend or condemn. One of your descriptions, therefore, represents *the way you really feel*. Your next task is to see this same scene from an opposing perspective. To get beyond your current assessment of the scene—to recognize aspects of it that are inconsistent with your beliefs—you need to "defamiliarize" it, to make it strange. Artists sometimes try to disrupt their ordinary ways of seeing by drawing something upside down or by imagining the scene from the perspective of a loathsome character—whatever it takes to wipe away "the film of habit" from the object.

The student who wrote the example on pages 98–99 worked from this last rationale. She disliked one of her classrooms, which she found unpleasant and detrimental to learning. In choosing this place, she discovered that she valued college classrooms that were well equipped, comfortable, quiet, modernized, reasonably roomy, and unaffected by outside weather conditions. She also thought that the university should spend money to modernize old classrooms to make them as attractive as the campus grounds. It was easy for her to write the negative description of this room, which used descriptive details showing how the scene violated all her criteria. However, she had trouble writing the positive description until she imagined being inside the head of someone totally different from herself.

Generating Details

Once you have chosen your scene, you need to compose descriptions that are rich in sensory detail. You might imagine yourself in descriptive partnership with a recently blinded friend in which you become your friend's eyes, while your friend—having a newly heightened sense of hearing, touch, and smell—can notice nonsight details that you might otherwise miss. In your writing, good description should be packed with sensory detail—sights, sounds, smells, textures, even on occasion tastes—all contributing to a dominant impression that gives the description focus.

After you have chosen a subject for your two descriptions, observe it intensely for fifteen or twenty minutes. One way to train yourself to notice sensory details is to create a sensory chart, with one column for your pleasant description and one column for your unpleasant description.

Pleasant Impression	Unpleasant Impression
Sight/eyes	Sight/eyes
Sound/ears	Sound/ears
Odor/nose	Odor/nose
Touch/fingers	Touch/fingers
Taste/tongue	Taste/tongue

As you observe your scene, note details that appeal to each of the senses and then try describing them, first positively (left column) and then negatively (right column). One student, observing a scene in a local tavern, made these notes in her sensory chart:

Positive Description	Negative Description
Taste/tongue	**Taste/tongue**
salted and buttered popcorn	salty, greasy popcorn
frosty pitchers of beer	half-drunk pitchers of stale, warm beer
big bowls of salted-in-the-shell peanuts on the tables	mess of peanut shells and discarded pretzel wrappers on tables and floor

Positive Description	Negative Description
Sound/ears	**Sound/ears**
hum of students laughing and chatting	din of high-pitched giggles and various obnoxious frat guys shouting at each other
the jukebox playing oldies but goodies from the early Beatles	jukebox blaring out-of-date music

Shaping and Drafting Your Two Descriptions

Once you have decided on your rationale for the two descriptions, observed your scene, and made your sensory chart, compose your two descriptions. You will need to decide on an ordering principle for your descriptions. It generally makes sense to begin with an overview of the scene to orient your reader.

> From the park bench near 23rd and Maple, one can watch the people strolling by the duck pond.

> By eight o'clock on any Friday night, Pagliacci's Pizzeria on Broadway becomes one of the city's most unusual gathering places.

Then you need a plan for arranging details. There are no hard-and-fast rules here, but there are some typical practices. You can arrange details in the following ways:

- By spatially scanning from left to right or from far to near
- By using the written equivalent of a movie zoom shot: begin with a broad overview of the scene, then move to close-up descriptions of specific details

Compose your pleasant description, selecting and focusing on details that convey a positive impression. Then compose your unpleasant description. Each description should comprise one fully developed paragraph (125–175 words).

Using *Show* Words Rather than *Tell* Words

In describing your scenes, use *show* words rather than *tell* words. *Tell* words interpret a scene without describing it. They name an interior, mental state, thus telling the reader what emotional reaction to draw from the scene.

Tell Words

There was a *pleasant* tree in the backyard.

There was an *unpleasant* tree in the backyard.

In contrast, *show* words describe a scene through sensory details appealing to sight, sound, smell, touch, and even taste. The description itself evokes the desired effect without requiring the writer to state it overtly.

Show Words

A *spreading elm* tree *bathed* the backyard with *shade*. [evokes positive feelings]

An *out-of-place elm, planted too close to the house, blocked our view* of the *mountains*.
[evokes negative feelings]

Whereas show words are particulars that evoke the writer's meaning through sensory detail, tell words are abstractions that announce the writer's intention directly (strategy 1 on pp. 96). An occasional tell word can be useful, but show words operating at the bottom of the "scale of abstraction" are the flesh and muscle of descriptive prose.

The "scale of abstraction" is explained in Chapter 3, pp. 50–51.

Inexperienced writers often try to create contrasting impressions of a scene simply by switching tell words.

Weak: Overuse of *Tell* Words

The smiling merchants happily talked with customers trying to get them to buy their products. [positive purpose]

The annoying merchants kept hassling customers trying to convince them to buy their products. [negative purpose]

In this example, the negative words *annoying* and *hassling* and the positive words *smiling* and *happily* are tell words; they state the writer's contrasting intentions, but they don't describe the scene. Here is how the student writer revised these passages using show words.

Strong: Conversion to *Show* Words

One of the merchants, selling thick-wooled Peruvian sweaters, nodded approvingly as a woman tried on a richly textured blue cardigan in front of the mirror. [positive purpose]

One of the merchants, hawking those Peruvian sweaters that you find in every open-air market, tried to convince a middle-aged woman that the lumpy, oversized cardigan she was trying on looked stylish. [negative purpose]

Here are some more examples taken from students' drafts before and after revision:

Draft with *Tell* Words	Revision with *Show* Words
Children laugh and point animatedly at all the surroundings.	Across the way, a small boy taps his friend's shoulder and points at a circus clown.
The wonderful smell of food cooking on the barbecue fills my nose.	The tantalizing smell of grilled hamburgers and buttered corn on the cob wafts from the barbecue area of the park, where men in their cookout aprons wield forks and spatulas and drink Budweisers.
The paintings on the wall are confusing, dark, abstract, demented, and convey feelings of unhappiness and suffering.	The paintings on the wall, viewed through the smoke-filled room, seem confusing and abstract—the work of a demented artist on a bad trip. Splotches of black paint are splattered over a greenish-yellow background like bugs on vomit.

Revising Your Two Descriptions

The following checklist of revision questions will help you improve your first draft:

1. *How can I make my two descriptions more parallel—that is, more clearly about the same place at the same time?* The rules for the assignment ask you to use only factual details observable in the same scene at the same time. It violates the spirit of the assignment to have one scene at a winning basketball game and the other at a losing game. Your readers' sense of pleasure in comparing your two descriptions will be enhanced if many of the same details appear in both descriptions.

2. *Where can I replace "tell" words with "show" words?* Inexperienced writers tend to rely on "tell" words rather than give the reader sensory details and visual impressions. Find words that deliver prepackaged ideas to the reader (*pleasant, happy, depressing, annoying, pretty,* and so forth) and rewrite those sentences by actually describing what you see, hear, smell, touch, and taste. Pay particular attention to this advice if you are choosing "different moods" as your rationale for two descriptions.

3. *How can I make the angle of vision in each description clearer? How can I clarify my focus on a dominant impression?* Where could you use words with vividly appropriate connotations? Where could you substitute specific words for general ones? For example, consider synonyms for the generic word *shoe*. Most people wear shoes, but only certain people wear spiked heels or thongs. Among words for kinds of sandals, *Birkenstocks* carries a different connotation from *Tevas* or *strappy espadrilles with faux-metallic finish.* Search your draft for places where you could substitute more colorful or precise words for generic words to convey your dominant impression more effectively.

Generating and Exploring Ideas for Your Rhetorical Analysis and Reflection

Part B of this Writing Project asks you to write a self-reflection on what you have learned from reading this chapter and writing your two descriptions. In the Table of Contents, we have categorized this assignment under the heading "writing-to-learn"; your self-reflection encourages you to articulate the learning, skills, and insights you have acquired from doing the assignment. Among the questions you might address are these:

Writing self-reflections constitutes a powerful learning strategy. See Chapter 27 on the practice and value of self-reflective writing.

■ What was your process in doing the assignment? How did you role-play your purpose for writing contrasting descriptions? How did you achieve your contrasting effects?

■ What did you find most difficult or challenging about the assignment?

■ What have you learned about the concept "angle of vision" and about ways writers can influence readers through their overt statement of purpose, their choice of words, their selection (or exclusion) of details, their use of figurative language, and their choices about sentence structure?

■ Throughout this text we urge you to read rhetorically, that is, to be aware of how a text is constructed to influence readers. How has this chapter advanced your ability to read rhetorically?

To illustrate self-reflection, we reproduce here a portion of the self-reflection written by the student who wrote the two descriptions on pages 98–99.

Selections from a Student's Self-Reflection

To write this assignment, I found it helpful both to imagine different moods and different rhetorical purposes. My composition class is held in one of the oldest buildings on our campus. Some days our classroom has struck me as quaint, a room with "character." Other days, I have gotten irritated with the problems in this room—the discomfort, inconvenience, and noise. I drew on and exaggerated the impressions I have of this room when I am in different moods. I also imagined that a fellow student was interviewing me on the question, How could the classroom facilities on our campus be improved? I role-played telling this person what I really like in a classroom and what I dislike.

Writing my two descriptions made me think about how much power writers have to influence readers' thinking. In deliberately changing my angle of vision from positive to negative, I realized how much the choice of individual words can convey particular ideas to readers. For example, to get across the idea of a comfortably studious environment in my first description, I used words such as "airy," "spacious," "focused," and "quiet harmony." But in my negative description, I wanted readers to feel the unpleasantness of this room so I used words like "cramped," "crammed," "blocked," and "bulky." What amazed me is that both of these descriptions are factually true depending on the observer's perspective. [. . .]

[In the rest of her self-reflection, this student analyzed other strategies she used for creating contrasting effects and then explored how she has begun to notice similar rhetorical strategies being used in some of her recent reading.]

■ GUIDELINES FOR PEER REVIEWS ■

Instructions for peer reviews are provided in Chapter 18 (pp. 490–496).

For the Writer

Prepare two or three questions you would like your peer reviewer to address while responding to your draft. The questions can focus on some aspect of your draft that you are uncertain about, on one or more sections where you particularly seek help or advice, on some feature that you particularly like about your draft, or on some part you especially wrestled with. Write out your questions and give them to your peer reviewer along with your draft.

For the Reviewer

To write a peer review for a classmate, use your own paper, numbering your responses to correspond to the question numbers. At the head of your paper, place the author's name and your own name, as shown.

Author's Name: _____

Peer Reviewer's Name: _____

I. Read the draft at a normal reading speed from beginning to end. As you read, do the following:

   A. Place a wavy line in the margin next to any passages that you find confusing, that contain something that doesn't seem to fit, or that otherwise slow down your reading.

   B. Place a "Good!" in the margin next to any passages where you think the writing is particularly strong or interesting.

II. Read the draft again slowly and answer the following questions by writing brief explanations of your answers:

   A. The two descriptions

      1. How could the two descriptions be made more parallel, sketched more boldly, or made more detailed and vivid?

      2. Which of the five senses are appealed to? How could the writer include more sensory details?

      3. Where could the writer replace *tell* words with *show* words? How could the writer use show words more effectively?

      4. If the writer has relied primarily on one or two strategies for creating contrast (overt interpretation, selection or omission of details), how might he or she use other strategies (contrasting word choice, contrasting figurative language, changes in sentence structure)?

      5. How might the writer sharpen or clarify the angle of vision in each description?

   B. Analysis and reflection

      1. How might the writer analyze more thoroughly and specifically the strategies used to create the different descriptions?

      2. Where could the writer use more or better examples to illustrate the chosen strategies?

      3. How could the writer explain what he or she has learned more surprisingly?

      4. What insights could be explained more clearly or developed more thoroughly?

   C. If the writer has prepared questions for you, respond to his or her inquiries.

   D. Sum up what you see as the chief strengths and problem areas of this draft.

      1. Strengths

      2. Problem areas

III. Read the draft one more time. Place a check mark in the margin wherever you notice problems in grammar, spelling, or mechanics (one check mark per problem).

CHAPTER 6

Reading Rhetorically
The Writer as Strong Reader

ABOUT READING RHETORICALLY

Many new college students are surprised by the amount, range, and difficulty of reading they have to do in college. Every day they are challenged by reading assignments ranging from scholarly articles and textbooks on complex subject matter to primary sources such as Plato's dialogues or Darwin's *Voyage of the Beagle*.

The goal of this chapter is to help you become a more powerful reader of academic texts, prepared to take part in the conversations of the disciplines you study. To this end, we explain two kinds of thinking and writing essential to your college reading:

- Your ability to listen carefully to a text, to recognize its parts and their functions, and to summarize its ideas
- Your ability to formulate strong responses to texts by interacting with them, either by agreeing with, interrogating, or actively opposing them

To interact strongly with texts, you must learn how to read them both with and against the grain. When you read *with the grain* of a text, you see the world through its author's perspective, open yourself to the author's argument, apply the text's insights to new contexts, and connect its ideas to your own experiences and personal knowledge. When you read *against the grain* of a text, you resist it by questioning its points, raising doubts, analyzing the limits of its perspective, or even refuting its argument. We say that readers who respond strongly to texts in this manner read *rhetorically;* that is, they are aware of the effect a text is intended to have on them, and they critically consider that effect, entering into or challenging the text's intentions.

EXPLORING RHETORICAL READING

As an introduction to rhetorical reading, we would like you to read Dr. Andrés Martin's "On Teenagers and Tattoos," which appeared in the *Journal of the American Academy of Child and Adolescent Psychiatry,* a scholarly publication. Before reading the article, complete the following opinion survey. Answer each question using a 1–5 scale, with 1 meaning "strongly agree" and 5 meaning "strongly disagree."

1. For teenagers, getting a tattoo is like following any other fad such as wearing the currently popular kind of shoe or hairstyle.
2. Teenagers get tattoos primarily as a form of asserting independence from parents and other adults.
3. Teenagers get tattoos on the spur of the moment and usually don't consider the irreversibility of marking their skin.
4. Teenagers who get tattoos are expressing deep psychological needs.
5. A psychiatry journal can provide useful insights into teen choices to tattoo their bodies.

When you have finished rating your degree of agreement with these statements, read Martin's article, using whatever note taking, underlining, or highlighting strategies you normally use when reading for a class. When you have finished reading, complete the exercises that follow.

Reading

■ ANDRÉS MARTIN, M.D. ■
ON TEENAGERS AND TATTOOS

The skeleton dimensions I shall now proceed to set down are copied verbatim from my right arm, where I had them tattooed: as in my wild wanderings at that period, there was no other secure way of preserving such valuable statistics.

—Melville/*Moby Dick CII*

1   Tattoos and piercings have become a part of our everyday landscape. They are ubiquitous, having entered the circles of glamour and the mainstream of fashion, and they have even become an increasingly common feature of our urban youth. Legislation in most states restricts professional tattooing to adults older than 18 years of age, so "high end" tattooing is rare in children and adolescents, but such tattoos are occasionally seen in older teenagers. Piercings, by comparison, as well as self-made or "jailhouse" type tattoos, are not at all rare among adolescents or even among schoolage children. Like hairdo, makeup, or baggy jeans, tattoos and piercings can be subject to fad influence or peer pressure in an effort toward group affiliation. As with any other fashion statement, they can be construed as bodily aids in the inner struggle toward identity consolidation, serving as adjuncts to the defining and sculpting of the self by means of external manipulations. But unlike most other body decorations, tattoos and piercings are set apart by their irreversible and permanent nature, a quality at the core of their magnetic appeal to adolescents.

2   Adolescents and their parents are often at odds over the acquisition of bodily decorations. For the adolescent, piercings or tattoos may be seen as personal and beautifying statements, while parents may construe them as oppositional and enraging affronts to their authority. Distinguishing bodily adornment from self-mutilation may indeed prove challenging, particularly

when a family is in disagreement over a teenager's motivations and a clinician is summoned as the final arbiter. At such times it may be most important to realize jointly that the skin can all too readily become but another battleground for the tensions of the age, arguments having less to do with tattoos and piercings than with core issues such as separation from the family matrix. Exploring the motivations and significance underlying tattoos (Grumet, 1983) and piercings can go a long way toward resolving such differences and can become a novel and additional way of getting to know teenagers. An interested and nonjudgmental appreciation of teenagers' surface presentations may become a way of making contact not only in their terms but on their turfs: quite literally on the territory of their skins.

The following three sections exemplify some of the complex psychological underpinnings of youth tattooing.   3

Identity and the Adolescent's Body

Tattoos and piercing can offer a concrete and readily available solution for many of the identity crises and conflicts normative to adolescent development. In using such decorations, and by marking out their bodily territories, adolescents can support their efforts at autonomy, privacy, and insulation. Seeking individuation, tattooed adolescents can become unambiguously demarcated from others and singled out as unique. The intense and often disturbing reactions that are mobilized in viewers can help to effectively keep them at bay, becoming tantamount to the proverbial "Keep Out" sign hanging from a teenager's door.   4

Alternatively, [when teenagers feel] prey to a rapidly evolving body over which they have no say, self-made and openly visible decorations may restore adolescents' sense of normalcy and control, a way of turning a passive experience into an active identity. By indelibly marking their bodies, adolescents can strive to reclaim their bearings within an environment experienced as alien, estranged, or suffocating or to lay claim over their evolving and increasingly unrecognizable bodies. In either case, the net outcome can be a resolution to unwelcome impositions: external, familial, or societal in one case; internal and hormonal in the other. In the words of a 16-year-old girl with several facial piercings, and who could have been referring to her body just as well as to the position within her family, "If I don't fit in, it is because *I* say so."   5

Incorporation and Ownership

Imagery of a religious, deathly, or skeletal nature, the likenesses of fierce animals or imagined creatures, and the simple inscription of names are some of the time-tested favorite contents for tattoos. In all instances, marks become not only memorials or recipients for clearly held persons or concepts: they strive for incorporation, with images and abstract symbols gaining substance on becoming a permanent part of the individual's skin. Thickly embedded in personally meaningful representations and object relations, tattoos can become not only the ongoing memento of a relationship,   6 but at times even the only evidence that there ever was such a bond. They can quite literally become the relationship itself. The turbulence and impulsivity of early attachments and infatuations may become grounded, effectively bridging oblivion through the visible reality of tattoos.

7　　*Case Vignette.* A, a 13-year-old boy, proudly showed me his tattooed deltoid. The coarsely depicted roll of the dice marked the day and month of his birth. Rather disappointed, he then uncovered an immaculate back, going on to draw for me the great "piece" he envisioned for it. A menacing figure held a hand of cards: two aces, two eights, and a card with two sets of dates. A's father had belonged to "Dead Man's Hand," a motorcycle gang named after the set of cards (aces and eights) that the legendary Wild Bill Hickock had held in the 1890s when shot dead over a poker table in Deadwood, South Dakota. A had only the vaguest memory of and sketchiest information about his father, but he knew he had died in a motorcycle accident: the fifth card marked the dates of his birth and death.

8　　The case vignette also serves to illustrate how tattoos are often the culmination of a long process of imagination, fantasy, and planning that can start at an early age. Limited markings, or relatively reversible ones such as piercings, can at a later time scaffold toward the more radical commitment of a permanent tattoo.

The Quest for Permanence

9　　The popularity of the anchor as a tattoo motif may historically have had to do less with guild identification among sailors than with an intense longing for rootedness and stability. In a similar vein, the recent increase in the popularity and acceptance of tattoos may be understood as an antidote or counterpoint to our urban and nomadic lifestyles. Within an increasingly mobile society, in which relationships are so often transient—as attested by the frequencies of divorce, abandonment, foster placement, and repeated moves, for example—tattoos can be a readily available source of grounding. Tattoos, unlike many relationships, can promise permanence and stability. A sense of constancy can be derived from unchanging marks that can be carried along no matter what the physical, temporal, or geographical vicissitudes at hand. Tattoos stay, while all else may change.

10　　*Case Vignette.* A proud father at 17, B had had the smiling face of his 3-month-old baby girl tattooed on his chest. As we talked at a tattoo convention, he proudly introduced her to me, explaining how he would "always know how beautiful she is today" when years from then he saw her semblance etched on himself.

11　　The quest for permanence may at other times prove misleading and offer premature closure to unresolved conflicts. At a time of normative uncertainties, adolescents may maladaptively and all too readily commit to a tattoo and its indefinite presence. A wish to hold on to a current certainty may lead the adolescent to lay down in ink what is valued and cherished one day but may not necessarily be in the future. The frequency of self-made tattoos among hospitalized, incarcerated, or gang-affiliated youths suggests such motivations: a sense of stability may be a particularly dire need under temporary, turbulent, or volatile conditions. In addition, through their designs teenagers may assert a sense of bonding and allegiance to a group larger than themselves. Tattoos may attest to powerful experiences, such as adolescence itself, lived and even survived together. As with *Moby Dick's* protagonist Ishmael, they may bear witness to the "valuable statistics" of one's "wild wandering(s)": those of adolescent exhilaration and excitement on the one hand; of growing pains, shared misfortune, or even incarceration on the other.

Adolescents' bodily decorations, at times radical and dramatic in their presentation, can be seen in terms of figuration rather than disfigurement, of the natural body being through them transformed into a personalized body (Brain, 1979). They can often be understood as self-constructive and adorning efforts, rather than prematurely subsumed as mutilatory and destructive acts. If we bear all of this in mind, we may not only arrive at a position to pass more reasoned clinical judgment, but become sensitized through our patients' skins to another level of their internal reality.

12

References

Brain, R. (1979). *The Decorated Body.* New York: Harper & Row.

Grumet, G. W. (1983). Psychodynamic implications of tattoos. *Am J Orthopsychiatry,* 53:482–492.

Thinking Critically about "On Teenagers and Tattoos"

1. Summarize in one or two sentences Martin's main points.

2. Freewrite a response to this question: In what way has Martin's article caused me to reconsider my answers to the opinion survey?

3. Working in small groups or as a whole class, compare the note taking strategies you used while reading this piece. (a) How many people wrote marginal notes? How many underlined or highlighted? (b) Compare the contents of these notes. Did people highlight the same passage or different passages? (c) Individually, look at your annotations and highlights and try to decide why you wrote or marked what you did. Share your reasons for making these annotations. The goal of this exercise is to make you more aware of your thinking processes as you read.

4. Working as a whole class or in small groups, share your responses to the questionnaire and to the postreading questions. To what extent did this article change people's thinking about the reasons teenagers choose to tattoo their bodies? What were the most insightful points in this article?

5. Assume that you are looking for substantial, detailed information about teenagers and tattooing. What parts of this article leave you with unanswered questions? Where is more explanation needed?

WRITING PROJECT

Write a "summary/strong response" essay that includes: (a) a summary (approximately 150–250 words) of a reading specified by your instructor and (b) a strong response to that reading in which you speak back to that reading from your own critical thinking, personal experience, and values. As you formulate your own response, consider both the author's rhetorical strategies and the author's ideas. Think of your response as your analysis of how the text tries to influence its readers rhetorically and how your wrestling with the text has expanded and deepened your thinking about its ideas.

The skills this assignment develops are crucial for academic writers. You will learn how to summarize an article (or book), including how to quote brief passages, how to use attributive tags to cue your reader that you are reporting someone else's ideas rather than your own, and how to cite the article using (in this case) the Modern Language Association (MLA) documentation system. Because writing summaries and producing strong responses are important writing-to-learn skills, you will draw on them any time you are asked to speak back to or critique a text. These skills are also needed for writing exploratory essays, analysis and synthesis essays, researched arguments, and any other scholarly work that uses sources. In learning how to summarize a text and interact with it in writing, you are learning how to contribute your own ideas to a conversation. Weak readers passively report what other people have said. Strong readers see themselves as contributors to the conversation, capable of analyzing and evaluating texts, speaking back to other authors, and thinking actively for themselves.

UNDERSTANDING RHETORICAL READING

In this section we explain why college-level reading is often difficult for new students and offer suggestions for improving your reading process based on the reading strategies of experts. We then show you the importance of reading a text both with the grain and against the grain—skills you need to summarize a text and respond to it strongly.

What Makes College-Level Reading Difficult?

The difficulty of college-level reading stems in part from the complexity of the subject matter. Whatever the subject—from international monetary policies to the intricacies of photosynthesis—you have to wrestle with new and complex materials that might perplex anyone. But in addition to the daunting subject matter, several other factors contribute to the difficulty of college-level reading:

■ *Vocabulary.* Many college-level readings—especially primary sources—contain unfamiliar technical language that may be specific to an academic discipline: for example, the terms *identity consolidation, normative, individuation,* and *object relations* in the Martin text or words like *existentialism* and

Neoplatonic in a philosophy textbook. In academia, words often carry specialized meanings that evoke a whole history of conversation and debate that may be inaccessible, even through a specialized dictionary. You will not fully understand them until you are initiated into the disciplinary conversations that gave rise to them.

■   *Unfamiliar rhetorical context.* As we explained in Part One, writers write to an audience for a purpose arising from some motivating occasion. Unless you know something about a text's purpose, occasion, and intended audience (that is, unless you know the conversation to which the text belongs), you may be confused. Sometimes the rhetorical context is easy to figure out, as in the case of the Martin article (he is offering advice to psychiatrists about how to counsel tattooed teens and their families effectively). But why did Plato write his dialogues? What conversation was the French philosopher and historian Michel Foucault joining when he began analyzing public executions? A text's internal clues can help you fill in the rhetorical context, but often you may need to do outside research.

■   *Unfamiliar genre.* In your college reading, you will encounter a range of genres such as textbooks, trade books, scholarly articles, scientific reports, historical documents, newspaper articles, op-ed pieces, and so forth. Each of these makes different demands on readers and requires a different reading strategy.

■   *Lack of background knowledge.* Writers necessarily make assumptions about what their readers already know. Your understanding of Martin, for example, would be more complete if you had a background in adolescent psychology and psychiatric therapy.

For Writing and Discussion

The importance of background knowledge can be easily demonstrated any time you dip into past issues of a newsmagazine or try to read articles about an unfamiliar culture. Consider the following passage from a 1986 *Newsweek* article. How much background knowledge do you need before you can fully comprehend this passage? What cultural knowledge about the United States would a student from Ethiopia or Indonesia need?

> Throughout the NATO countries last week, there were second thoughts about the prospect of a nuclear-free world. For 40 years nuclear weapons have been the backbone of the West's defense. For almost as long American presidents have ritually affirmed their desire to see the world rid of them. Then, suddenly, Ronald Reagan and Mikhail Gorbachev came close to actually doing it. Let's abolish all nuclear ballistic missiles in the next 10 years, Reagan said. Why not all nuclear weapons, countered Gorbachev. OK, the president responded, like a man agreeing to throw in the washer-dryer along with the house.
>
> What if the deal had gone through? On the one hand, Gorbachev would have returned to Moscow a hero. There is a belief in the United States that the Soviets

need nuclear arms because nuclear weapons are what make them a superpower. But according to Marxist-Leninist doctrine, capitalism's nuclear capability (unforeseen by Marx and Lenin) is the only thing that can prevent the inevitable triumph of communism. Therefore, an end to nuclear arms would put the engine of history back on its track.

On the other hand, Europeans fear, a nonnuclear United States would be tempted to retreat into neo-isolationism.

—Robert B. Cullen, "Dangers of Disarming," *Newsweek*

Working in small groups or as a class, identify words and passages in this text that depend on background information or knowledge of culture for complete comprehension.

Using the Reading Strategies of Experts

In Chapter 18, we describe the differences between the writing processes of experts and those of beginning college writers. There are parallel differences between the reading processes of experienced and inexperienced readers, especially when they encounter complex materials. In this section we describe some expert reading strategies that you can begin applying to your reading of any kind of college-level material.

Reconstruct the Text's Rhetorical Context

Before and as you read a text, ask questions such as these: Who is the author? What audience is he or she writing for? What occasion prompted this writing? What is the author's purpose? Any piece of writing makes more sense if you think of its author as a real person writing for some real purpose in a real historical context.

If you read an article that has been anthologized (as in the readings in this textbook), take note of any information you are given about the author, publication data, and genre. Try to reconstruct the author's original motivation for writing. How have audience, purpose, and genre shaped this text?

Make Marginal Notes as You Read

Expert readers seldom use highlighters, which encourage passive, inefficient reading; instead, they use pens or pencils to make extensive marginal notes as they read. (If they have borrowed the book or journal from the library, they take notes on paper or in a notebook.) Instead of passively highlighting whole passages and hoping you will remember what you were thinking as you read them, write in the margin why you think a passage is important. Next time you get the urge to highlight a passage, make notes that track your understanding of the text you are reading. Is the passage a major new point in the argument? A significant piece of support? A summary of the opposition? A particularly strong or particularly weak point? Use the margins to summarize, protest, question, or assent—but don't just color the pages.

Get in the Dictionary Habit

When you can't tell a word's meaning from context, get in the habit of looking it up. One strategy is to make small check marks next to words you're unsure of; then look them up after you're done so as not to break your concentration.

Try "Translating" Difficult Passages

When you stumble over a difficult passage, try "translating" it into your own words. Converting the passage into your own language forces you to focus on the precise meanings of words. Although your translation may not be exactly what the author intended, you will see more clearly where the sources of confusion lie and what the likely range of meanings might be.

Vary Your Reading Speed to Match Your Reading Goals

Unlike novices, experienced readers vary their reading speeds and strategies according to their goals. In other words, experienced readers know when to slow down or speed up. Robert Sternberg, a cognitive psychologist, discovered that novice readers tend to read everything at about the same pace, no matter what their purpose. In contrast, experienced readers vary their reading speed significantly depending on whether they are scanning for a piece of information, skimming for main ideas, reading deliberately for complete comprehension, or reading slowly for detailed analysis. Knowing when to speed up or slow down—especially if you are doing a research project and trying to cover lots of ground—can make your reading more efficient.

If a Text Is Complex, Read in a "Multidraft" Way

It may be comforting for you to know that expert readers struggle with difficult texts the same way you do. Often, experienced readers reread a text two or three times, treating their first readings like first drafts. They hold confusing passages in mental suspension, hoping that later parts of the essay will clarify earlier parts. The ironic point here is that sometimes you have to speed up to slow down. If you are lost in a passage, try skimming ahead rapidly, looking at the opening sentences of paragraphs and at any passages that sum up the writer's argument or that help clarify the argument's structure. Pay particular attention to the conclusion, which often ties the whole argument together. This rapid "first-draft reading" helps you see the text's main points and overall structure, thus providing a background for a second reading. The passage that puzzled you the first time might now be clearer.

Vary Your Reading Strategies to Match Genre

Experienced readers also match their reading strategies to the genre of the piece being read. They use conventions of the genre to select the portions of the text that are most important to their purposes. To illustrate, let's look at how experienced readers read scientific or technical reports, which typically contain five sections: introduction, methods, findings, discussion, and conclusions. Experts seldom read a scientific report from beginning to end. Instead, they might read the

For a discussion of the scientific research report genre, see pp. 68–69.

introduction to understand the research question being examined and then turn to the discussion section and conclusions to see the extent to which the study answered the research question. Most experts would turn to the methods and findings section only after determining that the research was relevant to their work and generally helpful. They would read these sections primarily to determine how carefully and thoughtfully the research was done. (Debates about scientific research often focus on the research design and methodology.)

Other genres, too, demand special ways of reading, which you will develop through experience. Learn to recognize that different genres use different conventions, which, in turn, invite different ways of reading.

Continue the Conversation after You Have Finished Reading

Expert readers continue thinking about a text after they have finished reading. When you've finished a text, in a journal or in your reading notes try exploring your responses to prompts like these:

■ This reading has influenced my views in these ways:

  _____

■ Although I agree with the author that _____, I still have these

  doubts: _____

■ The most significant questions this reading has raised for me are these:

  _____

■ The most important ideas that I will take away from this reading are these:

  _____

■ If I could meet this author at a party, I'd like to ask this question

  _____ or offer this perspective _____

  _____.

These questions help you remember the reading and urge you to respond actively to it.

Reading With the Grain and Against the Grain

The reading and thinking strategies that we have just described enable skilled readers to interact strongly with texts. Your purpose in using these strategies is to read texts both with the grain and against the grain, a way of reading that is analogous to the believing and doubting game we introduced in Chapter 2. This concept is so important that we have chosen to highlight it separately here.

When you read with the grain of a text, you practice what psychologist Carl Rogers calls "empathic listening," in which you try to see the world through the

For an explanation of the believing and doubting game, see pp. 37–39.

author's eyes, role-playing as much as possible the author's intended readers by adopting their beliefs and values and acquiring their background knowledge. Reading with the grain is the main strategy you use when you summarize a text, but it comes into play also when you develop a strong response. When making with-the-grain points, you support the author's thesis with your own arguments and examples, or apply or extend the author's argument in new ways.

When you read against the grain of a text, you challenge, question, resist, and perhaps even rebut the author's ideas. You are a resistant reader who asks unanticipated questions, pushes back, and reads the text in ways unforeseen by the author. Reading against the grain is a key part of creating a strong response. When you make against-the-grain points, you challenge the author's reasoning, sources, examples, or choice of language. You generate counterexamples, present alternative lines of reasoning, deny the writer's values, or raise points that the writer has overlooked or specific data that the writer has omitted.

Strong readers develop their ability to read in both ways—with the grain and against the grain. Throughout the rest of this chapter, we show you different ways to practice and apply these strategies.

UNDERSTANDING SUMMARY WRITING

In this section we explain techniques for writing an effective summary of a text. Summary writing fosters a close encounter between you and the text and demonstrates your understanding of it. When you write a summary, you practice reading with the grain of a text. You "listen" actively to the text's author, showing that you understand the author's point of view by restating his or her argument as completely and fairly as possible. Summary writing is an essential academic skill, regularly used in research writing of any kind, where you often present condensed views of other writers' arguments, either as support for your own view or as alternative views that you must analyze or respond to.

Reading for Structure and Content

In writing a summary, you must focus on both its structure and its content. In the following steps, we recommend a process that will help you condense a text's ideas into an accurate summary. As you become a more experienced reader and writer, you'll follow these steps without thinking about them.

Step 1: The first time through, read the text fairly quickly for general meaning. If you get confused, keep going; later parts of the text might clarify earlier parts.

Step 2: Reread the text carefully. As you read, write gist statements in the margins for each paragraph. A *gist statement* is a brief indication of the paragraph's function or purpose in the text or a brief summary of the paragraph's content. Sometimes it is helpful to think of these two kinds of gist statements as "what it does" statements and "what it says" statements.* A "what it does" statement speci-

---

* For our treatment of "what it does" and "what it says" statements, we are indebted to Kenneth A. Bruffee, *A Short Course in Writing,* 2nd ed. (Cambridge, MA: Winthrop, 1980).

fies the paragraph's function—for example, "summarizes an opposing view," "introduces another reason," "presents a supporting example," "provides statistical data in support of a point," and so on. A "what it says" statement captures the main idea of a paragraph by summarizing the paragraph's content. The "what it says" statement is the paragraph's main point, in contrast to its supporting ideas and examples. Sometimes an explicit topic sentence makes the main point easy to find, but often you have to extract the main point by shrinking an argument down to its essence. In some cases, you may be uncertain about the main point. If so, select the point that you think a majority of readers would agree is the main one.

When you first practice detailed readings of a text, you might find it helpful to write complete *does* and *says* statements on a separate sheet of paper rather than in the margins until you develop the internal habit of appreciating both the function and content of parts of an essay. Here are *does* and *says* statements for selected paragraphs of Andrés Martin's essay on teenage tattooing:

Paragraph 1: *Does:* Introduces the subject and sets up the argument. *Says:* The current popularity of tattoos and piercings is partly explained as an aid toward finding an identity, but the core of their appeal is their irreversible permanence.

Paragraph 2: *Does:* Narrows the focus and presents the thesis. *Says:* To counsel families in disagreement over tattoos, psychiatrists should exhibit a nonjudgmental appreciation of teen tattoos and use them to understand teenagers better.

Paragraph 4: *Does:* Discusses the first complex motivation behind youth tattooing. *Says:* Teens use tattoos to handle identity crises and to establish their uniqueness from others.

Paragraph 5: *Does:* Elaborates on the first motivation, the identity issue. *Says:* Tattoos provide teens with a sense of control over their changing bodies and over an environment perceived as adverse and domineering.

Paragraph 11: *Does:* Complicates the view of teens' use of tattoos to find permanence and belonging. *Says:* Although tattoos may unrealistically promise the resolution to larger conflicts, they may at least record the triumphs and miseries of adolescent turbulence, including gang and prison experience.

Paragraph 12: *Does:* Sums up the perspective and advice of the article. *Says:* Psychiatrists should regard adolescent tattoos positively as adornment and self-expression and employ tattoos to help understand teens' identities and sense of reality.

You may occasionally have difficulty writing a *says* statement for a paragraph because you may have trouble deciding what the main idea is, especially if the paragraph doesn't begin with a closed-form topic sentence. One way to respond to this problem is to formulate the question that you think the paragraph answers. If you think of chunks of the text as answers to a logical progression of questions, you can often follow the main ideas more easily. Rather than writing *says* statements in the margins, therefore, some readers prefer writing *says* questions. *Says* questions for the Martin text may include the following: What is the most constructive approach clinicians can take to teen tattooing when these tattoos have become the focus of family conflict? What psychological needs and problems are teenagers acting out through their tattoos? Why does the permanence of tattoos appeal to young people?

No matter which method you use—*says* statements or *says* questions—writing gist statements in the margins is far more effective than underlining or highlighting in helping you recall the text's structure and argument.

Step 3: After you have analyzed the article paragraph by paragraph, try locating the article's main divisions or parts. In longer closed-form articles, writers often forecast the shape of their essays in their introductions or use their conclusions to sum up main points. Although Martin's article is short, it uses both a forecasting statement and subheads to direct readers through its main points. The article is divided into several main chunks as follows:

- Introductory paragraphs, which establish the problem to be addressed and narrow the focus to a clinical perspective (paragraphs 1–2)
- A one-sentence organizing and predicting statement (paragraph 3)
- A section explaining how tattoos may help adolescents establish a unique identity (paragraphs 4–5)
- A section explaining how tattoos help teens incorporate onto their bodies a symbolic ownership of something important to them (paragraphs 6–8)
- A section explaining how tattoos represent and satisfy teens' search for permanence (paragraphs 9–11)
- A conclusion that states the thesis explicitly and sums up Martin's advice to fellow psychiatrists (paragraph 12)

Instead of listing the sections, you might prefer to make an outline or tree diagram of the article showing its main parts.

The same basic procedures can work for summarizing a book, but you will need to modify them to fit a much longer text. For instance, you might write "what it does" and "what it says" statements for chapters or parts of a book. In summarizing a book, you might pay special attention to the introduction and conclusion of the book. In the introduction, usually authors state their motivation for writing the book and often put forth their thesis and the sub-theses that the subsequent chapters of the book develop and explain. Chapter titles and chapter introductions often restate the author's sub-theses and can help you identify main ideas to include in a book summary.

Producing the Summary

Once you have written gist statements or questions in the margins and clarified the text's structure by creating an outline or diagram, you are ready to write a summary. Typically, summaries range from 100 to 250 words, but sometimes writers compose summaries as short as one sentence. The order and proportions of your summary can usually follow the order and proportions of the text. However, if the original article has a delayed thesis or other characteristics of open-form writing, you can rearrange the order and begin with the thesis. With prose that has many open-form features, you may also have to infer points that are more implied than expressed.

A summary of another author's writing—when it is incorporated into your own essay—makes particular demands on you, the writer. Most of all, writing a summary challenges you to convey the main ideas of a text—ideas that are often complex—in as few and as clear words as you can. We tell our students that writing a summary is like having a word budget: you only have so many words (say, a 250- or 100-word limit), and you have to spend them wisely. In addition, a successful summary should do all of the following:

- Represent the original article accurately and fairly.
- Be direct and concise, using words economically.
- Remain objective and neutral, not revealing your own ideas on the subject but, rather, only the original author's points.
- Give the original article balanced and proportional coverage.
- Use your own words to express the original author's ideas.
- Keep your reader informed through attributive tags (such as *according to Martin* or *Martin argues that*) that you are expressing someone else's ideas, not your own.
- Possibly include quotations for a few key terms or ideas from the original, but quote sparingly.
- Be a unified, coherent piece of writing in its own right.
- Be properly cited and documented so that the reader can find the original text.

Some of these criteria for a successful summary are challenging to meet. For instance, to avoid interjecting your own opinions, you need to choose your words carefully, including the verbs you use in attributive tags. Note the differences between these pairs of verbs: *Smith argues* versus *Smith rants; Jones criticizes* versus *Jones attacks; Brown asserts* versus *Brown leaps to the conclusion*. In each pair, the second verb, by moving beyond neutrality, reveals your own judgment of the author's ideas.

When you incorporate a summary into your own writing, it is particularly important to distinguish between the author's ideas and your own—hence the importance of frequent attributive tags, which tell the reader that these ideas belong to Smith or Jones or Brown rather than to you. If you choose to copy any of the author's words directly from the text, you need to use quotation marks and cite the quotation using an appropriate documentation system.

The following example, which summarizes Martin's article on teenagers and tattoos, uses the MLA documentation system.

Chapter 23 provides additional instruction on summarizing, paraphrasing, and quoting sources. It also explains how to work sources smoothly into your own writing and avoid plagiarism.

Summary of Martin Article

In "On Teenagers and Tattoos," published in the <u>Journal of the American Academy of Child and Adolescent Psychiatry</u>, Dr. Andrés Martin advises fellow psychiatrists to think of teenage tattooing not as a fad or as a form of self-mutilation but as an opportunity for clinicians to understand teenagers better. <u>Martin</u> examines

Identification of the article, journal, and author

Thesis of article

Attributive tag

Transition ——————

three different reasons that teenagers get tattoos. <u>First,</u>

he argues that tattoos help teenagers establish unique identities

Attributive tag ——————

Transition and attributive tag ——————

by giving them a sense of control over their evolving bodies and

over an environment perceived as adverse and domineering. <u>Second,</u>

he believes that a tattooed image often symbolizes the teen's

relationship to a significant concept or person, making the

Transition and attributive tag ——————

relationship more visible and real. <u>Finally, says Martin</u>, because

teens are disturbed by modern society's mobility and fragmentation

Inclusion of short quotation from article. MLA documentation style; number in parentheses indicates page number of original article where quotation is found

and because they have an "intense longing for rootedness and

stability" (861), the irreversible nature of tattoos may give

them a sense of permanence. <u>Martin concludes</u> that tattoos   *Attributive tag*

can be a meaningful record of survived teen experiences. <u>He</u>   *Attributive tag*

encourages therapists to regard teen tattoos as "self-constructive

and adorning efforts," rather than as "mutilatory and destructive

acts" (861) and suggests that tattoos can help therapists

Another short quotation

understand "another level of [teenagers'] internal reality" (861).

Brackets indicate that the writer changed the material inside the brackets to fit the grammar and context of the writer's own sentence

[195 words]

Works Cited

Martin, Andrés. "On Teenagers and Tattoos." <u>Journal of the</u>

    <u>American Academy of Child and Adolescent Psychiatry</u> 36

    (1997): 860–61.

Martin article cited completely using MLA documentation form; in a formal paper, the "works cited" list begins on a new page

---

For Writing and Discussion

Imagine that the context of a research paper you are writing calls for a shorter summary of the Martin article than the one presented here (which is approximately 195 words, including attributive tags). To practice distilling the main ideas of an article to produce summaries of different lengths, first write a 100-word summary of "On Teenagers and Tattoos." Then reduce your summary further to 50 words. Discuss the principles you followed in deciding what to eliminate or how to restructure sentences to convey the most information in the fewest number of words.

UNDERSTANDING STRONG RESPONSE WRITING

We have said that summary writing is an essential academic skill. Equally important is strong response writing in which you join the text's conversation and speak back to it. If a strong reading means to engage a text actively, both assenting to an author's ideas and questioning them, what exactly do you write about when you compose a strong response? To appreciate our answer to this question, you need to know the various ways that strong responses are assigned across the curriculum.

Kinds of Strong Responses

A strong response is one of the most common writing assignments you will encounter in college courses. However, teachers vary in what they mean by a "strong response," and they often use different terms for the same basic kind of assignment. Our conversations with instructors from across the disciplines suggest that there are three common kinds of strong response assignments:

- ▦ ***Analysis or critique assignment.*** Here your job is to analyze and critique the assigned reading. You discuss how a text is constructed, what rhetorical strategies it employs, and how effectively its argument is supported. Suppose, for example, that you are asked to critique an article, appearing in a conservative business journal, that advocates oil exploration in the Arctic National Wildlife Refuge (ANWR). For this kind of strong response, you'd be expected to analyze the article's rhetorical strategies (for example, How is it shaped to appeal to a conservative, business-oriented audience?) and evaluate its argument (for example, What are the underlying assumptions and beliefs on which the argument is based? Is the logic sound? Is the evidence accurate and up-to-date?). When you analyze and critique a reading, you focus on the text itself, giving it the same close attention that an art critic gives a painting, a football coach gives a game film, or a biologist gives a cell formation. This close attention can be with the grain, noting the effectiveness of the text's rhetorical strategies, or against the grain, discussing what is ineffective or problematic about these strategies. Or an analysis might point out both the strengths of and the problems with a text's rhetorical strategies.

- ▦ ***"Your own views" assignment.*** Here the instructor expects you to present your own views on the reading's topic or issue—for example, to give your own views on oil exploration in the ANWR, to support or challenge the writer's views, to raise new questions, and otherwise to add your voice to the ANWR conversation. This kind of strong response invites you to read both with and against the grain. A with-the-grain reading supports all or some of the article's arguments but supplies additional reasons or new evidence, directs the argument to a different audience, extends the argument to a different context, or otherwise adds your own support to the writer's views. An against-the-grain reading attempts to challenge all or part of the writer's argument, to raise doubts in the audience, to show flaws in the writer's reasoning, and to support your own views as they arise from your personal experience, observation, other reading, and wrestling with the author's ideas.

▪ *A blended assignment that mixes both kinds of responses.* Here the instructor expects you to respond in both ways—to analyze and critique the article but also to engage the writer's ideas by developing your own views on the topic. As a writer, you can emphasize what is most important to you, but the paper should contain elements of analysis and critique as well as your own views on the issue. The assignment for this chapter calls for this kind of blended strong response, but your instructor can specify what kind of emphasis he or she desires.

Instructors also vary in their preferences for the tone and structure of strong response essays. Some instructors prefer the term *reflection paper* rather than *strong response*—a term that invites you to write a personal response with an open-form structure and an expressive or exploratory purpose. In a reflection paper, the instructor is particularly interested in how the reading has affected you personally—what memories it has triggered, what personal experiences it relates to, what values and beliefs it has challenged, and so forth. Other instructors prefer closed-form strong responses with an explicit thesis statement, an analytical or persuasive purpose, and a more academic tone.

The assignment in this chapter calls for a closed-form strong response with a clear thesis statement. Your instructor, however, may modify the assignment to fit the goals of his or her course or the curriculum at your university.

Student Example of a Summary/Strong Response Essay

Before giving you some tips on how to discover ideas for your strong response, we show you an example of a student essay for this chapter: a summary/strong response essay. Note that the essay begins by identifying the question under discussion: Why do teenagers get tattoos? It then summarizes the article by Andrés Martin.* Immediately following the summary, the student writer states his thesis, followed by the strong response, which contains both rhetorical points and points about the causes of teenage tattooing.

Why Do Teenagers Get Tattoos? A Response to Andrés Martin

Sean Barry (student)

Introduces topic and sets context

My sister has one. My brother has one. I have one. Just take a stroll downtown and you will see how commonplace it is for someone to be decorated with tattoos and hung with piercings. In fact, hundreds of teenagers, every day, allow themselves to be etched upon or poked into. What's the cause of this phenomenon? Why do so many teenagers get tattoos?

Dr. Andrés Martin has answered this question from a psychiatrist's perspective in his article "On Teenagers and Tattoos," published in the *Journal of the American*

* In this essay the student writer uses a shortened version of his 195-word summary that was used as an illustration on pages 121–122.

Academy of Child and Adolescent Psychiatry. Martin advises fellow psychiatrists to think of teenage tattooing as a constructive opportunity for clinicians to understand teenagers better. Martin examines three different reasons that teenagers get tattoos. First, he argues that tattoos help teenagers establish unique identities by giving them a sense of control over their evolving bodies and over an environment perceived as adverse and domineering. Second, he believes that a tattooed image often symbolizes the teen's relationship to a significant concept or person, making the relationship more visible and real. Finally, says Martin, because teens are disturbed by modern society's mobility and fragmentation and because they have an "intense longing for rootedness and stability" (861), the irreversible nature of tattoos may give them a sense of permanence. Martin concludes that tattoos can be a meaningful record of survived teen experiences. Although Martin's analysis has relevance and some strengths, I think he overgeneralizes and over-romanticizes teenage tattooing, leading him to overlook other causes of teenage tattooing such as commercialization and teenagers' desire to identify with a peer group as well as achieve an individual identity.

Some of Martin's points seem relevant and realistic and match my own experiences. I agree that teenagers sometimes use tattoos to establish their own identities. When my brother, sister, and I all got our tattoos, we were partly asserting our own independence from our parents. Martin's point about the symbolic significance of a tattoo image also connects with my experiences. A Hawaiian guy in my dorm has a fish tattooed on his back, which he says represents his love of the ocean and the spiritual experience he has when he scuba dives.

Martin, speaking as a psychiatrist to other psychiatrists, also provides psychological insights into the topic of teen tattooing even though this psychological perspective brings some limitations, too. In this scholarly article, Martin's purpose is to persuade fellow psychiatrists to think of adolescent tattooing in positive rather than judgmental terms. Rather than condemn teens for getting tattoos, he argues that discussion of the tattoos can provide useful insights into the needs and behavior of troubled teens (especially males). But this perspective is also a limitation because the teenagers he sees are mostly youths in psychiatric counseling, particularly teens struggling with the absence of or violent loss of a parent and those who have experience with gangs and prison-terms. This perspective leads him to overgeneralize. As a psychological study of a specific group of troubled teens, the article is informative. However, it does not apply as well to most teenagers who are getting tattoos today.

Besides overgeneralizing, Martin also seems to romanticize teenage tattooing. Why else would a supposedly scientific article begin and end with quotations from *Moby Dick*? Martin seems to imply a similarity between today's teenagers and the sailor hero Ishmael who wandered the seas looking for personal identity. In quoting *Moby Dick,* Martin seems to value tattooing as a suitable way for teenagers to record their experiences. Every tattoo, for Martin, has deep significance. Thus, Martin casts tattooed teens as romantic outcasts, loners, and adventurers like Ishmael.

In contrast to Martin, I believe that teens are influenced by the commercial nature of tattooing, which has become big business aimed at their age group. Every movie or television star or beauty queen who sports a tattoo sends the commercial message that tattoos are cool: "A tattoo will help you be successful, sexy, handsome, or attractive like us." Tattoo parlors are no longer dark dives in seedy, dangerous parts of cities, but appear in lively commercial districts; in fact, there are several down the street from the university. Teenagers now buy tattoos the way they buy other consumer items.

Summary of Martin's article

Thesis statement

With-the-grain point in support of Martin's ideas

Rhetorical point about Martin's audience, purpose, and genre that has both with-the-grain and against-the-grain elements

Against-the-grain rhetorical point: Barry analyzes use of quotations from Moby Dick

Transition to writer's own analysis

Against-the-grain point: writer's alternative theory

Against-the-grain point: writer's second theory

Furthermore, Martin doesn't explore teenagers' desire not only for individuality but also for peer group acceptance. Tattooing is the "in" thing to do. Tattooing used to be defiant and daring, but now it is popular and more acceptable among teens. I even know a group of sorority women who went together to get tattoos on their ankles. As tattooing has become more mainstreamed, rebels/trendsetters have turned to newer and more outrageous practices, such as branding and extreme piercings. Meanwhile, tattoos bring middle-of-the-road teens the best of both worlds: a way to show their individuality and simultaneously to be accepted by peers.

Conclusion and summary

In sum, Martin's research is important because it examines psychological responses to teen's inner conflicts. It offers partial explanations for teens' attraction to tattoos and promotes a positive, noncritical attitude toward tattooing. But I think the article is limited by its overgeneralizations based on the psychiatric focus, by its tendency to romanticize tattooing, by its lack of recognition of the commercialization of tattooing, and by its underemphasis on group belonging and peer pressure. Teen tattooing is more complex than even Martin makes it.

Works Cited

Complete citation of article in MLA format

Martin, Andrés. "On Teenagers and Tattoos." *Journal of the American Academy of Child and Adolescent Psychiatry* 36 (1997): 860–61. Rpt. in *The Allyn and Bacon Guide to Writing.* John D. Ramage, John C. Bean, and June Johnson. 3rd ed. New York: Longman, 2003. 109–112.

In the student example just shown, Sean Barry illustrates a blended strong response that intermixes rhetorical analysis of the article with his own views on tattooing. He analyzes Martin's article rhetorically by pointing out some of the limitations of a psychiatric angle of vision and by showing the values implications of Martin's references to *Moby Dick.* He adds his own ideas to the conversation by supporting two of Martin's points using his own personal examples. But he also reads Martin against the grain by arguing that Martin, perhaps influenced by his romantic view of tattoos, fails to appreciate the impact on teenagers of the commercialization of tattooing and the importance of peer group acceptance. Clearly, Sean Barry illustrates what we mean by a strong reader. In the next section on question-asking strategies, we help you begin developing the same skills.

Questions for Analyzing and Critiquing a Text

Now that you have read a sample student essay, let's consider questions you can ask to generate ideas for your own strong response. This section focuses on analyzing and critiquing a text; the next section focuses on exploring your own views of the text's subject matter.

The concept of "angle of vision" is explained in Chapter 3, pp. 51–53. See also Chapter 5, pp. 93–99, where the concept is developed in more detail.

You may find that analyzing and critiquing a text represents a new kind of critical thinking challenge. At this stage in your academic career, we aren't expecting you to be an expert at this kind of thinking. Rather, the strong response assignment will help you begin learning this skill—to see how texts work, how they are written from an angle of vision, how they may reinforce or clash with your own views, and so forth.

A strong response focused on the rhetorical features of a text looks at how the text is constructed to achieve its writer's purpose. Here are sample questions you can ask to help you analyze and critique a text. (We have illustrated them with examples from a variety of texts read by our own students in recent years.) Of course, you don't have to address all these questions in your strong response. Your goal is to find a few of these questions that particularly illuminate the text you are critiquing.

Sample Questions for Analyzing and Critiquing

Questions about purpose and audience. What is the author's purpose and audience in this text? How clearly does this text convey its purpose and reach its audience?

WHAT TO WRITE ABOUT	HYPOTHETICAL EXAMPLE
Explain your author's purpose and intended audience and show how the author appeals to that audience. Explain how choice of language and use of examples appeal to the values and beliefs of the intended audience. In critiquing the text, you might show how the article is effective for the intended audience but has gaping holes for those who don't share these values and beliefs.	In "Why Johnny Can't Read, but Yoshio Can," Richard Lynn, writing for the conservative magazine the *National Review*, tries to persuade readers that the United States should adopt Japanese methods of education. He appeals to a conservative audience by using evidence and examples that support conservative beliefs favoring competition, discipline, and high academic achievement.

Questions about the credibility of the author. How does this author try to persuade readers that he or she is knowledgeable and reliable? Is the author successful in appearing credible and trustworthy?

WHAT TO WRITE ABOUT	HYPOTHETICAL EXAMPLE
Discuss features of the text that increase the reader's confidence in the author's knowledge and trustworthiness or that help the intended audience "identify" with the writer.	In her article "The Gender Blur" in the liberal magazine *Utne Reader*, Deborah Blum establishes credibility by citing numerous scientific studies showing that she has researched the issue carefully. She also tells personal anecdotes about her liberal views, establishing credibility with liberal audiences.

Questions about the text's genre. How has the genre of the text influenced the author's style, structure, and use of evidence? How might this genre be effective for certain audiences but not for others?

WHAT TO WRITE ABOUT	HYPOTHETICAL EXAMPLE
Show how certain features of the text can be explained by the genre of the work. Show how this genre contributes to the effectiveness of the piece for certain audiences but also has limitations.	Naomi Wolf's essay "The Beauty Myth" is actually the introduction to her book *The Beauty Myth*. Therefore, it presents her major thesis and subtheses for the whole book and only begins to provide supporting evidence for these points. This lack of development might make some readers question or reject her argument.

(continued)

Questions about the author's style. How do the author's language choices contribute to the overall impact of the text?

WHAT TO WRITE ABOUT

Discuss examples of images, figures of speech, and connotations of words that draw the reader into the writer's perspective and support the writer's points. In your critique, show how language choices can be effective for some audiences but not for others.

HYPOTHETICAL EXAMPLE

In his chapter "Where I Lived, and What I Lived For" from his book *Walden*, Henry David Thoreau describes his closeness to nature in vivid poetic language. His celebration of the beauty and wonder of nature makes readers reevaluate their indifference or utilitarian attitudes toward nature. Scientific readers might be put off, however, by his romanticism.

Questions about the logic of the argument. Does the argument seem reasonable? Do the points all relate to the thesis? Are the points well supported? Are there any obvious flaws or fallacies in the argument?

WHAT TO WRITE ABOUT

Describe the argument's logical structure and analyze whether it is reasonable and well supported. Also point out places where the argument is weak or fallacious.

HYPOTHETICAL EXAMPLE

Lynn attributes the success of Japanese students to three main causes: (1) High competition, (2) a national curriculum, and (3) strong cultural incentives to excel in school. These points are well supported with evidence. But his argument that this system should be adopted in the United States is flawed because he doesn't see the dangers in the Japanese system or appreciate the cultural differences between the two countries.

Questions about the author's use of evidence. Does the evidence come from reputable sources? Is it relevant to the points it supports? Is it appropriately up-to-date? Is it sufficiently broad and representative?

WHAT TO WRITE ABOUT

Describe the sources of evidence in an argument and determine their reliability. Pay particular attention to limitations or narrowness in these data. Point out whether the information is up to date, relevant, and compelling. Point out whether the author actually provides data for the argument.

HYPOTHETICAL EXAMPLE

In his book *The McDonaldization of Society*, sociologist George Ritzer elaborates on his thesis that the fast-food industry has come to dominate all of American society. Some readers might say that Ritzer pushes his provocative thesis too far. His discussion of health care, education, and reproductive technology is brief, general, and not developed with specific data.

Questions about the author's angle of vision. What does the text reveal about the author's values and beliefs? What is excluded from the author's text? What other perspectives could a writer take on this topic?

WHAT TO WRITE ABOUT

Analyze the author's angle of vision or interpretive filter. Show what the text emphasizes and what it leaves out. Show how this angle of vision is related to certain key values or beliefs.

HYPOTHETICAL EXAMPLE

Dr. Andrés Martin, a psychiatrist, takes a clinical perspective on tattooed adolescents. He writes for fellow psychiatrists, and he uses his teen patients as the subject of his analysis. He does not consider more typical tattooed teenagers who do not need psychiatric therapy. If he had interviewed a wider range of teenagers, he might have reached different conclusions.

Questions for Developing Your Own Views about the Text's Subject Matter

As you are analyzing and critiquing a text, you also want to imagine how you might speak back to the text's ideas. Look for ways to join the text's conversation using your own critical thinking, personal experience, observations, reading, and knowledge.

In responding to a text's ideas, you will most likely include both with- and against-the-grain points. Strong readers know how to build on a text's ideas and extend them to other contexts. They are also open to challenging or disturbing ideas and try to use them constructively rather than simply dismiss them. Strong readers, in other words, try to believe new ideas as well as doubt them. In speaking back to a text's ideas in your strong response, you will have to decide how affirming of or resistant to those ideas you want to be.

Here are questions you can use to help you generate ideas:

Sample Questions for Generating Your Own Views on the Topic

Question: Which of the author's points do you agree with?

WHAT TO WRITE ABOUT	HYPOTHETICAL EXAMPLE
Build on or extend the author's points with supporting evidence from personal experience or knowledge (with the grain).	Build on Dr. Andrés Martin's ideas by discussing examples of acquaintances who have marked significant moments in their lives (graduation, career changes, divorces) by getting tattoos.

Question: What new insights has the text given you?

WHAT TO WRITE ABOUT	HYPOTHETICAL EXAMPLE
Illustrate your insights with examples (with the grain).	Explore Martin's idea that some teens use tattoos as a form of bonding by discussing the phenomenon of women in college sororities getting tattoos together.

Question: Which of the author's points do you disagree with?

WHAT TO WRITE ABOUT	HYPOTHETICAL EXAMPLE
Provide your own counterpoints and counterexamples (against the grain).	Challenge Martin's views by showing that tattooing has become a commonplace mainstream, middle-class phenomenon among teens.

Question: What gaps or omissions do you see in the text? What has the author overlooked?

WHAT TO WRITE ABOUT	HYPOTHETICAL EXAMPLE
Point out gaps. Supply your own theory for why these gaps exist. Explain the value of your own perspective, which includes what the author has excluded or overlooked (against the grain).	Point out that Martin's views leave out the role that parents play in teens' decisions to get tattoos. Explain how rebellion has influenced some of your friends.

(continued)

Question: What questions or problems does the text raise for you? How has it troubled you or expanded your views?

WHAT TO WRITE ABOUT
Show how the text causes you to question your own values, assumptions, and beliefs; show also how you question the author's beliefs and values (with the grain and against the grain).

HYPOTHETICAL EXAMPLE
Martin's highly sympathetic attitude toward tattoos portrays body modification as positive, creative, and psychologically constructive, yet he glosses over health risks and long-term costs.

Question: In what contexts can you see the usefulness of the text? What applications can you envision for it?

WHAT TO WRITE ABOUT
Explore the applicability and consequences of the text or explore its limitations (with the grain or against the grain).

HYPOTHETICAL EXAMPLE
Martin's theory that troubled teens are seeking control over their bodies and their identities through getting tattoos is one important voice in the social conversation about tattoos. However, he doesn't explore why tattooing and piercing have become so popular in the last ten years. The relationship between fads and fashions and deeper psychological factors could lead to further research.

Rereading Strategies to Stimulate Thinking for a Strong Response

Earlier in the chapter, we presented general strategies to help you become an experienced reader. Now we turn to specific rereading strategies that will stimulate ideas for your strong response. Reread your assigned text, and as you do so, try the following strategies.

Step Up Your Marginal Note Taking, Making With-the-Grain and Against-the-Grain Comments

Writing a strong response requires a deep engagement with texts, calling on all your ability to read with the grain and against the grain. As you reread your text, make copious marginal notes looking for both with-the-grain and against-the-grain responses. Figure 6.1 shows Sean Barry's marginal comments on the opening page of Martin's article. Observe how the notes incorporate with-the-grain and against-the-grain responses and show the reader truly talking back to and interacting with the text.

Identify Hot Spots in the Text

Most texts will create "hot spots" for you (each reader's hot spots are apt to be different). By "hot spot" we mean a quotation or passage that you especially notice because you agree or disagree with it or because it triggers memories or other associations. Perhaps the hot spot strikes you as particularly thought provoking. Perhaps it raises a problem or is confusing yet suggestive. Mark all hot spots with marginal notes. After you've finished reading, find these hot spots and freewrite your responses to them in a reading journal.

■ ANDRÉS MARTIN, M.D. ■

ON TEENAGERS AND TATTOOS

The skeleton dimensions I shall now proceed to set down are copied verbatim from my right arm, where I had them tattooed: as in my wild wanderings at that period, there was no other secure way of preserving such valuable statistics.

Melville, *Moby Dick CII*

[margin: Quotation from a novel?]

[margin: A strange beginning for a scientific article]

[margin: What do 19th-century sailors have to do with 21st century teens?]

Tattoos and piercings have become a part of our everyday landscape. They are ubiquitous, having entered the circles of glamour and the mainstream of fashion, and they have even become an increasingly common feature of our urban youth. Legislation in most states restricts professional tattooing to adults older than 18 years of age, so "high end" tattooing is rare in children and adolescents, but such tattoos are occasionally seen in older teenagers. Piercings, by comparison, as well as self-made or "jailhouse" type tattoos, are not at all rare among adolescents or even among schoolage children. Like hairdo, makeup, or baggy jeans, tattoos and piercings can be subject to fad influence or peer pressure in an effort toward group affiliation. As with any other fashion statement, they can be construed as bodily aids in the inner struggle toward identity consolidation, serving as adjuncts to the defining and sculpting of the self by means of external manipulations. But unlike most other body decorations, tattoos and piercings are set apart by their irreversible and permanent nature, a quality at the core of their magnetic appeal to adolescents.

[margin: Larger tattooing scene?]

[margin: I like the phrase "the defining and sculpting of the self"—sounds creative, like art]

[margin: 1]

[margin: Idea here: the body as a concrete record of experience?]

[margin: This idea is surprising and interesting. It merits lots of discussion.]

Adolescents and their parents are often at odds over the acquisition of bodily decorations. For the adolescent, piercings or tattoos may be seen as personal and beautifying statements, while parents may construe them as oppositional and enraging affronts to their authority. Distinguishing bodily adornment from self-mutilation may indeed prove challenging, particularly when a family is in disagreement over a teenager's motivations and a clinician is summoned as the final arbiter. At such times it may be most important to realize jointly that the skin can all too readily become but another battleground for the tensions of the age, arguments having less to do with tattoos and piercings than with core issues such as separation from the family matrix. Exploring the motivations and significance underlying tattoos (Grumet, 1983) and piercings can go a long way toward resolving such differences and can become a novel and additional way of getting to know teenagers. An interested and nonjudgmental appreciation of teenagers' surface presentations may become a way of making contact not only in their terms but on their turfs: quite literally on the territory of their skins.

[margin: Which teenagers? All teenagers?]

[margin: Good open-minded, practical approach to teen tattoos]

[margin: 2]

[margin: These terms show the main opposing views on tattoos.]

[margin: Is he speaking only to psychiatrists? Does this clinical perspective have other applications?]

The following three sections exemplify some of the complex psychological underpinnings of youth tattooing.

[margin: 3 I like Martin's focus on complexity]

FIGURE 6.1 ■ Student Marginal Notes on Martin's Text

Write Questions Triggered by the Text

Almost any text triggers questions as you read. A good way to begin formulating a strong response is simply to write out several questions that the text caused you to think about. Then explore your responses to those questions through freewriting. Sometimes the freewrite will trigger more questions.

Articulate Your Difference from the Intended Audience

See pp. 66–67 for a discussion of audience analysis.

In some cases you can read strongly by articulating how you differ from the text's intended audience. As we showed in Chapter 4, experienced writers try to imagine their audience. They ask: What are my audience's values? How interested in and knowledgeable about my topic is my audience? Eventually, the author makes decisions about audience—in effect "creates" the audience—so that the text reveals both an image of the author and of its intended reader.

Your own experiences, arising from your gender, class, ethnicity, sexual orientation, political and religious beliefs, interests, values, and so forth may cause you to feel estranged from the author's imagined audience. If the text seems written for straight people and you are gay, or for Christians and you are a Muslim or an atheist, or for environmentalists and you grew up in a small logging community, you may well resist the text. Sometimes your sense of exclusion from the intended audience makes it difficult to read a text at all. For example, a female student of our acquaintance once brought a class to a standstill by slamming the course anthology on her desk and exclaiming, "How can you people stand reading this patriarchal garbage!" She had become so irritated by the authors' assumption that all readers shared their male-oriented values that she could no longer bear to read the selections.

When you differ significantly from the text's assumed audience, you can often use this difference to question the author's underlying assumptions, values, and beliefs.

For Writing and Discussion

What follows is a short passage by writer Annie Dillard in response to a question about how she chooses to spend her time. This passage often evokes heated responses from our students.

> I don't do housework. Life is too short. . . . I let almost all my indoor plants die from neglect while I was writing the book. There are all kinds of ways to live. You can take your choice. You can keep a tidy house, and when St. Peter asks you what you did with your life, you can say, "I kept a tidy house, I made my own cheese balls."

Individual task: Read the passage and then briefly freewrite your reaction to it.

Group task: Working in groups or as a whole class, develop answers to the following questions:

1. What values does Dillard assume her audience holds?
2. What kinds of readers are apt to feel excluded from that audience?
3. If you are not part of the intended audience for this passage, what in the text evokes resistance?

Articulate Your Own Purpose for Reading

You may sometimes read a text against the grain if your purposes for reading differ from what the author imagined. Normally you read a text because you share the author's interest in a question and want to know the author's answer. In other words, you usually read to join the author's conversation. But suppose that you wish to review the writings of nineteenth-century scientists to figure out what they assumed about nature (or women, or God, or race, or capitalism). Or suppose that you examine a politician's metaphors to see what they reveal about his or her values, or analyze *National Geographic* for evidence of political bias. In these cases, you will be reading against the grain of the text. In a sense, you would be blindsiding the authors—while they are talking about topic X, you are observing them for topic Y. This method of resistant reading is very common in academia.

Readings

This section contains three articles that invite strong responses. The first two articles are about controversies over smoking, and the last explores an environmental issue. One of the articles is distinctly closed form; however, several resist easy classification in that they include some features of open-form prose: lots of narrative elements and occasional implicit—rather than explicitly stated—points. Each piece will prompt your personal and intellectual grappling with the author's ideas and beliefs as well as attract your attention to the author's rhetorical strategies. Your instructor may choose one of these pieces as the subject of your assignment for this chapter. Because your task is to summarize your assigned piece and respond strongly to it, we omit the questions for analysis that typically accompany readings elsewhere in the text.

The first reading, by writer and journalist Florence King, first appeared in 1990 in the *National Review*, a news commentary magazine with a conservative readership.

■ FLORENCE KING ■
I'D RATHER SMOKE THAN KISS

1   I am a woman of 54 who started smoking at the late age of 26. I had no reason to start earlier; smoking as a gesture of teenage rebellion would have been pointless in my family. My mother started at 12. At first her preferred brands were the Fatimas and Sweet Caporals that were all the rage during World War I. Later she switched to Lucky Strike Greens and smoked four packs a day.

2   She made no effort to cut down while she was pregnant with me, but I was not a low-birth-weight baby. The Angel of Death saw the nicotine stains on our door and passed over. I weighed nine pounds. My smoke-filled childhood was remarkably healthy and safe except for the time Mama set fire to my Easter basket. That was all right, however, because I was not the Easter-basket type.

3   I probably wouldn't have started smoking if I had not been a writer. One day in the drugstore I happened to see a display of Du Maurier

English cigarettes in pretty red boxes with a tray that slid out like a little drawer. I thought the boxes would be ideal for keeping my paperclips in, so I bought two.

When I got home, I emptied out the cigarettes and replaced them with paperclips, putting the loose cigarettes in the desk drawer where the loose paperclips had been scattered. Now the cigarettes were scattered. One day, spurred by two of my best traits, neatness and thrift, I decided that the cigarettes were messing up the desk and going to waste, so I tried one.

It never would have happened if I had been able to offer the Du Mauriers to a lover who smoked, but I didn't get an addicted one until after I had become addicted myself. When he entered my life it was the beginning of a uniquely pleasurable footnote to sex, the post-coital cigarette.

Today when I see the truculent, joyless faces of anti-tobacco Puritans, I remember those easy-going smoking sessions with that man: the click of the lighter, the brief orange glow in the darkness, the ashtray between us— spilling sometimes because we laughed so much together that the bed shook.

A cigarette ad I remember from my childhood said: "One of life's great pleasures is smoking. Camels give you all of the excitement of choice tobaccos. Is enjoyment good for you? You just bet it is." My sentiments exactly. I believe life should be savored rather than lengthened, and I am ready to fight the misanthropes among us who are trying to make me switch.

A *misanthrope* is someone who hates people. Hatred of smokers is the most popular form of closet misanthropy in America today. Smokists don't hate the sin, they hate the sinner, and they don't care who knows it.

Their campaign never would have succeeded so well if the alleged dangers of smoking had remained a problem for smokers alone. We simply would have been allowed to invoke the Right to Die, always a favorite with democratic lovers of mankind, and that would have been that. To put a real damper on smoking and making it stick, the right of others not to die had to be invoked somehow so "passive smoking" was invented.

The name was a stroke of genius. Just about everybody in America is passive. Passive Americans have been taking it on the chin for years, but the concept of passive smoking offered them a chance to hate in the land of compulsory love, a chance to dish it out for a change with no fear of being called a bigot. The right of self-defense, long since gone up in smoke, was back.

Smokers on the Run

The big, brave Passive Americans responded with a vengeance. They began shouting at smokers in restaurants. They shuddered and grimaced and said "Ugh!" as they waved away the impure air. They put up little signs in their cars and homes: at first they said, "Thank You for Not Smoking," but now they feature a cigarette in a circle slashed with a red diagonal. Smokists even issue conditional invitations. I know—I got one. The woman said, "I'd love to have you to dinner, but I don't allow smoking in my home. Do you think you could refrain for a couple of hours?" I said, "Go — yourself," and she told everybody I was the rudest person she had ever met.

12   Smokists practice a sadistic brutality that would have done Vlad the Impaler proud. *Washington Times* columnist and smoker Jeremiah O'Leary was the target of two incredibly baleful letters to the editor after he defended the habit. The first letter said, "Smoke yourself to death, but please don't smoke me to death," but it was only a foretaste of the letter that followed:

> Jeremiah O'Leary's March 1 column, "Perilous persuaders . . . tenacious zealots," is a typical statement of a drug addict trying to defend his vice.
>
> To a cigarette smoker, all the world is an ashtray. A person who would never throw a candy wrapper or soda can will drop a lit cigarette without a thought.
>
> Mr. O'Leary is mistaken that nonsmokers are concerned about the damage smokers are inflicting on themselves. What arrogance! We care about living in a pleasant environment without the stench of tobacco smoke or the litter of smokers' trash.
>
> If Mr. O'Leary wants to kill himself, that is his choice. I ask only that he do so without imposing his drug or discarded filth on me. *It would be nice if he would die in such a way that would not increase my health-insurance rates* [my italics].

13   The expendability of smokers has also aroused the tender concern of the Federal Government. I was taking my first drag of the morning when I opened the *Washington Post* and found myself starting at this headline: NOT SMOKING COULD BE HAZARDOUS TO PENSION SYSTEM. MEDICARE, SOCIAL SECURITY MAY BE PINCHED IF ANTI-TOBACCO CAMPAIGN SUCCEEDS, REPORT SAYS.

14   The article explained that since smokers die younger than non-smokers, the Social Security we don't live to collect is put to good use, because we subsidize the pensions of our fellow citizens like a good American should. However, this convenient arrangement could end, for if too many smokers heed the Surgeon General's warnings and stop smoking, they will live too long and break the budget.

15   That, of course, is not how the government economists phrased it. They said:

> The implications of our results are that smokers "save" the Social Security system hundreds of billions of dollars. Certainly this does not mean that decreased smoking would not be socially beneficial. In fact, it is probably one of the most cost-effective ways of increasing average longevity. It does indicate, however, that if people alter their behavior in a manner which extends life expectancy, then this must be recognized by our national retirement program.

16   At this point the reporter steps in with the soothing reminder that "the war on tobacco is more appropriately cast as a public-health crusade than as

an attempt to save money." But then we hear from Health Policy Center economist Gio Gori, who says: "Prevention of disease is obviously something we should strive for. But it's not going to be cheap. We will have to pay for those who survive."

Something darkling crawls out of that last sentence. The whole article has a die-damn-you undertow that would make an honest misanthrope wonder if perhaps a cure for cancer was discovered years ago, but due to cost-effectiveness considerations . . .   17

But honest misanthropes are at a premium that no amount of Raleigh coupons can buy. Instead we have tinpot Torquemadas like Ahron Leichtman, president of Citizens against Tobacco Smoke, who announced after the airline smoking bans: "CATS will next launch its smoke-free airports project, which is the second phase of our smoke-free skies campaign." Representative Richard J. Durbin (D., Ill.) promised the next target will be "other forms of public transportation such as Amtrak, the inter-city bus system, and commuter lines that receive federal funding." His colleague, Senator Frank Lautenberg (D., N.J.), confessed, "We *are* gloating a little bit," and Fran Du Melle of the Coalition on Smoking OR Health, gave an ominous hint of things to come when she heralded the airline ban as "only one encouraging step on the road to a smoke-free society."   18

Health Nazis

These remarks manifest a sly, cowardly form of misanthropy that the Germans call *Schadenfreude:* pleasure in the unhappiness of others. It has always been the chief subconscious motivation of Puritans, but the smokists harbor several other subconscious motivations that are too egregious to bear close examination—which is precisely what I will now conduct.   19

Study their agitprop and you will find the same theme of pitiless revulsion running through nearly all of their so-called public-service ads. One of the earliest showed Brooke Shields toweling her wet hair and saying disgustedly, "I hate it when somebody smokes after I've just washed my hair. Yuk!" Another proclaimed, "Kissing a smoker is like licking an ashtray." The latest, a California radio spot, asks: "Why sell cigarettes? Why not just sell phlegm and cut out the middle man?"   20

Fear of being physically disgusting and smelling bad is the American's worst nightmare, which is why bathsoap commercials never include the controlled-force shower nozzles recommended by environmentalists in *their* public-service ads. The showering American uses oceans of hot water to get "ZESTfully clean" in a sudsy deluge that is often followed by a deodorant commercial.   21

"Raise your hand, raise your hand, raise your hand if you're SURE!" During this jingle we see an ecstatically happy assortment of people from all walks of life and representing every conceivable national origin, all obediently raising their hands, until the ad climaxes with a shot of the Statue of Liberty raising hers.   22

The New Greenhorns

23 The Statue of Liberty has become a symbol of immigration, the first aspect of American life the huddled masses experienced. The second was being called a "dirty little" something-or-other as soon as they got off the boat. Deodorant companies see the wisdom in reminding their descendants of the dirty-little period. You can sell a lot of deodorant that way. Ethnics get the point directly; WASPs get it by default in the subliminal reminder that, historically speaking, there is no such thing as a dirty little WASP.

24 Smokers have become the new greenhorns in the land of sweetness and health, scapegoats for a quintessentially American need, rooted in our fabled Great Diversity, to identify and punish the undesirables among us. Ethnic tobacco haters can get even for past slurs on their fastidiousness by refusing to inhale around dirty little smokers; WASP tobacco haters can once again savor the joys of being the "real Americans" by hurling with impunity the same dirty little insults their ancestors hurled with impunity.

25 The tobacco pogrom serves additionally as the basis for a class war in a nation afraid to mention the word "class" aloud. Hating smokers is an excellent way to hate the white working class without going on record as hating the white working class.

26 The anti-smoking campaign has enjoyed thumping success among the "data-receptive," a lovely euphemism describing the privilege of spending four years sitting in a classroom. The ubiquitous statistic that college graduates are two-and-a-half times as likely to be non-smokers as those who never went beyond high school is balm to the data-receptive, many of whom are only a generation or two removed from the lunch-bucket that smokers represent. Haunted by a fear of falling back down the ladder, and half-believing that they deserve to, they soothe their anxiety by kicking a smoker as the proverbial hen-pecked husband soothed his by kicking the dog.

27 The earnest shock that greeted the RJR Reynolds Uptown marketing scheme aimed at blacks cramped the vituperative style of the data-receptive. Looking down on blacks as smokers might be interpreted as looking down on blacks as blacks, so they settled for aping the compassionate concern they picked up from the media.

28 They got their sadism-receptive bona fides back when the same company announced plans to target Dakota cigarettes at a fearsome group called "virile females."

29 When I first saw the headline I thought surely they meant me: what other woman writer is sent off to a book-and-author luncheon with the warning, "Watch your language and don't wear your Baltimore Orioles warm-up jacket." But they didn't. Virile females are "Caucasian females, 18 to 24, with no education beyond high school and entry-level service or factory jobs."

30 Commentators could barely hide their smirks as they listed the tractor pulls, motorcycle races, and macho-man contests that comprise the leisure activities of the target group. Crocodile tears flowed copiously. "It's blue-collar people without enough education to understand what is happening

to them," mourned Virginia Ernster of the University of California School of Medicine. "It's pathetic that these companies would work so hard to get these women who may not feel much control over their lives." George Will, winner of the metaphor-man contest, wrote: "They use sophisticated marketing like a sniper's rifle, drawing beads on the most vulnerable, manipulable Americans." (I would walk a mile to see Virginia Ernster riding on the back of George Will's motorcycle.)

Hating smokers is also a guiltless way for a youth-worshipping country to hate old people, as well as those who are merely over the hill—especially middle-aged women. Smokers predominate in both groups because we saw Bette Davis's movies the same year they were released. Now we catch *Dark Victory* whenever it comes on television just for the pleasure of watching the scene in the staff lounge at the hospital when Dr. George Brent and all the other doctors light up.

31

Smoking is the only thing that the politically correct can't blame on white males. Red men started it, but the cowardly cossacks of the anti-tobacco crusade don't dare say so because it would be too close for comfort. They see no difference between tobacco and hard drugs like cocaine and crack because they don't wish to see any. Never mind that you will never be mugged by someone needing a cigarette; hatred of smokers is the conformist's substitute for the hatred that dare not speak its name. Condemning "substance abuse" out of hand, without picking and choosing or practicing discrimination, produces lofty sensations of democratic purity in those who keep moving farther and farther out in the suburbs to get away from . . . smokers.

32

The genre features of a scientific research report are explained in Chapter 4 on pp. 68–69.

The second reading is a scientific research report from the *American Journal of Public Health*. Note its multiple authors, its form, its use of tables, and its documentation style.*

■ Gina Escamilla, BA, Angie L. Cradock, MS, and Ichiro Kawachi, MD, PhD ■

WOMEN AND SMOKING IN HOLLYWOOD MOVIES: A Content Analysis

According to the Centers for Disease Control and Prevention, over one third (34.7%) of female high school students in a national survey reported smoking at least 1 cigarette in the previous month, up 10% since 1993 and

1

*The documentation style, common in the sciences, differs from the MLA and APA parenthetical citation systems explained in Chapter 23. For the article, each superscript refers to the similarly numbered source in "References" at the end of the article.

32% since 1991.[1] Cigarette smoking is initiated primarily in adolescence. Among adult regular smokers, 71% reported having formed the habit before the age of 18 years.[2]

2   Television and popular films have contributed to the allure of smoking. A recent study found that young adults smoked in about 75% of music videos.[3] Although tobacco industry documents suggest that manufacturers have not engaged in deliberate product placement in Hollywood movies since the late 1980s,[4] recent evidence indicates that smoking continues to be depicted at very high levels. Moreover, the gap between the prevalence of tobacco use in movies and in actual life has steadily widened through the 1990s.[5] A recent analysis of G-rated children's animated films found that more than two thirds featured tobacco or alcohol use in story plots, with no clear reference made to the adverse health consequences associated with these substances.[6]

3   Popular film actresses are likely to be role models for young women and adolescent girls. The way that movie stars portray cigarette smoking on the screen may influence young girls' attitudes toward the habit. In this study, we analyzed the portrayal of smoking by 10 leading Hollywood actresses.

Methods

Selection of Actresses

4   We selected 10 leading Hollywood actresses by surveying the 1997 issues of 5 popular magazines that had the highest readership among women aged 18 to 24 years, according to *Simmons Study of Media and Markets.*[7] Magazine titles from the "Special Interest" and "Women's Magazines" categories were selected if the editorial descriptions taken from *Bacon's Magazine Directory*[8] included 1 or more of the following key words or phrases: entertainment, contemporary or current, Hollywood, celebrity, film or movie, personality profiles, women in their 20s, or young women. All issues for the period January 1997 through December 1997 were obtained for the magazines *Cosmopolitan, Glamour, Vogue, Vanity Fair,* and *Rolling Stone.* Each issue was analyzed for the appearance of female film stars. Advertisements were excluded, and the search was limited to women whose careers are primarily in film. The number of magazine appearances was tallied for each actress, and the 10 actresses with the greatest number of appearances were selected.

Selection of Films

5   A list of films starring each selected actress was generated from the Web site www.tvguide.com. This Web site, maintained by TV Guide Entertainment Network, provides information on the cast, credits, and reviews for some 35,000 movies. Five titles released between 1993 and 1997 were randomly selected for each of the 10 actresses. We excluded period dramas as well as movies in which the actresses did not play a lead or major supporting role. The title, year of release, rating (R, NC-17, PG, PG-13, G), and genre of each film were recorded.

Content Analysis

We followed the analytic approach described by Hazan et al.[9] Each film was divided into 5-minute intervals. The occurrence of smoking episodes in each interval was recorded on a coding sheet. We recorded both actual and implied smoking behavior (e.g., holding or smoking a lit or unlit tobacco product); the presence of cigarettes or other smoking paraphernalia (e.g., cigars, matches, and ashtrays); and environmental messages, including "no smoking" signs, tobacco advertising, and tobacco merchandise. Additionally, we recorded smoker characteristics (e.g., gender; whether lead, supporting, or other character); location (i.e., outdoors or in a bar, restaurant, home, or car); the social context of the event (i.e., smoking alone or with others and whether consideration was shown to nonsmokers). We also noted verbal and nonverbal tobacco messages (i.e., positive or negative consequences of smoking behavior and discussion about tobacco products, including positive, negative, or mixed reference to tobacco use). To establish interrater reliability, 5 films (10% of total sample) were randomly selected and independently rated by graduate student coders (G. Escamilla and A. L. Cradock). The coders had 99% agreement on all of the parameters examined regarding the depiction of smoking.

6

After viewing each film, the coders also completed a qualitative assessment of smoking themes and behaviors, addressing contextual issues such as the emotional valence attached to the smoking behavior and the significance of smoking for the character portrayed. All statistical analyses were performed with Stata.[10]

7

Results

The 50 films, representing approximately 96 hours of footage, were broken down into 1116 5-minute intervals (excluding introductions and credits). Of these, 317 (28.4%) of the intervals depicted smoking behavior (Table 1). Cigarettes were the most common tobacco product shown (23.9%). Over half of the smoking episodes (58.7%) occurred in the presence of others who were not smoking.

8

As Table 2 indicates, smoking was significantly more likely to be depicted in R-rated or unrated films than in PG/PG-13-rated films ($P < .001$). Although the percentage of lead actors or supporting actors shown smoking was similar for men and women (38% and 42%, respectively), sex differences were apparent according to the film's rating. Males in lead or supporting roles were 2.5 times more likely to be shown smoking in R-rated/unrated movies than in PG/PG-13-rated films ($P < .001$). By contrast, the portrayal of smoking by a female lead or supporting character was not significantly different according to the movie's rating; that is, female actresses were *equally likely* to light up in movies aimed at juvenile audiences as in those aimed at mature audiences.

9

Smoking was also more likely to be depicted in the movies starring younger actresses. The mean age of the 10 actresses was 29.3 years (range = 21–40 years). When we categorized actresses according to quartiles by age,

10

movies starring actresses in the youngest quartile featured 3.6 times as many intervals depicting smoking as did movies starring actresses in the oldest age group (95% confidence interval [95% CI] = 2.4, 5.4).

TABLE 1 Depiction of Smoking Behavior and Paraphernalia, Smoking Context, and Location of Smoking Behaviors in 50 Hollywood Movies

	No. of 5-Min Intervals	Total 5-Min Movie Intervals, % (n = 1116)	Intervals Containing Smoking Behavior, % (n = 317)
Smoking behavior and paraphernalia			
Smoking (actual or implied) behavior	317	28.4	—
Cigarettes	267	23.9	—
Cigarette packs	64	5.7	—
Matches/lighter	108	9.7	—
Cigars, pipes, or smokeless tobacco	71	6.4	—
Ashtray	105	9.4	—
Social context of smoking behavior[a]			
Alone	46	—	14.5
With others (nonsmokers)	186	—	58.7
With others, including smokers and nonsmokers	71	—	22.4
Consideration shown to nonsmokers	5	—	1.6
Location of smoking behavior[b]			
Bar/lounge	25	—	7.9
Home/apartment	84	—	26.5
Restaurant	28	—	8.8
Car	40	—	12.6
Outside	103	—	32.5
Other location	69	—	21.8

[a]A total of 4.4% of intervals depicted incidental smoking of characters other than the lead/supporting actors.

[b]Percentages total more than 100 as smoking may have occurred in more than one context in the same interval.

TABLE 2 Odds Ratios (ORs) and 95% Confidence Intervals (95% CIs) for the Occurrence of Smoking Behavior in R-Rated/Unrated Movies

	OR[a]	95% CI
Overall smoking behavior	1.62	1.20–2.14
Smoking by male lead or supporting actor	2.48	1.55–3.97
Smoking by female lead or supporting actor	1.23	0.88–1.86

[a]Referent is PG/PG-13 movies.

Negative messages regarding tobacco product use (e.g., depictions of the   11
consequences of the use of tobacco products, such as coughing or grimacing
at the smell of smoke) were more common than positive messages (30 vs 23)
among the 50 films viewed. However, only 9 of 22 messages in PG/PG-13
films depicted smoking in a negative light, compared with 21 of 31 messages
in R-rated/unrated films; that is, movies aimed at young audiences were *less*
likely (odds ratio = 0.33; 95% CI = 0.11, 1.01) to carry negative messages
associated with tobacco use than were movies made for mature audiences.

In a qualitative analysis of the social context of smoking, sex differences   12
were detected in the themes associated with tobacco use. Women were likely to be portrayed using tobacco products to control their emotions, to manifest power and sex appeal, to enhance their body image or self-image, to
control weight, or to give themselves a sense of comfort and companionship. Men were more likely to be depicted using tobacco products to reinforce their masculine identity; to portray a character with power, prestige, or
significant authority; to show male bonding; or to signify their status as a
"protector" (the last 3 themes were associated with cigar smoking).

Discussion

The results of this study raise concerns about exposure to smoking in popu-   13
lar movies. According to social learning theory, by paying attention to the
behaviors of a person who possesses the qualities, skills, and capacities one
hopes to achieve, a young observer learns to model these behaviors.[11]
Among third- through sixth-grade students who had smoked, having role
models who smoked was more common, and having beliefs about the
adverse consequences of smoking was less common than among their peers
who never smoked.[12]

The prevalence of smoking by both female (42%) and male (38%) lead or   14
supporting actors was substantially higher than the national smoking prevalence for females (24.3%) and males (29.2%) aged 18 to 44.[13] This discrepancy is significant, given that adolescents who overestimate smoking prevalence among young people and adults are more likely to become smokers
themselves.[2] In the films viewed, over half of the smoking episodes occurred
in the presence of others who were not smoking, and in fewer than 2% of
the intervals was consideration shown to nonsmokers (e.g., smoker leaves
the room or asks permission to smoke). The depiction of smoking in
Hollywood would thus appear to reinforce smoking as an acceptable and
normative behavior in society. While most young people older than 18
years are able to acknowledge that on-screen smoking is part of a movie
role, this may be more difficult for younger females aged 12 to 17 years,
among whom smoking initiation is taking place.

Our qualitative analysis of smoking identified several themes related to   15
smoking. One of the most prominent themes was using smoking to control
emotion, which was specific to female characters and occurred during
times of stress or difficulty, when the character was trying to regain or

establish control, to repress or deny emotion, or to exit a negative or threatening situation.

16   Important limitations of this study should be noted. First, the sampling of magazine titles was limited to those with the highest readership among women aged 18 to 24 years. On the other hand, given the content and focus of the magazines, it is highly likely that they are widely read by adolescent girls. Surveying the issues of only 5 magazines may have biased our sample of actresses. However, a recent study on the influence of movie stars on adolescent smoking identified 6 of the 10 actresses in our sample as being the "most favorite" among girls.[14] Given that African American and Latina women have become targets for tobacco advertisements, it would also be informative to survey movies starring actresses of different racial/ethnic backgrounds. Future studies need to be extended to popular male actors as well. Finally, replication of our findings through the use of raters who are unaware of the hypotheses would be desirable, since the smoking-related themes emerging from our qualitative analyses may have been biased.

17   Our findings, in conjunction with those of others,[14] suggest the need for the development of policies—such as the adoption of a voluntary code of ethics by the entertainment industry—to eliminate the depiction of smoking in ways that appeal to adolescent audiences.

References

1. Centers for Disease Control and Prevention. Tobacco use among high school students—United States, 1997. *MMWR Morb Mortal Wkly Rep.* 1998; 47:229–233.
2. *Preventing Tobacco Use Among Young People: A Report of the Surgeon General.* Atlanta, Ga: National Center for Chronic Disease Prevention and Health Promotion, Office on Smoking and Health; 1994.
3. DuRant, RH, Rome ES, Rich M, Allred E, Emans SJ, Woods ER. Tobacco and alcohol use behaviors portrayed in music videos: a content analysis. *Am J Public Health,* 1997; 87:1131–1135.
4. http://www.philipmorris.com/getallimg.asp. DOC_ID = 2025863645/3659. Accessed July 1998.
5. Stockwell TF, Glantz SA. Tobacco use is increasing in popular films. *Tob Control.* 1997; 6:282–284.
6. Goldstein AO, Sobel RA, Newman GR. Tobacco and alcohol use in G-rated children's animated films. *JAMA.* 1999; 281:1131–1136.
7. Simmons Market Research Bureau. *Simmons Study of Media and Markets, M1.* New York, NY: Simmons Market Research Bureau; 1994; 0162–0163.
8. *Bacon's Magazine Directory: Directory of Magazines and Newsletters.* Chicago, Ill: Bacon's Information Inc; 1988.
9. Hazan AR, Lipton HL, Glantz S. Popular films do not reflect current tobacco use. *Am J Public Health.* 1994; 84:998–1000.
10. *Stata Statistical Software: Release 5.0.* College Station, Tex: Stata Corporation; 1997.
11. Greaves L. *Mixed Messages: Women, Tobacco and the Media.* Ottawa, Ontario: Health Canada; 1996.
12. Greenlund KJ, Johnson CC, Webber LS, Berenson GS. Cigarette smoking attitudes and first use among third- through sixth-grade students: the Bogalusa Heart Study. *Am J Public Health* 1997; 87:1345–1348.

13. Centers for Disease Control and Prevention. Cigarette smoking among adults—United States, 1995. *MMWR Morb Mortal Wkly Rep.* 1997; 46:1217–1220.
14. Distefan JM, Gilpin EA, Sargent JD, Pierce JP. Do movie stars encourage adolescents to start smoking? Evidence from California. *Prev Med.* 1999; 28:1–11.

The last reading, by prolific environmental writer Edward Abbey, first appeared in 1971 in *Beyond the Wall: Essays from the Outside.* His view of Lake Powell, a reservoir formed on the border of Utah and Arizona by the damming of Glen Canyon, has helped stimulate a growing anti-dam movement among environmentalists.

▪ EDWARD ABBEY ▪
THE DAMNATION OF A CANYON

There was a time when, in my search for essences, I concluded that the canyonland country has no heart. I was wrong. The canyonlands did have a heart, a living heart, and that heart was Glen Canyon and the golden, flowing Colorado River. 1

In the summer of 1959 a friend and I made a float trip in little rubber rafts down through the length of Glen Canyon, starting at Hite and getting off the river near Gunsight Butte—The Crossing of the Fathers. In this voyage of some 150 miles and ten days our only motive power, and all that we needed, was the current of the Colorado River. 2

In the summer and fall of 1967 I worked as a seasonal park ranger at the new Glen Canyon National Recreation Area. During my five-month tour of duty I worked at the main marina and headquarters area called Wahweap, at Bullfrog Basin toward the upper end of the reservoir, and finally at Lee's Ferry downriver from Glen Canyon Dam. In a number of powerboat tours I was privileged to see almost all of our nation's newest, biggest and most impressive "recreational facility." 3

Having thus seen Glen Canyon both before and after what we may fairly call its damnation, I feel that I am in a position to evaluate the transformation of the region caused by construction of the dam. I have had the unique opportunity to observe firsthand some of the differences between the environment of a free river and a powerplant reservoir. 4

One should admit at the outset to a certain bias. Indeed I am a "butterfly chaser, googly eyed bleeding heart and wild conservative." I take a dim view of dams; I find it hard to learn to love cement; I am poorly impressed by concrete aggregates and statistics in the cubic tons. But in this weakness I am not alone, for I belong to that ever-growing number of Americans, probably a good majority now, who have become aware that a fully industrial- 5 ized, thoroughly urbanized, elegantly computerized social system is not suitable for human habitation. Great for machines, yes: But unfit for people.

6   Lake Powell, formed by Glen Canyon Dam, is not a lake. It is a reservoir, with a constantly fluctuating water level—more like a bathtub that is never drained than a true lake. As at Hoover (or Boulder) Dam, the sole practical function of this impounded water is to drive the turbines that generate electricity in the powerhouse at the base of the dam. Recreational benefits were of secondary importance in the minds of those who conceived and built this dam. As a result the volume of water in the reservoir is continually being increased or decreased according to the requirements of the Basin States Compact and the power-grid system of which Glen Canyon Dam is a component.

7   The rising and falling water level entails various consequences. One of the most obvious, well known to all who have seen Lake Mead, is the "bathtub ring" left on the canyon walls after each drawdown of water, or what rangers at Glen Canyon call the Bathtub Foundation. This phenomenon is perhaps of no more than aesthetic importance; yet it is sufficient to dispel any illusion one might have, in contemplating the scene, that you are looking upon a natural lake.

8   The utter barrenness of the reservoir shoreline recalls by contrast the aspect of things before the dam, when Glen Canyon formed the course of the untamed Colorado. Then we had a wild and flowing river lined by boulder-strewn shores, sandy beaches, thickets of tamarisk and willow, and glades of cottonwoods.

9   The thickets teemed with songbirds: vireos, warblers, mockingbirds and thrushes. On the open beaches were killdeer, sandpipers, herons, ibises, egrets. Living in grottoes in the canyon walls were swallows, swifts, hawks, wrens, and owls. Beaver were common if not abundant: not an evening would pass, in drifting down the river, that we did not see them or at least hear the whack of their flat tails on the water. Above the river shores were the great recessed alcoves where water seeped from the sandstone, nourishing the semi-tropical hanging gardens of orchid, ivy and columbine, with their associated swarms of insects and birdlife.

10   Up most of the side canyon, before damnation, there were springs, sometimes flowing streams, waterfalls and plunge pools—the kind of marvels you can now find only in such small scale remnants of Glen Canyon as the Escalante area. In the rich flora of these laterals the larger mammals—mule deer, coyote, bobcat, ring-tailed cat, gray fox, kit fox, skunk, badger, and others—found a home. When the river was dammed almost all of these things were lost. Crowded out—or drowned and buried under mud.

11   The difference between the present reservoir, with its silent sterile shores and debris choked side canyons, and the original Glen Canyon, is the difference between death and life. Glen Canyon was alive. Lake Powell is a graveyard.

For those who may think I exaggerate the contrast between the former   12
river canyon and the present man-made impoundment, I suggest a trip on
Lake Powell followed immediately by another boat trip on the river below
the dam. Take a boat from Lee's Ferry up the river to within sight of the
dam, then shut off the motor and allow yourself the rare delight of a quiet,
effortless drifting down the stream. In that twelve-mile stretch of living
green, singing birds, flowing water and untarnished canyon walls—sights
and sounds a million years older and infinitely lovelier than the roar of
motorboats—you will rediscover a small and imperfect sampling of the kind
of experience that was taken away from everybody when the oligarchs and
politicians condemned our river for purposes of their own.

Lake Powell, though not a lake, may well be as its defenders assert the   13
most beautiful reservoir in the world. Certainly it has a photogenic backdrop of buttes and mesas projecting above the expansive surface of stag-
nant waters where the speedboats, houseboats and cabin cruisers play. But
it is no longer a wilderness. It is no longer a place of natural life. It is no
longer Glen Canyon.

The defenders of the dam argue that the recreational benefits available on   14
the surface of the reservoir outweigh the loss of Indian ruins, historical sites,
wildlife and wilderness adventure. Relying on the familiar quantitative logic
of business and bureaucracy, they assert that whereas only a few thousand
citizens even ventured down the river through Glen Canyon, now millions
can—or will—enjoy the motorized boating and hatchery fishing available
on the reservoir. They will also argue that the rising waters behind the dam
have made such places as Rainbow Bridge accessible by power-boat.
Formerly you could get there only by walking (six miles).

This argument appeals to the wheelchair ethos of the wealthy, upper-   15
middle-class American slob. If Rainbow Bridge is worth seeing at all, then by
God it should be easily, readily, immediately available to everybody with the
money to buy a big powerboat. Why should a trip to such a place be the
privilege only of those who are willing to walk six miles? Or if Pikes Peak is
worth getting to, then why not build a highway to the top of it so that anyone can get there? Anytime? Without effort? Or as my old man would say,
"By Christ, one man's just as good as another—if not a damn sight better."

It is quite true that the flooding of Glen Canyon has opened up to the   16
motorboat explorer parts of side canyons that formerly could be reached
only by people able to walk. But the sum total of terrain visible to the eye
and touchable by hand and foot has been greatly diminished, not increased.
Because of the dam the river is gone, the inner canyon is gone, the best
parts of the numerous side canyons are gone—all hidden beneath hundreds
of feet of polluted water, accumulating silt, and mounting tons of trash.
This portion of Glen Canyon—and who can estimate how many cubic miles
were lost?—*is no longer accessible to anybody.* (Except scuba divers.) And this,
do not forget, was the most valuable part of Glen Canyon, richest in
scenery, archaeology, history, flora, and fauna.

17   Not only has the heart of Glen Canyon been buried, but many of the side canyons above the fluctuating waterline are now rendered more difficult, not easier, to get into. This is because the debris brought down into them by desert storms, no longer carried away by the river, must unavoidably build up in the area where flood meets reservoir. Narrow Canyon, for example, at the head of the impounded waters, is already beginning to silt up and to amass huge quantities of driftwood, some of it floating on the surface, some of it half afloat beneath the surface. Anyone who has tried to pilot a motorboat through a raft of half-sunken logs and bloated dead cows will have his own thoughts on the accessibility of these waters.

18   Second, the question of costs. It is often stated that the dam and its reservoir have opened up to the many what was formerly restricted to the few, implying in this case that what was once expensive has now been made cheap. Exactly the opposite is true.

19   Before the dam, a float trip down the river through Glen Canyon would cost you a minimum of seven days' time, well within anyone's vacation allotment and a capital outlay of about forty dollars—the prevailing price of a two-man rubber boat with oars, available at any army-navy surplus store. A life jacket might be useful but not required, for there were no dangerous rapids in the 150 miles of Glen Canyon. As the name implies, this stretch of the river was in fact so easy and gentle that the trip could be and was made by all sorts of amateurs: by Boy Scouts, Camp Fire Girls, stenographers, schoolteachers, students, little old ladies in inner tubes. Guides, professional boatmen, giant pontoons, outboard motors, radios, rescue equipment were not needed. The Glen Canyon float trip was an adventure anyone could enjoy, on his own, for a cost less than that of spending two days and nights in a Page motel. Even food was there, in the water: the channel catfish were easier to catch and a lot better eating than the striped bass and rainbow trout dumped by the ton into the reservoir these days. And one other thing: at the end of the float trip you still owned your boat, usable for many more such casual and carefree expeditions.

20   What is the situation now? Float trips are no longer possible. The only way left for the exploration of the reservoir and what remains of Glen Canyon demands the use of a powerboat. Here you have three options: (1) buy your own boat and engine, the necessary auxiliary equipment, the fuel to keep it moving, the parts and repairs to keep it running, the permits and licenses required for legal operation, the trailer to transport it; (2) rent a boat; or (3) go on a commercial excursion boat, packed in with other sightseers, following a preplanned itinerary. This kind of play is only for the affluent.

21   The inescapable conclusion is that no matter how one attempts to calculate the cost in dollars and cents, a float trip down Glen Canyon was much cheaper than a powerboat tour of the reservoir. Being less expensive, as well as safer and easier, the float trip was an adventure open to far more people than will ever be able to afford motorboat excursions in the area now.

All of the foregoing would be nothing but a futile exercise in nostalgia (so much water over the dam) if I had nothing constructive and concrete to offer. But I do. As alternate methods of power generation are developed, such as solar, and as the nation establishes a way of life adapted to actual resources and basic needs, so that the demand for electrical power begins to diminish, we can shut down the Glen Canyon power plant, open the diversion tunnels, and drain the reservoir.   22

This will no doubt expose a dreary and hideous scene: immense mud flats and whole plateaus of sodden garbage strewn with dead trees, sunken boats, the skeletons of long-forgotten, decomposing water-skiers. But to those who find the prospect too appalling, I say give nature a little time. In five years, at most in ten, the sun and wind and storms will cleanse and sterilize the repellent mess. The inevitable floods will soon remove all that does not belong within the canyons. Fresh green willow, box elder and redbud will reappear; and the ancient drowned cottonwoods (noble monuments to themselves) will be replaced by young of their own kind. With the renewal of plant life will come the insects, the birds, the lizards and snakes, the mammals. Within a generation—thirty years—I predict the river and canyons will bear a decent resemblance to their former selves. Within the lifetime of our children Glen Canyon and the living river, heart of the canyonlands, will be restored to us. The wilderness will again belong to God, the people and the wild things that call it home.   23

COMPOSING YOUR SUMMARY/STRONG RESPONSE ESSAY

Generating and Exploring Ideas for Your Summary

After you have selected the piece you will use for this assignment, your first task is to read it carefully to get as accurate an understanding of the article as you can. Remember that summarizing is the most basic and preliminary form of reading with the grain of a text.

1. The first time through, read the piece for general meaning. Follow the argument's flow without judgment or criticism, trying to see the world as the author sees it.

2. Reread the piece slowly, paragraph by paragraph, writing "what it does" or "what it says" gist statements in the margins for each paragraph or writing out the question that you think each paragraph answers. We recommend that you supplement these marginal notations by writing out a complete paragraph by paragraph *does/says* analysis modeled after our example on pages 121–122.

3. After you've analyzed the piece paragraph by paragraph, locate the argument's main divisions or parts and create an outline or tree diagram of the main points.

Shaping, Drafting, and Revising Your Summary

Once you have analyzed the article carefully paragraph by paragraph and understand its structure, you are ready to write a draft. If the piece you are summarizing is closed form, you can generally follow the order of the original article, keeping the proportions of the summary roughly equivalent to the proportions of the article. Begin the essay by identifying the question or problem that the reading addresses. Then state the article's purpose or thesis and summarize its argument point by point. If the article has a delayed thesis or some features of open-form prose, then you may have to rearrange the original order to create a clear structure for readers.

Count the number of words in your first draft to see whether you are in the 150–250 word range specified by the assignment. When you revise your summary, follow the criteria presented on page 121. Also use the Guidelines for Peer Reviews (pp. 150–151) as a checklist for revision.

Generating and Exploring Ideas for Your Strong Response

After you have written your summary, which demonstrates your full understanding of the text, you are ready to write your strong response. Use the questions and specific reading strategies discussed on pages 126–133 to help you generate ideas. The following questions put this advice into a quick checklist. Look for the questions that most stimulate your thinking and try freewriting your responses.

- Who is the text's intended audience? How is the author trying to change that audience's view of his or her topic? What rhetorical strategies intended to influence the audience most stand out?
- How do I differ from the intended audience? How are my purposes for reading different from what the author imagined?
- How have the author's rhetorical strategies affected me?
- How have the author's ideas affected me? How have they extended or complicated my own thinking? What do I agree with? What can I support?
- How can I question the author's data, evidence, and supporting arguments? If I am not persuaded by the author's ideas and evidence, why not? What is missing? What can be called into question?
- What is excluded from the author's text? What do these exclusions tell me about the author's value system or angle of vision?
- How can I question the author's values, beliefs, and assumptions? Conversely, how does the text cause me to question my own values, beliefs, and assumptions?
- How has the author changed my view of the topic? What do I have to give up or lose in order to change my view? What do I gain?
- How can I use the author's ideas for my own purposes? What new insights have I gained? What new ways of thinking can I apply to another context?

Writing a Thesis for a Strong Response Essay

See Chapter 3, pp. 43–47, for a discussion of surprising thesis statements.

A thesis for a strong response essay should map out for readers the points that you want to develop and discuss. These points should be risky and contestable; your thesis should surprise your readers with something new or challenging. Your thesis might focus entirely on with-the-grain points or entirely on against-the-grain points, but most likely it will include some of both. Avoid tensionless thesis statements such as "This article has both good and bad points."

Here are some thesis statements that students have written for strong responses in our classes. Note that each thesis includes at least one point about the rhetorical strategies of the text.

Examples of Summary/Strong Response Thesis Statements

- In "The Beauty Myth," Naomi Wolf makes a very good case for her idea that the beauty myth prevents women from ever feeling that they are good enough; however, Wolf's argument is geared too much toward feminists to be persuasive for a general audience, and she neglects to acknowledge the strong social and physical pressures that I and other men feel.

- Although Naomi Wolf in "The Beauty Myth" uses rhetorical strategies persuasively to argue that the beauty industry oppresses women, I think that she overlooks women's individual resistance and responsibility.

- Although the images and figures of speech that Thoreau uses in his chapter "Where I Lived, and What I Lived For" from *Walden* wonderfully support his argument that nature has valuable spiritually renewing powers, I disagree with his antitechnology stance and with his extreme emphasis on isolation as a means to self-discovery.

- In "Where I Lived, and What I Lived For" from *Walden,* Thoreau's argument that society is missing spiritual reality through its preoccupation with details and its frantic pace is convincing, especially to twenty-first century audiences; however, Thoreau weakens his message by criticizing his readers and by completely dismissing technological advances.

Revising Your Strong Response

In revising your strong response, you will find that peer reviews are especially helpful, both in generating ideas and in locating places that need expansion and development. As you revise, think about how well you have incorporated ideas from your initial explorations and how you can make your essay clearer and more meaningful to readers.

▪ GUIDELINES FOR PEER REVIEWS ▪

Instructions for peer reviews are provided in Chapter 18 (pp. 490–496).

For the Writer

Prepare two or three questions you would like your peer reviewer to address while responding to your draft. The questions can focus on some aspect of your draft that you are uncertain about, on one or more sections where you particularly seek help or advice, on some feature that you particularly like about your draft, or on some part you especially wrestled with. Write out your questions and give them to your peer reviewer along with your draft.

For the Reviewer

I. Read the draft at normal reading speed from beginning to end. As you read, do the following:

    A. Place a wavy line in the margin next to any passages where you get confused or find something that doesn't seem to fit or otherwise slowed down your reading.

    B. Place a "Good!" in the margin next to any passages where you think the writing is particularly strong or interesting.

II. Read the draft again slowly and answer the following questions by writing brief explanations of your answers.

    A. The summary

        1. How could the summary be more comprehensive, balanced, and accurate?

        2. Where could it be more fair and neutral?

        3. How could it use attributive tags more effectively?

        4. How could it include and cite quotations more effectively?

        5. What would make the summary read more smoothly?

    B. The strong response

        1. How could the writer's thesis statement be clearer in setting up several focused points about the text's rhetorical strategies and ideas?

        2. How could the body of the strong response follow the thesis more closely?

        3. How could the rhetorical points and "your own views" points engage more specifically and deeply with the text?

        4. Where do you as a reader need more clarification or support for the writer's rhetorical points and subject-matter points?

        5. How could the strong response be improved by adding points, developing points, or making points in a different way?

    D. If the writer has prepared questions for you, respond to his or her inquiries.

    C. Sum up what you see as the chief strengths and problem areas of this draft.

        1. Strengths

        2. Problem areas

III. Finally, read the draft one more time. This time place a check mark in the margin next to any places where you noticed problems in grammar, spelling, or mechanics. (One check mark per problem.)

CHAPTER 7

Writing an Autobiographical Narrative

ABOUT AUTOBIOGRAPHICAL NARRATIVE

This chapter focuses on the rhetorical aim we have called "writing to express or share." This chapter's assignment asks you to write an autobiographical narrative about something significant in your own life. But rather than state the significance up front in a thesis, you let it unfold in storylike fashion. This narrative structure places autobiographical writing at the open end of the closed-to-open form continuum, making it more like literary nonfiction than a traditional academic essay. Consequently, we advise you to consult Chapter 20, which discusses the features of open-form prose, prior to writing your assignment for this chapter. The student essays in this chapter, as well as "Berkeley Blues" in Chapter 20 (pp. 545–547), were written for an assignment like the one in this chapter.

Don't let the term *literary* scare you. It simply refers to basic techniques such as dialogue, specific language, and scene-by-scene construction that you use when sharing stories, telling jokes, or recounting experiences to friends. These are the most natural and universal of techniques, the ones that peoples of all cultures have traditionally used to pass on their collective wisdom in myths, legends, and religious narratives.

Although most academic writing is closed form, it sometimes takes an open-form structure, especially when the writer tells the story of an intellectual discovery or narrates his or her wrestling with a problem. Some of the most profound and influential science writing for general audiences—for example, the work of Loren Eiseley, Jay Gould, Rachel Carson, and others—is narrative-based. Additionally, many kinds of academic prose have sections of narrative writing. For an example of the intellectual power of autobiographical narrative, consider freelance writer David Quammen's "The Face of a Spider" on pages 207–210 of this text. Although we have chosen to classify Quammen's essay as "informative" rather than "expressive" prose, it could just as easily be placed in this chapter as a professional example of autobiographical narrative. It shows how autobiographical writing can explore, deepen, and complicate our perception of the world.

In addition to telling stories to convey the complexity and significance of phenomena, we use them to reveal ourselves. In this regard, autobiographical writing, like certain forms of conversation, fills a very basic need in our daily lives—

See our explanation of rhetorical aims in Chapter 4, pp. 62–65.

The closed-to-open continuum is shown in Figure 1.1, page 16.

the need for intimacy or nontrivial human contact. One of the best measures we have of our closeness to other human beings is our willingness or reluctance to share with them our significant life stories, the ones that reveal our aspirations or humiliations.

We also use others' stories, particularly during adolescence, to monitor our own growth. Many of us once read (and still read) the stories of such people as Anne Frank, Maya Angelou, Helen Keller, Malcolm X, and Laura Ingalls Wilder in search of attitudes and behaviors to emulate. Reading their stories becomes a way of critiquing and understanding our own stories.

At this point, you might be thinking that your own life lacks the high drama needed for autobiographical prose. Perhaps you're thinking that unless you've dated a movie star, won an X-Game skateboard competition, starred on a reality TV show, or convinced a venture capitalist to fund your dot.com startup company devoted to Pez dispensers, you haven't done anything significant to write about. In this chapter we try to give you another view of significance—one that gets at the heart of what it means to write a story.

To our way of thinking, significance is not a quality somewhere out there in the events of your life: it's in the sensibility that you bring to those events and the way you write about them. When you mistakenly equate significance with singularity (it never happened to anyone else) or its public importance (what happened here made history), you misunderstand the power of a good writer to render any sort of event significant.

Many of the events your audience will find most interesting are those ordinary occurrences that happen to everyone. All of us have experienced a first day at a new school or job, a rival or sibling who seemed to best us at every turn, or a conflict with a parent, lover, spouse, or employer. But everyone enjoys hearing good writers describe their unique methods of coping with and understanding these universal situations. It is precisely because readers have experienced these things that they can project themselves easily into the writer's world. This chapter shows you how to write an autobiographical story by finding a significant moment in your life and writing about it compellingly using literary techniques.

EXPLORING AUTOBIOGRAPHICAL NARRATIVE

One of the premises of this book is that good writing is rooted in the writer's perception of a problem. Problems are at the center not only of thesis-based writing but also of narrative writing. In effective narration, the problem usually takes the form of a *contrary,* two or more things in opposition—ideas, characters, expectations, forces, worldviews, or whatever. Three kinds of contraries that frequently form the plots of autobiographical narratives are the following:

1. ***Old self versus new self.*** The writer perceives changes in himself or herself as a result of some transforming moment or event.

2. ***Old view of person X versus new view of person X.*** The writer's perception of a person (favorite uncle, friend, childhood hero) changes as a result of some

revealing moment; the change in the narrator's perception of person X also indicates growth in self-perception.

3. *Old values versus new values that threaten, challenge, or otherwise disrupt the old values.* The writer confronts an outsider who challenges his or her worldview, or the writer undergoes a crisis that creates a conflict in values.

Prior to class discussion, freewrite for ten minutes about episodes in your own life that fit one or more of these typical plots. Then, working in small groups or as a whole class, share your discoveries. Your goal is to begin seeing that each person's life is a rich source of stories.

For the moment think of *significant* not as "unusual" or "exciting" but as "revealing" or "conveying an unexpected meaning or insight." Thought of in this way, a significant moment in a story might be a gesture, a remark, a smile, a way of walking or tying a shoe, the wearing of a certain piece of clothing, or the carrying of a certain object in a purse or pocket. Invent a short scene in which a gesture, smile, or brief action reverses one character's feelings about, or understanding of, another character.

1. You think that Maria has led a sheltered life until _____
2. You think Pete is a gruff, intimidating thug until _____.
3. Marco (Julia) seemed the perfect date until _____.

In each case, think of specific details about one revealing moment that reverse your understanding. Here is an example of a scene:

> My dad seemed unforgivingly angry at me until he suddenly smiled, turned my baseball cap backward on my head, and held up his open palm for a high five. "Girl, if you don't change your ways, you're going to be as big a high school screw-up as your old man was."

WRITING PROJECT

Write a narrative essay about something significant in your life using the literary strategies of plot, character, and setting. Develop your story through the use of contraries, creating tension that moves the story forward and gives it significance. You can discuss the significance of your story explicitly, perhaps as a revelation, or you can imply it (we discuss and illustrate each of these strategies later in this chapter). Use specific details and develop contraries that create tension.

Pp. 549–553 explain the criteria for a "story."

This assignment calls for a *story.* In Chapter 20, we argue that a narrative qualifies as a story only when it depicts a series of connected events that create for the reader a sense of tension or conflict that is resolved through a new understanding or change in status. Your goal for this assignment is to write a story about your life that fulfills these criteria. The rest of this chapter will help you every step of the way.

UNDERSTANDING AUTOBIOGRAPHICAL WRITING

Autobiographical writing may include descriptions of places and people and depictions of events that are more entertaining than enlightening. However, the spine of most autobiographical writing is a key moment or event, or a series of key moments or events, that shapes or reveals the author's emerging character or growth in understanding.

Autobiographical Tension: The Opposition of Contraries

Key events in autobiography are characterized by a contrariety of opposing values or points of view. These oppositions are typically embodied in conflicts between characters or in divided feelings within the narrator. The contrariety in a story can often be summed up in statements such as these:

> My best friend from the eighth grade was suddenly an embarrassment in high school.
> My parents thought I was too young to drive to the movies when in fact I was ready to ride off with Iggy's Motorcycle Maniacs.
> My husband thought I was mad about his being late for dinner when in fact I was mad about things he had never understood.

An autobiographical piece without tension is like an academic piece without a problem or a surprising thesis. No writing is more tedious than a pointless "So what?" narrative that rambles on without tension. (You can read such a narrative in our discussion of the difference between a "story" and an "'and then' chronology" in Chapter 20. It is a good example of what *not* to do for this assignment.)

Like the risky thesis statement in closed-form writing, contrariety creates purpose and focus for open-form writing. It functions as an organizing principle, helping the writer determine what to include or omit. It also sets a direction for the writer. When a story is tightly wound and all the details contribute to the story line, the tension moves the plot forward as a mainspring moves the hands of a watch. The tension is typically resolved when the narrator experiences a moment of recognition or insight, vanquishes or is vanquished by a foe, or changes status.

Consider differences between "Berkeley Blues" (pp. 545–547) and "The Stolen Watch" (pp. 547–549).

Using the Elements of Literary Narrative to Generate Ideas

The basic elements of a literary narrative that work together to create a story are plot, character, setting, and theme. In this section we show how you can use each of these elements to help think of ideas for your autobiographical story.

Plot

By *plot* we mean the basic action of the story, including the selection and sequencing of scenes and events. Often stories don't open with the earliest chronological moment; they may start *in medias res* ("in the middle of things") at a moment of crisis and then flash backward to fill in earlier details that explain the origins of the crisis. What you choose to include in your story and where you place it are concerns of plot. The amount of detail you choose to devote to each scene is also a function of plot. How a writer varies the amount of detail in each scene is referred to as a plot's *pacing*.

Plots typically unfold in the following stages: (a) an arresting opening scene; (b) the introduction of characters and the filling in of background; (c) the building of tension or conflict through oppositions embedded in a series of events or scenes; (d) the climax or pivotal moment when the tension or conflict comes to a head; and (e) reflection on the events of the plot and their meaning.

To help you recognize story-worthy events in your own life, consider the following list of pivotal moments that have figured in numerous autobiographical narratives:

■ Moments of enlightenment or coming to knowledge: understanding a complex idea for the first time, recognizing what is meant by love or jealousy or justice, mastering a complex skill, seeing some truth about yourself or your family that you previously hadn't seen

■ Passages from one realm to the next: from innocence to experience, from outsider to insider or vice versa, from child to adult, from novice to expert, from what you once were to what you now are

■ Confrontation with the unknown or with people or situations that challenged or threatened your old identity and values

■ Moments of crisis or critical choice that tested your mettle or your system of values

■ Choices about the company you keep (friends, love interests, cliques, larger social groups) and the effects of those choices on your integrity and the persona you project to the world

■ Problems maintaining relationships without compromising your own growth or denying your own needs

■ Problems accepting limitations and necessities, such as the loss of dreams, the death of intimates, the failure to live up to ideals, or the difficulty of living with a chronic illness or disability

■ Contrasts between common wisdom and your own unique knowledge or experience: doing what people said couldn't be done, failing at something others said was easy, finding value in something rejected by society, finding bad consequences of something widely valued

For Writing and Discussion

Prior to class, use one or more of the above pivotal-moment categories as an aid to brainstorm ideas for your own autobiographical essay. Then choose one of your ideas to use for your plot, and freewrite possible answers to the following questions:

1. How might you begin your story?
2. What events and scenes might you include in your story?
3. How might you arrange them?
4. What would be the climax of your story (the pivotal moment or scene)?
5. What insights or meaning might you want your story to suggest?

Then share your ideas and explorations with classmates. Help each other explore possibilities for good autobiographical stories. Of course, you are not yet committed to any pivotal moment or plot.

Character

Which characters from your life will you choose to include in your autobiography? The answer to that question depends on the nature of the tension that moves your story forward. Characters who contribute significantly to that tension or who represent some aspect of that tension with special clarity belong in your story. Whatever the source of tension in a story, a writer typically chooses characters who exemplify the narrator's fears and desires or who forward or frustrate the narrator's growth in a significant way.

Sometimes writers develop characters not through description and sensory detail but through dialogue. Particularly if a story involves conflict between people, dialogue is a powerful means of letting the reader experience that conflict directly. The following piece of dialogue, taken from African-American writer Richard Wright's classic autobiography *Black Boy*, demonstrates how a skilled writer can let dialogue tell the story, without resorting to analysis and abstraction. In the following scene, young Wright approaches a librarian in an attempt to get a book by Baltimore author and journalist H. L. Mencken from a whites-only public library. He has forged a note and borrowed a library card from a sympathetic white coworker and is pretending to borrow the book in his coworker's name.

"What do you want, boy?"

As though I did not possess the power of speech, I stepped forward and simply handed her the forged note, not parting my lips.

"What books by Mencken does he want?" she asked.

"I don't know ma'am," I said avoiding her eyes.

"Who gave you this card?"

"Mr. Falk," I said.

"Where is he?"

"He's at work, at the M— Optical Company," I said. "I've been in here for him before."

"I remember," the woman said. "But he never wrote notes like this."

Oh, God, she's suspicious. Perhaps she would not let me have the books? If she had turned her back at that moment, I would have ducked out the door and never gone back. Then I thought of a bold idea.

"You can call him up, ma'am," I said, my heart pounding.

"You're not using these books are you?" she asked pointedly.

"Oh no ma'am. I can't read."

"I don't know what he wants by Mencken," she said under her breath.

I knew I had won; she was thinking of other things and the race question had gone out of her mind.

—Richard Wright, *Black Boy*

It's one thing to hear *about* racial prejudice and discrimination; it's another thing to *hear* it directly through dialogue such as this. In just one hundred or so words of conversation, Wright communicates the anguish and humiliation of being a "black boy" in the United States in the 1920s.

Another way to develop a character is to present a sequence of moments or scenes that reveal a variety of behaviors and moods. Imagine taking ten photographs of your character to represent his or her complexity and variety and then arranging them in a collage. Your narrative can create a similar collage using verbal descriptions. Sheila Madden uses this strategy in "Letting Go of Bart," a story in the Readings section of this chapter, pages 167–169.

For Writing and Discussion

If you currently have ideas for the story you plan to write, consider now the characters who will be in it. If you haven't yet settled on a story idea, think of memorable people in your life. Explore questions such as these: Why are these characters significant to you? What role did they play in forwarding or frustrating your progress? Given that role, which of their traits, mannerisms, modes of dress, and actions might you include in your account? Could you develop your character through dialogue? Through a collage of representative scenes? After you have considered these questions privately, share your responses to them either as a whole class or in groups. Help each other think of details to make your characters vivid and memorable.

Setting

Elements of setting are selected as characters are selected, according to how much they help readers understand the conflict or tension that drives the story. When you write about yourself, what you notice in the external world often reflects your inner world. In some moods you are apt to notice the expansive lawn, beautiful flowers, and swimming ducks in the city park; in other moods you might note the litter of paper cups, the blight on the roses, and the scum on the duck pond. The setting typically relates thematically to the other elements of a story. In "Berkeley Blues (pp. 545–547)" for example, the author contrasts the swimming pools and sunsets of his hometown to the grit and darkness of inner-city Berkeley. The contrast in settings mirrors the contrast in the worldviews of the high school debaters and the homeless person who confronts them.

For Writing and Discussion

On your own, freewrite about possible settings to include in your autobiographical narrative. Describe one of these settings fully. What do you see? Hear? Smell? Why is this setting appropriate for your story? Can you imagine two contrasting settings that reflect the contraries or oppositions in your story? Alternatively, picture in your mind one of the characters you thought of in the exercise above. Now, imagine this character in a setting that reveals his or her significance—in a kitchen baking a pie, on the front steps of a porch laughing with neighbors, in an open field running barefoot, in the backyard working on an old engine, in a cluttered office standing by the watercooler. Picture a photograph of your character in this setting. Freewrite your description of that photograph.

Then, share your descriptive freewrites with classmates, discussing how your settings might be used in your autobiographical narrative.

Theme

The word *theme* is difficult to define. Themes, like thesis statements, organize the other elements of the essay. But a theme is seldom stated explicitly and is never proved with reasons and factual evidence. Readers ponder—even argue about—themes, and often different readers are affected very differently by the same theme. Some literary critics view theme as simply a different way of thinking about plot. To use a phrase from critic Northrop Frye, a plot is "what happened" in a story, whereas the theme is "what happens" over and over again in this story and others like it. To illustrate this distinction, we summarize student writer Patrick José's autobiographical narrative "No Cats in America?", one of the essays in the Readings section of this chapter, from a plot perspective and from a theme perspective.

José's essay is on pp. 162–164.

> **Plot perspective** It's the story of a Filipino boy who emigrates with his family from the Philippines to the United States when he is in the eighth grade. On the first day of school, he is humiliated when classmates snicker at the lunch his mother packed for him. Feeling more and more alienated each day, he eventually proclaims, "I hate being Filipino!"
>
> **Theme perspective** It's the story of how personal identity is threatened when people are suddenly removed from their own cultures and immersed into new ones that don't understand or respect difference. The story reveals the psychic damage of cultural dislocation.

As you can see, the thematic summary goes beyond the events of the story to point toward the larger significance of those events. Although you may choose not to state your theme directly for your readers, you need to understand that theme to organize your story. This understanding usually precedes and guides your decisions about what events and characters to include, what details and dialogue to use, and what elements of setting to describe. But sometimes you need to reverse the process and start out with events and characters that, for whatever reason, force themselves on you, and then figure out your theme after you've written for a while. In other words, theme may be something you discover as you write.

For Writing and Discussion

Using the ideas you have brainstormed from previous exercises in this chapter, choose two possible ideas for an autobiographical narrative you might write. For each, freewrite your response to this question: What is the significance of this story for me? (Why did I choose this story? Why is it important to me? Why do I want to tell it? What am I trying to show my readers?)

In class, share your freewrites. All the exercises in this section are designed to generate discussion about the elements of autobiographical narrative and to encourage topic exploration.

Readings

Now that we have examined some of the key elements of autobiographical writing, let's look at some particular examples.

The first reading is by Kris Saknussemm, an American fiction writer whose short stories have appeared in such publications as *The Boston Review, New Letters, The Antioch Review,* and *ZYZZYVA.* He is the author of the forthcoming novel *Spiritcruiser.* This selection is taken from his autobiographical work in progress.

■ KRIS SAKNUSSEMM ■
PHANTOM LIMB PAIN

When I was 13 my sole purpose was to shed my baby fat and become the star halfback on our football team. That meant beating out Miller King, the best athlete at my school. He was my neighbor and that mythic kid we all know—the one who's forever better than us—the person we want to be.   1

Football practice started in September and all summer long I worked out. I ordered a set of barbells that came with complimentary brochures with titles like "How to Develop a He-Man Voice." Every morning before sunrise I lumbered around our neighborhood wearing ankle weights loaded with sand. I taught myself how to do Marine push-ups and carried my football everywhere so I'd learn not to fumble. But that wasn't enough. I performed a ceremony. During a full moon, I burned my favorite NFL trading cards and an Aurora model of the great quarterback Johnny Unitas in the walnut orchard behind our house, where Miller and I'd gotten into a fight when we were seven and I'd burst into tears before he even hit me.   2

Two days after my ceremony, Miller snuck out on his older brother's Suzuki and was struck by a car. He lost his right arm, just below the elbow. I went to see him the day after football practice started—after he'd come back from the hospital. He looked pale and surprised, but he didn't cry. It was hard to look at the stump of limb where his arm had been, so I kept glanc-   3 ing around his room. We only lived about 200 feet away, and yet I'd never been inside his house before. It had never occurred to me that he would also have on his wall a poster of Raquel Welch from One Million Years B.C.

4   I went on to break all his records that year. Miller watched the home games from the bench, wearing his jersey with the sleeve pinned shut. We went 10-1 and I was named MVP, but I was haunted by crazy dreams in which I was somehow responsible for the accident—that I'd found the mangled limb when it could've been sewn back on—and kept it in an aquarium full of vodka under my bed.

5   One afternoon several months later, toward the end of basketball season, I was crossing the field to go home and I saw Miller stuck going over the Cyclone fence—which wasn't hard to climb if you had both arms. I guess he'd gotten tired of walking around and hoped no one was looking. Or maybe it was a matter of pride. I'm sure I was the last person in the world he wanted to see—to have to accept assistance from. But even that challenge he accepted. I helped ease him down the fence, one diamond-shaped hole at a time. When we were finally safe on the other side, he said to me, "You know, I didn't tell you this during the season, but you did all right. Thanks for filling in for me."

6   We walked home together, not saying much. But together. Back to our houses 200 feet apart. His words freed me from my bad dreams. I thought to myself, how many things I hadn't told him. How even without an arm he was more of a leader. Damaged but not diminished, he was still ahead of me. I was right to have admired him. I grew bigger and a little more real from that day on.

Thinking Critically about "Phantom Limb Pain"

Perhaps the first thing the reader realizes about Saknussemm's narrative is that the climactic event is hardly an event at all—one boy helping another climb down a Cyclone fence. But the events leading to this moment have prepared us to understand the writer's revelation of his new relationship to his rival. Saknussemm's last paragraph comments on the preceding narrative, explicitly drawing out the theme by explaining the significance of the event.

■   Saknussemm chooses to leave a lot unsaid, depending on his readers to fill in the gaps. Why do you suppose that he had never been inside Miller King's house before? Why does he feel "somehow responsible for the accident"? What details does Saknussemm use to sketch in Miller's admirable traits?

■   What examples can you find in this narrative of revelatory words, memory-soaked words, and other concrete words low on the ladder of abstraction?

■   In closed-form prose, writers seldom use sentence fragments. In open-form prose, however, writers frequently use fragments for special effects. Note the two fragments in Saknussemm's final paragraph: "But together. Back to our houses 200 feet apart." Why does Saknussemm use these fragments? What is their rhetorical effect?

See Chapter 20, pp. 553-556, for a discussion of concrete language including revelatory words and memory-soaked words.

■ The sparseness of Saknussemm's narrative has already been noted. There are plenty of places where he could have added more descriptive or narrative detail—for example, a description of Miller trying to climb the fence with one arm or a more detailed account of his first visit to Miller's room after the accident. Do you agree with Saknussemm's decision to write in this minimalist style? Why?

For a different approach to narrative, consider student writer Patrick José's "No Cats in America?". Unlike Saknussemm's decision to write sparsely and include an overt thematic commentary, José devotes his essay almost entirely to scenes and events. His thematic commentary is short, subtle, and symbolically conveyed.

■ PATRICK JOSÉ (STUDENT) ■
NO CATS IN AMERICA?

"There are no cats in America." I remember growing up watching *An American Tail* with my sisters and cousins. Ever since I first saw that movie, I had always wanted to move to America. That one song, "There Are No Cats in America," in which the Mousekewitz family is singing with other immigrating mice, had the most profound effect on me. These were Russian mice going to America to find a better life—a life without cats. At first, I thought America really had no cats. Later, I learned that they meant that America was without any problems at all. I was taught about the American Dream with its promise of happiness and equality. If you wanted a better life, then you better pack up all your belongings and move to America. 1

However, I loved living in the Philippines. My family used to throw the best parties in Angeles City. For a great party, you need some delicious food. Of course there would be lechon, adobo, pancit, sinigang, lumpia, and rice. We eat rice for breakfast, lunch, and dinner, and rice even makes some of the best desserts. (My mom's bibingka and puto are perfect!) And you mustn't forget the drinks. San Miguel and Coke are usually sufficient. But we also had homemade mango juice and coconut milk. And a party wouldn't be a party without entertainment, right? So in one room, we had the gambling room. It's usually outside the house. Everybody would be smoking and drinking while playing mahjong. And sometimes, others would play pepito or pusoy dos. Music and dancing is always a must. And when there are firecrackers, better watch out because the children would go crazy with them. 2

Then one day, a mixed feeling came over me. My dad told us that he had gotten a job . . . in California. In the span of two months, we had moved to America, found a small apartment, and located a small private Catholic school for the kids. We did not know many people in California that first summer. We only had ourselves to depend on. We would go on car trips, go to the beach, cook, play games. In August, I thought we were living the American Dream. 3

4 But at the end of summer, school began. I was in the eighth grade. I had my book bag on one shoulder, stuffed with notebooks, folder paper, calculators, a ruler, a pencil box, and my lunch. I still can remember what I had for lunch on the first day of school—rice and tilapia and, in a small container, a mixture of vinegar, tomatoes, and bagoong. My mom placed everything in a big Tupperware box, knowing I eat a lot.

5 When I walked into the classroom, everyone became quiet and looked at me. I was the only Filipino in that room. Everyone was white. We began the day by introducing ourselves. When it got to my turn, I was really nervous. English was one of the courses that I took in the Philippines, and I thought I was pretty proficient at it. But when I first opened my mouth, everyone began to laugh. The teacher told everyone to hush. I sat down, smiling faintly not understanding what was so funny. I knew English, and yet I was laughed at. But it had nothing to do with the language. It was my accent.

6 Some students tried to be nice, especially during lunch. But it didn't last long. I was so hungry for my lunch. I followed a group of students to the cafeteria and sat down at an empty table. Some girls joined me. I didn't really talk to them, but they asked if they could join me. As I opened my Tupperware, I saw their heads turn away. They didn't like the smell of fish and bagoong. The girls left and moved to another table of girls. From the corner of my eye I saw them looking and laughing at me. I tried to ignore it, concentrating on eating my lunch as I heard them laugh. In the Philippines, the only way to eat fish and rice is with your hands. But that was in the Philippines. My manners were primitive here in America. I was embarrassed at the smell, was embarrassed at the way I ate, was embarrassed to be me.

7 When I got home, I lied to my parents. I told them school was great and that I was excited to go back. But deep down, I wanted to go back to the Philippines. When lunch came the next day, I was hungry. In my hand was my lunch. Five feet away was the trash. I stood up, taking my lunch in my hands. Slowly, I walked my way towards the trashcan, opened the lid, and watched as my lunch filled the trashcan. Again, I told my parents I enjoyed school.

8 When my grades began to suffer, the teacher called my parents and scheduled an appointment. The next day, my parents came to the classroom, and when they started talking to the teacher I heard laughter in the background. It humiliated me to have my classmates hear my parents talk.

9 That night, my parents and I had a private discussion. They asked why I lied to them. I told them everything, including my humiliation. They told me not to worry about it, but I pleaded for us to return to the Philippines. My parents said no. "Living here will provide a better future for you and your sisters," they said. Then the unexpected came. I didn't know what I was thinking. I yelled to them with so much anger, "I hate being Filipino!" Silence filled the room. Teardrops rolled down my cheeks. My parents were shocked, and so was I.

> I went to my room and cried. I didn't mean what I said. But I was tired of   10
> the humiliation. Lying on my bed, with my eyes closed, my mind began to
> wander. I found myself in the boat with the Mousekewitz family singing,
> "There are no cats in America." If only they knew how wrong they were.

Thinking Critically about "No Cats in America?"

Unlike Saknussemm, who comments explicitly on the significance of his experience, Patrick José lets the reader infer his essay's significance from the details of the narrative and from their connection to the framing story of the fictional mice and cats.

1. How do the settings help you understand José's theme at different points in the story?
2. What would you say is the story's climax or pivotal moment?
3. José's title, first paragraph, and last paragraph are about a children's movie that features the Mousekewitz's song proclaiming that there are no cats in America. How does the "no cats" image function as both part of the underlying tension of this narrative and as a symbolic vehicle for conveying the theme of José's essay? What is the insight that José has achieved at the end?
4. During a rough draft workshop, José asked his peer reviewers whether he should retain his description of parties in the Philippines, which he thought was perhaps unconnected to the rest of the story. His classmates urged him to keep those details. Do you agree with their advice? Why?

See Chapter 20, p. 556, for a discussion of the power of memory-soaked words.

5. For Filipinos and Filipinas, the specific names of foods and party games would be rich examples of memory-soaked words. For other readers, however, these names are foreign and strange. Do you agree with José's decision to use these specific ethnic names? Why?

For Writing and Discussion

Imagine a memorable party scene from your own life and experiences. It could be a family party, a neighborhood party, or a party from high school, college, or work. What specific words, revelatory words, and memory-soaked words will most likely make this party come to life in your readers' imagination? What details about food and drink, the activities of the party-goers, clothing and mannerisms, the party's setting (furniture, pictures on the walls, arrangement of rooms), and so on will trigger associations and memories for your readers? List these details and then share them with your classmates.

The next example was written in a first-year composition course by a student writer who wishes to remain anonymous.

MASKS

1   Her soft, blond hair was in piggytails, as usual, with ringlets that bounced whenever she turned her head. As if they were springs, they could stretch, then shrink, then bounce, excited by the merest movement of her head. Never was there a hair that wasn't enclosed in those glossy balls which always matched her dress. I knew the only reason she turned her head was so they'd bounce. Because it was cute. Today, she wore a pink dress with frills and lace and impeccably white tights. Her feet, which swayed back and forth underneath her chair, were pampered with shiny, black shoes without a single scuff. She was very wise, sophisticated beyond her kindergarten years.

2   I gazed at her and then looked down at my clothes. My green and red plaid pants and my yellow shirt with tiny, blue stars showed the day's wear between breakfast, lunch, and recess. Showing through the toe of my tenny runners was my red sock.

3   At paint time, I closely followed behind her, making sure I painted at the easel next to hers. She painted a big, white house with a white picket fence and a family: Mom, Dad, and Daughter. I painted my mom, my brother, and myself. I, then, painted the sky, but blue streaks ran down our faces, then our bodies, ruining the picture.

4   The next day, I wore my hair in piggytails. I had done it all by myself, which was obvious due to my craftsmanship. She pointed and giggled at me when I walked by. I also wore a dress that day but I didn't have any pretty white tights. The boys all gathered underneath me when I went on the monkeybars to peak at my underwear to chant, "I see London, I see France, I see Tiffy's underpants."

5   When the day was done, she ran to the arms of her mother that enveloped her in a loving and nurturing hug. She showed her mother her painting, which had a big, red star on it.

6   "We'll have to put this up on the refrigerator with all of your others," her mother said. I had thrown my painting away. I looked once more at the two of them as they walked hand in hand towards their big, white house with a white picket fence. I trudged to my babysitter's house. I wouldn't see my mother until six o'clock. She had no time for me, for my paintings, for my piggytails. She was too busy working to have enough money to feed my brother and me.

7   Digging absently through books and folders, I secretly stole a glance at her, three lockers down. Today she wore her Calvins and sported a brand new pair of Nikes. As always, at the cutting edge of fashion. If I wanted Nikes, I could pay for them myself, or so said my mother. In the meantime, I had to suffer with my cheap, treadless Scats. As I searched for a pen, her giggle caught my attention. Three of her friends had flocked around her locker. I continued searching for a pen but to no avail. I thought of approaching and borrowing one but I was fearful that they would make fun of me.

"Jim and Brad called me last night and both of them asked me to go to the show. Which one should I pick?" she asked. My mom wouldn't let me go out on dates until I was a sophomore in high school. We were only in seventh grade and she was always going out with guys. Not that it mattered that I couldn't date, yet. Nobody had ever asked me out.   8

"My hair turned out so yucky today. Ick," she commented. She bent down to grab a book and light danced among the gentle waves of her flowing, blond mane. Her radiant brown eyes and adorable smile captivated all who saw her. Once captured, however, none was allowed past the mask she'd so artfully constructed to lure them to her. We were all so close to her, so far away. She was so elusive, like a beautiful perfume you smell but can't name, like the whisper that wakes you from a dream and turns out to belong to the dream.   9

As she walked into the library, I heard a voice whisper, "There she is. God, she's beautiful." She was wearing her brown and gold cheerleader outfit. Her pleated skirt bounced off her thighs as she strutted by. Her name, "Kathy," was written on her sweater next to her heart and by it hung a corsage. As she rounded the corner, she flicked her long, blond curls and pivoted, sending a ripple through the pleats of the skirt. She held her head up high, befitting one of her social standing: top of the high school food chain. She casually searched the length of the library for friends. When she reached the end of the room, she carefully reexamined every table, this time less casually. Her smile shaded into a pout. She furrowed her face, knitting her eyebrows together, and saddening her eyes. People stared at her until she panicked.   10

She was bolting toward the door when she spotted me. She paused and approached my table. Putting on her biggest smile, she said, "Oh hi! Can I sit by you?" Thrilled at the possibility of at last befriending her, I was only too happy to have her sit with me. As she sat down, she again scanned the expanse of the library.   11

"So, who does the varsity basketball team play tonight?" I asked.   12

"Great Falls Central," she replied. "Make sure you're there! . . . How's the Algebra assignment today?!"   13

"Oh, it's okay. Not too tough," I said.   14

"John always does my assignments for me. I just hate Algebra. It's so hard."   15

We stood up in silence, suddenly painfully aware of our differences. She glanced in the reflection of the window behind us, checked her hair, then again scanned the room.   16

"There's Shelly! Well, I'll see you later," she said.   17

She rose from the table and fled to her more acceptable friend.   18

The next day, she walked down the hall surrounded by a platoon of friends. As we passed, I called out "Hi!" but she turned away as if she didn't know me, as if I didn't exist.   19

I, then, realized her cheerleader outfit, her golden locks, her smile were all a mask. Take them away and nothing but air would remain. Her friends and their adoration were her identity. Without them she was alone and vulnerable. I was the powerful one. I was independent.   20

Thinking Critically about "Masks"

1. What are the main contrarieties in this piece?

2. This piece focuses on the narrator's movement toward a significant recognition. What is it she recognizes? If you were a peer reviewer for this writer, would you recommend eliminating the last paragraph, expanding it, or leaving it as it is? Why?

3. In Chapter 20, we quote writer John McPhee's advice to prefer specific words over abstract ones—brand-names, for example, rather than generic names. This student writer follows this advice throughout her essay. Where does she use details and specific words with particular effectiveness?

The discussion of concrete language in Chapter 20 is on pp. 554–555.

The final example uses a collage technique. Here the emphasis is so much on the character Bart that the narrator seems relatively unimportant, and you may wonder whether this piece is biography (the story of Bart) or autobiography (the story of the narrator). We include "Letting Go of Bart" in the category of autobiographical narrative because the way in which the writer, Sheila Madden, tells the story reveals her own growth in understanding, her own deepening of character.

Collage technique is explained on p. 158.

▪ SHEILA MADDEN ▪
LETTING GO OF BART

1   Bart lies stiffly in bed, toes pointed downward like a dancer's, but Bart is far from dancing. When he tries to shift position, his limbs obey spasmodically because his nervous system has been whipsawed by the medications he has been taking for years to control the various manifestations of AIDS.

2   He is wearing diapers now, for incontinence—the ultimate indignity. An oxygen tube is hooked into his nose, morphine drips into his arm; his speech is slurred.

3   But Bart is not confused. He is intensely irritable and has been the terror of his nurses. Though he has a great self-deprecating grin, I haven't seen it for weeks.

4   I can't say a proper goodbye because he is never alone. I would like to pray silently by his bedside, meditating; but even if I could, he would barely tolerate it. Bart has no god.

5   I remember the day a tall, good-looking young man popped into the open door of the downstairs apartment I was fixing up in my San Francisco home. That late afternoon, I was tiredly putting the last coat of paint on the walls with the help of a couple of friends. Bart had seen the for-rent sign in the window and just walked in. Within moments he had all three of us laughing uproariously as he put a deposit in my hand. I had asked the

angels for help in finding a decent renter; the angels had responded. Bart and I would get on famously.

For one thing, Bart managed to fix or overlook the unfinished bits in the apartment. He and his father built a fine, much-needed deck on the back garden, charging me only for the lumber. He made the small apartment look spacious, arranging the furniture skillfully, backlighting the sofas. And he was prompt with the rent.   6

However, Bart was far more than a satisfactory renter. He was a fine singer and a member of the symphony chorus. When he practiced, his rich baritone would sail up the stairs, smoothing the airways, never ruffling them.   7

He asked permission to put a piano in his apartment, and I agreed nervously. Because he was a beginner on the instrument, I feared endless, fumbling scales disturbing my peace. It never happened. He played softly, sensitively, and always at reasonable hours.   8

I attended some of his concerts and met his friends. At times we joined forces at parties upstairs or downstairs, but somehow we never got in each other's hair.   9

He was a skillful ballroom dancer. Once he agreed to stand in as partner for my visiting sister when we attended a Friday dance at the Embarcadero Plaza—although the prospect could not have thrilled him.   10

Another time I disabled my tape deck by spraying it with WD-40 and ran downstairs for help. Bart came up immediately, scolding me roundly for putting oil on such a machine. Then he spent the better part of an hour wrapping matchsticks in cotton batting (for lack of a better tool), degreasing the heads with rubbing alcohol, and putting all to rights.   11

Bart had family problems; I had them. We commiserated. Bart was an ally, a compatriot, a brother.   12

I suspected Bart was gay; but we never talked about it, although he knew I was working in the AIDS fields as a counselor and that it was a nonissue with me.   13

Then one day he got a bad flu, which turned into a deep, wracking cough that did not go away. I worried about it, having heard such coughs in the AIDS patients I dealt with daily. I encouraged him to see a doctor, and he did, making light of his visit.   14

Finally the cough receded, but psychically so did Bart. I saw him hardly at all for the next three months. When I did, he seemed somber and abstracted.   15

However, my life was hectic at the time. I didn't pay attention, assuming his problem was job dissatisfaction; I knew his boss was a constant thorn in his side. One day he told me that he was changing jobs and moving to Napa, an hour's drive away. I rejoiced for him and cried for myself. I would miss Bart.   16

Our lives separated. Napa might as well have been the moon. Over a two-year period we talked once or twice on the phone, and I met him once for dinner in the city.   17

18   Then one night my doorbell rang unexpectedly, and Bart came in to tell me of his recovery from a recent bout of pneumocystis pneumonia. "I'm out of the closet, willy-nilly," he said.

19   I was stunned. I had put him in the "safe" category, stuffing my fears about the telltale cough. It must have been then that he learned his diagnosis. For the next 24 hours I cried off and on, inconsolably, for Bart and probably for all the others I had seen die.

20   Now he is at the end, an end so fierce there is nothing to do but pray it will come quickly. Bart is courageous, his anger masking fear. He has thus far refused to let the morphine dull his consciousness. His eyes, hawklike, monitor all that is going on around him. Angels, who once brought him, take him home.

Thinking Critically about "Letting Go of Bart"

1. Madden uses a series of scenes to create her portrait of Bart. Briefly list each of these scenes identifying its setting and events. How do these scenes function to reveal Bart's character? In other words, what does the reader learn through each scene?

2. How and how much does Madden as the narrator reveal about her own character? To what extent could you call this essay an "autobiographical narrative"?

3. How does Madden's collage technique create tension and resolution?

For Writing and Discussion

To generate more ideas for an autobiographical narrative, each class member should do the following exercise independently and then share the results with the rest of the class:

1. Have you ever had a moment of revelation when you suddenly realized that your own view of something (a person, a place, the world) was wrong, narrow, or distorted, as did Kris Saknussemm? If you have, freewrite about this experience.

2. Have you ever been suddenly whisked from a familiar to an unfamiliar setting and made to feel like an outsider, alienated and alone, as did Patrick José in "No Cats in America?"

3. Have you ever changed your view of a person in a way analogous to the narrator's reassessment of the cheerleader in "Masks"? If so, freewrite about this character. What details reveal this person before and after your moment of reassessment?

4. Have you ever known a person whose presence in your life made an important difference to you, as did Bart to Sheila Madden? If you have, freewrite about this character, imagining a series of scenes that might create a collage effect.

COMPOSING YOUR ESSAY

In deciding what to write about, keep in mind the basic requirement for a good story: it must portray a sequence of connected events driven forward by some tension or conflict that results in a recognition or new understanding. Not every memorable event in your life will lend itself to this sort of structure. The most common failing in faulty narratives is that the meaning of the event is clearer to the narrator than to the audience. "You had to be there," the writer comments, when a story just doesn't have the expected impact on an audience.

But it's the storyteller's job to *put the reader there* by providing enough detail and context for the reader to *see* why the event is significant. If an event didn't lead to any significant insight, understanding, knowledge, change, or other kind of difference in your life, and if you really had to be there to appreciate its significance, then it's a poor candidate for an autobiographical narrative.

Generating and Exploring Ideas

Choosing a Plot

For some of you, identifying a plot—a significant moment or insight arising out of contrariety—will present little problem; perhaps you have already settled on an idea you generated in one of the class discussion exercises earlier in this chapter. However, if you are still searching for a plot idea, you may find the following list helpful:

- ▨ A time when you took some sort of test that conferred new status on you (Red Cross lifesaving exam, driver's test, SAT, important school or work-related test, entrance exam, team tryout). If you failed, what did you learn from it or how did it shape you? If you succeeded, did the new status turn out to be as important as you expected it would be?

- ▨ A situation in which your normal assumptions about life were challenged (an encounter with a foreign culture, a time when a person you'd stereotyped surprised you).

- ▨ A time when you left your family for an extended period or forever (going to college, getting married, entering the military, leaving one parent for another after their divorce).

- ▨ A time that plunged you into a crisis (being the first person to discover a car crash, seeing a robbery in progress, being thrown in with people who are repugnant to you, facing an emergency).

- ▨ A situation in which you didn't fit or didn't fulfill others' expectations of you, or a situation in which you were acknowledged as a leader or exceeded others' expectations of you (call to jury duty, assignment to a new committee, being placed in charge of an unfamiliar project).

- ▨ A time when you overcame your fears to do something for the first time (first date, first public presentation, first challenge in a new setting).

- ▨ A situation in which you learned how to get along amicably with another human being, or a failed relationship that taught you something about life (your first extended romantic relationship; your relationship with a difficult sibling, relative, teacher, or boss; getting a divorce).

- A time when a person who mattered to you (parent, spouse, romantic interest, authority figure) rejected you or let you down, or a time when you rejected or let down someone who cared for you.

- A time when you made a sacrifice on behalf of someone else, or someone else made a sacrifice in your name (taking in a foster child, helping a homeless person, caring for a sick person).

- A time when you were irresponsible or violated a principle or law and thereby caused others pain (you shoplifted or drank when underage and were caught, you failed to look after someone entrusted to your care).

- A time when you were criticized unjustly or given a punishment you didn't deserve (you were accused of plagiarizing a paper that you'd written, you were blamed unjustly for a problem at work).

- A time when you were forced to accept defeat or death or the loss of a dream or otherwise learned to live with reduced expectations.

- A time when you experienced great joy (having a baby, getting your dream job) or lived out a fantasy.

Thickening the Plot

Once you've identified an event about which you'd like to write, you need to develop ways to show readers what makes that event particularly story worthy. In thinking about the event, consider the following questions:

- What makes the event so memorable? What particulars or physical details come most readily to mind when you think back on the event?

- What are the major contrarieties that gave the event tension? Did it raise a conflict between two or more people? Between their worldviews? Between before and after versions of yourself?

- How can you make the contrarieties memorable and vivid to the reader? What scenes can you create? What words could your characters exchange?

- Is there a moment of insight, recognition, or resolution that would give your plot a climax?

- What is the significance of the story? How does it touch on larger human issues and concerns? What makes it something your reader will relate to? What is its theme?

Shaping and Drafting

When stuck, writers often work their way into a narrative by describing in detail a vividly recalled scene, person, or object. This inductive approach is common with many creative processes. You may or may not include all the descriptive material in your final draft, but in the act of writing exhaustively about this one element, the rest of the story may begin to unfold for you, and forgotten items and incidents may resurface. In the course of describing scenes and characters, you will probably also begin reflecting on the significance of what you are saying. Try freewriting answers to such questions as "Why is this important?" and "What am I trying to do here?" Then continue with your rough draft.

Revising

Once you've written a draft, you need to get down to the real work of writing—rewriting. Revisit your prose critically, with an eye toward helping your reader share your experience and recognize its significance. Chapter 20, as well as the following guidelines for peer reviews, will be of particular help during revision.

■ GUIDELINES FOR PEER REVIEWS ■

Instructions for peer reviews are provided in Chapter 18 (pp. 490–496).

For the Writer

Prepare two or three questions you would like your peer reviewer to address while responding to your draft. The questions can focus on some aspect of your draft that you are uncertain about, on one or more sections where you particularly seek help or advice, or on some feature that you particularly like about your draft, or on some part you especially wrestled with. Write out your questions and give them to your peer reviewer along with your draft.

For the Reviewer

I. Read the draft at normal reading speed from beginning to end. As you read, do the following:

    A. Place a wavy line in the margin next to any passages that you find confusing, that contain something that doesn't seem to fit, or that otherwise slow down your reading.

    B. Place a "Good!" in the margin next to any passages where you think the writing is particularly strong or interesting.

II. Read the draft again slowly and answer the following questions by writing down brief explanations of your answers.

    A. Plot: What are the contrarieties, tensions, or conflicts in this story?

        1. How might the writer heighten or clarify the tension in the story?

        2. How might the writer improve the structure or pacing of scenes and the connection between these events? If you were to expand or reduce the treatment given to any events, which would you change and why?

        3. How could the writer use chronological order, flashbacks, or flashforwards more effectively?

B. Characters: How might the writer make the characters and their functions more vivid and compelling?

   1. Where might the writer provide more information about a character or describe the character more fully?

   2. Where might the writer use dialogue more effectively to reveal character?

C. Setting: How might the writer use setting more effectively to create contrasts or convey thematic significance? Where might the writer add or revise details about setting?

D. Theme: What do you see as the *So what?* or significance of this story?

   1. What insight or revelation do you get from this story?

   2. How could the story's thematic significance be made more memorable, powerful, or surprising? Should the writer comment more explicitly on the meaning or significance of the story or leave more for you to grasp on your own?

E. Title and opening paragraphs: How could the writer improve the title? How could the opening paragraphs be made more effective to hook the readers' interest and prepare them for the story to follow?

F. Language and details: Where do you find examples of specific language, including memory-soaked or revelatory words? Where and how could the writer use specific language more effectively?

G. If the writer has prepared questions for you, respond to his or her inquiries.

H. Briefly summarize in a list what you see as the chief strengths and problem areas in the draft.

   1. Strengths

   2. Problem Areas

III. Read the draft one more time. Place a check mark in the margin wherever you notice problems in grammar, spelling, or mechanics (one check mark per problem).

CHAPTER 8

Writing an Exploratory Essay

ABOUT EXPLORATORY WRITING

In Chapter 1, we said that to grow as a writer you need to love problems—to pose them and to live with them. Most academic writers testify that writing projects begin when they become engaged with a question or problem and commit themselves to an extensive period of exploration. During exploration, writers may radically redefine the problem and then later alter or even reverse their initial thesis.

As we noted in Chapters 2 and 3, however, inexperienced writers tend to truncate this exploratory process, committing themselves hastily to a thesis to avoid complexity. College professors say that this tendency hinders their students' intellectual growth. Asserting a thesis commits you to a position. Asking a question, on the other hand, invites you to contemplate multiple perspectives, entertain new ideas, and let your thinking evolve. As management professor A. Kimbrough Sherman puts it, to grow as thinkers, students need "to 'wallow in complexity' and work their way back out" (p. 24).

To illustrate his point, Sherman cites his experience in a management class where students were asked to write proposals for locating a new sports complex in a major U.S. city. To Sherman's disappointment, many students argued for a location without first considering all the variables—impact on neighborhoods, building costs and zoning, availability of parking, ease of access, attractiveness to tourists, aesthetics, and so forth—and without analyzing how various proposed locations stacked up against the criteria they were supposed to establish. The students reached closure without wallowing in complexity.

The assignment in this chapter asks you to dwell with a problem, even if you can't solve it. You will write an essay with an exploratory purpose; its focus will be a question rather than a thesis. The body of your paper will be a narrative account of your thinking about the problem—your attempt to examine its complexity, to explore alternative solutions, and to arrive at a solution or answer. Your exploration will generally require outside research, so many instructors will assign sections of Part Four, "A Rhetorical Guide to Research," along with this chapter. The paper will be relatively easy to organize because it follows a chronological structure, but you will have nothing to say—no process to report—unless you discover and examine your problem's complexity.

Exploratory essays can be composed in two ways—what we might call the "in-process" strategy and the "retrospective" strategy. When following the first strategy, writers compose the body of their essays during the actual process of thinking and researching. When writing page 4, for example, they don't know what they will be thinking by page 9. In contrast, when composing retrospectively, writers look back over their process from the vantage point of a completed journey. Their goal, when writing with an exploratory aim, is to reproduce their process, taking the readers, as it were, on the same intellectual and emotional journey they have just traveled. The first strategy yields genuine immediacy—like a sequence of journal entries written in the midst of the action. The second strategy, which allows for more selection and shaping of details, yields a more artistically designed essay.

Exploratory essays occur only occasionally in academic journals and almost never in business or professional life, where readers need thesis-driven arguments and reports. However, exploratory essays exist in embryo in the research journals or lab notebooks of scholars. Scholars sometimes revise their journals into stand-alone exploratory essays that take readers into the kitchen of academic discovery. The exploratory form underlies Plato's dialogues as well as the musings of the Renaissance French writer Michel de Montaigne, whose term "essai" (meaning a "try" or "attempt") leads to the English word *essay*. The power of exploratory writing as a stand-alone genre can be seen in such books as Jon Kraukauer's *Into the Wild*, which recounts the author's attempt to fathom the mystery of Chris McCandless, a bright young graduate from Emory University who abandoned conventional life and "disappeared" into the Alaska wilderness, where he was eventually found dead in an abandoned school bus. Who was Chris McCandless?, Krakauer asks. What motivated him? The book records Krakauer's exploration—a collage of personal narrative intermixed with interviews, musings on his reading, and frequent theorizing. This chapter introduces you to thinking processes behind this powerful form.

EXPLORING EXPLORATORY WRITING

Through our work in writing centers, we often encounter students disappointed with their grades on essay exams or papers. "I worked hard on this paper," they tell us, "but I still got a lousy grade. What am I doing wrong? What do college professors want?"

To help you answer this question, consider the following two essays written for a freshman placement examination in composition at the University of Pittsburgh, in response to the following assignment:

> Describe a time when you did something you felt to be creative. Then, on the basis of the incident you have described, go on to draw some general conclusions about "creativity."

How would you describe the differences in thinking exhibited by the two writers? Which essay do you think professors rated higher?

Essay A

I am very interested in music, and I try to be creative in my interpretation of music. While in high school, I was a member of a jazz ensemble. The members of the ensemble were given chances to improvise and be creative in various songs. I feel that this was a great experience for me, as well as the other members. I was proud to know that I could use my imagination and feelings to create music other than what was written.

Creativity to me means being free to express yourself in a way that is unique to you, not having to conform to certain rules and guidelines. Music is only one of the many areas in which people are given opportunities to show their creativity. Sculpting, carving, building, art, and acting are just a few more areas where people can show their creativity.

Through my music I conveyed feelings and thoughts which were important to me. Music was my means of showing creativity. In whatever form creativity takes, whether it be music, art, or science, it is an important aspect of our lives because it enables us to be individuals.

Essay B

Throughout my life, I have been interested and intrigued by music. My mother has often told me of the times, before I went to school, when I would "conduct" the orchestra on her records. I continued to listen to music and eventually started to play the guitar and the clarinet. Finally, at about the age of twelve, I started to sit down and to try to write songs. Even though my instrumental skills were far from my own high standards, I would spend much of my spare time during the day with a guitar around my neck, trying to produce a piece of music.

Each of these sessions, as I remember them, had a rather set format. I would sit in my bedroom, strumming different combinations of the five or six chords I could play, until I heard a series which sounded particularly good to me. After this, I set the music to a suitable rhythm (usually dependent on my mood at the time), and ran through the tune until I could play it fairly easily. Only after this section was complete did I go on to writing lyrics, which generally followed along the lines of the current popular songs on the radio.

At the time of the writing, I felt that my songs were, in themselves, an original creation of my own; that is, I, alone, made them. However, I now see that, in this sense of the word, I was not creative. The songs themselves seem to be an oversimplified form of the music I listened to at the time.

In a more fitting sense, however, I *was* being creative. Since I did not purposely copy my favorite songs, I was, effectively, originating my songs from my own "process of creativity." To achieve my goal, I needed what a composer would call "inspiration" for my piece. In this case the inspiration was the current hit on the radio. Perhaps, with my present point of view, I feel that I used too much "inspiration" in my songs, but, at that time, I did not.

Creativity, therefore, is a process which, in my case, involved a certain series of "small creations" if you like. As well, it is something the appreciation of which varies with one's point of view, that point of view being set by the person's experience, tastes, and his own personal view of creativity. The less experienced tend to allow for less originality, while the more experienced demand real originality to classify something a "creation." Either way, a term as abstract as this is perfectly correct, and open to interpretation.

Working as a whole class or in small groups, analyze the differences between Essay A and Essay B. What might cause college professors to rate one essay higher than the other? What would the writer of the weaker essay have to do to produce an essay more like the stronger?

WRITING PROJECT

Choose a question, problem, or issue that genuinely perplexes you. At the beginning of your exploratory essay, explain why you are interested in this chosen problem and why you have been unable to reach a satisfactory answer. Then write a first-person, chronologically organized, narrative account of your thinking process as you investigate your question through research, talking with others, and doing your own reflective thinking. Your research might involve reading articles or other sources assigned by your instructor, doing your own library or Internet research, or doing field research through interviews and observations. As you reflect on your research, you can also draw on your own memories and experiences. Your goal is to examine your question, problem, or issue from a variety of perspectives, assessing the strengths and weaknesses of different positions and points of view. By the end of your essay, you may or may not have reached a satisfactory solution to your problem. You will be rewarded for the quality of your exploration and thinking processes. In other words, your goal is not to answer your question but to report on the process of wrestling with it.

This assignment asks you to dwell on a problem—and not necessarily to solve that problem. Your problem may shift and evolve as your thinking progresses. What matters is that you are actively engaged with your problem and demonstrate why it is problematic.

Your instructor may choose to combine this writing project with a subsequent one (for example, a research paper based on one of the assignments in the remaining chapters in Part Two) to create a sustained project in which you write two pieces on the same topic. If so, then the essay for this chapter will prepare you to write a later analytical or persuasive piece. Check with your instructor to make sure that your chosen question for this project will work for the later assignment.

UNDERSTANDING EXPLORATORY WRITING

As we have explained, this assignment calls for an essay with an *exploratory purpose.* Exploratory writing generally has an open-form structure. The writer does not assert a thesis and forecast a structure in the introduction (typical features of closed-form prose) because the writer's purpose is to present the process of exploration itself—to write *thesis-seeking* rather than *thesis-supporting* prose. Instead of following a closed-form, points-first structure, the essay narrates chronologically the process of the author's thinking about the problem.

See the discussion of purposes in Chapter 4, pp. 61–65.

The Essence of Exploratory Prose: Considering Multiple Solutions

The essential move of an exploratory essay is to consider multiple solutions to a problem or multiple points of view on an issue. The writer defines a problem, poses a possible solution, explores its strengths and weaknesses, and then *moves* on to consider another possible solution.

To show a mind at work examining multiple solutions, let's return to the two student essays you examined in the previous exploratory activity (p. 176). The fundamental difference between Essay A and Essay B is that the writer of Essay B treats the concept of "creativity" as a true problem. Note that the writer of Essay A is satisfied with his or her initial definition:

> Creativity to me means being free to express yourself in a way that is unique to you, not having to conform to certain rules and guidelines.

The writer of Essay B, however, is *not* satisfied with his or her first answer and uses the essay to think through the problem. This writer remembers an early creative experience—composing songs as a twelve-year-old:

> At the time of the writing, I felt that my songs were, in themselves, an original creation of my own; that is, I, alone, made them. However, I now see that, in this sense of the word, I was not creative. The songs themselves seem to be an oversimplified form of the music I listened to at the time.

This writer distinguishes between two points of view: "On the one hand, I used to think *x*, but now, in retrospect, I think *y*." This move forces the writer to go beyond the initial answer to think of alternatives.

The key to effective exploratory writing is to create a tension between alternative views. When you start out, you might not know where your thinking process will end up; at the outset you might not have formulated an opposing, countering, or alternative view. Using a statement such as "I used to think . . . , but now I think" or "Part of me thinks this . . . , but another part thinks that . . ." forces you to find something additional to say; writing then becomes a process of inquiry and discovery.

The second writer's dissatisfaction with the initial answer initiates a dialectic process that plays one idea against another, creating a generative tension. In contrast, the writer of Essay A offers no alternative to his or her definition of creativity. This writer presents no specific illustrations of creative activity (such as the specific details in Essay B about strumming the guitar) but presents merely space-filling abstractions ("Sculpting, carving, building, art, and acting are just a few more areas where people can show their creativity."). The writer of Essay B scores a higher grade, not because the essay creates a brilliant (or even particularly clear) explanation of creativity; rather, the writer is rewarded for thinking about the problem dialectically.

We use the term *dialectic* to mean a thinking process often associated with the German philosopher Hegel, who said that each thesis ("My act was creative") gives rise to an antithesis ("My act was not creative") and that the clash of these opposing perspectives leads thinkers to develop a synthesis that incorporates some features of both theses ("My act was a series of 'small creations'"). You initiate dialectic thinking any time you play Elbow's believing and doubting game or use other strategies to place alternative possibilities side by side.

See Chapter 2, pp. 37–39, for an explanation of the believing and doubting game.

Essay B's writer uses a dialectic thinking strategy that we might characterize as follows:

1. Regards the assignment as a genuine problem worth puzzling over.
2. Considers alternative views and plays them off against each other.
3. Looks at specifics.
4. Continues the thinking process in search of some sort of resolution or synthesis of the alternative views.
5. Incorporates the stages of this dialectic process into the essay.

For Writing and Discussion

1. According to writing theorist David Bartholomae, who analyzed several hundred student essays in response to the placement examination question on page 175, almost all the highest scoring essays exhibited a similar kind of dialectic thinking. How might the writer of the first essay expand the essay by using the dialectic thinking processes just described?
2. Working individually, read each of the following questions and write out your initial opinion or one or two answers that come immediately to mind.

   ■ Given the easy availability of birth control information and the ready availability of condoms, why do you think there are so many teenage pregnancies?

   ■ Why do U.S. students, on average, lag so far behind their European and Asian counterparts in scholastic achievement?

   ■ Should women be assigned to combat roles in the military?

   ■ The most popular magazines sold on college campuses around the country are women's fashion and lifestyle magazines such as *Glamour*, *Seventeen*, and *Cosmopolitan*. Why are these magazines so popular? Is there a problem with these magazines being so popular? (Two separate questions, both of which are worth exploring dialectically.)

3. Choose one of these questions or one assigned by your instructor and freewrite for five or ten minutes using one or more of the following to stimulate dialectic thinking:

   I used to think _____, but now I think _____.

   Part of me thinks _____, but another part of me thinks_____ .

   On some days I think _____, but on other days I think _____.

   The first answers that come to mind are _____, but as I think further I see _____.

   My classmate thinks _____, but I think _____.

   (continued)

Your goal here is to explore potential weaknesses or inadequacies in your first answers, and then to push beyond them to think of new or different answers. Feel free to be wild and risky in posing possible alternative solutions.

4. As a whole class, take a poll to find out what the most common first-response answers are for each of the questions. Then share alternative solutions generated by class members during the freewriting. The goal is to pose and explore answers that go beyond or against the grain of the common answers. Remember, there is little point in arguing for an answer that everyone else already accepts.

Readings

In this section we include two student essays that illustrate writing with an exploratory purpose. In the first essay, student writer Christopher Leigh explores the problem of preventing school violence. You read about Christopher's early exploration of this problem in Chapter 1. By the end of his first-year writing course, he had developed his ideas into a researched argument opposing metal detectors in the schools. Christopher's argument against metal detectors is our sample student research paper in Chapter 23.

Christopher's early journal entry is shown on p. 10. His researched argument is on pp. 647–658.

■ CHRISTOPHER LEIGH (STUDENT) ■

AN EXPLORATION OF HOW TO PREVENT VIOLENCE IN SCHOOLS

The April 20, 1999, shootings at Columbine High School in Littleton, Colorado, left me, as well as people across America, in a state of shock and disbelief. The terrifying incidents made my friends and me wonder what had driven the two high school students to commit such a horrible crime. Most of all, we wanted to know what was being done to prevent incidents like this from happening again.   1

For the exploratory paper I knew I wanted to write on some aspect of school violence, such as what causes it or what can be done to prevent it, and I decided to focus on the ways that schools are working to prevent violence.   2

While I was searching through newspaper articles on Lexis-Nexis Academic Universe, I discovered a *New York Times* article by Timothy Egan that captured my interest. The article deals with the practice of profiling in high schools to identify potentially violent students. The profiles contain a list of behaviors and warning signs that may indicate that a student is troubled and prone to violence. Egan quotes former President Clinton, who said, "We must all do more to recognize and look for the early warning signals that deeply troubled young people send often before they explode into violence" (1). Within days, Egan writes, national organizations had distrib-   3 uted lists of characteristics, which included signs such as mood swings, drug/alcohol use, and fondness for violent television. I noted in my journal that the problem with these checklists is that they describe almost every person at some point in adolescence. However, I could also see why kids who fit the profiles for many of the traits should be closely watched; any adolescent who is often depressed and uses drugs or alcohol is likely to be troubled. But a kid could be depressed, troubled, and abusive of drugs or alcohol and yet pose no threat. Would being labeled as "potentially violent" only further alienate or anger the student?

4   The article really made me question how I felt about profiling. On the one hand, I believe that profiling in any form is wrong and defies the very principles upon which our country is built. Just as racial profiling singles out innocent people based on the color of their skin, profiling in schools targets those who do not fit social norms of acceptable behavior. On the other hand, I agree that violence in schools is a problem that needs to be addressed, and preventive measures that may help should be thoroughly considered.

5   After reading this article, I began to think about various issues surrounding profiling, such as whether profiling is effective and whether it violates students' rights. I decided to search for articles that specifically addressed these issues.

6   Unfortunately, after much searching I couldn't find any articles addressing whether or not profiling is effective, nor could I find any discussion of whether it violates civil rights. However, using Ebscohost I found an article in *US News and World Report* that raises another important issue related to profiling. Its author, Mary Lord, shows that many schools use profiling to identify kids who need counseling, but that fewer than ten percent of schools have mental health professionals available to deal with the kids once they have been identified (57). Lord also describes a student who was arrested for writing an essay about blowing up the school but then rebuilding it to make it state of the art (55). At this point I began to see more clearly why the issue of profiling is problematic. The student described in Lord's article had no intention of causing any harm, but his careless use of words in his essay resulted in an arrest and suspension, which was later rescinded when the school acknowledged its wrongdoing. The student then noted that he avoids writing essays and speaks less often in class as a result of the incident (Lord 55). I can understand that schools have good intentions—to prevent violence by providing troubled kids with counseling—but in this case, the school did not provide counseling and instead suspended him. Furthermore, if most schools do not have the resources to provide counseling, it seems pointless to try to identify potentially violent students.

7   Lord's article referred to an FBI report dealing with prevention of school violence, so I wanted to find out more about it. I found a newspaper article by David Vise and Kenneth Cooper, who write that the FBI report advises schools not to use profiling to identify potentially violent students because

actual incidents of school violence are so rare. Instead, they write, the report calls for the use of profiling only when some threat of violence has already occurred (Vise and Cooper A3). I was relieved to learn that the FBI is opposed to the general use of profiling. The article by Mary Lord that I had read earlier had given me the false impression that the FBI report supported profiling, but now I see that the FBI supports profiling only in the case of an actual threat. Nevertheless, many schools still misuse the profiles.

I decided that I shouldn't use any more magazines or newspapers due to their potential bias and omission of important information. I next went to find the full FBI report on school violence. The report, published by the FBI Academy's National Center for the Analysis of Violent Crime, can be found on the agency's Web site and can be read in its original format using Acrobat Reader. The report is written by Mary O'Toole, PhD, who headed the investigation. She proposes that schools set up a system of professionals who can be called in to assess threats and determine their severity and risk (United States 5). I found the report impressively comprehensive, even though it does not explain how schools should go about setting up a threat-assessment program. Although the report repeatedly warns schools not to use profiles alone, it still lists pages of characteristics of potentially violent kids, which seemed to me to be an invitation to misuse the report. The way I see it, school administrators will read the report, recognize the complexity of the proposal, and simply take the easiest course of action, which is to remove the profiles from context and use them on their own.

One aspect of O'Toole's report really struck me. She shows how the media misrepresent school violence by treating it as a widespread, frequent phenomenon and by portraying school shooters in a stereotypical way (United States 4). I have always felt strongly about the negative power of mass media, so I decided to investigate this lead. I found a brief article in *Professional School Counseling* entitled "Unsafe Schools: Perception or Reality?" The article's author, Tony Del Prete, writes that people tend to "overanalyze and sensationalize [incidents] to the point of hysteria" (375). He observes that the media inaccurately portray violence as a plague in American society, when in actuality school violence has steadily declined since 1993. After reading this article, I concluded that the media devote so much coverage to incidents such as the one at Columbine High that the public adopts an it-could-happen-to-anyone view of school violence. This attitude creates a panicked need to find a simplistic and crude solution, such as profiling or installing metal detectors in schools where there are no previous incidents of violence.

Despite my discovery that the frequency of school violence has been exaggerated, I believe that violence is a real problem, and methods of prevention should be implemented to maintain safe schools. Del Prete concludes his article by suggesting that the best approach is to create a more friendly community atmosphere in schools by eliminating harassment and reducing competition. Even though it too seems like a simplistic solution, I feel that making schools friendlier and educating teens about the harmful

8

9

10

effects of a hostile environment are keys to improving the state of our schools.

11   I then began to think about how other forms of preventing school violence, such as metal detectors, might have a negative impact on the school environment. Metal detectors are a popular form of violence prevention, yet their increasing presence in schools is troubling. I began searching the Web to find out more about metal detectors. One article, entitled "Districts Should Proceed Cautiously on Metal Detectors," from the New York State School Board's Web site, points out that most schools equipped with the devices cannot check every student due to the large numbers of people arriving at once, so it is practically impossible to ensure that weapons do not enter school buildings. The article also notes that metal detectors do not address the nature of the problem of violence, and that schools should be more concerned with "creating a climate that teaches peaceful resolution" ("Districts"). However, a poll conducted by Charlotte.com, a North Carolina newspaper-affiliated Web site, showed that eighty-one percent of local residents approved of metal detectors in schools (Ly and Toosi). Despite the public demand for metal detectors in schools, I feel that they might actually have a negative effect in reducing school violence because they make schools seem like prisons and damage the feeling of community. At this point I was becoming more and more convinced that the best way to reduce violence is to make schools more friendly and less hostile.

12   I decided to try to find one more article about ways to make schools less hostile environments. I went back to the educational journals and found an article by Scott Poland, whose name appeared in many of the other sources I found. The author, who is the president of the National Association of School Psychologists, also calls for an effort to personalize our schools and hire more professionals to help counsel kids who may be troubled (45). He writes that most counselors are already overworked and are required to do things such as scheduling that take away from their attention to the students. Poland also emphasizes that it is important for teachers to form strong relationships with their students. He suggests that teachers set aside a small amount of time each day to interact with students, and he discourages schools from cutting extracurricular programs that may help students feel connected to the school (46). From my point of view, Poland's article offers the most encouraging and perhaps the most promising solution to prevent school violence. Yet Poland's solution can't be done cheaply. I remembered an article that I had scanned briefly earlier in my research process, and I decided to return to it for a closer look. This article, "America Skips School," explains that until Americans recognize the importance of education by paying teachers higher salaries, public schools will continue to become less and less effective (Barber 45). My research on preventing violence in schools has shown me that now we have another big reason to invest more in public education. If teachers can and should play a significant role in creating a positive school community, then they should be compensated for this addi-

tional responsibility. After all, if teachers don't know the first thing about their students, there is no way they are going to be able to know who is in need of help and who is not. By developing relationships with students on a personal level, teachers will be able to sense when a student is in trouble and can take steps to reach out to that student. The need for more counselors is also crucial to provide students with help if a teacher thinks it is necessary.

I believe that this exploratory paper has helped me clarify my own thinking about school violence. I am now convinced that the media have instigated a panic about school violence, leading in many cases to counterproductive approaches like psychological profiling and metal detectors. When it comes time to write my major argument paper, I plan to show that these approaches only increase students' sense of alienation and hostility. The most important approach is to make schools more friendly, communal, and personal. We must ensure that troubled students are provided with the help they need, rather than treating them like criminals.

13

Works Cited

Barber, Benjamin. "America Skips School." Harper's Nov. 1993: 39–46.

Del Prete, Tony. "Unsafe Schools: Perception or Reality?" Professional School Counseling 3 (2000): 375–76.

"Districts Should Proceed Cautiously on Metal Detectors." New York State School Boards Association. 22 May 2000. 16 Aug. 2001 <http://www.nyssba.org/adnews/employee/employee052200.3.html>

Egan, Timothy. "The Trouble with Looking for Signs of Trouble." New York Times 25 Apr. 1999, sec. 4: 1.

Lord, Mary. "The Violent Kid Profile: A Controversial New Technique for Beating Violence in Schools." US News & World Report 11 Oct. 1999: 56–57.

Ly, Phuong, and Nahal Toosi. "Many Favor Metal Detectors." Charlotte Observer. 19 Nov. 2000. 16 Aug. 2001 <http://www.charlotte.com/observer/special/poll98/0804metal.htm>

Poland, Scott. "The Fourth R—Relationships." American School Board Journal 187.3 (2000): 45–46.

United States Dept. of Justice. Fed. Bureau of Investigation. The School Shooter: A Threat Assessment Perspective. By Mary O'Toole. 2000. 16 Aug. 2001 <http://www.fbi.gov/publications/school/school2.pdf>

Vise, David, and Kenneth Cooper. "FBI Opposes the Use of Profiling of Students." Washington Post 7 Sept. 2000: A3.

Thinking Critically about "An Exploration of How to Prevent Violence in Schools"

1. Exploratory papers usually narrate both the evolution of the writer's thinking and the physical actions the writer takes to do the actual research. In Christopher's case, approximately what percentage of the total paper focuses on Christopher's research processes and what percentage on ideas? When he switches from a summary of a research source to his own thinking or from his

own thinking to a description of his next action, how does he write transitions that keep the reader from getting lost?

2. Trace the evolution of Christopher's ideas in this paper. Does his thinking evolve in an ordered and understandable way, or does it seem random and directionless? Explain your reasoning.

3. Read Christopher's argument against metal detectors in the schools on pages 647–658. What connections do you see between his final argument and his earlier exploratory paper? What new research did he do for his final argument? What material from his exploratory paper is omitted from the final argument? In your own words, how does the difference in purpose (exploration versus persuasion) lead to different structures for the two papers?

4. What do you see as the chief strengths and weaknesses of Christopher's exploration of how to prevent school violence?

In this next essay, student writer Sheridan Botts explores problems related to the funding of hospices for the terminally ill. Because her professor assigned the exploratory essay as a first stage in writing a proposal argument (Chapter 17), this writer poses both content-oriented questions about hospices and rhetorical questions about the focus, purpose, and audience for her proposal paper.

Sheridan's proposal argument on hospices appears on pp. 456–459.

■ SHERIDAN BOTTS (STUDENT) ■
EXPLORING PROBLEMS ABOUT HOSPICES

1   Last fall my brother-in-law, Charles, lay dying, and his mother, Betty, was overwhelmed with grief and responsibility. Charles wanted to die at home, not connected to tubes in the hospital, so Betty cared for him in his home with the help of a home care agency. At the same time as she was caring for him—helping him get sips of water, trying to meet his every need—she was terribly depressed. She had already lost one son, and now she was losing another. But she was unable to talk about her depression with her friends. When I called the home care agency to seek counseling help for Betty, they said, "Is she the patient? We can only care for the patient." And then, after Charles died, and Betty was bereft, she was on her own. No services were available to her from the home care agency.

2   If Charles had been with a hospice agency instead of a home care agency, Betty would have had help. A hospice would have helped Charles stay comfortable at home, and, in addition to the visits by nurses, social workers, and home health aides provided by the home care agency, a hospice would have provided chaplain and volunteer helpers both for Charles and for Betty. Social workers or a chaplain would have helped Betty prepare for Charles's death—and after his death, helped her deal with her tremendous grief. Then, for the following year, a hospice would have offered Betty continuing help with grief—articles, a grief counseling group, and calls from volunteers.

So when I started thinking about what to do my paper on, I thought of   3
hospice. I wanted to learn more about the hospice movement and be able to
clearly articulate the benefit of hospice programs. I had two interconnected
writing assignments—this exploratory paper and then a follow-up persuasive argument. There were a lot of things I wanted to find out about hospice,
but what was there to argue about in a persuasive paper? Perhaps I could
persuade people about the benefits of hospice. But I already knew the benefits, and almost everyone agrees that hospices are valuable. So what issue
about hospices is there to argue about? What persuasive essay is crying to be
written?

I decided to find out more about the problems facing hospices, so I   4
looked in the phone book under "Hospice," called Hospice of Seattle, and
was referred to the Marketing Coordinator. I asked her if there was a hospice
question that needed arguing and she said:

> Yes! Convince the private insurance companies to bill on a per diem
> basis instead of fee-for-service. Fee-for-service doesn't pay for social work,
> chaplain visits, volunteers, and grief counseling. You could really help hos-
> pices if you wrote a persuasive paper on that subject!

Ah ha! This was it! A meaningful project. Here was an opportunity to make a
real difference, have an impact, learn more about hospices, and improve my
writing. Here was a subject that was important, and to which I didn't have a
ready answer. How could I convince insurance companies to pay for hospice
on a per diem basis?

I got excited about convincing a real entity to do something real about a   5
real issue. I called the National Hospice Organization and ordered information on hospice care. I then went to the library to see what else I could find.
I looked on Lycos and found Hospice Net. This Web page included a description of the hospice concept: a comprehensive program of care to patients
and families facing a life-threatening illness. From Hospice Net I found
Hospice Hands, from Hospice of North Central Florida. The Hospice Hands
Web page included links to other pages and articles on hospice services,
pain management, and ethical issues. These two pages were very helpful in
finding a variety of hospice information on the Web. In addition to information on the Web, the library had many books on hospice. I especially
enjoyed reading moving stories in *Final Passages: Positive Choices for the
Dying and Their Loved Ones* (Ahronheim) about men and women who had
received hospice care and how much it meant to them.

Although the Web sites and library books confirmed the value of hospice,   6
they did not help me understand the problem of funding, and I started feeling frustrated. I then conducted an article search on Infotrac using the keyword "hospice."

The problem was that I didn't quite know what to look for because I   7
didn't fully understand the implications of fee-for-service versus per diem
payment. Just what is the difference? Why is there such a distinct preference

for fee-for-service by insurance companies, and such a preference for per diem by hospices? Instead of seeking the answers in the library, I decided to try interviews. I made an appointment with a Medical Social Worker at Hospice of Seattle who helped patients sign up for insurance. She was great to talk to because she understood the issue clearly. She explained that with fee-for-service, each visit to the patient's home by a nurse, social worker, home health aide, or therapist is paid for separately, but fee-for-service doesn't pay for everything the patient needs. Fee-for-service doesn't pay for the volunteer program (which has a paid Volunteer Coordinator), chaplains, or grief care (the Grief Counselor coordinates volunteers to call on grief-stricken family members and mails packages throughout the year to family members). Also some insurance programs don't pay for social work. Hospice of Seattle pays for all these services, and tries to incorporate the cost into services that insurance *does* pay for. It seemed clear that fee-for-service did not benefit Hospice of Seattle.

8   According to the social worker, per diem payment works better for hospices. With per diem, the patient's insurance pays the hospice for each day of care the patient receives. This covers the costs better because the hospice can budget and plan better, can order the most appropriate services and supplies, can negotiate better rates with medical equipment companies, and can provide services not covered under fee-for-service. Per diem is also better for the family. They can be assured that their medical needs will be covered. There won't be unexpected surprises or mounting co-payments. This justification of per diem sounded good to me.

9   Per diem did not seem to benefit the insurance company, however. Insurance companies want to minimize the cost for each patient, and get the most for their money. As long as patients are getting the care they need, if the insurance company can get away without paying, well, that sounds pretty good for the insurance company.

10   Uh oh. What if I couldn't come up with good reasons for insurance companies to pay per diem? What if it is to the advantage of the hospice, but *not* to the insurance company, to pay per diem? I asked the Hospice of Seattle Director for help and he gave me a paper, "Accessing Reimbursement: How to Bill Private Insurance," by Brenda Horne. Ms. Horne says, "Billing on a per visit (fee-for-service) basis does not provide adequate reimbursement levels to cover costs for the entire range of hospice services. Only per diem rates take into consideration the fact that hospice offers a unique range of services not available through any other health provider" (2). Unfortunately, the rationale focuses on the value to hospices rather than for insurance companies. The article didn't help me as much as I had hoped it would.

11   This is where I am now, somewhat discouraged. I have learned quite a bit about hospice care and I am even more convinced of the importance of providing this care for dying people. I have been frustrated, however, that I was not able to find more literature analyzing per diem billing. I have more

papers to read, but I don't think they will shed light on this subject. The literature seems either to be about hospice care in general or on the cost saving of hospice care over traditional medicine. The Web pages, articles, and books don't get much into the specific question of the benefit of per diem over fee-for-service billing. Maybe that's why the Marketing Coordinator said that this would be a good paper to write.

I think my best hope in supporting per diem billing is to talk with more staff people at Hospice of Seattle. My guess is that per diem billing should have an advantage in keeping costs down; I need to investigate this justification for per diem billing and try to find other reasons that will persuade insurance companies to try the per diem approach. Now I have the question, but I still need to find a convincing answer.

12

Works Cited

Ahronheim, Judith, and Doron Weber. *Final Passages: Positive Choices for the Dying and Their Loved Ones*. New York: Simon, 1992.

Horne, Brenda. "Accessing Reimbursement: How to Bill Private Insurance." Unpublished essay. Annual Meeting and Symposium of the National Hospice Organization. Nashville. 30 Oct. 1992.

Hospice Hands. Hospice of North Central Florida. 31 July 1998 <http://www.hospice-cares.com/welcome.html>

Hospice Net. 1998. 31 July 1998 <http://www.hospicenet.org>

Thinking Critically about "Exploring Problems about Hospices"

1. In Part One, we distinguished between two kinds of problems that writers face: content problems and rhetorical problems. Sheridan Botts wrestles with both problems throughout this exploratory paper. In your own words, what are the content problems that Sheridan examines, and what are the rhetorical problems?
2. What are the chief strengths and chief weaknesses of her exploration so far?
3. What further research does Sheridan need to do before she can persuade insurance companies to pay hospices on a per diem basis?

COMPOSING YOUR EXPLORATORY ESSAY

Generating and Exploring Ideas

Your process of generating and exploring ideas is, in essence, the *subject matter* of your exploratory paper. This section helps you get started and keep going.

Keeping a Research Log

Since this assignment asks you to create a chronologically organized account of your thinking process, you need to keep a careful, detailed record of your investigation. The best tool for doing so is a research log or journal in which you take notes on your sources and record your thinking throughout the process.

As you investigate your issue, keep a chronologically organized account that includes notes on your readings, interviews, and significant conversations, as well as explorations of how each of these sources, new perspectives, or data influence your current thinking. Many writers keep a double-entry notebook that has a "notes" section in which to summarize key points, record data, copy potentially usable quotations verbatim, and so forth and a "reflections" section in which to write a strong response to each reading, exploring how it advanced your thinking, raised questions, or pulled you in one direction or another.

For an example of double-entry notes, see "Sam's Notes on *Newsweek* Article" on pp. 191–192.

As you write your exploratory essay, your research log will be your main source for details—evidence of what you were thinking at regular intervals throughout the process.*

Exploring Possible Problems for Your Essay

Your instructor may assign a specific problem to explore. If not, then your first step is to choose a question, problem, or issue that currently perplexes you. Perhaps a question is problematic to you because you haven't studied it (How serious is the problem of global warming? How can we keep pornography on the Internet away from children?) or because the available factual data seem conflicting and inconclusive (Should postmenopausal women take supplemental estrogen?) or because the problem or issue draws you into an uncomfortable conflict of values (Should we legalize drugs? Should the homeless mentally ill be placed involuntarily in state mental hospitals?).

The key to this assignment is to choose a question, problem, or issue *that truly perplexes you.* The more clearly readers sense your personal engagement with the problem, the more likely they are to be engaged by your writing. Note: If your instructor pairs this assignment with a later one, be sure that your question is appropriate for the later assignment. Check with your instructor.

Here are several exercises to help you think of ideas for this essay:

Exploration Exercise 1. In your research log, make a list of issues or problems that both interest and perplex you. Then choose two or three of your issues and freewrite about them for five minutes or so, exploring questions such as these: Why am I interested in this problem? What makes the problem problematic? What makes this problem significant? Share your list of questions and your freewrites with friends and classmates. Discussing questions with friends often stimulates you to think of more questions yourself or to sharpen the focus of questions you have already asked.

To show how a question is problematic and significant, see Chapter 1, pp. 20–22.

Exploration Exercise 2. If your exploratory essay is paired with a subsequent assignment, look at the invention exercises for that assignment to help you ask a question that fits the context of the final paper you will write.

---

*For those of you majoring in science or engineering, this research log is similar to the laboratory notebooks that are required parts of any original research in science or industry. Besides recording in detail the progress of your research, these notebooks often serve as crucial data in patent applications or liability lawsuits. Doctors and nurses keep similar logs in their medical records file for each patient. This is a time-honored practice. In Mary Shelley's early-nineteenth-century novel *Frankenstein,* the monster learns about the process of his creation by reading Dr. Frankenstein's laboratory journal.

Exploration Exercise 3. A particularly valuable kind of problem to explore for this assignment is a public controversy. Often such issues involve complex disagreements about facts and values that merit careful, open-ended exploration. This assignment invites you to explore and clarify where you stand on such complex public issues as gay marriages, overcrowded prisons, the Endangered Species Act, racial profiling, the electoral college, Internet censorship and privacy issues, and so forth. These issues make particularly good topics for persuasive papers or formal research papers, if either is required in your course. For this exercise, look through a current newspaper or weekly newsmagazine, and in your research log make a list of public issues that you would like to know more about. Use the following trigger question:

> I don't know where I stand on the issue of _____ .

Share your list with classmates and friends.

Formulating a Starting Point

After you've chosen a problem or issue, write a research log entry identifying the problem or issue you have chosen and explaining why you are perplexed by and interested in it. You might start out with a sharp, clearly focused question (for example, "Should the United States eliminate welfare payments for single mothers?"). Often, however, formulating the question turns out to be part of the *process* of writing the exploratory paper. Many writers don't start with a single, focused question but rather with a whole cluster of related questions swimming in their heads. This practice is all right—in fact, it is healthy—as long as you have a direction in which to move after the initial starting point. Even if you do start with a focused question, it is apt to evolve as your thinking progresses.

For this exercise, choose the question, problem, or issue you plan to investigate and write a research log entry explaining how you got interested in that question and why you find it both problematic and significant. This will be the *starting point* for your essay; it might even serve as the rough draft for your introduction. Many instructors will collect this exploration as a quick check on whether you have formulated a good question that promises fruitful results.

Here is how one student, Sam, wrote the starting point entry for his research log:

Sam's Starting Point Research Log Entry

I want to focus on the question of whether women should be allowed to serve in combat units in the military. I became interested in the issue of women in combat through my interest in gays in the military. While I saw that gays in the military was an important political issue for gay rights, I, like many gays, had no real desire to be in such a macho organization. But perhaps that was just the point—we had the opportunity to break stereotypes and attack areas most hostile to us.

Similarly, I wonder whether feminists see women in combat as a crucial symbolic issue for women's rights. (I wonder too whether it is a *good* symbol, since many women value a less masculine approach to the world.) I think my instinct right now is that women should be allowed to serve in combat units. I think it is wrong to discriminate against women. Yet I also think America needs to have a strong military. Therefore, I am in a quandary. If putting women in combat wouldn't harm our military power, then I am fully in favor of women in combat. But if it would hurt our military power, then I have to make a value judgment. So I guess I have a lot to think about as I research this issue. I decided to focus on the women issue rather than the gay issue because it poses more of a dilemma for me. I am absolutely in favor of gays in the military, so I am not very open-minded about *exploring* that issue. But the women's issue is more of a problem for me.

Continuing with Research and Dialectic Thinking

After you have formulated your starting point, you need to proceed with research, keeping a research log that records both your reading notes and your strong response reflections to each reading.

After Sam wrote his starting point entry, he created an initial bibliography by searching his college library's Infotrac. He decided to try keeping his research log in a double-entry, notes/reflections format. What follows is his research log entry for the first article he read, a piece from *Newsweek*.

For instruction on how to carry out library research, see Chapters 22–24.

Sam's Research Log Entry on *Newsweek* Article

Notes

Hackworth, David H. "War and the Second Sex." *Newsweek* 5 Aug. 1991: 24–28.

■ Ideals in conflict are equality and combat readiness.

■ Acknowledges women's bravery, competence, and education (uses the Gulf War as an example). Admits that there are some women as strong and fit as the strongest men (gives some examples), but then argues that allowing even these women in combat is the type of experimentation that the army doesn't need right now. (He says women already have plenty of jobs open to them in noncombat units.)

■ Biggest problem is "gender norming"—having different physical standards for men and women. A 22-year-old female is allowed three more minutes than a 22-year-old male to run two miles; men have to climb a 20-foot rope in 30 seconds; women can take 50 seconds.

■ One of Hackworth's big values is male bonding. He points to "male bonding" as a key to unit cohesion. Men have been socialized to think that women must be protected. He uses Israel as an example:

"The Israeli Army put women on the front lines in 1948. The experiment ended disastrously after only three weeks. It wasn't that the women couldn't fight. It was that they got blown apart. Female casualties demoralized the men and gutted unit cohesion." (pp. 26–27)

■ Another major problem is pregnancy causing women to leave a unit. He says that 10 to 15 percent of servicewomen wear maternity uniforms in a given year. During the Gulf War, pregnancy rates soared. 1200 pregnant women were evacuated from the gulf (p. 28) during the war. On one destroyer tender, 36 female crew members got pregnant (p. 28). These pregnancies leave vacancies in a unit that can destroy its effectiveness.

▪ He claims that women soldiers themselves had so many complaints about their experiences in the Gulf War (fraternization, sexual harassment, lack of privacy, primitive living conditions) that they said "don't rush to judgment on women in combat" (p. 28).

Reflections

Some challenging points, but not completely convincing. His biggest reason for opposing women in combat is harm to unit morale, but this isn't convincing to me. The Israeli example seems like unconvincing evidence seeing how those soldiers' attitudes in 1948 reflected a much different society.

Issue of pregnancy is more convincing. A pregnant woman, unlike a father-to-be, cannot continue to fill her role as a combat soldier. I was shocked by the number of pregnancies during the Gulf War and by the extent (although Hackworth doesn't give statistics) of the fraternization (he says the army passed out over a million condoms—p. 28).

I am also bothered by the gender-norming issue. It seems to me that there ought to be some absolute standards of strength and endurance needed for combat duty and the military ought to exclude both men and women who don't meet them. This would mean that a lower percentage of women than men would be eligible, but is that discrimination?

Where do I now stand? Well, I am still leaning toward believing that women should be allowed to serve in combat, but I see that there are a number of subquestions involved. Should physical standards for combat positions be the same for men and women? Will the presence of women really hurt morale in a mostly male unit? Should women be given special consideration for their roles as mothers? How serious a problem is pregnancy? I also see another problem: Should physically eligible women be *required* (e.g., drafted) to serve in combat the same way men are drafted into combat positions? And I still want to know whether this is a crucial issue for the women's rights movement.

In the next section we see how Sam converts material from his research log into a draft of his exploratory essay.

Shaping and Drafting

Your exploratory essay should offer accounts of your search procedures (useful conversations with friends, strategies for tracking down sources, use of indexes or computer searches, strokes of good fortune at stumbling on good leads, and so forth) and your thought processes (what you were discovering, how your ideas were evolving). Drawing on your research log, you can share your frustration when a promising source turned out to be off the mark or your perplexity when a conversation with a friend over late-night espresso forced you to rethink your views. Hook your readers by making your exploratory essay read like a detective story. Consider giving your account immediacy by quoting your thoughts at the very moment you wrote a log entry. The general shape of an exploratory essay can take the following pattern:

1. Starting point: you describe your initial problem, why you are interested in it, why it is problematic, why it is worth pursuing.
2. New input: you read an article, interview someone, pose an alternative solution.
   a. Summarize, describe, or explain the new input.
   b. Discuss the input, analyzing or evaluating it, playing the believing and doubting game with it, exploring how this input affects your thinking.
   c. Decide where to go next—find an alternative view, pursue a subquestion, seek more data, and so forth.
3. More new input: you repeat step 2 for your next piece of research.
4. Still more new input.
5. Ending point: you sum up where you stand at the point when the paper is due, how much your thinking about the issue has changed, whether or not you've reached a satisfactory solution.

Here is how Sam converted his starting point entry (pp. 190–191) and his first research entry (pp. 191–192) into the opening pages of his exploratory essay.

Should Women Be Allowed to Serve in Combat Units?

Sam Scofield

At first, I wanted to explore the issue of gays in the military. But since I am a gay man I already knew where I stood on that issue and didn't find it truly problematic *for myself*. So I decided to shift my question to whether women should be allowed to serve in combat units. I wasn't sure whether feminists see the issue of women in combat the same way that gays see the military issue. Is it important to the feminist cause for women to be in combat? Or should feminists seek a kind of political order that avoids combat and doesn't settle issues through macho male behavior? In my initial thinking, I was also concerned about maintaining our country's military strength. In my "starting point" entry of my research log, I recorded the following thoughts:

> If putting women in combat wouldn't harm our military power, then I am fully in favor of women in combat. But if it would hurt our military power, then I have to make a value judgment.

So I decided that what I should do first is find some general background reading on the women in combat question. I went to the library, plugged the key words "woman and combat" into our online Infotrac database, and found more than a dozen entries. I went to the stacks and found the most familiar magazine in my initial list: *Newsweek*.

I began with an article by a retired Air Force colonel, David H. Hackworth. Hackworth was opposed to women in combat and focused mainly on the standard argument I was expecting—namely that women in combat would destroy male bonding. He didn't provide any evidence, however, other than citing the case of Israel in 1948:

The Israeli Army put women on the front lines in 1948. The experiment ended disastrously after only three weeks. It wasn't that the women couldn't fight. It was that they got blown apart. Female casualties demoralized the men and gutted unit cohesion. (26–27)

However, this argument wasn't very persuasive to me. I thought that men's attitudes had changed a lot since 1948 and that cultural changes would allow us to get used to seeing both men and women as *people* so that it would be equally bad—or equally bearable—to see either men or women wounded and killed in combat.

But Hackworth did raise three points that I hadn't anticipated, and that really set me thinking. First he said that the military had different physical fitness requirements for men and women (for example, women had three minutes longer to run two miles than did men [25]). As I said in my research log, "It seems to me that there ought to be some absolute standards of strength and endurance needed for combat duty and the military ought to exclude both men and women who don't meet them." A second point was that an alarming number of female soldiers got pregnant in the Gulf War (1200 pregnant soldiers had to be evacuated [28]) and that prior to the war about ten to fifteen percent of female soldiers were pregnant at any given time (28). His point was that a pregnant woman, unlike a father-to-be, cannot continue to fill her role as a combat soldier. When she leaves her unit, she creates a dangerous gap that makes it hard for the unit to accomplish its mission. Finally, Hackworth cited lots of actual women soldiers in the Gulf War who were opposed to women in combat. They raised issues such as fraternization, sexual harassment, lack of privacy, and primitive living conditions.

Although Hackworth didn't turn me against wanting women to be able to serve in combat, he made the issue much more problematic for me. I now realized that this issue contained a lot of subissues, so I decided to focus first on the two major ones for me: (1) How important is this issue to feminists? This concern is crucial for me because I want to support equal rights for women just as I want to do so for gays or ethnic minorities. And (2) How serious are the pregnancy and strength-test issues in terms of maintaining military strength?

As I read the rest of the articles on my list, I began paying particular attention to these issues. The next article that advanced my thinking was. . . .

Revising

Because an exploratory essay describes the writer's research and thinking in chronological order, most writers have little trouble with organization. When they revise, their major concern is often to improve their essay's interest level by keeping it focused and lively. Exploratory essays grow tedious if the pace crawls too slowly or if extraneous details appear. They also tend to become too long, so that condensing and pruning become key revision tasks. The draft here is actually Sam's second draft; the first draft was a page longer and incorporated many more details and quotations from the Hackworth article. Sam eliminated these because he realized that his purpose was not to report on Hackworth but to describe the evolution of his own thinking. By condensing the Hackworth material, Sam saved room for the ideas he discovered later.

Peer reviewers can give you valuable feedback about the pace and interest level of an exploratory piece. They can also help you achieve the right balance between external details (how you did the research, to whom you talked, where you were) and mental details (what you were thinking about). As you revise, make sure you follow proper stylistic conventions for quotations and citations.

These conventions are explained in Chapter 23, pp. 631–645.

■ GUIDELINES FOR PEER REVIEWS ■

Instructions for peer reviews are provided in Chapter 18 (pp. 490–496).

For the Writer

Prepare two or three questions you would like your peer reviewer to address while responding to your draft. The questions can focus on some aspect of your draft that you are uncertain about, on one or more sections where you particularly seek help or advice, on some feature that you particularly like about your draft, or on some part you especially wrestled with. Write out your questions and give them to your peer reviewer along with your draft.

For the Reviewer

I. Read the draft at a normal reading speed from beginning to end. As you read, do the following:

    A. Place a wavy line in the margin next to any passages that you find confusing, that contain something that doesn't seem to fit, or that otherwise slow down your reading.

    B. Place a "Good!" in the margin next to any passages where you think the writing is particularly strong or interesting.

II. Read the draft again slowly and answer the following questions by writing brief explanations of your answers.

    A. Posing the problem:

        1. How might the title be improved to identify the problem more accurately or to better engage your interest?

        2. How has the writer tried to show that the problem is interesting, problematic, and significant? How could the writer engage you more fully with the initial problem?

        3. How does the writer provide cues that the writer's purpose is to explore a question rather than argue a thesis? How might the opening section of the paper be improved?

    B. Narrating the exploration:

        1. Is the body of the paper organized chronologically so that you see the gradual development of the writer's thinking? Where does the writer provide chronological transitions? Are there confusing shifts from past tense to present tense? If so, how might the chronological structure of the paper be made clearer?

        2. How has the writer revealed the stages or changes in his or her thinking about the problem?

3. Part of an exploratory paper involves summarizing the argument of each new research source. Where in this draft is a summary of a source particularly clear and well developed? Where are summary passages that seem undeveloped or unclear? How could these passages be improved?

4. Another part of an exploratory paper involves the writer's strong response to each source—evidence of the writer's own critical thinking and questioning. Where are the writer's own ideas particularly strong and effective? Where are the writer's own ideas undeveloped or weak? What additional ideas or perspectives do you think the writer should consider?

5. Has the writer done enough research to explore the problem? Can you make suggestions for further research?

6. How might the ending of the paper better sum up the evolution of the writer's thinking or better clarify why the writer has or has not resolved the problem?

C. If the writer has prepared questions for you, respond to his or her inquiries.

D. Sum up what you see as the chief strengths and problem areas of this draft:

1. Strengths

2. Problem areas

III. Read the draft one more time. Place a check mark in the margin wherever you notice problems in grammar, spelling, or mechanics (one check mark per problem).

CHAPTER 9

Writing an Informative (and Surprising) Essay

ABOUT INFORMATIVE (AND SURPRISING) WRITING

Throughout this text, we have encouraged the habit of considering alternative solutions to a problem. This chapter shows you how to amplify that habit through the use of a powerful rhetorical strategy for thesis-based essays: the pattern of *problem/common answer for your imagined audience/surprising reversal*. This pattern creates tension between your own thesis and one or more alternative views.

The concept of *surprising reversal* spurs you to go beyond the commonplace to change your reader's view of a topic. As we discussed in Chapters 3 and 4, writers of thesis-based prose usually try to change a reader's view in one of three ways, corresponding to three of the broadly defined purposes of writing.

1. *Informative purpose: enlarging* readers' views of a topic by providing new information or otherwise teaching them something about the topic they didn't know ("People my parents' age commonly think that men with tattoos are sleezy, macho bikers or waterfront sailors, but I will show them that many younger people get tattoos for deeply personal and spiritual reasons.")

2. *Analytical or interpretive purpose: clarifying* readers' views of a topic by bringing critical thinking to bear on problematic data or on a problematic text ("Most people think that this jeans ad reveals a liberated woman, but on closer inspection we see that the woman fulfills traditional gender stereotypes.")

3. *Persuasive purpose: restructuring* readers' views of a topic by causing them to choose the writer's position rather than a competing position on a controversial issue ("Many readers believe that the federal government should legalize cocaine and heroin, but I will show that legalizing such drugs would be disastrous.")

The surprising-reversal pattern occurs whenever you contrast your reader's original view of a topic with your own new or surprising view. The pattern's power isn't that it tells you what to say about the topic or how to organize the main body of your essay. Its power is that it automatically gives your thesis tension. It pushes your view up against the commonplace or expected views that are likely to be shared by your audience. Although the assignment in this chapter is limited to the first of the above purposes listed (writing to inform), the surprising-reversal pattern also works well for the purposes of analysis or persuasion. You may find yourself using variations of this pattern for the remaining essay assignments in Part Two.

EXPLORING INFORMATIVE (AND SURPRISING) WRITING

Your goal for this activity is to discover unique knowledge or experience that will give each member of your class an uncommon perspective on some topic for some audience. The key is to consider both a topic (something that you care about and that you have quite a bit of information about through personal experience or recent reading and research) and an audience (persons who have a mistaken or overly narrow view of your topic because they lack the information that you can provide).

For the first part of this task, work privately at your desk for five or ten minutes. Consider either of the following trigger questions:

> Based on my personal experience, reading, research, or observation, what information or knowledge do I have about X that is different from the common view of X held by my imagined audience?

or

> Although people within my imagined audience commonly regard X this way, my personal experience, observations, or research shows X to be this other way.

In response to these trigger questions, brainstorm as many possible topic/audience combinations as you can using freewriting, idea mapping, or simple list making. Here are some examples from recent students.

> Many of my friends think that having an alcoholic mother would be the worst thing that could happen to you, but my mother's disease forced our family closer together.
>
> A common misconception about Native Americans is that they lived in simple harmony with the earth, but my research reveals that they often "controlled" nature by setting fire to forests to make farming easier or to improve hunting.
>
> To the average person pawnshops are seen as sleazy, disreputable places, but my experience shows that pawn shops can be honest, wholesome businesses that perform a valuable social service.
>
> Most of my straight friends think of the film *Frankenstein* as a monster movie about science gone amuck, but to the gay community it holds a special and quite different meaning.
>
> Pit bulls have a bad reputation among those who don't know the breed, but I can show that pit bulls can make gentle and loving pets.

After everyone has brainstormed at several such statements, work in small groups or as a whole class to refine and share ideas. Most people discover many new ideas once they begin hearing what their classmates are saying. Keep helping classmates until everyone has at least one potential topic.

WRITING PROJECT

Write a short informative essay following the surprising-reversal pattern. Choose a topic about which you are reasonably informed, and imagine an audience of readers who hold a mistaken or overly narrow view of your topic. Your purpose is to give them a new, surprising view. Pose a question, provide your audience's commonly accepted answer to the question, and then give your own surprising answer, based on information derived from personal experience, observation, or research.

This assignment asks you to use your own personal experiences, observations, or research to enlarge your reader's view of a subject in a surprising way. The introduction of your essay should engage your reader's interest in a question and provide needed background or context. Do not put your thesis early in the introduction; instead, delay it until after you have explained your audience's common, expected answer to your opening question. This delay in presenting the thesis creates a slightly open-form feel that readers often find engaging.

You might wonder why we call this assignment "informative writing" rather than "persuasive writing," since we emphasize reversing a reader's view. The difference is in the kind of question posed and the reader's stance toward the writer. In persuasive writing the question being posed is controversial (Should drugs be legalized? Does rap music promote violence?), with strong, rational arguments on all sides. Often, disputes about values are as prevalent as disputes about facts. When writing persuasive prose, you imagine a resistant reader who may argue back.

With informative prose, the stakes are lower, and you can imagine a more trusting reader, willing to learn from your experiences or research. You are enlarging your reader's view of the topic by presenting unexpected or surprising information, but you aren't necessarily saying that your audience's view is wrong, nor are you initiating a debate. In the examples in the preceding exploratory activity, the student writers aren't arguing whether alcoholic mothers are good or bad, whether all pawnshops are honest, or whether everyone should get a pit bull. They are simply offering readers new, unexpected, and expanded views of their topics.

For this assignment, avoid disputed issues that engender debate (save these issues for the chapters on persuasion, Chapters 15–17), and focus on how you, through your personal experience or research, can enlarge your reader's view of a topic by providing unexpected or surprising information.

UNDERSTANDING INFORMATIVE (AND SURPRISING) WRITING

When we speak of informative writing aimed at surprise, we mean thesis-based prose that is consciously intended to surprise the reader with an unexpected view. Such an essay represents only one kind of informative writing. Other kinds include encyclopedia articles, technical manuals, budget reports, experimental observations, instruction sheets, and many kinds of college textbooks—all of which convey detailed information without being thesis based and without intending to surprise the reader with an unexpected view. Readers turn to these other forms of informative writing when they need straightforward, factual information. Often in your college and professional career, you will be called upon to write straightforward, informative prose without the surprising-reversal pattern.

The essay you will write for this assignment is thus more provocative, more like the kinds of self-contained essays published in magazines or journals, for which the audience isn't ready-made, as it is for a budget report or a case observation in nursing. Your essay will need to hook your readers and sustain their interest by showing them a surprising new way of seeing your subject.

Because of its power to hook and sustain readers, examples of surprising-reversal essays can be found in almost any publication—from scholarly journals to easy-reading magazines. Here, for example, are abstracts of several articles from the table of contents of the *Atlantic Monthly*.

"Reefer Madness" by Eric Schlosser

Marijuana has been pushed so far out of the public imagination by other drugs, and its use is so casually taken for granted in some quarters of society, that one might assume it had been effectively decriminalized. In truth, the government has never been tougher on marijuana offenders than it is today. In an era when violent criminals frequently walk free or receive modest jail terms, tens of thousands of people are serving long sentences for breaking marijuana laws.

"The Sex-Bias Myth in Medicine" by Andrew G. Kadar

A view has gained wide currency that men's health complaints are taken more seriously than those of women, and that medical research has benefited men more than it has women. "In fact," the author writes, "one sex does appear to be favored in the amount of attention devoted to its medical needs. . . . That sex is not men, however."

"'It's Not the Economy, Stupid'" by Charles R. Morris

The conventional assumption, on which national elections often turn, is that one of the President's jobs is to "manage" the American economy: to make detailed economic actions that have precise results. But the truth is, the author writes, that managing the economy in this sense is far beyond any President's power—and, indeed, beyond the power of economics.

"Midlife Myths" by Winifred Gallagher

The idea that middle age is a dismal stage of life—scarred by traumas of personal crisis and physical change—is both firmly entrenched and almost completely untrue. The image in many Americans' minds, the author writes, is derived "not from the ordinary experiences of most people but from the unusual experiences of a few."

Each of these articles asserts a surprising new position that counters a commonly held view.

Commonly Held Narrow or Inaccurate View	Surprising View
Because marijuana laws are no longer enforced, marijuana use has effectively become decriminalized	The government has never been tougher on marijuana offenders than it is today.
More research dollars are spent on men's diseases than on women's diseases.	The reverse is true: more money is spent on women's diseases.
One of the president's jobs is to manage the economy by taking detailed economic action.	The economy is too complicated to be controlled by presidential action.
Middle age is a dismal stage of life.	The widespread notion of midlife crises is a myth based on the unusual experiences of the few.

A similar pattern is often found in scholarly academic writing, which typically has the following underlying shape:

> Whereas scholar A says X, scholar B says Y, and scholar C says Z, my research reveals Q.

Because the purpose of academic research is to advance knowledge, an academic article almost always shows the writer's new view against a background of prevailing views (what previous scholars have said).

Readings

To help you understand the surprising-reversal pattern in more detail, let's look at some complete essays. We begin with an easy-reading piece from *America West Airlines Magazine*. The topic, tarantulas, is particularly relevant to travelers on America West Airlines, which has a hub in Arizona, where tarantulas are plentiful. Note that the writer's strategy is to sum up the common view of these creatures and then to counter it with his own thesis.

■ LEO W. BANKS ■
NOT GUILTY: Despite Its Fearsome Image, the Tarantula Is a Benign Beast

1   If an insect ever had an image problem, it is the tarantula. Big, dark and hairy, tarantulas cause even the bold among us to back up a little and shiver reflexively.

2   No doubt that's part of the reason why Hollywood has made the creepy crawlies a movie-industry tradition. In the not-so-subtle 1955 sci-fi film

Tarantula, for example, a scientist grows a 100-foot-tall version that chews up cars. The horror doesn't end until air force pilots hose the giant bug with napalm.

Science fiction isn't the only culprit. In *Dr. No,* the usually composed James Bond goes into a frenzy after being awakened by a tarantula crawling on his shoulder. Bond won the duel by frantically smashing the bug with a shoe.

These days Hollywood pays about $75 a day to rent a tarantula, a cheap price for such a grand and terrifying illusion. Illusion is the key word, for virtually everything the movies want the public to believe about tarantulas is false. The unexciting truth is that they are relatively benign insects. "The occurrence of humans being bitten by tarantulas is almost nonexistent," says Howard Lawler, curator of small animals at the Arizona-Sonora Desert Museum in Tucson, Arizona. "You have to practically hold one against your body or press it in your hand to make it bite you."

And when tarantulas do bite, the sensation is about as severe as an ant bite or bee sting. What's more, scientists say tarantula venom isn't especially potent and rarely is employed in defensive bites against humans. Instead, tarantulas save their venom, which is also a digestive enzyme, for use against natural prey. "Some people have a reaction to [the venom], but for others it's no problem," says Mike Carrington, a Tucson pet store owner. "I've been bitten several times and it doesn't bother me at all."

Found in much of the Southern and Western United States, tarantulas live in burrows—cylindrical foot-deep holes in the ground that usually are lined with silk. Life expectancy is 10 years for males and 25 years for females, who never venture farther than 6 feet from their burrows.

The spiders typically feed on crickets, grasshoppers and even small mice. Because of their bad eyesight, they rely on vibration-sensing organs in their feet to pick up the movements of passing prey. "In the darkness, if you drop a beetle from 6 feet above the head of a tarantula resting near its burrow, the tarantula will, in a millisecond, race out and grab it and return to the burrow," says Steve Prchal, president of Sonoran Arthropod Studies Inc., a non-profit organization in Tucson dedicated to public education about insects.

Predators, even large ones, often find tarantulas more than a match. If confronted by a curious fox, for example, a tarantula will scoop the hairs off its abdomen and toss them into the fox's eyes. The hairs, which are sharp and contain a venom, irritate and usually distract the animal long enough to allow the tarantula to escape.

Ironically, the male tarantula's worst enemy is probably the female. "If she is hungry enough, the female will sometimes try to eat the male during mating," Prchal says. As a defense, males have small hooks on their forelegs that can be used to grab the female's fangs to keep from being bitten.

10   Besides the bad rap they've received in Hollywood, these easygoing beasts also have been the villains of nursery rhymes—"Little Miss Muffet," for example—and folklore. One prominent superstition dates back to the Dark Ages in Europe, when people bitten by wolf spiders thought they had to dance hysterically and sweat out the creature's venom in order to survive. The ritual was called the Tarantula Dance.

11   But probably the biggest reason tarantulas are so feared is their appearance. Besides being ugly, they sport fangs that are sometimes a half-inch long and curled at the bottom. And, by spider standards, tarantulas are huge. "I have one male who, if you laid him flat, would reach 11 inches across," says Carrington, who keeps seven pet tarantulas. "Most people who come to the house don't mind my tarantulas, but my mother-in-law won't go anywhere near them."

12   Pet stores sell tarantulas, a practice discouraged by scientists, for between $7 and $35. But sales are irregular because the insects are commonly found in the wild, especially during the spring-summer mating season.

13   In fact, they're so plentiful that former Tucson bar owner Jack Sheaffer remembers some nights when he couldn't keep tarantulas from coming into his establishment. It made for some interesting encounters that speak not to the insect's Hollywood image, but to its true nature. "Tarantulas never hurt anything," Sheaffer says. "They just wanted to come in and say hello. Once I found one snoozing in a cash box. He was a friendly little critter."

Thinking Critically about "Not Guilty"

1. What audience does Banks imagine?
2. For this audience, what ideas does Banks present as the common view of tarantulas? Where and how does he present his thesis statement?
3. Banks's essay follows a formula frequently used in travel magazines: it gives travelers a new view of a local phenomenon. What popular misconceptions might there be about places, people, ways of life, or other phenomena in your own hometown or region? You might consider a similar topic for your own surprising-reversal essay. Working as a whole class or in small groups, brainstorm misconceptions that travelers or newcomers might have about phenomena in your area or about another area with which you are familiar.

     The next reading is by student writer Cheryl Carp, whose experience with volunteer outreach in a maximum security prison enabled her to reverse stereotyped ideas about prisoners. She wrote the following essay for her freshman English class.

■ CHERYL CARP (STUDENT) ■

BEHIND STONE WALLS

For about eight hours out of every month I am behind the stone walls of the Monroe State Penitentiary. No, that's not the sentencing procedure of some lenient judge; I am part of a group of inmates and outsiders who identify themselves as Concerned Lifers. Concerned Lifers is an organization operating both inside and outside of prison walls. Inside Monroe there are close to thirty men who take part in the organization and its activities, all of whom have been given life sentences. Concerned Lifers outside the prison visit the prisoners, take part in the organization's meetings, and then split into various small groups for personal conversation. I became involved in this exciting group as a personal sponsor (able to visit the prison alone for special activities) after attending my first meeting inside Monroe State Penitentiary. That first drive to Monroe seemed to take forever. Looking out the window of that twelve-seater van filled with apprehensive first-time volunteers, I kept my eyes on the evening sky and tried to imagine what it would be like to be shut up in prison for life, never to see this beautiful scenery again. I was not scared, but I was nervous and could feel my pulse rate steadily rise as I began to see the green and white road signs to the prison. As the van slowly climbed the hill to the guard tower at the top, I wondered what it would be like to visit this maximum security prison.

Many people believe that visiting a prison would be frightening. Most people typically picture dangerous men lurking in every corner. The guards are yelling and the men are fighting; the men are covered with tattoos, probably carrying concealed razor blades and scowling menacingly. People think that prisons are a haven for rampant homosexuality and illegal drugs. Common belief is that the inmates are like locked animals, reaching out between the iron bars of their cages. These men are seen as sex-starved, eagerly waiting for a female body to enter their domain. The atmosphere is one of suspense, with sub-human men ready at any moment to break free and run. People I've spoken to express a fear of danger to themselves and almost a threat to their lives. They wonder how I have the nerve to do it.

But visiting a prison to me is an uplifting experience, far from frightening. Since that initial visit, I have returned many times to organize and participate in a clown group. The clown group is made up of about twenty of the inmates in the Concerned Lifers group and myself. The prisoners meet and rehearse once a week, and I join them every other week to critique their progress, give them pointers, and do various exercises to improve their ability.

The only frightening part of a visit is getting through all the guards and their red tape. Last week I drove up the hill to the guard tower, identified myself and my affiliation, and was told to "park to the left" by a disembodied voice coming from a loudspeaker. After going through many metal security doors, being checked by a metal detector that even picks up the nails in your shoes, and being escorted by numerous guards, I finally got to be with the people I had come to see.

5   The most enjoyable, exciting, and friendly time I spend at the prison is the time I spend with the boys. These people are no longer "the prisoners" or "the inmates," but are now individuals. Visiting the prison is not a frightening experience because the men inside become people, people full of emotions, creativity, and kindness. These qualities are evident in the activities and projects these men become involved in or initiate themselves. For example, one young lifer named Ken became interested in Japanese paper folding—origami. In order to pursue his interest in origami, he requested a book on the subject from the prison librarian and proceeded to teach himself. A few weeks later, I saw origami creations everywhere—flowers, dragons, and birds—all made by the guys and all done carefully and beautifully. Ken had taught his fellow inmates. Another great thing that this group has undertaken is the sponsorship of four children through an orphan relief program. The men make almost nothing at their various jobs within the prison, but what they do make they are more than willing to share, something many of us never seem to "get around to."

6   It is true that the men value the presence of a female, but not for sexual reasons. The men inside Monroe are hungry for outside companionship and understanding. They're hungry for a woman's viewpoint and conversation. They have treated me as a friend, valued my conversation, and never made sexual advances. The men behind the walls are reaching through their bars not menacingly, but pleadingly—begging the outside world to take a good look at them. The men need to be looked at as people and as fellow humans in this world. Most of them are aching for a second chance at life and relationships. This is not a place for outsiders to fear, but a place to which outsiders can bring light, hope, and understanding.

7   My point is not to condone the crimes that these men may have committed in the past, but to look to the present and the future by seeing these men not as "inmates," but as individual people trying to succeed in the kind of life they now have to live.

Thinking Critically about "Behind Stone Walls"

1. What is the audience that Cheryl Carp imagines?
2. For this audience, what is the common view of prisoners that Cheryl Carp attempts to reverse?
3. What is her own surprising view?
4. What are the strengths and weaknesses of Cheryl's essay?

For Writing and Discussion

Perhaps reading the essays by Banks and Carp has stimulated you to think of possible essay topics that employ the surprising-reversal pattern. The goal of this exercise is to continue brainstorming possible topics.

Form small groups. Assign a group recorder to make a two-column list, with the left column titled "Mistaken or narrow view of X" and the right column titled "Groupmate's surprising view." Brainstorm ideas for surprising-reversal essay topics until every group member has generated at least one entry for the right-hand column. Avoid repeating the topics you developed in the opening exploratory activity (p. 198). Here is a sample list entry:

Mistaken or Narrow View of X	Groupmate's Surprising View
Football offensive lineman is a no-brain, repetitive job requiring size, strength, and only enough brains and athletic ability to push people out of the way.	Jeff can show that being an offensive lineman is an interesting job that requires mental smarts as well as size, strength, and athletic ability.

To help stimulate ideas, you might consider topic areas such as the following:

▪ *People:* computer programmers, homeless people, cheerleaders, skateboarders, gang members, priests or rabbis, feminists, house-spouses, mentally ill or developmentally disabled persons.

▪ *Activities:* washing dishes, climbing mountains, wrestling, modeling, gardening, living with a chronic disease or disability, owning a certain breed of dog, riding a subway at night, entering a dangerous part of a city.

▪ *Places:* particular neighborhoods, particular buildings or parts of buildings, local attractions, junkyards, places of entertainment, summer camps.

▪ *Other similar categories:* groups, animals and plants, and so forth; the list is endless.

Next, go around the room, sharing with the entire class the topics you have generated. Remember that you are not yet committed to writing about any of these topics.

Before we offer suggestions for composing your essay, let's look at one more example of a surprising-reversal essay. This one moves up the reading dial a bit from the easy-reading airline travel piece by Leo Banks to a more serious reading station. The article is by David Quammen, who regularly writes about nature for *Outside* magazine. As you will see shortly, this information is important to know because it gives you some clues about Quammen's intended audience. This article is also about Arizona spiders—written in Tucson, the same locale used by Banks—yet it couldn't be more different from Banks's article. Whereas Banks writes with a simple, informative purpose, Quammen combines his informative purpose with a more complex, exploratory one.

▪ DAVID QUAMMEN ▪

THE FACE OF A SPIDER:
Eyeball to Eyeball with the Good, the BAD, and the Ugly

1   One evening a few years ago I walked back into my office after dinner and found roughly a hundred black widow spiders frolicking on my desk. I am not speaking metaphorically and I am not making this up: a hundred black widows. It was a vision of ghastly, breathtaking beauty, and it brought on me a wave of nausea. It also brought on a small moral crisis—one that I dealt with briskly, maybe rashly, in the dizziness of the moment, and that I've been turning back over in my mind ever since. I won't say I'm *haunted* by those hundred black widows, but I do remember them vividly. To me, they stand for something. They stand, in their small synecdochical way, for a large and important question.

2   The question is, How should a human behave toward the members of other living species?

3   A hundred black widows probably sounds like a lot. It is—even for Tucson, Arizona, where I was living then, a habitat in which black widows breed like rabbits and prosper like cockroaches, the females of the species growing plump as huckleberries and stringing their ragged webs in every free corner of every old shed and basement window. In Tucson, during the height of the season, a person can always on short notice round up eight or ten big, robust black widows, if that's what a person wants to do. But a hundred in one room? So all right, yes, there was a catch: These in my office were newborn babies.

4   A hundred scuttering bambinos, each one no bigger than a poppyseed. Too small still for red hourglasses, too small even for red egg timers. They had the aesthetic virtue of being so tiny that even a person of good eyesight and patient disposition could not make out their hideous little faces.

5   Their mother had sneaked in when the rains began and set up a web in the corner beside my desk. I knew she was there—I got a reminder every time I dropped a pencil and went groping for it, jerking my hand back at the first touch of that distinctive, dry, high-strength web. But I hadn't made the necessary decision about dealing with her. I knew she would have to be either murdered or else captured adroitly in a pickle jar for relocation to the wild, and I didn't especially want to do either. (I had already squashed scores of black widows during those Tucson years but by this time, I guess, I was going soft.) In the meantime, she had gotten pregnant. She had laid her eggs into a silken egg sac the size of a Milk Dud and then protected that sac vigilantly, keeping it warm, fending off any threats, as black widow mothers do. While she was waiting for the eggs to come to term, she would have been particularly edgy, particularly unforgiving, and my hand would have been in particular danger each time I reached for a fallen pencil. Then the

great day arrived. The spiderlings hatched from their individual eggs, chewed their way out of the sac, and started crawling, brothers and sisters together, up toward the orange tensor lamp that was giving off heat and light on the desk of the nitwit who was their landlord.

By the time I stumbled in, fifty or sixty of them had reached the lamp- 6 shade and rappelled back down on dainty silk lines, leaving a net of gossamer rigging between the lamp and the Darwin book (it happened to be an old edition of *Insectivorous Plants,* with marbled endpapers) that sat on the desk. Some dozen others had already managed dispersal flights, letting out strands of buoyant silk and ballooning away on rising air, as spiderlings do— in this case dispersing as far as the bookshelves. It was too late for one man to face one spider with just a pickle jar and an index card and his two shaky hands. By now I was proprietor of a highly successful black widow hatchery.

And the question was, How should a human behave toward the members 7 of other living species?

The Jain religion of India has a strong teaching on that question. The 8 Sanskrit word is *ahimsa,* generally rendered in English as "noninjury" or the imperative "do no harm." *Ahimsa* is the ethical centerpiece of Jainism, an absolute stricture against the killing of living beings—*any* living beings—and it led the traditional Jains to some extreme forms of observance. A rigorously devout Jain would burn no candles or lights, for instance, if there was danger a moth might fly into them. The Jain would light no fire for heating or cooking, again because it might cause the death of insects. He would cover his mouth and nose with a cloth mask, so as not to inhale any gnats. He would refrain from cutting his hair, on grounds that the lice hiding in there might be gruesomely injured by the scissors. He could not plow a field, for fear of mutilating worms. He could not work as a carpenter or a mason, with all that dangerous sawing and crunching, nor could he engage in most types of industrial production. Consequently the traditional Jains formed a distinct socioeconomic class, composed almost entirely of monks and merchants. Their ethical canon was not without what you and I might take to be glaring contradictions (vegetarianism was sanctioned, plants as usual getting dismissive treatment in the matter of rights of life), but at least they took it seriously. They lived by it. They tried their best to do no harm.

And this in a country, remember, where 10,000 humans died every year 9 from snakebite, almost a million more from malaria carried in the bites of mosquitoes. The black widow spider, compared to those fellow creatures, seems a harmless and innocent beast.

But personally I hold no brief for *ahimsa,* because I don't delude myself 10 that it's even theoretically (let alone practically) possible. The basic processes of animal life, human or otherwise, do necessarily entail a fair bit of ruthless squashing and gobbling. Plants can sustain themselves on no more than sunlight and beauty and a hydroponic diet—but not we animals. I've only mentioned this Jainist ideal to suggest the range of possible viewpoints.

11   Modern philosophers of the "animal liberation" movement, most notably Peter Singer and Tom Regan, have proposed some other interesting answers to the same question. So have writers like Barry Lopez and Eugene Linden, and (by their example, as well as by their work) scientists like Jane Goodall and John Lilly and Dian Fossey. Most of the attention of each of these thinkers, though, has been devoted to what is popularly (but not necessarily by the thinkers themselves) considered the "upper" end of the "ladder" of life. To my mind, the question of appropriate relations is more tricky and intriguing—also more crucial in the long run, since this group accounts for most of the planet's species—as applied to the "lower" end, down there among the mosquitoes and worms and black widow spiders.

12   These are the extreme test cases. These are the alien species who experience human malice, or indifference, or tolerance, at its most automatic and elemental. To squash or not to squash? Mohandas Gandhi, whose own ethic of nonviolence owed much to *ahimsa,* was once asked about the propriety of an antimalaria campaign that involved killing mosquitoes with DDT, and he was careful to give no simple, presumptuous answer. These are the creatures whose treatment, by each of us, illuminates not just the strength of emotional affinity but the strength, if any, of principle.

13   But what is the principle? Pure *ahimsa,* as even Gandhi admitted, is unworkable. Vegetarianism is invidious. Anthropocentrism, conscious or otherwise, is smug and ruinously myopic. What else? Well, I have my own little notion of one measure that might usefully be applied in our relations with other species, and I offer it here seriously despite the fact that it will probably sound godawful stupid.

14   Eye contact.

15   Make eye contact with the beast, the Other, before you decide upon action. No kidding, now, I mean get down on your hands and knees right there in the vegetable garden, and look that snail in the face. Lock eyes with that bull snake. Trade stares with the carp. Gaze for a moment into the many-faceted eyes—the windows to its soul—of the house fly, as it licks its way innocently across your kitchen counter. Look for signs of embarrassment or rancor or guilt. Repeat the following formula silently, like a mantra: "This is some mother's darling, this is some mother's child." *Then* kill if you will, or if it seems you must.

16   I've been experimenting with the eye-contact approach for some time myself. I don't claim that it has made me gentle or holy or put me in tune with the cosmic hum, but definitely it has been interesting. The hardest cases—and therefore I think the most telling—are the spiders.

17   The face of a spider is unlike anything else a human will ever see. The word "ugly" doesn't even begin to serve. "Grotesque" and "menacing" are too mild. The only adequate way of communicating the effect of a spiderly countenance is to warn that it is "very different," and then offer a photograph. This trick should not be pulled on loved ones just before bedtime or when trying to persuade them to accompany you to the Amazon.

The special repugnant power of the spider physiognomy derives, I think, 18 from fangs and eyes. The former are too big and the latter are too many. But the fangs (actually the fangs are only terminal barbs on the *chelicerae,* as the real jaw limbs are called) need to be large, because all spiders are predators yet they have no pincers like a lobster or a scorpion, no talons like an eagle, no social behavior like a pack of wolves. Large clasping fangs armed with poison glands are just their required equipment for earning a living. And what about those eight eyes—big ones and little ones, arranged in two rows, all bugged-out and pointing every-whichway? (My wife the biologist offers a theory here: "They have an eye for each leg, like us—so they don't *step* in anything.") Well, a predator does need good eyesight, binocular focus, peripheral vision. Sensory perception is crucial to any animal that lives by the hunt and, unlike insects, arachnids possess no antennae. Beyond that, I don't know. I don't *know* why a spider has eight eyes.

I only know that, when I make eye contact with one, I feel a deep physi- 19 cal shudder of revulsion, and of fear, and of fascination; and I am reminded that the human style of face is only one accidental pattern among many, some of the others being quite drastically different. I remember that we aren't alone. I remember that we are the norm of goodness and comeliness only to ourselves. I wonder about how ugly I look to the spider.

The hundred baby black widows on my desk were too tiny for eye con- 20 tact. They were too numerous, it seemed, to be gathered one by one into a pickle jar and carried to freedom in the backyard. I killed them all with a can of Raid. I confess to that slaughter with more resignation than shame, the jostling struggle for life and space being what it is. I can't swear I would do differently today. But there is this lingering suspicion that I squandered an opportunity for some sort of moral growth.

I still keep their dead and dried mother, and their vacated egg sac, in a 21 plastic vial on an office shelf. It is supposed to remind me of something or other.

And the question continues to puzzle me: How should a human behave 22 toward the members of other living species?

Last week I tried to make eye contact with a tarantula. This was a huge 23 specimen, all hairy and handsomely colored, with a body as big as a hamster and legs the size of Bic pens. I ogled it through a sheet of plate glass. I smiled and winked. But the animal hid its face in distrust.

Thinking Critically about "The Face of a Spider"

This article is meaty enough to justify a closer look. Before we comment on it, take a few moments to explore your own reactions to the following questions:

1. This article is closer to the open end of our closed-to-open continuum than are the other readings in this chapter. Quammen poses two interconnected questions: (1) the narrow question, What should I do about this desk covered

with baby black widow spiders? and (2) the broad, philosophical question, "How should a human behave toward the members of other species?" He delays his answers until the end. His surprising answer to the first question is easy to understand: "I killed them all with a can of Raid." His answer to the second question is philosophically complex: "Make eye contact with the beast, the Other, before you decide upon action." Why does he ask two questions and give two answers? What is the effect of delaying his answers until the end of the article? How does the absence of a thesis up front affect your experience in reading the article?

2. We sometimes use Quammen's dilemma in our classes without having students read the article. We ask students what they would do if they found hundreds of baby black widow spiders crawling across their desks. The most common answer we get, by margins of ten to one, is, "Spray those suckers with a can of Raid." In other words, the surprising answer in Quammen's article is really the expected, common answer in our classes. So, to whom is Quammen writing?

3. Quammen's audience is apparently familiar with words such as *synecdochical* (we hope you looked it up), and they apparently know the people mentioned in paragraph 11 (animal liberationists Peter Singer and Tom Regan; nature writers Barry Lopez and Eugene Linden; and scientists Jane Goodall, John Lilly, and Dian Fossey). Quammen assumes that his readers are so familiar with these people's viewpoints that he needs only a single sentence to refresh their memories:

   Most of the attention of each of these thinkers . . . has been devoted to what is popularly (but not necessarily by the thinkers themselves) considered the 'upper' end of the 'ladder' of life.

   Are you familiar with any of these thinkers? If not, then what do you surmise their views are, based on the context of Quammen's piece?

4. What do you think Quammen is getting at when he uses the term *eye contact*? How is this a surprising reversal of what the audience expects? How does it lead to his decision to poison the spiders? How does it lead to his uncertainty as to whether Raid was the right answer?

Quammen's essay can teach us a lot about how writers work. By delaying his thesis, Quammen keeps us in suspense about how he is going to solve his problem and invites us to participate with him in thinking through it. The mood he creates—one of inquiring openness rather than confident certainty—is an effect of shifting from closed-form writing to more open-form writing.

In shaping his essay, Quammen sets up two interrelated problems: the immediate problem of what to do about the spiders, and the broad philosophical problem of how humans should behave toward other living species.

To appreciate this essay's surprising reversal, you have to appreciate Quammen's audience—well-educated, typically liberal environmentalists interested in such issues as the rift between humans and the earth's other living creatures. This audience is likely to be sympathetic toward Peter Singer's arguments against eating animals and to be familiar with Barry Lopez's essays on wolves, Jane Goodall's work with chimpanzees, and Dian Fossey's passionate defense of mountain gorillas against bounty hunters *(Gorillas in the Mist)*. Quammen's intention is to push such readers toward a dilemma. "I know," his prose implies, "that you ecologically minded readers won't bring harm to wolves, or salmon, or spotted owls, or mountain gorillas, but what about a deskful of black widow spiders?" To such an audience, a can of Raid has the same symbolic resonance as a chainsaw. Both symbolize Western man's (we use the patriarchal term intentionally) passion for control over nature. The essay thus raises profound questions about the boundaries of our concern for nonhumans. It surprises us—even haunts us—in any number of ways.

COMPOSING YOUR ESSAY

This assignment asks for an informative essay that surprises the reader with new information. Your new information can come either from your own personal experience (as Cheryl Carp uses her personal experience to reverse the common view of prison inmates) or from research (as Leo Banks uses both library and interview research to reverse the common view of tarantulas).

As you write your essay, keep in mind that *surprise* is a relative term based on the relationship between you and your intended audience. You don't have to surprise everyone in the world, just those who hold a mistaken or narrow view of your topic. Cheryl Carp writes to those classmates who have never been inside a prison; Leo Banks writes to airline travelers who have only a Hollywood understanding of tarantulas; and David Quammen writes to similar folks who have a philosophical bent toward animal liberation.

Additionally, your surprising view doesn't necessarily have to be diametrically opposed to the common view. Perhaps you think the common view is *incomplete* or *insufficient* rather than *dead wrong*. Instead of saying, "View X is wrong, whereas my view, Y, is correct," you can say, "View X is correct and good as far as it goes, but my view, Y, adds a new perspective." In other words, you can also create surprise by going a step beyond the common view to show readers something new.

Generating and Exploring Ideas

When you write something outside a school setting, you are usually prompted to do so in one of two ways: Sometimes you are prompted by a particular rhetorical occasion that dictates your subject matter and purpose—a notice from a collection agency prompting you to protest a bill; your boss needing a proposal for the next sales meeting; your grandmother complaining to your parents that you never write to her. On other occasions, you are motivated to write for your own internal reasons, creating your own context and selecting your own subject matter and purpose—you write in a daily journal to express your ideas and feelings; you write a poem or short story to satisfy a creative urge; you write to your representative in Congress to support or oppose impending legislation; or you write a freelance article on safety tips for hitchhikers to see whether you can be published in a magazine.

This present assignment, although it gives you an in-school mandate to write something, is designed to simulate the second kind of prompting. We'd like you to experience what it's like to write when you have an almost unlimited choice of subject matter and potential audiences. Part of the point of this assignment is to help you see how experienced writers finally settle on a particular topic under those circumstances. This assignment encourages you to determine how your unique experiences, observations, or research gives you an angle on a topic that differs from the common view held by some audiences.

The For Writing and Discussion exercise in this chapter has been designed to help you brainstorm and select a topic for this assignment. Look back over the exercise, and see whether it helps you choose a topic. If not, here is another exercise that might help you get started:

Exploration Task

With its emphasis on enlarging your audience's view through something unexpected or surprising, this assignment teaches you to imagine an audience when considering a topic. The key for this task is to imagine an audience less informed about your topic than you are. Suppose, as an illustration, that you have just completed an introductory economics course. You are less informed about economics than your professor, but more informed about economics than persons who have never had an econ class. You might therefore write a surprising reversal paper to the less informed audience:

> The average airplane traveler thinks that the widely varying ticket pricing for the same flight is chaotic and silly, but I can show how this pricing scheme makes perfect sense economically. [written to the "average airplane traveler," who hasn't taken an economics course]

This paper would be surprising to your intended audience, but not to the economics professor. From a different perspective, however, you could also write about economics to your professor because you might know more than your professor, say, about how students struggle with some concepts:

> Many economics professors assume that students can easily learn the concept of "elasticity of demand," but I can show why this concept was particularly confusing for me and my classmates. [written to economics professors who aren't aware of student difficulties with particular concepts]

The preceding examples prepare you for the following exercise. Think specifically about differences in knowledge levels between you and various audiences. Try this template:

> I know more about X than [specific person or persons].

Try the exercise first by naming topics that interest you and then thinking of less informed audiences:

I know more about cars/computer games/rats than [specific persons].

Then try the exercise by naming specific audiences and then thinking of topics about which you know more than they:

I know more about X than [my mother/the college registrar/students who don't commute/my boss at work]

Doing this exercise may help you discover an excellent topic for your essay.

Shaping and Drafting

The surprising-reversal pattern requires two main writing moves: an exposition of the common or expected answers to a question, and the development of your own surprising answer to that question. In addition, your essay needs an introduction that presents the question to be addressed and a separate conclusion that finishes it off.

Both Cheryl Carp and David Quammen use distinct introductory sections to provide a context and present the essay's focusing question. Carp's lead provokes curiosity ("For about eight hours out of every month I am behind the stone walls of the Monroe State Penitentiary"), provides explanatory background on Concerned Lifers, and then poses the question that gave rise to her essay—one that she imagines her readers are asking:

As the van slowly climbed the hill to the guard tower at the top, I wondered what it would be like to visit this maximum security prison.

Quammen opens his essay with a stunning lead ("One evening a few years ago I walked back into my office after dinner and found roughly a hundred black widow spiders frolicking on my desk"). He then explains how this event created "a small moral crisis" and presents, in its own separate paragraph, the essay's focusing question:

The question is, How should a human behave toward the members of other living species?

In contrast, Leo Banks uses the common view of tarantulas as his lead, fusing his introduction with his exposition of the common view. Rather than stating the essay's question explicitly ("What is the true nature of the tarantula?"), he simply implies it when he presents his thesis:

Illusion is the key word, for virtually everything the movies want the public to believe about tarantulas is false.

Both methods are effective.

As you go through these moves in your essay, your principal challenge is to maintain your reader's interest. You can do this by developing general statements with colorful, specific details. Cheryl Carp uses details from personal experience ("green-and-white road signs," "a disembodied voice coming from a loudspeaker," "origami creations"); Leo Banks uses research data about tarantulas (details about tarantula venom and so forth) as well as quotations from spider experts and local Arizonans; Quammen's essay is distinguished by its precise narrative and its descriptive sensory details (the explanation of how the baby spiders happened to be crawling on his desk and the description of the face of a spider, for example).

All three essays make extensive use of supporting examples. Banks uses a James Bond movie and a 1955 sci-fi film to support his point about the common Hollywood view of tarantulas; Carp uses the story of Ken's teaching his fellow inmates how to make origami flowers and dragons to illustrate her point about the inmates' humanity and creativity; Quammen provides a series of examples to make the point that devout Jains will not harm any animal (for example, they will not cut hair for fear of harming lice). Your essay will need these kinds of supporting examples and details.

As a way of helping you generate ideas and overcome writer's block, we offer the following five questions. Questions 1, 2, and 4 are planning questions that will help you create broad point sentences to form your essay's skeletal framework. These questions call for one-sentence generalizations. Questions 3 and 5 are freewriting prompts to help you generate supporting details. For these questions, freewrite rapidly, either on paper or at your computer. Following each question, we speculate about what Carp, Banks, and Quammen might have written if they had used the same questions to help them get started on their essays.

1. *What question does your essay address?* (Carp might have asked, "What is it like to visit inmates in a maximum security prison?" Banks might have asked, "Do tarantulas deserve their scary reputation?" Quammen might have asked, "How should I treat a deskful of baby black widow spiders? And how should humans behave toward other creatures?")

2. *What is the common, expected, or popular answer to this question held by your imagined audience?* (Carp might have said, "Visiting these prisoners will be scary because prisoners are sex-starved, dangerous people." Banks might have said, "Tarantulas are poisonous, nightmarish creatures." Quammen might have said, "My audience expects me to offer an ecologically sound solution to the spider problem that reflects my respect and concern for all of earth's creatures.")

3. *What examples and details support your audience's view?* Expand on these views by developing them with supporting examples and details. (Carp might have brainstormed details about concealed razor blades, drugs, prison violence, the fear of her friends, and so on. Banks's freewrites might have focused on the sci-fi and James Bond films and other misconceptions about tarantulas. Quammen's freewriting might have centered on the Jain religion and other respect-all-the-earth's-creatures movements.)

4. *What is your own surprising view?* (Carp might have answered, "Visiting the prison is uplifting because prisoners can be kind, creative, and generous." Banks might have answered, "Tarantulas are peaceful creatures with a largely painless bite and harmless venom." Quammen might have answered, "My look-them-in-the-eye theory allowed me to spray these spiders with Raid.")

5. *What examples and details support this view? Why do you hold this view? Why should a reader believe you?* Writing rapidly, spell out the evidence that supports your point. (Carp would have done a freewrite on all the experiences she had that changed her views about prisoners. Later she would have selected the most powerful ones and refined them for her readers. Banks would have spelled out all his evidence that tarantulas don't deserve their bad reputation. Quammen would have explored his theory about looking creatures in the eye, experimentally applying it to black widows.)

After you finish exploring your response to these five trigger questions, you will be well on your way to composing a first draft of your essay. Now finish writing your draft fairly rapidly without worrying about perfection.

Revising

Once you have your first draft on paper, the goal is to make it work better, first for yourself and then for your readers. If you discovered ideas as you wrote, you may need to do some major restructuring. Check to see that the question you are addressing is clear. Do you state it directly, as do Carp and Quammen, or simply imply it, as does Banks? Make sure that you distinguish between your audience's view and your own surprising view. Do you put your meanings up front, using point sentences at the head of each section and near the beginning of every paragraph? Carp's and Banks's essays are closed-form pieces with no narrative suspense about the writer's thesis or the essay's structure; Quammen purposely violates some of the rules for closed-form writing to create suspense. Which strategy are you using? Check to see that you have colorful details and plenty of examples and illustrations.

We conclude this chapter with peer review guidelines that sum up the features to look for in your essay and remind you of the criteria your instructor will use in evaluating your work.

■ GUIDELINES FOR PEER REVIEWS ■

Instructions for peer reviews are provided in Chapter 18 (pp. 490–496).

For the Writer
Prepare two or three questions you would like your peer reviewer to address while responding to your draft. The questions can focus on some aspect of your draft that you are uncertain about, on one or more sections where you particularly seek help or advice, on some feature that you particularly like about your draft, or on some part you especially wrestled with. Write out your questions and give them to your peer reviewer along with your draft.

For the Reviewer

I. Read the draft at a normal reading speed from beginning to end. As you read, do the following:

A. Place a wavy line in the margin next to any passages that you find confusing, that contain something that doesn't seem to fit, or that otherwise slow down your reading.

B. Place a "Good!" in the margin next to any passages where you think the writing is particularly strong or interesting.

II. Read the draft again slowly and answer the following questions by writing down brief explanations for your answers.

A. Introduction:

1. How does the title hook your interest in the essay and focus the subject? How might the title be improved?

2. How does the introduction capture your interest and set up the question to be addressed? How might the writer enliven or clarify the opening?

3. What details does the writer use to develop the audience's common view of the topic? What additional supporting examples, illustrations, or details might make the common view more vivid or compelling? Is this *your* view of the topic?

B. Thesis:

1. Identify the writer's thesis statement. Where does the writer locate the thesis? Would it be more effective located elsewhere?

2. Do you find the writer's thesis surprising? Why or why not?

C. Surprising view:

1. What details does the writer use to develop his or her surprising view? What additional supporting examples, illustrations, or details might help make the surprising view more vivid and compelling?

2. How might the writer improve the clarity or structure of the draft?

D. If the writer has prepared questions for you, respond to his or her inquiries.

E. Sum up what you see as the chief strengths and problem areas of this draft:

1. Strengths

2. Problem areas

III. Read the draft one more time. Place a check mark in the margin wherever you notice problems in grammar, spelling, or mechanics (one check mark per problem).

CHAPTER 10

Analyzing Images

ABOUT ANALYZING IMAGES

This chapter asks you to analyze images in order to understand their persuasive power—a skill often called "visual literacy." By *visual literacy,* we mean your awareness of the importance of visual communication and your ability to interpret or make meaning out of images and graphics (photos, pictures, illustrations, icons, charts, graphs, and other visual displays of data). In this chapter, we seek to enhance your visual literacy by focusing on the way that images influence our conceptual and emotional understanding of a phenomenon and the way that they validate, reveal, and construct the world.

See pp. 62–65 for an explanation of the aims of writing.

This chapter is the first of five assignment chapters on writing to analyze and synthesize. As you may recall from Chapter 4, when you write to analyze and synthesize, you apply your own critical thinking to a puzzling object or to puzzling data and offer your own new ideas to a conversation. Your goal is to raise interesting questions about the object or data being analyzed—questions that perhaps your reader hasn't thought to ask—and then to provide tentative answers to those questions, supported by points and particulars derived from your own close examination of the object or data. The word *analysis* derives from a Greek word meaning "to dissolve, loosen, undo." Metaphorically, analysis means to divide or dissolve the whole into its constituent parts, to examine these parts carefully, to look at the relationships among them, and then to use this understanding of the parts to better understand the whole—how it functions, what it means. Synonyms for writing to analyze might be writing to interpret, clarify, or explain. In this chapter, the objects being analyzed are photographs or other images as they appear in a rhetorical context—for example, as part of a news story, a television documentary, a public relations brochure, or an advertisement.

To appreciate the cultural importance of images, consider how British cultural critic John Berger, in his book *About Looking,* sketches the pervasive use of photographs shortly after the invention of the camera.

> The camera was invented by Fox Talbot in 1839. Within a mere 30 years of its invention as a gadget for an elite, photography was being used for police filing, war reporting, military reconnaissance, pornography, encyclopedic documentation, family albums, postcards, anthropological records (often, as with the Indians in the United States, accompanied by genocide), sentimental moralizing, inquisitive probing (the wrongly named "candid camera"), aesthetic effects, news reporting and for-

mal portraiture. The speed with which the possible uses of photography were seized upon is surely an indication of photography's profound, central applicability to industrial capitalism.

One of photography's purposes—as Berger hints—is to create images that "have designs on" us, that urge us to believe ideas, buy things, go places, or otherwise alter our views or behaviors. Information brochures use carefully selected photographs to enhance a product's image (consider how the photographs in your college's catalog or guidebook have been selected); news photographs editorialize their content (during the Vietnam War a newspaper photograph of a naked Vietnamese child running screaming toward the photographer while a napalm bomb explodes behind her turned many Americans against the war); social issue posters urge us to protest capital punishment or contribute money to save the salmon or sponsor a child in a third-world country; and advertisements urge us not only to buy a certain product but to be a certain kind of person with certain values.

Visual literacy is so important in our current world that we have already introduced it elsewhere in this text. In Chapter 3 we reproduced a photograph and a drawing that harmed Al Gore's presidential campaign in 2000 (pp. 56–57). In Chapter 5 we reproduced several photographs of the Arctic National Wildlife Refuge (ANWR) that were used to advance arguments for or against opening the ANWR to oil exploration (pp. 89–90). And for the Part Openers in this text, we have selected classic examples of the way images have been used with words for rhetorical effect. At appropriate moments in this chapter, we refer again to some of these images.

For the images in this chapter, we have selected those directly related to Berger's assertion that photographs often have a "profound, central applicability to industrial capitalism." We look specifically at how photographs and other images are used in "corporate image" advertisements and in product advertisements. We focus on advertisements because they are a wonderful source of images for analysis and because they raise important questions about how our own lives intersect with the processes of a free market economy. In addition to enhancing your visual literacy, studying advertising has other values as well. We suggest four benefits you will gain from your study of advertisements:

- You will appreciate more fully the fun, pleasure, and creativity of advertisements.
- You will become a more savvy consumer, better able to critique ads and make wise buying decisions.
- You will learn rhetorical strategies that you can use in your own career and civic life. (Your understanding of the relationship between words and images in advertising can be readily transferred to other rhetorical settings—for example, when you design a brochure or Web site or write any kind of document that incorporates images and depends on document design.)
- You will become a more perceptive cultural critic who understands how ads both convey and help construct our cultural values, our self-image, our sense of what is normal or ideal, and our ideas about gender, race, and class.

A study of advertisements can raise viewers' consciousness to counter prejudice, injustice, and discrimination.

EXPLORING IMAGE ANALYSIS

In this opening exercise we invite you to imagine that you are a member of an advertising design team hired by a major oil company to improve its corporate image. Here is some needed background.

Following the March 1989 Exxon Valdez oil spill, when an Exxon tanker dumped thousands of barrels of oil in Prince William Sound, Alaska, oil companies tried to refurbish their public image by portraying themselves as friends of the environment. The Valdez oil spill was a public relations disaster for oil companies. The most pervasive news media images from the Valdez spill were photographs of volunteers trying to remove oil from the feathers of dying coastal birds or photographs of oil-coated, dead wildlife. Figure 10.1 shows a typical media photograph of a bird killed by the oil.

During and after the cleanup period, one response of oil companies was to embark on advertising campaigns aimed at portraying oil companies as environmentally concerned corporate neighbors. These ads typically appeared (and still do) in upscale moderate-to-liberal intellectual magazines such as *Atlantic Monthly* and *Harpers* but not in *Sports Illustrated*, *Glamour*, or *Rolling Stone*. (Shortly we'll ask you to consider why oil companies choose these magazines.) *Atlantic Monthly*, one of the most typical outlets for corporate image advertisements from oil companies, features sophisticated articles on public affairs and cultural issues. Ads in the magazine are typically for upscale cars, cognacs and liqueurs, vacation resorts with spas and golf courses, mutual fund companies, and other high status items. In terms of the VALS categories discussed later in this chapter, these readers are generally "emulators" or "achievers."

See pp. 228–229 for a discussion of the VALS marketing research tool.

FIGURE 10.1 ■ Sea Bird Killed by Oil Spill

A typical ad may feature an oil company's charitable gift to organizations concerned with environmental preservation. It typically contains images of wildlife in a pristine natural setting, photographed in such a way as to create appropriately warm associations in the minds of viewers. (We were unable to obtain permission to reproduce an oil company's corporate image ad in this textbook. The company did not want its name associated with the name "Valdez," nor did it want to have its ad critiqued in an academic classroom.) The following exercise is based on an actual ad from a prominent oil company; it appeared in *Atlantic Monthly* in the mid-1990s. The company, in partnership with the U.S. Fish and Wildlife Service, with wildlife agencies in several Midwestern states, and with a duck hunting organization called "Ducks Unlimited, Inc.," contributed funding to a wetlands preservation project in the Midwest aimed at improving the breeding and migrating habitat for ducks and other birds.

Given this background, you are now ready for the role-playing exercise. Working in small groups or as a whole class, respond to the following questions.

1. Why did this particular company decide to contribute its charity dollars to an environmental project rather than, say, medical research or care of the homeless? Why birds? Particularly, why waterfowl and especially ducks?

2. Throughout the ad copy, the word "oil" never appears. Rather, the ad refers to the company as an "energy company," not an "oil company." Why does the adwriter use the term "energy company"? Why do your textbook authors use the term "oil company"?

3. The company bought ad space in *Atlantic Monthly* and other upscale, liberal-oriented magazines.

   a. Why did the company place these ads in a magazine such as *Atlantic Monthly* rather than in a wider circulation magazine such as *People*?

   b. Why did the company select primarily moderate-to-liberal magazines rather than conservative magazines?

4. The central image in the advertisement is a duck picture. The advertising agency chose the picture from a catalog of "stock photos" of ducks. We have reproduced in Figures 10.2, 10.3, 10.4, and 10.5 samples of typical stock photos of ducks. One of these four is the same photo chosen by the advertising agency for the oil company ad.

   a. As you examine the details of these photographs, what ideas about ducks, nature, and hunting do these images conjure up for you? How does each image create a different feeling?

   b. Which of the four duck images do you think most appealed to members of "Ducks Unlimited, Inc."—one of the sponsors of the wetlands preservation project?

   c. Which of these images do you think the agency chose for its *Atlantic Monthly* advertisement? Working in pairs or small groups, try duplicating the advertising team's conversation by making your own choice. Create the best arguments you can for your chosen photograph. (Later in this chapter we'll tell you which image the ad team chose.)

See Chapter 22, pp. 605–616, for further discussion of the images and layout of advocacy Web sites; see Chapter 17, pp. 448–450, for a discussion of public affairs advocacy advertisements.

FIGURE 10.2 ■ Duck Landing on Water

FIGURE 10.3 ■ Mother Duck Followed by Baby Ducks

FIGURE 10.4 ■ Duck Hunter at Sunrise

FIGURE 10.5 ■ Baby Ducks Followed by Mother Duck

WRITING PROJECT

Choose two print advertisements that sell the same kind of product but appeal to different audiences (for example, a car advertisement aimed at men and one aimed at women; a cigarette ad aimed at upper-middle-class consumers and one aimed at working-class consumers; a clothing ad from the *New Yorker* and one from *Rolling Stone*). Describe the ads in detail so that an audience can easily visualize them without actually seeing them. Analyze the advertisements and explain how each appeals to its target audience. To what values does each ad appeal? How is each ad constructed to appeal to those values? In addition to analyzing the rhetorical appeals made by each ad, you may also wish to evaluate or criticize the ads, commenting on the images of our culture they convey.

This writing assignment asks you to analyze how advertisers use words and images together to appeal to different audiences. By comparing ads for the same product targeted at different demographic groups, you learn how every aspect of an ad is chosen for an audience-specific rhetorical effect. You will discover, for example, that advertisers often vary their ads for female versus male audiences and that certain products or services are targeted at a specific socioeconomic class. Similarly, advertisers often vary their appeals to reach African-American, Hispanic, or Asian markets. This assignment asks you to explain how these appeals are targeted and created.

As a variation of this assignment, your instructor might ask you to analyze two photographs of a politician from magazines with different political biases; two news photographs from articles addressing the same story from different angles of vision; the images on the homepages of two Web sites presenting different perspectives on heated topics such as global warming, medical research using animals, and environmental protection; or two advocacy ads for corporations or political causes that represent opposing views. Although these images, articles, and Web sites are not selling you a product per se, they are "selling" you a viewpoint on an issue, and thus this chapter's explanations of how to analyze camera techniques and the use of details, props, and the posing of human figures in photographs can also be applied to visual images other than commercial advertisements.

UNDERSTANDING IMAGE ANALYSIS

Before we turn directly to advertising, let's look at some strategies you can use to analyze any image intended to have a specific rhetorical effect.

How Images Create a Rhetorical Effect

An image can be said to have a rhetorical effect whenever it moves us emotionally or intellectually. We might identify with the image or be repelled by it; the image might evoke our sympathies, trigger our fears, or call forth a web of interconnected ideas, memories, and associations. When the image is a photograph, its rhetorical effect derives from both the camera techniques that produced it and the composition of the image itself. Let's look at each in turn.

Analyzing Camera Techniques

The rhetorical effect of a photographic image often derives from skillful use of the camera and from the way the film is developed or the digital image is manipulated.* To analyze a photograph, begin by considering the photographer's choices about the camera's relationship to the subject:

▪ *Distance of camera from subject:* Note whether the photograph is a close-up, medium shot, or long shot. Close-ups tend to increase the intensity of the photograph and suggest the importance of the subject; long shots tend to blend the subject into the environment.

*Our ideas in this section are indebted to Paul Messaris, *Visual Persuasion: The Role of Images in Advertising* (Thousand Oaks, CA: Sage, 1997).

▨ *Orientation of the image and camera angle:* Note whether the camera is positioned in front of or behind the subject; note also whether the camera is positioned below the subject, looking up (a low-angle shot), or above the subject, looking down (a high-angle shot). Front view shots tend to emphasize the persons being photographed; rear view shots often emphasize the scene or setting. A low-angle camera tends to grant superiority, status, and power to the subject, while a high-angle camera can comically reduce the subject to childlike status. A level angle tends to imply equality.

▨ *Eye gaze:* Note which persons in the photograph, if any, gaze directly at the camera or look away. Looking directly at the camera implies power; looking away can imply deference or shyness.

▨ *Point of view:* Note whether the photographer strives for an "objective effect," in which the camera stands outside the scene and observes it, or a "subjective effect," in which the camera seems to be the eyes of someone inside the scene. Subjective shots tend to involve the viewer as an actor in the scene.

In addition, photographers often use other highly artistic film or digital techniques: making parts of an image crisp and in focus and others slightly blurred; using camera filters for special effects; distorting or merging images (a city that blends into a desert; a woman who blends into a tree); and creating visual parodies (a Greek statue wearing jeans).

There are also various ways that a photographic image can be manipulated or falsified. Be aware of the following devices used to create visual deception: staging images (scenes that appear to be documentaries but are really staged); altering images (for example, airbrushing, reshaping body parts, or constructing a composite image such as putting the head of one person on the body of another); selecting images or parts of images (such as cropping photographs so that only parts of the body are shown or only parts of a scene); and mislabeling (putting a caption on a photograph that misrepresents what it actually is).

For Writing and Discussion

Working as a whole class or in small groups, try to reach consensus answers to the following questions:

1. Look at the photograph of the ballot counter in Chapter 3 (Figure 3.3, p. 57). This photograph was widely published in national newspapers during the Florida ballot counting crisis that followed the November 2000 presidential election. Debate focused on how to count improperly punched ballots or ballots with hanging chads. What is the rhetorical effect of this photograph? How does the camera angle and point of view contribute to its rhetorical effect?

2. Earlier in this chapter (pp. 220–222), we asked you to select the photograph of ducks that you think the admakers chose for the oil company's corporate image ad. They selected Figure 10.5. Why do you think they chose an image of a mother duck with ducklings? Why do you think they selected Figure 10.5 rather than Figure 10.3? Why do you think they used a telephoto "close-up" image rather than a photograph showing more water and land-

scape? Also look at the buffalo image on the Yellowstone Flyer (Part Opener, p. 730). Why did the designer choose a drawing rather than a photograph? Why this style of drawing?

3. Look at three photographic images of bears: Figure 5.1 (Chapter 5, p. 88), Figure 5.3 (Chapter 5, p. 89), and the Nikon camera advertisement below. Analyze the camera techniques of each photograph, and explain how these techniques are rhetorically effective for the purpose of the message to which each is attached.

> *The camera for those who look at this picture and think, "Gosh, how'd they open up the shadows without blowing out the highlights?"*

When staring into the mouth of a 10 ft. grizzly bear, you tend to think about life. Limbs. And how handy legs are. Not the fill-flash ratio needed to expose teeth about to rip your leg off.

Nikon created the N90 specifically for complicated situations like this. When you have no time to think. A brown bear on brown earth, about to mangle a brown shoe. So instead of overexposing this picture like other cameras might, the N90™ works for you, properly analyzing the situation and delivering an accurate exposure.

Here's how it does it. The 3D Matrix Meter divides the scene into eight segments. It measures the brightness in each one of the segments and then compares them for contrast. D-type lenses incorporate the subject's distance which allows the N90 to calculate the proper ambient light exposure.

The SB-25 Speedlight fires a rapid series of imperceptible pre-flashes to determine the bear's reflectance. And then provides the precise amount of fill-flash needed to lighten the bear's dark brown fur, without overexposing his slightly yellow teeth.

The N90 can give you near-perfect exposures when other cameras would be fooled. Or, for that matter, eaten.

Professionals trust the N90. So you can too. Because it works just as well on children eating ice cream as it does on bears eating people.

The N90 System

Nikon.
We take the world's
greatest pictures.

See the Nikon N90 at authorized dealers where you see this symbol. Nikon Data Link System available Winter '93. For more on our MasterCard, call 1-800-NIKON-35.

FIGURE 10.6 ■ Nikon Ad

Analyzing the Compositional Features of the Image

In addition to analyzing camera and film or digital techniques, you need to analyze the compositional features of the photograph's subject. When photographs are used in ads, every detail down to the props in the photograph or the placement of a model's hands are consciously chosen.

1. *Examine the settings, furnishings, and props.*

   a. List all furnishings and props. If the photograph pictures a room, look carefully at such details as the kind and color of the rug; the subject matter of the paintings on the walls; furniture styles; objects on tables; and the general arrangement of the room. (Is it neat and tidy, or does it have a lived-in look? Is it formal or casual?) If the photograph is outdoors, observe the exact features of the landscape. (Why a mountain rather than a meadow? Why a robin rather than a crow or pigeon?)

   b. What social meanings are attached to the objects you listed? In a den, for example, duck decoys and fishing rods create a different emotional effect than computers and fax machines do. The choice of a breed of dog can signal differences in values, social class, or lifestyle—a Labrador retriever versus a groomed poodle; an English sheepdog versus a generic mutt. Even choice of flowers can have symbolic significance: A single rose connotes romance or elegance, a bouquet of daisies suggests freshness, and a hanging fuchsia suggests earthy naturalness.

2. *Consider the characters, roles, and actions.*

   a. Create the story behind the image. Who are these people in the photograph? Why are they here? What are they doing? In advertisements, models can be either *instrumental,* in which case they are acting out real-life roles, or *decorative,* in which case they are eye candy. A female model working on a car engine in grungy mechanics clothes would be instrumental; a female model in a bikini draped over the hood would be decorative.

   b. Note every detail about how models are posed, clothed, and accessorized. Note facial expressions, eye contact, gestures, activities, posed relationships among actors and among actors and objects, and relative sizes. (Who is looking at whom? Who is above or below whom? Who or what is in the foreground or background?) Pay special attention to hairstyles because popular culture endows hair with great significance.

   c. Ask what social roles are being played and what values appealed to. Are the gender roles traditional or nontraditional? Are the relationships romantic, erotic, friendly, formal, uncertain? What are the power relationships among characters?

3. *Analyze the rhetorical context of the image.*

   a. Images are always encountered in a rhetorical context: they accompany a news story, are part of a poster or Web site, or are used in an advertisement. Consider how the image functions within that context and how it contributes to the rhetorical effect of the whole to which it is a part.

b. In advertisements, consider carefully the relationship between the image and the words in the copy. The words in advertisements are chosen with the same care as the details in the image. Pay special attention to the document design of the copy, the style of the language, and the connotations, double entendres, and puns. Also note the kind of product information that is included or excluded from the ad.

See Chapter 4, pp. 74–79, for a discussion of document design.

How to Analyze an Advertisement

It is now time to move directly to advertising. In the previous section, we said that you should always analyze images within their specific rhetorical context. To analyze ads, you need to understand the context in which advertisers work—their specific goals and strategies.

Understanding an Advertiser's Goals and Strategies

Although some advertisements are primarily informational—explaining why the company believes its product is superior—most advertisements involve parity products such as soft drinks, deodorants, breakfast cereals, toothpaste, and jeans. (*Parity* products are products that are roughly equal in quality to their competitors and so can't be promoted through any rational or scientific proof of superiority.)

Advertisements for parity products usually use psychological and motivational strategies to associate a product with a target audience's (often subconscious) dreams, hopes, fears, desires, and wishes, suggesting that the product will magically dispel these fears and anxieties or magically deliver on values, desires, and dreams. Using sophisticated research techniques, advertisers study how people's fears, dreams, and values differ according to their ethnicity, gender, educational level, socioeconomic class, age, and so forth; this research allows advertisers to tailor their appeals precisely to the target audience.

Furthermore, advertisers often focus on long-range advertising campaigns rather than on just a single ad. Their goal is not simply to sell a product but to build brand loyalty or a relationship with consumers that will be long lasting. (Think of how the brand Marlboro has a different image from the brand Winston, or how Calvin Klein's "heroin chic" of the late 1990s differed from Tommy Hilfiger's "American freedom" image.) Advertisers try to convert a brand name from a label on a can or on the inside of a sweater to a field of qualities, values, and imagery that lives inside the heads of its targeted consumers. An ad campaign, therefore, uses subtle repetition of themes through a variety of individual ads aimed at building up a psychological link between the product and the consumer. Advertisers don't just want you to buy Nikes rather than Reeboks, but also to see yourself as a Nike kind of person who attributes part of your identity to Nikes. Some ad campaigns have been brilliant at turning whole segments of a population into loyal devotees of a brand. Among the most famous campaigns are the Volkswagen ads of the 1950s and early 1960s, the long-lived Marlboro cowboy ads, and the recent Pepsi blitz, culminating in a 2001 Britney Spears commercial featuring former presidential candidate (and Viagra spokesperson) Bob Dole saying, "Easy, boy" to his dog.

How Advertisers Target Specific Audiences

When advertisers produce an ad, they create images and copy intended to appeal to the values, hopes, and desires of a specific audience. How do they know the psychological attributes of a specific audience? Much of the market research on which advertisers rely is based on an influential demographic tool developed by SRI Research called the "VALS" (Values And Lifestyle System).* This system divides consumers into three basic categories with further subdivision:

1. ***Needs-driven consumers.*** Poor, with little disposable income, these consumers generally spend their money only on basic necessities.
   - ▓ *Survivors:* Live on fixed incomes or have no disposable income. Advertising seldom targets this group.
   - ▓ *Sustainers:* Have very little disposable income, but often spend what they have impulsively on low-end, mass-market items.

2. ***Outer-directed consumers.*** These consumers want to identify with certain in-groups, to "keep up with the Joneses," or to surpass them.
   - ▓ *Belongers:* Believe in traditional family values and are conforming, nonexperimental, nostalgic, and sentimental. They are typically blue collar or lower middle class, and they buy products associated with Mom, apple pie, and the American flag.
   - ▓ *Emulators:* Are ambitious and status conscious. They have a tremendous desire to associate with currently popular in-groups. They are typically young, have at least moderate disposable income, are urban and upwardly mobile, and buy conspicuous items that are considered "in."
   - ▓ *Achievers:* Have reached the top in a competitive environment. They buy to show off their status and wealth and to reward themselves for their hard climb up the ladder. They have high incomes and buy top-of-the-line luxury items that say "success." They regard themselves as leaders and persons of stature.

3. ***Inner-directed consumers.*** These consumers are individualistic and buy items to suit their own tastes rather than to symbolize their status.
   - ▓ *I-am-me types:* Are young, independent, and often from affluent backgrounds. They typically buy expensive items associated with their individual interests (such as mountain bikes, stereo equipment, or high-end camping gear), but may spend very little on clothes, cars, or furniture.
   - ▓ *Experiential types:* Are process-oriented and often reject the values of corporate America in favor of alternative lifestyles. They buy organic foods, make their own bread, do crafts and music, value holistic medicine, and send their children to alternative kindergartens.
   - ▓ *Socially conscious types:* Believe in simple living and are concerned about the environment and the poor. They emphasize the social responsibility of corporations, take on community service, and actively promote their

*Our discussion of VALS is adapted from Harold W. Berkman and Christopher Gibson, *Advertising,* 2nd ed. (New York: Random House, 1987), pp. 134–137.

favorite causes. They have middle to high incomes and are usually very well educated.

No one fits exactly into any one category, and most people exhibit traits of several categories, but advertisers are interested in statistical averages, not individuals. When a company markets an item, it enlists advertising specialists to help target the item to a particular market segment. Budweiser is aimed at belongers, while upscale microbeers are aimed at emulators or achievers. To understand more precisely the fears and values of a target group, researchers can analyze subgroups within each of these VALS segments by focusing specifically on women, men, children, teenagers, young adults, or retirees or on specified ethnic or regional minorities. Researchers also determine what kinds of families and relationships are valued in each of the VALS segments, who in a family initiates demand for a product, and who in a family makes the actual purchasing decisions. Thus, ads aimed at belongers depict traditional families; ads aimed at I-am-me types may depict more ambiguous sexual or family relationships. Advertisements aimed at women can be particularly complex because of women's conflicting social roles in our society. When advertisers target the broader category of gender, they sometimes sweep away VALS distinctions and try to evoke more deeply embedded emotional and psychological responses.

For Writing and Discussion

You own a successful futon factory that has marketed its product primarily to experiential types. Your advertisements have associated futons with holistic health, spiritualism (transcendental meditation, yoga), and organic wholesomeness (all-natural materials, gentle people working in the factory, incense and sitar music in your retail stores, and so forth). You have recently expanded your factory and now produce twice as many futons as you did six months ago. Unfortunately, demand hasn't increased correspondingly. Your market research suggests that if you are going to increase demand for futons, you have to reach other VALS segments.

Working in small groups, develop ideas for a magazine or TV advertisement that might sell futons to one or more of the other target segments in the VALS system. Your instructor can assign a different target segment to each group, or each group can decide for itself which target segment constitutes the likeliest new market for futons.

Groups should then share their ideas with the whole class.

Sample Analysis of an Advertisement

With an understanding of possible photographic effects and the compositional features of ads, you now have all the background knowledge needed to begin doing your own analysis of ads. To illustrate how an analysis of an ad can reveal the ad's persuasive strategies, we show you our analysis of an ad for Coors Light (Figure 10.7) that ran in a variety of women's magazines. First, consider the

FIGURE 10.7 ■ Beer Ad Aimed at Women

contrast between the typical beer ads that are aimed at men (showing women in bikinis fulfilling adolescent male sexual fantasies or men on fishing trips or in sports bars, representing male comradeship and bonding) and this Coors Light ad with its "Sam and Me" theme.

Rather than associating beer drinking with a wild party, this ad associates beer drinking with the warm friendship of a man and a woman, with just a hint of potential romance. The ad shows a man and a woman, probably in their early- to mid-twenties, in relaxed conversation; they are sitting casually on a tabletop, with their legs resting on chair seats. The woman is wearing casual pants, a summery cotton top, and informal shoes. Her braided, shoulder-length hair has a healthy, mussed appearance, and one braid comes across the front of her shoulder. She is turned away from the man, leans on her knees, and holds a bottle of Coors Light. Her sparkling eyes are looking up, and she smiles happily, as if reliving a pleasant memory. The man is wearing slacks, a cotton shirt with the sleeves rolled up, and scuffed tennis shoes with white socks. He also has a reminiscing smile on his face, and he leans on the woman's shoulder. The words "Coors Light. Just between friends." appear immediately below the picture next to a Coors Light can.

This ad appeals to women's desire for close friendships and relationships. Everything about the picture signifies long-established closeness and intimacy— old friends rather than lovers. The way the man leans on the woman shows her strength and independence. Additionally, the way they pose, with the woman slightly forward and sitting up more than the man, results in their taking up equal space in the picture. In many ads featuring male-female couples, the man appears larger and taller than the woman; this picture signifies mutuality and equality.

The words of the ad help interpret the relationship. Sam and the woman have been friends since the first grade, and they are reminiscing about old times. The relationship is thoroughly mutual. Sometimes he brings the Coors Light and sometimes she brings it; sometimes she does the listening and sometimes he does; sometimes she leans on his shoulder and sometimes he leans on hers. Sometimes the ad says, "Sam and me"; sometimes it says, "me and Sam." Even the "bad grammar" of "Sam and me" (rather than "Sam and I") suggests the lazy, relaxed absence of pretense or formality.

These two are reliable, old buddies. But the last three lines of the copy give just a hint of potential romance. "Me and Sam? Together? I've never even thought about it. Okay, so I've thought about it." Whereas beer ads targeting men portray women as sex objects, this ad appeals to many women's desire for relationships and for romance that is rooted in friendship rather than sex.

And why the name "Sam"? Students in our classes have hypothesized that Sam is a "buddy" kind of name rather than a romantic hero name. Yet it is more modern and more interesting than other buddy names such as "Bob" or "Bill" or "Dave." "A 'Sam,'" said one of our students, "is more mysterious than a 'Bill.'" Whatever associations the name strikes in you, be assured that the ad makers spent hours debating possible names until they hit on this one. For an additional example of an ad analysis, see the sample student essay (pp. 242–245).

For Writing and Discussion

1. Examine any of the ads reprinted in this chapter or in the Part Openers (the Hoover ad on p. 2 or the Malboro "Adbuster" ad on p. 84) or magazine ads brought to class by students or your instructor, and analyze them in detail, paying particular attention to setting, furnishings, and props; characters, roles, and actions; photographic effects; and words and copy. Prior to discussion, freewrite your own analysis of the chosen ad.

(continued)

2. An excellent way to learn how to analyze ads is to create your own advertisement. Read the following introduction to a brief article with the headline "Attention Advertisers: Real Men Do Laundry." This article appeared in an issue of *American Demographics,* a magazine that helps advertisers target particular audiences based on demographic analysis of the population.

> Commercials almost never show men doing the laundry, but nearly one-fifth of men do at least seven loads a week. Men don't do as much laundry as women, but the washday gap may be closing. In the dual-career 1990's laundry is going unisex.
>
> Forty-three percent of women wash at least seven loads of laundry a week, compared with 19 percent of men, according to a survey conducted for Lever Brothers Company, manufacturers of Wisk detergent. Men do 29 percent of the 419 million loads of laundry Americans wash each week. Yet virtually all laundry-detergent advertising is aimed at women.

Working in small groups, create an idea for a laundry detergent ad to be placed in a men's magazine such as *Men's Health, Sports Illustrated, Field and Stream,* or *Esquire.* Draw a rough sketch of your ad that includes the picture, the placement of words, and a rough idea of the content of the words. Pay particular attention to the visual features of your ad—the models, their ages, ethnicity, social status or class, and dress; the setting, such as a self-service laundry or a home laundry room; and other features. When you have designed a possible approach, explain why you think your ad will be successful.

Cultural Perspectives on Advertisements

There isn't space here to examine in depth the numerous cultural issues raised by advertisements, but we can introduce you to a few of them and provide some thought-provoking tasks for exploratory writing and talking. The key issue we want you to think about in this section is how advertisements not only reflect the cultural values and the economic and political structures of the society that produces them but also actively construct and reproduce that society.

As one way to look at the cultural implications of advertisements, consider the way that ads might shape our conception of gender. In 1979, the influential sociologist and semiotician* Erving Goffman published a book called *Gender Advertisements,* arguing that the way in which women are pictured in advertisements removes them from serious power. In many cases, Goffman's point seems self-evident: Women in advertisements are often depicted in frivolous, childlike, exhibitionistic, sexual, or silly poses that would be considered undignified for a man. However, the picture Goffman paints is complicated by some new ads—for example, the new genre of physical fitness ads that emphasize women's physical strength and capabilities as well as their sexuality and femininity. Ads for athletic products feature models with beautiful hair and faces, tanned skin, and strong, trim, and shapely bodies. These ads strike different balances between female

---

*A *semiotician* is a person who studies the meanings of signs in a culture. A *sign* is any human-produced artifact or gesture that conveys meaning. It can be anything from a word to a facial expression to the arrangement of chairs at a dinner table.

FIGURE 10.8 ■ Burn-A-Genics Ad

athleticism and sexuality, leaving the question of empowerment up to the viewer. (See the ad for Burn-A-Genics above.)

A decade later, another cultural critic, researcher Jean Kilbourne, made a more explicit argument against the way advertisements negatively construct women. In her films *Still Killing Us Softly* (1987) and *Slim Hopes: Advertising and the Obsession with Thinness* (1995), Kilbourne argues that our culture's fear of powerful women is embodied in advertisements that entrap women in futile pursuit of an impossible, flawless standard of beauty. Advertisements help construct the social values that pressure women (particularly middle-class white women) to stay thin, frail, and little-girlish and thus become perfect objects. In *Slim Hopes*, she claims that basically only one body type is preferred (the waif look or the waif-made-voluptuous-with-reconstructed-breasts look). Further, the dismemberment of women in ads—the focus on individual body parts—both objectifies women and intensifies women's anxious concentration on trying to perfect each part of their bodies. Kilbourne asserts that ads distort women's attitudes toward

FIGURE 10.9 ■ Zenith Ad

food through harmful and contradictory messages that encourage binging while equating moral goodness with thinness and control over eating. Ads convert women into lifelong consumers of beauty and diet products while undermining their self-esteem and health.

For Writing and Discussion

To see what Goffman and Kilbourne are getting at, we invite you to explore this issue in the following sequence of activities, which combine class discussion with invitations for exploratory writing.

1. Examine the following four ads that feature photographs of women: the Hoover ad in the Part Opener on page 2; the Burn-A-Genics video ad (Figure 10.8); the "Of Sound Body" Zenith ad (Figure 10.9); and the AT&T Calling Card ad (Figure 10.10). To what extent do each of these ads construct women as lacking in power in the economic, political, and professional structures of our culture? Which ads, if any, treat women as powerful? Freewrite your responses to the way women are constructed in these ads as preparation for class discussion.

2. Consider again the Burn-A-Genics ad (Figure 10.8) and the Zenith ad (Figure 10.9). Both these ads have a striking—even memorable—composition with bold, attractive shapes. But are the women featured in these ads instrumental or decorative? What social roles are these women playing? How do camera techniques contribute to the depiction of these women? Would you say these ads portray women in a positive or negative way? How would Goffman and Kilbourne respond?

For an explanation of "instrumental" and "decorative," see p. 226.

3. Bring to class advertisements for women's clothing, perfumes, or accessories from recent fashion and beauty magazines such as *Glamour, Elle, InStyle,* and *Vogue.* Study the ways that female models are typically posed in these ads. Then have male students assume the postures of the female models. How many of the postures, which look natural for women, seem ludicrous when adopted by men? To what extent are these postures really natural for women? To what extent do these postures illustrate Goffman's point that advertisements don't take women seriously?

4. Bring to class examples of two kinds of advertisements from contemporary magazines: (1) ads that portray women in trivialized, demeaning, or objectified ways and that support the points that Erving Goffman and Jean Kilbourne make about women in advertising; and (2) ads that portray women in a particularly positive and empowered way—ads that you think neither Goffman nor Kilbourne could deconstruct to show the subordination of women in our culture. Share your examples with the class and see whether your classmates agree with your assessment of these ads.

5. After you have discussed your responses to the five ads and after everyone in the class has examined several recent advertisements in a variety of magazines, hold an all-class dialectic discussion addressing the following claim: "In recent years, advertising has made enormous gains in portraying women as strong, independent, intelligent, and equal with men in their potential for professional status."

See Chapter 2, p. 34, for an explanation of dialectic discussion.

FIGURE 10.10 ■ AT&T Calling Card Ad

Readings

Our first reading is an excerpt from Paul Messaris's book, *Visual Persuasion: The Role of Images in Advertising.* Messaris, a communications professor at the University of Pennsylvania, intended this book for an academic audience (hence his frequent parenthetical references to other scholars). His purpose is to analyze the distinctive features of visual communication and to examine the role of visual images in political campaigns and commercial advertising. In the following excerpt, Messaris explains his position on the ethical responsibility of advertisers. The particular question at issue is whether advertisers are being unethical when they display certain groups of people—in this passage, adolescents and African-Americans—in ways that are stereotypical, unrealistic, or potentially harmful to individuals or society.

■ PAUL MESSARIS ■

From VISUAL PERSUASION: The Role of Images in Advertising

1   As we have seen, the iconicity[1] of images makes it possible for ads to elicit our attention and emotions by simulating various significant features of our real-world visual experiences. By virtue of their iconicity, visual ads are able to erect before our eyes a mirror world, with whose inhabitants we are invited to identify or to imagine that we are interacting. These acts of identification and imaginary interaction have real-world consequences. Some of the most revealing analyses of advertising have described the ways in which viewers use the characters they see in ads as reference points for their own evolving identities (Barthel, 1988; Ewen, 1988; Ewen & Ewen, 1982). For example, Carol Moog (1990) recalls how, as a young girl, she studied the posture of a woman in a refrigerator commercial to learn how to carry herself as an adult (p. 13). Together with fictional movies and TV programs, ads are a major source of images that young people can use to previsualize their places in the world of sexual and status relationships. It can be argued that advertisers have an ethical responsibility to take these circumstances into account in fashioning the images that they place before the public.

2   What might constitute a violation of this ethical responsibility? Critics of advertising images often focus on the discrepancy between the vision of life offered in ads and the needs or abilities of real people. Drawing on her practice as a psychotherapist, Moog (1990) cites the story of a young lawyer who expressed dissatisfaction with her life because she had not lived up to her potential as a member of "the Pepsi generation"—that is, "beautiful, sexy, happy, young people . . . a generation that didn't slog through law school, work twelve-hour days, or break up with fiancés" (p. 15). Moog presents this vignette as a reminder of the fact that "advertisers are not in the business of making people feel better about themselves, they're in the *selling* business" (p. 16). As this statement implies, commercial advertising often does create a vision of a fantasy world that may become a source of dissatisfaction in people's real lives, and this is especially true of ads that use sex or status as

---

[1]*Iconicity* is an academic term (related to *icon*, meaning "image") referring to the power of images to influence a viewer. When you desire, for example, to meet a stranger in a Parisian café or to ride a horse through the pounding surf because you saw characters do these things in an ad, you experience the *iconic power* of the image.

part of their appeal. Some people may find this practice objectionable in and of itself, although in my view it would be rather fatuous, as well as somewhat puritanical, to suggest that advertisers should stop purveying the images of "beautiful, sexy, happy young people" that led to Moog's client's distress. However, there is a related trend in advertising that does seem to me to raise especially troublesome ethical issues.

In recent years, ads aimed at young people have increasingly sought to appeal to an adolescent sense of frustration and resentment at the constricting demands of adult society. There may be a lingering element of this type of sentiment in the dissatisfaction expressed by Moog's client, but the kind of advertising to which I am referring is quite different from the old, Pepsi-generation style of happy, carefree images. Instead, these more recent ads, for products such as athletic shoes, off-road vehicles, or video games, often make a point of displaying abrasive, belligerent behavior and physical recklessness (cf. Lull, 1995, pp. 73–81). A defender of such ads might argue that they are simply being honest. Adolescents often have good reason to chafe at the standards imposed on them by older people and to recoil from the vision of the future that many of them face. The aggression and recklessness depicted in some of these ads are no doubt authentic expressions of how many young people feel. To put a happy face on those feelings could be considered hypocritical. Nevertheless, with due respect for such views, I would argue that the type of resentment exploited in these ads is unproductive at best, counterproductive at worst. Dissatisfaction that leads to impulsiveness and disregard for other people gains nothing from being expressed openly. In that sense, I would say that the ethics of this genre of advertising are certainly questionable.

This is not to say, however, that advertising aimed at young people should necessarily revert to the untroubled imagery of earlier times. It should be possible to portray and address youth honestly without pandering to the irresponsible tendencies that are sometimes associated with adolescence. For instance, despite the criticism that has recently been directed at the advertising of Calvin Klein, it seems to me that there are many Calvin Klein ads that manage to strike this balance quite effectively. In particular, the print ads for cK one fragrance have generated record-breaking sales while presenting a view of youthful sexuality that is remarkably unglamorized (compared to most other ads) and, furthermore, notably inclusive both racially and in terms of sexual orientation. This inclusiveness deserves special mention. The cK one ads are among the few examples of mass-produced imagery in which the mingling of people from different backgrounds appears relatively natural, rather than an artificial (albeit well-meaning) concoction of the media.

But, again, this comment should not be interpreted as a blanket endorsement of unvarnished naturalism in all of advertising. In a recent discussion of the portrayal of blacks and whites in the mass media, DeMott (1995) has argued that movies and ads present a phony picture of harmony between the races that serves to obscure the unpleasant truth about race relations in the United States. I do not find this argument persuasive. For one thing, information about racial friction is abundantly available elsewhere in the media. More importantly, though, I think it is a mistake to assume that people always look at advertising images expecting to see the way things really are in society. Almost by definition, the portrayals of the good life presented in ads carry with them the implicit understanding that they are idealizations, not documentary reports (cf. Schudson, 1984). What people look for in such ads is a vision of the way things ought to be. Furthermore, when an ad is produced by a large corporation, people are likely to see this vision as an indicator of socially approved values—even though it also may be understood tacitly that those values do not correspond very closely to current social reality. From this perspective, the kinds of advertisements that DeMott criticizes—depictions of people from different racial and ethnic backgrounds living together in harmony and prosperity—are actually highly desirable. For example, an American Express Gold Card ad (attacked by DeMott) shows elegantly dressed blacks and whites occupying adjacent box seats in an opulent-looking theater or concert hall, while an ad for Chubb Insurance portrays two suburban families, one black, one white, posing together in a setting of obvious wealth. Such ads should be praised, not subjected to carping objections. In my view, they are models of the responsible use of advertising's iconic powers.

Thinking Critically about "Visual Persuasion"

1. Messaris seeks to establish a middle position between two additional extreme views of advertisers' responsibility to viewers and consumers. How would you describe his view and the extremes he is reacting against?

2. Can you find examples of adolescent-directed ads portraying, in Messaris's words, "abrasive, belligerent behavior and physical recklessness"? What points can you raise in support of or against his censure of this type of ad?

3. Over the last two decades, the number of magazine ads featuring persons of color has increased substantially. Sometimes ads show multiracial groups. At other times, especially in middlebrow magazines such as *Parents' Magazine, Working Mother, Good Housekeeping,* or *Sports Illustrated,* ads now feature models from minority groups, where formerly the models would have been white. Observe closely the ads shown in Figures 10.11 through 10.14. To what extent do these ads present a harmonious multiracial and multicultural society? Do any of them contain racial or ethnic stereotypes? What vision of social reality, race, and class are these ads constructing?

4. Messaris refers to the argument of Benjamin DeMott that buddy movies featuring pals from different races or "happy harmony" ads showing blacks and whites together create a false sense that America no longer has a race problem. How do you think Messaris and DeMott would analyze the ads in Figures 10.11

FIGURE 10.12 ■ PINE-SOL® Household Cleaner Ad

©2001 The Clorox Company. Reprinted with permission.

FIGURE 10.11 ■ MetLife Ad

PEANUTS © United Feature Syndicate, Inc.

FIGURE 10.13 ■ Vokal by Nelly Ad

FIGURE 10.14 ■ Skechers Ad

through 10.14? Do you think the Skechers ad (Figure 10.14) illustrates DeMott's concept of a "happy harmony" ad? How would you describe the difference in the image of black males in the MetLife ad (Figure 10.11) and the Vokal ad (Figure 10.13)? How would the effect of the MetLife ad differ if the model were dressed like Nelly? Why doesn't Nelly dress like the MetLife model?

5. Messaris distinguishes between ads that include people of different races "naturally" and those that appear "artificial" and "concocted." Do the ads in Figures 10.11 through 10.14 seem to you to be natural or artificially concocted? Why or why not?

6. These ads also raise questions about the intersection of race and gender. We have asked how Messaris and DeMott might analyze these ads. Now ask how Goffman and Kilbourne might analyze them. Imagine the PINE-SOL® Household Cleaner ad (Figure 10.12) using a white model rather than a black model (same pose, clothing, and body type with only the skin color changed). Would the ad work? Why or why not? Try a similar experiment with the Skechers ad (Figure 10.14). Why did they choose a white model for the central figure? How would the effect of the ad be different if the black male model on the left and the white male model in the center were reversed so that the black male dominated the ad? What if the woman on the right were the central figure? The admakers obviously could have made these choices, so why did they pose the models as they did? Look also at the insert pictures at the bottom and top of the ad in Figure 10.14. Why did the admakers choose those models and those poses?

PINE-SOL® is a registered trademark of the Clorox Company. Used with permission.

The final reading is a student essay written in response to the assignment in this chapter. It contrasts the strategies of two different cigarette ads to make smoking appear socially desirable despite public sentiment to the contrary.

■ STEPHEN BEAN (STUDENT) ■
HOW CIGARETTE ADVERTISERS ADDRESS THE STIGMA AGAINST SMOKING:
A Tale of Two Ads

Any smoker can tell you there's a social stigma attached to smoking in this country. With smokers being pushed out of restaurants, airports, and many office buildings, how could anyone not feel like a pariah lighting up? While never associated with the churchgoing crowd, smoking is increasingly viewed as lower class or as a symbol of rebellion. Smoking has significantly decreased among adults while increasing among teenagers and young adults in recent years—a testament to its growing status as an affront to middle- and upper-class values. Cigarette advertisers are sharply tuned into this cultural attitude. They must decide whether to overcome the working-class/rebellious image of smoking in their advertisements or use it to their advantage. The answer to this question lies in what type of people they want an ad to target—the young? the rich? the poor?—and in what values, insecurities, and desires they think this group shares. Two contrasting answers to these questions are apparent in recent magazine ads for Benson & Hedges cigarettes and for Richland cigarettes.

2 The ad for Benson & Hedges consists of a main picture and a small insert picture below the main one. The main picture shows five women (perhaps thirty years old) sitting around, talking, and laughing in the living room of a comfortable and urbane home or upscale apartment. The room is filled with natural light and is tastefully decorated with antique lamps and Persian rugs. The women have opened a bottle of wine, and a couple of glasses have been poured. They are dressed casually but fashionably, ranging from slightly hip to slightly conservative. One woman wears a loose, black, sleeveless dress; another wears grungesque boots with a sweater and skirt. One of the women, apparently the hostess, sits on a sofa a bit apart from the others, smiles with pleasure at the conversation and laughter of her friends, and knits. Two of the women are smoking, and three aren't. No smoke is visible coming from the cigarettes. Underneath the main picture is a small insert photograph of the hostess—the one knitting in the main picture—in a different pose. She is now leaning back in pleasure, apparently after the party, and this time she is smoking a cigarette. Underneath the photos reads the slogan "For people who like to smoke."

3 The ad for Richland cigarettes shows a couple in their late twenties sitting in a diner or perhaps a tavern off the freeway. The remains of their lunch—empty burger and fries baskets, a couple of beer bottles—lie on the table. They seem to be talking leisurely, sharing an after-meal smoke. The man is wearing black jeans and a black T-shirt. The woman is wearing a pinkish skirt and tank top. Leaning back with her legs apart she sits in a position that signals sexuality. The slogan reads, "It's all right here." And at the bottom of the ad, "Classic taste. Right price." Outside the window of the diner you can see a freeway sign slightly blurred as if from heated air currents.

4 Whom do these different advertisements target? What about them might people find appealing? Clearly the Benson & Hedges ad is aimed at women, especially upper-middle-class women who wish to appear successful. As the media have noted lately, the social stigma against smoking is strongest among middle- and upper-class adults. My sense of the B&H ad is that it is targeting younger, college-educated women who feel social pressure to quit smoking. To them the ad is saying, "Smoking makes you no less sophisticated; it only shows that you have a fun side too. Be comfortable doing whatever makes you happy."

5 What choices did the advertisers make in constructing this scene to create this message? The living room—with its antique lamps and vases, its Persian rugs and hardcover books, and its wall hanging thrown over what

appears to be an old trunk—creates a sense of comfortable, tasteful, upscale living. But figuring out the people in the room is more difficult. Who are these women? What is their story? What brought them together this afternoon? Where did their money come from? Are these professional women with high-paying jobs, or are they the wives of young bankers, attorneys, and stockbrokers? One woman has a strong business look—short hair feathered back, black sleeveless dress—but why is she dressed this way on what is apparently a Saturday afternoon? In contrast, another woman has a more hip, almost grunge look—slightly spiky hair that's long in the back, a loose sweater, a black skirt, and heavy black boots. Only one woman wears a wedding ring. It seems everything about these women resists easy definition or categorization. The most striking image in the ad is the hostess knitting. She looks remarkably domestic, almost motherly, with her knees drawn close, leaning over her knitting and smiling to herself as others laugh out loud. Her presence gives the scene a feeling of safety and old-fashioned values amidst the images of independence. Interestingly, we get a much different image of the hostess in the second insert picture placed just above the B&H logo. This picture shows the hostess leaning back pleasurably on the couch and smoking. The image is undeniably sexual. Her arms are back; she's deeply relaxed; the two top buttons of her blouse are open; her hair is slightly mussed; she smokes languidly, taking full pleasure in the cigarette, basking in the party's afterglow.

The opposing images in the advertisement (knitting/smoking, conservative/hip, wife/career, safe/independent, domestic/sexual) mean that these women can't easily be defined—as smokers or as anything else. For an ad promoting smoking, the cigarettes themselves take a back seat. In the main picture the cigarettes are hardly noticeable; the two women holding cigarettes do so inconspicuously and there is no visible smoke. The ad doesn't say so much that it is good to smoke, but that it is okay to smoke. Smoking will not make you less sophisticated. If anything, it only shows that you have an element of youth and fun. The slogan, "For people who like to smoke," targets nonsmokers as much as it does smokers—not so much to take up smoking but to be more tolerant of those who choose to smoke. The emphasis is on choice, independence, and acceptance of others' choices. The ad attacks the social stigma against smoking; it eases the conscience of "people who like to smoke."

While the B&H ad hopes to remove the stigma attached to smoking, the Richland ad feasts on it. Richland cigarettes aren't for those cultivating the upper-class look. The ad goes for a rebellious, gritty image, for beer drinkers, not wine sippers. While the story of the women in the B&H ad is difficult to figure out, the Richland ad gives us a classic image: a couple on the road who have stopped at a diner or tavern. Here the story is simpler: a man and woman being cool. They are going down the freeway to the big city. I picture a heavy American cruising car parked out front.

Everything about the ad has a gritty, blue-collar feel. They sit at a booth with a Formica tabletop; the walls are bare, green-painted wood. The man is dressed in black with a combed-back, James Dean haircut. The woman wears a pink skirt with a tank top; her shoulder-length hair hasn't been fussed over, and she wears a touch of makeup. Empty baskets and bottles cluttering the table indicate they had a classic American meal—hamburgers, fries, and a beer—eaten for pleasure without politically correct worries about calories, polyunsaturated fats, cruelty to animals, or cancer. While the sexual imagery in the B&H ad is subtle, in the Richland ad it is blatant. The man is leaning forward with his elbows on the table; the woman is leaning back with her legs spread and her skirt pushed up slightly. Her eyes are closed. They smoke leisurely, and the woman holds the cigarette a couple of inches from her expecting lips. The slogan, "It's all right here," is centered beneath the woman's skirt. Smoking, like sex, is about pure pleasure—something to be done slowly. Far from avoiding working-class associations with smoking, this ad aims to reinforce them. The cigarettes are clearly visible, and, unlike the cigarettes in the B&H ad, show rings of rising smoke. This ad promotes living for the moment. The more rebellious, the better.

8   So we see, then, two different ways that cigarette companies address the stigma against smoking. The B&H ad tries to eliminate it by targeting middle-class, college-educated women. It appeals to upscale values, associating cigarette smoking with choice, and showing that "people who like to smoke" can also knit (evoking warm, safe images of domestic life) or lean back in postparty pleasure (evoking a somewhat wilder, more sexual image). In contrast, the Richland ad exploits the stigma. It associates smoking with on-the-road freedom, rebellion, sexuality, and enjoyment of the moment. The smoke visibly rising from the cigarettes in the Richland ad and noticeably absent from the Benson & Hedges ad tells the difference.

Thinking Critically about "How Cigarette Advertisers Address the Stigma against Smoking"

1. Stephen Bean argues that the Benson & Hedges and the Richland ads use very different appeals to encourage their target audiences to smoke. What are the appeals he cites? Do you agree with Stephen's analysis?

2. Collect a variety of cigarette ads from current magazines, and analyze their various appeals. How do the ads vary according to their intended audiences? Consider ads targeted at men versus women or at audiences from different VALS segments.

3. What do you see as the strengths and weaknesses of Stephen's essay?

COMPOSING YOUR ESSAY

Generating and Exploring Ideas

Your first task is to find two ads that sell the same general product to different target audiences or that make appeals to noticeably different value systems. Look for ads that are complex enough to invite detailed analysis. Then, analyze the ads carefully, using the strategies suggested earlier in this chapter. The sample student essay (pp. 242–245) provides an example of the kind of approach you can take.

If you get stuck, try freewriting your responses to the following questions: (a) What attracted your attention to this ad? (b) Whom do you think this ad targets? Why? (c) What photographic techniques, visual devices, and camera angles are used in this ad? (d) What props and furnishings are in this ad, and what values or meanings are attached to them? (e) What are the characters like, what are they doing, and why are they wearing what they are wearing and posed the way they are posed? (f) How do the words of the ad interplay with the picture? (g) How would the ad be less effective if its key features were changed in some way? (h) Overall, to what fears, values, hopes, or dreams is this ad appealing?

Shaping and Drafting

Your essay should be fairly easy to organize at the big-picture level, but each part will require its own organic organization depending on the main points of your analysis. At the big-picture level, you can generally follow a structure like this:

I. Introduction (hooks readers' interest, gives background on how ads vary their appeals, asks the question your paper will address, and ends with initial mapping in the form of a purpose or thesis statement)

II. General description of the two ads

A. Description of ad 1

B. Description of ad 2

III. Analysis of the two ads

A. Analysis of ad 1

B. Analysis of ad 2

IV. Conclusion (returns to the big picture for a sense of closure; makes final comments about the significance of your analysis or touches in some way on larger issues raised by the analysis)

We recommend that you write your rough draft rapidly, without worrying about gracefulness, correctness, or even getting all your ideas said at once. Many people like to begin with the description of the ads and then write the analysis before writing the introduction and the conclusion. After you have written your draft, put it aside for a while before you begin revising. We recommend that you ask classmates for a peer review of your draft early in the revising process.

Revising

Most experienced writers make global changes in their final drafts when they revise, especially when they are doing analytical writing. The act of writing a rough draft generally leads to the discovery of more ideas. You may also realize that many of your original ideas aren't clearly developed or that the draft feels scattered and unorganized.

■ GUIDELINES FOR PEER REVIEWS ■

Instructions for peer reviews are provided in Chapter 18 (pp. 490–496).

For the Writer

Prepare two or three questions you would like your peer reviewer to address while responding to your draft. The questions can focus on some aspect of your draft that you are uncertain about, on one or more sections where you particularly seek help or advice, on some feature that you particularly like about your draft, or on some part you especially wrestled with. Write out your questions and give them to your peer reviewer along with your draft.

For the Reviewer

  I. Read the draft at a normal reading speed from beginning to end. As you read, do the following:

   A. Place a wavy line in the margin next to any passages that you find confusing, that contain something that doesn't seem to fit, or that otherwise slow down your reading.

   B. Place a "Good!" in the margin next to any passages where you think the writing is particularly strong or interesting.

 II. Read the draft again slowly and answer the following questions by writing brief explanations of your answers.

   A. Introduction:

    1. Is the title appropriate for an academic analysis? Does it suggest the thesis and focus of the paper and pique your interest? How might the title be improved?

    2. What does the writer do to capture your interest, provide needed background, and set up the question to be addressed?

    3. How does the thesis statement, purpose statement, or forecasting statement provide the big picture for both the description and the analysis of the two ads? How might the writer improve the introduction?

   B. Description of the ads:

    1. Does the writer describe the ads in an interesting and vivid manner? How could this description help you "see" the ads more clearly?

    2. In what ways do the ads appeal to different audiences or have differ-ent value systems? What makes the ads complex enough to justify an analysis?

  C. Analysis of the ads:

    1. How does the analysis of the ads shed light on and build on the description of the ads?

    2. How many of the following features does the writer discuss? Which could be added to deepen and complicate the analysis?

      a. Setting, props, and furnishings: how they indicate lifestyle and socioeconomic status; appeal to certain values; carry certain cul-tural associations or meanings; serve as symbols.

      b. Characters, roles, and actions: the story of the ad; power rela-tionships and status of the characters; gender, age, or ethnic roles followed or violated; the significance of clothing and accessories, of hair and facial expressions, and of posing, positioning, and gestures.

      c. Photographic effects: lighting, camera angle, cropping, focus.

      d. Language and wording of the ad's copy: its overt message; feel-ings, mood, and values communicated through connotations, double entendres, and so forth; visual layout of copy.

    3. What portions of the analysis are convincing? Which details of the ads contradict the analysis? Do you disagree with the writer's view of these ads?

    4. How could the body of the paper be made clearer, better organized, or easier to follow? Where might the writer better apply the princi-ples of clarity from Chapter 19 (starting with the big picture; putting points before particulars; using transitions; following the old/new contract)?

  D. If the writer has prepared questions for you, respond to his or her inquiries.

  E. Sum up what you see as the chief strengths and problem areas of this draft:

    1. Strengths

    2. Problem areas

III. Read the draft one more time. Place a check mark in the margin wherever you notice problems in grammar, spelling, or mechanics (one check mark per problem).

CHAPTER 11

Analyzing Numerical Data

ABOUT NUMERICAL ANALYSIS

The ability to analyze numbers and to use numbers effectively in your own writing—often displayed visually in tables, graphs, and charts—is an important thinking and communicating skill in today's world.* A quick look at any modern newspaper reveals the frequent inclusion of graphs and pie charts in newspaper stories. In fact some newspapers, such as the *Wall Street Journal* and *USA Today,* are particularly known for their distinctive use of quantitative graphics. (The conservative *Wall Street Journal* has staid, scientific-looking graphics in contrast to the flashy, eye-catching charts in *USA Today.*)

Additionally many modern arguments use numbers extensively as evidence. Writers present numerical data on everything from the crime rate to the cost of drugs, from the decline of frog populations to the effect of a tax cut on the federal deficit. In making arguments, writers filter numerical data through the screen of their own perspective or angle of vision—an interpretive process that, as we have seen, is characteristic of how evidence is used in all thesis-based prose. As a critical thinker, you need to be aware of how writers select and present numbers and how their choices support their own perspectives while de-emphasizing others.

As a writer, you also need to be able to use numbers effectively in your own arguments. Many people, of course, are skeptical of numbers. They believe that writers manipulate data for their own ends. Such sayings as "You can make numbers say anything you want" or "There are three kinds of lies: lies, damned lies, and statistics" suggest our fear that writers regularly tweak, massage, or even cook the data to deceive us. But we want to show in this chapter that a writer can use numbers ethically and responsibly, just as a writer can and should use other kinds of evidence in an ethical way. By understanding how numbers tell a story and by recognizing how writers select numbers to support the story they want to tell, you will always be aware that other stories are also possible. Ethical use of numbers means using reputable sources for basic data, not inventing or intentionally distorting numbers, and not ignoring alternative points of view.

In this chapter we have two related purposes. First, we want to show you how to analyze the numbers you encounter in other people's arguments—to see, for example, how the numbers have been selected, arranged, and presented for

The concept of "angle of vision" is introduced and explained in Chapter 3, pp. 51–53, and throughout Chapter 5.

*Our revised treatment of numerical analysis in this edition has been influenced by Tim McGee and Michael Hassett, "Showing to Tell: Integrating Quantitative Graphics into Composition Instruction," *Journal of Teaching Writing* 17.1 (Summer 2001). We would also like to thank Dean Peterson, Department of Finance and Economics at Seattle University, for his professional and technical expertise in providing and analyzing data on income distribution used as an illustration in this chapter.

rhetorical effect. Second, we want to show you how to use numbers effectively in your own writing. We particularly want to introduce you to the power of quantitative graphics (tables, graphs, and charts) for increasing the explanatory and persuasive power of your own arguments.

EXPLORING NUMERICAL ANALYSIS

Because we have two interconnected purposes in this chapter, we present two initial exercises that will introduce you to each goal.

Task 1: Analyzing the Use of Numbers in an Article

Suppose that you are researching changes over the last two decades in the public image of teenagers. As part of your research, you wish to examine the way teenagers are portrayed in the media. You come across the following article in *USA Today* from November 8, 1985. Read this brief article, and then answer the questions that follow.

HELP TROUBLED TEENS— DON'T FORGET THEM

The USA's teenagers are in trouble.   1

Too many of them are pregnant. Too many are drunk. Too many are   2
strung out on drugs. Too many are criminals. Too many die because of homicide or suicide.

Some are poor kids, on the street corners of The Bronx or Watts, sneaking   3
marijuana cigarettes and wobbling off to school. Some are rich kids, in San Rafael or Scarsdale, raiding the liquor closet, mixing booze and pills.

Some are young and pregnant. In the high schools of small towns or large   4
cities. Some will never see 18, victims of homicide or suicide in Detroit or Dallas.

Last week a blue-ribbon committee, the Business Advisory Commission   5
of the Education Commission of the States, released some startling statistics about teenagers.

Twenty-two percent of them—14 million—live in poverty. More than 1   6
million get pregnant each year, and most do not marry. About 700,000 dropped out of school last year.

On Wednesday, a new survey of high school seniors showed 30 percent   7
had used illegal drugs in the past month; 37 percent had indulged in heavy drinking.

People under 21 account for more than half of all arrests in serious   8
crimes. And the teen-age suicide rate is up 150 percent since 1950.

Why would a group of business and government leaders worry about the   9
USA's young people?

10   They worry that if too many of our kids are lost to drugs or booze, there will be a shortage of skilled labor. But beyond that, they realize that if these mixed-up kids don't get help, huge numbers of them will never lead productive lives. And the rest of us will pay the bill for their failures.

11   Business already spends $40 billion a year to train workers. In some cases, it has been forced to teach young people things they should have learned in elementary school.

12   The business group calls these kids "disconnected"—cut off from school or work. As many as 15 percent of all teens may be in trouble, lost, unable to live productive lives.

13   What can be done about it?

14   Nothing, some say. They argue there will always be a small number of underachievers or misfits—so don't waste time, energy, or money helping them.

15   That view, besides being callous, is terribly short-sighted. If today's teens don't contribute to our society, then they will take from it—and the rest of us will pay for it.

16   Some solutions are just common sense. Restore discipline and accountability in the schools. Get parents involved in education. Crack down on drug and alcohol abuse. Give them a sense of values.

Working in small groups or as a whole class, explore your answers to the following questions:

1. What view of U.S. teenagers emerges from this article?

2. How does the writer's use of statistical data contribute to the rhetorical effect of the article?

3. Consider some of the writer's specific uses of statistics:

   ■ "More than 1 million get pregnant each year, and most do not marry." Why does the writer use a raw number here (1 million) rather than a percentage? What percent of all teenagers get pregnant? [*Note:* A clue early in the article will help you compute the total number of teenagers. The writer says that 14 million equals 22 percent of the whole.] What does the writer mean by "most"?

   ■ "And the teen-age suicide rate is up 150 percent since 1950." The writer has several choices here: citing the actual raw number of teenage suicides; citing the percentage of teenagers who committed suicide; or citing the increase in the rate of suicide measured from any base year. Why does the writer choose the last option? Why do you suppose he or she starts from the base year 1950 rather than, say, 1930 or 1960?

   ■ "People under 21 account for more than half of all arrests in serious crimes." Why does the writer choose to focus on *arrests* for serious crimes rather than *convictions*? (Can you think of occasions where the police automatically suspect teenagers, arrest them, and then later release them?) How serious is "serious"?

TABLE 11.1 ■ Before-tax Family Income for Previous Year, by Selected Characteristics of Families, 1989, 1992, 1995, and 1998 (Thousands of 1998 dollars, except as noted)

Family Characteristic	1989			1992			1995			1998		
	Median	Mean	Percent of Families	Median	Mean	Percent of Families	Median	Mean	Percent of Families	Median	Mean	Percent of Families
All families	33.2	52.2	100.0	30.4	45.6	100.0	32.7	47.4	100.0	33.4	53.0	100.0
Income (1998 $)												
Less than 10,000	6.6	6.2	14.7	6.4	6.0	14.8	6.2	4.7	15.1	6.2	5.2	12.7
10,000–24,999	15.9	16.7	23.8	17.5	17.3	27.1	17.4	17.4	25.1	17.2	17.1	24.7
25,000–49,999	35.9	36.1	30.0	36.3	36.7	29.5	37.1	36.5	31.1	35.5	35.9	29.0
50,000–99,999	66.4	68.9	22.7	65.5	68.7	20.9	66.5	69.1	21.3	65.9	68.7	25.0
100,00 or more	144.8	239.3	8.7	140.4	195.3	7.6	148.3	219.5	7.4	141.9	237.0	8.7
Age of head (years)												
Less than 35	26.6	35.5	28.1	28.1	34.6	25.8	27.3	33.3	24.8	27.4	36.1	23.3
35–44	46.5	63.3	21.5	40.9	53.2	22.8	40.3	51.7	23.0	42.6	59.8	23.3
45–54	49.2	76.9	15.1	48.0	64.6	16.2	42.5	70.4	17.9	50.7	69.5	19.2
55–64	33.2	60.7	13.9	33.9	56.4	13.2	36.0	57.1	12.5	38.5	71.4	12.8
65–74	21.3	45.5	12.6	19.9	33.0	12.6	20.7	39.8	12.0	24.3	46.4	11.2
75 and more	17.3	32.5	8.9	15.2	26.6	9.4	17.4	28.2	9.8	16.2	28.9	10.2
Education of head												
No high school diploma	17.3	24.9	24.3	14.0	19.9	20.3	15.3	22.1	18.5	15.2	21.7	16.5
High school diploma	29.2	38.1	32.1	26.9	34.3	30.0	27.3	37.3	31.7	29.4	37.0	31.9
Some college	37.2	51.8	15.6	31.6	42.2	17.8	32.7	43.1	19.0	35.5	50.7	18.5
College degree	53.1	92.3	28.0	51.5	74.6	31.9	49.1	75.8	30.7	54.7	85.2	33.2
Race or ethnicity of head												
White non-Hispanic	38.5	59.9	74.8	35.1	50.4	75.3	34.9	52.1	77.6	37.5	58.6	77.7
Nonwhite or Hispanic	18.6	29.3	25.2	21.1	31.1	24.7	21.8	31.0	22.4	23.3	33.5	22.3
Work status of head												
Working for someone else	41.2	52.3	57.0	39.8	50.0	54.8	39.3	51.6	58.3	40.5	53.4	59.2
Self-employed	47.8	120.9	11.1	51.5	86.5	10.9	40.3	84.1	10.3	52.7	108.3	11.3
Retired	18.6	30.7	25.2	17.5	26.1	26.0	17.4	29.7	25.0	19.3	32.6	24.4
Other not working	9.3	18.0	6.7	12.9	23.9	8.3	12.0	19.8	6.5	11.1	23.2	5.2
Housing status												
Own	42.5	65.8	63.9	39.8	55.9	63.9	40.3	58.7	64.7	43.6	66.3	66.3
Rent	17.3	28.2	36.1	19.9	27.5	36.1	19.6	26.7	35.3	20.3	26.7	33.7
Net worth (percentile)												
Bottom 25%	13.3	19.0	24.9	15.2	19.9	25.0	15.3	19.8	25.0	16.2	20.4	25.0
25–49.9	27.9	31.9	25.1	28.1	31.6	25.0	30.5	33.4	25.0	30.4	33.8	25.0
50–74.9	39.9	46.0	25.0	37.4	41.6	25.0	38.2	43.3	25.0	40.5	46.8	25.0
75–89.9	53.1	65.0	15.0	49.1	58.0	15.0	45.8	55.9	15.0	56.8	67.4	15.0
Top 10%	99.6	182.1	10.0	92.4	136.8	10.0	86.1	148.8	10.0	88.2	176.0	10.0

NOTE: In this and following tables, percent distributions may not sum to 100 because of rounding. Dollars have been converted to 1998 values using the current methods CPI for all urban consumers. In providing data on income, respondents were asked to base their answers on the calendar year preceding the interview.
Source: Federal Reserve Board "1998 Survey of Consumer Finances"

◼ "As many as 15 percent of all teens may be in trouble, lost, unable to live pro-ductive lives?" This sentence is powerful rhetorically, but when you examine it, what does it really say? Where did the 15 percent come from? What about the weasel words *as many as* and *may*? How would you define "in trouble"?

4. How could you derive data from this article to argue that teenagers are not in trouble?

Task 2: Analyzing Quantitative Graphics

Peruse carefully the data shown in Table 11.1. This table presents data on the mean and median* incomes of American families, subdivided into several differ-ent categories, in the years 1989, 1992, 1995, and 1998. (All the income figures are reported in 1998 dollars, so none of the differences is due to inflation.) As we explain later in this chapter, a table like this provides an intensely rich field of data for telling different stories—in this case, stories about economic life in America. This table tells you how income and wealth are distributed in the United States, how education and race or ethnicity enter into that picture, how families' incomes tend to rise and then fall as the head of household gets older,** and how the econ-omy changed from 1989 to 1998. (When this edition went to press in 2002, 1998 was the most recent data year available; these data are compiled by the Federal Reserve Board every three years and published both on the Web and in print bul-letins.) As we later explain, when writers focus on a story told with numbers, they usually extract data from tables such as this and display the data in more dramatic forms such as line graphs, bar charts, or pie charts. The effective construction of such graphics contributes to the rhetorical effect of the writer's analysis.

For this exercise, begin looking for different stories summarized quantitatively in the table.

1. In 1989, the median income of all American families was $33,200, while the mean income was $52,200—a fairly dramatic difference. In your own words, explain why these numbers are different. What does this difference tell you about how income is distributed in America?

2. If you look at the median income of all American families in 1989, 1992, 1995, and 1998, you will discover that America had a recession in 1992 and that American families didn't recover to their 1989 position until 1998. The numbers tell the story: In 1989 the median income for all American families

---

*You will recall from your math classes that the "mean" is the average of all numbers in a specific category, while the "median" is the middle number of all the numbers arranged in ascending or descending order. Sometimes there can be a large difference between the mean and the median. Suppose you have five friends reporting their incomes over the summer. Friend 1 reports $500; friend 2 reports $1,000; friend 3 reports $1,500; friend 4 reports $2,000; and friend 5 reports $50,000 (let's say he won the lottery or received royalties on a new video game he invented). The median summer income of your friends is $1,500 (two friends made less than $1,500 and two friends made more). But the average summer income is $11,000.

**This table focuses on total family income without distinguishing between single- and dual-income families. In dual-income families, the "head of household" is considered to be the family member with the higher income.

was $33,200; in 1992 the median income dropped to $30,400, then climbed to $32,700 in 1995, and finally reached $33,400 in 1998 ($200 over 1989).

a. Now look at how families headed by high school dropouts or headed by college graduates fared during this same period. What happens to the median income for families in each of those groups?

b. Look at how families headed by white non-Hispanics fared compared to families headed by nonwhites or Hispanics during this same period. (Again look at median income.) How might you explain these different economic stories for families in each of these categories?

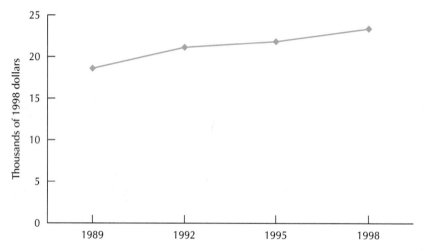

FIGURE 11.1 ▪ Income of Families Headed by Nonwhites or Hispanics, 1989–1998

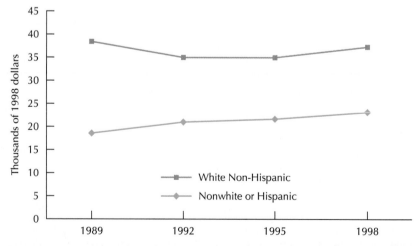

FIGURE 11.2 ▪ Income of Families Headed by White Non-Hispanics Versus Families Headed by Nonwhites or Hispanics, 1989–1998

c. As a percentage of the total population, did the number of families headed by high school dropouts increase or decrease from 1989–1998? How about the percentage of families that owned their own homes? To what extent were Americans better off financially in 1998 than they were in 1989?

3. Look at the graphs in Figures 11.1 and 11.2. One graph puts a "good news" effect on the income of nonwhites and Hispanics. The other puts a "bad news" effect on that income. Both graphs accurately portray data from Table 11.1. How do the two graphs tell different stories? What gives the two graphs different rhetorical effects? Are the graphs equally ethical?

WRITING PROJECT

Option A: Find a recent short article, editorial, or op-ed piece that relies heavily on numerical data for its argument. In your paper, analyze the writer's rhetorical choices in selecting and shaping the data. How do the writer's decisions about the selection and representation of data help persuade readers toward the writer's point of view?

In using numerical data, writers regularly make decisions about what data to select (and hence to omit) and how to display it (raw numbers versus percentages, real numbers versus adjusted numbers, pie charts versus tables, and so forth). Your task for the Option A assignment is to analyze a writer's rhetorical decisions in selecting and displaying numerical data. Vicki Alexander's paper (pp. 268–270) is an example of a student essay written for this assignment. It analyzes the *USA Today* article on teenagers that you just read.

Option B: Write a short "microtheme" (fewer than 300 words) that tells a story based on data you select from Table 11.1 or from another table provided by your instructor.* Include in your microtheme at least one quantitative visual (table, line graph, bar graph, pie chart), which should be labeled and referenced according to standard conventions.

Option B asks you to convert a numerical "story" embedded in a table into verbal language and to support it with one or more quantitative graphics. This assignment will teach you how to import a graphic into your own document and reference it properly. These are essential skills for students majoring in scientific or technical fields as well as for writers examining civic issues where quantitative data are important. Jean Fleming's microtheme (pp. 270–271) illustrates this assignment.

*We particularly recommend the tables on labor force, employment, and earnings from the reference work *Statistical Abstracts of the United States*, which is available in the reference section of any library or online at <http://www.census.gov/prod/www/statistical-abstract-us.html>

UNDERSTANDING NUMERICAL ANALYSIS

What Do We Mean by "Data"?

Before we discuss more specifically the basic tools of data analysis and the rhetorical strategies that get data to tell their stories, we need to explain what we mean by "data" and where they fit into our picture of reality. *Data* are representations, in the form of numbers, words, or graphics, of facts or events in the real world. In its raw form, each piece of data represents one fact or event. For example, each piece of raw data used to calculate the Consumer Price Index (CPI) represents the current price of one of several hundred types of consumer goods based on samples from a variety of stores. Similarly, the wealth distribution data in Table 11.1 is based on raw data derived from thousands of interviews with a random sample of American families.

Data are rarely used in raw form. Their power derives from our ability to compress and combine them to express a profusion of raw data as a single number. Consider how data become progressively transformed in the process of creating the Consumer Price Index. Figure 11.3 shows how data are gradually transformed from raw data to intermediate data to cumulative data to comparative data. The resulting CPI is a single number that represents a given year's price level as compared to a previously established base year. An increase in the CPI means that inflation has occurred.

The value of a statistic such as the CPI is that it can make a powerful generalization about what is happening in the world. The CPI, for example, functions as a gauge by which to measure increases in the cost of living. Workers in many industries use the CPI to determine whether their wages are keeping up with inflation. If you were a union worker arguing for increased wages at the Amalgamated Mudflaps factory, a line graph plotting percentage increase of wages against the rate of inflation could convey the workers' plight in a powerful "see-the-story-in-one-glance" way (see Figure 11.4 for a hypothetical example).

FIGURE 11.3 ■ Types of Data Used to Create Consumer Price Index (CPI)

Raw Data	Bread X	Detergent Y
Store A	$1.04	$1.89
Store B	$1.29	$1.75
Store C	$1.43	$1.59
Intermediate Data	**Bread X**	**Detergent Y**
Average Price		
Stores A–Z	$1.25	$1.74
Cumulative Data		
Combined average current price of all products.		
Comparative Data		
Current average combined price of all sampled products measured against average combined price of similarly sampled products in months or years past; expressed as percentage of current year over a specified base year.		

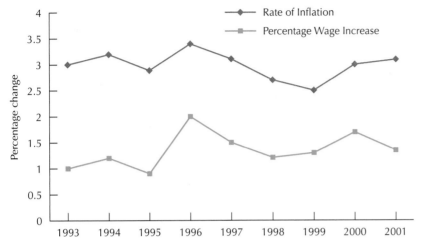

FIGURE 11.4 ■ Rate of Inflation Versus Percentage Increase in Wages at Amalgamated Mudflaps, 1993–2001

Basic Tools of Data Analysis

In this section, we discuss some of the most common tools for data analysis and offer advice on when to use them and how to read them. We look specifically at tables, line graphs, bar graphs, and pie charts and discuss the rhetorical effects created by each. For illustration, we show you how each of these kinds of quantitative graphics can be used to tell a story about the distribution of income and wealth in America.

Tables

One of the simplest ways to make data visible to your audience is to arrange them in a table. Halfway between a picture and a list, a table presents data in columns (vertical groupings) and rows (horizontal groupings), thereby allowing us to see relationships relatively quickly.

When you read a quantitative table, avoid the temptation simply to plunge into all the numbers. After you've read the title and headings to make basic sense of what the table is telling you, try randomly selecting several numbers in the table and saying aloud what those numbers mean to be sure you understand what the table is really about. For example, in Table 11.1, which you have already examined in some detail, you might choose the row for a family whose head of household is less than 35 years old. In 1989 the median income for this group of families was $26,600, while the mean income was $35,500. Families in this group accounted for 28.1 percent of the total number of families participating in the 1989 survey.

Dense tables, such as Table 11.1, contain dozens of potential stories, none of which is highlighted. Analysts pore over such tables in close detail, looking for all the stories the tables tell. If you want to use a table rather than a graph or chart to highlight one story for your readers, you can do so by constructing a smaller table that isolates just the data relevant to your story. If, for example, you want to show how a person's income level tends to rise with level of education, you could construct a table like Table 11.2.

TABLE 11.2 ▨   Median Income of Families by Education Level of Head of Household, 1989, 1992, 1995, and 1998

Education of Head	Median Income (in Thousands of 1998 Dollars)			
	1989	1992	1995	1998
No high school diploma	17.3	14.0	15.3	15.2
High school diploma	29.2	26.9	27.3	29.4
Some college	37.2	31.6	32.7	35.5
College degree	53.1	51.5	49.1	54.7

This small table focuses attention on just those data that tell your story: the more educated you are in America, the more money you tend to make. It also shows that people with college degrees fully recovered from the 1992 recession, while people in other categories did not recover or just barely recovered.

For Writing and Discussion

It is obvious from Table 11.1 that income in the United States is unequally distributed. Looking at the table we see that median and mean income vary depending on age, education levels, race and ethnicity, job status, housing status, and net worth. Much political debate is focused on how to interpret this inequality. Does the unequal distribution of income suggest that America is an unjust society or not? Using the information contained in Table 11.1, which pieces of data would you point toward to argue that the distribution of income raises serious questions about social justice? Which data from the table suggest that the distribution of income does not raise serious questions about justice?

Line Graphs

Line graphs can tell a story much more dramatically than a table because we can often see the significance of a line graph at first glance. A line graph achieves this effect by converting numerical data into a series of points on a grid and connecting them to create flat, rising, or falling lines. The result gives us a picture of the relationship between the variables represented on the horizontal and vertical axes. Although they are extremely economical, graphs can't convey the same richness of information that tables can. They are most useful when your focus is on a single relationship that tells a significant story.

To illustrate how graphs work, consider Figure 11.5, which contains a graphic representation of one relationship from the data in Table 11.1—in this case, median family income and its relationship to the age of the head of household.

To determine what this graphic is telling you, you must first clarify what's represented on the two axes. By convention, the horizontal axis of a graph contains the predictable, known variable that has no surprises—what researchers call the "independent variable." In this case the horizontal axis represents "Age of head" and is arranged predictably by years in ascending order. The vertical axis contains the unpredictable variable that forms the graph's story—what researchers call the "dependent variable"—in this case, the median income of families in each age

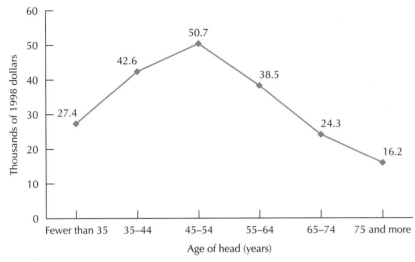

FIGURE 11.5 ■ 1998 Median Income by Age of Head of Household

category.* As the graph shows, the median income for a family with a head of household less than 35 years old is $27,400. For a family with a head of household between 45 and 54 years old, however, the median income is much higher—$50,700. For a family with a head of household who is 75 or more years old, however, median income is only $16,200.

So what does this graph tell us? In simplest terms, it tells us that people generally have low income early in life, high income in the middle, and low income in retirement. Young families, with individuals just beginning their careers, often have trouble making ends meet. Later in life, after they have become established in their careers, income levels rise. Finally, people who have retired earn no salary but still receive some income in the form of social security, pension payments, stock dividends, or interest payments on savings. Political conservatives often use this relationship to argue that the inequality of income in the United States is not a significant social problem. They argue that the inequality of income simply reflects a natural pattern of lifetime income earnings. The average person in America will get his or her share of the American earnings pie during the high earning years of late middle age.

For Writing and Discussion

The graph in Figure 11.5 argues that individuals make more money as their careers advance. But what happens in old age? Return to Table 11.1 and look at the difference between the median and the mean income for families headed
(continued)

*If we said, "The longer Jim stays on the Internet, the angrier his dad gets," we'd plot "Length of time on the Internet" on the horizontal axis and "Dad's anger level" (measured, say, in number of angry looks per minute) on the vertical axis. We know what goes on the horizontal axis: a time sequence (30 minutes, 45 minutes, 60 minutes, 75 minutes, 90 minutes, etc.). This is the predictable variable. We plot "Dad's anger level" on the vertical axis. This is the unknown, new information that the graph tells us. Does Dad explode after 60 minutes?

by persons aged 65–74. What do you think is the main source of income for persons below the median (that is, for half of all American families in that age bracket)? Why is the mean income in this bracket so much higher than the median? What do you imagine is the main source of income for families in this age category as they get further and further above the median?

Another powerful use of line graphs is to chart two or more variables on the same graph so that readers can instantly see different patterns for each variable. This is the strategy we use in Figure 11.2 where we plot the income patterns for both white non-Hispanics and for nonwhites or Hispanics on the same axes. Although it is good news that the income of nonwhites or Hispanics is slowly rising (the story of the bottom line in Figure 11.2), it remains bad news that the discrepancy between whites and people of color is so great (the story of the difference between the two lines in Figure 11.2).

Bar Graphs

Bar graphs use bars of varying lengths, extending either horizontally or vertically, to contrast two or more quantities. As with any graphic presentation, begin by reading the title, which tells you what is being compared. Most bar graphs also have *legends,* which explain what the different features on the graph represent. Bars are typically distinguished from each other by use of different colors, shades, or patterns of crosshatching.

The bar graph in Figure 11.6 is based on data contained in Table 11.1. The title tells us that the graph contrasts median income by race or ethnicity in 1989, 1992, 1995, and 1998. The legend, in turn, shows us which quantity each of the bars in the graph represents: the green bars represent median income for nonwhites or Hispanics, while the purple bars represent median income for non-Hispanic whites.

The power of bar graphs is that they can help readers make quick comparisons between different groups across a variable such as time. For example, Figure 11.6 allows us to see how income was correlated with ethnicity in four different years.

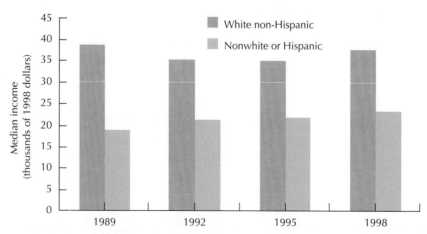

FIGURE 11.6 ■ Median Income by Race or Ethnicity of Head of Household, 1989, 1992, 1995, 1998

It shows that non-Hispanic white median income is significantly higher than the median income of nonwhites or Hispanics, even though the gap might be diminishing slightly. Liberals often use comparisons such as this to argue that the income inequality in the United States is a serious problem that is at least partially related to racial discrimination.

For Writing and Discussion

The bar graph in Figure 11.6 tells essentially the same story as the line graph in Figure 11.2. How would you describe the different effects of the two graphics in terms of drama, immediate comprehension, precision, and overall impact? Under what rhetorical circumstances would the bar graph be more effective? When might the line graph be more effective?

Pie Charts

Pie charts, as their name suggests, depict different percentages of a total (the "pie") in the form of slices. At tax time, pie charts are a favorite way of depicting all the different places that your tax dollars go. If your main point is to demonstrate that a particular portion of a whole is disproportionately large or small—perhaps you're arguing that too many of our tax dollars are spent on road construction and not enough on schools or children's health—the pie chart can demonstrate that at a glance. The effectiveness of pie charts diminishes as we add more slices, however. In most cases, you'll begin to confuse readers if you include more than five or six slices.

Figures 11.7 and 11.8 show two side-by-side pie charts based on data taken from Table 11.1. Figure 11.7 presents the percentages of family heads from the 1998 sample according to level of education. Figure 11.8 shows the percentage of

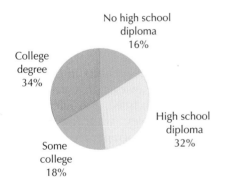

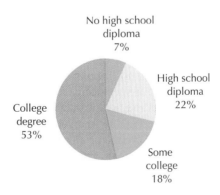

FIGURE 11.7 ■ Percentage of Families Grouped by Head of Household Education Level

FIGURE 11.8 ■ Percentage of Income Grouped by Head of Household Education Level

income received by family heads within those same education levels. Thus, from Figure 11.7 we see that 34 percent of the family heads from the 1998 sample had college degrees. From Figure 11.8, we see that that same group received 53 percent of the total income from the 1998 sample. Similarly, 16 percent of the sample had no high school education, and that group earned only 7 percent of the income. This presentation of the data contained in Table 11.1 strongly highlights the importance of a college education. It could be used further to support an argument for increased financial support for higher education.

For Writing and Discussion

Compare the pie chart in Figure 11.8 with Table 11.2 (p. 258). Both graphics deal with distribution of income by educational level of the head of household. How do the two graphics differ in rhetorical effect?

Incorporating Quantitative Graphics into Your Own Writing

Today, writers working with quantitative data usually use graphing software that automatically creates tables, graphs, or charts from data entered into the cells of a spreadsheet. (It is beyond the scope of this textbook to explain how to use these graphing utilities. For the purposes of the microtheme in this chapter, you can also make your graphics with pencil and ruler and tape them into your document.)

Designing the Graphic

When you design your graphic, your goal is to have a specific rhetorical effect on your readers, not to demonstrate all the bells and whistles available on your software. Adding extraneous data in the graphic or using such features as 3-D effects can often call attention away from the story you are trying to tell. Keep the graphic as uncluttered and simple as possible and design it so that it reinforces the point you are making in your text.

Numbering, Labeling, and Titling Graphics

In newspapers and popular magazines, writers often include graphics in boxes or sidebars without specifically referring to them in the text. However, in academic or workplace writing, graphics are always labeled, numbered, titled, and referred to directly in the text. By convention, tables are listed as "Tables," while line graphs, bar graphs, pie charts, or any other kinds of drawings or photographs are labeled as "Figures." Suppose you create a document that includes four graphics—a table, a bar graph, a pie chart, and an imported photograph. The table would be labeled Table 1." The rest of the graphics would be labeled "Figure 1," "Figure 2," and "Figure 3."

In addition to numbering and labeling, every graphic needs a title that explains fully what information is being displayed. Look back over the tables and figures in this chapter and compare their titles to the information in the graphics. In a line graph showing changes over time, for example, a typical title identifies the information on both the horizontal and vertical axes and the years covered. Bar graphs also add a "legend" explaining how the bars are coded. When you import the graphic into your own text, be consistent in where you place the title—either above the graphic or below it.

Referencing the Graphic in Your Text

Academic and professional writers follow a referencing convention called "independent redundancy." The general rule is this: The graphic should be understandable without the text; the text should be understandable without the graphic; the text should repeat the most important information in the graphic.

You can easily understand the principle of independent redundancy if you imagine yourself giving an oral presentation using graphics as slides and saying something like this:

> As you can see on the next slide, income is not evenly distributed in the United States. *[Using your pointer you point at the appropriate places on the graphic as you talk.]* Note that in 1998 the median income of persons of color was more than a third less than that of white non-Hispanics.

In the above scenario, you talk your listeners through the graphic, saying in your own words what you want them to see. The same principle applies in writing as shown in Figure 11.9.

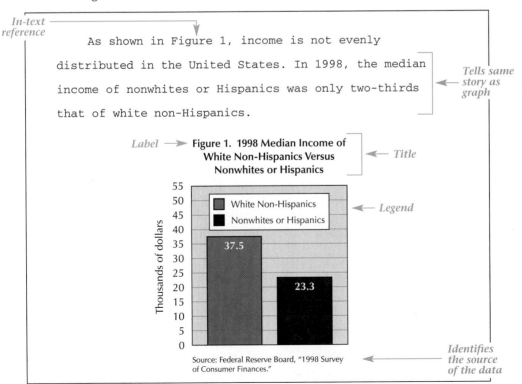

FIGURE 11.9 ■ Example of Student Text with Referenced Graphic

Shaping Data for Specific Effects

As a reader and daily consumer of numerical data, and as a writer who uses numerical data, you need to be aware of how data are being selected and displayed for rhetorical effect. In the section that follows, we review several choices that writers make in shaping their data. The difference between shaping such data legitimately and shaping it intentionally to mislead an audience is a matter of degree, not kind. To put it another way, everyone inevitably *shapes* data according to his or her goals and perspectives; the question is, How much shaping is legitimate?

Using Data Selectively

Throughout this book, we've remarked on the human tendency to see the world selectively, depending upon the viewer's situation and purpose in observing or seeking out information. We've seen this principle at work in previous examples in this chapter. Figure 11.1 (p. 254), for example, focuses on the income growth of nonwhites and Hispanics from 1989 to 1998. It paints a fairly rosy picture of progress and could be part of an optimistic article on the gradual movement of minorities toward middle-class status. Figure 11.2, in contrast, adds more data—this time, the parallel data about the income of white non-Hispanics. This graphic paints a less rosy picture and could be part of a more pessimistic article showing the continuing existence of unequal income distribution by race. When you look at data as a reader, therefore, always ask: What data are *not* displayed here? What has been included and excluded from this picture?

Using Graphics for Effect

Any time you present numerical data pictorially, the potential for enhancing the rhetorical presence of your argument, or for manipulating your audience outright, increases markedly. By *presence,* we mean the immediacy and impact of your material. As you have seen, raw numbers by their nature are abstract. But numbers turned into pictures are very immediate. Graphs, charts, and tables help an audience see at a glance what long strings of statistics can only hint at.

You can have markedly different effects on your audience according to how you design and construct a graphic. For example, by coloring one variable prominently and enlarging it slightly, a graphic artist can greatly distort the importance of that variable. Although such depictions may carry warnings that they are not to scale, the visual impact is often more memorable than the warning.

One of the subtlest ways of controlling an audience's perception of a numerical relationship is through the presentation of the grids on the horizontal and vertical axes of a line graph. Consider the graph in Figure 11.10, which depicts the monthly net profits of an ice cream sandwich retailer. Looking at this graph, you'd think that the net profits of Bite O' Heaven were themselves shooting heavenward. But if you were considering investing in an ice cream sandwich franchise, you would want to consider how the graph was constructed. Note the quantity assigned to each line on the vertical axis. Although the graph does represent the correct quantities, the designer's choice of increments leads to a wildly inflated depiction of

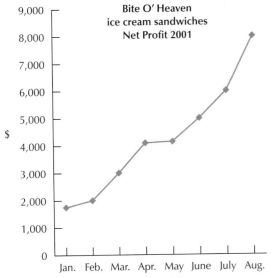

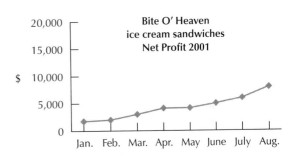

FIGURE 11.10 ■ A Line Graph That Distorts the Data

FIGURE 11.11 ■ A Line Graph That More Accurately Depicts Data

success. If the Bite O' Heaven folks had chosen a larger increment for each line on the vertical axis—say, $5,000 instead of $1,000—the company's rise in profitability would appear as in Figure 11.11. You can easily distort or overstate a rate of change on a graph by consciously selecting the quantities assigned to each scale unit on the horizontal or vertical axis.

Another way to create a rhetorical effect with a line graph is to vary the scope of time it covers. Note that the graphs in Figures 11.10 and 11.11 cover net sales from January through August. What do you think might be typical sales figures for this company from September through December?

Using Numbers Strategically

The choice and design of a graphic can markedly affect your audience's perception of your subject. You can also influence your audience through the kinds of numbers you use: raw numbers versus percentages; raw numbers versus adjusted numbers (for example, wages "adjusted for inflation"); use of a mean versus a median; or a statistical presentation versus a narrative one. The choice always depends on the audience you are addressing and the purpose you want to achieve.

One of the most frequent choices you have to make as a writer is whether to cite raw numbers or percentages, rates, or some sort of adjusted numbers. In some cases a raw number will be more persuasive than a percentage. In the summer of 2001, for example, users of Florida's beaches became panicked by shark attacks—a panic intensified by the media's use of raw numbers. A widely quoted figure was that there were 220 shark attacks off Florida beaches in the 1990s. However, if we calculated the percentage of swimmers who were attacked by sharks, the number would be infinitesimally low. Often, as in this instance, the presentation of the data shapes the identification and representation of a problem.

For Writing and Discussion

A proposal to build a new ballpark in Seattle, Washington, yielded a wide range of statistical arguments. The following statements are all reasonably faithful to the same facts:

- The ballpark will be funded by raising the sales tax from 8.2 percent to 8.3 percent for a twenty-year period.
- The sales tax increase is one-tenth of one percent.
- This increase represents an average of $7.50 per person per year—about the price of a movie ticket.
- This increase represents $750 per five-person family over the twenty-year period of the tax.
- This is a $250-million tax increase for the residents of the Seattle area.

How would you describe the costs of the proposed ballpark if you opposed the proposal? How would you describe the costs if you supported the proposal?

Readings

The first reading is taken from a question/answer column in which science writer Bryant Stamford explains how the labels on low-fat milk can mislead consumers.

■ BRYANT STAMFORD ■
UNDERSTAND CALORIES, FAT CONTENT IN FOOD

Q: *There was a story in the national news on 2 percent low-fat milk. I think I understand the* 1 *concept about the difference between fat content as weight and as calories. Something about this conversion still escapes me, however. In plain English, can you explain the conflict surrounding low-fat milk?*

—J. H., St. Johns, Mich.

A: Millions of Americans think that 2 percent milk is low in fat. The label 2 even says "low-fat." Sorry, but 2 percent milk actually is very high in fat, with 37.5 percent of its calories (kcals) coming from fat.

How can they get away with trying to pass off this fatty product as low- 3 fat? The answer has to do with how the fat content is reported. Food manufacturers who don't want you to know their products are loaded with fat will report the fat content by weight.

4   Here is a simple example: Let's assume a bottle contains 99 grams of water. Water has no calories and passes through the body quickly and easily. We add 1 gram of fat to the water, making 100 total grams. The 1 gram of fat contains calories and stays in the body after being digested. The water, in effect, serves merely as a carrier for the fat.

5   In reporting the fat content of this watery mix, we can report it by weight or by calories. The choice makes a profound difference in our perception of the mix.

6   If we report fat content by weight, we see that, because only 1 gram out of 100 is fat, the mix is only 1 percent fat, or 99 percent fat-free. This is the way a manufacturer would want you to see it, and that's why they would tell you the fat content by weight.

7   But when fat is reported by calories, it is a much different story. This product contains 9 calories, because 1 gram of fat contains 9 calories.

8   Since all 9 calories are in the form of fat, this product is 100 percent fat. The difference between reporting a product as 1 percent fat (by weight) vs. 100 percent fat (by calories) speaks for itself.

9   Now let's apply this concept to milk. Since milk is mostly water, reporting fat by weight will always grossly underestimate the actual fat content. In 2 percent milk, out of 100 grams of total weight, 2 grams will be fat. Thus, it can be reported as 98 percent fat-free.

10   It's an entirely different story when reporting fat content by calories.

11   One cup of 2 percent milk contains 5 grams of fat and 120 calories. Here is the calculation for determining fat content by calories.

12   Five grams of fat times 9 calories equal 45 calories of fat. Of the 120 total calories, 45 are from fat. Forty-five divided by 120 equals .375. Then, .375 times 100 equals 37.5 percent fat.

13   The story is just as bad for whole milk, which is 3.3 percent fat by weight, but 48 percent fat by calories.

14   You can apply this formula to other food as well.

15   Meat, for example, may contain a high proportion of water, and, therefore, reporting fat content by weight grossly underestimates the actual fat content. Your confusion may arise from the fact that there is no "typical" conversion factor, or constant, that can be applied to all food to convert the fat content by weight to fat content by calories.

16   The reason is that foods vary in water content. The greater the water content, the more diluted will be the fat content when reported by weight.

17   Thus, you must use the formula for each food to determine the actual fat content by calories.

18   The bottom line is buyer beware. Unless you are armed with a little information, chances are you will be misled every time.

Thinking Critically about "Understand Calories, Fat Content in Food"

1. In calling 2 percent milk "low fat," do you think the manufacturer is telling the truth, tweaking the data, massaging the data, or cooking the data? Why?
2. Reporting fat content as a percentage of weight or calories is analogous to numerous other statistical dilemmas. What other situations can you think of in which different ways of calculating the numbers lead to significant differences in results?

The second reading, by Vicki Alexander, was written for the assignment in this chapter. It analyzes the article on teenagers in *USA Today* on pages 250–251.

▪ VICKI ALEXANDER (STUDENT) ▪
TROUBLE WITH TEENS OR WITH NUMBERS?

The author of the *USA Today* editorial "Help Troubled Teens—Don't Forget Them" argues that the nation's teens are besieged with problems. The editorial primarily uses statistics to support its claims. Initially, the editorial may seem persuasive, but if readers examine it closely, they may discern ways the editorial distorts perceptions of the teen population.

The first specific statistic offered about teens is that "[t]wenty-two percent of them—14 million—live in poverty." This is a grim statistic, but it is hard to tell what it means. How many of these are teenagers living in families below the poverty level and how many are teenagers who are independent of their parents but not yet earning very much money? It's logical to expect that teenagers working part time or full time at low-paying jobs wouldn't earn enough money to be above the poverty level. As teens age and gain experience, their incomes will certainly increase. Thus, while this statistic may seem disturbing, it is likely that for lots of teens, their poverty is only temporary. Certainly it doesn't mean that they are "underachievers" or "misfits" as the article seems to imply.

The next statistic the editorial presents is "[m]ore than 1 million get pregnant each year." A million pregnancies sounds alarming; however, the percentage this number represents is actually surprisingly low. The percentage can be calculated by using the information in an earlier statistic that 14 million teenagers comprise 22 percent of the teen population. Rounded off, the total size of the teen population is 63 million. Therefore, the 1 million referred to here constitutes only about 1.6 percent of the teen population. The writer chooses to say 1 million rather than 1.6 percent because the raw number has a greater persuasive impact. The writer again uses only a raw number—700,000—when reporting how many teens dropped out of school last year. When this number is converted to a percentage, the statistic is surprising but only because it is so small: just about 1 percent dropped out of school.

4   The editorial's next piece of evidence to support its thesis that teens are troubled is this statement: "On Wednesday, a new survey of high school seniors showed 30 percent had used illegal drugs in the past month; 37 percent had indulged in heavy drinking." Who conducted this survey? These figures seem not to be part of the study done by the "blue-ribbon committee" identified earlier. Research can only be as credible as its source, but no source of this study is identified. Furthermore, although the editorial is supposedly about teenagers in general, this statistic focuses just on high school seniors, a quite different population. High school seniors are more likely than younger teens to use illegal drugs and excessive alcohol, so limiting the statistics to only high school seniors may falsely inflate these statistics. Other information is excluded that could also help readers better interpret the statistics on high school seniors' drug and alcohol use. What constitutes "heavy drinking"? And when was the study done? Perhaps it was conducted soon after prom or graduation, when seniors would be especially tempted to use illegal drugs or excessive alcohol at parties marking these events.

5   The statistic that "[p]eople under 21 account for more than half of all arrests in serious crimes" changes the population group once more: from all teens to just high school seniors to those up through age 20. The source of these findings is also unclear: Is it the blue-ribbon committee first cited, or another study? "[M]ore than half" is imprecise, perhaps representing a number just minimally greater than half. Also, the statistic refers to arrests, not convictions. If police officers have the same negative assumptions about teens that the writer of this editorial has, innocent teens may often be subjected to arrests which do not result in convictions.

6   The final statistic given presents information using a unit of measurement not used before in the editorial: "[T]he teen-age suicide rate is up 150 percent since 1950." Why didn't the writer use raw numbers or percentages as elsewhere in the editorial? According to the U.S. Department of Health and Human Services, the teen suicide rate when this editorial was published was .01 percent, that is, one-hundredth of 1 percent. Clearly it is more alarming to say the suicide rate has gone up 150 percent than to say it has risen from .0067 percent to .01 percent. One must wonder too why the writer selected 1950 as the year for comparison. Perhaps the teen suicide rate has stayed the same or decreased in recent years, and the writer could only make the problem seem significantly worse by stretching back many decades. Finally, the suicide figures for 1950 may not be accurate. Because of the conservatism of the time, it's likely that suicide was underreported as a cause of death more often than it would be now.

Ideally, teens would not have any of the problems referred to in this *USA Today* editorial. Teens deserve social support even if only a few of them are poor, pregnant, drug or alcohol addicted, or convicted of crimes. Clearly, even one teen suicide is too many. Yet this is not the writer's point. Instead, the writer distorts readers' perceptions of the teen population. By changing the units of statistical measurement, the identity of the population being studied, and the source of the statistics, as well as by omitting important information that can put the statistics about teens into perspective, the editorial reinforces falsely negative stereotypes of most teenagers.

7

Thinking Critically about "Trouble with Teens or with Numbers?"

1. Read again the article that student writer Vicki Alexander analyzes—the *USA Today* editorial "Help Troubled Teens—Don't Forget Them" (pp. 250–251). Most readers find that article persuasive in its depiction of teenagers in trouble. How does the editorialist use statistics persuasively?

2. How does Vicki Alexander's analysis undermine the persuasiveness of the editorial's statistics?

3. Which parts of Alexander's analysis seem strongest to you? Which parts are weakest?

The third reading, by student writer Jean Fleming, illustrates the Option B microtheme assignment on page 255. It is based on the data in Table 11.1.

▪ JEAN FLEMING (STUDENT) ▪
HOW WELL-OFF ARE RETIRED PEOPLE?

Data provided by the federal government's survey of family income show that income drops off remarkably when a person retires. As shown in Figure 1, the median income for working families in 1998 was $40,500 (if the head of household worked for an employer) or $52,700 (if the head of household was self-employed). In contrast, median income for retired families in 1998 was $19,300. Since 1989, the median income of retired persons has been only slightly higher than that of high school dropouts and some $13,000 below the average for all American families (see Figure 2). Of course, all retired persons aren't pinching pennies. The mean income of retired families ($32,600 in 1998) is considerably higher than the median. This figure means that wealthy retired persons supplement social security with income from stocks, real estate, or other investments. But by definition half of all retired families have incomes below the median, and they must be living on very tight budgets.

1

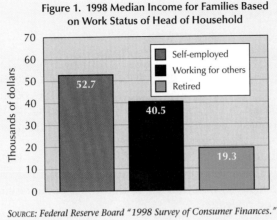

Figure 1. 1998 Median Income for Families Based
on Work Status of Head of Household

SOURCE: *Federal Reserve Board "1998 Survey of Consumer Finances."*

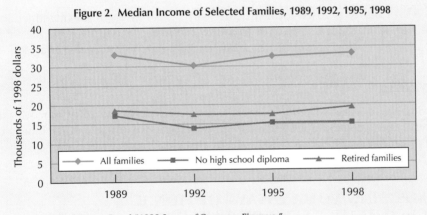

Figure 2. Median Income of Selected Families, 1989, 1992, 1995, 1998

SOURCE: *Federal Reserve Board "1998 Survey of Consumer Finances."*

Thinking Critically about "How Well-Off Are Retired People?"

1. Fleming's purpose is to show that many retired people live on low budgets. How effective is Fleming's choice of statistics to support her point? How effective are her bar graph and line graph?

2. In trying to help readers understand the significance of the low income of retired people, Fleming decided to compare the median income of families whose head of household is retired with that of families headed by high school dropouts and with "all families." How effective do you find these choices?

COMPOSING YOUR ESSAY—OPTION A, ARTICLE ANALYSIS

Generating and Exploring Ideas

The first step in composing this essay is to analyze your chosen article carefully, isolating all the statistics. Pick out representative examples of data that contribute to the persuasiveness of the article. Then consider alternative ways that the data could have been presented—as raw numbers, say, rather than as percentages, or as a line graph rather than a pie chart.

Pay particular attention to what is not included and to various contexts that may suggest a different interpretation or explanation of the data from that presented in the article. Also question the source of the data, looking especially at its recency, scope, and relevance.

Shaping and Drafting

This essay calls for a closed-form structure with a clear thesis in the introduction. A good way to organize this essay is to follow the strategy used by Vicki Alexander, who devotes a paragraph or block of paragraphs to each statistic she analyzes.

Revising

Once you've developed a thesis and written a draft, you are ready to road-test it on readers to determine what works and what is confusing or undeveloped. The Guidelines for Peer Reviews can serve as a checklist for your revision.

COMPOSING YOUR ESSAY—OPTION B, MICROTHEME BASED ON TABLE 11.1

Generating and Exploring Ideas

You get ideas for this microtheme by studying the table and looking for a "story" embedded within it. Your goal is to tell that story verbally in a brief, closed-form essay headed by a thesis statement that is supported primarily by numerical data drawn from the table. You will then create one or more graphics to tell the same story visually. At the idea-generating stage, discuss the table with classmates, looking for interesting patterns and relationships.

Shaping and Drafting

Your challenge is to tell the same story twice—once verbally and once visually. The fun of this assignment is designing the graphic—trying to decide whether to use a table, line graph, bar graph, or pie chart. Your decision turns on what you are trying to show, what relationships are important, and how many variables are involved. If you use a graphing program on your computer, you can quickly make a number of different versions to try out on readers. (If you are making graphics by hand, sketch them quickly at first so that you can have several different versions to show readers.) Without telling the reader what the graphic is supposed to show, ask him or her to explain the graphic's message to you. Any confusion your reader has will provide clues on how to make the graphic clearer and more effective.

Revising

At the revising stage, make sure that the text and the graphic tell the same story and that each tells the story independently (the principle of *independent redundancy*). Check to be sure that you have properly referenced the graphic in the text and that the graphic has a label, number, and title. Position the graphic neatly into the text so that the whole document is visually attractive.

The principle of *independent redundancy* is explained on p. 263.

▪ GUIDELINES FOR PEER REVIEWS ▪

Instructions for peer reviews are provided in Chapter 18 (pp. 490–496).

For the Writer

Prepare two or three questions you would like your peer reviewer to address while responding to your draft. The questions can focus on some aspect of your draft that you are uncertain about, on one or more sections where you particularly seek help or advice, on some feature that you particularly like about your draft, or on some part you especially wrestled with. Write out your questions and give them to your peer reviewer along with your draft.

For the Reviewer

I. Read the draft at a normal reading speed from beginning to end. As you read, do the following:

    A. Place a wavy line in the margin next to any passages that you find confusing, that contain something that doesn't seem to fit, or that otherwise slow down your reading.

    B. Place a "Good!" in the margin next to any passages where you think the writing is particularly strong or interesting.

II. Read the draft again slowly and answer the following questions by writing down brief explanations of your answers.

Assignment Option A

    A. Introduction:

        1. Can you suggest improvements to the title to better focus the paper and pique interest?

        2. Where does the writer briefly summarize the article? How could the summary be improved?

3. The introduction should end with a clear thesis about how the use of statistics creates a rhetorical effect. How could the thesis be improved?

B. Analysis:

1. Where does the author choose specific examples of statistics from the article? How does the author analyze these examples? Where could the analysis be improved?

2. To what extent do you agree with the author's analysis? What additional details from the article do you think the author should discuss? Where are the ideas weak, undeveloped, or confusing?

3. How could the author improve the clarity or structure of the draft?

Assignment Option B

A. Text:

1. What is the thesis of the microtheme?

2. What data does the writer select from the table to support the thesis?

3. Is the "story" or thesis of the microtheme true to the table? Is the use of numbers accurate?

4. Where does the writer tell verbally the same story told by the graphic? (This is the principle of redundancy.)

5. How and where does the writer clearly reference each graphic in the text?

B. Graphics:

1. What kind of graphics has the author chosen (table, line graph, bar graph, pie chart)? How appropriate is the author's choice? What story does each graphic tell? Is it the same story told in the microtheme's text? How might the author improve the rhetorical impact of each graphic?

2. How would you improve the clarity of each graphic with regard to label, numbering, title, legends, and other details?

3. Does the graphic adequately make its case without the text? (This is again the principle of redundancy.)

III. If the writer has prepared questions for you, respond to his or her inquiries.

IV. Sum up what you see as the chief strengths and problem areas of this draft:

A. Strengths

B. Problem Areas

V. Read the draft one more time. Place a check mark in the margin wherever you notice problems in grammar, spelling, or mechanics (one check mark per problem).

CHAPTER 12

Analyzing a Short Story

ABOUT LITERARY ANALYSIS

You've no doubt had more than one experience analyzing literature. For some students, such analysis is fun. It gives you a welcome break from densely packed textbook pages while stimulating your imagination. For others, the very word *literary* might trigger memories of mystifying class discussions and teachers' seemingly arbitrary decrees about the "hidden meaning" of something. Our goal in this chapter is to demonstrate that analyzing literature need not be either mystifying or arbitrary. In fact, analyzing literature is quite similar to analyzing just about any type of text or event: asking questions that you think will intrigue your reader as well as yourself and studying the text to find what answers it provides. What's different about literary analysis is that it opens up imaginative possibilities that can entertain and delight readers as well as inform them.

To begin understanding literary analysis, try to think of literature not so much as a collection of great books to be read, but rather as a way of reading. Or, put another way, you can choose to read anything literally or literarily. When you read something *literally,* you attempt to reduce its meaning to one clear set of statements and disregard other possible ways of reading the text. When you read something *literarily,* you read it playfully and openly, trying to see in it a wide range of possible meanings.

To help you understand the distinction we're drawing, consider the following analogy: A literal reading of an imaginative text is like a packaged bus tour of an unfamiliar city. Picture a bus filled with out-of-town conventioneers going from one landmark to the next, but missing the details of the city's lived life. The bus turns here and there, sweeping past a neighborhood market, past cemeteries dotted with crumbling headstones, past the smells of coffee, fish, spicy foods, and bakery goods. These tourists may catch a brief glimpse of a vibrant city waiting to be explored, but mostly they are looking ahead to the standardized comforts of their Quality Inn, Hilton, or Sheraton rooms.

The first step in moving beyond a literal to a literary understanding of a text, or a city, is to get off the bus. Stop being a tourist and become instead a traveler. Open yourself up to the otherness of a text the way travelers on foot open up to the sights and sounds of a new place to understand the diverse ways that humans create their lives. Reading literarily, experience the text on its own terms; that is, read it carefully, noticing and examining your reactions to what you have read. Travelers aren't driven by a desire to have been somewhere so they can tell others that they were there. Instead, they are driven by curiosity, a sense of wonder, a knack for recognizing resemblances in a world of apparent differences, and a capacity for being enthralled by the differences they do find.

To be a traveler rather than a tourist, you need to be an active participant in the process of constructing meaning from a text. Whereas tourists tend to write brief "We're here!" notes on postcards to friends, travelers are more likely to keep extensive journals to help them remember and understand their experiences. They reflect on what they see and on relationships between what they see, do, and feel one day to what they've seen, done, or felt in the past or to what others have reported seeing, doing, and feeling in the same place.

In this way, travelers interpret what they experience. Interpretive writing differs from other forms of writing most notably in its degree of tentativeness. An interpretation focuses on an ambiguous aspect of a text or experience and says, "Here's what I think is most probable." Unlike a traditional argument, which obligates the writer to refute other points of view, an interpretation may simply point out alternative explanations of the ambiguity and then focus on the writer's own interpretation and the evidence that supports it.

EXPLORING LITERARY ANALYSIS

As we have noted, any sort of text can be read either literally or literarily. However, texts do tend to invite one kind of reading over another. The following Navajo legend contains several signals that invite us to read literarily rather than literally. As you read through this piece, note where those signals occur.

R e a d i n g

▪ RETOLD BY EVELYN DAHL REED ▪
THE MEDICINE MAN

There is a telling that, in the beginning, when the animals first came up from the darkness to live above the ground, Coyote was sent ahead by Thought Woman to carry a buckskin pouch far to the south.   1

"You must be very careful not to open the pouch," she told him, "or you will be punished."   2

For many days, Coyote ran southward with the pouch on his back. But the world was new, and there was nothing to eat along the way, so he grew very hungry. He wondered if there might be food in the pouch. At last, he took it from his back and untied the thongs. He looked inside and saw nothing but stars. Of course, as soon as he opened the pouch the stars all flew up into the sky, and there they are to this day.   3

"Now look what you've done," said Thought Woman. "For now you shall always get into trouble everywhere you go."   4

And because Coyote disobeyed, he was also made to suffer with the toothache. When the other animals were asleep, he could only sit and howl at the stars. Thus, he has been crying ever since the beginning of the world.   5

6   Sometimes he would ask the other animals to cure him, but they would only catch the toothache from him, and they, too, would cry.

7   One day he met Mouse, who lived in a little mound under the chaparral bush. "Friend Mouse," begged Coyote, "can you cure me of this toothache?"

8   Now it happened that while digging underground, as is his habit, Mouse had come upon a sweet-smelling root and had put it with the other herbs in the pouch he always carried. He was said to be very wise in the use of herbs.

9   "I don't know," said Mouse, "but I have just found a new root, and it may be that it will help you." He rubbed the root on Coyote's swollen cheek, and in a little while the toothache was gone.

10   This is how it happened that coyotes never hunt or kill field mice.

Thinking Critically about "The Medicine Man"

1. List the signals in the text that led you to read this story literally as opposed to literally. Summarize the most important differences between how you read this story and how you read the introduction to this chapter.

2. Devise questions about the legend that you think might produce different responses among your classmates. For example: Why is the woman named Thought Woman? Why is Thought Woman a female and not a male?

3. Explain why you think these questions will evoke different responses.

WRITING PROJECT

Your writing project for this chapter has two parts—a formal essay about a short story and a series of reading log entries that will prepare you to write your essay. Your entries in your reading log will give you an opportunity to explore your own understanding of the story, pose questions about it, and then compare your ways of reading and responding to it with your classmates' experiences of it. This process of writing about and discussing the story will help you find places in the text where readers' understandings differ, where ambiguities lead to uncertainties about some aspect of the story. These places will prompt *interpretive questions*— that is, questions for which the text contains evidence that supports more than one good thesis regarding, for example, events, motives, or meaning. Such questions are the perfect starting points for an interpretive paper like the one called for in the following assignment.

For help choosing or framing such questions, you may wish to review the advice in Chapter 1 about posing interesting, problematic, and significant questions.

Essay Assignment

Pose an interpretive question about a short story and respond to it analytically, showing your readers where and how the text of the story supports your interpretation. In the introduction to your essay, pose an interesting, problematic, and significant question about the story, one that can be answered several different ways according to the evidence in the text. Look for a question that might lead to differences in opinion among your classmates and that offers readers new insights into the story. Your task in this assignment is not to discover the right way to interpret the text, but to explain *your* way of reading some aspect of it.

Using a closed-form structure, present your thesis about the story and your supporting arguments. Before you give your thesis, make clear just what question you are putting to the text and why. It is this question that engages your readers' interest and makes them look forward to your analysis. Then, in the body of your paper, explain your own responses to this question, contrasting your answer with other possible interpretations that have been proposed by your classmates or that you yourself have considered. Without disputing the alternative interpretations, concentrate on showing your reader how you arrived at *your* interpretation and why you think that that interpretation is valuable. Use details from the story for support.

Reading Log Assignment

To help you settle on a good question for your paper and to develop and share ideas, we have interspersed throughout the chapter a series of reading log questions for you to use in exploring the text. Your reading log will help you the most if you write in response to each freewriting task when you come to it in the text. (There are fifteen in all.) The sequence and timing of the early entries are important, so do not read ahead. Keep your notebook and pen with you as you read, and when you come to a reading log question, stop and respond to it at that time.

The reading log entries will help you pose a good question about your assigned short story. Good literary questions call attention to problematic details of the text, stimulate conversation, and provoke readers to return to the text to reread and rethink. You know you have a good question if your classmates disagree about the answer and contribute their own differing views to the conversation. Sharing your reading log entries with classmates will help you generate and sustain a productive discussion about the short story.

UNDERSTANDING LITERARY ANALYSIS
The Truth of Literary Events

As an introduction to literary analysis, let's return to "The Medicine Man" and consider several questions that it, and other texts of its sort, pose to the reader. First, in what sense is the story true? What advantages are there to expressing a view of truth in a literary, rather than in a literal, way? Why might someone choose to tell such a story rather than approach the world scientifically? What other stories does "The Medicine Man" remind you of? How is it different from those stories? How are the characters in the story like and unlike characters you've known in real life?

"The Medicine Man" is immediately recognizable as literary; it's difficult, if not impossible, to read it literally. Animals can't talk, and galaxies can't be carted about in a buckskin pouch. We either make a leap of faith and license the author to play fast and loose with our conventional understanding of reality, or we put the story down, dismayed that anyone could think we'd be gullible enough to buy this twaddle.

The events of the story are presented to us as if they actually happened. We know better, but we go along with the ruse in order to enjoy the story. We know that when we read these sorts of texts, we can't demand a one-to-one correspondence between the words we read and the things, persons, and events to which they supposedly refer. We must read instead with what the poet Coleridge called "a Willing Suspension of Disbelief."

Suspending disbelief does not mean erasing it. While we're reading literarily, we are to some degree consciously suppressing skepticism and nagging doubts, leftovers of our literal-minded selves. Both ways of looking at the story—literal and literary—are open to us, and we consciously choose one over the other. While we're reading "The Medicine Man," we never really forget that coyotes can't talk. But if coyotes could talk, we can imagine them talking as this coyote talks.

Choosing between a literary and a literal reading is similar to looking at an optical illusion. Consider, for example, the photograph in Figure 12.1 of painter

FIGURE 12.1 ■ Muralist Richard Haas's 1983 *Trompe l'oeil* Classical Alcove on Cincinnati's Brotherhood Building

Courtesy of Richard Haas, Inc. Photography by Peter Mauss/Esto Photographics.

Richard Haas's *trompe l'oeil* (fool-the-eye) mural on the Brotherhood Building in downtown Cincinnati. In the center of one of the seven-story building's flat walls, Haas has used paint to "carve out" an alcove complete with marble statue and eternal flame honoring Roman general Cincinnatus. Passersby (and people who view the photo) know that the alcove's curves—its sweeping staircase, multiple columns, domed roof, and upward curling smoke—are an illusion. (*This can't be classical Rome. Look at all the cars driving by.*) Yet the images persuade onlookers to set aside their skepticism and see something other than what they know to be physical reality. As we gaze, we conspire with the artist to compose the illusory image he designed for us. The façade is flat, but as we look, it curves inward; the tension between these perceptions makes looking itself pleasurable.

So it is with the language of literature. The both/and principle that allows us to see the roundness of images carved into a flat façade allows us to become engrossed in the events in a fictional story, while at the same time standing back from the story to analyze how it works. To read literarily isn't to cease reading literally as much as it is to read both/and—*both* literally *and* literarily. The image that fools the eye in Figure 12.1 is both a painted wall of an ordinary building in present-day Cincinnati and a deep marble alcove honoring a hero of ancient Rome.

Reading the Story

We ask you now to read the short story your instructor has designated for this assignment. Let the following reading log tasks help you become a traveler in the story rather than a tourist. Task 1 asks you to stop several times along the way as you read. Tasks 2 and 3 should be written immediately after you finish reading.

Reading Log Task 1: As you read your assigned story, stop at several points and predict what you think will happen in the rest of the story. Make your first stop fairly early in the story, choose a second stopping place in the middle, and stop a third time near the end. In each case, predict what is going to happen next and note what in the text causes you to make your prediction. Freewrite for three or four minutes each time you stop.

Reading Log Task 2: As soon as you finish your reading, write down your immediate responses to the text—how it made you feel or think, what emotions it triggered, what issues it raised. Freewrite for five minutes.

Reading Log Task 3: Write down (a) what most interested you about the story and (b) the most important question you're left with after reading the text. Freewrite for a couple of minutes after several minutes of reflecting.

For Writing and Discussion

As a whole class or in small groups, share your responses to the reading log tasks. Because you need to begin your formal essay for this assignment with a problematic question, pay particular attention to your classmates' responses to (b) in Task 3—the most important question raised by the text. Perhaps you have a tentative answer that you would like to propose to someone else's question.

Writing (about) Literature

We put "about" in parentheses in this heading because in a sense, to write about literature is to write literature. When you read literarily you are an active cocreator of the text just as a musician is a cocreator of a concerto. Musicians and literary readers don't completely reinvent composers' notes and authors' words every time they play or read them. Composers and writers provide abundant cues to signal how they wish their works to be played or read and to limit possible interpretations of their works. But in the process of performing another's text or music, readers and musicians give those words and notes a meaning unique to that particular performance. And in some cases, their renditions may depart considerably from the originator's intentions.

This reading as performance is quite different from the more passive process of literal reading. Whereas the literal reader expects to find unambiguous, universally shared meaning in the text, the literary reader anticipates having to create meaning, which then must be justified to other readers and modified by them. For the literal reader, meaning is a commodity that is extracted intact from the text much as gold nuggets are sluiced from a stream. For the literary reader, meaning is more like a quilt constructed from bits and pieces of the text by many people who consult and argue and admire each other's skill and change each other's minds about which pieces to include and where to put them.

To participate in the reading process actively, to "write" your version of a text, you need to know the kinds of questions you might ask of it. To help you, we briefly summarize five critical elements of a literary text and the kinds of questions each element suggests.

For additional discussion of these elements and of open-form writing in general, refer to Chapter 7 and Chapter 20.

Asking Questions about Plot

Plot refers to the sequence of critical events in the story. The key term here is *critical*. A plot summary does not include everything that happens in a story; it focuses on the elements that most directly move the action of the story forward. One method of analyzing the plot is to begin by identifying what you see as the most critical single event or moment in a story. What is the most pivotal point, the one that prior events lead up to and that subsequent events derive from? Different readers are apt to pick different moments, indicating differences in the way they read the story. Your task is to identify your own choice and to be prepared to defend it. Remember, you are *performing* the story, not trying to figure out some unambiguous right meaning. As long as you have a rationale for your decision, you are acting as a literary critic.

Reading Log Task 4: What is the single most important moment or event in your assigned story? Why do you see this moment as important or crucial? Freewrite for about ten minutes.

For Writing and Discussion

As a whole class or in small groups, share your responses to Task 4. Which events did you choose and what are your arguments for selecting them? Take notes about how your classmates' interpretations differ.

Asking Questions about Setting

Although a setting is sometimes little more than a backdrop, like a black curtain behind a speaker on a stage, it can also serve to amplify or help explain the events and motivations of a story. Sometimes the setting acts as a symbol or serves the same function in a story that theme music serves in a movie, underscoring the text's primary themes and moods. A story could be set at the edge of a dark forest, on an ascent up a mountain, or in an inner city, with action moving back and forth between remote vacant lots and a warm kitchen. Sometimes setting plays an active role in the text, functioning almost as a character. A setting could thwart the protagonist's efforts to bring about change or to survive; for example, the collapse of a bridge could prevent a character from crossing a river. Does setting play a role in the story you are analyzing? If so, how would you characterize that role? Could you picture the events of the text taking place in a significantly different setting? Why or why not?

> **Reading Log Task 5:** What is worth noting about your assigned story's setting? What is the setting? How does it change? Consider multiple aspects of time, location, atmosphere, and so forth to discern the role that setting plays in the unfolding events. Freewrite for ten minutes on your ideas about the importance of setting in the story.

Asking Questions about Characters

Characters are the people who make the decisions that forward the plot and whose fortunes change as a result of the plot. You can understand characters in a text only in relationship to each other and to the direction of change in the text. The major character, sometimes called the *protagonist,* is typically the one most responsible for forwarding the plot. In action stories, these characters are pretty static: Dirty Harry or Batman may undergo occasional physical changes and disguises, but their characters tend not to grow or deepen. In other kinds of stories, the major character may change significantly in terms of fortune, insight, or understanding. Which characters change in the story you are examining? How do they change? Which characters do not change? Why do the characters change or not change?

To examine the characters' relationships with each other, you might start with the protagonist and consider the other characters according to how they help or hinder the protagonist. Characters may contribute to the plot by overt action or inaction, by recognizing or failing to recognize something of significance, by adapting to the situation of the story or by being inflexible. They can guide or misguide the protagonist, be a friend or foe, share or threaten the protagonist's values or beliefs, and so forth. What tensions, contrasts, and differing points of view do you see among the characters?

Reading Log Task 6: Who do you think is the most important character in the story? How does this character change or grow as the story progresses? How do the other characters promote or inhibit change in the main character? How do they help you see and understand the changes? Freewrite for ten to fifteen minutes.

For Writing and Discussion

Share your reading log entries and note differences in the interpretations of various members of the class. Remember that you are not seeking the one right answer to these questions. You are trying to determine how *you* read this story.

Asking Questions about Point of View

Perhaps the toughest element to perceive in a fictional work is point of view. It does not exist out there on the page as do character and plot. Point of view is the filter through which the reader views the action of a story. In some cases the impact of point of view on your perception of a character or event is obvious; in other cases it is not. The point of view can trick you into seeing an event in a particular way that you will have to revise when you realize that the narrator's perspective was limited, biased, or ironic. Often the narrator's values and perceptions are different from those of the author; you should never assume that the narrator of the story and the author are the same.

The two primary elements of point of view are time and person. Most stories are told in the past tense, a significant number in the present tense, and a few in the future tense. An almost equal number of stories are told in the first person (in which case the narrator is usually an actor in the story, although not always the main character) as in the third person (in which case the narrator tells the story from a position outside the tale). All choices of tense and person affect the reader's perception of a story. For example, a story told in the first-person present tense ("We ride back from the hunt at dusk") has an immediacy that a story told in the third-person past ("They rode back from the hunt at dusk") does not have. You learn about a first-person narrator both from what the narrator does or says in the plot and from how the narrator tells the story—what he or she includes or omits, the sentence structure, tone, or figures of speech that he or she adopts, and so forth. A third-person narrator may be objective (the narrator sees only the external actions of characters) or omniscient (the narrator can enter the minds and feelings of various characters). Sometimes a third-person narrator is omniscient with respect to one character but objective toward others.

Narrators can provide a full and complete sense of a given character (by entering that character's mind as an omniscient narrator) or a partial view only (by observing the character from the outside). Some stories feature multiple points of view through multiple narrators. For example, one character may discover a journal written by another character or may listen to a story told by another character.

The surest path to understanding point of view is to start with your feelings and attitudes toward characters and events and then to examine the extent to which point of view contributes to those attitudes. Do you trust the narrator? Do you like the narrator? Has the narrator loaded the dice, causing you to see characters or events in strongly slanted ways? Is the narrator scrupulously objective or ironic to the point that you're not quite sure what to make of his or her observations?

To ask questions about point of view, begin by asking whether the narrative is first or third person. Then ask whether the narrator's perspective is omniscient or limited. Does the narrator reveal bias or irony? Do you feel that there is more to the story than the narrator is telling you? What does the narrator leave out? How are the narrator's perceptions different from your own?

Reading Log Task 7: What is the story's point of view? What is the narrator's role in the unfolding of events? How do the narrator's perceptions filter your understanding of the story? Do you consider the narrator's perceptions reliable, or does the text suggest alternative understandings? Is the narrator's way of seeing part of what the story is about? Freewrite for ten minutes on ideas you generate by contemplating the story's point of view.

For Writing and Discussion

Share your reading log entries with your class and note differences in interpretations.

Asking Questions about Theme

If a plot is what happens in a story, then theme is the significance of what happens. Your response to the question "So what?" after reading a story represents your notion of the story's theme. Sometimes, a theme is obvious—the main characters might discuss it, or the author might even state it outright. Often, however, a theme is veiled, and you have to infer it from the words and deeds of the characters.

One way to discover theme is simply to reflect on your immediate responses to characters or on passages that affected you particularly strongly. Consider questions such as these: How did this story change your view of something or the way you feel about something? Is this story trying to reveal something about racism? About endurance in time of trial? About growth from one phase of life to another? About appearance versus reality? About conflicts between the individual and family? About exterior loss and interior gain? About rebellion from society? About what's really valuable versus what appears to be valuable? About establishing values in a confusing world?

Reading Log Task 8: Reread your response to Task 2, your first attempt to articulate ideas related to the story's theme. Then complete one of the following statements: (a) After further reflection on my assigned story, I think the author is trying to say something to readers about _____. (b) Here is what this story makes me think about and see: _____. Freewrite for ten minutes.

You can often gain valuable insights into a story's theme by examining the connections among the various literary elements we have been discussing. These points of intersection may also help you generate significant interpretive questions.

Reading Log Task 9: Look again at the place in the story that you identified in Task 4 as its most important moment or event. (a) What role do the elements of *character* that you identified in Task 6 play in this crucial passage? (b) Do elements of the story's *setting* contribute to your understanding of the importance of this passage? How do these details add to its impact? (c) How does *point of view* contribute to a reader's sense of the importance of the events and/or description in this passage? (d) Does your analysis of the interconnections of these literary elements give you new ideas or raise new questions for you about the story's *theme*? Freewrite for ten minutes.

For Writing and Discussion

Share your responses to Reading Log Tasks 8 and 9 with your class and note differences in the ways members of the class read this story.

Readings

We include in this section two short stories to test your analytical skills. Because analyzing short stories requires you to pose your own interesting questions about a text, we do not provide any analysis questions following the stories. In addition, we include a student essay written for this chapter's assignment.

The first reading is "Everyday Use (for Your Grandmama)" by contemporary African-American writer Alice Walker. It appeared in *In Love and Trouble: Stories of Black Women* in 1973.

■ ALICE WALKER ■

EVERYDAY USE (FOR YOUR GRANDMAMA)

1   I will wait for her in the yard that Maggie and I made so clean and wavy yesterday afternoon. A yard like this is more comfortable than most people know. It is not just a yard. It is like an extended living room. When the hard clay is swept clean as a floor and the fine sand around the edges lined with tiny, irregular grooves, anyone can come and sit and look up into the elm tree and wait for the breezes that never come inside the house.

2   Maggie will be nervous until after her sister goes: she will stand hopelessly in corners, homely and ashamed of the burn scars down her arms and legs, eying her sister with a mixture of envy and awe. She thinks her sister has held life always in the palm of one hand, that "no" is a word the world never learned to say to her.

3   You've no doubt seen those TV shows where the child who has "made it" is confronted, as a surprise, by her own mother and father, tottering in weakly from backstage. (A pleasant surprise, of course: What would they do if parent and child came on the show only to curse out and insult each other?) On TV mother and child embrace and smile into each other's faces.

Sometimes the mother and father weep; the child wraps them in her arms and leans across the table to tell how she would not have made it without their help. I have seen these programs.

Sometimes I dream a dream in which Dee and I are suddenly brought together on a TV program of this sort. Out of a dark and soft-seated limousine I am ushered into a bright room filled with many people. There I meet a smiling, gray, sporty man like Johnny Carson who shakes my hand and tells me what a fine girl I have. Then we are on the stage and Dee is embracing me with tears in her eyes. She pins on my dress a large orchid, even though she has told me once that she thinks orchids are tacky flowers.   4

In real life I am a large, big-boned woman with rough, man-working hands. In the winter I wear flannel nightgowns to bed and overalls during the day. I can kill and clean a hog as mercilessly as a man. My fat keeps me hot in zero weather. I can work outside all day, breaking once to get water for washing; I can eat pork liver cooked over the open fire minutes after it comes steaming from the hog. One winter I knocked a bull calf straight in the brain between the eyes with a sledge hammer and had the meat hung up to chill before nightfall. But of course all this does not show on television. I am the way my daughter would want me to be: a hundred pounds lighter, my skin like an uncooked barley pancake. My hair glistens in the hot bright lights. Johnny Carson has much to do to keep up with my quick and witty tongue.   5

But that is a mistake. I know even before I wake up. Who ever knew a Johnson with a quick tongue? Who can even imagine me looking a strange white man in the eye? It seems to me I have talked to them always with one foot raised in flight, with my head turned in whichever way is farthest from them. Dee, though. She would always look anyone in the eye. Hesitation was no part of her nature.   6

"How do I look, Mama?" Maggie says, showing just enough of her thin body enveloped in pink skirt and red blouse for me to know she's there, almost hidden by the door.   7

"Come out into the yard," I say.   8

Have you ever seen a lame animal, perhaps a dog run over by some careless person rich enough to own a car, sidle up to someone who is ignorant enough to be kind to him? That is the way my Maggie walks. She has been like this, chin on chest, eyes on ground, feet in shuffle, ever since the fire that burned the other house to the ground.   9

Dee is lighter than Maggie, with nicer hair and a fuller figure. She's a woman now, though sometimes I forget. How long ago was it that the other house burned? Ten, twelve years? Sometimes I can still hear the flames and feel Maggie's arms sticking to me, her hair smoking and her dress falling off her in little black papery flakes. Her eyes seemed stretched open, blazed open by the flames reflected in them. And Dee. I see her standing off under the sweet gum tree she used to dig gum out of; a look of concentration on   10 her face as she watched the last dingy gray board of the house fall in toward the red-hot brick chimney. Why don't you do a dance around the ashes? I'd wanted to ask her. She had hated the house that much.

11   I used to think she hated Maggie, too. But that was before we raised the money, the church and me, to send her to Augusta to school. She used to read to us without pity; forcing words, lies, other folks' habits, whole lives upon us two, sitting trapped and ignorant underneath her voice. She washed us in a river of make-believe, burned us with a lot of knowledge we didn't necessarily need to know. Pressed us to her with the serious way she read, to shove us away at just the moment, like dimwits, we seemed about to understand.

12   Dee wanted nice things. A yellow organdy dress to wear to her graduation from high school; black pumps to match a green suit she'd made from an old suit somebody gave me. She was determined to stare down any disaster in her efforts. Her eyelids would not flicker for minutes at a time. Often I fought off the temptation to shake her. At sixteen she had a style of her own: and she knew what style was.

13   I never had an education myself. After second grade the school was closed down. Don't ask me why: in 1927 colored asked fewer questions than they do now. Sometimes Maggie reads to me. She stumbles along good-naturedly but can't see well. She knows she is not bright. Like good looks and money, quickness passed her by. She will marry John Thomas (who has mossy teeth in an earnest face) and then I'll be free to sit here and I guess just sing church songs to myself. Although I never was a good singer. Never could carry a tune. I was always better at a man's job. I used to love to milk till I was hooked in the side in '49. Cows are soothing and slow and don't bother you, unless you try to milk them the wrong way.

14   I have deliberately turned my back on the house. It is three rooms, just like the one that burned, except the roof is tin; they don't make shingle roofs any more. There are no real windows, just some holes cut in the sides, like the portholes in a ship, but not round and not square, with rawhide holding the shutters up on the outside. This house is in a pasture, too, like the other one. No doubt when Dee sees it she will want to tear it down. She wrote me once that no matter where we "choose" to live, she will manage to come see us. But she will never bring her friends. Maggie and I thought about this and Maggie asked me, "Mama, when did Dee ever *have* any friends?"

15   She had a few. Furtive boys in pink shirts hanging about on washday after school. Nervous girls who never laughed. Impressed with her they worshipped the well-turned phrase, the cute shape, the scalding humor that erupted like bubbles in lye. She read to them.

16   When she was courting Jimmy T she didn't have much time to pay to us, but turned all her faultfinding power on him. He *flew* to marry a cheap city girl from a family of ignorant flashy people. She hardly had time to recompose herself.

When she comes I will meet—but there they are!   17

Maggie attempts to make a dash for the house, in her shuffling way, but I   18
stay her with my hand. "Come back here," I say. And she stops and tries to
dig a well in the sand with her toe.

It is hard to see them clearly through the strong sun. But even the first   19
glimpse of leg out of the car tells me it is Dee. Her feet were always neat-
looking, as if God himself had shaped them with a certain style. From the
other side of the car comes a short, stocky man. Hair is all over his head a
foot long and hanging from his chin like a kinky mule tail. I hear Maggie
suck in her breath. "Uhnnnh," is what it sounds like. Like when you see the
wriggling end of a snake just in front of your foot on the road. "Uhnnnh."

Dee next. A dress down to the ground, in this hot weather. A dress so   20
loud it hurts my eyes. There are yellows and oranges enough to throw back
the light of the sun. I feel my whole face warming from the heat waves it
throws out. Earrings gold, too, and hanging down to her shoulders.
Bracelets dangling and making noises when she moves her arm up to shake
the folds of the dress out of her armpits. The dress is loose and flows, and as
she walks closer, I like it. I hear Maggie go "Uhnnnh" again. It is her sister's
hair. It stands straight up like the wool on a sheep. It is black as night and
around the edges are two long ponytails that rope about like small lizards
disappearing behind her ears.

"Wa-su-zo-Tean-o!" she says, coming in on that gliding way the dress   21
makes her move. The short stocky fellow with the hair to his navel is all
grinning and he follows up with "Asalamalakim, my mother and sister!" He
moves to hug Maggie but she falls back, right up against the back of my
chair. I feel her trembling there and when I look up I see the perspiration
falling off her chin.

"Don't get up," says Dee. Since I am stout it takes something of a push.   22
You can see me trying to move a second or two before I make it. She turns,
showing white heels through her sandals, and goes back to the car. Out she
peeks next with a Polaroid. She stoops down quickly and lines up picture
after picture of me sitting there in front of the house with Maggie cowering
behind me. She never takes a shot without making sure the house is included. When a cow comes nibbling around the edge of the yard she snaps it
and me and Maggie *and* the house. Then she puts the Polaroid in the back
seat of the car, and comes up and kisses me on the forehead.

Meanwhile Asalamalakim is going through the motions with Maggie's   23
hand. Maggie's hand is as limp as a fish, and probably cold, despite the
sweat, and she keeps trying to pull it back. It looks like Asalamalakim wants
to shake hands but wants to do it fancy. Or maybe he don't know how people shake hands. Anyhow, he soon gives up on Maggie.

"Well," I say. "Dee."   24

"No, Mama," she says. "Not 'Dee,' Wangero Leewanika Kemanjo!"   25

"What happened to 'Dee'?" I wanted to know.   26

27 "She's dead," Wangero said. "I couldn't bear it any longer, being named after the people who oppress me."

28 "You know as well as me you was named after your aunt Dicie," I said. Dicie is my sister. She named Dee. We called her "Big Dee" after Dee was born.

29 "But who was she named after?" asked Wangero.

30 "I guess after Grandma Dee," I said.

31 "And who was she named after?" asked Wangero.

32 "Her mother," I said, and saw Wangero was getting tired. "That's about as far back as I can trace it," I said. Though, in fact, I probably could have carried it back beyond the Civil War through the branches.

33 "Well," said Asalamalakim, "there you are."

34 "Uhnnnh," I heard Maggie say.

35 "There I was not," I said, "before 'Dicie' cropped up in our family, so why should I try to trace it that far back?"

36 He just stood there grinning, looking down on me like somebody inspecting a Model A car. Every once in a while he and Wangero sent eye signals over my head.

37 "How do you pronounce this name?" I asked.

38 "You don't have to call me by it if you don't want to," said Wangero.

39 "Why shouldn't I?" I asked. "If that's what you want us to call you, we'll call you."

40 "I know it might sound awkward at first," said Wangero.

41 "I'll get used to it," I said. "Ream it out again."

42 Well, soon we got the name out of the way. Asalamalakim had a name twice as long and three times as hard. After I tripped over it two or three times he told me to just call him Hakim-a-barber. I wanted to ask him was he a barber, but I didn't really think he was, so I didn't ask.

43 "You must belong to those beef-cattle peoples down the road," I said. They said "Asalamalakim" when they met you, too, but they didn't shake hands. Always too busy: feeding the cattle, fixing the fences, putting up salt-lick shelters, throwing down hay. When the white folks poisoned some of the herd the men stayed up all night with rifles in their hands. I walked a mile and a half just to see the sight.

44 Hakim-a-barber said, "I accept some of their doctrines, but farming and raising cattle is not my style." (They didn't tell me, and I didn't ask, whether Wangero (Dee) had really gone and married him.)

45 We sat down to eat and right away he said he didn't eat collards and pork was unclean. Wangero, though, went on through the chitlins and corn bread, the greens and everything else. She talked a blue streak over the sweet potatoes. Everything delighted her. Even the fact that we still used the benches her daddy made for the table when we couldn't afford to buy chairs.

46 "Oh, Mama!" she cried. Then turned to Hakim-a-barber. "I never knew how lovely these benches are. You can feel the rump prints," she said, running her hands underneath her and along the bench. Then she gave a sigh

and her hand closed over Grandma Dee's butter dish. "That's it!" she said. "I knew there was something I wanted to ask you if I could have." She jumped up from the table and went over in the corner where the churn stood, the milk in it clabber by now. She looked at the churn and looked at it.

"This churn top is what I need," she said. "Didn't Uncle Buddy whittle it out of a tree you all used to have?"   47

"Yes," I said.   48

"Uh huh," she said happily. "And I want the dasher, too."   49

"Uncle Buddy whittle that, too?" asked the barber.   50

Dee (Wangero) looked up at me.   51

"Aunt Dee's first husband whittled the dash," said Maggie so low you almost couldn't hear her. "His name was Henry, but they called him Stash."   52

"Maggie's brain is like an elephant's," Wangero said, laughing. "I can use the churn top as a centerpiece for the alcove table," she said, sliding a plate over the churn, "and I'll think of something artistic to do with the dasher."   53

When she finished wrapping the dasher the handle stuck out. I took it for a moment in my hands. You didn't even have to look close to see where hands pushing the dasher up and down to make butter had left a kind of sink in the wood. In fact, there were a lot of small sinks; you could see where thumbs and fingers had sunk into the wood. It was beautiful light yellow wood, from a tree that grew in the yard where Big Dee and Stash had lived.   54

After dinner Dee (Wangero) went to the trunk at the foot of my bed and started rifling through it. Maggie hung back in the kitchen over the dishpan. Out came Wangero with two quilts. They had been pieced by Grandma Dee and then Big Dee and me had hung them on the quilt frames on the front porch and quilted them. One was in the Lone Star pattern. The other was Walk Around the Mountain. In both of them were scraps of dresses Grandma Dee had worn fifty and more years ago. Bits and pieces of Grandma Jarrell's Paisley shirts. And one teeny faded blue piece, about the size of a penny matchbox, that was from Great Grandpa Ezra's uniform that he wore in the Civil War.   55

"Mama," Wangero said sweet as a bird. "Can I have these old quilts?"   56

I heard something fall in the kitchen, and a minute later the kitchen door slammed.   57

"Why don't you take one or two of the others?" I asked. "These old things was just done by me and Big Dee from some tops your grandma pieced before she died."   58

"No," said Wangero. "I don't want those. They are stitched around the borders by machine."   59

"That'll make them last better," I said.   60

"That's not the point," said Wangero. "These are all pieces of dresses Grandma used to wear. She did all this stitching by hand. Imagine!" She held the quilts securely in her arms, stroking them.   61

62 "Some of the pieces, like those lavender ones, come from old clothes her mother handed down to her," I said, moving up to touch the quilts. Dee (Wangero) moved back just enough so that I couldn't reach the quilts. They already belonged to her.

63 "Imagine!" she breathed again, clutching them closely to her bosom.

64 "The truth is," I said, "I promised to give them quilts to Maggie, for when she marries John Thomas."

65 She gasped like a bee had stung her.

66 "Maggie can't appreciate these quilts!" she said. "She'd probably be backward enough to put them to everyday use."

67 "I reckon she would," I said. "God knows I been saving 'em for long enough with nobody using 'em. I hope she will!" I didn't want to bring up how I had offered Dee (Wangero) a quilt when she went away to college. Then she had told me they were old-fashioned, out of style.

68 "But they're *priceless!*" she was saying now, furiously; for she has a temper. "Maggie would put them on the bed and in five years they'd be in rags. Less than that!"

69 "She can always make some more," I said. "Maggie knows how to quilt."

70 Dee (Wangero) looked at me with hatred. "You just will not understand. The point is these quilts, *these* quilts!"

71 "Well," I said, stumped. "What would *you* do with them?"

72 "Hang them," she said. As if that was the only thing you *could* do with quilts.

73 Maggie by now was standing in the door. I could almost hear the sound her feet made as they scraped over each other.

74 "She can have them, Mama," she said, like somebody used to never winning anything, or having anything reserved for her. "I can 'member Grandma Dee without the quilts."

75 I looked at her hard. She had filled her bottom lip with checkerberry snuff and it gave her face a kind of dopey, hangdog look. It was Grandma Dee and Big Dee who taught her how to quilt herself. She stood there with her hands hidden in the folds of her skirt. She looked at her sister with something like fear but she wasn't mad at her. This was Maggie's portion. This was the way she knew God to work.

76 When I looked at her like that something hit me in the top of my head and ran down to the soles of my feet. Just like when I'm in church and the spirit of God touches me and I get happy and shout. I did something I never had done before: hugged Maggie to me, then dragged her on into the room, snatched the quilts out of Miss Wangero's hands and dumped them into Maggie's lap. Maggie just sat there on my bed with her mouth open.

77 "Take one or two of the others," I said to Dee.

78 But she turned without a word and went out to Hakim-a-barber.

79 "You just don't understand," she said, as Maggie and I came out to the car.

80 "What don't I understand?" I wanted to know.

"Your heritage," she said. And then she turned to Maggie, kissed her, and said, "You ought to try to make something of yourself, too, Maggie. It's really a new day for us. But from the way you and Mama still live you'd never know it." 81

She put on some sunglasses that hid everything above the tip of her nose and her chin. 82

Maggie smiled; maybe at the sunglasses. But a real smile, not scared. After we watched the car dust settle I asked Maggie to me bring me a dip of snuff. And then the two of us sat there just enjoying, until it was time to go in the house and go to bed. 83

The second reading is David Updike's story "Summer." Updike, the son of novelist John Updike, has published several children's books as well as stories and essays in magazines such as the *New Yorker* and *Doubletake*. "Summer" is from his 1988 collection *Out on the Marsh*.

▪ DAVID UPDIKE ▪
SUMMER

It was the first week in August, the time when summer briefly pauses, shifting between its beginning and its end: the light had not yet begun to change, the leaves were still full and green on the trees, the nights were still warm. From the woods and fields came the hiss of crickets; the line of distant mountains was still dulled by the edge of summer haze, the echo of fireworks was replaced by the rumble of thunder and the hollow premonition of school, too far off to imagine though dimly, dully felt. His senses were consumed by the joy of their own fulfillment: the satisfying swat of a tennis ball, the dappled damp and light of the dirt road after rain, the alternating sensations of sand, mossy stone, and pine needles under bare feet. His days were spent in the adolescent pursuit of childhood pleasures: tennis, a haphazard round of golf, a variant of baseball adapted to the local geography: two pine trees as foul poles, a broomstick as the bat, the apex of the small, secluded house the dividing line between home runs and outs. On rainy days they swatted bottle tops across the living room floor, and at night vented budding cerebral energy with games of chess thoughtfully played over glasses of iced tea. After dinner they would paddle the canoe to the middle of the lake and drift beneath the vast, blue-black dome above them, looking at the stars and speaking softly in tones which, with the waning summer, became increasingly philosophical: the sky's blue vastness, the distance and magnitude of stars, an endless succession of numbers, gave way to a rising sensation of infinity, eternity, an imagined universe with no bounds. But the sound of the paddle hitting against the side of the canoe, the faint shadow of surrounding mountains, the cry of a nocturnal bird brought them back to the happy, cloistered finity of their world, and they paddled slowly home and went to bed. 1

2   Homer woke to the slant and shadow of a summer morning, dressing in their shared cabin, and went into the house where Mrs. Thyme sat alone, looking out across the flat, blue stillness of the lake. She poured him a cup of coffee and they quietly talked, and it was then that his happiness seemed most tangible. In this summer month with the Thymes, freed from the complications of his own family, he had released himself to them and, as interim member—friend, brother, surrogate son—he lived in a blessed realm between two worlds.

3   From the cool darkness of the porch, smelling faintly of moldy books and kerosene and the tobacco of burning pipes, he sat looking through the screen to the lake, shimmering beneath the heat of a summer afternoon: a dog lay sleeping in the sun, a bird hopped along a swaying branch, sunlight came in through the trees and collapsed on the sandy soil beside a patch of moss, or mimicked the shade and cadence of stones as they stepped to the edge of a lake where small waves lapped a damp rock and washed onto a sandy shore. An inverted boat lay decaying under a tree, a drooping American flag hung from its gnarled pole, a haphazard dock started out across the cove toward distant islands through which the white triangle of a sail silently moved.

4   The yellowed pages of the book from which he occasionally read swam before him: "... Holmes clapped the hat upon his head. It came right over the forehead and settled on the bridge of his nose. 'It is a question of cubic capacity' said he ..." Homer looked up. The texture of the smooth, unbroken air was cleanly divided by the sound of a slamming door, echoing up into the woods around him. Through the screen he watched Fred's sister Sandra as she came ambling down the path, stepping lightly between the stones in her bare feet. She held a towel in one had, a book in the other, and wore a pair of pale blue shorts—faded relics of another era. At the end of the dock she stopped, raised her hands above her head, stretching, and then sat down. She rolled over onto her stomach and, using the book as a pillow, fell asleep.

5   Homer was amused by the fact that although she did this every day, she didn't get any tanner. When she first came in her face was faintly flushed, and there was a pinkish line around the snowy band where her bathing suit strap had been, but the back of her legs remained an endearing, pale white, the color of eggshells, and her back acquired only the softest, brownish blur. Sometime she kept her shoes on, other times a shirt, or sweater, or just collapsed onto the seat of the boat, her pale eyelids turned upward toward the pale sun and then, as silently as she arrived, she would leave, walking back through the stones with the same, casual sway of indifference. He would watch her, hear the distant door slam, the shower running in the far corner of the house; other times he would just look up and she would be gone.

6   On the tennis court she was strangely indifferent to his heroics. When the crucial moment arrived—Homer serving in the final game of the final set— the match would pause while she left, walking across the court, stopping to

call the dog, swaying out through the gate. Homer watched her as she went down the path—her pale legs in the mottled light—and, impetus suddenly lost, he double faulted, stroked a routine backhand over the back fence and the match was over.

When he arrived back at the house she asked him who won, but didn't seem to hear his answer. "I wish I could go sailing," she said, looking distractedly out over the lake.

At night, when he went out to the cottage where he and Fred slept, he could see her through the window as she lay on her bed, reading, her arm folded beneath her head like a leaf. Her nightgown, pulled and buttoned to her chin, pierced him with a regret that had no source or resolution, and its imagined texture floated in the air above him as he lay in bed at night, suspended in the surrounding darkness, the scent of pine, the hypnotic cadence of his best friend's breathing.

Was it that he had known her all his life, and as such had grown up in the shadow of her subtle beauty? Was it the condensed world of the lake, the silent reverence of surrounding woods, mountains, which heightened his sense of her and brought the warm glow of her presence into soft, amorous focus? She had the hair of a baby, the freckles of a child, and the sway of motherhood. Like his love, her beauty rose up in the world that spawned and nurtured it, and found in the family the medium in which it thrived, and in Homer distilled to a pure distant longing for something he had never had.

One day they climbed a mountain, and as the components of family and friends strung out along the path on their laborious upward hike, he found himself tromping along through the woods with her with nobody else in sight. Now and then they would stop by a stream, or sit on a stump, or stone, and he would speak to her, and then they would set off again, he following her. But in the end this day exhausted him, following her pale legs and tripping sneakers over the ruts and stones and a thousand roots, all the while trying to suppress a wordless, inarticulate passion, and the last mile or so he left her, sprinting down the path in a reckless, solitary release, howling into the woods around him. He was lying on the grass, staring up into the patterns of drifting clouds when she came ambling down. "Where'd you go I thought I'd lost you," she said, and sat heavily down in the seat of the car. On the ride home, his elbow hopelessly held in the warm crook of her arm, he resolved to release his love, give it up, on the grounds that it was too disruptive to his otherwise placid life. But in the days to follow he discovered that his resolution had done little to change her, and her life went on its oblivious, happy course without him.

His friendship with Fred, meanwhile, continued on its course of athletic and boyhood fulfillment. Alcohol seeped into their diet, and an occasional cigarette, and at night they would drive into town, buy two enormous cans of Australian beer and sit at a small cove by the lake, talking. One night on the ride home Fred accelerated over a small bridge, and as the family station wagon left the ground their heads floated up to the ceiling, touched, and then came crashing down as they landed, and Fred wrestled the car back onto course. Other times they would take the motorboat out onto the lake and make sudden racing turns around buoys, sending a plume of water into the air and everything in the boat, including them, crashing to one side. But always with these adventures Homer felt a pang of absence, and was always relieved when they headed back toward the familiar cove, and home.

12   As August ran its merciless succession of beautiful days, Sandra drifted in and out of his presence in rising oscillations of sorrow and desire. She worked at a bowling alley on the other side of the lake, and in the evening Homer and Fred would drive the boat over, bowl a couple of strings, and wait for her to get off work. Homer sat at the counter and watched her serve up sloshing cups of coffee, secretly loathing the leering gazes of whiskered truck drivers, and loving her oblivious vacant stare in answer, hip cocked, hand on counter, gazing up into the neon air above their heads. When she was finished, they would pile into the boat and skim through darkness the four or five miles home, and it was then, bundled beneath sweaters and blankets, the white hem of her waitressing dress showing through the darkness, their hair swept in the wind and their voices swallowed by the engine's slow, steady growl, that he felt most powerless to her attraction. As the boat rounded corners he would close his eyes and release himself to gravity, his body's warmth swaying into hers, guising his attraction in the thin veil of centrifugal force. Now and then he would lean into the floating strands of her hair and speak into her fragrance, watching her smile swell in the pale half-light of the moon, the amber glow of the boat's rear light, her laughter spilling backward over the swirling "V" of wake.

13   Into the humid days of August a sudden rain fell, leaving the sky a hard, unbroken blue and the nights clear and cool. In the morning when he woke, leaving Fred a heap of sighing covers in his bed, he stepped out into the first rays of sunlight that came through the branches of the trees and sensed, in the cool vapor that rose from damp pine needles, the piercing cry of a blue jay, that something had changed. That night as they ate dinner—hamburgers and squash and corn on the cob—everyone wore sweaters, and as the sun set behind the undulating line of distant mountains—burnt, like a filament of summer into his blinking eyes—it was with an autumnal tint, a reddish glow. Several days later the tree at the end of the point bloomed with a sprig of russet leaves, one or two of which occasionally fell, and their lives became filled with an unspoken urgency. Life of summer went on in the silent knowledge that, with the slow inexorable seepage of an hourglass, it was turning into fall. Another mountain was climbed, annual tennis matches were arranged and played. Homer and Fred became unofficial champions of the lake by trouncing the elder Dewitt boys, unbeaten in several years. "Youth, youth," glum Billy Dewitt kept saying over iced tea afterward, in jest, though Homer could tell he was hiding some greater sense of loss.

And the moment, the conjunction of circumstance that, through the 14 steady exertion of will, minor adjustments of time and place, he had often tried to induce, never happened. She received his veiled attentions with a kind of amused curiosity, as if smiling back on innocence. One night they had been the last ones up, and there was a fleeting, shimmering moment before he stepped through the woods to his cabin and she went to her bed that he recognized, in a distant sort of way, as the moment of truth. But to touch her, or kiss her, seemed suddenly incongruous, absurd, contrary to something he could not put his finger on. He looked down at the floor and softly said good night. The screen door shut quietly behind him and he went out into the darkness and made his way through the unseen sticks and stones, and it was only then, tripping drunkenly on a fallen branch, that he realized he had never been able to imagine the moment he distantly longed for.

The Preacher gave a familiar sermon about another summer having run 15 its course, the harvest of friendship reaped, and a concluding prayer that, "God willing, we will all meet again in June." That afternoon Homer and Fred went sailing, and as they swept past a neighboring cove Homer saw in its sullen shadows a girl sitting alone in a canoe, and in an eternal, melancholy signal of parting, she waved to them as they passed. And there was something in the way that she raised her arm which, when added to the distant impression of her fullness, beauty, youth, filled him with desire but their boat moved inexorably past anyway, slapping the waves, and she disappeared behind a crop of trees.

The night before they were to leave they were all sitting in the living 16 room after dinner—Mrs. Thyme sewing, Fred folded up with the morning paper, Homer reading on the other end of the couch where Sandra was lying—when the dog leapt up and things shifted in such a way that Sandra's bare foot was lightly touching Homer's back. Mrs. Thyme came over with a roll of newspaper hit the dog on the head and he leapt off. But to Homer's surprise Sandra's foot remained, and he felt, in the faint sensation of exerted pressure, the passive emanation of its warmth, a distant signal of acquiescence. And as the family scene continued as before it was with the accompanying drama of Homer's hand, shielded from the family by a haphazard wall of pillows migrating over the couch to where, in a moment of breathless abandon, it settled softly on the cool hollow of her arch. She laughed at something her mother had said, her toe twitched, but her foot remained. It was only then, in the presence of the entire family, that he realized she was his accomplice, and that, though this was as far as it would ever go, his love had been returned.

The following student essay on Walker's "Everyday Use (for Your Grandmama)" was written in response to this chapter's assignment. As you read it, consider what questions and comments you would have for its writer if you were in a peer review session together.

■ Betsy Weiler (student) ■

WHO DO YOU WANT TO BE? Finding Heritage in Walker's "Everyday Use"

"You just don't understand."
"What don't I understand?"
"Your heritage" (291–292).*

1   Whose heritage is Dee talking about? Is it her family's heritage or her ethnic heritage?

2   This exchange takes place near the end of Alice Walker's short story, "Everyday Use," when Dee is saying goodbye to her mother and her sister Maggie after a brief visit and an argument about some quilts. That visit was almost like a treasure hunt for Dee. It seems that Dee, who now has the name Wangero Leewanika Kemanjo, came to visit because she wants to try to identify herself with the past. She wants to take parts of a butter churn and some family quilts back home with her, but Mama says "no" about the quilts because she promised them to Maggie. Dee thinks that Maggie can't "appreciate" the quilts and is "backward enough to put them to everyday use" (291). This confrontation over the quilts suggests that Dee may have learned a lot in college about her ethnic background as an African American, but she does not understand or appreciate her own family's heritage.

3   At first, a reader might think that Dee/Wangero has come home to express her appreciation for her family's heritage. While Mama is waiting for her, she expects that Dee will want to tear down the family house because it is just like the one that burned down when she was a child there. Dee hated that house. But when Dee arrives, before she even tells her mother her new name, she begins taking "picture after picture" of her mother and Maggie, "making sure the house is included" in every one (288). It seems that Dee is proud to include the house in her heritage—but is it her ethnic heritage or her family heritage? What will she do with the pictures? Are they something to remember her family with or are they something "artistic" that she will use to display her ethnic heritage?

4   When Dee explains her new name to her mother, she seems to have forgotten part of her family heritage. Wangero says that "Dee" is "dead" because "I couldn't bear it any longer, being named after the people who oppress me" (289). After her mother explains that she is actually named after Aunt Dee and Grandma Dee, Wangero Leewanika Kemanjo may gain some appreciation of the family tradition because she says that Mama doesn't have to call her the new name "if you don't want to." But Mama shows her own respect for her own daughter by saying "I'll get used to it."

*Numbers in parentheses indicate page numbers on which the quotation is found (in this case, page numbers in this text). This parenthetical citation system follows the MLA format. See Chapter 23 for a complete explanation.

When the treasure hunt part of the visit begins after the dinner, Dee's concern for ethnic heritage becomes clear. Dee wants items from the past that she identifies with her ethnic heritage. She jumps up from the table and declares that she needs the churn top. She asks, "Didn't Uncle Buddy whittle it [the churn] out of a tree you all used to have?" (290). She is talking about the churn top in terms of family heritage, but when she says that she intends to use it as a centerpiece on an alcove table, the reader understands that for Dee the churn is more significant for the ethnic heritage it represents. Many blacks could not afford to buy butter, so they had to make it themselves. (In fact, her mother is still using that churn to make butter.) She also wants the dasher from the churn. For Maggie and Mama, it is a tool in the present that represents family history. Maggie explains that Aunt Dee's first husband, Stash, whittled it; when Mama (the narrator) looks it over she notices the "small sinks" in the wood from the hands of people who had used it (including her own, no doubt). There is a strong contrast between their attitude toward the heirloom and Dee/Wangero's. She laughs at Maggie's story (family heritage), saying Maggie has a "brain like an elephant's" and announces that she herself will "think of something artistic to do with the dasher" (290). For all of them, the dasher represents the hard work blacks have had to struggle through, but for Mama and Maggie, it is a tool made by a family member to help with that work today. For Wangero it is an ethnic heritage object to display.

The final two items that Dee wants are the hand-stitched quilts that she digs out of Mama's trunk. They represent family heritage because they contain pieces of her ancestors' clothing, including a tiny piece from the blue uniform of a great-grandfather who fought in the Civil War. That family heritage is very strong for Mama, who was planning to give the quilts to Maggie as a wedding present. She remembers, but doesn't say anything, that Dee/Wangero had refused to take a quilt with her to college because they were old fashioned. Dee loses her temper over the idea of Maggie using the quilts on a bed because "in five years they'd be rags" (291). Mama says that then Maggie would make new ones. But Dee wants "*these* quilts," the ones with pieces of her own family's clothing. This may appear to be an appreciation of family heritage, but since Dee/Wangero wants to hang the quilts on the wall, not use them for a practical purpose, it seems that she wants to display a heritage that she doesn't want to live anymore.

Maggie is willing to give up the quilts, saying she can remember Grandma Dee without them, but Mama grabs the quilts back from Dee. The conflict here is not only about remembering but also about how to remember. Although Dee wants to preserve the original quilts with their antique pieces, she keeps separating herself from the family heritage that created them.

As Dee gets into the car to leave, she puts on a pair of sunglasses that hide "everything above the tip of her nose and her chin" (292). If, as the saying goes, the eyes are the windows to the soul, then Dee is hiding her soul. By wearing the sunglasses, Dee is hiding who she truly is and just wants to be identified with the color of her skin, her ethnic heritage. She tells Maggie that "[i]t's really a new day for us" although "from the way you[. . .]live, you'd never know it" (292).

9   Mama and Maggie may live in a very old-fashioned setting, using old-fashioned tools every day, but Dee/Wangero's attitude about her family and its heirlooms shows that actually she is the person who does not understand her heritage.

Thinking Critically about "Who Do You Want to Be? Finding Heritage in Walker's 'Everyday Use'"

1. The assignment for this chapter asks for an essay built around a problematic and significant interpretive question. Do you think that Betsy Weiler adequately addresses the assignment? Has she been successful in articulating a problematic question and indicating its importance for our understanding of the story?

2. Does Weiler's thesis statement respond adequately to the question? Does she supply enough details from the Walker story as evidence to support her analysis? Would the paper be better with more analysis of literary elements? What would you suggest that she add? Should she cut some material?

3. What alternative answers to Weiler's interpretive question occur to you besides the ones she brings up? What evidence do you find in the text to support your analysis and interpretation?

4. What are the strengths and weaknesses of Weiler's essay? What recommendations would you have for improving this draft of the essay?

COMPOSING YOUR ESSAY

The reading log entries you've completed in conjunction with your assigned story should help you considerably when you start planning your essay. Begin that planning by writing out the question you will pose and explore in your paper. As we have seen, a good question, one that is problematic and significant, is one that promotes engaged conversation and differing points of view. To help you decide on a question, the reading log tasks in this section ask you to freewrite in response to several different "starter questions." After you decide on a question, you will need to explore ways to answer it, using textual details for support.

Generating and Exploring Ideas

To help you settle on a good problematic question for the introduction of your formal essay, we list several starter questions that focus on *turning points*—major changes in a story's character, plot, language, and point of view. You may want to begin with one of these questions and then refine it to make it more specific to the story.

After reviewing these questions, complete the two reading log tasks that follow.

Turning-Point Starter Questions about a Short Story

1. Changes in character
   a. How do circumstances change for each character? What sets each change of circumstance in motion?
   b. How does each character's understanding or knowledge change?
   c. How does your attitude toward each character change?
   d. How does each character's relationship to other characters change?

2. Changes in language
   a. How does the dialogue change? Do characters talk to each other differently at any point?
   b. How does the tone of the language change? Does it become lighter or darker at given points?
   c. How do the metaphors and similes change? Is there a pattern to that change?

3. Changes in point of view
   a. How does the narrator's attitude toward the characters and events change? Does the narrator move closer or farther away from characters and events at any point?
   b. How trustworthy or credible is the narrator? If the narrator is not credible, at what point do you first suspect him or her of unreliability?

4. Changes in setting
   a. How does the time or place depicted in the text change? How are other changes in the text related to these changes?

Reading Log Task 10: Using the turning-point starter questions to stimulate your thinking, pose five or six specific turning-point questions about your assigned story.

Reading Log Task 11: Choose one of our turning-point questions and explore your own answer to it.

Looking at turning points is not the only way to pose questions about a text. A second list of starter questions focuses on other considerations, such as theme, values, and character. Review the questions and then complete the two reading log tasks that follow.

Additional Starter Questions

1. How does the story's title contribute to your understanding of the story?
2. What does each of the major characters seek and want? What are each character's values?
3. Which character's beliefs and values are closest to your own? How so?

4. What or who blocks the characters from reaching their goals (remember, sometimes what blocks them may be inside them), and how much control do they have over achieving their ends?

5. How successful are the characters in achieving their goals and how do they respond to the outcome?

6. Among all the characters, who seems best to understand what happens and why?

Reading Log Task 12: Use these additional starter questions to post two or three specific questions about your assigned story.

Reading Log Task 13: Choose one of your questions and explore your responses to it through freewriting or idea mapping.

Choosing Your Problematic Question and Exploring Your Answer

You're now ready to choose the question that will initiate your essay and to explore your answer. For the final reading log tasks, freewrite rapidly to spill your ideas onto the paper and avoid writer's block. Before you begin, read over what you have written so far in your reading log to help you get the juices flowing.

Reading Log Task 14: Write out the question that you want to ask in your essay about your assigned short story. What makes this an interesting and significant question? Why don't you and your classmates immediately agree on the answer?

Reading Log Task 15: Freewriting as rapidly as you can, explore your answer to the question you asked in Task 14. Use textual details and your own critical thinking to create an argument supporting your answer.

Shaping and Drafting

Reading Log Tasks 14 and 15 give you a head start on a rough draft. The best way to organize your literary analysis is to follow the problem-thesis pattern of closed-form prose:

First, begin with an introduction that poses your question about the text and shows readers why it is an interesting, problematic, and significant question. To show why your question is problematic, you may want to refer briefly to differing interpretations your classmates have suggested or you have considered. At the end of your introduction, be sure to include a thesis statement—a one-sentence summary answer to your question. Early in the introduction you may need to supply background about the story so that readers can understand your question.

Second, write the main body of your essay, in which you develop and support your thesis using textual details and argument. There is no formula for organizing the body. The major sections depend on your argument and the steps needed to make your case. If you haven't already summarized alternative interpretations in the introduction, you may choose to do so in the body. The key here is to create tension for your thesis and to demonstrate the significance of your interpretation.

Conclude by returning to your essay's big picture and suggesting why your answer to your opening question is significant. What larger implications does your analysis have for the story? What kind of changed view of the story do you want to bring about in your readers' minds? Why is this view important? You may choose to write about different value systems or different ways of reading that distinguish *your* analysis of the story from that of some of your classmates.

Revising

After you have produced a good rough draft, let it sit for a while. Then try it out on readers, who can follow the Guidelines for Peer Reviews. Based on your readers' advice, begin revising your draft, making it as clear as possible for your readers. Remember to start with the big issues and major changes and then work your way down to the smaller issues and minor changes.

■ GUIDELINES FOR PEER REVIEWS ■

Instructions for peer reviews are provided in Chapter 18 (pp. 490–496).

For the Writer

Prepare two or three questions you would like your peer reviewer to address while responding to your draft. The questions can focus on some aspect of your draft that you are uncertain about, on one or more sections where you particularly seek help or advice, on some feature that you particularly like about your draft, or on some part you especially wrestled with. Write out your questions and give them to your peer reviewer along with your draft.

For the Reviewer

I. Read the draft at a normal reading speed from beginning to end. As you read, do the following:

   A. Place a wavy line in the margin next to any passages that you find confusing, that contain something that doesn't seem to fit, or that otherwise slow down your reading.

   B. Place a "Good!" in the margin next to any passages where you think the writing is particularly strong or interesting.

II. Read the draft again slowly and answer the following questions by writing down brief explanations of your answers.

   A. Introduction:

      1. Does the title arouse interest and forecast the problem to be addressed? How might the author improve the title?

2. How does the introduction capture your interest, explain the question to be addressed, and suggest why it is both problematic and significant?

3. Does the introduction conclude with the writer's thesis? Is the thesis surprising? How might the author improve the introduction?

B. Analysis and interpretation:

1. How has the writer shown that his or her thesis is in tension with alternative interpretations or views?

2. How is the essay organized? Does the writer helpfully forecast the whole, place points before particulars, use transitions, and follow the old/new contract as explained in Chapter 19? How might the author improve or clarify the organization?

3. Where does the author quote from the story (or use paraphrase or other specific references to the text)? How are each of the author's points grounded in the text? What passages not cited might better support the argument? What recommendations do you have for improving the author's use of supporting details?

4. Where do you disagree with the author's analysis? What aspects of the story are left unexplained? What doesn't fit?

C. If the writer has prepared questions for you, respond to his or her inquiries.

D. Sum up what you see as the chief strengths and problem areas of this draft:

1. Strengths

2. Problem areas

III. Finally, read the draft one more time. Place a check mark in the margin next to any places where you notice problems in grammar, spelling, or mechanics (one check mark per problem).

CHAPTER 13

Analyzing and Synthesizing Ideas

ABOUT THE ANALYSIS AND SYNTHESIS OF IDEAS

In many of your college courses, you'll be asked to explore connections and contradictions among groups of texts. Distilling main points from more than one text, seeing connections among texts, commenting on meaningful relationships, and showing how the texts have influenced your own thinking on a question are all part of the thinking and writing involved in synthesis.

Synthesis, which is a way of seeing and coming to terms with complexities, is a counterpart to *analysis.* When you analyze something, you break it down into its parts to see the relationships among them. When you synthesize, you take one more step, putting parts together in some new fashion. The cognitive researcher Benjamin Bloom has schematized "synthesis" as the fifth of six levels of thinking processes, ranked in order of complexity and challenge: knowledge, comprehension, application, analysis, *synthesis,* and evaluation. Bloom defined synthesis in these terms: "putting together of constituent elements or parts to form a whole requiring original creative thinking."* Synthesis drives those light-bulb moments when you exclaim, "Ah! Now I see how these ideas are related!"

A second useful and related way to think of synthesis is as a dialectical thinking process. Throughout this text, we have explained that college writing involves posing a significant question that often forces you to encounter clashing or contradictory ideas. Such conflicts intrigued the German philosopher Hegel, who posited that thinking proceeds dialectically when a thesis clashes against an antithesis, leading the thinker to formulate a synthesis encompassing dimensions of both the original thesis and the antithesis. When you write a synthesis essay, your interaction with a group of related texts exemplifies this dialectical process. From your encounter with alternative perspectives on an issue, you emerge with a new, enlarged perspective of your own.

Synthesis is an especially important component of research writing, where you use synthesis to carve out your own thinking space on a research question while sifting through the writings of others. Synthesis, then, is the skill of wrestling

This Hegelian view is also discussed in Chapter 8, pp. 178–179.

---

*Benjamin Bloom, *Taxonomy of Educational Objectives: Handbook I: Cognitive Domain* (New York: David McKay, 1956).

with ideas from different texts or sources, trying to forge a new whole out of potentially confusing parts. It is the principle way you enter into a conversation on a social, civic, or scholarly issue.

College synthesis assignments sometimes specify the readings and the questions you are to explore, or they may, as in the case of research assignments, ask you to originate your own questions and find your own readings. Here are examples of synthesis assignments that you might encounter in different disciplines. In these sample assignments, note that the readings and focusing questions are provided in each case.

Environmental Politics Course

Texts to Be Analyzed

Garrett Hardin's essay on over-population, "The Tragedy of the Commons," from *Science* (1968)

Kenneth E. Boulding's essay "Economics of the Coming Spaceship Earth" (1966)

A chapter from Dixie Lee Ray's *Trashing the Planet* (1992)

A chapter from Ron Bailey's *The True State of the Planet* (1995)

Synthesis Questions

Are there any common assumptions about the world's environment in these readings?

What problems and solutions appear in these readings?

What direction would you take in proposing a solution?

American Literature Survey Course

Texts to Be Analyzed

Selections from the *Lowell Offering,* a publication produced in Lowell, Massachusetts, in the 1840s, featuring the writings of young female factory workers

Historian Gerda Lerner's essay "The Lady and the Mill Girl: Changes in the Status of Women in the Age of Jackson 1800–1840" (1969)

Herman Melville's short story "The Paradise of Bachelors and the Tartarus of Maids" (1835)

Synthesis Questions

What common questions about changes in women's social roles in the 1800s emerge in these texts?

Which text gives you the clearest understanding of the problems with women's changing roles and why?

Film Criticism Course

Films to Be Analyzed

Drums along the Mohawk (1939)

Fort Apache (1948)

Dances with Wolves (1990)

Smoke Signals (1998)

Synthesis Questions

What similarities and differences do you see in these films' representations of Native Americans?

How do you explain these differences?

The assignment for this chapter is modeled after assignments like those just shown and draws on the kinds of readings you will typically be asked to synthesize in your college courses. As an introduction to synthesis thinking, this chapter provides extended examples of student writers who are analyzing and synthesizing readings on the impact of technology. Specifically, the students are asked to address a focusing question that many cultural critics are pondering: *To what extent does technology enrich or dehumanize our lives?* As one contemporary critic puts it, "Does technology liberate or enslave us?"*

EXPLORING THE ANALYSIS AND SYNTHESIS OF IDEAS

In this exercise, we ask you to read two pieces about the value and effects of technology. The first reading, "Young Entrepreneurs Disdain for Time Off" by John Gallagher appeared in the Business section of *The Seattle Times*, July 4, 2001. The second, "The Late, Great Outdoors" by Keith Goetzman, is from the September–October 2001 *Utne Reader*. Read these pieces carefully and then do the exercises that follow.

Readings

▪ JOHN GALLAGHER ▪
YOUNG ENTREPRENEURS' DISDAIN FOR TIME OFF

A weeklong cruise in the Caribbean this spring left Detroit software executive John Lauer feeling so cut off from his work that he couldn't wait to get to an island. 1

"I'll pull into the port and all of a sudden get a voice-mail alert because they had cellular connectivity and I'd be, like, 'Thank God!'" He recalled, "The only reason I was glad to be on land is because my cell phone was working again." 2

The 26-year-old Lauer typifies the gigabyte lifestyle of young entrepreneurs. It's a life gladly given to stretched workdays and little time off. 3

"I hate to not be at the office," said the sandal- and T-shirt-clad chief executive and founder of rootlevel, a Web application-service firm based in Detroit. "Fortunately, I'm as connected at home now as I am at work." 4

A compulsive workaholic? Not necessarily. Some experts think working on vacation is growing more common. Lauer's disdain for time off reflects 5

*This quotation come from Bernd Herzogenrath, "The Question Concerning Humanity: Obsolete Bodies and (Post)Digital Flesh" in the on-line journal, *Enculturation: A Journal of Rhetoric, Writing, and Culture* 3.1 (Fall 2000). We accessed this article on March 27, 2002 at *http://www.uta.edu/huma/enculturation/3_1/herzogenrath/*.

not just a choice of the computer elite but a growing trend for many Americans, for good or for ill.

6 Once conceived of as an extended time of renewal and exploration, vacation today too often means a cramped few days juggling kids at the beach and calls to the office.

7 The New York-based Families and Work Institute reported in May that 26 percent of 1,003 adults surveyed do not take all the vacation to which they are entitled. They blamed the demands of their jobs.

8 Among the managerial class, the toll looks even worse. A 1999 survey of 5,000 executives by the Cleveland-based Management Recruiters International reported that 82 percent said they checked in with their office while on vacation.

9

Vacation Time
Average annual vacation days per employee, by country:

U.S.	13
Japan	25
S. Korea	25
Canada	26
Britain	28
Brazil	34
Germany	35
France	37
Italy	42

Such behavior can take a toll. Some 55 percent of employees who skip some or all of their vacation say they experience feelings of being overworked, vs. 27 percent of those who use all their vacation, the Families and Work Institute study found.

Perhaps worst of all, paid vacation isn't even an option for most of the nation's working poor.

Eileen Appelbaum, an economist with the Washington, D.C.-based Economic Policy Institute, a think tank that studies poverty issues, said that of the people who make less than $10 an hour—roughly one in five workers—two-thirds either have had no paid vacation for the past five years or had some years with no time off.

12 When the working poor do get paid time off, it's usually one week or less per year.

13 "Paid vacation is definitely a middle-class-or-better benefit," Appelbaum said.

14 Americans clearly are of two minds about working during vacation. Many bemoan the trend. Others, like Lauer, don't seem to care.

15 "I cannot be disconnected," Lauer said. "Going on vacation is horrible. "It's absolutely miserable."

16 Today's connectivity encourages working on vacation. Vince Webb, senior vice president of marketing and strategy for Management Recruiters, said the profusion of laptops, cell phones, pagers and other devices make it too easy to stay plugged in thousands of miles from the office.

17 "You can get sucked in so easily 365 days a year, 24/7," Webb said.

18 And it's only going to get worse. Airline maker Boeing said last month that it's going into business with three major airlines to let fliers access e-mail and the Internet in aircraft cabins.

American Airlines, United Airlines and Delta Air Lines—the nation's three largest carriers—are the first three to sign up, but Boeing is also in talks with 30 other airlines. . . . 19

If technology helps the overworked stay plugged in, it can also help would-be vacationers tune out. E-mail programs like Microsoft's Outlook have an "out-of-office" feature that responds to incoming e-mails with an announcement that the recipient is away. 20

Ron Watson, vice president of human resources for Compuware, the Farmington Hills, Mich.-based software firm, urges employees to use such features to smooth the transition to time off. 21

"At Compuware, we really encourage people to separate themselves when they go on vacation," Watson said. "In order to be effective, they really need to get out and recharge." 22

But even those who know better sometimes get caught up in vacation work. Gary Baker, an Ann Arbor, Mich.-based partner with the Andersen consulting firm and host of the radio show "Internet Adviser," recalls the sideways glances his wife shot him when he made cell-phone calls in between rides at Walt Disney World in Florida. 23

"There's so much going on that you need to stay in touch with," he explained. 24

Baker said he tries to schedule his work time on vacation when it will least disrupt his family. "Your kids are playing in the surf, so you go upstairs and make the call." 25

But like many a New Year's Eve resolution, promising to take more time off doesn't always stick. "We have the same kind of rules that everybody else has," Baker said. "Leave the cell phone at home; take the time off." Yet Baker left unused all but a day and a half of his four weeks of vacation last year. 26

For those truly dedicated to work, vacationing may always be more burden than boon. 27

Describing plans for his wedding, Lauer outlines a three-week honeymoon with Ribiat in Europe this fall. The itinerary includes Britain, France, Spain, Italy and Greece. But then Lauer added, "Once that's done, there's no way we're going to be taking any huge vacations like that until we're old and gray." 28

His voice dropped, and he added softly, "Kind of sad, in a way." 29

■ Keith Goetzman ■

THE LATE, GREAT OUTDOORS

In the 2000 Sydney Olympics, whitewater kayaking competitors bucked through an artificial channel surging with machine-pumped water, then rode conveyor belts back upstream without ever getting out of their boats. In Chamonix, France, gateway to the Alps and a mountaineering mecca, ice 1 climbers in the 2001 Ice World Cup ascended not nearby peaks but an elaborate ice-covered structure erected in the middle of town.

2   The artificial outdoors isn't just for world-class competitors, though. At the $130 million Gotcha Glacier sports complex being built in Anaheim, California, everyone will be able to surf faux waves, climb imitation cliffs, "skydive," ski, snowboard, skateboard—and, of course, shop—under one gigantic roof.

3   Gotcha may be just the tip of the glacier when it comes to the future of recreation. Increasingly, the great outdoors are being brought indoors or altered considerably to produce more accessible venues for adventure seekers. Indoor climbing walls are sprouting everywhere, artificial whitewater courses are on the drawing boards in dozens of cities, and several "snow-domes" are being built in Europe and the United States.

4   The phenomenon is generating considerable debate within the outdoor sports world. Some feel that something is lost when the rapids are always just right and the view at the top of the climb is the checkout line. Many of these are conservationists who oppose manipulating or re-creating natural environments. But for the "extreme" sports crowd—whose allies include much of the outdoor gear industry—the more places to play, the better.

5   Witness a recent exchange between paddlers on an Internet message board. "I am opposed to taking a backhoe and cement truck to the river, to supposedly make it more 'fun.' It strikes me as obscene," wrote "dancewater."

6   But "paddleboy" was unapologetic: "Artificial courses are for convenience, not getting in touch with the flow. We don't eat at McDonald's because the burgers taste good. Most 'natural' rivers aren't natural. . . . We paddle what's wet."

7   Similar differences exist among rock climbers, says Lloyd Athearn, deputy director of the American Alpine Club in Golden, Colorado. "For some people, climbing is about achieving the greatest level of technical difficulty they can achieve. There are people who climb at just obscene levels of difficulty, and they may not care at all about the scenery," he explains. "Others prefer being out on a remote peak someplace where they've bushwhacked 10 miles to get to the base of it. To them the inspiration of the environment is as important as the technical difficulties, if not more so."

8   Artificial environments have caught on for various reasons, says Professor Alan Ewert, who teaches outdoor leadership at Indiana University. For some participants, they are simply places to train for "real" outdoor experiences. Others are seeking a nontraditional athletic workout in a controlled, safe setting. And a growing number of people are using climbing walls and the like as social gathering spots. Says Athearn: "As the whole climbing gym scene evolved, there ended up being some people who like that environment, and they don't really climb outside."

9   Proponents of artificial environments, which are usually in metropolitan areas, say it's all about access, convenience, and a good time. "This is a fun sport. Why should we have to drive 200 miles to participate?" says Damon

Peters, an avid kayaker and owner of L'eau Vive Paddlesports, a kayak accessory distributor based in Portland, Maine.

Backers of artificial environments often point out that they're helping   10
expose urban dwellers to outdoor recreation. Gotcha Glacier's marketing and
operations chief, Mike Gerard, told the *Los Angeles Times* he's performing a
service. "It costs money to get to the mountains," he said. "Snowboarding is
a sport with huge growth potential. We just need to get it to the people. I
want to see kids of all ages and ethnic groups have a chance to do this."

Ewert says it's not yet clear whether artificial environments are instilling   11
a desire for real wilderness experience in city dwellers. "We hope that's happening, but we're not really sure," he says. What is happening, he believes,
is that indoor adventurers are being connected with organizations that can
take them to the next step, and they may be more likely to develop an environmental consciousness.

And the outdoors may need some help in attracting new enthusiasts.   12
Athearn points to a recent study that attempted to determine why younger
people weren't as interested in wilderness experiences as the previous generation. One teen responded, "If I'm in the mountains, I'm out of cell-phone
coverage, and I can't do that."

Individual Tasks

1. How would you describe each writer's perspective or angle of vision on technology? In one or two sentences, summarize each writer's main points in these passages.
2. List ideas that these pieces have in common.
3. List any contradictions or differences you see in these pieces.
4. Freewrite your own response to these passages for five minutes, exploring what questions they raise for you or personal experiences that they might remind you of.

Group or Whole-Class Tasks

5. Working in small groups or as a whole class, try to reach consensus answers to questions 1, 2, and 3.
6. Share your individual responses to question 4. What are the major questions and issues raised by your group or the whole class? What different views of technology emerged?

WRITING PROJECT

The writing project for this chapter has two parts—a formal essay and a series of five learning log exploratory pieces that will prepare you to write your formal essay.

Essay Assignment

Write a synthesis essay that meets the following criteria:

■ It addresses a focusing question that your instructor provides or that you formulate for yourself.

■ It summarizes and analyzes the views of at least two writers on this question.

■ It shows how you have wrestled with different perspectives on the question and have synthesized these ideas to arrive at your own new view of the question.

This assignment asks you to take apart, make sense of, assess, and recombine—that is, synthesize—the ideas from two or more readings. In the introduction to your essay, present the focusing question to your readers so that they become interested in it, see its problematic nature, and appreciate its significance. Then present your own thesis that grows out of your analysis and synthesis of your chosen or assigned readings. Early in your essay, you need to summarize these readings briefly because you should assume that your audience has not read them.

In the body of your paper, you have two main goals: (1) through analysis, show how the pieces you have selected provide different perspectives on the focusing question based on differing values, assumptions, beliefs, or framing of the question; and (2) through synthesis, add your own perspective and independent thinking by making your own connections among the ideas in the readings. In other words, create a new view by combining ideas gathered from readings with your own ideas.

Learning Log Assignments

To help you develop ideas for your synthesis essay, we have included five learning log tasks. These tasks will guide you gradually from understanding through analysis to synthesis and will provide thinking that you can use directly in your formal essay. On several occasions you will have an opportunity to share your learning log explorations with classmates and to use them for the basis of discussions that will help you generate more ideas for your formal essay. Your instructor will specify the amount of time to spend on these learning log responses. Keep your writing informal and exploratory with an emphasis on idea generation rather than correctness and polish.

Chapter 2, p. 33, explains "focused freewriting," which is appropriate for these learning log tasks.

Suggested Ideas for Synthesis Questions and Readings

This text provides a number of options from which your instructor can choose. Many instructors will follow our own approach, which is to assign both the readings and the focusing question. Others may assign the readings but invite students to formulate their own focusing questions. Still others may leave both the focusing question and the readings up to the student.

The articles in the "Readings" section of this chapter raise questions about the lifestyle changes we should make to combat global warming. But there are other readings throughout the text that can be successfully combined for a synthesis essay. Here is a list of possible focusing questions and readings:

In addition, your instructor might assign readings not found in this text.

Reading Options for This Assignment

Focusing Question	Possible Readings
What lifestyle changes should we make to combat global warming and the depletion of nonrenewable resources?	▓ Bill McKibben, "The Environmental Issue from Hell," pp. 323–326
	▓ Alan Durning, "Land of the Free . . . Parking," pp. 330–332
	▓ Bjørn Lomborg, "Global Warming—Are We Doing the Right Thing?" pp. 326–330
	▓ Evar D. Nering, "The Mirage of a Growing Fuel Supply," pp. 351–352
What social attitude should we take toward smoking?	▓ Gina Escamilla, et al., "Women and Smoking in Hollywood Movies: A Content Analysis," pp. 138–143
	▓ Florence King, "I'd Rather Smoke than Kiss," pp. 133–138
	▓ "Malboro Country" spoof ad, p. 84
What position should our nation take on capital punishment?	▓ Edward I. Koch, "Death and Justice: How Capital Punishment Affirms Life," pp. 394–398
	▓ David Bruck, "The Death Penalty," pp. 399–403
What social attitude should we take toward guns?	▓ Richard F. Corlin, "The Secrets of Gun Violence in America," pp. 462–470
	▓ The homepage for "Women Against Gun Control," p. 572
	▓ Various advocacy Web sites on gun issues discussed in Chapter 22, pp. 609–615

An Explanation of the Student Examples in This Chapter

The student examples in this chapter focus on the technological question—"To what extent does technology enrich or dehumanize our lives?". These examples enable you to role-play the same sort of audience stipulated in the assignment—readers who have not read the articles being discussed. You will need to depend, then, on the writers' summaries of these readings. The two student writers, Kara Watterson and Kate MacAulay, are working with the following texts:

- George Ritzer, "The Irrationality of Rationality: Traffic Jams on Those 'Happy Trails.'" This is a chapter from Ritzer's widely discussed book *The McDonaldization of Society*, New Century Edition (Thousand Oaks, CA: Pine Forge Press, 2000).

- Sherry Turkle, "Who Am We?" published in the magazine *Wired* 4.1 (January 1996): 148–52, 194–99.

UNDERSTANDING ANALYSIS AND SYNTHESIS
The Challenge of Synthesizing Ideas

The need to synthesize ideas usually begins when you pose a problematic question that sends you off on an intellectual journey through a group of texts. Your goal is to achieve your own informed view on that question, a view that reflects your intellectual wrestling with the ideas in your sources and in some way integrates ideas from these sources with your own independent thinking.

The most efficient and productive way to handle this multitask challenge is to break it into a series of incremental thinking steps that take you gradually from understanding your chosen texts, to an analysis of them, to a synthesis of their ideas with your own. The learning log tasks in each of the sections that follow show you a series of thinking steps to guide you through this process.

Understanding Your Texts Through Summary Writing

> **Learning Log Task 1:** Write a 200–250-word summary of each of the main texts you will use in your final paper.

As a starting point for grappling with a writer's ideas, writing careful summaries prompts you to read texts with the grain, adopting each text's perspective and walking in each author's shoes. When you summarize a text, you try to achieve an accurate, thorough understanding of it by stating its main ideas in a tightly distilled format.

Instructions on how to write a summary are found on pp. 118–122.

What follows are Kara's summary of the book chapter by Ritzer and Kate's summary of Turkle's article—the two readings they will use in their synthesis essays. Notice how they use attributive tags to show that they are representing Ritzer's and Turkle's ideas as objectively as they can and that these ideas belong to Ritzer or Turkle, not to them.

Instructions on how to use attributive tags are found on pp. 121 and 626–629.

Kara's Summary of Ritzer's Chapter

In "The Irrationality of Rationality," the seventh chapter in *The McDonaldization of Society*, sociologist George Ritzer identifies a major sociological and economic problem: in an effort to find the most efficient way to run a business (what Ritzer calls "rationalizing"), more and more companies are following the franchise model pioneered by McDonald's. Although McDonaldization is efficient and economical for the companies, Ritzer argues it can be irrational, inconvenient, inefficient, and costly for consumers who often stand in long lines at fast-food restaurants and supermarkets. Ritzer also claims that McDonaldized systems cause people to forfeit real fun for manufactured fun and illusion. He cites the example of fake international villages at amusement parks and the fake friendliness of the "scripted interactions" (138) that employees are supposed to have with customers. Ritzer explains that our McDonaldized society has begun focusing more on quantity than quality. He believes that McDonaldized systems are dehumanizing: jobs "don't offer much in the way of satisfaction or stability" (137) and families hardly ever eat together any more, a situation that is contributing to the "disintegration of the family" (141). Ritzer also argues that by franchising everywhere, we are losing cultural distinctions. Whether you are in Japan or the United States, products are beginning to look the same. Finally, Ritzer shows that when companies become rationalized, they limit the possibility of connection between human beings. Citing examples from fast-food restaurants to hospitals, he states that there are many serious drawbacks to "our fast-paced and impersonal society" (140).

Kate's Summary of Turkle's Article

In her *Wired* article "Who Am We?" psychologist and MIT professor Sherry Turkle explores how computers and the Internet are transforming our views of ourselves and the way we interact socially. Turkle believes that the Internet is moving us toward a "decentered" (149) sense of the self. She says that computers used to be thought of as "calculating machines" (149), but they are increasingly now seen as intelligent objects capable of interaction and simulation. She uses children's interactive computer games to illustrate how some people now think of computers as having personalities and psyches, which make them "fitting partners for dialog and relationship" (150). In the second half of her article, she argues that virtual life raises new moral issues. She uses the example of MUDs (multiuser domains), which allow people to create multiple and often simultaneous virtual identities by playing different characters. She presents examples of the relationships of cyber characters—often cyber-sex—that raise the question of whether cyber-sex is an act of real-life infidelity or adultery. Turkle concludes that it is easy for people to lose themselves between the real world and these virtual worlds. Because we have the ability to create better "selves" in the virtual world, it is possible to become addicted to virtual life and be "imprisoned by the screens" (199). According to Turkle, we are moving toward a "postmodernist culture of simulation" (149), and she cautions that it is more important than ever that we are very self-aware.

For Writing and Discussion

Working in small groups or as a whole class, share your summaries of your two chosen or assigned readings. What important main ideas does your group agree must be included in a summary of each text? What points are secondary and can be left out?

Examining the Rhetorical Strategies Used in Your Texts

Learning Log Task 2: Analyze the rhetorical strategies used in each of your texts (for example, purpose, audience, genre, angle of vision, and use of reasoning and evidence).

Explanations of these terms and concepts are found in Chapters 3 and 4.

In order to analyze a text and synthesize its ideas, you need to consider the text rhetorically. To whom is the author writing and why? Do you see how the genre of each text influences some of the author's choices about language and structure? What angle of vision shapes each text and accounts for what is included and excluded? Do you share the values of the author or of his or her intended audience?

Here is Kara's learning log entry exploring the rhetorical contexts of the Ritzer and Turkle texts:

Instructions on how to write a rhetorical analysis of a text are found in Chapter 6 on pp. 126–133.

Kara's Response to Learning Log Task 2

Although both George Ritzer and Sherry Turkle are scholars, their texts are not really written for scholarly audiences. Both would fall in the category of nonfiction books (articles) written for general audiences and both are written to raise audience awareness of sociological/cultural problems—in this case, the way that technological advances and the fast-food model of business are affecting the quality of life and the way that the Internet is affecting our sense of ourselves and our relationships.

Both Ritzer and Turkle have chosen to write in accessible language so that their ideas can easily be understood by a general audience, and both use many examples to build credibility. Still, because I had no previous personal background with multiuser domains, I found it challenging to imagine some of Turkle's descriptions of the virtual world of MUDs, but I did have previous experience with all of Ritzer's examples so I never felt in over my head while reading his chapters.

From Ritzer's angle of vision, McDonaldization has had a damaging and irreversible effect on the quality of contemporary life, and he is trying to prompt people to slow down this destructive process. His approach is quite one-sided, though. He does admit that "we undoubtedly have gained much from the rationalization of society in general" (132), but he does not develop this idea any further. He refuses to make any further concessions to the rationalization he is fighting. Instead of acknowledging contradicting ideas, Ritzer hammers his point strongly with example after example. By the end of the chapter, the reader is left with a glazed-over feeling, not really taking in the information.

Turkle's angle of vision seems to include curiosity and exploration as well as concern about the way computers are transforming society. She seems to analyze more than argue. She is trying to get across her notion that the Internet lets people adopt many different characters and have multiple selves, for example when they play in MUDs and simulation games. So maybe, in claiming that computers are no longer calculating machines, Turkle, like Ritzer, is only presenting one limited view of her subject, the view that interests her as a psychologist who has written many books and articles on computers, and our changing sense of identity and community.

For Writing and Discussion

Working in small groups or as a whole class, share what each of you discovered in Learning Log Task 2. Try to reach consensus on the most important rhetorical features of each of the texts you are using for your synthesis essay.

Identifying Main Themes and Examining Similarities and Differences in the Ideas in Your Texts

Learning Log Task 3: Identify main issues or themes in your assigned or chosen texts. Then explore the similarities and differences in their ideas.

This learning log task asks you to identify main issues, ideas, or themes that surface in your texts as preparation for looking for similarities and differences among your texts. This process of thinking—comparison and contrast—will help you clarify your understanding of each reading and promote analysis of the underlying values, assumptions, and ideas of each author. Here are some questions that can guide your learning log writing at this stage of your thinking:

Questions to Help You Grapple with Similarities and Differences in Your Texts

- ▦ What main ideas or themes do you see in each text?
- ▦ What similarities and differences do you see in the way the authors choose to frame the issue they are writing about? How do their theses (either implied or stated) differ?
- ▦ What are the main similarities and differences in their angles of vision?
- ▦ What commonalities and intersections do you see in their ideas? What contradictions and clashes do you see in their ideas?
- ▦ What similarities and differences do you see in the authors' underlying values and assumptions?
- ▦ What overlap, if any, is there in these authors' examples and uses of terms?
- ▦ How would Author A respond to Author B?

Here are excerpts from Kara's and Kate's learning logs, showing their exploratory analyses of Ritzer's and Turkle's texts. Note how they each begin to organize comparisons by points, to make analytical connections among them, and to push themselves to think out exactly where these authors agree and differ.

Excerpt from Kara's Response to Learning Log Task 3

Both Ritzer and Turkle make strong comments about health problems that may be caused by the particular type of technology they are dealing with. For Ritzer, the dangers that arise from McDonaldization can most easily be seen in fast-food restaurants and their fatty, unhealthy foods: "such meals are the last things many Americans need, suffering as they do from obesity, high cholesterol levels, high blood pressure, and perhaps diabetes"(133). He also considers the high level of stress created by our high-speed society that can cause heart attacks, panic attacks, maybe nervous breakdowns. Turkle, too, is concerned about the effects of technology on people's health, but her focus is people's psyches and minds. One person in her research study who creates different identities on the Internet thinks that "MUDding has ultimately made him feel worse about himself"(196). For Turkle, the Internet can be dangerous for what it can do to a person's psyche.

Both authors agree that technological advances are causing a loss of real human connection. McDonaldization fosters fake contact; employees are given guidelines about how to interact with customers and are programmed with what to say and what not to say: "rule Number 17 for Burger King workers is 'Smiles at all times'"(Ritzer 130). Quick sales, not real customer relations, are the main concern. For Turkle too, this loss of human contact is a dilemma. MUDs are not places where you truly get to know a person; they are places where people are acting out characters. These are not real friends that can aid you when you are feeling ill or down. Also, people are spending vast quantities of time logging on, spending time with a computer screen instead of family and friends. [. . .]

Excerpt from Kate's Response to Learning Log Task 3

[. . .] Last, I think that Turkle and Ritzer have very different attitudes about what they observe and claim is happening to society. Turkle seems to be a little more optimistic than Ritzer. While she sees the changes that advanced technology is causing in society, she seems to think that we, as human beings, have the ability to adjust to the changes facing us and to change ourselves in order to preserve our humanity. In contrast to that view, Ritzer seems to take the position that we are on a downward spiral and McDonaldized systems are destroying us and society as a whole. Ritzer and Turkle would have a really great discussion about all the negative effects that technology and rationality are having on individuals and society, but they would probably largely disagree on society's ability to bounce back and fix itself.

For Writing and Discussion

Working as a whole class or in small groups, share your analyses of similarities and differences in your chosen or assigned texts. Pay close attention to these two overarching questions: How are the texts similar and different? How do each author's assumptions, beliefs, purposes, and values account for these similarities and differences?

Moving Toward Your Own Views

Learning Log Task 4: In light of what you have read and thought about so far, explore your own views on the original focusing question that has guided your probing of the texts.

One of your biggest challenges in writing a synthesis essay is to move beyond analysis to synthesis. A successful synthesis essay incorporates ideas from your texts and yet represents your own independent thinking, showing evidence of the dialectic process. You need to think about how the differing perspectives of Texts A and B have led you to new realizations that will let you enter the conversation of these texts. As you begin to formulate your synthesis views, you will also need to reassert your personal/intellectual investment in the conversation of the texts. You will need to take ownership of the ideas and to emerge with a clearer sense of your own views. You may also want to consider which text—in your mind—makes the most significant contribution to the question you are exploring. You may want to evaluate the texts to determine which has influenced your thinking the most and why. The following questions should help you think of ideas for Learning Log 4:

Questions to Help You Develop Your Own Views

- ▪ What do I agree with and disagree with in the texts I have analyzed?
- ▪ How have these texts changed my perception and understanding of an issue, question, or problem? You might want to use this prompt: "I used to think _____, but now I think _____."
- ▪ Although these texts have persuaded me that _____, I still have doubts about _____.
- ▪ What do I see or think now that I didn't see or think before I read these texts?
- ▪ What new significant questions do these texts raise for me?
- ▪ What do I now see as the main controversies?
- ▪ What is my current view on the focusing question that connects my texts and that all my texts explore?
- ▪ How would I position myself in the conversation of the texts?
- ▪ If I find one author's perspective more valid, accurate, interesting, or useful than another's, why is that?

To illustrate this learning log task, we show you excerpts from the explorations of both Kara and Kate.

Excerpt from Kara's Response to Learning Log Task 4

When I was in Puerto Rico one spring break, I remember how excited my friend and I were to go to a burger place for dinner one night. It was so nice to have American food after days of eating fajitas and enchiladas. At the time, I did not think about how this American restaurant got to Puerto Rico; I was just glad it was there. However, after reading "The Irrationality of Rationality" by George Ritzer, I began to take a closer look at this experience. Both this article and "Who Am We?" have caused me to take a closer look at our society. [. . .] What is it that causes people to surf the Internet for hours on end, to chat with people they have never met? What is this doing to our culture? Are we losing the distinctions evident when you travel from one region to the next, from one country to another? [. . .]

Excerpt from Kate's Response to Learning Log Task 4

Reading the articles by Ritzer and Turkle made me much more aware of a social problem that I didn't really pay attention to before. I didn't realize how much modern technology is changing our human relationships. For example, the other night I was at a family gathering, and some of my cousins began discussing the idea of purchasing a new car. After talking for a short while about how much it would cost and how to get the best deal, one of my cousins had that modern craving for wanting to know the answer immediately. He logged on to the Internet and spent the remainder of the evening looking at cars and prices, and had limited interaction with the family. It made me think about the articles and how things were becoming more immediate and less personal, and how interactions between machines and humans are decreasing the interactions between people. Why speak with another person who might not know the answer to a question or the solution to a problem when you can just log on to the Internet and find the right answer immediately? It makes me wonder what the Internet does not offer. [. . .]

Taking Your Position in the Conversation: Your Synthesis

Learning Log Task 5: Reread your first four learning logs and consider how your own views on the focusing question have evolved and emerged. Think about the risky, surprising, or new views that you can bring to your readers. In light of your reading and thinking, explore what you want to say in your own voice to show the connections you have made and the new insights you now have.

After you have discovered what you think about the texts you have analyzed—what ideas you accept and reject, what new questions you have formulated, how your ideas have been modified and transformed through your reading experience—you need to find a way to pull your ideas together. Your synthesis view should be the fruit of your intellectual work, a perspective that you have come to after reading the ideas of other writers, pondering them reflectively and keenly. Here are some synthesis questions that can help you articulate the points that you want to develop in your essay:

Questions to Help You Formulate and Develop Your Synthesis Views

■ What discoveries have I made after much thought?

■ What are the most important insights I have gotten from these readings?

■ What is my intellectual or personal investment with the focusing question at this point?

■ Where can I step out on my own, even take a risk, in my thinking about the ideas discussed in these texts?

■ What new perspective do I want to share with my readers?

What follows is an excerpt from Kara's learning log. Note how she is beginning to find her stance on the focusing question of whether technology enriches or dehumanizes our lives.

Excerpt from Kara's Response to Learning Log Task 5

What is technology doing to our relationships with one another? Both Ritzer and Turkle seem to be urging us away from dependency on technology, and these authors have made me aware of my complacence in accepting technology, but still I see value in technology that these writers don't discuss. [. . .]

I find myself questioning these writers' views. Ritzer seems to believe that families go to McDonald's rather than eat family meals together. He doesn't consider that it is when people are on the road or out already that these restaurants are visited, not when they are sitting at home deciding what is for dinner. Turkle also speaks of the loss of connection that can arise from people constantly at their computers. She raises some very important questions about what technology is doing to our relationships and self-image, but I think she focuses too much on MUDs. How many people actually are doing this MUDding? Also, there are some valid things that come out of relationships on the Internet. I know of several examples of people who have met their future spouses through chat rooms. When I left for college, I was not sure whom I would stay in touch with, but because of the Internet, I am able to stay connected to people I would have drifted away from otherwise.

Also, while we note the dangers of technology, I think we need to remember the benefits as well. I agree that cell phones are overused, but how often have cell phones saved people in emergencies or aided people stranded on the road with car problems? I hope to be a doctor. I have great appreciation for the way that cameras can see inside a patient as surgeons are operating and thus reduce the risk of many surgeries. [. . .]

For Writing and Discussion

Prior to the start of this task, work individually to write two or three main points that you want to make in the synthesis portion of your final essay. Working in small groups or as a whole class, share your short list of main points. Briefly explain to your group or to the whole class why these points interest you. Take notes on group ideas.

Student Example of a Synthesis Essay

We conclude this section by showing you Kate's final synthesis essay. Note that Kate begins by presenting the focusing question that connects the texts she is analyzing. She then summarizes these texts and presents her mapping thesis statement. She devotes more than half of the body of the essay to a close analysis of the texts before she moves on to present her own independent thinking in the synthesis section of the essay.

Technology's Peril and Potential

Kate MacAulay (student)

Introduces focusing questions and context

Recently in English class, we have been focusing on the question, What effect is technology having on humanity and the quality of life in the twenty-first century? We have had heated discussions about the use of cell phones, palm pilots, beepers, e-mail, chat rooms, and the Web. As part of my investigation of this question, I read two texts: a chapter from George Ritzer's book *The McDonaldization of Society*, entitled "The Irrationality of Rationality: Traffic Jams on Those 'Happy Trails'", and an article published in the magazine *Wired* entitled "Who Am We?", by Sherry Turkle. In his chapter, Ritzer, a sociology professor, explains how technology has rationalized businesses and many facets of society following the McDonald's model. He argues that modern technology is causing loss of quality products, time, and relationships. In the McDonaldized system, where everything is designed logically for economy and convenience, things have become more artificial, and our relationships have become more superficial. In her article "Who Am We?", Sherry Turkle, a psychology professor at MIT, shows how computers and the Internet are transforming our views of ourselves and the way we interact socially. Focusing on computers' capacities for simulation and promoting interaction, Turkle has explored MUDs (multiuser domains), which allow people to create virtual identities. MUDs, Turkle believes, contribute to the formation of postmodern multiple selves and raise new questions about personal identity and morality. Although both Turkle and Ritzer identify problems in technology's influence and in society's responses to it, Turkle sees more potential and gain where Ritzer sees mostly peril and loss. Both articles made me question how we define our values and morality in this postmodern, technologically advanced world and persuaded me of the need for caution in embracing technology.

Although Ritzer and Turkle both see technology as having some negative effects on human relations and the quality of life, they disagree about exactly where the most interesting and serious problems lie. Ritzer believes that the problems caused by technology are not problems within the individual, but problems imposed on the individual by McDonaldized systems. For example, Ritzer claims that fast-food restaurants encourage us to eat unhealthy food quickly and also contribute to "the disintegration of the family" (141) by taking away family time. He also believes that rationalized systems create illusions of fun, reality, and friendliness. He talks about the "scripted interactions" (138) that employees are supposed to have with customers, where they are told exactly what to say to every customer, making interactions less real. Further, rationalized systems are dehumanizing in the kinds of jobs they create that "don't offer much in the way of satisfaction or stability" (137), benefiting only stockholders, owners, and employers.

In contrast, Turkle responds to technology's threat by focusing inward on technology's effect on the self and on relationships. While she is clearly intrigued by such Internet capabilities as multiuser domains, she acknowledges that this potential for multiple simultaneous identities threatens the wholeness of individuals, possibly damaging our emotional and psychological selves. Her concern is that people become addicted to these games because in the virtual world it is easy to create better "selves," to be what you wish you were. Turkle shows that people can lose themselves between the real world and the virtual world and be "imprisoned by the screens" (199). Although the virtual world is exciting and fun, she notes that "[o]ur experiences there are serious play" (199). She also examines cases of virtual characters who get into relationships with other characters, including cyber-sex relationships. She ponders the issue of cyber-sex immorality and adultery.

Despite Turkle and Ritzer's agreement that technology can damage us as a society, they disagree on their overall outlook and on our power to respond positively to technology's influence. I find Ritzer's views almost entirely negative. He believes that we are irreversibly damaged by technological advances because we are completely

Introduces the texts to be analyzed

Brief summary of Ritzer's text

Brief summary of Turkle's text

Thesis statement with analytical points and synthesis points

Analytical point: compares and contrasts Ritzer's and Turkle's ideas

Analyzes and elaborates on Ritzer's ideas

Analyzes, contrasts, and elaborates on Turkle's ideas

Analytical point: compares and contrasts Ritzer's and Turkle's ideas

Analyzes and elaborates on Ritzer's ideas

Presents writer's independent thinking

Analyzes, contrasts, and elaborates on Turkle's ideas

Presents writer's independent thinking

Transition to writer's synthesis. Synthesis point discusses writer's own view

Elaborates on the connections the writer is making

Synthesis point discusses writer's own view

Synthesis point discusses writer's own view

Presents connections the writer is making

Transition and final connections

caught up in the McDonaldized system, with few parts of society left unchanged. Almost all of the family-owned neighborhood restaurants or mom-and-pop grocery stores have been taken over by franchises like Red Robin or Safeway. The costs of these rationalized systems, he says, are "inefficiency, illusions of various types, disenchantment, dehumanization, and homogenization" (124). In this chapter of his book, Ritzer doesn't mention any ways that our lives could be improved by these systems; he gives only examples of the way we are misled and damaged by them.

Turkle's approach strikes me as much more positive and balanced than Ritzer's. Optimistically, she explains that MUDs can give people self-knowledge that they can apply to real life: "[t]he anonymity of MUDs gives people the chance to express multiple and often unexplored aspects of the self, to play with their identity and to try out new ones" (152). Turkle sees an opportunity for us to grow as individuals and to learn to use technology in a positive way: "If we can cultivate awareness of what stands behind our screen personae, we are more likely to succeed in using virtual experience for personal transformation" (199). I think Turkle's views are more complex than Ritzer's. She believes that we have to take responsibility for our own habits and psychological responses to technology. She encourages us to be aware of how we interact with technology and believes that we can grow as individuals using this technology.

After reading these articles, I have realized how the continuing advancement of technology raises new moral questions. In a McDonaldized system, where everything is designed for convenience, there seem to be many places for morals to be left out of the picture. For example, is it okay for us to exchange real human interaction for convenience and saving time? Is there something wrong with our ethics when interesting and fulfilling jobs are eliminated by machines or replaced by dead-end, low-paying Mcjobs? Turkle too shows us how virtual worlds pose new moral questions for us. In MUDs, people can form virtual relationships, even cyber-sex relationships. The people behind the characters are real people, even if they are acting as someone else. If a married person has a cyber-sex relationship on a MUD, is he or she cheating? If a person commits a virtual assault or other crime that has no real-world, physical effects, should he or she feel guilty or sinful for the intention? Ritzer and Turkle have made me see how important these questions are.

Reading the articles made me strongly believe that we must use this technology in moderation in order to preserve individual qualities and our relationships. From our class discussions, I remember what Scott said about the way that the Internet connects people. He said that people like his uncle, who was severely injured on the job, use the Internet as a way of "getting out" to meet people and socialize. He pointed out how the Microsoft Gaming Zone has brought his uncle into an ongoing backgammon tournament through which he has made friends. Meanwhile his aunt has gotten a lot of pleasure out of playing and problem solving in the world of MUDs.

But my own experience has left me concerned about the danger we face as emotional, social beings in the face of technology. The other night at a family gathering, one of my cousins, after discussing car buying with some of the relatives, got the urge to research new car prices. He left the room, logged onto the Internet, and spent the rest of the evening looking at cars and prices. We saw him only once the whole evening when he came out to get a slice of pie. My cousin's withdrawal from the conversation made me think about Ritzer's and Turkle's concerns that technology decreases real interactions among people.

Ritzer and Turkle offer us a warning that technology can be damaging if we don't recognize and overcome its dangers. I would encourage us not to let ourselves become dominated by technology, not to let it take our full attention just because it is there, and not to overlook the complex moral questions that technology poses. The convenience that technology offers—our e-mail, cell phones, and debit cards—should help us save time that can be spent in nurturing our relationships with other people. The real challenge is to find ways to become even better people because of technology.

Conclusion

Works Cited

Ritzer, George. <u>The McDonaldization of Society</u>. Thousand Oaks: Pine Forge, 2000.

Turkle, Sherry. "Who Am We?" *Wired* Jan. 1996: 148+.

Complete citation of articles in MLA format

Readings

The readings in this chapter immerse you in the question of whether citizens of First World countries such as the United States should alter their way of life to combat global warming, and if so, how or how much. Although some scientific disagreement remains about the existence and potential threat of global warming, these readings all assume that human-influenced global warming is occurring. They invite you to think about your own ethical stance toward the environment, toward people in impoverished countries, and toward future generations. Your instructor may assign two or all three of these readings as the focus of your synthesis essay. (Another relevant article is Evar D. Nering, "The Mirage of a Growing Fuel Supply," on pages 351–353.) We have framed the focusing question for a synthesis essay on these readings as follows: *What lifestyle changes should we make to combat global warming and the depletion of nonrenewable resources?* To avoid influencing your own analysis of these readings, we omit the discussion questions that typically follow readings in other chapters.

The first reading, by Bill McKibben, appeared in the liberal news magazine *In These Times* in April 2001 and in the September–October 2001 issue of the *Utne Reader*. McKibben is the author of the books *The End of Nature* and *Long Distance*.

■ BILL MCKIBBEN ■

THE ENVIRONMENTAL ISSUE FROM HELL

1   When global warming first emerged as a potential crisis in the late 1980s, one academic analyst called it "the public policy program from hell." The years since have only proven him more astute: Fifteen years into our understanding of climate change, we have yet to figure out how we're going to tackle it. And environmentalists are just as clueless as anyone else: Do we need to work on lifestyle or on lobbying, on photovoltaics or on politics? And is there a difference? How well we handle global warming will determine what kind of century we inhabit—and indeed what kind of place we leave behind. The issue cuts close to home and also floats off easily into the abstract. So far it has been the ultimate "can't get there from here" problem, but the time has come to draw a roadmap—one that may

help us deal with the handful of other issues on the list of real world-shattering problems.

Typically, when you're mounting a campaign, you look for self-interest, you scare people by saying what will happen to us if we don't do something: All the birds will dies, the canyon will disappear beneath a reservoir, we will choke to death on smog. But in the case of global warming, that doesn't exactly do the trick, at least in the time frame we're discussing. In temperate latitudes, climate change will creep up on us. Severe storms already have grown more frequent and more damaging. The progression of seasons is less steady. Some agriculture is less reliable. But face it: Our economy is so enormous that it takes those changes in stride. Economists who work on this stuff talk about how it will shave a percentage or two off the GNP over the next few decades. And most of us live lives so divorced from the natural world that we hardly notice the changes anyway. Hotter? Turn up the air-conditioning. Stormier? Well, an enormous percentage of Americans commute from remote-controlled garage to office parking garage—it may have been some time since they got good and wet in a rainstorm. By the time the magnitude of the change is truly in our faces, it will be too late to do much about it: There's such a lag time to increased levels of carbon dioxide in the atmosphere that we need to be making the switch to solar and wind and hydrogen power right now to prevent disaster decades away. Yesterday, in fact.

So maybe we should think of global warming in a different way—as the great moral crisis of our time, the equivalent of the civil rights movement of the 1960s.

Why a moral question? In the first place, no one's ever figured out a more effective way to screw the marginalized and poor of this planet than climate change. Having taken their dignity, their resources, and their freedom under a variety of other schemes, we now are taking the very physical stability on which their already difficult lives depend.

Our economy can absorb these changes for a while, but consider Bangladesh for a moment. In 1998 the sea level in the Bay of Bengal was higher than normal, just the sort of thing we can expect to become more frequent and severe. The waters sweeping down the Ganges and the Brahmaputra rivers from the Himalayas could not drain easily into the ocean—they backed up across the country, forcing most of its inhabitants to spend three months in thigh-deep water. The fall rice crop didn't get planted. We've seen this same kind of disaster over the past few years in Mozambique and Honduras and Venezuela and other places.

And global warming is a moral crisis, too, if you place any value on the rest of creation. Coral reef researchers indicate that these spectacularly intricate ecosystems are also spectacularly vulnerable. Rising water temperatures are likely to bleach them to extinction by mid-century. In the Arctic, polar bears are 20 percent scrawnier than they were a decade ago: As pack ice melts, so does the opportunity for hunting seals. All in all, the 21st century seems poised to see extinctions at a rate not observed since the last big asteroid slammed into the planet. But this time the asteroid is us.

7　　It's a moral question, finally, if you think we owe any debt to the future. No one has ever figured out a more thoroughgoing way to strip-mine the present and degrade what comes after—all the people who will ever be related to you. Ever. No generation yet to come will ever forget us—we are the ones present at the moment when the temperature starts to spike, and so far we have not reacted. If it had been done to us, we would loathe the generation that did it, precisely as we will one day be loathed.

8　　But trying to launch a moral campaign is no easy task. In most moral crises, there is a villain—some person or class or institution that must be overcome. Once the villain is identified, the battle can commence. But you can't really get angry at carbon dioxide, and the people responsible for its production are, well, us. So perhaps we need some symbols to get us started, some places to sharpen the debate and rally ourselves to action. There are plenty to choose from: our taste for ever bigger houses and the heating and cooling bills that come with them, our penchant for jumping on airplanes at the drop of a hat. But if you wanted one glaring example of our lack of balance, you could do worse than point the finger at sport utility vehicles.

9　　SUVs are more than mere symbols. They are a major part of the problem—we emit so much more carbon dioxide now than we did a decade ago in part because our fleet of cars and trucks actually has gotten steadily less fuel efficient for the past 10 years. If you switched today from the average American car to a big SUV, and drove it for just one year, the difference in carbon dioxide that you produced would be the equivalent of opening your refrigerator door and then forgetting to close it for six years. SUVs essentially are machines for burning fossil fuel that just happen to also move you and your stuff around.

10　　But what makes them such a perfect symbol is the brute fact that they are simply unnecessary. Go to the parking lot of the nearest suburban supermarket and look around: The only conclusion you can draw is that to reach the grocery, people must drive through three or four raging rivers and up the side of a canyon. These are semi-military machines, armored trucks on a slight diet. While they do not keep their occupants appreciably safer, they do wreck whatever they plow into, making them the perfect metaphor for a heedless, supersized society.

11　　That's why we need a much broader politics than the Washington lobbying that's occupied the big environmental groups for the past decade. We need to take all the brilliant and energetic strategies of local grassroots groups fighting dumps and cleaning up rivers and apply those tactics in the national and international arenas. That's why some pastors are starting to talk with their congregations about what cars to buy, and why some college seniors are passing around petitions pledging to stay away from the Ford

Explorers and Excursions, and why some auto dealers have begun to notice informational picketers outside their showrooms on Saturday mornings urging customers to think about gas mileage when they look at cars.

The point is not that such actions by themselves—any individual actions—will make any real dent in the levels of carbon dioxide pouring into our atmosphere. Even if you got 10 percent of Americans really committed to changing their energy use, their solar homes wouldn't make much of a difference in our national totals. But 10 percent would be enough to change the politics around the issue, enough to pressure politicians to pass laws that would cause us all to shift our habits. And so we need to begin to take an issue that is now the province of technicians and turn it into a political issue, just as bus boycotts began to make public the issue of race, forcing the system to respond. That response is likely to be ugly—there are huge companies with a lot to lose, and many people so tied in to their current ways of life that advocating change smacks of subversion. But this has to become a political issue—and fast. The only way that may happen, short of a hideous drought or monster flood, is if it becomes a personal issue first.   12

The second reading, by Danish political scientist Bjørn Lomborg, was written for the online journal *Guardian Unlimited* (http://www.guardian.co.uk/globalwarming), which we accessed January 13, 2002. Lomborg, a former member of Greenpeace and a professor of political science and statistics at the University of Aarhus, Denmark, is the author of *The Skeptical Environmentalist: Measuring the Real State of the World* (2001)—probably the most persuasive of recent works arguing that human material well-being is actually improving and that human ingenuity can solve environmental problems. In this online article, shortened here to focus on Lomborg's key points, Lomborg refers to the Kyoto Protocol and the decisions made at Bonn, Germany—two international efforts to confront the problem of global warming.

▩ Bjørn Lomborg ▩

GLOBAL WARMING—Are We Doing the Right Thing?*

Last month in Bonn, most of the world's nations (minus the US) reached an agreement to cut carbon emissions. Generally, the deal was widely reported as almost saving the world. Yet, not only is this untrue in the scientific sense—the deal will do almost no good—but it is also unclear whether carbon emission cuts are really the best way for the world to ensure progress on its most important areas.   1

Global warming is important, environmentally, politically and economically. There is no doubt that mankind has influenced and is still increasing   2

*This article is extensively documented with scientific references as well as citations to economic and cultural studies. For the purposes of this assignment, which focuses on Lomborg's ideas rather than on his research sources, we have eliminated the numerous scholarly references as well as one of the figures.

atmospheric concentrations of CO_2 and that this will increase temperature. I will not discuss all the scientific uncertainty, but basically accept the models and predictions from the 2001 report of the UN Climate Panel (IPCC). Yet, we will need to separate hyperbole from realities in order to choose our future optimally. [. . .]

3   [G]lobal warming will have serious costs—the total cost is estimated at about $5 trillion. Such estimates are unavoidably uncertain but derive from models assessing the cost of global warming to a wide variety of societal areas such as agriculture, forestry, fisheries, energy, water supply, infrastructure, hurricane damage, drought damage, coast protection, land loss caused by a rise in sea level, loss of wetlands, forest loss, loss of species, loss of human life, pollution and migration.

4   The consequences of global warming will hit hardest on the developing countries, whereas the industrialized countries may actually benefit from a warming lower than 2–3°C. The developing countries are harder hit primarily because they are poor—giving them less adaptive capacity.

5   Despite our intuition that we naturally need to do something drastic about such a costly global warming, we should not implement a cure that is actually more costly than the original affliction. Here, economic analyses clearly show that it will be far more expensive to cut CO_2 emissions radically, than to pay the costs of adaptation to the increased temperatures. [. . .]

6   So is it not curious, then, that the typical reporting on global warming tells us all the bad things that could happen from CO_2 emissions, but few or none of the bad things that could come from overly zealous regulation of such emissions? Indeed, why is it that global warming is not discussed with an open attitude, carefully attuned to avoid making big and costly mistakes to be paid for by our descendants, but rather with a fervor more fitting for preachers of opposing religions?

7   This is an indication that the discussion of global warming is not just a question of choosing the optimal economic path for humanity, but has much deeper, political roots as to what kind of future society we would like. This understanding is clearly laid out in the new 2001 IPCC report. Here IPCC tells us that we should build cars and trains with lower top speeds, and extol the qualities of sail ships, biomass (which "has been the renewable resource base for humankind since time immemorial") and bicycles. Likewise, it is suggested that in order to avoid demand for transport, we should obtain a regionalized economy.

8   Essentially, what the IPCC suggests—and openly admits—is that we need to change the individual lifestyles, and move away from consumption. We must focus on sharing resources (e.g. through co-ownership), choosing free time instead of wealth, quality instead of quantity, and "increase freedom while containing consumption." Because of climate change we have to remodel our world, and find more "appropriate lifestyles."

9   The problem—as seen by the IPCC—is, that "the conditions of public acceptance of such options are not often present at the requisite large scale."

Actually, it is even "difficult to convince local actors of the significance of climate change and the need for corrective action." IPCC goes as far as suggesting that the reason why we are unwilling to accept slower (or no) cars and regionalized economies with bicycles but no international travel, is that we have been indoctrinated by the media, where we see the TV characters as reference points for our own lives, shaping our values and identities. Consequently, IPCC finds that the media could also help form the path towards a more sustainable world: "Raising awareness among media professionals of the need for greenhouse gas mitigation and the role of the media in shaping lifestyles and aspirations could be an effective way to encourage a wider cultural shift."

But, of course, while using global warming as a springboard for other wider policy goals is entirely legitimate, such goals should in all honesty be made explicit. Moreover, it is problematic to have an organization which often quite successfully gathers the most relevant scientific information about global warming, also so clearly promoting a political agenda, which seldom reaches the news headlines.

Thus, the important lesson of the global warming debate is fivefold. First, we have to realize what we are arguing about—do we want to handle global warming in the most efficient way or do we want to use global warming as a stepping stone to other political projects? Before we make this clear to ourselves and others, the debate will continue to be muddled. Personally, I believe that in order to think clearly we should try to the utmost to separate issues, not the least because trying to solve all problems at one go may likely result in making bad solutions for all areas. Thus, I try to address just the issue of global warming.

Second, we should not spend vast amounts of money to cut a tiny slice of the global temperature increase when this constitutes a poor use of resources and when we could probably use these funds far more effectively in the developing world. This connection between resource use on global warming and aiding the Third World actually goes much deeper, because the developing world will experience by far the most damage from global warming. Thus, when we spend resources to mitigate global warming we are in fact and to a large extent helping future inhabitants in the developing world. However, if we spend the same money directly in the Third World we would be helping present inhabitants in the developing world, and through them also their descendants. Since the inhabitants of the Third World are likely to be much richer in the future, and since the return on investments in the developing countries is much higher than those on global warming (about 16 percent to 2 percent), the question really boils down to: *Do we want to help more well-off inhabitants in the Third World a hundred years from now a little or do we want to help poorer inhabitants in the present Third World much more?* To give a feel for the size of the problem—the Kyoto Protocol will likely cost at least $150 billion a year, and possibly much more. UNICEF estimates that just $70–80 billion a year could give all Third World inhabitants access to the basics like health, education, water and sanitation. More important still is the fact that if we could muster such a massive investment in the present-day developing countries this would also give them a much better future position in terms of resources and infrastructure from which to manage a future global warming.

13   Third, we should realize that the cost of global warming will be substantial—about $5 trillion. Since cutting back CO_2 emissions quickly turns very costly and easily counterproductive, we should focus more of our effort at finding ways of easing the emission of greenhouse gases over the long run. Partly, this means that we need to invest much more in research and development of solar power, fusion and other likely power sources of the future. Given a current US investment in renewable energy research and development of just $200 million, a considerable increase would seem a promising investment to achieve a possible conversion to renewable energy towards the latter part of the century. Partly, this also means that we should be much more open towards other techno-fixes (so-called geoengineering). These suggestions range from fertilizing the ocean (making more algae bind carbon when they die and fall to the ocean floor) and putting sulfur particles into the stratosphere (cooling the earth) to capturing CO_2 from fossil fuels use and returning it to storage in geological formations. Again, if one of these approaches could indeed mitigate (part of) CO_2 emissions or global warming, this would be of tremendous value to the world.

14   Fourth, we ought to have a look at the cost of global warming in relation to the total world economy. Analysis shows that even if we should choose some of the most inefficient programs to cut carbon emissions, the costs will at most defer growth a couple of years in the middle of the century. Global warming is in this respect still a limited and manageable problem.

15   Finally, this also underscores that *global warming is not anywhere the most important problem in the world.* What matters is making the developing countries rich and allowing the citizens of developed countries even greater opportunities. In Figure 1 we see the total income over the coming century as envisaged in the four main scenarios from the new IPCC report. If we choose a world focused on economic development within a global setting, the total income over the coming century will be some $900 trillion. However, should we go down a path focusing on the environment, even if

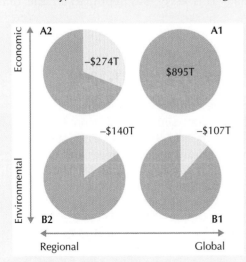

FIGURE 1 ■ The Four Main Scenarios in IPCC, along the Main Future Directions: Global-Regional and Economic-Environmental. (All amounts in trillion 2000 US$.)

we stay within a global setting, humanity will lose some $107 trillion or 12 percent of the total, potential income. And should we choose a more regional approach to solving the problems of the twenty-first century, we would stand to lose $140–274 trillion or even more than a quarter of the potential income. Moreover, the loss will mainly be to the detriment of the developing countries—switching from A1 to B1 would cost the developing world a quarter of its total income, forgoing a developing per capita income some 75 percent higher. Again, this should be seen in the light of a total cost of global warming at about $5 trillion and that the optimal global warming policy can save us just $0.3 trillion.

What this illustrates is that if we want to leave a planet with the most possibilities for our descendants, both in the developing and developed world, it is imperative that we focus primarily on the economy and solving our problems in a global context rather than focusing on the environment in a regionalized context. Basically, this puts the spotlight on securing economic growth, especially in the third world while ensuring a global economy, both tasks which the world has set itself within the framework of the World Trade Organization (WTO). If we succeed here, we could increase world income with $107–274 trillion, whereas even if we achieve the absolutely most efficient global warming policies, we can increase wealth with just $0.3 trillion. To put it squarely, what matters to our and our children's future is not primarily decided within the IPCC framework but within the WTO framework. 16

The third reading by Alan Durning, executive director of the Seattle-based research center Northwest Environmental Watch, first appeared in the Elm Street Writers Group, an online news service that focuses on preserving the environment and making communities livable. This essay was reprinted in the *Utne Reader,* September–October 2001.

▪ ALAN DURNING ▪

LAND OF THE FREE . . . PARKING

President Bush's answer to soaring gasoline prices and allegedly dwindling energy supplies is to drill for oil from the Arctic National Wildlife Refuge to the Gulf of Mexico. But he'd find a much larger source of untapped energy, and a solution to rising transportation woes and expanding sprawl, by looking somewhere else: in the zoning and tax codes that make America the land of the free parking place. 1

Free parking, it turns out, is a major cause of the nation's unquenchable thirst for gasoline and automobile use. And this thirst drives an array of national concerns: not just rising fuel prices but also global climate change, dependence on foreign oil, tightening traffic snarls, relentless sprawl, and worsening urban smog. 2

3   More than 90 percent of all car trips end in free parking spaces. But they aren't really free. In fact, as a nation we pay more to store our vehicles during the 23 hours a day when they're immobile than we do to keep their tanks full.

4   Fully 50 percent of the cost of parking is paid by employers, businesses, and taxpayers. Another 40 percent is paid through rent and mortgages for off-street parking at home. With everybody splitting the cost of free parking, it's no wonder that drivers have almost nothing to gain by leaving their cars at home.

5   The remaining 10 percent of the nation's parking bill is pay-per-use at meters, lots, or garages—a far smaller share than most nations. Pay parking is rare outside the center of big cities because antiquated provisions in zoning and tax codes—along with auto-centered street designs—bloat the parking supply and glut the market. Most zoning codes require a surplus of parking spaces. In the Pacific Northwest, for example, office buildings are required to provide up to four spots per 1,000 square feet of floor space. Many stores provide enough parking to accommodate cars on the Friday after Thanksgiving—the busiest shopping day of the year—and most of the lot is empty (and the land is wasted) for the next 364 days.

6   The resulting oceans of parking give employees and customers a big incentive to drive; they also discourage transit, bike, and pedestrian travel by interposing vast parking lots between streets and buildings and by spreading out the destinations people want to reach.

7   A few communities have recently begun reforming parking policies. Portland, Oregon, exempts downtown residential development from off-street parking requirements. Downtown Olympia, Washington, has no minimum parking requirements.

8   But here's a simpler reform: Strike all off-street parking requirements from the law books and leave it to property owners to decide how much parking to provide. Many owners, especially real estate developers, would devote less land to cars and more to buildings, increasing the supply of housing and commercial space.

9   In new communities, streets can be made more narrow, eliminating on-street parking. Olympia plans to build residential streets as skinny as 13 feet in one fast-growing neighborhood—one-third the conventional width—while Missoula, Montana, Eugene, Oregon, and Kirkland, Washington, have reduced some streets down to 20 or 24 feet.

10   Changes like these can also work in existing developments. With no parking requirements, the owners of buildings now surrounded by concrete have new choices: They can expand their businesses, sell land to others for development, or turn parking into plazas.

11   It might take 10 years to absorb all the excess parking places across America, but scarcity—and a market—would develop. Free parking would dwindle as higher-value uses take over space currently devoted to car storage. And, as drivers begin to face the full environmental and social costs of their decisions, auto use would decrease.

Finally, the United States could eliminate inequitable tax provisions that favor cars over other transportation. At present, taxes encourage employers to supply free parking by treating it as a nontaxable fringe benefit. Employers may give employees parking worth $175 a month as an untaxed fringe benefit—equivalent to pretax income exceeding $2,500 a year. 12

"Cashing out" employer-paid parking would further dampen driving. A full-fledged cash-out policy requires that employers who give workers free parking let them choose to receive the parking space's dollar value in cash instead. Tests of this policy in Los Angeles show that as many as two in five commuters take the money and leave their wheels at home. 13

By shepherding a full-fledged cash-out provision into federal law, President Bush could save more oil than we're likely to find by drilling. If tens of millions of workers across the country left their cars at home and tacked an extra $2,500 onto their paychecks, it would save 2.5 million barrels of oil a day or more than twice what the Department of Energy estimates we can recover from the Alaska wildlife refuge. Subjecting parking to the free market so revered by the president can diminish the need for new oil wells—and safeguard the livability of so many communities. 14

COMPOSING YOUR SYNTHESIS ESSAY

The main project of composing your synthesis essay is to move from the kernels of good ideas that you generated in your learning logs to the fully developed and logically organized discussion of these ideas.

Generating and Exploring Ideas

If you have speculated about, responded to, and explored your texts using the progression of learning logs, you should now have a body of ideas to use in the development of your synthesis essay. Your task in the production of your essay is to sort through, make decisions about, and pursue further both the analysis ideas and the synthesis ideas that you have generated.

At this point, you should return to the writing you did for your learning logs. For the analysis part of your essay, identify the points in Learning Logs 2 and 3 that strike you as the most interesting, lively, profound, or significant. For the synthesis part of your essay, identify the points in Learning Logs 4 and 5 that you feel most excited about or interested in. In both cases, add new ideas generated by class discussion and further reflection.

Shaping and Drafting

Both focusing and organizing your ideas for a synthesis essay are challenging writing tasks. We offer some suggestions for formulating a thesis that will direct and hold together your essay. There are also several plans you can use for developing your essay.

Analysis Section: About two-thirds of your essay should focus on analyzing the texts. This part of the body of your essay should compare and contrast what the texts claim and argue, how they frame the problem you are exploring, how they present different angles of vision, and where they intersect or differ in their perspectives or approaches. The analysis part of your essay should show how you have wallowed in the complexity of the texts. What do the authors of the texts do to make their readers think? How rhetorically effective are these texts? How and how well do the authors' examples and approaches support their theses and advance their views?

Synthesis section: About one-third of your essay should be your synthesis. Where do the texts and their authors leave you in your thinking? What have you discovered or realized after studying these texts? What new perspectives have you gained through the contrast and/or clash of different ideas? How much or how little have these texts changed your views and why?

Writing a Thesis for a Synthesis Essay

It is often difficult to write a one-sentence, high-level thesis statement for a synthesis essay that encompasses all your analysis and synthesis points. In such cases you can write two lower-level thesis statements—one for your analysis section and one for your synthesis section—and simply join them together. What is important is that your thesis forecasts your main analysis and synthesis points and creates a map for your reader. This is the strategy used by Kate at the end of her introduction:

For a full explanation of thesis statements, purpose statements, and mapping statements, see pp. 515–516.

Kate's Thesis

Although both Turkle and Ritzer identify problems in technology's influence and in society's responses to it, Turkle sees more potential and gain where Ritzer sees mostly peril and loss. Both articles made me question how we define our values and morality in this postmodern, technologically advanced world and persuaded me of the need for caution in embracing technology.

Lower-level thesis for analysis

Lower-level thesis for synthesis

Your thesis statement should be clear, specific, focused, and risky. It should be the product of earnest intellectual work, insights achieved through serious reflection, and your own original connecting of ideas. Avoid noncontestable thesis statements such as "These articles have both good points and bad points." Try to formulate your thesis so that it challenges or surprises your reader.

See pp. 512–515 for a discussion of how to avoid unsurprising, noncontestable thesis statements.

Here are some more examples:

Example 1

Whereas Ritzer focuses on the way high-tech society makes us homogeneous and superficial, Turkle focuses on how the Internet unsettles traditional views of the self. Although I agree with Ritzer's argument that McDonaldization is dehumanizing, I think that role-playing in MUDs is actually a healthy way to oppose McDonaldization and expresses human desire to be creative, to develop the self, and to make human connections.

Lower-level thesis for analysis

Lower-level thesis for synthesis

*Writer chooses
high-level,
one-sentence
thesis rather
than two
lower-level
theses*

Example 2

Ritzer's attack on technological society and Turkle's more optimistic belief that it offers opportunity for growth and discovery have together forced me to consider the superficiality and vulnerability of human relationships in our high-tech society.

Possible Organizations for Synthesis Essays

The biggest organizational decision you have to make in writing a synthesis essay is how much to summarize your texts and how to incorporate these summaries into your essay. Your decision should be guided by your audience's familiarity with the texts you are discussing and the complexity of the points you are making.

Plan 1

- ▓ Introductory paragraph that presents the focusing question and hooks the reader
- ▓ Summaries of the texts you are examining (unless your instructor posits that readers have already read the texts, in which case you can omit the summaries or reduce them to one or two sentences each)
- ▓ A thesis that maps out your main analytical points and your main synthesis points. Your thesis can come at the end of the paragraph(s) with your summaries or in a miniparagraph of its own.
- ▓ Paragraphs discussing and developing your analytical points
- ▓ Synthesis section consisting of paragraphs discussing and developing your synthesis points
- ▓ Concluding paragraph that reiterates the values and limitations of the texts you have analyzed, pulls together your new insights, and leaves readers thinking about your views

Plan 2

- ▓ Introductory paragraph that presents the focusing question and hooks the reader
- ▓ A thesis that maps out your main analytical points and your main synthesis points
- ▓ Summary and analysis of the first text
- ▓ Summary and analysis of the second text
- ▓ Synthesis section that develops several main synthesis points
- ▓ Concluding paragraph that reiterates the values and limitations of the texts you have analyzed, pulls together your new insights, and leaves readers thinking about your views

Revising

As you revise your synthesis essay, focus on exploring even stronger ways to set up the focusing question that connects your texts and on ways to make your essay a stronger and more lively engagement with these texts by clarifying and developing your analytical points. Also consider how to make your synthesis views more clearly reflect your wrestling with the texts' ideas. Think about finding the most interesting ways to show how these texts have enlarged and deepened your own views on technology's effect on us. The following Guidelines for Peer Reviews can both help your peer reviewers and direct you as you think of ways to revise your paper.

▪ GUIDELINES FOR PEER REVIEWS ▪

Instructions for peer reviews are provided in Chapter 18 (pp. 490–496).

For the Writer
Prepare two or three questions you would like your peer reviewer to address while responding to your draft. The questions can focus on some aspect of your draft that you are uncertain about, on one or more sections where you particularly seek help or advice, on some feature that you particulary like about your draft, or on some part you especially wrestled with. Write out your questions and give them to your peer reviewer along with your draft.

For the Reviewer
I. Read the draft at a normal reading speed from beginning to end. As you read, do the following:

   A. Place a wavy line in the margin next to any passages that you find confusing, that contain some idea or word that doesn't seem to fit, or that otherwise slow down your reading.

   B. Place a "Good!" in the margin next to any passages where you think the writing is particularly strong or interesting.

II. Read the draft again slowly and answer the following questions by writing brief explanations of your answers.

   A. Introduction and summaries of the texts:

      1. How could the introduction present the focusing question more powerfully, showing its significance, relevance, and problematic nature?

      2. How could the summaries be expanded or condensed to suit more closely the audience's knowledge of these texts? In other words, does this audience need longer or shorter summaries of the texts in order to understand the writer's analysis and synthesis?

      3. How could the placement of the summaries—in the introductory paragraph or woven into the analysis section of the paper—be improved?

      4. How could the summaries be made more accurate, fair, and clear?

      5. How could the thesis be made more focused, risky, and clear in setting up the writer's analytical and synthesis points?

B. Analytical section of the essay:

1. How could the analytical points more clearly compare and contrast the authors' values, assumptions, angles of vision, or rhetorical strategies in addressing the question of the problem of technology?

2. What further textual evidence could the writer add to develop these analytical points and make them more interesting or comprehensive?

C. Synthesis section of the essay:

1. How could the writer's synthesis points more clearly demonstrate the writer's thoughtful interaction with these texts and with the question of technology's influence?

2. What examples or other specifics could the writer include to develop these synthesis points more effectively?

3. How could the writer conclude this essay more effectively to leave readers with a new perspective on the texts and on the underlying question?

D. If the writer has prepared questions for you, respond to his or her inquiries.

E. Sum up what you see as the main strengths and problem areas of the draft:

1. Strengths

2. Problem areas

III. Read the draft one more time. Place a check mark in the margin wherever you notice problems in grammar, spelling, or mechanics (one check mark per problem).

CHAPTER 14

Investigating Cause and Consequence

ABOUT CAUSAL ANALYSIS

Puzzling over causes and consequences is one of the most common kinds of thinking. Take, for example, the case of Robert, an exceptionally shy teenager whose older brother is a party animal and extrovert. What caused Robert, but not his brother, to become shy? Was it something in the family dynamics—perhaps related to birth order or to changes in his parents' marriage—that caused his parents to treat Robert differently from his brother? Was it the result of some bad childhood experience when Robert was made fun of or mocked? Is it perhaps genetic, in which case Robert, unlike his brother, inherited a "shyness" gene? Or might Robert's shyness be related to brain chemistry? Starting in the late 1990s, psychiatrists began treating shyness with selected antidepressants, often with encouraging success. Soon pharmaceutical companies began targeting shy people in their advertisements. The ads identified shyness as a symptom of "social anxiety disorder" and promised pills that could get shy people out of their houses and into the social whirl. The result was a stunning increase in the sale of antidepressants as shy people by the droves redefined their shyness as a treatable brain condition rather than a personality trait. Critics of the drug companies complained about the power of advertising to cause perfectly normal (and mentally healthy) shy people to believe they had a personality disorder requiring drugs. Meanwhile, psychiatrists explained how debilitating severe cases of shyness can be, robbing afflicted persons of a full life.

The controversy over shyness illustrates the fascination and complexity of causal analysis. When you analyze the causes or consequences of something, you try to show how one event or phenomenon brings about another. The investigation of causes and consequences is the main business of the physical and social sciences. How does the HIV virus destroy the immune system? Why are white teenage females seven times more likely to smoke than black teenage females? Why are sea otter populations declining precipitously in Alaskan waters? What causes one person to be gay and another straight?

Questions about cause and consequence also dominate business and public life, where answers to causal questions shape important public decisions. What is causing the rising illegitimacy rate in the United States? Will a federal tax cut stimulate spending? How would the legalization of marijuana change the police and court systems?

Throughout college, many of your assignments will focus on causal questions. In a chemistry lab, you might have to determine experimentally why a solution turns blue, or in a psychology course you might try to determine what variables in study methods affect students' retention of textbook information. You will also engage in a variety of other activities—observing, reading, testing, surveying, comparing—to help you understand why and how things happen in nature and in culture. In this chapter, we prepare you for these future activities by showing you various ways to analyze causes or predict consequences and to make compelling cases for your ideas.

EXPLORING CAUSAL ANALYSIS

To help you appreciate why cause or consequence questions can stimulate critical thinking, we invite you to consider some causal problems. Working in small groups or as a whole class, brainstorm as many possible causes or consequences as you can for each of the following cases. As you conduct your discussion, note moments of controversy when people disagree about a cause or consequence or moments of surprising insight when someone argues for an unsuspected or over-looked cause or consequence.

1. Until fairly recently in Western culture, women considered beautiful were ample, rounded, and fleshy. Titian's famous *Venus Anadyomene* (Figure 14.1)

FIGURE 14.1 ■ Titian's Venus Anadyomene, c. 1520. Oil on canvas.

suggests a standard of beauty entirely different from the super slender look. Why did thinness in women come to be considered attractive? To what extent is the ideal of thinness related to race and class? Why?

2. Why did rap music become popular? Consider first why it arose within urban black culture. Then consider why its popularity spread rapidly into white middle-class youth culture. What have the consequences been of this popularity?

3. What are some causes of frustration, anxiety, or stress on your campus for one or more of the following categories of students?

Students in general
Commuting (or residential) students
Students with jobs
Students with learning or physical disabilities
Students belonging to racial, ethnic, or religious minorities

Students with preschool or school-age children
Gay or lesbian students
Science majors (humanities, nursing, business, or other majors)
Older students (student athletes, conservative or liberal students)
Another category of your choice

For discussion of proposal arguments, which are often built on an analysis of causes and consequences, see Chapter 17.

Often students in one of these categories have little knowledge of campus issues faced by students in other categories. Your analyses of the causes of stress for different categories of students might lead eventually to a proposal for solving a particular problem.

WRITING PROJECT

Write an essay in which you analyze the causes or consequences of an event, trend, or phenomenon, or in which you argue for an unusual, overlooked, or unexpected cause or consequence.

Your writing assignment for this chapter is to analyze the causes or consequences of an event, trend, or phenomenon. Your essay must bring something new to the reader. Sometimes your purpose is to enlarge your reader's view of an event or phenomenon by pointing out an unexpected or surprising cause or consequence. In such a case, your underlying purpose might be to change your reader's initial evaluation of the phenomenon. (My reader thinks that the consequences of X are good, but my paper will reveal several surprising bad consequences.) At other times, your purpose is to clarify your reader's view by explaining the causes or consequences of a phenomenon that your reader initially finds baffling or puzzling. (My reader is puzzled by the causes of X; my paper will explain these causes.) At still other times, your purpose is to restructure your reader's understanding of a causal link by arguing against your reader's initial beliefs about the causes or consequences of a phenomenon. In this case you would treat your causal question as controversial. (My reader thinks that the primary cause of X is Y, but I am going to show the primary cause is Z.) Causal analyses can thus serve a variety of rhetorical aims.

For further discussion of how writers can enlarge, clarify, or restructure an audience's view of a topic, see Chapter 3, pp. 44–45.

Depending on your instructor's purposes and goals for this assignment, you may be asked to write a relatively short paper drawing primarily on your own experiences and observations or a longer documented paper using research sources. The two student essays in this chapter illustrate each kind of paper.

UNDERSTANDING CAUSAL ANALYSIS

Now that you have been introduced to questions of cause and consequence, we next provide a fuller explanation of causal reasoning and, along the way, provide examples that should help you produce your own analysis of a causal problem.

Kinds of Phenomena That Give Rise to Causal Questions

Most questions about causes and consequences can be classified into three categories: one-time events, repeatable or recurring events, and trends. We look at each in turn.

One-time events

One-time events, as the name implies, happen only once in time. They can't be repeated to permit scientific study. Examples of puzzling one-time events that have sparked extensive causal analysis are the crash of John F. Kennedy, Jr.'s private airplane en route to Martha's Vineyard in 1999 or each discrete incident in the anthrax scare beginning shortly after the September 11, 2001, terrorist attacks. One-time events can also lead to questions about consequences. For example, "What will the consequences be of instituting a mandatory service learning course on our campus?" Although one-time events can be compared to other similar events (other crashes of private planes, other anthrax scares, other universities that have mandated service learning), they don't give you the opportunity to study the same phenomenon over multiple repetitions. Here is a student example of a causal argument addressing a one-time event:

Why did the Tiger basketball team lose the division play-offs? (posed by a basketball fan proposing an unanticipated or surprising cause)

Most persons feel that losing the series was bad luck, but I want to show the cause was bad coaching:

- Failure to anticipate the opponent's trapping full court press
- Too much reliance throughout the season on the three-point shot instead of the inside game
- Failure to make key substitutions in the fourth quarter

Repeatable Events or Recurring Phenomena

Unlike one-time events, repeatable events occur again and again, thus making it possible to conduct a scientific study of causes. When an event is repeatable, scientists can study it over time, looking for the relative contribution of different variables and determining each link in a causal chain. Typical examples posed by professional researchers are these: What causes math anxiety among females? or What are the consequences of excessive television watching on children? Student Susan Meyers' paper on the causes of anorexia (pp. 356–366) fits this category as does Edgar Lobaton's paper on the causes of Latino stereotypes (pp. 353–355). Here is another student example:

> ### *What are the consequences of cell phone usage?* (posed by a mountain climber proposing an unanticipated or surprising consequence, which he saves for last)

- ▨ Cell phones keep people easily in touch with each other. (common view)
- ▨ They are useful in emergencies. (another common view)
- ▨ But, surprisingly, they cause adventurers to take greater risks leading to an increase in accidents and death (unexpected negative consequence)

Trends

Trends are marked by an increase or decrease in the frequency of a phenomenon. Some trends probably happen only once in time such as the hula hoop craze of the 1950s, while others recur in cycles (such as the popularity of bell bottom pants or long hair for men). You can study both the causes and consequences of trends. What are the causes (or consequences) of the increasing contempt for women in rap lyrics? What are the causes (or consequences) of the growing popularity of transgender role-playing in cyberspace MUDs? Here is how a student constructed a causal argument addressing a trend:

> ### *Why are herbal medicines gaining popularity?* (posed by a nursing student who imagined an audience puzzled by this question)

- ▨ Herbal remedies are less expensive than prescription drugs.
- ▨ Herbal remedies come from a medical tradition that treats the whole person.
- ▨ Immigrants are bringing in their medical traditions.
- ▨ Rising interest in multiculturalism and diversity causes recognition of cultures and their remedies that are thousands of years old (Chinese, Native American).

Special Difficulty of Examining Causality in Humans

Causal analysis faces special difficulties whenever a phenomenon involves humans. First of all, humans have (or appear to have) free will, which means they don't always respond to external forces predictably. Whereas any two rocks, if dropped from a roof, will always accelerate at precisely the same rate, any two human beings placed in identical circumstances may react in a bewildering variety of ways. Sometimes human beings will respond oddly out of pure perversity, precisely to disappoint expectations.

The problem we have just raised—the philosophic problem of freedom versus determinism—shows that human beings aren't predictable in the same way that billiard balls or laboratory rats are predictable. We must therefore be cautious when we say that X caused a person to do Y. Do we mean that X "forced" that person to do Y (as if some powerful drug overwhelmed the person's will)? Or do we mean simply that X "motivated" the person to do Y so that doing Y is still an act of freedom?

Even when human beings are acted upon by forces outside their control, it may be difficult to sort out the influences of nature versus nurture. We raised this issue at the beginning of this chapter with the case of Robert's shyness. Is Robert shy because of his upbringing and environment (nurture) or because of his genetic structure or brain chemistry (nature)? Or is it some combination of both? Questions of nature versus nurture arise in the most vexing ways whenever scientists discuss the causes of alcoholism, schizophrenia, generosity, aggressiveness, tendency toward criminal behavior, musical talent, and almost any other human trait.

The Law of Unexpected Consequences

Another way to appreciate the complexity of causal questions is to consider the "law of unintended consequences." Whenever you propose a solution to a problem, you should conduct a cost-benefit analysis to see whether the good consequences outweigh the bad. But how accurately can you predict the consequences? The law of unexpected consequences raises a warning. Consider these examples:

- ▨ *Stonewashed jeans and strip-mining.* When the fad for stonewashed jeans reached its height, the clothing industry's demand for pumice—a rocklike substance that produces the stonewashed effect—caused its price to jump from $7 per cubic yard to $60 per cubic yard. According to an article in *Environment* magazine, this increased market demand caused a profit-seeking New Mexico mining company to strip-mine pumice from thousands of acres that were being considered for designation as a national recreational area.

- ▨ *Oil crisis and SUVs.* In 1977, during the height of a national oil shortage, the federal government passed the "Corporate Average Fuel Economy" standards act (CAFE), which mandated that Detroit carmakers make their automobiles more fuel efficient. It set a high-efficiency standard for passenger cars and a lower standard for pickups. Detroit responded by making its pickups more comfortable—and the SUV was born. Considered pickups rather than cars, SUVs are allowed to guzzle gasoline like a truck. According to journalist Doron Levin, the ironic consequence of CAFE was to get America hooked on SUVs and burn more gas rather than less.

Now that you have looked at some of the complexities of causal analysis, let's turn to various ways of arguing that one event causes another.

Three Methods for Arguing That One Event Causes Another

How much you need to develop your analysis of any given causal link is a function of your readers' degree of skepticism. If you imagine your readers' accepting your speculation that Event A helps cause Event B, you don't have to develop an extended demonstration of the causal link. Both you and your readers see its plausibility. However, if you imagine a skeptical audience, a more extensive explanation may be required. In this section we examine three different methods for arguing that one event is linked causally to another: directly, indirectly, or analogically.

Method 1: Explain the Causal Mechanism Directly

The most compelling form of causal argument explains directly, step-by-step, how one event causes another. For example, in a recent newspaper article on the health problems of female athletes, author Monica Yant noted the alarming tendency of top female athletes to develop severe health problems. This claim is surprising because people typically associate athletes with vigorous health. Yant used a carefully constructed argument to show how a successful young female athlete could become a victim of osteoporosis, a disease of the bones associated with elderly females. She forged the following chain of causes and consequences:

Starting Point	Successful young female athletes are driven by a fierce competitiveness to achieve at the highest levels.
Link A	A female athlete may diet rigorously to keep her weight down to give her an edge over the competition and to please her coach.
Link B	Rigorous dieting gradually becomes obsessive, leading to an abnormal loss of body fat.
Link C	Loss of body fat leads to decreased production of estrogen, which leads in turn to amenorrhea, an absence or marked decrease in menstrual periods.
Link D	Amenorrhea leads to a further drop in the woman's estrogen levels.
End Point	A low estrogen level leads to diminished bone mass and, in extreme cases, to osteoporosis.

Certainly you could raise additional questions about this causal chain. You could start further back, asking how these young athletes became so competitive and so concerned with their achievements, why they care so much about what their coaches think of them, and why they need that external validation. Or you might want to know more precisely *how* low body fat leads to low estrogen and *how* low estrogen brings about low bone mass.

Even in a largely scientific study concerning osteoporosis, for instance, causal chains are always open to more questioning. Arguing for direct links between events becomes even more difficult when you look at broad historical questions. Consider, for example, the causal dilemma that engrossed American citizens following the September 11, 2001, terrorism attacks in New York City and Washington, D.C. Many Americans couldn't fathom a hatred of the United States so severe that it inspired suicide terrorist missions, apparent rejoicing in the streets in Palestine, or massive anti-American demonstrations in Pakistan and other Muslim countries. "Why do they hate us?" became an almost universally debated question in the American press. Here are some of the proposed answers:

■ Osama bin Laden and his al Queda terrorists hate the United States because it is a "beacon of freedom" (one of President Bush's favorite terms). The United States is a multi-ethnic, diverse, and open society founded on constitutionally protected rights and governed by civil laws that separate church and state. It is this very diversity and openness that terrorists fear and hate.

■ The hatred comes from the United States' support of Israel and its failure to promote an independent Palestinian state. Videotapes from Osama bin Laden following the terrorist attacks mentioned this cause explicitly.

■ The hatred comes from American military presence in Saudi Arabia, which desecrates the holy Islamic sites of Mecca and Medina. This military presence, in turn, comes from America's need for a stable oil supply, which was perceived by many Muslims as the chief motivation for the Gulf war.

■ The hatred can be explained by worldwide fundamentalist movements opposing modernism. The United States is perceived as a decadent society characterized by materialism, sex-obsessed youth, secular values, drugs, and pornography. These decadent values invade Islam through advertising, movies, television, and music. American culture corrupts Islamic youth and erodes the principles of morality, discipline, and order essential to faith.

■ The hatred comes from American bullying and hypocrisy. From the perspective of the world's poor, the United States has no real desire to promote democracy, but instead supports dictators in the Middle East and Africa as long as they keep the oil flowing; U.S. economic sanctions against Iraq have contributed to the deaths of hundreds of thousands of Iraqi children, which is worse than the deaths of the 3,000 or more Americans on September 11; the United States consumes most of the world's resources and cares nothing for the world's poor.

As you can see, these competing causal explanations—all of which probably contain some truth—illustrate why causal questions provide a rich field for analysis, critical thinking, and argument.

For Writing and Discussion

Suppose you are writing a causal analysis identifying personal choices that contribute to global warming. You want readers to blame themselves for global warming instead of complaining abstractly about greedy corporations. In your paper you want to show how the following three actions all contribute to global warming.

■ Needlessly driving your car when other options are available

■ Buying an SUV

■ Eating beef (especially buying hamburgers from fast-food restaurants)

Working as a whole class or in small groups, develop consensus answers to the following questions:

1. Which of the above causal links requires the most explanation? (That is, which will seem initially plausible to your imagined audience and which will seem far-fetched?) The more your audience can be expected to doubt your proposed cause, the more you have to develop your causal explanation.
2. Develop causal chains linking each of the above causes to global warming.
3. Using the direct causal chain method, write a passage explaining the link you think your audience is most apt to doubt. (We expect the "eating beef" link needs the most explanation. Hint: A major cause for cutting down tropical rain forests is to clear space for cattle grazing; the cattle market is driven by an appetite for beef. How does cutting down rain forests contribute to global warming?)

Method 2: Explain the Causal Link Through Inductive Methods

Induction is a form of reasoning by generalizing from a limited number of specific cases. If you regularly get a headache after eating white rice but not after eating brown rice, you might conclude *inductively* that white rice causes you to get headaches, even though you can't explain the causal mechanism directly. However, it is also possible that unusual coincidences are at work. Because inductive reasoning yields only probable truths, not certain ones, it can mislead you into false assumptions. We discuss this caution in more detail later in this chapter.

When you conduct an investigation of causes using inductive methods, you can take one of several approaches:

Observation of samples. One way to analyze causes inductively is to act like an anthropologist or ethnographer and observe representative instances of the phenomenon you are investigating. For example, if you wanted to figure out why people subject themselves to mosh pits at rock concerts, you could hurl yourself into a mosh pit and interview various concertgoers as a source of data and insights for your causal analysis.

For example, two German neurologists, puzzled by the fact that so many teenage girls faint at rock concerts, attended a concert and interviewed nearly four hundred fainters. Their conclusion? The biggest culprit was lack of sleep—the fainters had been too excited to sleep the night before the concert.

Scientific experimentation. You can reach more precise inductive conclusions by designing scientific experiments to control variables and test them one at a time. For example, scientists conducted a study to determine whether a tendency toward obesity is caused by some inherited metabolic defect, by lifestyle and diet choices, or by some combination of both. The medical team randomly selected people to participate in an experiment designed to identify which of many variables affect weight gain. Researchers placed all subjects in the same environment and gave each the same amount of food, proportioned by body weight, for a prolonged period of time. Some subjects gained weight; others lost weight.

The team noticed that two important variables seemed to have the greatest effect on weight gain or loss: gender and activity level. Women tended to gain more weight than men because they burned fewer calories (a finding that was already well established), and those who lost weight moved around more than those who gained weight (a finding that was less well established and, thanks to the study, assumed greater importance).

Correlation. *Correlation* is a statistical term indicating the probability that two events or phenomenon will occur together. The higher the correlation, the greater the chance that the two events or phenomenon are linked causally rather than coincidentally. But correlation can't tell us the direction of causality. X may cause Y, Y may cause X, or some unknown factor, Z, may cause both of them.

For example, various studies have shown a correlation between creativity and left-handedness. That is, when we compare the percentage of left-handed people in the general population to the percentage of left-handed people in the population of creative people, the latter percentage is two or three times higher than we'd expect. That's too high to be coincidental. (Folk wisdom appears to have arrived at a similar conclusion: in folk tales left-handedness is often associated with eccentricity and imaginative behavior.) But does creativity cause left-handedness, or vice versa? Or is there some third factor that accounts for both? Some researchers have suggested that right brain dominance accounts for both left-handedness and creativity, although many scientists are unsatisfied with that explanation.

Method 3: Cite Precedents or Analogies

One of the most common ways to construct a causal argument is to compare the case you are analyzing to something else that is better known and less controversial to your audience. For example, when baseball fans in Seattle and Cincinnati wanted new ballparks built, they argued that new ballparks can revitalize downtown areas. As proof, they cited the Baltimore Orioles' Camden Yards ballpark, which had spurred a dramatic revitalization in Baltimore. Or to take an example from analogy rather than precedent, people who argue that high-density apartments can cause stress disorders in humans cite studies that prove that mice develop stress disorders when placed in overcrowded cages. But causal arguments by analogy and precedent usually are logically weaker than direct or inductive arguments because the *dissimilarities* between the things being compared often outweigh the similarities. Seattle and Cincinnati might be very different from Baltimore; humans are not mice.

But for all their logical and empirical limitations, analogies and precedents often have a great emotional impact in that they explain unfamiliar or puzzling phenomena by connecting them to phenomena that people understand well. As long as they are plausible, analogies and precedents can be extremely persuasive. To make an important point, however, a writer rarely relies on analogy or precedent alone. Most writers provide additional evidence from direct or inductive arguments to strengthen a case.

For Writing and Discussion

Suppose your state legislature proposes to legalize marijuana and sell it in state liquor stores. As part of an argument against this proposal, one of your class-mates—let's call him Sam—wants to show negative consequences of legalizing marijuana. So far Sam has developed the following list:

■ Legalizing marijuana will cause more people to move on to more dangerous drugs like cocaine and heroin.

■ Legalizing marijuana will lead to a less productive society.

■ Legalizing marijuana will lead to dangerous health risks for individuals who mistakenly believe that marijuana is harmless.

Working in small groups or as a whole class, consider various ways that Sam might support each of these causal assertions. Where might Sam use the direct causal link method? Where might Sam look for empirical studies in the scientific literature (which use experimental or correlation data)? Where might Sam make analogies to other experiences or phenomena?

Glossary of Causal Terms

When analyzing causes, you may find it helpful to know some of the specialized terms that occur in causal arguments.

The Fallacy of the Oversimplified Cause. When conducting a causal analysis, a writer may be tempted to look for *the* cause of a phenomenon. But rarely is an event or phenomenon caused by a single factor; almost always multiple factors work together. A carefully constructed causal analysis explains why one causal factor made a more or less important contribution than another; rarely does the writer try to convince us that a single factor is solely responsible for an effect.

Immediate versus Remote Causes. Every causal chain links backward into the indefinite past. Immediate causes are those closest in time to the effect you are studying; remote causes are those further away in time. An immediate cause of Ken's failing an exam might be his wild partying on Saturday night followed by a throbbing headache on Sunday. A more remote cause might be his relationship with his parents that led to partying behavior in college. The more remote in time the cause is from its purported effect, the greater the arguer's burden of proof. On the flip side, it's all too easy to overemphasize an immediate cause and treat it as *the* cause rather than one among many.

Precipitating versus Contributing Causes. Whereas remote and immediate caus-es have different temporal relationships to their effects, precipitating and con-tributing causes may coexist simultaneously. Contributing causes give rise to a precipitating cause, which triggers the effect. In Ken's case, the precipitating cause of his failing the exam was his failure to study throughout the weekend, which was itself a result of his partying; contributing causes were all the conditions that make partying a part of the college environment—a social structure that values partying, the availability of liquor, films such as *Animal House* that make partying cool, friends who kept bringing Ken another drink, and so on.

Necessary versus Sufficient Causes. A necessary cause is one that must be present for a given effect to occur. In Ken's case, the presence of liquor was a necessary cause of Ken's hangover that kept him from studying the day after the party. A sufficient cause is one that, if present, always triggers the given effect. In Ken's case, the existence of liquor wasn't a sufficient cause for Ken's hangover. (On many occasions, Ken has gone to parties and chosen not to drink at all.) Another cause had to be present—perhaps Ken had just broken up with Barbie and was drowning his sorrow. In this case the existence of a party and the breakup of a romantic relationship are together sufficient causes of his wild behavior. Sometimes a cause can be sufficient without being necessary. Ken's wild partying was a sufficient cause of his failing the examination, but it wasn't a necessary cause. (Ken could have failed the examination for many other reasons besides partying.)

Constraints. Sometimes an effect occurs not because X happened, but because another factor—a constraint—was removed. A constraint is a kind of negative cause, a factor whose presence limits possibilities and choices. Ken's partying may have been caused by the removal of a constraint. Perhaps his relationship with Barbie had previously constrained his partying behavior because she disapproved of drinking and valued high grades; when they broke up, this constraint was gone. Likewise, if Ken's college had instituted severe penalties for partying, these rules may have constrained Ken from partying, and he would have aced his exam.

The Post Hoc, Ergo Propter Hoc Fallacy ("After this, therefore because of this"). The *post hoc* fallacy is the most common reasoning fallacy associated with causal arguments. You fall victim to this fallacy when you assume that Event A causes Event B because Event A precedes Event B. Perhaps Ken would accuse us of *post hoc* reasoning when we assumed that his failing the exam was caused by his partying the weekend before (the partying occurred and then the exam occurred). But, Ken might claim, he had studied thoroughly for the exam the week before, was well rested, and had a migraine rather than a hangover on the day after the party. He flunked the test because he didn't see a whole set of questions on the back of the test sheet.

See Chapter 15, pp. 392–394, for further discussion of reasoning fallacies.

R e a d i n g s

The following readings show examples of student and professional writers analyzing causal questions and proposing causal or consequence claims. The first reading, by Webzine author Steven E. Landsburg, addresses a puzzling trend—the increasing obesity of U.S. citizens. This article appeared in the online magazine *Slate* on May 1, 2001.

■ STEVEN E. LANDSBURG ■

WHY ARE WE GETTING SO FAT?
A Few Theories on America's Weight Problem

1   Georgia is the home state of cornbread, barbecue, peach pie, and a whole lot of really fat people—21.1 percent of the state's population, to be exact, is obese. Ten years ago, the cornbread, barbecue, and peach pie were all just as good as they are now, but only 9.5 percent of Georgians were obese. What changed?

2   Whatever changed, it changed everywhere. Obesity is skyrocketing in every age group, in every race, in both genders, and in every state of the union. The most obese region in the country remains the South—four of the five most obese states are below the Mason-Dixon line—but the spectacular recent *growth* in obesity is nationwide, led by Georgia but followed by New Mexico, Virginia, California, and Vermont. In 1991, a little over 12 percent of the country was obese; by 1999, it was almost 20 percent.

3   OK, so what's changed in the past decade or so? Well, one thing that's changed is the portion sizes at fast food joints like McDonald's. In 1970, McDonald's offered one size of French fries; today that size is called "small." Eventually, it introduced a new size and called it "large"; today that size is called "medium." There's a new larger large size, but you don't have to settle for that—you can always "supersize it" and go a step beyond large.

4   So, are we fatter because we're being fed more? Not so fast: Bigger portions don't necessarily translate into bigger meals. When portions were small, you could buy two orders of fries and eat them both; now that portions are enormous, you can buy one supersized order and share it with your family. How much of that goes on? We simply have no idea.

5   And even if people *are* eating more fries these days, there's still a which-came-first-the-chicken-tenders-or-the-Egg-McMuffin question: Do big meals cause obesity or does obesity cause big meals? Did McDonald's decide on a whim to fatten us up or did its market research reveal that bigger customers were demanding bigger portions? My money's on the latter. After all, McDonald's was presumably just as greedy in 1970 as it is today, so if we had wanted supersizes back then, we'd presumably have gotten them. That means we still have to figure out why people want to be fatter now than in the recent past.

6   Well, what else has changed? Here's a thought: Ten years ago, you couldn't read a magazine without walking to the newsstand or at least to the mailbox; today you're reading *Slate* from the same chair where you work, chat with friends, and do half your shopping. Did Bill Gates make us fat?

7   The facts suggest otherwise: Obesity tends to be highest in states where computer ownership is lowest, and that's true even after you control for income. Furthermore, *increases* in obesity tend to be highest in states where

increases in computer ownership are lowest. So, the evidence goes against the computers-as-instruments-of-the-devil theory. Instead, computers seem to keep us trim—maybe because they're so fascinating that we forget to eat, or maybe because we burn calories in silent rage every time the system crashes.

What about smoking habits? A lot of people have quit smoking lately, and maybe that's what's making them fat. After all, those who quit often eat more to satisfy their oral fixation. But the numbers tell a different story. It's true that in the 25 states where smoking fell during the '90s, obesity rose 55 percent—but in the 25 states where smoking increased, obesity rose by an even greater 59 percent. Minnesota, where smoking plummeted faster than anywhere else, ranked only 38th in obesity growth. New Mexico, which led the nation in new smokers, ranked second in obesity growth. 8

So, what else has changed? Incomes have risen, but that cuts both ways: As we get richer, we can afford more food, but we can also afford better quality food and better quality health clubs. On net, there is no statistically significant correlation (in either direction) between changes in income and changes in obesity. 9

Which brings us back to the same question: What else changed? What happened in the early '90s that could have triggered an obesity epidemic? Did the advent of Rush Limbaugh make obesity stylish? Did the Americans With Disabilities Act make obesity less of a handicap in the job market? 10

Here's one plausible story: The '90s saw the advent of drugs like Pravachol and Lipitor that can dramatically cut your cholesterol and increase your life expectancy. With medical advances like that, who needs to be thin? Of course obesity is still bad for you—but it's not as bad for you as it used to be. The price of obesity (measured in health risks) is down, so rational consumers will choose more of it. 11

With the success of the human genome project, even greater advances are just over the horizon, making obesity an even greater bargain. Today's expanding waistlines might reflect nothing more than a rational expectation of future progress against heart disease. 12

If you don't like that story, here's another: The '90s were the era of low-fat foods. At fewer calories per serving, it makes sense to eat more servings. The net effect can be either an increase or a decrease in weight. For example: Suppose a scoop of ice cream a night would add 10 pounds to your weight, and you've decided that's not worth it, so you don't eat ice cream. Now along comes a low-fat ice cream that allows you to eat *two* scoops a night and add 10 pounds to your weight. That's a better deal, and a perfectly rational being might well opt for it. So when low-fat foods come along, some people sensibly decide to become fatter. (Other people, equally sensibly, use low-fat foods to become thinner. Therefore, the overall impact of low-fat foods on obesity could in principle go in either direction.) 13

That's my theory or rather my pair of theories: The obesity epidemic is caused by some combination of medical advances and low-fat foods. Can some reader do better? 14

Thinking Critically about "Why Are We Getting So Fat?"

1. Landsburg begins with some startling statistics about how Americans are getting more obese. He doesn't, however, provide a source for those statistics. We decided to look up "obesity" on the Web to see whether we could verify his figures. We quickly discovered—through the Web site of the Centers for Disease Control, a federal agency—that Landsburg's statistics are accurate. How does the introduction convince you that a puzzling trend toward obesity has occurred?

2. Landsburg's subtitle is "A Few Theories on America's Weight Problem," yet the conclusion identifies a "pair of theories." Landsburg's strategy in the body of the paper is to posit a theory, make it seem initially plausible, and then reject it. List each of the theories proposed by Landsburg. Then, in your own words, explain his argument for rejecting each one (except his final two). What are his final two theories—the ones he apparently doesn't reject?

3. Landsburg raises some interesting questions about correlation versus causation. For example, he shows that there seems to be an inverse correlation between computer ownership and obesity. People who own computers are less apt to be obese than people who don't. Landsburg humorously proposes a direct causal link: Computers make us thinner because we "burn calories in silent rage every time the [computer] crashes." But he probably wants us to contemplate some other factor that causes a correlation between computer ownership and a lower level of obesity. How might you explain that correlation?

4. What are your own theories about why Americans are getting more obese?

The next reading is a brief consequence argument showing that the best long-range solution to preserving natural resources is to reduce the rate of consumption. Written by Evar D. Nering, a retired mathematics professor at Arizona State University, this important article appeared as an op-ed piece in the *New York Times* on June 4, 2001.

■ EVAR D. NERING ■
THE MIRAGE OF A GROWING FUEL SUPPLY

1   When I discussed the exponential function in the first-semester calculus classes that I taught, I invariably used consumption of a nonrenewable natural resource as an example. Since we are now engaged in a national debate about energy policy, it may be useful to talk about the mathematics involved in making a rational decision about resource use.

2   In my classes, I described the following hypothetical situation. We have a 100-year supply of a resource, say oil—that is, the oil would last 100 years if it were consumed at its current rate. But the oil is consumed at a rate that

grows by 5 percent each year. How long would it last under these circumstances? This is an easy calculation; the answer is about 36 years.

Oh, but let's say we underestimated the supply, and we actually have a 1,000-year supply. At the same annual 5 percent growth rate in use, how long will this last? The answer is about 79 years.

3

Then let us say we make a striking discovery of more oil yet—a bonanza—and we now have a 10,000-year supply. At our same rate of growing use, how long would it last? Answer: 125 years.

4

Estimates vary for how long currently known oil reserves will last, though they are usually considerably less than 100 years. But the point of this analysis is that it really doesn't matter what the estimates are. There is no way that a supply-side attack on America's energy problem can work.

5

The exponential function describes the behavior of any quantity whose rate of change is proportional to its size. Compound interest is the most commonly encountered example—it would produce exponential growth if the interest were calculated at a continuing rate. I have heard public statements that use "exponential" as though it describes a large or sudden increase. But exponential growth does not have to be large, and it is never sudden. Rather, it is inexorable.

6

Calculations also show that if consumption of an energy resource is allowed to grow at a steady 5 percent annual rate, a full doubling of the available supply will not be as effective as reducing that growth rate by half—to 2.5 percent. Doubling the size of the oil reserve will add at most 14 years to the life expectancy of the resource if we continue to use it at the currently increasing rate, no matter how large it is currently. On the other hand, halving the growth of consumption will almost double the life expectancy of the supply, no matter what it is.

7

This mathematical reality seems to have escaped the politicians pushing to solve our energy problem by simply increasing supply. Building more power plants and drilling for more oil is exactly the wrong thing to do, because it will encourage more use. If we want to avoid dire consequences, we need to find the political will to reduce the growth in energy consumption to zero—or even begin to consume less.

8

I must emphasize that reducing the growth rate is not what most people are talking about now when they advocate conservation; the steps they recommend are just Band-Aids. If we increase the gas mileage of our automobiles and then drive more miles, for example, that will not reduce the growth rate.

9

Reducing the growth of consumption means living closer to where we work or play. It means telecommuting. It means controlling population growth. It means shifting to renewable energy sources.

10

It is not, perhaps, necessary to cut our use of oil, but it is essential that we cut the rate of increase at which we consume it. To do otherwise is to leave our descendants in an impoverished world.

11

Thinking Critically about "The Mirage of a Growing Fuel Supply"

1. Nering's purpose in this article is to show how the rate of consumption is critical in determining how long the supply of oil (or any other nonrenewable resource) will last under various scenarios. He proceeds by examining the consequences of several hypothetical one-time events. What would happen if we doubled the oil supply? What would happen if we went from a 100-year supply to a 1,000-year supply? In your own words, what are his answers to these questions?

2. The analysis of consequences is often a crucial part of proposal arguments, where it is important to predict the consequences of a proposed action and weigh their benefits and costs. What energy proposals would Nering be most apt to support? Which proposals would he oppose?

3. How convincing do you find Nering's argument?

The next reading, written for a first-year college composition course, addresses the causes of Latino stereotypes in the United States. As student writer Edgar Lobaton explains, he became interested in this question when he first encountered Latino stereotypes as a high school student who had moved with his family from Peru to the United States.

■ EDGAR LOBATON (STUDENT) ■
WHAT CAUSES LATINO STEREOTYPES IN THE UNITED STATES?

1   I moved with my family from Peru to the United States when I was in high school. The adjustment to this new culture was difficult, and when I first heard of Latino stereotypes, I was surprised and troubled. In Peru, of course, almost all people are Latinos, and there are no Latino stereotypes. That is why I found it so confusing in the United States to realize that some people associated me with gangs and violence. Others were even surprised when they discovered I wanted to go to college and get a good education. Because these stereotypes can be so damaging to the self-image of Latino people, I decided to find out how pervasive these stereotypes are and to analyze what causes them.

2   To determine the pervasiveness of Latino stereotypes, I distributed a questionnaire to twenty-five persons in my residence hall asking the question "What image do you think most people have of Latinos and Hispanics?" Of the various views or images of Latinos mentioned on the responses, only 10 percent were positive (see Figure 1). The positive images noted were "strong family values" and "hard-working—e.g., farm workers." Of the negative images, the most frequently mentioned was "gang members" followed by

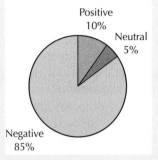

Figure 1. View of Latinos by Percentage of Responses

Positive 10%

Neutral 5%

Negative 85%

"uneducated," "looking for an easy life," "drug dealers," and "rude and dirty."

What causes people in America to stereotype Latinos as gang members or as rude and lazy uneducated persons looking for the easy life? Anyone who knows Latino and Hispanic communities understands that these images are unfounded. In reality, most Latinos are hard-working people trying to make progress in life. So what has caused these images to arise in America? I have three theories.

First the stereotypes come from Americans' view of poverty. Most Latino immigrants in the United States come from the lower classes. In Peru, in contrast, there are many wealthy upper-class Latinos, a growing middle class, and a large lower class of very poor people. In Peru, it is understood that poverty is part of the class system, but in America poor people are often stereotyped as being lazy and unmotivated. This image does not fit Latinos. Most Latinos immigrate to the United States to find a better life, and they are very hard working. Agricultural workers, for example, can work sixty or more hours per week, and they often send their earnings back to families in Mexico or elsewhere. Many industries value Latino immigrants (or even illegal immigrants) because they will work so hard for so little pay. It is ironic then that the poverty of Latinos causes Americans to stereotype them as lazy.

A second cause of these stereotypes is the portrayal of Latinos in TV shows and films. Movies such as *Blood In Blood Out* and *Mi Vida Loca* depict the negative aspects of a complex culture. These films only show one side of the coin. In both films Latinos are shown as violent people with problems. They are either gang members, drug dealers, or criminals. In the case of *Blood In Blood Out,* two half-brothers, Paco and Cruz, grow up with their cousin Miklo, and each one is influenced by their violent environment and the prevalence of drugs on the streets. In a similar way, *Mi Vida Loca* tells the struggle of young Hispanic women in a life of gangs, drugs, and betrayal. These two films present Latinos as a culture with problems who struggle even in their own families.

A final cause of stereotypes is the way news is reported. Generally news stories focus on problems rather than on the everyday life of people. When Latinos show up in the news, it is because they are associated with problems such as gangs, illegal immigration, or the expense of schools having to provide bilingual education. Probably when newspaper readers or TV news watchers think of Latinos, their first image is pictures of Mexicans trying to sneak across the border, stories about illegal aliens living off American welfare, or stories about the English Only movement, where Latinos are seen as a threat to the American way. The actual stories of hard work, of close family values, and of taking care of relatives back in the home country never get told.

7   These stereotypes seem to arise because Latinos are a largely impoverished minority culture trying to survive in a country that basically has not learned to value multiculturalism completely—a country that finds ways to dislike people of color whose native language isn't English. In contrast, stereotypes don't arise back in Peru because Latinos are the majority culture and not a minority.

Thinking Critically about "What Causes Latino Stereotypes in the United States?"

1. To show the pervasiveness of Latino stereotypes, Lobaton creates a survey and displays the results in a pie chart. How effective do you find his approach? Why?
2. When you read Lobaton's essay, did you think he provided any new insights into the causes of Latino stereotypes? What did you find new or surprising in his analysis? Where might you say he enlarged your view of possible causes of stereotypes? Where did he clarify your view? Did he in any sense restructure your view?
3. What additional explanations might you have for the causes of Latino stereotypes or for the process of stereotyping in general?

The final essay, by student writer Susan Meyers, was written for the assignment in this chapter. We have reproduced it exactly to demonstrate the manuscript form and documentation style of the APA (American Psychological Association) system for research papers. Papers written in this style often include an abstract (summary) between the title page and the first page of the body. We have not included an abstract.

For a description of the APA system, see pp. 659–667.

Denying Desire   1

Denying Desire:

The Anorexic Struggle with Image, Self, and Sexuality

Susan Meyers

English 110

November 1, 1998

Note: Format of this student page follows the guidelines of the American Psychological Association (APA).

Denying Desire:

The Anorexic Struggle with Image, Self, and Sexuality

Imagine a disease without a clear diagnosis or cure, a disease caused by neither a virus nor a cancer, a disease with no enemy to trace and root out of the body. Imagine a self-inflicted disease that haunts you minute-by-minute--a disease that you control, just as it controls you.

Anorexia nervosa, a psychological disorder with physical consequences, is such a disease. As of 1998, according to the National Academy of Anorexia Nervosa and Associated Disorders, this eating disorder currently plagues more than 7 million American teenage girls. In its online article "Anorexia Nervosa," the American Academy of Neurology describes anorexia as "a pathological fear of weight gain leading to faulty eating patterns, malnutrition, and usually excessive weight loss." Typical anorexics are healthy, attractive girls from successful families. Although public awareness of anorexia has risen since the 1980s, its cause and cure have continued to baffle

Denying Desire   3

physicians and psychologists, as well as parents,
friends, and victims themselves (Landau, 1983).

Many theories about the cause of anorexia have
been proposed. Some experts blame the advertising and
entertainment industries for their startlingly thin
models and actresses. Others argue that girls monitor
their food intake because they lack control in other
areas of their lives. Still others blame perfectionist
families or cite depression and low self-esteem as
causes for anorexia. All these theories, however,
lack a key element--the complex relationship that
teenage girls have with sexual desire and
desirability.

Blaming the media's thin role models is an
especially popular explanation for anorexia in
teenage girls (Zerbe, 1993). Sleek, slim, 5 ft 10 in.,
115-lb women are not good role models for girls just
coming into an understanding about their bodies, say
feminists and parents. As they reach their early
teens, girls begin to flirt, date, and worry about
their physical appearance. When the only images they
have to compare themselves with are grossly

3

4

Denying Desire   4

disproportioned, it is not surprising that many girls
develop unrealistic goals for their appearance.

5   Further, teens encourage each other to uphold and
follow the standards set up by the media. Exercise
and dieting are common topics of discussion among
teenage girls, as are grooming and dating. While boys
are encouraged to compete in football or hockey, girls
tend to compete for the best bodies and boyfriends.
The popular "blame the media and peer pressure"
explanation, however, does not by itself fully address
the reasons that girls value beauty and sexual
desirability so highly.

6   A different theory about teenage anorexia
cites the drastic changes during adolescence as a
source of anxiety and illness. According to this
theory, teenagers feel out of control as they make
the shift from childhood to adulthood, so they seek
to control the only thing they think they can: their
bodies (Landau, 1983). Undoubtedly, girls (and boys)
face many changes during adolescence: shifts in
relationships with parents, new social standing and
worries about the future, introduction to dating and

Denying Desire   5

sexuality, as well as physical and hormonal changes.
So much upheaval could certainly lead one to feel
panicked, helpless, or out of control. Such feelings,
coupled with sexual peer pressure and the idealized
female image described above, likewise could certainly
lead some girls to starve themselves. They want both
to reach the new standard that has been set for them
(a 5 ft 10 in., 115-lb toned body), and they want to
hold onto and shape some part of their lives.

A more specific pressure that many anorexic girls
may be responding to is family. Statistically,
anorexics tend to be high-achieving "good girls
[and] dutiful daughters" (Pipher, 1994, p.174). Their
families are strict, close-knit, and success-driven,
and often it is difficult for these daughters to
separate psychologically from their parents (Stierlin
& Weber, 1989). Anorexia, then, becomes both a way to
strive for high goals (female beauty expressed through
extreme thinness) and a means to act autonomously. As
Melissa Dean, a former anorexic and the daughter of a
successful business owner, explains, "My parents were
really strict. I did everything [for them]. I

Denying Desire   6

accomplished everything. I felt like I had to do all
this stuff. But [dieting] was the one thing I could
do by myself . . . I could make myself not eat"
(personal communication, August 25, 1998). The theory
of familial pressure has become very popular during
the 1980s and 1990s, and deservedly so, since so many
anorexic girls come from traditional middle- and
upper-class homes. Like the theory of media pressure,
however, it does not explain why girls choose
starvation and/or beauty to seek their autonomy.

    Still another theory is that anorexia stems from
depression or low self-esteem. Proponents of this
theory suggest that uncertainty about physical,
emotional, or relational changes may cause many
teenagers to lose self-confidence and, possibly, to
collapse into depression. Once these girls feel
depressed or inadequate, they look for a way to
redeem themselves: physical perfection (Kinoy, Miller,
Atchley, & American Anorexia/Bulimia Association
1984). However, although depression and low
self-esteem might be present in an anorexic, they
do not necessarily cause anorexia. Depression, for

Denying Desire   7

example, sometimes causes people to overeat rather
than to starve themselves. Furthermore, this theory,
like the control theory, does not consider why
physical perfection becomes the chosen means of
dealing with depression or feelings of inadequacy.
The question still remains: Why is being physically
desirable so intensely important to some adolescent
girls?

Perhaps a fuller understanding lies in a
different direction. Perhaps anorexics don't pursue
desirability but are rather avoiding it. Part of the
traumatic shift from girlhood to womanhood is a
movement from a presexual "neutral" self to a
sexualized self that is an object of desire. During
adolescence, American girls learn that in order to be
good, successful women, they must inspire male desire
while repressing their own; they are introduced to a
double standard that favors male sexuality and
represses women's desires. On the one hand, girls
learn to seek male attention because having dates and
boyfriends can increase their popularity or social
status. But on the other hand, giving in to sexual

9

Denying Desire   8

pressures can turn them into outcasts; they may be
labeled "sluts" (Orenstein & American Association of
University Women, 1994). Further, they learn that,
since men cannot be expected to control their sexual
appetites, women must use mental willpower to overcome
male pressures, as well as their own physical desires.
As one mother explained to her daughter, "'Your body
wants one thing and your mind says another and you'll
always feel that way'" (Orenstein & American
Association of University Women, 1994, p. 211). In
this way, girls learn to hide their own desire while
tantalizing it in males.

   The shift from a largely desexualized girlhood
to a highly sexualized adolescence and womanhood can
easily lead to confusion, upset, and anger. Such
stress can also compound anxieties about changes at
home, school, and in the body. Indeed, it can create
a need to control something, to hold onto something;
and sometimes that thing, whether victims know it or
not, is girlhood. It has been argued that anorexics
starve themselves in an unconscious effort to stunt
their growth in order to remain girls (Landau, 1983),

10

Denying Desire   9

and, certainly, teenage anorexia does interfere with
maturation and hormonal development. The thing that
such girls resist, however, may not simply be physical
change but rather the shift from a neutral self to
an object of desire. As Sarah Lasseter, a former
anorexic, related, "I hated the thought of sex. I
didn't want a gender. I didn't want a body. I just
wanted to be me" (personal communication, July 22,
1998). Such comments are heart-breaking, and it is a
great misfortune that girls--and their teachers,
parents, and doctors--do not consider the traumatic
social conditioning that accompanies adolescence
when they search out causes for anorexia. Instead of
seeking desirability, some girls may actually be trying to escape it.

Denying Desire   10

References

American Academy of Neurology. Anorexia nervosa.

Retrieved October 10, 1998, from

http://www.aan.com/res/pig6.html.

Kinoy, B., Miller, E. B., Atchley, J. A., & American

Anorexia/Bulimia Association. (1984). *When will*

we laugh again? Living and dealing with anorexia

nervosa and bulimia. New York: Columbia

University Press.

Landau, E. (1983). *Why are they starving themselves?*

Understanding anorexia and bulimia. New York:

Julian Messner.

National Academy of Anorexia Nervosa and Associated

Disorders. (1998). Who suffers from anorexia?

Retrieved October 11, 1998, from

http://www.healthtouch.com/level1/special/

4Health.htm.

Orenstein, P., & American Association of University

Women. (1994). *Schoolgirls: Young women, self-*

esteem, and the confidence gap. New York:

Doubleday.

Pipher, M. B. (1994). *Reviving Ophelia: Saving the selves of adolescent girls*. New York: Putnam.

Stierlin, H., & Weber, G. (1989). *Unlocking the family door: A systematic approach to the understanding and treatment of anorexia nervosa*. New York: Brunner/Mazel.

Zerbe, K. J. (1993). *The body betrayed: Women, eating disorders, and treatment*. Washington, DC: American Psychiatric Press.

Thinking Critically about "Denying Desire"

1. Meyers argues for a surprising cause of anorexia that she hints at but doesn't reveal until near the end. Does this organizational strategy work for you? Is her argument convincing?
2. In your own words, what did you find new or surprising in this paper?
3. What do you see as the strengths and weaknesses of this paper?

COMPOSING YOUR ESSAY

This assignment asks you to write a causal analysis in which you pose a question about a puzzling event, trend, or phenomenon and then explain and support your own understanding of its causes or consequences.

Generating and Exploring Ideas

The first stage of your thinking is to discover a question about the cause or consequence of a phenomenon and an audience to whom you can bring something new. Here are three starter questions you can use to help stimulate thinking:

- What one-time event, recurring event, or trend raises puzzling questions for my readers about cause or consequence? (My goal will be to explain the causes or consequences through my own analysis.)
- How can I unsettle or change my readers' current view of a one-time event, recurring event, or trend by showing an unexpected or surprising cause or consequence?
- How do my readers currently misunderstand the causes or consequences of a one-time event, recurring event, or trend? How can I argue for a different causal explanation?

To help you think of ideas for your paper, try the following brainstorming strategies:

- *Make a list of people's unusual likes and dislikes.* One fruitful subject for a causal analysis is to examine the causes of people's likes or dislikes that would seem unusual to your intended audience. Typical examples might be: Why did eating sushi become popular among upscale urban Americans? Why do Canadians like curling? How could you explain to your grandparents the popularity of teenage horror movies (rap music, body piercing, snow boarding)? Despite their environmental destructiveness, why have SUVs become more popular than mini-vans? Freewrite for five minutes or so about likes or dislikes that would seem unusual for some audience.
- *Make lists of one-time events, repeatable phenomena, or trends.* Simply brainstorming lists of events in these categories can give you ideas for your

paper. You'll quickly come across events that are puzzling for some audiences. Consider working together with classmates since two heads (or three or four) are often better than one at the brainstorming stage.

■ *Brainstorm unexpected or surprising causes or consequences of a phenomenon.* When speculating about causes or consequences of a phenomenon, recognize that your first ideas are likely to be the common explanations that your readers will also think of. To bring something new to your reader, search for an unexpected or surprising cause or effect. Try the following exercise:

For your imagined audience, think of unexpected or surprising causes of:	**For your imagined audience, think of unexpected or surprising consequences of:**
Teenage smoking	A change in a specific rule or regulation for a sport
The popularity of reality TV	Establishing a four-day workweek
Low-level American interest in professional soccer	Giving credit cards to young people
The appeal of a specific advertising campaign	Some proposed action on your campus or in your city, state, or region
Your own one-time event, recurring phenomenon, or trend	Your own one-time event, recurring phenomenon, or trend

■ *Explore your chosen phenomenon through rapid freewriting.* To generate ideas for your paper, overcome writer's block, and discover areas where you may need to do some research, freewrite your responses to the following invention questions:

1. Describe the phenomenon you will be analyzing.

2. What personal experiences have you had with this phenomenon, either as a participant or as an observer? Describe those experiences.

3. What makes the causes or consequences of this phenomenon puzzling?

4. What are the most common causal explanations for this phenomenon? (That is, what explanations do you think will first pop into your readers' minds?)

5. Do you think these causes (consequences) fully explain your phenomenon? What may be wrong, missing, or inadequate?

6. What do you see as the most important causes or consequences of this phenomenon? What is your evidence or support?

7. Are there alternative explanations that you think need to be examined and rejected? Why?

8. "My ideas about the causes or consequences of this phenomenon will bring something new to my reader because _____."

Shaping and Drafting

Your goal at this early discovery stage of drafting is to get your developing argument onto paper. It is useful, therefore, to know some of the standard ways that a causal argument can be organized. Later, you may decide to adopt quite a different organizational pattern, but these standard ways will help you get started.

Plan 1   When your intention is to link your phenomenon to a cause (or consequence) by describing and explaining the links in a causal chain:

- Introduce the phenomenon and show why it is problematic. Get your reader interested in the puzzle.
- Present your thesis about the causal chain that accounts for this phenomenon or leads to a certain consequence.
- Describe and explain each link in the causal chain.

Plan 2   When your intention is to explore the relative contributions of several different causes of a phenomenon or to predict a variety of consequences:

- Introduce the phenomenon to be explained and show why it is problematic or controversial. Engage your reader's interest.
- Devote one section to each possible cause/consequence and support it with evidence or arguments. (Arrange sections so that those causes most familiar to the audience come first and the most surprising ones come last.)
- If appropriate, describe alternative hypotheses and show why you are rejecting them.

Plan 3   When your purpose is to change your reader's view by arguing for a surprising or unexpected cause or consequence:

- Introduce your phenomenon, engage your reader's interest in the question, and summarize the commonplace view of the causes or consequences that you assume your audience holds.
- One by one, examine and reject (or show as inadequate or insufficient) the causes or consequences your audience would normally assume or expect.
- Introduce your unexpected or surprising cause(s) or consequence(s) and argue for it (them).

Revising

Once you've selected your puzzling phenomenon, written your draft, and discussed it with readers, you're ready to do the major work of revising—converting your draft from something that works for you to something that works for readers. Because you will probably write this paper near the closed end of the closed-to-open continuum, the revision suggestions in Chapter 19 are especially relevant: Give the big picture first and refer to it often; place points before particulars; use frequent transitions; and follow the old/new contract.

You should also seek out peer reviews, using the following guidelines:

▪ GUIDELINES FOR PEER REVIEWS ▪

Instructions for peer reviews are provided in Chapter 18 (pp. 490–496).

For the Writer

Prepare two or three questions you would like your peer reviewer to address while responding to your draft. The questions can focus on some aspect of your draft that you are uncertain about, on one or more sections where you particularly seek help or advice, on some feature that you particularly like about your draft, or on some part you especially wrestled with. Write out your questions and give them to your peer reviewer along with your draft.

For the Reviewer

I. Read the draft at a normal reading speed from beginning to end. As you read, do the following:

   A. Place a wavy line in the margin next to any passages that you find confusing, that contain something that doesn't seem to fit, or that otherwise slow down your reading.

   B. Place a "Good!" in the margin next to any passages where you think the writing is particularly strong or interesting.

II. Read the draft again slowly and answer the following questions by writing brief explanations of your answers.

   A. Introduction

      1. How does the title create interest and focus the essay?

      2. At what point is it clear to you what causal question is being addressed? How could the writer improve the presentation of the problem or question?

      3. What is the writer's thesis? What seems new or surprising in the thesis?

   B. Analyzing the causes or consequences

      1. For each part of the argument, how does the writer show that X helps cause Y?

         a. If the writer describes the links in the causal chain, where could these links be developed more convincingly?

         b. If the writer uses indirect methods such as observation, citing of scientific research, or correlation studies, where could these strategies be improved?

         c. If the writer uses an analogy or precedent, how could the analogy be made more persuasive?

      2. How might the writer improve the structure and clarity of this draft? Are there parts of the argument that need more development? Are there parts that could be shortened?

3. Where do you disagree with the writer's argument or have doubts or queries?

C. If the writer has prepared questions for you, respond to his or her inquiries.

D. Sum up what you see as the chief strengths and problem areas of this draft.

   1. Strengths

   2. Problem areas

III. Read the draft one more time. Place a check mark in the margin wherever you notice problems in grammar, spelling, or mechanics (one check mark per problem).

CHAPTER 15

Writing a Classical Argument

ABOUT CLASSICAL ARGUMENT

The assignment for this chapter introduces you to a classical way of arguing in which you take a stand on an issue, offer reasons and evidence in support of your position, and summarize and respond to alternative views. Your goal is to persuade your audience, who can be initially perceived as either opposed to your position or undecided about it, to adopt your position or at least to regard it more openly or favorably.

The need for argument arises whenever members of a community disagree on an issue. Classical rhetoricians believed that the art of arguing was essential for good citizenship. If disputes can be resolved through exchange of perspectives, negotiation of differences, and flexible seeking of the best solutions to a problem, then nations won't have to resort to war or individuals to fisticuffs.

The study of argumentation involves two components: truth seeking and persuasion. By *truth seeking,* we mean a diligent, open-minded, and responsible search for the best course of action or solution to a problem, taking into account all the available information and alternative points of view. By *persuasion,* we mean the art of making a claim* on an issue and justifying it convincingly so that the audience's initial resistance to your position is overcome and they are moved toward your position.

These two components of argument seem paradoxically at odds: Truth seeking asks us to relax our certainties and be willing to change our views; persuasion asks us to be certain, to be committed to our claims, and to get others to change their views. We can overcome this paradox if we dispel two common but misleading views of argument. The most common view is that argument is a fight as in "I just got into a horrible argument with my roommate." This view of argument as a fist-waving, shouting match in which you ridicule anyone who disagrees with you (popularized by radio and television talk shows) entirely disregards argument as truth seeking, but it also misrepresents argument as persuasion because it polarizes people, rather than promoting understanding, new ways of seeing, and change.

Another common but misleading view is that argument is a pro/con debate modeled after high school or college debate matches or presidential debates. Although debating can be an excellent way to develop critical thinking skills, it misrepresents argument as a two-sided contest with winners and losers. Because

*By longstanding tradition, the thesis statement of an argument is often called its "claim."

controversial issues involve many different points of view, not just two, reducing an issue to pro/con positions distorts the complexity of the disagreement. Instead of thinking of *both* sides of an issue, we need to think of *all* sides. Equally troublesome, the debate image invites us to ask, "Who won the debate?" rather than "What is the best solution to the question that divides us?" The best solution might be a compromise between the two debaters or an undiscovered third position. The debate image tends to privilege the confident extremes in a controversy rather than the complex and muddled middle.

From our perspective, the best image for understanding argument is neither "fight" nor "debate" but the deliberations of a committee representing a wide spectrum of community voices charged with finding the best solution to a problem. From this perspective, argument is both a *process* and a *product*. As a process, argument is an act of inquiry characterized by fact finding, information gathering, and consideration of alternative points of view. As a product, it is someone's contribution to the conversation at any one moment—a turn taking in a conversation, a formal speech, or a written position paper such as the one you will write for this chapter. The goal of argument as process is truth seeking; the goal of argument as product is persuasion. When members of a diverse committee are willing to argue persuasively for their respective points of view but are simultaneously willing to listen to other points of view and to change or modify their positions in light of new information or better arguments, then both components of argument are fully in play.

We cannot overemphasize the importance of both truth seeking and persuasion to your professional and civic life. Truth seeking makes you an informed and judicious employee and a citizen who delays decisions until a full range of evidence and alternative views are aired and examined. Persuasion gives you the power to influence the world around you, whether through letters to the editor on political issues or through convincing position papers for professional life. Whenever an organization needs to make a major decision, those who can think flexibly and write persuasively can wield great influence.

EXPLORING CLASSICAL ARGUMENT

An effective way to appreciate argument as both truth seeking and persuasion is to address an issue that is new to you and then watch how your own views evolve. Your initial position will probably reflect what social scientists sometimes call your personal *ideology*—that is, a network of basic values, beliefs, and assumptions that tend to guide your view of the world. However, if you adopt a truth-seeking attitude, your initial position may evolve as the conversation progresses. In fact, the conversation may even cause changes in some of your basic beliefs, since ideologies aren't set in stone and since many of us have unresolved allegiance to competing ideologies that may be logically inconsistent (for example, a belief in freedom of speech combined with a belief that hate speech should be banned). In this exercise we ask you to keep track of how your views change and to note what causes the change.

The case we present for discussion involves ethical treatment of animals.

> *Situation:* A bunch of starlings build nests in the attic of a family's house, gaining access to the attic through a torn vent screen. Soon the eggs hatch, and every morning at sunrise the family is awakened by the sound of birds squawking and wings beating against rafters as the starlings fly in and out of the house to feed the hatchlings. After losing considerable early morning sleep, the family repairs the screen. Unable to get in and out, the parent birds are unable to feed their young. The birds die within a day. Is this cruelty to animals?

1. Freewrite your initial response to this question. Was the family's act an instance of cruelty to animals (that is, was their act ethically justifiable or not)?

2. Working in small groups or as a whole class, share your freewrites and then try to reach a group consensus on the issue. During this conversation (argument as process), listen carefully to your classmates' views and note places where your own initial views begin to evolve.

3. So far we have framed this issue as an after-the-fact yes/no question: Is the family guilty of cruelty to animals? But we can also frame it as an open-ended, before-the-fact question: "What should the family have done about the starlings in the attic?" Suppose you are a family member discussing the starlings at dinner, prior to the decision to fix the vent screen. Make a list of your family's other options and try to reach class consensus on the two or three best alternative solutions.

4. At the end of the discussion, do another freewrite exploring how your ideas evolved during the discussion. What insights did you get about the twin components of argument, truth seeking and persuasion?

WRITING PROJECT

Write a position paper that takes a stand on a controversial issue. Your introduction should present your issue, provide background, and state the claim you intend to support. The body of your argument will summarize and respond to opposing views as well as present reasons and evidence in support of your own position. You need to choose whether to summarize and refute opposing views before or after you have made your own case. Try to end your essay with your strongest arguments.

We sometimes call this assignment an argument in the *classical style* because it is patterned after the persuasive speeches of ancient Greek and Roman orators. In the terms of ancient rhetoricians, the main parts of a persuasive speech are the *exordium*, in which the speaker gets the audience's attention; the *narratio*, which provides needed background; the *propositio*, the speaker's proposition or thesis; the *partitio*, a forecast of the main parts of the speech, equivalent to a blueprint statement; the *confirmatio*, the speaker's arguments in favor of the proposition; the *confutatio*, the refutation of opposing views; and the *peroratio*, the conclusion that sums up the argument, calls for action, and leaves a strong lasting impression.

We cite these tongue-twisting Latin terms only to assure you that in writing a classical argument you are joining a time-honored tradition that links you to Roman senators on the capitol steps. From their discourse arose the ideal of a democratic society based on superior arguments rather than on superior weaponry. Although there are many other ways to persuade audiences, the classical approach is a particularly effective introduction to persuasive writing.

UNDERSTANDING CLASSICAL ARGUMENT

Having introduced you to argument as both process and product, we now turn to the details of effective argumentation. To help orient you, we begin by describing the typical stages that mark students' growth as arguers.

Stages of Development: Your Growth as an Arguer

We have found that when we teach argument in our classes, students typically proceed through identifiable stages as their argumentative skills increase. While these stages may or may not describe your own development, they suggest the skills you should strive to acquire.

- *Stage 1: Argument as personal opinion.* At the beginning of instruction in argument, students typically express strong personal opinions but have trouble justifying their opinions with reasons and evidence and often create short, undeveloped arguments that are circular, lacking in evidence, and insulting to those who disagree. The following freewrite, written by a student first confronting the starling case (p. 374), illustrates this stage:

   The family shouldn't have killed the starlings because that is really wrong! I mean that act was disgusting. It makes me sick to think how so many people are just willing to kill something for no reason at all. How are these parents going to teach their children values if they just go out and kill little birds for no good reason?!! This whole family is what's wrong with America!

This writer's opinion is passionate and heartfelt, but it provides neither reasons nor evidence why someone else should hold the same opinion.

- *Stage 2: Argument structured as claim supported by one or more reasons.* This stage represents a quantum leap in argumentative skill because the writer can now produce a rational plan containing point sentences (the reasons) and particulars (the evidence). The writer who produced the previous freewrite later developed a structure like this:

The family's act constituted cruelty to animals

- because the starlings were doing minimal harm

- because other options were available

- because the way they killed the birds caused needless suffering

- ▓ *Stage 3: Increased attention to truth seeking.* In stage 3 students become increasingly engaged with the complexity of the issue as they listen to their classmates' views, conduct research, and evaluate alternative perspectives and stances. They are often willing to change their positions when they see the power of other arguments.

- ▓ *Stage 4: Ability to articulate the unstated assumptions underlying their arguments.* As we show later in this chapter, each reason in a writer's argument is based on an assumption, value, or belief (often unstated) that the audience must accept if the argument is to be persuasive. Often the writer needs to state these assumptions explicitly and support them. At this stage students identify and analyze their own assumptions and those of their intended audiences. Students gain increased skill at accommodating alternative views through refutation or concession.

- ▓ *Stage 5: Ability to link an argument to the values and beliefs of the intended audience.* In this stage writers are increasingly able to link their arguments to their audience's values and beliefs and to adapt structure and tone to the resistance level of their audience. Writers also appreciate how delayed-thesis arguments or other psychological strategies can be more effective than closed-form arguments when addressing hostile audiences.

The rest of this chapter helps you progress through these stages. Although you can read the remainder in one sitting, we recommend that you break your reading into sections, going over the material slowly and applying it to your own ideas in progress. Let the chapter's concepts and explanations sink in gradually, and return to them periodically for review. This section on "Understanding Classical Argument" contains the chapter's key instructional material and comprises a compact but comprehensive course in argumentation.

Creating an Argument Frame: A Claim with Reasons

Somewhere in the writing process, whether early or late, you need to create a frame for your argument. This frame includes a clear question that focuses the argument, your claim, and one or more supporting reasons. Often your reasons, stated as *because* clauses, can be attached to your claim to provide a working thesis statement.

Finding an Arguable Issue

At the heart of any argument is an issue, which we can define as a question that invites more than one reasonable answer and thus leads to perplexity or disagreement. This requirement excludes disagreements based on personal tastes, where no shared criteria could be developed ("Baseball is more fun than soccer"). It also excludes purely private questions because issues arise out of disagreements in communities. When you are thinking of issues, ask what questions are currently being contested in one of the communities to which you belong (your family, neighborhood, religious or social group, workplace, classroom, dormitory, campus, hometown, state, region, nation, and so forth).

Issue questions are often framed as yes/no choices, especially when they appear on ballots or in courtrooms: Should gay marriage be legalized? Should the city pass the new school bond proposal? Is this defendant guilty of armed robbery? Just as frequently, they can be framed openly, inviting many different possible answers: What should our city do about skateboarders in downtown pedestrian areas? How can children be kept from pornography on the Internet?

It is important to remember that framing an issue as a yes/no question does not mean that all points of view fall neatly into pro/con categories. Although citizens may be forced to vote yes or no on a proposed ballot initiative, they can support or oppose the initiative for a variety of reasons. Some may vote happily for the initiative, others vote for it only by holding their noses, and still others oppose it vehemently but for entirely different reasons. To argue effectively, you need to appreciate the wide range of perspectives from which people approach the yes/no choice.

How you frame your question necessarily affects the scope and shape of your argument itself. In our exploratory exercise we framed the starling question in two ways: (1) Was the family guilty of cruelty to animals? and (2) What should the family do about the starlings? Framed in the first way, your argument would have to develop criteria for "cruelty to animals" and then argue whether the family's actions met those criteria. Framed in the second way, you could argue for your own solution to the problem, ranging from doing nothing (waiting for the birds to grow up and leave, then fixing the screen) to climbing into the attic and drowning the birds so that their deaths are quick and painless. Or you could word the question in a broader, more philosophical way: When are humans justified in killing animals? Or you could focus on a subissue: When can an animal be labeled a "pest"?

For Writing and Discussion

1. Working individually, make a list of several communities that you belong to and then identify one or more questions currently being contested within those communities. (If you have trouble, get a copy of your local campus and city newspapers or an organizational newsletter; you'll quickly discover a wealth of contested issues.) Then share your list with classmates.

2. Pick two or three issues of particular interest to you, and try framing them in different ways: as broad or narrow questions, as open-ended or yes/no questions. Place several examples on the chalkboard for class discussion.

Stating a Claim

Your claim is the position you want to take on the issue. It is your brief, one-sentence answer to your issue question:

> The family was not ethically justified in killing the starlings.

> The city should build skateboarding areas with ramps in all city parks.

You will appreciate argument as truth seeking if you find that your claim evolves as you think more deeply about your issue and listen to alternative views. Be willing to rephrase your claim to soften it or refocus it or even to reverse it as you progress through the writing process.

Articulating Reasons

Your claim, which is the position you take on an issue, needs to be supported by reasons and evidence. A *reason* (sometimes called a *premise*) is a subclaim that supports your main claim. In speaking or writing, a reason is usually linked to the claim with such connecting words as *because, therefore, so, consequently,* and *thus*. In planning your argument, a powerful strategy for developing reasons is to harness the grammatical power of the conjunction *because*; think of your reasons as *because* clauses attached to your claim. Formulating your reasons in this way allows you to create a thesis statement that breaks your argument into smaller parts, each part devoted to one of the reasons.[*]

Suppose, for example, that you are examining the issue "Should the government legalize hard drugs such as heroin and cocaine?" Here are several different points of view on this issue, each expressed as a claim with because clauses:

One View

Cocaine and heroin should be legalized

- because legalizing drugs will keep the government out of people's private lives.
- because keeping these drugs illegal has the same negative effects on our society that alcohol prohibition did in the 1920s.

Another View

Cocaine and heroin should be legalized

- because the subsequent elimination of the black market would cut down on muggings and robberies.
- because decriminalization would cut down on prison overcrowding and free police to concentrate on dangerous crime rather than on finding drug dealers.
- because elimination of underworld profits would change the economic structure of the underclass and promote shifts to socially productive jobs and careers.

Still Another View

The government should not legalize heroin and cocaine

- because doing so will lead to an increase in drug users.
- because doing so will send the message that it is okay to use hard drugs.

Although the yes/no framing of this question seems to reduce the issue to a two-position debate, many different value systems are at work here. The first pro-legalization argument, libertarian in perspective, values maximum individual freedom. The second argument—although it too supports legalization—takes a community

---

[*]The thesis statement for your essay could be your claim by itself or you could include in your thesis statement your main supporting reasons. For advice on how much of your supporting argument you should summarize in your thesis statement, see Chapter 19, pp. 515–516.

perspective valuing the social benefits of eliminating the black market. In the same way, individuals could oppose legalization for a variety of reasons.

For Writing and Discussion

Working in small groups or as a whole class, generate a list of reasons for and against one or more of the following yes/no claims. State your reasons as *because* clauses. Think of as many because clauses as possible by imagining a wide variety of perspectives on the issue.

1. The school year for grades 1 through 12 should be lengthened to eleven months.
2. Eminem (and other such iconoclastic entertainers) serves a valuable social function.
3. Women's fashion and style magazines (such as *Glamour* and *Seventeen*) are harmful influences on teenage females.
4. The United States should replace its income tax with a national sales tax.
5. Medical insurance should cover alternative medicine (massage therapy, acupuncture, herbal treatments, and so forth).

Articulating Unstated Assumptions

So far, we have focused on the frame of an argument as a claim supported with one or more reasons. Shortly, we will proceed to the flesh and muscle of an argument, which is the evidence you use to support your reasons. But before turning to evidence, we need to look at another crucial part of an argument's frame: its *unstated assumptions*.

What Do We Mean by an Unstated Assumption?

Every time you link together a claim with a reason, you make a silent assumption that may need to be articulated and examined. Consider this argument:

The family was justified in killing the starlings because starlings are pests.

To support this argument, the writer would first need to provide evidence that starlings are pests (examples of the damage they do and so forth). But the persuasiveness of the argument rests on the unstated assumption that it is okay to kill pests. If an audience doesn't agree with that assumption, then the argument flounders unless the writer articulates the assumption and defends it. The complete frame of the argument must therefore include the unstated assumption.

Claim: The family was justified in killing the starlings.
Reason: Because starlings are pests.
Unstated assumption: It is ethically justifiable to kill pests.

It is important to examine the unstated assumption behind any claim with reason *because you must determine whether your audience will accept that assumption. If not, you need to make it explicit and support it.* Think of the unstated assumption as a general principle, rule, belief, or value that connects the reason to the claim. It answers your reader's question, "Why, if I accept your reason, should I accept your claim?"

Here are a few more examples:

Claim with reason: Women should be allowed to join combat units because the image of women as combat soldiers would help society overcome gender stereotyping.

Unstated assumption: It is good to overcome gender stereotyping.

Claim with reason: The government should not legalize heroin and cocaine because doing so will lead to an increase in drug users.

Unstated assumption: It is bad to increase the number of drug users.

Claim with reason: The family was guilty of cruelty to animals in the starling case because less drastic means of solving the problem were available.

Unstated assumption: A person should choose the least-drastic means to solve a problem.

For Writing and Discussion

Identify the unstated assumptions for each of the following claims with reasons.

1. Cocaine and heroin should be legalized because legalizing drugs will keep the government out of people's private lives.
2. The government should eliminate welfare payments to unwed mothers because doing so will reduce the illegitimacy rate.
3. After-school jobs are bad for high school students because they use up valuable study time.
4. We should strengthen the Endangered Species Act because doing so will preserve genetic diversity on the planet.
5. The Endangered Species Act is too stringent because it severely damages the economy.

Using Toulmin Terminology to Describe an Argument's Structure

Our explanation of argument structure is influenced by the work of philosopher Stephen Toulmin, who viewed argumentation as a dynamic courtroom drama where opposing attorneys exchange arguments and cross-examinations before a judge and jury. The terms used by Toulmin to describe the structure of argument are widely accepted in rhetoric and composition studies and provide a handy vocabulary for discussing arguments. Toulmin called the unstated assumption behind a claim with reason the argument's *warrant,* based on our common word *warranty* for guarantee. If the audience accepts your warrant—that is, if they agree with your unstated assumption—then your argument is sound, or guaranteed. To put it another way, if your audience accepts your warrant, and if you can convince them that your reason is true, then they will accept your claim.

Besides the term *warrant,* Toulmin also uses the terms *grounds, backing, conditions of rebuttal,* and *qualifier.* We will explain these terms to you at the appropriate moments as we proceed.

Using Evidence Effectively

In Chapter 3 we showed you that the majority of words in a closed-form essay are particulars used to support points. If you think of reasons and warrants as the main points of your argument, then think of evidence as the supporting particulars. Each of your reasons needs to be supported by evidence. Toulmin's term for evidence in support of a reason is *grounds,* which we can think of as all the facts, data, testimony, statistics, subarguments, and other details a writer can find to support a reason. Toulmin calls the evidence and arguments used to support a warrant its *backing.* In this section we survey different kinds of evidence and show you how to incorporate that evidence into an argument, either as grounds to support a reason or as backing to support a warrant. Some arguments can be fleshed out with evidence based on your personal experience and observations. But most arguments require more formal evidence—the kind you gather from library or field research.

Part Four, "A Rhetorical Guide to Research," treats research writing in detail.

Kinds of Evidence

The kinds of evidence most often used for the grounds and backing are the following:

Examples. An example from personal experience can often be used to support a reason. Here is how one student writer, arguing that her church building needs to be remodeled, used a personal example to support a reason.

> Finally, Sacred Heart Church must be renovated immediately because the terrazzo floor that covers the entire church is very dangerous. Four Sundays ago, during 11:00 Mass, nine Eucharistic Ministers went up to the altar to prepare for distributing communion. As they carefully walked to their assigned post on the recently buffed terrazzo floor, a loud crash of crystal echoed through the church. A woman moving to her post slipped on the recently buffed floor, fell to the ground, hit her head on the marble, and was knocked unconscious. People rushed to her aid, thinking she was dead. Fortunately she was alive, only badly hurt. This woman was my mother.

Besides specific examples like this, writers sometimes invent hypothetical examples, or *scenarios,* to illustrate an issue or hypothesize about the consequences of an event. (Of course, you must tell your reader that the example or scenario is hypothetical.)

Summaries of Research. Another common way to support an argument is to summarize research studies. Here is how a student writer used a summary statement to support his opposition to mandatory helmet laws for motorcycle riders:

> However, a helmet won't protect against head injury when one is traveling at normal traffic speeds. According to a U.S. Department of Transportation study,

"There is no evidence that any helmet thus far, regardless of cost or design, is capable of rejecting impact stress above 13 mph" (Transportation Study, 1988, p. 8).*

For a discussion of statistics in argument, see Chapter 11.

Statistics. Another common form of evidence is statistics. Here is how one writer uses statistics to argue that alcohol poses a more serious social problem than heroin or cocaine:

> The uproar about drugs is itself odd. In 1987, according to the Kerry subcommittee, there were 1,400 deaths from cocaine; in 1988, that figure had increased to 3,308. Deaths from *all* forms of illegal drugs total under 6,000. By contrast, 320,000 to 390,000 people die prematurely each year from tobacco and 100,000 to 200,000 from misuse of alcohol. Alcohol is associated with 40 percent of all suicide attempts, 40 percent of all traffic deaths, 54 percent of all violent crimes and 10 percent of all work-related injuries.

Testimony. Writers can also use expert testimony to bolster a case. The following student essay uses testimony to support "comparable worth"—an economic policy intended to redress salary inequities between traditionally "male" and "female" job fields.

> Barbara Bergmann, professor of economics at the University of Maryland, has studied the comparable worth issue at length. If comparable worth were enacted, she points out, "Nobody's pay need go down. Nor will budgets or profits be wiped out" (9).**

Subarguments. Sometimes writers support reasons not directly through data but through sequences of subarguments. Sometimes these subarguments develop a persuasive analogy, hypothesize about consequences, or simply advance the argument through a chain of connected points. In the following passage, taken from a philosophic article justifying torture under certain conditions, the author uses a subargument to support one of his main points—that a terrorist holding victims hostage has no "rights":

> There is an important difference between terrorists and their victims that should mute talk of the terrorist's "rights." The terrorist's victims are at risk unintentionally, not having asked to be endangered. But the terrorist knowingly initiated his actions. Unlike his victims, he volunteered for the risks of his deed. By threatening to kill for profit or idealism, he renounces civilized standards, and he can have no complaint if civilization tries to thwart him by whatever means necessary.

Rather than using direct empirical evidence, the author supports his point with a subargument showing how terrorists differ from victims and thus relinquish their claim to rights.

---

*This student is using the APA (American Psychological Association) style for documenting sources. This quotation is found on page 8 of a document listed as "Transportation Study" in the References list at the end of the essay. See Chapter 23.
**This student is using the MLA (Modern Language Association) style for documenting sources. This quotation will be found on page 9 of an article authored by Barbara Bergmann that is listed under "Bergmann" in the Works Cited list at the end of the essay.

Reliability of Evidence

When you use empirical evidence, you can increase its persuasiveness by monitoring its recency, relevance, impartiality, and scope.

Recency. As much as possible, and especially if you are addressing current issues in science, technology, politics, or social trends, use the most recent evidence you can find.

Relevance. Ensure that the evidence you cite is relevant to the point you are making. For example, for many decades the medical profession offered advice about heart disease to their female patients based on studies of male patients. No matter how extensive or how recent those studies, some of their conclusions were bound to be irrelevant for female patients.

Impartiality. While all data must be interpreted and hence are never completely impartial, careful readers are aware of how easily data can be skewed. Newspapers, magazine, and journals often have political biases and different levels of respectability. Generally, evidence from peer reviewed scholarly journals is more highly regarded than evidence from secondhand sources. Particularly problematic is information gathered from Internet Web sites, which can vary wildly in reliability and degree of bias.

See pp. 603–604 for a discussion of political slant in the media and for advice on evaluating sources for reliability and bias. See pp. 605–616 for help on evaluating Web sites.

Sufficiency. One of the most common reasoning fallacies is to make a sweeping generalization based on only one or two instances. The criterion of sufficiency (which means having enough examples to justify your point) helps you guard against hasty generalizations.

Addressing Objections and Counterarguments

Having looked at the frame of an argument (claim, reasons, and warrants) and at the kinds of evidence used to flesh out the frame, let's turn now to the important concern of anticipating and responding to objections and counterarguments. In this section, we show you an extended example of a student anticipating and responding to a reader's objection. We then describe a planning schema that can help you anticipate objections and show you how to respond to counterarguments, either through refutation or concession. Finally we show how your active imagining of alternative views can lead you to qualify your claim.

Anticipating Objections: An Extended Example

In our earlier discussions of the starling case, we saw how readers might object to the argument "The family was justified in killing the starlings because starlings are pests." What rankles these readers is the unstated assumption (warrant) that it is okay to kill pests. Imagine an objecting reader saying something like this:

It is *not* okay to get annoyed with a living creature, label it a "pest," and then kill it. This whole use of the term "pest" suggests that humans have the right to dominate nature. We need to have more reverence for nature. The ease with which the family solved their problem by killing living things sets a bad example for children. The family could have waited until fall and then fixed the screen.

Imagining such an objection might lead a writer to modify his or her claim. But if the writer remains committed to that claim, then he or she must develop a response. In the following example in which a student writer argues that it is okay to kill the starlings, note (1) how the writer uses evidence to show that starlings are pests, (2) how he summarizes a possible objection to his warrant, and (3) how he supports his warrant with backing.

Student Argument Defending Reason and Warrant

Claim with reason

The family was justified in killing the starlings because starlings are pests. Starlings are nonindigenous birds that drive out native species and multiply rapidly. When I searched "starlings and pests" on the Alta Vista search engine, I discovered 161 Web sites dealing with starlings as pests. Starlings are hated by farmers and gardeners because huge flocks of them devour newly planted seeds in spring as well as fruits and berries at harvest. A flock of starlings can devastate a cherry orchard in a few days. As invasive nesters, starlings can also damage attics by tearing up insulation and defecating on stored items. Many of the Web site articles focused on ways to kill off starling populations. In killing the starlings, the family was protecting its own property and reducing the population of these pests.

Evidence that starlings are pests

Summary of a possible objection

Many readers might object to my argument, saying that humans should have a reverence for nature and not quickly try to kill off any creature they label a pest. Further, these readers might say that even if starlings are pests, the family could have waited until fall to repair the attic or found some other means of protecting their property without having to kill the baby starlings. I too would have waited until fall if the birds in the attic had been swallows or some other native species without starlings' destructiveness and propensity for unchecked population growth. But starlings should be compared to rats or mice. We set traps for rodents because we know the damage they cause when they nest in walls and attics. We don't get sentimental trying to save the orphaned rat babies. In the same way, we are justified in eliminating starlings as soon as they begin infesting our houses. Think of them not as chirpy little songsters but as rats of the bird world.

Response to the objection

In the preceding example, we see how the writer uses grounds to support his reason and then, anticipating his readers' objection to his warrant, summarizes that objection and offers backing. One might not be convinced by the argument, but the writer has done a good job trying to support both the reason and the warrant.

Using a Planning Schema to Anticipate Objections

The arguing strategy used by the previous writer was triggered by his anticipation of objections—what Toulmin calls *conditions of rebuttal*. Under conditions of rebuttal, Toulmin asks arguers to imagine various ways skeptical readers might object to a writer's argument or specific conditions under which the argument might not hold. The Toulmin system lets us create a planning schema that can help writers develop a persuasive argument.

This schema encourages writers to articulate their argument frame (reason and warrant) and then to imagine what could be used for grounds (to support the reason) and backing (to support the warrant). Equally important, the schema encourages writers to anticipate counterarguments by imagining how skeptical readers might object to the writer's reason or warrant or both. To create the schema, simply make a chart headed by your claim with reason and then make slots for grounds, warrant, backing, and conditions of rebuttal. Then brainstorm ideas to put into each slot. Here is how another student writer used this schema to plan an argument on the starling case:

Claim with Reason

The family showed cruelty to animals because the way they killed the birds caused needless suffering.

Grounds

I've got to show how the birds suffered and also how the suffering was needless. The way of killing the birds caused the birds to suffer. The hatchlings starved to death, as did the parent birds if they were trapped inside the attic. Starvation is very slow and agonizing. The suffering was also needless since other means were available such as calling an exterminator who would remove the birds and either relocate them or kill them painlessly. If no other alternative was available, someone should have crawled into the attic and found a painless way to kill the birds.

Warrant

If it is not necessary to kill an animal, then don't; if it is necessary, then the killing should be done in the least painful way possible.

Backing

I've got to convince readers it is wrong to make an animal suffer if you don't have to. Humans have a natural antipathy to needless suffering—our feeling of unease if we imagine cattle or chickens caused to suffer for our food rather than being cleanly and quickly killed. If a horse is incurably wounded, we put it to sleep rather then let it suffer. We are morally obligated to cause the least pain possible.

Conditions of Rebuttal

How could a reader object to my reason? A reader could say that killing the starlings did not cause suffering. Perhaps hatchling starlings don't feel pain of starvation and die very quickly. Perhaps a reader could object to my claim that other means were available: There is no other way to kill the starlings—impossibility of catching a bunch of adult starlings flying around an attic. Poison may cause just as much suffering. Cost of exterminator is prohibitive.

How could a reader object to my warrant? Perhaps the reader would say that my rule to cause the least pain possible does not apply to animal pests. In class, someone said that worrying about the baby starlings was sentimental. Laws of nature condemn millions of animals each year to death by starvation or by being eaten alive by other animals. Humans occasionally have to take their place within this tooth-and-claw natural system.

How many of the ideas from this schema would the writer use in her actual paper? That is a judgment call based on the writer's analysis of the audience. In every case, the writer should support the reason with evidence because supporting a claim with reasons and evidence is the minimal requirement of argument.

But it is not necessary to state the warrant explicitly or provide backing for it unless the writer anticipates readers who doubt it.

The same rule of thumb applies to the need for summarizing and responding to objections and counterarguments: Let your analysis of audience be your guide. If we imagined the preceding argument aimed at readers who thought it was sentimental to worry about the suffering of animal pests, the writer should make her warrant explicit and back it up. Her task would be to convince readers that humans have ethical responsibilities that exclude them from tooth-and-claw morality.

For Writing and Discussion

Working individually or in small groups, create a planning schema for the following arguments. For each claim with reason: (a) imagine the kinds of evidence needed as grounds to support the reason; (b) identify the warrant; (c) imagine a strategy for supporting the warrant (backing); and (d) anticipate possible objections to the reason and to the warrant (conditions of rebuttal).

1. *Claim with reason:* Now that we are buying our first car together, we should buy a Jupiter 500 sedan because it is the most economical car on the road. (Imagine this argument aimed at your significant other, who wants to buy a Phantomjet 1000 sports car.)

2. *Claim with reason:* Gay marriage should be legalized because doing so will promote faithful monogamous relationships among lesbians and gay men. (Imagine this argument aimed at a homophobic audience.)

3. *Claim with reason:* The government should eliminate welfare payments for unwed mothers because doing so would reduce the illegitimacy rate. (Imagine this argument aimed at liberals who support welfare payments to single mothers.)

4. *Claim with reason:* After-school jobs are bad for high school students because they use up valuable study time. (Aim this argument at a middle-class teenager who wants to get a job to earn extra spending money.)

Responding to Objections, Counterarguments, and Alternative Views Through Refutation or Concession

We have seen how a writer needs to anticipate alternative views that give rise to objections and counterarguments. Surprisingly, one of the best ways to approach counterarguments is to summarize them fairly. Make your imagined reader's best case against your argument. By resisting the temptation to distort a counterargument, you demonstrate a willingness to consider the issue from all sides. Moreover, summarizing a counterargument reduces your reader's tendency to say, "Yes, but have you thought of . . . ?" After you have summarized an objection or counterargument fairly and charitably, you must then decide how to respond to it. Your two main choices are to rebut it or concede to it.

Rebutting Opposing Views

When rebutting or refuting an argument, you can question the argument's reasons/grounds or warrant or both. In the following student example, the writer summarizes her classmates' objections to abstract art and then analyzes shortcomings in their reasons and grounds.

> Some of my classmates object to abstract art because it apparently takes no technical drawing talent. They feel that historically artists turned to abstract art because they lacked the technical drafting skills exhibited by Remington, Russell, and Rockwell. Therefore these abstract artists created an art form that anyone was capable of and that was less time consuming, and then they paraded it as artistic progress. But I object to the notion that these artists turned to abstraction because they could not do representative drawing. Many abstract artists, such as Picasso, were excellent draftsmen, and their early pieces show very realistic drawing skill. As his work matured, Picasso became more abstract in order to increase the expressive quality of his work. *Guernica* was meant as a protest against the bombing of that city by the Germans. To express the terror and suffering of the victims more vividly, he distorted the figures and presented them in a black and white journalistic manner. If he had used representational images and color—which he had the skill to do—much of the emotional content would have been lost and the piece probably would not have caused the demand for justice that it did.

Conceding to Counterarguments

In some cases, an alternative view can be very strong. If so, don't hide that view from your readers; summarize it and concede to it.

Making concessions to opposing views is not necessarily a sign of weakness; in many cases, a concession simply acknowledges that the issue is complex and that your position is tentative. In turn, a concession can enhance a reader's respect for you and invite the reader to follow your example and weigh the strengths of your own argument charitably. Writers typically concede to opposing views with transitional expressions such as the following:

admittedly	I must admit that	I agree that	granted
even though	I concede that	while it is true that	

After conceding to an opposing view, you should shift to a different field of values where your position is strong and then argue for those new values. For example, adversaries of drug legalization argue plausibly that legalizing drugs would increase the number of users and addicts. If you support legalization, here is how you might deal with this point without fatally damaging your own argument:

> Opponents of legalization claim—and rightly so—that legalization will lead to an increase in drug users and addicts. I wish this weren't so, but it is. Nevertheless, the other benefits of legalizing drugs—eliminating the black market, reducing street crime, and freeing up thousands of police from fighting the war on drugs—more than outweigh the social costs of increased drug use and addiction, especially if tax revenues from drug sales are plowed back into drug education and rehabilitation programs.

The writer concedes that legalization will increase addiction (one reason for opposing legalization) and that drug addiction is bad (the warrant for that reason).

But then the writer redeems the case for legalization by shifting the argument to another field of values (the benefits of eliminating the black market, reducing crime, and so forth).

Qualifying Your Claim

The need to summarize and respond to alternative views lets the writer see an issue's complexity and appreciate that no one position has a total monopoly on the truth. Consequently, in the argument schema that we have adapted from Toulmin, there is one final term that is important to know: the *qualifier*. This term refers to words that limit the scope or force of a claim to make it less sweeping and therefore less vulnerable. Consider the difference between the sentences "After-school jobs are bad for teenagers" and "After-school jobs are often bad for teenagers." The first claim can be refuted by one counterexample of a teenager who benefited from an after-school job. Because the second claim admits exceptions, it is much harder to refute. Unless your argument is airtight, you will want to limit your claim with qualifiers such as the following:

perhaps	maybe
in many cases	generally
tentatively	sometimes
often	usually
probably	likely
may or might (rather than is)	

You can also qualify a claim with an opening "unless" clause ("*Unless* your apartment is well soundproofed, you should not buy such a powerful stereo system").

Appealing to *Ethos* and *Pathos*

When the classical rhetoricians examined ways that orators could persuade listeners, they focused on three kinds of proofs: *logos,* the appeal to reason; *ethos,* the appeal to the speaker's character; and *pathos,* the appeal to the emotions and the sympathetic imagination. So far in this chapter we have focused on the logical appeals of *logos.* In this section we examine *ethos* and *pathos.* You can see how these three appeals are connected by visualizing a triangle with interrelated points labeled *message, audience, and/or writer/speaker* (Figure 15.1). Effective arguments consider all three points of this *rhetorical triangle.*

Appeal to *Ethos*

A powerful way to increase the persuasiveness of an argument is to gain your readers' trust. You appeal to *ethos* whenever you present yourself as credible and trustworthy. In Chapter 4 we discussed how readers develop an image of the writer—the writer's *persona*—based on features of the writer's prose. For readers to accept your argument, they must perceive a persona that's knowledgeable, trustworthy, and fair. We suggest three ways to enhance your argument's ethos:

1. Demonstrate that you know your subject well. If you have personal experience with the subject, cite that experience. Reflect thoughtfully on your sub-

Message

Logos: How can I make the argument internally consistent and logical? How can I find the best reasons and support them with the best evidence?

Audience

Pathos: How can I make the readers open to my message? How can I best engage my readers' emotions and imaginations? How can I appeal to my readers' values and interests?

Writer or Speaker

Ethos: How can I present myself effectively? How can I enhance my credibility and trustworthiness?

FIGURE 15.1 ■ Rhetorical Triangle

ject, citing research as well as personal experience, accurately and carefully summarize a range of viewpoints.

2. Be fair to alternative points of view. Scorning an opposing view may occasionally win you favor with an audience predisposed toward your position, but it will offend others and hinder critical analysis. As a general rule, treating opposing views respectfully is the best strategy.

3. Build bridges toward your audience by grounding your argument in shared values and assumptions. Doing so will demonstrate your concern for your audience and enhance your trustworthiness. Moreover, rooting your argument in the audience's values and assumptions has a strong emotional appeal, as we explain in the next section.

Appeals to *Pathos*

Besides basing your argument on appeals to logos and ethos, you might also base it on an appeal to what the Greeks called *pathos*. Sometimes pathos is interpreted narrowly as an appeal to the emotions. This interpretation effectively devalues pathos because popular culture generally values reason above emotion. Although appeals to pathos can sometimes be irrational and irrelevant ("You can't give me a C! I need a B to get into medical school, and if I don't it'll break my ill grandmother's heart"), they can also arouse audience interest and deepen understanding of an argument's human dimensions. Here are some ways to use pathos in your arguments:

Use Vivid Language and Examples. One way to create pathos is to use vivid language and powerful examples. If you are arguing in favor of homeless shelters, for example, you can humanize your appeal by describing one homeless person.

He is huddled over the sewer grate, his feet wrapped in newspapers. He blows on his hands, then tucks them under his armpits and lies down on the sidewalk with his shoulders over the grate, his bed for the night.

But if you are arguing for tougher laws against panhandling, you might let your reader see the issue through the eyes of downtown shoppers intimidated by "ratty, urine-soaked derelicts drinking fortified wine from a shared sack."

Find Audience-Based Reasons. The best way to think of *pathos* is not as an appeal to emotions but rather as an appeal to the audience's values and beliefs. With its emphasis on warrants, Toulmin's system of analysis naturally encourages this kind of appeal. For example, in engineer David Rockwood's argument against wind-generated power, Rockwood's final reason is that constructing wind-generation facilities will damage the environment. To environmentalists, this reason has emotional as well as rational power because its warrant ("Preserving the environment is good") appeals to their values. It is an example of an audience-based reason, which we can define simply as any reason whose warrant the audience already accepts and endorses. Such reasons, because they hook into the beliefs and values of the audience, appeal to *pathos*.

See Chapter 1, pp. 13–14.

When you plan your argument, seek audience-based reasons whenever possible. Suppose, for example, that you are advocating the legalization of heroin and cocaine. If you know that your audience is concerned about their own safety in the streets, then you can argue that legalization of drugs will cut down on crime:

> We should legalize drugs because doing so will make our streets safer: It will cut down radically on street criminals seeking drug money, and it will free up narcotics police to focus on other kinds of crime.

If your audience is concerned about improving the quality of life for youths in inner cities, you might argue that legalization of drugs will lead to better lives for the current underclass:

> We should legalize drugs because doing so will eliminate the lure of drug trafficking that tempts so many inner-city youth away from honest jobs and into crime.

Or if your audience is concerned about high taxes and government debt, you might say:

> We should legalize drugs because doing so will help us balance federal and state budgets: It will decrease police and prison costs by decriminalizing narcotics; and it will eliminate the black market in drugs, allowing us to collect taxes on drug sales.

In each case, you move people toward your position by connecting your argument to their beliefs and values.

Some Advanced Considerations

You have now finished reading what we might call a "basic course in argumentation." In this final section, we briefly discuss some more-advanced ideas about argumentation. Your instructor may want to expand on these in class, simply ask you to read them, or not assign this section at all. The three concepts we explore briefly are argument types, delayed-thesis and Rogerian arguments, and informal fallacies.

Argument Types

The advice we have given you so far in this chapter applies to any type of argument. However, scholars of argumentation have categorized arguments into several different types, each of which uses its own characteristic structures and ways of development. One way to talk about argument types is to divide them into truth issues and values issues.

Truth issues stem from questions about the way reality is (or was or will be). Unlike questions of fact, which can be proved or disproved by agreed-on empirical measures, issues of truth require interpretation of the facts. "Does Linda smoke an average of twenty or more cigarettes per day?" is a question of fact, answerable with a yes or a no. But "Why did Linda start smoking when she was fifteen?" is a question of truth with many possible answers. Was it because of cigarette advertising? Peer pressure? The dynamics of Linda's family? Dynamics in the culture (for example, white American youths are seven times more likely to smoke than are African-American youths)? Truth issues generally take one of the three following forms:

1. *Definitional issues.* Does this particular case fit into a particular category? (Is bungee jumping a "carnival ride" for purposes of state safety regulations? Is tobacco a "drug" and therefore under the jurisdiction of the Federal Drug Administration?)
2. *Causal issues.* What are the causes or consequences of this phenomenon? (Does the current welfare system encourage teenage pregnancy? Will the "three strikes and you're out" rule reduce violent crime?*)
3. *Resemblance or precedence issues.* Is this phenomenon like or analogous to some other phenomenon? (Was U.S. involvement in Bosnia like U.S. involvement in Vietnam? Is killing a starling like killing a rat?)

Rational arguments can involve disputes about values as well as truth. Family disagreements about what car to buy typically revolve around competing values: What is most important? Looks? Performance? Safety? Economy? Comfort? Dependability? Prestige? Similarly, many public issues ask people to choose among competing value systems: Whose values should be adopted in a given situation: Those of corporations or environmentalists? Of the fetus or the pregnant woman? Of owners or laborers? Of the individual or the state? Values issues usually fall in one of the following two categories:

1. *Evaluation issues.* How good is this particular member of its class? Is this action morally good or bad? (How effective was President Bush's first year in

---

*Although we placed the chapter on causes and consequences (Chapter 14) in the "writing to analyze" category, we could have placed it just as logically under "writing to persuade." The difference concerns the writer's perceived relationship to the audience. If you imagine your readers as decidedly skeptical of your thesis and actively weighing alternative theses, then your purpose is persuasive. However, if you imagine your readers as puzzled and curious—reading your essay primarily to clarify their own thinking on a causal question—then your purpose is analytical. The distinction here is a matter of degree, not of kind.

See Chapter 16 for a fuller discussion of evaluation arguments and Chapter 17 for more on policy issues.

office? Which computer system best meets the company's needs? Is the death penalty morally wrong?)

2. *Policy issues.* Should we take this action? (Should Congress pass stricter gun control laws? Should health insurance policies cover eating disorders?)

Delayed-Thesis and Rogerian Argument

Classical arguments are usually closed form with the writer's thesis stated prominently at the end of the introduction. Classical argument works best for neutral audiences weighing all sides of an issue or for somewhat-opposed audiences who are willing to listen to other views. However, when you address a highly resistant audience, one where your point of view seems especially threatening to your audience's values and beliefs, classical argument can seem too blunt and aggressive. In such cases, a *delayed-thesis argument* works best. In such an argument you don't state your actual thesis until the conclusion. The body of the paper extends your sympathy to the reader's views, shows how troubling the issue is to you, and leads the reader gradually toward your position.

A special kind of delayed-thesis argument is called *Rogerian argument,* named after psychologist Carl Rogers, who specialized in helping people with widely divergent views learn to talk to each other. The principle of Rogerian communication is that listeners must show empathy toward each other's worldviews and make every attempt to build bridges toward each other. In planning a Rogerian argument, instead of asking, "What reasons and evidence will convince my reader to adopt my claim?" you ask, "What is it about my view that especially threatens my reader? How can I reduce this threat?" Using a Rogerian strategy, the writer summarizes the audience's point of view fairly and charitably, demonstrating the ability to listen and understand the audience's views. The writer then reduces the threat of his or her own position by showing how both writer and resistant audience share many basic values. The key to successful Rogerian argument, besides the art of listening, is the ability to point out areas of agreement between the writer's and the reader's positions. Then the writer seeks a compromise between the two views.

As an example, if you support a woman's right to choose abortion and you are arguing with someone completely opposed to abortion, you're unlikely to convert your reader, but you may reduce the level of resistance. You begin this process by summarizing your reader's position sympathetically, stressing your shared values. You might say, for example, that you also value babies; that you also are appalled by people who treat abortion as a form of birth control; that you also worry that the easy acceptance of abortion diminishes the value society places on human life; and that you also agree that accepting abortion lightly can lead to lack of sexual responsibility. Building bridges like these between you and your readers makes it more likely that they will listen to you when you present your own position.

Avoiding Informal Fallacies

Informal fallacies are instances of murky reasoning that can cloud an argument and lead to unsound conclusions. Because they can crop up unintentionally in anyone's writing, and because advertisers and hucksters often use them intentionally to deceive, it is a good idea to learn to recognize the more common fallacies.

*Post Hoc, Ergo Propter Hoc (**After This, Therefore Because of This**).* This fallacy involves mistaking sequence for cause. Just because one event happens before another event doesn't mean the first event caused the second. The connection may be coincidental, or some unknown third event may have caused both of these events.

> **Example** For years I suffered from agonizing abdominal itching. Then I tried Smith's pills. Almost overnight my abdominal itching ceased. Smith's pills work wonders.

Hasty Generalization. Closely related to the *post hoc* fallacy is the hasty generalization, which refers to claims based on insufficient or unrepresentative data.

> **Example** The food stamp program supports mostly freeloaders. Let me tell you about my worthless neighbor.

False Analogy. Analogical arguments are tricky because there are, almost always, significant differences between the two things being compared. If the two things differ greatly, the analogy can mislead rather than clarify.

> **Example** You can't force a kid to become a musician any more than you can force a tulip to become a rose.

Either/Or Reasoning. This fallacy occurs when a complex, multisided issue is reduced to two positions without acknowledging the possibility of other alternatives.

> **Example** Either you are pro-choice on abortion or you are against the advancement of women in our culture.

*Ad Hominem ("**Against the Person**").* When people can't find fault with an argument, they sometimes attack the arguer, substituting irrelevant assertions about that person's character for an analysis of the argument itself.

> **Example** Don't pay any attention to Fulke's views on sexual harassment in the workplace. I just learned that he subscribes to *Playboy.*

Appeals to False Authority and Bandwagon Appeals. These fallacies offer as support the fact that a famous person or "many people" already support it. Unless the supporters are themselves authorities in the field, their support is irrelevant.

> **Example** Buy Freeble oil because Joe Quarterback always uses it in his fleet of cars.

> **Example** How can abortion be wrong if millions of people support a woman's right to choose?

*Non Sequitur ("**It Does Not Follow**").* This fallacy occurs when there is no evident connection between a claim and its reason. Sometimes a *non sequitur* can be repaired by filling in gaps in the reasoning; at other times, the reasoning is simply fallacious.

Example   I don't deserve a B for this course because I am a straight-A student.

Circular Reasoning. This fallacy occurs when you state your claim and then, usually after rewording it, you state it again as your reason.

Example   Marijuana is injurious to your health because it harms your body.

Red Herring. This fallacy refers to the practice of raising an unrelated or irrelevant point deliberately to throw an audience off track. Politicians often employ this fallacy when they field questions from the public or press.

Example   You raise a good question about my support for sending ground troops into Afghanistan. Let me tell you about my admiration for the bravery of our soldiers.

Slippery Slope. The slippery slope fallacy is based on the fear that one step in a direction we don't like inevitably leads to the next with no stopping place.

Example   We don't dare send weapons to these guerrillas. If we do, we will next send in military advisers, then a Special Forces battalion, and then large numbers of troops. Finally, we will be in all-out war.

R e a d i n g s

The first reading is by Edward I. Koch, former mayor of New York and longtime active member of the Democratic Party. Generally associated with liberal politics, Koch here takes a conservative position on the death penalty, arguing that capital punishment affirms life. This article originally appeared in the *New Republic* in 1985.

■ EDWARD I. KOCH ■
DEATH AND JUSTICE:
How Capital Punishment Affirms Life

Last December a man named Robert Lee Willie, who had been convicted of raping and murdering an eighteen-year-old woman, was executed in the Louisiana state prison. In a statement issued several minutes before his death, Mr. Willie said: "Killing people is wrong. . . . It makes no difference whether it's citizens, countries, or governments. Killing is wrong." Two weeks later in South Carolina, an admitted killer named Joseph Carl Shaw was put to death for murdering two teenagers. In an appeal to the governor for clemency, Mr Shaw wrote: "Killing is wrong when I did it. Killing is wrong when you do it. I hope you have the courage and moral strength to stop the killing." 1

It is a curiosity of modern life that we find ourselves being lectured on morality by cold-blooded killers. Mr. Willie previously had been convicted of aggravated rape, aggravated kidnapping, and the murders of a Louisiana deputy and a man from Missouri. Mr. Shaw committed another murder a 2 week before the two for which he was executed, and admitted mutilating the body of the fourteen-year-old girl he killed. I can't help wondering what prompted these murderers to speak out against killing as they entered the deathhouse door. Did their newfound reverence for life stem from the realization that they were about to lose their own?

3 Life is indeed precious, and I believe the death penalty helps to affirm this fact. Had the death penalty been a real possibility in the minds of these murderers, they might well have stayed their hand. They might have shown moral awareness before their victims died, and not after. Consider the tragic death of Rosa Velez, who happened to be home when a man named Luis Vera burglarized her apartment in Brooklyn. "Yeah, I shot her," Vera admitted. "She knew me, and I knew I wouldn't go to the chair."

4 During [my] twenty-two years in public service, I have heard the pros and cons of capital punishment expressed with special intensity. As a district leader, councilman, congressman, and mayor, I have represented constituencies generally thought of as liberal. Because I support the death penalty for heinous crimes of murder, I have sometimes been the subject of emotional and outraged attacks by voters who find my position reprehensible or worse. I have listened to their ideas. I have weighed their objections carefully. I still support the death penalty. The reasons I maintain my position can be best understood by examining the arguments most frequently heard in opposition.

1. The death penalty is "barbaric."

5 Sometimes opponents of capital punishment horrify with tales of lingering death on the gallows, of faulty electric chairs, or of agony in the gas chamber. Partly in response to such protests, several states such as North Carolina and Texas switched to execution by lethal injection. The condemned person is put to death painlessly, without ropes, voltage, bullets, or gas. Did this answer the objections of death penalty opponents? Of course not. On June 22, 1984, the *New York Times* published an editorial that sarcastically attacked the new "hygienic" method of death by injection, and stated that "execution can never be made humane through science." So it's not the method that really troubles opponents. It's the death itself they consider barbaric.

6 Admittedly, capital punishment is not a pleasant topic. However, one does not have to like the death penalty in order to support it any more than one must like radical surgery, radiation, or chemotherapy in order to find necessary these attempts at curing cancer. Ultimately we may learn how to cure cancer with a simple pill. Unfortunately, that day has not yet arrived. Today we are faced with the choice of letting the cancer spread or trying to cure it with the methods available, methods that one day will almost certainly be considered barbaric. But to give up and do nothing would be far more barbaric and would certainly delay the discovery of an eventual cure. The analogy between cancer and murder is imperfect, because murder is not

the "disease" we are trying to cure. The disease is injustice. We may not like the death penalty, but it must be available to punish crimes of cold-blooded murder, cases in which any other form of punishment would be inadequate and, therefore, unjust. If we create a society in which injustice is not tolerated, incidents of murder—the most flagrant form of injustice—will diminish.

2. No other major democracy uses the death penalty.

No other major democracy—in fact, few other countries of any description—are plagued by a murder rate such as that in the United States. Fewer and fewer Americans can remember the days when unlocked doors were the norm and murder was a rare and terrible offense. In America the murder rate climbed 122 percent between 1963 and 1980. During the same period, the murder rate in New York City increased by almost 400 percent, and the statistics are even worse in many other cities. A study at M.I.T. showed that based on 1970 homicide rates a person who lived in a large American city ran a greater risk of being murdered than an American soldier in World War II ran of being killed in combat. It is not surprising that the laws of each country differ according to differing conditions and traditions. If other countries had our murder problem, the cry for capital punishment would be just as loud as it is here. And I daresay that any other major democracy where 75 percent of the people supported the death penalty would soon enact it into law.

3. An innocent person might be executed by mistake.

Consider the work of Hugo Adam Bedau, one of the most implacable foes of capital punishment in this country. According to Mr. Bedau, it is "false sentimentality to argue that the death penalty should be abolished because of the abstract possibility that an innocent person might be executed." He cites a study of the 7,000 executions in this country from 1893 to 1971, and concludes that the record fails to show that such cases occur. The main point, however, is this. If government functioned only when the possibility of error didn't exist, government wouldn't function at all. Human life deserves special protection, and one of the best ways to guarantee that protection is to assure that convicted murders do not kill again. Only the death penalty can accomplish this end. In a recent case in New Jersey, a man named Richard Biegenwald was freed from prison after serving eighteen years for murder; since his release he has been convicted of committing four murders. A prisoner named Lemuel Smith, who, while serving four life sentences for murder (plus two life sentences for kidnapping and robbery) in New York's Green Haven Prison, lured a woman corrections officer into the chaplain's office and strangled her. He then mutilated and dismembered her body. An additional life sentence for Smith is meaningless. Because New York has no death penalty statute, Smith has effectively been given a license to kill.

But the problem of multiple murder is not confined to the nation's penitentiaries. In 1981, 91 police officers were killed in the line of duty in this country. Seven percent of those arrested in the cases that have been solved had a previous arrest for murder. In New York City in 1976 and 1977, 85 persons arrested for homicide had a previous arrest for murder. Six of these individuals had two previous arrests for murder, and one had four previous murder arrests. During those two years the New York police were arresting for murder persons with a previous arrest for murder on the average of one every 8.5 days. This is not surprising when we learn that in 1975, for example, the median time served in Massachusetts for homicide was less than two and a half years. In 1976 a study sponsored by the Twentieth Century Fund found that the average time served in the United States for first-degree murder is ten years. The median time served may be considerably lower.

4. Capital punishment cheapens the value of human life.

10   In the contrary, it can be easily demonstrated that the death penalty strengthens the value of human life. If the penalty for rape were lowered, clearly it would signal a lessened regard for the victim's suffering, humiliation, and personal integrity. It would cheapen their horrible experience, and expose them to an increased danger of recurrence. When we lower the penalty for murder, it signals a lessened regard for the value of the victim's life. Some critics of capital punishment, such as columnist Jimmy Breslin, have suggested that a life sentence is actually a harsher penalty for murder than death. This is sophistic nonsense. A few killers may decide not to appeal a death sentence, but the overwhelming majority make every effort to stay alive. It is by exacting the highest penalty for the taking of human life that we affirm the highest value of human life.

5. The death penalty is applied in a discriminatory manner.

11   This factor no longer seems to be the problem it once was. The appeals process for a condemned prisoner is lengthy and painstaking. Every effort is made to see that the verdict and sentence were fairly arrived at. However, assertions of discrimination are not an argument for ending the death penalty but for extending it. It is not justice to exclude everyone from the penalty of the law if a few are found to be so favored. Justice requires that the law be applied equally to all.

6. Thou Shalt Not Kill.

12   The Bible is our greatest source of moral inspiration. Opponents of the death penalty frequently cite the sixth of the Ten Commandments in an attempt to prove that capital punishment is divinely proscribed. In the original Hebrew, however, the Sixth Commandment reads "Thou Shalt Not Commit Murder," and the Torah specifies capital punishment for a variety of offenses. The biblical viewpoint has been upheld by philosophers throughout history. The greatest thinkers of the nineteenth century—Kant, Locke, Hobbes, Rousseau, Montesquieu, and Mill—agreed that natural law properly authorizes the sovereign to take life in order to vindicate justice. Only Jeremy Bentham was ambivalent. Washington, Jefferson, and Franklin endorsed it. Abraham Lincoln authorized executions for deserters in wartime. Alexis

de Tocqueville, who expressed profound respect for American institutions, believed that the death penalty was indispensable to the support of social order. The United States Constitution, widely admired as one of the seminal achievements in the history of humanity, condemns cruel and inhuman punishment, but does not condemn capital punishment.

7. The death penalty is state-sanctioned murder.

This is the defense with which Messrs. Willie and Shaw hoped to soften the resolve of those who sentenced them to death. By saying in effect, "You're no better than I am," the murderer seeks to bring his accusers down to his own level. It is also a popular argument among opponents of capital punishment, but a transparently false one. Simply put, the state has rights that the private individual does not. In a democracy, those rights are given to the state by the electorate. The execution of a lawfully condemned killer is no more an act of murder than is legal imprisonment an act of kidnapping. If an individual forces a neighbor to pay him money under threat of punishment, it's called extortion. If the state does it, it's called taxation. Rights and responsibilities surrendered by the individual are what give the state its power to govern. This contract is the foundation of civilization itself.   13

Everyone wants his or her rights, and will defend them jealously. Not everyone, however, wants responsibilities, especially the painful responsibilities that come with law enforcement. Twenty-one years ago a woman named Kitty Genovese was assaulted and murdered on a street in New York. Dozens of neighbors heard her cries for help but did nothing to assist her. They didn't even call the police. In such a climate the criminal understandably grows bolder. In the presence of moral cowardice, he lectures us on our supposed failings and tries to equate his crimes with our quest for justice.   14

The death of anyone—even a convicted killer—diminishes us all. But we are diminished even more by a justice system that fails to function. It is an illusion to let ourselves believe that doing away with capital punishment removes the murderer's deed from our conscience. The rights of society are paramount. When we protect guilty lives, we give up innocent lives in exchange. When opponents of capital punishment say to the state, "I will not let you kill in my name," they are also saying to murderers: "You can kill in your *own* name as long as I have an excuse for not getting involved."   15

It is hard to imagine anything worse than being murdered while neighbors do nothing. But something worse exists. When those same neighbors shrink back from justly punishing the murderer, the victim dies twice.   16

Thinking Critically about "Death and Justice"

1. Skilled arguers use opening attention grabbers to create a desired rhetorical effect. Why does Koch begin with the material on Robert Lee Willie and Joseph Carl Shaw? What effect does he hope for? Does the opening work?

2. In supporting capital punishment, why does Koch choose to rebut opposing arguments rather than arguing more directly for his own position?

3. Consider carefully Koch's use of evidence. Sometimes he uses empirical evidence based on scholarly studies (for example, the study cited by Hugo Adam Bedau under point 3); sometimes he focuses on a single example (the cases of Biegenwald and Smith in point 3); sometimes he uses analogies (the comparison of murder to cancer under point 1). Where is his evidence most persuasive? Where is it least persuasive?

4. In citing the case of Lemuel Smith, Koch's logical point is complete once he tells us that Smith killed a corrections officer while serving a life sentence. Why does Koch also inform us that he strangled her and mutilated and dismembered her body?

5. In paragraph 3 Koch states: "Had the death penalty been a real possibility in the minds of these murderers, they might well have stayed their hand." Although Koch's statement seems intuitively logical, most statistical studies show that the death penalty does not deter murder. Having no hard data to support his claim, Koch instead quotes Luis Vera. What is the rhetorical purpose of that quotation?

6. Koch chooses to list and number the objections to capital punishment. What is the rhetorical effect of having a numbered list?

The next argument is a direct response to Koch. It also appeared in the *New Republic* in 1985. Its author, David Bruck, is a practicing attorney specializing in the legal defense of persons facing a death sentence. He has written numerous articles opposing the death penalty and particularly studies the problem of racial bias in sentencing.

▪ DAVID BRUCK ▪
THE DEATH PENALTY

1   Mayor Ed Koch contends that the death penalty "affirms life." By failing to execute murderers, he says, we "signal a lessened regard for the value of the victim's life." Koch suggests that people who oppose the death penalty are like Kitty Genovese's neighbors, who heard her cries for help but did nothing while an attacker stabbed her to death.

2   This is the standard "moral" defense of death as punishment: even if executions don't deter violent crime any more effectively than imprisonment, they are still required as the only means we have of doing justice in response to the worst of crimes.

3   Until recently, this "moral" argument had to be considered in the abstract, since no one was being executed in the United States. But the death penalty is back now, at least in the southern states, where every one of

the more than thirty executions carried out over the last two years has taken place. Those of us who live in those states are getting to see the difference between the death penalty in theory, and what happens when you actually try to use it.

South Carolina resumed executing prisoners in January with the electro- 4
cution of Joseph Carl Shaw. Shaw was condemned to death for helping to murder two teenagers while he was serving as a military policeman at Fort Jackson, South Carolina. His crime, propelled by mental illness and PCP, was one of terrible brutality. It is Shaw's last words ("Killing was wrong when I did it. It is wrong when you do it. . . .") that so outraged Mayor Koch: he finds it "a curiosity of modern life that we are being lectured on morality by cold-blooded killers." And so it is.

But it was not "modern life" that brought this curiosity into being. It was 5
capital punishment. The electric chair was J. C. Shaw's platform. (The mayor mistakenly writes that Shaw's statement came in the form of a plea to the governor for clemency: Actually Shaw made it only seconds before his death, as he waited, shaved and strapped into the chair, for the switch to be thrown.) It was the chair that provided Shaw with celebrity and an opportunity to lecture us on right and wrong. What made this weird moral reversal even worse is that J. C. Shaw faced his own death with undeniable dignity and courage. And while Shaw died, the TV crews recorded another "curiosity" of the death penalty—the crowd gathered outside the death-house to cheer on the executioner. Whoops of elation greeted the announcement of Shaw's death. Waiting at the penitentiary gates for the appearance of the hearse bearing Shaw's remains, one demonstrator started yelling, "Where's the beef?"

For those who had to see the execution of J. C. Shaw, it wasn't easy to 6
keep in mind that the purpose of the whole spectacle was to affirm life. It will be harder still when Florida executes a cop-killer named Alvin Ford. Ford has lost his mind during his years of death-row confinement, and now spends his days trembling, rocking back and forth, and muttering unintelligible prayers. This has led to litigation over whether Ford meets a centuries-old legal standard for mental competency. Since the Middle Ages, the Anglo-American legal system has generally prohibited the execution of anyone who is too mentally ill to understand what is about to be done to him and why. If Florida wins its case, it will have earned the right to electrocute Ford in his present condition. If it loses, he will not be executed until the state has first nursed him back to some semblance of mental health.*

We can at least be thankful that this demoralizing spectacle involves a 7
prisoner who is actually guilty of murder. But this may not always be so. The ordeal of Lenell Jeter—the young black engineer who recently served more than a year of a life sentence for a Texas armed robbery that he didn't commit—should remind us that the system is quite capable of making the very

*Authors' Note: On June 26, 1986, the Supreme Court ruled against the State of Florida.

worst sort of mistake. That Jeter was eventually cleared is a fluke. If the robbery had occurred at 7 P.M. rather than 3 P.M., he'd have had no alibi, and would still be in prison today. And if someone had been killed in that robbery, Jeter probably would have been sentenced to death. We'd have seen the usual execution-day interviews with state officials and the victim's relatives, all complaining that Jeter's appeals took too long. And Jeter's last words from the gurney would have taken their place among the growing literature of death-house oration that so irritates the mayor.

8   Koch quotes Hugo Adam Bedau, a prominent abolitionist, to the effect that the record fails to establish that innocent defendants have been executed in the past. But this doesn't mean, as Koch implies, that it hasn't happened. All Bedau was saying was that doubts concerning executed prisoners' guilt are almost never resolved. Bedau is at work now on an effort to determine how many wrongful death sentences may have been imposed: his list of murder convictions since 1900 in which the state eventually *admitted* error is some four hundred cases long. Of course, very few of these cases involved actual executions: the mistakes that Bedau documents were uncovered precisely because the prisoner was alive and able to fight for his vindication. The cases where someone is executed are the very cases in which we're least likely to learn that we got the wrong man.

9   I don't claim that executions of entirely innocent people will occur very often. But they will occur. And other sorts of mistakes already have. Roosevelt Green was executed in Georgia two days before J. C. Shaw. Green and an accomplice kidnapped a young woman. Green swore that his companion shot her to death after Green had left, and that he knew nothing about the murder. Green's claim was supported by a statement that his accomplice made to a witness after the crime. The jury never resolved whether Green was telling the truth, and when he tried to take a polygraph examination a few days before his scheduled execution, the state of Georgia refused to allow the examiner into the prison. As the pressure for symbolic retribution mounts, the courts, like the public, are losing patience with such details. Green was electrocuted on January 9, while members of the Ku Klux Klan rallied outside the prison.

10   Then there is another sort of arbitrariness that happens all the time. Last October, Louisiana executed a man named Ernest Knighton. Knighton had killed a gas station owner during a robbery. Like any murder, this was a terrible crime. But it was not premeditated, and is the sort of crime that very rarely results in a death sentence. Why was Knighton electrocuted when almost everyone else who committed the same offense was not? Was it because he was black? Was it because his victim and all 12 members of the jury that sentenced him were white? Was it because Knighton's court-appointed lawyer presented no evidence on his behalf at his sentencing hearing? Or maybe there's no reason except bad luck. One thing is clear: Ernest Knighton was picked out to die the way a fisherman takes a cricket out of a bait jar. No one cares which cricket gets impaled on the hook.

Not every prisoner executed recently was chosen that randomly. But many were. And having selected these men so casually, so blindly, the death penalty system asks us to accept that the purpose of killing each of them is to affirm the sanctity of human life.   11

The death penalty states are also learning that the death penalty is easier to advocate than it is to administer. In Florida, where executions have become almost routine, the governor reports that nearly a third of his time is spent reviewing the clemency requests of condemned prisoners. The Florida Supreme Court is hopelessly backlogged with death cases. Some have taken five years to decide, and the rest of the Court's work waits in line behind the death appeals. Florida's death row currently holds more than 230 prisoners. State officials are reportedly considering building a special "death prison" devoted entirely to the isolation and electrocution of the condemned. The state is also considering the creation of a special public defender unit that will do nothing else but handle death penalty appeals. The death penalty, in short, is spawning death agencies.   12

And what is Florida getting for all of this? The state went through almost all of 1983 without executing anyone: its rate of intentional homicide declined by 17 percent. Last year Florida executed eight people—the most of any state, and the sixth highest total for any year since Florida started electrocuting people back in 1924. Elsewhere in the U.S. last year, the homicide rate continued to decline. But in Florida, it actually rose by 5.1 percent.   13

But these are just the tiresome facts. The electric chair has been a centerpiece of each of Koch's recent political campaigns, and he knows better than anyone how little the facts have to do with the public's support for capital punishment. What really fuels the death penalty is the justifiable frustration and rage of people who see that the government is not coping with violent crime. So what if the death penalty doesn't work? At least it gives us the satisfaction of knowing that we got one or two of the sons of bitches.   14

Perhaps we want retribution on the flesh and bone of a handful of convicted murderers so badly that we're willing to close our eyes to all of the demoralization and danger that come with it. A lot of politicians think so, and they may be right. But if they are, then let's at least look honestly at what we're doing. This lottery of death both comes from and encourages an attitude toward human life that is not reverent, but reckless.   15

And that is why the mayor is dead wrong when he confuses such fury with justice. He suggests that we trivialize murder unless we kill murderers. By that logic, we also trivialize rape unless we sodomize rapists. The sin of Kitty Genovese's neighbors wasn't that they failed to stab her attacker to death. Justice does demand that murderers be punished. And common sense demands that society be protected from them. But neither justice nor self-preservation demands that we kill men whom we have already imprisoned.   16

The electric chair in which J. C. Shaw died earlier this year was built in 1912 at the suggestion of South Carolina's governor at the time, Cole Blease. Governor Blease's other criminal justice initiative was an impassioned cru-   17 sade in favor of lynch law. Any lesser response, the governor insisted, trivial-ized the loathsome crimes of interracial rape and murder. In 1912 a lot of people agreed with Governor Blease that a proper regard for justice required both lynching and the electric chair. Eventually we are going to learn that justice requires neither.

Thinking Critically about "The Death Penalty"

1. In this essay Bruck partly refutes Koch and partly makes his own arguments opposing the death penalty. In your own words, why does Bruck oppose capi-tal punishment? Make a list of the reasons he uses.

2. Koch claims that the death penalty "affirms life." What rhetorical strategies does Bruck employ to persuade readers that the death penalty degrades life?

3. Imagine that Bruck and Koch are in the same room engaged not in a pro/con debate but in a search for the best understanding of each other's perspective. What common ground can you find between Koch and Bruck? Which of Koch's arguments would Bruck be most apt to agree with? Which of Bruck's arguments would be most compelling to Koch?

4. Why is it important to Bruck *when* J. C. Shaw uttered his condemnation of capital punishment?

5. A frequent claim-with-reason cited by opponents of capital punishment is this: "Capital punishment should be outlawed because innocent persons may be put to death." How does Koch rebut this argument? Where does Koch attack the reason and grounds and where does he attack the warrant? How does Bruck rebut Koch?

6. Before you read these two arguments, you probably had your own views on capital punishment. Locate one or two places where either Koch or Bruck caused you to change slightly your initial view.

The third reading is an op-ed piece by *Miami Herald* columnist Leonard Pitts, Jr., that appeared in the *Seattle Times* in September 2001. In this editorial, Pitts jumps into the ongoing controversy over corporal punishment, children's rights, child-rearing practices, and spanking.

■ LEONARD PITTS, JR. ■
SPARE THE ROD, SPOIL THE PARENTING

1   I hate to tell you this, but your kid is spoiled. Mine aren't much better.
2   That, in essence, is the finding of a recent Time/CNN poll. Most of us think most of our kids are overindulged, materialistic brats.

If you're waiting for me to argue the point, you're in the wrong column.   3

No, I only bring it up as context to talk about a controversial study   4
released late last month. It deals with corporal punishment—spanking—and
it has outraged those who oppose the practice while rearming those who
support it.

It seems that Dr. Diana Baumrind, a psychologist at the University of   5
California at Berkeley, followed 164 middle-class families from the time
their children were in preschool until they reached their 20s. She found that
most used some form of corporal punishment. She further found that, contrary to what we've been told for years, giving a child a mild spanking
(defined as open-handed swats on the backside, arm or legs) does not leave
the child scarred for life.

Baumrind, by the way, opposes spanking. Still, it's to her credit as an aca-   6
demic that her research draws a distinction other opponents refuse to. That
is, a distinction between the minor punishments practiced by most parents
who spank and the harsher variants practiced by a tiny minority (shaking
and blows to the head or face, for example).

Yes, children whose parents treat them that severely are, indeed, more   7
likely to be maladjusted by the time they reach adolescence. And, yes, the
parents themselves are teetering dangerously close to child abuse.

But does the same hold true in cases where corporal punishment means   8
little more than swatting a misbehaving backside?

For years, the official consensus from the nation's child-rearing experts   9
was that it did. Maybe that's about to change. We can only hope.

For my money, there was always something spurious about the ortho-   10
doxy that assured us all corporal punishment, regardless of severity, was de
facto abuse. Nevertheless, we bought into it, with the result being that parents who admitted to spanking were treated as primitive dolts and heaped
with scorn. They were encouraged to negotiate with misbehaving children
in order to nurture their self-esteem.

But the orthodoxy was wrong on several fronts.   11

In the first place, it's plainly ridiculous—and offensive—to equate a child   12
who has been swatted on the butt with one who has been stomped, scalded
or punched. In the second, the argument that reasonable corporal punishment leads inevitably to mental instability always seemed insupportable
and has just been proven so by Baumrind's study. And in the third, have
you ever tried to "negotiate" with a screaming 5-year-old? It may do wonders for the child's self-esteem, but, I promise, it's going to kill yours. Your
sanity, too.

Don't get me wrong, contrary to what its proponents sometimes claim,   13
corporal punishment is not a panacea for misbehavior. Rearing a child
requires not just discipline, but also humor, love and some luck.

Yet the very fact that spanking must be exonerated by a university study   14
suggests how far afield we've wandered from what used to be the central

tenet of family life: parents in charge. Ultimately, it probably doesn't matter whether that tenet is enforced by spanking or other corrective measures, so long as it is enforced.

15   I've seen too many children behave with too grand a sense of entitlement to believe that it is. Heard too many teachers tell horror stories of dealing with kids from households where parents are not sovereign, adult authority not respected. As a culture, we seem to have forgotten that the family is not a democracy, but a benign dictatorship.

16   Small wonder our kids are brats.

17   So the pertinent question isn't: To spank or not to spank? Rather, it's: Who's in charge here? Who is teaching whom? Who is guiding whom?

18   The answer used to be obvious. It's obvious no more. And is it so difficult to see where that road leads? To understand that it is possible to be poisoned by self-esteem, and that a spoiled child becomes a self-centered adult ill-equipped to deal with the vagaries and reversals of life?

19   Some folks think it's abuse when you swat a child's backside. But maybe, sometimes, it's abuse when you don't.

Thinking Critically about "Spare the Rod, Spoil the Parenting"

1. In the introductory paragraphs of this op-ed piece, Leonard Pitts, Jr., mentions the rhetorical situation that has called forth his argument. What contemporary research is prompting Pitts's column?

2. Pitts's argument takes a stand on the issue question "Is spanking a good child-rearing practice?" What claim does he make in this argument? What reasons and evidence does he offer to support this claim?

3. Where does Pitts acknowledge and respond to opposing views?

4. To understand the intensity of the social controversy on this issue, we suggest that you search the key words "spanking" and "corporal punishment" using an online database and the Web. What different positions do you find represented in articles and by advocacy Web sites such as the site for the Center for Effective Discipline? How would these sources challenge Pitts's position and evidence?

The next reading is by Dan Savage, a nationally syndicated author of a sex-advice column and of "The Kid," a memoir about adoption. This op-ed piece appeared in the *New York Times* on September 8, 2001. Written during a time of public controversy over gay rights and gay marriage, this article is Savage's response to a Federal District Court ruling upholding a Florida law banning adoption of children by gay men and lesbians.

■ Dan Savage ■

IS NO ADOPTION REALLY BETTER THAN A GAY ADOPTION?

"I pray my correspondence does not offend you, but it is my understanding that you are a practicing homosexual," the message in my e-mail said. "It is also my understanding that you and your partner have adopted a child into your home." The author, a fundamentalist Christian who lives in West Virginia, was deeply concerned for the physical and spiritual well-being of my 3-year-old son. He walked me through some familiar Bible quotations and ended his letter with this startling offer: "My wife and I would be very willing to adopt the child you have adopted." 1

I imagine this man was pleased by a Federal District Court decision handed down last week. Judge James Lawrence King upheld a 1977 Florida law that bans adoptions by gay men and lesbians. "It is arguable that placing children in married homes is in the best interest of Florida's children," Judge King wrote. 2

Any state that uses a married-home standard to prevent gay people from adopting would also, a reasonable person might assume, ban adoptions by unmarried heterosexuals. But that's not the case in Florida, where a quarter of all the children adopted every year go to single heterosexual adults. How can Florida justify the creation of hundreds of new single-parent families every year if lawmakers there believe every child should have a married mom and dad? 3

Florida's adoption laws would be laughable if they weren't so tragic. And make no mistake, the tragedy is not for gay men and lesbians: those who want to start families are free to move to other states. The law's real victims are the thousands of children trapped in Florida's foster care system. These children can't pick up and move to states that don't exclude perfectly fit single people and loving couples from pools of potential adoptive parents. 4

The religious right in the United States has sought to frame the debate over gay adoption as a choice between gay parents and straight parents. It's a false choice. The real choice for children waiting to be adopted in Florida and elsewhere isn't between gay and straight parents, but between parents and no parents. There are more children out there who need to be adopted than there are people seeking to adopt them. 5

Gay and lesbian couples in New York, New Jersey, Oregon, Illinois and other states that allow them to adopt are not snapping up all the available babies or even the "best" babies. It is an open secret among social workers that gay and lesbian couples are often willing to adopt children whom most heterosexual couples won't touch: H.I.V.-positive children, mixed-race children, disabled children and children who have been abused or neglected. 6

It's highly unlikely, for example, that a straight couple is going to step forward and adopt the three African-American children—two of whom are 7

H.I.V.-positive—that one of the gay plaintiffs in Florida has been caring for practically since birth. What purpose is serviced in denying children like these the security of a legally formalized relationship with adults who want to raise them?

8   My own son was turned down by a married heterosexual couple before he was offered to us. This couple didn't want to take a chance on him because his birth mother, a homeless teenager, drank and took drugs during the early stages of her pregnancy. We wouldn't have been able to adopt him if he had had the bad luck to be born in Florida. And if social workers in Florida couldn't find a heterosexual person or couple willing to adopt a drug- and alcohol-exposed infant from a homeless teenager who wanted to stay in contact with her child, well, he might still be bouncing around the state's foster care system.

9   Finally, if the people from West Virginia who were eager to adopt my son are reading this, I have some advice for them: There are plenty of kids out there who need loving homes. My child already has one. But there are kids in Florida who don't, and the State of Florida is dead set on making it more difficult for these children to find homes. If you're "deeply concerned" about children, I suggest you adopt one of Florida's unlucky kids.

Thinking Critically about "Is No Adoption Really Better Than a Gay Adoption?"

1. Summarize Savage's argument as a claim with attached "because" clauses. How many main reasons does Savage develop in support of his claim? (There is no single right answer to this question. Some readers will find one major reason with subparts. Others will break the argument into several separate reasons.)

2. Analyze how Savage summarizes and responds to opposing views:
   a. Why does he identify his opposition with the Christian Right?
   b. Might there be reasons to oppose gay adoption other than those he mentions? If so, what are they?
   c. Why does he choose not to mention these other views?
   d. Who do you think is Savage's intended audience?

3. What does Savage use as evidence to support his own position?

4. What is the main warrant behind this argument? (That is, what is the primary belief, value, or assumption that Savage believes he and his audience will share?)

5. How effective is Savage's argument?

In this last essay, first-year student Tiffany Linder enters an argument fiercely debated by environmentalists and the timber industry: the logging of old-growth forests.

■ TIFFANY LINDER (STUDENT) ■

SALVAGING OUR OLD-GROWTH FORESTS

It's been so long since I've been there I can't clearly remember what it's like. I can only look at the pictures in my family photo album. I found the pictures of me when I was a little girl standing in front of a towering tree with what seems like endless miles and miles of forest in the background. My mom is standing on one side of me holding my hand, and my older brother is standing on the other side of me, making a strange face. The faded pictures don't do justice to the real-life magnificence of the forest in which they were taken—the Olympic National Forest—but they capture the awe my parents felt when they took their children to the ancient forest.

Today these forests are threatened by timber companies that want state and federal governments to open protected old-growth forests to commercial logging. The timber industry's lobbying attempts must be rejected because the logging of old-growth forests is unnecessary, because it will destroy a delicate and valuable ecosystem, and because these rare forests are a sacred trust.

Those who promote logging of old-growth forests offer several reasons, but when closely examined, none is substantial. First, forest industry spokespeople tell us the forest will regenerate after logging is finished. This argument is flawed. In reality, the logging industry clear-cuts forests on a 50–80 year cycle, so that the ecosystem being destroyed—one built up over more than 250 years—will never be replaced. At most, the replanted trees will reach only one-third the age of original trees. Because the same ecosystem cannot rebuild if the trees do not develop to full maturity, the plants and animals that depend on the complex ecosystem—with its incredibly tall canopies and trees of all sizes and ages—cannot survive. The forest industry brags about replaceable trees but doesn't mention a thing about the irreplaceable ecosystems.

Another argument used by the timber industry, as forestry engineer D. Alan Rockwood has said in personal correspondence, is that "an old-growth forest is basically a forest in decline. . . . The biomass is decomposing at a higher rate than tree growth." According to Rockwood, preserving old-growth forests is "wasting a resource" since the land should be used to grow trees rather than let old ones slowly rot away, especially when harvesting the trees before they rot would provide valuable lumber. But the timber industry looks only at the trees, not at the incredibly diverse biosystem which the ancient trees create and nourish. The mixture of young and old-growth trees creates a unique habitat that logging would destroy.

Perhaps the main argument used by the logging industry is economic. Using the plight of loggers to their own advantage, the industry claims that logging old-growth forests will provide jobs. They make all of us feel sorry for the loggers by giving us an image of a hardworking man put out of work and unable to support his family. They make us imagine the sad eyes of the logger's children. We think, "How's he going to pay the electricity bill? How's he going to pay his mortgage? Will his family become homeless?" We all see these images in our minds and want to give the logger his job so his family won't suffer, but in reality giving him his job back is only a temporary solution to a long-term problem. Logging in the old-growth forest couldn't possibly give the logger his job for long. For example, according to Peter Morrison of the Wilderness Society, all the old-growth forest in the Gifford Pinchot National Forest would be gone in three years if it were opened to logging (vi). What will the loggers do then? Loggers need to worry about finding new jobs now and not wait until there are no old-growth trees left.

6   Having looked at the views of those who favor logging of old-growth forests, let's turn to the arguments for preserving all old growth. Three main reasons can be cited. First, it is simply unnecessary to log these forests to supply the world's lumber. According to environmentalist Mark Sagoff, we have plenty of new-growth forest from which timber can be taken (89–90). Recently, there have been major reforestation efforts all over the United States, and it is common practice now for loggers to replant every tree that is harvested. These new-growth forests, combined with extensive planting of tree farms, provide more than enough wood for the world's needs. According to forestry expert Robert Sedjo (qtd. in Sagoff 90), tree farms alone can supply the world's demand for industrial lumber. Although tree farms are ugly and possess little diversity in their ecology, expanding tree farms is far preferable to destroying old-growth forests.

7   Moreover, we can reduce the demand for lumber. Recycling, for example, can cut down on the use of trees for paper products. Another way to reduce the amount of trees used for paper is with a promising new innovation, kenaf, a fast-growing, 15-foot-tall, annual herb that is native to Africa. According to Jack Page in *Planet Earth, Forest,* kenaf has long been used to make rope, and it has been found to work just as well for paper pulp (158).

8   Another reason to protect old-growth forests is the value of its complex and very delicate ecosystem. The threat of logging to the northern spotted owl is well known. Although loggers say "people before owls," ecologists consider the owls to be warnings, like canaries in mine shafts, that signal the health of the whole ecosystem. Evidence provided by the World Resource Institute shows that continuing logging will endanger other species. Also, Dr. David Brubaker, an environmental biologist at Seattle University, has said in a personal interview that the long-term effects of logging will be severe. Loss of the spotted owl, for example, may affect the small rodent population, which at the moment is kept in check by the predator owl. Dr. Brubaker also explained that the old-growth forests also connect to salmon runs. When dead timber falls into the streams, it creates a habitat conducive to spawning. If the dead logs are removed, the habitat is destroyed. These are only two examples in a long list of animals that would be harmed by logging of old-growth forests.

Finally, it is wrong to log in old-growth forests because of their sacred beauty. When you walk in an old-growth forest, you are touched by a feeling that ordinary forests can't evoke. As you look up to the sky, all you see is branch after branch in a canopy of towering trees. Each of these amazingly tall trees feels inhabited by a spirit; it has its own personality. "For spiritual bliss take a few moments and sit quietly in the Grove of the Patriarchs near Mount Rainier or the redwood forests of Northern California," said Richard Linder, environmental activist and member of the National Wildlife Federation. "Sit silently," he said, "and look at the giant living organisms you're surrounded by; you can feel the history of your own species." Although Linder is obviously biased in favor of preserving the forests, the spiritual awe he feels for ancient trees is shared by millions of other people who recognize that we destroy something of the world's spirit when we destroy ancient trees, or great whales, or native runs of salmon. According to Al Gore, "We have become so successful at controlling nature that we have lost our connection to it" (qtd. in Sagoff 96). We need to find that connection again, and one place we can find it is in the old-growth forests.

9

The old-growth forests are part of the web of life. If we cut this delicate strand of the web, we may end up destroying the whole. Once the old trees are gone, they are gone forever. Even if foresters replanted every tree and waited 250 years for the trees to grow to ancient size, the genetic pool would be lost. We'd have a 250-year-old tree farm, not an old-growth forest. If we want to maintain a healthy earth, we must respect the beauty and sacredness of the old-growth forests.

10

Works Cited

Brubaker, David. Personal interview. 25 Sept. 1998.

Linder, Richard. Personal interview. 12 Sept. 1998.

Morrison, Peter. *Old Growth in the Pacific Northwest: A Status Report.* Alexandria: Global Printing, 1988.

Page, Jack. *Planet Earth, Forest.* Alexandria: Time-Life, 1983.

Rockwood, D. Alan. E-mail to the author. 24 Sept. 1998.

Sagoff, Mark. "Do We Consume Too Much?" *Atlantic Monthly* June 1997: 80–96.

World Resource Institute. "Old-Growth Forests in the United States Pacific Northwest." 13 Sept. 1998 <http://www.wri.org/biodiv>.

Thinking Critically about "Salvaging Our Old-Growth Forests"

1. What is the issue addressed in this argument? What is the writer's claim? What are the writer's main reasons in support of the claim?

2. How does this writer structure her argument to respond to alternative viewpoints? Does her summary of these arguments seem fair?

3. How does the writer appeal to readers' emotions, beliefs, and values?

4. What do you see as the strengths and weaknesses of this argument?

COMPOSING YOUR ESSAY

Writing arguments deepens our thinking by forcing us to consider alternative views and to question the assumptions underlying our reasons and claims. Consequently, it is not unusual for a writer's position on an issue to shift—and even to reverse itself—during the writing process. If this happens to you, take it as a healthy sign of your openness to change, complexity, and alternative points of view. If writing a draft causes you to modify your views, it will be an act of discovery, not a concession of defeat.

Generating and Exploring Ideas

The tasks that follow are intended to help you generate ideas for your argument. Our goal is to help you build up a storehouse of possible issues, explore several of these possibilities, and then choose one for deeper exploration before you write your initial draft.

Make an Inventory of Issues That Interest You

Following the lead of the For Writing and Discussion exercise on page 377, make a list of various communities that you belong to and then brainstorm contested issues in those communities. You might try a trigger question like this: "When members of [X community] get together, what contested questions cause disagreements?" What decisions need to be made? What values are in conflict? What problems need to be solved?

Explore Several Issues

For this task, choose two or three possible issues from your previous list and explore them through freewriting or idea mapping. Try responding quickly to the following questions:

1. What is my position on this issue and why?
2. What are alternative points of view on this issue?
3. Why do people disagree about this issue? (Do people disagree about the facts of the case? About key definitions? About underlying values, assumptions, and beliefs?)
4. If I were to argue my position on this issue, what evidence would I need to gather and what research might I need to do?

Brainstorm Claims and Reasons

For *because* clauses, see pp. 378–379.

Choose one issue that particularly interests you and work with classmates to brainstorm possible claims that you could make on the issue. Imagining different perspectives, brainstorm possible reasons to support each claim, stating them as because clauses.

Conduct and Respond to Initial Research

If your issue requires research, do a quick bibliographic survey of what is available and do enough initial reading to get a good sense of the kinds of arguments that surround your issue and of the alternative views that people have taken. Then freewrite your responses to the following questions:

1. What are the different points of view on this issue? Why do people disagree with each other?

2. Explore the evolution of your thinking as you did this initial reading. What new questions have the readings raised for you? What changes have occurred in your own thinking?

Conduct an In-Depth Exploration Prior to Drafting

The following set of tasks is designed to help you explore your issue in depth. Most students take one or two hours to complete these tasks; the time will pay off, however, because most of the ideas that you need for your rough draft will be on paper.

See the discussion of issues questions on pp. 376–377.

1. Write out the issue your argument will address. Try phrasing your issue in several different ways, perhaps as a yes/no question and as an open-ended question. Try making the question broader, then narrower. Finally, frame the question in the way that most appeals to you.

2. Now write out your tentative answer to the question. This will be your beginning thesis statement or claim. Put a box around this answer. Next, write out one or more different answers to your question. These will be alternative claims that a neutral audience might consider.

3. Why is this a controversial issue? Is there insufficient evidence to resolve the issue, or is the evidence ambiguous or contradictory? Are definitions in dispute? Do the parties disagree about basic values, assumptions, or beliefs?

4. What personal interest do you have in this issue? How does the issue affect you? Why do you care about it? (Knowing why you care about it might help you get your audience to care about it.)

5. What reasons and evidence support your position on this issue? Freewrite everything that comes to mind that might help you support your case. This freewrite will eventually provide the bulk of your argument. For now, freewrite rapidly without worrying whether your argument makes sense. Just get ideas on paper.

6. Imagine all the counterarguments your audience might make. Summarize the main arguments against your position and then freewrite your response to each of the counterarguments. What are the flaws in the alternative points of view?

7. What kinds of appeals to *ethos* and *pathos* might you use to support your argument? How can you increase your audience's perception of your credibility and trustworthiness? How can you tie your argument to your audience's beliefs and values?

8. Why is this an important issue? What are the broader implications and consequences? What other issues does it relate to? Thinking of possible answers to these questions may prove useful when you write your introduction or conclusion.

Shaping and Drafting

Once you have explored your ideas, create a plan. Here is a suggested procedure:

Begin your planning by analyzing your intended audience. You could imagine an audience deeply resistant to your views or a more neutral, undecided audience acting like a jury. In some cases, your audience might be a single person, as when you petition your department chair to take an upper-division course when you are a sophomore. At other times, your audience might be the general readership of a newspaper, church bulletin, or magazine. When the audience is a general readership, you need to imagine from the start the kinds of readers you particularly want to sway. Here are some questions you can ask:

- ▓ *How much does your audience know or care about your issue?* Will you need to provide background? Will you need to convince them that your issue is important? Do you need to hook their interest? Your answers to these questions will particularly influence your introduction and conclusion.

- ▓ *What is your audience's current attitude toward your issue?* Are they deeply opposed to your position? If so, why? Are they neutral and undecided? If so, what other views will they be listening to? Classical argument works best with neutral or moderately dissenting audiences. Deeply skeptical audiences are best addressed with delayed-thesis or Rogerian approaches.

For Rogerian approaches, see p.392

- ▓ *How do your audience's values, assumptions, and beliefs differ from your own?* What aspects of your position will be threatening to your audience? Why? How does your position on the issue challenge your imagined reader's world view or identity? What objections will your audience raise toward your argument? Your answers to these questions will help determine the content of your argument and alert you to the extra research you may have to do to respond to audience objections.

- ▓ *What values, beliefs, or assumptions about the world do you and your audience share?* Despite your differences with your audience, where can you find common links? How might you use these links to build bridges to your audience?

Your next step is to plan out an audience-based argument by seeking audience-based reasons or reasons whose warrants you can defend. Here is a process you can use:

1. Create a skeleton, tree diagram, outline, or flowchart for your argument by stating your reasons as one or more "because" clauses attached to your claim. Each because clause will become the head of a main section or *line of reasoning* in your argument.

2. Use the planning schema to plan each line of reasoning. If your audience accepts your warrant, concentrate on supporting your reason with grounds. If your warrant is doubtful, support it with backing. Try to anticipate audience objections by exploring conditions for rebuttal, and brainstorm ways of addressing those objections.

For planning schema, see pp. 384–386.

3. Using the skeleton you created, finish developing an outline or tree diagram for your argument. Although the organization for each part of your argument will grow organically from its content, the main parts of a classical argument are as follows:

a. *An introduction,* in which you engage your reader's attention, introduce your issue, and state your own position.

b. *Background and preliminary material,* in which you place your issue in a current context and provide whatever background knowledge and definitions of key terms or concepts that your reader will need. (If this background is short, it can often be incorporated into the introduction.)

c. *Arguments supporting your own position,* in which you make the best case possible for your views by developing your claim with reasons and evidence. This is usually the longest part of your argument, with a separate section for each line of reasoning.

d. *Anticipation of objections and counterarguments,* in which you summarize fairly key arguments against your position. This section not only helps the reader understand the issue more clearly, but also establishes your *ethos* as a fair-minded writer willing to acknowledge complexity.

e. *Response to objections through refutation or concession,* in which you point out weaknesses in opposing arguments or concede to their strengths.

f. *A conclusion,* in which you place your argument in a larger context, perhaps by summarizing your main points and showing why this issue is an important one or by issuing a call to action.

This classical model can be modified in numerous ways. A question that often arises is where to summarize and respond to objections and counterarguments. Writers generally have three choices. One option is to handle opposing positions before you present your own argument. The rationale for this approach is that skeptical audiences may be more inclined to listen attentively to your argument if they have been assured that you understand their point of view. A second option is to place this material after you have presented your argument. This approach is effective for neutral audiences who don't start off with strong opposing views. A final option is to intersperse opposing views throughout your argument at appropriate moments. Any of these possibilities, or a combination of all of them, can be effective.

Another question often asked is the best way to order one's reasons. A general rule of thumb when ordering your own argument is to put your strongest reason last and your second strongest reason first. The idea here is to start and end with your most powerful arguments. If you imagine a quite skeptical audience, build bridges to your audience by summarizing alternative views early in the paper and concede to those that are especially strong. If your audience is neutral or undecided, you can summarize and respond to possible objections after you have presented your own case.

Revising

As you revise your argument, you need to attend both to the clarity of your writing (all the principles of closed-form prose described in Chapter 19) and also to the persuasiveness of your argument. As always, peer reviews are valuable, and especially so in argumentation if you ask your peer reviewers to role-play an opposing audience. The following Guidelines for Peer Reviews can both assist your peer reviewers and help you with revision.

▪ GUIDELINES FOR PEER REVIEWS ▪

Instructions for peer reviews are provided in Chapter 18 (pp. 490–496).

For the Writer

Prepare two or three questions you would like your peer reviewer to address while responding to your draft. The questions can focus on some aspect of your draft that you are uncertain about, on one or more sections where you particularly seek help or advice, on some feature that you particularly like about your draft, or on some part you especially wrestled with. Write out your questions and give them to your peer reviewer along with your draft.

For the Reviewer

I. Read the draft at a normal reading speed from beginning to end. As you read, do the following:

   A. Place a wavy line in the margin next to any passages that you find confusing, that contain something that doesn't seem to fit, or that otherwise slow down your reading.

   B. Place a "Good!" in the margin next to any passages where you think the writing is particularly strong or interesting.

II. Read the draft again slowly and answer the following questions by writing brief explanations of your answers.

   A. Introduction

   1. How could the title be improved so that it announces the issue, reveals the writer's claim, or otherwise focuses your expectations and piques interest?

   2. What strategies does the writer use to introduce the issue, engage your interest, and convince you that the issue is significant and problematic? What would add clarity and appeal?

   3. How could the introduction more effectively forecast the argument and present the writer's claim? What would make the statement of the claim more focused, clear, or risky?

    B. Arguing for the claim

        1. Consider the overall structure: What strategies does the writer use to make the structure of the paper clear and easy to follow? How could the structure of the argument be improved?

        2. Consider the support for the reasons: Where could the writer provide better evidence or support for each line of reasoning? Look for the grounds in each line of reasoning by noting the writer's use of facts, examples, statistics, testimony, or other evidence. Where could the writer supply more evidence or use existing evidence more effectively?

        3. Consider the support for the warrants: For each line of reasoning, determine the assumptions (warrants) that the audience needs to grant for the argument to be effective. Are there places where these warrants need to be stated directly and supported with backing? How could the use of backing be improved?

        4. Consider *ethos* and *pathos:* What strategies does the writer use to appear credible and trustworthy? What strategies does the writer use to appeal to the audience's imagination, emotions, and values? Where and how could the writer improve his or her appeals to *ethos* and *pathos?*

        5. Consider the writer's summary of and response to alternative viewpoints: Where does the writer treat alternative views? Are there additional alternative views that the writer should consider? What strategies does the writer use to respond to alternative views? How could the writer's treatment of alternative views be improved?

    C. Conclusion: How might the conclusion more effectively bring completeness or closure to the argument?

    D. If the writer has prepared questions for you, respond to his or her inquiries.

    E. Sum up what you see as the main strengths and problem areas of the draft:

        1. Strengths

        2. Problem areas

III. Read the draft one more time. Place a check mark in the margin wherever you notice problems in grammar, spelling, or mechanics (one check mark per problem).

CHAPTER 16

Making an Evaluation

ABOUT EVALUATIVE WRITING

In everyday life you make evaluations all the time. You do so through a critical thinking process in which you match the thing being evaluated against criteria that you deem important. Consider how you might choose between two elective courses for your class schedule next term. You'll decide by matching each course against criteria that matter to you, such as the course's projected interest level, the course's workload and level of difficulty, the reputation of the teacher, the course's usefulness to your future career, or the attractiveness of the course's time slot.

In many evaluative decisions, the stakes will be high. In professional life you may have to write evaluations of a subordinate's work performance or create an argument for investing substantial company funds into Project A or Project B—decisions with enormous consequences. In fact, making evaluative arguments may be among the most important writing you will ever do.

This chapter instructs you in a systematic procedure for evaluating an object, person, or other phenomenon. Research suggests that most college assignments require some form of evaluative thinking. According to one study, college assignments often take the form of "good/better/best" questions:*

Good: Is X good or bad? (Based on your current perspective, how effective was the U.S. response to the terrorist acts of September 11, 2001?)

Better: Which is better—X or Y? (Which is the better theoretical model for designing a treatment program for social anxiety disorder—a medical/biological model or an environmental model?)

Best: Among available options, which is the best solution to the problem? (For this engineering application, what is the best solution: conventional steel roller bearings, ceramic bearings, air bearings, or magnetic bearings? Why?)

You can write evaluations for different rhetorical purposes such as an informative purpose, an analytic purpose, or a persuasive purpose. A typical informative evaluation might be an article in *Consumer Reports,* where, for example, a prospective buyer of a used car might find independent data about a car's reliability, fuel economy, safety, and other factors. Typical analytical evaluations include movie, book, or restaurant reviews. In a typical restaurant review, for example, the writer might

Chapter 4, pp. 61–65, discusses the different purposes writers can have.

*See Barbara E. Walvoord and Lucille P. McCarthy, *Thinking and Writing in College: A Naturalistic Study of Students in Four Disciplines* (Urbana, IL: National Council of Teachers of English, 1990), p. 7.

describe the good and bad features of Elvis's House of Chili using such criteria as quality of cuisine, seating and atmosphere, friendliness of service, cost, and so forth.

In this book we have chosen to treat evaluative writing as persuasion, in which case you imagine a skeptical audience with some degree of initial resistance to your evaluation. Because evaluation issues frequently cause the most disagreements within communities, many students writing classical arguments for Chapter 15 may have already addressed an evaluation issue in their arguments. (The starling case used as an example in Chapter 15 is an evaluation issue.) All the classical arguing skills covered in Chapter 15 apply as well to this chapter, which simply looks at this specific kind of argument in more depth. (The next chapter looks in depth at proposal arguments, which are another very common kind of argument.) Because evaluative arguments help communities make choices about actions, beliefs, or values, they are among the most important kinds of arguments to understand.

EXPLORING EVALUATIVE WRITING

To introduce you to evaluative thinking, we ask you to resolve a provocative evaluative question that at first looks innocuous. As you apply the principles of truth seeking and persuasion to this issue, be aware of your thinking processes.

Situation: You are a tenth-grade social studies teacher. In your school building, the history and social studies classrooms have a large map of the Americas prominently displayed on a side wall. At a teachers' meeting, one of your colleagues proposes that in the history and social studies classrooms, this traditional map of the Americas be replaced with an equivalent-sized *inverted map* like the one shown in Figure 16.1. The question becomes, "Which of these two kinds of maps—the traditional one or the inverted one—is better for the front of a social studies classroom?" (As a class you may wish to establish a fuller context for this discussion by stipulating the size and location of the high school, thereby giving you more information about the class, ethnicity, and politics of its community.)

1. Freewrite your initial thoughts on this question and then share your freewrites in small groups or as a whole class.

2. Working in small groups or as a whole class, create the best arguments you can in favor of each map, framing each argument as a claim with reasons. State each reason as a *because* clause (for example, "The traditional map is better because . . . , because . . . ," etc.; then do the same for the inverted map).

3. Role-playing the teachers in this high school, reach consensus on this issue by holding a truth-seeking discussion in which participants make their best persuasive cases for their points of view but listen empathically to other points of view.

4. When the class reaches consensus on the issue, write the frame of the deciding argument on the chalkboard as a claim with *because* clauses. If you wish, you can also write a dissenting argument on the board. Then write out the warrant that links each reason to the claim (that is, the unstated assumption that the audience has to accept for the reason to have any force). As we show in the next section, these warrants are actually statements of evaluative criteria for the argument.

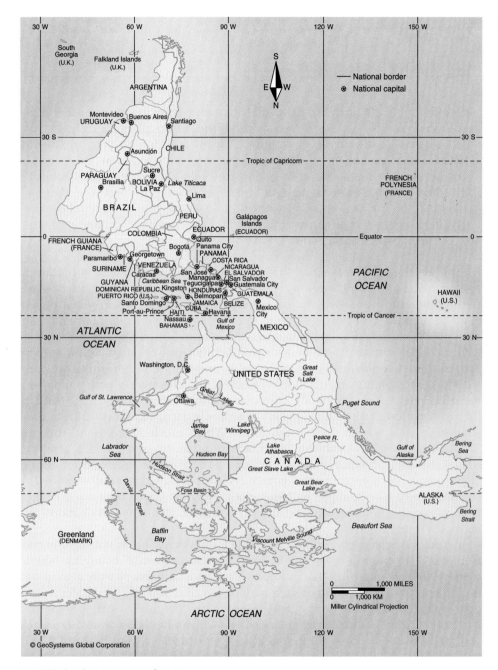

FIGURE 16.1 ■ An Inverted Map

Map makers have traditionally placed north at the top of maps and south at the bottom. However, putting north on top is an arbitrary and conventional decision that has a subtle rhetorical effect. Because words like *top, above,* and *up* suggest superiority over words like *bottom, below,* and *down,* a conventional map makes the northern hemisphere seem more important than the southern. An inverted map reverses this effect, placing the southern hemisphere in the privileged "upper" position. Geographically, the inverted map is completely accurate. All that changes is the viewer's perspective.

WRITING PROJECT

Write an argument in which you use evaluative thinking to persuade your audience to see the value (or lack of value) of the person, place, thing, event, or phenomenon that you are evaluating. The introduction to your argument should hook your audience's interest in your evaluation question. The body of your argument should establish criteria for evaluating your chosen subject, and then show how your subject meets or does not meet the criteria. Depending on the degree of controversy surrounding your subject, follow the procedure for other arguments by summarizing alternative views and responding to them through either concession or refutation.

For this assignment you need to pose an evaluative question that is important to your audience and invites multiple views. This question can arise from any of the various communities to which you belong: family, school, work, social or religious communities, or the civic communities of town, city, region, or nation. For example: What telephone plan (automobile, method of paying for your college education, day care facility) is best for your family? How effective is your school's general studies curriculum (intramural sports program, service-learning program, writing center, online registration system)? How effective is your employer's incentive program (office layout, customer relations office, dress code)? Is establishing a national ID system (profiling airline passengers, federalizing airport security) a good way to combat terrorism? Which movie deserves an Academy Award? Is art therapy a valuable contribution to clinical psychological practice?

In some cases, you may choose to evaluate a controversial person, event, thing, or phenomenon—something that engenders lively disagreement within a particular community. (For example: Is "Nimbletoes" Nelson a good quarterback?) When your subject is controversial, you need to consider alternative evaluations and show why yours is better.

In other cases, you may choose to evaluate something that is not directly controversial. Your purpose might be to help a specific audience determine how to spend their time or money. For example, is taking an art gallery walk a good way for students to spend a Saturday afternoon in your city? You might consider writing your evaluation within a specific genre. For example, you might write a review for a parents magazine evaluating whether *Lord of the Rings* is a good family movie. Or you might write an editorial for your school newspaper explaining why tutoring with the local children's literacy project is a good experience for education majors.

UNDERSTANDING EVALUATION ARGUMENTS

The Criteria-Match Process of Evaluation Arguments

Evaluation arguments involve what we call a *criteria-match* process. The first step in this process is to establish criteria; the second step is to show how well your subject matches these criteria. Here are several examples:

- Which students should be awarded the prestigious presidential scholarships?

  Criteria task: What are the criteria for the presidential scholarship?

  Match task: Which of the candidates best meets the criteria?

- Is hospitalization an effective treatment program for eating disorders?

  Criteria task: What are the criteria for an effective treatment for eating disorders?

  Match task: Does hospitalization meet these criteria?

- Is *Nightmare on Elm Street* a great horror film?

  Criteria task: What are the criteria for a great horror film?

  Match task: Does *Nightmare on Elm Street* meet these criteria?

- Which is the better map for this high school's social studies classroom—a traditional map or an inverted one?

  Criteria task: What are the criteria for a better map in this context?

  Match task: Which map best meets the criteria?

In each of these cases, it is possible to articulate criteria, even though stakeholders in each issue might argue for different criteria or weight the criteria differently. For example, on the map issue, one set of stakeholders might have argued this way:

Argument in Favor of Traditional Map

The traditional map is the better choice

- because it follows standard conventions for map making.
- because it is easier to comprehend quickly and will facilitate more thorough learning.
- because no costs are involved (we already own these maps and don't have to buy replacements).

The unstated assumptions (warrants) behind these reasons are that in choosing a map it is good to follow standard conventions, it is good to facilitate ease of comprehension, and it is good to keep costs low. In other words, this argument states that a good map should meet three criteria: (1) standard conventions, (2) ease of comprehension, and (3) minimal cost. Based on these criteria, the traditional map wins the argument hands down.

Chapter 15, p. 380, introduces *warrant* as one of Toulmin's terms for the structure of an argument.

But another group of stakeholders might present a different argument:

Argument in Favor of Inverted Map

The inverted map is the better choice

- because it reveals how certain arbitrary conventions of map making (e.g., putting north on top) can have a rhetorical effect on how we read the map.
- because it exposes Americans' ethnocentric assumptions about the "top" being superior to the "bottom."
- because it better promotes multicultural awareness and respect.

The warrants behind this argument establish a quite different set of criteria. To these stakeholders, a good map (1) reveals the rhetorical effect of arbitrary map conventions, (2) exposes ethnocentric assumptions, and (3) promotes multiculturalism. Based on these criteria, the inverted map wins hands down. Clearly, what is at issue in this dispute are the criteria themselves.

In other evaluation disputes, it is the application of criteria (the match argument) that causes disagreement. Consider a family deciding what used car to buy. They might agree on the criteria—let's say, (1) low cost, (2) safety, and (3) reliability. But they might disagree whether a specific car meets the criteria. In terms of cost, Car A may be initially cheaper than Car B but may get lower gas mileage and have a higher frequency-of-repair record. It would not be clear, then, whether Car A or Car B best meets the cost criterion.

For Writing and Discussion

Whenever you evaluate something you first need to establish criteria—that is, for any given class of items, you have to determine the qualities, traits, behaviors, or features that constitute excellence for members of that class. Then you need to match those criteria to a single member of that class—the thing you are evaluating. The following simple exercise will give you practice in thinking in this systematic, two-stage way.

1. Working individually, make a list of criteria that are important to you in choosing a career. These criteria are apt to differ from person to person. Some people might place "high income" at the top of their list, while others might put "adventure" or "being outdoors" or "time for family and leisure" at the top. Then rank your criteria from highest to lowest priority.

2. Share your criteria lists in small groups or as a whole class. Then write on the chalkboard two or three representative lists of criteria.

3. Finally, write several different careers on the board and match them to the lists of criteria. Which possible careers come out on top for you? Which ones come out on top based on the criteria lists placed on the board? Possible careers to consider include these: grade school/high school teacher, lawyer, auto mechanic, airplane pilot, bus driver, military officer, engineer, computer technician, insurance salesperson, accountant, small business owner, plumber, commercial artist, homemaker, nurse/physician/dentist, chiropractor/optometrist, social worker, police officer.

4. When disagreements arise, try to identify whether they are disagreements about criteria or disagreements about the facts of a given career.

The Role of Purpose and Context in Determining Criteria

Ordinarily, criteria are based on the purpose of the class to which the thing being evaluated belongs. For example, if you asked a professor to write a recommendation for you, he or she would need to know what you were applying for—A scholarship? Internship in a law office? Peace Corps volunteer? Summer job in a national park? The qualities of a successful law office intern differ substantially from those of a successful Peace Corps worker in Uganda. The recommendation isn't about you in the abstract but about you fulfilling the purposes of the class "law office intern" or "Peace Corps volunteer." Similarly, if you were evaluating a car, you would need to ask, "a car for what purpose?"—Reliable family transportation? Social status (if so, what social group?)? Environmental friendliness?

Decisions about purpose are often affected by context. For example, a union member, in buying a car, might specify an American-made car while a subscriber to *Mother Jones* magazine might specify high gas mileage and low pollution. To see how context influences criteria, consider a recent review of Seattle's soup kitchens appearing in a newspaper produced by homeless people. In most contexts, restaurant reviews focus on the quality of food. But in this review the highest criterion was the sense of dignity and love extended to homeless people by the staff.

Or consider the wider context of the map issue discussed earlier. The teachers might well pay attention to how administrators, parents, and school board members would react to a change of maps in the history classrooms. Would some people ridicule the teachers for their politically correct agenda? Would others applaud the teachers for championing multiculturalism and diversity? Would new, untenured teachers, drawn into the conflict, risk alienating key administrators or powerful senior teachers? Sometimes a tiny act that seems inconsequential at the time can become a symbolic battleground for clashing political forces.

For Writing and Discussion

1. Working in small groups or as a whole class, decide how you would evaluate a local eatery as a place to study. How would you evaluate it as a place to take a date, a place to hang out with friends, or a place to buy a nutritious meal?

2. Working in small groups or as a whole class, decide how you would evaluate Britney Spears, Christina Aguilera, or Madonna in the class "popular entertainer." How about the class "role model for women"?

3. Working individually, identify several different classes that you belong to such as the class "son or daughter," "math student," "employee," "party animal," "friend." Choose one category in which you would rate yourself high or low. What are the criteria for excellence in that category? How do you meet or not meet these criteria? (You do not need to share your results unless you want to.)

4. As a whole class or in small groups, discuss how this individual exercise helped you realize how criteria for excellence vary when you place the same item into different classes with different purposes.

Other Considerations in Establishing Criteria

Establishing the criteria for evaluation arguments can entail other considerations besides purpose and context. We examine these considerations in this section.

The Problem of Apples and Oranges

To avoid the problem of mixing apples and oranges, try to place the thing you are evaluating into the smallest applicable class. That way, apples compete only with other apples, not with other members of the next larger class "fruit" where they have to go head-to-head against bananas, peaches, and oranges. You would therefore evaluate Kobe Bryant against other basketball players rather than against golfers and race car drivers. And if you were to evaluate a less talented basketball player, you might do so within the subclass of "point guard" or "power forward" or "off-the-bench scorer" rather than the general class "basketball player."

In the readings for this chapter, the student writer evaluating the film *Picnic at Hanging Rock* had to place it in the narrow class of "art film" to distinguish it from Hollywood blockbuster films or other subclasses of film. Clearly, the criteria for a successful art film are different from those for a horror film, an action film, or a dramatic comedy.

The Problem of Standards: What's Commonplace Versus What's Ideal

When we determine criteria, we often encounter the problem of what's commonplace versus what's ideal. Do we praise something because it is better than average, or do we condemn it because it is less than ideal? Do we hold it to absolute standards or to common practice? Do we censure someone for paying a housekeeper under the table to avoid taxes (failure to live up to an ideal), or do we overlook this behavior because it is so common? Is it better for high schools to pass out free contraceptives because teenagers are having sex anyway (what's *commonplace*), or is it better not to pass them out in order to support abstinence (what's *ideal*)?

There is no easy way to decide which standard to use. The problem with the "ideal" is that nothing may ever measure up. The problem with the "commonplace" is that we may lower our standards and slip into a morally dangerous relativism. In deciding which standard to follow, we need to recognize the limitations of each, to make the best choice we can, and to use the same standard for all items being evaluated.

The Problems of Necessary, Sufficient, and Accidental Criteria

In identifying criteria, we often recognize that some are more important than others. Suppose you said, "I will be happy with any job as long as it puts food on my table and gives me time for my family." In this case the criteria "adequate income" and "time for family," taken together, are *sufficient*, meaning that once these criteria are met, the thing being rated meets your standard for excellence. Suppose you said instead, "I am hard to please in my choice of a career, which must meet many criteria. But I definitely will reject any career that doesn't put enough food on my table or allow me time for my family." In this case the criteria of "adequate income" and "time for family" are *necessary* but not *sufficient*, meaning that these two criteria have to be met for a career to meet your standards, but that other criteria must be met also.

Besides necessary and sufficient criteria, there are also *accidental* criteria, which are added bonuses but not essential. For example, you might say something like, "Although it's not essential, having a career that would allow me to be outside a lot would be nice." In this case "being outside" is an *accidental* criteria (nice but not required).

The terms *necessary* and *sufficient* are also used in causal arguments; see p. 348.

The Problem of Seductive Empirical Measures

Empirical data can help you evaluate all sorts of things. If you are buying an automobile, you can be helped a great deal by knowing the numbers for its horsepower and acceleration, for its fuel economy and frequency-of-repair record, and for its potential resale value. But sometimes the need to make defensible evaluative decisions leads people to empirical measures that disastrously oversimplify complex matters. Every year, for example, new crops of potential professional athletes are scrutinized minutely for their records in the forty-yard dash, the bench press, the vertical jump, and so forth. Every year, some of the people who max out on these empirical measures flop ingloriously in actual competition because they lack qualities that are difficult if not impossible to measure empirically, whereas other athletes, with more modest scores, achieve great success thanks to these same invisible qualities.

Quantifiable measures can be helpful, of course. But they are so concrete and they make comparisons so easy that they can seduce you into believing that you can make complex judgments by comparing numbers. It's all too easy to fall into the trap of basing college admissions on SAT scores, scholarships on grade point averages, or the success of a government policy on tax dollars saved.

The Problem of Cost

A final problem in establishing criteria is cost. A given X may be far superior to any other Xs in its class, but it may also cost far more. Before you move from evaluating an X to acting on your evaluation (by buying, hiring, or doing X), you must consider cost, whether it is expressed as dollars, time, or lost opportunity. There's little question, for example, that a Lexus is superior to a Nissan Sentra according to most automotive criteria. But are the differences sufficient to justify the additional thirty thousand or so dollars that the Lexus costs?

Using Toulmin's System to Develop Evaluation Arguments

In Chapter 15, we presented a language for talking about argument based on the terminology of philosopher Stephen Toulmin. We explained how you can examine any claim–with–reason from the perspective of *grounds* (evidence to support the reason), *warrant* (the unstated assumption that links the reason to your claim), *backing* (an argument to support the warrant if needed), *conditions of rebuttal* (ways that a skeptical audience might refute your argument by attacking your reason and grounds or your warrant), and *qualifier* (a limiting phrase to reduce the sweep of your claim). Because the warrants for an evaluation argument are typically statements of your criteria, this system can easily be applied to evaluation arguments.

Chapter 15, pp. 384–386, explains how the Toulmin system can help writers map out and structure an argument to connect with their audience.

Let's say that you are the student member of a committee to select a professor for an outstanding teaching award. Several members of the committee want to give the award to Professor M. Mouse, a popular sociology professor at your institution. You are opposed. One of your lines of reasoning is that Professor Mouse's courses aren't rigorous. Here is how you could develop this line of reasoning using the planning schema explained in Chapter 15.

Claim with Reason

Professor Mouse does not deserve the teaching award because his courses aren't rigorous.

Grounds

I need to provide evidence that his courses aren't rigorous. From the dean's office records, I have discovered that 80 percent of his students get As or high Bs; a review of his syllabi shows that he requires little outside reading and only one short paper; he has a reputation in my dorm of being fun and easy.

Warrant

Having rigorous academic standards is a necessary criterion for the university teaching award.

Backing

I need to show why I think rigorous academic standards are necessary. Quality of teaching should be measured by the amount that students learn. Good teaching is more than a popularity contest. Good teachers draw high-level performance from their students and motivate them to put time and energy into learning. High standards lead to the development of skills that are demanded in society.

Conditions of Rebuttal

How could someone attack my reason and grounds? Might a person say that Mouse has high standards? Could someone show that students really earned the high grades? Are the students I talked to not representative? Could someone say that Mouse's workload and grading patterns meet or exceed the commonplace behavior of faculty in his department? *How could someone attack my warrant?* Could someone argue that rigorous academic standards aren't as important as other criteria—that this is an accidental not a necessary criterion? Could a person say that Mouse's goal—to inspire interest in sociology—is best achieved by not loading students down with too many papers and too much reading, which can appear like busy-work? (I'll need to refute this argument.) Could someone say that the purpose of giving the university teaching award is public relations and it is therefore important to recognize widely popular teachers who will be excellent speakers at banquets and other public forums?

Qualifier

Rather than saying that Professor Mouse doesn't deserve the award, perhaps it would be better for me to say that he is a weak candidate or even a generally strong candidate except for one notable weakness.

Conducting an Evaluation Argument: An Extended Example of Evaluating a Museum

Now that we have explored some potential difficulties in establishing and defending criteria for an evaluation, let's consider in more detail the process of making an evaluation argument.

The student examples in this section focus on the evaluation of a rock and roll museum in Seattle, Washington, called Experience Music Project (EMP). Designed by world-famous architect Frank Gehry (who is known for his creation of the Guggenheim Museum in Bilbao, Spain, the Aerospace Hall in Los Angeles, and other famous buildings around the world), EMP was sponsored by Microsoft cofounder Paul Allen as a tribute to rock singer Jimi Hendrix and to rock music itself, especially in the Pacific Northwest. In Figure 16.2, you can see this innovative structure which has sparked much controversy (is it a wonder or an eyesore?). Sharing some characteristics with the Rock and Roll Hall of Fame and Museum in Cleveland, Ohio, EMP features some permanent exhibits—the Hendrix Gallery, the Guitar Gallery (tracing the development of guitars from the 1500s to the electric guitars of today), Milestones (including displays from rhythm and blues to hip-hop and current rap artists), and Northwest Passage (focusing on popular music in Seattle, from jazz and rhythm and blues to heavy metal, punk, grunge, and the contemporary music scene). EMP also includes Sound Lab (where visitors can play instruments using interactive technology), On Stage (where visitors can pretend to be rock stars playing before a cheering crowd), Artist's Journey (a ride involving motion platform technology), three restaurants, and a store. (To see for yourself what EMP is and how it looks on the inside, you can go to its Web site at www.emplive.com. A Web search on Frank Gehry will show you photos of his prizewinning architecture.)

For an extended example of how to evaluate Web sites for academic purposes, see Chapter 22, pp. 605–616.

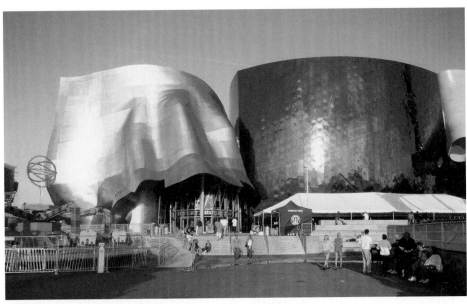

FIGURE 16.2 ■ Experience Music Project, Seattle, Washington

Let's now turn to the specific steps of making an evaluation argument.

Step 1: Determining the Class to Which X Belongs and the Purposes of That Class

When you conduct an evaluation argument, you must first assign your person/object/phenomenon (the X you are evaluating) to a category or class and then determine the purposes of that class. Often people disagree about an evaluation because they disagree about the arguer's choice of category for X. EMP, as students soon discovered, could be placed in several different categories, leading to different criteria for evaluation. Here are typical classes proposed by students:

- A tourist attraction (for an audience of visitors to Seattle)
- A museum of rock history (for people interested in the development of rock as an art form)
- A rock and roll shrine (for rock fans who want to revere their favorite artists and feel part of the rock scene for a day)

Clearly these classes have different purposes. The purpose of a tourist attraction is to offer a unique, fun place to spend the day during a visit to Seattle. The purpose of a rock museum is to teach about the history of its subject in an informative, interesting, and accessible way. The purpose of a rock and roll shrine is to honor famous rock stars, bring visitors into their lives and work, and let them experience the music scene.

Step 2: Determining and Weighting Criteria

The criteria for your evaluation are directly connected to the purposes of the class to which X belongs. The following lists show typical criteria chosen by different students for each of the classes listed in Step 1:

- A good *tourist attraction* should
  - be entertaining and enjoyable.
  - be affordable and worth the price, not simply out to gouge tourists' wallets.
  - be unique—something the tourist wouldn't find in another city.
- A good *museum of rock history* should
  - have a clear, well-organized layout that is easy to navigate.
  - display objects of clear aesthetic or historical significance.
  - teach the public by providing clear, meaningful information about rock music.
  - arouse interest in rock as an art form and encourage the public's appreciation and involvement.
- A good *rock and roll shrine* should
  - take fans up close and personal into the lives of major artists.
  - encourage fans to appreciate the complexity of rock and the skills of artists.
  - help fans experience the rock scene and fantasize about being rock stars themselves.

In addition to identifying criteria, you should arrange them in order of importance so that you build to your most important criterion. In each of the preceding examples, students placed their most important criterion last.

Step 3: Determining the Extent to Which X Meets Your Criteria for the Class

A third step in constructing an evaluation argument is to make your match argument: To what extent does X meet or not meet the criteria you have formulated? The following examples show how three students framed the match part of their evaluation arguments on EMP. Note how each student matches EMP to the specific criteria he or she has selected.

- Experience Music Project is a tourist trap rather than an attraction because
    - the headphones and heavy computerized MEGs (Museum Exhibit Guides) keep everyone isolated, making companionship difficult.
    - the arrangement of exhibits is chaotic, leading to frustration and repetition of the same experiences.
    - it doesn't give any substance, just endless music trivia.
    - it's too expensive and commercial, leaving the tourist feeling ripped-off.
- Experience Music Project is a good museum of rock and roll history because
    - it covers a range of popular music styles from jazz and blues to reggae, punk, grunge, and hip-hop.
    - it provides interesting information on musicians, musical styles, and key moments in popular music history.
    - it makes people excited about popular music and its history through the museum's interactive exhibits and technologically advanced museum guide devices.
- For rock fans, Experience Music Project is a good rock and roll shrine because
    - it gives illuminating insights into the lives and artistry of many rock musicians.
    - it gives an in-depth look at some of the greats like Jimi Hendrix and helps fans really appreciate the talent of these musicians.
    - the "onstage" room lets fans fulfill a fantasy by pretending they are rock stars.

Step 4: Determining What Alternative Views You Must Respond to in Your Evaluation Argument

Finally, in constructing your evaluation argument you need to determine whether your intended audience is likely to object to (1) the class in which you have placed your object; (2) the criteria you have developed for assessing your object; or (3) the degree to which your object matches the criteria you have chosen. You have numerous options for accommodating your audience's doubts or objections. For example, if your proposed class is controversial, you might choose to justify it in your introduction. If your criteria might be controversial, you could address objections before you start the match part of your argument. If you think your match argument will raise doubts, you could intersperse alternative views throughout or treat them separately near the end of your argument. Any of these methods can work.

In the readings section of this chapter, we include a student writer's complete evaluation argument on the Experience Music Project. ▪

For Writing and Discussion

Consider how student writer Katie Tiehen confronts and responds to alternative views. After reading the passage typical from her argument, answer these questions:

1. What objections to her argument does Katie anticipate (doubts about her proposed class for EMP, her criteria, or her match argument)?
2. How does Katie respond to alternative views—by conceding points and shifting back to her own perspective or by refuting alternative views with counterreasons and counterexamples?

> . . . Some may challenge my contention that EMP is an ineffective museum of rock history by arguing that a day spent at EMP is entertaining and fun. I'll be the first to admit that EMP is fun. From a rock and roll fan's perspective, EMP is nonstop entertainment, a musical paradise. I felt like a five-year-old on Christmas morning when I saw Eric Clapton's guitar, Jimi Hendrix's personal journals, and walls plastered in punk memorabilia. These items, coupled with video documentaries and hands-on activities, provided hours of enjoyment. Because of the fun factor, it's easy for people to jump to EMP's defense. However, it is not the entertainment value of EMP that I am questioning. There's no doubt that it is a fun and amusing place to visit. The problem arises when one tries to classify EMP as an historical museum, which should provide visitors with access to objects of lasting historical significance. Some entertainment is fine, but not to the point that it clouds the true purpose of the museum as it does in EMP's case. After two visits, I still couldn't tell you where rock and roll originated, but I could tell you that the line to play the drums in Sound Lab is really long. Entertainment is the main purpose of EMP and it shouldn't be.

Readings

The first reading is a student essay by Jackie Wyngaard evaluating the Experience Music Project in Seattle, Washington.

▪ JACKIE WYNGAARD (STUDENT) ▪
EMP: Music History or Music Trivia?

Along with other college students new to Seattle, I wanted to see what cultural opportunities the area offers. I especially wanted to see billionaire Paul

1

Allen's controversial Experience Music Project (known as EMP), a huge, bizarre, shiny, multicolored structure that is supposed to resemble a smashed guitar. Brochures say that EMP celebrates the creativity of American popular music, but it has prompted heated discussions among architects, Seattle residents, museumgoers, and music lovers, who have questioned its commercialism and the real value of its exhibits. My sister recommended this museum to me because she knows I am a big music lover and a rock and roll fan. Also, as an active choir member since the sixth grade, I have always been intrigued by the history of music. I went to EMP expecting to learn more about music history from exhibits that showed a range of popular musical styles, that traced historical connections and influences, and that enjoyably conveyed useful information. However, as a museum of rock history, EMP is a disappointing failure.

2   EMP claims that it covers the history of rock and roll from its roots to the styles of today, but it fails at this task because it isolates musicians and styles without explaining historical progressions or cultural influences. For instance, the museum doesn't show how Elvis Presley's musical style was influenced by his predecessors like Chuck Berry and Muddy Waters. It doesn't show how early folk and blues influenced Bob Dylan's music. It doesn't show how early jazz paved the way for rock and roll. How are these isolated and separate EMP exhibits connected? How did rock and roll progress from the '50s "Let's Go to the Hop" beats to the laid-back guitar riffs of the '60s and '70s? How did '70s music become the heavy metal, head-banger rock of the '80s and '90s? How did these styles lead to rap? The exhibits show the existence of these different styles, but they don't help viewers understand the historical developments or historical context. While it is interesting to see a peace patch once owned by Janis Joplin, this exhibit does not explain either the social and political events of the time or Joplin's political views.

3   Another fault of EMP is that it omits many influential groups and musicians, particularly women. For example, there is no display about the Beatles, the Rolling Stones, Led Zeppelin, or the Doors. The exhibits also exclude many major female artists who made substantial contributions to popular music. I found nothing about Joan Baez, Ella Fitzgerald, Aretha Franklin, Carly Simon, or Joni Mitchell. I was also surprised that there were few women mentioned in the Northwest Passage exhibit. Weren't more women involved in the Seattle music scene? As a woman interested in music, I felt left out by EMP's overall neglect of women musicians.

4   Perhaps most frustrating about EMP is the way exhibits are explained through the awkward, difficult-to-use handheld computer called a Museum Exhibit Guide (MEG). The explanations are hard to access and then disappointing in their content. I wanted to hear a landmark song that an artist wrote or an interesting analysis of the artist's musical style. Instead, I listened to "how Elvis made the leather jacket famous" and other random trivia. The MEG also offers too many choices for each exhibit, like a Web

page with a dozen links. But after all the time and effort, you learn nothing that increases your understanding or stimulates your thinking about music history. The MEGs themselves are very heavy, clunky, and inconvenient. If you don't point this gadget exactly at the activator, nothing happens. It took me a good ten minutes to figure out how to get the device to play information for me, and many of my classmates had to keep going back to the booth to get new batteries or other repairs. The museum would be much more effective if visitors had the option of just reading about the displays from plaques on the walls.

I know that many people will disagree with my assessment of EMP.   5
They'll point to the fun of the interactive exhibits and the interesting collection of album covers, crushed velvet costumes, concert clips, famous guitars, and old jukeboxes. But a good museum has to be more than a display of artifacts and an array of hands-on activities. Pretending you're a rock star by performing on stage with instruments doesn't tell you how a certain style of music came about. Displaying trivial information about Elvis's leather jacket or Janis Joplin's feather boa doesn't help you appreciate the importance of their music. Devoting half an exhibit to punk rock without any analysis of that style doesn't teach you anything. In short, the museum displays frivolous trivia tidbits without educational substance.

Music lovers hoping for an educational experience about the rock and   6
roll era of musical history will be disappointed by EMP. And this is without the additional insult of having to shell out $19.95 to get in the door. Speaking for serious music lovers and students of music history, I have to say that EMP is a failure.

Thinking Critically about "EMP: Music History or Music Trivia?"

1. What strategies particularly appropriate for evaluation arguments does Jackie Wyngaard use in her introduction?
2. How has Jackie chosen to classify Experience Music Project? What criteria does she choose?
3. In the match part of her argument, what evidence does Jackie use to support her assessment of Experience Music Project?
4. What alternative views does she acknowledge and where in her argument does she choose to treat them? Does she anticipate objections to her criteria or to the match part of her argument? What other objections might people raise to her argument?
5. What do you find persuasive about her arguments? How might this evaluation argument be improved?

The second reading aims at changing its readers' assessment of the children's television program *Sesame Street*. It posits just one criterion—a good children's program should not be sexist—and then focuses exclusively on demonstrating that *Sesame Street* is sexist. Its authors are both attorneys and mothers of young children.

■ Diane Helman and Phyllis Bookspan ■

SESAME STREET: Brought to You by the Letters M-A-L-E

1   A recent report released by the American Association of University Women, "How Schools Shortchange Women," finds that teachers, textbooks, and tests are, whether intentionally or unintentionally, giving preferential treatment to elementary-school boys. As a result, girls who enter school with equal or better academic potential than their male counterparts lose confidence and do not perform as well.

2   An earlier study about law students, published in the *Journal of Legal Education,* found a similar disparity. "Gender Bias in the Classroom" found that male law students are called upon in class more frequently than females, speak for longer periods of time, and are given more positive feedback by law professors.

3   The article raised some disturbing questions about whether women and men receive truly equal education in American law schools.

4   Unfortunately, this insidious gender bias appears long before our children enter school and pervades even the television show *Sesame Street.* Yes, *Sesame Street* is sexist! But, just as in the story of the emperor and his new clothes, many of us do not notice the obvious.

5   The puppet stars of the show, Bert and Ernie, and all the other major *Sesame Street* animal characters—Big Bird, Cookie Monster, Grover, Oscar the Grouch, Kermit the Frog, and Mr. Snuffleupagus—are male. Among the secondary characters, including Elmo, Herry Monster, Count VonCount, Telemonster, Prairie Dawn, and Betty Lou, only a very few are girls.

6   The female Muppets always play children, while the males play adult parts in various scenes. In a recently aired skit "Squeal of Fortune," this disparity is evident when the host of the show introduces the two contestants. Of Count VonCount of Transylvania the host asks, "What do you do for a living?" to which the count responds authoritatively, "I count!" Of Prairie Dawn, he inquires, "And how do you spend your day?" Sure, it would be silly to ask a schoolgirl what she does for a living. But none of the female Muppets on *Sesame Street* are even old enough to earn a living.

7   Further, almost all the baby puppet characters on *Sesame Street* are girls. For example, Snuffie's sibling is Baby Alice; in books, Grover's baby cousin is

a girl, and when Herry Monster's mother brings home the new baby—it's a girl. Since babies are totally dependent and fairly passive, the older (male) relatives take care of them and provide leadership.

Also, the female Muppets almost never interact with each other. In sharp contrast, consequential and caring friendships have been fully developed between male Muppets: Ernie and Bert; Big Bird and Snuffie; even Oscar the Grouch and his (male) worm, Squirmy.   8

Any parent of toddlers or preschoolers can testify that the "girls" on *Sesame Street* are not very popular. Children ask their parents for Bert and Ernie dolls, not Baby Alice. Is this just because the girls are not marketed via books, tapes, placemats and toy dolls the same way the boys are? Or is it that the *Sesame Street* writers simply have not developed the girls into the same types of lovable, adorable personalities that belong to the main characters?   9

Interestingly and peculiarly, the minor "girls" look more human than most of the well-loved animal roles. They are not physically cuddly, colorful or bizarre, as are the more important male characters. Prairie Dawn has ordinary blonde hair and brown eyes—nothing even remotely similar to Big Bird's soft yellow feathers or Cookie Monster's wild, bright blue, mane.   10

Yes, we believe that *Sesame Street* is one of the best shows on television for small children. Our children—boys and girls—are regular viewers. In addition to its educational value, lack of violence and emphasis on cooperation, the adult characters on the show are admirably balanced in terms of avoiding sexual stereotypes.   11

But even the best of the bunch has room for improvement. Just as elementary through professional school educators must learn to be more sensitive to subtle and unintentional gender bias, so too should the folks at Children's Television Network. We can stop sexism from seeping into our children's first "formal" educational experience.   12

The message was brought to you by the letter F: fairness for females.   13

Thinking Critically about "Sesame Street"

1. This essay spends no time on the criteria part of the argument ("Sexism is bad") and all its time on the match argument ("*Sesame Street* exhibits sexism"). Why do the authors feel no need to defend the criterion?

2. Do the authors convince you that *Sesame Street* is sexist?

3. If you agree with the argument that *Sesame Street* is sexist, should that criterion be sufficient for undermining the popular assessment of *Sesame Street* as a model educational program for children?

The final essay, by student writer Sarah Erickson, evaluates the film *Picnic at Hanging Rock* as an art film.

■ SARAH ERICKSON (STUDENT) ■
PICNIC AT HANGING ROCK AS AN ART FILM

1   Peter Weir's film *Picnic at Hanging Rock* (1975) opens ambiguously. A silent announcement informs viewers that three girls and their teacher disappeared without a trace while on a picnic in 1901. The camera focuses on the Australian bush and a monolithic rock on a hot summer day. Eerie pan-pipe music strikes up. Several teenage schoolgirls in their nightshifts and corsets are shown dressing for the day. Unlike Weir's recent American films—*The Dead Poets Society* (1989) and *The Truman Show* (1998)—and definitely unlike blockbuster thrillers, *Picnic at Hanging Rock* immediately defies mainstream classification. Some people in our class thought the film was "strange," "slow," or "hard to understand," and they evaluated it as an unsuccessful movie. However, this Australian film should be evaluated as an art film because of its nonformulaic and unpredictable plot and its heavy use of symbolism to convey its themes and characters. Moreover, it is an excellent art film because it uses the elements effectively to provoke thought and create ambiguity.

2   While most mainstream popular films feature action-packed plots that follow a problem-climax-resolution pattern and clear, boldly developed characters, successful art films meet distinctly different criteria. An art film has no defined form. It is original, often unpredictable, and can be interpreted in many different ways depending on the viewers. Symbolism is used to connect ideas, but the interpretation is left up to the imagination of the viewer. In order to make sense of an art film, the viewer must analyze the characters, settings, and recurring themes. A good art film is original, mysterious, and ambiguous.

3   *Picnic at Hanging Rock* takes place in 1901 in Australia at two main locations: Appleyard College, a boarding school for wealthy girls, and Hanging Rock, an ancient geological formation. When the girls go on a Valentine's Day picnic to Hanging Rock, four girls—Marion, Irma, Edith, and their leader, beautiful, adventurous Miranda—disregard the prohibitions and explore Hanging Rock. Miss McCraw, the mathematics teacher, also heads up to the towering cliffs. While the girls are climbing, they seem to be in a trance. Later in the afternoon Miss McCraw and these girls, except for Edith who has fled back to the picnic, have vanished. One girl, Sarah, the school's only charity case, has been forced to miss the picnic by Mrs. Appleyard, the headmistress. Sarah, an orphan, depends on Miranda, but before leaving for the picnic, Miranda has cryptically advised Sarah to learn to live without her. In the second half of the film, two

young men—Michael Fitzhubert and his coachman Albert Crundall—search exhaustively for the girls, whom they had seen earlier, and eventually Albert finds Irma unconscious in a cave. Irma is unable to explain what happened that dreadful day, and the school, the townspeople who have formed a search party, and the audience are left to wonder about the disappearance. When the school's reputation suffers from this incident and Sarah is unable to pay her tuition, Mrs. Appleyard becomes increasingly cruel to her. At the end of the movie, both Sarah and Mrs. Appleyard die strangely.

Picnic at Hanging Rock meets the first criterion of a good art film in that it follows no set formula and is unpredictable. The mysterious deaths or disappearances of the characters leave the ending of the movie up to the viewer's imagination. Nobody knows exactly what has happened. The possible conclusions are endless. Did the three girls and Miss McCraw commit suicide? Were they kidnapped and molested? Did they discover another world at the top of the mysterious rock? Did they find, or become, a part of a higher state of being? Who knows? The viewer must decide. Sarah is found dead in the greenhouse, and the headmistress dies at the base of Hanging Rock. Did they commit suicide? Did one kill the other? These questions do not have definite answers, either. These unresolved questions illustrate the open-endedness and thought-provoking unpredictability, which are appropriate for a successful art film. 4

A good art film also relies on symbolism more than direct statements and action to convey its themes. Symbolism permeates *Picnic at Hanging Rock*. Miranda is the most symbolic character. While climbing the rock, she is the first one to take off her stockings, something totally inappropriate for women in the early 1900s. She represents sensuality; perhaps that is why she mesmerizes Michael Fitzhubert, who cannot forget her. Miranda also has an adventurous spirit that refuses to be bound by class and gender restrictions. After shooting a scene of Miranda, the camera often focuses on a swan. Weir uses the swan to symbolize Miranda: both are beautiful, wild, and free, showing female sexuality at odds with restrictive Victorian standards. The swan is also elusive—appearing and flying away. Similarly, Miranda and reality are elusive and illusory in this film. 5

Another set of interrelated symbols are prominent in this film. Appleyard College is used to represent the sophisticated, wealthy British elite. Hanging Rock, on the other hand, represents Australia. In its raw form, the rock is magnificent, mysterious, untamed, and dangerous. As powerful nature, it dominates the action and overwhelms the civilized British intruders. Like the bush and the Aborigines, the rock is wild, free, and original. Unlike the beauty that Miranda portrays, the rock is beautiful in its own sense. The symbolism shows the clash between Appleyard College and the rock, which hardly seem able to exist in the same vicinity. 6

The film also displays the difference between the wealthy English elite and the poorer Australian-born characters. The lower-class Australians are subordinate in their own land and yet, as Albert's success in finding Irma on 7

8 the rock indicates, are more able to survive than the upper-class British, who are imperiled in this harsh, mysterious land that is not their own.

Many mysteries and questions arise in this film. In the opening scenes, Miranda speaks Edgar Allan Poe's line: "What we see and what we seem, are but a dream. A dream within a dream." Later the Australian-born gardener at Appleyard College comments: "Some questions got answers and some haven't." With lines like these and all its scenes, the film challenges basic artistic formulas and sparks curiosity in the viewer's mind while it maintains its focus on illusion, contrasts, and mystery. In its lack of resolution and its symbolism, the film preserves its ambiguity. Weir's film meets and exceeds all the criteria for a good art film. So what did actually happen at Hanging Rock?

Thinking Critically about "*Picnic at Hanging Rock* as an Art Film"

1. What criteria does Sarah Erickson use for evaluating *Picnic at Hanging Rock*?

2. In writing about literature, students are generally advised not to include plot summaries of the story they are analyzing. Why do you suppose Erickson chooses to summarize the plot of this film?

3. What evidence does she supply to support the idea that this movie is "an excellent example of an art film"?

4. Where do you find this argument convincing? What weaknesses do you see, and how could this evaluative argument be made stronger?

COMPOSING YOUR ESSAY

Generating and Exploring Ideas

For your evaluation essay, you will try either to change your readers' assessment of a controversial person, event, thing, or phenomenon or help your readers decide whether an event or thing is worth their time or money.

If you have not already chosen an evaluation issue, try thinking about evaluation questions within the various communities to which you belong:

Local civic community: evaluative questions about transportation, land use, historical monuments, current leaders, political bills or petitions, housing, parking policies, effectiveness of police

National civic community: evaluative questions about public education, environmental concerns, economic policies, responses to terrorism, Supreme Court decisions, foreign policies, political leaders

Your university community: evaluative questions about academic or sports programs, campus life programs, first-year or transfer student orientation, clubs, dorm life, campus facilities, financial-aid programs, campus security, parking, cultural programs

Your scholarly community or disciplinary community in your major: evaluative questions about internships, study abroad programs, general studies programs, course requirements, first-year studies, major curriculum, advising, course sequences, teaching methods, homework requirements, academic standards, recent books or articles, new theories in a field, library resources, laboratory facilities, Web site sources of primary documents or numerical data in a field

Culture and entertainment issues within your social or family communities: evaluative questions about restaurants, movies, plays, museums, TV shows, musicians, video games, entertainment Web sites, concerts, books, paintings, sports figures, buildings

Consumer issues within your social or family communities: evaluative questions about computer systems, CDs, cars, clothing brands, stores, products, e-commerce

Work communities: Evaluative questions about supervisors or subordinates, office efficiency, customer relations, advertising and marketing, production or sales, record keeping and finance, personnel policies

Another good strategy for finding a topic is to think about a recent review or critique with which you disagree—a movie or restaurant review, a sportswriter's assessment of a team or player, an op-ed column assessing a government official or proposed legislation. How would you evaluate this controversial subject differently?

Once you have chosen a possible topic, freewrite your response to each of the following questions as a means of exploring ideas for your argument.

1. For the audience you have in mind, what is the most meaningful and most specific category in which you can place your X? Choose the smallest relevant class. (Instead of asking, "Is the Super Eye 2000 a good digital camera?" ask "Is the Super Eye 2000 a good low-cost digital camera for novices?")

2. Determine the criteria you will use to make your evaluation meaningful and helpful to your audience. Begin by listing the purposes of the class you have placed your subject in and then use freewriting or idea mapping to explore the qualities a member of that class needs to have to achieve those purposes. If your subject is highly disputed, what objections might your audience raise about your criteria? How will you justify your criteria?

3. Which of your criteria is the most important? Why?

4. Evaluate your subject by matching it to each of the criteria. Explore why your subject does or does not match each of the criteria. Your freewriting for this exercise will yield most of the ideas you need for your argument.

Shaping and Drafting

For your first draft, consider trying the following format. Many evaluation arguments follow this shape, and you can always alter the shape later if it seems too formulaic for you.

1. Introduce your issue and show why evaluating X is problematic or controversial.
2. Summarize and respond to opposing or alternative views.
3. Present your own argument.
    a. State criterion 1 and defend it if necessary.
    b. Show that X meets/does not meet the criterion.
    c. State criterion 2 and defend it if necessary.
    d. Show that X meets/does not meet the criterion.
    e. Continue with additional criteria and match arguments.
4. Sum up your evaluation.

Revising

If your essay is an evaluation intended to help your audience make a decision, think about the clarity and usefulness of your criteria and the match part of your evaluation for that audience.

If you have written about a controversial topic, a good way to revise an evaluation argument, as well as other kinds of arguments, is to analyze your lines of reasoning using Toulmin's system. Look particularly at your reasons and grounds (the match part of your argument) and your warrants (your criteria in an evaluation argument) to determine how persuasively you have structured and supported these parts for your chosen audience.

■ GUIDELINES FOR PEER REVIEWS ■

Instructions for peer reviews are provided in Chapter 18 (pp. 490–496).

For the Writer
Prepare two or three questions you would like your peer reviewer to address while responding to your draft. The questions can focus on some aspect of your draft that you are uncertain about, on one or more sections where you particularly seek help or advice, on some feature that you particularly like about your draft, or on some part you especially wrestled with. Write out your questions and give them to your peer reviewer along with your draft.

For the Reviewer
    I. Read the draft at a normal reading speed from beginning to end. As you read, do the following:
        A. Place a wavy line in the margin next to any passages that you find confusing, that contain something that doesn't seem to fit, or that otherwise slow down your reading.
        B. Place a "Good!" in the margin next to any passages where you think the writing is particularly strong or interesting.

II. Read the draft again slowly and answer the following questions by writing brief explanations of your answers.

A. Introduction

1. What expectations does the title set up for you? How does it grab your interest?

2. What does the introduction do to capture your interest, provide needed background, and identify the controversy or importance of the subject?

3. What is the evaluative question being addressed? Who is the intended audience? What is the writer's claim?

4. How might the writer improve the introduction or make the claim more focused?

B. The Criteria-Match Argument

1. What criteria does the writer use for evaluating X? How could the writer establish or defend these criteria more clearly or persuasively?

2. Do you accept the writer's criteria and agree with the way the writer has weighted their relative importance? How could the writer improve the criteria argument?

3. What evidence does the writer present to show that the X being evaluated meets or fails to meet each criterion? How could the writer make the evidence more compelling? How could the writer improve the match argument?

4. Where does the writer anticipate and summarize alternative views? Is the summary fair? How does the writer respond to these alternative views? How could the writer's refutation or response be improved?

5. How might the writer better apply the ideas from Chapter 19 to achieve more clarity?

C. If the writer has prepared questions for you, respond to his or her inquiries.

D. Sum up what you see as the chief strengths and problem areas of this draft.

1. Strengths

2. Problem areas

III. Read the draft one more time. Place a check mark in the margin wherever you notice problems in grammar, spelling, or mechanics (one check mark per problem).

CHAPTER 17

Proposing a Solution

ABOUT PROPOSAL WRITING

Proposal arguments call an audience to action. They make a claim that some action *should* or *ought* to be taken. Sometimes referred to informally as *should arguments,* proposals are among the most common kinds of arguments that you will write or read.

Some proposals aim to solve local, practical matters. For example, Rebekah Taylor's proposal in this chapter (pp. 451–456) advocates that campus stores carry products that are not tested on animals. Practical proposals generally target a specific audience (usually the person with the power to act on the proposal) and are typically introduced with a "letter of transmittal," in which the writer briefly summarizes the proposal, explains its purpose, and courteously invites the reader to consider it.

The rhetorical context of practical proposals makes effective document design essential. An effective design (appropriate layout, overall neatness, clear headings, flawless editing) helps establish the writer's *ethos* as a quality-oriented professional and makes reading the proposal as easy as possible. In business and industry, effective practical proposals are crucial for financial success. Many kinds of businesses—construction and engineering firms, ad agencies, university research teams, nonprofit agencies, and others—generate most of their revenue from effective, competitive proposals.

Another kind of proposal (often called a *policy proposal*) is aimed at more general audiences instead of specific decision makers. These proposals typically address issues of public policy with the aim of swaying public support toward the writer's proposed solution. Policy proposals might address the problems of prison overcrowding, out-of-control health costs, children's access to Internet pornography, national security and terrorism, and so forth.

A third kind of proposal argument takes the form of condensed *public affairs advocacy advertisements.* These are usually very focused arguments making direct appeals to an audience to take action. These arguments appear as flyers, one-page advertisements in newspapers and magazines, posters, brochures, and Web pages in advocacy Web sites. Because advocacy advertisements are brief and must be catchy, clear, and lively, they often employ document design—type, layout, graphic images, and color—to maximum advantage.

If the problem you are addressing is already known to your audience, then proposal arguments can follow the shape of classical arguments described in Chapter 15, in which you introduce the issue, present the claim, provide supporting reasons

441

for the claim, summarize and respond to alternative views, and provide a conclusion. If you wrote an argument for Chapter 15, you may have chosen a proposal issue. Tiffany Linder's argument in that chapter, in which she argues that "logging of old-growth forests should be banned," is a proposal argument (pp. 408–410).

In many cases, however, the problem you wish to address is not known to your audience (or the audience doesn't take the problem seriously). The writer, in effect, must *create* the issue being addressed by calling the readers' attention to the problem and then proposing a course of action. The rest of this chapter focuses on strategies for the second type of proposal, in which part of the writer's task is to convince readers that a problem exists, that it is serious, and that some action should be taken to resolve it.

EXPLORING PROPOSAL WRITING

The following activity introduces you to the thinking processes involved in writing a proposal argument.

1. In small groups, identify and list several major problems facing students in your college or university.
2. Decide among yourselves which problems are most important and rank them in order of importance.
3. Choose your group's number one problem and explore answers to the following questions. Group recorders should be prepared to present answers to the class as a whole.
   a. Why is the problem a problem?
   b. For whom is the problem a problem?
   c. How will these people suffer if the problem is not solved? Give specific examples.
   d. Who has the power to solve the problem?
   e. Why hasn't the problem been solved up to this point?
   f. How can the problem be solved? Create a proposal for a solution.
   g. What are the probable benefits of acting on your proposal?
   h. What costs are associated with your proposal?
   i. Who will bear these costs?
   j. Why should this proposal be enacted?
   k. What makes this proposal better than alternative proposals?
4. As a group, draft an outline for a proposal argument in which you do the following:
   a. Describe the problem and its significance.
   b. Propose your solution to the problem.
   c. Justify your proposal by showing how the benefits of adopting it outweigh the costs.

5. Recorders for each group should write the group's outline on the board and be prepared to present the group's argument orally to the class.

Writing Project

Call your audience's attention to a problem, propose a solution to that problem, and present a justification for your solution. You have three choices (your instructor may limit you to just one): (a) create a *practical proposal*, with a letter of transmittal, proposing a nuts-and-bolts solution to a local problem; (b) write a more general *policy proposal*, addressing a public issue, in the form of a feature editorial for a particular (state, local, or college) newspaper; or (c) create a *public affairs advocacy advertisement* that takes a proposed stand on a public issue. If you choose (b), your instructor might ask you to do substantial research and model your proposal after a magazine or journal article.

All proposals have one feature in common—they offer a solution to a problem. For every proposal, there is always an alternative course of action, including doing nothing. Your task as a proposal writer is threefold: You must demonstrate that a significant problem exists; propose a solution to the problem; and justify the solution, showing that benefits outweigh costs and that the proposed solution will fix the problem better than alternative solutions would. Accordingly, a proposal argument typically has three main parts.

1. *Description of the problem.* The description often begins with background. Where does the problem show up? Who is affected by the problem? How long has the problem been around? Is it getting worse? You may add an anecdote or some kind of startling information or statistics to give the problem *presence*. Typically, this section also analyzes the problem. What are its elements? What are its causes? Why hasn't it been solved before? Why are obvious solutions not adequate or workable? Finally, the description shows the problem's significance. What are the negative consequences of not solving the problem?

2. *Proposal for a solution.* This section describes your solution and shows how it would work. If you don't yet have a solution, you may choose to generate a *planning proposal,* calling for a committee or task force to study the problem and propose solutions at a later date. The purpose of a planning proposal is to call attention to a serious problem. In most cases, however, this section should propose a detailed solution, showing step-by-step how it would solve the problem and at what cost.

3. *Justification.* Here you persuade your audience that your proposal should be enacted. Typically you show that the benefits of your proposal outweigh the costs. You also need to show why your proposed solution is better than alternatives. Point out why other possible approaches would not solve the problem, would provide fewer benefits, or would cost significantly more than your proposal.

UNDERSTANDING PROPOSAL WRITING

As we have noted, proposal arguments focus on identifying a problem and then proposing and justifying a solution. In this section we look first at some of the distinctive demands of proposal writing. We then show you a powerful strategy for developing the justification section of a proposal.

Special Demands of Proposal Arguments

To get the reader to take action—the ultimate purpose of a proposal—requires you to overcome some difficult challenges. Here we examine the special demands that proposal arguments make on writers and offer suggestions for meeting them.

Creating Presence

To convince readers that a problem really exists, you must give it *presence;* that is, you must help readers *see* and *feel* the problem. Writers often use anecdotes or examples of people suffering from the problem or cite startling facts or statistics to dramatize the problem. For example, a student proposing streamlined check-out procedures in the hotel where she worked gave presence to her problem by describing a family that missed its flight home because of a slow checkout line. Her description of this family's frustration—including angry complaints over-heard by people waiting to check in—convinced her boss that the problem was worth solving. To persuade your readers to act on your proposal, you need to involve them both mentally *and* emotionally in your argument.

Appealing to the Interest and Values of Decision Makers

Proposal writers sometimes appeal directly to readers' idealism, urging them to do the right thing. But writers also need to show how doing the right thing converges with their readers' own best interests. Show decision makers how acting on your proposal will benefit *them* directly. The author of the hotel checkout proposal argued that her solution would enhance customer satisfaction, an idea that her boss would find more compelling than the notion of making life easier for desk clerks.

Overcoming Inherent Conservatism

People are inherently resistant to change. One of the most famous proposals of all time, the Declaration of Independence, is notable for the way in which it antici-pates its audience's resistance to change: "Prudence, indeed, will dictate that gov-ernments long established should not be changed for light and transient causes; and accordingly, all experience hath shown, that mankind are more disposed to suffer, while evils are sufferable, than to right themselves by abolishing the forms to which they are accustomed."

To restate this passage as folk wisdom, "Better the devil you know than the one you don't know." Most people expect the status quo to have its problems, flaws, and frustrations. They live with and adapt to familiar imperfections. Unless they can be persuaded that change will make things markedly better, they will "suffer, while evils are sufferable" rather than risk creating new, possibly insufferable evils.

The challenge of proving that something needs to be changed is compounded by the fact that the status quo often appears to be working. If its shortcomings were readily apparent, people would probably already have fixed them. It is much harder to stir an audience to action when the problem you depict entails lost potential (things could be better), rather than palpable evil (look at all the suffering).

Predicting Consequences

People also resist change because they fear unforeseen bad consequences and doubt predictions of good consequences. Everyone has experienced the disappointment of failed proposals: your favorite sports team makes a major trade—and then does worse; a company you invested in went through a major reorganization—and promptly went into the red; voters elect a new leader who promises major reforms—and nothing happens. Although most people do not become true cynics, they are understandably cautious about accepting the rosy scenarios contained in most proposals.

The more uncertain your proposal's consequences, the more clearly you must show *how* the proposal will bring about those consequences. To persuade your audience that your predictions are realistic, follow the strategies outlined in Chapter 14 for causal arguments. Show the links in the chain and how each one leads to the next. Whenever possible, cite similar proposals that yielded the sorts of results you are predicting.

Evaluating Consequences

Compounding the problem of predicting consequences is the difficulty of figuring out whether those consequences are good or bad and for whom. For example, any alternative to the current health care system will contain changes that simultaneously advantage one segment of your audience (say, patients) and disadvantage another (say, doctors, insurance companies, or taxpayers). Indeed, if any health care proposal benefited all segments of your audience, it would probably have been adopted long ago.

It can also be difficult to identify the appropriate standard of measurement to use in calculating a proposal's costs and benefits. Often you must try to balance benefits measured in apples against costs measured in oranges. For instance, suppose that a health care proposal will reduce the cost of insurance by limiting coverage. How would you balance the dollars saved on your insurance bill against the suffering of persons denied a potentially lifesaving medical procedure? Some cost-benefit analyses try to reduce all consequences to one scale of measure—usually money. This scale may work well in some circumstances, but it can lead to grotesquely inappropriate conclusions in others.

With these challenges in mind, we now set forth some strategies for making proposals as effective as possible.

Developing an Effective Justification Section

The distinctions between proposals and other kinds of arguments dictate a special variety of support for proposals. Experienced proposal writers often use a *three-approach* strategy to help them develop their justification sections. They

brainstorm justifying reasons by focusing sequentially on principles, consequences, and precedents or analogies. Figure 17.1 explains each element in the
sequence.

Each of these argumentation strategies was clearly evident in a recent public
debate in Seattle, Washington, over a proposal to raise county sales taxes to
build a new baseball stadium. Those favoring the stadium put forth arguments
such as these:

> We should build the new stadium because preserving our national pastime for
> our children is important (*argument from principle*), because building the stadium will
> create new jobs and revitalize the adjacent Pioneer Square district (*arguments from
> consequence*), and because building the stadium will have the same beneficial effects
> on the city that building Camden Yards had in Baltimore (*argument from precedent*).

Those opposing the stadium created arguments using the same strategies:

> We should not build the stadium because it is wrong to subsidize rich owners and
> players with tax dollars (*argument from principle*), because building a stadium diverts
> tax money from more important concerns such as low-income housing (*argument
> from consequence*), and because Toronto's experience with Skydome shows that once
> the novelty of a new stadium wears off, attendance declines dramatically (*argument
> from precedent*).

For Writing and Discussion

Working individually or in small groups, use the strategies of principle, consequence, and precedent/analogy to create *because* clauses that support (or
oppose) the following proposals. Try to have at least one *because* clause from
each of the strategies, but generate as many reasons as possible.

Example:

Claim	Spanking children should be made illegal.
Principle	Because it is wrong to cause bodily pain to children.
Consequence	Because it teaches children that it is okay to hit someone out of anger; because it causes children to obey rules out of fear rather than respect; because it can lead children to be abusive parents.
Precedent/ analogy	Because spanking a child is like throwing dishes or banging your fists against a wall—it relieves your anger but turns the child into an object.

1. Service-learning courses should/should not be required for graduation.
2. Medical insurance should/should not cover psychological counseling for eating disorders.
3. Marijuana should/should not be legalized.
4. The school year for grades K through 12 should/should not be extended to eleven months.

Approach 1: Argument from Principle

Using this strategy, you argue that a particular action should be taken because doing so is right according to some value, assumption, principle, or belief that you share with your audience. For example, you might argue, "We should create publicly financed jobs for poor people because doing so is both charitable and just." The formula for this strategy is as follows:

> We should (should not) do (this action) because (this action) is
>
> _____.

Fill in the blank with an appropriate adjective or noun specifying a belief or value that the audience holds: good, just, right, ethical, honest, charitable, equitable, fair, and so forth.

Approach 2: Argument from Consequence

Using this strategy, you argue that a particular action should (should not) be taken because doing so will lead to consequences that you and your audience believe are good (bad). For example, you might say, "We should create publicly financed jobs for poor people because doing so will provide them money for food and housing, promote a work ethic, and produce needed goods and services." The formula for this strategy is as follows:

> We should (should not) do (this action) because (this action) will lead to these good (bad) consequences: _____, _____, _____, etc.

Think of consequences that your audience will agree are good or bad, as your argument requires.

Approach 3: Argument from Precedent or Analogy

Using a precedent strategy, you argue that a particular action should (should not) be taken because doing so is similar to what was done in another case, which proved to be successful (unsuccessful). For example, you might say, "We should create publicly financed jobs for poor people because doing so will alleviate poverty in this country just as a similar program has helped poor people in Upper Magnesia." Using an analogy strategy, you compare the proposed action with a similar action that your audience already accepts as good or bad. For example, "We should create publicly financed jobs for poor people because doing so is like teaching the poor how to fish rather than giving them fish." The formula for either strategy is as follows:

> We should (should not) do (this action) because doing (this action) is like
>
> _____, which turned out to be good (bad).

Think of precedents or analogies that are similar to your proposed action and that have definite good (bad) associations for your audience.

FIGURE 17.1 ▪ The Three-Approach Strategy for a Justification Section

PROPOSAL ARGUMENTS AS PUBLIC AFFAIRS ADVOCACY ADVERTISEMENTS

Understanding the Power of Condensed Advocacy Arguments

As the volume of information bombarding us grows, we are increasingly met by condensed, attention-grabbing advocacy ads promoting a cause and seeking our support. These condensed arguments appear as posters or flyers, as paid advertisements in newspapers or magazines, as brochures filling our mailboxes, and as Web pages in advocacy Web sites.

These condensed advocacy ads are marked by their bold, abbreviated, tightly planned format. The creators of these arguments know they must work fast to capture our attention, give presence to a problem, advocate a solution, and enlist our support. These advocacy ads frequently use photographs, images, or icons that are arresting or in some way memorable and that appeal to a reader's emotions and imagination. For example, consider the one-page advocacy advertisement in Figure 17.2, which appeared in the *Progressive* magazine.

As part of a campaign to decriminalize drugs, the ad is sponsored by an organization calling itself "Common Sense for Drug Policy." Note how the advocacy advertisement makes its view of the problem real and urgent to readers by using disturbing black-and-white drawings, varied type sizes and fonts, and powerful lists of evidence, and gains credibility through its documentation of sources, presented at the bottom of the page.

As another example, observe the advocacy ad appealing for charitable donations to feed children in Afghanistan (the introduction to Part Five, p. 476). This advertisement appeared on the Web site of an advocacy organization.

Document Design Features of Advocacy Advertisements

To interpret and drive home the problem presented in photos or drawings, advocacy ads employ different type sizes and fonts. Large-type text in these documents frequently takes the form of slogans or condensed thesis statements written in an arresting style. Here are some examples of large bold-faced copy from advocacy literature that the authors of this text have encountered recently:

▓ "Abstinence: It works every time...." (from a newspaper advocacy ad sponsored by Focus on the Family, asking readers to donate money to promote abstinence education)

▓ "Educating, Organizing, Fighting to end the barbarism, racism, unfairness, and shame of judicial homicide in our lifetime" (from an advocacy ad in the *Progressive* asking readers to donate money to Death Penalty Focus to end capital punishment)

WHITE KIDS ARE MUCH MORE LIKELY TO BE USING (AND SELLING) DRUGS!

CAN YOU FIND ANYTHING WRONG WITH THESE PICTURES??

According to the federal Centers for Disease Control, he's 4 times more likely than his African-American classmate to be a regular cocaine user.

According to the Justice Department, if he's arrested on drug charges, he's 1-1/2 times more likely than his white classmate to be sent to prison.

White high-school students who are current users of cocaine: 4.1%[1]

African-American high-school students who are current users of cocaine: 1.1%[1]

Chance of a white person ever trying an illicit drug in their lifetime: 42%[2]

Chance of an African-American person ever trying an illicit drug in their lifetime: 37.7%[2]

Percent of felony drug defendants in state courts who are white: 37%[3]

Percent of felony drug defendants in state courts who are black: 61%[3]

Percent of white drug felons given probation or nonincarceration sentence by state courts: 32%[4]

Percent of black drug felons given probation or nonincarceration sentence by state courts: 25%[4]

Percent of white drug felons sentenced to prison by state courts each year: 27%[5]

Percent of black drug felons sentenced to prison by state courts each year: 43%[5]

BLACK KIDS ARE MORE LIKELY TO GO TO PRISON!

Note:
According to the US Justice Department and the Office of National Drug Control Policy, drug users typically buy their drugs from sellers of their own racial or ethnic background. Research of Ethnicity & Race of Drug Sellers and Users: US Dept. of Justice National Institute of Justice & the Office of National Drug Control Policy, "Crack, Powder Cocaine, and Heroin: Drug Purchase and Use Patterns in Six U.S. Cities, " December 1997, p.1, 16, and p. 15, Table 16.

Sources:
[1] Data on drug use by high-school students: Youth Risk Behavior Survey 1999, Centers for Disease Control, reported in Morbidity and Mortality Weekly Report, Vol. 49, No. SS-5, p. 66, Table 24.
[2] Data on lifetime prevalence of drug use: US Dept. of HHS Substance Abuse and Mental Health Services Administration, "Summary of Findings from the 1999 National Household Survey on Drug Abuse," August 2000, p. G-13, Table G-13.
[3] Demogaphic data on felony drug defendants in state courts: US Dept. of Justice Bureau of Justice Statistics. "Felony Defendants in Large Urban Counties, 1996," October 1999, p.4, Table 3
[4] Demographic data on felony drug defendants in state courts: US Dept. of Justice Bureau of Justice Statistics, "State Court Sentencing of Convicted Felons, 1996," February 2000, p. 13, Table 2.5
[5] Demographic data on felony drug defendants in state courts: US Dept. of Justice Bureau of Justice Statistics, "State Court Sentencing of Convicted Felons, 1996," February 2000, p. 13, Table 2.5

Kevin B. Zeese, President, Common Sense for Drug Policy
3220 "N" Street, NW, #141, Washington, D.C. 20007 * 703-354-9050 * fax 703-354-5695 * info@csdp.org
For more information, visit www.csdp.org and www.drugwarfacts.org

FIGURE 17.2 ■ A One-Page Advocacy Advertisement from a Magazine

■ "Expectant Mothers Deserve Compassionate Health Care—Not Prison!" (an advocacy advertisement from "Common Sense for Drug Policy." This one appeared in the *National Review.*)

To outline and justify their solutions, creators of advocacy ads often put main supporting reasons in bulleted lists and sometimes enclose carefully selected facts and quotations in boxed sidebars. To add an authoritative ethos, the ads often include footnotes and bibliographies in fine print.

Another prominent feature of these condensed, highly visual arguments is their direct call for a course of action: Go to an advocacy Web site to find out more information on how to support a cause; cut out a postcard-like form to send to a decision maker; vote for or against the proposition or the candidate; write a letter to a political representative; or donate money to a cause.

Creating an Advocacy Poster, Flyer, Brochure, One-Page Advertisement, or Web Page

As an alternative to a traditional written argument, your instructor may ask you to create a one-page or brochure-length advocacy flyer, ad, poster, or Web page. The first stage of your invention process should be the same as for a longer proposal argument. Choose a controversial public issue that needs immediate attention or a neglected issue about which you want to arouse public passion. As with a longer proposal argument, consider your audience in order to identify the values and beliefs on which you will base your appeal.

When you construct your argument, the limited space available puts high demands on you, the writer, to be efficient in your choice of words and in your use of document design. Your goal is to have a memorable impact on your readers in order to promote the action you advocate. When creating a condensed advocacy ad, we suggest that you consider the following invention questions:

1. Will your advocacy argument be a poster, a flyer, a one-page advertisement in a newspaper or magazine, a brochure, or a Web page? How will your chosen medium be appropriate for your rhetorical purpose?
2. How could photos or other graphic elements establish and give presence to the problem?
3. How can type size and font and layout be used to present the core of your proposal, including the justifying reasons, in the most powerful way for the intended audience?
4. Could any part of this argument be presented as a slogan or in an otherwise memorable style? What key phrases could highlight the parts or the main points of this argument?
5. How can document design clarify the course of action and the direct demand on the audience that this argument is proposing?
6. How could use of color enhance the overall impact of your advocacy argument? (*Note:* One-page newspaper advertisements are expensive to reproduce in color, but you might make effective use of color in posters, brochures, flyers, or Web pages.)

For Writing and Discussion

1. Working as a whole class or in small groups, reach consensus answers to the following questions:

   a. What features do the condensed advocacy ads in Figure 17.2 and on page 476 share with traditional verbal argument?

   b. What features do they share with advertising?

   c. How do these advocacy ads make appeals from logos, ethos, and pathos as discussed in Chapter 15, pages 388–390?

2. Working in small groups, create a mock-up for a one-page advocacy ad on an issue chosen by your instructor. (Some suggestions: Arguments for or against capital punishment, adapted from the readings on pp. 394–403; an argument for or against removing the Glen Canyon Dam, adapted from the reading on pp. 144–148; or arguments for or against a national ID card, adapted from the reading on pp. 460–461.) Use freehand drawings to sketch your ideas for visual images.

Readings

The first reading is a practical proposal by a student writer. Because practical proposals are aimed at a specific audience, they are often accompanied by a letter of transmittal that introduces the writer, sets the context, and summarizes the proposal.

_____ Hall, Room 356
May 15, 2001

Mr. Charles Ramos
Director of Residence Life
_____ University
Street
City, State, Zip

Dear Mr. Ramos:

1   Enclosed is my proposal that the campus store add cruelty-free products to its inventory. Currently, there are no toiletry or household products sold on campus that are not tested on animals, forcing students like myself, who are concerned about animal welfare, to go off-campus.

2   My proposal would provide concerned students with needed products that are clearly designated as "cruelty free."

3   I believe that if these new products were offered on campus, they would be popular with students, would bring attention to the issue of animal testing, and would be in strong accordance with our university's mission statement.

Thank you for taking the time to read and consider this proposal.   4

Sincerely,
Rebekah Taylor

Following the letter of transmittal is the proposal's cover or title page.

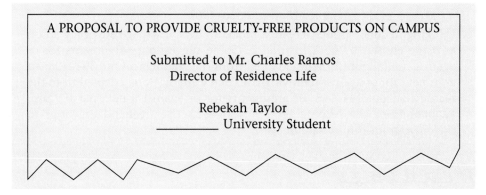

A PROPOSAL TO PROVIDE CRUELTY-FREE PRODUCTS ON CAMPUS

Submitted to Mr. Charles Ramos
Director of Residence Life

Rebekah Taylor
_____ University Student

If this were the actual proposal, the first page would begin on a new page following the cover page.

PROBLEM

The _____ University campus store does not offer toiletry or household products that are not tested on animals. Students who desire to purchase cruelty-free products on campus cannot do so.   1

A quick look inside the campus store reveals nearly every kind of product a student might desire or need. Shampoo, deodorant, soap, detergent, toothpaste, and eyedrops crowd shelves. Most of these products, manufactured by respected companies such as*_____ and others, have well-known names: _____, _____, _____, _____. Unfortunately, these companies all test their products on animals.   2

Those who understand that cruelty to animals runs rampant in these companies try their hardest not to buy from them. These conscientious shoppers support companies such as _____ and _____ that have made staunch commitments to quality product testing without the use of animals. To buy these cruelty-free products, conscientious students now have to go off-campus—a situation that is problematic in two ways: 3

---

*In the proposal argument that Rebekah Taylor actually submitted, she named specific companies and specific brand names. For textbook publication, these names had to be deleted.

■ *First, students without cars have to walk or take the bus, potentially jeopardizing their safety.* Many students attending this university do not own cars, and the nearest store that carries cruelty-free products is about five blocks away from campus. Although this walk is safe during the day, at night it can be dangerous, especially for women, but when students desperately need toiletry products, they'll often go to the store after dark to get them.

■ *Second, many students cannot afford to spend money off-campus.* Many students are not employed and don't have any real money to speak of. Frequently students find themselves flat broke, except for the money on their campus cards. They need to be able to use their cards on campus to buy personal and household products.

So conscientious students face a dilemma because they have no on-campus options for buying cruelty-free products. Often students must go against their principles by buying products made by companies that they strongly do not want to support.

4   In the past I have asked campus store personnel to stock cruelty-free items, but I was told that none of their purveyors offer this service and that the expense would be too great. However, I believe the benefits of solving this problem would outweigh the costs. The following proposal explains an approach the university can take.

PROPOSAL

5   The campus store should offer students basic toiletry and household products that are not tested on animals. These products should be clearly distinguished on the shelves with a placard reading, 'NOT TESTED ON ANIMALS.'

6   If enacted, this proposal would provide students with cruelty-free options for such products as toothpaste, deodorant, shampoo, soap, shaving products, laundry detergent, dish soap, and all-purpose cleaner. One cruelty-free brand of each of these products would be sufficient. This proposal would not prevent students from buying the products they normally do because it would add new products to the store inventories; it would not replace any existing products.

7   To enact this proposal, the campus store can select among numerous producers of cruelty-free brands. _____ could provide toothpaste and floss, shampoos, deodorants, and soap. _____ offers excellent shaving products that are cruelty free. A conscientious company called "_____" could provide laundry detergent, dish soap, and cleaning sprays.

8   Perhaps one of the university's many purveyors could be persuaded to carry brands like these. If that is the case, providing cruelty-free products would only require adding new inventory from an already existing source.

This situation would be ideal because the products could be easily delivered to campus along with other goods that the store already provides. If the university's purveyors will not offer such brands, they might still be easily acquired from a new purveyor, or from a local warehouse store. Based on phone calls I have made, I know of several warehouse stores in our area that offer natural and cruelty-free products in bulk. These companies might provide delivery services just as the university's current purveyors do.

If a new purveyor could not be found, and if the warehouse stores in the area could not deliver, concerned students might volunteer to personally obtain cruelty-free products from neighborhood stores and transport them to the school.   9

An important part of my proposal is that designated areas on campus store shelves would be provided for cruelty-free products. These areas would be clearly identified with a sign so that compassionate students would know which products are cruelty free. This aspect of the proposal is very important because it would draw the attention of students to the issue of animal testing and encourage them to consider seriously which products they want to buy. The hope is not only to offer cruelty-free products on campus, but to create a dialogue on the issue of animal testing.   10

JUSTIFICATION

There are four important reasons why _____ University should act on this proposal.   11

Success at Other Universities

First, other colleges and universities have enacted similar proposals to help combat animal testing and have had great success with the new products. I have researched two such places—_____ College and _____ College—and have discovered that cruelty-free products are very popular with students.   12

For example, the campus stores at _____ College in Iowa underwent a massive product change about five years ago in response to student protests against the _____ products sold on campus. These students knew that _____ is one of the corporate world's most ardent supporters of animal testing. The cruelty-free products that replaced _____ sold exceedingly well. Similarly, at _____ College in Colorado students raised an outcry when one of these cruelty-free products was almost pulled from the shelves. Our university should look to success stories such as these when considering whether or not to offer cruelty-free products on campus.   13

In Line with University Mission

Second, offering cruelty-free products on campus would be an action in line with our university's efforts to be a progressively minded, service- and   14

value-oriented school. In many ways, _____ University has shown itself
to be a leader in social change. This university has proved eager to become
involved in struggles against all kinds of injustice. The most recent examples are the mission to Iraq to help people impoverished by U.N. sanctions
and the addition of environmentally friendly, shade-grown coffee in the
university coffee shops. These actions challenged current social practices
and demonstrated clearly that many of our students are willing to fight for
human rights and for the global ecosystem and endangered species. These
actions are consistent with _____ University's official mission "to look
critically at the society in which we live and at its institutions" (Mission
Statement). It is time now to look critically at corporations that contribute
to the suffering of animals by subjecting them to cruel, unnecessary experiments. At the very least, _____ University should allow its students the
right to choose not to support such corporations.

Student Convenience and Safety

15   Third, offering cruelty-free products would allow students to purchase
needed items on campus and to use the money on their University One
Cards to do so. Simply put, if cruelty-free products were offered on campus,
students would be safer and less inconvenienced because they would not
have to worry about off-campus transportation or security. In addition, the
ability to purchase such products with the One Card would allow numerous
students who otherwise could not have afforded to do so to buy what they
need.

Promise of Economic Success

16   Finally, many students at this university would choose cruelty-free products over other brands if they were available on campus. In a short survey I
conducted winter quarter, many students said they would support a proposal to introduce cruelty-free products to the stores on campus. This survey of
fifty randomly selected students revealed that over half (56%) are more than
"somewhat concerned" about animal testing. The survey also showed that
almost three-quarters (72%) would buy cruelty-free products instead of
products tested on animals if they were offered on campus. Additionally,
compassionate students who have gone off-campus to buy cruelty-free products would start spending their money at the campus store.

CONCLUSION

17   Past social actions by the students, faculty, and administration of
_____ University reveal a long-held belief that real progress means real
change. In hope of bettering the school and society, this university has
always been willing to challenge the status quo. It is time to challenge the

status quo again. To continue the university's efforts to fight injustice in the world, to take conscientious action on the issue of animal testing as other respected colleges have, and to honor the wishes of many students, the university's campus store should offer cruelty-free products. Taking this action would help our university remain faithful to its mission.

Thinking Critically about "A Proposal to Provide Cruelty-Free Products on Campus"

1. What strategies does Rebekah Taylor use to convince the Director of Residence Life that a problem exists?
2. What strategies (including arguments from principle, consequence, and precedent) does Rebekah employ to persuade university administrators that her proposal is workable and that the benefits outweigh the costs?
3. How does Rebekah tie her proposal to the values and beliefs of her audience— the Director of Residence Life in particular and university administrators in general?
4. If you were Mr. Charles Ramos, the Director of Residence Life to whom this proposal is addressed, how effective would you find this proposal? What are its chief strengths and weaknesses?

The second proposal, also by a student writer, is a researched policy argument that addresses the issue of funding for hospices. To appreciate the origins of Sheridan Botts's argument, read her exploratory essay in Chapter 8 (pp. 185–188). The exploratory essay describes how Botts became interested in hospices, how she discovered the issue of funding (fee-for-service versus per diem funding), and how she wrestled to find an appropriate audience and focus for her ideas. The proposal argument that follows is the final product that emerged from her struggling with the problem. Because Botts imagined her argument as an op-ed piece in a newspaper, she has used informal documentation style. She supplied a separate reference page to her instructor.

■ SHERIDAN BOTTS (STUDENT) ■
SAVING HOSPICES:
A Plea to the Insurance Industry

Last fall my brother-in-law Charles lay dying, not in a sterile hospital room but in the warm and familiar surroundings of his own home, cared for

1

by his mother Betty. Although the home care provision of Charles's private insurance paid for his medical expenses, it provided no services for Betty, who was overwhelmed with responsibility and grief. Tending her son hour by hour, Betty became terribly depressed. She had already lost one son and now had to watch another slowly die before her eyes.

2   If Charles's care had come from a hospice agency instead of a home care agency, Betty would have had help. Home care provides at-home clinician visits for nursing services, some social work, and personal attendant care. It is generally directed toward helping the patient get better and is strictly oriented toward the patient, not the family. In contrast, hospice care is holistic, comprehensive, and family centered, addressing the emotional needs of caregivers as well as the patient's medical needs. In Charles's case, hospice care would have provided, in addition to Charles's medical expenses, grief counseling for Betty, chaplain's visits, a variety of volunteer services, and assistance in helping the family make the dying person's last days a time of emotional bonding and support rather than loneliness and isolation.

3   Unfortunately, hospice care may not be available to the public in the future as long as the present system of insurance funding continues. Insurance companies often pay on a fee-for-service basis, meaning that each provided service must be preapproved and reimbursed separately. According to Rodney Smith, a local hospice director, the agency loses $900 per month for each hospice patient served on a fee-for-service basis. Hospices continue to provide services not reimbursed by private insurance because they are committed to holistic care regardless of the family's ability to pay. However, as the cost of medical care increases, hospices risk insolvency if private insurance companies refuse to reimburse them fairly.

4   The solution to this problem is for private insurance companies to fund hospices on a per diem rather than fee-for-service basis. With per diem, the patient's insurance pays the hospice for each day of care. Per diem rates are based on the total costs of providing hospice services divided by the total number of patients and days that services are provided. Medicare (the primary insurer of citizens 65 and older) has reimbursed hospices on a per diem basis for many years. This fair system now needs to be adopted by private insurance companies.

5   Although per diem funding would benefit the general public, insurance companies fight it tooth and nail. Claims representatives from two different insurance companies told me that paying on a per diem basis would be giving hospices blank checks to provide all kinds of unnecessary services.

6   First, they explained that fee-for-service controls costs by allowing insurance companies to specify in advance which services will be funded and to limit indiscriminant spending. But in actuality per diem payments would not give hospice agencies more money than they need. The per diem rate paid by Medicare averages the costs of care for patients who need few services with patients who need many services. It is true that a per diem rate

would give hospices too much money for *some* patients, but also not nearly enough for other patients. Fair rates could be established that provided hospices with average costs.

The second objection to per diem payments raised by insurance companies is their belief that medical insurance should pay only for the medical needs of the insured patient. They say that it is simply beyond the intended scope of medical insurance to pay for nonmedical care or for counseling for the patient's family.

7

I would say that this objection is based on an outdated view of medicine that treats the patient as an isolated entity rather than as a human being in a network of family. Moreover, this view is shortsighted, since providing nonmedical services to the family can keep the patient at home, where costs are relatively cheap, rather than sending the patient to the hospital.

8

As an example of how helping the family can save an insurance company money, consider the case of Randy and his daughter Sharon (not their real names) as told to me by a staff member of a local hospice. Randy, 85 years old, was dying of heart and lung disease and wanted to die at home, where Sharon cared for him. Having never been exposed to seriously ill persons, Sharon panicked in emergencies. Fortunately, their hospice provided Sharon with nursing consultation twenty-four hours a day, seven days a week. Several times in the middle of the night, Sharon phoned with terror in her voice. "I think Dad needs to go back to the hospital," she would say. "He's looking really bad." Over the phone the on-call nurse calmed Sharon, helped her figure out the right dose of pain medication, and convinced her that Randy would be better off at home. Moreover, counseling from a social worker helped Sharon accept the process of her father's dying. Without on-call nursing and counseling help—provided by hospice but not paid for by private insurance companies—Sharon would have called 911 during these emergencies and Randy would have been back in the hospital. The insurance company would have been stuck with huge hospital bills and Randy would have died in a strange place attached to tubes and machines.

9

Luckily for the future of hospices, studies are providing convincing data that per diem reimbursement is cheaper for insurance companies in the long run. According to a 1994 study by Manard and Perrone, private insurance companies who adopted per diem payments to hospices saved money while increasing benefits. In another study the same year, Mitchell compared hospice and nonhospice patient costs in the last three months of life. The average cost of medical care for hospice patients was $986, compared with $7,731 for nonhospice patients. These cost savings were attributed to the hospice team's teaching the family how to manage the patient at home

10

(a nonmedical cost), providing constant, ongoing support for the family (another nonmedical cost), and providing optimal comfort care for the patient in the home setting. The enormous cost for nonhospice patients was caused by the frequency with which families sent the patient back to the hospital. Still another study, cited by Manard and Perrone, found that the grief counseling and support services offered to family members by hospices led to reduced use of hospital and clinic services.

11   But there is another reason why insurance companies should reimburse hospices equitably: It is the right and just thing to do. The psychological value of hospice care for the terminally ill and their families is undisputed. It is time that insurance companies recognized the value of psychological as well as physical care. There is something wrong with current medical practice when insurance companies will fund without question expensive technological treatments for a dying patient but will quibble at paying grief counseling for the patient's loved ones. Because the general public values hospice care, most private insurance companies in their advertising brochures boast of covering hospice care. But by excluding "nonmedical" services, they actually provide only home care, not hospice. If insurance companies claim they believe in the holistic care of hospices, then they ought to pay for it. If enough insurance customers complain loudly enough, perhaps insurance companies will hear the message.

Thinking Critically about "Saving Hospices"

1. Compare Sheridan Botts's proposal argument with her exploratory essay on pages 185–188. How did she solve the problems she confronted in the exploratory essay? In your view, how effective are these solutions?

2. One of Sheridan's rhetorical problems is that few audiences are inherently interested in technical issues such as fee-for-service versus per diem payments. Moreover, differences between the two forms of payment are hard to explain succinctly. How does Sheridan try to make her proposal interesting? Does she succeed?

3. Another rhetorical problem is how to make the argument appeal to the values of insurance companies. It is easy to see how this proposal could benefit hospices, patients, and patients' families, but since it would increase the direct costs of hospice care for insurance companies, Sheridan must show how it would benefit insurance companies. Does she do so successfully?

4. How persuasive do you find Sheridan's argument? From your perspective, what are the strengths and weaknesses of her proposal?

The third reading appeared on the editorial page of the *Seattle Times* on October 4, 2001. The authors of this editorial—Nicholas G. Jenkins, cofounder of TheFence.com, an Internet debate site, and Amit Rind, a staff writer for the site—propose a course of action for the United States in the aftermath of the September 11, 2001, attacks on New York City and Washington, D.C.

☒ NICHOLAS G. JENKINS AND AMIT RIND ☒

NATIONAL ID CARDS WOULD BE THE DRAGNET WE NEED

Flip around the news channels and you will find politicians talking about what America must do to prevent Sept. 11, 2001, from happening again. "We'll get tough," they all say, but we will also make sure to safeguard our civil liberties. They know the buzzwords we like to hear. That's why they got elected. 1

So far, we like most of what we see. Banning knives from airplane cabins will certainly make it harder to hijack planes. Stronger money-laundering laws and increased surveillance powers for people suspected of terrorist activities will undoubtedly make domestic terrorism a tougher business. But nothing we have seen so far does anything about the would-be terrorists who quietly reside in the United States illegally who aren't yet terrorist suspects. How many of them there are among the estimated 8 million illegal residents in this country we do not know: We do know that 15 of them are no longer with us—they were among the 19 Islamic fundamentalists who killed some 6,000 innocent people on that fateful day. 2

Short of a knock-on-every-door dragnet, there is no easy way to find them. But a dragnet is needed. The one we favor is one that Germany, Austria, France, Greece, Spain, Hong Kong, Belgium and the Netherlands have already, and Australia and England are seriously considering—a national citizenship/identification card. 3

Here's how it would work. By some date certain, every citizen and lawful resident would be required to obtain a tamper-proof national identification card. To protect against counterfeiting, the card would be encoded with some type of biometric data—a fingerprint, retina scan, voice pattern, or blood sample—and include a hologram, like we see today on most driver's licenses. 4

Temporary residents' and visitors' cards would include expiration dates. The governing federal agency would offer an incentive to illegal immigrants to come forward by agreeing not to immediately deport them, or by giving amnesty or permanent work visas to select immigrants who meet certain criteria. By doing this, we would learn the whereabouts of millions of illegal immigrants that the Immigration and Naturalization Service admits it has lost track of. If you think this sounds like a roundup, you're right. It is. 5

After our date certain, ID cards would weed out people illegally here in two ways. First and foremost, it will be impossible for people without ID 6 cards to move unseen through the American landscape. Getting on a plane? Collecting federal benefits? Opening a bank account? Activating utilities? Obtaining health care? Cashing a check? Getting a job? Not possible without a card, and just as most activities are in many European countries.

7   Second, not having an ID card would be grounds for immediate deportation. Federal, state and local law enforcement would play key roles here. For all stops, detentions and arrests, police would require ID cards. A person unable to produce his card would be detained, whereby law enforcement would determine whether he is legally in the United States by accessing a national database. People not determined legal would be arrested and given a hearing post haste to show cause why they should not be deported. Long branded the stuff of Big Brother by opponents, ID cards would make little difference to legal U.S. citizens. Police would still need reasonable suspicion to stop us for suspected unlawful activity. This comprehensive program would do more than find illegal residents. It would save taxpaying American citizens billions in tax and welfare fraud by eliminating a major incentive for illegal immigration—free government benefits. (Australia estimates that ID cards would save it $1 billion annually in welfare benefits.) Plastic ID cards are not the only weapons needed to combat domestic terrorism, and they are not a catchall. They would not catch the Timothy McVeighs of the world—U.S. citizens who also happen to be terrorists. They would also not be problem-free. The program will certainly pose administrative challenges. And insofar as it might lead to the deportations of migrant workers who pose no security threat to the United States, a national ID card will also probably lead to marginal increases in the price of goods they produce—namely textiles and produce.

8   We can live with paying more for T-shirts and apples. What we cannot live with is knowing that next year we may break bread with a guy who is planning to poison our water supply, but who remains in this country because our tough-talking politicians are too addicted to the rhetoric of rights to require citizens to carry around a three-inch piece of plastic.

9   We're all for "smokin' 'em out," as President Bush put it. If our eyes get just a little irritated, so be it.

Thinking Critically about "National ID Cards Would Be the Dragnet We Need"

1. What is the specific problem that Nicholas G. Jenkins and Amit Rind are proposing to solve?

2. In addition to justifying the need for a particular proposal, a proposal argument must make a case for the benefits of enacting a proposal. What gains do Jenkins and Rind offer?

3. How do Jenkins and Rind address the costs of implementing their proposal? Where do they concede points to alternative views? How do they rebut some

of these views? Can you think of other objections that might be used to challenge this proposal?

4. In order for readers to accept this argument, what assumptions and values must they have?

5. How successful is this argument in overcoming people's conservatism, in predicting consequences, and in moving decision makers to consider this proposal?

The final reading is a speech that Richard F. Corlin, the president of the American Medical Association, delivered at the 2001 annual meeting in Chicago, Illinois, on June 20, 2001. In this policy proposal, Corlin seeks to enlist the resources and dedication of the AMA in stopping the "epidemic" of gun violence in America.

▪ RICHARD F. CORLIN ▪
THE SECRETS OF GUN VIOLENCE IN AMERICA:
What We Don't Know Is Killing Us

Thank you for joining me tonight. It's my great pleasure to introduce to you the friends, colleagues and family members, without whom, I would not have made it here tonight. And without whose presence, this wouldn't be a special evening for me.   1

I grew up in East Orange, New Jersey, in the 1940s and 1950s. My high school was a mosaic of racial and ethnic diversity—equal numbers of blacks and whites, some Puerto Ricans, and a few Asians. We'd fight among ourselves from time to time—sometimes between kids of the same race, sometimes equal opportunity battles between kids of different races and nationalities. Our fights were basically all the same: some yelling and shouting, then some shoving, a couple of punches, and then some amateur wrestling. They weren't gang fights—everyone but the two combatants just stood around and watched—until one of our teachers came over and broke it up.   2

My old high school reminds me a little of "West Side Story" only without the switchblades or a Leonard Bernstein score. And there were no Sharks or Jets. Remember, those were the days of James Dean and Elvis Presley. Nobody pulled out a gun—none of us had them and no one even thought of having one. The worst wound anyone had after one of these fights was a split lip or a black eye.   3

It was just like kids have always been—until today. Back then, no parents in that town of mostly lower-middle class blue collar workers had to worry that their children might get shot at school, in the park or on the front stoop at home. But then again, that was also a time when we thought of a Columbine as a desert flower, not a high school in Littleton, Colorado.   4

5   Even in my first encounter with medicine, when I was only 14 years old and got a summer job at Presbyterian Hospital in Newark, New Jersey, there were no guns. I worked on what was called the utility team—moving patients back to their own rooms after surgery, starting IVs, taking EKGs and passing N-G tubes. I told them I wanted to be a doctor and—unbelievably at the age of 14—they let me help the pathologist perform autopsies. I was so excited about helping with the autopsies that I used to repeat the details to my Mom and Dad over dinner. Before long, they made me eat by myself in the kitchen.

6   When I was old enough to get a driver's license, I got a job working as an emergency room aide and ambulance driver at Elizabeth General Hospital. In all that time, in five summers of working in two center city hospitals—in the recovery room, in the morgue, in the emergency room, and driving the ambulance—I never saw even one gun-shot victim.

7   Today, it's very different. Guns are so available and violence so common- place that some doctors now see gunshot wounds every week—if not every day. It's as if guns have replaced fists as the playground weapon of choice. The kids certainly think so. In a nationwide poll taken in March after two students were shot to death at Santana High School near San Diego, almost half of the 500 high school students surveyed said it wouldn't be difficult for them to get a gun. And one in five high school boys said they had carried a weapon to school in the last 12 months. One in five. Frightening, isn't it?

8   I began by telling you how I grew up in a world without guns. That has changed for me—as it has for so many Americans. Recently, the violence of guns touched me personally. Not long ago, Trish, one of our office staff members in my practice—a vibrant, hard-working young woman from Belize—was gunned down while leaving a holiday party at her aunt's home in Los Angeles.

9   Trish had done nothing wrong—some might say that she was in the wrong place at the wrong time—but I don't buy into that. Here was a woman who was where she should be—leaving a relative's home—when she was gunned down. Someone drove down the street randomly firing an assault weapon out the car window, and he put a bullet through her eye. Trish lingered in a coma for eight days—and then she died, an innocent vic- tim of gun violence.

10   With the preponderance of weapons these days, it comes as no surprise that gun violence—both self-inflicted and against others—is now a serious public health crisis. No one can avoid its brutal and ugly presence. No one. Not physicians. Not the public. And most certainly—not the politicians—no matter how much they might want to.

11   Let me tell you about part of the problem. In the 1990s, the CDC [Centers for Disease Control] had a system in place for collecting data about the results of gun violence. But Congress took away its funding, thanks to heavy lobbying by the anti-gun control groups. You see, the gun lobby doesn't want gun violence addressed as a public health issue. Because that

data would define the very public health crisis that these powerful interests don't want acknowledged. And they fear that such evidence-based data could be used to gain support to stop the violence. Which, of course, means talking about guns and the deaths and injuries associated with them.

We all know that violence of every kind is a pervasive threat to our socie-ty. And the greatest risk factor associated with that violence—is access to firearms. Because—there's no doubt about it—guns make the violence more violent and deadlier.   12

Now my speech today is not a polemic. It is not an attack on the politics or the profits or the personalities associated with guns in our society. It isn't even about gun control. I want to talk to you about the public health crisis itself— and how we can work to address it; in the same way we have worked to address other public health crises such as polio, tobacco, and drunk driving.   13

At the AMA, we acknowledged the epidemic of gun violence when—in 1987—our House of Delegates first set policy on firearms. The House recog-nized the irrefutable truth that "uncontrolled ownership and use of firearms, especially handguns, is a serious threat to the public's health inasmuch as the weapons are one of the main causes of intentional and unintentional injuries and death." In 1993 and 1994, we resolved that the AMA would, among oth-er actions, "support scientific research and objective discussion aimed at iden-tifying causes of and solutions to the crime and violence problem."   14

Scientific research and objective discussion because we as physicians are—first and foremost—scientists. We need to look at the science of the subject, the data, and—if you will—the micro-data, before we make a diag-nosis. Not until then can we agree upon the prognosis or decide upon a course of treatment.   15

First, let's go straight to the science that we do know. How does this dis-ease present itself? Since 1962, more than a million Americans have died in firearm suicides, homicides and unintentional injuries. In 1998 alone, 30,708 Americans died by gunfire: 16

- 17,424 in firearm suicides
- 12,102 in firearm homicides
- 866 in unintentional shootings

Also in 1998, more than 64,000 people were treated in emergency rooms for non-fatal firearm injuries.   17

This is a uniquely American epidemic. In the same year that more than 30,000 people were killed by guns in America, the number in Germany was 1,164, in Canada, it was 1,034, in Australia 391, in England and Wales 211, and in Japan, the number for the entire year was 83.   18

Next, let's look at how the disease spreads, what is its vector, or delivery system. To do that, we need to look at the gun market today. Where the hard, cold reality is—guns are more deadly than ever. Gun manufacturers— in the pursuit of technological innovation and profit—have steadily increased the lethality of firearms. The gun industry's need for new products   19 and new models to stimulate markets that are already oversupplied with guns—has driven their push to innovate. Newer firearms mean more profits. With the American gun manufacturers producing more than 4.2 million new guns per year—and imports adding another 2.2 million annually— you'd think the market would be saturated.

20   But that's why they have to sell gun owners new guns for their collections—because guns rarely wear out. Hardly anyone here is driving their grandfather's 1952 Plymouth. But a lot of people probably have their grandfather's 1952 revolver. So gun manufacturers make guns that hold more rounds of ammunition, increase the power of that ammunition, and make guns smaller and easier to conceal.

21   These changes make guns better suited for crime, because they are easy to carry and more likely to kill or maim whether they are used intentionally or unintentionally. In fact, one of the most popular handgun types today is the so-called "pocket rocket": a palm-sized gun that is easy to conceal, has a large capacity for ammunition and comes in a high caliber.

22   The *Chicago Tribune* reported that the number of pocket rockets found at crime scenes nationwide almost tripled from 1995 to 1997. It was a pocket rocket in the hands of a self-proclaimed white supremacist that shot 5 children at the North Valley Jewish Community Center and killed a Filipino-American postal worker outside of Los Angeles in August of 1999.

23   Now, we don't regulate guns in America. We do regulate other dangerous products like cars and prescription drugs and tobacco and alcohol—but not guns. Gun sales information is not public. Gun manufacturers are exempt by federal law from the standard health and safety regulations that are applied to all other consumer products manufactured and sold in the United States.

24   No federal agency is allowed to exercise oversight over the gun industry to ensure consumer safety. In fact, no other consumer industry in the United States—not even the tobacco industry—has been allowed to so totally evade accountability for the harm their products cause to human beings. Just the gun industry.

25   In a similar pattern to the marketing of tobacco—which kills its best customers in the United States at a rate of 430,000 per year—the spread of gun-related injuries and death is especially tragic when it involves our children. Like young lungs and tar and nicotine—young minds are especially responsive to the deadliness of gun violence.

26   Lieutenant Colonel Dave Grossman, a West Point professor of psychology and military science, has documented how video games act as killing simulators, teaching our children not just to shoot—but to kill. Grossman, who calls himself an expert in "killology," cites as evidence the marksmanship of the two children, aged 11 and 13, in the Jonesboro, Arkansas, shootings in 1998. Both shooters were avid video game players. And just like in a video game—they fired off 27 shots—and hit 15 people. Killing four of their fellow students—and a teacher. Such deadly accuracy is rare and hard to achieve—even by well-trained police and military marksmen.

I want you to imagine with me a computer game called "Puppy Shoot."   27
In this game puppies run across the screen. Using a joystick, the game player aims a gun that shoots the puppies. The player is awarded one point for a
flesh wound, three points for a body shot, and ten points for a head shot.
Blood spurts out each time a puppy is hit—and brain tissue splatters all over
whenever there's a head shot. The dead puppies pile up at the bottom of the
screen. When the shooter gets to 1000 points, he gets to exchange his pistol
for an Uzi, and the point values go up.

If a game as disgusting as that were to be developed, every animal rights   28
group in the country, along with a lot of other organizations, would protest,
and there would be all sorts of attempts made to get the game taken off the
market. Yet, if you just change puppies to people in the game I described,
there are dozens of them already on the market—sold under such names as
"Blood Bath," "Psycho Toxic," "Redneck Rampage," and "Soldier of
Fortune." These games are not only doing a very good business—they are
also supported by their own Web sites. Web sites that offer strategy tips,
showing players how to get to hidden features, like unlimited ammunition,
access more weapons, and something called "first shot kill," which enables
you to kill your opponent with a single shot.

We do not let the children who play these games drive because they are   29
too young. We do not let them drink because they are too young. We do not
let them smoke because they are too young. But we do let them be trained to
be shooters at an age when they have not yet developed their impulse control and have none of the maturity and discipline to safely use the weapons
they are playing with. Perhaps worst of all, they do this in an environment
in which violence has no consequences. These kids shoot people for an hour,
turn off the computer—then go down for dinner and do their homework.

We need to teach our children from the beginning that violence does   30
have consequences—serious consequences—all the time. Gunfire kills 10
children a day in America. In fact, the United States leads the world in the
rate at which its children die from firearms. The CDC recently analyzed
firearm-related deaths in 26 countries for children under the age of 15—and
found that 86 percent of all those deaths—occurred in the United States.

If this was a virus—or a defective car seat or an undercooked hamburg-   31
er—killing our children, there would be a massive uproar within a week.
Instead, our capacity to feel a sense of national shame has been diminished
by the pervasiveness and numbing effect of all this violence.

We all are well aware of the extent of this threat to the nation's health.   32
So why doesn't someone do something about it? Fortunately, people are.
People we know, people we don't know, and people we have only heard
about are working hard to abolish the menace of gun violence—of all forms
of violence—from the American scene. Some of them are with us tonight.

One of them is Elizabeth Kagan, the newly inaugurated president of our   33
AMA Alliance. Elizabeth will head the Alliance campaign for Safe Gun Storage.

34   Another is Dr. William Schwab, chief of trauma surgery at the University of Pennsylvania in Philadelphia. He is truly one of the heroes in this battle. His work has shown us just the kind of information we really need to reduce this violence. We are extremely pleased that he has agreed to be one of our ongoing advisors in this activity.

35   These are the people who stand and deliver when it comes to educating the nation about the threat of gun violence. Elizabeth and Bill, will you please stand? They certainly deserve a hand.

36   Elizabeth and Bill will be with us through the evening, and I urge as many of you as possible to spend a few minutes with them. They came here because they understand that gun violence in the United States is a problem that is bigger than every one of us. And the blood in America's streets—and classrooms—is a problem for all of us.

37   I was gratified when—earlier today—Terry Hillard, Superintendent of the Chicago Police Department, stopped by to join me in talking with reporters. We discussed the importance of data collection and how the physician community can work together with law enforcement to tackle this important issue of gun violence.

38   The question remains, what are we—the physician community—going to do about it? I can tell you first what we're not going to do. We're not going to advocate changing or abolishing the Second Amendment to the Constitution. We really don't have to, to make our point.

39   The gun lobby loves to use the Second Amendment as a smokescreen—to hide the reality of the damage that guns do—and to prevent our looking any deeper into the facts and statistics of that damage. We've all heard that tired old statement: Guns don't kill people—people kill people. But how does that explain these facts? A gun kept in the home for self-defense is 22 times more likely to be used to kill a family member or a friend than an intruder. The presence of a gun in the home triples the risk of homicide— and increases the risk of suicide fivefold.

40   And listen to this quote: ". . . the Second Amendment has been the subject of one of the greatest pieces of fraud, I repeat the word fraud, on the American people by special interest groups that I have ever seen in my lifetime. The very language of the Second Amendment refutes any argument that it was intended to guarantee every citizen an unfettered right to any kind of weapon. Surely the Second Amendment does not remotely guarantee every person the constitutional right to have a Saturday night special or a machine gun. There is no support in the Constitution for the argument that federal and state governments are powerless to regulate the purchase of such firearms."

41   These are the words of a respected conservative jurist, the late Chief Justice of the Supreme Court, Warren Burger.

42   As I said, our mission is not to abolish all guns from the hands of our fellow citizens. We're not advocating any limitations on hunting or the legitimate use of long guns, or for that matter, any other specific item of

gun control. And we won't even be keeping a scorecard of legislative victories against guns in Congress and in the statehouses.

Why not? Because all these well-intentioned efforts have been tried by good people—and they have not met with success. Instead, they have been met with a well-organized, aggressive protest against their efforts by powerful lobbies in Washington and at the state and community levels. We—the American Medical Association—are going to take a different route—not just calls for advocacy—but for diplomacy and for statesmanship and for research as well. And make no mistake about this: We will not be co-opted by either the rhetoric or the agendas of the public policy "left" or "right" in this national debate about the safety and health of our citizens.   43

One of the ways we will do this is—to help assemble the data. Current, consistent, credible data are at the heart of epidemiology. What we don't know about violence—and guns—is literally killing us. And yet, very little is spent on researching gun-related injuries and deaths.   44

A recent study shows that for every year of life lost to heart disease, we spend $441 on research. For every year of life lost to cancer, we spend $794 on research. Yet for every year of life lost to gun violence, we spend only $31 on research—less than the cost of a taxi ride from here to the airport.   45

That's bad public policy. It's bad fiscal policy. And it is certainly is bad medical policy. If we are to fight this epidemic of violence, the Centers for Disease Control must have the budget and the authority to gather the data we need. As I mentioned earlier, the CDC's National Center for Injury Prevention and Control researched the causes and prevention of many kinds of injuries. But in the mid-90's the gun lobby targeted the NCIPC—and scored a bulls eye when Congress eliminated its funding. It wasn't a lot of money—just $2.6 million—budget dust to the Federal government. But it meant the difference between existence and extinction for the project.   46

Just think—gun injuries cost our nation $2.3 billion dollars in medical costs each year—yet some people think $2.6 million dollars is too much to spend on tracking them. Every dollar spent on this research has the potential to reduce medical costs by $885.   47

The CDC is intent on doing its job and is now heading up the planning for a National Violent Death Reporting System—coordinated and funded at the federal level—and collecting data at the state level. Because knowing more about the who, what, when, where, why and how violent homicides, suicides, and deaths—will help public health officials, law enforcement, and policy makers prevent unnecessary deaths.   48

We must further insist that such a system be expanded to cover data about non-fatal gunshot injuries so that we can prevent these as well. Such a system of data collection and analysis has already helped us address another national epidemic—motor vehicle fatalities. Prompting preventive measures like mandatory seat belt laws, air bags, improved highway signage, and better designed entry and exit ramps—not the confiscation of cars. The establish-   49 ment of a National Violent Death and Injury Reporting System would help us establish similar preventive measures against violence. And help us fill in all the blanks about violent death and injury in America. Including such basics as:

- How do kids with guns get their weapons?
- Do trigger locks work?
- What can we do to reduce accidental, self-inflicted gun injuries?
- What are the warning signs of workplace or school shootings?
- During which hours of the week and in what specific parts of town (down to individual blocks—not just neighborhoods) do the shootings occur?
- Do we need to work with Police Departments to change patrolling patterns based on these data?
- And finally, the realization that the answers to these questions are apt to be different from one town to the next.

50   Today, we can't answer these questions—because we are not allowed to collect the data. Collecting and considering the facts isn't a matter of opinion or politics, it's essential. It's a matter of working with other committed leaders to get the job done.

51   The good news is that we have HELP—the Handgun Epidemic Lowering Plan—with membership of 130 organizations including the AMA, and, among others, the Rehabilitation Institute of Chicago, and the Minnesota Department of Health. We also have the Surgeon General's National Strategy for Suicide Prevention, released last month, which also supports the National Violent Death Reporting System.

52   We will not advocate any changes at all based on urban legend, anecdote or hunch. We will only base our conclusions on evidence-based data and facts. It's just good, common sense—the kind of solid epidemiology that has been brought to bear on other public health hazards—from Legionnaire's Disease to food-borne illnesses to exposure to dioxin or DDT. Trustworthy science that can help us prevent harm before it happens. For, as we physicians know, prevention is usually the best cure.

53   One of the giants of American medicine, Dr. William Osler, proposed using preventive medicine against serious public health threats like malaria and yellow fever. And the tools he advocated—education, organization and cooperation—sound like a pretty good definition of diplomacy to me. We will put these same tools to use in removing the threat of gun violence from our society.

54   As we have in the past, we have already sought the cooperation of the American Bar Association—and we are grateful that our invitation has been accepted. We will be working with the ABA on their Forum on Justice Improvements, taking place this October in Washington, D.C. The forum, set up by their Justice Initiatives Group, will focus on gun violence.

55   We are being advised by a panel of physicians and other experts, who have worked long and hard in tackling the many-headed monster of gun violence and its grisly outcomes. They have welcomed our involvement in

this issue and look forward to a newly configured playing field with allies that command such clout as the ABA and the AMA.

People have told me that this is a dangerous path to follow. That I am crazy to do it. That I am putting our organization in jeopardy. They say we'll lose members. They say we'll be the target of smear campaigns. They say that the most extremist of the gun supporters will seek to destroy us. But I believe that this is a battle we cannot not take on.   56

While there are indeed risks—the far greater risk for the health of the public, for us in this room, and for the AMA, is to do nothing. We, as physicians, and as the American Medical Association, have an ethical and moral responsibility to do this—as our mission statement says—"to promote the science and art of medicine and the betterment of public health." If removing the scourge of gun violence isn't bettering the public health—what is?   57

As physicians, we are accustomed to doing what is right for our patients—and not worrying about our comfort, ease or popularity. Our goal is to help cure an epidemic, not to win a victory over some real or imagined political enemy. Anyone who helps us in this fight is an ally—anyone.   58

We don't pretend to have all the answers. Nor do we expect the solution to be quick—and we certainly don't expect it to be easy. In fact, I am certain that we will not reach the solution during my term as your president. But, together as the American Medical Association—guided by our stated mission—we recognize our obligation to contribute our voice, our effort and our moral imperative to this battle. And we will.   59

Almost a century ago, in his book *Confessio Medici*, Stephen Paget, the British physician and author, referred to medicine as a divine vocation. This is part of what he said: 60

"Every year young people enter the medical profession . . . and they stick to it . . . not only from necessity, but from pride, honor, and conviction. And Heaven, sooner or later, lets them know what it thinks of them. This information comes quite as a surprise to them . . . that they were indeed called to be doctors. . . . Surely a diploma . . . obtained by hard work . . . cannot be a summons from Heaven. But it may be. For, if a doctor's life may not be a divine vocation, then no life is a vocation, and nothing is divine."   61

We are here today as the guardians of the divine vocation and as such are dedicated to do what is right, whether or not it is comfortable, whether or not it is easy, and whether or not it is popular. Stephen Paget, you can rest well tonight. Your divine vocation is in good hands. We will guard it well. We will live up to our mission—we will do what is right.   62

Thank you.   63

Thinking Critically about "The Secrets of Gun Violence in America"

1. How does Richard F. Corlin use appeals to ethos and pathos to create presence and to persuade his audience that a problem exists?

2. One of Corlin's major strategies is to redefine gun violence as a public health issue. Where does Corlin use arguments from resemblance (precedence or analogy) both to establish the seriousness of the problem and to argue for his solution—in this case, the course of action he wants the American Medical Association to take?

3. How does Corlin use numerical data to support his identification of the problem and his proposed solution? Where do you see him weighing benefits against costs? How might resistant readers question his data?

4. What strategies does Corlin employ for considering alternative proposals and for acknowledging and responding to opposing views?

5. Unlike arguments in print, speeches have an immediacy and live connection with their audiences. They also must be easily comprehensible to listeners. What features in this spoken proposal argument strike you as particularly effective in connecting with the values, interests, and attention of an audience composed of physicians?

COMPOSING YOUR ESSAY
Generating and Exploring Ideas

If you are having trouble thinking of a proposal topic, try making an idea map of local problems you would like to see solved. For your spokes, consider some of the following starting points:

Finding a Proposal Issue

Problems at your university: dorm, parking, registration system, grading system, campus appearance, clubs, curriculum, intramural program

Problems in your city or town: dangerous intersections, ugly areas, inadequate lighting, a poorly designed store, a shopping center that needs a specific improvement

Problems at your place of work: office design, flow of customer traffic, merchandise display, company policies, customer relations

Problems related to other aspects of your life: hobbies, recreational time, life as a consumer, and so forth

Another approach is to freewrite your response to these trigger statements:

I would really like to solve the problem of _____.

I believe that X should _____. (Substitute for X words such as *my instructor, the president, the school administration, Congress, my boss,* and so forth.)

Note that the problem you pose for this paper can be personal, but shouldn't be private; that is, others should be able to benefit from a solution to your personal problem. For example, your inability to find child care for your daughter is a private problem. But if you focus your proposal on how zoning laws discourage development of in-home day care—and propose a change in those zoning laws to permit more in-home day care centers—then your proposal will benefit others.

Using Stock Issues to Explore Your Problem

Once you have decided on a proposal issue, explore it by freewriting your responses to the following questions. These questions are often called *stock issues,* since they represent generic, or stock, questions that apply to almost any kind of proposal.

1. Is there a problem here that has to be solved?
2. Will the proposed solution really solve this problem?
3. Can the problem be solved in a simpler way without disturbing the status quo?
4. Is the proposed solution practical enough that it really stands a chance of being implemented?
5. What will be the positive and negative consequences of the proposal?

You might also try freewriting your responses to the questions in the exploratory exercise on page 442. Although these questions cover much the same territory as the stock issues, their different presentation might stimulate additional thought.

Finally, try thinking of justifications for your solution by using the three-approach strategy described earlier in this chapter.

Avoid Presupposing Your Solution in Your Problem Statement

A common mistake of inexperienced proposal writers is to write problem statements that presuppose their solutions. As a restaurant server, suppose you notice that customers want coffee refills faster than servers can provide them. To solve this problem, you propose placing carafes of hot coffee at each table. When describing your problem, don't presuppose your solution: "The problem is that we don't have carafes of hot coffee at the tables." Rather, describe the problematic situation itself: annoyed customers clamoring for coffee and harassed servers trying to bring around refills. Only by giving presence to the original problem can you interest readers in your proposed solution, which readers will compare to other possible approaches (including doing nothing).

Here are some more examples:

> **Weak:** The problem is that our medical office doesn't have an answering machine during closed hours.

> **Actual Problem:** The problem is that (1) we are overwhelmed with calls from patients canceling appointments during the first few hours every morning; (2) employees can't phone in emergency messages early in the morning (illness, car trouble); and (3) because we are on the West Coast, East Coast insurance companies can't communicate with us until after 12:00 p.m. their time.

> **Weak:** Our supermarket doesn't give new employees a location index for store items.

Actual problem: Customers often ask employees where to find an item and are given a bad first impression when a new employee doesn't know the answer; it wastes valuable time when the new employee walks with the customer to find an experienced employee to actually answer the question.

Weak: The Campus Coffee House doesn't stay open late enough at night.

Actual problem: Students who study late at night don't have an attractive, convenient place to socialize or study; off-campus coffee houses are too far to walk to at night; dorm lounges aren't attractive or conducive to study; late-nighters make noise in the dorms instead of going to a convenient place.

Shaping and Drafting

The following is a typical organizational plan for a proposal argument that you might turn to if you get stuck in composing the first draft of your essay.

1. Presentation of a problem that needs solving
   a. Description of the problem (give it presence)
   b. Additional background, including previous attempts to solve the problem
   c. Argument that the problem is solvable (optional)
2. Presentation of the proposed solution
   a. Succinct statement of the proposed solution
   b. Explanation of specifics for the proposed solution
3. Summary and rebuttal of opposing views (in practical proposals, this section is often a summary and rejection of alternative ways of solving the problem)
4. Justification—persuades reader that proposal should be enacted
   a. Reason 1 presented and developed
   b. Reason 2 presented and developed
   c. And so forth
5. Conclusion—exhorts audience to act (sometimes incorporated into the last sentences of the final supporting reason)

Revising

After you have completed your first draft and begun to clarify your argument for yourself, you are ready to start making your argument clear and persuasive for your readers. Use the strategies for clear closed-form prose outlined in Chapter 19. At this stage, feedback from peer readers can be very helpful. Use the following guidelines for peer reviews:

▪ GUIDELINES FOR PEER REVIEWS ▪

Instructions for peer reviews are provided in Chapter 18 (pp. 490–496).

For the Writer

Prepare two or three questions you would like your peer reviewer to address while responding to your draft. The questions can focus on some aspect of your draft that you are uncertain about, on one or more sections where you particularly seek help or advice, on some feature that you particularly like about your draft, or on some part you especially wrestled with. Write out your questions and give them to your peer reviewer along with your draft.

For the Reviewer

   I. Read the draft at a normal reading speed from beginning to end. As you read, do the following:

   A. Place a wavy line in the margin next to any passages that you find confusing, that contain something that doesn't seem to fit, or that otherwise slow down your reading.

   B. Place a "Good!" in the margin next to any passages where you think the writing is particularly strong or interesting.

   II. Read the draft again slowly and answer the following questions by writing brief explanations of your answers.

   A. Introduction and statement of problem:

   1. How could the title more effectively focus the paper and pique your interest? How could the title be improved?

   2. How does the writer convince you that a problem exists and that it is significant (worth solving) and solvable? How does the writer give the problem presence? How could the writer improve the presentation of the problem?

   B. Proposed solution:

   1. How could the writer's thesis more clearly propose a solution to the problem? Could the thesis be made more precise?

   2. Could the writer give you more details about the solution so that you can understand it and see how it works? How could the writer make the solution clearer?

   C. Justification:

   1. In the justification section, how could the writer provide stronger reasons for acting on the proposal? Where could the reasons be better supported with more details and evidence? How could the reasons appeal more to the values and beliefs of the audience?

   2. Can you help the writer think of additional justifying arguments (arguments from principle, from consequences, from precedent or analogy)? How could the writer improve support for the proposal?

   3. Where does the writer anticipate and address opposing views or alternative solutions? How does the writer convince you that the proposed solution is superior to alternative solutions?

4. Has the writer persuaded you that the benefits of this proposal will outweigh the costs? Who will pay the costs and who will get the benefits? What do you think the gut reaction of a typical decision maker will be to the writer's proposal?

5. Can you think of other unforeseen costs that the writer should acknowledge and address? What unforeseen benefits could the writer mention?

6. How might the writer improve the structure and clarity of the argument? Where might the writer better apply the principles of clarity from Chapter 19?

D. If the writer has prepared questions for you, respond to his or her inquiries.

E. Sum up what you see as the chief strengths and problem areas in this draft:

1. Strengths

2. Problem areas

III. Read the draft one more time. Place a check mark in the margin wherever you notice problems in grammar, spelling, or mechanics (one check mark per problem).

**Your Help Is Needed Now
To Feed Starving Children in Afghanistan**

Donate

$20 will feed one child for a month. Please respond now!

Click for
earthquake update

Afghanistan Links:

>> Updates on refugees
>> Refugee photos
>> Press releases
>> Shocking malnutrition levels
>> The anguish of Afghanistan
>> Rough life for returnees
>> Conditions in Herat
>> Food relief in Herat

Contact Us
--
Our Privacy Policy
--
Uniform Disclosure Statement
--
About Credit Card Security

Children in Afghanistan are starving. And with a brutal winter setting in, the situation could become even worse.

World Vision workers on the ground estimate that 7.5 million people are currently in danger of starvation, with 15% of small children severely malnourished.

As weather conditions grow worse, it will become increasingly difficult to transport emergency food for refugee children and their families. In a recent alert, World Vision's Dr. Doris Knoechel stated:

*"People are starving. It is urgent we get aid in. Otherwise, people will die.
There is only limited time before the roads are filled with snow and we can't get in."*

That is why World Vision is responding now to help the people of Afghanistan. Relief centers have been opened in Herat and Mazar-e-Sharif. Additional feeding programs are planned in Farah, Ghor and Badghis.

Now your support is urgently needed to provide emergency food including high-protein Unimix to the starving children of Afghanistan. Twenty dollars will feed one child for a month. One hundred dollars will feed an entire family. But we must respond immediately.

You can make your secure donation using the online form below. Or you can call us at our special Afghanistan hotline, 1-888-511-6571. Please give generously ‹ the lives of innocent children hang in the balance.

Please use my gift of:
- ○ $20 ○ $80
- ○ $40 ○ $100
- ○ $60 ● Other: $ [   ]

In order to:
- ○ help Afghan refugees
- ○ help where most needed

About WV
- Contact Us
- Our Mission and History
- What Your Gifts Accomplish
- Global Projects

Resources
- News Room
- Gift Planning

Get Involved
- Sponsor / Pray / Volunteer / Intern
- Speak Out

PART THREE

A Guide to Composing and Revising

Dedicated to responding to humanitarian emergencies and ending cycles of poverty, World Vision, founded in 1950, is the world's largest Christian international relief and development agency. World Vision's commitment to hunger relief, water programs, health care education, and agricultural and economic development is explained on its Web site. One of the organization's many campaign links, this World Vision public affairs advocacy ad—"Your Help Is Needed Now To Feed Starving Children in Afghanistan"—presents an abbreviated proposal argument that employs a simple layout and photo, different font styles, and bold statements of both the problem and the appeal to promote its cause and convey its direct call to action. To discuss and analyze this advocacy ad, see the questions in the section entitled "Using the Part Opener Images" that follows the Preface.

477

CHAPTER 18

Writing as a Problem-Solving Process

I rewrite as I write. It is hard to tell what is a first draft because it is not determined by time. In one draft, I might cross out three pages, write two, cross out a fourth, rewrite it, and call it a draft. I am constantly writing and rewriting. I can only conceptualize so much in my first draft—only so much information can be held in my head at one time; my rewriting efforts are a reflection of how much information I can encompass at one time. There are levels and agenda which I have to attend to in each draft.

—Description of Revision by an Experienced Writer

*I read what I have written and I cross out a word and put another word in; a more decent word or a better word. Then if there is somewhere to use a sentence that I have crossed out, I will put it there.**

—Description of Revision by an Inexperienced Writer

Blot out, correct, insert, refine,
Enlarge, diminish, interline;
Be mindful, when invention fails,
To scratch your head, and bite your nails.

—Jonathan Swift

I n Part One of this text we focused on writing as a problem-solving process in which writers pose and solve both subject-matter problems and rhetorical problems. Part Three shows you how to translate these basic principles into effective strategies for composing and revising your writing along the continuum from closed to open forms. The three self-contained chapters, which can be read in whatever sequence best fits your instructor's course plan, will help you compose and revise the essays you write for the assignments in Part Two.

---

*From Nancy Sommers, "Revision Strategies of Student Writers and Experienced Adult Writers," *College Composition and Communication* 31 (October 1980): 291–300.

This chapter explains how experienced writers use multiple drafts to manage the complexities of writing and suggests ways for you to improve your own writing processes. Chapter 19, which takes the form of ten self-contained lessons, focuses on key strategies for composing and revising closed-form prose. Chapter 20 switches from closed to open forms, showing you how, when appropriate, to open your prose by creating surprises of style and structure that engage readers and involve them in the process of completing your text's meaning.

UNDERSTANDING HOW EXPERTS COMPOSE AND REVISE

We begin this chapter with a close look at how experienced writers compose, explaining what they think about when they write and why they often need multiple drafts. In Chapter 3 we quoted Peter Elbow's assertion that "meaning is not what you start out with" but "what you end up with" (p. 40). Thus composing is a discovery process. In the early stages of writing, experienced writers typically discover what they are trying to say, often deepening and complicating their ideas rather than clarifying them. Only in the last drafts will such writers be in sufficient control of their ideas to shape them elegantly for readers.

It's important not to overgeneralize, however, because no two writers compose exactly the same way; moreover, the same writer may use different processes for different kinds of prose. Some writers outline their ideas before they write; others need to write extensively before they can outline. Some write their first drafts very slowly, devoting extensive thought and planning to each emerging paragraph; others write first drafts rapidly, to be sure to get all their ideas on paper, and then rework the material part by part. Some prefer to work independently, without discussing or sharing their ideas; others seek out classmates or colleagues to help them hash out ideas and rehearse their arguments before writing them down. Some seek out the stillness of a library or private room; others do their best writing in noisy cafeterias or coffee shops.

The actual mechanics of composing differ from writer to writer as well. Some writers create first drafts directly at a keyboard, whereas others require the reassuring heft of a pen or pencil. Among writers who begin by planning the structure of their work, some make traditional outlines (perhaps using the flexible outline feature on their word processors), whereas others prefer tree diagrams or flowcharts. Some of those who use word processors revise directly at the computer, whereas others print out a hard copy, revise with pen, and then type the changes into the computer.

Also, writers often vary their composing processes from project to project. A writer might complete one project with a single draft and a quick editing job, but produce a half dozen or more drafts for another project.

What experienced writers do have in common is a willingness to keep revising their work until they feel it is ready to go public. They typically work much harder at drafting and revising than do inexperienced writers, taking more runs at their subject. And experienced writers generally make more substantial alter-

Minoan/Assyrian/Etruscan
too—check dates of gold bees,
procession fibulae, etc!—
contemp.? earlier?
Story of Jewelry

as in other parts of the Classical world, goldsmithing

Work it—
wooden

later?

In Ancient Greece, ~~the craft of jewelry making~~ was raised to a

high art. Classical goldsmiths worked the metal in its unrefined

state, as it was extracted from the earth. Usually, the natural

alloy was roughly equivalent to 22 karat gold. Using pine resin as

goldsmiths

an organic glue, mouth blow-pipes, and brick furnaces, ~~they~~ bonded

surfaces without the use of solder, creating jewels of fabulous

All later

delicacy and seeming fragility. Yet many of these bonds ~~were~~

have   d

~~strong enough to~~ endure more than two millennia, withstanding the

ravages of entombment, grave robbers, dozens of wearers, and

misguided   attempts

finally, ~~curatorial~~ conservation. Today, as museum-goers marvel at

delicately

the repoussed and richly (granulated) surfaces of a rosette earring

or a ram's head necklace finial, they may wonder whether these

were the creations of earthly beings or of angels. In fact,

Was this
system
or slavery?

historical evidence seems to indicate that most of the Greek

live children, not angels, were the agency of   *—children indentured*

Lead?

~~godsmiths used children to do the intricate work,~~ perhaps ~~at~~

at the tender age of (nine or ten) and ~~condem~~ often rendered sightless before they reached maturity.

~~great expense to the children's health and especially their~~

pressed
into service

~~eyesight.~~

verify

more
trasnstion

Check
accent—sp?

here or later?

have to
explain—size of
granules, control
required, etc.
Have to have
pix!

(cringe)

to bathe their
houng faces in
flames

Backing into corner? Want disc. of
technology as well as social evils_maybe frame??
Beauty/acheivements framed by sadness
of human cost??

FIGURE 18.1 ■ Draft Page of Experienced Writer

ations in their drafts during revision. (Compare the first two quotations that open this chapter—one from an experienced and one from an inexperienced writer.) An experienced writer will sometimes throw away a first draft and start over; a beginning writer tends to be more satisfied with early drafts and to think of revision as primarily cleaning up errors. Figure 18.1 shows the first page of a first draft for a magazine article written by an experienced writer.

WHY EXPERIENCED WRITERS REVISE SO EXTENSIVELY

To help you understand the puzzling difference between beginning and experienced writers, let's consider *why* experienced writers revise. If they are such good writers, why don't they get it right the first time? Why so many drafts? To use the language of Part One, experienced writers need multiple drafts to help them pose, pursue, and solve problems—both subject-matter problems and related rhetorical problems. Faced with many choices, experienced writers use multiple drafts to break a complex task into manageable subtasks. Let's look more closely at some of the functions that revising can perform for writers.

Revising to Overcome Limits of Short-Term Memory

A writer's need for multiple drafts results partly from the limitations of memory. Cognitive psychologists have shown that working memory—often called *short-term memory*—has remarkably little storage space. People use short-term memory to hold the data on which they are actively focusing at any given moment while solving problems, reading texts, writing a draft, or performing other cognitive tasks. People also have long-term memories, which can store an almost infinite amount of material. The trouble is that much of the material held temporarily in short-term memory never gets transferred to long-term memory. (Try closing this book for a moment and writing out this paragraph from memory.)

You can conceptualize short-term memory as a small tabletop surrounded by filing cabinets (long-term memory). To use the ideas and data you generate while writing a draft, you have to place them on the tabletop, which can hold only a few items at once.* As you generate ideas for your draft, you pile on your tabletop more data than it can hold. You need some means of holding on to your thoughts in process, lest ideas spill off the table and become permanently lost.

This analogy illustrates why experienced writers rely on multiple drafts. Because of the limitations of short-term memory, you can actively engage only a few chunks of material at any given moment—a few sentences of a draft or several ideas in an outline. The remaining portions of the evolving essay quickly recede from consciousness without being stored in long-term memory. (Think of your horror when your computer eats your draft or when you accidentally leave your nearly finished term paper on the bus—proof that you can't rely on long-term memory to restore what you wrote.) Writing a draft, however, captures these ideas from short-term memory and stores them on paper. When you reread these stored ideas, you can note problem areas, think of new ideas, see material that

---

*A famous study conducted by psychologist George Miller revealed that the average person's short-term memory can hold "seven plus or minus two" chunks of information at a time. When given, say, a thirty-item list of random words or numbers, the average person can remember between five and nine of them. The items will quickly be lost from short-term memory unless the person actively rehearses them over and over (as when you repeat a new phone number to yourself so that you won't forget it before you write it down).

doesn't fit, recall additional information, and so forth. You can then begin working on a new draft, focusing on one problem at a time.

What kinds of problems do experienced writers locate in a draft? What triggers further rounds of rewriting? We continue with more reasons experienced writers revise.

Revising to Accommodate Shifts and Changes in a Writer's Ideas

Early in the writing process, experienced writers often are unsure of what they want to say or where their ideas are leading; they find their ideas shifting and evolving as their drafts progress. Sometimes writing a draft leads the writer to reformulate the initial problem. Just as frequently, the solution that may have seemed exciting at the beginning of the process may seem less satisfactory once it is written out. A writer's ideas deepen or shift under pressure of new insights stimulated by the act of writing. A professional writer's finished product often is radically different from the first draft—not simply in form and style but in actual content.

Revising to Clarify Audience and Purpose

As we noted in Chapters 3 and 4, writers need to say something significant to an audience for a purpose. When a writer's sense of audience or purpose shifts, an entire piece may need to be restructured. As they draft, experienced writers pose questions such as these: Who am I picturing as my readers? What is my purpose in writing to them? What effect do I want this piece of writing to have on them? How much background will they need? To which of their values and beliefs should I appeal? What tone and style are appropriate for this audience? What objections will they raise to my argument? In the process of writing, the answers to these questions may evolve so that each new draft reflects a deeper or clearer understanding of audience and purpose.

Revising to Clarify Structure and Create Coherence

Few writers can create detailed outlines before drafting. Those who can, typically set aside their outlines as their drafts take on lives of their own, spilling over the boundaries the writers have laid out. Whereas early drafts usually reflect the order in which writers conceived their ideas, later drafts are often reordered— sometimes radically—in consideration of readers' needs. To help them see their drafts from a reader's perspective, experienced writers regularly put aside those drafts for a time. When they return to a draft, the ideas no longer so familiar, they can more readily see where the material is disjointed, underdeveloped, or irrelevant. Writing teachers sometimes call this transformation a movement from writer-based to reader-based prose.* The lessons in Chapter 19 will help you develop the skills of seeing your drafts from a reader's perspective.

*The terms *writer-based* and *reader-based* prose come from Linda Flower, "Writer-Based Prose: A Cognitive Basis for Problems in Writing," *College English,* 41.1 (1979): 19–37.

Revising to Improve Gracefulness and Correctness

Finally, writers have to perfect their grammar, punctuate effectively, spell correctly, and compose sentences that are concise, clear, graceful, and pleasing to the ear. Late in the revision process, experienced writers focus extensively on these matters. Often this stage of revision involves more than stylistic polishing. Making a single sentence more graceful may entail rewriting surrounding sentences. If an awkward sentence is symptomatic of confused thinking, correcting the sentence may require generating and exploring more ideas.

A WORKING DESCRIPTION OF THE WRITING PROCESS

The writing process we have just described may be considerably different from what you have previously been taught. For many years—before researchers began studying the composing processes of experienced writers—writing teachers typically taught a model something like this:

Old Model of the Writing Process

1. Choose a topic
2. Narrow it
3. Write a thesis
4. Make an outline
5. Write a draft
6. Revise
7. Edit

The major problem with this model is that hardly anyone writes this way. Few experienced writers begin by choosing a topic and then narrowing it—a process that seems passionless, arbitrary, and mechanical. As we explained in Part One, experienced writers begin by looking at the world with a wondering and critical eye; they pose problems and explore ideas; they become dissatisfied with the answers or explanations given by others; they identify questions that impel them to add their own voice to a conversation. Nor is the process neatly linear, as the old model implies. Sometimes writers settle on a thesis early in the writing process. But just as frequently they formulate a thesis during an "Aha!" moment of discovery later in the process, perhaps after several drafts. (So *this* is my point! Here is my argument in a nutshell!) Even very late in the process, while checking spelling and punctuation, experienced writers are apt to think of new ideas, thus triggering more revision.

Rather than dividing the writing process into distinct, sequential steps, let's review the kinds of things experienced writers are likely to do early, midway, and late in the process of writing an essay.

Early in the Process

The activities in which writers engage early in the process are recursive—writing a draft sends the writer back for further exploring, researching, and talking.

Writers Sense a Question or Problem. Initially, the question or problem may not be well-defined, but the writers sense something unknown about the topic, disagree with someone else's view of it, or otherwise notice something confusing or problematic. In college, the instructor often assigns the problem or question to be addressed. Sometimes, the instructor assigns only a general topic area, leaving students to find their own questions or problems.

Writers Explore the Problem, Seeking Focus. Writers gather data from various sources, and through exploratory writing and talking, they search for an effective response to the problem. They consider what they want their readers to know about the topic and how their ideas might surprise the readers, given the readers' background knowledge and point of view. Writers may also take time off from the problem and do other things, letting ideas cook in their unconscious.

Writers Compose a First Draft. At some point writers put ideas on paper in a whole or partial draft. Some writers make an informal outline prior to writing. Others discover direction as they write, putting aside concerns about coherence to pursue different branches of ideas. In either case, they don't try to make the draft perfect as they go. One of the major causes of writer's block among less experienced writers is the inability to live with temporary imperfection and confusion. Experienced writers know their first drafts are often messy and unfocused, and they lower their expectations accordingly. Writing a first draft often leads writers to discover new ideas, to complicate or refocus the problem, to reimagine audience or purpose, and sometimes to change directions.

Midway Through the Process

Writers Begin to Revise and Reformulate. Once they have written a first draft, writers are in a better position to view the whole territory and are better able to recognize relationships among the parts. Some writers begin again, selecting insights from the first draft and reshaping them into a new draft with a different approach and structure; others keep much of the original draft but incorporate newfound ideas. Writers often find that the conclusion of the first draft is much clearer than its introduction—proof that they discovered and clarified their ideas as they wrote. At this point writers begin a second draft, often by going slowly through the first draft, adding, deleting, reordering, or completely rewriting passages.

Writers Increasingly Consider the Needs of Readers. As writers clarify their ideas for themselves, they increasingly focus on their readers' needs. They reorganize material and insert mapping statements, transitions, and cue words to help readers follow their ideas. In particular, they try to write effective introductions to hook readers' attention, explain the problem to be examined, and preview the whole of the essay.

Writers Seek Feedback from Readers. Midway through the writing process, experienced writers often ask colleagues to read their drafts and offer feedback. They seek readers' responses to such questions as these: Where do you get lost or confused? Where do you disagree with my ideas? Where do I need to put in more evidence or support? They then revise their drafts in response to readers' queries and suggestions.

Late in the Process

Writers begin to shift from discovery, shaping, and development to editing. Eventually, the writer's sense of purpose and audience stabilizes, and the ideas become increasingly clear, well organized, and developed. At this point writers begin shifting their attention to the craft of writing—getting each word, phrase, sentence, and paragraph just right so that the prose is clear, graceful, lively, and correct. Even as writers struggle with issues of style and correctness, however, they may discover new meanings and intentions that impel them to rethink parts of the essay.

For Writing and Discussion

When you write, do you follow a process resembling the one we just described? Have you ever

- ▓ had a writing project grow out of your engagement with a problem or question?
- ▓ explored ideas by talking with others or by doing exploratory writing?
- ▓ made major changes to a draft because you changed your mind or otherwise discovered new ideas?
- ▓ revised a draft from a reader's perspective by consciously trying to imagine and respond to a reader's questions, confusions, and other reactions?
- ▓ road-tested a draft by trying it out on readers and then revising it as a result of what they told you?

Working in groups or as a whole class, share stories about previous writing experiences that match or do not match the description of experienced writers' processes. To the extent that your present process differs, what strategies of experienced writers might you like to try?

IMPROVING YOUR OWN WRITING PROCESSES

The previous section describes the many ways in which experienced writers compose. Although it is difficult for beginning writers simply to duplicate these processes, which evolve from much experience, practice, and trial and error, beginning writers can take steps to develop more effective composing habits. Some nuts-and-bolts suggestions for improving your writing processes are given next.

Recognize Kinds of Changes Typically Made in Drafts

We begin by classifying the kinds of changes writers typically make in drafts and explaining their reasons for making each sort of change.

Kinds of Changes	Reasons for Change
Crossing out whole passage and rewriting from scratch	Original passage was unfocused; ideas have changed.
	New sense of purpose or point meant that whole passage needed reshaping.
	Original passage was too confused or jumbled for mere editing.
Cutting and pasting; moving parts around	Original was disorganized.
	Points weren't connected to particulars.
	Conclusion was clearer than introduction; part of conclusion had to be moved to introduction.
	Rewriting introduction led to discovery of more effective plan of development; new forecasting required different order in body.
Deletions	Material not needed or irrelevant.
	Deleted material was good but went off on a tangent.
Additions	Supporting particulars needed to be added: examples, facts, illustrations, statistics, evidence (usually added to bodies or paragraphs).
	Points and transitions needed to be supplied (often added to openings of paragraphs).
	New section needed to be added or a brief point expanded.
Recasting of sentences (crossing out and rewriting portions of sentences; combining sentences; rephrasing; starting sentences with a different grammatical structure)	Passage violated old/new contract (see pp. 525–531).
	Passage was wordy or choppy.
	Passage lacked rhythm and voice.
	Grammar was tangled, diction odd, meaning confused.
Editing sentences to correct mistakes	Words were misspelled or mistyped.
	Comma splices, fragments, dangling participles, other grammatical errors were found.

For Writing and Discussion

Choose an important paragraph in the body of a draft you are currently working on. Then write out your answers to these questions about that paragraph.

1. Why is this an important paragraph?
2. What is its main point?
3. Where is that main point stated?

Now—as an exercise only—write the main point at the top of a blank sheet of paper, put away your original draft, and, without looking at the original, write a new paragraph with the sole purpose of developing the point you wrote at the top of the page.

When you are finished, compare your new paragraph to the original. What have you learned that might help you revise your original?

Here are some typical responses of writers who have tried this exercise:

> I recognized that my original paragraph was unfocused. I couldn't find a main point.
>
> I recognized that my original paragraph was underdeveloped. I had a main point but not enough particulars supporting it.
>
> I began to see that my draft was scattered and that I had too many short paragraphs.
>
> I recognized that I was making a couple of different points in my original paragraph and that I needed to break it into separate paragraphs.
>
> I recognized that I hadn't stated my main point (or that I had buried it in the middle of the paragraph).
>
> I recognized that there was a big difference in style between my two versions and that I had to choose which version I liked best. (It's not always the "new" version!)

Practice the Composing Strategies of Experienced Writers

In addition to knowing the kinds of changes writers typically make in drafts, you can also improve your composing processes by practicing the strategies used by experienced writers.

Use Exploratory Writing and Talking to Discover and Clarify Ideas

Use the exploratory strategies described in detail in Chapter 2 (pp. 24–39). Don't let your first draft be the first time you put your ideas into written words. Also seek out opportunities to talk about your ideas with classmates or friends. Exchange ideas on topics so that you can appreciate alternative points of view. Whenever possible, talk through your draft with a friend; rehearse your argument in conversation as practice for putting it in writing.

Schedule Your Time

Plan for exploration, drafting, revision, and editing. Don't begin your paper the night before it is due. Give ideas time to ruminate in your mind. Recognize that your ideas will shift, branch out, even turn around as you write. Allow some time off between writing the first draft and beginning revision. Experienced writers build in time for revision.

Exchange Drafts with Others

Get other people's reactions to your work in exchange for your reactions to theirs. The next section explains procedures for peer review of drafts.

Discover What Methods of Drafting Work Best for You

Some people compose rough drafts directly on a computer; others write long-hand. Of those who write longhand, some find that a certain kind of paper or pen best stimulates thought. Different people prefer different surroundings, also. Discover what works best for you.

Revise on Double- or Triple-Spaced Hard Copy

Although some people can revise directly on the computer, research suggests that writers are more apt to make large-scale changes in a draft if they work from hard copy. Double- or triple-space your drafts and write on one side of the page only. Cross out text to be changed and write new text in the blank spaces between the lines. When a draft gets too messy, enter your changes into the computer and print out another hard copy for another round of revision.

Save Correctness for Last

To revise productively, concentrate first on the big questions: Do I have good ideas in this draft? Am I responding appropriately to the assignment? Are my ideas adequately organized and developed? Save questions about exact wording, grammar, and mechanics for later. These concerns are important, but they cannot be efficiently attended to until after higher-order concerns are met. Your first goal is to create a thoughtful, richly developed draft.

To Meet Deadlines and Bring the Process to a Close, Learn How to *Satisfice*

Our description of the writing process may seem pretty formidable. Potentially, it seems, you could go on revising forever. How can you ever know when to stop? There's no ready answer to that question, but in our opinion it is much more a psychological than a technical problem. The best advice we can offer is to "satisfice."

Satisficing doesn't require that you be perfectly satisfied with your writing. To *satisfice* is to make it as good as you can under the circumstances—your rhetorical situation, your time constraints, and the pressures of other demands on you. So our best advice for finishing a project is to write a rough draft as early in the process as possible and to allow time for feedback from peers or other readers. Then let the deadline give you the energy for intensive revision. From lawyers preparing briefs for court to engineers developing design proposals, writers have used deadlines to help them put aside doubts and anxieties and conclude their work, as every writer must. "Okay, it's not perfect, but it's the best I can do" (a good definition of *satisficing*).

USING PEER REVIEWS TO STIMULATE REVISION

One of the best ways to become a better reviser is to see your draft from a *reader's* rather than a *writer's* perspective. As a writer, you know what you mean; you are already inside your own head. But you need to see what your draft looks like to someone outside your head.

The best way to learn this skill is to practice reading your classmates' drafts and have them read yours. In this section we offer advice on how to respond candidly to your classmates' drafts and how to participate in peer reviews.

Becoming a Helpful Reader of Classmates' Drafts

When you respond to a writer's draft, learn to make readerly rather than writerly comments; describe your mental experience in trying to understand the draft rather than pointing out problems or errors in the draft. For example, instead of saying, "Your draft is disorganized," say, "I got lost when. . . ." Instead of saying, "This paragraph needs a topic sentence," say, "I had trouble seeing the point of this paragraph."

When you help a writer with a draft, your goal is both to point out where the draft needs more work and to brainstorm with the writer possible ways to improve the draft. Begin by reading the draft all the way through at a normal reading speed. As you read, take mental notes to help focus your feedback. We suggest that you make wavy lines in the margin next to passages that you find confusing; write "Good!" in the margin where you like something; and write "?" in the margin where you want to ask questions.

After you have read the draft, use the following strategies for making helpful responses:

If the ideas in the draft seem thin or undeveloped, or if the draft is too short:

- help the writer brainstorm for more ideas.
- help the writer add more examples, better details, more supporting data or arguments.

If you get confused or lost:

- have the writer talk through ideas to clear up confusing spots.
- help the writer sharpen the thesis: suggest that the writer view the thesis as the answer to a controversial or problematic question; ask the writer to articulate the question that the thesis answers.
- help the writer create an outline, tree diagram, or flowchart.
- help the writer clarify the focus by asking him or her to complete these statements about purpose:

  My purpose in this paper is _____.

  My purpose in this section (paragraph) is _____.

See Chapter 19 for a detailed explanation of these revision strategies.

Before reading my paper, the reader will have this view of my topic: _____; after reading my paper, my reader will have this different view of my topic: _____.

■ show the writer where you got confused or miscued in reading the draft ("I started getting lost here because I couldn't see why you were giving me this information" or "I thought you were going to say X, but then you said Y").

If you can understand the sentences but can't see the point:

■ help the writer articulate the meaning by asking "So what?" questions, making the writer bring the point to the surface by stating it directly. ("I can understand what you are saying here but I don't quite understand why you are saying it. I read all these facts, and I say, 'So what?' What do these facts have to do with your thesis?")

If you disagree with the ideas or think the writer has avoided alternative points of view:

■ play devil's advocate to help the writer deepen and complicate ideas.
■ show the writer specific places where you had queries or doubts.

For Writing and Discussion

In the following exercise, we ask you to respond to a student's draft ("Should the University Carpet the Dorm Rooms?" on pp. 492–493). The assignment asked students to take a stand on a local campus issue. Imagine that you have exchanged drafts with this student and that your task is to help this student improve the draft.

Read the draft carefully; make wavy lines in the margins where you get confused, write "Good!" for something you like, and write "?" where you want to ask questions.

On your own, complete the following tasks:

1. Identify one specific place in the draft where you got confused. Freewrite a brief explanation for why you got confused. Make readerly rather than writerly comments.
2. Identify one place in the draft where you think the ideas are thin or need more development.
3. Identify one place where you might write "So what?" in the margins. These are places where you understand the sentences but don't see the point the writer is getting at.
4. Identify at least one place where you could play devil's advocate or otherwise object to the writer's ideas. Freewrite your objections.

In groups or as a whole class, share your responses. Then turn to the following tasks:

1. With the instructor serving as a guide, practice explaining to the writer where or how you got confused while reading the draft. Readers often have difficulty explaining their reading experience to a writer. Let several class members role-play being the reader. Practice using language such as "I like the way this draft started because. . . ." "I got confused when. . . ." "I had to back up and reread when. . . ." "I saw your point here, but then I got lost again because. . . ." Writing theorist Peter Elbow calls such language a "movie of your mind."

2. Have several class members role-play being devil's advocates by arguing against the writer's thesis. Where are the ideas thin or weak?

Should the University Carpet the Dorm Rooms?

Tricia, a university student, came home exhausted from her work-study job. She took a blueberry pie from the refrigerator to satisfy her hunger and a tall glass of milk to quench her thirst. While trying to get comfortable on her bed, she tipped her snack over onto the floor. She cleaned the mess, but the blueberry and milk stains on her brand-new carpet could not be removed.

Tricia didn't realize how hard it was to clean up stains on a carpet. Luckily this was her own carpet.

A lot of students don't want carpets. Students constantly change rooms. The next person may not want carpet.

Some students say that since they pay to live on campus, the rooms should reflect a comfortable home atmosphere. Carpets will make the dorm more comfortable. The carpet will act as insulation and as a soundproofing system.

Paint stains cannot be removed from carpets. If the university carpets the rooms, the students will lose the privilege they have of painting their rooms any color. This would limit students' self-expression.

The carpets would be an institutional brown or gray. This would be ugly. With tile floors, the students can choose and purchase their own carpets to match their taste. You can't be an individual if you can't decorate your room to fit your personality.

According to Rachel Jones, Assistant Director of Housing Services, the cost will be $300 per room for the carpet and installation. Also the university will have to buy more vacuum cleaners. But will vacuum cleaners be all that is necessary to keep the carpets clean? We'll need shampoo machines too.

What about those stains that won't come off even with a shampoo machine? That's where the student will have to pay damage deposit costs.

There will be many stains on the carpet due to shaving cream fights, food fights, beverage parties, and smoking, all of which can damage the carpets.

Students don't take care of the dorms now. They don't follow the rules of maintaining their rooms. They drill holes into the walls, break mirrors, beds, and closet doors, and leave their food trays all over the floor.

If the university buys carpets our room rates will skyrocket. In conclusion, it is a bad idea for the university to buy carpets.

Conducting a Peer Review Workshop

If you are willing to respond candidly to a classmate's draft—in a readerly rather than a writerly way—you will be a valuable participant in peer review workshops. In a typical workshop, classmates work in groups of two to six to respond to each other's rough drafts and offer suggestions for revisions. These workshops are most helpful when group members have developed sufficient levels of professionalism and trust to exchange candid responses. A frequent problem in peer review workshops is that classmates try so hard to avoid hurting each other's feelings that they provide vague, meaningless feedback. Saying, "Your paper's great. I really liked it. Maybe you could make it flow a little better" is much less helpful than saying, "Your issue about environmental pollution in the Antarctic is well defined in the first paragraph, but I got lost in the second paragraph when you began discussing penguin coloration."

Chapter 25 (pp. 685–700) discusses additional ways to use groups and improve group dynamics.

Responsibilities of Peer Reviewers and Writers

Learning to respond conscientiously and carefully to others' work may be the single most important thing you can do to improve your own writing. When you review a classmate's draft, you should prepare as follows:

1. ***Understand how experienced writers revise their drafts.*** Prior to reviewing a classmate's draft, review the material in this chapter. Pay particular attention to pages 490–491, which provide general guidelines about what to look for when reading a draft, and to page 487, which summarizes the kinds of changes writers often make in response to reviews: additions, deletions, reordering, complete refocusing and rewriting, and so forth.

2. ***Understand the assignment and the guidelines for peer reviewers.*** For assignments in Part Two of this text, carefully read both the assignment itself and the Guidelines for Peer Reviews at the end of the chapter in which the assignment appears. These guidelines will help both the writer and you, as peer reviewer, to understand the demands of the assignment and the criteria on which it should be evaluated.

3. ***Understand that you are not acting as a teacher.*** A peer reviewer's role is that of a fresh reader. You can help the writer appreciate what it's like to encounter his or her text for the first time. Your primary responsibility is to articulate your understanding of what the writer's words say to you and to identify places where you get confused, where you need more details, where you have doubts or queries, and so on. Although the specific kinds of evaluations called for in the Guidelines for Peer Reviews will be helpful, you don't need to be an expert offering solutions to every problem.

When you play the role of writer during a workshop session, your responsibilities parallel those of your peer reviewers. You need to provide a legible rough draft, preferably typed and double-spaced, that doesn't baffle the reader with illegible handwriting, crossouts, arrows, and confusing pagination. Your instructor may ask you to bring photocopies of your draft for all group members. During the workshop, your primary responsibility is to *listen,* taking in how others respond to your draft without becoming defensive. Many instructors also ask writers to formulate two or three specific questions about their drafts—questions they particularly want their reviewers to address. These questions might focus on something writers particularly like about their drafts or on specific problem areas or concerns.

Exchanging Drafts

An excellent system for exchanging drafts is to have each writer read his or her draft aloud while group members follow along in their own photocopies. We value reading drafts aloud when time allows. Reading expressively, with appropriate emphasis, helps writers distance themselves from their work and hear it anew. When you read your work silently to yourself, it's all too easy to patch up bits of broken prose in your head or to slide through confusing passages. But if you stumble over a passage while reading aloud, you can place a check mark in the margin to indicate where further attention is needed. Another benefit to reading aloud is perhaps more symbolic than pragmatic: Reading your work to others means that you are claiming responsibility for it, displaying your intention to reach a range of readers other than the teacher. And knowing that you will have to read your work aloud will encourage you to have that work in the best possible shape before bringing it to class.

Types of Peer Review Workshops

After you've read your draft aloud, the next stage of your peer review may take one of several forms, depending on your instructor's preference. We describe here two basic strategies: response-centered workshops, and advice-centered workshops. Additional strategies often build on these approaches.

Response-Centered Workshops

This process-oriented, non-intrusive approach places maximum responsibility on the writer for making decisions about what to change in a draft. After the writer reads the draft aloud, group members follow this procedure:

1. All participants take several minutes to make notes on their copies of the manuscript. We recommend using the wavy line, "Good!", "?" system described in the Guidelines for Peer Reviews.
2. Group members take turns describing to the writer their responses to the piece—where they agreed or disagreed with the writer's ideas, where they got confused, where they wanted more development, and so forth. Group members do not give advice; they simply describe their own personal response to the draft as written.
3. The writer takes notes during each response but does not enter into a discussion. The writer listens without trying to defend the piece or explain what he or she intended.

No one gives the writer explicit advice. Group members simply describe their reactions to the piece and leave it to the writer to make appropriate changes.

Advice-Centered Workshops

In this more product-oriented and directive approach, peer reviewers typically work in pairs. Each writer exchanges drafts with a partner, reviews the draft carefully, and then writes specific advice on how to improve the draft. This method works best when peer reviewers use the Guidelines for Peer Reviews that conclude each chapter in Part Two, either addressing all the questions in the guidelines or focusing on specific questions specified by the instructor.

A variation on this approach, which allows peer reviewers to collaborate in pairs when analyzing a draft, uses the following process:

1. The instructor divides the class into initial groups of four.
2. Each group then divides into pairs; each pair exchanges drafts with the other pair.
3. The members of each pair collaborate to compose jointly written reviews of the two drafts they have received.
4. The drafts and the collaboratively written reviews are then returned to the original writers. If time remains, the two pairs meet to discuss their reviews.

When two students collaborate to review a draft, they often produce more useful and insightful reviews than when working individually. In sharing observations and negotiating their responses, they can write their reviews with more confidence and reduce the chances of idiosyncratic advice.

However, because each pair has received two drafts and has to write two peer reviews, this approach takes more class time. Instructors can speed this process by setting up the groups of four in advance and asking pairs to exchange and read drafts prior to the class meeting. Class time can then be focused on collaborative writing of the reviews.

Responding to Peer Reviews

After you and your classmates have gone over each other's papers and walked each other through the responses, everyone should identify two or three things about his or her draft that particularly need work. Before you leave the session, you should have some notion about how you want to revise your paper.

You may get mixed or contradictory responses from different reviewers. One reviewer may praise a passage that another finds confusing or illogical. Conflicting advice is a frustrating fact of life for all writers, whether students or professionals. Such disagreements reveal how readers cocreate a text with a writer: each brings to the text a different background, set of values, and way of reading.

It is important to remember that you are in charge of your own writing. If several readers offer the same critique of a passage, then no matter how much you love that passage, you probably need to follow their advice. But when readers disagree, you have to make your own best judgment about whom to heed.

Once you have received advice from others, reread your draft again slowly and then develop a revision plan, allowing yourself time to make sweeping, global changes if needed. You also need to remember that you can never make your draft perfect. Plan when you will bring the process to a close so that you can turn in a finished product on time and get on with your other classes and your life. (See our advice on *satisficing* on p. 489.)

CHAPTER SUMMARY

This chapter has focused on the writing processes of experts, showing how experienced writers use multiple drafts to solve subject-matter and rhetorical problems. We have also offered advice on how to improve your own writing processes. Particularly, beginning college writers need to understand the kinds of changes writers typically make in drafts, to role-play a reader's perspective when they revise, and to practice the revision strategies of experts. Because peer reviewing is a powerful strategy for learning how to revise, we showed you how to make "readerly" rather than "writerly" comments on a rough draft and how to participate productively in peer review workshops.

CHAPTER 19

Composing and Revising Closed-Form Prose

[Form is] an arousing and fulfillment of desires. A work has form insofar as one part of it leads a reader to anticipate another part, to be gratified by the sequence.
—Kenneth Burke, Rhetorician

I think the writer ought to help the reader as much as he can without damaging what he wants to say; and I don't think it ever hurts the writer to sort of stand back now and then and look at his stuff as if he were reading it instead of writing it.
—James Jones, Writer

Chapter 18 explained the composing processes of experienced writers and suggested ways that you can improve your own writing processes. In this chapter we present ten lessons in composing and revising closed-form prose. This chapter is not intended to be read in one sitting, lest you suffer from information overload. To help you learn the material efficiently, we have made each lesson a self-contained unit that can be read comfortably in half an hour or less and discussed in class as part of a day's session. You will benefit most from these lessons if you focus on one lesson at a time and then return to the lessons periodically as you progress through the term. Each lesson's advice will become increasingly meaningful and relevant as you gain experience as a writer.

The first lesson—on reader expectations—is intended as a theoretical overview to the rest of the chapter. The remaining nine lessons can then be assigned and read in any order your instructor desires. You will learn how to convert loose structures into thesis/support structures (Lesson 2); how to plan and visualize your structure (Lesson 3); how to create effective titles and introductions (Lesson 4); how to use topic sentences, transitions, and the old/new contract to guide your readers through the twists and turns of your prose (Lessons 5–7); how to create an effective document design (Lesson 8); how to perform several common writer's "moves" for developing your ideas (Lesson 9); and, finally, how to write good conclusions (Lesson 10). Together these lessons will teach you strategies for making your closed-form prose reader-friendly, well structured, clear, and persuasive.

LESSON 1: UNDERSTANDING READER EXPECTATIONS

In this opening lesson, we show you how to think like a reader. Imagine for a moment that your readers have only so much *reader energy,* which they can use either to follow and respond to your ideas (the result you want) or to puzzle over what you are trying to say (the result you don't want).* Skilled readers make predictions about where a text is heading based on clues provided by the writer. When readers get lost, the writer has often failed to give clues about where the text is going or has failed to do what the reader predicted. "Whoa, you lost me on the turn," a reader might say. "How does this passage relate to what you just said?" To write effective closed-form prose, you need to help readers see how each part of your text is related to what came before. (Sometimes with open-form prose, surprise or puzzlement may be the very effect you want to create. But with closed-form prose this kind of puzzlement is fatal.)

In this lesson we explain what readers of closed-form prose need in order to predict where a text is heading. Specifically we show you that readers need three things in a closed-form text:

- ▦ They need unity and coherence.
- ▦ They need old information before new information.
- ▦ They need forecasting and fulfillment.

Let's look at each in turn.

Unity and Coherence

Together the terms *unity* and *coherence* are defining characteristics of closed-form prose. *Unity* refers to the relationship between each part of an essay and the larger whole. *Coherence* refers to the relationship between adjacent sentences, paragraphs, and parts. The following thought exercise will illustrate your own expectations for unity and coherence:

Thought Exercise 1

Read the following two passages and try to explain why each fails to satisfy your expectations as a reader:

A. Recent research has given us much deeper—and more surprising—insights into the father's role in childrearing. My family is typical of the east side in that we never had much money. Their tongues became black and hung out of their mouths. The

---

*For the useful term *reader energy,* we are indebted to George Gopen and Judith Swan, "The Science of Scientific Writing," *American Scientist* 78 (1990): 550–559. In addition, much of our discussion of writing in this chapter is indebted to the work of Joseph Williams, George Gopen, and Gregory Colomb. See especially Gregory G. Colomb and Joseph M. Williams, "Perceiving Structure in Professional Prose: A Multiply Determined Experience," in Lee Odell and Dixie Goswamie (eds.), *Writing in Nonacademic Settings* (New York: The Guilford Press, 1985), pp. 87–128.

back-to-basics movement got a lot of press, fueled as it was by fears of growing illit-
eracy and cultural demise.

    B. Recent research has given us much deeper—and more surprising—insights into
the father's role in childrearing. Childrearing is a complex process that is frequently
investigated by psychologists. Psychologists have also investigated sleep patterns
and dreams. When we are dreaming, psychologists have shown, we are often reviewing recent events in our lives.

If you are like most readers, Passage A comically frustrates your expectations
because it is a string of random sentences. Because the sentences don't relate
either to each other or to a larger point, Passage A is neither unified nor coherent.

Passage B frustrates expectations in a subtler way. If you aren't paying attention, Passage B may seem to make sense because each sentence is linked to the
one before it. But the individual sentences don't develop a larger whole: the topics switch from a father's role in childrearing to psychology to sleep patterns to
the function of dreams.

To fulfill a reader's expectations, then, a closed-form passage must be both unified and coherent:

    C. *(Unified and coherent)* Recent research has given us much deeper—and more
surprising—insights into the father's role in childrearing. It shows that in almost
all of their interactions with children, fathers do things a little differently from
mothers. What fathers do—their special parenting style—is not only highly complementary to what mothers do but is by all indications important in its own
right. [The passage continues by showing the special ways that fathers contribute
to childrearing.]

This passage makes a unified point—that fathers have an important role in childrearing. Because all the parts relate to that whole (unity) and because the connections from sentence to sentence are clear (coherence), the passage satisfies our
expectations: It makes sense.

Because achieving unity and coherence is a major goal in revising closed-form
prose, we'll refer frequently to these concepts in later lessons.

Old Before New

One dominant way that readers process information and register ideas is by moving from already known (old) information to new information. In a nutshell, this
concept means that new material is meaningful to a reader only if it is linked to
old material that is already meaningful. To illustrate this concept, consider the
arrangement of names and numbers in a telephone directory. Because we read
from left to right, we want people's names in the left column and the telephone
numbers in the right column. A person's name is the old, familiar information we
already know and the number is the new, unknown information that we seek. If
the numbers were in the left column and the names in the right, we would have
to read backward.

    You can see the same old-before-new principle at work in the following
thought exercise:

Thought Exercise 2

You are a passenger on an airplane flight into Chicago and need to transfer to Flight 29 to Atlanta. As you descend into Chicago, the flight attendant announces transfer gates. Which of the following formats is easier for you to process? Why?

Option A	Option B
To Memphis on Flight 16 Gate B20	Gate B20 Flight 16 to Memphis
To Dallas on Flight 35 Gate C25	Gate C25 Flight 35 to Dallas
To Atlanta on Flight 29 Gate C12	Gate C12 Flight 29 to Atlanta

If you are like most readers, you prefer Option A, which puts old information before new. In this case, the old/known information is our destination and per- haps our flight number (To Atlanta on Flight 29). The new/unknown information is Gate C12. Option B causes us to expend more energy than does Option A because it forces us to hold the number of each gate in memory until we hear its corresponding city and flight number. Whereas Option A allows us to relax until we hear the word "Atlanta," Option B forces us to concentrate intensely on each gate number until we find the meaningful one.

The principle of old before new has great explanatory power for writers. At the level of the whole essay, this principle helps writers establish the main structural frame and ordering principle of their argument. An argument's frame derives from the writer's purpose to change some aspect of the reader's view of the topic. The reader's original view of the topic—what we might call the common, expect- ed, or ordinary view—constitutes old/known/familiar material. The writer's sur- prising view constitutes the new/unknown/unfamiliar material. The writer's hope is to move readers from their original view to the writer's new and different view. By understanding what constitutes old/familiar information to readers, the writer can determine how much background to provide, how to anticipate read- ers' objections, and how to structure material by moving from the old to the new. We discuss these matters in more depth in Lesson 4, on writing effective introductions.

At the sentence level, the principle of old before new also helps writers create coherence between adjacent parts and sentences. Most sentences in an essay should contain both an old element and a new element. To create coherence, the writer begins with the old material, which links back to something earlier, and then puts the new material at the end of the sentence. (See the discussion of the old/new contract in Lesson 7.)

Forecasting and Fulfillment

Finally, readers of closed-form prose expect writers to forecast what is coming and then to fulfill those forecasts. To appreciate what we mean by forecasting and ful- fillment, try one more thought exercise:

Thought Exercise 3

Although the following paragraph describes a simple procedure in easy-to-follow sentences, most readers still scratch their heads in bewilderment. Why? What makes the passage difficult to understand?

> The procedure is actually quite simple. First, you arrange things into different groups. Of course, one pile may be sufficient depending on how much there is to do. If you have to go somewhere else due to lack of facilities, that is the next step; otherwise, you are pretty well set. Next you operate the machines according to the instructions. After the procedure is completed, one arranges the materials into different groups again. Then they can be put in their appropriate places. Eventually, they will be used once more and the whole cycle will have to be repeated. However, that is part of life.

Most readers report being puzzled about the paragraph's topic. Because the opening sentence doesn't provide enough context to tell them what to expect, the paragraph makes no forecast that can be fulfilled. Now try rereading the paragraph, but this time substitute the following opening sentence:

> The procedure for washing clothes is actually quite simple.

With the addition of "for washing clothes," the sentence provides a context that allows you to predict and understand what's coming. In the language of cognitive psychologists, this new opening sentence provides a schema for interpretation. A *schema* is the reader's mental picture of a structure for upcoming material. The new opening sentence allows you as reader to say mentally, "This paragraph will describe a procedure for washing clothes and argue that it is simple." When the schema proves accurate, you experience the pleasure of prediction and fulfillment. In the language of rhetorician Kenneth Burke, the reader's experience of form is "an arousing and fulfillment of desires."

What readers expect from a closed-form text, then, is an ability to predict what is coming as well as regular fulfillment of those predictions. Writers forecast what is coming in a variety of ways: by writing effective titles and introductions, by putting points at the beginning of paragraphs, by creating effective transitions and mapping statements, and by using effective headings and subheadings if appropriate for the genre. To meet their readers' needs for predictions and fulfillment, closed-form writers start and end with the big picture. They tell readers where they are going before they start the journey, they refer to this big picture at key transition points, and they refocus on the big picture in their conclusion.

Summary

In this lesson we explained that to think like a reader, you need to understand a reader's needs and expectations. The three needs we explained—unity and coherence, old before new, and prediction and fulfillment—all work together when a reader construes meaning from a text. Your knowledge of these expectations will give you a theoretical basis for understanding the practical advice in the lessons that follow.

LESSON 2: CONVERTING LOOSE STRUCTURES INTO THESIS/SUPPORT STRUCTURES

In Lesson 1 we described readers' expectations for unity and coherence, old information before new, and forecasting and fulfillment. In academic contexts, readers also expect closed-form prose to have a thesis/support structure. As we explained in Chapter 3, most closed-form academic writing—especially writing with the aim of analysis or persuasion—is governed by a contestable or risky thesis statement. Because developing and supporting a thesis is complex work requiring much critical thought, writers sometimes retreat into loose structures that are easier to compose than a thesis-based argument with points and particulars.

In this lesson we help you better understand thesis-based writing by contrasting it with prose that looks like thesis-based writing but isn't. We show you three common ways in which inexperienced writers give the appearance of writing thesis-based prose while actually retreating from the rigors of making and developing an argument. Avoiding the pitfalls of these loose structures can go a long way toward improving your performance on most college writing assignments.

And Then Writing, or Chronological Structure

Chronological structure, often called *narrative,* is the most common organizing principle of open-form prose. It may also be used selectively in closed-form prose to support a point. But sometimes the writer begins recounting the details of a story until chronological order takes over, driving out the thesis-based structure of points and particulars.

To a large degree, chronological order is the default mode we fall into when we aren't sure how to organize material. For example, if you were asked to analyze a fictional character, you might slip into a plot summary instead. In much the same way, you might substitute historical chronology ("First A happened, then B happened . . .") for historical analysis ("B happened because A happened . . ."); or you might give a chronological recounting of your research ("First I discovered A, then I discovered B . . .") instead of organizing your material into an argument ("I question A's account of this phenomenon on the grounds of B's recent findings . . .").

The tendency toward loose chronological structure is revealed in the following example from a student's essay on Shakespeare's *The Tempest.* This excerpt is from the introduction of the student's first draft:

Plot Summary—*And Then* Writing

Prospero cares deeply for his daughter. In the middle of the play Prospero acts like a gruff father and makes Ferdinand carry logs in order to test his love for Miranda and Miranda's love for him. In the end, though, Prospero is a loving father who rejoices in his daughter's marriage to a good man.

Here the student seems simply to retell the play's plot without any apparent thesis. (The body of her rough draft primarily retold the same story in more detail.) However, during an office conference, the instructor discovered that the student regarded her sentence about Prospero's being a loving father as her thesis. In fact, the student had gotten in an argument with a classmate over whether Prospero was a good person or an evil one. The instructor helped her convert her draft into a thesis/support structure:

Revised Introduction—Thesis/Support Structure

Many persons believe that Prospero is an evil person in the play. They claim that Prospero exhibits a harsh, destructive control over Miranda and also, like Faust, seeks superhuman knowledge through his magic. However, I contend that Prospero is a kind and loving father.

This revised version implies a problem (What kind of father is Prospero?), presents a view that the writer wishes to change (Prospero is harsh and hateful), and asserts a contestable thesis (Prospero is a loving father). The body of her paper can now be converted from plot summary to an argument with reasons and evidence supporting her claim that Prospero is loving.

This student's revision from an *and then* to a thesis/support structure is typical of many writers' experience. Because recounting events chronologically is a natural way to organize, many writers—even very experienced ones—lapse into long stretches of *and then* writing in their rough drafts. However, experienced writers have learned to recognize these *and then* sections in their drafts and to rework this material into a closed-form, thesis-based structure.

All About Writing, or Encyclopedic Structure

Whereas *and then* writing turns essays into stories by organizing details chronologically, *all about* writing turns essays into encyclopedia articles by piling up details in heaps. When *all about* writing organizes these heaps into categories, it can appear to be well organized: "Having told you everything I learned about educational opportunities in Cleveland, I will now tell you everything I learned about the Rock and Roll Hall of Fame." But the categories do not function as points and particulars in support of a thesis. Rather, like the shelving system in a library, they are simply ways of arranging information for convenient retrieval, not a means of building a hierarchical structure.

To illustrate the differences between *all about* writing and thesis-based writing, consider the case of two students choosing to write term papers on the subject of female police officers. One student is asked simply to write "all about" the topic; the other is asked to pose and investigate some problem related to female police officers and to support a thesis addressing that problem. In all likelihood, the first student would produce an initial outline with headings such as the following:

I. History of women in police roles

    A. Female police or soldiers in ancient times

    B. 19th century (Calamity Jane)

    C. 1900s–1960

    D. 1960–present

II. How female police officers are selected and trained

III. A typical day in the life of a female police officer

IV. Achievements and acts of heroism of female police officers

V. What the future holds for female police officers

Such a paper is a data dump that places into categories all the information the writer has uncovered. It is riskless, and, except for occasional new information, surpriseless. In contrast, when a student focuses on a significant question—one that grows out of the writer's own interests and demands engagement—the writing can be quite compelling.

Consider the case of a student, Lynnea, who wrote a research paper entitled "Women Police Officers: Should Size and Strength Be Criteria for Patrol Duty?" Her essay begins with a group of male police officers complaining about being assigned to patrol duty with a new female officer, Connie Jones (not her real name), who is four feet ten inches tall and weighs ninety pounds. Here is the rest of the introduction to Lynnea's essay.

> Connie Jones has just completed police academy training and has been assigned to patrol duty in _____. Because she is so small, she has to have a booster seat in her patrol car and has been given a special gun, since she can barely manage to pull the trigger of a standard police-issue .38 revolver. Although she passed the physical requirements at the academy, which involved speed and endurance running, situps, and monkey bar tests, most of the officers in her department doubt her ability to perform competently as a patrol officer. But nevertheless she is on patrol because men and women receive equal assignments in most of today's police forces. But is this a good policy? Can a person who is significantly smaller and weaker than her peers make an effective patrol officer?

Lynnea examined all the evidence she could find—through library and field research (interviewing police officers) and arrived at the following thesis: "Because concern for public safety overrides all other concerns, police departments should set stringent size and strength requirements for patrol officers, even if these criteria exclude many women." This thesis has plenty of tension because it sets limits on equal rights for women. Because Lynnea considers herself a feminist, it caused her considerable distress to advocate setting these limits and placing public safety ahead of gender equity. The resulting essay is engaging precisely because of the tension it creates and the controversy it engenders.

Engfish Writing, or Structure without Surprise

Unlike the chronological story and the *all about* paper, the *engfish* essay has a thesis.* But the thesis is a riskless truism supported with predictable reasons—often structured as the three body paragraphs in a traditional five-paragraph theme. It is fill-in-the-blank writing: "The food service is bad for three reasons. First, it is bad because the food is not tasty. Blah, blah, blah about tasteless food. Second, it is bad because it is too expensive. Blah, blah, blah about the expense." And so on. The writer is on autopilot and is not contributing to a real conversation about a real question. In some situations, writers use engfish intentionally: bureaucrats and politicians may want to avoid saying something risky; students may want to avoid writing about complex matters that they fear they do not fully understand.

---

*The term *engfish* was coined by the textbook writer Ken Macrorie to describe a fishy kind of canned prose that bright but bored students mechanically produce to please their teachers. See Ken Macrorie, *Telling Writing* (Rochelle Park, NJ: Hayden Press, 1970).

In the end, using engfish is bad not because what you say is *wrong,* but because what you say couldn't *possibly be* wrong. To avoid engfish, stay focused on the need to surprise your reader.

Summary

This lesson has explained strategies for converting *and then, all about,* and engfish writing into thesis/support writing. Your goal as a closed-form academic writer is to pose a problematic question about your topic and, in response to it, assert a contestable thesis that you must support with points and particulars.

For Writing and Discussion

As a class, choose a topic from popular culture such as TV talk shows, tattooing, eating disorders, rock lyrics, or something similar.

1. Working as a whole class or in small groups, give examples of how you might write about this topic in an *and then* way, an *all about* way, and an engfish way.
2. Then develop one or more questions about the topic that could lead to thesis/support writing. What contestable theses can your class create?

LESSON 3: PLANNING AND VISUALIZING YOUR STRUCTURE

As we explained in Lesson 2, closed-form writing supports a contestable thesis through a hierarchical network of points and particulars. One way to visualize this structure is to outline its skeleton, an exercise that makes visually clear that not all points are on equal levels. The highest-level point is an essay's thesis statement, which is usually supported by several main points that are in turn supported by subpoints and sub-subpoints, all of which are supported by their own particulars. In this lesson we show you how to create such a hierarchical structure for your own papers and how to visualize this structure through an outline, tree diagram, or flowchart.

At the outset, we want to emphasize two important points. First, structural diagrams are not rigid molds, but flexible planning devices that evolve as your thinking shifts and changes. The structure of your final draft may be substantially different from your initial scratch outline. In fact, we want to show you how your outlines or diagrams can help you generate more ideas and reshape your structure.

Second, outlines or diagrams organize *meanings,* not topics. Note that in all our examples of outlines, diagrams, and flowcharts, we write *complete sentences* rather than phrases in the high-level slots. We do so because sentences can make a point, which conveys meaning, unlike a phrase, which identifies a topic but doesn't make an assertion about it. Any point—whether a thesis, a main point, or a subpoint—is a contestable assertion that requires its own particulars for support.

By using complete sentences rather than phrases in an outline, the writer is forced to articulate the point of each section of the emerging argument.

With this background, we now proceed to a sequence of steps you can take to plan and visualize a structure.

Use Scratch Outlines Early in the Writing Process

Many writers can't make a detailed outline of their arguments until they have written exploratory drafts. At these early stages, writers often make brief scratch outlines that list the main ideas they want to develop initially or they make a list of points that emerged from a freewrite or a very early draft. Here is student writer Christopher Leigh's initial scratch outline for his argument against metal detectors in schools.

> Schools should not use metal detectors as a way of reducing violence.

▧ Media have created a panic.

▧ Metal detectors are easily defeated.

▧ Students hate them.

▧ Should I put in a section on whether they violate rights???

▧ Poland article shows we should put the money into creating better school atmosphere.

We first introduced Christopher's research problem in Chapter 1, p 10. Christopher's final paper is shown in Chapter 23, pp. 647–658.

Before Making a Detailed Outline, "Nutshell" Your Argument

As you explore your topic and begin drafting, your ideas will gradually become clearer and more structured. You can accelerate this process through a series of short exercises that will help you "nutshell" your argument (see Figure 19.1).

The six exercises in this figure cause you to look at your argument from different perspectives, helping you clarify the question you are addressing, articulate the kind of change you want to make in your audience's view of your topic, and directly state your purpose, thesis, and tentative title. The authors of this text often use this exercise in one-on-one writing conferences to help students create an initial focus from a swirl of ideas. We recommend that you write out your responses to each exercise as a preliminary step in helping you visualize your structure. Here are Christopher Leigh's responses to these questions:

> **Exercise 1:** I was initially puzzled by how best to reduce school violence. When I found that many schools were using metal detectors, I wondered whether this was a good approach.
>
> **Exercise 2:** Before reading my paper, my readers will believe that metal detectors are a good way to reduce school violence. After reading my paper, my readers will realize that there are many problems with metal detectors and will want to put money instead into improving the school environment.
>
> **Exercise 3:** The purpose of my paper is to argue against metal detectors and to argue for a better school environment.

Exercise 1	What puzzle or problem initiated your thinking about X?
Exercise 2	*(Paradigm: Many people think X, but I am going to argue Y.)*

Before reading my paper, my readers will think this about my topic:

_____.

But after reading my paper, my readers will think this new way about my topic:

_____.

Exercise 3	The purpose of my paper is _____.
Exercise 4	My paper addresses the following question: _____.
Exercise 5	My one-sentence summary answer to the above question is this:

_____.

Exercise 6	A tentative title for my paper is this: _____.

FIGURE 19.1 ■ Exercises for Nutshelling Your Argument

Exercise 4: Should schools use metal detectors? Are metal detectors a good way to reduce school violence?

Exercise 5: Metal detectors should not be used in schools because there are other, more effective, and less costly alternatives for violence prevention.

Exercise 6: The Case Against Metal Detectors in Schools.

Articulate a Working Thesis and Main Points

Once you have nutshelled your argument, you are ready to visualize a structure containing several sections, parts, or chunks, each of which is headed by a main point and supported with particulars. Try answering these questions:

1. *My working thesis statement is:*
2. *The main sections or chunks needed in my paper are:*

Here are Christopher Leigh's answers to these questions:

1. Metal detectors should not be used in schools because there is no basis for panic about violence and because there are other, more effective, and less costly alternatives for violence prevention.
2. (a) A section on the media's having created a panic; (b) a big section on the arguments against metal detectors; (c) a section on my solution, which is to improve the school atmosphere.

Sketch Your Structure Using an Outline, Tree Diagram, or Flowchart

At this point you can make an initial structural sketch of your argument and use the sketch to plan out the subpoints and particulars necessary to support the main points. We offer you three different ways to visualize your argument: outlines, tree diagrams, and flowcharts. Use whichever strategy best fits your way of thinking and perceiving.

Outlines

The most common way of visualizing structure is the traditional outline, which uses letters and numerals to indicate levels of points, subpoints, and particulars. If you prefer outlines, we recommend that you use the outlining feature of your word processing program, which allows you to move and insert material and change heading levels with great flexibility. Here is Christopher Leigh's detailed outline of his argument:

> Thesis: Except for schools with severe threats of danger, metal detectors should not be used because there is no basis for panic and because there are other, more effective, and less costly alternatives for violence prevention in schools.
>
> I. Media have created panic over school violence.
>
>   A. School violence is actually quite rare.
>
>   B. Frequency of weapons being brought to school has declined since 1993.
>
> II. There are many strong arguments against use of metal detectors.
>
>   A. Metal detectors may violate student rights.
>
>   1. Quotations from students reveal belief that metal detectors violate their rights.
>
>   2. Court rulings leave gray areas.
>
>   B. Metal detectors are easily defeated.
>
>   1. They can't close off all entrances.
>
>   2. A shooter can always find a way to get guns inside.
>
>   C. Metal detectors are costly.
>
>   D. Metal detectors have bad psychological consequences for students.
>
>   1. Quotations from students show students' dislike of prison atmosphere.
>
>   2. Metal detectors create feeling of distrust and humiliation.
>
> III. A better solution is to use the money spent on metal detectors to provide a better school atmosphere.
>
>   A. Quotation from high school senior Malik Barry-Buchanan shows need to create respect and caring in the schools.
>
>   B. Article by Poland shows need to make schools more personal and to provide more counseling.

      1. Teachers should make efforts to know each student as an individual.

      2. Extracurricular activities should not be cut.

      3. Schools should provide more counseling.

IV. Conclusion

Tree Diagrams

A tree diagram displays a hierarchical structure visually, using horizontal and vertical space instead of letters and numbers. Figure 19.2 shows Christopher's argument as a tree diagram. His thesis is at the top of the tree. His main reasons, written as point sentences, appear as branches beneath his claim. Supporting evidence and arguments are displayed as subbranches beneath each reason.

Unlike outlines, tree diagrams allow us to *see* the hierarchical relationship of points and particulars. When you develop a point with subpoints or particulars, you move down the tree. When you switch to a new point, you move across the tree to make a new branch. Our own teaching experience suggests that for many writers, this visual/spatial technique, which engages more areas of the brain than the more purely verbal outline, produces fuller, more detailed, and more logical arguments than does a traditional outline.

Flowcharts

Many writers prefer an informal, hand-sketched flowchart as an alternative to an outline or tree diagram. The flowchart presents the sequence of sections as separate boxes, inside which (or next to which) the writer notes the material needed to fill each box. A flowchart of Christopher's essay is shown in Figure 19.3.

Let the Structure Evolve

Once you have sketched out an initial structural diagram, use it to generate ideas. Tree diagrams are particularly helpful because they invite you to place question marks on branches to "hold open" spots for new points or for supporting particulars. If you have only two main points, for example, you could draw a third main branch and place a question mark under it to encourage you to think of another supporting idea. Likewise, if a branch has few supporting particulars, add question marks beneath it. The trick is to think of your structural diagrams as evolving sketches rather than rigid blueprints. As your ideas grow and change, revise your structural diagram, adding or removing points, consolidating and refocusing sections, moving parts around, or filling in details.

Summary

This lesson has shown you the value of nutshelling your argument as a preliminary step toward visualizing a structure. The nutshelling exercise helps you articulate the change you are trying to bring about in your reader and clarify your

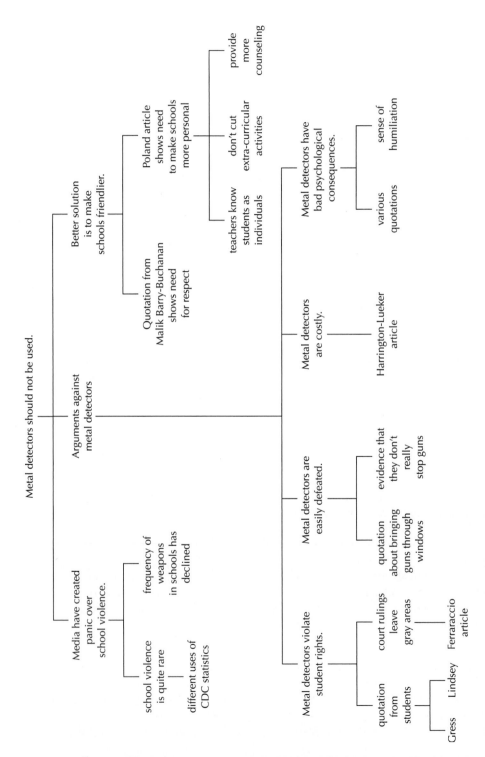

FIGURE 19.2 ■ Christopher's Tree Diagram

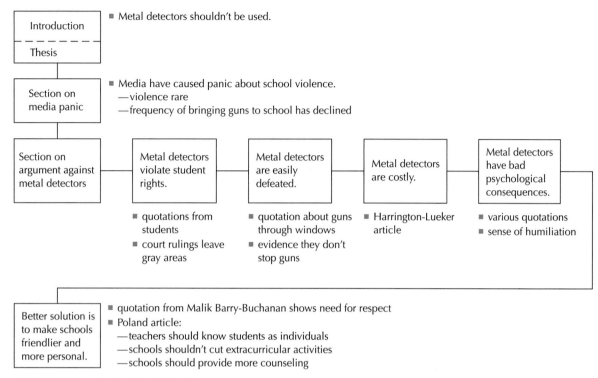

FIGURE 19.3 ■ Christopher's Flowchart

purpose, thesis, and main supporting points. You can then use outlines, tree diagrams, or flowcharts to help you visualize your structure and use it to develop new ideas. Outlines or diagrams are most powerful if you write complete sentences rather than phrases at the top levels of the structure.

For Writing and Discussion

1. Working individually or in small groups, make a traditional outline, a tree diagram, and a flowchart of David Rockwood's argument against wind-generated electricity on pages 13–14. Which method of representing structure works best for you?

2. **Individual task:** For a current writing project, visualize the structure of your ideas by creating an outline, tree diagram, or flowchart. To help you organize *meanings* rather than *topics,* write complete sentences for your higher level points. Add place-holding question marks at locations where you may wish to add more ideas or details. If you haven't yet written a draft, you might choose to start with a scratch list of main points or sections. If you have already written a draft, use your outline, tree diagram, or flowchart to analyze its present structure and plan revisions.

(continued)

> **Group task:** Working with a partner or in small groups, show how you visualized your structure and share insights or discoveries you learned from the process. What did you find most difficult or challenging? What did you learn that was helpful?

LESSON 4: WRITING EFFECTIVE TITLES AND INTRODUCTIONS

Because effective titles and introductions give readers a big-picture overview of a paper's argument, writers often can't compose them until they have finished one or more exploratory drafts. But as soon as you know your essay's big picture, you'll find that writing titles and introductions follows some general principles that are easy to learn.

What Not to Do: The "Funnel Introduction"

Some students have been taught an opening strategy, sometimes called the "funnel," that encourages students to start with broad generalizations and then narrow down to their topics. This strategy often leads to vapid generalizations in the opening sentences, as the following example shows:

> Since time immemorial people have pondered the question of freedom. What it means to be free was asked by the great philosophers of ancient Greece and Rome, and the question has echoed through the ages up until the present day. One modern psychologist who asked this question was B. F. Skinner, who wanted to study whether humans had free will or were programmed by their environment to act the way they did. . . .

Here the writer eventually gets to his subject, B. F. Skinner. But the opening sentences are snoozers. A better approach, as we will show, is to hook immediately into your readers' interests.

From Old to New: The General Principle of Closed-Form Introductions

We introduced the principle of old before new in Lesson 1. See pp. 499–500.

Whereas the broad-to-narrow strategy is mechanical, the strategy we show you in this lesson, based on the principle of old information before new information, is dynamic and powerful. Old information is something your readers already know and find interesting before they start reading your essay. New information is the surprise of your argument, the unfamiliar material that you add to your readers' understanding.

Because the writer's thesis statement forecasts the new information the paper will present, a thesis statement for a closed-form essay typically comes *at the end of the introduction*. What precedes the thesis is typically the old, familiar information that the reader needs in order to understand the conversation that the thesis joins. In most closed-form prose, particularly in academic prose, this old information is the problem or question that the thesis addresses. A typical closed-form introduction has the following shape:

See the explanation of a prototypical academic introduction in Chapter 2, pp. 29–31.

PROBLEM
[old information]
↓
THESIS
[new information]

The length and complexity of your introduction is a function of how much your reader already knows and cares about the question or problem your paper addresses. The function of an introduction is to capture the reader's interest in the first few sentences, to identify and explain the question or problem that the essay addresses, to provide any needed background information, and to present the thesis. You can leave out any of the first three elements if the reader is already hooked on your topic and already knows the question you are addressing. For example, in an essay exam you can usually start with your thesis statement because you can assume the instructor already knows the question and finds it interesting.

To illustrate how an effective closed-form introduction takes the reader from the question to the thesis, consider how the following student writer revised his introduction to a paper on Napster.com.

Original Introduction (Confusing)

Napster is all about sharing, not stealing, as record companies and some musicians would like us to think. Napster is an online program that was released in October of '99. Napster lets users easily search for and trade mp3s—compressed, high-quality music files that can be produced from a CD. Napster is the leading file sharing community; it allows users to locate and share music. It also provides instant messaging, chat rooms, an outlet for fans to identify new artists, and a forum to communicate their interests.

Thesis statement

Background on Napster

Most readers find this introduction confusing. The writer begins with his thesis statement before the reader is introduced to the question that the thesis addresses. He seems to assume that his reader is already a part of the Napster conversation, and yet in the next sentences, he gives background on Napster. If the reader needs background on Napster, then the reader also needs background on the Napster controversy. In rethinking his assumptions about old-versus-new information for his audience, this writer decides he wants to reach general newspaper readers who may have heard about a lawsuit against Napster and are interested in the issue but aren't sure of what Napster is or how it works. Here is his revised introduction.

Revised Introduction (Clearer)

Several months ago the rock band Metallica filed a lawsuit against Napster.com, an online program that lets users easily search for and trade mp3s—compressed, high-quality music files that can be produced from a CD. Napster.com has been wildly popular among music lovers because it creates a virtual community where

Triggers readers' memory of lawsuit

Background on Napster

Clarification of problem (Implied question: Should Napster be shut down?)

Thesis —

users can locate and share music. It also provides instant messaging, chat rooms, an outlet for fans to identify new artists, and a forum to communicate their interests. But big-name bands like Metallica, alarmed at what they see as lost revenues, claim that Napster.com is stealing their royalties. However, Napster is all about sharing, not stealing, as some musicians would like us to think.

This revised introduction fills in the old information the reader needs in order to recall and understand the problem; then it presents the thesis.

Typical Elements of a Closed-Form Introduction

Now that you understand the general principle of closed-form introductions, let's look more closely at its four typical features or elements.

An Opening Attention-Grabber. The first few sentences in an introduction have to capture your reader's interest. If you aren't sure your reader is already interested in your problem, you can begin with an attention-grabber (what journalists call the "hook" or "lead"), which is typically a dramatic vignette, a startling fact or statistic, an arresting quotation, an interesting scene, or something else that taps into your reader's interests. Attention-grabbers are uncommon in academic prose (where you assume your reader will be initially engaged by the problem itself) but frequently used in popular prose. The student writer of the Napster paper initially toyed with the following attention-grabber to begin his essay:

> How many times have you liked one or two songs on a CD but thought the rest of it was garbage? How many times have you burned your own customized CDs by finding your favorite music on Napster.com? Well, that opportunity is about to be lost if Metallica wins its lawsuit against Napster.

He decided not to use this attention-grabber, however, because he wanted to reach audiences who weren't already users of Napster. He decided that these general readers were already interested in the lawsuit and didn't need the extra zing of an attention-grabber.

Explanation of the Question to Be Investigated. If you assume that your reader already knows about the problem and cares about it, then you need merely to summarize it. This problem or question is the starting point of your argument. Closed-form writers often state the question directly in a single sentence ending with a question mark, but sometimes they imply it, letting the reader formulate it from context. If you aren't sure whether your audience fully understands the question or fully cares about it, then you need to explain it in more detail showing why it is both problematic and significant.

Background Information. In order to understand the conversation you are joining, readers sometimes need background information—perhaps a definition of key terms, a summary of events leading up to the problem you're presenting, factual details needed for basic understanding of the problem, and so forth. In scientific papers, this background often includes a review of the preexisting literature on the problem. In the Napster introduction, the writer devotes several sentences to background on Napster.com.

The Brief Writing Project in Chapter 1 teaches you how to show that a question is problematic and significant. See pp. 19–23.

A Preview of the Whole. The final element of a closed-form introduction sketches the big picture of your essay by giving readers a sense of the whole. This preview is initially new information for your readers (this is why it comes at the end of the introduction). Once stated, however, it becomes old information that readers will use to locate their position in their journey through your argument. By predicting what's coming, this preview initiates the pleasurable process of prediction/fulfillment that we discussed in Lesson 1. Writers typically forecast the whole by stating their thesis, but they can also use a purpose statement or a blueprint statement to accomplish the same end. These strategies are the subject of the next section.

See this chapter's opening epigraph from rhetorician Kenneth Burke, p. 497.

Forecasting the Whole with a Thesis Statement, Purpose Statement, or Blueprint Statement

The most succinct way to forecast the whole is to state your thesis directly. Student writers often ask how detailed their thesis statements should be and whether it is permissible, sometimes, to delay revealing the thesis until the conclusion—an open-form move that gives papers a more exploratory, mystery-novel feel. It is useful, then, to outline briefly some of your choices as a writer. To illustrate a writer's options for forecasting the whole, we use Christopher Leigh's essay on metal detectors in schools that we discussed in Lesson 3.

To see the choices Christopher Leigh actually made, see his complete essay on pp. 647–658.

Options for Forecasting the Whole		
Option	**Explanation**	**Example**
Short thesis	State claim without summarizing your supporting argument or forecasting your structure.	Schools should not use metal detectors to reduce school violence.
Detailed thesis	Summarize whole argument; may begin with an "although" clause that summarizes the view you are trying to change.	Although metal detectors may be justified in schools with severe threats of danger, they should generally not be used because there is no basis for panic and because there are other, more effective and less costly alternatives for violence prevention in schools.
Purpose statement	State your purpose or intention without summarizing the argument. A purpose statement typically begins with a phrase such as "My purpose is to . . ." or "In the following paragraphs I wish to . . . :"	My purpose in this essay is to make a case against using metal detectors in schools.
Blueprint or mapping statement	Describe the structure of your essay by announcing the number of main parts and describing the function or purpose of each one.	First I show that the media have created a false panic about school violence. Next I present four reasons metal detectors have bad consequences. Finally I outline a better approach—making schools friendlier and more personal.

In addition you have at least two other options.

- *Multisentence summary.* In long articles, academic writers often use all three kinds of statements—a purpose statement, a thesis statement, and a blueprint statement. While this sort of extensive forecasting is common in academic and business writing, it occurs less frequently in informal or popular essays. Christopher decided that his paper wasn't complex enough to justify an extensive multisentence overview.

- *Thesis question.* When writers wish to delay their thesis until the middle or the end of their essays, letting their arguments slowly unfold and keeping their stance a mystery, they often end the introduction with a question. This open-form strategy invites readers to join the writer in a mutual search for the answer.

> Although I would prefer having no metal detectors in schools, I am strongly in favor of making schools safer. So the question of whether metal detectors are justified leaves me baffled and puzzled. Should schools use them or not? [This approach would have required a very different structure from the paper Christopher actually wrote.]

Which of these options should a writer choose? There are no firm rules to help you answer this question. How much you forecast in the introduction and where you reveal your thesis is a function of your purpose, audience, and genre. The more you forecast, the clearer your argument is and the easier it is to read quickly. You minimize the demands on readers' time by giving them the gist of your argument in the introduction, making it easier to skim your essay if they don't have time for a thorough reading. The less you forecast, the more demands you make on readers' time: you invite them, in effect, to accompany you through the twists and turns of your own thinking process, and you risk losing them if they become confused, lost, or bored. For these reasons, academic writing is generally closed form and aims at maximum clarity. In many rhetorical contexts, however, more open forms are appropriate.

Chapter 4, pp. 70–71, gives more advice on when to choose closed or open forms.

If you choose a closed-form structure, we can offer some advice on how much to forecast. Readers sometimes feel insulted by too much forecasting, so include only what is needed for clarity. For short papers, readers usually don't need to have the complete supporting argument forecast in the introduction. In longer papers, however, or in especially complex ones, readers appreciate having the whole argument forecast at the outset. Academic writing in particular tends to favor explicit and often detailed forecasting.

Writing Effective Titles

The strategies we have suggested for a closed-form introduction apply equally well to a closed-form title. A good title needs to have something old (a word or phrase that hooks into a reader's existing interests) and something new (a hint of the writer's thesis or purpose). Here is an example of an academic title:

> "Style as Politics: A Feminist Approach to the Teaching of Writing" [This title attracts scholars interested either in style or in feminist issues in writing (old); it promises to analyze the political implications of style (new).]

As this example shows, your title should provide a brief but detailed overview of what your paper is about. Academic titles are typically longer and more detailed than are titles in popular magazines. They usually follow one of four conventions:

1. Some titles simply state the question that the essay addresses:

   "Will Patriarchal Management Survive Beyond the Decade?"

2. Some titles state, often in abbreviated form, the essay's thesis:

   "The Writer's Audience Is Always a Fiction"

3. Very often the title is the last part of the essay's purpose statement:

   "The Relationship Between Client Expectation of Improvement and Psychotherapy Outcome"

4. Many titles consist of two parts separated by a colon. To the left of the colon the writer presents key words from the essay's issue or problem or a "mystery phrase" that arouses interest; to the right the author places the essay's question, thesis, or summary of purpose:

   "Money and Growth: An Alternative Approach"; "Deep Play: Notes on a Balinese Cockfight"; or "Fine Cloth, Cut Carefully: Cooperative Learning in British Columbia"

Although such titles might seem overly formal to you, they indicate how much a closed-form writer wishes to preview an article's big picture. Although their titles may be more informal, popular magazines often use these same strategies. Here are some titles from *Redbook* and the business magazine *Forbes:*

   "Is the Coffee Bar Trend About to Peak?" (question)
   "A Man *Can* Take Maternity Leave—And Love It" (abbreviated thesis)
   "Why the Department of Education Shouldn't Take Over the Student Loan Program" (last part of purpose statement)
   "Feed Your Face: Why Your Complexion Needs Vitamins" (two parts linked by colon)

Composing a title for your essay can help you find your focus when you get bogged down in the middle of a draft. Thinking about your title forces you to *nutshell* your ideas by seeing your project's big picture. It causes you to reconsider your purpose and to think about what's old and what's new for your audience.

Summary

In this lesson we have shown that titles and introductions must include old information that links to your readers' interests and new information that forecasts what is new, surprising, or challenging in your essay. The typical features of a closed-form introduction are the opening attention-grabber, an explanation of the problem to be investigated, background information, and a forecasting of the whole by means of a thesis statement, purpose statement, blueprint statement, or predictive question. Any element except the last can be omitted if the reader doesn't need it. Titles follow the same old/new principle as do introductions.

For Writing and Discussion

Individual task: Choose an essay you are currently working on or have recently completed and examine your title and introduction based on the advice in this lesson. Ask yourself these questions:

- ▩ What audience am I imagining? What do I assume are my readers' initial interests that will lead them to read my essay (the old information I must hook into)? What is new in my essay?
- ▩ Do I have an attention-grabber? Why or why not?
- ▩ Where do I state or imply the question or problem that my essay addresses?
- ▩ Do I explain why the question is problematic and significant? Why or why not?
- ▩ For my audience to understand the problem, do I provide too much background information, not enough, or just the right amount?
- ▩ What strategies do I use to forecast the whole?

Based on your analysis of your present title and introduction, revise as appropriate.

Group task: Working with a partner or in small groups, share the changes you made in your title or introduction and explain why you made the changes.

LESSON 5: PLACING POINTS BEFORE PARTICULARS

In our lesson on outlining (Lesson 3), we suggested that you write complete sentences rather than phrases for the high-level slots of the outline in order to articulate the *meaning* or *point* of each section of your argument. In this lesson we show you how to place these points where readers expect them: near the beginning of the sections or paragraphs they govern.

When you place points before particulars, you follow the same principle illustrated in Lesson 1 with the flight attendant announcing the name of the city before the departure gate (the city is the old information, the departure gate the new information). When you first state the point, it is the new information that the next paragraph or section will develop. Once you have stated it, it becomes old information that helps readers understand the meaning of the particulars that follow. If you withhold the point until later, the reader has to keep all the particulars in short-term memory until you finally reveal the point that the particulars are supposed to support or develop.

Place Topic Sentences at the Beginning of Paragraphs

Readers of closed-form prose need to have point sentences (usually called "topic sentences") at the beginnings of paragraphs. However, writers of rough drafts often don't fulfill this need because, as we explained in Chapter 18, drafting is an exploratory process in which writers are often still searching for their points as they compose. Consequently, in their rough drafts writers often omit topic sentences entirely or place them at the ends of paragraphs, or they write topic sentences that misrepresent what the paragraphs actually say. During revision, then, you should check your body paragraphs carefully to be sure you have placed accurate topic sentences near the beginning.

What follow are examples of the kinds of revisions writers typically make. We have annotated the examples to explain the changes the writer has made to make the paragraphs unified and clear to readers. The first example is from a later draft of the essay on dorm room carpets from Chapter 18 (pp. 492–493).

Revision—Topic Sentence First

Another reason for the university not to buy carpets is the cost.
According to Rachel Jones, Assistant Director of Housing Services, the initial purchase and installation of carpeting would cost $300 per room. Considering the number of rooms in the three residence halls, carpeting amounts to a substantial investment. Additionally, once the carpets are installed, the university would need to maintain them through the purchase of more vacuum cleaners and shampoo machines. This money would be better spent on other dorm improvements that would benefit more residents, such as expanded kitchen facilities and improved recreational space. ~~Thus carpets would be too expensive.~~

Topic sentence placed first

In the original draft, the writer states the point at the end of the paragraph. In his revision he states the point in an opening topic sentence that links back to the thesis statement, which promises "several reasons" that the university should not buy carpets for the dorms. The words "another reason" thus link the topic sentence to the argument's big picture.

Revise Paragraphs for Unity

In addition to placing topic sentences at the heads of paragraphs, writers often need to revise topic sentences to better match what the paragraph actually says, or revise the paragraph to better match the topic sentence. Paragraphs have unity when all their sentences develop the point stated in the topic sentence. Paragraphs in rough drafts are often not unified because they reflect the writer's shifting, evolving, thinking-while-writing process. Consider the following paragraph from an early draft of an argument against euthanasia by student writer Dao Do. Her peer reviewer labeled it "confusing." What makes it confusing?

We look at more examples from Dao's essay later in this chapter.

Early Draft—Confusing

First, euthanasia is wrong because no one has the right to take the life of another person. Some people say that euthanasia or suicide will end suffering and pain. But what proofs do they have for such a claim? Death is still mysterious to us; therefore, we do not know whether death will end suffering and pain or not. What seems to be the real claim is that death to those with illnesses will end our pain. Such pain involves worrying over them, paying their medical bills, and giving up so much of our time. Their deaths end our pain rather than theirs. And for that reason, euthanasia is a selfish act, for the outcome of euthanasia benefits us, the nonsufferers, more. Once the sufferers pass away, we can go back to our normal lives.

The paragraph opens with an apparent topic sentence: "Euthanasia is wrong because no one has the right to take the life of another person." But the rest of the paragraph doesn't focus on that point. Instead, it focuses on how euthanasia benefits the survivors more than the sick person. Dao had two choices: to revise the paragraph to fit the topic sentence or to revise the topic sentence to fit the paragraph. Here is her revision, which includes a different topic sentence and an additional sentence midparagraph to keep particulars focused on the opening point.

Revision for Unity

Revised topic sentence better forecasts focus of paragraph

First, euthanasia is wrong because it benefits the survivors more than the sick person. ~~First, euthanasia is wrong because no one has the right to take the life of another person.~~ Some people say that euthanasia

Keeps focus on "sick person"

or suicide will end *the sick person's* suffering and pain. But what proofs do they have for such a claim? Death is still mysterious to us; therefore,

Concludes subpoint about sick person

Moreover, modern pain killers can relieve most ~~most~~ *of the pain a sick person has to endure.* we do not know whether death will end suffering and pain or not.

Supports subpoint about how euthanasia benefits survivors

What seems to be the real claim is that death to those with illnesses will end our pain. Such pain involves worrying over them, paying their medical bills, and giving up so much of our time. Their deaths end our pain rather than theirs. And for that reason, euthanasia is a selfish act, for the outcome of euthanasia benefits us, the nonsufferers, more. Once the sufferers pass away, we can go back to our normal lives.

Dao unifies this paragraph by keeping all its parts focused on her main point: "Euthanasia . . . benefits the survivors more than the sick person."

A paragraph may lack unity for a variety of reasons. It may shift to a new direction in the middle, or one or two sentences may simply be irrelevant to the point. The key is to make sure that all the sentences in the paragraph fulfill the reader's expectations based on the topic sentence.

Add Particulars to Support Points

Just as writers of rough drafts often omit point sentences from paragraphs, they also sometimes leave out the particulars needed to support a point. In such cases, the writer needs to add particulars such as facts, statistics, quotations, research summaries, examples, or further subpoints. Consider how adding additional particulars to the following draft paragraph strengthens student writer Tiffany Linder's argument opposing the logging of old-growth forests.

Tiffany's complete essay is on pp. 408–410.

Draft Paragraph: Particulars Missing

One reason that it is not necessary to log old-growth forests is that the timber industry can supply the world's lumber needs without doing so. For example, we have plenty of new-growth forest from which timber can be taken (Sagoff 89). We could also reduce the amount of trees used for paper products by using other materials besides wood for paper pulp. In light of the fact that we have plenty of trees and ways of reducing our wood demands, there is no need to harvest old-growth forests.

Revised Paragraph: Particulars Added

One reason that it is not necessary to log old-growth forests is that the timber industry can supply the world's lumber needs without doing so. For example, we have plenty of new-growth forest from which timber can be taken as a result of major reforestation efforts all over the United States (Sagoff 89). In the Northwest, for instance, Oregon law requires every acre of timber harvested to be replanted. According to Robert Sedjo, a forestry expert, the world's demand for industrial wood could be met by a widely implemented tree farming system (Sagoff 90). We could also reduce the amount of trees used for paper products by using a promising new innovation called Kenaf, a fast-growing annual herb which is fifteen feet tall and is native to Africa. It has been used for making rope for many years, but recently it was found to work just as well for paper pulp. In light of the fact that we have plenty of trees and ways of reducing our wood demands, there is no need to harvest old-growth forests.

Added particulars support subpoint that we have plenty of new-growth forest

Added particulars support second subpoint that wood alternatives are available

Summary

Point sentences form the structural core of an argument. In this lesson, we stressed the reader's need to have point sentences placed at the heads of sections and paragraphs. In revising, writers often need to recast point sentences or restructure paragraphs to create unity. We also stressed the reader's need for particulars, which make points vivid and persuasive.

For Writing and Discussion

Individual task: Bring to class a draft-in-progress for a closed-form essay. Pick out several paragraphs in the body of your essay and analyze them for "points first" structure. For each paragraph, ask the following questions:

- Does my paragraph have a topic sentence near the beginning?
- If so, does my topic sentence accurately forecast what the paragraph says?
- Does my topic sentence link to my thesis statement or to a higher order point that my paragraph develops?
- Does my paragraph have enough particulars to develop and support my topic sentence?

Group task: Then exchange your draft with a partner and do a similar analysis of your partner's selected paragraphs. Discuss your analyses of each other's paragraphs and then help each other plan appropriate revision strategies. If time permits, revise your paragraphs and show your results to your partner. [Note: Sometimes you can revise simply by adding a topic sentence to a paragraph, rewording a topic sentence, or making other kinds of local revisions. At other times, you may need to cross out whole paragraphs and start over, rewriting from scratch after you rethink your ideas.]

LESSON 6: SIGNALING RELATIONSHIPS WITH TRANSITIONS

As we have explained in previous lessons, when readers read closed-form prose, they expect each new sentence, paragraph, and section to link clearly to what they have already read. They need a well-marked trail with signposts signaling the twists and turns along the way. They also need resting spots at major junctions where they can review where they've been and survey what's coming. In this lesson, we show you how transition words as well as summary and forecasting passages can keep your readers securely on the trail.

Use Common Transition Words to Signal Relationships

Transitions are like signposts that signal where the road is turning and limit the possible directions that an unfolding argument might take. Consider how the use of "therefore" and "nevertheless" limits the range of possibilities in the following examples:

> While on vacation, Suzie caught the chicken pox. Therefore, _____.

> While on vacation, Suzie caught the chicken pox. Nevertheless, _____.

"Therefore" signals to the reader that what follows is a consequence. Most readers will imagine a sentence similar to this one:

Therefore, she spent her vacation lying in bed itching, feverish, and miserable.

In contrast, "nevertheless" signals an unexpected or denied consequence, so the reader might anticipate a sentence such as this:

Nevertheless, she enjoyed her two weeks off, thanks to a couple of bottles of calamine lotion, some good books, and a big easy chair overlooking the ocean.

Here is a list of the most common transition words and phrases and what they signal to the reader:*

Words or Phrases	What They Signal
first, second, third, next, finally, earlier, later, meanwhile, afterwards	*sequence*—First we went to dinner; then we went to the movies.
that is, in other words, to put it another way,—(dash), :(colon)	*restatement*—He's so hypocritical that you can't trust a word he says. To put it another way, he's a complete phony.
rather, instead	*replacement*—We shouldn't use the money to buy opera tickets; rather, we should use it for a nice gift.
for example, for instance, a case in point	*example*—Mr. Carlysle is very generous. For example, he gave the janitors a special holiday gift.
because, since, for	*reason*—Taxes on cigarettes are unfair because they place a higher tax burden on the working class.
therefore, hence, so, consequently, thus, then, as a result, accordingly, as a consequence	*consequences*—I failed to turn in the essay; therefore I flunked the course.
still, nevertheless	*denied consequence*—The teacher always seemed grumpy in class; nevertheless, I really enjoyed the course.
although, even though, granted that (*with* still)	*concession*—Even though the teacher was always grumpy, I still enjoyed the course.
in comparison, likewise, similarly	*similarity*—Teaching engineering takes a lot of patience. Likewise, so does teaching accounting.
however, in contrast, conversely, on the other hand, but	*contrast*—I disliked my old backpack immensely; however, I really like this new one.
in addition, also, too, moreover, furthermore	*addition*—Today's cars are much safer than those of ten years ago. In addition, they get better gas mileage.
in brief, in sum, in conclusion, finally, to sum up, to conclude	*conclusion or summary*—In sum, the plan presented by Mary is the best choice.

*Although all the words on the list serve as transitions or connectives, grammatically they are not all equivalent, nor are they all punctuated the same way.

For Writing and Discussion

This exercise is designed to show you how transition words govern relation-ships between ideas. Working in groups or on your own, finish each of the fol-lowing statements using ideas of your own invention. Make sure what you add fits the logic of the transition word.

1. Writing is difficult; therefore _____.
2. Writing is difficult; however, _____.
3. Writing is difficult because _____.
4. Writing is difficult. For example, _____.
5. Writing is difficult. To put it another way, _____.
6. Writing is difficult. Likewise, _____.
7. Although writing is difficult, _____.
8. _____. In sum, writing is difficult.

In the following paragraph, various kinds of linking devices have been omit-ted. Fill in the blanks with words or phrases that would make the paragraph coherent. Clues are provided in brackets.

Writing an essay is a difficult process for most people. _____ [contrast] the process can be made easier if you learn to practice three simple techniques. _____ [sequence] learn the technique of nonstop writing. When you are first trying to think of ideas for an essay, put your pen to your paper and write nonstop for ten or fifteen minutes without letting your pen leave the paper. Stay loose and free. Let your pen follow the waves of thought. Don't worry about grammar or spelling. _____ [concession] this technique won't work for everyone, it helps many people get a good cache of ideas to draw on. A _____ [sequence] technique is to write your rough draft rapidly without worrying about being perfect. Too many writers try to get their drafts right the first time. _____ [contrast] by learning to live with imperfection, you will save yourself headaches and a wastepaper basket full of crumpled paper. Think of your first rough draft as a path hacked out of the jungle—as part of an explo-ration, not as a completed highway. As a _____ [sequence] technique, try printing out a triple-spaced copy to allow space for revision. Many beginning writers don't leave enough space to revise. _____ [consequence] these writers never get in the habit of crossing out chunks of their rough draft and writing revisions in the blank spaces. After you have revised your rough draft until it is too messy to work from any more, you can _____ [sequence] enter your changes into your word processor and print out a fresh draft, again setting your text on triple-space. The resulting blank space invites you to revise.

Write Major Transitions Between Parts

In long closed-form pieces, writers often put *resting places* between major parts—transitional passages that allow readers to shift their attention momentarily away from the matter at hand to a sense of where they've been and where they're going. Often such passages sum up the preceding major section, refer back to the essay's thesis statement or opening blueprint plan, and then preview the next major section. Here are three typical examples:

> So far I have looked at a number of techniques that can help people identify debilitating assumptions that block their self-growth. In the next section, I examine ways to question and overcome these assumptions.

> Now that the difficulty of the problem is fully apparent, our next step is to examine some of the solutions that have been proposed.

> These, then, are the major theories explaining why Hamlet delays. But let's see what happens to Hamlet if we ask the question in a slightly different way. In this next section, we shift our critical focus, looking not at Hamlet's actions, but at his language.

Signal Transitions with Headings and Subheadings

In many genres, particularly scientific and technical reports, government documents, business proposals, textbooks, and long articles in magazines or scholarly journals, writers conventionally break up long stretches of text with headings and subheadings. Headings are often set in different type sizes and fonts and mark transition points between major parts and subparts of the argument. We discuss headings in detail in Lesson 8 on document design.

Summary

In this brief lesson we explained some simple yet effective strategies for keeping your readers on track:

- Mark your trail with appropriate transition words.
- Write major transitions between sections.
- If the genre allows, use headings and subheadings.

Effective use of these strategies will help your readers follow your ideas with ease and confidence.

LESSON 7: BINDING SENTENCES TOGETHER BY FOLLOWING THE OLD/NEW CONTRACT

In the previous lesson we showed you how to mark the reader's trail with transitions. In this lesson we show you how to build a smooth trail without potholes or washed-out bridges.

An Explanation of the Old/New Contract

A powerful way to prevent gaps is to follow the old/new contract—a writing strategy derived from the principle of old before new that we explained and illustrated in Lesson 1. Simply put, the old/new contract asks writers to begin sentences with something old—something that links to what has gone before—and then to end sentences with new information.

To understand the old/new contract more fully, try the following thought exercise. We'll show you two passages, both of which explain the old/new contract. One of them, however, follows the principle it describes; the other violates it.

Thought Exercise

Which of these passages follows the old/new contract?

Version 1

The old/new contract is another principle for writing clear closed-form prose. Beginning your sentences with something old—something that links to what has gone before—and then ending your sentence with new information that advances the argument is what the old/new contract asks writers to do. An effect called *coherence*, which is closely related to *unity*, is created by following this principle. Whereas the clear relationship between the topic sentence and the body of the paragraph and between the parts and the whole is what *unity* refers to, the clear relationship between one sentence and the next is what *coherence* relates to.

Version 2

Another principle for writing clear closed-form prose is the old/new contract. The old/new contract asks writers to begin sentences with something old—something that links to what has gone before—and then to end sentences with new information that advances the argument. Following this principle creates an effect called *coherence*, which is closely related to unity. Whereas *unity* refers to the clear relationship between the body of a paragraph and its topic sentence and between the parts and the whole, *coherence* refers to the clear relationship between one sentence and the next, between part and part.

If you are like most readers, you have to concentrate much harder to understand Version 1 than Version 2 because it violates the old-before-new way that our minds normally process information. When a writer doesn't begin a sentence with old material, readers have to hold the new material in suspension until they have figured out how it connects to what has gone before. They can stay on the trail, but they have to keep jumping over the potholes between sentences.

To follow the old/new contract, place old information near the beginning of sentences in what we call the *topic position* and new information that advances the argument in the predicate or *stress position* at the end of the sentence. We associate topics with the beginnings of sentences simply because in the standard English sentence, the topic (or subject) comes before the predicate. Hence the notion of a "contract" by which we agree not to fool or frustrate our readers by breaking with the "normal" order of things. The contract says that the old, backward-linking material comes at the beginning of the sentence and that the new, argument-advancing material comes at the end.

For Writing and Discussion

What follow are two more passages, one of which obeys the old/new contract while the other violates it. Working in small groups or as a whole class, reach consensus on which of these passages follows the old/new contract. Explain your reasoning by showing how the beginning of each sentence links to something old.

Passage A

Play is an often-overlooked dimension of fathering. From the time a child is born until its adolescence, fathers emphasize caretaking less than play. Egalitarian feminists may be troubled by this, and spending more time in caretaking may be wise for fathers. There seems to be unusual significance in the father's style of play. Physical excitement and stimulation are likely to be part of it. With older children more physical games and teamwork that require the competitive testing of physical and mental skills are also what it involves. Resemblance to an apprenticeship or teaching relationship is also a characteristic of fathers' play: Come on, let me show you how.

Passage B

An often-overlooked dimension of fathering is play. From their children's birth through adolescence, fathers tend to emphasize play more than caretaking. This may be troubling to egalitarian feminists, and it would indeed be wise for most fathers to spend more time in caretaking. Yet the fathers' style of play seems to have unusual significance. It is likely to be both physically stimulating and exciting. With older children it involves more physical games and teamwork that require the competitive testing of physical and mental skills. It frequently resembles an apprenticeship or teaching relationship: Come on, let me show you how.

How to Make Links to the "Old"

To understand how to link to "old information," you need to understand more fully what we mean by "old" or "familiar." In the context of sentence-level coherence, we mean everything in the text that the reader has read so far. Any upcoming sentence is new information, but once the reader has read it, it becomes old information. For example, when a reader is halfway through a text, everything previously read—the title, the introduction, half the body—is old information to which you can link to meet your readers' expectations for unity and coherence.

In making these backward links, writers have three targets:

1. They can link to a key word or concept in the immediately preceding sentence (creating coherence).

2. They can link to a key word or concept in a preceding point sentence (creating unity).

3. They can link to a preceding forecasting statement about structure (helping readers map their location in the text).

Writers have a number of textual strategies for making these links. In Figure 19.4 our annotations show how a professional writer links to old information within the first five or six words of each sentence. What follows is a compendium of these strategies:

- ■ *Repeat a key word.* The most common way to open with something old is to repeat a key word from the preceding sentence or an earlier point sentence. In our example, note the number of sentences that open with "father," "father's," or "fathering." Note also the frequent repetitions of "play."

- ■ *Use a pronoun to substitute for a key word.* In our example, the second sentence opens with the pronouns "it," referring to "research," and "their" referring to "fathers." The last three sentences open with the pronoun "it," referring to "father's style of play."

- ■ *Summarize, rephrase, or restate earlier concepts.* Writers can link to a preceding sentence by using a word or phrase that summarizes or restates a key concept. In the second sentence, "interactions with children" restates the concept of childrearing. Similarly, the phrase "an often-overlooked dimension" refers to a concept implied in the preceding paragraph—that recent

---

Refers to "fathers" in previous sentence

Transition tells us new paragraph will be an example of previous concept

Refers to fathers

New information that becomes topic of this paragraph

Repeats words "father" and "play" from the topic sentence of the paragraph

Recent research has given us much deeper—and more surprising—insights into the father's role in childrearing. It shows that in almost all of their interactions with children, fathers do things a little differently from mothers. What fathers do—their special parenting style—is not only highly complementary to what mothers do but is by all indications important in its own right.

For example, an often-overlooked dimension of fathering is play. From their children's birth through adolescence, fathers tend to emphasize play more than caretaking. This may be troubling to egalitarian feminists, and it would indeed be wise for most fathers to spend more time in caretaking. Yet the fathers' style of play seems to have unusual significance. It is likely to be both physically stimulating and exciting. With older children it involves more physical games and teamwork that require the competitive testing of physical and mental skills. It frequently resembles an apprenticeship or teaching relationship: Come on, let me show you how.

Refers to "research" in previous sentence

Rephrases idea of "childrearing"

Repeats "fathers" from previous sentence

Rephrases concept in previous paragraph

Pronoun sums up previous concept

"It" refers to fathers' style of play

(David Popenoe, "Where's Papa?" from *Life Without Father: Compelling New Evidence that Fatherhood and Marriage Are Indispensable for the Good of Children and Society.*)

FIGURE 19.4 ■ How a Professional Writer Follows the Old/New Contract

research reveals something significant and not widely known about a father's role in childrearing. An "often-overlooked dimension" sums up this idea. Finally, note that the pronoun "this" in the second paragraph sums up the main concept of the previous two sentences. (But see our warning below about the overuse of "this" as a pronoun.)

- ■ *Use a transition word.* Writers can also use transition words such as *first . . . , second . . . , third . . .* or *therefore* or *however* to cue the reader about the logical relationship between an upcoming sentence and the preceding ones. Note how the second paragraph opens with "For example," indicating that the upcoming paragraph will illustrate the concept identified in the preceding paragraph.

These strategies give you a powerful way to check and revise your prose. Comb your drafts for gaps between sentences where you have violated the old/new contract. If the opening of a new sentence doesn't refer back to an earlier word, phrase, or concept, your readers could derail, so use what you have learned to repair the tracks.

For Writing and Discussion

Individual task: Bring to class a draft-in-progress for a closed-form essay. On a selected page, examine the opening of each sentence. Place a vertical slash in front of any sentence that doesn't contain near the beginning some backward-looking element that links to old, familiar material. Then revise these sentences to follow the old/new contract.

Group task: Working with a partner, share the changes you each made on your drafts. Then on each other's pages, work together to identify the kinds of links made at the beginning of each sentence. (For example, does the opening of a sentence repeat a key word, use a pronoun to substitute for a key word, rephrase or restate an earlier concept, or use a transition word?)

As we discussed in Lesson 1, the principle of old before new has great explanatory power in helping writers understand their choices when they compose. In this last section, we give you some further insights into the old/new contract.

Avoid Ambiguous Use of "This" to Fulfill the Old/New Contract

Some writers try to fulfill the old/new contract by frequent use of the pronoun *this* to sum up a preceding concept. Occasionally such usage is effective, as in our example passage on fathers' style of play when the writer says: "*This* may be troubling to egalitarian feminists." But frequent use of *this* as a pronoun creates lazy and often ambiguous prose. Consider how our example passage might read if many of the explicit links were replaced by *this*.

Lazy Use of *This* as Pronoun

Recent research has given us much deeper—and more surprising—insights into **this**. It shows that in doing **this**, fathers do things a little differently from mothers. **This** is not only highly complementary to what mothers do but is by all indications important in its own right.

For example, an often-overlooked dimension of **this** is play.

Perhaps this passage helps you see why we refer to *this* (used by itself as a pronoun) as "the lazy person's all-purpose noun-slot filler."*

How the Old/New Contract Modifies the Rule "Avoid Weak Repetition"

Many students have been warned against repetition of the same word (or *weak repetition,* as your teacher may have called it). Consequently, you may not be aware that repetition of key words is a vital aspect of unity and coherence. The repeated words create what linguists call *lexical strings* that keep a passage focused on a particular point. Note in our passage about the importance of fathers' style of play the frequent repetitions of the words *father* and *play.* What if the writer worried about repeating *father* too much and reached for his thesaurus?

Unnecessary Attempt to Avoid Repetition

Recent research has given us much deeper—and more surprising—insights into the **male parent's** role in childrearing. It shows that in almost all of their interactions with children, **patriarchs** do things a little differently from mothers. What **sires** do. . . .

For example, an often-overlooked dimension of **male gender parenting** is. . . .

You get the picture. Keep your reader on familiar ground through repetition of key words.

How the Old/New Contract Modifies the Rule "Prefer Active over Passive Voice"

Another rule that you may have learned is to use the active voice rather than the passive voice. In the active voice the doer of the action is in the subject slot of the sentence, and the receiver is in the direct object slot, as in the following examples:

The dog caught the Frisbee.
The women wrote letters of complaint to the boss.
The landlord raised the rent.

In the passive voice the receiver of the action becomes the subject and the doer of the action either becomes the object of the preposition *by* or disappears from the sentence.

*It's acceptable to use *this* as an adjective, in "this usage"; we refer only to *this* used by itself as a pronoun.

The Frisbee was caught by the dog.
Letters of complaint were written (by the women) to the boss.
The rent was raised (by the landlord).

Other things being equal, the active voice is indeed preferable to the passive because it is more direct and forceful. But in some cases, other things *aren't* equal, and the passive voice is preferable. *What the old/new contract asks you to consider is whether the doer or the receiver represents the old information in a sentence.* Consider the difference between the following passages:

Second Sentence,   My great-grandfather was a skilled cabinetmaker. He made
Active Voice   this dining room table near the turn of the century.

Second Sentence,   I am pleased that you stopped to admire our dining room
Passive Voice   table. It was made by my great-grandfather near the turn of
                        the century.

In the first passage, the opening sentence is about *my great-grandfather.* To begin the second sentence with old information ("he," referring to "grandfather"), the writer uses the active voice. The opening sentence of the second passage is about the *dining room table.* To begin the second sentence with old information ("it," referring to "table"), the writer must use the passive voice, since the table is the receiver of the action. In both cases, the sentences are structured to begin with old information.

Summary

This lesson has focused on the power of the old/new contract to bind sentences together and eliminate gaps that the reader must leap over. We have shown various ways that writers can link to old information by repeating key words, using a pronoun, summarizing or restating an earlier concept, or using a transition word. Additionally, we have advised against the ambiguous use of *this* as a pronoun to link back to old information and have shown how the principle of old before new modifies rules about the avoidance of *weak repetition* and *passive voice.*

LESSON 8: USING DOCUMENT DESIGN EFFECTIVELY

Throughout this text, we have emphasized that rhetorical context, subject matter, and document design are closely connected. In Chapter 4, we discussed document design as four components of the visual appearance of a piece of writing: use of type, use of space on the page, use of color, and use of graphics (pp. 75–77). In this chapter we ask you to consider what part document design should play in the composing and revising of your closed-form prose. Our advice is eminently practical: good document design serves the whole communication, and good document design enhances—but does not substitute for—the quality of thinking and writing in a document. Beneath these overriding concepts, we offer four principles of document design that can make your closed-form writing effective for your intended audience:

■ Match your document design to the genre expectations of your audience.

■ Consider document design an important part of your ethos.

■ Use document design components for clarity and emphasis.

■ Use design elements to highlight and reinforce—but not replace—transitions, topic sentences, and key explanations in the text itself.

In this lesson, we explain how attention to document design can make your closed-form documents more effective and your ethos more professional.

Match Your Document Design to the Genre Expectations of Your Audience

In Chapter 4 (pp. 67–68) we discussed how genres or kinds of writing have their own conventions for approaching subject matter, structure, and style. These conventions function as agreements with readers that a particular kind of writing will meet certain reader expectations, including expectations for the way a document will look.

The closed-form genres you are likely to be assigned in college include academic research papers, experimental/scientific reports, various civic genres (letters to the editor, op-ed pieces, proposals, advocacy posters), and various academic or workplace genres inside your major (nursing logs, marketing proposals, informational letters to clients, technical documentation, public relations brochures or Web sites, or research proposals). In this textbook, you find examples of a wide variety of closed-form genres including an MLA style research paper (pp. 647–658), an APA style research paper (pp. 356–366), a practical proposal (pp. 451–456), letters to the editor (pp. 54–55), an experimental report (pp. 138–144), an advocacy poster (p. 449), and various kinds of advocacy or informational Web sites (see especially Chapter 22).

A common principle of document design for closed-form genres is to keep the design functional—not decorative—with an emphasis on what you are communicating. You should use conventional fonts such as Times New Roman, CG Times, or Courier and 11- or 12-point font sizes. As part of your functional design, you should use standard black ink.

Where academic genres vary is in the layout of documents. Long research papers, experimental reports, and practical proposals are likely to call for certain features such as these:

■ Separate title page or cover sheet (but not for MLA documents, which call for the title on the first page of text)

■ Table of contents page (for long proposals or reports)

■ Inclusion of an initial freestanding abstract of the document (for APA documents and most scientific papers; in a business setting, "executive summaries" are common for longer proposals and reports)

- Headings and subheadings throughout the document to highlight parts of the document and their purposes
- The use of numbered or bulleted items in lists
- Quantitative graphics where appropriate
- Documentation of sources according to appropriate conventions
- Separate "Works Cited" page

Familiarizing yourself in advance with the specific document design requirements of a genre can help you throughout the invention, drafting, and revising stages of your writing by letting you envision the structure and appearance of your final product.

Consider Document Design an Important Part of Your Ethos

The appearance of your document communicates to your audience in another way by helping you establish your professional ethos. As you prepare your final document, ask yourself these questions: Does the appearance of my document convey that I am responsible, serious, credible, and knowledgeable about the genre? Does my document design show consideration for my audience's time as well as appreciation of their background and expectations?

Use Document Design Components for Clarity and Emphasis

You can often increase the clarity and persuasiveness of documents through effective use of headings, graphics, or other visuals.

Headings and subheadings can add clarity to your documents by providing readers with a mental frame for processing your ideas. Some genres employ standard part headings. For example, experimental reports have the conventional headings of "Introduction," "Methods," "Findings," and "Discussion." Grant proposals and other proposal arguments often have the standard headings "Statement of Problem," "Proposed Solution," and "Justification."

In other genres, writers often create their own headings, especially in papers more than six pages long. These headings show readers at a glance not only the structure of the paper but also a capsule of the argument. Each heading serves the same forecasting function as a bulleted main point on a PowerPoint slide. For example, one of our students claimed, in a researched argument, that coastal Indian tribes should not be allowed to hunt whales for cultural reasons, even on a limited basis. She organized her argument using the following headings and subheadings:

THE NATIVE PERSPECTIVE: WHALING AS A CULTURAL TRADITION	First-level head
CULTURAL WHALING AS A STEP TOWARD COMMERCIAL WHALING	First-level head
THE HARM OF COMMERCIAL WHALING	First-level head
Increase in Demand for Whale Meat	Second-level head

Second-level head | Difficulty in Sustaining Whale Stocks
Second-level head | Decrease in Biodiversity
First-level head | INTRINSIC VALUE OF WHALES

When creating heads, develop and follow the same font style for each level of head and make all the heads at each level grammatically parallel. (All the headings in the previous example are nouns or noun phrases.)

Like headings, graphics and images can enhance clarity and emphasize ideas by creating a visually interesting contrast to the written text, by focusing the readers' attention on the points you are making, and by giving your points presence and impact. Graphics and images should contribute to your intended rhetorical effect rather than show off the bells and whistles of your computer's graphics program. To avoid decorative and distracting use of graphics, ask yourself these questions: What point or story do I want this graphic or image to emphasize? What does this graphic add to my written text?

Chapter 11 explains when and how to construct quantitative graphics; see also Chapter 3, pp. 55–57, and Chapter 10 throughout.

Use Design Elements to Highlight and Reinforce—But Not Replace—Transitions, Topic Sentences, and Key Explanations in the Text Itself

Graphics and design elements should enhance a written text but never replace the verbal explanations of the same points. While headings and subheadings can guide readers through a document and direct them to particular points, you need to repeat the point, topic sentence, or transition in the text itself. Your text should make complete sense with headings and graphics removed.

See Chapter 11 on independent redundancy of text and graphics, p. 263.

Summary

In this lesson we have explained four principles of document design that can make your closed-form prose more effective: (1) matching your document design to the genre expectations of your audience; (2) considering document design as an important part of your ethos; (3) using document design for clarity and emphasis; and (4) using design components to highlight and reinforce—but not replace—transitions, topic sentences, and key explanations in the text itself.

For Writing and Discussion

1. Individually, in groups, or as a whole class, consider the following writing scenarios. What document design features can you imagine being used in the final document? How will advance consideration of these design features help the writers at the invention, drafting, and revising stages of their writing?

Scenario 1: Mara has been assigned a research project for an interdisciplinary English and sociology course that must include field research and take the form of an experimental report. Her research question is this: What kind of environment does our campus provide for gay male and lesbian students?

Scenario 2: Spencer works in a drug rehabilitation center as an aide. He is writing an argument that the United States should divert money currently being spent on the "War on Drugs" into rehabilitation programs. Spencer wants to influence his fellow students to vote in favor of a state initiative to spend more money on drug rehabilitation. If the paper is good enough, he wants to send it to his local newspaper as a possible op-ed column.

2. If you have a writing assignment this term that invites special consideration of document design (for example, a research paper following MLA or APA style; a practical proposal; a paper with graphics; or a paper imagined in desktop published style for a particular magazine), discuss with classmates the design features that you are considering. Note how advanced consideration of design features can help you at the invention, drafting, and revising stages of your work.

LESSON 9: LEARNING FOUR EXPERT MOVES FOR ORGANIZING AND DEVELOPING IDEAS

In this lesson we show you that writers of closed-form prose often employ a conventional set of moves to organize parts of an essay. In using the term *moves,* we are making an analogy with the "set moves" or "set plays" in such sports as basketball, volleyball, and soccer. For example, a common set move in basketball is the "pick," in which an offensive player without the ball stands motionless in order to block the path of a defensive player who is guarding the dribbler. Similarly, certain organizational patterns in writing occur frequently enough to act as set plays for writers. These patterns set up expectations in the reader's mind about the shape of an upcoming stretch of prose, anything from a few sentences to a paragraph to a large block of paragraphs. As you will see, these moves also stimulate the invention of ideas. Next, we describe four of the most powerful set plays.*

The *For Example* Move

Perhaps the most common set play occurs when a writer makes an assertion and then illustrates it with one or more examples, often signaling the move explicitly with transitions such as *for example, for instance,* or *a case in point is.* . . . Here is how student writer Dao Do used the "for example" move to support her third reason for opposing euthanasia.

An earlier example of Dao's paragraphs is on pp. 519–521.

*You might find it helpful to follow the set plays we used to write this section. This last sentence is the opening move of a play we call *division into parallel parts.* It sets up the expectation that we will develop four set plays in order. Watch for the way we chunk them and signal transitions between them.

***For Example* Move**

Topic sentence ⟶ My third objection to euthanasia is that it fails to see the value in suffering. Suffering is a part of life. We see the value of suffering only if we look deeply within our suffering. *Transition signaling the move* For example, I never thought my crippled uncle from Vietnam was a blessing to my grandmother until I talked to her. My mother's little brother was born prematurely. As a result of oxygen and nutrition deficiency, he was born crippled. His tiny arms and legs were twisted around his body, preventing him from any normal movements such as walking, picking up things, and lying down. He could only sit. Therefore, his world was very limited, for it consisted of his own room and the garden viewed through his window. Because of his disabilities, my grandmother had to wash him, feed him, and watch him constantly. It was hard, but she managed to care for him for forty-three years. He passed away after the death of my grandfather in 1982. Bringing this situation out of Vietnam and into Western society shows the difference between Vietnamese and Western views. In the West, my uncle might have been euthanized as a baby. Supporters of euthanasia would have said he wouldn't have any quality of life and that he would have been a great burden. But he was not a burden on my grandmother. She enjoyed taking care of him, and he was always her company after her other children got married and moved away. Neither one of them saw his defect as meaningless suffering because it brought them closer together.

Extended example supporting point

This passage uses a single, extended example to support a point. You could also use several shorter examples or other kinds of illustrating evidence such as facts or statistics. In all cases the *for example* move creates a pattern of expectation and fulfillment. This pattern drives the invention of ideas in one of two ways: it urges the writer either to find examples to develop a generalization or to formulate a generalization that shows the point of an example.

For Writing and Discussion

Working individually or in groups, develop a plan for supporting one or more of the following generalizations using the *for example* move.

1. Another objection to state sales taxes is that they are so annoying.
2. Although assertiveness training has definite benefits, it can sometimes get you into real trouble.
3. Sometimes effective leaders are indecisive.

The *Summary/However* Move

This move occurs whenever a writer sums up another person's viewpoint in order to qualify or contradict it or to introduce an opposing view. Typically, writers use transition words such as *but, however, in contrast,* or *on the other hand* between the parts of this move. This move is particularly common in academic writing, which often contrasts the writer's new view with prevailing views. Here is how Dao uses a *summary/however* move in the introduction of her essay opposing euthanasia.

Summary/However Move

Should euthanasia be legalized? My classmate Martha and her family think it should be. Martha's aunt was blind from diabetes. For three years she was constantly in and out of the hospital, but then her kidneys shut down and she became a victim of life support. After three months of suffering, she finally gave up. Martha believes this three-month period was unnecessary, for her aunt didn't have to go through all of that suffering. If euthanasia were legalized, her family would have put her to sleep the minute her condition worsened. Then, she wouldn't have had to feel pain, and she would have died in peace and with dignity. However, despite Martha's strong argument for legalizing euthanasia, I find it wrong.

Issue over which there is disagreement

Summary of opposing viewpoint

Transition to writer's viewpoint

Statement of writer's view

The first sentence of this introduction poses the question that the essay addresses. The main body of the paragraph summarizes Martha's opposing view on euthanasia, and the final sentence, introduced by the transition "however," presents Dao's thesis.

For Writing and Discussion

For this exercise, assume that you favor development of wind-generated electricity. Use the *summary/however* move to acknowledge the view of civil engineer David Rockwood, whose letter opposing wind-generated electricity you read in Chapter 1 (pp. 13–14). Assume that you are writing the opening paragraph of your own essay. Follow the pattern of Dao's introduction: (a) begin with a one-sentence issue or question; (b) summarize Rockwood's view in approximately one hundred words; and (c) state your own view, using *however* or *in contrast* as a transition. Write out your paragraph on your own, or work in groups to write a consensus paragraph. Then share and critique your paragraphs.

The *Division-into-Parallel-Parts* Move

Among the most frequently encountered and powerful of the set plays is the *division-into-parallel-parts* move. To initiate the move, a writer begins with an umbrella sentence that forecasts the structure and creates a framework. (For example, "Freud's theory differs from Jung's in three essential ways" or "The decline of the U.S. space program can be attributed to several factors.") Typical overview sentences either specify the number of parts that follow by using phrases such as "two ways," "three differences," or "five kinds," or they leave the number unspecified, using words such as *several, a few,* or *many.* Alternatively, the writer may ask a rhetorical question that implies the framework: "What are some main differences, then, between Freud's theory and Jung's? One difference is. . . ."

To signal transitions from one part to the next, writers use two kinds of signposts in tandem. The first is a series of transition words or bullets to introduce each of the parallel parts. Here are typical series of transition words:

First . . . Second . . . Third . . . Finally . . .

First . . . Another . . . Still another . . . Finally . . .

One . . . In addition . . . Furthermore . . . Also

Instead of transition words, writers can also use bullets followed by indented text:

> The Wolf Recovery Program is rigidly opposed by a vociferous group of ranchers who pose three main objections to increasing wolf populations:

- They perceive wolves as a threat to livestock. [development]

- They fear the wolves will attack humans. [development]

- They believe ranchers will not be compensated by the government for their loss of profits. [development]

The second kind of signpost, usually used in conjunction with transitions, is an echolike repetition of the same grammatical structure to begin each parallel part.

> I learned several things from this class. First, *I learned that* [development]. Second, *I learned that* [development]. Finally, *I learned that* [development].

The division-into-parallel-parts move can be used within a single paragraph, or it can control larger stretches of text in which a dozen or more paragraphs may work together to complete a parallel series of parts. (For example, you are currently in the third part of a parallel series introduced by the mapping sentence on page 535: "Next, we describe four of the most powerful set plays.") Here are some more examples of common situations in which writers use this move:

Classification. When writers want to divide a concept into various categories— a thinking process often called *classification*— they regularly devote a major piece of the essay to each of the classes or categories.

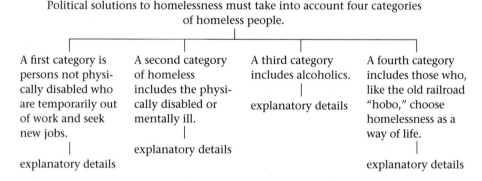

Process Analysis. Writers often explain a process by dividing it into a number of separate stages or steps.

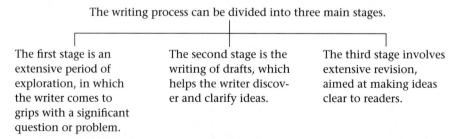

Argumentation. When writers of arguments offer two or more parallel reasons for adhering to a particular view or course of action, they typically use the *division-into-parallel-parts* move. Dao used this large-scale strategy to organize her argument against euthanasia.

Despite Martha's strong argument for legalizing euthanasia, I find it is wrong for several reasons.

First, euthanasia is wrong because it benefits survivors more than the sick person.	Second, euthanasia is wrong because of its unfavorable consequences.	Third, euthanasia is wrong because it fails to see the value in suffering.

Ordering the Parallel Parts

Whenever you create two or more parallel parts, you must decide which to put first, which to put in the middle, and which to put last. If the parts are of equal weight and interest, or if you are just exploring their significance, the order doesn't really matter. But if the parts are of different importance, significance, or complexity, their order can be rhetorically important. As a general rule, save the best for last. What constitutes "best" depends on the circumstances. In an argument, the best reason is usually the strongest or the one most apt to appeal to the intended audience. In other cases, the best is usually the most unusual, the most surprising, the most thought provoking, or the most complex, in keeping with the general rule that writers proceed from the familiar to the unfamiliar and from the least surprising to the most surprising.

For Writing and Discussion

Working individually or in small groups, use the *division-into-parallel-parts* move to create, organize, and develop ideas to support one or more of the following point sentences. Try using a tree diagram to help guide and stimulate your invention.

1. To study for an exam effectively, a student should follow these (specify a number) steps.
2. Why do U.S. schoolchildren lag so far behind European and Asian children on standardized tests of mathematics and science? One possible cause is . . . (continue).
3. Constant dieting is unhealthy for several reasons.

The *Comparison/Contrast* Move

A common variation on the division-into-parallel-parts move is the *comparison/contrast* move. To compare or contrast two items, you must first decide on the points of comparison (or contrast). If you are contrasting the political views of two presidential candidates, you might choose to focus on four points of comparison:

differences in their foreign policy, differences in economic policy, differences in social policy, and differences in judicial philosophy. You then have two choices for organizing the parts: the *side-by-side pattern,* in which you discuss all of candidate A's views and then all of candidate B's views; or the *back-and-forth pattern,* in which you discuss foreign policy, contrasting A's views with B's views, then move on to economic policy, then social policy, and then judicial philosophy. Here is how these two patterns would appear on a tree diagram.

Side-by-side pattern

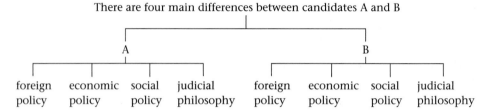

Back-and-forth pattern

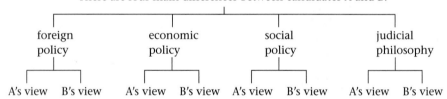

There are no cut-and-dried rules that dictate when to use the side-by-side pattern or the back-and-forth pattern. However, for lengthy comparisons, the back-and-forth pattern is often more effective because the reader doesn't have to store great amounts of information in memory. The side-by-side pattern requires readers to remember all the material about A when they get to B, and it is sometimes difficult to keep all the points of comparison clearly in mind.

For Writing and Discussion

Working individually or in groups, create tree diagrams for stretches of text based on one or more of the following point sentences, all of which call for the *comparison/contrast* move. Make at least one diagram follow the back-and-forth pattern and at least one diagram follow the side-by-side pattern.

1. To understand U.S. politics, an outsider needs to appreciate some basic differences between Republicans and Democrats.
2. Although they are obviously different on the surface, there are many similarities between the Boy Scouts and a street gang.
3. There are several important differences between closed-form and open-form writing.

Summary

In this lesson we have shown you how practicing experts' set moves extends your repertoire of strategies for organizing and developing ideas. In particular, we have explained how to add an example to support a point; how to sum up an alternative view and then switch to your own; how to develop an idea by announcing a series of parallel subparts; and how to compare or contrast two ideas or phenomena. These moves can be used on a large or small scale, wherever appropriate in a paper.

LESSON 10: WRITING EFFECTIVE CONCLUSIONS

Conclusions can best be understood as complements to introductions. In both the introduction and the conclusion, writers are concerned with the essay as a whole more than with any given part. In a conclusion, the writer attempts to bring a sense of completeness and closure to the profusion of points and particulars laid out in the body of the essay. The writer is particularly concerned with helping the reader move from the parts back to the big picture and to understand the importance or significance of the essay.

If you are having trouble figuring out how to conclude an essay, consider the following guide questions, which are designed to stimulate thought about how to conclude and to help you determine which model best suits your situation.

1. How long and complex is your essay? Is it long enough or complex enough that readers might benefit from a summary of your main points?
2. What's the most important point (or points) you want your readers to remember about your essay? How long ago in the essay did you state that point? Would it be useful to restate that point as succinctly and powerfully as possible?
3. Do you know of an actual instance, illustration, or example of your main point that would give it added weight?
4. What larger principle stands behind your main point? Or what must your audience accept as true in order to accept your main point? How would you defend that assumption if someone were to call it into question?
5. Why is your main point significant? Why are the ideas in your paper important and worth your audience's consideration? What larger issues does your topic relate to or touch on? Could you show how your topic relates to a larger and more significant topic? What might that topic be?
6. If your audience accepts your thesis, where do you go next? What is the next issue or question to be examined? What further research is needed? Conversely, do you have any major reservations, unexpressed doubts, or "All bets are off if X is the case" provisos you'd like to admit? What do you *not* know about your topic that reduces your certainty in your thesis?
7. How much antagonism or skepticism toward your position do you anticipate? If it's a great deal, would it be feasible to delay your thesis, solution, or proposal until the very end of the paper?

Because many writers find conclusions challenging to write, we offer the following six possible models:

The *Simple Summary* Conclusion

The most common, though often not the most effective, kind of conclusion is a simple summary, in which the writer recaps what has just been said. This approach is useful in a long or complex essay or in an instructional text that focuses on concepts to be learned. We use *summary* conclusions for most of the chapters in this text. In a short, easy-to-follow essay, however, a summary conclusion can be dull and may even annoy readers who are expecting something more significant, but a brief summary followed by a more artful concluding strategy can often be effective.

The *Larger Significance* Conclusion

A particularly effective concluding strategy is to draw the reader's attention to the *larger significance* of your argument. In our discussion of academic problems (see Chapter 1), we explained that a good academic question needs to be significant (worth pursuing). Although readers need to be convinced from the outset that the problem investigated in your paper is significant, the conclusion is a good place to elaborate on that significance by showing how your argument now leads to additional benefits for the reader. If you started off asking a pure-knowledge question, you could show in your conclusion how your thesis leads to potential understanding of a larger, more significant question. If you asked an applied-knowledge question, your conclusion could point out the practical benefits of your ideas. If you posed a values question, you could show how your argument clarifies the stance you might take when facing a related problem. Your goal in writing this kind of conclusion is to show how your answer to the question posed in your paper leads to a larger or more significant understanding.

The *Proposal* Conclusion

Another option, often used in analyses and arguments, is the *proposal* conclusion, which calls for action. A proposal conclusion states the action that the writer believes needs to be taken and briefly demonstrates the advantages of this action over alternative actions or describes its beneficial consequences. If your paper analyzes the negative consequences of shifting from a graduated to a flat-rate income tax, your conclusion may recommend an action such as modifying or opposing the flat tax. A slight variation is the *call-for-future-study* conclusion, which indicates what else needs to be known or resolved before a proposal can be offered. Such conclusions are especially common in scientific writing.

The *Scenic* or *Anecdotal* Conclusion

Popular writers often use a *scenic* or *anecdotal* conclusion, in which a scene or brief story illustrates the theme's significance without stating it explicitly. A paper opposing the current trend against involuntary hospitalization of the homeless mentally ill might end by describing a former mental patient, now an itinerant homeless person, collecting bottles in a park. Such scenes can help the reader experience directly the emotional significance of the topic analyzed in the body of the paper.

The *Hook and Return* Conclusion

A related variety of conclusion is the *hook and return,* in which the ending of the essay returns to something introduced in the opening hook or lead. If the lead of your essay is a vivid illustration of a problem—perhaps a scene or an anecdote— then your conclusion might return to the same scene or story, but with some variation to illustrate the significance of the essay. This sense of return can give your essay a strong feeling of unity.

The *Delayed-Thesis* Conclusion

This type of conclusion delays the thesis until the end of the essay. Rather than stating the thesis, the introduction merely states the problem, giving the body of the essay an open, exploratory, "let's think through this together" feel. Typically, the body of the paper examines alternative solutions or approaches to the problem and leaves the writer's own answer—the thesis—unstated until the end. This approach is especially effective when writing about highly complex or divisive issues on which you want to avoid taking a stand until all sides have been fairly presented.

For Writing and Discussion

Choose a paper you have just written and write an alternative conclusion using one of the strategies discussed in this lesson. Then share your original and revised conclusions in groups. Have group members discuss which one they consider most effective and why.

Summary

These six types of conclusions are neither exhaustive nor mutually exclusive. It is possible to imagine a conclusion that mixes several of these types—a few sentences summarizing your essay, a short passage showing the relationship of your topic to some broader issues, a brief call to action, and a final concluding scene. In determining an effective conclusion, you need to assess your audience's attitude toward your thesis, its understanding of your topic, the length and complexity of your essay, and your desired final effect. Review the guide questions at the beginning of this section to help determine the most appropriate conclusion for you.

CHAPTER 20

Composing and Revising Open-Form Prose

Good writing is supposed to evoke sensation in the reader—not the fact that it's raining, but the feel of being rained upon.

—E. L. DOCTOROW, *NOVELIST*

M uch of this book focuses on closed-form prose where "good writing" means having a surprising thesis supported with effective points and particulars arranged hierarchically into unified and coherent paragraphs. But there are many kinds of good writing, and we probably all share the desire at times to write in ways other than tightly argued, thesis-governed, closed-form prose. In our epigraph, novelist E. L. Doctorow suggests another way to think of "good writing": Writing that evokes sensations, that triggers in the reader's imagination the very feel of the rain.

Chapter 7 on autobiographical narrative discusses plot, characterization, setting, and theme.

In this chapter, we shift our attention from closed- to open-form writing. Open-form prose differs from closed-form prose in its basic features, in the challenges and options it presents writers, in the demands it places on its readers, and in the mental and emotional pleasures it creates. Open-form writing, of the kind we discuss here, is often called *literary nonfiction* because it uses literary techniques and strategies such as story, plot, characterization, setting, and theme.

Of course, it should be remembered that writing exists on a continuum from closed to open forms and that many features of open-form prose can appear in primarily closed-form texts. In fact, many of the example essays in this book combine elements of both open and closed styles. At the extremes of the continuum, closed- and open-form writing are markedly different, but the styles can be blended in pleasing combinations.

For essays that blend open and closed elements, see Cheryl Carp's "Behind Stone Walls" (pp. 204–205), David Quammen's "The Face of a Spider" (pp. 207–210), Florence King's "I'd Rather Smoke than Kiss" (pp. 133–138), or Edward Abbey's "The Damnation of a Canyon" (pp. 144–148).

As we have discussed throughout this text, writing at the closed end of the spectrum seeks to be efficient and reader-friendly. By forecasting what's coming, placing points first, using clear transitions, and putting old information before new, closed-form writers place maximum emphasis on delivering clear ideas that readers can grasp quickly. In contrast, open-form writers, by violating or simply stretching those same conventions, set up a different kind of relationship with readers. They often provide more pleasure in reading, but just as often demand more patience and tolerance of ambiguity. They are likely to take readers backstage to share the process of their thinking. They often cast themselves in the role of narrators or characters reporting their quest for understanding and all the coincidences, disappointments, puzzling advice, and confusion they experienced along the way. In this process of sharing, they make readers codiscoverers of ideas and insights.

Open-form prose is also characterized by its emphasis on an aesthetic use of language—that is, language used to please and entertain. Without the benefit of a thesis or points appearing first to convey meaning, open-form prose depends on the very specificity of words, the ability of words to create mental pictures, to appeal to readers' senses and emotions, and to conjure up memories.

Our goal in this chapter is to give you some practical lessons on how to write effective open-form prose. But we need to acknowledge at the outset that, whereas closed-form prose is governed by a few widely accepted conventions, one of the main features of open-form prose is its freedom to play with conventions in a bewildering variety of ways. Consequently, our discussion of open-form writing seeks more to introduce you to guiding principles rather than to treat open-form writing exhaustively.

LESSON 1: MAKE YOUR NARRATIVE A STORY, NOT AN *AND THEN* CHRONOLOGY

We have said that open-form prose is narrative-based and uses the strategies of a story. In this first lesson we want you to think more deeply about the concept of a story—particularly how a story differs from an *and then* chronology. Both a story and an *and then* chronology depict events happening in time. But there are important differences between them. At the start of this lesson, we'd like you to try your own hand at articulating the differences between a story and an *and then* chronology. Read the following example of a student's autobiographical narrative and then respond to the questions that follow.

And then writing is also discussed in Chapter 19, pp. 502–503.

Readings

■ Patrick Klein (Student) ■
BERKELEY BLUES

1   It was a cold night. That is nothing new in San Francisco, but something made this night particularly frigid. It was early February and the whole city, including the Berkeley section where we were staying, was still held tight in the firm grip of winter. It had also rained that afternoon and the air, having been cleared by the storm, was cold and sharp. It hurt the back of your throat when you inhaled and turned into mist when you exhaled. As the six of us hurriedly walked in a huddled mass, the water that was lying in puddles on the dimly lit sidewalk jumped out of our way as we slammed our dress shoes down into its dregs. We silently decided on our destination and slipped into the grungy, closet-like pizza joint. We took the only seats the

place had and as we pulled them into a circle, we all breathed a sigh of relief.

This was our first night at Berkeley. We were there for a debate tourna-   2
ment to be held the next day at the university. On this night, however, we were six high school sophomores in search of food. So, dressed in our suits and ties (we were required to wear them) and heavy coats, we ventured out of the university and entered the city of Berkeley.

Berkeley is an interesting place. Many might have romantic notions of a   3
bunch of shaggy intellectuals discussing French existentialism while sipping cappuccino, but while this might have been the case a few decades ago, the reality is that Berkeley is a ghetto. The place is filled with grungy closet shops while newspapers cover the sidewalks and the people lying on them. The university is divided from this ghetto by a two-lane street.

As the six of us crossed the two-lane street that fateful night, my   4
thoughts drifted to my own neighborhood, which up until that moment had been the extent of my world.

McCormick Ranch, Arizona, is a sheltered place. To a certain extent it's   5
mostly white, with little crime and few domestic problems. Everybody has a pool, at least two cars, and a beautiful desert sunset every night. I had every-thing I ever wanted. It seemed very gentle and dreamlike compared to the harsh slum we found ourselves in.

When we made it into the pizza place and moved the chairs into a pro-   6
tective circle around a square table, anxiety about our "hostile" environ-ment was quickly swept away with hot, greasy pizza. We ate until we were content and were trying to decide how to divide the few remaining pieces among ourselves when it happened.

The pizza place was separated from the rest of humanity by a large win-   7
dow. Our table was directly in front of that window and two feet from the door. People had been passing the window and probably remarking on the six well-dressed kids inside, but we paid them no mind and they all walked by without incident. Still, our hearts were seized with terror every time a human being would pass that window, and we hoped with all that we could muster that every one of them would continue on. We were almost right.

On this night, when six young yuppie kids from an upper middle-class   8
world decided to risk it and go eat pizza in a ghetto, he walked by. He didn't look any different from others we'd seen that night. Black. Dirty. Tired. Cold. His clothes consisted of a grimy, newspaper-stained jacket, a T-shirt with who-knows-how-old dirt on it, flimsy pants with holes at the knees, and tattered excuses for shoes. He was not quite up to par with our Gucci loafers and Armani jackets.

He shuffled past the window and glanced in. We didn't notice. He   9
stopped. We noticed. Twelve eyes glanced up as casually as they could and six hearts stopped beating for a second. Yep, still there. All eyes went back to the floor, except for two. Those eyes belonged to Chad, and in some act of defiance, his eyes met the poor man's eyes and glared.

10   The man opened the door. "We're all going to die," I thought. "All my hopes and dreams are going to end here, in a stupid pizza place, at the hands of a crazy black bum."

11   He took something out of his pocket.

12   It was shiny.

13   I couldn't look.

14   A knife.

15   No. It was a flask. He took a swig from it, and, still propping the door open with his sagging frame, spoke the most jolting, burning words I've ever heard.

16   "I love you," he said. "All of you." He glanced at Chad, "Even you." He stepped back and said, "I know what you think of me, but I still love you." I will probably never forget those words or how he said them with a steady, steely voice.

17   Then he left. That was it. Gone. It took about five minutes for anyone to talk. When the talking started, we exchanged jokes and responded with empty, devastating laughter.

18   We soon left the shop. It had grown colder outside and we quickly returned to our climate-controlled hotel room. We had just eaten a filling meal and paid for it with our own money. We were all about fifteen. The man we had encountered was probably in his fifties. He had no roof, no money, or food. It seemed strange that I owned more than an adult, but in truth, he had more than I. He was able to love us when we ostracized him and thought stereotypically about him.

19   I remember later trying to rationalize my sickening behavior by thinking that there is nothing wrong with being and acting afraid in a strange environment. I tried to use my age as an excuse. Nothing worked. I was guilty of fearing a fellow human being because of his color and my preset notions of bums.

20   To this day I still think about what difference, if any, it would have made if we had given him our leftover pizza. It might have eased my conscience. It was a very cold night and we had made it colder.

For Writing and Discussion

Individual task: Now that you have read "Berkeley Blues," read the following autobiographical narrative entitled "The Stolen Watch," which was submitted by a student as a draft for an assignment on narrative writing.

The Stolen Watch

Last fall and winter I was living in Spokane with my

brother, who during this time had a platonic girlfriend come

(continued)

over from Seattle and stay for a weekend. Her name was Karen, and we became interested in each other and I went over to see her at the first of the year. She then invited me to, supposedly, the biggest party of the year, called the Aristocrats' Ball. I said sure and made my way back to Seattle in February. It started out bad on Friday, the day my brother and I left Spokane. We left town an hour late, but what's new. Then my brother had to stop along the way and pick up some parts; we stayed there for an hour trying to find this guy. It all started out bad because we arrived in Seattle and I forgot to call Karen. We were staying at her brother's house and after we brought all our things in, we decided to go to a few bars. Later that night we ran into Karen in one of the bars, and needless to say she was not happy with me. When I got up the next morning I knew I should have stayed in Spokane, because I felt bad vibes. Karen made it over about an hour before the party. By the time we reached the party, which drove me crazy, she wound up with another guy, so her friends and I decided to go to a few bars. The next morning when I was packing, I could not find my watch and decided that someone had to have taken it. We decided that it had to have been the goon that Karen had wound up with the night before, because she was at her brother's house with him before she went home. So how was I going to get my watch back?

We decided the direct and honest approach to the problem would work out the best. We got in contact and confronted him. This turned out to be quite a chore. It turned out that he was visiting some of his family during that weekend and lived in Little Harbor, California. It turned out that Karen knew his half brother and got some information on him, which was not pretty. He had just been released by the army and was trained in a special forces unit, in the field of Martial Arts. He was a trained killer! This information did not help matters at all, but the next bit of information was just as bad if not worse. Believe it or not, he was up on charges of attempted murder and breaking and entering. In a way, it turned out lucky for me, because he was in enough trouble with the police and did not need any more. Karen got in contact with him and threatened him that I would bring him up on charges if he did not return the watch. His mother decided that he was in enough trouble and sent me the watch. I was astounded, it was still working and looked fine. The moral of the story is don't drive 400 miles to see a girl you hardly know, and whatever you do, don't leave your valuables out in the open.

Group task: Share your responses to the following questions:

1. How does your experience of reading "Berkeley Blues" differ from your experience of reading "The Stolen Watch"? Try to articulate the different ways you reacted to the two pieces while in the process of reading them.

2. Based on the differences between these two pieces, how would you define a "story"? Begin by brainstorming all the ways that the two pieces differ. Then try to identify the essential differences that make one a "story" and the other an *and then* chronology.

Now that you have tried to define a story for yourselves, we would like to explain our own four criteria for a story: depiction of events through time, connectedness, tension, and resolution. If we combine these criteria into a sentence, it would read like this: A story depicts events that are connected causally or thematically to create a sense of tension that is resolved through action, insight, or understanding. These four criteria occurring together turn a chronology into a story.

Depiction of Events Through Time

The essence of storytelling is the depiction of events through time. Whereas thesis-based writing descends from problem to thesis to supporting reasons and evidence, stories unfold linearly, temporally, from event to event. You may start in the middle of the action and then jump backward and forward, but you always encounter some sequence of events happening in time. This temporal focus creates a sense of "onceness." Things that happen at a point in time happen only once, as the classic fairy-tale opening "Once upon a time" suggests. When you compose and revise a narrative, you want to try to capture the "oneness" of that experience. As the essayist E. B. White once advised a young writer, "Don't write about Man but about a man."

Consider how Val Plumwood, a professor of women's studies and author of the book *Feminism and the Mastery of Nature,* depicts the events leading up to a disturbing encounter with a crocodile that dramatically shapes her understanding of humans' place in the food chain and the need for a respectful, rather than a dominating, attitude toward other animals.

> In the early wet season, Kakadu's paper-bark wetlands are especially stunning, as the water lilies weave white, pink, and blue patterns of dreamlike beauty over the shining thunderclouds reflected in their still waters. Yesterday, the water lilies and the wonderful bird life had enticed me into a joyous afternoon's idyll as I ventured onto the East Alligator Lagoon for the first time in a canoe lent by the park service. "You can play about on the backwaters," the ranger had said, "but don't go onto the main river channel. The current's too swift, and if you get into trouble, there are the crocodiles. Lots of them along the river!" I followed his advice and glutted myself on the magical beauty and bird life of the lily lagoons, untroubled by crocodiles.
>
> Today, I wanted to repeat the experience despite the drizzle beginning to fall as I neared the canoe launch site. I set off on a day trip in search of an Aboriginal rock art site across the lagoon and up a side channel. The drizzle turned to a warm rain within a few hours, and the magic was lost. The birds were invisible, the water lilies were sparser, and the lagoon seemed even a little menacing. I noticed now how low the 14-foot canoe sat in the water, just a few inches of fiberglass between me and the great saurians, close relatives of the ancient dinosaurs. [. . .]
>
> After hours of searching the maze of shallow channels in the swamp, I had not found the clear channel leading to the rock art site, as shown on the ranger's sketch map. When I pulled my canoe over in driving rain to a rock outcrop for a hasty, sodden lunch, I experienced the unfamiliar sensation of being watched. Having never been one for timidity, in philosophy or in life, I decided, rather than return defeated to my sticky trailer, to explore a clear, deep channel closer to the river I had traveled the previous day.
>
> The rain and wind grew more severe, and several times I pulled over to tip water from the canoe. The channel soon developed steep mud banks and snags. Farther on, the channel opened up and was eventually blocked by a large sandy bar. I pushed the canoe toward the bank, looking around carefully before getting out of the shallow and pulling the canoe up. I would be safe from crocodiles in the canoe—I had been told—but swimming and standing or wading at the water's edge were dangerous. Edges are one of the crocodile's favorite food-capturing places. I saw nothing, but the feeling of unease that had been with me all day intensified.

In this example of literary nonfiction, Plumwood persuades readers to appreciate the beauties of the exotic Australian rain forest as well as its dangers. Note how her method includes the depicting of events that happen once in time—her wondrous first day of exploration, the ranger's warning to stay away from the main river, her second day's unsuccessful search by canoe for a site of Aboriginal rock art, and then her emerging discovery that in the increasing intensity of the rainstorm, she had reached the junction with the main river. Plumwood's powerful narrative becomes the basis for a profound concluding reflection on what she calls humans' "ecological identity."

Connectedness

The events of a story must also be connected, not merely spatially or sequentially, but causally or thematically. When discussing "The Stolen Watch" in the previous exercise, you might have asked yourselves, "What does all that stuff about forgetting to call Karen and stopping for parts, etc., have to do with the stolen watch? Is this story about the watch or about confronting a potential killer?" If so, you instinctively understood the concept of connectedness. Stories are more than just chronicles of events. Novelist E. M. Forster offered the simplest definition of a story when he rejected "The king dies and then the queen died," but accepted "The king died and then the queen died . . . of grief." The words "of grief" connect the two events to each other in a causal relationship, converting a series of events into a patterned, meaningfully related sequence of events. Now examine this passage to see the connections the writer establishes between the scenes.

Thematic and Causal Connectedness

I have been so totally erased from nature lately, like a blackboard before school starts, that yesterday when I was in the Japanese section of San Francisco, Japantown, I saw the sidewalk littered with chocolate wrappers.

There were hundreds of them. Who in the hell has been eating all these chocolates? I thought. A convention of Japanese chocolate eaters must have passed this way.

Then I noticed some plum trees on the street. Then I noticed that it was autumn. Then I noticed that the leaves were falling as they will and as they must every year. Where had I gone wrong?

—Richard Brautigan, "Leaves"

Brautigan's narrative becomes a story only when you realize that the "chocolate wrappers" are really plum leaves; the two images are connected by the writer's changed perception, which illuminates the thematic question raised at the beginning and end: Why has he become "so totally erased from nature"? As you write, connect the elements of your narrative causally and thematically.

Tension or Conflict

The third criterion for a story—tension or conflict—creates the anticipation and potential significance that keep the reader reading. In whodunit stories, the tension follows from attempts to identify the murderer or to prevent the murderer from doing in yet another victim. In many comic works, the tension is generated by confusion or misunderstanding that drives a wedge between people who would normally be close. Tension always involves contraries, such as those between one belief and another, between opposing values, between the individual and the environment or the social order, between where I am now and where I want to be or used to be. In the following passage, see how the contraries create dramatic tension that engages readers.

Dramatic Tensions

Straddling the top of the world, one foot in China and the other in Nepal, I cleared the ice from my oxygen mask, hunched a shoulder against the wind, and stared absently down at the vastness of Tibet. I understood on some dim, detached level that the sweep of earth beneath my feet was a spectacular sight. I'd been fantasizing about this moment, and the release of emotion that would accompany it, for many months. But now that I was finally here, actually standing on the summit of Mount Everest, I just couldn't summon the energy to care.

It was early in the afternoon of May 10, 1996. I hadn't slept in fifty-seven hours. The only food I'd been able to force down over the preceding three days was a bowl of ramen soup and a handful of peanut M&M's. Weeks of violent coughing had left me with two separated ribs that made ordinary breathing an excruciating trial. At 29,028 feet up in the troposphere, so little oxygen was reaching my brain that my mental capacity was that of a slow child. Under the circumstances, I was incapable of feeling much of anything except cold and tired.

—Jon Krakauer, *Into Thin Air*

Notice how this passage presents several contraries or conflicts: the opposition between the narrator's expectation of what it would be like to stand on the top of Mount Everest and the actuality once he's there; and the opposition between the physical strength and stamina of the climber and the extreme danger of climbing this mountain. The reader wonders how Krakauer reached the summit with no sleep, almost no food, and a violent and agonizing cough; more important, the reader wonders why he kept on climbing. We can ask this important query of any narrative: What conflicts and tensions are prompting readers' ongoing questions and holding their interest?

Resolution, Recognition, or Retrospective Interpretation

The final criterion for a story is the resolution or retrospective interpretation of events. The resolution may be stated explicitly or implied. Fables typically sum up the story's significance with an explicit moral at the end. In contrast, the interpretation of events in poetry is almost always implicit. Note how the following haiku collapses events and resolution.

Resolution

A strange old man
stops me,
Looking out of my deep mirror.

—Hitomaro, *One Hundred Poems from the Japanese*

In this tiny story, two things happen simultaneously. The narrator is stopped by a "strange old man" and the narrator looks into a mirror. The narrator's *recognition* is that he is that same old man. This recognition—"That's me in the mirror; when I wasn't looking, I grew old!"—in turn ties the singular event of the story back to more universal concerns and the reader's world.

The typical direction of a story, from singular event(s) to general conclusion, reverses the usual points-first direction of closed-form essays. Stories force readers to read inductively, gathering information and looking for a pattern that's confirmed or unconfirmed by the story's resolution. This resolution is the point *toward* which readers read. It often drives home the significance of the narrative. Typically, a reader's satisfaction or dissatisfaction with a story hinges on how well the resolution manages to explain or justify the events that precede it. Writers need to ask: How does my resolution grow out of my narrative and fit with the resolution the reader has been forming?

Summary

In this lesson we have shown how you can make your narrative a story rather than an *and then* chronology by depicting events through time, by connecting the events thematically, by creating tension or conflict, and by providing a resolution or retrospective interpretation of the events.

For Writing and Discussion

1. Working as a whole class or in small groups, return to Patrick Klein's essay "Berkeley Blues" and explain how it qualifies as a story rather than an *and then* chronology. How does it meet all four of the criteria: depiction of events through time, connectedness, tension, and resolution?

2. Consider again "The Stolen Watch." It seems to meet the criterion of "depiction of events through time," but it is weak in connectedness, tension, and resolution. How could the writer revise the chronology to make it a story? Brainstorm several different ways that this potentially exciting early draft could be rewritten.

3. If you are working on your own open-form narrative, exchange drafts with a classmate. Discuss each others' drafts in light of this lesson's focus on story. To what extent do your drafts exhibit the features of a story rather than of an *and then* chronology? Working together, develop revision plans that might increase the story elements in your narratives.

LESSON 2: WRITE LOW ON THE LADDER OF ABSTRACTION

In Chapter 3 we introduced the concept of "ladder of abstraction," in which words can be arranged from the very abstract (living creatures, clothing) down to the very specific (our dog Charley, a Rhodesian Ridgeback with floppy ears; my hippie Birkenstocks with the saltwater stains; see pp. 50–51). In this lesson we show why and how open-form writers stay low on the ladder of abstraction through their use of concrete words, revelatory words, and memory-soaked words.

Concrete Words Evoke Images and Sensations

To appreciate the impact of specific, concrete language, look again at the opening sentence of Val Plumwood's narrative about her encounter with crocodiles (p. 550):

> In the early wet season, Kakadu's paper-bark wetlands are especially stunning, as the water lilies weave white, pink, and blue patterns of dreamlike beauty over the shining thunderclouds reflected in their still waters.

Here is how that same passage might sound if rewritten a rung higher on the ladder of abstraction:

> In the early wet season the Kakadu landscape is especially stunning as the water plants weave their colorful patterns of dreamlike beauty over the clouds reflected in the water's surface.

See also Chapter 5, pp. 102–103, for further discussion of specific, sensory words.

This is still quite a nice sentence. But something is lost when you say "landscape" rather than "paper-bark wetlands," "clouds" rather than "thunderclouds," or "colorful" rather than "white, pink, and blue." The lower you write on the ladder of abstraction, the more you tap into your readers' storehouse of particular memories and images.

The power of concrete words has been analyzed by writer John McPhee in a widely quoted and cited interview. When asked why he wrote the sentence "Old white oaks are rare because they had a tendency to become bowsprits, barrel staves, and queen-post trusses" instead of a more generic sentence such as, "Old white oaks are rare because they were used as lumber," he responded in a way that reveals his love of the particular.

> There isn't much life in [the alternative version of the sentence]. If you can find a specific, firm, and correct image, it's always going to be better than a generality, and hence I tend, for example, to put in trade names and company names and, in an instance like this, the names of wood products instead of a general term like "lumber." You'd say "Sony" instead of "tape recorder" if the context made it clear you meant to say tape recorder. It's not because you're on the take from Sony, it's because the image, at least to this writer or reader, strikes a clearer note.

Some readers might complain that the particulars "bowsprits, barrel staves, and queen-post trusses" don't help readers' understanding, as do particulars in closed-form prose, but instead give most readers a moment's pause. Today most barrel staves and bowsprits are made of metal, not oak, and few contemporary readers encounter them on a regular basis no matter what they're made of. Furthermore, few readers at any time could readily identify "queen-post trusses," a technical term from the building trade. Instead of smoothly completing the reader's understanding of a point, McPhee's particulars tend to arrest and even sidetrack, sending the reader in pursuit of a dictionary.

But if McPhee's examples momentarily puzzle, it's the sort of puzzlement that can lead to greater understanding. Precisely because they are exotic terms, these words arouse the reader's curiosity and imagination. "Exotic language is of value," says McPhee. "A queen-post truss is great just because of the sound of the words and what they call to mind. The 'queen,' the 'truss'—the ramifications in everything."

For McPhee, the fact that these words trip up the reader is a point in their favor. If McPhee had said that old white oaks are rare these days because they became parts of "ships, barrels, and roofs," no one would blink or notice. If you were to visualize the items, you'd probably call up some ready-made pictures that leave little trace in your mind. You also wouldn't hear the sounds of the words. (In this regard, notice McPhee's emphasis on images sounding "a clearer note.") Your forward progress toward the point would be unimpeded, but what would be lost? A new glimpse into a lost time when oak trees were used to make exotic items that today exist mostly in old books and memories.

Another quality also recommends words that readers trip over, words such as *bowsprit, barrel stave,* and *queen-post truss*: their power to persuade the reader to believe in the world being described. Tripping over things, whether they're made of steel or words, forces the reader to acknowledge their independence, the reality of a world outside the reader's own head. For this reason, writers of formula fiction—thrillers, westerns, romances, and the like—will load their texts with lots of little details and bits of technical information from the time and place they describe. Because their stories are otherwise implausible (e.g., the description of the Evil Empire's doomsday machine), they need all the help they can get from their details (the size of the toggle bolts used to keep the machine in place while it's blasting out intergalactic death rays) to convince readers that the story is real.

Using Revelatory Words

We use the term *revelatory words* for specific details that reveal the social status, lifestyle, beliefs, and values of people. According to writer Tom Wolfe, carefully chosen details can reveal a person's *status life*—"the entire pattern of behavior and possessions through which people express their position in the world or what they think it is or hope it to be."

Wolfe favors writing that records "everyday gestures, habits, manners, customs, styles of furniture, clothing, decoration, styles of traveling, eating, keeping house, modes of behaving toward children, servants, superiors, inferiors, peers, plus the various looks, glances, poses, styles of walking and other symbolic details that might exist within a scene." For example, Patrick Klein and his classmates are economically revealed as upper middle-class people by their attire—"Armani jackets" and "Gucci loafers."

For Writing and Discussion

Try your own hand at using descriptive details that reveal status life. Working in small groups or as a whole class, create a list of specific details that you might associate with each of the following: junior high boys standing on a street corner; a college professor's office; the kitchen of an upscale apartment of a two-profession couple; the kitchen of a lower-middle-class blue-collar family; the kitchen of an apartment shared by college students.

(continued)

> *Example:* Junior high boys standing on a street corner might be associated with baggy pants with crotch at the knee level and exposed boxer shorts; Nike Air Jordans with the top laces loose; Camel cigarettes; San Jose Sharks cap on backward; ears studded with silver rings.

Using Memory-Soaked Words

Wolfe offers a psychological explanation for the pleasure people take in exotic or revelatory language: "Print (as opposed to film or theater) is an indirect medium that does not so much 'create' images or emotions as jog the reader's memories." The best way to jog that memory and evoke sensations, according to Wolfe, is through careful selection of very specific words and images that evoke complex responses in the brain; the "human memory seems to be made up of *sets* of meaningful data" (emphasis ours) as opposed to separate bits of data that people consciously combine. In the following passage, Wolfe describes the complex interplay between writers' words and readers' responses.

> These memory sets often combine a complete image and an emotion. The power of a single image in a story or song to evoke a complex feeling is well known. I have always enjoyed the opening lines of a country and western song by Roger Miller called "King of the Road." "Trailers for Sale or Rent," it begins, "Room to Let Fifty Cents." It is not the part about trailers that I enjoy so much as the "Room to Let." This is the sort of archaic wording that, in my experience, is found only in windows or on door frames in the oldest and most run-down section of a city. It immediately triggers in my memory a particular view of a particular street near Worcester Square in New Haven, Connecticut. The emotion it calls up is one of loneliness and deprivation but of a rather romantic sort (bohemia). One's memory is apparently made up of millions of such sets, which work together. . . . The most gifted writers are those who manipulate the memory sets of the reader in such a rich fashion that they create within the mind of the reader an entire world that resonates with the reader's own real emotions.
>
> —Tom Wolfe, *New Journalism*

Had Miller opened his song with "Room *for Rent* Fifty Cents," there would have been no loss of clarity; if anything, most people would process the more familiar "rent" more rapidly than "let." The loss would have been associational and emotional. "For Rent" signs are too common to evoke any particular set of associations for most people. "To Let" signs, however, are rare enough that they are much more likely to evoke particular times and places for those who've encountered them. People who have never heard the phrase "to let" will either puzzle over it and eventually experience the pleasure of making sense of it or not notice the substitution and pass over it.

Summary

This lesson has focused on the value of specific details low on the ladder of abstraction. Particularly, you can improve your drafts by using concrete words that appeal to the senses, revelatory words that show social status and values, and memory-soaked words that trigger networks of associations in your readers' minds.

For Writing and Discussion

1. Make a list of specific words and names associated with your childhood that you now rarely hear or see. Share your list with others in your group and identify the items that provoke the strongest associations. People who grew up in the '50s, for example, might have deep associations with *Flexible Flyer* (a sled), *45-RPM records, tail fins, duck tails,* and the *Ed Sullivan Show.* In recent years, our students have come up with these memory-soaked words from their own childhoods: *Teenage Mutant Ninja Turtles, American Girl dolls, Nintendo 64, Ghostbusters action figures,* and *Uno* (card game). The idea is to think of specific words that are soaked with memories. Identify the emotions you associate with these words.

2. If you are working on your own open-form narrative, exchange drafts with a classmate and, working together, find specific examples where each of you have successfully used concrete, revelatory, or memory-soaked words. Then find passages that could be profitably revised by stepping down a rung on the ladder of abstraction or by adding concrete details that follow the advice in this lesson.

LESSON 3: DISRUPT YOUR READER'S DESIRE FOR DIRECTION AND CLARITY

The epigraph to Chapter 19 by the philosopher Kenneth Burke speaks about form as "an arousing and fulfillment of desires." In closed-form prose, we can easily see this process at work: The writer previews what he or she is going to say, arousing the reader's desire to see the general outline fleshed out with specifics, and then fulfills that desire speedily through a presentation of pertinent points and particulars.

In more open-form prose, the fulfillment of desire follows a less straightforward path. Writers offer fewer overviews and clues, leaving readers less sure of where they're headed; or writers mention an idea and then put it aside for a while as they pursue some other point, whose relevance may seem tenuous. Rather than establish the direction or point of their prose, writers suspend that direction, waiting until later in the prose to show how the ideas are meaningfully related. In other words, the period of arousal is longer and more drawn out; the fulfillment of desire is delayed until the end, when the reader finally sees how the pieces fit together.

Open-form prose gives you the opportunity to overlay your narrative core with other patterns of ideas—to move associatively from idea to idea, to weave a complex pattern of meaning in which the complete picture emerges later. Often the way you achieve these surprising twists and turns of structure and meaning is by playing with the conventions of closed-form prose. For example, in the autobiographical narrative "Berkeley Blues," Patrick Klein breaks the cardinal closed-form rule that pronouns should refer only to previously stated antecedents; he introduces the stranger only as *he* and gradually reveals that person's identity. This violation creates an aura of mystery and suspense. Here in this lesson we describe some of your open-form options for surprising your readers and delaying their fulfillment of desires.

Disrupting Predictions and Making Odd Juxtapositions

Open-form writers frequently violate the principle of forecasting and mapping that we stressed in Chapter 19. Consider the following introduction to an essay:

Passage with Disrupted Predictions and Odd Juxtapositions

Whose bones?
What feathers?

Birds? What birds?
What do birds have to do with how the brain works? Where is this writer going?

I suppose their little bones have years ago been lost among the stones and winds of those high glacial pastures. I suppose their feathers blew eventually into the piles of tumbleweed beneath the straggling cattle fences and rotted there in the mountain snows, along with dead steers and all the other things that drift to an end in the corners of the wire. I do not quite know why I should be thinking of birds over the *New York Times* at breakfast, particularly the birds of my youth half a continent away. It is a funny thing what the brain will do with memories and how it will treasure them and finally bring them into odd juxtapositions with other things, as though it wanted to make a design, or get some meaning out of them, whether you want it or not, or even see it.

—Loren Eisley, "The Bird and the Machine"

Note the sequence of ideas from bones to birds to breakfast over the *New York Times* to comments about the workings of the brain. In fact, in this essay it takes Eisley six full paragraphs in which he discusses mechanical inventions to return to the birds with the line: ". . . or those birds, I'll never forget those birds. . . ."

Throughout these paragraphs, what drives the reader forward is curiosity to discover the connections between the parts and to understand the meaning of the essay's title "The Bird and the Machine." Actually, Eisley's comment about the brain's "odd juxtapositions" of memories with "other things, as though it wanted to make a design, or get some meaning out of them" could be a description of this open-form technique we've called *disrupting predictions and making odd juxtapositions*. Open-form writers can choose when "odd juxtapositions" are an appropriate strategy for inviting the reader to accompany the discovering, reflecting writer on a journey toward meaning.

Leaving Gaps

An important convention of closed-form prose is the old/new contract, which specifies that the opening of every sentence should link in some way to what has gone before. Open-form prose often violates this convention, leaving *gaps* in the text, forcing the reader to puzzle over the connection between one part and the next.

The following passage clearly violates the old/new contract. This example recounts the writer's thoughts after startling a weasel in the woods and exchanging glances with it.

Passage with Intentional Gaps

Gap caused by unexplained or unpredicted shift from weasel to philosophic musing

What goes on in [a weasel's brain] the rest of the time? What does a weasel think about? He won't say. His journal is tracks in clay, a spray of feathers, mouse blood and bone: uncollected, unconnnected, loose-leaf, and blown.

I would like to learn, or remember, how to live. I come to Hollins Pond not so much to learn how to live as, frankly, to forget about it.

—Annie Dillard, "Living Like Weasels"

Dillard suddenly switches, without transition, from musing about the mental life of a weasel to asserting that she would like to learn how to live. What is the connection between her encounter with the weasel and her own search for how to live? Dillard's open-form techniques leave these gaps for readers to ponder and fill in, inviting us to participate in the process of arriving at meaning. Just as open-form writers can deliberately avoid predicting or mapping statements, they also have the liberty to leave gaps in a text when it suits their purpose.

Employing Unstable or Ironic Points of View

Whereas the closed-form style encourages a single sort of viewpoint—rational, trustworthy, thoughtful—the open-form style tolerates a variety of viewpoints, including some that are more perplexing than reassuring. In open-form prose, writers are free to don masks and play around with different personae, including some that the writer may question or even loathe. A particular favorite of open-form writers is the ironic point of view. In this context, *irony* means saying one thing while intending other things, one of which may be the exact opposite of what's being said.

Consider the following bit of irony from eighteenth-century writer Jonathan Swift:

> I have been assured by a very knowing American of my acquaintance in London, that a young healthy child well nursed is at a year old a most delicious, nourishing, and wholesome food, whether stewed, roasted, baked, or boiled; and I make no doubt that it will equally serve in a fricassee or a ragout.

The shock of this passage comes in part from the narrator's sudden change of direction. Previously, the writer had seemed to point toward some elevating discussion of child wellness. Then, without warning, the reader is plunged into a grotesque treatise on the tastiness of cooked children.

Clearly the narrator's values are not shared by Swift, a religious Irishman who spent much of his life protesting the very sort of inhumanity he presents in this passage. What does Swift gain by adopting the persona of a moral monster and proposing that poor Irish people sell their children to English gentry for food in order to reduce Ireland's population and make some money? For one thing, he gains immediacy.

By stepping inside the persona that he reviles, Swift dramatizes what he sees as the snobbish, self-assured, and predatory English "gentleman." He doesn't talk about his enemy; he *becomes* that enemy so that the reader can see him as Swift sees him. Swift could have written an essay condemning the callous attitudes that were causing the Irish people so much suffering. But consider what would happen to the passage if Swift were to speak for himself.

> The landed English gentry who control Ireland treat the Irish people like consumer goods to be bought, sold, and used up in the service of their self-interests. For all the English care, we Irish could be chunks of mutton to be tossed into their nightly stew.

That's still pretty strong, but it leaves the reader outside the evil that Swift describes. The audience hears about "landed English gentry" but doesn't experience their attitudes, values, and language directly, as in the original passage. The difference in the two passages is the difference between being told that someone is really hideous and spending half an hour trapped in an elevator with that person.

Unstable viewpoints aren't always this dramatic. But they always offer writers the freedom to present directly, through dialogue and perspective, points of view that they might otherwise have to represent via summary and argument. Such viewpoints also require readers to be more attentive in order to distinguish the author's point of view from that of the narrator.

Summary

This lesson has shown how open-form narratives often violate the structural principles of closed-form prose by disrupting predictions, by leaving gaps, and by employing unstable or ironic points of view.

For Writing and Discussion

If you are currently working on an open-form narrative, exchange drafts with a classmate. Discuss in what way the strategies explained in this lesson might be appropriate for your purposes. Where might you currently "explain too much" and benefit by juxtaposing scenes without explanatory filler? Where might you use other strategies from this lesson?

LESSON 4: TAP THE POWER OF FIGURATIVE LANGUAGE

Open-form writers often use figurative language in situations in which closed-form writers would use literal language. In this brief lesson, we show you some of the power of figurative language.

When journalist Nicholas Tomalin describes a captured Vietnamese prisoner as young and slight, the reader understands him in a literal way, but when, a moment later, he compares the prisoner to "a tiny, fine-boned wild animal," the reader understands him in a different way; the reader understands not only what the subject looks like—his general physical attributes—but how that particular boy appears in that moment to those around him—fierce, frightened, trapped.

Metaphors abound when literal words fail. When writers encounter eccentric people or are overwhelmed by the strangeness of their experiences, they use *figurative language*—imaginative comparisons—to explain their situation and their reactions to it. Figurative language—similes, metaphors, and personifications—enables the writer to describe an unfamiliar thing in terms of different, more familiar things. The surprise of yoking two very unlike things evokes from the reader a perception, insight, or emotional experience that could not otherwise be communicated. The originality and vividness of the imaginative comparison frequently resonates with meaning for readers and sticks in their minds long afterwards.

In the following passage, Isak Dinesen describes an experience that most of us have not had—seeing iguanas in the jungle and shooting one. After reading this passage, however, we have a striking picture in our minds of what she saw and a strong understanding of what she felt and realized.

Passage Using Figurative Language

In the Reserve I have sometimes come upon the Iguana, the big lizards, as they were sunning themselves upon a flat stone in a riverbed. They are not pretty in shape, but nothing can be imagined more beautiful than their coloring. They shine like a heap of precious stones or like a pane cut out of an old church window. When, as you approach, they swish away, there is a flash of azure, green and purple over the stones, the color seems to be standing behind them in the air, like a comet's luminous tail.

Similes heaped up

Simile

Once I shot an Iguana. I thought that I should be able to make some pretty things from his skin. A strange thing happened then, that I have never afterwards forgotten. As I went up to him, where he was lying dead upon his stone, and actually while I was walking a few steps, he faded and grew pale, all color died out of him as in one long sigh, and by the time that I touched him he was gray and dull like a lump of concrete. It was the live impetuous blood pulsating within the animal, which had radiated out all that glow and splendor. Now that the flame was put out, and the soul had flown, the Iguana was as dead as a sandbag.

Metaphor of dying applied to color simile

Metaphor

Simile

—Isak Dinesen, "The Iguana"

The figurative language in this passage enables readers to share Dinesen's experience. It also compacts a large amount of information into sharp, memorable images.

Summary

This lesson has shown the power of figurative language, which yokes together two realms of experience—the familiar and the unfamiliar—to help readers understand imaginatively what the writer can't say directly. Figurative language is a frequent strategy in much open-form prose.

For Writing and Discussion

1. Figurative language can fall flat when it takes the form of clichés ("I stood transfixed like a bump on a log") or mixed metaphors ("Exposed like a caterpillar on a leaf, he wolfed down his lunch before taking flight.") But when used effectively, figurative language adds powerfully compressed and meaningful images to a passage. Working individually or in small groups, find examples of figurative language in one or more of the example essays in this chapter or in Chapter 7 (pp. 160–169). See if you can reach consensus on what makes a particular instance of figurative language effective or ineffective. As an initial example, consider this passage from the student essay "Masks" (pp. 165–166): "She was so elusive, like a beautiful perfume you smell but can't name, like the whisper that wakes you from a dream and turns out to belong to the dream."

(continued)

2. If you are currently working on an open-form narrative, exchange drafts with a classmate. See if you can find instances of figurative language in your current drafts and analyze their effectiveness. Perhaps you can also discover places where figurative language could be profitably added to the text.

LESSON 5: EXPAND YOUR REPERTOIRE OF STYLES

See pp. 71–73 for a discussion of style.

In Chapter 4, we introduced you to the concept of style, which is a combination of sentence structure, word choice, and rhythm that allows writers to vary their emphasis and tone in a variety of ways. In this lesson, we show you how to expand your repertoire of styles through a classic method of teaching in which you try to imitate other writers' styles. This rhetorical practice—called *creative imitation*—has a long history beginning with the rhetoricians of classical Greece and Rome. When you do creative imitation, you examine a passage from an expert stylist and try to emulate it. You substitute your own subject matter, but you try to imitate the exact grammatical structures, lengths and rhythms of the sentences, and the tones of the original passage. The long-range effect of creative imitation is to expand your stylistic choices; the more immediate effect is to increase your skill at analyzing a writer's style. Most practitioners find that creative imitation encourages surprising insights into their own subject matter (when seen through the lens of the original writer's style) as well as a new understanding of how a particular piece of writing creates its special effects.

You begin a creative imitation by asking questions such as these: What is distinctive about the sentences in this passage of writing? How do choices about sentence length and complexity, kinds of words, figures of speech, and so forth create a writer's voice? After close examination of the passage, you then think of your own subject matter that could be appropriately adapted to this writer's style.

To help you understand creative imitation, we provide the following example. In this passage, the writer, Victoria Register-Freeman, is exploring how relations between young men and women today threaten to undo some of the twentieth century's progress toward gender equality. In the section of her article that precedes this passage, Register-Freeman explains how she, as a single mother, taught her boys to cook, sew, do laundry, and "carry their weight domestically." But then, as she explains in this passage, teenage girls undid her attempts at creating gender equality:

Register-Freeman Passage

Then came puberty and hunkhood. Over the last few years, the boys' domestic skills have atrophied because handmaidens have appeared en masse. The damsels have driven by, beeped, phoned and faxed. Some appeared so frequently outside the front door they began to remind me of the suction-footed Garfields spread-eagled on car windows. While the girls varied according to height, hair color and basic body type, they shared one characteric. They were ever eager to help the guys out.

—Victoria Register-Freeman, "My Turn: Hunks and Handmaidens"

Register-Freeman's voice projects the image of a concerned mother and feminist social critic. Her tone includes a range of attitudes: serious, personal, factual, ironic, frustrated. Note how this passage begins and ends with short, clipped sentences. The second sentence states a problem that the next three sentences develop with various kinds of details. The third sentence includes a series of colorful verbs; the fourth uses a metaphor (the ever-present girls compared to Garfields on car windows). The fifth sentence builds to the point in the sixth sentence, which is delivered bluntly and simply.

Here is one writer's attempt at a creative imitation:

Creative Imitation of Register-Freeman

Then came prosperity and popularity. Over the last ten years, Seattle's special charms have faded because expansion has occurred too rapidly. Traffic has multiplied, thickened, amplified, and slowed. Traffic jams appeared so often on the freeways and arterials they began to remind me of ants swarming over spilled syrup. While the congestion varied according to time, seasons, and weather conditions, it had one dominant effect. It increasingly threatened to spoil the city's beauty.

For Writing and Discussion

1. Do your own creative imitation of the passage from Register-Freeman.
2. Choose one or both of the following passages for creative imitation. Begin by jotting down all the specific observations you can make about the stylistic features of the passage. Then choose a topic that matches the topic of the original in its degree of lightness or seriousness and its depth. Explore your topic by presenting it using the sentence structures and kinds of words used in the original. Try to imitate the original phrase by phrase and sentence by sentence. You may find it helpful to use a dictionary and thesaurus.

   a. Africa is mystic; it is wild; it is a sweltering inferno; it is a photographer's paradise, a hunter's Valhalla, an escapist's Utopia. It is what you will, and it withstands all interpretations. It is the last vestige of a dead world or the cradle of a shiny new one. To a lot of people, as to myself, it is just "home." It is all of these things but one thing—it is never dull.
      —Beryl Markham, "Flying Elsewhere," *West with the Night*

   b. The disease was bubonic plague, present in two forms: one that infected the bloodstream, causing the buboes and internal bleeding, and was spread by contact; and a second, more virulent pneumonic type that infected the lungs and was spread by respiratory infection. The presence of both at once caused the high mortality and speed of contagion. So lethal was the disease that cases were known of persons going to bed well and dying before they woke, of doctors catching the illness at bedside and dying before the patient.
      —Barbara Tuchman, "This Is the End of the World," *A Distant Mirror*

Summary

This lesson has introduced you to "creative imitation" as a classic technique for expanding one's stylistic flexibility. With practice, you can transfer your new skills to your own writing in both open and closed forms.

LESSON 6: USE OPEN-FORM ELEMENTS TO CREATE "VOICE" IN CLOSED-FORM PROSE

So far we have been talking about features of open-form prose in its purer forms. Sometimes, however, writers wish simply to loosen basically closed-form prose by combining it with some features of open-form prose. If, for example, an academic wanted to share new developments in a field with a popular audience, he or she would be well-advised to leaven his or her prose with some elements of open-form writing. In this final lesson, we offer several pieces of advice for loosening up closed-form prose.

Introducing Some Humor

Humor is rare in tightly closed prose because humor is nonfunctional—it doesn't *have* to be there for a writer to make a point—and closed-form prose values efficiency, getting what you have to say said in the most economical fashion.

Humor is closely related to one of the mainsprings of open-form style, surprise. Humor typically depends on sudden twists and abrupt changes in direction. In physical comedy, pratfalls are funny in direct proportion to the audience's inability to see them coming. In verbal humor, the less clearly the audience sees the punch line coming, the more it makes the audience laugh.

Humor is particularly valuable in that it can make imposing subjects more manageable for readers. Just as humor can deflate pretensions and bring down the high and the mighty in an instant, it can make difficult and foreign subjects less anxiety producing. Formal, abstract language can put readers off, estranging them from the subject; humor has the power to "de-strange" a subject, to allow the audience to look at it long enough to understand it. Many popular books on science and many of the best instructional books on car repair, cooking, money management, and others of life's drearier necessities use a humorous style to help their phobic readers get on with life.

To appreciate the effect of humor, consider the following passages from two different instructional books on how to operate the database program Paradox. The first passage, from *Windows in 21 Days,* uses a clear, humor-free, closed-form style.

> In this book, you learn by following detailed step-by-step exercises based on real-world problems in database application design. Every exercise leads you further into the power of "Paradox for Windows" as you develop the components of an automated application. This section does the following: explains the assumptions and conventions used in this book; lists the hardware and software requirements and setup needed to run Paradox for Windows and use this book efficiently; and offers

some suggestions for strategies to get the most from this book. The step-by-step exercises make it easy.

Now note the different effect produced by the following passage from one of the hugely popular *Dummies* books:

> Welcome to *Paradox for Windows for Dummies,* a book that's not afraid to ask the tough questions like "When's lunch?" and "Who finished the cookie dough ice cream?" If you're more interested in food (or Australian Wombats, for that matter) than you are in Paradox for Windows, this book is for you. If you're more interested in Paradox for Windows, please get some professional help before going out into society again.
>
> My goal is to help you get things done despite the fact that you're using Paradox. Whether you're at home, in your office, or at home in your office (or even if you just *feel* like you live at work) *Paradox for Windows for Dummies* is your all-in-one guidebook through the treacherous, frustrating, and appallingly technical world of the relational database.

For Writing and Discussion

1. Which of these two instructional books would you prefer to read?

2. The second passage says that the world of relational databases is "treacherous, frustrating, and appallingly technical," whereas the first stresses that the "step-by-step exercises [in the book] make it easy." Why do you suppose the humorous passage stresses the difficulty of databases whereas the humorless passage stresses the ease of a step-by-step approach? Is it good strategy for the humorous writer to stress the difficulty of Paradox?

3. Under what rhetorical circumstances are humorous instructions better than strictly serious instructions? When is a strictly serious approach better?

Using Techniques from Popular Magazines

Writers who publish regularly for popular audiences develop a vigorous, easy-reading style that differs from the style of much academic writing. The effect of this difference is illustrated by the results of a famous research study conducted by Michael Graves and Wayne Slater at the University of Michigan. For this study, teams of writers revised passages from a high school history textbook.* One team consisted of linguists and technical writers trained in producing closed-form texts using the strategies discussed in Chapter 19 (forecasting structure, putting points first, following the old/new contract, using transitions). A second team consisted of two *Time-Life* book editors.

Whereas the linguists aimed at making the passages clearer, the *Time-Life* writers were more concerned with making them livelier. The result? One hundred eleven-grade students found the *Time-Life* editors' version both more

---

*The study involved three teams, but for purposes of simplification we limit our discussion to two.

comprehensible and more memorable. Lack of clarity wasn't the problem with the original textbook; unbearable dryness was the problem. According to the researchers, the *Time-Life* editors did not limit themselves

> to making the passages lucid, well-organized, coherent, and easy to read. Their revisions went beyond such matters and were intended to make the texts interesting, exciting, vivid, rich in human drama, and filled with colorful language.

To see how they achieved this effect, let's look at their revision. Here is a passage about the Vietnam War taken from the original history text.

Original History Text

The most serious threat to world peace developed in Southeast Asia. Communist guerrillas threatened the independence of the countries carved out of French Indo-China by the Geneva conference of 1954. In South Vietnam, Communist guerrillas (the Viet Cong) were aided by forces from Communist North Vietnam in a struggle to overthrow the American-supported government. . . .

Shortly after the election of 1964, Communist gains prompted President Johnson to alter his policy concerning Vietnam. American military forces in Vietnam were increased from about 20,000 men in 1964 to more than 500,000 by 1968. Even so, North Vietnamese troops and supplies continued to pour into South Vietnam.

Here is the *Time-Life* editors' revision.

History Presented in Popular Magazine Style

In the early 1960's the greatest threat to world peace was just a small splotch of color on Kennedy's map, one of the fledgling nations sculpted out of French Indo-China by the Geneva peacemakers of 1954. It was a country so tiny and remote that most Americans had never uttered its name: South Vietnam. . . .

Aided by Communist North Vietnam, the Viet Cong guerrillas were eroding the ground beneath South Vietnam's American-backed government. Village by village, road by road, these jungle-wise rebels were waging a war of ambush and mining: They darted out of tunnels to head off patrols, buried exploding booby traps beneath the mud floors of huts, and hid razor-sharp bamboo sticks in holes. . . .

No sooner had Johnson won the election than Communist gains prompted Johnson to go back on his campaign promise. The number of American soldiers in Vietnam skyrocketed from 20,000 in 1964 to more than 500,000 by 1968. But in spite of GI patrols, leech-infested jungles, swarms of buzzing insects, and flash floods that made men cling to trees to escape being washed away—North Vietnamese troops streamed southward without letup along the Ho Chi Minh Trail.

What can this revision teach you about envigorating closed-form prose? What specifically are the editors doing here?

First, notice how far the level of abstraction drops in the revision. The original is barren of sensory words; the revision is alive with them ("South Vietnam" becomes a "small splotch of color on Kennedy's map"; "a struggle to overthrow the American-supported government" becomes "[They] buried exploding booby traps beneath the mud floors of huts and hid razor-sharp bamboo sticks in holes").

Second, notice how much more dramatic the revision is. Actual scenes, including a vision of men clinging to trees to escape being washed away by flash floods, replace a chronological account of the war's general progress. According to the editors, such scenes, or "nuggets"—vivid events that encapsulate complex processes or principles—are the lifeblood of *Time-Life* prose.

Finally, notice how the revision tends to delay critical information for dramatic effect, moving information you would normally expect to find early on into a later position. In the first paragraph, the *Time-Life* writers talk about "the greatest threat to world peace" in the early 1960s for five lines before revealing the identity of that threat—South Vietnam.

Summary

In this lesson we suggest open-form strategies you can use to enliven closed-form prose, especially when you are trying to reach popular audiences rather than strictly academic ones. We suggested two strategies: Using humor and using the stylistic devices of popular magazine writers such as narrative elements and specific details that are low on the ladder of abstraction.

For Writing and Discussion

Here is a passage from a student argument opposing women's serving on submarines. Working individually or in small groups, enliven this passage by using some of the techniques of the *Time-Life* writers.

> Not only would it be very expensive to refit submarines for women personnel, but having women on submarines would hurt the morale of the sailors. In order for a crew to work effectively, they must have good morale or their discontent begins to show through in their performance. This is especially crucial on submarines, where if any problem occurs, it affects the safety of the whole ship. Women would hurt morale by creating sexual tension. Sexual tension can take many forms. One form is couples' working and living in a close space with all of the crew. When a problem occurs within the relationship, it could affect the morale of those directly involved and in the workplace. This would create an environment that is not conducive to good productivity. Tension would also occur if one of the women became pregnant or if there were complaints of sexual harassment. It would be easier to deal with these problems on a surface ship, but in the small confines of a submarine these problems would cause more trouble.

CHAPTER SUMMARY

In this chapter we have presented six lessons for composing and revising open-form prose:

1. Make your narrative a story, not an *and then* chronology.
2. Write low on the ladder of abstraction.
3. Disrupt your reader's desire for direction and clarity.
4. Tap the power of figurative language.

5. Expand your repertoire of styles.

6. Use open-form elements to create "voice" in closed-form prose.

As a final exercise, we'd like you to read a famous short example of open-form prose—Annie Dillard's "Living Like Weasels." The exercises that follow the reading will help you review the lessons in this chapter.

R e a d i n g

■ ANNIE DILLARD ■

LIVING LIKE WEASELS

A weasel is wild. Who knows what he thinks? He sleeps in his underground den, his tail draped over his nose. Sometimes he lives in his den for two days without leaving. Outside, he stalks rabbits, mice, muskrats, and birds, killing more bodies than he can eat warm, and often dragging the carcasses home. Obedient to instinct, he bites his prey at the neck, either splitting the jugular vein at the throat or crunching the brain at the base of the skull, and he does not let go. One naturalist refused to kill a weasel who was socketed into his hand deeply as a rattlesnake. The man could in no way pry the tiny weasel off, and he had to walk half a mile to water, the weasel dangling from his palm, and soak him off like a stubborn label.   1

And once, says Ernest Thompson Seton—once, a man shot an eagle out of the sky. He examined the eagle and found the dry skull of a weasel fixed by the jaws to his throat. The supposition is that the eagle had pounced on the weasel and the weasel swiveled and bit as instinct taught him, tooth to neck, and nearly won. I would like to have seen that eagle from the air a few weeks or months before he was shot: was the whole weasel still attached to his feathered throat, a fur pendant? Or did the eagle eat what he could reach, gutting the living weasel with his talons before his breast, bending his beak, cleaning the beautiful airborne bones?   2

I have been reading about weasels because I saw one last week. I startled a weasel who startled me, and we exchanged a long glance.   3

Twenty minutes from my house, through the woods by the quarry and across the highway, is Hollins Pond, a remarkable piece of shallowness, where I like to go at sunset and sit on a tree trunk. Hollins Pond is also called Murray's Pond; it covers two acres of bottomland near Tinker Creek with six inches of water and six thousand lily pads. In winter, brown-and-white steers stand in the middle of it, merely dampening their hooves; from the distant shore they look like miracle itself, complete with miracle's nonchalance. Now, in summer, the steers are gone. The water lilies have blossomed and spread to a green horizontal plane that is terra firma to plodding blackbirds, and tremulous ceiling to black leeches, crayfish, and carp.   4

5   This is, mind you, suburbia. It is a five-minute walk in three directions to rows of houses, though none is visible here. There's a 55 mph highway at one end of the pond, and a nesting pair of wood ducks at the other. Under every bush is a muskrat hole or a beer can. The far end is an alternating series of fields and woods, fields and woods, threaded everywhere with motorcycle tracks—in whose bare clay wild turtles lay eggs.

6   So. I had crossed the highway, stepped over two low barbed-wire fences, and traced the motorcycle path in all gratitude through the wild rose and poison ivy of the pond's shoreline up into high grassy fields. Then I cut down through the woods to the mossy fallen tree where I sit. This tree is excellent. It makes a dry, upholstered bench at the upper, marshy end of the pond, a plush jetty raised from the thorny shore between a shallow blue body of water and a deep blue body of sky.

7   The sun had just set. I was relaxed on the tree trunk, ensconced in the lap of lichen, watching the lily pads at my feet tremble and part dreamily over the thrusting path of a carp. A yellow bird appeared to my right and flew behind me. It caught my eye. I swiveled around—and the next instant, inexplicably, I was looking down at a weasel, who was looking up at me.

8   Weasel! I'd never seen one wild before. He was ten inches long, thin as a curve, a muscled ribbon, brown as fruitwood, soft-furred, alert. His face was fierce, small and pointed as a lizard's; he would have made a good arrowhead. There was just a dot of chin, maybe two brown hairs' worth, and then the pure white fur began that spread down his underside. He had two black eyes I didn't see, any more than you see a window.

9   The weasel was stunned into stillness as he was emerging from beneath an enormous shaggy wild rose bush four feet away. I was stunned into stillness twisted backward on the tree trunk. Our eyes locked, and someone threw away the key.

10   Our look was as if two lovers, or deadly enemies, met unexpectedly on an overgrown path when each had been thinking of something else: a clearing blow to the gut. It was also a bright blow to the brain, or a sudden beating of brains, with all the charge and intimate grate of rubbed balloons. It emptied our lungs. It felled the forest, moved the fields, and drained the pond; the world dismantled and tumbled into that black hole of eyes. If you and I looked at each other that way, our skulls would split and drop to our shoulders. But we don't. We keep our skulls. So.

11   He disappeared. This was only last week, and already I don't remember what shattered the enchantment. I think I blinked, I think I retrieved my brain from the weasel's brain, and tried to memorize what I was seeing, and the weasel felt the yank of separation, the careening splashdown into real life and the urgent current of instinct. He vanished under the wild rose. I waited motionless, my mind suddenly full of data and my spirit with pleadings, but he didn't return.

Please do not tell me about "approach-avoidance conflicts." I tell you I've   12
been in that weasel's brain for sixty seconds, and he was in mine. Brains are
private places, muttering through unique and secret tapes—but the weasel
and I both plugged into another tape simultaneously, for a sweet and shocking time. Can I help it if it was a blank?

What goes on in his brain the rest of the time? What does a weasel think   13
about? He won't say. His journal is tracks in clay, a spray of feathers, mouse
blood and bone: uncollected, unconnected, loose-leaf, and blown.

I would like to learn, or remember, how to live. I come to Hollins Pond not   14
so much to learn how to live as, frankly, to forget about it. That is, I don't
think I can learn from a wild animal how to live in particular—shall I suck
warm blood, hold my tail high, walk with my footprints precisely over the
prints of my hands?—but I might learn something of mindlessness, something of the purity of living in the physical senses and the dignity of living
without bias or motive. The weasel lives in necessity and we live in choice,
hating necessity and dying at the last ignobly in its talons. I would like to live
as I should, as the weasel lives as he should. And I suspect that for me the way
is like the weasel's: open to time and death painlessly, noticing everything,
remembering nothing, choosing the given with a fierce and pointed will.

I missed my chance. I should have gone for the throat. I should have   15
lunged for that streak of white under the weasel's chin and held on, held on
through mud and into the wild rose, held on for a dearer life. We could live
under the wild rose wild as weasels, mute and uncomprehending. I could
very calmly go wild. I could live two days in the den, curled, leaning on
mouse fur, sniffing bird bones, blinking, licking, breathing musk, my hair
tangled in the roots of grasses. Down is a good place to go, where the mind
is single. Down is out, out of your ever-loving mind and back to your careless senses. I remember muteness as a prolonged and giddy fast, where every
moment is a feast of utterance received. Time and events are merely poured,
unremarked, and ingested directly, like blood pulsed into my gut through a
jugular vein. Could two live that way? Could two live under the wild rose,
and explore by the pond, so that the smooth mind of each is as everywhere
present to the other, and as received and as unchallenged, as falling snow?

We could, you know. We can live any way we want. People take vows of   16
poverty, chastity, and obedience—even of silence—by choice. The thing is
to stalk your calling in a certain skilled and supple way, to locate the most
tender and live spot and plug into that pulse. This is yielding, not fighting.
A weasel doesn't "attack" anything; a weasel lives as he's meant to, yielding
at every moment to the perfect freedom of single necessity.

I think it would be well, and proper, and obedient, and pure, to grasp   17
your one necessity and not let it go, to dangle from it limp wherever it takes
you. Then even death, where you're going no matter how you live, cannot

you part. Seize it and let it seize you up aloft even, till your eyes burn out and drop; let your musky flesh fall off in shreds, and let your very bones unhinge and scatter, loosened over fields, over fields and woods, lightly, thoughtless, from any height at all, from as high as eagles.

For Writing and Discussion

Working in small groups or as a whole class, use the questions that follow to guide your close examination of Dillard's structural and stylistic choices.

1. How does Dillard's essay meet the criteria for a story—events depicted in time, connectedness, tension, and resolution? What final resolution or interpretation does Dillard offer?

2. Find ten examples of Dillard's use of specific words and concrete language. Try rewording some of these examples at a higher level of abstraction and then compare Dillard's "low on the scale" version with your "higher on the scale" version.

3. Choose three consecutive paragraphs in this essay and examine how Dillard employs gaps between sentences to stimulate readers to think actively about the questions she is raising. Try tracking her ideas from sentence to sentence in these paragraphs. Where does she disrupt readers' expectations by violating conventions of closed-form prose? Also, how does Dillard experiment with viewpoint, and how is this shifting of perspective part of the significance of her narrative?

4. Find ten examples of figurative language and explain how these are particularly effective in holding the reader's interest and portraying the intensity or meaning of her experience.

5. Suppose that you were going to do a stylistic imitation of one of Dillard's passages. Choose a passage that you think is particularly interesting stylistically and explain why you have chosen it.

6. Imagine the entry on "weasels" in an encyclopedia. How could you use some of Dillard's strategies to make a typical closed-form encyclopedia article more lively?

Ladies of High-Calibre

Protect Your Rights!

Join Now!

Click Here for the 10 Commandments of gun safety!

Home

WAGC Information

WAGC Features

WAGC Boycotts

WAGC Links

WAGC Site map

WAGC Contact

Women Against Gun Control

"The Second Amendment IS the Equal Rights Am

Click here to sign and read our new forum board!

Click here for a special message from WAGC President, Janalee Tobias

Contact Us

Postal Address

- WAGC
  PO Box 95357
  South Jordan, UT
  84095

Telephone

- 801-328-9660

E-Mail

- info@wagc.com

It's a Fact:

RECENT RESEARCH INDICATES THAT GUNS ARE USED DEFENSIVELY 2.5 MILLION TIMES PER YEAR.

It's not surprising then, that more women than ever want to keep their rights to own and carry a gun.
The reason is simple: Women **are** concerned about becoming victims of crime. Guns give women a fighting chance against crime.

Join Women Against Gun Control. Take the Women Against Gun Control Pledge and you qualify for a membership in Women Against Gun Control, a grass roots volunteer organization dedicated to preserving our gun rights.

Join thousands of women (and men) in sending a powerful message throughout the world.

"Guns **SAVE** Lives. We do **NOT** support gun control. Gun Control does **NOT** control crime!"

2nd Amendment
A well regulated Militia being necessary to the security of a free State, the right of the people to keep and bear Arms shall not be infringed.

Special Article
Have gun, will not fear it anymore

Rosie O' Donnel

Hillary Clinton

Janet Reno

Diane Feinstein

Want Americans to believe all women support gun control...

Let's BLOW HOLES in this MYTH!

If women are disarmed, a rapist will never fear...

"STOP OR I'LL SHOOT!"

Gun Control: The theory that a woman found dead in an alley, raped and strangled with her panty hose, is somehow morally superior to a woman explaining to police how her attacker got that fatal bullet wound.

PART FOUR

A Rhetorical Guide to Research

This screen capture shows the home page of Women Against Gun Control (www.wagc.com), a grassroots organization dedicated to supporting women's right to defend themselves. This organization participates in pro-gun political activism, legislative research, media awareness, distribution of print resources, and gun-related education. The Web site itself uses color, images, other design features, and bold text to stake out its position in the complex controversy over women's role in the hotly contested, larger issue of gun control. To discuss and analyze this home page, see the questions in the section entitled "Using the Part Opener Images" that follows the Preface.

CHAPTER 21

An Introduction to Research

AN OVERVIEW OF PART FOUR, "A RHETORICAL GUIDE TO RESEARCH"

Our goal in Part Four is to help you become an effective writer of college-level research papers. This chapter, "An Introduction to Research," gives you a big-picture overview of how to approach research writing using rhetorical skills. It explains some of the challenges research writing poses for college students who are new to academic scholarship. It ends by identifying seven essential skills that you should develop in order to become a successful writer of research papers across the curriculum.

Chapters 22 and 23, "Finding and Evaluating Sources" and "Using, Citing, and Documenting Sources," help you learn these skills through a sequence of seven self-contained sections or lessons. Each one focuses on a specific aspect of the research process and forms a discrete unit for class discussion or for application to your own research writing. Finally, Chapter 24 presents some advanced or specialized research skills, such as field research or specialized reference work, that can be useful to you in specific situations.

INTRODUCTION TO RESEARCH WRITING

Although the research paper is a common writing assignment in college, students are often baffled by their professor's expectations. Many students think of research writing as finding information on a topic or as finding quotations to support a thesis rather than as wrestling with a question or problem. One of our colleagues calls these sorts of papers "data dumps": The student backs a truckload of data up to the professor's desk, unloads it, and says, "Here's what I found out about sweatshops, Professor Jones. Enjoy!" Another colleague calls papers full of long quotations "choo-choo train papers": big boxcars of quotations coupled together with little patches of the students' own writing.

But a research paper shouldn't be a data dump or a train of boxcar quotations. Instead, it should follow the same principles of writing discussed throughout this text. In a research paper, the writer poses an interesting and significant problem and responds to it with a contestable thesis. In addition, in a formal research paper the writer must grapple with research sources and document them in a formal, academic style.

Much popular writing has the characteristics of a research paper, but without the documentation. Consider the following excerpt from an article in *Glamour*.

> Subliminal self-help tapes—which promise everything from instant relaxation to higher earning power—are a big business: Industry watchers estimate they generate about $60 million in sales annually. But a number of recent studies show no evidence that they work.
>
> . . . Philip Merkle, Ph.D., of the University of Waterloo, analyzed commercially available tapes using a spectrograph that reveals patterns of auditory signals. He found no evidence of speech-associated patterns on the tapes. The messages embedded in the tapes are so completely masked by the other sounds that they cannot be heard *even subliminally.**

As does a good research paper, this article has a thesis (subliminal self-help tapes are not effective) and uses research data for development and support (a statistic about the size of the subliminal self-help tape industry and a summary of the research by Philip Merkle). But if you doubt the sales figure of $60 million, you have no way to check the author's accuracy, nor can you easily find Merkle's work to read it for yourself. You might be able to contact the researcher through e-mail at the University of Waterloo, but that would be an inefficient approach to tracking down his work.

In academic research, the purpose of in-text citations and a bibliography is to enable readers to follow the trail of the author's research. But the problems faced by beginning college-level researchers are more complex and subtle than the mere handling of citation and documentation. In the interests of full disclosure— and of our own desire to bring you into the kitchen of academic life—let's explore for a moment some of the difficulties of undergraduate research.

WHY RESEARCH WRITING POSES DIFFICULTIES FOR NOVICE WRITERS

Although research writing has much in common with the shorter papers you have already written in college, meeting instructors' expectations for research papers requires knowledge about how academic discourse works. Many of you reading this text—as first-year college students—are novices standing outside the research culture of your professors. Our goal is to help you begin to enter that culture. Once you are inside it, you'll learn habits of critical reading and thinking that will help you excel in your careers as well as in college. Here is a list of difficulties almost all new researchers face.

Learning How to Ask Research Questions

Unless your previous teachers have emphasized question asking and inquiry in a variety of courses, you may be new to this text's emphasis on problem posing as

---

*Pamela Erens, "Are Subliminal Self-help Tapes a Hoax?" *Glamour* (October 1994): 62.

the starting point of the writing process. To complicate your initiation into academic culture, each new discipline you encounter in college asks different kinds of questions and frames them in different ways. The first section in Chapter 22 explains how to pose a good research question for your particular project.

Learning How to Find Sources

We live in an information-saturated culture. Novice researchers are often overwhelmed by the sheer volume of information that is available on many topics, especially now that the world's computers share information through the Internet. Novice researchers are often unaware of how the print and video resources of a library differ significantly from cyberspace resources or of how searching licensed databases leased by libraries differs from searching the World Wide Web. Moreover, because material from both licensed database and Web searches can be downloaded and printed, retrieved material from both sources has the same basic appearance. When they emerge from your printer, an article downloaded from Wacky Wally's Web page looks just like an authoritative article downloaded from a licensed database. To separate the gold of good material from the gravel of everything available, you need to understand how sources differ and how the different kinds are stored, indexed, and searched. The sequenced sections in Chapter 22 teach you these skills. They show you how to conduct efficient searches by thinking rhetorically about the whole search process.

Learning *Why* to Find Sources

Perhaps the most subtle problem is learning *why* an academic writer needs to find sources. For people outside the culture of scholarship, research can seem like a mechanical process of jumping through the professor's hoops. To many students, research means paraphrasing an encyclopedia, padding a term paper to include "five required sources," or scouring articles to find quotations to support a thesis.

But all these views reveal a beginner's confusion about how academic discourse works. Once you are inside the culture, you will recognize that research is propelled by genuine curiosity and intellectual wrestling. In looking for sources, skilled researchers have two kinds of goals:

▨ First, they conduct research to uncover information, data, and evidence that bear on their research problems—the raw material of primary data that they analyze and synthesize in search of a thesis and an argument.

▨ Second, they conduct research to position themselves in the conversation surrounding the topic, trying to figure out how their views relate to what others have written about the same problem.

In other words, a scholar doesn't do research to *find* an answer to her research question. She does research to *make* an answer. Scholars always see themselves as critical thinkers working toward something new, surprising, or challenging for their intended readers. You see this point emphasized throughout Chapters 22 and 23.

Learning How to Read Sources Rhetorically

Beginning researchers often treat all sources as having equal and objective status—a quotation from writer A is as good as a quotation from writer B. But, as we have shown throughout this text, all writers have an angle of vision (or interpretive filter) that causes them to choose and present data in ways that advance their own purposes and points of view. You therefore need to think rhetorically about your research sources. You need to ask of each source: Who wrote this piece, for what audience, and for what purpose?

"Angle of vision" is first introduced in Chapter 3, pp. 51–53.

In order to analyze a source's bias and perspective, you often need to determine its writer's original context. This problem is particularly troublesome for sources retrieved from the Web. Chapter 22 deals specifically with reading sources rhetorically and evaluating their biases.

Learning How to Work Sources into Your Own Writing

Another major difficulty is figuring out what to do with your sources—when to quote, when to paraphrase, and when to summarize a part of or the whole of an argument. Moreover, you need to work these quotations and paraphrases into the texture of your own prose so that you carry the argument in your own voice and make it easy for readers to distinguish between your ideas and those of your sources. If you quote long passages or include extensive paraphrasing, you are not in control of your sources but are simply reproducing them. In contrast, your own voice will dominate your writing after you learn how to use sources purposefully. The first section of Chapter 23 focuses on these skills.

Learning How to Cite and Document Sources

From a mechanical point of view, the problems of citing and documenting sources should be relatively easy to solve. In actual practice, however, documentation can seem bewildering. First of all, conventions for citing sources differ from discipline to discipline. Literature teachers prefer the MLA (Modern Language Association) system, social scientists the APA (American Psychological Association) system, historians the University of Chicago *Manual of Style,* and chemists the ACS (American Chemical Society) system. Novice researchers, then, have to keep shifting formats when they move from discipline to discipline.

Additionally, citing Web sources can be frustrating. These sources often come and go, disembodied and free-floating in cyberspace. It is often hard to tell who wrote a Web document, when, under what circumstances, and for what audience.

Finally, the details of citing can seem pointlessly arcane and nitpicky. Does it really matter, you might ask, whether you put a period after the parenthesis or not? As we try to show, the details of citing are as much a matter of the writer's projected ethos as of objective correctness. Are you trying to project yourself as an insider or an outsider to this discipline? The last section in Chapter 23 deals with these skills.

SEVEN ESSENTIAL SKILLS FOR NOVICE RESEARCHERS

Now that we have laid out some of the problems you can expect to encounter as a researcher, let us reassure you that you can develop skills to deal with them. In fact, you could probably develop these skills on your own through trial and error over a period of several years. What we hope to do in the next chapters is to accelerate your learning. In the following bulleted list, we identify seven essential skills you need to learn. Then in the next two chapters, we devote one section to each skill.

- **Skill 1: Argue your own thesis.** By arguing your own thesis, we mean the ability to pose a research question, to create your own answer, and to compose an argument in your own voice using research. In doing research, your purpose is twofold: to find information and data relevant to your research question and to position yourself in a conversation with other voices that have addressed the same question.

- **Skill 2: Understand the different kinds of sources.** As you look at books, periodicals, and Web sites, you need to understand how scholarly books differ from trade books, how peer-reviewed journals differ from magazines, and how print sources differ from cyberspace-only sources.

- **Skill 3: Use purposeful strategies for searching libraries, databases, and Web sites.** By using your rhetorical knowledge during a search, you can efficiently tap the resources of libraries and the Internet to find books, articles, and Web sites relevant to your research question. Specifically, you need to learn how to use your library's online catalog, how to search a licensed database such as EBSCOhost or Lexis-Nexis Academic Universe, and how to search the World Wide Web using a search engine such as Yahoo! or Google.

- **Skill 4: Use rhetorical knowledge to read and evaluate sources.** This skill, which helps you read sources rhetorically, includes the ability to evaluate sources for angle of vision, degree of advocacy, credibility, and reliability.

- **Skill 5: Understand the rhetoric of Web sites.** In the dozen years since the World Wide Web was formed, its store of information has expanded exponentially. It is now an indispensable resource for almost all researchers, but it is also a conundrum. To use the Web with sophistication, you need to know how its welter of advocacy sites, its use of images and hypertext structure, and its democratic openness to anyone with a cause make the Web substantively and rhetorically different from print media. Understanding the rhetoric of Web sites will help you make expert decisions when you evaluate and use Web sources.

- **Skill 6: Use sources purposively through clearly attributed summary, paraphrase, or quotation.** Incorporating sources into your own prose through purposeful summary, paraphrase, or quotation is a hallmark of an experienced writer. To help your reader separate your own voice from the voice of your sources, you need to write effective attributive tags and use in-text citations. Together these skills protect you from any hint of plagiarism.

■ **Skill 7: Cite and document sources effectively according to appropriate conventions.** A final skill you need is the ability to cite and document sources according to the conventions appropriate to your purpose, genre, and audience. Chapter 23 explains two common systems—the Modern Language Association (MLA) and the American Psychological Association (APA). When you cite and document according to appropriate conventions, you help your readers follow the track of your research while you project a competent and professional image.

CHAPTER SUMMARY

This chapter has presented a brief overview of the difficulties novice writers can expect to face when conducting college-level research. The chapter concludes with an overview of seven essential skills that first-year students must develop in order to write effective research papers across the curriculum.

CHAPTER 22

Finding and Evaluating Sources

The previous chapter explained some of the difficulties that novice research writers regularly encounter and introduced seven essential skills you need to become an effective research writer. This chapter focuses on the first five of these skills. To help you avoid information overload, we cover each skill in a relatively short, self-contained section that can be read comfortably in one sitting.

These seven skills are listed on pp. 579–580.

SKILL 1: ARGUE YOUR OWN THESIS

This skill, which enables you to take charge of your own writing, means that you need to pose your own research question and write a thesis-based argument in your own voice. In doing so, you use research for two connected purposes: to find information and data relevant to your research question and to position yourself in a conversation with other voices.

Formulating a Research Question

The best way to avoid writing a data dump or a jumble of quotations is to begin with a good research question. A good question keeps you in charge of your writing. It reminds you that your task is to answer this question for yourself, in your own voice, through your own critical thinking, applied to your own research sources. Skilled researchers don't seek the "perfect source" that answers their question. Rather, they know that they must create an answer themselves out of a welter of data and conflicting points of view.

See the discussion of data dumps and "choo-choo train papers" on pp. 575–576. Question asking is introduced in Chapter 1.

To stay in charge of your writing, you need to focus your research on a question rather than on a topic. Suppose a friend sees you doing research in the library and asks what your research paper is about. Consider differences in the following answers.

> **Topic Focus:** I am doing a paper on eating disorders.
> **Question Focus:** I'm trying to sort out what the experts say is the best way to treat severe anorexia nervosa. Is inpatient or outpatient treatment more effective?

> **Topic Focus:** I am doing my paper on gender-specific toys for children.
> **Question Focus:** I am puzzled about some of the effects of gender-specific toys. Do boys' toys, such as video games, toy weapons, and construction sets, develop intellectual and physical skills more than girls' toys do?

As these scenarios suggest, a topic focus invites you to collect information without a clear purpose—a sure road toward data dumping. In contrast, a question focus requires you to be a critical thinker who must assess and weigh data and understand multiple points of view. A topic focus encourages passive collection of information. A question focus encourages active construction of meaning.

How do you arrive at a research question? Ideally, good research questions arise from your own intellectual curiosity—a desire to resolve something that truly puzzles you. Often questions emerge from conflicting points of view in class discussions or from controversies or unknowns you encounter while reading. In most cases your initial research question will evolve as you do your research. You may make it broader or narrower, or refocus it on a newly discovered aspect of your original problem. You can test the initial feasibility of your research question by considering the following prompts:

For a discussion of problematic and significant questions, see Chapter 1, pp. 7–12.

■ Are you personally interested in this question?

■ Is the question both problematic and significant?

■ Is the question limited enough for the intended length of your paper?

■ Is there a reasonable possibility of finding information on this question based on the time and resources you have available?

■ Is the question appropriate for your level of expertise?

Establishing Your Role as a Researcher

After you have formulated your research question, you need to consider the possible roles you might play as a researcher. Your role is connected to the aim or purpose of your paper—to explore, to inform, to analyze, or to persuade. To help you see more fully what we mean by "role," here are some of the typical roles that writers of academic research papers might take.

■ **Reporter of the Current Best Thinking on a Problem:** In this role, the writer researches the current thinking of experts on some important problem and reports what the experts think. The paper has primarily an informative purpose. For example, *What are the current views of experts on the causes of homosexuality?*

■ **Reviewer of a Controversy:** In this role, the writer investigates and reports the differing arguments on various sides of a controversy. If the writer simply reports alternative arguments, the purpose is informative. If the writer decides to evaluate these arguments, the paper takes on an analytical or persuasive purpose. A typical example is, *What are the arguments for and against creating a five-year undergraduate engineering curriculum?*

■ **Advocate in a Controversy:** Here the writer shifts from an informative or analytical to a persuasive purpose. The paper asserts a position using research data for support, with the aim of persuading skeptical readers toward the writer's position: *Should U. S. citizens be required to carry a national ID card?* This purpose and role are particularly common in civic discourse where writers use reason and argument to influence decision making in a democratic society.

■ **Analyzer/Synthesizer Positioned Within a Conversation:** When writers adopt this role, they devote much of their paper to their own original analyses of a text, phenomenon, or data source, but they must also relate their views to what others have said about the same or similar questions. *How does Hobbes's view of the effective prince differ from Machiavelli's? What view of the self emerges from inventing identities in a cyberspace MUD or MOO?* This is perhaps the most common role taken by scholars in academic discourse.

■ **Original Field or Laboratory Researcher:** Here the writer poses a problem that requires field or laboratory research. In this case, research papers often take the form of a five-section scientific report. Field research, particularly common in the social sciences, involves collecting data through observation, interviews, and questionnaires. A typical field research question might be: *How did the war on terrorism following the September 11, 2001, disaster affect the lives of Muslim students on our campus?* A typical laboratory question might be: *Does topsoil downwind from the copper refinery show dangerous levels of heavy metals?* For questions of this kind, library research is often also required in order to determine what others have said about the same or similar problems (often called a "review of the literature"). Papers in this category generally combine an informative and an analytic purpose.

The structure of experimental reports is explained on p. 69.

See pp. 675–681 for advice about conducting field research.

■ **Narrator of One's Research Process:** Most academic research papers follow a closed-form, question-thesis-support structure. Occasionally, however, readers may be interested in the researcher's thinking processes (exploratory purpose), so the paper will read like a detective story with the thesis or further questions emerging at the end. In adopting an exploratory stance, the researcher narrates chronologically his or her engagement with the problem. Although this role is rare in academic and professional writing, it is becoming more common in some academic disciplines and is frequently used in popular writing aimed at showing the process of discovery. It is also an effective tool for generating complex thought about a question.

For Writing and Discussion

Working individually or in small groups, develop research questions on one general topic area such as music, health, sports, or some other topic specified by your instructor. Develop questions that would be appropriate for each of the following roles:

1. Reporter of the current best thinking on a problem
2. Reviewer of a controversy
3. Advocate in a controversy
4. Analyzer/synthesizer positioned within a conversation
5. Original field or laboratory researcher
6. Miscellaneous (good questions that don't fit neatly into any of these roles)

Seeing Your Research Process as Purposeful

After you understand the typical roles that academic researchers can play, you will know more clearly what you are looking for when you read research sources. When you read, keep in mind that you are trying to accomplish two connected goals. First, you read sources to find data and information that will help you develop your own answer to your research question—facts, statistics, examples, anecdotes, testimony, and so forth. If your purpose is informative, your paper will select and organize this information for effective presentation. If your purpose is analytic, you will look for meaningful patterns in the data, seeking new ways to understand or interpret the material you are investigating. If your purpose is persuasive, the data will become supporting evidence for your argument or counterevidence that complicates the issue and may support opposing views.

Second, you read sources to position yourself in a conversation. You want to find out what others have said about your research question, to learn who the experts are, to discover various perspectives and points of view, to find out what is agreed upon and what is controversial, and so forth. As you learn about different points of view, you also try to determine how each writer's perspective on an event, analysis of a phenomenon, or position on an issue may be similar to or different from your own.

A Case Study: Christopher Leigh's Research on School Violence

To illustrate how a student writer stays in charge of his writing by arguing his own thesis, let's return to Christopher Leigh's research on school violence, which we introduced in Chapter 1. Christopher's concern, as you will recall, grew out of his distress from the Columbine High School massacre in April 1999, which led to a nationwide debate: What causes school violence? How can we prevent it? Dozens of possible causes were bandied about in the media, such as unsupervised teenagers, violent video games, rap lyrics, a proliferation of guns, Internet chat rooms, the overuse of psychotropic medications, bullying, cliquish high schools, and the disintegration of the two-parent family. Likewise, promoted solutions ranged from banning violent video games to putting metal detectors in schools. As he began reading about this controversy, trying to make sense of it for himself, Christopher read an article on psychological profiling. His initial reaction to this article was recorded in a journal entry, which we reprinted on page 10.

At the start of his research project, Christopher narrowed the broad question "How can school violence be reduced?" down to the more limited question, "Is psychological profiling an effective means of reducing school violence?" He knew he was opposed to psychological profiling, but he also knew that something needed to be done to reduce school violence. Christopher's research process is narrated in his exploratory essay (pp. 180–184), in which he wrestles with different points of view on school violence.

As the exploratory essay makes clear, Christopher's center of interest gradually shifts from psychological profiling to the use of metal detectors in schools. Throughout this process you can observe Christopher thinking for himself, questioning different points of view, searching for different perspectives, struggling to find his own position.

In the conclusion of his exploratory narrative, Christopher sums up what he has learned so far in his research:

> I believe that this exploratory paper has helped me clarify my own thinking about school violence. I am now convinced that the media have instigated a panic about school violence, leading in many cases to counterproductive approaches like psychological profiling and metal detectors. When it comes time to write my major argument paper, I plan to show that these approaches only increase students' sense of alienation and hostility. The most important approach is to make schools more friendly, communal, and personal. We must ensure that troubled students are provided with help they need, rather than treating them like criminals.

Christopher's exploratory research gave him a solid background on school violence, allowing him to explore his own point of view against those of other voices in the conversation. In order to convert his exploratory narrative into a closed-form, question-thesis-support research paper, he decided to create an argument against metal detectors in schools. He had already clarified his own beliefs that schools need to be made more personal, so his remaining research primarily involved finding arguments in favor of metal detectors, in order to build a well-structured argument that attended to opposing views. You can read his final research paper in Chapter 23, pages 647–658.

For Writing and Discussion

Working individually, read Christopher's exploratory paper (pp. 180–184) and his final research paper (pp. 647–658). Then, working in small groups or as a whole class, try to reach consensus answers to the following questions:

1. Trace the steps in Christopher's thinking from the time he first becomes interested in psychological profiling until he finally settles on metal detectors as the topic of his final paper. What were the key moments that shaped his thinking? How did his thinking evolve?

2. We have used Christopher's story as an example of a student in charge of his own writing. Where do you see Christopher doing active critical thinking? Where do you see instances of what we have called "rhetorical reading"—that is, places where Christopher asks questions about an author's purpose, angle of vision, and selection of evidence? How is his final paper different from a data dump or a choo-choo train paper?

See pp. 575–576 for a description of data dumps and choo-choo train papers.

Summary

This section has focused on the importance of arguing your own thesis by posing a good research question, establishing a clear research role, and understanding your research purpose. We presented the case of Christopher Leigh to illustrate an effective research process used by a student writer.

SKILL 2: UNDERSTAND THE DIFFERENT KINDS OF SOURCES

To be an effective researcher, you need to understand the differences among the many kinds of books, articles, and Web sites you are apt to encounter. For example, you need to understand how scholarly books differ from trade books, how peer-reviewed scholarly journals differ from magazines, and how print sources differ from cyberspace-only sources. Before we explain strategies for finding sources (the skill covered in the section devoted to Skill 3), we want to explain more fully the concept of "sources." More specifically, we want you to understand that sources fall into different categories and that knowing these categories is important for the following reasons:

- Different categories require different kinds of searches.
- For any particular research question, some categories of sources are more useful than others.
- Knowing these categories speeds your learning of search strategies, making you a more efficient and sophisticated researcher.
- Knowing a source's category helps you read it rhetorically.

Looking at Sources Rhetorically

The best way to understand different categories of sources is to view them rhetorically. Table 22.1, "A Rhetorical Overview of Print Sources," shows how print sources (books, scholarly journals, magazines, newspapers) can be categorized according to genre, publisher, author, and angle of vision. The last column in Table 22.1 identifies contextual clues that will help you recognize what category a print source belongs to. Table 22.2, "A Rhetorical Overview of Web Sites," provides the same kind of information for Web sites. Take a few moments to peruse the information in Tables 22.1 and 22.2. As you do so, you will begin to appreciate the significance of the following terms and concepts.

Books Versus Periodicals Versus Web Sites

When you conduct library research, you often leave the library with an armload of books and a stack of articles that you have either photocopied from journals or magazines or downloaded from a computer and printed. At home, you will have no trouble determining who wrote the books and for what purpose, but your photocopied or downloaded articles can pose problems. What is the original source of the article in your hands? If you photocopied the articles from actual journals or magazines in your library, then you can be sure that they are "periodical print sources" (*periodical* means a publication, such as a scholarly journal or magazine, issued at regular intervals—that is, periodically). If you downloaded them from a computer—which may have been connected either to a licensed database leased by the library or to the World Wide Web—they may be electronic copies of periodical print sources or they may be material posted on the Web but never published in a print periodical.

The difference between licensed databases and the Web is explained later in this chapter, pp. 592–593.

TABLE 22.1 ■ A Rhetorical Overview of Print Sources

Genre and Publisher	Author and Angle of Vision	How to Recognize Them
Books		
SCHOLARLY BOOKS ■ University/academic presses ■ Nonprofit ■ Selected through peer review	**Author:** Professors, researchers **Angle of vision:** Scholarly advancement of knowledge	■ University press on title page ■ Specialized academic style ■ Documentation and bibliography
TRADE BOOKS (NONFICTION) ■ Commercial publishers (for example, Penguin Putnam) ■ Selected for profit potential	**Author:** Journalists, freelancers, scholars aiming at popular audience **Angle of vision:** Varies from informative to persuasive; often well researched and respected, but sometimes shoddy and aimed for quick sale	■ Covers designed for marketing appeal ■ Popular style ■ Usually documented in an informal rather than academic style
REFERENCE BOOKS ■ Publishers specializing in reference material ■ For-profit through library sales	**Author:** Commissioned scholars **Angle of vision:** Balanced, factual overview	■ Titles containing words such as *encyclopedia, dictionary,* or *guide* ■ Found in reference section of library
Periodicals		
SCHOLARLY JOURNALS ■ University/academic presses ■ Nonprofit ■ Articles chosen through peer review ■ Examples: *Journal of Abnormal Psychology, Review of Metaphysics*	**Author:** Professors, researchers, independent scholars **Angle of vision:** Scholarly advancement of knowledge; presentation of research findings; development of new theories and applications	■ Not sold on magazine racks ■ No commercial advertising ■ Specialized academic style ■ Documentation and bibliography ■ Cover often has table of contents
PUBLIC AFFAIRS MAGAZINES ■ Commercial, "for-profit" presses ■ Manuscripts reviewed by editors ■ Examples: *Harper's, Commonweal, National Review*	**Author:** Staff writers, freelancers; scholars writing for general audiences **Angle of vision:** Aims to deepen public understanding of issues; magazines often have political bias of left, center, or right	■ Long, well-researched articles ■ Ads aimed at upscale professionals ■ Often has reviews of books, theater, film, and the arts
TRADE MAGAZINES ■ Commercial, "for-profit" presses ■ Focused on a profession or trade ■ Examples: *Advertising Age, Automotive Rebuilder, Farm Journal*	**Author:** Staff writers, industry specialists **Angle of vision:** Informative articles for practitioners; advocacy for the profession or trade	■ Title indicating trade or profession ■ Articles on practical job concerns ■ Ads geared toward a particular trade or profession

TABLE 22.1 ▨ A Rhetorical Overview of Print Sources (Continued)

Genre and Publisher	Author and Angle of Vision	How to Recognize Them
Periodicals (continued)		
NEWSMAGAZINES AND NEWSPAPERS ▪ Newspaper chains and publishers ▪ Examples: *Time, Newsweek, Washington Post*	**Author:** Staff writers and journalists; occasional freelance pieces **Angle of vision:** News reports aimed at balance and objectivity; editorial pages reflect perspective of editors; op-ed pieces reflect different perspectives	▪ Readily familiar by name, distinctive cover style ▪ Widely available on newsstands and by subscription ▪ Ads aimed at broad, general audience
POPULAR NICHE MAGAZINES ▪ Large conglomerates or small presses with clear target audience ▪ Focused on special interests of target audience ▪ Examples: *Seventeen, People, TV Guide, Car and Driver, Golf Digest*	**Author:** Staff or freelance writers **Angle of vision:** Varies—in some cases content and point of view are dictated by advertisers or the politics of publisher	▪ Glossy paper, extensive ads, lots of visuals ▪ Popular, often distinctive style ▪ Short, undocumented articles ▪ Credentials of writer often not mentioned

TABLE 22.2 ▨ A Rhetorical Overview of Web Sites

Type of Site	Author/Sponsor and Angle of Vision	What to Watch Out For
.COM OR .NET (A COMMERCIAL SITE CREATED BY A BUSINESS OR CORPORATION) ▪ Purpose is to enhance image, attract customers, market products and services, provide customer service ▪ Creators are paid by salary or fees and often motivated by desire to design innovative sites	**Author:** Difficult to identify individual writers; sponsoring company often considered the author **Angle of vision:** Obvious bias to promote the point of view of the corporation or business; links are to sites that promote same values	▪ Links are often to other products and services provided by company ▪ Photographs and other visuals used to enhance corporate image
.ORG (NONPROFIT ORGANIZATIONS OR ADVOCACY GROUPS) ▪ Sometimes purpose is to provide accurate, balanced information (for example, the American Red Cross site) ▪ Frequently, purpose is to advocate the organization's political views (for example, the Persons for the Ethical Treatment of Animals [PETA] site)	**Author:** Often hard to identify individual writers; sponsoring organization often considered the author; some sites produced by amateurs with passionate views; others produced by well-paid professionals **Angle of vision:** Advocacy sites promote views of sponsoring organization and aim to influence public opinion and policy	▪ Advocacy sites sometimes don't announce purpose on home page ▪ You may enter a node of an advocacy site through a link from another site and not realize the political slant ▪ Facts/data selected and filtered by site's angle of vision ▪ Often uses visuals for emotional appeal

TABLE 22.2 ■ A Rhetorical Overview of Web Sites

Type of Site	Author/Sponsor and Angle of Vision	What to Watch Out For
.EDU (AN EDUCATIONAL SITE ASSOCIATED WITH A COLLEGE OR UNIVERSITY) ■ Wide range of purposes ■ Home page aimed at attracting prospective students and donors ■ Inside the site are numerous subsites devoted to research, pedagogy, libraries, student work, and so forth	**Author:** Professors, staff, students **Angle of vision:** Varies enormously from personal sites of professors and students to organizational sites of research centers and libraries; can vary from scholarly and objective to strong advocacy on issues	■ Often an .edu site has numerous "subsites" sponsored by the university library, art programs, research units ■ It is often difficult to determine where you are in the site—e.g., professor's course site, student site
.GOV OR .MIL (SPONSORED BY GOVERNMENT AGENCIES OR MILITARY UNITS) ■ Provides enormous range of basic data about government policy, bills in Congress, economic forecasts, and so forth ■ Aims to create good public relations for agency or military unit	**Author:** Development teams employed by the agency; sponsoring agency is usually considered the author **Angle of vision:** varies—informational sites publish data and government documents with an objective point of view; agency sites also promote agency's point of view—e.g., Dept. of Energy, Dept. of Labor	■ Typical sites (for example, www.energy.gov, the site of the U.S. Dept. of Energy) are extremely layered and complex and provide hundreds of links to other sites ■ Valuable for research ■ Sites often promote values/ assumptions of sponsoring agency
PERSONAL WEB SITES (An individual contracts with server to publish the site; many personal Web sites also have .edu affiliation)	**Author:** Anyone can create a personal Web site **Angle of vision:** Varies from person to person	■ Home page URL ends with initials of Web server rather than .com, .org, .mil, or .gov ■ Credentials/bias of author often hard to determine ■ Irresponsible sites might have links to excellent sites; tracing links is complicated

When you download a print article from a computer, you should be aware that you lose many contextual clues about the author's purpose and bias—clues that you can pick up from the original magazine or journal itself by its appearance, title, advertisements (if any), table of contents, and statement of editorial policy. When you download something from the Web that has never appeared in print, you have to be wary about its source. Because print publications are costly to produce, print articles generally go through some level of editorial review. In contrast, anyone can post almost anything on the Web. You need to become savvy at recognizing these distinctions in order to read sources rhetorically and to document them accurately in your bibliography.

How to document Web sources is explained in Chapter 23, pp. 642–644 (MLA) and pp. 665–666 (APA).

Scholarly Books Versus Trade Books

Note in Table 22.1 the distinction between scholarly books, which are peer-reviewed and published by nonprofit academic presses, and trade books, which are published by for-profit presses with the intention of making money. By "peer review," which is a highly prized concept in academia, we mean the selection process by which scholarly manuscripts get chosen for publication. When manuscripts are submitted to an academic publisher, the editor sends them for independent review to experienced scholars who judge the rigor and accuracy of the research and the significance and value of the argument. The process is highly competitive and weeds out much shoddy or trivial work.

In contrast, trade books are not peer-reviewed by independent scholars. Instead, they are selected for publication by editors whose business is to make a profit. Fortunately, it can be profitable for popular presses to publish superbly researched and argued intellectual material because college-educated people, as lifelong learners, create a demand for intellectually satisfying trade books written for the general reader rather than for the highly specialized reader. These can be excellent sources for undergraduate research, but you need to separate the trash from the treasure. Trade books are aimed at many different audiences and market segments and can include sloppy, unreliable, and heavily biased material.

Scholarly Journals Versus Magazines

Like scholarly books, scholarly journals are academic, peer-reviewed publications. Although they may look like magazines, they almost never appear on newsstands; they are nonprofit publications subsidized by universities for disseminating high-level research and scholarship.

In contrast, magazines are intended to make a profit through sales and advertising revenues. Fortunately for researchers, a demand exists for intellectually satisfying magazines, just as for sophisticated trade books. Many for-profit magazines publish highly respectable, useful material for undergraduate or professional researchers, but many magazines publish shoddy material. As Table 22.1 shows, magazines fall in various categories aimed at different audiences.

Print Sources Versus Cyberspace Sources

Another crucial distinction exists between print sources and cyberspace sources. Much of what you can retrieve from a computer was originally published in print. What you download is simply an electronic copy of a print source, either from a library-leased database or from someone's Web site. (The next section shows you how to tell the difference.) In such cases, you often need to consider the article's original print origins for appropriate cues about its rhetorical context and purpose. But much cyberspace material, having never appeared in print, may never have undergone either peer review or editorial review. To distinguish between these two kinds of cyberspace sources, we call one kind a "print/cyberspace source" (something that has appeared in print and is made available on the Web or through library-leased databases) and the other a "cyberspace-only source." When you use a cyberspace-only source, you've got to take special care in figuring out who wrote it, why, and for what audience. Also, you document cyberspace-only material differently from print material retrieved electronically.

These distinctions are explained in Chapter 23, pp. 633–634.

For Writing and Discussion

Your instructor will bring to class a variety of sources—different kinds of books, scholarly journals, magazines, and downloaded material. Working individually or in small groups, try to decide which category in Tables 22.1 and 22.2 each piece belongs to. Be prepared to justify your decisions on the basis of the cues you used to make your decision.

Summary

This section has explained the different kinds of sources—particularly the categories of books, periodicals, and Web sites. Knowledge of these differences will help you read sources rhetorically and document them properly.

SKILL 3: USE PURPOSEFUL STRATEGIES FOR SEARCHING LIBRARIES, DATABASES, AND WEB SITES

In the previous section we explained differences among the kinds of sources you may encounter in a research project. In this section, we explain how to find these sources by using your library's online catalog (for locating books and other library resources), library-leased electronic databases (for finding articles in journals and magazines), and Web search engines (for finding material on the World Wide Web). An additional research skill—using specialized reference books and encyclopedias from your library's reference collection—is discussed in Chapter 24.

Finding Books: Searching Your Library's Online Catalog

Your library's holdings are listed in its online catalog. Most of the entries are for books, but an academic library also has a wealth of other resources such as periodical collections, government records and reports, newspapers, videos and cassettes, maps, encyclopedias, and hundreds of specialized reference works that your reference librarian can help you use.

Indexed by subject, title, and author, the online catalog gives you titles of books and other library-owned resources relevant to your research area. Note that the catalog lists the titles of journals and magazines in the library's periodical collection (for example, *Journal of Abnormal Psychology, Atlantic Monthly*), but does *not* list the titles of individual articles within these periodicals. As we explain later in this section, you can search the contents of periodicals by using a licensed database. Methods of accessing and using online catalogs vary from institution to institution, so you'll need to learn the specifics of your library's catalog through direct experience.

Subject Searches Versus Keyword Searches

At the start of a research project, before researchers know the names of specific authors or book titles, they typically search by subject or by keywords. Your own research process will be speedier if you understand the difference between these kinds of searches.

- ■ *Subject searches.* Subject searches use predetermined categories published in the reference work *Library of Congress Subject Headings*. This work informs you that, for example, material on "street people" would be classified under the heading "homeless persons." If the words you use for a subject search don't yield results, seek help from a librarian, who can show you how to use the subject heading guide to find the best word or phrase.

- ■ *Keyword searches.* Keyword searches are not based on predetermined subject categories. Rather, the computer locates the keywords you provide in titles, abstracts, introductions, and sometimes bodies of text. Keyword searches in online catalogs are usually limited to finding words and phrases in titles. We explain more about keyword searches in the upcoming section on using licensed databases, whose search engines look for keywords in bodies of text as well as in titles.

Learning Your Library's Shelving System

After you have found possible sources in the online catalog, you need to jot down their call numbers and then become familiar with the organization of your library's shelving system. Most college and university libraries use the Library of Congress classification system, but some may have an older book collection classified in the Dewey Decimal System.

Finding Print Articles: Searching a Licensed Database

For many research projects, useful sources are print articles from your library's periodical collection, including scholarly journals, public affairs magazines, newspapers or newsmagazines, and niche magazines related to your research area. Some of these articles are available free on the World Wide Web, but most of them are not. Rather, they may be located physically in your library's periodical collection (or in that of another library and available through interlibrary loan) or located electronically in vast databases leased by your library.

What Is a Licensed Database?

Electronic databases of periodical sources are produced by for-profit companies that index articles in thousands of periodicals and construct engines that can search the database by author, title, subject, keyword, date, genre, and other characteristics. In most cases the database contains an abstract of each article, and in many cases it contains the complete text of the article that you can download and print. These databases are referred to by several different generic names: "licensed databases" (our preferred term), "general databases," or "subscription services." Because access to these databases is restricted to fee-paying customers, they can't be searched through Web engines like Yahoo! or Google. Most university libraries allow students to access these databases from a remote computer by using a password. You can therefore use the Internet to connect your computer to licensed databases as well as to the World Wide Web (see Figure 22.1).

Although the methods of accessing licensed databases vary from institution to institution, we can offer some widely applicable guidelines. Most likely your library has online one or more of the following databases:

- *EBSCOhost:* Includes citations and abstracts from journals in most disciplines as well as many full-text articles from over three thousand journals; its *Academic Search Elite* function covers material published as long ago as the early 1980s.
- *UMI ProQuest Direct:* Gives access to the full text of articles from journals in a variety of subject areas; includes full-text articles from newspapers.
- *InfoTrac:* Is often called "Expanded Academic Index," and is similar to EBSCOhost and UMI ProQuest in its coverage of interdisciplinary subjects.
- *FirstSearch Databases:* Incorporates multiple specialized databases in many subject areas, including WorldCat, which contains records of books, periodicals, and multimedia formats from libraries worldwide.
- *Lexis-Nexis Academic Universe:* Is primarily a full-text database covering current events, business and financial news; includes company profiles and legal, medical and reference information.

Generally, one of these databases is the "default database" chosen by your library for most article searches. Your reference librarian will be able to direct you to the most useful licensed database for your purpose.

More on Keyword Searching

To use an online database, you need to be adept at keyword searching, which we introduced on page 592. When you type a word or phrase into a search box, the computer will find sources that contain the same words or phrases. If you want the computer to search for a phrase, put it in quotation marks. Thus if you type *"street people"* using quotation marks, the computer will search for those two words occurring together. If you type in *street people* without quotation marks, the

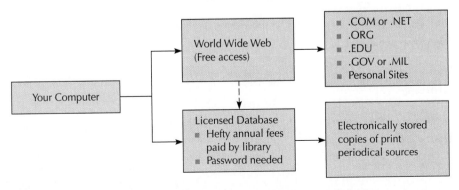

FIGURE 22.1 ■ Licensed Database Versus Free-Access Portions of Internet

TABLE 22.3 ▪ Boolean Search Commands

Command and Function	Research Example	What to Type	Search Result
X OR Y (Expands your search)	You are researching Barbie dolls and decide to include G.I. Joe figures.	"Barbie doll" OR "GI Joe"	Articles that contain either phrase
X AND Y (Narrows your search)	You are researching the psychological effects of Barbie dolls and are getting too many hits under *Barbie dolls*.	"Barbie dolls" AND psychology	Articles that include both the phrase "Barbie dolls" and the word *psychology*
X NOT Y (Limits your search)	You are researching girls' toys and are tired of reading about Barbie dolls. You want to look at other popular girls' toys.	"girl toys" NOT Barbie	Articles that include the phrase "girl toys" but exclude *Barbie*

computer will look for the word *street* and the word *people* occurring in the same document but not necessarily together. Use your imagination to try a number of related terms. If you are researching gendered toys and you get too many hits using the keyword *toys*, try *gender toys, Barbie, G.I. Joe, girl toys, boy toys, toys psychology,* and so forth. You can increase the flexibility of your searches by using Boolean terms to expand, narrow, or limit your search (see Table 22.3 for an explanation of Boolean searches).

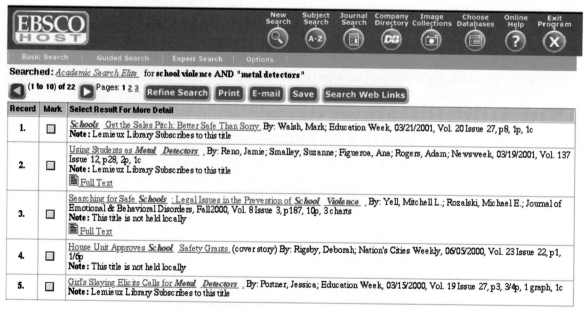

FIGURE 22.2 ▪ Sample Results List from a Search Using EBSCOhost

Illustration of a Database Search

As an illustration, Figure 22.2 shows a screen from the Results List for a search under the keywords *school violence AND "metal detectors"* in the database EBSCOhost. In the third column, the appearance of a page icon followed by "Full Text" (for example, Records 2 and 3) indicates that the full text of the article is available on the database. The line marked "Note" under each entry indicates whether your particular library subscribes to the magazine or journal. If you click on a specific article in the Results list, you will get a full display page showing complete publication data about that article. Figure 22.3 shows a full display page for the fifth article, "Girl's Slaying Elicits Calls for Metal Detectors." This page provides an abstract of the article—useful for helping you decide whether you want to read the entire text. But note that the article is only three-quarters of a page long (one column), indicating that it won't give you an in-depth discussion. Note also that a box at the top of the page lets you refine the search. With a little practice you will learn how to limit the search in useful ways—either by asking only for articles in peer-reviewed journals or only for articles of certain lengths.

After you've identified articles you'd like to read, locate physically all those available in your library's periodical collection. (This way you won't lose important con-

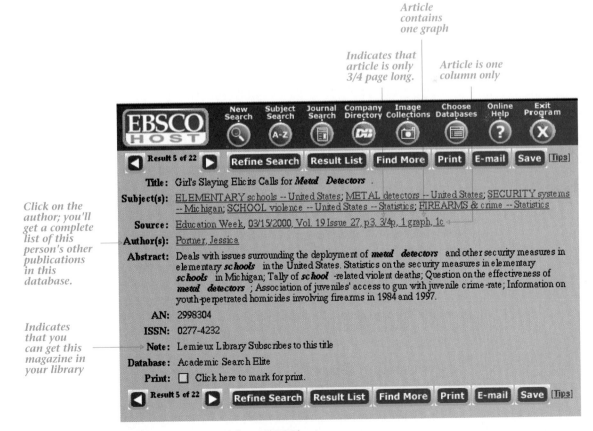

FIGURE 22.3 ■ Sample Full Display for an Article on EBSCOhost

textual cues for reading them rhetorically.) For those unavailable in your library, print them from the database, if possible, or order them from interlibrary loan.

Finding Cyberspace Sources: Searching the World Wide Web

Another valuable resource is the World Wide Web. In this section we begin by explaining in more detail the logic of the Internet—the difference between restricted portions of the Internet, such as licensed databases, and the amorphous, ever changing, "free-access" portion, commonly called the "World Wide Web" (see again Figure 22.1). We then offer suggestions for searching the Web.

The Logic of the Internet

To understand the logic of Web search engines, you need to know that the Internet is divided into restricted sections open only to those with special access rights and a "free-access" section. Web engines such as Yahoo! or Google search only the free-access portion of the Internet. When you type keywords into a Web search engine, it searches for matches in material made available on the Web by all the users of the world's network of computers—government agencies, corporations, advocacy groups, information services, individuals with their own Web sites, and many others.

The following example will quickly show you the difference between a licensed database search and a Web search. When we entered the keywords *school violence AND "metal detectors"* into EBSCOhost, we received twenty-two "hits"—the titles of twenty-two recent articles on the subject of metal detectors in schools (see Figure 22.2). In contrast, when we entered the same keywords into the Web search engine AltaVista, we received 5,934 hits—all the files available to AltaVista that had the words *school, violence,* and *metal detectors* appearing somewhere in the file. When we plugged the same words into Google, we received 11,400 hits, but none of the first ten hits from AltaVista matched the first ten hits from Google.

For Writing and Class Discussion

Figure 22.4 shows the first screen of hits for the keywords *school violence AND "metal detectors"* retrieved by the search engine AltaVista. Working in small groups or as a whole class, compare these items with those retrieved from the equivalent search using the licensed database EBSCOhost (Figure 22.2). Then explain in your own words why the results for the Web searches are different from the licensed database search.

Using Web Search Engines

Although the hits you receive from a Web search frequently include useless, shoddy, trivial, or irrelevant material, the Web's resources for researchers are breathtak-

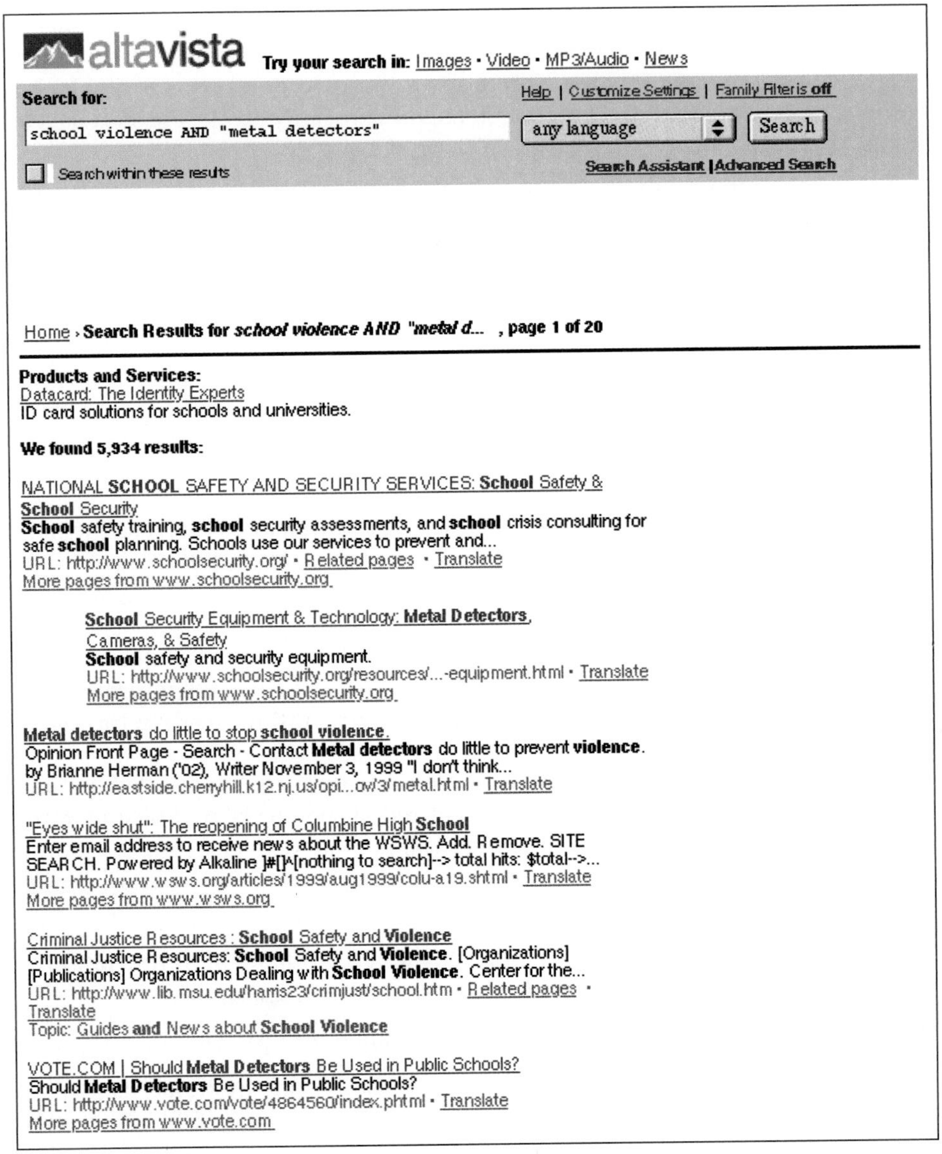

altavista Try your search in: Images · Video · MP3/Audio · News

Search for: Help | Customize Settings | Family Filter is off

school violence AND "metal detectors"   any language ⬍   Search

☐ Search within these results   Search Assistant | Advanced Search

Home › **Search Results for** *school violence AND "metal d...* , page 1 of 20

Products and Services:
Datacard: The Identity Experts
ID card solutions for schools and universities.

We found 5,934 results:

NATIONAL **SCHOOL** SAFETY AND SECURITY SERVICES: **School** Safety &
School Security
School safety training, **school** security assessments, and **school** crisis consulting for
safe **school** planning. Schools use our services to prevent and...
URL: http://www.schoolsecurity.org/ · Related pages · Translate
More pages from www.schoolsecurity.org

    School Security Equipment & Technology: **Metal Detectors**,
    Cameras, & Safety
    School safety and security equipment.
    URL: http://www.schoolsecurity.org/resources/...-equipment.html · Translate
    More pages from www.schoolsecurity.org

Metal detectors do little to stop **school violence**.
Opinion Front Page - Search - Contact **Metal detectors** do little to prevent **violence**.
by Brianne Herman ('02), Writer November 3, 1999 "I don't think...
URL: http://eastside.cherryhill.k12.nj.us/opi...ov/3/metal.html · Translate

"Eyes wide shut": The reopening of Columbine High **School**
Enter email address to receive news about the WSWS. Add. Remove. SITE
SEARCH. Powered by Alkaline]#[]^[nothing to search]--> total hits: $total-->...
URL: http://www.wsws.org/articles/1999/aug1999/colu-a19.shtml · Translate
More pages from www.wsws.org

Criminal Justice Resources : **School** Safety and **Violence**
Criminal Justice Resources: **School** Safety and **Violence**. [Organizations]
[Publications] Organizations Dealing with **School Violence**. Center for the...
URL: http://www.lib.msu.edu/harris23/crimjust/school.htm · Related pages ·
Translate
Topic: Guides **and** News about **School Violence**

VOTE.COM | Should **Metal Detectors** Be Used in Public Schools?
Should **Metal Detectors** Be Used in Public Schools?
URL: http://www.vote.com/vote/4864560/index.phtml · Translate
More pages from www.vote.com

FIGURE 22.4 ■ First Screen of Hits from AltaVista

ing. At your fingertips you have access to government documents and statistics,
legislative and corporate white papers, court cases, persuasive appeals of advocacy
groups, consumer information—the list is almost endless.

The World Wide Web can be searched by a variety of engines that collect and
categorize individual Web files and search them for keywords. Most of these
engines will find not only text files but also graphic, audio, and video files. Some

look through the titles of files, whereas others scan the entire text of documents. Different engines search the Web in different ways, so it is important that you try a variety of search engines when you look for information. Although the Web is evolving rapidly, some of the best search engines are fairly stable. For starters, you might try the following:

Google (http://www.google.com)

HotBot (http://www.hotbot.com)

Yahoo! (http://yahoo.com)

Lycos (http://www.lycos.com)

WebCrawler (http://www.webcrawler.com)

AltaVista (http://www.altavista.com)

GoTo (http://www.goto.com)

Ask Jeeves (http://www.askjeeves.com)

Again, if you are in doubt, your reference librarian can help you choose the most productive search engine for your needs.

Determining Where You Are on the Web

As you browse the Web looking for resources, clicking from link to link, try to figure out what site you are actually in at any given moment. This information is crucial, both for properly documenting a Web source and for reading the source rhetorically.

To know where you are on the Web, begin by recognizing typical designations for home pages. When a new Web site is created, it may be hosted by an already existing site (in which case the home page will be that of the existing site), or its creator may register the site for its own URL (universal resource locator). Typical home page URLs look like this:

www.monash.com (home page of Monash, Inc., an information technology firm)

www.nea.org (home page of the National Education Association)

www.usdoj.gov (home page of the U.S. Department of Justice)

The site designer then creates hyperlinks that branch off the home page. Each hyperlink opens a new file, which is identified by the home page URL followed by extension codes that are separated by slashes. The generic structure of a typical URL looks like this:

http://www.servername.domain/directory/subdirectory/filename.filetype

Here is a specific example:

Stands for "hypertext transfer protocol"

Server name   *Domain type*   *File name*

Directory   *Subdirectory*   *File Type*

http://www.nea.org/issues/safescho/resources.html#state

The file named "resources" is linked through a series of directories and subdirectories to the home page of the National Education Association (www.nea.org).

Often, when you click on a link in one site, you will be sent to a totally different site. To determine the home page of this new site, simply note the root URL immediately following the "www."* To view the home page directly, delete the codes to the right of the initial home page URL in your computer's location window and hit Enter. You will then be linked directly to the site's home page. As you will see later in this chapter and in Chapter 23, being able to examine a site's home page helps you read the site rhetorically and document it properly.

In navigating where you are on the Web, there is one hitch you should be aware of. Some highly commercialized search engines don't give you a site's actual URL. These engines generate revenue by displaying advertising banners on the pages that give search results. The designers of these search engine sites don't want the banners to disappear when users click on a link to look at a new site. They therefore create alias links to the new site that cause the new site to be displayed inside the advertising frame of the engine's site. You'll be able to recognize when this problem occurs by the following cues:

- The advertising banners in the engine site won't disappear when you go to the new site.
- The URL in the location window will be very long and very strange looking.

If this problem happens to you, switch to a different search engine.

Summary

In this section we have focused on strategies used by expert researchers to locate books, articles, and Web sites. Specifically, we have explained how to use your library's online catalog to locate books and other library resources; how to use licensed databases to find articles in print periodicals; and how to use Web search engines to find useful material from the World Wide Web.

SKILL 4: USE RHETORICAL KNOWLEDGE TO READ AND EVALUATE SOURCES

Now that you know expert strategies for searching library catalogs, licensed databases, and the Web, we turn in this section to strategies for reading and evaluating sources. Specifically, we focus on reading sources rhetorically, taking useful and efficient notes, and evaluating sources for credibility and bias.

---

*Not all URLs begin with "www" after the first set of double slashes. Our description doesn't include variations from the most typical URL types. You can generally find the home page of any site by eliminating all codes to the right of the first slash mark following the initial set of double slashes.

Reading Your Sources Rhetorically

Even when you have a research question that interests you, it's easy to feel overwhelmed when you return from a library with a stack of books and magazine or journal articles. How do you begin reading all this material? There is no one right answer to this question. At times you need to read slowly with analytical closeness, as we discussed in Chapter 6. At other times you can skim a source, looking only for its gist or for a needed piece of information.

See our discussion of Leigh's process on pp. 584–585. See also his exploratory paper on pp. 180–184.

Reading with Your Own Goals in Mind

How you read a source depends to a certain extent on where you are in the research process. Early in the process, when you are in the thesis-seeking, exploratory stage, your goal is to achieve a basic understanding about your research problem. You need to become aware of different points of view, learn what is unknown or controversial about your research question, see what values or assumptions are in conflict, and build up your store of background knowledge. As we saw in the case of Christopher Leigh, your initial research question often evolves as your knowledge increases and your interests shift.

An annotated list of reference works can be found on pp. 668–670.

Given these goals, at the early stages of research you should select, where possible, easy-to-read, overview kinds of sources to get you into the conversation. In some cases, even an encyclopedia or specialized reference work can be a good start for getting general background.

As you get deeper into your research, your questions become more focused, and the sources you read become more specialized. Once you formulate a thesis and plan a structure for your paper, you can determine more clearly the sources you need and read them with purpose and direction. For example, after Christopher Leigh decided to argue against metal detectors in the schools, he knew that he needed to find research sources in three different areas:

- Arguments in favor of metal detectors (He knew he would need to summarize opposing views and respond in some way to their arguments.)
- Testimony, data, research studies, and other information that would help him support his own case against metal detectors
- Ideas and supporting data for ways of reducing school violence other than metal detectors

Reading with Rhetorical Awareness

To read your sources rhetorically, you should keep two basic questions in mind: (1) What was the source author's purpose in writing this piece? And (2) What might be my purpose in using this piece? Table 22.4 sums up the kinds of questions a rhetorical reader typically considers.

This chart reinforces a point we've made throughout this text: All writing is produced from an angle of vision that privileges some ways of seeing and filters out other ways. You should guard against reading your sources as if they present hard, undisputed facts or universal truths. For example, if one of your sources says

TABLE 22.4 ■ Questions Asked by Rhetorical Readers

What was the source author's purpose in writing this piece?	What might be my purpose in using this piece in my own argument?

■ Who is this author? What are his or her credentials and affiliations?
 ■ What audience was this person addressing?
 ■ What is the genre of this piece? (If you downloaded the piece from the World Wide Web, did it originally appear in print?)
 ■ If this piece appeared in print, what is the reputation and bias of the journal, magazine, or press? Was the piece peer-reviewed?
 ■ If this piece appeared only on the Web, who or what organization sponsors the Web site (check the home page)? What is the reputation and bias of the sponsor?
 ■ What is the author's thesis or purpose?
 ■ How does this author try to change his or her audience's view?
 ■ What is this writer's angle of vision or bias?
 ■ What is omitted or censored from this text?
 ■ How reliable and credible is this author?
 ■ What facts, data, and other evidence does this author use and what are the sources of these data?
 ■ What are this author's underlying values, assumptions, and beliefs?
	■ How has this piece influenced or complicated my own thinking?
	 ■ How does this piece relate to my research question?
	 ■ How will my own intended audience react to this author?
	 ■ How might I use this piece in my own argument?
	   ■ Is it an opposing view that I might summarize?
	   ■ Is it an alternative point of view that I might compare to other points of view?
	   ■ Does it have facts and data that I might use?
	   ■ Would a summary of all or part of this argument support or oppose one or more of my own points?
	   ■ Could I use this author for testimony? (If so, how should I indicate this author's credentials?)
	 ■ If I use this source, will I need to acknowledge the author's bias and angle of vision?

that "Saint-John's-wort [an herb] has been shown to be an effective treatment for depression," some of your readers might accept that statement as fact; but many wouldn't. Skeptical readers would want to know who the author is, where his views have been published, and what he uses for evidence. Let's say the author is someone named Samuel Jones. Skeptical readers would ask whether Jones is relying on published research, and if so, whether the studies have been peer-reviewed in reputable, scholarly journals and whether the research has been replicated by other scientists. They would also want to know whether Jones has financial connections to companies that produce herbal remedies and supplements. Rather than settling the question about Saint-John's-wort as a treatment for depression, a quotation from Jones might open up a heated controversy about medical research.

Reading rhetorically is thus a way of thinking critically about your sources. It influences the way you take notes, evaluate sources, and shape your argument.

Taking Effective Notes

Taking good research notes serves two functions: First, it encourages you to read actively because you must summarize your sources' arguments, record usable information, and extract short quotations. Second, taking notes encourages you to do exploratory thinking—to write down ideas as they occur to you, to analyze sources as you read them, and to join your sources in conversation.

Dialectic journals are explained on pp. 188–190; for an example of dialectic note taking, see Chapter 8, pp. 191–192.

There are many ways to take notes, but we can offer several techniques that have worked especially well for other writers. First of all, you can try using a dialectic or double-entry journal. Divide a page in half, entering your informational notes on one side and your exploratory writing on the other. Another system is to record notes on index cards or in a computer file and then write out your exploratory thinking in a separate research journal. Still another method is to record informational notes on your computer in a regular font and then to use a boldfaced font for exploratory writing. Your objective here is to create a visual way to distinguish your informational notes from your exploratory thinking.

A common practice of beginning researchers—one that experienced researchers almost never use—is *not* taking notes as they read and *not* doing any exploratory writing. We've seen students photocopy a dozen or more articles, but then write

---

Note Taking According to Purpose

How Source Might Be Used in Your Paper	Notes to Take
Background information about research problem or issue	Summarize the information; record specific data.
Part of a section reviewing different points of view on your question	Summarize the source's argument; note its bias and perspective. In exploratory notes, jot down ideas on how and why different sources disagree.
As an opposing view that you must summarize and respond to	Summarize the argument fully and fairly. In exploratory notes, speculate about why you disagree with the source and whether you can refute the argument, concede to it, or compromise with it.
As data, information, or testimony to be used as evidence to support your thesis	Record the data or information; summarize or paraphrase the supporting argument with occasional quotations of key phrases; directly quote short passages for supporting testimony; note the credentials of the writer or person quoted. In exploratory notes, record new ideas as they occur to you.
As data, information, or testimony that counters your position or raises doubts about your thesis	Take notes on counterevidence. In exploratory notes, speculate on how you might respond to the counterevidence.

nothing as they read (sometimes they highlight passages with a marker), planning to rely later on memory to navigate through the sources. This practice reduces your ability to synthesize your sources and create your argument. When you begin drafting your paper, you'll have no notes to refer to, no record of your thinking-in-progress. Your only recourse is to revisit all your sources, thumbing through them one at a time—a practice that leads to passive cutting and pasting.

To make your notes purposeful, you need to imagine how a given source might be used in your research paper. The chart on page 602 shows how notes are a function of your purpose.

When you use a source's exact words, be meticulous in copying them exactly and marking the quoted passage with prominent quotation marks. If you record information without directly quoting it, be sure that you restate it completely in your own words to avoid later problems with plagiarism. Next, check that you have all the bibliographic information you may need for a citation including the page numbers for each entry in your notes. (Citing page numbers for articles downloaded from the Web or a licensed database is problematic—see Chapter 23, pp. 633–634.)

For a discussion of plagiarism, see Chapter 23, pp. 629–631.

Evaluating Sources

When you read sources for your research project, you need to evaluate them as you go along. As you read each potential source, ask yourself questions about the author's angle of vision, degree of advocacy, reliability, and credibility.

Angle of Vision

By "angle of vision," we mean the way that a piece of writing gets shaped by the underlying values, assumptions, and beliefs of the author so that the text reflects a certain perspective, worldview, or belief system. The angle of vision is revealed by internal factors such as the author's word choice (especially notice the connotations of words), selection and omission of details, overt statements, figurative language, and grammatical emphasis, and by external factors such as the politics of the author, the genre of the source, the politics of the publisher, and so forth. When reading a source, see whether you can detect underlying assumptions or beliefs that suggest a writer's values or political views: Is this writer conservative or liberal? Predisposed toward traditional "family values" or new family structures? Toward technology or toward the simple life? Toward free markets or social controls on the economy? Toward business interests or labor? Toward the environment or jobs? Toward order or freedom?

The concept "angle of vision" was first introduced in Chapter 3, pp. 51–55, and further developed in Chapter 5.

You can also get useful clues about a writer's angle of vision by looking at external data. What are the writer's credentials? Is the writer affiliated with an advocacy group or known for a certain ideology? (If you know nothing about an author who seems important to your research, try typing the author's name into a Web search engine. You might discover useful information about the author's other publications or about the writer's reputation in various fields.) Also pay attention to publishing data. Where was this source originally published? What is the reputation and editorial slant of the publication in which the source appears?

TABLE 22.5 ■ Political Bias of Media

Far Left	Left Liberal	Left Center	Right Center	Right Conservative	Far Right
Media					

People's World
The Guardian
	The Nation
	Mother Jones
	The Progressive
	Utne Reader
		Village Voice
		LA Times
		NY Times
		Atlantic
		Newsweek
		Harper's
		PBS
		NPR
			Time
			Washington
			  Post
			New Republic
			CBS
			NBC
			ABC
				U.S. News and
				  World Report
				Reader's Digest
				The Wall Street
				  Journal
				American
				  Spectator
				National Review
					New American
					Plain Truth
					Washington Times

Commentators					

Alexander
  Cockburn
Edward Said
Noam
  Chomsky
	Gore Vidal
	Barbara
	  Ehrenreich
	Jesse Jackson
	Molly Ivins
	Ralph Nader
		Michael
		  Kinsley
		Anthony
		  Lewis
		Bill Moyers
		Ted Koppel
		Ellen
		  Goodman
		Mark Shields
		Jonathan Alter
		Anna
		  Quindlen
			David Broder
			William Saffire*
				George Will
				Charles
				  Krauthammer
				John Leo
				William Buckley
				Milton Friedman
				Thomas Sowell
				Paul Gigot
					Rush Limbaugh
					Pat Buchanan
					Pat Robertson
					Phyllis Schlafly
					Paul Harvey

*Safire is a right-center columnist employed by the New York Times, a left-center newspaper.

Our ideas in this table are adapted from Donald Lazere, "Teaching the Political Conflicts: A Rhetorical Schema," College Composition and Communication 43 (May 1992): 194–213.

For example, editorial slants of magazines can range from very liberal to very conservative. Likewise, publications affiliated with advocacy organizations (the Sierra Club, the National Rifle Association) will have a clear editorial bias.* Table 22.5 shows our own assessment of the political biases of various popular magazines and media commentators.

Degree of Advocacy

By "degree of advocacy" we mean the extent to which an author unabashedly takes a persuasive stance on a contested position as opposed to adopting a more neutral, objective, or exploratory stance. When a writer has an ax to grind, you need to weigh carefully the writer's selection of evidence, interpretation of data, and fairness to opposing views. Although objectivity is itself an "angle of vision" and no one can be completely neutral, it is always useful to seek out authors who offer a balanced assessment of the evidence. Evidence from a more detached and

*If you are uncertain about the editorial bias of a particular magazine or newspaper, consult the Gale Directory of Publications and Broadcast Media or Magazines for Libraries, which, among other things, identifies the intended audience and political biases of a wide range of magazines and newspapers.

neutral writer may be more trusted by your readers than the arguments of a committed advocate. For example, if you want to persuade corporate executives on the dangers of global warming, evidence from scholarly journals may be more persuasive than evidence from an environmentalist Web site or from a freelance writer in a leftist popular magazine like *Mother Jones.*

Reliability

"Reliability" refers to the accuracy of factual data in a source as determined by external validation. If you check a writer's "facts" against other sources, do you find that the facts are correct? Does the writer distort facts, take them out of context, or otherwise use them unreasonably? In some controversies, key data are highly disputed—-for example, the number of homeless people in the United States, the frequency of date rape, or the risk factors for many diseases. A reliable writer acknowledges these controversies and doesn't treat disputed data as fact. Furthermore, if you check out the sources used by a reliable writer, they'll reveal accurate and careful research—respected primary sources rather than hearsay or secondhand reports. Journalists of reputable newspapers (not tabloids) pride themselves in meticulously checking out their facts, as do editors of serious popular magazines. Web sources, however, can be notoriously unreliable. As you gain knowledge of your research question, you'll develop a good ear for writers who play fast and loose with data.

Credibility

"Credibility" is similar to "reliability" but is based on internal rather than external factors. It refers to the reader's trust in the writer's honesty, goodwill, and trustworthiness and is apparent in the writer's tone, reasonableness, fairness in summarizing opposing views, and respect for different perspectives. Audiences differ in how much credibility they will grant to certain authors. Nevertheless a writer can achieve a reputation for credibility, even among bitter political opponents, by applying to issues a sense of moral courage, integrity, and consistency of principle.

"Credibility" is synonymous with the classical term *ethos* in argument. See pp. 388–389.

Summary

This section has focused on reading your sources rhetorically. It has shown you how to take notes efficiently by considering your purposes for using a source. It has also shown you how to evaluate sources for angle of vision, degree of advocacy, reliability, and credibility.

SKILL 5: UNDERSTAND THE RHETORIC OF WEB SITES

In the previous section we focused on reading sources rhetorically by asking questions about a source's angle of vision, degree of advocacy, reliability, and credibility. In this section we turn to the skills of effectively evaluating and using Web sources by understanding the special rhetoric of Web sites.

The Web as a Unique Rhetorical Environment

The resources available on the World Wide Web are mind-boggling. Some Web sites are historical archives, functioning like major research libraries. For example, a professional association of medieval historians has created a site that gives scholars access to thousands of rare historical documents, enabling a scholar to do research without traveling to Paris or Madrid. Or, consider a site created by the Federal Bureau of Investigation that gives detailed information about its latest investigations, posts pictures of its "most wanted" criminals and terrorists, solicits public help on unsolved cases, and provides a series of children's detective games.

The sites just mentioned are highly professional and expensive to produce. But the Web is also a great vehicle for democracy, giving voice to the otherwise voiceless. Anyone with a cause and a rudimentary knowledge of Web page design can create a Web site. Before the invention of the Web, people with a message had to stand on street corners passing out flyers or put money into newsletters or advocacy advertisements. The Web, in contrast, is cheap. The result is a rhetorical medium that differs in significant ways from print.

Consider, for example, the difference in the way writers attract readers. Magazines displayed on racks attract readers through interest-grabbing covers and teaser headlines inviting readers to look inside. Web sites, however, can't begin attracting readers until the readers have found them through links from another site or through a "hit" on a Web search. Research suggests that Web surfers stay connected to a site for no more than thirty seconds unless something immediately attracts their interest; moreover they seldom scroll down to see the bottom of a page. The design of the home page—the arrangement and size of the print, the use of images and colors, the locations and labels of navigational buttons—must hook readers immediately and send a clear message about the purpose and contents of the site. If the home page is a confused jumble or simply a long, printed text, the average surfer will take one look and leave.

The biggest difference between the Web and print is the Web's hypertext structure. Users click from link to link rather than read linearly down the page. Users often "read" a Web page as a configuration of images and strategically arranged text that is frequently bulleted or enclosed in boxes. Long stretches of straight text are effective only deep within a site where a user purposively chooses to read something in a conventional, linear way.

Analyzing the Purpose of a Site and Your Own Research Purpose

For instructions on how to find a site's home page, see pp. 598–599.

When you conduct research on the Web, your first question should be, Who placed this piece on the Web and why? You can begin answering this question by analyzing the site's home page, where you will often find navigational buttons linking to "Mission," "About Us," or other identifying information about the site's sponsors. You can also get hints about the site's purpose by asking, What kind of Web site is it? As we explained earlier, different kinds of Web sites have different purposes, often revealed by the domain identifier following the server name (.com, .net, .org, .edu, .gov, .mil). As you evaluate the Web site, also consider your own purpose for using it. For instance, are you trying to get an initial understanding of various points of view on an issue, or are you looking for reliable information? An advocacy site may be an excellent place for researching a point of view but a doubtful source of data and evidence for your own argument.

See Table 22.2, "A Rhetorical Overview of Web Sites."

An Illustration: Examining the Rhetoric of "Women and Gun Control" Web Sites

In this section we show you strategies used by experts to research an issue on the Web and evaluate Web sources. As an illustration, we imagine ourselves as student researchers exploring the following research question: How are women represented and involved in the public controversy over gun control? We launched our search by entering "gun control and women" into Google and got more than 357,000 hits. (We calculated that if we worked nonstop around the clock spending one minute per hit, it would take more than eight months to examine every site—hence the need to approach Web research efficiently.) When we began looking at representative samples of these sites, we encountered a vigorous national conversation on gun control in which women's groups and traditionally male-dominated groups seeking support or membership from women carried on a lively debate.

To understand more clearly the individuals and groups who post gun control material on the Web, we decided to determine how these 357,000 hits on "women and gun control" were subdivided by domain types. Using the advanced search strategies in Google,* we determined the number of hits from each domain type and then explored the typical kinds of sites associated with each domain. Our results are shown in Table 22.6. As this table shows, knowing the distribution of domain types gives a researcher a useful overview of the kinds of sources available on a given issue. For our purposes, we stayed primarily in .org sites and occasionally in .com or .net sites because we wanted to see how advocacy organizations supporting or opposing gun control created appeals to women.

Our next step was to examine the rhetoric of these sites to understand the ways that women frame their interests and represent themselves on sites for or against gun control. We discovered that the angle of vision of each kind of site—whether pro–gun control or anti–gun control—filters data in distinctive ways. For example, women's groups advocating gun control emphasize accidental deaths from guns (particularly of children), suicides from easy access to guns, domestic violence turned deadly, guns in schools, and gun-related crime (particularly juvenile crime). In contrast, women's groups opposing gun control emphasize armed resistance to assaults and rapes, the inadequacy of the police to respond to crime, the right of individuals to protect themselves and their families, and generalized appeals to the second amendment. (Women's anti–gun control sites often frame the gun control

---

*Almost all search engines have an "advanced search" feature that allows you to sort sites by domain type or make other kinds of specialized searches. These strategies are generally easy to learn and are clearly explained within the site when you click on "Advanced Search" or "Help."

TABLE 22.6 ▨ Women and Gun Control Sites by Domain Type

Domain	Number of Hits	Typical Kinds of Sites
.com or .net	219,000	▨ Articles in newspapers or magazines accessed through publication's .com site ▨ Threads in chat rooms and newsgroups posted on host's .com site ▨ Marketing sites for firing ranges, gun shops, firearm instructors, etc. (Many included anti–gun control arguments and data and links to anti–gun control sites.)
.org	65,800	▨ Advocacy sites by nonprofit organizations supporting or opposing gun control (anti–gun control sites outnumbered pro–gun control sites by a considerable margin)
.edu	22,900	▨ Student sites posting student papers on gun control ▨ Scholarly sites by professors researching gun control issues (often had valuable, balanced bibliographies)
.gov	3,550	▨ Congressional sites giving details about pending gun control legislation ▨ Sites analyzing gun control issues ▨ Sites of individual congresspersons posting white papers and speeches on gun control
Other	45,750	▨ Personal home pages, local advocacy group sites, and other sites whose URLs are created through small Web servers

issue as pro-self-defense versus anti-self-defense.) We also noted that most of these sites make powerful use of visual elements—icons, colors, and well-known symbols to enhance their emotional appeals. For instance, anti–gun control sites often have patriotic themes with images of waving American flags, stern-eyed eagles, and colonial patriots with muskets. Pro–gun control sites often have pictures of children about to find a gun in Mommy's or Daddy's dresser drawer.

Most of the sites we examined tailor their appeals directly to women. We started our search with the site of the most well-known women's group advocating gun control—the Million Mom March organization. Its home page, featuring a picture of a march on the Capitol Mall in Washington, D.C., is shown in Figure 22.5.

For another pro–gun control perspective, see the speech by the president of the American Medical Association, reprinted on pp. 462–470.

A click on the button labeled "About Us" links to the mission statement, which announces that the organization is "dedicated to preventing gun death and injury and supporting victims and survivors of gun violence." In a memorable last sentence, the mission states: "With one loud voice, we will continue to cry out that we love our children more than the gun lobby loves its guns."

The Million Mom March Web site capitalizes on the connotations of motherhood. The sentence immediately beneath the Capitol Mall picture says, "Ask your neighbor if there is a gun where your children play." In the same spirit, the organization gives a monthly award called "Mom's Apple Pie Award" to a person or organization that advances the cause of gun legislation. It also gives a "Time Out" award to individuals who set back the cause. (Note that these nonviolent moms have time-outs rather than spankings.) The whole site emphasizes mothers'

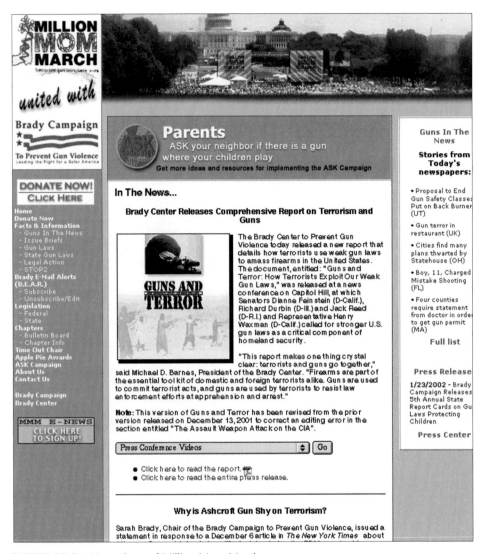

FIGURE 22.5 ■ Home Page of Million Mom March

bonding with children and protecting children from the violence of guns. Note how the links on the right side of the home page provide access to the kinds of stories and data emphasized in pro-gun-control sites: stories about gun terror in a restaurant, an eleven-year-old boy charged with a shooting, and four counties in Massachusetts that now require a doctor's statement to get a gun permit.

At this point, we wondered: How do women who oppose gun control represent themselves? Do they also portray themselves as nurturing mothers or as something else? We invite you now to consider the home pages of the Second Amendment Sisters (Figure 22.6) and Women Against Gun Control (see p. 572).

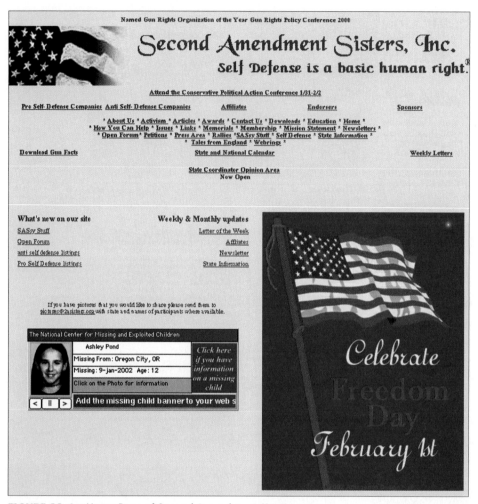

FIGURE 22.6 ■ Home Page of Second Amendment Sisters

For Writing and Discussion

Working in small groups or as a whole class, try to reach consensus answers to the following questions:

1. How is the image of women in each of these home pages different from that of the Million Mom March home page?

2. What is the Web designer's intention in the use of color, curved background lines, and images in the Women Against Gun Control home page?

3. What images of women are conveyed by words like "SASsy Stuff" in the Second Amendment Sisters (SAS) home page or "Ladies of High-Caliber" in the WAGC home page?

4. Why does the home page of the SAS site contain the picture of a missing child?

5. Why do American flags show up much more frequently on anti–gun control sites than on pro–gun control sites?

Now that you have had an opportunity to consider these sites, we offer our own rhetorical analysis. We noticed that the Second Amendment Sisters site positions itself openly against the Million Mom March organization. In its "About Us" link accessed from the home page, it voices its scorn of that group:

> THE SECOND AMENDMENT SISTERS, Inc. came about when a group of women decided they had enough: Enough of the distortion, enough of the misrepresentation, enough of the reproach from the anti-Second Amendment crowd. Learning of the Million Mom March [. . .] was the last straw.

Significantly, however, this site and other anti–gun control sites also portray women as protectors of children—but not as nurturing mothers reducing gun violence but as combatant mothers defending their homes against intruders with firearms. The image of the missing child in the Second Amendment Sisters (SAS) home page appeals to this pro-child sentiment. The Second Amendment Sisters home page thus spins off the Million Mom March home page and tries to outdo it in its concern for children.

When we looked at the Women Against Gun Control (WAGC) home page (p. 572), we noticed that it, too, talks back to the Million Mom March home page and takes ironic delight in antagonizing feminists. Its bold, pink colors and provocatively curved lines use traditional symbols of coy seductiveness to create an in-your-face, Annie Oakley-style message: This gun-toting cowgirl won't take any guff. The messages are complex: Women can be sexy and feminine while simultaneously being powerful and independent if they own and carry a gun. The language in the home page is vigorous and powerful, associating women with self-defense and protection of second amendment rights. This home page purports to "BLOW HOLES" in the myth that all women support gun control. Instead, these women seek, through guns, "a fighting chance against crime" and yell "STOP OR I'LL SHOOT" at burglars. The statistic next to the Annie Oakley figure says that "guns are used defensively 2.5 million times per year"—a factoid meant to startle the reader into getting a gun for self-defense. The gritty realism of these no-nonsense women is brought out in the caption at the bottom of the home page:

> Gun Control: The theory that a woman found dead in an alley, raped and strangled with her panty hose, is somehow morally superior to a woman explaining to police how her attacker got that fatal bullet wound.

Whereas the home page of the Million Mom March site ends with a "Mom's Apple Pie Award," the WAGC home page ends with the verbal image of a raped woman dead in the street (the implied consequence of gun control) versus the image of a heroic woman shooting the assailant dead (the implied consequence of empowering women with guns). These sites are in conversation with both gun control sites and feminist sites—redefining the gun-carrying woman as defiant, sexy, and independent, and yet protective of the family.

Just as we have done here, when you conduct your own research on the Web, you need to be aware that you might be stepping into a heated controversy. To read a site rhetorically, you've got to understand its position within the larger social conversation in order to interpret its use of both visual and textual elements.

Evaluating a Web Source

Once you've considered your reasons for using a source and the rhetorical context of your issue on the Web, you are ready to evaluate a site's angle of vision, degree of advocacy, reliability, and credibility. As we show, part of evaluating a source is evaluating the site in which it is posted. In the following chart, we offer five criteria developed by scholars and librarians as points to consider when you are evaluating Web sites.

Criteria for Evaluating Web Sites

Criteria	Questions to Ask
1. Authority	■ Is the Web site author or sponsor clearly identified? ■ Does the site identify the occupation, position, education, experience, and credentials of the site's author? ■ Does the home page or a clear link from the home page reveal the author's or sponsor's motivation for establishing the site? ■ Does the site provide contact information for the author or sponsor such as an e-mail or organization address?
2. Objectivity or Clear Disclosure of Advocacy	■ Is the site's purpose clear (for example, to inform, entertain, or persuade)? ■ Is the site explicit about declaring its point of view? ■ Does the site indicate whether the author is affiliated with a specific organization, institution, or association? ■ Does the site indicate whether it is directed toward a specific audience?
3. Coverage	■ Are the topics covered by the site clear? ■ Does the site exhibit a suitable depth and comprehensiveness for its purpose? ■ Is sufficient evidence provided to support the ideas and opinions presented?
4. Accuracy	■ Are the sources of information stated? ■ Do the facts appear to be accurate? ■ Can you verify this information by comparing this source with other sources in the field?
5. Currency	■ Are dates included in the Web site? ■ Do the dates apply to the material itself, to its placement on the Web, or to the time the site was last revised and updated? ■ Is the information current, or at least still relevant, for the site's purpose?

An Example: Applying Evaluation Criteria

In this section we offer a brief example of the thinking processes used to evaluate a potential Web source. Suppose, for illustrative purposes, that you are trying to determine your own stance on gun control from a woman's perspective. In doing a Web search, you click on a link that takes you to the following site: http://www.armedandsafe.com/women.htm. What appears on your screen is an article entitled "Women Are the Real Victims of Handgun Control" by Kelly Ann Connolly, who is identified as the director of the Nevada State Rifle and Pistol Association. (See Figure 22.7 which shows the first screen of this article.) The site includes a biographical note indicating that she is a public school teacher with a master's degree and that her husband is a former California Deputy Sheriff and police officer.

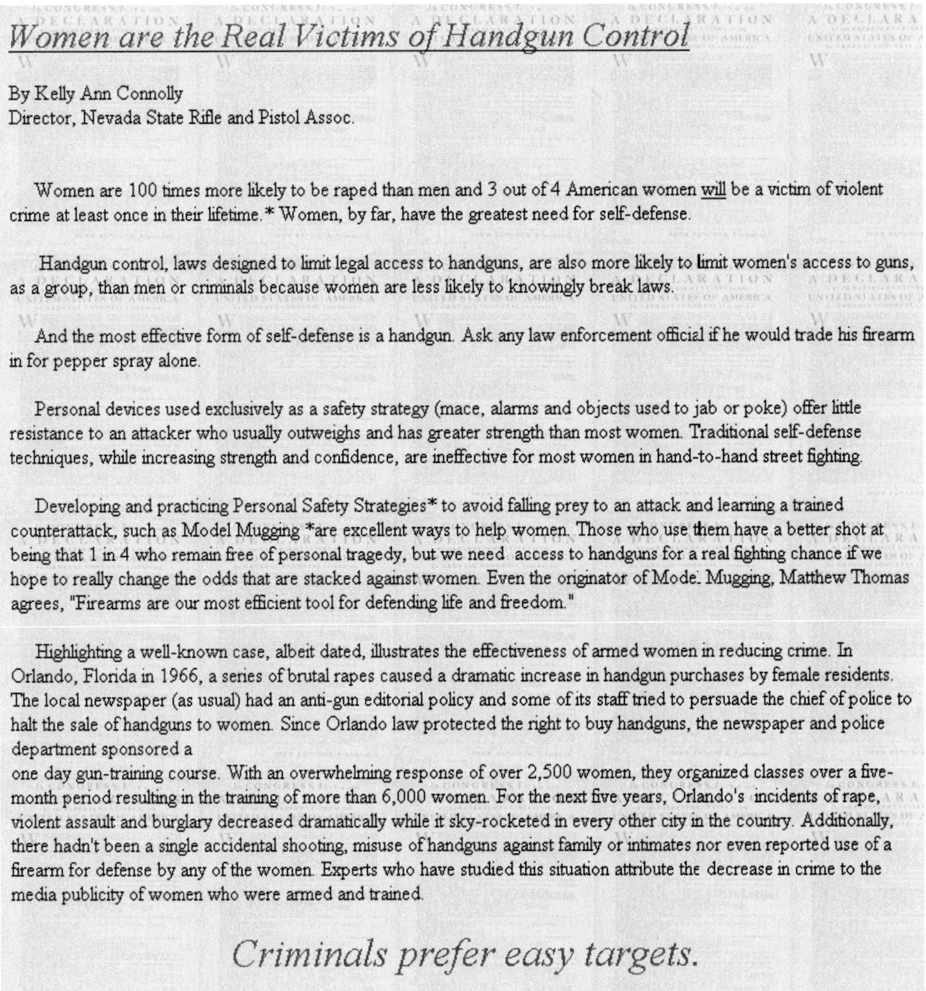

Women are the Real Victims of Handgun Control

By Kelly Ann Connolly
Director, Nevada State Rifle and Pistol Assoc.

Women are 100 times more likely to be raped than men and 3 out of 4 American women will be a victim of violent crime at least once in their lifetime.* Women, by far, have the greatest need for self-defense.

Handgun control, laws designed to limit legal access to handguns, are also more likely to limit women's access to guns, as a group, than men or criminals because women are less likely to knowingly break laws.

And the most effective form of self-defense is a handgun. Ask any law enforcement official if he would trade his firearm in for pepper spray alone.

Personal devices used exclusively as a safety strategy (mace, alarms and objects used to jab or poke) offer little resistance to an attacker who usually outweighs and has greater strength than most women. Traditional self-defense techniques, while increasing strength and confidence, are ineffective for most women in hand-to-hand street fighting.

Developing and practicing Personal Safety Strategies* to avoid falling prey to an attack and learning a trained counterattack, such as Model Mugging *are excellent ways to help women. Those who use them have a better shot at being that 1 in 4 who remain free of personal tragedy, but we need access to handguns for a real fighting chance if we hope to really change the odds that are stacked against women. Even the originator of Model Mugging, Matthew Thomas agrees, "Firearms are our most efficient tool for defending life and freedom."

Highlighting a well-known case, albeit dated, illustrates the effectiveness of armed women in reducing crime. In Orlando, Florida in 1966, a series of brutal rapes caused a dramatic increase in handgun purchases by female residents. The local newspaper (as usual) had an anti-gun editorial policy and some of its staff tried to persuade the chief of police to halt the sale of handguns to women. Since Orlando law protected the right to buy handguns, the newspaper and police department sponsored a
one day gun-training course. With an overwhelming response of over 2,500 women, they organized classes over a five-month period resulting in the training of more than 6,000 women. For the next five years, Orlando's incidents of rape, violent assault and burglary decreased dramatically while it sky-rocketed in every other city in the country. Additionally, there hadn't been a single accidental shooting, misuse of handguns against family or intimates nor even reported use of a firearm for defense by any of the women. Experts who have studied this situation attribute the decrease in crime to the media publicity of women who were armed and trained.

Criminals prefer easy targets.

FIGURE 22.7 ■ First Screen of "Women Are the Real Victims of Handgun Control"

Connolly argues that a woman can walk confidently down any street in America if she is carrying a concealed weapon and is skilled in using it. She offers as support anecdotal cases of women who fought off rapists and cites numerous statistics, attributing the sources to "Bureau of Justice Statistics (1999)." Here are some examples from later screens in the article:

- "3 out of 4 American women <u>will</u> be a victim of violent crime at least once in their lifetime."
- 2 million women are raped each year, one every 15 seconds.
- Rapists know they have only a 1 in 605 chance of being caught, charged, convicted, and sentenced to serving time.

The effect of these statistics is to inform women about the prevalence of rape and to reduce women's confidence in the police or justice system to protect them. The implied solution is to buy a pistol and learn how to use it.

How might you evaluate such an article for your own research purposes? A first step is to evaluate the site itself. We found the home page by deleting "/women.htm" from the URL and looking directly at www.armedandsafe.com. The screen that appeared is shown in Figure 22.8. This is the commercial site of a husband-and-wife team who run a firing range and give lessons in the use of rifles, pistols, and machine guns. The site obviously advocates second amendment rights and promotes gun ownership as a means of domestic and personal security. The fierce eagle emerging from a collage of the American flag, the burning World Trade Center towers, and an aircraft carrier appeals to the patriotic sentiments that tend to dominate pro-gun Web sites. (On the day we accessed it, the site also played a John Wayne rendition of "America the Beautiful.") It is easy to evaluate this site against the five criteria:

1. *Authority:* You can clearly tell who created the site and is responsible for its contents.
2. *Advocacy:* The site clearly advocates second amendment rights and gun ownership.
3. *Coverage:* The site will not cover gun control issues in a complex way. Every aspect of the site will be filtered to support its pro-gun vision.
4. *Accuracy:* You still need to check its facts against other sources, but you can predict that the information will be rhetorically filtered and selected to promote the site's position.
5. *Currency:* Because the site supports a pro-gun stance, it will use data that are most effective in promoting its view. Dates are included in the material and the Web site. Some dates cited are not recent (1996 Florida example), but appear relevant to the issue presented.

How might you therefore use Connolly's article posted on the site? The article could be very useful to you as one point of view on the gun control controversy. It is a fairly typical example of the argument that guns can increase a woman's sense of confidence and well-being, and it clearly shows the kinds of rhetorical

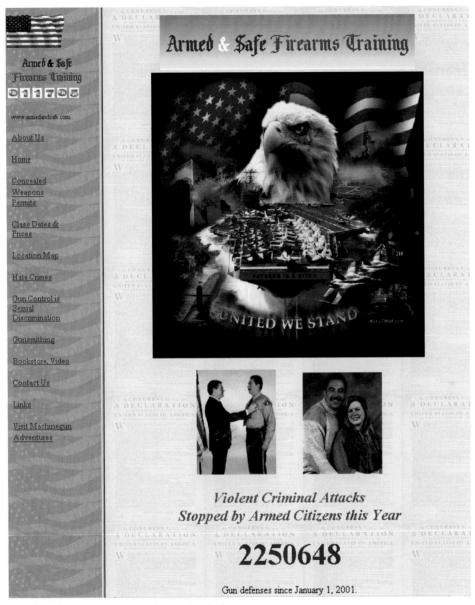

FIGURE 22.8 ■ Home page of armedandsafe.com

strategies such articles use—statistics on rape, descriptions of guns as equalizers in empowering women, and so forth.

As a source of factual data, however, the article is questionable. The sources used are not well documented, and the data appear to be filtered through the writer's pro-gun lens. As a responsible researcher, you need to find primary sources of statistics about gun usage and crime. You will also want to see how data are used in other sites, including those that take on the gun-control issue.

Summary

In this section we have examined the rhetoric of Web sites, showing the range of information and points of view available on the Web and the rhetorical complexity of Web research. Constructed in hypertext format, Web sites demand reading strategies different from those for print sources and rely heavily on visual images and multimedia effects. The Web has given rise to numerous advocacy sites promoting various points of view on public issues. We have shown ways of reading Web sites by understanding how they are positioned in a conversation. Finally we offered criteria for evaluating Web sites.

Using, Citing, and Documenting Sources

The previous chapter focused on the first five of seven research skills listed at the end of Chapter 21 (see pp. 579–580). In Chapter 22, you learned how to conduct an argument in your own voice, how to use appropriate search engines to find different kinds of research sources, and how to read and evaluate those sources using the skills of rhetorical reading emphasized throughout this text. We also examined the special problems of evaluating Web sources.

In this chapter we turn to the final two skills on our list: how to incorporate sources into your writing and how to cite and document them properly.

SKILL 6: USE SOURCES PURPOSIVELY THROUGH CLEARLY ATTRIBUTED SUMMARY, PARAPHRASE, OR QUOTATION

One of the essential skills you need as a researcher is the ability to incorporate research sources purposively into your prose. This section shows you how to do so. Specifically we show you how to use sources for your own purposes and how to weave them gracefully into your prose through effective summary, paraphrase, and quotation. We also show you how to shape your readers' response to these sources through rhetorically effective attributive tags. Finally, we show you how to recognize and scrupulously avoid plagiarism.

Using Sources for Your Own Purposes

In Chapter 22, we explained how you should remain aware of your research goals when you take notes and evaluate sources. To use sources purposively, you need to understand why you are using any given source and how it functions in your argument. Keep in mind the following reasons for using research sources:

See the chart "Note Taking According to Purpose" on p. 602.

- To provide direct evidence, such as facts, information, statistics, and other data, in support of your reasons and points
- To provide indirect evidence through testimony of experts

- ■ To show conflicting or puzzling data that you will analyze or interpret
- ■ To show your understanding of alternative views
- ■ To provide big-picture overviews and background
- ■ To convey your general knowledge, credibility, and authority

The most typical way that inexperienced researchers use sources is through block quotations—a method that often seems amateurish because it simply reproduces a source without foregrounding the writer's voice and purpose.

To illustrate the difference between reproducing a source and using a source purposively, we show you the hypothetical case of three writers using the same article for different purposes. Read carefully the following short article about violence in the Old West. Then proceed to the examples of three writers who use this article for their own different purposes.

Reading

■ ROGER D. MCGRATH ■
THE MYTH OF VIOLENCE IN THE OLD WEST

It is commonly assumed that violence is part of our frontier heritage. But the historical record shows that frontier violence was very different from violence today. Robbery and burglary, two of our most common crimes, were of no great significance in the frontier towns of the Old West, and rape was seemingly nonexistent. [1]

Bodie, one of the principal towns on the trans-Sierra frontier, illustrates the point. Nestled high in the mountains of eastern California, Bodie, which boomed in the late 1870s and early 1880s, ranked among the most notorious frontier towns of the Old West. It was, as one prospector put it, the last of the old-time mining camps. [2]

Like the trans-Sierra frontier in general, Bodie was indisputably violent and lawless, yet most people were not affected. Fistfights and gunfights among willing combatants—gamblers, miners, and the like—were regular events, and stagecoach holdups were not unusual. But the old, the young, the weak, and the female—so often the victims of crime today—were generally not harmed. [3]

Robbery was more often aimed at stagecoaches than at individuals. Highwaymen usually took only the express box and left the passengers alone. There were eleven stagecoach robberies in Bodie between 1878 and 1882, and in only two instances were passengers robbed. (In one instance, the highwaymen later apologized for their conduct.) [4]

5   There were only ten robberies and three attempted robberies of individuals in Bodie during its boom years, and in nearly every case the circumstances were the same: the victim had spent the evening in a gambling den, saloon, or brothel; he had revealed that he had on his person a significant sum of money; and he was staggering home drunk when the attack occurred.

6   Bodie's total of twenty-one robberies—eleven of stages and ten of individuals—over a five-year period converts to a rate of eighty-four robberies per 100,000 inhabitants per year. On this scale—the same scale used by the FBI to index crime—New York City's robbery rate in 1980 was 1,140, Miami's was 995, and Los Angeles's was 628. The rate for the United States as a whole was 243. Thus Bodie's robbery rate was significantly below the national average in 1980.

7   Perhaps the greatest deterrent to crime in Bodie was the fact that so many people were armed. Armed guards prevented bank robberies and holdups of stagecoaches carrying shipments of bullion, and armed homeowners and merchants discouraged burglary. Between 1878 and 1882, there were only thirty-two burglaries—seventeen of homes and fifteen of businesses—in Bodie. At least a half-dozen burglaries were thwarted by the presence of armed citizens. The newspapers regularly advocated shooting burglars on sight, and several burglars were, in fact, shot at.

8   Using the FBI scale, Bodie's burglary rate for those five years was 128. Miami's rate in 1980 was 3,282, New York's was 2,661, and Los Angeles's was 2,602. The rate of the United States as a whole was 1,668, thirteen times that of Bodie.

9   Bodie's law enforcement institutions were certainly not responsible for these low rates. Rarely were robbers or burglars arrested, and even less often were they convicted. Moreover, many law enforcement officers operated on both sides of the law.

10   It was the armed citizens themselves who were the most potent—though not the only—deterrent to larcenous crime. Another was the threat of vigilantism. Highwaymen, for example, understood that while they could take the express box from a stagecoach without arousing the citizens, they risked inciting the entire populace to action if they robbed the passengers.

11   There is considerable evidence that women in Bodie were rarely the victims of crime. Between 1878 and 1882 only one woman, a prostitute, was robbed, and there were no reported cases of rape. (There is no evidence that rapes occurred but were not reported.)

12   Finally, juvenile crime, which accounts for a significant portion of the violent crime in the United States today, was limited in Bodie to pranks and malicious mischief.

13   If robbery, burglary, crimes against women, and juvenile crime were relatively rare on the trans-Sierra frontier, homicide was not: thirty-one Bodieites were shot, stabbed, or beaten to death during the boom years, for a homicide rate of 116. No U.S. city today comes close to this rate. In 1980,

Miami led the nation with a homicide rate of 32.7; Las Vegas was a distant second at 23.4. A half-dozen cities had rates of zero. The rate for the United States as a whole in that year was a mere 10.2.

Several factors contributed to Bodie's high homicide rate. A majority of the town's residents were young, adventurous, single males who adhered to a code of conduct that frequently required them to fight even if, or perhaps especially if, it could mean death. Courage was admired above all else. Alcohol also played a major role in fostering the settlement of disputes by violence.   14

If the men's code of conduct and their consumption of alcohol made fighting inevitable, their sidearms often made it fatal. While the carrying of guns probably reduced the incidence of robbery and burglary, it undoubtedly increased the number of homicides.   15

For the most part, the citizens of Bodie were not troubled by the great number of killings; nor were they troubled that only one man was ever convicted of murder. They accepted the killings and the lack of convictions because most of those killed had been willing combatants.   16

Thus the violence and lawlessness of the trans-Sierra frontier bear little relation to the violence and lawlessness that pervade American society today. If Bodie is at all representative of frontier towns, there is little justification for blaming contemporary American violence on our frontier heritage.   17

What we want to show in this section is that there is no one right way to use this article in your research paper. What you use depends on your research question and your purpose in using the source. Sometimes you will summarize a source's whole argument; sometimes you will summarize only a part; at other times you will use an isolated fact or statistic from the source or quote a sentence or two as testimonial evidence. In what follows we show how three hypothetical writers, addressing three different research questions, use this source in different ways.

Writer 1: Summary for an Analytical Paper on Causes of Violence

For an explanation of numbers in parenthesis, see the discussion of MLA in text documentation on pp. 634–635.

The first hypothetical writer is analyzing the causes of violence in contemporary U.S. society. She wants to reject one possible cause—that contemporary violence grows out of our violent past. To make this point in her argument, she summarizes McGrath's article.

Many people believe that violence is part of our Wild West heritage. But Roger McGrath, in his article "The Myth of Violence in the Old West," shows that frontier violence was very different from contemporary violence. He explains that in a typical frontier town, violence involved gunslingers who were "willing combatants," whereas today's typical victims—"the old, the young, the weak, and the female"—were unaffected by crime (618). Because the presence of an armed populace deterred robbery and burglary, theft was much less common in the Old West than today. On the other hand, McGrath explains, killings were fueled by guns, alcohol, and a code of conduct that invited fighting, so murders were much more frequent than in any U.S. city today (619–20). Thus, according to McGrath, there is little resemblance between violence on the frontier and violence in today's cities, so we cannot blame current violence on our tumultuous frontier past.

In this passage the author summarizes McGrath's argument in order to refute the violent-frontier theory about the causes of contemporary violence. Presumably, this author will proceed to other causes of violence and will not return again to McGrath.

Writer 2: Partial Summary for a Persuasive Paper in Support of Gun Control

In our next case, the hypothetical writer uses McGrath's article in an argument supporting gun control. He wants to refute the popular anti–gun control argument that law-abiding citizens need to be armed to protect themselves against crime.

> Opponents of gun control often argue that guns benefit society by providing protection against intruders. But such protection is deadly, as Roger McGrath shows in his study of violence in the frontier town of Bodie, California. Although guns reduced theft, as seen in the low rate of theft in the well-armed town of Bodie, the presence of guns also led to a homicide rate far above that of the most violent city in the U.S. today. The homicide rate in the frontier town of Bodie, California, for example, was 116 per 100,000, compared to the current national average of 10.2 per 100,000 (619–620). True, Bodie citizens reduced the theft rate by being heavily armed, but at a cost of a homicide rate more than ten times the current national average. To protect our consumer goods at the cost of so much human life is counter to the values of most Americans.

McGrath's article contains data that could be used on either side of the gun control debate. This writer acknowledges the evidence showing that gun possession reduces theft and then works that potentially damaging information into an argument for gun control. How might you use the McGrath article to oppose gun control?

Writer 3: Partial Summary for an Analytical Paper on Shifting Definitions of Crime

Looking at another facet of McGrath's article, the last hypothetical writer summarizes part of McGrath's article to support her thesis that a community's definition of crime is constantly shifting.

> Our notion of criminal activity shifts over time. For example, only a short time ago on the American frontier, murder was often ignored by law enforcement. Roger McGrath, in his discussion of violence in the frontier town of Bodie, California, during the 1870s and 1880s, showed that the townspeople accepted homicides as long as both the murderer and the victim were "willing combatants" who freely participated in gunfights (618). These young males who were the "willing combatants" in Bodie share many characteristics with modern gang members in that they were encouraged to fight by a "code of conduct": "A majority of the town's residents were young, adventurous, single males who adhered to a code of conduct that frequently

required them to fight even if [. . .] it could mean death" (620). Today's gang members also follow a code of conduct that requires violence—often in the form of vengeance. Although joining a gang certainly makes youths "willing combatants," that status doesn't prevent prosecution in court. Today's "willing combatants" are criminals, but yesterday's "willing combatants" were not.

This writer uses McGrath's article to make a point completely different from McGrath's. But by extending and applying information from McGrath's article to a new context, the writer gathers fuel for her own argument about shifting definitions of the word *criminal*.

For Writing and Discussion

Each of the hypothetical writers uses McGrath's article for a different purpose. Working individually or in groups, answer the following questions. Be ready to elaborate on and defend your answers.

1. What are the differences in the ways the writers use the original article? How are these differences related to differences in each writer's purpose?
2. What differences would you expect to find in the research notes each writer took on the McGrath article?
3. What makes each writer's paragraph different from a purposeless listing of random information?

Working Sources into Your Own Prose

As a research writer, you need to incorporate sources gracefully into your own prose so that your paper's focus stays on your own argument. In this section we examine some of the techniques that the three hypothetical writers used to adapt the McGrath article to their own purposes: summarizing a source's argument, paraphrasing a relevant portion of a source, or quoting the source directly. Let's look at each of these options.

Summarizing

See Chapter 6, pp. 118–122, for detailed advice on summary writing.

Writing a summary of a source's argument (either of the whole argument or of a relevant section) is an appropriate strategy when the source represents an opposing or alternative view or when it supports or advances one of your own points. Summaries can be as short as a single sentence or as long as a paragraph. Writer 1's summary of the McGrath article on pages 618–620 is a good example of a graceful summary.

Paraphrasing

We explain how to cite sources later in this chapter; see pp. 631–667.

Unlike a summary, which is a condensation of a source's whole argument, a paraphrase translates a short passage from a source's words into the writer's own words. You should paraphrase when you are using brief, specific information from a source and don't want to interrupt the flow of your own voice with a quotation. Of course, you must still acknowledge the source through a citation.

When you paraphrase, be careful to avoid the original writer's grammatical structure and syntax. If you mirror the original sentence structure while replacing some words with synonyms, you are plagiarizing rather than paraphrasing. Here is an acceptable paraphrase of a short passage from the McGrath article:

Original

There is considerable evidence that women in Bodie were rarely the victims of crime. Between 1878 and 1882 only one woman, a prostitute, was robbed, and there were no reported cases of rape. (There is no evidence that rapes occurred but were not reported.)

Paraphrase

According to McGrath, women in Bodie seldom suffered at the hands of criminals. Between 1878 and 1882, the only female robbery victim in Bodie was a prostitute. Also rape seemed nonexistent, with no reported cases and no evidence that unreported cases occurred (619).

Note that to avoid plagiarism, the writer has changed the sentence structure substantially. However, the writer still acknowledges the original source with the phrase "According to McGrath" and also provides the page number.

Quoting Directly

Occasionally, you will want to quote an author's words directly. Avoid quoting too much because the effect, from your reader's perspective, is a collage of quotations rather than an argument. Quote only when doing so strengthens your argument. Here are some occasions when a direct quotation is appropriate:

- When the quotation comes from a respected authority and, in a pithy way, supports one of your points. (Your use of the quotation is like expert testimony in a trial.)
- When you are summarizing an opposing or alternative view and want to use brief quotations to show that you have listened carefully and accurately.
- When you want to give readers the flavor of a source's voice, particularly if the language is striking or memorable.
- When you want to analyze the writer's choice of words or metaphors. (You would first quote the passage and then begin your analysis.)

When you quote, you must be meticulous in copying the passage *exactly,* including punctuation. When the quoted material takes up more than four lines in your paper, use the following block quotation method:

Example of a Block Quotation

McGrath describes the people most affected by violence in the frontier town of Bodie:

> Fistfights and gunfights among willing combatants—gamblers, miners, and the like—were regular events, and stagecoach holdups were not unusual. But the old, the young, the weak, and the female—so often the victims of crime today—were generally not harmed. (618)

Explanation*

- ▩ The block quotation is indented one inch or ten spaces.

- ▩ There are *no quotation marks*. The block indentation itself signals a quotation.

- ▩ The number in parentheses indicates the page number where the quotation is found in the original source. Note that the parentheses come after the closing period.

- ▩ Because the line introducing the block quotation is a complete sentence, it ends with a colon.

If the quoted passage is fewer than four lines in your own text, insert it directly into your paragraph using quotation marks. How you punctuate depends on whether the inserted quotation is a complete sentence or part of a sentence.

Example of an Inserted Quotation
When the Quotation Is a Complete Sentence

According to McGrath, "It was the armed citizens themselves who were the most potent—though not the only—deterrent to larcenous crime" (619).

Explanation

- ▩ The page number in parentheses is inserted *after* the quotation mark but *before* the closing period.

- ▩ Because the quotation is a complete sentence, it starts with a capital letter and is separated from the introductory phrase by a comma.

Often you won't want to quote a complete sentence but instead work brief words and phrases from your source into your own grammatical structure.

Example of an Inserted Quotation
When the Quotation Is Not a Complete Sentence

McGrath contrasts frontier violence to crime today, pointing out that today's typical crime victims are "the old, the young, the weak, and the female" and showing that these groups were not molested in Bodie (618).

Explanation

- ▩ Because the quoted material is not a complete sentence, it is worked into the grammar of the writer's own sentence.

- ▩ No comma introduces the quotation; commas should be used to fit the grammar of the writer's own sentence.

- ▩ The number in parentheses is the page number where the quotation is found in the original source. Note that it comes wherever the borrowed idea ends.

Modifying Quotations to Fit Your Grammatical Structure

Occasionally the grammar of a desired quotation doesn't match the grammatical structure of your own sentence, or the meaning of a quoted word will not be

---

*This and subsequent examples follow the guidelines of the MLA (Modern Language Association) style. We explain this style in detail in the last half of this chapter (Skill 7), where we also explain APA (American Psychological Association) style.

clear because the passage has been removed from its original context. In these cases, use brackets to modify the quotation's grammar or to add a clarifying explanation: Change the quotation, placing your changes in brackets to indicate that the bracketed material is not part of the original wording. You should also use brackets to show a change in capitalization.

Original Passage

The newspapers regularly advocated shooting burglars on sight, and several burglars were, in fact, shot at.

Quotation Modified to Fit the Grammar of the Writer's Sentence

In Bodie, an armed citizenry successfully eliminated burglaries, aided by newspapers "regularly advocat[ing] shooting burglars on sight" (McGrath 619).

Original Passage

Highwaymen, for example, understood that while they could take the express box from a stagecoach without arousing the citizens, they risked inciting the entire populace to action if they robbed the passengers.

Use of Brackets to Change the Capitalization and Explain Missing Referents

Public sentiment influenced what laws were likely to be broken. According to McGrath, "[W]hile they [highwaymen] could take the express box from a stagecoach without arousing the citizens, they risked inciting the entire populace to action if they robbed the passengers" (619).

Perhaps the most frequent modification writers make is omitting portions of a quotation. To indicate an omission in a quotation in MLA style, use three spaced periods, called an *ellipsis*, enclosed in a pair of brackets.

Original Passage

Finally, juvenile crime, which accounts for a significant portion of the violent crime in the United States today, was limited in Bodie to pranks and malicious mischief.

Using Ellipses to Indicate Omission

"Finally, juvenile crime [. . .] was limited in Bodie to pranks and malicious mischief" (McGrath 619).

When your ellipsis comes at the boundary between sentences, use an additional period to mark the end of the sentence. Do not place this period inside the brackets. Placement of the ellipsis depends on where the omitted material occurs.

Original   Bodie's law enforcement institutions were certainly not responsible for these low rates. Rarely were robbers or burglars arrested, and even less often were they convicted. Moreover, many law enforcement officers operated on both sides of the law.

| Omitting Sentence Within Quotation | According to McGrath, "Bodie's law enforcement institutions were certainly not responsible for these low rates. [. . .] Moreover, many law enforcement officers operated on both sides of the law" (619). |
| Omitting End of Quoted Sentence | According to McGrath, "Bodie's law enforcement institutions were certainly not responsible for these low rates. Rarely were robbers or burglars arrested [. . .]. Moreover, many law enforcement officers operated on both sides of the law" (619). |

Quotations Within Quotations

Occasionally a passage that you wish to quote will already contain quotation marks. If you use block indentation, keep the quotation marks exactly as they are in the original. If you set the passage within your own quotation marks, however, change the original double marks (") into single marks (') to indicate the quotation within the quotation. The same procedure works whether the quotation marks are used for quoted words or for a title.

Original Passage: Robert Heilbroner Quoting William James

And finally, we tend to stereotype because it helps us make sense out of a highly confusing world, a world which William James once described as "one great, blooming, buzzing confusion."

Quoted Passage: Writer Quoting Heilbroner

Robert Heilbroner explains why people tend to create stereotypes: "And finally, we tend to stereotype because it helps us make sense out of a highly confusing world, a world which William James once described as 'one great, blooming, buzzing confusion'" (22).

Creating Rhetorically Effective Attributive Tags

As we have shown in this section, whenever you use sources in your writing, you need to distinguish your source's words and ideas from your own. The most precise way of doing so is to use strategically placed attributive tags—short phrases like "according to McGrath," "McGrath says," "in McGrath's view," and so on. As we show in a moment, attributive tags can have a powerful rhetorical effect by letting you create the angle of vision from which you want your readers to view a source.

Using Attributive Tags to Separate Your Ideas from Your Source's

The previous examples of citing, summarizing, paraphrasing, and quoting used attributive tags to signal which ideas are the writer's and which are taken from another source. Here, for example, are excerpts from Writer 1's summary of McGrath, in which we have highlighted the attributive tags with boldfaced font. (The complete summary appears on pp. 620–621.)

Use of Attributive Tags

Many people believe that violence is part of our Wild West heritage. But **Roger McGrath, in his article "The Myth of Violence in the Old West,"** shows that frontier violence was very different from contemporary violence. **He explains** that [. . .]. On the other hand, **McGrath explains**, killings were fueled [. . .]. Thus, **according to McGrath,** there is little resemblance between violence on the frontier and violence in today's cities [. . .].

Using Parenthetical Citations Without Attributive Tags and the Resulting Ambiguities

You can also indicate borrowed material by inserting the source author's name and appropriate page number in a parenthetical citation at the end of the borrowed material:

> (McGrath 619)

However, this approach—which is common in some academic writing, particularly in the social sciences—can introduce two kinds of ambiguity. First, it doesn't clearly mark where the borrowed material begins or how far it extends. Second, it tends to imply that the borrowed material is a "fact" as opposed to an author's argument filtered through the author's angle of vision. Note these ambiguities in the following passage where parenthetical citations are used without attributive tags:

Ambiguous Attribution

There are many arguments in favor of preserving old-growth forests. First, it is simply unnecessary to log these forests to supply the world's lumber. We have plenty of new-growth forest from which lumber can be taken (Sagoff 89–90). Recently there have been major reforestation efforts all over the United States, and it is common practice now for loggers to replant every tree that is harvested. These new-growth forests, combined with extensive planting of tree farms, provide more than enough wood for the world's needs. Tree farms alone can supply the world's demand for industrial lumber (Sedjo 90).

When confronted with this passage, skeptical readers might ask, "Who are Sagoff and Sedjo? I've never heard of them." It is also difficult to tell how much of the passage is the writer's own argument and how much is borrowed from Sagoff and Sedjo. Is this whole passage a paraphrase? Finally, the writer tends to treat Sagoff's and Sedjo's assertions as uncontested facts rather than as professional opinions. Compare the preceding version with this one in which attributive tags are added:

Clear Attribution

There are many arguments in favor of preserving old-growth forests. First, it is simply unnecessary to log these forests to supply the world's lumber. **According to environmentalist Carl Sagoff,** we have plenty of new-growth forest from which lumber can be taken (89–90). Recently there have been major reforestation efforts all over the United States, and it is common practice now for loggers to replant every tree that is harvested. These new-growth forests, combined with extensive planting of tree farms, provide more than enough wood for the world's needs. **According to**

forestry expert Robert Sedjo, tree farms alone can supply the world's demand for industrial lumber (90).

We can now see that most of the paragraph is the writer's own argument, into which she has inserted the expert testimony of Sagoff and Sedjo, whose views are treated not as indisputable facts but as the opinions of authorities in this field.

Using Attributive Tags to Create Context and Shape Reader Response

When you introduce a source for the first time, you can use the attributive tag not only to introduce the source but also to shape your readers' attitudes toward the source. In the previous example, the writer wants readers to respect Sagoff and Sedjo, so she identifies Sagoff as an "environmentalist" and Sedjo as a "forestry expert." If the writer favored logging old-growth forests and supported the logging industry's desire to create more jobs, she might have used different tags: "Carl Sagoff, an outspoken advocate for spotted owls over people," or "Robert Sedjo, a forester with limited knowledge of world lumber markets."

When you compose an initial tag, you can add to it any combination of the following kinds of information, depending on your purpose, your audience's values, and your sense of what the audience already knows or doesn't know about the source:

Add to Attributive Tag	*Example*
Author's credentials or relevant specialty (enhances credibility)	Civil engineer David Rockwood, a noted authority on stream flow in rivers
Author's lack of credentials (decreases credibility)	City Council member Dilbert Weasel, a local politician with no expertise in international affairs
Author's political or social views	Left wing columnist Alexander Cockburn [has negative feeling]; Alexander Cockburn, a longtime champion of labor [has positive feeling]
Title of source if it provides context	In her book *Fasting Girls: The History of Anorexia Nervosa*, Joan Jacobs Brumberg shows that [establishes credentials for comments on eating disorders]
Publisher of source if it adds prestige or otherwise shapes audience response	Dr. Carl Patrona, in an article published in the prestigious *New England Journal of Medicine*
Historical or cultural information about a source that provides context or background	In his 1960s book popularizing the hippie movement, Charles Reich claims that
Indication of source's purpose or angle of vision	Feminist author Naomi Wolfe, writing a blistering attack on the beauty industry, argues that

Our point here is that you can use attributive tags rhetorically to help your readers understand the significance and context of a source when you first introduce it and to guide your readers' attitudes toward the source.

For Writing and Discussion

What follow are four different ways that a writer can use the same passage from a source to support a point about the greenhouse effect. Working in groups or as a whole class, rank the four methods from "most effective" to "least effective." Assume that you are writing a researched argument addressed to your college classmates.

1. *Quotation without attributive tag*

   The greenhouse effect will have a devastating effect on the earth's environment: "Potential impacts include increased mortality and illness due to heat stress and worsened air pollution, as in the 1995 Chicago heat wave that killed hundreds of people. [. . .] Infants, children and other vulnerable populations—especially in already-stressed regions of the world—would likely suffer disproportionately from these impacts" (Hall 19).

2. *Quotation with attributive tag*

   The greenhouse effect will have a devastating effect on the earth's environment. David C. Hall, president of Physicians for Social Responsibility, claims the following: "Potential impacts include increased mortality and illness due to heat stress and worsened air pollution, as in the 1995 Chicago heat wave that killed hundreds of people. [. . .] Infants, children and other vulnerable populations—especially in already-stressed regions of the world—would likely suffer disproportionately from these impacts" (19).

3. *Paraphrase without attributive tag*

   The greenhouse effect will have a devastating effect on the earth's environment. One of the most frightening effects is the threat of diseases stemming from increased air pollution and heat stress. Infants and children would be most at risk (Hall 19).

4. *Paraphrase with attributive tag*

   The greenhouse effect will have a devastating effect on the earth's environment. One of the most frightening effects, according to David C. Hall, president of Physicians for Social Responsibility, is the threat of diseases stemming from increased air pollution and heat stress. Infants and children would be most at risk (19).

Avoiding Plagiarism

Before we proceed to the nuts and bolts of documenting sources, we'd like you to understand the ethical issue of plagiarism. As you know from writing your own papers, developing ideas and putting them into words is hard work. *Plagiarism* occurs whenever you take someone else's work and pass it off as your own. Plagiarism has two forms: borrowing another person's ideas without giving credit through proper citation and borrowing another writer's language without giving credit through quotation marks or block indentation.

The second kind of plagiarism is far more common than the first, perhaps because inexperienced writers don't appreciate how much they need to change the wording of a source to make the writing their own. It is not enough just to change the order of phrases in a sentence or to replace a few words with synonyms. In the following example, compare the satisfactory paraphrase of a passage from McGrath's piece with a plagiarized version.

Original	There is considerable evidence that women in Bodie were rarely the victims of crime. Between 1878 and 1882 only one woman, a prostitute, was robbed, and there were no reported cases of rape. (There is no evidence that rapes occurred but were not reported.)
Acceptable Paraphrase	According to McGrath (619), women in Bodie rarely suffered at the hands of criminals. Between 1878 and 1882, the only female robbery victim in Bodie was a prostitute. Also, rape seemed nonexistent, with no reported cases and no evidence that unreported cases occurred.
Plagiarism	According to McGrath (619), there is much evidence that women in Bodie were seldom crime victims. Between 1878 and 1882 only one woman, a prostitute, was robbed, and there were no reported rapes. There is no evidence that unreported cases of rape occurred (619).

For Writing and Discussion

The writer of the plagiarized passage perhaps assumed that the accurate citation of McGrath is all that is needed to avoid plagiarism. Yet this writer is guilty of plagiarism. Why? How has the writer attempted to change the wording of the original? Why aren't these changes enough?

The best way to avoid plagiarism is to be especially careful at the note-taking stage. If you copy from your source, copy exactly, word for word, and put quotation marks around the copied material or otherwise indicate that it is not your own wording. If you paraphrase or summarize material, be sure that you don't borrow any of the original wording. Also be sure to change the grammatical structure of the original. Lazy note taking, in which you follow the arrangement and grammatical structure of the original passage and merely substitute occasional synonyms, leads directly to plagiarism.

Also remember that you cannot borrow another writer's ideas without citing them. If you summarize or paraphrase another writer's thinking about a subject, you should indicate in your notes that the ideas are not your own and be sure to record all the information you need for a citation. If you do exploratory reflection to accompany your notes, then the distinction between other writers' ideas and your own should be easy to recognize when it's time to incorporate the source material into your paper.

For Writing and Discussion

The following exercise asks you to apply all the research and writing skills that you have learned in this part of the chapter. After reading Edward Abbey's article "The Damnation of a Canyon" (pp. 144–148), imagine that you are going to use Abbey's article in an essay of your own. Working individually or in small groups, write an appropriate passage for each of the following scenarios. You will need to decide how much you will quote from Abbey's article and how you will use attributive tags to create a context and to shape your readers' responses to your source.

Scenario 1 You are a supporter of dams and wish to write an article supporting the Glen Canyon Dam and opposing Abbey's article. Write a one-paragraph summary of Abbey's views to include in your own essay.

Scenario 2 You are doing research on the ecological effects of dams and want to use Abbey's article as one source. For your essay, write a paragraph, citing Abbey's article, on how building the Glen Canyon Dam changed the river's ecology.

Scenario 3 You are investigating the socioeconomic status of people who use Lake Powell for recreation. You particularly want to investigate Abbey's claim that the lake is used only by the wealthy. For your essay, write a short passage that reports Abbey's view of the socioeconomic status of the lake's recreational users.

Summary

This lesson has shown you how to use sources purposively and to work them into your own writing through summarizing, paraphrasing, and quoting. It has also shown you how to help readers separate your ideas from those of sources through the use of rhetorically effective attributive tags. Finally, it has defined plagiarism and showed you how to avoid it.

SKILL 7: CITE AND DOCUMENT SOURCES EFFECTIVELY ACCORDING TO APPROPRIATE CONVENTIONS

In this final section we focus on the nuts and bolts of documentation that is appropriate for your purpose, audience, and genre. As we have explained, proper documentation helps other researchers locate your sources while contributing substantially to your own ethos as a writer. Specifically, this section helps you understand the general logic of parenthetical citation systems, the MLA and APA

An example of a research paper written in MLA style is Christopher Leigh's paper on pp. 647–658. An example of a research paper written in APA style is Susan Meyers's on pp. 356–366.

methods for in-text citations, the MLA and APA methods for documenting sources in a "Works Cited" and "References" list, respectively, and the MLA and APA styles for formatting academic papers.*

Understanding the Logic of Parenthetical Citation Systems

Not too many years ago, most academic disciplines used footnotes or endnotes to document sources. Today, however, both the MLA (Modern Language Association) system, used primarily in the humanities, and the APA (American Psychological Association) system, used primarily in the social sciences, use parenthetical citations instead of footnotes or endnotes. Before we examine the details of MLA and APA styles, we want to explain the logic of parenthetical citation systems.

Connecting the Body of the Paper to the Bibliography

In both the MLA and APA systems, the writer places a complete bibliography at the end of the paper. In the MLA system this bibliography is called "Works Cited." In the APA system it is called "References." The bibliography is arranged alphabetically by author or by title (if an author is not named). The key to the system's logic is this:

- Every source in the bibliography must be mentioned in the body of the paper.
- Conversely, every source mentioned in the body of the paper must be listed in the bibliography.
- There must be a one-to-one correspondence between the first word in each bibliographic entry (usually, but not always, an author's last name)** and the name used to identify the source in the body of the paper.

Suppose a reader sees this phrase in your paper: "According to Debra Goldstein [. . .]." The reader should be able to turn to your bibliography and find an alphabetized entry beginning with "Goldstein, Debra." Similarly, suppose that in looking over your bibliography, your reader sees an article by "Guillen, Manuel." This means that the name "Guillen" has to occur in your paper in one of two ways:

- As an attributive tag: "Economics professor Manuel Guillen argues that. . . ."
- As a parenthetical citation, often following a quotation: ". . . changes in fiscal policy" (Guillen 49).

---

*Our discussion of MLA style is based on Joseph Gibaldi, *MLA Handbook for Writers of Research Papers,* 5th ed. (New York: Modern Language Association of America, 1999). Our discussion of APA style is based on the *Publication Manual of the American Psychological Association,* 5th ed. (Washington, D.C.: American Psychological Association, 2001).

**Sometimes a source has a corporate author (especially common with Web sites), in which case the entry would begin with the corporation's name (for example, "Centers for Disease Control") rather than an author's last name. Occasionally a source won't have any named author. In such cases you identify the source by the title rather than by the author and begin the bibliographic entry with the title (for example, "Guidelines for School Safety").

Because this one-to-one correspondence is so important, let's illustrate it with some complete examples using the MLA formatting style:

If the body of your paper has this:	Then the "Works Cited" list must have this:
According to linguist Deborah Tannen, political debate in America leaves out the complex middle ground where most solutions must be developed. [author cited in an attributive tag]	Tannen, Deborah. <u>The Argument Culture: Moving From Debate to Dialogue</u>. New York: Random, 1998.
In the 1980s, cigarette advertising revealed a noticeable pattern of racial stereotyping (Pollay, Lee, and Carter-Whitney). [authors cited in parentheses]	Pollay, Richard W., Jung S. Lee, and David Carter-Whitney. "Separate, but Not Equal: Racial Segmentation in Cigarette Advertising." <u>Journal of Advertising</u> 21.1 (1992): 45–57.
In its award-winning Web site, the National Men's Resource Center offers advice to parents whose teenagers want to get a nose stud or other form of body piercing. [corporate author identified in attributive tag]	National Men's Resource Center. "Ouch! Body Piercing." <u>Menstuff</u> 1 Feb. 2001. 17 July 2001 <http:// www.menstuff.org/ issues/byissue/tattoo.html>.

Special Citation Problems with Downloaded Sources

Now that you understand the concept of connecting the body of your text to your bibliography, you need to understand some special citation problems associated with sources downloaded from a licensed database or the Web. It is easy to cite a print source that you read in its original form (books, articles from the actual magazine or journal) because these sources can be retrieved in the same paper format from library to library all over the world. Both the MLA and APA systems have a basic format for citing books and articles. Although you'll encounter variations on the basic formats—more than one author, a revised edition, a translation, and so forth—in general, you simply find a bibliographic model that matches your source and plug the information into the correct slots.

The case is more difficult when you download an article from a licensed database or the Web. First of all, scholarly organizations usually expect researchers to find the original print version rather than use the downloaded version. But for college students, it is often difficult to locate the original print source if their libraries don't have it. There are three main problems with the downloaded articles: (1) you can't be sure the electronic article is a completely accurate version of the print article; (2) the downloaded version often doesn't reproduce the visual images that appear in the print version and that may be important; (3) the downloaded version usually doesn't reproduce the page numbering of the original source, so there is no clear way to cite pages.* (The formatting of downloaded printouts varies

---

*Databases are increasingly offering some sources in pdf format, which reproduces the original look of the article. In these cases, images are usually reproduced, and the original page formatting is maintained.

from computer to computer, so you can't simply number the printout pages and cite those numbers.) Because downloaded versions are unstable, you must include in your bibliographic entry all the publication information about the original print version of the article *plus* information about the electronic source.

You will encounter the most difficulty when citing Web sources. The World Wide Web is a citation nightmare for scholarly organizations because the material on it is unstable and ephemeral. (But there are important exceptions. For example, totally electronic, peer-reviewed scholarly journals are now being published online. The publisher archives all accepted articles, making them stable and electronically available to future scholars.) In general, though, you can't be sure that material available today from the Web will still be available tomorrow, not to mention twenty or more years from now. Another problem with Web sources, as we saw in Chapter 22, is that it is often hard to determine publication dates and authorship of material. Also, as with licensed database sources, page numbers are usually impossible to specify for Web sites. Sometimes the only certain thing you'll know about a Web site is the URL in your computer's location window and the date you accessed the site. At the very minimum, you have to include this information in the citation.

From this point on, we separate our discussions of the MLA and APA systems. We begin with the MLA system because it is the one most commonly used in writing courses. We then explain the APA system.

Understanding the MLA Method of In-Text Citation

To cite sources in your text using the MLA system, place the author's last name and the page reference in parentheses immediately after the material being cited. If an attributive tag already identifies the author, give only the page number in parentheses. Once you have cited the author and it is clear that the same author's material is being used, you need cite only the page references in parentheses. The following examples show parenthetical documentation with and without an attributive tag. Note that the citation precedes the period. If you are citing a quotation, the parenthetical citation follows the quotation mark but precedes the final period.

> The Spanish tried to reduce the status of Filipina women who had been able to do business, get divorced, and sometimes become village chiefs (Karnow 41).

> According to Karnow, the Spanish tried to reduce the status of Filipina women who had been able to do business, get divorced, and sometimes become village chiefs (41).

> "And, to this day," Karnow continues, "women play a decisive role in Filipino families" (41).

A reader who wishes to look up the source will find the bibliographic information in the Works Cited section by looking for the entry under "Karnow." If more than one work by Karnow was used in the paper, the writer would include in the in-text citation an abbreviated title of the book or article following Karnow's name.

(Karnow, "In Our Image" 41)

Special Case 1: Citing from an Indirect Source

Occasionally you may wish to use a quotation that you have seen cited in one of your sources. You read Jones, who has a nice quotation from Smith, and you want to use Smith's quotation. What do you do? Whenever possible, find the quotation in its original source and cite that source. But if the original source is not available, cite the source indirectly by using the terms "qtd. in"; and list only the indirect source in your "Works Cited" list. In the following example, the writer wishes to quote a Buddhist monk, Thich Nhat Hanh, who has written a book entitled *Living Buddha, Living Christ.* However, the writer is unable to locate the actual book and instead has to quote from a review of the book by newspaper critic Lee Moriwaki. Here is how he would make the in-text citation:

> A Buddhist monk, Thich Nhat Hanh, stresses the importance of inner peace: "If we can learn ways to touch the peace, joy, and happiness that are already there, we will become healthy and strong, and a resource for others" (qtd. in Moriwaki C4).

The "Works Cited" list will have an entry for "Moriwaki" but not for "Thich Nhat Hanh."

Special Case 2: Citing Page Numbers for Downloaded Material

There is no satisfactory solution to the problem of citing page numbers for sources retrieved electronically from a database or the Web. Because different computers and printers will format the same source in different ways, the page numbers on a printout won't be consistent from user to user. Sometimes, a downloaded article will indicate page numbers from the original print source, in which case you can cite page numbers in the ordinary way. At other times downloaded material will have numbered paragraphs, in which case you can cite the paragraph number (preceded by *par.*) or numbers (preceded by *pars.*): (Jones, *pars.* 22–24). Most typically, however, downloaded sources will indicate neither page nor paragraph numbers. In such cases, MLA says to omit page references from the parenthetical citation. They assume that researchers can locate the source on a computer and then use a search engine to find a specific quotation or passage.

Documenting Sources in a "Works Cited" List (MLA)

In the MLA system, you place a complete bibliography, titled "Works Cited," at the end of the paper. The list includes all the sources that you mention in your paper. However, it does not include works you read but did not use. Entries in the Works Cited list are arranged alphabetically by author, or by title if there is no author.

To see what citations look like when typed in a manuscript, see Christopher Leigh's Work Cited list on pp. 657–658. The MLA example citations on pp. 636–645 show the correct elements, sequence, and punctuation, but not typing formats.

Here are some general formatting guidelines for the Works Cited list:

■ Begin the list on a new sheet of paper with the words "Works Cited" centered one inch from the top of the page.

■ Sources are listed alphabetically, the first line flush with the left margin and succeeding lines indented one-half inch or five spaces. (Use the "hanging indentation" feature on your word processor.)

■ MLA formatting style uses abbreviations for months of the year (except for May, June, and July) and publishers' names (for example, Random House is shortened to "Random" and "University Press" is shortened to "UP"). For a complete list of abbreviations, consult the fifth edition of the *MLA Handbook for Writers of Research Papers*.

■ Author entries include the name as it appears in the article by-line or on the book's title page.

■ MLA style recommends underlines rather than italics for book titles and names of journals and magazines (because underlines stand out better on the page). Do not underline any punctuation marks following an underlined title.

Here is a typical example of a work, in this case a book, cited in MLA form.

Karnow, Stanley. <u>In Our Image: America's Empire in the Philippines</u>. New York: Random, 1989.

Special Case: Two or More Listings for One Author

When two or more works by one author are cited, the works are listed alphabetically by title. For the second and all additional entries, type three hyphens and a period in place of the author's name.

Dombrowski, Daniel A. <u>Babies and Beasts: The Argument from Marginal Cases</u>. Urbana: U of Illinois P, 1997.

---. <u>The Philosophy of Vegetarianism</u>. Amherst: U of Massachusetts P, 1984.

The remaining pages in this section show examples of MLA formats for different kinds of sources. We begin with a "Quick Reference Guide" for the most common citations. We then explain these citations in more depth and give the most frequently encountered variations and source types.

MLA Quick Reference Guide for the Most Common Citations

Table 23.1 provides MLA models for the most common kinds of citations. This table will help you distinguish the forest from the trees when you try to cite sources. All the major categories of sources are displayed on this table. For further explanation of these citations, along with instructions on citing variations and sources not listed in the Quick Reference Guide, see the page indicated in the third column.

TABLE 23.1 ■ Quick Reference Guide for MLA Citations

Kind of Source	Basic Citation Model	Index for Variations
Print Sources When You Have Used the Original Print Version		
Book	Tannen, Deborah. <u>The Argument Culture: Moving From Debate to Dialogue</u>. New York: Random, 1998.	One author, 638 Two or more authors, 639 Second, later, or revised edition, 639 Republished book, 639 Multivolume work, 639 Articles in reference works, 639 Translation, 639 Corporate author, 639 Anonymous author, 640
Article in anthology with an editor	Shamoon, Linda. "International E-mail Debate." <u>Electronic Communication Across the Curriculum</u>. Ed. Donna Reiss, Dickie Self, and Art Young. Urbana: NCTE, 1998. 151–61.	Citing the editor, 640 Citing an individual article, 640
Article in scholarly journal	Pollay, Richard W., Jung S. Lee, and David Carter-Whitney. "Separate, but Not Equal: Racial Segmentation in Cigarette Advertising." <u>Journal of Advertising</u> 21.1 (1992): 45–57.	Scholarly journal that numbers pages continuously, 640 Scholarly journal that restarts page numbering with each issue, 641
Article in magazine or newspaper	Beam, Alex. "The Mad Poets Society." <u>Atlantic Monthly</u> July–Aug. 2001: 96–103. Lemonick, Michael D. "Teens Before Their Time." <u>Time</u> 30 Oct. 2000: 66–74. Cauvin, Henri E. "Political Climate Complicates Food Shortage in Zimbabwe." <u>New York Times</u> 18 July 2001: A13.	Magazine article with named author, 641 Anonymous magazine article, 641 Review of book, film, or performance, 641 Newspaper article, 641 Newspaper editorial, 642 Letter to the editor, 642
Print Sources That You Have Downloaded from a Database or the Web		
Article downloaded from database	Barr, Bob. "Liberal Media Adored Gun-Control Marchers." <u>Insight on the News</u> 5 June 2000: 44. ProQuest. Lemieux Lib., Seattle U. 15 Aug. 2001 <http://proquest.umi.com>.	Print article downloaded from licensed database, 642
Article downloaded from Web	Goodman, Ellen. "The Big Hole in Health Debate." <u>Boston Globe Online</u> 24 June 2001: D7. 18 July 2001 <http://www.boston.com/dailyglobe2/175/oped/The_big_hole_in_health_debate+.shtml>.	Article or book available online or from an information service, 642 Print article downloaded from Web, 642

(continued)

TABLE 23.1 ▨ Quick Reference Guide for MLA Citations (continued)

Kind of Source	Basic Citation Model	Index for Variations
Web Sources That Haven't Appeared in Print		
Home Page (use for citing an entire Web site)	Duck Unlimited. Home page. 14 Mar. 2002 <http://www.ducks.org/>.	Whole Web site, 643
Authored document within a Web site	Tobin, Sally. "Getting the Word Out on the Human Genome Project: A Course for Physicians." Stanford University Center for Biomedical Ethics. 2000. 18 July 2001 <http://scbe.stanford.edu/research/current_programs.html#genomics>.	Authored document within a Web site, 643 Article from a scholarly e-journal, 644
Document with corporate or unnamed author within a Web site	National Men's Resource Center. "Ouch! Body Piercing." Menstuff 1 Feb. 2001. 17 July 2001 <http:// www.menstuff.org/issues/byissue/tattoo.html>.	Document without identified author within a Web site, 643
Other		E-book, 644 Online reference database, 644 E-mail, 644 Bulletin board or newsgroup postings, 644
Miscellaneous Sources		
Interview	Van der Peet, Rob. Personal interview. 24 June 2001.	Interview, 645
Lecture, Address, or Speech	Jancoski, Loretta. "I Believe in God, and She's a Salmon." University Congregational United Church of Christ. Seattle. 30 Oct. 2001.	Lecture, speech, conference presentation, 645
Other		Television or radio program, 644 Film or videorecording, 644 Sound or recording, 645 Cartoon or advertisement, 645 Government publications, 645

MLA Citations

Books

General Format for Books

Author. Title. City of publication: Publisher, year of publication.

One author

Brumberg, Joan J. The Body Project: An Intimate History of American Girls. New York: Vintage, 1997.

Two or more authors

Dombrowski, Daniel A., and Robert J. Deltete. <u>A Brief, Liberal, Catholic Defense of Abortion</u>. Urbana: U of Illinois P, 2000.

Belenky, Mary, et al. <u>Women's Ways of Knowing: The Development of Self, Voice, and Mind</u>. New York: Basic, 1986.

If there are four or more authors, you have the choice of listing all the authors in the order in which they appear on the title page or using "et al." (meaning "and others") to replace all but the first author.

Second, later, or revised edition

Montagu, Ashley. <u>Touching: The Human Significance of the Skin</u>. 3rd ed. New York: Perennial, 1986.

In place of "3rd ed.," you can include abbreviations for other kinds of editions: "Rev. ed." (for "Revised edition") or "Abr. ed." (for "Abridged edition").

Republished book (for example, a paperback published after the original hardback edition or a modern edition of an older work)

Hill, Christopher. <u>The World Turned Upside Down: Radical Ideas During the English Revolution</u>. 1972. London: Penguin, 1991.

Wollstonecraft, Mary. <u>The Vindication of the Rights of Woman, with Strictures on Political and Moral Subjects</u>. 1792. Rutland: Tuttle, 1995.

The date immediately following the title is the original publication date of the work.

Multivolume work

Churchill, Winston S. <u>A History of the English-Speaking Peoples</u>. 4 vols. New York: Dodd, 1956–58.

Churchill, Winston S. <u>The Great Democracies</u>. New York: Dodd, 1957. Vol. 4 of <u>A History of the English-Speaking Peoples</u>. 4 vols. 1956–58.

Use the first method when you cite the whole work; use the second method when you cite one specific volume of the work.

Article in familiar reference work

"Mau Mau." <u>The New Encyclopedia Britannica</u>. 15th ed. 2002.

Article in less familiar reference work

Ling, Trevor O. "Buddhism in Burma." <u>Dictionary of Comparative Religion</u>. Ed. S. G. F. Brandon. New York: Scribner's, 1970.

Translation

De Beauvoir, Simone. <u>The Second Sex</u>. 1949. Trans. H. M. Parshley. New York: Bantam, 1961.

Corporate author (a commission, committee, or other group)

American Red Cross. <u>Standard First Aid</u>. St. Louis: Mosby Lifeline, 1993.

Anonymous author

The *New Yorker* Cartoon Album: 1975–1985. New York: Penguin, 1987.

Edited Anthologies

An edited anthology looks like a regular book but has an editor rather than an author, and the contents are separate articles written by individual scholars. Anthology editors might also produce collections of short stories, poems, artworks, cartoons, or other kinds of documents. When you refer to the whole book, you cite the editor. When you refer to an individual article, you cite the author of that article.

Citing the editor

O'Connell, David F., and Charles N. Alexander, eds. Self Recovery: Treating Addictions
    Using Transcendental Meditation and Maharishi Ayur-Veda. New York: Haworth,
    1994.

Citing an individual article

Royer, Ann. "The Role of the Transcendental Meditation Technique in Promoting
    Smoking Cessation: A Longitudinal Study." Self Recovery: Treating Addictions
    Using Transcendental Meditation and Maharishi Ayur-Veda. Eds. David F.
    O'Connell and Charles N. Alexander. New York: Haworth, 1994. 221–39.

In the above examples, O'Connell and Alexander are the editors of the anthology. Ann Royer is the author of the article on smoking cessation. When you cite an individual article, the inclusive page numbers for the article come at the end of the citation.

Articles in Scholarly Journals Accessed in Print

The differences between a scholarly journal and a magazine are explained on page 590. When citing scholarly journals, you need to determine how the journal numbers its pages. Typically, separate issues of a journal are published four times per year. The library then binds the four separate issues into one "annual volume." Some journals restart the page numbering with each issue, which means that during the year there would be four instances of, say, page 31. Other journals number the pages consecutively throughout the year. In such a case, the fall issue might begin with page 253 rather than page 1. When pages are numbered sequentially throughout the year, you need to include only the volume number in the volume slot (for example, "25"). When page numbering starts over with each issue, you need to include in the volume slot both the volume and the issue number, separated by a period (for example, "25.3").

General Format for Scholarly Journals

Author. "Article Title." Journal Title volume number.issue number (year): page numbers.

Scholarly journal that numbers pages continuously

Barton, Ellen L. "Evidentials, Argumentation, and Epistemological Stance." College
    English 55 (1993): 745–69.

Scholarly journal that restarts page numbering with each issue

Pollay, Richard W., Jung S. Lee, and David Carter-Whitney. "Separate, but Not Equal: Racial Segmentation in Cigarette Advertising." <u>Journal of Advertising</u> 21.1 (1992): 45–57.

Articles in Magazines and Newspapers Accessed in Print

Magazine and newspaper articles are easy to cite. If no author is identified, begin the entry with the title or headline. Distinguish between news stories and editorials by putting the word "Editorial" after the title. If a magazine comes out weekly or biweekly, include the complete date (27 Sept. 1998). If it comes out monthly, then state the month only (Sept. 1998).

General Format for Magazines and Newspapers

Author. "Article Title." <u>Magazine Title</u> [day] Month year: page numbers.

Note: If the article continues in another part of the magazine or newspaper, add "+" to the number of the first page to indicate the nonsequential pages.

Magazine article with named author

Snyder, Rachel L. "A Daughter of Cambodia Remembers: Loung Ung's Journey." <u>Ms</u>. Aug.–Sept. 2001: 62–67.

Hall, Stephen S. "Prescription for Profit." <u>New York Times Magazine</u> 11 Mar. 2001: 40+.

Anonymous magazine article

"Daddy, Daddy." <u>New Republic</u> 30 July 2001: 2–13.

Review of book, film, or performance

Schwarz, Benjamin. "A Bit of Bunting: A New History of the British Empire Elevates Expediency to Principle." Rev. of <u>Ornamentalism: How the British Saw Their Empire</u>, by David Cannadine. <u>Atlantic Monthly</u> Nov. 2001: 126–35.

Kaufman, Stanley. "Polishing a Gem." Rev. of <u>The Blue Angel</u>, dir. Josef von Sternberg. <u>New Republic</u> 30 July 2001: 28–29.

Lahr, John. "Nobody's Darling: Fascism and the Drama of Human Connection in <u>Ashes to Ashes</u>." Rev. of <u>Ashes to Ashes</u>, by Harold Pinter. The Roundabout Theater Co. Gramercy Theater, New York. <u>New Yorker</u> 22 Feb. 1999: 182–83.

Follow this general model: Name of reviewer. "Title of Review." Rev. of <u>book, film, or play</u>, by Author/Playright [for films, use name of director preceded by "dir."; for play add production data as in last example.] <u>Magazine Title</u> [day] month year: inclusive pages.

Newspaper article

Henriques, Diana B. "Hero's Fall Teaches Wall Street a Lesson." <u>Seattle Times</u> 27 Sept. 1998: A1+.

Page numbers in newspapers are preceded by the section letter: "A1" means "section A, page 1." The "+" indicates that the article is completed on one or more pages later in the newspaper.

Newspaper editorial

"Dr. Frankenstein on the Hill." Editorial. New York Times 18 May 2002: A22.

Letter to the editor of a magazine or newspaper

Tomsovic, Kevin. Letter. New Yorker 13 July 1998: 7.

Print Articles or Books Downloaded from a Database or the Web

As we explained earlier, it is often impossible to determine original page numbers from downloaded articles, nor can you be sure that the electronic version is exactly like the print version. Therefore, citations in this category begin with complete print information, followed by the electronic information.

Print article downloaded from licensed database

Portner, Jessica. "Girl's Slaying Elicits Calls for Metal Detectors." Education Week 14
    Mar. 2000: 3. Academic Search Elite. EBSCO Publishing. Lemieux Lib., Seattle U.
    17 July 2001 <http://www.epnet.com>.

Begin with the original print information; then cite the database used (underlined), the name of the database company if different, the name and location of the library leasing the service, your date of access, and the URL home page of the service.

Article or book available online or on microfiche from an information service

These services, such as ERIC (Educational Resources Information Center) or NTIS (National Technical Information Service), provide material to your library on microfiche or online with indexes on CD-ROM or online. Much of the material from these services has not been published in major journals or magazines. Frequently they are typescripts of conference papers or other scholarly work disseminated on microfiche.

Eddy, P. A. The Effects of Foreign Language Study in High School on Verbal Ability as
    Measured by the Scholastic Aptitude Test—Verbal. Washington, DC: Center for
    Applied Linguistics, 1981. ERIC ED 196 312.

The ERIC code at the end tells researchers that this work is available on microfiche.

Print article downloaded from Web

Kane, Joe. "Arrested Development." Outside Online May 2001: 5 pp. 17 Nov. 2001
    <http://www.outsidemag.com/magazine/200105/200105molokai1.html>.

If the online magazine indicates the page numbers of the original print source, cite them after the date of publication; if it doesn't give the number of pages in the online version, if they are numbered, followed by "pp."

Web Sources and Other Electronically Retrieved Sources

While rules for formatting electronic sources are still being developed, the principle that governs electronic citations is the same as that for print sources: give enough information so that the reader can find the source you used. If the reader cannot locate the Web page, Listserv, or other electronic source based on inform-taion in your citation, you haven't given enough details. It is also important to give in your citation the date that you accessed the material, since Web sites are frequently updated, altered, or dropped.

The MLA has developed general guidelines for citing electronic sources, which we apply here to specific examples. Nevertheless, you have more freedom of judgment in this area than in the area of print media citations because electronic sources are in constant development and flux. When in doubt, always make your entries as clear and informative as possible.

General Format for Electronic Sources

Author of the page or document, either individual or corporate. "Title of page or document." <u>Title of the overall site, usually taken from the home page</u>. Date of publication online or last update of site. Total length of piece, if known. Name of site sponsor if not already stated. Date you accessed the site <URL of the specific document>.

Whole Web site

National Men's Resource Center. <u>Menstuff: The National Men's Resource</u>. 17 Mar. 2002 <http://www.menstuff.org/>.

National School Safety and Security Services. Home page. 23 Aug. 2001 <http://www.schoolsecurity.org/>.

When citing an entire Web site, cite the home page. If the home page has a distinctive title, cite the title and underline it. If not, use the words "Home page."

Authored document within a Web site

Lithwick, Dahlia. "Creche Test Dummies: Nativity Scenes on Public Lands Are Illegal, Rules the Supreme Court. Except When They're Not." <u>Slate</u> 21 Dec. 2001. 22 Dec. 2001 <http://slate.msn.com/?id=2060070>.

In this case, the first date indicates when the article was posted on the Web. The second date indicates the researcher's date of accessing the article.

Document without an identified author within a Web site

The Interdisciplinary Center, Herzliya. "Palestine Liberation Front (PLF)." <u>International Policy Institution for Counter-Terrorism</u>. 21 Dec. 2001 <http://www.ict.org.il/ inter_ter/orgdet.cfm?orgid=29>.

When citing a document without a named author, use the following generic format: Name of corporate author. "Title of document." <u>Title of Web site on home page</u>. Date of publication, if available. Date you accessed the document <URL of site>. In many cases the name of the Web site and the name of the sponsor are the same. In this case, begin the entry with the name of the Web site underlined.

Article from a scholarly e-journal

Welch, John R., and Ramon Riley. "Reclaiming Land and Spirit in the Western Apache
Homeland." <u>American Indian Quarterly</u> 25 (2001): 5–14. 19 Dec. 2001
<http://muse.jhu.edu/journals/american_indian_quarterly/v025/25.1welch.pdf>.

E-book

Hoffman, Frank W. <u>The Literature of Rock: 1954–1978</u>. Metuchen: Scarecrow, 1981.
<u>NetLibrary</u>. Lemieux Lib., Seattle U. 19 Dec. 2001 <http://www.netlibrary.com/
ebook_info.asl?product_id=24355>.

Online reference database

"Uses and Ethics of Cloning." <u>Encyclopedia Britannica Online</u>. Year in Review 1997. 22
Dec. 2001 <http://www.eb.com:180/bol/topic?eu=124355&sctn=1>.

E-mail

Daffinrud, Sue. "Scoring Guide for Class Participation." E-mail to the author. 12 Dec.
2001.

Bulletin board or newsgroup postings

Dermody, Tony. "Re: Can We Have It All or Was It a Lie?" Online posting. 19 Dec. 2001.
Google newsgroup soc.feminism. 22 Dec. 2001 <http://groups.google.com/
groups?hl=en&selm=n7os1us9ue4k8th1vtvlbepgtbun2booqk%404ax.com>.

For a bulletin board, newsgroup, or chat room posting, follow this format: Author
name. "Title of Posting." Online posting. Date of posting. Name of forum. Date of
access <URL>.

Miscellaneous Sources

Television or radio program

"Lie Like a Rug." <u>NYPD Blue</u>. Dir. Steven Bochco and David Milch. ABC. KOMO,
Seattle. 6 Nov. 2001.

For a program with episodes, begin with the episode name in quotation marks followed by the program name, underlined. If the program is part of a series (such as
Masterpiece Theatre), add the series name without quotation marks or underlines.

Film or video recording

<u>Shakespeare in Love</u>. Dir. John Madden. Perf. Joseph Fiennes and Gwyneth Paltrow.
Screenplay by Marc Norman and Tom Stoppard. Universal Miramax, 1998.

A minimal citation begins with the name of the film, underlined, and includes
the name of the film company or the distributor and distribution date. Most citations also include the name of the director and may include the names of major
performers and writers.

<u>Shakespeare in Love</u>. Dir. John Madden. Perf. Joseph Fiennes and Gwyneth Paltrow.
Screenplay by Marc Norman and Tom Stoppard. 1998. Videocassette. Universal
Miramax, 1999.

Cite the original film data. Then cite the recording medium (videocassette, laser disc, or DVD), name of recording company, and date of the videocassette or disc.

Sound recording

Dylan, Bob. "Rainy Day Woman." Bob Dylan MTV Unplugged. Columbia, 1995.

For sound recordings begin the entry with what your paper emphasizes—for example, the artist's name, composer's name, or conductor's name—and adjust the elements accordingly.

Cartoon or advertisement

Trudeau, Garry. "Doonesbury." Cartoon. Seattle Times 19 Nov. 2001: B4.

Banana Republic. Advertisement. Details Oct. 2001: 37.

Interview

Castellucci, Marion. Personal interview. 7 Oct. 2001.

Lecture, speech, or conference presentation

Sharples, Mike. "Authors of the Future." Conference of European Teachers of Academic Writing. U of Groningen. Groningen, Neth. 20 June 2001.

Government publications

Government publications are often difficult to cite because there are so many varieties. In general, follow these guidelines:

■ Usually cite as author the government agency that produced the document. Begin with the highest level and then branch down to the specific agency:

United States. Dept. of Justice. FBI

Idaho. Dept. of Motor Vehicles

■ Follow this with the title of the document, underlined.

■ If a specific person is clearly identified as the author, you may begin the citation with that person's name, or you may list the author (preceded by the word "By") after the title of the document.

■ Follow standard procedures for citing publication information for print sources or retrieval information for Web sources.

United States. Dept. of Justice. FBI. The School Shooter: A Threat Assessment Perspective. By Mary O'Toole. 2000. 16 Aug. 2001 <http://www.fbi.gov/publications/school/school2.pdf>.

The in-text citation would be: (United States). If you have more than one U.S. government document, continue to narrow down the in-text citation: (United States. Dept. of Justice. FBI. School Shooter). Had this document been published in print rather than online, you would list the standard publishing information found on the title page. Typically the press would be the GPO (Government Printing Office).

Formatting an Academic Paper in MLA Style

An example research paper in MLA style is shown on pages 647–658. Here are the distinctive formatting features of MLA papers.

- Double-space throughout including block quotations and the Works Cited list.
- Use one-inch margins top and bottom, left and right. Indent one-half inch or five spaces from the left margin at the beginning of each paragraph.
- Number pages consecutively throughout the manuscript including the Works Cited list, which begins on a new page. Page numbers go in the upper right-hand corner, flush with the right margin, and one-half inch from the top of the page. The page number should be preceded by your last name. The text begins one inch from the top of the page.
- Do *not* create a separate title page. Type your name, professor's name, course number, and date in the upper left-hand corner of your paper (all double-spaced), beginning one inch from the top of the page; then double-space and type your title, centered, without underlines or any distinctive fonts (capitalize the first word and important words only); then double-space and begin your text.
- Start a new page for the Works Cited list. Type "Works Cited" centered, one inch from the top of the page in the same font as the rest of the paper; do not enclose it in quotation marks. Use hanging indentation of five spaces or one half inch for each entry longer than one line. Format entries according to the instructions on pages 635–646.

Student Example of an MLA-Style Research Paper

As an illustration of a student research paper written in MLA style, we present Christopher Leigh's paper on metal detectors in schools. Christopher's process in producing this paper has been discussed in various places throughout the text.

Leigh 1

Christopher Leigh

Professor Grosshans

English 110

September 1, 2001

The Case Against Metal Detectors in Public Schools

One of the most watched news stories of the last decade took place on April 20, 1999, when two students walked into their suburban Colorado high school and shot twelve students and one teacher before shooting themselves. The brutal slayings sent shock waves around the country, leaving everyone asking the same questions. What drove them to commit such a horrible crime? What can we do to prevent something like this from happening again?

Panic over school safety has caused school boards from coast to coast to take action. Though their use is far from widespread, many schools are installing metal detectors to keep guns and knives out of school. Unfortunately, such measures do not address the causes of violence and are simply an ill-considered quick fix that may do more harm than good. Except for schools with very severe threats of danger, metal detectors should not be used because there is no basis for panic and because there are other more effective and less costly alternatives for violence prevention in schools.

An important point to realize about school violence is that the media have created a public outcry

over school safety when in fact violent incidents are
extremely rare. The media have taken uncommon incidents
like the one at Columbine High and, according to school
psychologist Tony Del Prete, "overanalyze[d] and
sensationalize[d] them to the point of hysteria" (375).

Statistics and studies regarding school violence
are astonishingly conflicting and reported in
sensationalized ways. For example, one study conducted
by the Centers for Disease Control and Prevention
(United States) reports percentages of youths who
carried a gun or weapon to school from 1993 to 1999
(Table 1).

Table 1

Percentage of Youths Carrying Weapon or Gun to School,
1993-1999

	1993	1995	1997	1999
Carried a weapon	11.8%	9.8%	8.5%	6.9%
Carried a gun	7.9%	7.6%	5.9%	4.9%

Source: United States. Dept. of Health and Human
Services. Centers for Disease Control and Prevention.

These numbers can be cited in a frightening way ("In
1993 nearly 8 percent of teenagers reported carrying a
gun to school"). But it is also possible to display
these numbers in a graph (see Figure 1) and report them
in a more comforting way: "As shown in Figure 1,

Leigh 3

between 1993 and 1999 the number of students who carried a gun to school has dropped 38 percent from 7.9 percent to 4.9 percent." Proponents of metal detectors generally cite the figures in the most alarming way. For example, advocates of metal detectors claim that 100,000 students carry guns to school each day (Wilson and Zirkel 32), but they fail to note that these statistics are based on data before 1993. Since 1993, violence incidents in schools have declined steadily each year, and youth homicide has dropped by over 50 percent (Barr 44). Of course it is true that weapons and violence are undeniably present in schools. But the percentage of schools in which violence is a recurring problem is perceived to be exponentially larger than it actually is. As a result, metal detectors have been installed in schools that have had no problems with weapons and violence simply to appease a panicked and irrational public.

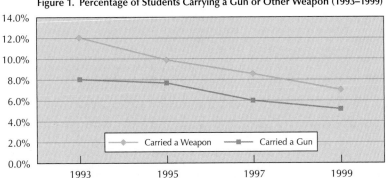

Figure 1. Percentage of Students Carrying a Gun or Other Weapon (1993–1999)

Leigh 4

Although metal detectors may seem like a quick and tangible way to fight violence in schools, there are many strong arguments against them based on students' rights, the ease of defeating metal detectors, the cost, and the psychological consequences that the devices have on the school environment.

Many students believe that metal detectors violate their rights. According to Arizona student Jon Gress, the use of metal detectors

> invades the student's personal space, permitting anyone to see into their bags and purses. And if the detector went off, they would be required to subject their bags and body to a more thorough search. This act alone seems to infringe on the Fourth Amendment right of unwarranted search and seizure.

Another student, Lindsey, in a message posted on the juvenile.net message board, says,

> [L]earning in such a threatening environment is not good for the students. [. . .] Does anyone else believe [besides me] that [use of metal detectors] disrupts the 'good' students and is [a] violation against student's rights [. . .]?

So far the few court cases involving metal detectors have ruled in favor of the schools, saying that the benefit of public safety outweighs the right to privacy. According to Michael Ferraraccio, the Supreme

Leigh 5

Court has said metal detectors in schools are legal.
However, he says, the Supreme Court decision "seemed to
indicate that generally some level of individualized
suspicion is necessary for a search to be reasonable
under the Fourth Amendment" (215). Although this case
does not address generalized metal detector searches,
legal experts believe that minimally invasive
"administrative" searches will be permitted by the
courts (Stefkovich and O'Brien 155). Judges liken them
to searches used in airports where people are searched
for weapons without reasonable suspicion. But I think
there is a key distinction between the two situations.
People are not required to travel through airports and
may walk away from a search, but students are required
by law to attend school and do not have the option of
refusing a search. Despite court rulings so far, many
students will continue to believe their constitutional
rights are being violated.

Besides possibly violating students' rights, metal
detectors have another serious problem: they can be
easily defeated. As <u>American School Board Journal</u>
contributor Donna Harrington-Lueker points out, schools
have many entrances that can't be locked due to fire
codes, windows that can be opened, "and legions of
youngsters arriving en masse at the same time each day"
(26). As she forcefully puts it, a "permanent, full
time metal detector at the front door isn't going to

stop a youngster from passing a gun to a buddy through
the side window" (26).

Also, metal detectors are often used only at the
beginning of the day and sometimes not every day, which
creates a false sense of security. In 1992, a student
in a New York school was shot and killed on a day when
the metal detectors were not in use (Yarbrough 586).
Other shootings have taken place in schools despite the
use of metal detectors. In Los Angeles, ten shooting
incidents occurred after the school district began
using metal detectors in schools, and not a single gun
was confiscated through the searches (Stecklow A1).
Similar conditions exist in a Washington, D.C., school
district, which left one security guard "convinced that
the [metal] detectors were useless" (Stecklow A6).
Dennis Cunningham, a spokesman for a metal detector
manufacturer, notes that the devices are a "'Band Aid'
solution that 'an innovative student' could foil 'very
easily'" (qtd. in Stecklow A1). Some students
interviewed note that "[A]nyone could sneak in a knife
[. . .] or a gun" (qtd. in Stecklow A6). Even
organizations that strongly advocate metal detectors,
such as the National School Safety and Security
Services, warn on their Web site that metal detectors
are "not a panacea for solving safety concerns." Yet
schools continue to use the devices despite the

Leigh 7

compelling evidence that indicates that they are not
working.

Another major concern surrounding the use of metal
detectors is cost. Airport-style units cost anywhere
between four and ten thousand dollars (Harrington-
Lueker 27). Handheld units are cheaper and therefore
considerably more common, but they are much more time
consuming and much less effective. Personnel are also
required to operate the machinery, and large schools
will often require upwards of fifteen officers to
conduct the searches. According to Harrington-Lueker,
it is not unusual for school districts to spend
several million dollars to implement a comprehensive
metal detector system in their schools (27). Parents
and citizens argue that the safety of our children
shouldn't carry a price tag, but when metal detectors
prove ineffective, alternatives need to be
investigated.

Perhaps the most harmful effect of metal detectors is
their psychological impact on students subjected to daily
searches. Student essays posted on the Web, along with
dozens of postings on electronic message boards, show
students' dismay at being subjected to metal detectors.
"Guards, cameras, scanners, and metal detectors every day
take over our schools," says a Philadelphia high school
senior (qtd. in Lee). Another student, using the nickname

Leigh 8

"ummm" on a message board, says:

> It's not actually walking through the metal
> detectors that I'm against [. . .]. It's much
> more the principle of the thing. These damn
> things, and the people the school board has
> hired to run them, cost so much freaking money
> that could be used for useful things. Metal
> detectors will not stop a shooting in [this
> high school]. If someone wanted to kill people
> then they could just as well shoot people in
> the damn line to get through them.

Metal detectors not only reinforce the feeling that
schools are unsafe, but they also instill a sense of
humiliation in students and, as a result, a feeling of
distrust between students and school administrators.
These feelings of distrust and susceptibility erode the
atmosphere of learning that is so important to a
student's education, and schools begin to feel more
like prisons than schools.

If metal detectors are an inappropriate means to
curb violence in our schools, what is a better
approach? If we look again at student postings on the
Web, we see a consistently recurring suggestion:
friendlier schools, personal relationships, and better
counseling. Says one student, "City kids get metal
detectors, suburban kids get counselors" (qtd. in Lee).
Atlanta high school senior Malik Barry-Buchanan was

Leigh 9

asked how the school environment can be changed "so
people don't feel the need to bring a weapon to
school." Here is his answer:

> Well, for starters, we need to find ways for
> students to respect each other, have teachers
> go through training to encourage them to make
> even the smallest attempt at getting in touch
> with the students, and have school admin-
> istrators look at students as independent,
> free-thinking young adults and not 5-year-old
> rug rats.

In order to combat the problem of school violence
head-on, it is essential to provide students with
better counseling and to work towards improving the
overall school environment. Scott Poland, the
president of the National Association of School
Psychologists, writes that administrators need to do
more to personalize schools and provide better
counseling services to students who may be troubled
(45). He writes that most counselors are already
overworked and are required to do things such as
scheduling that take away from their attention to the
students. Poland also emphasizes that it is important
for teachers to form strong relationships with each
and every student. He suggests that teachers set aside
a small amount of time each day to interact with
students, and discourages schools from cutting

Leigh 10

extracurricular programs that may help students feel connected to the school (46).

In my opinion, Poland's article offers the most encouraging and perhaps the best advice for the prevention of school violence. Teachers might complain that they do not have the time to spend getting to know every student. But getting to know each student should be part of the job requirement. If teachers know their students on a personal level, they will be able to sense when a student is in trouble, reach out to that student, and create an atmosphere of care and trust rather than suspicion and surveillance.

Violence does undoubtedly exist in schools, but the percentage of schools where the level of violence justifies metal detectors is extremely small. The problem of school violence is simply a reflection of the high level of violence in American society in general, and the problem is not the schools, but society as a whole. Metal detectors may deter some students from bringing weapons to school, but they can't prevent violence and they create an atmosphere of fear and suspicion rather than trust and community. The key to preventing school violence is to focus on improving students' relationships with teachers and, more importantly, themselves, rather than treat them like potential criminals.

Leigh 11

Works Cited

Barr, Bob. "Liberal Media Adored Gun-Control Marchers."

    Insight on the News 5 June 2000: 44. ProQuest.

    Lemieux Lib., Seattle U. 15 Aug. 2001

    <http://proquest.umi.com>.

Barry-Buchanan, Malik. "More Rules + More Security =

    Feelings of Safety." Alternet.org 16 Aug. 2001

    <http://alternet.org/print.html?StoryID=9623>.

Del Prete, Tony. "Unsafe Schools: Perception or Reality?"

    Professional School Counseling 3 (2000): 375-76.

Ferraraccio, Michael. "Metal Detectors in the Public

    Schools: Fourth Amendment Concerns." Journal of

    Law and Education 28 (1999): 209-29.

Gress, Jon. "School Violence: How to Stop the Crime of

    Today's Youth." Gecko—The Student Server 5 May

    2000. 16 Aug. 2001 <http://gecko.gc.maricopa.edu/

    ~jtgress/argue2.htm>.

Harrington-Lueker, Donna. "Metal Detectors." American

    School Board Journal 179.5 (1992): 26-27.

Lee, Venture. "Detectors Alarm Some Students." Said &

    Done. Urban Journalism Workshop. Summer 2000. 16

    Aug. 2001 <http://ujw.philly.com/2000/

    detector.htm>.

Lindsey. "Re: School Security." Online posting. 23 Oct.

    1999. Juvenile Information Network. 16 Aug. 2001

    <http://www.juvenilenet.org/messages/27.html>.

Leigh 12

National School Safety and Security Services. "School
    Security Equipment and Technology." 23 Aug. 2001
    <http://www.schoolsecurity.org/resources/
    security-equipment.html>.

Poland, Scott. "The Fourth R--Relationships." <u>American
    School Board Journal</u> 187.3 (2000): 45-46.

Stecklow, Steve. "Metal Detectors Find a Growing
    Market, But Not Many Guns." <u>The Wall Street
    Journal</u> 7 Sept. 1993: A1+.

Stefkovich, Jacqueline, and G. M. O'Brien. "Students'
    Fourth Amendment Rights and School Safety."
    <u>Education and Urban Society</u> 29 (1997): 149-59.

Ummm. "Alright." Online posting. 27 May 2000. ezboard.
    16 Aug. 2001 <http://pub6.ezboard.com/
    fmastermanschool.showMessage?topicID=99.topic>.

United States. Dept. of Health and Human Services. Centers
    for Disease Control and Prevention. "Youth Risk
    Behavior Trends from CDC's 1991, 1993, 1995, 1997,
    and 1999 Youth Risk Behavior Surveys." <u>Adolescent and
    School Health</u> 6 Aug. 2001. 11 Aug. 2001
    <http://www.cdc.gov/nccdphp/dash/yrbs/trend.htm>.

Wilson, Joseph M., and Perry Zirkel. "When Guns Come to
    School." <u>American School Board Journal</u> 181.1
    (1994): 32-34.

Yarbrough, Jonathan W. "Are Metal Detectors the Answer
    to Handguns in Public Schools?" <u>Journal of Law and
    Education</u> 22 (1993): 584-87.

Understanding APA Style and Formatting

In many respects, the APA style and the MLA style are similar and the basic logic is the same. However, the APA style has a few distinguishing features:

- APA style emphasizes dates of books and articles and de-emphasizes the names of authors. Therefore the date of publication appears in parenthetical citations and is the second item mentioned in each entry in the "References" list (the name of the bibliography at the end of a paper).

- Only published or retrievable documents are included in the "References" list. Personal correspondence, e-mail messages, interviews, and lectures or speeches are referenced in text citations only.

- APA style uses fewer abbreviations and spells out the complete names of university presses. It uses an ampersand (&) instead of the word *and* for items in a series in the reference list and in text citations.

- APA style uses italics rather than underlines for titles and capitalizes only the first word of titles and subtitles of books and articles. It doesn't place titles of articles in quotation marks.

- APA style uses only an initial for authors' or editors' first names in "Reference" citations.

- APA style has a distinctive format for title pages and frequently includes an "abstract" of the paper immediately following the title page.

- Page numbers are placed at the top right-hand margin and are preceded by a "running head" (a short version of the title).

- APA uses block indentation for quotations when they are longer than forty words. Quotations shorter than forty words are worked into your own text using quotation marks as in the MLA system.

For an example of a student paper in APA style, see Susan Meyers' research paper on pp. 356–366.

APA Formatting for In-Text Citations

To cite sources in the APA system, you follow procedures very similar to those in the MLA system. When you make an in-text citation in APA style, you place inside the parentheses the author's last name and the year of the source as well as the page number if a particular passage or table is cited. The elements in the citation are separated by commas and a "p." or "pp." precedes the page number(s). If a source has more than one author, use an ampersand (&) to join their names. When the author is mentioned in an attributive tag, you include only the date (and page if applicable). The following examples show parenthetical documentation with and without attributive tags according to APA style.

> The Spanish tried to reduce the status of women who had been able to do business, get divorced, and sometimes become village chiefs (Karnow, 1989, p. 41).

> According to Karnow (1989), the Spanish tried to reduce the status of women who had been able to do business, get divorced, and sometimes become village chiefs (p. 41).

Just as with MLA style, readers of APA style look for sources in the list of references at the end of the paper if they wish to find full bibliographic information. In the APA system, this bibliographic list is titled "References" and includes only the sources cited in the body of the paper. If your sources include two works by the same author published in the same year, place an "a" after the date for the first work and a "b" after the date for the second, ordering the works alphabetically by title in the References list. If Karnow had published two different works in 1989, your in-text citation would look like this:

> (Karnow, 1989a, p. 41)
>
> or
>
> (Karnow, 1989b, p. 41)

APA style also makes provisions for quoting or using data from an indirect source. Use the same procedures as for MLA style (see the example on p. 635), but in your parenthetical citation use "as cited in" rather than the MLA's "qtd. in." Here is the APA equivalent of the example on page 635:

> A Buddhist monk, Thich Nhat Hanh, stresses the importance of inner peace: "If we can learn ways to touch the peace, joy, and happiness that are already there, we will become healthy and strong, and a resource for others" (as cited in Moriwaki, 1995, p. C4).

Documenting Sources in a "References" List (APA)

Like the MLA system, the APA system includes a complete bibliography, called "References," at the end of the paper. Entries are listed alphabetically, with a similar kind of hanging indentation to that used in MLA style. If you list more than one item for an author, repeat the author's name each time and arrange the items in chronological order beginning with the earliest. If two works appeared in the same year, arrange them alphabetically, adding an "a" and a "b" after the year for purposes of in-text citation. Here is a hypothetical illustration:

Smith, R. (1995). *Body image in Western cultures, 1750–Present.* London: Bonanza Press.

Smith, R. (1999a). *Body image in non-Western cultures.* London: Bonanza Press.

Smith, R. (1999b). Eating disorders reconsidered. *Journal of Appetite Studies, 45,* 295–300.

APA Quick Reference Guide for the Most Common Citations

Table 23.2 provides examples in APA style for the most common kinds of citations to be placed in a "References" list at the end of the paper. It also provides, in the third column, an index to other kinds of APA citations explained in the text.

TABLE 23.2 ■ Quick Reference Guide for APA Citations

Kind of Source	Basic Citation Model	Index for Variations
Print Sources When You Have Used the Original Print Version		
Book	Tannen, D. (1998). *The argument culture: Moving from debate to dialogue.* New York: Random House.	One author, 662 Two or more authors, 662 Second, later, or revised edition, 663 Republished book, 663 Multivolume work, 663 Articles in reference works, 663 Translation, 663 Corporate author, 663 Anonymous author, 663
Article in anthology with an editor	Shamoon, L. (1998). International e-mail debate. In D. Reiss, D. Self, & A. Young (Eds.), *Electronic communication across the curriculum* (pp. 151–161). Urbana, IL: National Council of Teachers of English.	Citing the editor, 664 Citing an individual article, 664
Article in scholarly journal	Pollay, R. W., Lee, J. S., & Carter-Whitney, D. (1992). Separate, but not equal: Racial segmentation in cigarette advertising. *Journal of Advertising, 21*(1),45–57.	Scholarly journal that numbers pages continuously, 664 Scholarly journal that restarts page numbering with each issue, 664
Article in magazine or newspaper	Beam, A. (2001, July–August). The mad poets society. *Atlantic Monthly, 288,* 96–103. Lemonick, M. D. (2000, October 30). Teens before their time. *Time, 156,* 66–74. Cauvin, H. E. (2001, July 18). Political climate complicates food shortage in Zimbabwe. *The New York Times,* p. A13.	Magazine article with named author, 664 Anonymous magazine article, 664 Review of book or film, 665 Newspaper article, 665 Newspaper editorial, 665 Letter to the editor, 665
Print Sources That You Have Downloaded from a Database or the Web		
Article downloaded from database	Barr, B. (2000, June 5). Liberal media adored gun-control marchers. *Insight on the News,* 44. Retrieved August 15, 2001, from ProQuest database.	Print article downloaded from licensed database, 665
Article downloaded from Web	Goodman, E. (2001, June 24). The big hole in health debate. *Boston Globe Online,* p. D7. Retrieved July 18, 2001, from http://www.boston.com/dailyglobe2/175/oped/The_big_hole_in_health_debate+.shtml	Article or book available online or from an information service, 665 Print article downloaded from the Web, 665

(continued)

TABLE 23.2 ▪ Quick Reference Guide for APA Citations (Continued)

Kind of Source	Basic Citation Model	Index for Variations
Web Sources That Haven't Appeared in Print		
Authored document within a Web site	Tobin, S. (2000). Getting the word out on the human genome project: A course for physicians. Retrieved July 18, 2001, from Stanford University, Center for Biomedical Ethics Web site: http://scbe.stanford.edu/research/current_programs. html#genomics	Authored document within a Web site, 665 Article from scholarly e-journal, 666
Document with corporate or unnamed author within a Web site	National Men's Resource Center. (2001, February 1). Ouch! Body piercing. Retrieved July 17, 2001, from http:// www.menstuff.org/issues/byissue/tattoo.html	Document without an identified author within a Web site, 665
Other		E-book, 666 Online reference database, 666 Bulletin board or newsgroup postings, 666
Miscellaneous Sources		
Interview, personal communication	Van der Peet (personal communication, June 24, 2001) stated that . . . [In-text citation only; not included in References]	E-mail, interviews, and personal correspondence, 666
Lecture, address, or speech	According to Jancoski (speech to University Congregational United Church of Christ, Seattle, October 30, 2001), salmon . . . [In-text citation only; not included in References; further details about speech can be included in text]	Lecture or conference presentation, 666
Other		Television program, 666 Film, 666 Sound recording, 666 Government publications, 667

APA Citations

Books

One author

Brumberg, J. J. (1997). *The body project: An intimate history of American girls*. New York: Vintage.

Two or more authors

Dombrowski, D. A., & Deltete, R. J. (2000). *A brief, liberal, Catholic defense of abortion*. Urbana: University of Illinois Press.

Belenky, M., Clinchy, B. M., Goldberger, N. R., & Tarule, J. M. (1986). *Women's ways of knowing: The development of self, voice, and mind.* New York: Basic Books.

APA style uses "et al." only for books with more than six authors.

Second, later, or revised edition

Montagu, A. (1986). *Touching: The human significance of the skin* (3rd ed.). New York: Perennial Press.

The number of the edition goes in parentheses. One could also say "Rev. ed." for "Revised edition."

Republished book (for example, a paperback published after the original hardback edition or a modern edition of an older work)

Hill, C. (1991). *The world turned upside down: Radical ideas during the English revolution.* London: Penguin. (Original work published 1972)

The in-text citation should read: (Hill, 1972/1991).

Wollstonecraft, M. (1995). *The vindication of the rights of woman, with strictures on political and moral subjects.* Rutland, VT: Tuttle. (Original work published 1792)

The in-text citation should read: (Wollstonecraft, 1792/1995).

Multivolume work

Churchill, W. S. (1956–1958). *A history of the English-speaking peoples* (Vols. 1–4). New York: Dodd, Mead.

Citation for all the volumes together. The in-text citation should read: (Churchill, 1956–1958).

Churchill, W. S. (1957). *A history of the English-speaking peoples: Vol. 4. The great democracies.* New York: Dodd, Mead.

Citation for a specific volume. The in-text citation should read: (Churchill, 1957).

Article in reference work

Ling, T. O. (1970). Buddhism in Burma. In S. G. F. Brandon (Ed.), *Dictionary of comparative religion.* New York: Scribner's.

Translation

De Beauvoir, S. (1961). *The second sex* (H. M. Parshley, Trans.). New York: Bantam Books. (Original work published 1949)

The in-text citation should read: (DeBeauvoir, 1949/1961).

Corporate author (a commission, committee, or other group)

American Red Cross. (1993). *Standard first aid.* St. Louis, MO: Mosby Lifeline.

Anonymous author

The New Yorker Cartoon Album: 1975–1985. (1987). New York: Penguin Books.

The in-text citation should be a shortened version of the title as follows: (*New Yorker Cartoon Album,* 1987).

Edited Anthologies

Citing the editor

O'Connell, D. F., & Alexander, C. N. (Eds.). (1994). *Self recovery: Treating addictions using transcendental meditation and Maharishi Ayur-Veda.* New York: Haworth Press.

Citing an individual article

Royer, A. (1994). The role of the transcendental meditation technique in promoting smoking cessation: A longitudinal study. In D. F. O'Connell & C. N. Alexander (Eds.), *Self recovery: Treating addictions using transcendental meditation and Maharishi Ayur-Veda* (pp. 221–239). New York: Haworth Press.

The pattern is as follows: Author of article. (Year of publication). Title of article. In Name of editor (Ed.), *Title of anthology* (pp. inclusive page numbers of article). Place of publication: Name of press.

Articles in Scholarly Journals Accessed in Print

Scholarly journal that numbers pages continuously

Barton, E. L. (1993). Evidentials, argumentation, and epistemological stance. *College English, 55,* 745–769.

The pattern is as follows: Author. (Year of publication). Article title. *Name of Journal, volume number,* inclusive page numbers. Note that the volume number is italicized along with the title of the journal.

Scholarly journal that restarts page numbering with each issue

Pollay, R. W., Lee, J. S. , & Carter-Whitney, D. (1992). Separate, but not equal: Racial segmentation in cigarette advertising. *Journal of Advertising, 21*(1), 45–57.

The citation includes the issue number in parentheses as well as the volume number. Note that the issue number and the parentheses are *not* italicized.

Articles in Magazines and Newspapers Accessed in Print

Magazine article with named author

Snyder, R. L. (2001, August–September). A daughter of Cambodia remembers: Loung Ung's journey. *Ms., 12,* 62–67.

Hall, S. S. (2001, March 11). Prescription for profit. *New York Times Magazine,* 40–45, 59, 91–92, 100.

The pattern is as follows: Author. (Year, Month [Day]). Title of article. *Name of Magazine, volume number [if stated in magazine],* inclusive pages. If page numbers are discontinuous, identify every page.

Anonymous magazine article

Daddy, Daddy. (2001, July 30). *New Republic, 225,* 12–13.

Review of book or film

Schwarz, B. (2001, November). A bit of bunting: A new history of the British empire elevates expediency to principle [Review of the book *Ornamentalism: How the British
Saw Their Empire*]. *Atlantic Monthly, 288,* 126–135.

Kaufman, S. (2001, July 30). Polishing a gem [Review of the motion picture *The blue
angel*]. *New Republic, 225,* 28–29.

Newspaper article

Henriques, D. B. (1998, September 27). Hero's fall teaches Wall Street a lesson. *Seattle
Times,* pp. A1, A24.

Newspaper editorial

Dr. Frankenstein on the hill [Editorial]. (2002, May 18). *The New York Times,* p. A22.

Letter to the editor of a magazine or newspaper

Tomsovic, K. (1998, July 13). Culture clash [Letter to the editor]. *New Yorker,* p. 7.

Print Articles or Books Downloaded from a Database or the Web

Print article downloaded from licensed database

Portner, J. (2000, March 14). Girl's slaying elicits calls for metal detectors. *Education
Week,* p. 3. Retrieved July 17, 2001, from EBSCO Academic Search Elite database.

Article or book available online or on microfiche from an information service
These services, such as ERIC (Educational Resources Information Center) or NTIS
(National Technical Information Service), provide material to your library on
microfiche or online with indexes on CD-ROM or online. Much of the material
from these services has not been published in major journals or magazines.
Frequently they are typescripts of conference papers or other scholarly work disseminated on microfiche.

Eddy, P. A. (1981). *The effects of foreign language study in high school on verbal ability as
measured by the Scholastic Aptitude Test—verbal.* Washington, DC: Center for Applied
Linguistics. (ERIC Document Reproduction Service No. ED 196 312)

Print article downloaded from the Web

Kane, J. (2001, May). Arrested development. *Outside Online.* Retrieved November 17,
2001, from http://www.outsidemag.com/magazine/200105/200105molokai1.html

Web Sources and Other Electronically Retrieved Sources

Authored document within a Web site

Lithwick, D. (2001, December 21). Creche test dummies: Nativity scenes on public
lands are illegal, rules the Supreme Court. Except when they're not. *Slate.* Retrieved
December 22, 2001, from http://slate.msn.com/?id=2060070

Document without an identified author within a Web site

The Interdisciplinary Center, Herzliya. (n.d.). Palestine Liberation Front (PLF). Retrieved
December 21, 2001, from http://www.ict.org.il/inter_ter/orgdet.cfm?orgid=29

Choose for the author slot the name of the organization that produced the document, if identified. If not, use the home page name of the Web site. The abbreviation "n.d." stands for "no date."

Article from a scholarly E-journal

Welch, J. R., & Riley, R. (2001). Reclaiming land and spirit in the western Apache homeland. *American Indian Quarterly, 25,* 5–14. Retrieved December 19, 2001, from http://muse.jhu.edu/journals/american_indian_quarterly/v025/25.1welch.pdf

E-book

Hoffman, F. W. (1981). *The literature of rock: 1954–1978.* Retrieved December 19, 2001, from http://www.netlibrary.com/ebook_info.asl?product_id=24355

The *Publication Manual of the American Psychological Association,* 5th ed., has no example of an E-book. We followed the manual's advice about how to proceed when an unusual case arises.

Online reference database

Uses and ethics of cloning. (1997). *Encyclopedia Britannica online.* (Year in Review 1997). Retrieved December 22, 2001, from http://www.eb.com:180/bol/topic?eu=124355&sctn=1

The *Publication Manual of the American Psychological Association,* 5th ed., has no example of an online reference database. We followed the manual's advice about how to proceed when an unusual case arises.

E-mail, interviews, and personal correspondence

APA guidelines limit the "References" list to published or retrievable information. Cite personal correspondence in the body of your text, but not in the References list: "Daffinrud (personal communication, December 12, 2001) claims that. . . ."

Bulletin board or newsgroup posting

Dermody, T. (2001, December 19). Re: Can we have it all or was it a lie? Message posted to soc.feminism group http://groups.google.com/groups?hl=en&selm=n7os1us9ue4k8th1vtvlbepgtbun2booqk%404ax.com

Miscellaneous Sources

Television program

Bochco, S., & Milch, D. (Directors). (2001, November 6). Lie like a rug [Television series episode]. In *NYPD blue.* New York: American Broadcasting Company.

Film

Madden, J. (Director). (1998). *Shakespeare in love* [Motion picture]. United States: Universal Miramax.

Sound recording

Dwarf Music. (1966). Rainy day woman [Recorded by B. Dylan]. On *Bob Dylan MTV unplugged* [CD]. New York: Columbia. (1995).

Follow this format: Writer of song or copyright holder. (Date of copyright). Title of song [Recorded by artist if different from writer]. On *Title of album* [Medium such as CD, record, or cassette]. Location: Label. (Date of album if different from date of song)

Unpublished paper presented at a meeting

Sharples, M. (2001, June 20). *Authors of the future.* Keynote address presented at Conference of European Teachers of Academic Writing, Groningen, the Netherlands.

Government publications

O'Toole, M. (2000). *The school shooter: A threat assessment perspective.* Washington, D C: U.S. Federal Bureau of Investigation. Retrieved August 16, 2001, from http://www.fbi.gov/publications/school/school2.pdf

Student Example of an APA paper

An example of a paper in APA style is shown on pages 356–366.

Summary

This section has shown you the nuts and bolts of citing and documenting sources in both the MLA and APA styles. It has explained the logic of parenthetical citation systems, showing you how to cite sources in your text using parenthetical references and how to create a bibliographic list at the end of your paper that exactly matches the information cited in the text. It has also provided "quick reference" tables, in both MLA and APA styles, for the most commonly cited sources.

CHAPTER 24

Advanced or Specialized Research Skills

Once you are familiar with searching your library's online catalog and licensed databases and the World Wide Web and have a general familiarity with academic research, you can benefit by learning a few advanced or specialized research skills. In this chapter, we introduce you to the following resources and strategies for research:

- Using specialized library resources such as specialized indexes, reference works, and local libraries and organizations
- Exploring ideas through listserv discussions, Usenet newsgroups, and real-time chat rooms or MOOs
- Conducting field research through observation, interviews, and questionnaires

USING SPECIALIZED LIBRARY RESOURCES

Using Specialized Indexes

Depending on the subject area of your research, you may find that specialized indexes can give you more useful information than general databases. Formerly, specialized indexes, which list articles in more narrow and specific areas than do general databases, appeared as hard-copy volumes housed in the reference area of libraries. Today many of these specialized indexes are online as well as in print, and the online versions are substantially easier to use. In the following list, we briefly describe some of the specialized indexes that writers might find useful. The information given after each index title indicates whether the index exists in both book (noted as "print") and online form.

ABI/Inform. (Online). Includes citations on business and management topics in U.S. and international publications.

America: History and Life. (Print and online). Includes abstracts and scholarly articles on the history of the United States and Canada.

ERIC Database. (CD-ROM and online). Consists of references to thousands of educational topics and includes journal articles, books, theses, curricula, conference papers, and standards and guidelines.

General Science Abstracts. (Print and online). Includes journals and magazines from the United States and Great Britain, covering such subjects as anthropology, astronomy, biology, computers, earth sciences, medicine, and health; includes articles, reviews, biographical sketches, and letters to the editor.

Historical Abstracts. (Print and online). Includes abstracts of scholarly articles on world history (excluding U.S. and Canadian) from 1775 to 1945.

Humanities Abstracts. (Print and online). Includes periodicals in archeology, art, the classics, film, folklore, journalism, linguistics, music, the performing arts, philosophy, religion, world history, and world literature.

Medline. (Online). Includes journals published internationally covering all areas of medicine.

MLA (Modern Language Association) International Bibliography. (Print and online). Indexes scholarly articles on literature, languages, linguistics, and folklore published worldwide.

New York Times Index. (Print and online). Covers international, national, business, and New York regional news as well as sciences, medicine, arts, sports, and lifestyle news; provides the full text of articles from the last ninety days.

Public Affairs Information Service (PAIS) International. (Print and online). Consists of articles, books, conference proceedings, government documents, book chapters, and statistical directories about public affairs.

Social Sciences Abstracts. (Print and online). Covers international English-language periodicals in sociology, anthropology, geography, economics, political science, and law; concentrates on articles published in scholarly journals aimed at professional scholars rather than the general public.

UMI Newspaper Abstracts. (Online). Covers national and regional newspapers, including *The Wall Street Journal.*

Awareness of these specialized indexes might increase the efficiency of your research as well as expand your skill and power as a researcher.

Using Library Reference Materials

Besides being a storehouse for books and periodicals, your library has a wealth of material in the reference section that may be useful to you in finding background information, statistics, and other kinds of data or evidence. Here are some sources that we have found particularly useful in our own research.

Encyclopedias: For getting quick background information on a research question, you will often find that a good encyclopedia is your best bet. In addition to the well-known general-purpose encyclopedias such as the *Encyclopedia Britannica,* there are excellent specialized encyclopedias devoted to in-depth coverage of specific fields. Among the ones you might find most useful are these:

- *The International Encyclopedia of the Social Sciences*
- *Dictionary of American History*

- *Encyclopedia of World Art*
- *McGraw-Hill Encyclopedia of Science and Technology*

Facts on File: These interesting volumes give you a year-by-year summary of important news stories. If you wish to assemble a chronological summary of a news event such as the disputed Bush/Gore vote count in Florida, the protests and riots at World Trade Association meetings, or Slobodan Milosevic's human rights trial at The Hague, *Facts on File* gives you a summary of the events along with information about exact dates so that you can find the full stories in newspapers. A special feature is a series of excellent maps in the back of each volume, allowing you to find all geographical place-names that occur in the year's news stories. The front cover of each volume explains how to use the series.

Statistical Abstracts of the United States: If you don't have spare time, don't even consider picking up one of these fascinating volumes, because you'll get hooked on the illuminating graphs, charts, and tables compiled by the Bureau of Statistics. For statistical data about birthrates and abortions, marriages and divorces, trends in health care, trends in employment and unemployment, nutritional habits, and a host of other topics, these yearly volumes are a primary source of quantitative information about life in the United States.

Congressional Abstracts: For people working on current or historical events related to politics or any controversy related to the public sector, this index can guide you to all debates about the topic in the Senate or the House of Representatives.

Book Review Digest: For research writers wanting to discover whether a certain book might be useful to them, this series is a treasure trove, providing not only a brief summary of the book but also excerpts from a variety of reviews of the book, allowing the writer to size up quickly the conversation surrounding the book's ideas.

Using Specialized Libraries and Local Organizations

Sometimes a search of your college library doesn't give you the information you need. In these cases, don't give up. If your college or university is in or near a large city, there may be small, specialized libraries that can help you. Often these focus on local history or on ethnic culture and heritage. The public libraries in many cities house directories of specialized libraries.

Businesses and organizations also have libraries and information services. Public relations departments can provide brochures and pamphlets. For example, if you were writing about diabetes, you could ask the American Diabetes Association for books and articles available to the public. Check the Yellow Pages in your telephone directory for businesses or organizations that might be good sources of information. Student writer Sheridan Botts, who wrote an exploratory paper (pp. 185–188) and a research paper (pp. 456–459) on the funding of hospices, obtained much of her information from materials provided by local hospices and insurance companies.

Be aware, however, that businesses and organizations that provide information to the public do so for a reason. Often the reason is benign. The American Diabetes Association, for example, wants to provide helpful information to persons afflicted with diabetes. But it is wise to keep in mind the bias of any organization whose information you use. Bias does not mean that the information is wrong, but bias does affect the slant of writing and the choice of aspects of a question that are discussed. A good researcher looks at many points of view with an open and questioning mind. If you are researching whether to cut old-growth timber, you will want to read publications of both the environmentalists and the timber industry, keeping in mind the goals and values of each group. If the "facts" of either group seem hazy, you will need to seek more reliable data from a disinterested source. In one respect, you have an advantage when working with data provided by organizations because their biases are readily visible.

EXPLORING IDEAS ON THE INTERNET

In addition to giving you access to the World Wide Web, the Internet lets you join listserv discussions, Usenet newsgroups, and real-time chat rooms and MOOS. These can provide useful information and give you a forum for exploring ideas.

Listserv Discussions

For many researchers, a productive way to explore ideas is to join a listserv interest group through your e-mail account. A listserv compiles any number of e-mail accounts into a mailing list and forwards copies of messages to all people on the list. There are thousands of well-established listservs about a wide variety of topics. You need to know the address of a list in order to join. Specific information about joining various listservs and an index of active lists can be found by entering either the uniform resource locator (URL) address http://tile.net/lists/ or http://www.liszt.com once you are on the World Wide Web and in a browser. After you have subscribed to a listserv, you will receive all messages sent to the list, and any message you send to the list address will be forwarded to the other members.

A message sent to a listserv interest group is sure to find a responsible audience because all members on the list have chosen to take part in an ongoing discussion on the list's specific topic. Often lists archive and periodically post important messages or frequently asked questions (FAQs) for you to study. Most lists are for those seriously interested in the list's topic, so to avoid offending any list members, learn the conventions for posting a message before you jump in.

Although you might find all kinds of interactions on a listserv, many users expect thoughtful, well-organized statements. If you are posting a message that introduces a new thread of discussion, you should clearly state your position (or question) and summarize those of others. Here is a sample posting to a listserv on the environment.

```
To: environL@brahms.usdg.org

From: alan@armadillo.edu (Alan Whigum)

Subject: Acid Rain and Action

I've been doing research on acid rain and am troubled by some
of the things I've found. For instance, I've learned that
washing coal gases with limestone before they are released
could reduce sulfur emissions. I know that the government has
the power to mandate such devices, but the real problem seems
to be lack of public pressure on the government. Why don't
people push for better legislation to help end acid rain? I
suppose it's an economic issue.
```

In turn, you can expect cogent, thoughtful responses from the list members. Here's a possible reply to the preceding message.

```
To: environL@brahms.usdg.org

From: bboston@armadillo.edu

Subject: Re Acid Rain and Action

I think you are right in pointing out that it is ultimately
public pressure that will need to be applied to reduce acid
rain. I've heard the argument that it is cost that prevents
steps from being taken; people will pay more for goods and
services if these measures are taken, so they resist. However,
judging from the people I've talked to about the subject, I
would say that a bigger problem may be knowledge. Most of them
said they would be willing to pay a little bit more for their
electricity if it meant a safer environment. People aren't
aware that action needs to be taken now, because the problem
seems remote.
```

When you join a listserv, you are granted instant access to a discourse community that is committed and knowledgeable about its topic. You can join one of the discussions already taking place on the list or post a request to get information and clarification about your own interests.

Listservs can take your ideas through a productive dialectic process as your message is seconded, refuted, complicated, and reclarified by the various list members. Listservs also afford valuable opportunities to practice your summarizing skills as you respond to messages or provide additional information in a second posting. For example, suppose you take issue with a long message that placed the blame for youth violence on the music industry. Rather than reproducing that entire message, you might provide a brief summary of the main points. The summary would not only give the readers enough background information to appreciate fully your response but would also help you determine the main points of the original message and pinpoint the issues on which you disagree.

Usenet Newsgroups

Among the most useful sections of the Internet for writers are the bulletin-board-like forums of Usenet newsgroups. Newsgroups are electronic forums that allow you to post or respond to messages about virtually any topic imaginable. Newsgroups can be powerful tools for exploring problems and considering alternative viewpoints. The news server at your school determines the organization and number of groups available to you. Some schools carry groups that provide articles from professional news services such as AP, Reuters, and UPI. Others provide topic-centered discussion groups. Your campus system may also offer class newsgroups for exchanging messages and drafts with others at your school.

The majority of newsgroups are used by members of the larger Internet community. Although some groups are devoted to subjects that don't lend themselves directly to the work you are probably undertaking in the composition class, many are frequented by regulars who are professionals in their fields or individuals deeply interested in the topic of the newsgroup. One key to successfully interacting on newsgroups, then, is finding a group that is appropriate to your work. Most of the newsreading programs that are built into Web browsers have a search function that can help you select appropriate groups. Another strategy is to spend some time searching through the archives of newsgroup postings at the DejaNews site (http://www.dejanews.com). Using keywords, you can comb through postings either to tap into preexisting conversations or to pinpoint newsgroups that seem to take up the issues that you are interested in.

Once you find an appropriate group, you will need to work through the logistics of accessing the newsgroup, reading messages, and, perhaps, posting messages of your own. Check with your instructor or computer center to find out how to access and interact with the groups available to you.

Although you may be tempted to begin participating in a group immediately, you should familiarize yourself with some of the style conventions and the audience for that particular newsgroup before jumping in. Take time to read and listen in ("lurk") to the group's postings. Debate on Usenet can become fairly heated, and a message that ignores previous postings can elicit angry responses ("flames"). In addition, a message that doesn't consider the newsgroup's audience or its favored style will likely be challenged. For example, if you want to post something in the "alt.fan.rush-limbaugh" group, you should be cautious about composing a message that openly contradicts Rush Limbaugh's brand of politics. If you send a message to the newsgroup "soc.history," you might be able to tread less carefully—this list is more politically diverse—but members of this group might take offense if asked an obvious factual question.

Regardless of their makeup, most groups resent being asked questions that have already been answered. Some groups provide an archive of frequently asked questions. If your interest is in something practical that is likely to be covered in the FAQ files, refer to them before posting a query. You should use the expertise of the group to find information that you might not be able to uncover otherwise.

When you are ready to post a message, use some of the strategies given for composing a message to a listserv: try to summarize and synthesize your own position as well as those of others; highlight what you see as the most problematic or murky aspects of the topic. Carefully constructed messages are more likely to receive useful responses.

When you do receive feedback, evaluate it with special care. The unfiltered nature of all Internet media makes critical reading an essential skill. Because anyone with an Internet connection can take part in a discussion or post a message or article, you need to evaluate this information differently than how you would articles from national newsmagazines, which are professionally written, edited for clarity, and checked for accuracy.

Although most postings are thoughtful, you will also find carelessly written messages that misconstrue an argument, personal rants that offer few, if any, stated reasons for their claims, and propaganda and offensive speech of many kinds in certain newsgroups. It is your responsibility, and unique opportunity, to read newsgroup messages critically, looking for their various biases and making decisions about their relative authority.

Of course, printed sources are marked by their own biases. Deadlines and space constraints may limit the depth and accuracy of printed coverage, and firsthand insights may be screened by authors and editors. If you were studying attitudes toward the Middle East peace process, a newsgroup exchange between a conservative Jew in Israel and a Palestinian student in the United States might provide better insight than a news article. As you read through newsgroup messages, take time to evaluate the users' personal investments in the issues. Compare their comments to those in traditional sources, check for accuracy, and look for differing perspectives. Work these perspectives into your own thinking and writing about the topic. Treat information and points of view gathered from the Internet as primary rather than as secondary material; many of the people who contribute such material care passionately about an issue. It is up to you to place this material in context and edit it for your own audience.

Real-Time Discussions (Chat) or MOOs

Real-time discussions, or "chats," are synchronous exchanges that take place on a network. Chat rooms are like cyberspace cocktail parties in which people come and go, interacting with each other through lively discussion. A MOO (multiuser domain, object-oriented) is like a chat room except that the site attempts to create a physical environment.

Like other Internet forums, chat groups and MOOs are organized around common interests, but real-time sessions are more spontaneous and informal than the communication through newsgroups or listservs. In a chat room or MOO you communicate with people who are logged on at the same time. For example, one of our students researching the question, "Should teen mothers put their babies up for adoption?" logged on to a chat room and carried on an illuminating discussion with a teen mother who had decided to keep her baby and who agreed to talk about the challenges of her pregnancy. In these online conversations, typographical and spelling errors are mostly overlooked, and abbreviations are an acceptable part of real-time style. The pace can be extremely fast, so users generally focus on getting their thoughts out rather than on producing highly polished messages. In MOOs, participants often invent a character and play different roles, even assuming a cross-gender identity.

It is beyond the scope of this book to explain how to access and use chat rooms and MOOs, but if you try them out, you'll discover how they promote brainstorming and freewriting. Be aware, however, that discussions tend to heat up rapidly. Many real-time forums on the Internet allow users to take on pseudonyms, and some people use the opportunity to become irresponsible in what they say and write.

Real-time interactions give rise to several ethical issues. In these uncensored forums, you will at times encounter discussions and materials that aren't appropriate to your assignments and class work. You may be challenged to assert your own feelings about censorship, pornography, hate speech, and free speech. And you will need to consider the impact of your persona and words on others as you take on a character or act out an idea.

CONDUCTING FIELD RESEARCH

Your academic assignments, professional training, and career itself may require you to gather data directly through field research—for example, through observations, interviews, and questionnaires. Academic majors that depend on field research—particularly physical sciences, social sciences, health sciences, engineering, education, and many branches of business—will give you specific training in how to conduct such research. Often, however, students have an opportunity to use some field research in their first-year writing courses. Many of the assignments in this text, for example, can use evidence gathered from field research. In this section, we offer a brief introduction to the strategies of observation, interviewing, and questionnaire construction.

Using Observation to Gather Information

Many academic assignments or workplace writing projects depend on data gathered from observation. Laboratory experiments, for example, require precise observation and measurement of an observed phenomenon. Psychology courses might ask you to observe children's interactions with their peers or with certain kinds of toys. Fields such as anthropology, sociology, and rhetoric/composition often use ethnographic research to observe the behavior of individuals or groups over time in their natural environments.

In writing courses, students can often use observational data to support one or more of their points. Here, for example, is how one student used observational data to support an argument that a certain street crossing was dangerous:

> The intersection at Vine and Stephenson is particularly dangerous. Traffic volume on Vine is so heavy that pedestrians almost never find a comfortable break in the flow of cars. On November 12, I watched fifty-seven pedestrians cross this intersection. Not once did cars in both directions stop before the pedestrian stepped off the sidewalk onto the street. Typically, the pedestrian had to move into the street, start tentatively to cross, and wait until a car finally stopped. On fifteen occasions, pedestrians had to stop halfway across the street, with cars speeding by in both directions, waiting for cars in the far lanes to stop before they could complete their crossing.

The key to successful observation is having a clear sense of your purpose, planning and organizing well ahead of time, and being systematic and thorough. We offer the following practical suggestions for carrying out productive observations:

1. ***Determine the purpose and scope of your observation.*** Think ahead about what you will be observing and what kinds of details, behaviors, or processes you will want to take note of. Can you observe your phenomenon only once or will you need to observe regularly over a period of days? If you plan to conduct a series of observations, the first one could provide an overview or baseline, while subsequent observations could enable you to explore parts of your subject in more detail or note changes over time.

2. ***Make timely arrangements.*** In some cases, you may need to ask permission or get special clearance for your observation. Be sure to make the necessary arrangements long before you start the observation. In making requests, state clearly who you are and what the purpose of your visit is. Be cordial in your requests and in your thanks after your observations.

3. ***Come prepared with the appropriate tools and take clear, usable notes.*** You will need note-taking materials—either a laptop computer or plenty of paper, a clipboard or binder with a hard surface for writing, and good writing utensils. Make sure that your notes are easy to read and well labeled with helpful headings. Document your notes with exact indications of location, time, and names and titles of people (if relevant).

4. ***Go through your notes soon after your observation.*** Don't count on your memory to reconstruct details or recapture thoughts you had while observing. You might actually produce a draft of this segment of your paper while the results of your observation are still fresh in your mind.

Conducting Interviews

An interview is often an effective way to gather specialized information. Although asking a busy professional for an interview can be intimidating, many experts are generous with their time when they encounter a student who is interested in their work. Depending on the circumstances, your interview can be formal or informal; you may even conduct an interview over the telephone, without a face-to-face meeting. To make interviews as useful as possible, we suggest several strategies.

Tiffany Linder's paper on pp. 408–410 shows several examples of the use of interview data.

Preparing for Interviews

Preparing for an interview is crucial because you want to make a good first impression and not waste anyone's time. The following are some key preparatory steps:

1. *Consider your purpose.* Determine in advance what you hope to learn from the interview. Think about your research question and the aim of the paper you are planning to write.

2. *Do background reading.* Prepare for the interview by researching important subjects related to your research question and to the person you will be interviewing. Ideally, interviews should give you knowledge or perspectives unavailable in books or articles. Although you needn't be an expert at the time of the interview, you should be conversant about your subject.

3. *Formulate well-thought-out questions.* Be as thorough with your questions as possible. Most likely you will have only one chance to interview this person. Develop a range of questions, including short-answer questions like the following: How long have you been working in this field? What are the typical qualifications for this job? Give special thought to creating open-ended questions, which should be the heart of your interview. Here are some typical examples of open-ended questions: What changes have you seen in this field? What solutions have you found to be most successful in dealing with . . . ? What do you see as the causes of . . . ? Questions framed in this way will elicit the information you need but still allow the interviewee to answer freely. Avoid yes-or-no questions that can stall conversation with a one-word answer. Also, avoid leading questions. For example, instead of asking a social worker, "What do you think about infringing on the rights of the homeless by making them take antipsychotic medication?" ask instead, "What are your views on requiring the mentally ill homeless to take antipsychotic medications as a condition for welfare assistance?" The more you lead the interviewee to the answers you want, the less valid your research becomes.

4. *Gather your supplies.* Before the interview, decide how you plan to record the information. Many people like to use a portable tape recorder, but be sure to ask your interviewee's permission if you plan to do so. Taping allows you to focus your attention on the interaction, following the speaker's train of

thought and planning in your head what else you need to ask. Most likely, you will want to take notes even if you are taping.

Managing the Interview

Here are some practical suggestions for conducting successful interviews.

1. *Be prompt.* Arrive for the interview on time to show respect for your interviewee's time.
2. *Be courteous and alert.* Your attitude during the interview can help set up a cordial and comfortable relationship between you and the person you are interviewing.
3. *Take brief but clear notes.* Try to record all the main ideas and to be accurate with quoted material. Don't hesitate to ask if you are unsure about a fact or statement or if you need to double-check what the person intended to say.
4. *Have your questions clearly in mind but be flexible.* Ask your questions in a logical order, but also be sensitive to the flow of the conversation. If the interviewee rambles away from the question, don't jump in too fast. You may learn something valuable from the seeming digression. You may even want to ask unanticipated questions if you have delved into new ideas.

Processing and Using Material from Interviews

You will probably leave the interview feeling immersed in what you heard. No matter how vivid the words are in your mind, take time *very* soon after the interview to go over your notes or to transcribe your tape. What may seem unforgettable at the moment is all too easy to forget later. If you do your reviewing soon after, you can usually fill in gaps in your notes or explain unclear passages on the tape. Do not trust your memory alone.

For Writing and Discussion

You can practice interview techniques by interviewing fellow students. Imagine that your class is conducting field research to answer the following question: What are the chief problems that students encounter in producing college-level research papers? Working in small groups, develop a short sequence of interview questions that will elicit the information you seek. Outside class, each class member should interview a fellow student, preferably one not in your current writing class. In the next class, you should all report the results of your interviews to the class, discussing any difficulties in conducting the interviews and sharing insights into how to improve interviewing techniques.

Using Questionnaires

In some writing situations, you can use data collected from questionnaires. Consider, for example, how student writer Rebekah Taylor used questionnaire data to support her practical proposal asking the manager of her university's campus store to stock personal and household products that had not been tested on animals.

> In a short survey I conducted winter quarter, many students said they would support a proposal to introduce cruelty-free products to the stores on campus. This survey of fifty randomly selected students revealed that over half (56%) are more than "somewhat concerned" about animal testing. The survey also showed that almost three-quarters (72%) would buy cruelty-free products instead of products tested on animals if they were offered on campus. Additionally, compassionate students who have gone off-campus to buy cruelty-free products would start spending their money at the campus bookstore.

Rebekah Taylor's practical proposal is found in Chapter 17, pp. 451–456.

These data, which she obtained from constructing a short questionnaire, provided timely evidence of student support for her proposal.

Constructing a Useful Questionnaire

In constructing a questionnaire, you want to elicit responses that are concrete, useful, and directly related to your overall purpose. The construction of a questionnaire—both its wording and its arrangement on the page—is crucial to its success. Although questionnaires often raise concerns of bias and statistical validity, careful planning and accurate reporting can alleviate most of the concerns. You will probably want to include both closed-response questions that require checking a box or number on a scale and open-response questions that allow narrative answers. The former yield quantitative data that can be reported statistically; the latter can provide fresh insights and can make your respondents feel that you value their input.

As you construct your questionnaire, think about the psychology of your targeted audience. Keep your questionnaire clear and easy to complete, and avoid ambiguous questions. Proofread it carefully, and road-test it on a few volunteer respondents before you make your final version. When you have settled on the exact questions you will ask, write an introduction that explains the questionnaire's purpose. If possible, encourage response by explaining why the knowledge gained from the questionnaire will be beneficial to others. As your final step, prepare a neatly typed, easy-to-read version of your questionnaire. Figure 24.1 shows a cover letter and questionnaire prepared by a student investigating the parking problems of commuter students on her campus.

When you distribute a questionnaire, take special care to get a random sample. Typically, people who feel strongly about an issue are more likely to complete a questionnaire than those who don't feel strongly. The student who prepared the parking questionnaire, for example, is likely to get the highest rate of response from those most angry about parking issues, and thus her sample might not be representative of all commuter students. Rather than collecting completed questionnaires in a box outside the student union (see the introductory paragraph in Figure 24.1), she might have considered distributing questionnaires at places where commuter students gather (the library, student union cafeteria) and then returned shortly to collect them in an effort to get a fuller response.

Dear Commuter Student:

I am conducting a study aimed at improving the parking situation for commuter students. Please take a few moments to complete the following questionnaire, which will provide valuable information that may lead to specific proposals for easing the parking problems of commuters. If we commuter students work together with the university administration, we may be able to find equitable solutions to the serious parking issues we face. Please return the questionnaires to the box I have placed at the south entrance to the Student Union Building.

1. When do you typically arrive on campus?

   Before 8 A.M. _____   Between 1 P.M. and 5 P.M. _____
   Between 8 A.M. and 9 A.M. _____   Between 5 P.M. and 7 P.M. _____
   Between 9 A.M. and noon _____   After 7 P.M. _____
   During noon hour _____

2. How frequently do you have problems finding a place to park?

   Nearly every day ____
   About half the time ____
   Occasionally ____
   Almost never ____

3. When the first lot you try is full, how long does it typically take you to find a place to park (for those who buy a commuter parking permit)?

   Less than 10 minutes ___
   10–15 minutes ___
   More than 15 minutes ___

4. For those who use street parking only, how long does it take you to find a place to park?

   Less than 10 minutes ___
   10–15 minutes ___
   More than 15 minutes ___

5. Do you currently carpool?

   Yes ____
   No ____

6. The university is considering a proposal to raise parking fees for single-driver cars and lower them for car pools. If you don't currently carpool, how difficult would it be to find a car-pool partner?

   Impossible ___
   Very difficult ___
   Somewhat difficult ___
   Fairly easy ___

7. If finding a car-pool partner would be difficult, why?

   Few fellow students live in my neighborhood ___
   Few fellow students match my commuting hours ___
   Other ___

8. What suggestions do you have for improving the parking situation for commuter students?

FIGURE 24.1 ▪ Questionnaire on Parking

Incorporating Data from Questionnaires into Your Writing

After your questionnaire has supplied you with representative responses, you should tally them and formulate clear summary statements of the information you have gathered. You may report them in a brief, narrative format, as Rebekah Taylor did in the example cited earlier, or you may choose to display the results in tables or graphs as student writer Edgar Lobaton did in his causal analysis of stereotypes of Latinos.

See Edgar Lobaton's causal analysis on pp. 353–355. Chapter 11 provides instruction on creating graphs and tables.

CHAPTER SUMMARY

This chapter has explained some of the advanced or specialized resources of your library or community. It has described specialized indexes, library reference materials, and local libraries or businesses with specialized collections. It has given you a brief overview of using listservs, Usenet newsgroups, and real-time chat rooms or MOOs to explore ideas. Finally, it has introduced you to field research involving observations, interviews, and questionnaires.

PART FIVE

A Guide to Special Writing and Speaking Occasions

During the Great Depression of the 1930s, misuse of land, overgrazing, and years of drought turned the southwestern plains of the United States into the "Dust Bowl," forcing hundreds of thousands of people off their farms. To help these displaced farmers as well as unemployed artists, President Franklin Roosevelt's New Deal promoted projects for economic recovery. Commissioned in 1937 by Roosevelt's Resettlement Administration, the classic poster *Years of Dust* by social realist artist Ben Shahn (1899–1969) graphically embodies a problem-solution message. The poster conveys Shahn's sympathy for impoverished Americans and the government's efforts to address the social and economic problems.

To discuss and analyze this classic poster, see the questions in the section entitled "Using the Part Opener Images" that follows the Preface.

CHAPTER 25

Oral Communication
Working in Groups and Giving Speeches

The consensual process of truth seeking is based on the simple assumption that all
of us thinking together are smarter than any one of us thinking alone.

        —PARKER PALMER, *EDUCATOR*

I n this chapter we focus on thinking, writing, and speaking as social activities that involve specific kinds of interaction. The first half of this chapter encourages you to discover how working in groups can deepen your thinking and enrich your writing. The second half shows you how preparing and giving formal—and sometimes impromptu—speeches can build on and extend what you have learned about effective writing for audiences.

ABOUT WORKING IN GROUPS

Although images of the solitary writer are part of the cultural mystique of writing, most writers, as we have stressed throughout this book, seek out communities of peers with whom they test and share ideas and exchange drafts.

 Writing communities are especially important in academic, business, and professional settings. The vast majority of scientific and technical articles are written by a team, often with three or more authors. And increasingly, professional proposals, research reports, legal briefs, ad campaigns, brochures to stockholders, and other documents in the academic and business worlds are team-produced efforts.

 The reasons for this trend are readily apparent. First, much contemporary work is so complex and technical that no single person has enough expertise to compose a nonroutine document. Second, many large businesses now use self-directed teams without middle managers, and these teams are responsible for multiple tasks, many of which require the production of documents. And perhaps most important, much professional writing is now produced on networked computers, making joint authorship of documents procedurally convenient. Clearly, the ability to write effectively as part of a team is an increasingly critical skill for career advancement. Many businesses now regard group skills as one of the three or four most important determinants of employee success.

Besides these economic and career reasons, the ability to participate in writing communities is important for other reasons. Humans construct knowledge through interaction with others. Throughout this text, we have said that to write an essay is to join a conversation about a question; the back-and-forth dialogue involved in group work is a real-time version of the conversations embodied in printed texts. Through discourse with others, you gather multiple perspectives on phenomena, which you synthesize through the filter of your own perspective. In other words, you construct your knowledge by exposing yourself to alternative views. Moreover, purposeful, thoughtful group interaction is a source not only of knowledge of the world around you, but also of self-knowledge because groups enable you to see the products of your mind the way that others see them. The kind of thinking that you practice in groups, therefore, is the kind you must exhibit in writing.

BASIC PRINCIPLES OF SUCCESSFUL GROUP INTERACTION

If the thought of group work makes you uncomfortable, you are not alone. Experiences of unpleasant or unproductive groups and unwieldy, time-consuming committees have generated such jokes as "A zebra is a horse designed by a committee" and "Committees keep minutes and waste hours." However, we suggest a different vision of groups. We prefer to think of groups as problem-solving teams like engineering design teams or the marketing teams that plan new sales strategies. You might also recall that one of the world's most influential documents—the Declaration of Independence—was written as a small-group project.

To help you form efficient and productive teams, we recommend that you and your group members practice the following principles.

Avoid Clone-Think and Ego-Think

Many group tasks ask you to propose and justify a solution to a problem. A group consensus is not the same as a majority view. Although a consensus is a form of agreement, a good one grows out of respectful and productive *disagreement.* The best small groups build solutions thoughtfully, beginning with different points of view and encouraging dissent along the way. Weak groups either reach closure too early or bicker endlessly, never building on disagreement to reach consensus.

To steer a middle ground between early closure and endless bickering, you need to avoid two common problems of group interaction: clone-think and ego-think. When groups lapse into *clone-think,* discussions degenerate into "feel-good sessions" guaranteed to produce safe, superficial solutions. Everyone agrees with the first opinion expressed to avoid conflict and difficult work. At the other extreme is the *ego-think* group, in which group members go their own way, producing a collection of minority views. Whereas clone-thinkers view their task as conformity to a norm, ego-thinkers see their goal as safeguarding the autonomy of individual group members. At both extremes, group members fail to take one another's ideas seriously.

When we talk about taking other people's ideas seriously or about reaching consensus, we don't mean that group discussions should transform people's fundamental values and attitudes. But we do mean that they should bring about realistic changes: softening a position, complicating an understanding, or simply acknowledging an alternative possibility. These sorts of changes in understanding happen only when people learn how to present and consider alternative views in a constructive, nonthreatening manner. One approach to avoiding both clone-thinking and ego-thinking is to practice our next principle, empathic listening.

Listen Empathically

Sometimes called "Rogerian listening," after the psychologist Carl Rogers, who popularized the technique, empathic listening is a powerful strategy for helping people resolve conflicts. To be *empathic* is to try to stand in the other person's shoes—to understand the values, beliefs, and fears underlying that person's position. Empathic listeners are *active,* not passive; they interpret not only the speaker's words, but also the speaker's tone of voice, body language, and even silences. Empathic listeners invite speech from others by maintaining eye contact, avoiding disapproving frowns or gestures, asking clarifying questions, and nodding or taking notes.

The rules of empathic listening are simple. Before you respond to someone else's position on an issue, summarize that person's viewpoint fairly in your own words. Carl Rogers discovered that when negotiating parties in a dispute (or couples in marital therapy) were required to summarize each other's views, the experience often defused their anger and encouraged them toward compromise or synthesis. In small groups, empathic listening can deepen conversation. If there is a dispute, the acting group leader might ask one disputant to summarize the other's position. For example: "Irwin, what do you understand Beth's position to be here and how do you see your position differing from hers?" Once Irwin and Beth understand their differences, they will be better able to reconcile them.

When a group becomes skilled at listening, here's what happens.

1. *There are fewer interruptions.* Group members have more "space" in which to complete their thoughts. They take turns speaking. To get the floor, one person doesn't have to interrupt another.

2. *Participation is more equitable.* Group discussions are less apt to be dominated by one or two group members. The group draws out shy or quiet group members and values their contributions.

3. *Discussions are more connected.* Speakers are apt to begin their contributions by referring to what previous speakers have said. "I really liked Pam's point about . . ." or "I see what Paul was saying when . . . , but . . ."

For Writing and Discussion

Freewrite your response to the following questions:

1. In the group work we have done so far in this class, how well do I think the group members have listened to and understood my views?

2. How good a listener have I been?

(continued)

3. What might our group do differently to promote better listening?

Then share your freewrites in groups and take turns summarizing each other's views. Reach consensus on several ways in which the group might improve its listening skills.

Play Assigned Roles

Writing groups accomplish tasks more efficiently when members take turns playing two distinct roles.

1. *Leader/Coordinator.* This person's job is to ensure that the assigned task is clearly understood by all, to set clear goals for the session, to monitor the time, to keep the group on task, and to make sure that the group has its assigned product completed in the time allocated by the instructor. To prevent early closure or endless bickering, the leader/coordinator must draw out divergent views, promote good listening, and help the group achieve a consensus, without ever being dictatorial.

2. *Recorder/Reporter.* The recorder keeps notes on the group's decision-making process, constantly asking group members for clarification, and reads back what he or she understands group members to have said and decided. The recorder also synthesizes the group's deliberations and reports the results to the class.

In writing classrooms, we have found that groups work best when each student takes a rotation in each of these roles. Some instructors prefer to combine the two roles so that a group recorder serves as both leader and note taker.

Be Sensitive to Body Language

Groups can often learn to function more effectively by reading body language. Groups that draw their chairs close together are more effective than groups that maintain distance from each other or marginalize some members through irregular placement of chairs. Group members should note potential problems signaled by body language. A person who sits with arms folded across the chest staring out a window is signaling alienation. Other signs of dysfunction include side conversations, division of the group into subgroups, and domination of the discussion by one or two people who ignore others.

Invest Time in Group Maintenance

Group members periodically need to reflect on and think critically about their performance, a process called *group maintenance*. Group maintenance may be as simple as taking several minutes at the completion of a task to discuss the things the group did well or not so well and to identify steps for improvement.

Occasionally a more extensive and formal sort of group-maintenance task is required. One such task calls for each member to do a self-assessment by freewriting responses to questions such as the following:

Our group performs best when _____.

Our group's effectiveness could be improved if _____.

My greatest strength as a group member is _____.

Another thing I could contribute is _____.

The members then share these self-assessments with the whole group.

Recognize How Personality and Culture Affect Group Participation

Group interaction can often be improved if group members understand the influence of personality and culture on a person's behavior in a group. Psychologists have discovered that people with different personality types have different reactions to working in groups. According to interpreters of the Myers-Briggs Type Indicator,* one of the most highly regarded personality assessment tests, people who test as *extroverts* like to think through an issue by talking out their ideas with others; they tend to be vocal and highly engaged during group discussions. People who test as *introverts* prefer thinking privately about an issue before talking about it and are often uncomfortable discussing their ideas in groups, although they listen carefully and take in what everyone is saying. Often, quiet group members are listening more carefully and thinking more deeply than more-vocal people realize. Until the group gently encourages them to contribute, however, they may be silent.

Judgers like to reach decisions rapidly, and they often grow impatient if the group wants to extend discussion of an issue. In contrast, *perceivers* resist early closure and want to talk through all possible points of view on an issue before reaching a decision. If you understand such personality differences, then you might better tolerate classmates' behaviors that are different from your own.

Other important differences are related to culture. Most U.S.-born students are used to talking in class, holding class debates, and even disagreeing with the teacher. In many cultures, however, it is disrespectful to argue with the teacher or to speak in class unless called on. Students are socialized to listen and not to talk. They can find group work in a North American college extremely painful.

Speech habits also vary widely. Typically, North Americans state their desires bluntly and assertively in ways that would seem rude to people from Asian cultures, who are taught to mask their statements of desire in roundabout conversation.

---

*The Myers-Briggs Type Indicator locates persons along four different continuums: introversion/extroversion, thinking/feeling, sensing/intuition, perceiving/judging. Composition researchers have used the Myers-Briggs inventory to reveal fascinating differences among writers that throw valuable light on students' behavior in groups. See G. H. Jensen and J. K. DiTiberio, *Personality and the Teaching of Composition* (Norwood, NJ: Ablex, 1989).

Some cultures have a strong oral tradition of storytelling or speech making, whereas others have a tradition of silence. If your institution has a diverse student body that includes members of ethnic minority groups and international students, then group work can be a fascinating laboratory for the study of cultural differences.

Manage Conflict by Dealing with an "Impossible Group Member"

Occasionally groups face a critical test of their ability to manage conflict: the Impossible Group Member, or IGM. IGMs may dominate group discussions; they may be rude or intimidating, trying to turn every discussion into a conflict; they may sit sullenly, draining off group enthusiasm; or they may be generally unprepared or fail to do the work assigned to them outside class.

Although it's not easy to deal with an IGM (sometimes the instructor has to intervene), most impossible group members may simply need encouragement and direction. The root of most IGMs' problems is their difficulty in recognizing the effects they're having on other people. Direct criticism of their behaviors will likely surprise them—they won't see it coming—and cause them to react defensively. IGMs need to see the consequences of their actions and they need to see positive behaviors modeled for them. If IGMs dominate discussions, they need to learn to listen. If they are sullenly silent, they need to have their input actively solicited and their responses taken seriously. They have to take their turns in leadership positions and learn to appreciate the difficulties of consensus building and decision making. And they must be made aware that their actions are bothering the other group members.

The best way to deal with IGMs is to discuss the problem candidly, perhaps during a group-maintenance session (see pp. 688–689). If group members reflect on and evaluate *how* the group did its task, focusing on group shortcomings ("What could we do better next time?") rather than on individuals' failures ("Martine, you drive me crazy!"), then it becomes easier for errant group members to accept responsibility for their actions. In explaining a problem to an IGM, try using what communication experts call *I statements* rather than *you statements*. Keep the focus on your own feelings and avoid launching accusations. Note the different tones in the following examples:

You Statement	Martine, you're always insulting us by looking out the window.
I Statement	Martine, when you look out the window, it makes me feel like I'm a boring person.
You Statement	Pete and Valencia are always dominating the discussion.
I Statement	On some days I want to say something in the group but there is never a break in the conversation where I can join.

Using *I* statements helps defuse defensiveness by calling attention to the consequences of behaviors without attaching blame or censure.

We are now ready to turn to productive group strategies for addressing three kinds of tasks: consensus-seeking, brainstorming, and orally rehearsing drafts.

THINKING IN GROUPS

Group work is one of the most effective ways to practice critical thinking. This section examines three ways that groups can think together.

Seeking Consensus

Most of the problems posed in the For Writing and Discussion exercises in this text have alternative solutions—there is no single "right" answer. Seeking a consensus answer—especially when group members have different views—can lead to highly productive critical thought. When different group members propose different answers to the same problem, how does a group reach a consensus?*

First, don't assume that every group member has to be completely satisfied with the group's final solution. Instead, everyone should agree that the proposed solution is feasible and rationally supportable. Your solution must be achieved through *consensus* rather than through majority vote, coin flip, or taking turns. This approach means that each group member has veto power over the final solution. But this option should be used sparingly, and only if a person truly cannot live with the proposed solution. After an initial discussion to be sure that everyone understands the task, you can use the following guidelines to embark on a problem-solving procedure that encourages consensus:

1. *Ask every group member to propose at least one tentative solution for discussion.* Members should present justifying arguments as well so that group members can appreciate the reasoning behind each approach.

2. *Once you have presented a possible solution, avoid arguing for it a second time.* Your goal now is to be flexible and listen to other viewpoints rather than to press for adoption of your own position. Remember, however, not to give up your viewpoint quickly just to avoid conflict. Yield only if you see legitimate strengths in other approaches.

3. *If none of the proposed solutions wins everyone's approval, begin brainstorming for alternatives that synthesize good features from various proposals.* Sometimes you can formulate a lowest-common-denominator solution—one that everyone grudgingly accepts but that no one really likes—and brainstorm ways to improve it.

4. *Don't think in terms of winners and losers* ("If Lenore's solution wins, then Pete's must lose"). Rather, try to negotiate win/win solutions in which all parties give up something but also retain something.

5. *Accept disagreement and conflict as a strength rather than a weakness.* Chances are that the disagreements in your group mirror disagreements in the larger community to which your solution must appeal. From these disagreements you can forge a synthesis that is much stronger than any individual's private solution. As Parker Palmer says in the epigraph to this chapter, "The consensual process of truth seeking is based on the simple assumption that all of us thinking together are smarter than any one of us thinking alone."

*The discussion of consensus making is adapted from Parker Palmer, *To Know as We Are Known: Education as a Spiritual Journey* (San Francisco: Harper & Row, 1983), pp. 94–96.

Brainstorming

Group brainstorming uses intuitive, unstructured thinking. During a brainstorming session, everyone is encouraged to suggest ideas, however outlandish they may seem on the surface, and to build on, without criticizing or questioning, all other suggestions generated by group members. Groups often begin brainstorming by asking individual members to take turns offering ideas. Frequently, a high-energy, almost frantic atmosphere develops. In its zanier moments, brainstorming crosses over into free association.

For a writer exploring topic ideas, brainstorming sessions can provide a variety of options to consider as well as clues about an audience's potential reaction to a topic and ideas about how the writer might change those views. Brainstorming can also generate arguments in support of a thesis. When the class is assigned a persuasive paper, playing the believing and doubting game with each group member's proposed thesis can help writers anticipate alternative possibilities and counterevidence as well as think of new support for a position.

The believing and doubting game is explained on pp. 37–39.

Oral Rehearsal of Drafts

Rehearsing a draft orally is an excellent way to generate and clarify ideas. A good procedure for doing so is to interview one another in pairs or in groups of three early in the writing process. One-on-one or one-on-two interviews that enable writers to talk through their ideas can help clarify the writers' sense of direction and stimulate new ideas. When you are the interviewer, use the following set of generic questions, modifying them to fit each assignment.

- ▉ What problem or question is your paper going to address?
- ▉ Why is this an interesting question? What makes it problematic and significant?
- ▉ How is your paper going to surprise your readers?
- ▉ What is your thesis statement? (If the writer doesn't have a good thesis statement yet, go on to the next question and then come back to this one. Perhaps you can help the writer figure out a thesis.)
- ▉ Talk me (us) through your whole argument or through your ideas so far.

When you conduct your interview, get the writer to do most of the talking. Respond by offering suggestions, bringing up additional ideas, playing devil's advocate, and so forth. The goal is for the writer to rehearse the whole paper orally. Whenever the writer gets stuck for ideas, arguments, or supporting details, help brainstorm possibilities.

During these sessions, it is best for writers not to look at notes or drafts. They should try to reformulate their ideas conversationally. We recommend that each student talk actively for fifteen to twenty minutes as the interviewer asks probing questions, plays devil's advocate, or helps the writer think of ideas.

We now turn to a more formal kind of social interaction, that of making a speech in front of an audience.

ABOUT ORAL PRESENTATIONS

This section explains how to prepare and deliver the kinds of oral presentations that you are most likely to give in academic, business, or professional settings. We focus mostly on formal speeches, but we also provide tips for handling impromptu speeches that you might have to produce on the spot.

The idea that oral communication is spoken instead of written might seem too obvious to mention; less apparent, however, is the difference from the audience's perspective: heard versus seen. That difference points to the special needs of an audience of listeners. What kinds of messages can listeners really follow? The answer to that question will guide the adjustments you should make to your writing as you compose speeches.

Just as you can use writing for a wide variety of purposes, you can also use speaking for a wide variety of purposes; however, the range of oral presentations that people actually deliver in academic and professional settings is quite limited. Formal speeches are usually arguments, reports, or ceremonial orations. Less formal speech opportunities include giving input at an open forum and answering questions. We start by explaining the process of preparing a formal speech and then show how to accelerate that process for impromptu speaking.

PREPARING FORMAL SPEECHES

Most formal speeches are delivered extemporaneously. That means that the speaker has spent ample time preparing a well-arranged speech, but does not end up reading from a script or reciting from memory. Instead, the speaker talks directly to the audience with the aid of note cards or an outline that may be projected from transparencies or a computer.

Long before the delivery of the speech, the speaker should have engaged in the same sort of writing process that precedes a finished essay, including the production of multiple drafts to solve subject-matter and rhetorical problems. However, in the case of a speech, the drafts may consist mostly of revised versions of a sentence outline, with very few fully composed paragraphs written out in detail. That does not mean that you should draft an outline and then wing it. Effective speakers regularly spend an hour of preparation time per minute of speaking time; that preparation includes revising the outline and saying aloud the details that flesh out the skeleton. Such spoken composition helps keep a speech "oral" and prevents you from accidentally composing a text that is too "written" and therefore begs for an audience of readers.

One way that well-composed speeches accommodate the needs of listeners is that the closed forms associated with written discourse close up even more when the message is to be spoken. The most common formula for a speech is sometimes called the "tell 'em rule." It says: Tell 'em what you are about to say, say it, then tell 'em what you just said. While such redundancy may seem ridiculous, it greatly enhances an audience's ability to follow a spoken argument without a text. This "tell 'em rule" serves audience-based needs for unity and coherence, for receiving old information before new information, and for forecasting and fulfillment. These essentials are especially valuable to listeners, who, unlike readers, cannot back up to reread a sentence or a whole paragraph.

Speech Outlines as Multipurpose Tools

While an outline may be optional for an essay consisting of several paragraphs of polished prose, it is vital for a formal speech delivered extemporaneously. A speech outline serves as a composing tool and as an essential aid to your delivery, and it may, in fact, be the only "finished" text that the audience ever sees—if they see any written text at all. It, plus some note cards for reading exact quotations or precise figures, often represents the fullest "written" form that some speeches ever take, as most formal speaking rarely requires a full text of polished prose—just a polished delivery of a well-planned talk.

Whether you use traditional outlines or different fonts and indentations to indicate a hierarchy of main points and subpoints, you should be aware of the two essential features of any well-arranged message: coordination and subordination. What are your main points, and what other points are subordinate to them? Often speakers provide outlines of their speeches through a handout or slide projection. However, even if the only thing your audience gets is the sound of your voice, you can still clearly indicate coordinate and subordinate ideas by using parallel sentence structures. When you do this, your audience "sees" the structure of your message through what they hear.

The following simple outline uses parallel syntactic structures so that the relationships of coordination and subordination can be heard:

- The proposed amendment will cost too much.
  - It will increase expenses.
  - It will decrease revenues.
- The proposed amendment will worsen conditions.
  - It will not eliminate the old problems.
    - The noise problem
    - The safety problem
  - It will add new problems.
    - The problem of accountability
    - The problem of sustainability
    - The problem of legality

While the outline above may take only twenty seconds to read aloud, it could represent the entire structure of a ten-minute speech. The speaker fills the rest of the airtime by fleshing out each of the points. For example, the claim that the proposed amendment will increase expenses could be sustained first with a quotation from a financial expert, followed by dollar amounts comparing current expenses with projected increases. Both the quotation and the figures can be printed on an index card clearly labeled "Increased Expenses" to be read at the appropriate moment. Remember, however, that every time you read from a text, you lose eye contact with your audience while also running the risk of presenting some of that "writerly" prose that may not suit an audience of listeners.

Contents and Arrangement

What your speech has to include depends upon the rhetorical situation. If you are making an argument, then the classical form suggests that you not only provide support for your claim but that you also anticipate objections, rebut those that you can, and concede what you must. If you are delivering a report, then you need to determine what your audience already knows and provide the information they lack. In addition to a global structure, your speech will probably include several local structures, each with its own arrangement of ideas and information: problem/solution, cause/effect, cost/benefit, or past/present/future.

See Chapter 15 for an explanation of classical argument.

If you are concerned about boring your audience by keeping your arrangement utterly predictable, you can always choose to defy some of their expectations. Just remember that each time you do, you increase the information processing burden upon your audience while simultaneously drawing attention to your arrangement itself rather than to your message. Yes, some of the best stories are told through multiple flashbacks instead of using chronological order. However, whenever you employ an unusual arrangement, you also create the need for more signposting with phrases like "as I stated earlier." Such convoluted messages are harder for your audience to follow and harder for you to give. So, rather than relying on artful twists to maintain the audience's interest, keep the structure simple, and maintain their interest with strong content and an enthusiastic delivery.

For Writing and Discussion

Working in groups or as a whole class, examine the full text of the speech by Richard F. Corlin delivered at the 2001 Annual Meeting of the American Medical Association and entitled "The Secrets of Gun Violence in America," (pp. 462–470). Then answer the following questions about the speech.

1. Where can you "see" the structure of this speech?
2. Where does Corlin follow the "tell 'em rule"?
3. Create an after-the-fact outline for this speech.
4. How does Corlin adapt the presentation of his points to the needs of listeners? In other words, how can you tell that this piece is a speech?
5. This speech is actually quite long. What might Corlin have omitted and still conveyed the same message and achieved the same effect?

Using Visual Aids to Support Your Presentation

Long before the arrival of presentation software such as Microsoft PowerPoint, speakers developed simple rules for the effective use of visual aids. Nowadays, these commonsense rules are programmed into the software: your visuals should be simple, neat, and big enough for everyone to see clearly; additionally, any single slide should contain only a few lines of text. The default settings in PowerPoint guarantee that you adhere to these rules. If you find yourself wanting to reduce the font size so that you can fit more text onto a slide, resist the temptation, because it indicates that you are trying to use the program as a word processor, not a slide processor.

The programs allow you to work on your presentation in several different views, including Outline and Slide View. Outline View provides the same advantages as the outlining feature in a word processor, with the added benefit that slide size promotes the short phrases and key words that provide effective memory aids. Slide View is particularly effective when you are using charts or other graphical features to support your presentation because it lets you edit the slide for maximum visual impact. Figure 25.1 shows a portion of the simple outline used earlier as it would appear in Slide View. Note that the phrase "The problem of . . ." was not repeated in the slide as it was in the outline because, now that the audience can see the relationships of coordination and subordination with their eyes, it is not as important that you help them "see" these relationships with their ears.

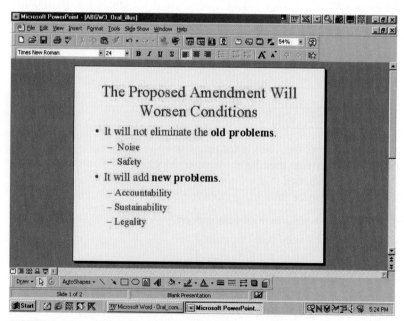

FIGURE 25.1 ▪ "Slide View" in PowerPoint lets you edit all aspects of a slide while simultaneously displaying the visual effects that will result.

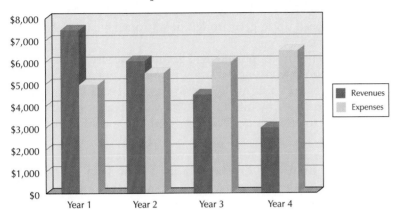

Financial Impact of Amendment

FIGURE 25.2 ■ "Slide Show View" allows you to preview what the audience will see.

"Slide Show View" is what your audience will see when you project the slide onto a screen. Figure 25.2 shows a bar graph produced using the graphing utility included within PowerPoint.

Another view, Slide Sorter, lets you rearrange your speech at the global level by simply shuffling individual portions of your presentation. Finally, these programs help you produce attractive handouts so that your audience can follow your presentation and walk away with a record of your talk in outline form or printed as multiple slides on one sheet of paper. If you produce any detailed graphs, you should provide your audience with handouts just in case they cannot read some parts of the projected images from where they are sitting.

If a computer projection system is not available in the room where you will give your speech, PowerPoint and similar programs let you print attractive transparencies for use with an overhead projector. With either approach, you need to remember to look at and talk to your audience, not the slide projected on the screen, and to be sure to familiarize yourself with any equipment you will be using well before you start your speech.

Delivering a Formal Speech

When the moment finally arrives to give your speech, you will be delivering much of it for the umpteenth time, because your composing process included saying it aloud while timing yourself, preferably in front of a mirror. If possible, you have recorded it on audio- or videotape and practiced it in front of a group of friends, revising all the way. Now it's show time, so you need to attend to what will show—what the audience will see and hear. The aspects of delivery that you need to consider are volume and pace, posture and gesture, eye contact, enthusiasm, use of notes, and integration of presentation aids if you use any.

Because delivery style has become less dramatic and more natural over the years, the only vocal aspects you need to control are your volume and pace. As long as you speak loud enough to be heard, you can add emphasis by speaking louder or softer. You can speed up to get through details quickly and slow down for points you want to stress.

Like delivery style, conventions for posture and gesture have also become more natural, but you should hold yourself as straight and as open as you can. Nervousness might make you try to shrink down to a smaller target, but a slouching form will weaken your delivery by interfering with your breathing and projection. No one is ever going to criticize a speaker for standing too straight or projecting too well.

Gestures, however, are another matter. The sweeping gestures of yesteryear now look contrived, but a death grip on the podium doesn't help either. Some people use their hands a lot when they speak, while others rarely move them. Too many gestures can be distracting, but if you tend not to talk with your hands, then a few planned gestures, even something as simple as holding up two fingers when you turn to your second main point, can help your delivery.

The most important visible aspect of your delivery is your eye contact. You should try to make as much eye contact as possible and be sure to spread it around. Don't deliver your entire speech to just one member of the audience or glance around so quickly that you never actually meet anyone's gaze.

Your enthusiasm counts for a lot. If, out of nervousness or a desire to look cool, you appear not to care about your message, your audience probably won't care about it either. Rather than claim that your topic is important, show that by the energy you put into your delivery.

Finally, your delivery will be affected by how well you use your notes and any presentation aids you might include. If you read more than a very small amount, you are going to lose contact with your audience. If you have handouts, transparencies, or PowerPoint slides, you need to control the flow of information so that your supports match what you say when you say it. If you want your audience to listen to what you have to say, it is a bad idea to give them something to read unless it repeats, summarizes, or exemplifies your point. And you certainly don't want your audience looking at the slide that summarizes an opposing viewpoint five minutes after you have dispensed with that argument.

PREPARING AND DELIVERING IMPROMPTU SPEECHES

Impromptu speaking, where you receive little or no warning that you have to deliver some remarks, is considered so challenging that some textbooks recommend that you avoid it. That may be good advice when you have a choice in the matter, but when a professor calls on you with a question, you probably shouldn't say, "Sorry, I don't do impromptus."

The real challenge with impromptu speaking is that the preparation and delivery stages get collapsed into one, and you literally have to be inventing much of your speech as you give it. However, if you can remember three simple techniques, you should be able to produce impromptu speeches that are clear and intelligible, instead of a series of awkward pauses punctuated mostly by "um."

First, use the "tell 'em rule." While short speeches may not need an organizational preview and a follow-up summary, it never hurts to announce what your point is going to be before you actually make it.

Second, try the principle of "define and divide." By "define" we mean that you should specify the scope of your remarks by asserting what you will address and what you will not. ("I will limit my remarks to the economic causes of this problem and not attempt to address the more complex personnel issues at this time.")

The "divide" principle refers again to your audience's need for structure. Give your remarks a structure with obvious divisions like problem/solution, cause/effect, or past/present/future. By quickly choosing such an arrangement, you buy yourself time to invent the solution portion while you are articulating some aspect of the problem.

Finally, we come to the "vocalized pause." When called upon to speak, most people keep making sounds even when they don't have something to say. Consequently, they often fill the air with a series of linguistic tics such as "ya know," "like," "really," and the ubiquitous "um." Rather than fill the void with "*um*'s," use a silent pause or two. If a moment's silence could cost you the floor, hold up your index finger to indicate that your next point is about to be uttered, while you use that moment to come up with it. Furthermore, effective impromptu speakers regularly use a whole series of vocalized pauses to buy time to discover their next point, while sounding fairly articulate in the process. For example, say "actually" in lieu of "really" and substitute "as you may be aware" for "ya know." Combine the "tell 'em rule" with the articulate pause and you can buy ten seconds of thinking time: "If we consider, now, for a moment, what some solutions to this problem might actually be, I am confident that some of you may well be aware that they would most probably include at least these two."

HANDLING SPEECH ANXIETY

If you are like most people, giving a formal presentation will make you nervous; however, there are things you can do to minimize the jitters. Remember that speech anxiety is a universal phenomenon; also realize that your nervousness is largely invisible. Your racing pulse, the butterflies in your stomach, and that knot in your shoulders all feel very intense to you, but the audience can't see any of them. So, instead of letting the slight tremor in your hands become magnified by holding a visibly trembling outline, rest your paper on the podium and gently grasp its sides. Instead of letting your voice get high and reedy because you are taking short, shallow breaths, take deep breaths and speak slightly louder than usual. Finally, you should know that the path that connects your psychological state of anxiety to your physical reactions of discomfort is a two-way street. You can engage in breathing exercises that relax all the major muscle groups in your body, making them less able to tense up involuntarily, and you can be doing this quite invisibly as you sit awaiting your turn to speak. The net result will be an overall physical relaxation that will also reduce your level of anxiety. But the most effective thing you can do about speech anxiety is to use that nervousness about your performance as an incentive to prepare your presentation diligently and practice it repeatedly.

For Writing and Discussion

Convert one of your writing projects for this course from an essay to a speech. Using the principles in this chapter, prepare a speech outline and drafts of appropriate slides or transparencies. Then, working in groups, do a practice run-through of your speech, using your outline. Group members who are playing the role of audience should answer the following questions on each practice speech:

1. How could the speaker help the audience "see" the structure of the speech more clearly with their ears using the "tell 'em rule" and parallel syntactic structures for parallel points? How could the speaker's thesis and hierarchy of coordinate points and subordinate points be clearer?
2. What other ways could the speaker accommodate the audience's ability to process information delivered orally?
3. How could the visual aids better help the audience understand and enjoy this speech? How could these be more effectively integrated?
4. How could the speaker improve his or her volume, emphasis, posture, gestures, eye contact, use of notes, and use of visual aids?

CHAPTER SUMMARY

This chapter has focused on oral communication in small groups and in speeches given before an audience. In the group section, we explained basic principles for successful group interaction: avoiding clone-think and ego-think, listening empathically, playing assigned roles, being sensitive to body language, investing time in group maintenance, recognizing how personality and culture affect group participation, and managing conflict by dealing with "an impossible group member." We have also showed you how to use groups for seeking consensus, brainstorming ideas, and rehearsing drafts orally. In the speech section, we explained similarities and differences between speeches and writing and showed you how to prepare and deliver a formal speech using speech outlines and visual aids designed to meet the needs of your audience. We also offered suggestions for impromptu speaking and for overcoming speech anxiety.

CHAPTER 26

Essay Examinations
Writing Well Under Pressure

*I'm pretty good at writing research essays, but when I have to write under pressure,
I freeze. Last time I took an essay test, I wrote two pages before I realized that I'd
left out an important piece of my argument. By the time I had scratched out, made
additions, and drawn arrows all over the page, my paper was such a mess that I
couldn't decipher it. Needless to say, the instructor couldn't either.*

—STUDENT A

*For me, the worst thing about exams is trying to figure out what the professor
wants. The final in my European literature course was a perfect example: There
was only one question. It started with a difficult-to-follow quotation from an
author we hadn't studied, which we were supposed to apply to a whole slew of
questions about novels we had read during the semester. The question went on for
half a page (single-spaced!) and had at least five or six subsections. By the time I
finished reading it, I didn't have a clue about where to start or how to cover so
much ground in a single essay.*

—STUDENT B

*(Anonymous undergraduate students at the University of Oklahoma, paraphrased
from responses written when asked to comment on their experiences with essay
examinations)*

As these students' comments about essay exams indicate, taking essay
exams, with the extra demands that exams place on writers, can be
stressful and frustrating experiences. When instructors give essay exams,
they want to see how well students can restate, apply, and assess course
material. Just as important, they want to see whether students can discuss in their
own words what they have studied—whether they can participate in that discipline's discourse community. These twin demands make essay exams doubly
challenging. Furthermore, not only must students master course material, but
they must also write about it quickly and confidently.

Although you will rarely take exams after you leave college (unless you plan to
attend graduate school), writing essay tests can help you develop skills relevant to
many real-world situations. For example, in such fields as journalism, advertising,

marketing, publishing, engineering, and teaching, you will need to compose documents on tight deadlines.

Even when you accept that it's important to learn how to write essay exams, you may wonder how you can possibly prepare for the kinds of exams you will face in all your college courses. These diverse courses will require that you adapt your exam essays to the course, instructor, and test question at hand. However, we can give you some useful guidelines and strategies that you can apply. This chapter shows you how to plan and draft an essay exam and how to adapt to the unique requirements of in-class essay writing.

HOW EXAMS WRITTEN UNDER PRESSURE DIFFER FROM OTHER ESSAYS

Essay exams do share similarities to other assignments. Most of the instructions in this book apply to exam writing. For instance, you have learned how to respond to rhetorical context—audience, purpose, and genre—as you write an essay. Your audience for an essay exam is your instructor, so you need to ask yourself what your instructor values and wants. Does your instructor stress analysis of material or application of roles? Does your instructor encourage individual interpretations? Just as analyzing an audience helps you focus an out-of-class essay, so too analyzing your instructor's expectations can help you focus an exam response.

You also know the importance of knowing what you're talking about. Even the most brilliant writers will stumble on a test if they haven't bothered to attend class regularly, take notes, participate in class discussions, and keep up with the reading. Familiarity with the material lays the groundwork for a successful exam performance, just as thorough research and exploratory writing grounds a good paper.

However, not all the writing strategies you use for papers will serve you well in a test situation. Writing researcher Randall Popken, after reviewing more than two hundred sample exams in various disciplines, identified three skills unique to essay exam writing.

1. The ability to store, access, and translate appropriate knowledge into an organized essay
2. The ability to analyze quickly the specific requirements of an exam question and formulate a response to those requirements
3. The ability to deal with time pressure, test anxiety, and other logistical constraints of the exam situation

We examine each of these skills in the next section.

PREPARING FOR AN EXAM: LEARNING AND REMEMBERING SUBJECT MATTER

One of the biggest differences between writing a paper and writing an exam essay involves how you access material. For essays written outside of class, in addition to your own personal knowledge of the topic, you have access to other sources—the library, course readings, your classmates' and instructor's input. But in an exam, you're on your own. You won't know beforehand which of the many pages of material you have studied in a class you'll be asked to synthesize and comment on. Although you may have studied hard and learned a great deal, you will have to display your knowledge in rapid, on-the-spot writing. Preparing for an exam involves finding efficient ways to organize and recall your knowledge so that you can easily construct an intelligent discussion on paper.

Identifying and Learning Main Ideas

No instructor will expect you to remember every single piece of information covered in class. Most instructors are happy if you can remember main ideas and theories, key terminology, and a few supporting examples. The best strategy when you study for an essay exam is to figure out what is most important and learn it first.

How do you determine the main ideas and key concepts? Sometimes they're obvious. Many professors outline their lectures on the board or distribute review sheets before each exam. If your professor does not provide explicit instructions, listen for a thesis statement, main points, and transitions in each lecture to determine the key ideas and relationships among them. For example,

The *most important critics* of the welfare state are . . .

Four developments contributed to the reemergence of the English after the Norman invasion . . .

Hegel's dialectic was *most influenced by* Kant . . .

Look for similar signals in your textbook and pay special attention to chapter summaries, subheadings, and highlighted terms. If the course involves a lot of discussion or if your professor prefers informal remarks to highly structured lectures, you may have to work harder to identify major points. But streamlining and organizing your knowledge in this way will keep you from feeling overwhelmed when you sit down to study.

Chapter 19, Lesson 9, explains some of the main organizing moves writers use in the bodies of essays to clarify and develop their points.

Most instructors expect you to master more than the information they cover in class. Essay exams in humanities, social science, and fine arts courses often ask for an individual interpretation, argument, or critique. To prepare for such questions, practice talking back to course readings by developing your own positions on the viewpoints they express. If the professor has lectured on factors involved in mainstreaming schoolchildren with physical disabilities, look at your notes and try to define your own position on mainstreaming. If the textbook identifies salient features of Caravaggio's art, decide how you think his paintings compare to and differ from his contemporaries' work. Questioning texts and lectures in this way will help you personalize the material, expand your understanding, and take ownership of your education. Remember, though, that professors won't be impressed by purely subjective opinions; as you explore your views, search for evidence and arguments, not just from your own experience but the course as well, that you can use to support your ideas in the exam.

For specific strategies to help you understand and respond to reading material, review Chapter 6 and Chapter 13.

Applying Your Knowledge

In business, science, social science, and education courses, professors may ask you to apply a theory or method to a new situation; for example, they might ask you to show how "first in, last out" accounting might work in bookkeeping for a washing machine factory or how you might use Freudian concepts to analyze a hypothetical psychiatric case. If you suspect that such a question might appear, use some study time to practice this kind of thinking. Brainstorm two or three current situations to which you could apply the theories or concepts you've been learning. Check local newspapers or browse the World Wide Web for ideas. Then freewrite for a few minutes on how you might organize an essay that puts the theory to work. For instance, if you've studied federal affirmative action law in a public administration course, you might ask the following questions: How does the law apply to the recent decision by the California regents to abolish race as a factor in college admissions? How might it apply to a local controversy over hiring female firefighters? You won't be able to predict exactly what will appear on the exam, but you can become skilled at transferring ideas into new settings.

Making a Study Plan

Once you've identified crucial subject matter, you need to develop a study plan. If you're a novice at studying for a major exam, try following some tried-and-true approaches. Review your instructor's previous exams. Don't be afraid to ask your instructor for general guidelines about the type, length, and format of questions he or she normally includes on tests. Then generate your own practice questions and compose responses. If you can, organize group study sessions with two to four classmates. Meet regularly to discuss readings, exchange practice questions, test each other informally, and critique each other's essays.

Avoid study techniques that are almost universally ineffective: Don't waste time trying to reread all the material or memorize passages word for word (unless the exam will require you to produce specific formulas or quotations). Don't set an unreasonable schedule. You can seldom learn the material adequately in one or two nights, and the anxiety produced by cramming can hurt your performance even more. Most important, don't stay up all night studying. Doing so can be worse than not studying at all, since sleep deprivation impairs your ability to recall and process information.

No matter how you decide to study, remember that the point of developing exam-preparation strategies isn't simply to do well on a single test, but to become comfortable with learning difficult, complex material and to acquire a level of intellectual confidence that will help you grow as a writer.

ANALYZING EXAM QUESTIONS

Whereas paper assignments typically ask you to address broad problems that can be solved in numerous possible ways, essay exams usually require much more narrowly focused responses. Think about some of your paper assignments. They might have read, "Write a persuasive research paper in which you propose a solution to a current local controversy" or "Write a ten-page essay exploring an ethical issue in the field of vertebrate biology"; they might have called for either closed- or open-form prose; but in virtually all cases you were free to choose from among several possible approaches to your topic. Essay exams, in contrast, feature well-defined problems with a very narrow range of right answers. They require you to recall a particular body of information and present it in a highly specific way. However, what your instructors are asking you to recall and how they want it presented will not always be clear to you. Exam questions often require interpretation.

Although the language of essay exams varies considerably across disciplines, professors typically draw on a set of conventional moves when they write exam prompts. Consider the following question from an undergraduate course in the history of the English language:

> Walt Whitman once wrote that English was not "an abstract construction of dictionary makers" but a language that had "its basis broad and low, close to the ground." Whitman reminds us that English is a richly expressive language because it comes from a variety of cultural sources. One of these is African-American culture. Write an essay discussing the major ways in which African-American culture and dialect have influenced the English language in the United States. Identify and illustrate at least three important influences: What were the historical circumstances? What important events and people were involved? What were the specific linguistic contributions?

This question presents an intimidating array of instructions, but it becomes manageable if you recognize some standard organizational features.

Outside Quotations. First, like many exam questions, this sample opens with a quotation from an author or work not covered in the course. Many students panic when they encounter such questions. "Whitman?! We didn't even study Whitman. What am I supposed to do now?" Don't worry. The primary function of such quotations is to encapsulate a general issue that the instructor wants you to address in your response. When you encounter an unfamiliar quotation, look carefully at the rest of the question for clues about what role the quotation should play in your essay. The point of the Whitman quotation is restated in the very next sentence—English is shaped by numerous cultural influences—and the function of the quotation is simply to reinforce that point. Because the rest of the question tells you specifically what kinds of cultural influences your response should address (African-American culture, three major linguistic contributions), you don't need to consider this quotation when you write your essay.

Sometimes professors will ask you to take a position on an unfamiliar quotation and support your argument with material covered in the course. Suppose that the question was, "What is your position on Whitman's view? Do you believe that English is enriched or corrupted by multicultural influences?" In this case the quotation is presented as the basis for a thesis statement, which you would then explain and support. A successful response might begin, "Whitman believes that multicultural influences make our language better, but this view is hopelessly naive for the following reasons. . . ." or "Whitman correctly argues that the contributions of different cultures enrich our language. Take these three examples. . . ."

Organizational Cues. The question itself can show you the best way to organize your response. Questions tend to begin with general themes that often suggest a thesis statement. Subsequent divisions tell you how to organize the essay into sections and in what order to introduce supporting points. For example, a successful response that follows the organization of our sample might be arranged as follows:

- A thesis stating that several contributions from African-American language and culture have enriched English
- Three supporting paragraphs, each discussing a different area of influence by
  1. summarizing historical circumstances
  2. noting important people and events
  3. providing one or two examples of linguistic contributions

Key Terms. As do all exam questions, this one asks you to write about a specific body of information in a specific way. When you encounter a lengthy question such as this, first pick out the *noun phrases* that direct you to specific areas of knowledge: "African-American culture," "major influences on the English language in the United States," "historical circumstances," "important events and people," "linguistic contributions." Pay careful attention to words that modify these noun phrases. Does the question tell you how many influences to discuss? What kinds of examples to cite? Does the instructor include conjunctions, such as *or*, to give you a choice of topics, or does he or she use words such as *and* or *as well as* that require you to address all areas mentioned? Words such as *who, what, where,* and *why* also point to particular kinds of information.

After you've determined the specific areas you need to address, look for *directive verbs* that tell you what to do: *discuss, identify,* or *illustrate,* for example. These verbs define the horizons of your response. Table 26.1 defines some key directives that frequently appear in essay exams and provides sample questions for each. Meanings vary somewhat according to the course, the context of the question, and the professor's expectations, but you'll feel more confident if you have basic working definitions.

In some questions, directives are implied rather than stated directly. If a question asks, "Discuss the effects of Ronald Reagan's tax policies on the U.S. economy during the 1980s," you'll need to summarize what those policies were before you can assess their effects. Before you can take a position on an issue, you have

TABLE 26.1   ■   Strategies for Responding to Common Essay-Question Verbs

Verb	How to Respond	Example
Analyze	Break an argument, concept, or approach into parts and examine the relations among them; discuss causes and effects; evaluate; or explain your interpretation. Look at the rest of the question to determine which strategies to pursue.	*Analyze* the various technical, acoustic, and aesthetic factors that might lead a musician to choose analog over digital recording for a live performance. Be sure to include the strengths and weaknesses of both methods in your discussion.

TABLE 26.1 ■ Strategies for Responding to Common Essay-Question Verbs *(continued)*

Verb	How to Respond	Example
Apply	Take a concept, formula, theory, or approach and adapt it to another situation.	Imagine that you've been hired to reengineer the management structure of a major U.S. automaker. How might you *apply* the principles of Total Quality Management in your recommendations?
Argue	Take a position for or against an issue and give reasons and evidence to support that position.	*Argue* whether or not cloning should be pursued as a method of human reproduction. Be sure to account for the relationship between cloning and mitosis in your discussion.
Compare/ Contrast	Note the similarities (compare) or differences (contrast) between two or more objects or ideas.	*Compare* and *contrast* the leadership styles of Franklin Delano Roosevelt, John F. Kennedy, and Ronald Reagan, focusing on their uses of popular media and political rhetoric.
Construct	Assemble a model, diagram, or other organized presentation of your knowledge about a subject.	*Construct* a model of the writing process that illustrates the major stages writers go through when developing an idea into a finished text.
Critique	Analyze and evaluate an argument or idea, pointing out and explaining both strengths and weaknesses.	Dinesh D'Souza's "Illiberal Education" sparked widespread controversy when it was published in 1991. Write an essay *critiquing* D'Souza's arguments against affirmative action, identifying both the strengths and weaknesses of his position. Use examples from the text, class discussion, and other class readings to illustrate your points.
Define	Provide a clear, concise, authoritative meaning for an object or idea. The response may include describing the object or idea, distinguishing it clearly from other objects or ideas, and providing one or more supporting examples.	How was "equality" *defined* by the Supreme Court in *Plessy v. Ferguson* (1896)? How did that definition influence subsequent educational policy in the United States?
Discuss	Comprehensively present and analyze important concepts, supported by examples or evidence. Cover several key points or examine the topic from several perspectives. Check the question for guidelines about what to include in your response.	*Discuss* the controversy that surrounded Stanley Milgram's studies of authority and state your own position on the relevance and validity of the experiments.

(continued)

TABLE 26.1 ■ Strategies for Responding to Common Essay-Question Verbs[*](concluded)

Verb	How to Respond	Example
Enumerate (or List)	List steps, components, or events pertaining to a larger phenomenon, perhaps briefly explaining and commenting on each item.	A two-year-old child falls from a swing on the playground and lies unconscious. As the head preschool teacher, *enumerate* the steps you would take from the time of the accident until the ambulance arrives.
Evaluate	Make a judgment about the worth of an object or idea, examining both strengths and weaknesses.	*Evaluate* William Whyte's "Street Corner Society" as an ethnographic study. What are its methodological strengths and weaknesses? Do you believe the weaknesses make Whyte's research obsolete?
Explain	Clarify and state reasons to show how some object or idea relates to a more general topic.	*Explain* the relationship of centri-petal force to mass and velocity and give an example to illustrate this relationship.
Identify	Describe some object or idea and explain its significance to a larger topic.	*Identify* the major phonetic characteristics of each of the following language groups of Africa, and provide illustrative examples: Koisan, Niger-Kordofanian, and Nilo-Saharan.
Illustrate	Give one or more examples, cases, or other concrete instances to clarify a general concept.	Define "monopoly," "public utility," and "competition," and give specific *illustrations* of each.
Prove	Produce reasons and evidence to establish that a position is logical, supportable, or factual.	Use your knowledge about the findings of the National Assessment of Educational Progress to *prove* that public schools either are or are not doing an adequate job of educating children to become productive U.S. citizens.
Review	Briefly survey or summarize something.	*Review* the major differences between Socrates' conception of ethics and the ethical theories of his contemporaries in the fifth century B.C.E.
Summarize	Lay out the main points of a theory, argument, or event in a concise and organized manner.	*Summarize* Mill's definition of justice and explain how it differs from Kant's. Which definition comes closest to your own, and why?
Trace	Explain chronologically a series of events or the development of an idea.	Write an essay that *traces* the pathway of a nerve impulse through the nervous system, being sure to explain neuron structure, action potential, and the production and reception of neurotransmitters.

[*]*Our thanks to Michael C. Flanigan, who suggested some of the terms for this table.*

to define what the controversy is about. In general, when you answer any question, you should include sufficient background information about the topic to convince your instructor that you're making an informed argument, whether or not the question specifically asks for background information.

For Writing and Discussion

This exercise will hone your ability to analyze essay questions. Each of the following student essays, which received an A, was a response to one of the four closely related questions that follow it. Each essay may address issues raised in two or more questions, but each is an A response to only one. Your task is to figure out which question the essay answers best. Although you have not read the specific material from which each essay draws, you should nonetheless be able to match the responses to the questions based on the kinds of information included and how the information is used.

Decide on your answer independently; then compare answers in small groups. Try to come to a group consensus, referring to Table 26.1 to help resolve disagreements. As you discuss your responses, note any successful strategies that you may be able to adapt to your own writing.

From a Library Science Course

Bandura's social learning theory breaks from the behaviorist learning theory developed by B. F. Skinner. Behaviorists believe that humans learn only those behaviors that are positively reinforced; behaviors that are not reinforced become "extinct." Bandura, however, argued that some learning happens vicariously, as a child models the behaviors of people around him or her. Such learning does not depend on direct reinforcement, but on observation and imitation. For example, a child from a violent family may behave aggressively toward his or her friends, not because there is a reward for behaving that way, but because he or she has seen the behavior continually at home.

Many variables affect whether a child will learn from a model, according to Bandura. These include the type of behavior, whether the model is someone the child admires, and whether the behavior is punished or reinforced. For example, if a movie villain slapped a woman, a child might not imitate the behavior, since the model is not someone he or she wants to identify with. But if the hero of the movie did the same thing, especially if the woman responded by passionately kissing him (a reward), the child would be more likely to repeat the behavior.

Bandura's theory has clear implications for library staff in selecting children's books. It is important that children have available a variety of positive role models to identify with and imitate—especially to provide a balance to the violent, sexist role models often presented in television and movies. School-age boys who survive on a TV diet of Arnold Schwarzenegger and Power Rangers need to also read about males who are admirable without being violent. Biographies of men like Abraham Lincoln and Mahatma Gandhi, and novels like *Johnny Tremain* and *Encyclopedia Brown* that show characters who succeed by helping others, give boys some positive behaviors to imitate. Stories about strong, independent girl characters, such as *Caddie Woodlawn* and *The Summer of the Swans*, give young girls whose ideas are shaped by Barbie and *Beverly Hills 90210* more admirable role models.

(continued)

These are just a few examples. Many books give both boy and girl readers characters to look up to. Bandura's theory shows us just how important that is to children's social learning.

Which question does this response address most successfully?

1. Summarize the learning theories of Skinner and Bandura, and explain how each might inform book selections at a children's library.

2. Review the major components of Bandura's theory of social learning. Then discuss the following: How might these principles apply if you were responsible for selecting children's books for a public library system? What kinds of books might Bandura's theory lead you to choose?

3. Bandura's social learning theory proposes that children learn partly from imitating the behavior of role models. Based on what you know about children's reading preferences, do you believe this is the case? Support your position with examples of particular books, characters, and themes.

4. Compare and contrast Skinner's learning theory, Bandura's theory of social learning, and current theories on children's book selection.

From a British Literature Course

Gulliver's Travels and *Frankenstein* portray characters whose adventures bring them face to face with the innate weaknesses and limitations of humankind. Victor Frankenstein and Lemuel Gulliver find out during their travels that humans are limited in reasoning capacity and easily corruptible, traits that cause even their best-intentioned projects to go awry. These characters reflect the critical view that Swift and Shelley take of human nature. Both believe that humans have a "dark side" that leads to disastrous effects.

In *Gulliver's Travels,* Gulliver's sea voyages expose him to the best and worst aspects of human civilization. Through Gulliver's eyes, readers come to share Swift's perception that no matter how good people's original intentions, their innate selfishness corrupts everything they attempt. All the societies Gulliver visits give evidence of this. For example, Lilliput has a system of laws once grounded on justice and morality, but that slowly were perverted by greedy politicians into petty applications. Even the most advanced society, Brobdingnag, has to maintain a militia even though the country is currently peaceful—since they acknowledge that because humans are basically warlike, peace can't last forever. By showing examples of varied cultures with common faults, Swift demonstrates what he believes to be innate human weaknesses. He seems to believe that no matter how much progress we make, human societies will eventually fall back into the same old traps.

Victor Frankenstein also experiences human limitations, this time in his own personality, as he pushes to gain knowledge beyond what any human has ever possessed. When he first begins his experiments to manufacture life in the laboratory, his goals are noble—to expand scientific knowledge and to help people. As he continues, he becomes more concerned with the power that his discovery will bring him. He desires to be a "god to a new race of men." Later, when the creature he creates wreaks havoc, Frankenstein's pride and selfishness keep him from confessing and preventing further deaths. Like the societies Gulliver observed, Frankenstein is a clear example of how human frailties corrupt potentially good projects.

Even though Swift and Shelley wrote during two different historical periods, they share a critical view of human nature. However, several unambiguously good characters in *Frankenstein*—including the old man and his daughter—suggest that Shelley feels more optimism that people are capable of overcoming their weaknesses, while Swift seems adamant that humans will eternally backslide into greed and violence. Basically, however, both works demonstrate vividly to readers the ever present flaws that prevent people and their societies from ever attaining perfection.

Which question does this essay address most successfully?

1. Contrast Swift's and Shelley's views of human nature, illustrating your points with specific examples from *Gulliver's Travels* and *Frankenstein*.

2. Analyze the use Swift and Shelley make of scientific knowledge to show the limits of human progress in *Gulliver's Travels* and *Frankenstein,* citing specific illustrations from each work.

3. Discuss the characters of Lemuel Gulliver in *Gulliver's Travels* and Victor Frankenstein in *Frankenstein:* What purpose does each serve in the text? How does each author use the character to illustrate important traits or concepts?

4. Many of the writers we've studied this semester explored the limitations of human potential in their work. Write an essay showing how any two of the following works deal with this idea: William Blake's *Songs of Innocence and Experience,* Jonathan Swift's *Gulliver's Travels,* Mary Shelley's *Frankenstein,* Percy Shelley's "Prometheus Unbound." Does each writer suggest a pessimistic or optimistic view of human nature? Be sure to support your argument with specific illustrations from each text.

DEALING WITH CONSTRAINTS: TAKING AN ESSAY EXAM

Suppose that you've organized the course material, studied faithfully, analyzed the exam questions, and know generally how you'll respond. You still need one more skill to succeed: the ability to thrive within the limits of a test situation. Here are some suggestions for handling the pressure.

First, you need to minimize test anxiety. Many students feel anxious if a test question looks unfamiliar or difficult. Others freeze up if they lose their train of thought midway through an essay. Still others panic when time begins to run out. But you can learn to anticipate potential disasters and brainstorm ways to handle them. If you tend to panic when a test question looks impossible on first reading, make a deal with yourself to close your eyes and count to ten and then read it again and try to block off the parts that you don't have to consider. If you usually run out of time, set a time limit when writing some practice questions so that you can get used to performing under pressure. Finally, make sure that you're in top form to take the exam: organize your supplies—including extra exam booklets and scratch paper, pens, and any testing aids your instructor allows—the night before; get plenty of sleep; eat breakfast; arrive at class a few minutes early; give yourself a pep talk. These measures will increase your confidence and head off debilitating nerves.

Lack of time when writing an essay exam is perhaps the hardest constraint for most people to deal with. Most writers produce their best work only after writing several drafts. You won't be able to compose a perfectly polished essay in an exam—there simply isn't time—so you will need to streamline your writing process through planning. After you have analyzed the exam question carefully, take a few minutes to jot down a quick outline or a list of key concepts you want to discuss. Exploratory writing techniques, such as tree diagrams and freewriting, can help you generate and arrange ideas. Prewriting gives you a sense of direction and helps you remember where the essay is going as you write.

For example, one undergraduate student jotted down this five-minute scratch outline in response to the following exam question in a Texas government course:

> What are the relative advantages and disadvantages of the district method versus the at-large method in municipal elections? Analyze the strengths and weaknesses of each and then either argue in favor of one method over the other or propose a different plan that avoids the limitations of both.

Thesis
District method
Advantages—history of discrimination and underrepresentation of minorities (examples)
　　—race consciousness important for overcoming injustice
Disadvantages—encourages racial divisions
　　—not necessary because much racism has been overcome; minorities may
　　now be freely elected (ex. Sen. Barrientos, Ann Richards) **BUT**
At-large
Advantages—all citizens can work together for common good, not just concerned with narrow group interests
Disadvantages—majority rule may ignore important minority needs (ex. East Austin)
THESIS—B/c minories have been and are still underrepresented in local government, the district method of local elections, while flawed, offers the best chance for these communities' voices to be heard.

Once you have a plan, you need to determine how much time to give to each answer. Many students' grades suffer because they blow all their time on the first question and then race through the rest of the exam. To determine how much time to allot each response, you need to solve a quick ratio problem. Divide the points assigned to a given question by the points for the whole exam; the result equals the percentage of time you should spend on that question. When you write your answer, follow the example of journalists and load critical information into your lead. Write a first paragraph that summarizes your whole answer (the second student response in the For Writing and Discussion exercise on pp. 710–711 does this beautifully). Add examples and details to the extent that you have time, moving from more important to less important. If you can't finish a response in time, stop, but don't panic. You may have time to return to it later. If not, write a brief note directing the professor to your original notes or outline; let your professor know that you intended to write more but ran out of time. Many instructors will award partial credit for outlined responses.

You can save time by focusing only on elements important to your grade. Instructors don't expect dramatic, polished introductions and conclusions or artistically constructed sentences in an exam. They would rather you provide a clear thesis statement and explain your main points fully. Most instructors also value organization, although some grade almost entirely on content.

Instructors differ in how they treat errors in grammar, spelling, and punctuation. Some believe it's unfair to expect students to edit their work thoroughly in a short time and don't penalize such errors unless they interfere with the argument (as do garbled or fragmented sentences, for example). Other instructors deduct points for grammatical errors on the grounds that correct usage is always important. If your instructor is a stickler for these details, you may want to save the last five or ten minutes of the exam period for proofreading.

Even if you know a lot about a question, avoid writing more than it asks—unless, perhaps, you know absolutely nothing about one question and want to demonstrate extreme depth of understanding about the others to compensate. Extraneous material may make it difficult for your instructor to find the core of your argument.

Guidelines for Producing Successful Responses

No matter how committed you are to studying, planning, analyzing exam questions, and managing time constraints, your worries about essay tests probably come down to a single, inevitable question: What does an A response look like? Research suggests that most professors want closed-form, thesis-based prose that develops key ideas fully, drawing on supporting facts and examples. Although your essay's shape will be influenced by your individual writing style and the particular rhetorical context, the following summary of the points covered in this chapter can serve as a template for a successful essay.

Clear thesis statement. Show your professor that you understand the big picture that the question addresses by including a thesis statement early on. Many professors recommend that you state your thesis clearly, though not necessarily stylishly, in the very first sentence.

Coherent organization. Although a few instructors will read your essay only to see whether you've included important facts and concepts, most expect a logical presentation. Each paragraph should develop and illustrate one main point. Use transition words and phrases to connect each paragraph clearly to the thesis of the essay: "Another factor that led to the economic decline of the South was . . ."; "In contrast to Hegel, Mill believed. . . ." Show your instructor that you know where the essay's going, that you're developing your thesis.

Support and evidence. When the question calls for supporting facts and examples, be specific. Don't assert or generalize unless you present names, dates, studies, examples, diagrams, or quotations from your reading as support.

Independent analysis and argument. Your response should not be a pedestrian rehash of the textbook. When the question allows, present your own insights, criticisms, or proposals, making sure to support these statements with course material and relate them clearly to your thesis.

Conclusion. Even if you're running short of time, write a sentence or two to tie together main points and restate your thesis. Your conclusion, even if brief, serves an important rhetorical function. It confirms that you've dealt adequately with the question and proved your point.

Clearly we can't teach you everything you need to know about exam writing in one chapter. Becoming comfortable with any genre of writing requires patience and experience. Practicing the suggestions in this chapter for preparing for essay exams, comprehending exam questions, and organizing your answers will help you build your mastery of this kind of writing.

For Writing and Discussion

To gain some practical experience, your instructor may ask you to write an essay exam on one of the following topics. Use the preparation and prewriting strategies you've practiced in this chapter and any other strategies you find useful to prepare for the exam. Review the guidelines for writing a successful response presented on page 713 and, if possible, organize and conduct group study sessions with your classmates.

Exam Option 1   Imagine that you've been appointed to a campus committee charged with developing minimum requirements for writing assignments in undergraduate courses. Specifically, the committee is trying to decide whether to require professors to assign a final essay exam or a major research paper in core-curriculum courses. Write an essay in which you argue in favor of mandatory essay exams or mandatory research papers, using examples from your own experience and material from Chapters 1 through 4 and this chapter to support your position. You may want to consider some or all of the following questions in your discussion: Which kind of writing helps students learn the most? Which kind of writing most accurately gauges how well students know course material? Which kind of writing develops skills students are most likely to need in the future?

Exam Option 2   Explain the difference between closed-form and open-form prose as presented in Chapter 1 and Chapters 19–20. Illustrate your answer with examples taken from Tiffany Linder's "Salvaging Our Old-Growth Forests" (pp. 408–410) and Annie Dillard's "Living Like Weasels" (pp. 568–571). Why does Linder choose to write near the closed end of the closed-to-open continuum, whereas Dillard chooses to write near the open end?

Exam Option 3   Write an essay on a topic of your instructor's choice.

CHAPTER SUMMARY

This chapter has discussed strategies for writing effective examination essays under time pressure. We have shown how exam essays differ from essays written outside class and have suggested strategies for learning and remembering subject matter, for analyzing exam questions, and for dealing with the constraints of an exam situation. We have also provided guidelines for producing successful examination essays: a clear thesis statement, coherent organization, specific support and evidence, independent analysis and argument, and an effective conclusion.

CHAPTER 27

Assembling a Portfolio and Writing a Reflective Self-Evaluation

Reflection becomes a habit of mind, one that transforms.
— KATHLEEN BLAKE YANCEY, *WRITING AND COMPOSITION THEORIST*

Being an adult student, returning after a twelve-year layoff, working full-time and taking a twelve-credit load, I found that I really had to make time to reinvent my writing. These were times of incredible discovery and frustration. Odd as it seems, frustration breeds discovery.

— WILLIAM JENSEN, *STUDENT*

Before we explain in detail what we mean by a reflective self-evaluation, let's begin with some examples. Consider the following scenarios:

Scenario 1: Your boss sends you to a one-week professional development seminar in Chicago. Upon your return, she asks you to write a memo reflecting on what you learned from the seminar, how you might apply it to your current job, and how it has helped you grow professionally.

Scenario 2: Your history professor has assigned a major term paper and is willing to read and comment on a rough draft. When you submit your draft, the professor asks you to write out your answers to three questions: What do you like best about this draft? What has been your greatest difficulty in composing this draft? If you were on your own, how would you revise this current draft?

Scenario 3: The composition program at your college requires students to submit a portfolio of their work at the end of the term. You have been given the following assignment:

Write a reflective letter, addressed to other instructors of this course, that will introduce you and your portfolio. It may describe and compare the process used in creating the out-of-class essays contained in your portfolio, explain why you chose these pieces as your best work for the semester, assess the strengths and weaknesses of your writing, discuss how the writing for this course fits in with previous or future writing, or combine these approaches. Your letter should provide readers with a clearer understanding of who you are as a writer. It should be approximately 500 to 750 words.

All these assignments ask you to look back over a recently completed process; to think reflectively about that process; and to evaluate critically what went well, what didn't go well, what you might have done differently, and how you might change in the future. Our aim in this chapter is to explain in more detail this kind of reflective, self-evaluative writing. We begin by explaining what we mean by reflective writing, how reflective writing is assigned in writing courses, and why reflective writing is important. We then give examples of different kinds of reflective assignments and describe strategies for composing good reflections. We conclude this chapter by explaining how to assemble a writing portfolio and compose an accompanying reflective self-evaluation.

UNDERSTANDING REFLECTIVE WRITING

What Is Reflective Writing?

Broadly defined, reflective writing is writing that describes, explains, interprets, and evaluates any past performance, action, belief, feeling, or experience. To *reflect* is to turn or look back, to reconsider something thought or done in the past from the perspective of the present.

Whether or not you record your thinking on paper, you think reflectively all the time. Suppose you ask your boss for a raise and get turned down. An hour later, as you cool your anger over coffee and a doughnut, you think of a particular point you could have made more effectively. On a larger scale, this kind of informal reflective thinking can be made more formal, systematic, and purposeful. Consider, for example, a football team that systematically reviews game tapes to evaluate their own and their opponents' strategies and patterns of play. The camera's eye offers players and coaches new perspectives on their performance; it enables them to isolate, analyze, and evaluate specific moves that were unconsciously performed in the heat of the game.

Similar ways of thinking can be applied to any past performance. Writing reflectively encourages you to train your own camera's eye, metaphorically speaking, on the past. Reflective writing is now required in many jobs where employees are asked to write an annual self-reflective review of their job performance. The following example comes from the performance review of a student who worked for a health maintenance organization. In this excerpt, she describes how she plans to make herself more productive in her job and then considers how this improvement will help the company's efficiency generally:

Excerpt from a Self-Evaluation of Job Performance

To improve my claims processing knowledge, I signed up to take a CPT4 coding class. This will allow me to answer coding questions quickly without having to contact our Cost Containment Department. The Cost Containment Department will have more time to work on their projects if our department does not have to continually call to get answers to simple coding questions.

Similarly, a writer can look back reflectively on a writing performance. The following example is from an e-mail message sent by student writer Susan Meyers to her writing instructor concerning his comments on a draft she had submitted. (The topic is the causes of anorexia; you can read Meyers's final version of the paper on pp. 356–366.) On the draft, the instructor had puzzled over a confusing sentence and suggested a revised version. Here is her e-mail response.

Excerpt from a Student Reflection on a Draft

I think that your suggested revision changes what I intended. I'd like that sentence to read: "Perhaps anorexics don't pursue desirability but are rather avoiding it." I am arguing not that anorexics want to be "undesirable" (as your sentence suggests) but rather that they want to avoid the whole issue; they want to be neutral. Sexuality and desire can be tremendously scary if you're in a position that places the value of your body over the value of your self/personage; one can feel that, by entering the sexual world of mature adults, one will lose hold of one's essential self. This is the idea I'm trying to express. Perhaps I should try to draft it some more [. . .] At any rate, thank you for pointing out the inadequacies of the topic sentence of this paragraph. I struggled with it, and I think your impulse is right: it needs to encompass more of a transition.

As these examples suggest, reflection involves viewing your writing from different perspectives, looking back on the past from the present, achieving a critical distance. Just as light waves are thrown or bent back from the surface of a mirror, so, too, reflective writing throws our experience, action, or performance back to us, allowing us to see it differently.

This process resembles the kind of dialectical thinking introduced in Chapter 8 on exploratory writing, where we explained how juxtaposing one thesis against its opposite can lead to synthesis that incorporates some aspects of each of the opposing views. Similarly, the process of reexamining one's writing from a new perspective yields new insights and an enriched, more complicated understanding of a particular action, question, problem, or choice.

The synthesizing strategies in Chapter 13 for responding to multiple readings and arriving at your own enlarged views can also be applied to your own pieces of writing.

For Writing and Discussion

Working individually, think of a past experience that you can evaluate reflectively. This experience could be your performance in a job; participation in a sport, play, music recital, or other activity; development of a skill (learning to play the piano, juggle a soccer ball, perform a complex dance movement); or problem with an institution (a coach, your dorm resident assistant, job supervisor). To encourage you to think about the past from the perspective of the present, try the formula, "How do I see the experience differently now from the way I saw it then?" Imagine you are doing a debriefing of your participation in the experience. Working on your own for ten minutes, freewrite reflectively about your performance. What did you do well? What wasn't working for you? What could you have done better?

Then in groups or as a whole class, share what you have learned through your reflective freewrites. How did the process of looking back give you a new perspective on your experience? How might reflective writing help you bring about changes and improvements in future performances?

Reflective Writing in the Writing Classroom

Reflective writing in college writing courses can take several forms. One common type of reflective assignment asks you to write a brief, informal reflection on a particular draft in progress or a recently completed essay. Susan Meyers's e-mail reflection on her anorexia draft is an example of this type of reflective writing.

Perhaps the type most frequently assigned is the reflective letter or essay that accompanies a writing portfolio handed in at the end of a term. This final portfolio is a collection of representative work produced for a particular course. Sometimes this work includes rough drafts and informal writing such as freewrites and journal entries as well as polished final drafts; at other times, it includes just the polished final products. Almost always, however, writers have some or complete say in what goes into the final portfolio. Just as architects select their best designs or photographers their best photographs to put into a portfolio to show a potential employer, so, too, do student writers assemble their best writing to demonstrate to the instructor or portfolio readers what they have learned and accomplished during the term. The role of the accompanying reflective letter or essay is to offer the author's perspective on the writing in the portfolio, to give a behind-the-scenes account of the thinking and writing that went into the work, and to assess the writer's struggles and achievements during the term. The last section of this chapter discusses writing portfolios further and offers suggestions for assembling such a portfolio.

To distinguish the two types of reflective writing, we use the terms *single reflection* and *comprehensive reflection*. When you write a single reflection, you focus on one piece of writing, either recently completed or in-process; you formulate your ideas primarily for yourself and perhaps for a friendly, nonjudgmental audience. When you write a comprehensive reflection, you offer your perspective on a series of completed writing projects for presentation to an outside audience, either your instructor or a portfolio reader. The aim of a single reflection is to learn about a particular piece of writing in order to understand and often to revise it in the present or near future. The aim of a comprehensive reflection is to demonstrate what you have learned from your writing over the course of the term in order to transfer that learning to future writing situations.

Why Is Reflective Writing Important?

According to learning theorists, reflective writing can substantially enhance both your learning and your performance.* Reflective writing helps you gain the insights needed to transfer current knowledge to new situations. For example, one of our students recently reported that the most important thing she had learned in her first-year writing course was that research could be used in the service of her own argument. In high school, she had thought of research as merely assembling and reporting information she had found in various sources. Now she realized that writers must make their own arguments, and she saw how research could help her do so. Clearly, this new understanding of the relationship between argument and research will help this student do the kind of research writing expected in upper-level college courses.

Learning theorists call this kind of thinking *metacognition:* the ability to monitor consciously one's intellectual processes or, in other words, to be aware of how one "does" intellectual work. Reflection enables you to control more consciously the thinking processes that go into your writing, and it enables you to gain the critical distance you need to evaluate and revise your writing successfully.

REFLECTIVE WRITING ASSIGNMENTS

In this section we describe the kinds of reflective writing that your instructors across the disciplines may ask of you.

Single Reflection Assignments

Single reflection assignments are usually informal exploratory pieces, similar to other kinds of informal writing you have done. Like the exploratory writing described in Chapter 2, single reflections are conversational in tone, open in form, and written mainly for yourself and, perhaps, a friendly, nonjudgmental audience. However, single reflections differ from most other kinds of exploratory writing in timing, focus, and purpose.

Whereas exploratory writing helps you generate ideas early in the writing process, reflective writing is usually assigned between drafts or after you have completed an essay. Its focus is your writing itself, both the draft and the processes that produced it. Its aim is critical understanding, usually for the purpose of revision. In it, you think about what's working or not working in the draft, what

---

*Learning theorists who have made this general claim include J. H. Flavel, "Metacognitive Aspects of Problem-Solving," in L. B. Resnick (ed.), *The Nature of Intelligence* (Hillsdale, NJ: Erlbaum, 1976); Donald Schon, *Educating the Reflective Practitioner* (San Francisco: Jossey-Bass, 1987); and Stephen Brookfield, *Becoming a Critically Reflective Teacher* (San Francisco: Jossey-Bass, 1995). Throughout this chapter we are indebted to Kathleen Blake Yancey, *Reflection in the Writing Classroom* (Logan, UT: Utah State UP, 1998), who has translated and extended this work on reflection for writing instructors. We are also indebted to Donna Qualley, *Turns of Thought: Teaching Composition as Reflexive Inquiry* (Portsmouth, NH: Boynton/Cook, Heinemann, 1997), who draws on feminist and other critical theorists to argue for the value of reflexive approaches to writing instruction.

thinking and writing processes went into producing it, and what possibilities you see for revising it.

Instructors use a variety of assignments to prompt single reflections. Some examples of assignments are the following:

- ▩ *Process log:* Your instructor asks you to keep a process log in which you describe the writing processes and decisions made for each essay you write throughout the term. In particular, you should offer a detailed and specific account of the problems you encountered (your "wallowing in complexity") and the rhetorical and subject-related alternatives considered and choices made.

- ▩ *Writer's memo:* Your instructor asks you to write a memorandum to turn in with your draft. In it, you answer a series of questions: How did you go about composing this draft? What problems did you encounter? What do you see as this draft's greatest strengths? What are its greatest weaknesses? What questions about your draft would you like the instructor to address?

- ▩ *Companion piece:* Less structured than a formal memorandum, a companion piece asks you to reflect briefly on one or two questions. A typical assignment might be this: "Please turn over your draft and on the back tell me what you would do with this draft if you had more time."

- ▩ *Talk-To:* In this type of companion piece, your instructor asks you to do four things: (1) believe this is the best paper you've ever written and explain why; (2) doubt that this paper is any good at all and explain why; (3) predict your instructor's response to this paper; and (4) agree or disagree with what you expect your instructor's response to be.

- ▩ *Talk-Back:* In another type of companion piece, the instructor asks you to respond to his or her comments after you get the paper back: (1) What did I value in this text as a reader? (2) Do you agree with my reading? and (3) What else would you like for me to know?*

Guidelines for Single Reflection Assignments

If you are inexperienced with reflective writing, your tendency at first may be to generalize about your writing. That is, you may be tempted to narrate your writing process in generic, blow-by-blow procedural terms ("First I took some notes. Then I wrote a first draft and showed it to my roommate, who gave me some suggestions. Then I revised") or to describe your rhetorical choices in general, prescriptive terms ("I started with a catchy introduction because it's important to grab your reader's attention").

---

*We are indebted to Kathleen Blake Yancey and Donna Qualley for a number of the definitions, specific assignments, and suggestions for single and comprehensive reflection tasks that are discussed in the rest of this chapter. Yancey explains the "Talk-To" and "Talk-Back" assignments in her book *Reflection in the Writing Classroom* (Logan, UT: Utah State UP, 1998). Donna Qualley draws on feminist and other critical theorists to argue for the value of reflexive approaches to writing instruction. See her book *Turns of Thought: Teaching Composition as Reflexive Inquiry* (Portsmouth, NH: Boynton/Cook, Heinemann, 1997).

To write an effective single reflection, select only a few ideas to focus on, look at specific aspects of a specific paper, explore dialectically your past thinking against your present thinking, and support your analysis with adequate details. We suggest the following questions as a guide to producing such reflections. But don't answer them all. Rather, pick out the two or three questions that best apply to your performance and text. (Try to select your questions from at least two different categories.) Your goal should be depth, not a broad survey. The key criteria are these: be *selective,* be *specific,* show *dialectic thinking,* and include *adequate details.*

Process questions: What specific writing strategies did I use to complete this paper?

- Which strategies were the most or least productive?
- Did this writing project require new strategies or did I rely on past strategies?
- What was the biggest problem I faced in writing this paper, and how successful was I in solving that problem?
- What was my major content-level revision so far?
- What were my favorite sentence- or word-level revisions?
- What did I learn about myself as a writer or about writing in general by writing this paper?

Subject-related questions: How did the subject of my paper cause me to "wallow in complexity"?

- What tensions did I encounter between my ideas/experiences and those of others? Between the competing ideas about the subject in my own mind?
- Did I change my mind or come to see something differently as a result of writing this paper?
- What passages in the paper show my independent thinking about the subject? My unresolved problems or mixed feelings about it?
- What were the major content problems I had with this paper, and how successful was I in solving them?
- What did writing about this subject teach me?

Rhetoric-related questions: How did the audience I imagined influence me in writing this paper?

- What do I want readers to take away from reading my paper?
- What rhetorical strategies please me most (my use of evidence, my examples, my delayed thesis, etc.)? What effect do I hope these strategies have on my audience?
- How would I describe my voice in this paper? Is this voice appropriate? Similar to my everyday voice or to the voices I have used in other kinds of writing?
- Did I take any risks in writing this paper?
- What do readers expect from this kind of paper, and did I fulfill those expectations?

Self-assessment questions: What are the most significant strengths and weaknesses in this essay?

- Do I think others will also see these as important strengths or weaknesses? Why or why not?
- What specific ideas and plans do I have for revision?

Student Example of a Single Reflection

In the following companion piece, a student, Jaime, writes about what she sees as the strengths and weaknesses of an exploratory essay in which she was asked to pose a question raised but not clearly answered in a collection of essays on issues of race and class. (She posed the question: "What motivates people to behave as they do?") She was then asked to investigate various perspectives on the question that were offered by the readings, to consider other perspectives drawn from her own knowledge and experience, and to assess the strengths and weaknesses of differing points of view.

Jaime's Single Reflection

Although this paper was harder than the first one, I believe I have a good opening question. I like how I divided her [the author of the essays] ideas about motivation into two parts—individual and social. I also like how I used examples from many different essays (this proves I really read the whole book!). Another thing I like about this essay is how I include some examples of my own, like the Michael Jordan example of how he did not make the basketball team in his freshman year and that motivated him to practice every day for a year before making the team his sophomore year. I wonder if he ever would have been as good as he is if he had made the team his freshman year? I wish I could or would have added more of my own examples like this one.

What I'm not sure about is if I later ask too many other questions, like when I ask, "If someone is doing something because of society's pressures, is he responsible for that behavior?" and "How much are we responsible to other people like the homeless?" I felt that I piled up questions, and also felt I drifted from my original questions. The paper was confusing for me to write, and I feel that it jumps around. Maybe it doesn't, but I don't know.

Since *Alchemy* [the title of the essay collection] was such a hard book, I'm kind of happy with my paper (although after hearing some of the others in my peer group, I don't know if it's up to par!!).

For Writing and Discussion

Working as a whole class or in small groups, consider the following questions:

1. To what extent does this reflection show that Jaime has deepened her thinking about the question "What motivates people to behave as they do?"
2. Where does Jaime show an awareness of audience and purpose in her self-reflection on her essay?

3. To what extent does Jaime show us that she can identify strengths and weaknesses of her essay?
4. What are Jaime's most important insights about her essay?
5. How would you characterize Jaime's voice in this reflection? Does this voice seem appropriate for this kind of reflective writing? Why or why not?
6. What are the greatest strengths and weaknesses in Jaime's single reflection?

Comprehensive Reflection Assignments

You may also be asked to write a final, comprehensive reflection on your development as a writer over a whole term. Although end-of-the-term reflective essays differ in scope and audience from single reflections, similar qualities are valued in both: selectivity, specificity, dialectical thinking, and adequate detail.

In some cases, the reflective essay will introduce the contents of a final portfolio; in other cases, this will be a stand-alone assignment. Either way, your goal is to help your readers understand more knowledgeably how you developed as a writer. Most important, in explaining what you have learned from this review of your work, you also make new self-discoveries.

Guidelines for Comprehensive Reflection Assignments

Instructors look for four kinds of knowledge in comprehensive reflections: self-knowledge, content knowledge, rhetorical knowledge, and critical knowledge or judgment. Here we suggest questions that you can use to generate ideas for your comprehensive reflective letter or essay. Choose only a few of the questions to respond to, questions that allow you to explain and demonstrate your most important learning of the course. Also, choose experiences to narrate and passages to cite that illustrate more than one kind of knowledge.

Self-Knowledge
By *self-knowledge,* we mean your understanding of how you are developing as a writer. Think about the writer you were, are, or hope to be. You can also contemplate how the subjects you have chosen to write about (or the way you have approached your subjects) relate to you personally beyond the scope of your papers. Self-knowledge questions you might ask are the following:

- What knowledge of myself as a writer have I gained from the writing I did in this course?
- What changes, if any, have occurred in my writing practices or my sense of myself as a writer?
- What patterns or discontinuities can I identify between the way I approached one writing project versus another?
- How can I best illustrate and explain the self-knowledge I have gained through reference to specific writing projects?

Content Knowledge

Content knowledge refers to what you have learned by writing about various subjects. It also includes the intellectual work that has gone into the writing and the insights gained from considering multiple points of view and from grappling with your own conflicting ideas. Perhaps you have grasped ideas about your subjects that you have not shown in your papers. These questions about content knowledge can prod your thinking:

- ▨ What kinds of content complexities did I grapple with this semester?
- ▨ What *earned insights** did I arrive at through confronting clashing ideas?
- ▨ What new perspectives did I gain about particular subjects from my considerations of multiple or alternate viewpoints?
- ▨ What new ideas or perspectives did I gain that may not be evident in the essays themselves?
- ▨ What passages from various essays best illustrate the critical thinking I did in my writing projects for this course?

Rhetorical Knowledge

Our third category, *rhetorical knowledge,* focuses on your awareness of your rhetorical decisions—how your contemplation of purpose, audience, and genre affected your choices about content, structure, style, and document design. The following questions about rhetorical choices can help you assess this area of your knowledge:

- ▨ What important rhetorical choices did I make in various essays to accomplish my purpose or to appeal to my audience? What passages from my various essays best illustrate these choices? Which of these choices are particularly effective and why? About which choices am I uncertain and why?
- ▨ What have I learned about the rhetorical demands of audience, purpose, and genre, and how has that knowledge affected my writing and reading practices?
- ▨ How do I expect to use this learning in the future?

Critical Knowledge or Judgment

A fourth area of knowledge, *critical knowledge* or *judgment,* concerns your awareness of significant strengths and weaknesses in your writing. This area also encompasses your ability to identify what you like or value in various pieces of writing and to explain why. You could ask yourself these questions about your critical knowledge:

- ▨ Of the papers in my portfolio, which is the best and why? Which is the weakest paper and why?
- ▨ How has my ability to identify strengths and weaknesses changed during this course?

*Thomas Newkirk, in *Critical Thinking and Writing: Reclaiming the Essay* (Urbana, IL: NCTE, 1989), coined the phrase "earned insights," a phrase that Donna Qualley also refers to in *Turns of Thought: Teaching Composition as Reflexive Inquiry* (Portsmouth, NH: Boynton/Cook, Heinemann, 1997), pp. 35–37.

- What role has peer, instructor, or other reader feedback had on my assessments of my work?
- What improvements would I make in the enclosed papers if I had more time?
- How has my writing changed over the term? What new abilities will I take away from this course?
- What are the most important things I still have to work on as a writer?
- What is the most important thing I have learned in this course?
- How do I expect to use what I've learned from this course in the future?

THE WRITING PORTFOLIO AS AN OPPORTUNITY FOR REFLECTIVE SELF-EVALUATION

Assembling a portfolio of your writing at the end of a composition course, in which you are invited to select and present what work you think best shows your progress or what work represents your best writing for the term, engages you deeply in reflective self-evaluation. Typically, writing portfolios include a reflective letter or essay in which you discuss your portfolio choices and the learning they represent.

Portfolios offer many advantages to writers. You have more time to revise before presenting your work for evaluation since many instructors who assign portfolios do not assign grades to individual drafts. Through your comprehensive reflection, you can assess and comment on your writing and learning before someone else passes judgment. Further, the portfolio process helps you develop the metacognitive insights we mentioned earlier in this chapter, insights that can help you transfer this learning to new writing situations. Finally, this experience can prepare you for work-related tasks because portfolios are increasingly used in job applications as well as in assessments for job promotions or merit-based increases.

Specific guidelines for preparing a writing portfolio vary from course to course, so you will need to check with each individual instructor for directions about what to include and how to organize your portfolio. You may be given a lot of choice in what you include in your portfolio, or you may be required to submit a specific number or type of work. You may be asked to include only polished final essays, or you may be asked to include other work such as process work, multiple drafts, journal entries, peer responses, research notes, and so on. However, no matter what the specific requirements entail, the following general suggestions can help you manage the portfolio process.

Keeping Track of Your Work

Crucial to your success in assembling a portfolio is careful organization of your work throughout the term. This way, you will avoid the headache and wasted time caused by trying to hunt down lost or misplaced work. If you are in a conventional, non-computer-based course, we recommend that you purchase an accordion-type file folder to keep and organize all of your work for the course. You can use the dividers to separate your work for individual writing projects. Include everything that contributed to your work on a particular writing project: the original assignment sheet, process work, multiple drafts, peer response sheets, teacher comments, reflective writing about the project, research notes, photocopied research articles, and so on. In addition to careful organization and storage of your work, you need to date and label all work so that you can reconstruct your work on a particular project and identify which draft is second or third, which peer response goes with which draft, and so on.

If you are in a computer-based course where most of the work is submitted electronically, then your portfolio will take electronic form. In this case, you will need to develop an electronic storage system. Specifically, you will need to establish separate electronic files for all work related to specific writing projects and to save, label, and back up all of that work. You will probably want to save your work on a disk as well as on a hard drive. You may also have hard copy you need to save—say, of in-class handwritten peer responses. If this is the case, you will need to develop two storage systems.

Besides the practical need to keep track of all your work in order to review and select the writing that you will include in your portfolio, the process of saving and organizing your work causes you to attend to writing processes throughout the term, one of the key goals of portfolio teaching.

Selecting Work for Your Portfolio

Even if you are given explicit instructions about the number and type of writing to include in your portfolio, you will still have important choices to make about which completed pieces to include or which pieces to revise for inclusion. We suggest three general guidelines to consider as you review your writing and select work for your portfolio presentation.

■ *Variety:* One purpose of portfolio assessment is to offer a fuller picture of a writer's abilities. Therefore, it is important that you choose work that demonstrates your versatility—your ability to make effective rhetorical choices according to purpose, audience, and genre. What combination of writing samples best illustrates your ability to write effectively for different rhetorical situations?

■ *Course Goals:* A second consideration is course goals. The goals are likely to be stated in the course syllabus and may include such things as "ability to demonstrate critical thinking in writing"; "ability to use multiple strategies for generating ideas, drafting, revising, and editing"; and "ability to demonstrate control over surface features such as syntax, grammar, punctuation, and spelling." Which pieces of writing most clearly demonstrate the abilities given as your course's goals or which pieces can be revised to offer such a demonstration?

■ *Personal Investment:* Finally, be sure to consider which pieces of writing best reflect your personal investment and interest. If you are going to be revising the selected pieces multiple times during the last few weeks of class, you want to make sure you choose work that holds your interest and has ideas you care about. Which pieces are you proudest of? Which were the most challenging or satisfying to write? Which present ideas you'd like to explore further?

Writing a Comprehensive Reflective Letter

Because the letter (sometimes an essay) that you write to introduce your portfolio shows your insights not only about your writing abilities but also about your abilities as a reflective learner, it may be one of the most important pieces of writing you do for the course. Earlier in this chapter, we offered guidelines for writing a comprehensive reflection. Here we offer some additional suggestions geared specifically toward introducing your writing portfolio:

■ Review the single reflections you have written about specific writing projects during the term. As you reread these process-log entries, writer's memos, companion pieces, and so on, what do you discover about yourself as a writer?

■ Consider key rhetorical concepts and terms that you have learned in this course. Use this book's index to refresh your memory about these concepts. How can you show that you understand these terms and have applied them in your writing?

■ Take notes on your own writing as you review your work and reconstruct your writing processes for particular writing projects. What patterns do you see? What surprises you? How can you show the process behind the product? How can you show your growth as a writer through specific examples?

■ Be honest. Identifying weaknesses is as important as identifying strengths. How can you use this opportunity to discover more about yourself as a writer or learner?

Student Example of a Comprehensive Reflective Letter

Now let's look at the draft of a reflective letter written by a student, Bruce, for a second-semester composition course that involved a large-scale portfolio assessment. Bruce's portfolio as a whole will be read and scored (Pass or Fail) by two outside readers (and a third if the first two disagree). The contents of Bruce's portfolio include two essays written outside of class and revised extensively and one essay written in class under test conditions. As his letter suggests, his two out-of-class essays were classical arguments (see Chapter 15) written in response to the nonfiction texts that his class read during the semester. The assignment he was given for this comprehensive reflection is similar to the one on pages 715–716.

Dear Portfolio Reader:

This is my first college course in five years. I left school for financial reasons and a career opportunity that I couldn't pass up. I thought of contesting the requirement of this course because I had completed its equivalent back in 1993. But, as I reflected on the past few years, I realized that the only books I have read have been manuals for production machinery. My writing has consisted of shorthand, abbreviated notes that summarize a shift's events. Someday, after I finish my degree and move up in my company, I'm going to have to write a presentation to the directors on why we should spend millions of dollars on new machinery to improve productivity. I need this course if I expect to make a persuasive case.

I was very intimidated after I read the first book in the course, *No Contest: The Case Against Competition,* by Alfie Kohn. The author used what seemed to me a million outside sources to hammer home his thesis that competition is unhealthy in our society and that cooperation is the correct route. I felt very frustrated with Kohn and found myself disagreeing with him although I wasn't always sure why. I actually liked many of his ideas, but he seemed so detached from his argument. Kohn's sources did all the arguing for him. I tried to take a fresh perspective by writing about my own personal experience. I also used evidence from an interview I conducted with a school psychologist to back up my argument about the validity of my own experiences with cooperative education. The weakness of this paper is my lack of opposing opinions.

For my second essay, on Terry Tempest Williams's *Refuge: An Unnatural History of Family and Place,* I certainly could not use any personal experience. Williams, a Mormon woman, writes about the deaths of her mother, grandmother, and other female relatives from breast cancer, believed to be caused by the atomic testing in Utah. I argued that the author, Williams, unfairly blamed men and the role women play in the Mormon religion for the tragic death of her mother and other relatives. She thinks that if the Mormon Church had not discouraged women from questioning authority, maybe some of them would have protested the nuclear testing. But I think this reasoning ignores the military and government pressures at the time and the fact that women in general didn't have much power back in the 50s. Since I didn't know anything about the subject, I asked a Mormon woman that I know to comment on these ideas. Also, my critique group in class was comprised of myself and three women. I received quite a bit of verbal feedback from them on this essay. I deal with men at work all day. This change, both for this essay and the entire semester, was welcome.

In-class, timed essay writing was my biggest downfall. I have not been trained to develop an idea and present support for it on the fly. Thoughts would race through my head as I tried to put them on paper. I thought I was getting better, but the in-class essay in this portfolio is just awful. I really wish I could have had more practice in this area. I'm just not comfortable with my writing unless I've had lots of time to reflect on it.

A few weeks ago, I found a disk that had some of my old papers from years ago stored on it. After reading some of them, I feel that the content of my writing has improved since then. I know my writing has leaped huge steps since my first draft back in September. As a student not far from graduation, I know I will value the skills practiced in this course.

For Writing and Discussion

Working individually or in groups, discuss your responses to the following questions:

1. What kinds of self-knowledge does Bruce display in his reflective letter?

2. Does Bruce demonstrate dialectical thinking about himself as a writer? If so, where? What multiple writing selves does Bruce identify in his letter?

3. What has Bruce learned from writing about *No Contest* and *Refuge*? What specific examples does he give of "earned insights" or dialectical thinking regarding his subjects?

4. Does Bruce demonstrate his ability to make judgments about his essays' strengths and weaknesses?

5. What learning from this course do you think Bruce is likely to use in the future?

6. Which of the four kinds of writer's knowledge would you like Bruce to address more closely in revising this reflective letter? What kinds of questions does he overlook? Which points could he build up more? Where could his comments be more text specific and adequately detailed?

CHAPTER SUMMARY

In this chapter, we have introduced you to the value of reflective thinking as a path to self-discovery and improvement as a writer. We have shown how single reflections enable you to reexamine your writing processes, subject-matter choices, and rhetorical choices for individual pieces of writing, often with the goal of targeting problems to resolve in your revision of that writing. We have explained how comprehensive reflections, in contrast, sum up and give you more of a long-range, wide-angle view of your writing over the course of a term, encouraging you to consider your growth as a writer, your intellectual and personal discoveries as you wrestled with subjects, your understanding of the effectiveness of rhetorical choices, and the development of your critical reading and writing skills. Finally, we have shown how writing portfolios work and how they emphasize reflective learning. We have suggested ways to manage the portfolio process by organizing, selecting, and presenting your writing to display your progress in the course. Throughout this chapter, we have shown you the value of making your reflective writing selective, specific, dialectical, and adequately detailed.

 # WARNING

MANY VISITORS HAVE BEEN GORED BY BUFFALO

BUFFALO CAN WEIGH 2000 POUNDS AND CAN SPRINT AT 30 MPH, THREE TIMES FASTER THAN YOU CAN RUN

THESE ANIMALS MAY APPEAR TAME BUT ARE WILD, UNPREDICTABLE, AND DANGEROUS

DO NOT APPROACH BUFFALO

PART SIX

A Guide to Editing

Yellowstone National Park is the oldest national park in the country. Located in Wyoming, Montana, and Idaho, the park boasts "the largest concentration of free-ranging wildlife in the lower 48 states." In Yellowstone, "it is against the law to approach within 100 yards of bears and within 25 yards of other wildlife" (http://www.nps.gov/yell/planvisit/rules/impact.htm). At the park gates, rangers hand this $5^{1}/_{2}$-by-8-inch flyer, along with a map and park news, to visitors purchasing a pass to enter the park.

To discuss and analyze this flyer, see the questions in the section entitled "Using the Part Opener Images" that follows the Preface.

HANDBOOK 1

Improving Your Editing Skills

WHY EDITING IS IMPORTANT

In our discussion of the writing process in Chapter 18, we recommend saving editing for last. We do so not because editing is unimportant but because fine-tuning a manuscript requires that the main features of the text—its ideas and organization—be relatively stable. There is no point in correcting mistakes in a passage that is going to be deleted or completely rewritten.

Of course, no text is completely stable. During the late stages of editing, you may well make some revisions by moving sentences, by rewriting passages to improve clarity or coherence, or even by reformulating an entire section. Eventually, however, you will reach a stage at which you focus primarily on finding and eliminating errors—catching a nonparallel construction, untangling a garbled sentence, deciding between a comma and a semicolon, repairing sentence fragments, or double-checking the spelling of an author's name.

This late-stage concern for clarity and correctness is a crucial part of the writing process because editing and proofreading errors reflect directly on your *ethos*, that is, on the reader's image of you as a writer. The problem with sentence-level errors is that they inevitably show up to embarrass us whenever we let our guard down. They are like the grinning tricks of an Idiot Twin Sibling in Algonquin mythology. This character is a screwup, an oaf, a goofmeister who can take over when you're not alert. Remember when you stood in front of your eighth-grade class to deliver that stirring science report on fish parasites? After a few minutes you noticed that a lot of your classmates were inexplicably snickering. When you returned to your desk, Velda Sleeth, whom you'd worshiped from afar for six months, said in a stage whisper, "You might want to pick that big hunk of lettuce outta your teeth, John." Well, that lettuce was the work of your Idiot Twin Sibling.

Think of editing and proofreading as a way to foil this jokester's attempts at undermining your successes. If you're writing something with real-world consequences—a job application letter, a grant proposal, a letter to a client, a field report for your boss—then typos, misspellings, sentence fragments, and dangling participles are like a piece of lettuce between your teeth. Instead of focusing on your message, your readers may not even take you seriously enough to finish reading what you have written.

Another reason to edit is more existential than rhetorical. It has to do with the care we devote to the details of something that matters to us. In Robert Pirsig's philosophical novel about writing, *Zen and the Art of Motorcycle Maintenance,* editing and

733

proofreading belong to the "motorcycle maintenance" side of writing, not to the Zen side. For Pirsig, motorcycle maintenance is a metaphor for the unglamorous but essential aspect of any thoughtful enterprise. It requires discipline; you must give yourself up to the object before you, whether it is a motorcycle, a philosophical system, or the draft of an essay. Editing and proofreading, like motorcycle maintenance, require us to focus painstakingly on the parts. It can seem unrelentingly, oppressively nitpicky, but in a complex engine or complex essay, misfires and mistakes among the parts keep the whole from realizing its full potential. Even if you are the only one aware of these failures, you gain an innate satisfaction in making the parts function perfectly—the sort of satisfaction that carries over into larger pursuits.

OVERVIEW OF THIS GUIDE TO EDITING

We are not about to call this guide "The Joy of Grammar" or "Zen and the Art of Punctuation." But we do believe that you will find satisfaction in gaining control over the details of sentence structure and punctuation. The six handbook chapters of this guide are intended to help you master various aspects of editing.

In the rest of this chapter, Handbook 1, we suggest ways to improve your editing processes. The chapter concludes with a series of short microthemes that your instructor might use for writing assignments, group miniprojects, or in-class problem-solving tasks.

Handbook 2, "Understanding Sentence Structure," provides a brief review of grammar, including a discussion of sentence patterns, parts of speech, and various kinds of phrases and clauses. Knowledge of these primary sentence elements will help you better apply the principles of punctuation and usage presented throughout this editing guide.

Handbook 3, "Punctuating Boundaries of Sentences, Clauses, and Phrases," describes the main punctuation system for signaling to readers where sentences begin and end and for guiding them through the internal structure of sentences. We focus on three common sentence-boundary problems—fragments, run-ons, and comma splices. We also describe how writers use internal punctuation to signal the boundaries of clauses and phrases.

Handbook 4, "Editing for Standard English Usage," focuses on the most common kinds of sentence-level errors: grammatical tangles, errors in agreement and consistency, lack of parallel structure, dangling or misplaced modifiers, and other errors in the use of pronouns, verbs, adjectives, and adverbs.

Handbook 5, "Editing for Style," explains how to make your prose more lively and readable. We offer suggestions for pruning your prose (by eliminating wordiness), enlivening it (by avoiding nominalizations and clichés and adding sentence variety and details), and making it more coherent (by putting old information before new). In the chapter we also review the active and passive voice and provide guidelines for using inclusive language.

Finally, Handbook 6, "Editing for Punctuation and Mechanics," presents a comprehensive overview of the rules governing the use of terminal punctuation or endmarks, commas, semicolons, colons, dashes, and other punctuation marks. The chapter concludes with a brief discussion of manuscript form.

IMPROVING YOUR EDITING AND PROOFREADING PROCESSES

You can become a more attentive editor and proofreader of your own prose if you practice the kinds of editing strategies we suggest in this section.

Keep a List of Your Own Characteristic Errors

When one of your papers is returned, look carefully at the kinds of sentence-level errors noted by your instructor. A paper with numerous errors might actually contain only two or three *kinds* of errors repeated several times. For example, some writers consistently omit apostrophes from possessives or add them to plurals; others regularly create comma splices when they use such words as *therefore* or *however* at the beginning of an independent clause. Try to classify the kinds of errors you made on the paper, and then try to avoid these errors on your next paper.

Do a Self-Assessment of Your Editing Knowledge

Look over the detailed table of contents for this editing guide and note the various topics covered. Which of these topics are familiar to you from previous instruction? In which areas are you most confident? In which areas are you most shaky? We generally recommend that students study the topics in Handbook 3 early in a course because the chapter explains the main punctuation codes that let you avoid fragments and comma splices and that help you make decisions about comma placement within a sentence. The remaining handbook chapters can function as handy references when specific questions arise. Become familiar with the organization of this guide so that you can find information rapidly.

Read Your Draft Aloud

A key to good editing is noting every word. An especially helpful strategy is to read your paper aloud—really aloud, not half-aloud, mumbling to yourself, but at full volume, as if you were reading to a room full of people. When you stumble over a sentence or have to go back to fit sound to sense, mark the spot. Something is probably wrong there and you will want to return to it later. Make sure that the words you read aloud are actually on the page. When reading aloud, people often unconsciously fill in missing words or glide over mispunctuated passages, so check carefully to see that what you say matches what you wrote. Some writers like to read aloud into a tape recorder and then reread their draft silently while playing back the recording. If you haven't tried the tape recorder technique, consider doing so at least once; it is a surprisingly powerful way to improve your editing skills.

Read Your Draft Backward

Another powerful editing technique—strange as it might seem—is to read your paper backward, word by word, from end to beginning. When you read forward, you tend to focus on meaning and often read right past mistakes. Reading backward estranges you from the paper's message and allows you to focus on the details of the essay—the words and sentences. As you read backward, keep a dictionary and this handbook close by. Focus on each word, looking for typos, spelling errors, misused apostrophes, pronoun case errors, and so forth, and attend to each sentence unit, making sure that it is a complete sentence and that its boundaries have been properly marked with punctuation.

See Handbook 3.

Use a Spell Checker and (Perhaps) Other Editing Programs

The advent of powerful spell checkers means that if you have access to a computer, you have almost no excuse for including misspelled words or typos in a formal paper. Become a skilled operator of your computer's spell checker, and always allow yourself time to run the program before printing your final draft.

Be aware, however, that a spell checker isn't foolproof. These programs match strings of letters in a document against strings stored in memory. A spell checker may not contain some of the specialized words you use (authors' names or special course terms), nor can it tell whether a correctly spelled word is used correctly in context (*it's, its; their, there,* or *they're; to, too,* or *two*).

Many writers use "grammar" checkers, also called *style* or *usage* checkers. We place "grammar" in quotation marks because these programs do not really check grammar. They can perform only countable or matchable functions such as identifying *be* verbs and passive constructions, noting extremely long sentences, identifying clichés and wordy expressions, and so forth. Although these programs can be useful by drawing your attention to some areas where you may be able to tighten or enliven your prose, they have to be used with caution. So-called grammar checkers can't catch most of the most common errors in usage and grammar that writers make, and they often flag nonexistent problems.

Summary

We have explained that careful editing and proofreading are important, not only to improve the clarity of your writing but also to ensure that you project an ethos of professionalism and responsibility. We have suggested several ways to improve your editing processes: keep track of your own characteristic errors; do a self-assessment of your editing knowledge; read your draft aloud; read your draft backward; and run your draft through a spell checking program (and perhaps a grammar checking program as well).

MICROTHEME PROJECTS ON EDITING

The following microtheme assignments focus on selected problems of editing and style. Since you never know a concept as well as when you have to teach it to someone else, these assignments place you in a teaching role. They ask you to solve an editing problem and to explain your solution in your own words to a hypothetical audience that has turned to you for instruction.

Your instructor can use these microtheme assignments as individual or group writing projects or as prompts for classroom discussion.

Microtheme 1: Apostrophe Madness

Your friend Elmer Fuddnick has decided to switch majors from engineering to creative writing. Poor Elmer has a great imagination, but he forgot to study basic punctuation when he was in high school. He's just sent you the first draft of his latest short story, "The Revenge of the Hedgehogs." Here are his opening sentences.

> The hedgehogs' scrambled from behind the rock's at the deserts edge, emitted what sounded like a series of cats scream's and then rolled themselve's into spiny balls. One of the hedgehogs hunched it's back and crept slowly toward a cactus' shadow.

Although you can't wait to finish Elmer's story, you are a bit annoyed by his misuse of apostrophes. Your job is to explain to Elmer how to use apostrophes correctly. Begin by correcting Elmer's sentences; then explain to Elmer the principles you used to make your corrections. Your explanation of apostrophes should be clear enough so that Elmer can learn their use from your explanation. In other words, you are the teacher. Use your own language and make up your own examples.

Microtheme 2: Stumped by *However*

You are putting yourself through college by operating an online grammar hot line and charging people for your advice. One day you receive the following e-mail message:

> Dear Grammarperson:
>
> I get really confused on how to punctuate words like "however" and "on the other hand." Sometimes these words have commas on both sides of them, but at other times they have a comma in back and a semicolon in front. What's the deal here? How can I know whether to use a comma or a semicolon in front of a "however"?
>
> Bewildered in Boston

Write a response to Bewildered explaining why words such as *however* are sometimes preceded by a comma and sometimes by a semicolon (or a period, in which case *however* starts with a capital letter). Use your own language and invent your own examples.

Microtheme 3: The Comic Dangler

Here is another message received at the grammar hot line (see Microtheme 2).

> Dear Grammarperson:
>
> My history teacher was telling us the other day that editing our papers before we submitted them was really important. And then she mentioned in passing that some editing mistakes often create comic effects. She said that the dangling participle was her favorite because it often produced really funny sentences. Well, maybe so, but I didn't know what she was talking about. What are dangling participles and why are they funny?
>
> Not Laughing in Louisville

Explain to Not Laughing what dangling participles are and why they are often funny. Illustrate with some examples of your own and then show Not Laughing how to correct them.

Microtheme 4: How's That Again?
The grammar hot line is doing a great business (see Microtheme 2). Here is another e-mail message.

> Dear Grammarperson:
>
> It has often been said by some instructors that I have had in the various educational institutions that I have attended that a deadening effect is achievable in the prose produced by writers through the transformation of verbs into nouns and through the overuse of words that are considered empty in content or otherwise produce a redundant effect by the restating of the same idea in more words than are necessary for the reader's understanding of the aforementioned ideas. Could these teachers' allegations against the sentence structure of many writers be considered to be at least partially true in the minds of those persons who read these writers' prose?
>
> Verbose in Vermont

Help Verbose out by rewriting this question in a crisper style. Then explain briefly, using your own language and examples, the concepts of wordiness and nominalization.

Microtheme 5: The Intentional Fragment
Advertisers frequently use sentence fragments purposely. Find an advertisement that makes extensive use of fragments in its copy. Rewrite the copy to eliminate all sentence fragments. Then write a one-paragraph microtheme in which you speculate why the advertiser used fragments rather than complete sentences. Try to suggest at least two possible reasons.

Microtheme 6: Create Your Own
Following the model of the five preceding assignments, create your own microtheme assignment on an editing problem related to any section of this handbook (or to a section assigned by your instructor). Then exchange assignments with a classmate and write a microtheme in response to your classmate's assignment. Be prepared to write a microtheme in response to your own assignment also.

HANDBOOK 2

Understanding Sentence Structure

This chapter provides a basic review of English grammar. Throughout, we emphasize that you already have an innate understanding of grammar, based on your ability to speak and understand English. In this chapter we want to give you a more conscious understanding of the structures you subconsciously use all the time. We also introduce some useful terms and labels that will facilitate your learning of the rules for usage and punctuation. Handbook 2 covers the following elements:

- An explanation of your innate knowledge of grammar
- The concept of the sentence
- Basic sentence patterns
- Parts of speech
- Types of phrases
- Types of clauses
- Types of sentences

WHAT YOU ALREADY KNOW ABOUT GRAMMAR

By *grammar* we mean the set of rules in any language for combining words into patterns that can convey meanings. In English, these rules govern both the order of words and the endings added to words. Students often complain that they don't understand grammar. The truth is that you learned grammar when you learned to talk. If you didn't know grammar, neither of the following groups of words would make sense:

1. Complain don't that grammar often they understand all at students.
2. Students often complain that they don't understand grammar at all.

If sentence 2 makes more sense to you than sentence 1, you understand English grammar; that is, you understand the required order of English words ("The dog chased the cat" has a different meaning from "The cat chased the dog"), and you understand the meaning of endings placed on words (*cats* is different from *cat, chased* from *chase*). What people mean when they say they don't understand grammar is that they don't understand the terms that language teachers use to describe grammatical structures, even though they internalized those structures when they first learned to talk. Be aware that you know English grammar at a much deeper level than you may appreciate—far deeper than any computer has yet been programmed to understand it. You can rely on that innate knowledge of grammar to help you understand the terms and concepts covered in the rest of this chapter.

THE CONCEPT OF THE SENTENCE

The *sentence* is perhaps the most crucial grammatical concept for writers to understand. A sentence is a group of related words with a complete subject and a complete predicate. The subject names something, and the predicate makes an assertion about the thing named.

Name Something	Make an Assertion about It
Cheese	tastes good on crackers.
Lizards and snakes	are both kinds of reptiles.
Capital punishment	has been outlawed in many countries.

Every sentence must include at least one subject and one predicate. These components answer two different questions: (1) Who or what is the sentence about? (subject); and (2) What assertion does the sentence make about the subject? (predicate). Consider the following example:

Tree ants in Southeast Asia construct nests by sewing leaves together.

What is this sentence about? *Tree ants in Southeast Asia* (subject). What assertion is made about tree ants? (They) *construct nests by sewing leaves together* (predicate).

Grammarians sometimes distinguish between simple and complete subjects and between simple and complete predicates. A simple subject is the single word or phrase that the sentence is about. In our example, *ants* is the simple subject and *tree ants in Southeast Asia* is the complete subject (the simple subject plus all its modifiers). A simple predicate is the main verb (along with its helping or auxiliary verbs) that makes the assertion about the subject. In our example, *construct* is the simple predicate (the verb) and *construct nests by sewing leaves together* is the complete predicate (the main verb plus modifiers and nouns needed to complete its meaning).

Ordinarily a sentence begins with the subject, followed by the verb. Sometimes, however, word order can be changed. In the following examples, the subjects are underlined once and the verbs are underlined twice.

Normal Word Order	The most terrifying <u>insects</u> <u>wander</u> through the countryside seeking prey.
Question	<u>What</u> <u>are</u> the most terrifying insects?
Imperative	<u>Watch</u> for the driver ants. ("You" is understood as the subject.)
"There" Opening	There <u>are</u> various <u>kinds</u> of terrifying insects.
Inverted Order	Across the jungles of Africa <u>marched</u> the driver <u>ants</u>.

Sentences can also have more than one subject or predicate.

Compound Subject	The army <u>ants</u> of South America and the driver <u>ants</u> of Africa <u>march</u> in long columns.
Compound Predicate	The <u>hunters</u> at the head of a column <u>discover</u> a prey, <u>swarm</u> all over it, and eventually <u>cut</u> it apart.

BASIC SENTENCE PATTERNS

All sentences must have a complete subject and a complete predicate. However, the predicates of sentences can take several different shapes, depending on whether the verb needs a following noun, pronoun, or adjective to complete its meaning. These words are called *complements*. The four kinds of complements are *direct objects, indirect objects, subject complements,* and *object complements.*

Pattern One: Subject + Verb (+ Optional Adverb Modifiers)

                               adverb modifiers

The <u>eagle</u> <u>soared</u> gracefully across the summer sky.

In this pattern, the predicate contains only a verb and optional adverbial modifiers. Because the verb in this pattern does not transfer any action from a doer to a receiver, it is called *intransitive.*

Pattern Two: Subject + Verb + Direct Object (DO)

                        DO

<u>Peter</u> <u>was fixing</u> a flat tire over in Bronco County at the very moment of the crime.

Direct objects occur with *transitive verbs,* which transfer action from a doer (the subject) to a receiver (the direct object). Transitive verbs don't seem complete in themselves; they need a noun or pronoun following the verb to answer the question What? or Whom? Peter was fixing *what? The flat tire.*

Pattern Three: Subject + Verb + Subject Complement (SC)

SC

My <u>mother</u> <u>is</u> a professor.

SC

The <u>engine</u> in this car <u>seems</u> sluggish.

In this pattern, verbs are *linking verbs,* which are followed by subject complements rather than direct objects. Unlike direct objects, which receive the action of the verb, subject complements either rename the subject (a noun) or describe the subject (an adjective). You can best understand a subject complement if you think of the linking verb as an equal sign (=).

Pattern Four: Subject + Verb + Direct Object + Object Complement (OC)

DO   OC

That <u>woman</u> <u>called</u> me an idiot.

Whereas a subject complement describes the subject of the sentence, an object complement describes the direct object, either by modifying it or by renaming it. Compare the patterns.

Pattern Three	SC I <u>am</u> an idiot.
Pattern Four	DO OC The <u>woman</u> <u>called</u> me an idiot.

Pattern Five: Subject + Verb + Indirect Object (IDO) + Direct Object

IDO   DO

My <u>mother</u> <u>sent</u> the professor an angry letter.

IDO DO

My <u>father</u> <u>baked</u> me a cake on Valentine's Day.

Sometimes transitive verbs take an *indirect object* as well as a direct object. Whereas the direct object answers the question What? or Whom? following the verb, the indirect object answers the question To what or whom? or For what or whom? My mother sent *what*? *A letter* (direct object). She sent a letter *to whom*? *The professor* (indirect object). My father baked what? *A cake* (direct object). My father baked a cake for whom? *For me* (indirect object).

PARTS OF SPEECH

Although linguists argue about the best way to classify the functions of words in a sentence, the traditional eight parts of speech listed here are most often used in dictionaries and basic introductions to grammar.

Parts of Speech

nouns (N)	adverbs (Adv)
pronouns (PN)	prepositions (P)
verbs (V)	conjunctions (C)
adjectives (Adj)	interjections (I)

Each part of speech serves a different function in a sentence and also possesses structural features that distinguish it from the other parts of speech. Because many words can serve as different parts of speech in different circumstances, you can determine what part of speech a word plays only within the context of the sentence you are examining.

Nouns

Nouns are the names we give to persons (Samuel, mechanic), places (Yellowstone, the forest), things (a rock, potatoes), and abstract concepts (love, happiness). Nouns can be identified by structure as words that follow the articles *a, an,* or *the*; as words that change their form to indicate number; and as words that change their form to indicate possession.

a rock   several rock*s*   the rock*'s* hardness

But not: a *from*; several *from*s; the *from*'s coat.

Pronouns

Pronouns take the place of nouns in sentences. The noun that a pronoun replaces is called the pronoun's *antecedent.* English has the following types of pronouns:

Type of Pronoun	Examples
Personal	I, me, you, he, him, she, her, it, we, us, they, them
Possessive (with Noun)	my, your, his, her, its, our, their
Possessive (no Noun)	mine, yours, his, hers, ours, theirs
Demonstrative	this, that, these, those
Indefinite	any, anybody, someone, everyone, each, nobody
Reflexive/Intensive	myself, yourself, himself, herself, itself, ourselves, yourselves, themselves
Interrogative	who, what, whom, whose, which, whoever, whomever
Relative	who, whom, whose, which, that

Verbs

Verbs are words that express action (*run, laugh*) or state of being (*is, seem*). Structurally, they change form to indicate tense and sometimes to indicate person and number. A word can function as a verb if it can fit the following frames:

I want to _____.   I will _____.

I want to *throw*.   I will *throw*.

But not: I want to *from;* I will *from*.

Verbs are used as complete verbs or as incomplete verbs, often called *verbals*. When used as complete verbs, they fill the predicate slot in a sentence. When used as incomplete verbs, they fill a noun's, adjective's, or adverb's slot in a sentence. Verbs often require helping verbs, also called *auxiliary verbs,* to fulfill their function.

Person and Number

In many instances, verbs change form to agree with the person or number of the subject.

Person	Singular	Plural
First person	I give. I am giving.	We give. We are giving.
Second person	You give. You are giving.	You give. You are giving.
Third person	He (she, it) gives.	They give. They are giving.
	He (she, it) is giving.	

Principal Parts

Verbs have five principal parts, which vary depending on whether the verb is *regular* or *irregular.*

Principal Part	Regular Verb Examples	Irregular Verb Examples
Infinitive or Present Stem (infinitives begin with *to;* the word following the *to* is the *present stem*)	to love to borrow	to begin to get
Present Stem + -*s* (used for third-person singular, present tense)	loves borrows	begins gets
Past Stem (regular verbs add -*ed* to present stem; irregular verbs have different form)	loved borrowed	began got
Past Participle (same as past stem for regular verbs; usually a different form for irregular verbs)	loved borrowed	begun gotten
Present Participle (add -*ing* to present stem)	loving borrowing	beginning getting

The irregular verb *to be* has more forms than do other verbs.

Infinitive	to be
Present Forms	am, is, are
Past Forms	was, were
Past Participle	been
Present Participle	being

Tenses

Verbs change their forms to reflect differences in time. A verb's time is called its *tense.* There are six main tenses, each with three forms, sometimes called *aspects*— simple, progressive, and emphatic. For two of the tenses—the simple present and simple past—a complete verb is formed by using one word only. For all other tenses, two or more words are needed to form a complete verb. The additional words are called *helping,* or *auxiliary,* verbs. In some tenses the main verb or one of the helping verbs changes form to agree with its subject in person and number.

See pp. 765–768 on subject-verb agreement.

Simple Form. Here are regular and irregular examples of the simple form of the six main tenses.

Simple Present	She *enjoys* the pizza. They *begin* the race.
Simple Past	She *enjoyed* the pizza. They *began* the race.
Simple Future	She *will enjoy* the pizza. They *will begin* the race.
Present Perfect	She *has enjoyed* the pizza. They *have begun* the race.
Past Perfect	She *had enjoyed* the pizza. They *had begun* the race.
Future Perfect	She *will have enjoyed* the pizza. They *will have begun* the race.

Progressive Form. Each tense also has a progressive form to indicate actions that are ongoing or in-process.

Present Progressive	Sally *is eating* her sandwich.
Past Progressive	Sally *was eating* her sandwich.
Future Progressive	Sally *will be eating* her sandwich.
Present Perfect Progressive	Sally *has been eating* her sandwich.
Past Perfect Progressive	Sally *had been eating* her sandwich.
Future Perfect Progressive	Sally *will have been eating* her sandwich.

Emphatic Form. Several tenses have an emphatic form, which uses the helping verb *to do* combined with the present stem. The emphatic form is used for giving special stress, for asking questions, and for making negations.

I *do go.* I *did go.*

Did the dog *bark*?

Do you *like* peanuts?

The child *does* not *sit* still.

Modal Forms. Additionally, a variety of other helping verbs, often called *modals,* can be used to form complete verbs with different senses of time and attitude.

See the section on subjunctive mood, p. 746.

will, would	may, might
can, could	must
shall, should	

Mood

Verbs have three moods: indicative (by far the most common), subjunctive, and imperative. These three moods indicate the attitude of the writer toward the statement the verb makes.

Indicative Mood. The indicative mood is so common that you might call it the default mood. It is used for both statements and questions.

The dog *rode* in the back of the pickup. Where *is* Sally?

Subjunctive Mood. The subjunctive mood is used to indicate that a condition is contrary to fact and, in certain cases, to express desire, hope, or demand. The subjunctive is formed in the present tense by using the infinitive stem.

I request that Joe *pay* the bill.

Compare with the indicative: Joe *pays* the bill.

In the past tense, only the verb *to be* has a distinctive subjective form, which is always *were*.

If I *were* the teacher, I would give you an A for that project.

Here the subjunctive *were* means "I am *not* the teacher"; it expresses a condition contrary to fact.

The subjunctive frequently causes problems for writers in sentences with *if* clauses. If an *if* clause uses the indicative mood, then the independent clause uses the simple present or the simple future. However, if an *if* clause uses the subjunctive mood, then the independent clause uses a modal auxiliary such as *would, could, might,* or *should.*

Indicative in *If* Clause	If he *takes* chemistry from Dr. Jones, he *will learn* a great deal.
Subjunctive in *If* Clause	If he *were* a serious science student, he *would have taken* chemistry from Dr. Jones.

The subjunctive in the second sentence implies the following meaning: "He is not a serious science student, so he didn't take chemistry from Dr. Jones."

Imperative Mood. Finally, the imperative mood conveys a command or request. For most verbs the imperative form is the same as the second-person present tense. An exception is the verb *to be,* which uses *be.*

Be here by noon. *Pay* the bill immediately.

Voice

The voice of a verb indicates whether the subject of the verb acts or is acted on. The concept of voice applies only to *transitive* verbs, which transfer action from a doer to a receiver. In the active voice, the subject is the doer of the action and the direct object is the receiver.

Active Voice   The professor graded the paper.

For advice on when to use active and passive voice, see pp. 784–785.

In the passive voice, the subject is the receiver of the action; the actor is either omitted from the sentence or made the object of the preposition *by.* The passive voice is formed with the past participle and some form of the helping verb *to be.*

Passive Voice   The paper was graded (by the professor).

Adjectives and Adverbs

Adjectives and adverbs describe or *modify* other words.

Adjectives

Adjectives modify nouns by answering such questions as Which one? (*those* rabbits); What kind? (*gentle* rabbits); How many? (*four* rabbits); What size? (*tiny* rabbits); What color? (*white* rabbits); What condition? (*contented* rabbits); and Whose? (*Jim's* rabbits).

Articles (*a, an, the*) form a special class of adjectives. *A* and *an* are indefinite and singular, referring to any representative member of a general class of objects.

I would like *an* apple and *a* sandwich.

The is definite and can be singular or plural. It always specifies that a particular object is meant.

I want *the* apple and *the* sandwich that were sitting on my desk a few minutes ago.

Adverbs

Adverbs modify verbs, adjectives, or other adverbs. They answer the questions How? (he petted the rabbit *gently*); How often? (he petted the rabbit *frequently*); Where? (he petted the rabbit *there* in the corner of the room); When? (he petted the rabbit *early*); and To what degree? (he petted the rabbit *very* gently).

Conjunctive adverbs, such as *therefore, however,* and *moreover,* modify whole clauses by showing logical relationships between clauses or sentences.

Positive, Comparative, and Superlative Forms

A distinctive structural feature of adjectives and adverbs is that they take positive, comparative, and superlative forms.

Positive	This is a *quick* turtle. It moves *quickly.*
Comparative	My turtle is *quicker* than yours. It moves *more quickly* than yours.
Superlative	Of the three turtles, mine is the *quickest.* Of all the turtles in the race, mine moves *most quickly.*

Conjunctions

Conjunctions join elements within a sentence. *Coordinating* conjunctions (*and, or, nor, but, for, yet,* and *so*) join elements of equal importance.

John *and* Mary went to town.

The city rejoiced, *for* the rats had finally been exterminated.

Subordinating conjunctions (such as *when, unless, if, because, after, while, although*) turn an independent sentence into a subordinate clause and then join it to an independent clause.

For more on coordinating and subordinating conjunctions, see pp. 754–755.

After I get off work, I will buy you a soda.

She won't show him how to use the Internet *unless* he apologizes.

If you are going to the city, please get me a new CD at Caesar's.

Prepositions

Prepositions show the relationship between a noun or pronoun (the object of the preposition) and the rest of the sentence. The preposition and its object together are called a *prepositional phrase*. Common prepositions include *about, above, across, among, behind, between, from, in, into, of, on, toward,* and *with*.

The cat walked *under* the table.

The vase was *on* the table.

The table is a mixture *of* cherry and walnut woods.

Interjections

Interjections (*Yippee! Baloney! Ouch!*) are forceful expressions, usually followed by exclamation marks, that express emotion. They can be removed from a sentence without affecting the sentence grammatically.

Hooray, school's out! *Ah, shucks,* I'm sorry!

TYPES OF PHRASES

A phrase is a group of related words that does not contain a complete subject and a complete verb. There are four main kinds of phrases:

1. prepositional
2. appositive
3. verbal (participial, gerund, and infinitive)
4. absolute

Prepositional Phrases

A preposition connects a noun, pronoun, or group of words acting as a noun to the rest of the sentence, thereby creating a prepositional phrase that serves as a modifying element within the sentence. Prepositional phrases usually begin with the preposition and end with the noun or noun substitute, called the *object of the preposition*.

We watched the baby crawl *under the table*.

The man *in the gray suit* is my father.

Appositive Phrases

Appositive phrases give additional information about a preceding noun or pronoun. They sometimes consist of only one word.

Jill saw her friend *Susan* in the café.

We stopped for a mocha latte at Adolpho's, *the most famous espresso bar in the city.*

Verbal Phrases

Verbals are incomplete forms of verbs that can't function as predicates in a sentence. They function instead as other parts of speech—nouns, adjectives, and adverbs. Verbals are somewhat similar to verbs in that they can show tense and can take complements, but they also function as other parts of speech in that they fill noun, adjective, or adverb slots in a sentence. When a verbal is accompanied by modifiers or complements, the word group is called a *verbal phrase.* There are three kinds of verbals and verbal phrases:

1. participial
2. gerund
3. infinitive

Participial Phrases

Participles have two forms: the present participle and the past participle. The present participle is the *-ing* form (*swimming, laughing*); the past participle is the *-ed* form for regular verbs (*laughed*) and an irregular form for irregular verbs (*swum*). Participles and participial phrases always act as adjectives in a sentence. In the following examples, the noun modified by the participle is indicated by an arrow.

I saw some ducks *swimming in the lake.*

Laughing happily, Molly squeezed Jake's arm.

The 100-meter freestyle, a race *swum by more than twenty competitors last year,* was won by a thirteen-year-old boy.

Gerund Phrases

Gerunds are always the *-ing* form of the verb, and they always serve as nouns in a sentence.

Swimming is my favorite sport.   *[serves as subject]*

I love *swimming in the lake.*   *[serves as direct object]*

I am not happy about *losing my chemistry notebook in the student union.*   *[serves as object of preposition]*

Infinitive Phrases

An infinitive is the dictionary form of a verb preceded by the word *to* (*to run, to swim, to laugh*). Infinitives or infinitive phrases can serve as nouns, adjectives, or adverbs in a sentence.

To complete college with a major in electrical engineering is my primary goal at the moment.

The person *to help you with that math* is Molly Malone.

Absolute Phrases

An absolute phrase is comprised of a noun or noun substitute, followed by a participle. It is *absolute* because it doesn't act as a noun, adverb, or adjective; rather, it modifies the whole clause or sentence to which it is attached.

> *Her face flushed with sweat,* the runner headed down Grant Street.

> The secretary hunched over the keyboard, *his fingers typing madly.*

TYPES OF CLAUSES

Clauses have complete subjects and complete predicates. Some clauses can stand alone as sentences (*independent,* or *main,* clauses), whereas others (*dependent,* or *subordinate,* clauses) cannot stand alone as sentences because they are introduced by a *subordinating conjunction* or a *relative pronoun.*

Here are two independent sentences that could serve as independent clauses.

> Sam broke the window.

> Lucy studied the violin for thirteen years.

Now here are the same two sentences converted to subordinate clauses.

> because Sam broke the window

> who studied the violin for thirteen years

In the first example, the subordinating conjunction *because* reduces the independent clause to a subordinate clause. In the second example, the relative pronoun *who,* which replaces *Lucy,* also reduces the independent clause to a subordinate clause.

Finally, here are these subordinated clauses attached to independent clauses to form complete sentences.

> Because Sam broke the window, he had to pay for it out of his allowance.

> Lucy, who studied the violin for thirteen years, won a music scholarship to a prestigious college.

Subordinate clauses always act as nouns, adjectives, or adverbs in another clause.

Noun Clauses

A noun clause is a subordinate clause that functions as a noun in a sentence. Noun clauses act as subjects, objects, or complements.

> He promised *that he would study harder.*   *[serves as direct object]*

> *Why he came here* is a mystery.   *[serves as subject]*

> He lied about *what he did last summer.*   *[serves as object of preposition]*

Adjective Clauses

An adjective clause is a subordinate clause that modifies a noun or a pronoun. Adjective clauses are formed with the relative pronouns *who, whom, whose, which,* and *that.* For this reason they are sometimes called *relative clauses.*

> Peter, *who is a star athlete,* has trouble with reading.
>
> The future threat *that I most fear* is a stock market collapse.

Adverb Clauses

An adverb clause is a subordinate clause that modifies a verb, an adjective, or another adverb. Adverb clauses begin with subordinating conjunctions, such as *although, because, if,* and *when* (see p. 747 for a list of subordinating conjunctions).

> *Because he had broken his leg,* he danced all night using crutches.
>
> *When he got home,* he noticed unusual blisters.

TYPES OF SENTENCES

Sentences are often classified by the number and kinds of clauses they contain. There are four kinds of sentences:

1. simple
2. compound
3. complex
4. compound-complex

Simple Sentences

A sentence is *simple* if it consists of a single independent clause. The clause may contain modifying phrases and have a compound subject and a compound predicate.

> John laughed.
>
> John and Mary laughed and sang.
>
> modifying phrase
> Laughing happily and holding hands in the moonlight, John and Mary walked
> independent clause (with compound subject and predicate)
> along the beach, wrote their names in the sand, and threw pebbles into the crashing waves.

Compound Sentences

See the discussion of comma splices and run-ons, pp. 758–760.

A sentence is *compound* if it consists of two independent clauses linked either by a semicolon or by a comma and a coordinating conjunction. Each clause may contain modifying phrases as well as compound subjects and predicates.

independent clause   independent clause

John laughed, and Mary sang.

modifying phrase   independent clause (with compound subject)

Laughing happily, John and Mary walked hand in hand toward the kitchen, but

independent clause

they weren't prepared for the surprise on the countertop.

Complex Sentences

A sentence is *complex* if it contains one independent clause and one or more subordinate clauses.

independent clause   subordinate clause

John smiled to himself while Mary sang.

subordinate clause   independent clause

When John and Mary saw the surprise on the countertop, they screamed uncontrol-

subordinate clause

lably until John fainted.

Compound-Complex Sentences

A *compound-complex sentence* has at least one subordinate clause and two or more independent clauses joined by a semicolon or by a comma and a coordinating conjunction.

independent clause   subordinate clause   independent clause

John smiled to himself while Mary sang, for he was happy.

subordinate clause   independent clause

When John and Mary saw the surprise on the countertop, they screamed uncontrol-

independent clause

lably; soon John collapsed on the floor in a dead faint.

HANDBOOK 3

Punctuating Boundaries of Sentences, Clauses, and Phrases

Readers can quickly get lost if writers fail to signal sentence boundaries accurately. Readers also rely on internal punctuation, primarily commas, to help them recognize the boundaries of clauses and phrases within a sentence. Periods, capital letters, commas, and, occasionally, semicolons are to readers what stop signs and yield signs are to drivers: they guide the reader through the twists and turns of prose.

This chapter focuses on punctuation rules that help readers recognize the boundaries of sentences and of clauses and phrases within sentences. Here's what you'll find.

- A demonstration of why readers need punctuation
- Four basic punctuation rules for signaling internal sentence elements
- Guidelines for identifying and correcting sentence fragments
- Guidelines for identifying and correcting comma splices and run-on sentences
- A reference chart summarizing the rules for joining clauses within a sentence

Additional punctuation rules are covered in detail in Handbook 6.

You will have mastered the skills of this chapter if you can create sentences of your own that follow these patterns.

_____ . _____ .

_____ ; _____ .

_____ ; however, _____ .

_____ ; _____ , however, _____ .

_____ , and _____ .

_____ and _____ .

_____ , _____ .

Because_____ , _____ .

_____ because _____ .

WHY READERS NEED PUNCTUATION

To understand why it is important to punctuate sentence and clause boundaries, try to read the following passage:

> RECENTLY A GROWING NUMBER OF COMMENTATORS HAVE BEEN FOCUSING ON THE MENTALLY ILL HOMELESS IN RESPONSE TO THE VIOLENT MURDER OF AN ELDERLY PERSON BY A HOMELESS MENTALLY ILL MAN NEW YORK CITY RECENTLY INCREASED ITS EFFORTS TO LOCATE AND HOSPITALIZE DANGEROUS HOMELESS MENTALLY ILL INDIVIDUALS THEIR PLAN WILL INCLUDE AGGRESSIVE OUTREACH SUCH AS ACTIVELY GOING OUT INTO THE STREETS AND SHELTERS TO LOCATE MENTALLY ILL INDIVIDUALS AND THEN INVOLUNTARILY HOSPITALIZING THOSE DEEMED DANGEROUS ALTHOUGH MANY CRITICS OBJECT TO THIS APPROACH MANY APPLAUD THE CITY'S ACTION.

In this passage the use of all capital letters and the deletion of punctuation eliminates all visual clues for sentence boundaries. How many complete sentences do you find in this passage? Where do they begin and end?

RULES FOR PUNCTUATING CLAUSES AND PHRASES WITHIN A SENTENCE

If writers used nothing but short, simple sentences, a capital letter and a period would suffice to signal sentence structure. But when writers combine clauses to form compound, complex, or compound-complex sentences, they must use internal punctuation to help readers perceive the boundaries of these elements. This section explains four main punctuation rules for marking the boundaries of clauses and phrases within a sentence. Once you understand these rules, you will find it easier to mark the boundaries of complete sentences and thus to avoid fragments, run-ons, and comma splices.

Rule 1: Join two independent sentences with a semicolon or with a comma and a coordinating conjunction

You can join two complete sentences to form a compound sentence in two ways: (1) with a semicolon, or (2) with a comma and a coordinating conjunction. You should learn the seven coordinating conjunctions.

and   but   or   nor   for   yet   so

When you join two sentences using either of these methods, each sentence becomes an independent clause in the compound sentence; the punctuation signals the joining point.

Two Sentences	Melissa hasn't changed the oil in her car. However, she is still willing to take it to the game.
Joined with Semicolon	Melissa hasn't changed the oil in her car; however, she is still willing to take it to the game.

Joined with Comma and Coordinating Conjunction	Melissa hasn't changed the oil in her car, but she is still willing to take it to the game.

Rule 2: Use a single comma to set off an introductory adverb clause

Another common way to join sentences is to use a subordinating conjunction to convert one sentence to an adverb clause. Subordinating conjunctions are words such as *because, when, if, although,* and *until.* If the resulting adverb clause opens the sentence, set it off from the independent clause with a comma. If it follows the independent clause, don't set it off.

See p. 747 for a longer list of subordinating conjunctions.

Adverb Clause Preceding Independent Clause	If the sun is shining in the morning, we'll go for the hike.
Adverb Clause Following Independent Clause	We'll go for the hike if the sun is shining in the morning.

Note that no comma is used in the latter example because the adverb clause follows, rather than precedes, the independent clause.

An exception to this rule occurs with the subordinating conjunction *although.* You should use a comma to set off a clause introduced by *although* even if it comes at the end of a sentence.

> The police officer still gave me a ticket, although I explained to her that my speedometer was broken.

Rule 3: Inside a sentence core, use pairs of commas to set off interrupting elements

The core of a sentence consists of the subject, verb, and direct object or subject complement. Within the core of a sentence, never use a single comma; either omit commas or use commas *in pairs* to set off interrupting elements.

Sentence Core	My dog chased the cat around the room.
Interrupting Element Inside the Core	My dog, barking loudly and snapping his teeth, chased the cat around the room.

Note that *a pair* of commas—a comma preceding the element and a comma following the element—marks the boundaries of the interrupting element.

Sentence Core	The police officer still gave me a ticket.
Interrupting Element Inside the Core	The police officer, however, still gave me a ticket.

Rule 4: Use a single comma to set off some introductory or concluding phrases

An introductory phrase often precedes the core of a sentence. Set off an introductory phrase if it is long or if your voice pauses noticeably between the phrase (or single word such as *however*) and the start of the sentence core. Similarly, use a single comma to set off long concluding elements if your voice pauses noticeably after the core. In either case, the comma signals the boundary between the sentence core and the introductory or concluding element.

Introductory Element

Barking loudly and snapping his teeth, my dog chased the cat around the room.

According to many authorities, this author's treatment of women is historically inaccurate.

However, I disagree.

Concluding Element

My dog chased the cat around the room, his jaws snapping angrily.

The scholar's claim bothered Jensen, leaving him bewildered and possibly angry.

Your familiarity with these four rules will help you understand the logic for punctuating sentences that combine two or more clauses or that include introductory, interrupting, or concluding phrases. Knowing these rules, in turn, will help you learn to signal sentence boundaries to readers.

Exercise

Return to the sentence templates on page 753 that show blank lines punctuated with commas and semicolons and use the words *and, however,* and *because.* On a separate sheet of paper, create sentences of your own to fill in these templates. Share your sentences with class members.

Next we turn to three common sentence-boundary errors:

1. *Sentence fragment:* a nonsentence punctuated as a sentence or an independent clause
2. *Run-on:* two sentences fused together without punctuation
3. *Comma splice:* two sentences joined with a comma

IDENTIFYING AND CORRECTING SENTENCE FRAGMENTS

A sentence fragment is a nonsentence (any structure lacking a complete subject or a complete predicate) that is punctuated either as a sentence or as an independent clause.

Types of Fragments

There are two kinds of sentence fragments.

1. *Phrase fragments* may lack either a subject or a complete predicate or both. In the following passage, the phrase fragments are italicized.

Paul and Sarah love their mountain home. *Going fishing in the morning. Watching the deer graze in the meadows.* Outside their cabin, a pair of majestic eagles nest in the top of a lone pine; *with only the starry sky as a night roof.*

The first two fragments are participial phrases punctuated as complete sentences. The last fragment is a prepositional phrase punctuated as an independent clause. The semicolon signals to readers that two independent clauses are joined together.

2. *Subordinate clause fragments* have a subject and a complete predicate, but they begin with either a subordinating conjunction or a relative pronoun, which prevents them from standing alone as a sentence. In the following examples, the subordinate clause fragments are italicized.

Sarah and Paul often go for a hike. *As soon as the sun comes up.* At night they love to watch the eyes of owls. *Which blink at them from the branches of nearby trees.*

The first fragment is created by the subordinating conjunction *as soon as*; the second is created by the relative pronoun *which*.

Methods for Correcting Sentence Fragments

There are various ways to correct a fragment; each method produces a slightly different variation in meaning and emphasis.

Method 1: Change a phrase fragment to a complete sentence by converting an incomplete verb into a complete verb or by adding a verb

This method emphasizes the material in the fragment by giving it the weight of a full sentence.

Fragment	The buffalo began to stampede. Their heads flailing wildly.
Revised	The buffalo began to stampede. Their heads flailed wildly.

The fragment has been converted to a complete sentence by changing the participle *flailing* to the complete verb *flailed*.

Method 2: Change a clause fragment to a complete sentence by removing the subordinator

This method also emphasizes the ideas in the original fragment.

Fragment	For Native Americans, killing buffalo was very dangerous. Because the stampeding buffalo herd had to be guided toward the cliff by braves shaking wolf skins.
Revised	For Native Americans, killing buffalo was very dangerous. The stampeding buffalo herd had to be guided toward the cliff by braves shaking wolf skins.

Removing the subordinating conjunction *because* converts the fragment into a complete sentence.

Method 3: Correct the fragment by joining it to the sentence that precedes or follows it, whichever makes more sense

This method subordinates the material in the fragment and can work for either phrase or clause fragments. With this method, you may need to use a comma to signal the joining point.

Fragment   The buffalo crashed to their deaths. Although the braves killed the animals that were still alive. The squaws did most of the work in preparing the hides and meat.

Revised   The buffalo crashed to their deaths. Although the braves killed the animals that were still alive, the squaws did most of the work in preparing the hides and meat.

The original passage contains a subordinate clause fragment beginning with *although.* The revised passage attaches the *although* clause to the second sentence.

Exercise

Proofread the following passage adapted from a student paper. Underline all of the sentence fragments. Then, on a separate sheet of paper, revise the fragments using one of the main correction methods—turn the fragment into a complete sentence or connect the fragment to a neighboring sentence. Choose the correction method that seems most appropriate for the context of the passage.

Another difference between a taxi driver and other occupations being the way that taxi drivers interact with people. Driving a taxi is one of the few jobs where you really get to "know the customer." In other service jobs, you rarely get to know the customer's name. Such as waiter or bartender. In those jobs you can wait on one hundred people in a night or mix drinks for two hundred. Without personally talking to five of them. In a taxi, however, each customer spends at least ten to fifteen minutes in a quiet car. Having nothing else to do but talk with the driver.

IDENTIFYING AND CORRECTING RUN-ONS AND COMMA SPLICES

Writers make run-on errors or comma splices whenever they fail to show where one sentence ends and the next begins.

A *run-on error* occurs when two sentences are fused together without any punctuation.

I explained to the police officer that my speedometer was broken she still gave me a ticket.

Two sentences come together between *broken* and *she,* but no period or capital letter marks the boundary.

A *comma splice* occurs when a writer marks the end of a sentence with a comma instead of with a period and a capital letter.

I explained to the police officer that my speedometer was broken, she still gave me a ticket.

A comma by itself cannot mark the boundary between two sentences.

Methods for Correcting Run-ons and Comma Splices

Run-ons and comma splices can be corrected in a variety of ways, depending on the meaning you wish to convey. You may choose to separate the ideas by placing them in two separate sentences, or you may wish to join the ideas into a single sentence. To choose the most appropriate method, consider the rhetorical context of the passage you are writing.

Method 1: Separate the sentences with a period and a capital letter

This method gives equal emphasis to both sentences. If you wish to indicate a logical relationship between the two sentences, you can add a conjunctive adverb (such as *therefore* or *nevertheless*) somewhere in the second sentence.

Revised   I explained to the police officer that my speedometer was broken. She still gave me a ticket.

Revised   I explained to the police officer that my speedometer was broken. However, she still gave me a ticket.

Method 2: Join the sentences with a semicolon

This method creates a compound sentence with two equally strong independent clauses.

Revised   I explained to the police officer that my speedometer was broken; however, she still gave me a ticket.

Method 3: Join the sentences with a comma and a coordinating conjunction

This method also creates a compound sentence with two equally strong independent clauses.

Revised   I explained to the police officer that my speedometer was broken, but she still gave me a ticket.

Method 4: Join the sentences with a subordinating conjunction or a relative pronoun

This method creates a complex sentence with an independent clause and a subordinate clause. The material in the independent clause receives more emphasis than the subordinated material does.

Revised   Although I explained to the police officer that my speedometer was broken, she still gave me a ticket.

Method 5: Convert one of the sentences into a phrase

This method creates a simple sentence with an added or embedded phrase. The phrase has less importance than the rest of the sentence.

Revised   Despite my explanation of the broken speedometer, the police officer gave me a ticket.

Choosing the Most Appropriate Method for Correction

Although each of these methods of correcting run-ons and comma splices will produce a grammatically correct solution, the method used in a given situation depends on the meaning and emphasis you intend. Consider the following example:

Comma Splice   The weather is beautiful, my neighbor is washing her car.

To determine the best way to correct this comma splice, you need to consider the passage in which it occurs. Different correction methods create different effects.

Revised   It is a great day. The weather is beautiful. My neighbor is washing her car. Kids are playing in the street. The dog is sleeping in the sun.

Here the focus is on the writer's sense of a great day. The beautiful weather and the neighbor washing her car are only two of four separate pieces of evidence the writer uses to support the feeling. By putting them all in separate sentences, the writer emphasizes each one.

But consider how the comma splice might be corrected in a different context.

Revised   I was hoping to invite my neighbor over to watch the football game with me this afternoon. But because the weather is beautiful, she is washing her car.

In this version, the main point is the writer's disappointment that the neighbor isn't coming over to watch football. The beautiful weather is the cause of her washing the car, but the subordinating conjunction *because* makes that information secondary. The writer isn't interested in the beautiful weather for its own sake, so a separate sentence such as the one in the first example would be inappropriate.

These differences illustrate that punctuation is a way of controlling and signaling meaning for readers. As you learn ways of correcting comma splices and run-ons, you will also become aware of the wide variety of options available to convey subtleties of thought and feeling.

Exercise

In the following sentences, underline the comma splices or run-ons (some sentences may be correct). Then, on a separate sheet of paper, revise the underlined sentences.

1. I love to hear coffee perking in the pot on lazy Saturday mornings another of my favorite sounds is rain on a tin roof.
2. When the ice cream wagon begins playing its song in our neighborhood, the children run to greet it, clasping their dimes and quarters in grubby little hands.
3. Freud assumed that the unconscious was the basis for human behavior, therefore, he believed that the pleasure audiences receive from art comes from art's embodiment of unconscious material.

4. Because St. Augustine's conception of God was Neoplatonic, Augustine believed that existence in itself is good.

5. Although scientists don't know for sure how much dinosaurs actually ate, they know that the food intake of the great reptiles must have been enormous, a question they ask themselves, therefore, is what the dinosaurs actually ate.

6. The doctor told me that my X ray revealed nothing to be alarmed about, nevertheless, she wants me to come back in six months for another checkup.

7. Juan and Alicia began taking the engine apart they worked diligently for four hours and then discovered that they didn't have the right tools to continue.

8. I should apologize for the snide letter I wrote you last week, although I must admit that I am still angry.

9. In a home aquarium fish will sometimes die from overeating the instructions on fish food boxes, therefore, stress that you feed fish a specified amount on a strict schedule.

10. The upgrade on Manuel's word processing program seems more trouble han it's worth, so he has decided to return it.

OVERVIEW OF METHODS FOR JOINING CLAUSES

Figure HB3.1 (on p. 762) summarizes the methods used in standard written English to join two sentences.

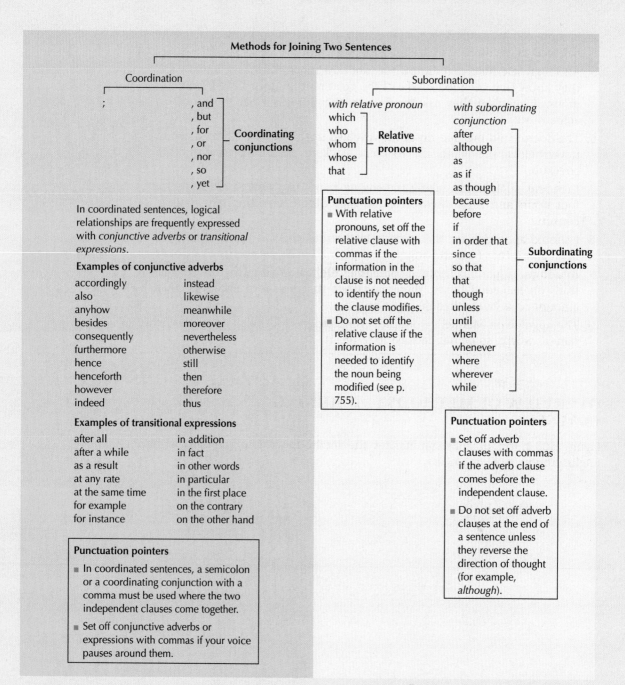

Methods for Joining Two Sentences

Coordination

; , and
, but
, for
, or
, nor
, so
, yet

Coordinating conjunctions

In coordinated sentences, logical relationships are frequently expressed with *conjunctive adverbs* or *transitional expressions*.

Examples of conjunctive adverbs

accordingly	instead
also	likewise
anyhow	meanwhile
besides	moreover
consequently	nevertheless
furthermore	otherwise
hence	still
henceforth	then
however	therefore
indeed	thus

Examples of transitional expressions

after all	in addition
after a while	in fact
as a result	in other words
at any rate	in particular
at the same time	in the first place
for example	on the contrary
for instance	on the other hand

Punctuation pointers

■ In coordinated sentences, a semicolon or a coordinating conjunction with a comma must be used where the two independent clauses come together.

■ Set off conjunctive adverbs or expressions with commas if your voice pauses around them.

Subordination

with relative pronoun
which
who
whom
whose
that

Relative pronouns

Punctuation pointers
■ With relative pronouns, set off the relative clause with commas if the information in the clause is not needed to identify the noun the clause modifies.

■ Do not set off the relative clause if the information is needed to identify the noun being modified (see p. 755).

with subordinating conjunction
after
although
as
as if
as though
because
before
if
in order that
since
so that
that
though
unless
until
when
whenever
where
wherever
while

Subordinating conjunctions

Punctuation pointers

■ Set off adverb clauses with commas if the adverb clause comes before the independent clause.

■ Do not set off adverb clauses at the end of a sentence unless they reverse the direction of thought (for example, *although*).

FIGURE HB 3.1 ■ Methods for Joining Sentences

HANDBOOK 4

Editing for Standard English Usage

In this chapter we address common errors in sentence structure, or usage. This chapter will help you recognize and correct the following kinds of errors:

- Grammatical tangles such as mixed constructions or faulty predication
- Consistency errors (unnecessary shifts in verb tense or pronoun person)
- Agreement errors (lack of subject-verb agreement or pronoun-antecedent agreement)
- Nonparallel constructions
- Dangling or misplaced modifiers
- Pronoun case errors
- Verb form errors
- Adjective/adverb errors

FIXING GRAMMATICAL TANGLES

Among the most frequent errors in rough drafts are grammatically tangled sentences that result in *mixed constructions* or *faulty predication.*

Mixed Constructions

In the heat of composing a first draft, a writer sometimes starts a sentence with one kind of construction and shifts midway to another construction.

Faulty   By buying a year's supply of laundry soap at one time saves lots of money.

This sentence opens with a prepositional phrase that cannot serve as a sentence subject. The writer can correct the error by eliminating the preposition or by supplying a subject.

Revised   Buying a year's supply of laundry soap at one time saves lots of money.

        or

    By buying a year's supply of laundry soap at one time, the average consumer can save lots of money.

Faulty Predication

Another kind of grammatical tangle, called *faulty predication,* occurs when the action specified by the verb can't logically be performed by the subject.

Faulty   Throughout *The Scarlet Letter,* Hester Prynne's "A" is imbibed with symbolic significance.

Imbibe means "to drink," so its use makes no sense in this sentence.

Revised   Throughout *The Scarlet Letter,* Hester Prynne's "A" is invested with symbolic significance.

MAINTAINING CONSISTENCY

Consistency errors occur whenever a writer illogically shifts verb tenses or shifts the person or number of pronouns.

Shifts in Tense

Readers can become confused when writers change tenses without explanation. You should avoid shifting verb tenses in a passage unless you mean to signal a shift in time.

Faulty   The display cases of the little bakery were filled with cakes, pies, doughnuts, and special pastries. From the heated ovens against the back wall *drifts* the aroma of buttery croissants.

The verbs in the first sentence are all in the past tense. The verb in the second sentence shifts to the present without an explanation.

Revised   The display cases of the little bakery were filled with cakes, pies, doughnuts, and special pastries. From the heated ovens against the back wall *drifted* the aroma of buttery croissants.

Shifts in the Person and Number of Pronouns

For advice on avoiding sexist language when using third-person pronouns, see pp. 786–787.

Pronouns have three persons: first (*I, we*); second (*you*); and third (*he, she, it, one, they*). Keep your point of view consistent by avoiding confusing shifts from one person to another or from singular to plural.

Confusing   As readers, we are not prepared for Hamlet's change in the last act. When one sees Hamlet joking with the grave diggers, you forget momentarily about his earlier despair.

The pronouns shift from first to third to second person.

Revised   As readers, we are not prepared for Hamlet's change in the last act. When we see Hamlet joking with the grave diggers, we forget momentarily about his earlier despair.

MAINTAINING AGREEMENT

Writers often have to choose between singular and plural forms of verbs and pronouns to ensure that verbs match their subjects and pronouns match their antecedents. In some cases, special rules determine whether a subject or an antecedent is singular or plural.

Subject-Verb Agreement

In many tenses a verb changes its form to agree in number with its subject.

Singular This violin *is* beautiful.

Plural These violins *are* beautiful.

In most cases, it is easy to determine whether the subject is singular or plural, but some cases are tricky. The following rules cover most cases.

Plural Words Between Subject and Verb

It may be difficult to find the subject when it is separated from the verb by intervening words, phrases, or embedded clauses or when an indefinite word such as *one, each,* or *kind* is followed by a prepositional phrase beginning with *of.* In the latter case the object of the preposition is often mistaken for the subject.

Faulty One of the recent shipments of boxes containing computers, printers, and modems *were* delayed.

Revised One of the recent shipments of boxes containing computers, printers, and modems *was* delayed.

In this sentence, *one* is the subject, not any of the intervening plural words.

Similarly, prepositional phrases beginning with *as well as, in addition to, along with,* and *including* can trick writers into thinking that a singular subject is plural.

Faulty My mother, along with several of her coworkers, *are* getting a special award for excellence in customer relations.

Revised My mother, along with several of her coworkers, *is* getting a special award for excellence in customer relations.

In this sentence the subject is *mother;* the intervening prepositional phrase should be ignored.

Compound Subjects Joined by *and*

Use a plural verb for singular or plural subjects joined by *and* unless the nouns joined by *and* are thought of as one unit, in which case the verb is singular. Notice the different meanings of the following sentences:

My brother and my best friend *is* with me now.

This sentence means that my brother is with me now and that my brother is my best friend.

My brother and my best friend *are* with me now.

This sentence means that two people are with me—my brother and my best friend.

Compound Subjects Joined by *or, nor, either . . . or, neither . . . nor*

The coordinating conjunctions *or, nor, either . . . or,* and *neither . . . nor* take singular verbs if they join singular subjects and plural verbs if they join plural subjects.

If they join a singular subject to a plural subject, the verb agrees with the nearer subject.

Either a coyote or a dog *is* getting into the chicken coop.

Both subjects are singular, so the verb is singular.

Either coyotes or dogs *are* getting into the chicken coop.

Both subjects are plural, so the verb is plural.

Either some coyotes or a dog *is* getting into the chicken coop.

The subject closest to the verb is singular, so the verb is singular.

Indefinite Pronoun as Subject

Some indefinite pronouns are always singular; others can be singular or plural depending on context.

Always Singular		Singular or Plural
anybody	none	all
anyone	each	any
anything	everybody	some
either	neither	
nobody		

The indefinite pronouns in the left-hand columns are always singular.

Faulty   Each of the dogs *are* thirsty.

Revised   Each of the dogs *is* thirsty.

The indefinite pronouns in the right-hand column can be singular or plural. These words are generally followed by a prepositional phrase beginning with *of*. The number of the pronoun depends on whether the object of the preposition is singular or plural.

Some of the table *is* sanded.

The object of the preposition (*table*) is singular, so the verb is singular.

Some of the tables *are* sanded.

The object of the preposition (*tables*) is plural, so the verb is plural.

Inversion of Subject and Verb

Locating the subject may be tricky in inverted sentences, in which the subject comes after the verb.

Just beyond the fence line on the other side of the road are some pheasants.

The subject is *pheasants*, so the verb is plural.

Be especially careful with inverted sentences that begin with *here*, *there*, or *where*. Errors occur most frequently when a writer uses these words in contractions or in questions.

Faulty   Where's my belt and sweater?

The subject is *belt and sweater,* so the verb should be plural.

Revised   Where are my belt and sweater?

Relative Pronoun as Subject

Relative pronouns used as subjects (*who, that, which*) are singular or plural depending on their antecedents.

A person who *builds* glass houses shouldn't throw stones.

Who is singular because its antecedent, *person,* is singular; hence the verb should be singular.

People who *build* glass houses shouldn't throw stones.

Who is plural because its antecedent, *people,* is plural; hence the verb should be plural.

Be especially careful when the antecedent is the object of the preposition *of.*

One of the reasons that *are* frequently given is inflation.

The verb of the main clause (*is*) is singular because its subject is the singular pronoun *one.* But the verb of the relative clause (*are*) is plural because its subject (*that*) has a plural antecedent (*reasons*).

Subject Followed by Linking Verb and Subject Complement

Linking verbs should agree with the subject of the sentence, not with the subject complement.

Sleeping, eating, and drinking *are* his whole life.

The verb *are* agrees with the plural subject, not with the singular subject complement.

His whole life *is* sleeping, eating, and drinking.

In this case, the verb agrees with the singular subject, not with the plural subjective complement.

Collective Noun as Subject

With collective nouns such as *group, committee, crew, crowd, faculty, majority,* and *audience,* use a singular verb if the collective group acts as one unit; use a plural verb if the members of the group act individually.

The faculty at Hogwash College *is* delighted with the new president.

Here the faculty functions as a single unit.

The faculty at Hogwash College *are* arguing at this very moment.

Here *faculty* refers to individuals who act independently.

Some collective nouns present special problems or follow special rules, for instance, *a number* versus *the number. A number* refers to a collection of individual items and takes a plural verb. *The number* refers to a unit and takes a singular verb.

A number of students *are* studying grammar this semester.

The number of students studying grammar *is* declining every year.

Titles or words referred to as words use singular verbs.

Snow White and the Seven Dwarfs is a famous Disney movie.

The italics indicates a title, which takes a singular verb. If you were referring to the characters rather than the title, the verb would be plural: "Snow White and the seven dwarfs are my favorite Disney characters."

Exercise

In the following sentences, underline the true subject or subjects of the verb in parentheses. Then underline the correct verb form twice.

1. Under a pile of old rags in the corner of the basement (is/are) a mother mouse and a squirming family of baby mice.
2. Hard work, together with intelligence, initiative, and a bit of good luck, (explains/explain) the success of many wealthy businesspeople.
3. The first thing she emphasized (was/were) the differences between Pacific and Atlantic breeding patterns of these fish.
4. The myth, legend, prayer, and ritual of primitive religions (contains/contain) many common themes.
5. Unfortunately, neither of the interviewers for the local TV station (has/have) read any of her works.
6. There (is/are) a number of students who (is/are) waiting to see the teacher.
7. (Does/Do) one of the students still have my notebook?
8. One of the students who (is/are) trying out for the play (wants/want) to become a professional actor.
9. He is the only one of all the students in the theater arts class who really (has/have) professional ambitions.
10. The committee (is/are) writing individual letters to the judge.

Pronoun-Antecedent Agreement

Just as a subject must agree in number with its verb, so must a pronoun agree in number with its antecedent (the noun that the pronoun stands for). To apply this rule, you must first determine the antecedent of the pronoun and then decide whether the antecedent is singular or plural, following the rules presented in the previous section. Pronoun-antecedent agreement occasionally presents some difficulties. The following rules cover most cases.

Compound Construction as Antecedent

If a compound antecedent is joined by *and,* choose a plural pronoun; if a compound antecedent is joined by *or,* the pronoun should agree in number with the closest antecedent.

Rebecca and Paul invited us to their party.

Either Brian or Luis will bring his volleyball to the party.

Either Brian or his sisters will bring their volleyball.

Collective Noun as Antecedent

Use a singular pronoun to refer to a collective noun that acts as one unit; use a plural pronoun if members of the group act individually.

The committee reported its opinion.

The committee began arguing among themselves.

Indefinite Pronoun as Antecedent

Generally, if the antecedent is an indefinite pronoun such as *either, neither, everyone, everybody, someone, somebody, anyone,* or *anybody,* you use a singular pronoun.

Everybody coming to the party should bring his or her own drinks.

Note: Sentence constructions such as this one can lead to the use of non-inclusive language.

See pp. 786–787 for suggestions on alternative constructions.

MAINTAINING PARALLEL STRUCTURE

When joining items in series or lists, make sure that each item has the same grammatical structure: nouns should be joined to nouns, verbs to verbs, prepositional phrases to prepositional phrases, clauses to clauses, and so forth. Parallelism greatly increases the clarity and force of your sentences.

A nonparallel construction occurs whenever a writer fails to maintain the same grammatical structure for each item in a series.

Faulty   Shanelle likes playing soccer and to roller-skate.

Here the writer has joined a gerund phrase (*playing soccer*) to an infinitive (*to roller-skate*). The problem can be solved by making both items gerunds or both infinitives.

Revised   Shanelle likes playing soccer and roller-skating.

            or

            Shanelle likes to play soccer and to roller-skate.

Faulty   As a teacher, he was a courteous listener, helpful during office hours, and he lectured in an exciting way.

Revised   As a teacher, he was a courteous listener, a good helper during office hours, and an exciting lecturer.

In this revision the writer converts all items in the series to nouns.

Faulty   This term paper is illogical, poorly documented, and should have used more primary sources.

Here the first two items are parallel (the adjectives *illogical* and *poorly documented*), but the last item is a verb phrase (*should have used more primary sources*).

Revised	This term paper is illogical, poorly documented, and poorly researched.
	or
	This term paper, which should have used more primary sources, is illogical and poorly documented.

To increase clarity, writers often repeat function words such as articles, prepositions, conjunctions, or the infinitive word *to* at the beginning of each item in a parallel series.

Confusing	The drill sergeant told the recruits that there would be no weekend passes and they would be on KP instead.
Revised	The drill sergeant told the recruits that there would be no weekend passes and that they would be on KP instead.

The repetition of *that* clarifies the writer's intention: to report two things the drill sergeant told the recruits.

Placement of Correlative Conjunctions

When using correlative conjunctions (such as *either . . . or, neither . . . nor, both . . . and,* and *not only . . . but also*), make sure that each unit of the correlative precedes the same grammatical structure.

Faulty	I not only like ice cream but also root beer.

Here the writer places *not only* in front of a verb (*like*), but places *but also* in front of a noun (*root beer*).

Revised	I like not only ice cream but also root beer.

Use of *and which/that* or *and who/whom*

Be sure that a clause beginning with *and which, and that, and who,* or *and whom* is preceded by a parallel clause beginning with *which, that, who,* or *whom.*

Faulty	Of all my friends, Paul is the one with the greatest sense of courage and who most believes in honesty.

The writer links a pronoun (*one*) to a relative clause (*who most believes . . .*), creating a nonparallel structure.

Revised	Of all my friends, Paul is the one who has the greatest sense of courage and who most believes in honesty.

Exercise

In the following sentences, underline the nonparallel constructions. Then, on a separate sheet of paper, revise the sentences to create parallel structures.

1. We improved our old car's acceleration by resetting the spark plug gaps and also we boiled out the carburetor.

2. Race car driving requires much practical experience, and your reactions must be quick.

3. After reading the events calendar, we decided to go to a festival of Japanese art and on attending the symphony afterward.

4. I want to read a biography of a flamboyant figure working in volunteer organizations and who has altered history.

5. Sasha not only does volunteer work in the school, but also coaching soccer every fall.

6. Either you must leave early or leave after the major rush hour.

7. The harvest moon shone brightly, pouring its light over the surrounding water, and which made the evening a special moment in their lives.

8. You can avoid a comma splice by joining main clauses with a comma and a coordinating conjunction, with a semicolon, or by changing one of the main clauses to a subordinate clause.

9. Again and again psychologists explore the same questions: Are we shaped by our heredity, by our environment, or do we have free will?

10. To make friends you must first be a friend and then listening carefully.

AVOIDING DANGLING OR MISPLACED MODIFIERS

Dangling Modifiers

When a sentence opens with a modifying phrase, the phrase must be followed immediately by the noun it modifies, which is usually the grammatical subject of the sentence; otherwise, the phrase is said to dangle. You can correct a dangling modifier by (a) recasting the sentence so that the subject is the word modified by the opening modifier; or (b) expanding the modifying phrase into a clause that has its own subject.

                          modifier   subject

Faulty   Walking down the street, a flowerpot fell on my head.

This sentence brings to mind a walking flowerpot.

                          modifier   subject

Revised   Walking down the street, I was struck on the head by a flowerpot.

          or

                    modifying clause with subject

          While *I* was walking down the street, a flowerpot fell on my head.

                        modifier   subject

Faulty   With only a dollar in change, the meal was too expensive.

Does the meal have only a dollar in change?

modifier   subject

Revised   With only a dollar in change, I couldn't afford the meal.

or

modifying clause with subject

Because *I* had only a dollar in change, the meal was too expensive.

Misplaced Modifiers

A misplaced modifier occurs when a modifying word or phrase is separated from the element it modifies. To correct this type of error, change the location of the modifier so that it is next to the word or phrase it modifies.

Faulty   The students gave a present to their teacher in a big box.

This sentence suggests that the teacher is in a big box.

Revised   The students gave their teacher a present in a big box.

Note: Be careful to place limiting adverbs, such as *only, just,* and *merely,* next to the words they limit. As the following example shows, changing the location of *only* can often change the meaning of a sentence.

Only I baked the cake. (I am the person solely responsible for baking the cake.)
I only baked the cake. (I baked it, but I didn't put the frosting on it.)
I baked only the cake. (Someone else baked the cookies.)

Place limiting adverbs *directly in front of* the words they modify.

Faulty   I should get a higher grade because I only failed one exam.

The writer intends to modify *one exam* rather than *failed* and thus needs to move *only.*

Revised   I should get a higher grade because I failed only one exam.

Exercise

In the following sentences, underline the dangling or misplaced modifiers (some sentences may be correct). Then, on a separate sheet of paper, revise the faulty sentences.

1. Feeling cold, tired, and depressed, tears streamed from my friend's eyes.
2. Their heads tilted back in awe, the children on this summer's night began trying to count the stars.
3. Seen through a telescope that magnifies things sixty times, Jupiter appears as big as the moon.
4. By studying the light reflected by Jupiter, its clouds are a poisonous mixture of ammonia floating in hydrogen.

5. Having long expected to return to Harlem after graduation, the young accountant was not prepared for the changes he saw on Lennox Avenue.

6. While cruising at 10,000 feet 45 miles east of Albuquerque, New Mexico, on July 16, 1945, at approximately 5:30 A.M., a brilliant flash of light, brighter than the sun, blazed across the horizon.

7. We were absolutely startled, unable to explain the sunlike flash or to grasp the meaning of the huge mushroom cloud that soon appeared above the desert floor.

8. Reporting what we had seen by radio to ground authorities, no satisfactory explanation could be found.

9. The following morning, still plagued by the event, the newspapers only reported that an ammunition dump had exploded in the approximate area where we had seen the flash.

10. Listening to the radio on August 6, 1945, a similar flash of light occurred over Hiroshima, Japan; then we realized what we had seen several weeks earlier—the first explosion of an atomic bomb.

CHOOSING CORRECT PRONOUN CASES

Many pronouns change their form according to the grammatical slot they fill in a sentence.

Case Name	Used for These Slots	Personal Pronouns	Relative Pronouns
subjective	subject, subject complement	I, we, he, she, they	who, whoever
objective	direct object, indirect object, object of preposition, subject of infinitive	me, us, him, her, them	whom, whomever
possessive	adjective showing possession	my, our, his, her, their	whose

The case of a pronoun is determined by its slot in the sentence.

She and *I* are good friends. *[subjects]*

Paul likes *her* and *me*. *[direct objects]*

Give *her* and *me* the present. *[indirect objects]*

Paul did it for *her* and *me*. *[objects of preposition]*

The winners were *she* and *I*. *[subject complements]*

Patricia asked *her* and *me* to write the final report. *[subjects of infinitive]*

Although writers generally handle pronoun cases accurately, the following instances give special trouble.

Cases of Relative Pronouns

In relative or noun clauses, the pronouns *who, whom, whoever,* or *whomever* take their case from their function in their own clause, not from the function of that clause in the rest of the sentence.

Faulty   Give the prize to *whomever* says the secret word.

Although *whomever* at first seems to be the object of the preposition *to,* it is actually the subject of the verb *says* and should be in the subjective case. The object of the preposition *to* is actually the whole noun clause.

Revised   Give the prize to *whoever* says the secret word.

Faulty   I voted against Ralph Winkley, *who* big business especially supports.

In this case the relative pronoun fills a direct object slot in its own clause. Compare: Big business especially supports *him.* The writer should choose *whom.*

Revised   I voted against Ralph Winkley, *whom* big business especially supports.

Intervening Parenthetical Clauses

When choosing the case of relative pronouns, don't let such words as *I think* or *he supposes* influence your choice. These are parenthetical expressions that can be discarded from the sentence.

Faulty   I voted for Marion Fudge, *whom* I think is the most honest candidate.

Here the relative pronoun is the subject of the verb *is,* not the direct object of *I think,* and hence it should be subjective.

Revised   I voted for Marion Fudge, *who* I think is the most honest candidate.

Pronouns as Parts of Compound Constructions

Case errors are especially frequent in compound constructions. Many people who were reprimanded as children for saying "Him and me are going outside" overcorrect by using "he and I" even when "him and me" is warranted. Pronouns that fill object slots (or subjects of infinitives) must be in the objective case. You can usually avoid case errors in compound constructions by choosing the same case that you would select if you were using the pronoun alone.

Faulty   Isobel appointed Ralph and *I* to the committee.

The pronoun is a direct object and should be in the objective case. Compare: Isobel appointed *me* to the committee.

Revised   Isobel appointed Ralph and *me* to the committee.

Note that subjects of infinitives are in the objective case.

Faulty   The dean of students wants *she* and *I* to represent the student council at the convention.

Compare: The dean of students wants *me* to represent the student council. . . ."

Revised   The dean of students wants *her* and *me* to represent the student council at the convention.

Be especially careful with pronouns appearing in front of infinitives that omit the *to*.

Faulty   Let's you and *I* go to the show this evening.

The pronoun is the subject of the infinitive *(to) go* and should be in the objective case. Compare: Let *me* go to the show.

Revised   Let's you and *me* go to the show this evening.

Pronouns in Appositive Constructions

In appositive constructions, in which the pronoun is followed by an identifying noun, use the pronoun case that would be correct if the noun were not there:

The principal told *us* boys to go home.

Compare: The principal told us to go home.

We boys hid around the corner until the principal went back to her office.

Compare: We hid around the corner.

Pronouns as Parts of Implied Clauses

When a pronoun occurs after a *than* that is introducing an implied clause, choose the pronoun's case according to the pronoun's use in the implied clause. Both of the following sentences are correct, but their meanings are different.

I like Paul better than he.

This sentence means "I like Paul better than he likes Paul."

I like Paul better than him.

This sentence means "I like Paul better than I like him."

Pronouns Preceding Gerunds or Participles

Use the possessive case before gerunds (*-ing* verbals used as nouns) and the subjective or objective case before present participles (*-ing* verbals used as adjectives).

I saw *him* running away from the police.

In this sentence, *running* is a participle modifying the direct object *him*.

I think *his* running away from the police was his biggest mistake.

Here, *running* is a gerund, the subject of *was*.

Exercise

In the following sentences, underline the correct pronoun from the choices given in parentheses.

(continued)

1. (We/Us) girls want to bike to the store.
2. Natalie, (who/whom) received the scholarship, will study microbiology.
3. If you and (he/him) can visit Tim and (I/me) next month, we will tour the national park.
4. Jessica and Lin-Ju will bring (her/their) skis.
5. (His/Him) playing loud music annoyed the neighbors.
6. He is the racer (who/whom) I believe fell at the finish line.
7. This vacation was necessary for you and (I/me).
8. A burglar stole our computer, but no one saw (his/him) entering the house.
9. Stephen or Tom will do (his/her/their) practicing before school.
10. Emily and Amy do (his/her/their) practicing faithfully every day.

CHOOSING CORRECT VERB FORMS

As we explained in Handbook 2 (pp. 744–745), English verbs change structure to make different tenses. *Regular* verbs add *-ed* to the base form to create the past and past participle; *irregular* verbs form the past and past participle through internal spelling changes.

Verb form errors occur when the writer uses a nonstandard form, often with irregular verbs.

Faulty   I *seen* Aram in the back room at 8:00.

The past form of *to see* is *saw*.

Revised   I *saw* Aram in the back room at 8:00.

Another verb form error arises when the preposition *of* is substituted for the auxiliary verb *have*. In spoken English, *have* often sounds like *of*, especially in contractions: "I should've finished my paper earlier." In written English, be sure not to confuse the two words.

Faulty   I should *of* finished my paper earlier.
Revised   I should *have* finished my paper earlier.

CHOOSING CORRECT ADJECTIVE AND ADVERB FORMS

For more on adjectives and adverbs, see p. 747.

Although adjectives and adverbs are both modifiers, they cannot be used interchangeably because adjectives modify nouns or pronouns whereas adverbs modify verbs, adjectives, other adverbs, and sometimes whole phrases, clauses, or sentences.

Problems with adjectives and adverbs can occur in the following cases.

Confusion of Adjective and Adverb Forms

Do not use adjectives when adverbs are warranted.

Faulty   I did *real good* on that test.

The adverb form is *well*, not *good*. Similarly, *real* is an adjective, which cannot modify an adverb.

Revised   I did *really well* on that test.

Be careful to use the appropriate modifier after verbs that can be either linking verbs or action verbs. Linking verbs (such as *is, are,* and *seem*) take subject complements, which are either nouns or adjectives. Certain linking verbs, especially the sense verbs *feel, look, taste, smell,* and *sound* as well as a few others, can also be action verbs. After such verbs choose an adjective if the word modifies the subject and an adverb if it modifies the verb.

The captain looked *angry.*

Here, *angry* is an adjective modifying *captain.* Compare: The angry captain . . .

The captain looked *angrily* at the crew.

Here, *angrily* is an adverb telling how the captain did the looking.

Problems with Comparative and Superlative Forms

Short adjectives (with one syllable or two syllables ending in *-y* or *-le*) form their comparative and superlative degrees by adding *-er* and *-est* to the simple form. Other adjectives and most adverbs generally use *more* (or *less*) for the comparative and *most* (or *least*) for the superlative. A few modifiers are irregular.

Choosing Comparatives Versus Superlatives

Use the comparative degree for two persons or things and the superlative for three or more.

Of the two players, Maria is the *better.*

Of the whole team, Maria is the *best.*

Misuse of Comparatives with Absolute Adjectives

Do not use comparative and superlative degrees with absolute adjectives, such as *unique* or *impossible.*

Faulty   Her dress was the *most unique* one I had ever seen.

Unique already means "one of a kind" and can't be further modified.

Revised   Her dress was *unique.*

        or

        Her dress was the *most unusual* one I had ever seen.

Double Comparatives
Avoid double comparatives or superlatives.

Faulty   Raphael is *more smarter* than George.

Revised   Raphael is *smarter* than George.

Illogical Comparisons
Avoid making illogical comparisons between items that are not actually compara-ble. Sometimes illogical comparisons result from a missing word such as *other*.

Faulty   Our Volvo is better than any car on the road.

This sentence inadvertently implies that this Volvo isn't on the road.

Revised   Our Volvo is better than any *other* car on the road.

At other times an illogical comparison arises when the grammar of the sentence mixes apples and oranges.

Faulty   Handwritten papers are harder to read than typing.

Papers cannot be compared with typing.

Revised   Handwritten papers are harder to read than typed papers.

Ambiguous Adverbs

Problems rarely occur with adverbs except when they are used ambiguously to modify whole sentences. Normally an adverb modifies a single word or a group of words in a sentence. Sometimes, however, writers use an adverb to modify an entire sentence. Occasionally such sentences are ambiguous.

Ambiguous   Unluckily, the wide receiver dropped the pass.

Who has the bad luck here? The wide receiver? Or the speaker of the sentence who hopes her team will win? The ambiguity can be eliminated by clarifying what *unluckily* modifies.

Revised   The wide receiver unluckily dropped the pass.

   or

   Unluckily for us, the wide receiver dropped the pass.

HANDBOOK 5

Editing for Style

I n Handbook 4 we focused on sentence-level errors. In this chapter we consider stylistic concerns, with the goal of making your prose more lively, interesting, and clear. The problems we address in this chapter are not errors. Rather, they are more like noise or interference in a radio broadcast; they annoy your reader and can sometimes distort your message.

This chapter teaches you to do the following:

- Prune your prose to cut out deadwood
- Enliven your prose by eliminating nominalizations, noun pileups, pretentious diction, and clichés and by varying sentence structure and using specific details
- Avoid broad or unclear pronoun references
- Put old information before new
- Make informed decisions about the use of the active or passive voice
- Use inclusive language

PRUNING YOUR PROSE

In most rhetorical contexts, conciseness is a virtue. Readers like efficient prose that makes its point without padding. Avoiding wordiness does not mean eliminating details or cutting into the muscle of an essay; it means eliminating inefficient words and bulky phrases that take up space without adding meaning.

Cutting Out Deadwood

Good writers typically write first drafts that are much longer than their final versions. Eliminating unneeded words and phrases is an essential part of revision.

Wordy	At the present time it can be considered a truism that families with incomes neither too far above nor too far below the median income can send their children to expensive colleges with no more out-of-pocket charges and expenses than it would cost to send these same children to colleges whose tuition and related expenses are much lower.
Revised	The truth is that for average-income families an expensive college costs no more than a cheap one.

When eliminating deadwood, watch out for common wordy phrases such as the following:

at the present time (use *now*)

because of the fact that (use *because*)

are of the opinion that (use *believe*)

have the ability to (use *can*)

in spite of the fact that (use *although*)

You can easily delete these expressions—and dozens more like them—without sacrificing meaning.

Combining Sentences

Another cause of wordiness is the inefficient use of short, choppy sentences. Try to recast a choppy passage by combining sentences, thus saving words while creating more complex and graceful structures.

Wordy   Jim Maxwell took two years to build his solar building. Building his solar building included nearly one year of planning. His solar building was intended mainly as a grain drier. But it also provided a warm winter shop. Additionally he had the advantage of a machinery shed. This shed kept his machinery dry. His new solar building would pay dividends for years to come.

Revised   It took two years to build, including nearly one year of planning, but when Jim Maxwell finished his solar building, he had a grain drier, a warm winter shop, and a dry machinery shed that would pay dividends for years to come.

Exercise

On a separate sheet of paper, improve the style of the following sentences by cutting out deadwood, recasting the words, or combining elements to eliminate wordiness.

1. It appears to me that he seems to be an unusually quiet person but also that he is the kind of person who really cares a lot about other people.

2. If a person is the kind of person who hurries rapidly when that person tries to do things, then that person is apt to find that he or she has wasted a lot of valuable time and material by trying to do the events too rapidly.

3. Ilana was interested in finding out the answer to a question that she had recently been puzzling about. The question was this: What is the important and essential difference between a disease that most people would call "mental illness" and a disease that is simply a disease of the brain?

4. It is unfortunate that the mayor acted in this manner. The mayor settled the issue. But before he settled the issue he made a mistake. He fostered a public debate that was very bitter. The debate pitted some of his subordinates

against each other (and these were key subordinates, too). It also caused many other people to feel inflamed passions and fears as a result of the way the mayor handled the whole affair.

ENLIVENING YOUR PROSE

You can often revise your prose to make the tone livelier and more interesting.

Avoiding Nominalizations

Lively writers express actions with verbs. Lifeless writers often *nominalize* their sentences by converting actions into nouns (for example, by writing, "arrive at a conclusion" rather than "conclude"). A highly nominalized style characterizes much bureaucratic and administrative prose, making it sound stilted, impersonal, and dead.

Nominalized	For the production of effective writing, the expression of an action through the use of a verb is the method most highly preferred.
Revised	Effective writers express actions with verbs.

A nominalized sentence is not only long and dull, but also confusing. Nominalized sentences often include two additional problems: overuse of the verb *to be* and a pileup of prepositional phrases. To revise a nominalized sentence, ask yourself who is doing what; then make the doer of the action the subject and make the action a verb.

Nominalized	Jim's receiving of this low grade was the result of his reading of the material too quickly.
Revised	Jim received a low grade because he read the material too quickly.

By putting *Jim* in the subject slot, the writer eliminates the weak verb *was* as well as three prepositional phrases.

Exercise

On a separate sheet of paper, revise the following sentences to eliminate nominalizations.

1. The person who received the rewards is the person who was the victor.
2. The killing of a goose from which the laying of golden eggs is frequent is usually seen to be a mistake.
3. The socialization of children in the avoidance of risky behaviors often results in their timidity as adults.
4. Juanita came to the realization that her preference of major was changing from history to mathematics.
5. The teacher's examination of the student's locker was caused by the teacher's suspicion of the possibility of the hiding of drugs by the student.

Avoiding Noun Pileups

Noun pileups result from the tendency, again common in bureaucratic prose, to use nouns as adjectives.

Noun Pileup	Consideration of an applicant physical disability access plan by the student services reform committee will occur forthwith.
Revised	The committee to reform student services will soon consider a plan for improving access to buildings for physically disabled applicants.

Avoiding Pretentious Language

Unless you are intentionally imitating a long-winded style, strive for language that sounds natural and clear rather than pretentious (or developed through over-use of a thesaurus).

Stilted	The tyro in the field of artistic endeavors commenced to ascertain the suitability of different constituencies of pigment.
Revised	The student artist began wondering which color paint would be most suitable.

Avoiding Clichés, Jargon, and Slang

Clichés are tired, frequently repeated phrases such as "last but not least," "easier said than done," or "a chill ran up my spine." Replace them with fresh language.

Deciding when to avoid jargon and slang is more problematic because their use may be appropriate depending on your audience, purpose, and genre. Technical jargon is acceptable if you are writing for an audience that understands it within a genre that uses it; slang is also fine if it suits your purpose, audience, and genre. In general, you should avoid jargon that may not be understood by your audience, and you should avoid slang in most formal contexts.

Inappropriate Jargon for a Teacher's Letter to Parents

Your child displays maladaptive socialization behaviors.

Revised	Your child is sometimes rude to classmates.

Inappropriate Slang for a College Essay

The gods are all bent out of shape because Oedipus killed his dad.

Revised	The gods are angry because Oedipus killed his father.

Creating Sentence Variety

Prose can feel wooden or choppy if each sentence has the same construction and length. Skilled writers combine sentences in various ways for emphasis and grace.

Monotonous	Martin watched carefully for loose rocks. He picked his way along the edge of the cliff. Martin didn't hear the rattles at first. Then he suddenly froze with fear when he heard them. A timber rattler was about two feet away. It was coiled like a garden hose. The rattler's neck was arched. Its fangs looked like twin needles of death.

In this passage, each sentence starts with the subject, and all the sentences are approximately the same length.

Revised   Watching carefully for loose rocks as he picked his way along the edge of the cliff, Martin suddenly froze with fear. At first he didn't hear the rattles. Then he heard them for sure. About two feet away, coiled like a garden hose, was a timber rattler, its neck arched, its fangs looking like twin needles of death.

Here the longest sentence is twenty-four words and the shortest is six words. The two short sentences emphasize dramatically important moments.

Using Specific Details

Except in philosophical or theoretical writing, which uses abstract language precisely, abstract prose can be dull. You can enliven abstract prose by replacing abstract terms with concrete words or by adding specific, colorful details for support.

Abstract   The poor are often stereotyped as beggars, drunks, or people with uncared-for children. We think of them as being without spirit or hope.

Revised   We often stereotype poor people as panhandlers demanding our spare change, as scruffy drunks holding a bottle in a paper bag, or as barefoot children with matted hair, filthy clothes, and tears streaking down their dirty faces as they tug on their mother's arm. We picture the poor as spiritless or hopeless, isolated in their own world, eyes glazed with despair.

Note that in this example, adding concrete language makes the passage *longer,* whereas pruning deadwood makes a passage shorter. What is the difference between deadwood and detail?

AVOIDING BROAD OR UNCLEAR PRONOUN REFERENCE

Each time you use a pronoun, make sure that the noun to which it refers, its *antecedent,* is clearly apparent. Unclear use of pronouns can confuse readers.

Avoiding Broad Reference

A broad reference occurs whenever a pronoun—usually *this, that,* or *it*—stands for an idea or a whole group of words rather than for a single noun. Although this usage is sometimes acceptable, it is often ambiguous or vague.

For more on *this* as a pronoun, see pp. 529–530.

Broad   Harold Krebs in Hemingway's "Soldier's Home" rebels against his
Reference   his parents. He does *this* by refusing to accept their values, and *this* is why his parents are so upset by *it.*

In this sentence the italicized pronouns refer not to specific nouns but to ideas, which shift with each pronoun, confusing the reader.

Revised   Harold Krebs in Hemingway's "Soldier's Home" rebels against his parents by refusing to accept their way of life. His rejection of their values explains why his parents are so upset by his later actions.

Do not make broad references with the pronoun *which,* which must have a single noun for its antecedent.

Faulty	He drinks a lot, which is something I disapprove of.
Revised	I disapprove of his heavy drinking.

In the original sentence, *which* has no noun antecedent.

Avoiding Unclear Antecedents

To avoid confusing your readers, make sure that every pronoun has a clear antecedent. Avoid using pronouns that seem to stand for two different antecedents.

Unclear Antecedent	Chris explained to his son the reasons he couldn't go to the meeting.
Revised	Chris explained the reasons his son couldn't go to the meeting.

In the original sentence, *he* could stand for either *Chris* or *son,* making it unclear whether Chris or his son couldn't go to the meeting.

PUTTING OLD INFORMATION BEFORE NEW INFORMATION

The old/new contract is one of the chief principles of clarity in closed-form prose. See Chapter 19, pp. 525–529, for more details.

In closed-form prose, clear writers begin sentences with old information—a key word or concept from the previous sentence, from the paragraph's topic sentence, or from the essay's thesis, purpose, or thesis statement—to keep their readers on track. Revise the structure of sentences that violate this rule.

New Information Before Old	When the experts disagree, therefore, what advice can be given? Ferreting out the facts that all sides agree on is a first step that we can take.
Revised	What advice can we give, therefore, when the experts disagree? First, we try to ferret out the facts that all sides agree on.

DECIDING BETWEEN ACTIVE AND PASSIVE VOICE

See p. 746, for further discussion of active and passive voice.

You must choose active or passive voice whenever you use a transitive verb—an action verb that has a receiver of the action as well as a doer. The active voice makes the doer of the action the subject and the receiver of the action the direct object; the passive voice makes the receiver of the action the subject and either omits the doer or makes the doer the object of the preposition *by.*

Active Voice	Our cat just caught a mouse.
Passive Voice	A mouse was just caught by our cat.

Strength of the Active Voice

Experienced writers usually prefer the active voice because it is stronger and more economical. The passive voice requires *to be* helping verbs and prepositional phrases for the doer of the action.

Weak   The cake and ice cream were eaten, and then games were played.

Revised   The children ate the cake and ice cream and then played games.

However, the passive voice isn't always inappropriate. The choice of voice depends on the context of your sentence.

When to Use the Passive Voice

Writers sometimes choose the passive voice to create appropriate emphasis or to evade responsibility.

Passive Voice When Doer Is Unimportant

The passive voice is appropriate whenever the receiver of the action is more important than the doer. It is often used in scientific writing, which tends to emphasize the material acted on rather than the doer of the action.

The distillate is then removed from the liquid.

Passive Voice to Place Old Information Before New

The passive voice is also appropriate when the old information in a sentence is the receiver of the action rather than the doer.

Graphs are essential tools for economic analysis. They *are* commonly *used* by economists to display both concrete economic data and abstract economic concepts.

In the second sentence, the passive voice allows the writer to begin with old information. The pronoun *they* refers to *graphs* in the previous sentence.

For more on the use of the passive voice, see pp. 530–531.

Passive Voice to Evade Responsibility

Sometimes writers use the passive voice intentionally to avoid naming a responsible party. This practice is ethically questionable. Avoid it when you can.

Evasive   The decision has been made to raise the dues.

Forthright   The president and the treasurer have decided to raise the dues.

Exercise

On a separate sheet of paper, convert the transitive passive sentences to transitive active, and convert the transitive active sentences to transitive passive. Leave the intransitive sentences unchanged. In converting some transitive passive sentences to transitive active, you may have to add an actor or agent. For each sentence, explain in which rhetorical situations the active-voice version would be better and in which the passive would be better.

(continued)

1. The wrong carpets were installed by the carpet layers while the owners were away.
2. Smoke rose in thick billows above the burning house.
3. Beth ladled hot liquid blackberry jelly into sterilized jars.
4. The little girl in the green sunsuit slowly covered her sleeping father with piles of sand.
5. Some of the most important scientific principles have been discovered accidentally.
6. The motor was probably ruined by the turbine bearing's being rusted out.

USING INCLUSIVE LANGUAGE

For much of the history of the English language, grammarians accepted the use of masculine pronouns ("Everyone should bring *his* own lunch") and the use of *man* ("Peace and goodwill to *men* everywhere") as generic references for both men and women. Many contemporary writers believe that these usages reflect pro-male bias. Many writers are also now aware of other ways in which language subtly reflects attitudes toward gender, culture, and ethnicity. In this section, we offer suggestions that will help you construct sentences free of biased language.

Avoiding Sexist Labels and Stereotypes

Avoid language that labels or stereotypes women. Referring to women as "the weaker sex," "the ladies," "the girls," or "the distaff side" implies that women are not equal to men. Similarly, it is inappropriate to identify women as wives or mothers in a context where their professional or work status is more relevant or to refer to a woman's appearance unless the context demands it. Let the same considerations guide you whether you are describing a man or a woman.

Sexist	Janet Peterson, stunning in her new, blue-sequined evening gown, gave the keynote address at the annual mayors' conference.
	Would you say, "Robert Peterson, stunning in his new tuxedo, ruffled shirtfront, and cumberbund, gave the keynote address at the annual mayors' conference"?
Revised	Janet Peterson, newly elected mayor of the state's third-largest city, gave the keynote address at the annual mayors' conference.

Avoiding Use of Masculine Pronouns to Refer to Both Sexes

Whenever possible, revise sentences to avoid using the masculine pronouns *he, him, his,* and *himself* to refer to people of both sexes. Often you can use plural pronouns (*they, them, their,* and *themselves*), which do not indicate gender.

Problematic	If a student wants to bring his text to the exam, he may.
Revised	If students want to bring their texts to the exam, they may.

In informal writing, you can also use *you* and *your* to avoid sexist language; in formal prose you can use *one* and *one's,* although this usage sometimes sounds stilted.

Revised   If you want to bring your texts to the exam, you may.

Revised   If one wants to bring one's text to the exam, one may.

Another strategy is to alternate between masculine and feminine forms.

> At the revising stage, the writer should go over *his* draft carefully, making sure that the central idea of each paragraph is clear. At the editing stage a writer's focus shifts. Now *she* should check for sentence-level problems, paying particular attention to spelling, punctuation, and problems of usage.

(*Note:* This practice, although common in some academic journals, is not yet widely accepted in the popular media.)

Avoid bureaucratic constructions such as *him/her* or *s/he,* which are cumbersome and inelegant. Occasional use of the combined forms *he or she* or *him or her* is acceptable, but overuse of this construction is tiresome.

Avoiding Inappropriate Use of the Suffix *-man*

Use of *-man* as a suffix in such words as *repairman, mailman,* and *policeman* or as a prefix in *mankind* seems to ignore the presence of women in the workforce and in the human race. The suffix *-person* may be an acceptable substitute; *chairperson* and *salesperson* are becoming increasingly common in formal usage. However, *weatherperson* still sounds odd, as does "Joan is a new *freshperson* at state college." Look for alternative expressions.

Avoid	Prefer
chairman	chairperson
coed	student
congressman	representative, member of congress
forefathers	ancestors
mailman	mail carrier
man (generic)	person, people, humans, human beings
wives, husbands	spouses
manmade	synthetic
policeman	police officer
salesman	sales representative, salesclerk
waiter, waitress	waitperson, server
newsman	reporter, journalist
fireman	firefighter
weatherman	weather announcer, meteorologist
sportsman	sports enthusiast, athlete
stewardess	flight attendant

Avoiding Language Biased Against Ethnic or Other Minorities

Avoid language that reflects stereotypes against ethnic or other minorities. Language referring to minorities evolves rapidly. In the 1980s *black* and *Afro-American* were preferred terms, but in the 1990s these largely gave way to *African-American*. Similarly, the terms *Latino* and *Latina* are replacing *Hispanic*. Homosexual people now prefer the terms *gay man* and *lesbian* and in some contexts are reviving the word *queer*. Today the term *people of color* is in favor, but the term *colored person* is an intense insult.

As a writer, you need to be sensitive to the subtle ways in which language can make people feel included and welcomed or excluded and insulted. Nowhere is the evolving and charged nature of language more evident than in the connotations of words referring to cultural minorities.

HANDBOOK 6

Editing for Punctuation and Mechanics

This chapter provides a handy compendium of rules and guidelines for using punctuation marks, underlining (italics), and capital letters. It also includes a section on manuscript form. The following main topics are covered:

- Periods, question marks, and exclamation points
- Commas
- Semicolons
- Colons, dashes, and parentheses
- Apostrophes
- Quotation marks
- Underlining (italics)
- Brackets, ellipses, and slashes
- Capital letters
- Numbers
- Abbreviations
- Manuscript form

PERIODS, QUESTION MARKS, AND EXCLAMATION POINTS

Periods, question marks, and exclamation points, sometimes called *terminal punctuation* or *endmarks,* signal the end of a sentence. These marks generally raise few problems for writers except in the case of sentence fragments (when an endmark follows a nonsentence), comma splices (when a comma is substituted for an endmark), and run-ons (when two sentences are fused together without an endmark).

A few other situations that sometimes pose problems for writers are discussed next.

For a full discussion of sentence boundaries, including advice for avoiding fragments, comma splices, and run-ons, see Handbook 3.

Courtesy Questions

Courtesy questions—mild commands phrased politely as questions—normally end with a period.

> Would you please return the form in the enclosed envelope.
>
> The absence of a question mark makes this a mild command, not a real question.

Indirect Questions

Although direct questions require a question mark, indirect questions end with a period.

Direct Question   He asked me, "Where are you going?"

Indirect Question   He asked me where I was going.

Placement of Question Marks with Quotations

If quotation marks and a question mark appear together, the question mark goes inside the quotation marks when only the quotation is a question and outside when the whole sentence is a question.

Quotation Is Question

The professor asked, "Can you solve the fox-and-chicken puzzle?"

Entire Sentence Is Question

Did you hear the professor talk about the "fox-and-chicken puzzle"?

Note: When the question mark goes inside the quotation marks, do not follow the question mark with a comma or period.

Faulty   "Can we go with you?," she asked.

Revised   "Can we go with you?" she asked.

Exclamation Points

An exclamation point is used after a sentence or word group to express strong emotion. Exclamation points are used primarily in dialogue to indicate shouting or an especially strong feeling. Avoid using them in most other instances—especially academic prose—because they rarely have the effect on a reader that the writer intends. Expressing emotion through word choice, sentence structure, and tone is more effective. When an exclamation point goes inside a quotation, do not follow the exclamation point with a comma or period.

COMMAS

The comma is the most frequently used mark of internal punctuation. A comma mistakenly used as an endmark creates a comma splice. The main rules for use of commas to mark the boundaries of phrases, clauses, and sentences are covered in depth in Handbook 3. These rules are reviewed in this section, along with additional guidelines.

For comma splices, see Handbook 3, pp. 758–760.

Using Commas

Using Commas with Coordinating Conjunctions

Use a comma and a coordinating conjunction (*and, or, nor, for, but, yet,* and *so*) to join two independent clauses.

I released the dog's leash, and the dog trotted off across the field.

If the main clauses are very short, it is acceptable to omit the comma before the coordinating conjunction, but it is never acceptable to omit the coordinating conjunction; doing so will create a comma splice.

Comma Splice   We crossed the meadow, then we headed toward the mountain.

Revised   We crossed the meadow, and then we headed toward the mountain.

Comma after Introductory Adverb Clauses and Long Introductory Phrases

Use a comma to set off introductory adverb clauses and long introductory phrases from the rest of the sentence.

Introductory Adverb Clause   When I get home from work, I always fix myself a big sardine sandwich.

Introductory Phrase   Having lost my balance, I began waving my arms frantically.

Note: Initial gerund phrases or infinitive phrases used as sentence subjects should not be set off because they are part of the sentence core.

Faulty   To know him, is to love him. Playing her guitar every evening, is Sally's way of relaxing.

These introductory phrases serve as the subjects of their sentences and should not be set off.

Revised   To know him is to love him. Playing her guitar every evening is Sally's way of relaxing.

Comma after Introductory Transitional Words and Expressions

Set off most introductory transitional words and phrases such as *on the other hand, in sum, however, moreover,* and *for example* with a comma.

On the other hand, bicycle racing involves an astonishing amount of strategy.

Writers often do not use a comma to set off *thus* and *therefore* and some other transitional expressions that do not noticeably interrupt the flow of the sentence. In such cases let your voice be your guide. If you pause noticeably after the transitional expression, set it off with a comma.

See Figure HB3.1 on p. 762 for a list of transitional expressions.

Commas to Set Off Absolute Phrases

An absolute phrase comprises a noun followed by a participle or participial phrase. These phrases are *absolute* because they are complete in themselves; they modify the entire sentence rather than an individual word within the sentence. Absolute phrases are always set off with commas.

See p. 750, for an explanation of verbal phrases.

His hand wrapped in a blanket, Harvey hobbled toward the ambulance.

The bear reared on its hind legs, *its teeth looking razor sharp in the glaring sun.*

Comma Before Concluding Participial Phrases

Use commas to set off participial phrases at the ends of sentences if they modify the subjects.

The doctor rushed quickly toward the accident victim, fumbling to open his black bag.

In this example, it is the doctor who fumbles to open his bag. The comma indicates that *fumbling* modifies *doctor* (the sentence subject) and not *victim* (the noun immediately preceding the participle).

Do not use a comma to set off a participial phrase at the end of a sentence if the phrase modifies the immediately preceding noun.

The doctor rushed quickly toward the accident victim lying face forward on the soft shoulder of the road.

Here the participial phrase modifies the preceding noun, *victim,* instead of the sentence subject. It is not set off with commas.

Commas to Avoid Confusion

Use commas to separate sentence elements if failure to separate them would create confusion.

Confusing	Every time John ate his dog wanted to be fed too.
Revised	Every time John ate, his dog wanted to be fed too.

Commas to Set Off Nonrestrictive Clauses and Phrases

Adjective modifiers following a noun are either *restrictive* or *nonrestrictive,* depending on whether they are needed to identify the noun they modify. Use commas to set off nonrestrictive clauses and phrases.

Restrictive and Nonrestrictive Clauses. An adjective clause is *nonrestrictive* if it is not needed to identify the noun it modifies. In such cases, set off the clause or phrase with commas.

Nonrestrictive Clause	My father dislikes Bill Jones, who rides a noisy motorcycle.

In this case, you know whom the father dislikes: Bill Jones. The fact that Bill rides a noisy motorcycle is additional information about him.

If the modifying clause is needed to identify the noun it is modifying, then it is *restrictive* and is not set off with commas.

Restrictive Clause	My father dislikes people who ride noisy motorcycles.

Here the meaning is "My father doesn't dislike all people, just those people who ride noisy motorcycles." The adjective clause restricts the meaning of *people;* that is, it narrows down the class "people" to the subclass of "people who ride motorcycles." Because the phrase is needed to identify which people the father dislikes, it is a restrictive clause used *without* commas.

To help you remember this rule, think of this saying: Extra information, extra commas; needed information, no commas.

Nonrestrictive Clause	My grandmother, who graduated from college when she was eighty-two years old, deserves a special award.

You know who deserves a special award: my grandmother. The adjective clause provides extra information, so the sentence needs extra commas.

Restrictive Clause	Anyone who graduates from college at age eighty-two deserves a special award.

Here, *who graduates from college* is needed information. Otherwise the sentence would mean that "anyone" deserves a special award, rather than only those people who graduate from college at age eighty-two. This sentence follows the rule "needed information, no commas."

Restrictive and Nonrestrictive Phrases. The same extra information/needed information rule holds for adjective phrases.

Restrictive Phrase	The man wearing the double-breasted suit is an accountant.

Here the phrase *wearing the double-breasted suit* identifies which man is an accountant. The sentence implies that there are two or more men. (Which man is the accountant? The one wearing the double-breasted suit.) Because the phrase is needed to identify which man is meant, it is not set off with commas.

Nonrestrictive Phrase	Elvis Dweezle, wearing a double-breasted suit, looked at himself briefly in the mirror before knocking on his boss's door.

Here the phrase *wearing a double-breasted suit* merely adds extra information about the already-identified Elvis Dweezle.

Commas to Set Off Nonrestrictive Appositives

An *appositive* is a noun or noun phrase that immediately follows another noun, renaming it or otherwise referring to it. Appositives also follow the extra information/needed information rule. An appositive is restrictive (needed information) if it serves to identify the preceding noun; it is nonrestrictive (extra information) if it simply contributes additional information to an already-identified noun. As with nonrestrictive adjective clauses and phrases, set off nonrestrictive appositives with commas.

Nonrestrictive Appositive	Angela, a good friend of mine, has just been promoted to chief accountant.

In this example you know who has just been promoted: Angela. The appositive *a good friend of mine* adds extra information about Angela.

Restrictive Appositive	My friend Angela offered to do my income taxes for me.

Here the appositive *Angela* is needed to identify which friend offered to do the taxes. No commas are used.

Commas to Separate Items in a Series

Use commas to separate items in a series of three or more words, phrases, or clauses. The first comma leads readers to anticipate a list, with the last two elements joined by *and* or *or.* Place commas after each item in the series except the last.

He especially likes golf, jogging, and swimming.

We went to the movies, had dinner downtown, and then went bowling.

(*Note:* Although British writers and some American writers omit the comma before the coordinating conjunction in a series, sentences are generally clearer if the comma is included.)

Confusing	I like three kinds of pizza: pepperoni, Canadian bacon and pineapple and Italian sausage.
Clearer	I like three kinds of pizza: pepperoni, Canadian bacon and pineapple, and Italian sausage.

In the first version, the reader initially thinks that the first *and* marks the end of the series when it simply joins one of the elements (*Canadian bacon and pineapple*). Placing a comma before the final *and* in the series clarifies the sentence.

Commas to Separate Coordinate Adjectives Preceding a Noun

Coordinate adjectives in a series are separated by commas. Adjectives are coordinate if they can be separated by *and* or if they can be placed in a different order.

Coordinate Adjectives	A nearsighted, tall, thin, grumpy-looking man walked slowly down the street.

In this case you could say a "thin and grumpy-looking and nearsighted and tall man," thus separating the elements with *and* and placing them in a different order. These are coordinate adjectives separated by commas.

Noncoordinate Adjectives	Three aluminum-plated frying pans sat on the shelf.

These adjectives are not coordinate because you cannot say "frying and aluminum-plated and three pans." Hence these adjectives are not separated by commas.

Note: Do not place a comma after the last coordinate adjective in a series.

Faulty	A lightweight, sleekly designed, racing, bicycle was my summer's dream.
Revised	A lightweight, sleekly designed, racing bicycle was my summer's dream.

Commas to Set Off Parenthetical or Interrupting Elements

Use commas to set off parenthetical words, phrases, or clauses and other similar elements that interrupt the flow of the sentence. By reading your sentences aloud in a natural voice, you can generally identify parenthetical material that interrupts the flow of a sentence. Such material should be set off by pairs of commas. The following are common examples of interrupting material:

Contrasting Elements Introduced by *but, not,* or *although*

The man at the front desk, not the mechanic, was the one who quoted me the price.

Words of Direct Address, *yes* and *no,* and Mild Interjections

I tell you, Jennifer, your plan won't work.

Transition Words and Expressions

She will, however, demand more money.

Tag Phrases Citing Sources

This new car, according to the latest government reports, gets below-average mileage.

Attributive Tags Identifying Speakers

"To be a successful student," my adviser told me, "you have to enjoy learning."

Commas to Set Off Elements of Places, Addresses, and Dates

Use commas to set off each separate element in a date, place, or address.

He drove to Grand Forks, North Dakota, on July 5, 1971, in an old blue Ford.

Do not place a comma in front of zip codes in addresses.

I live on 23 Elm Street, Seattle, WA 98115.

Omitting Commas

Many beginning writers tend to use too many commas rather than too few. Do not use a comma unless a specific rule calls for one. "When in doubt, leave commas out" is a good rule of thumb. Learn to recognize the following situations that do *not* require commas. These are frequently sources of error in student papers.

Do Not Use a Comma to Separate a Subject from Its Verb or a Verb from Its Complements

Faulty   The man in the apartment next to mine, swallowed a goldfish.

Here a comma mistakenly separates the subject from the verb.

Revised   The man in the apartment next to mine swallowed a goldfish.

Do Not Use a Single Comma Within a Sentence Core

Faulty   My brother, who recently won a pole-sitting contest swallowed a goldfish.

Here a comma occurs on one side of a nonrestrictive clause but not on the other side.

Revised   My brother, who recently won a pole-sitting contest, swallowed a goldfish.

Do Not Use a Comma Before *and* If It Joins Only Two Words or Phrases

Faulty   She pedaled uphill for twenty minutes, and won the race by several lengths.

The *and* joins two verbs rather than two main clauses.

Revised   She pedaled uphill for twenty minutes straight and won the race by several lengths.

Do Not Use a Comma after *such as*

Faulty   They forgot some key supplies such as, candles, matches, and trail mix.

Revised   They forgot some key supplies such as candles, matches, and trail mix.

Exercise

Insert commas where needed in the following sentences.

1. Whenever I go home to Bismarck North Dakota for Christmas vacation the dinner conversation turns to cross-country skiing.

2. On my last visit during dessert my dad who is an expert skier asked me if I wanted to try dogsled racing.

3. "I've wanted to try dogsledding for years" Dad said "but we've never had the equipment or the dogs. Now however my friend Jake Jackson the new agent for Smith Insurance has just bought a team and wants his friend to give it a try."

4. Rock shrimp unlike some other species have hard shells that make them difficult to peel.

5. Hiking or biking through southern Germany you will discover a rich mosaic of towns regional foods colors sounds and smells of the rural countryside and historic Black Forest region.

6. Instead of riding on busy boulevards you can pedal on a network of narrow paved roads built for farm vehicles or on graveled paths through lush green forests.

7. According to historian Daniel T. Rodgers a central question that divided workers and employers in the nineteenth and early twentieth centuries was how many hours a day the average worker should work.

8. Believing strongly in tradition the early factory owners thought their workers should follow the old sunrise to sunset work schedule of agricultural laborers.

9. This schedule which meant fourteen-hour workdays during the summer could also be maintained during the winter thanks to the invention of artificial light which owners rapidly installed in their factories.

10. Spurred on by their desire to create a shorter working day laborers began to organize into forerunners of today's labor unions and used their collective powers to strive for change.

SEMICOLONS

A semicolon is stronger than a comma. It can be used to join two independent clauses to form a single sentence or to separate the main items in a list that already contains commas.

Semicolon to Join Main Clauses

When a semicolon is used to join main clauses, it signals a close relationship between the meanings of the two main clauses and creates a sentence with two balanced, equal parts.

> I asked the professor for an extension on my essay; she told me I was out of luck.

Semicolons are frequently used to connect main clauses when the second clause contains a conjunctive adverb or transitional phrase such as *however, therefore, nevertheless,* and *on the other hand.*

> The new airport won't be finished until June; therefore we'll have to land at Fitzsimmons Field.

Note: Joining two main clauses with only a comma creates a comma splice.

For more on comma splices, see pp. 758–760.

Comma Splice	He spent all morning baking the pie, however, nobody seemed to appreciate his efforts.
Revised	He spent all morning baking the pie; however, nobody seemed to appreciate his efforts.

Semicolon in a Series Containing Commas

Use a semicolon to separate elements in a series when some of those elements already contain commas.

> On vacation we went to Laramie, Wyoming; Denver, Colorado; Salt Lake City, Utah; and Boise, Idaho.
>
> Since commas are used to separate the cities from the states, the semicolons are needed to separate the elements of the series.

Exercise

In the following sentences, insert semicolons and commas as needed. Some sentences may need no additional punctuation. Make sure that your marks of punctuation can be easily read.

1. The two men defended themselves before the justice of the peace in Bilford across the river a similar case was being tried with attorneys and a full jury.
2. She claimed that most teenage shoplifters are never caught moreover those who are caught are seldom punished.
3. I admit that I went to the party I did not however enjoy it.
4. I admit that I went to the party but I did not enjoy it.
5. Although I went to the party I did not enjoy it.
6. When the party ended our apartment was in chaos from one end of the living room to the other end of the bedroom a fine layer of confetti blanketed everything like snow.

(continued)

7. Within twenty minutes of leaving the trail we saw an antelope two elk one of which had begun to shed the velvet on its antlers an assortment of squirrels gophers and chipmunks and most startling of all a large black bear with two cubs.

8. An effective education does not consist of passive rote learning rather it consists of active problem solving.

9. Failure to introduce and to use calculators and computers in school creates needless barriers for teachers and learners furthermore computer literacy is a basic skill in the new millennium.

10. We watched the slides of their vacation for what seemed like an eternity— Toledo Ohio Columbus Missouri Topeka Kansas Omaha Nebraska and on and on across the continent.

COLONS, DASHES, AND PARENTHESES

Colons

The most frequent uses of a colon are to introduce a list; to announce a word, clause, or phrase predicted in a preceding main clause; or to introduce a block quotation. Colons are generally preceded by main clauses and are not used as internal punctuation within a clause.

Colon to Introduce a List

Use a colon to introduce a list when the list follows a grammatically complete independent clause.

> We can win in two ways: changing our defense or adding Jones to the offensive lineup.

Do not use a colon in the middle of a clause or after the words *such as, for example,* or *including.*

Faulty	The things you should bring to the party are: chips, salsa, and your own drinks.
Revised	The things you should bring to the party are chips, salsa, and your own drinks.
	or
	Please bring to the party the following: chips, salsa, and your own drinks.

In the first example the offending colon is removed. In the second, the structure preceding the colon has been expanded to a main clause by adding *the following,* which serves as the direct object of *bring.*

| Faulty | We have many opportunities to improve our score, such as: retaking the exam, doing an extra credit project, or doing a longer paper. |
| Revised | We have many opportunities to improve our score, such as retaking the exam, doing an extra credit project, or doing a longer paper. |

Colon to Introduce a Predicted Element Following an Independent Clause

Following an independent clause, use a colon to introduce a predicted element, which can be a word, a phrase, or a clause.

> The professor agreed to something remarkable: grading contracts for all students.

> The professor agreed to something remarkable: He allowed Jack to submit a late paper.

Note on capitalization: If what follows the colon is a main clause, you have the option of beginning the clause with a capital letter; if what follows the colon is not a complete sentence, use a lowercase letter.

Colon to Introduce Block Quotations or Quotations Receiving Special Emphasis

A colon is used to introduce a block quotation if what precedes the colon is a main clause. You can also use a colon to introduce a short quotation that you want to emphasize.

For an explanation of block quotations, see pp. 623–624.

> His father replied slowly, carefully, thoughtfully: "Buying the tractor now, when we are already too deeply in debt, is not a good idea."

> A comma could also be used to introduce this quotation; a colon is more formal and emphatic.

Colon in Salutations, Time Notations, Titles, and Biblical Citations

Colons are sometimes used in letter salutations and within titles. They are also used in time expressions and biblical notations.

Salutation	Dear Sarah:
Time Notation	4:30 a.m.
Titles	*Teaching Critical Thinking Skills: Theory and Practice*
Biblical Citations	John 3:16

Dashes

Think of the dash as a strong comma that gives special emphasis to the material being set off. (To make a dash, type two hyphens; leave no space before, after, or between the hyphens.)

> Sir Walter Raleigh brought the potato--as well as tobacco--to Queen Elizabeth I on his return from Virginia.

> In this example a pair of commas could replace the pair of dashes. The dashes emphasize the material between them by calling for a greater pause when reading.

Sometimes a dash is used to set off nouns placed for special emphasis at the beginning of a sentence. The nouns are then summarized by a pronoun following the dash.

> Joy, happiness, prosperity--all this is promised to investors in the new Veggi-burger fast-food chain.

Parentheses

Parentheses are used to enclose nonessential, supplemental information and to enclose citations or list numbers.

Supplemental Information

The most common use of parentheses is to enclose supplemental information.

> He took one look at my computer (an old Kaypro from the early 1980s) and started to laugh.

Citations and Numbered Items in a List

For an explanation of the MLA and APA documentation systems, see pp. 631–667.

Parentheses are also used to enclose citations in many documentation systems and to enclose numbers or letters identifying parts of a list.

> To graduate, a student must fill out three forms: (1) the transcript summary, (2) the request form, and (3) the adviser's sign-off sheet (*Junebug State Bulletin* 32).
>
> Parentheses enclose the list numbers and the citation to the *Junebug State Bulletin*, page 32, where this information is found.

Punctuating Sentences That Include Parentheses

When you place a complete sentence within parentheses, the concluding endmark goes inside the parentheses. When you end a sentence with parenthetical elements, the endmark goes outside the parentheses.

> When visiting England, we watched a lot of cricket (a British game somewhat similar to American baseball).
>
> When visiting England, we watched a lot of cricket. (Cricket is a British game something like American baseball.)

APOSTROPHES

The apostrophe is used mainly for showing possession, but it is also used to indicate missing letters in contractions and to form special plurals.

Apostrophe to Show Possession

Use the apostrophe to indicate possession of nouns and indefinite pronouns. Possessive constructions show both a possessor and a thing possessed: the thing possessed occurs last in the construction; the person or thing that possesses (the possessor) comes first and contains an apostrophe.

Possessor	Thing Possessed	Alternative Construction
Sally's	car	car belonging to Sally
men's	coats	coats for men
cats'	fur	fur of cats
three minutes'	work	work lasting three minutes

Because plurals and possessives both add an *s* sound to words, they are identical to the ear. To the eye, however, they are easily distinguished by the use of the apostrophe in the possessive. Be sure that you don't confuse your reader by mixing possessives and plurals.

Faulty	Our neighbor's have two horse's and ten cat's on their grandfathers old farm.
Revised	Our neighbors have two horses and ten cats on their grandfather's old farm.

Neighbors, horses, and *cats* are plurals, not possessives; *grandfather's* is a possessive, not a plural.

Forming the Possessive

To make a noun possessive, you must first determine whether it is singular or plural. Add an apostrophe and an *s* (*'s*) to singular nouns and to plural nouns that do not end in *s*; add an apostrophe only (*'*) to plural nouns that end in *s*.

The man's car   *[the car belonging to the man]*

The men's cars   *[the cars belonging to the men]*

The cats' food dish   *[the food dish belonging to the cats]*

The cat's food dish   *[the food dish belonging to the cat]*

To form the possessive of hyphenated words, compound words, and word groups, add an apostrophe and an *s* (*'s*) to the last word only.

her mother-in-law's lawn mower

the ladies-in-waiting's formal gowns

Do Not Use Apostrophes for Possessives of Personal Pronouns

Do not use apostrophes with the possessive forms of personal and relative pronouns (*yours, his, hers, ours, theirs, its, whose*). When an apostrophe is used with personal or relative pronouns, it indicates a contraction. Be especially careful to distinguish between *it's* ("it is") and *its* (possessive).

Possessive	Contraction
The dog chases its tail.	It's (it is) a funny dog.
Your tie is crooked.	You're (you are) a sloppy dresser.
Whose dog is that?	Who's (who is) at the door?

Apostrophes with Contractions

Use an apostrophe (*'*) to indicate omitted letters in contractions.

you're (you are)	isn't (is not)
it's (it is)	spring of '34 (spring of 1934)

Note: Be sure to insert the apostrophe exactly where the missing letters would be.

Faulty   is'nt

Revised   isn't

Apostrophes to Form Plurals

See p. 805 on underlining.

Use an apostrophe and an *s* (*'s*) to form the plural of letters and words used as words. Underline (italicize) the letter or word but not the plural ending.

> On your test I can't distinguish between your *t*'s and your *E*'s. You also use too many *very*'s and *extremely*'s.

QUOTATION MARKS

See Chapter 23, pp. 629–631, for details on how to quote sources and avoid plagiarism.

Use quotation marks to enclose words, phrases, and sentences that are someone's spoken words or that you have copied from a source. Also use quotation marks to set off titles of short works and to indicate words used in a special sense. Quotation marks always occur in pairs, one marking the beginning and the other the ending of the quoted material.

Punctuating the Start of a Quotation

When a quotation is introduced with an attributive tag (such as "my instructor says" or "Sharon Smith acknowledges"), the tag can be followed by a comma, a colon, or *that.* If you use a comma or a colon, begin the quotation with a capital letter. If you introduce a quotation with *that,* do not capitalize the first letter of the quotation even if it is capitalized in the original. In this case, you do not precede the quotation with a comma.

For use of brackets, see pp. 624–626 and 806.

> Columnist E. J. Dionne says, "Terror is designed to paralyze."
>
> Columnist E. J. Dionne says that : "[t]error is designed to paralyze."

If you work a short quotation into the structure of your own sentence, use no punctuation other than a quotation mark to introduce the quoted passage.

> According to E. J. Dionne, all acts of terror are "designed to paralyze."

Placement of Attributive Tags

Attributive tags can be placed before, inside, or after the quotation. When an attributive tag is placed between the two halves of a quotation, the second half is not capitalized unless it begins a new sentence.

> Michael Karnok says, "To be a father is to know the meaning of failure."
>
> "To be a father," says Michael Karnok, "is to know the meaning of failure."
>
> "To be a father is to know the meaning of failure," says Michael Karnok.

Punctuating the End of a Quotation

Put commas and periods inside quotation marks.

> He told me to "buzz off," and then he went about his business.

> He told me to "buzz off." Then he went about his business.

> Note that both the comma (first sentence) and the period (second sentence) go inside the quotation mark.

In documented papers that place citations inside parentheses at the end of the quotation, put the comma or period after the parenthetical citation.

> According to Immunex Chief Executive Edward Fritzky, "Genetic Institute is doing very, very well" (Lim C5).

> Note the order: quotation mark, parenthetical citation, final period.

Place colons and semicolons outside the ending quotation mark.

> He told me to "buzz off"; then he went about his business.

> My sexist husband wants his "privileges": Monday night football and no household chores.

> Note that the semicolon (first sentence) and the colon (second sentence) go outside the quotation mark.

Place question marks and exclamation points inside quotation marks if they belong to the quotation; place them outside the ending quotation mark if they belong to the whole sentence.

See p. 790 for an example.

Indirect Quotations

Use quotation marks for *direct* quotations—the actual words spoken by someone—but not for *indirect* quotations, which report what someone said without using the exact words.

Direct Quotation	"Do you want to go to the library?" Sally asked Harry.
Indirect Quotation	Sally asked Harry whether he wanted to go to the library.

Indented Block Method for Long Quotations

When quoting more than four typed lines (MLA style) or forty words (APA style), use the indented block method rather than quotation marks to indicate direct quotations. Double-space the quotation for both styles. For the MLA style, indent each line ten spaces from the left margin. Indent five spaces for the APA style. Do *not* put quotation marks around the blocked passage.

See p. 650 for an example.

Single Quotation Marks

In American practice, use a single quotation mark, made with an apostrophe on most keyboards, to enclose a quotation within a quotation.

Molly angrily told her discussion group, "Every time I ask my husband to help me with the ironing, he says that 'men don't iron clothes' and stalks out of the room in a huff."

Inside Molly's directly quoted words is a direct quotation from Molly's husband: *men don't iron clothes*. The husband's words in this case are enclosed in single quotation marks.

With the block indentation method, use regular quotation marks to enclose a quotation within a quotation.

Quotation Marks for Titles of Short Works

Use quotation marks for titles of essays, short stories, short poems, songs, book chapters, and other sections that occur within books or periodicals.

I liked Spenser's sonnet "Most Glorious Lord of Lyfe" better than *The Faerie Queene*.

In this sentence, both the sonnet and *The Faerie Queene* are poems, but the former is in quotation marks because it is short, and the latter is underlined (italicized) because it is long.

Quotation Marks for Words Used in a Special Sense

Use quotation marks to call attention to a word or phrase used in a special sense. Often your intention is to show that you disagree with how someone else uses the word or phrase.

My husband refuses to do what he considers "woman's work."

In this example, the quotation marks indicate that the writer would not use the phrase *woman's work* and that she and her husband have different ideas about what the phrase means.

Although you may set off words used in a special sense with quotation marks, avoid using quotation marks for slang and clichés as an attempt to apologize for them. Rephrase your sentence to eliminate the triteness.

Weak   I've been "busy as a bee" all week, so I'm exhausted.

Revised I've been so busy this week that I'm exhausted.

Exercise

In the following sentences, insert apostrophes and single or double quotation marks as needed.

1. My mother told me that she didn't want me to buy a car until I had a permanent part-time job.
2. Jake has his little quirks, as Molly calls them, but he is still lovable.

3. My adviser recently remarked: The nervous student who encounters a professor who states, Twenty percent of this class usually fails, must learn to say, Not I, instead of giving up.

4. Did your friends teacher really say Attendance is necessary in this class?

5. We are guilty of gross misuse of language, continued the speaker, whenever we use disinterested to mean uninterested.

6. I spent two hours worth of good homework time, complained Thomas friend Karen, trying to invent a tongue twister that would make people stand up and shout, "That's a masterpiece."

UNDERLINING (ITALICS)

In handwritten papers, indicate italics with underlining. In papers prepared using a word processing program, either underlining or italicizing is usually acceptable. Check with your instructor.

Underlines or Italics for Titles of Long Complete Works

Use underlines or italics for titles of books, magazines, journals, newspapers, plays, films, works of art, long poems, pamphlets, and musical works. Capitalize and underline *a*, *an*, and *the* only if they are part of the title.

Moby-Dick	Michaelangelo's David
Newsweek	the Encyclopaedia Britannica
Star Wars	The Sound and the Fury

Note: Books of the Bible and the Bible itself are not underlined or italicized.

Exodus   Revelations   Luke   the Bible

Underlines or Italics for Foreign Words and Phrases

Use underlines or italics for foreign words and phrases.

You should avoid the post hoc ergo propter hoc fallacy.

Underlines or Italics for Letters, Numbers, and Words Used as Words

Use underlines or italics for letters, for numbers, and for words when they are referred to as words and phrases and not as what they represent.

To spell the word separate correctly, remember there is a rat in separate.

BRACKETS, ELLIPSES, AND SLASHES

Brackets and ellipses (three spaced dots) indicate changes within quotations and occasionally have other uses. Slashes are used primarily to indicate line breaks in quoted poetry or, in informal or bureaucratic prose, to indicate an option of alternative words or phrases.

Brackets

Brackets [ ] are made with straight lines and should not be confused with parentheses ( ), which use curved lines.

Brackets to Set Off Explanatory Material Inserted into Quotations

Use brackets to set off explanatory material inserted into a quotation.

> According to Joseph Menosky, "Courses offered to teach these skills [computer literacy] have popped up everywhere."

The original source of this quotation did not contain the words *computer literacy*, since the context of the original source explained what *these skills* meant. In this example, *computer literacy* is inserted in brackets to make up for the missing context. The brackets indicate that the material they enclose did not occur in the original version.

Brackets to Indicate the Writer's Alteration of the Grammar of a Quotation

Use brackets when you need to change the grammar of a quotation to make it fit the grammar of your own sentence.

Original Source	I see electric cars as our best hope for reducing air pollution.
	—Jean Haricot
Correct Use of Brackets	Jean Haricot says that "electric cars [are] our best hope for reducing air pollution."

In this example the writer has to change the original *as* to *are* to make the quotation fit the grammar of his or her own sentence. This change is placed in brackets.

Brackets to Enclose *Sic* to Indicate a Mistake in a Quotation

If you quote a source that contains an obvious mistake, you can insert *sic* in brackets to indicate that the mistake is in the original source and is not your own.

> According to Vernon Tweeble, not your greatest sportswriter, the home-run king is still "Baby [*sic*] Ruth."

Here the *sic* indicates that Tweeble said "Baby Ruth," not "Babe Ruth." The mistake belongs to Tweeble, not to the writer.

Brackets to Enclose the Spaced Periods of an Ellipsis

Whenever you use an ellipsis to indicate omitted material in a quotation, enclose the three spaced periods in a pair of brackets. See the next section on ellipses.

Ellipses

An ellipsis, made with three spaced periods, is used to indicate an omission within a quotation. In MLA style, the ellipsis is enclosed in a pair of brackets unless the ellipsis was already in the original. (In APA style, brackets are not needed around an ellipsis.) When an ellipsis occurs at the end of a sentence, a fourth period is used to mark the sentence boundary. Place this period outside the brackets.

For more on the use of ellipses in quotations, see pp. 625–626.

Original	Before the dam, a float trip down the river through Glen Canyon would cost you a minimum of seven days' time, well within anyone's vacation allotment, and a capital outlay of about forty dollars—the prevailing price of a two-man rubber boat with oars, available at any army-navy surplus store. A life jacket might be useful but not required, for there were no dangerous rapids in the 150 miles of Glen Canyon. —Edward Abbey, "The Damnation of a Canyon"
Correct Use of Ellipses in MLA style	According to Edward Abbey, before the dam was built "a float trip down the river through Glen Canyon would cost you a minimum of seven days' time [. . .] and a capital outlay of about forty dollars [. . .]. A life jacket might be useful but not required [. . .]" (351).

Here the first ellipsis indicates words omitted in the middle of a sentence. The second ellipsis shows words omitted at the end of a sentence and hence includes a fourth period to mark the sentence boundary. In the last example, the period marking the sentence boundary occurs after the parenthetical citation, which indicates the page number of the source.

When quoting poetry, use a line of dots to indicate that one or more full lines of the poem have been omitted, as in this example using Ben Jonson's "Come, My Celia":

Come, my Celia, let us prove,
While we can, the sports of love;
. . . .
Why should we defer our joys?
Fame and rumor are but toys.

Slashes

The main use of the slash is to divide lines of poetry written as a quotation within a sentence.

For the use of the block indentation method for long quotations, see p. 803.

Ben Jonson evokes the *carpe diem* tradition when he says: "Come, my Celia, let us prove, / While we can, the sports of love."

If you quote more than four lines of poetry, use the indented block method rather than quotation marks with slashes.

Slashes are sometimes used to indicate options, but this use is too informal for most essays.

Informal   He told me to take algebra and/or trigonometry.

Formal   He told me to take either algebra or trigonometry or both.

CAPITAL LETTERS

Most writers agree on the conventions for using capital letters, but on occasion usage varies. When in doubt about whether to capitalize a particular word, consult a good dictionary.

Capitals for First Letters of Sentences and Intentional Fragments

Capitalize the first letter of the first word in every sentence and also in sentence fragments used intentionally for effect. In fragmentary questions in a series, initial capital letters are optional.

That man is a liar and a scoundrel. What do you want me to do? Like him? Invite him to dinner? Offer him my money?

or

What do you want me to do? like him? invite him to dinner? offer him my money?

Capitals for Proper Nouns

Use capitals for all proper nouns. The following rules cover most cases you will encounter.

Capitalize the names of people.	Pete Rose; Muhammed Ali; Ho Chi Minh
Capitalize titles of people when the title precedes the name or when the title follows the name without an article.	Doctor Sarah Smith; John Jones, Professor of Mathematics
Do not capitalize titles of people that include an article (*a* or *an*).	Sarah Smith, a medical doctor; John Jones, a mathematics professor
Capitalize family relationship names (Mother, Uncle) when used with a name. When used in place of a name, capitalization is optional.	Please, Aunt Eloise, tell Grandfather (or grandfather) that dinner is ready.
Do not capitalize relationship words when not used with a name or as a name.	I hear that my uncle and your father are going to visit Tony's grandfather.
Capitalize the names of specific geographic locations, areas, and regions, including compass directions if they are part of a name.	Mount Everest; the Pacific Northwest; Idaho; Main Street; the Salmon River; the South

Do not capitalize geographic locations indicated by compass directions but not considered actual names	the northwest part of the United States; a mountain south of here
Capitalize historical events, names, movements, and writings.	the Korean War; the Oregon Territory; Articles of Confederation; the Renaissance; the Impressionist Period
Capitalize the names of ships and buildings and capitalize brand names.	USS *Missouri;* the Empire State Building; Sanka
Capitalize specific academic courses but not academic subject areas, except English and foreign languages.	This term I am taking Chemistry 101, Integral Calculus, and French. But: This term I am taking chemistry, calculus, and French. (In the first sentence, the writer names specific courses; in the second sentence, the writer names subject areas only.)
Capitalize specific times, days, months, and holidays, but not names of seasons.	Monday; the Fourth of July; Halloween; last year; autumn; winter
Capitalize abbreviations derived from proper names.	NFL U.S.A. RCA NAFTA U. of W.

Capitals for Important Words in Titles

In titles of books, articles, plays, musical works, and so forth, capitalize the first and last words, any word following a colon or a semicolon, and all other words except articles, prepositions, and conjunctions of fewer than five letters.

"Ain't No Such Thing as a Montana Cowboy"

Famous Myths and Legends of the World: Stories of Gods and Heroes

Capitals in Quotations and Spoken Dialogue

Capitalize the first word of spoken dialogue, but do not capitalize the first word in the second half of a broken quotation that follows an attributive tag.

She said, "Because it is raining, we won't go."

"Because it is raining," she said, "we won't go."

Do not capitalize indirect quotations.

She said that we wouldn't go because it is raining.

Consistency in Use of Capitals

Use capitals consistently and avoid unnecessary capitals. Contemporary writers generally use capitals sparingly. Once you make a decision in optional or ambiguous cases, stick with it throughout your essay.

NUMBERS

Writers often have to decide whether to write numbers as words (ten) or as numerals (10). Follow the conventions of the genre in which you are writing.

Numbers in Scientific and Technical Writing

Scientific and technical writers generally use numerals for all numbers. Check with your instructor about how to handle numbers in lab reports and other formal papers in science, mathematics, and engineering.

Numbers in Formal Writing for Nontechnical Fields

In the humanities and other nontechnical fields and in most business and professional writing, writers usually adhere to the following conventions:

Use Words Instead of Numerals

For single-word number	eight dogs; a hundred doughnuts
For common fractions	one-third of a cup; half a pie
In the humanities, for two-word numbers	twenty-three students (however, business and professional writers prefer numerals for two-word numbers—23 students)
For numbers greater than a million, use a combination of words and numerals	72 billion dollars

Use Numerals Instead of Words

For addresses	1420 Heron Street
For times and dates	I'll be there at 10:00 A.M. on November 5th.
For percentages and statistics	At least 30 percent of the students scored above 15 on the standardized test.
With decimals	The average score was 29.63
For amounts of money that include cents	That notebook cost around $3.95.
With symbols	20° C, 5'4"
For scores	The Yankees beat the Indians 5 to 3.
To refer to chapters, pages, and lines	You'll find that statistic in Chapter 12 on page 100 at line 8.

Numbers at the Beginning of a Sentence

Spell out in words any number that begins a sentence. If the result is awkward, rewrite the sentence.

Faulty	375 students showed up for the exam.
Revised	Three hundred seventy-five students showed up for the exam.
	or
	We counted 375 students at the exam.

Plurals of Numbers

Do not use an apostrophe for the plural form of numbers.

Faulty	Most of my golf scores are in the low 90's.
Revised	Most of my golf scores are in the low 90s.

Numbers in a Series for Comparison

Use numerals instead of words to express numbers in a series when easy comparison is important.

There were 700 persons at the professor's first public lecture, 270 at the second, and 40 at the third.

ABBREVIATIONS

Whenever it is necessary to save space, such as in tables, indexes, and footnotes, you may use abbreviations. In the main text of formal writing, however, you should generally spell out rather than abbreviate words. Abbreviations are acceptable in the following cases.

Abbreviations for Academic Degrees and Titles

Use abbreviations for academic degrees and for the following common titles when used with a person's name: Mr., Ms., Mrs., Dr., Jr., Sr., St. (Saint). Other titles, such as governor, colonel, professor, and reverend, are spelled out.

The doctor asked Colonel Jones, Ms. Hemmings, and Professor Pruitt to present the portrait of St. Thomas to Judge Hogkins on the occasion of her receiving a Ph.D. in religious studies.

Abbreviations for Agencies, Institutions, and Other Entities

Use abbreviations for agencies, groups, people, places, or objects that are commonly known by capitalized initials.

FBI	UCLA
IOOF	DNA molecules
Washington, D.C.	CD-ROM

If you wish to use a specialized abbreviation that may be unclear to your audience, write out the term in full the first time it occurs and place in parentheses the abbreviation that you will use subsequently.

> The Modern Language Association (MLA) recently issued new guidelines for citing electronic sources.
>
> This example indicates that the writer will henceforth use the abbreviation *MLA*.

Abbreviations for Terms Used with Numbers

Use abbreviations for terms commonly used with numbers, especially times, dates,* amounts, and other units of measure.

1200 C.E.	$15.05
500 B.C.E.	no. 12 in a series
2:45 P.M.	

Note that you should use abbreviations for units of measure only when they appear with numbers; never use abbreviations by themselves.

Faulty   I will meet you sometime in the P.M.

Revised   I will meet you sometime in the afternoon.

There is no clear rule about when to use a period with abbreviations (*U.S.A.* or *USA; kg.* or *kg*). Most publishing houses establish their own guidelines, which they follow consistently.

Abbreviations for Common Latin Terms

Use abbreviations for common Latin terms used in footnotes, bibliographies, or parenthetical comments. In the main text, spell out the English equivalents.

e.g.	for example
i.e.	that is
c.f.	compare

This rule applies also to *etc.* (*et cetera,* meaning "and so forth"). Avoid using *etc.* in formal writing. Instead, use the English *and so forth* or *and so on,* or rewrite your sentence to make it more inclusive, thus eliminating the need for *and so forth.* Never write *and etc.,* because *et* is Latin for "and."

Weak   During my year in London I went to ballets, the opera, Shakespeare plays, etc.

---

*If used, A.D. always precedes the date while B.C. follows it. The abbreviations B.C. ("before Christ") and A.D. (*anno domini* "in the year of the Lord") are now often replaced with B.C.E. ("before the common era") and C.E. ("common era"). In both cases the abbreviation appears after the date. Thus A.D. 500 would be rewritten 500 C.E.

Revised	During my year in London I saw many cultural events, including two ballets, one opera, and four Shakespeare plays.

Plurals of Abbreviations

Do not use an apostrophe when forming the plural of an abbreviation.

Faulty	I've misplaced two of my CD's.
Revised	I've misplaced two of my CDs.

MANUSCRIPT FORM

An attractive manuscript contributes to your *ethos* as a writer. A sloppily prepared, visually unattractive manuscript, or one that violates standard conventions or your instructor's special instructions, creates a negative first impression and weakens the rhetorical effectiveness of your writing.

For more on *ethos,* see Chapters 15 and 23.

Unless told otherwise by your instructor, use the following format for all your college papers:

1. Use white, twenty-pound, 8½-by-11-inch paper.
2. Print the paper in black using an inkjet or laser printer. The type should be dark and readable. Do not use colored inks. Do not use a dot matrix printer, which produces poor quality type, unless you check with your instructor first.
3. Avoid fancy typefaces and icons. Make the text look like a typed manuscript rather than a published document unless the assignment calls for such an appearance.
4. Double-space the text throughout, including quotations and notes.
5. Use one-inch margins at the top and bottom, and left and right sides.
6. Indent five spaces for paragraphs. Leave two spaces after periods and other terminal punctuation; leave one space after commas and other marks of punctuation.
7. Make a dash with two unspaced hyphens so that it looks like this--a proper dash.
8. Distinguish between brackets [ ] and parentheses ( ) and make ellipses with spaced periods.

For rules on the use of brackets, parentheses, and ellipses, see pp. 800 and 806–807.

9. Proofread carefully. Type in your corrections, and print a clean copy of the paper. If you can't use a computer to make the corrections, write them neatly in ink by crossing out typographical errors and writing corrections above the crossouts.
10. Do *not* make a separate title page unless you are using the APA style or have been given special directions by your instructor. Rather, follow the MLA style, which places "cover page" information on the first page of the paper itself.
11. Staple your pages in the upper-left-hand corner. Do *not* place your essay in a binder unless your instructor requests you to do so.

For MLA formatting instructions, see p. 646; for an example of an opening page, see p. 647; for a cover page in APA style, see p. 356.

Acknowledgments

Page 5. Rodney Kilcup, "A Modest Proposal for Reluctant Writers," *Newsletter of the Pacific Northwest Writing Consortium 2*, no. 3 (September 1982): 5.

Page 5. Stephen D. Brookfield, *Developing Critical Thinkers: Challenging Adults to Explore Alternative Ways of Thinking and Acting* (San Francisco: Jossey-Bass, 1987):5.

Page 6. Andrea Lunsford and Lisa Ede, *Singular Texts/Plural Authors: Perspective on Collaborative Writing* (Carbondale and Edwardsville, IL: Southern Illinois University Press, 1992): 21, 45–48.

Page 7. Excerpts from a workshop for new faculty members, Jeffrey R. Stephens (Department of Chemistry, Seattle University), Bridget Carney (School of Nursing, Seattle University), and Tomas Guillen (Department of Speech Communication and Journalism, Seattle University).

Page 9. Paulo Freire, *Pedagogy of the Oppressed* (New York: Continuum, 1989).

Page 10. Christopher Leigh, 2 journal entries, student writing. Reprinted with the permission of the author.

Page 13. David M. Rockwood, letter to editor, *The Oregonian* (January 1, 1993): E4. Reprinted with the permission of David M. Rockwood.

Page 14. Thomas Merton, "Rain and the Rhinoceros," from *Raids on the Unspeakable*, copyright © 1966 by The Abbey of Gethsemani, Inc. Reprinted by permission of New Directions Publishing Corp.

Page 19. Amanda Higgins, "Country Music Cool?," student essay. Reprinted with the permission of the author.

Page 24. David Wallechinsky, "This Land of Ours," *Parade Magazine* (July 5, 1992): 4.

Page 24. A. Kimbrough Sherman, in *Thinking and Writing in College: A Naturalistic Study of Students in Four Disciplines* by Barbara E. Walvord and Lucille P. McCarthy (Urbana, IL: NCTE, 1990): 51.

Page 25. William G. Perry, *Forms of Intellectual and Ethical Development in the College Years* (Troy, MO: Holt, Rinehart & Winston, 1970).

Page 29. Evelyn Fox Keller, "Women in Science: An Analysis of a Social Problem," *Harvard Magazine* (1974).

Page 32. Stephen Bean, student writing.

Page 35. "Proposed Law Calls for Fines, Arrests," from "Will Tougher Panhandling Laws Work?" *The Seattle Times* (October 1, 1993). Copyright © 2001 Seattle Times Company. Used by permission.

Page 37. Peter Elbow, *Writing Without Teachers* (New York: Oxford University Press, 1973): 147–190.

Page 38. Paul Theroux, *Sunrise with Seamonsters* (Boston: Houghton Mifflin, 1985).

Pages 40 and 41. Peter Elbow, *Writing Without Teachers* (New York: Oxford University Press, 1973): 14–15.

Page 54. Peter M. Hosinski, letter to editor, *The New York Times* (July 21, 2001). Reprinted by permission of Peter M. Hosinski.

Page 54. Marcus J. Wiesner, letter to editor, *The New York Times* (July 21, 2001). Reprinted by permission of Marcus J. Wiesner.

Page 55. Robert R. Sullivan, letter to editor, *The New York Times* (July 21, 2001). Reprinted by permission of Robert R. Sullivan.

Page 55. Carol Belford, letter to editor, *The New York Times* (July 21, 2001).

Page 60. James Moffett, *Active Voice: A Writing Program Across the Curriculum* (Montclair, NJ: Boynton/Cook Publishers, 1981).

Pages 72 and 78. Dale Kunkel, Kristie M. Cope, and Erica Biely, from "Sexual Messages on Television," *The Journal of Sex Research*, Vol. 36, No. 3 (August 1999): 230. Reprinted with permission.

Pages 73 and 79. Deborah A. Lott, from "The New Flirting Game," *Psychology Today* (January/February 1999). Reprinted with permission from *Psychology Today* Magazine, copyright © 1999 Sussex Publishers, Inc.

Page 73. Lisa Sussman and Tracey Cox, from "I'd Never Be Unfaithful, But…," *Cosmopolitan* (Australian ed.) (January 2001): 108ff.

Page 83. Penny Parker, "For Teeth, Say Cheese," from *New Scientist* (April 6, 1991). Copyright © 1991. Reprinted with the permission of *New Scientist*.

Page 83. Carlo Patrono, "Aspirin as an Antiplatelet Drug," *The New England Journal of Medicine* 330, (May 5, 1994): 1287–1294. Copyright © 1994 by the Massachusetts Medical Society. Reprinted by permission of *The New England Journal of Medicine*.

Page 89. From "ANWR Information Brief" from www.anwr.org/tech-facts.pdf, accessed September 24, 2001. Reprinted by permission of Arctic Power.

Page 90. Randal Rubini, from "A Vicious Cycle," *The Seattle Times* (August 27, 1992): G1+.

Page 91. From "Which One Is the Real ANWR" from www.anwr.org/features/pdfs/realanwr.pdf, accessed September 24, 2001. Reprinted by permission of Arctic Power.

Page 91. Jimmy Carter, from "Make This Natural Treasure a National Monument." *The New York Times* (December 28, 2000): A23. Copyright © 2000. Reprinted by permission of The New York Times Company.

Page 91. From "An Open Letter to the Honorable Jimmy Carter, Former President of the United States," by Alaska Governor Tony Knowles, at http://www.anwr.org/features/gov-carter.htm, accessed September 24, 2001. Reprinted by permission.

Page 95. Lorna Marshal, *The !Kung of Nyae Nyae* (Cambridge: Harvard University Press, 1976): 177–178.

Page 95. P. Draper, "!Kung Women: Contrasts in Sexual Egalitarianism in Foraging and Sedentary Contexts," in *Toward an Anthropology of Women*, ed. R. Reiter (New York: Monthly Review Press, 1975): 82–83.

Page 99. Henry Morton Stanley, "Henry Morton Stanley's Account" from "A Classroom Laboratory for Writing History" from *Social Studies Review* 31, no. 1 (1991). Copyright © 1991. Reprinted with permission.

Page 99. Donald C. Holsinger, "A Classroom Laboratory for Writing History," *Social Studies Review* 31, no. 1 (1991): 59–64.

Pages 109 and 131. Andrés Martin, M.D., "On Teenagers and Tattoos," *Journal of the American Academy of Child and Adolescent Psychiatry* 36, no. 6 (June

1997): 860–861. Reprinted with the permission of Williams & Wilkins.

Page 114. Robert B. Cullen with Sullivan, "Dangers of Disarming," *Newsweek* (October 27, 1986). Copyright © 1986 by Newsweek Inc. All rights reserved. Reprinted with the permission of *Newsweek*.

Page 117. Carl Rogers, *On Becoming a Person: A Therapist's View of Psychotherapy*, 3rd ed. (Boston: Houghton Mifflin, 1961).

Page 124. Sean Barry, "Why Do Teenagers Get Tattoos? A Response to Andrés Martin," student essay. Reprinted with the permission of the author.

Page 133. Florence King, "I'd Rather Smoke Than Kiss," *National Review* (July 9, 1990): 32, 34–36. Copyright © 1990 by National Review, Inc., 215 Lexington Avenue, New York, NY 10016. Reprinted by permission.

Page 138. Gina Escamilla, Angie L. Cradock, and Ichiro Kawachi, "Women and Smoking in Hollywood Movies: A Content Analysis," *American Journal of Public Health*, Vol. 90, Issue 3 (March 2000): 412ff. Copyright © 2000 by APHA. Reprinted with permission of The American Public Health Association.

Page 144. Edward Abbey, "The Damnation of a Canyon" from *Beyond the Wall* by Edward Abbey, © 1971, 1976, 1977, 1979, 1984 by Edward Abbey. Reprinted by permission of Henry Holt and Company, LLC.

Page 157. Richard Wright, excerpt from *Black Boy* by Richard Wright, pp. 216–217. Copyright © 1937, 1942, 1944, 1945 by Richard Wright. Copyright renewed 1973 by Ellen Wright. Reprinted by permission of HarperCollins Publishers Inc.

Page 160. Kris Saknussemm, "Phantom Limb Pain." Reprinted by permission of Kris Saknussemm.

Page 162. Patrick José, "No Cats in America?," student essay. Reprinted with the permission of the author.

Page 167. Sheila Madden, "Letting Go of Bart," *Santa Clara Magazine* (Summer 1994). Copyright © 1994 by Sheila Madden. Reprinted with the permission of the author.

Page 176. Anonymous, "Essay A/Essay B" from "Inventing the University," in *When A Writer Can't Write* by David Bartholomae. Reprinted with the permission of The Guilford Press.

Page 180. Christopher Leigh, "An Exploration of How to Prevent Violence in Schools," student essay. Reprinted with the permission of the author.

Page 185. Sheridan Hopper Botts, "Exploring Problems About Hospices," student essay. Reprinted with the permission of the author.

Pages 190 and 193. Stephen Bean, "Sam" journal entries and "Should Women Be Allowed to Serve in Combat Units?", student writing. Reprinted with the permission of the author.

Page 200. Article abstract of "Reefer Madness" by Eric Schlosser (August 1994). Abstract reprinted with the permission of *The Atlantic Monthly*.

Page 200. Article abstract of "The Sex-Bias Myth in Medicine" by Andrew G. Kadar, M.D. (August 1994). Abstract reprinted with the permission of *The Atlantic Monthly*.

Page 200. Article abstract of "It's Not the Economy, Stupid" by Charles R. Morris (July 1993). Abstract reprinted with the permission of *The Atlantic Monthly*.

Page 200. Article abstract of "Midlife Myths" by Winifred Gallagher (May 1993). Abstract reprinted with the permission of *The Atlantic Monthly*.

Page 201. Leo W. Banks, "Not Guilty: Despite Its Fearsome Image, the Tarantula Is a Benign Beast," *America West Airlines Magazine* (February 1988). Copyright © 1988 by Leo Banks. Reprinted with the permission of the author.

Page 204. Cheryl Carp, "Behind Stone Walls," student essay. Reprinted with the permission of the author.

Page 207. David Quammen, "The Face of a Spider: Eyeball to Eyeball with the Good, the Bad, and the Ugly," from *Outside Magazine* (March 1987). Reprinted by permission of David Quammen. All rights reserved. Copyright © 1987 by David Quammen.

Page 218. John Berger, *About Looking* (New York: Vintage Books, 1980), p. 52.

Page 232. "Attention Advertisers: Real Men Do Laundry," *American Demographics* (March 1994): 13–14.

Page 232. Erving Goffman, *Gender Advertisements* (New York: Harper & Row, 1979).

Page 237. Paul Messaris, from *Visual Persuasion: The Role of Images in Advertising* by Paul Messaris (Thousand Oaks, CA: Sage, 1997). Reprinted by permission of Sage Publications, Inc.

Page 242. Stephen Bean, "How Cigarette Advertisers Address the Stigma Against Smoking: A Tale of Two Ads," student essay. Reprinted with the permission of the author.

Page 250. "Help Troubled Teens—Don't Forget Them," *USA Today* (November 8, 1985).

Page 252. The Federal Reserve Board, "1998 Survey of Consumer Finances." http://www.federalreserve.gov/pubs/oss/oss2/98/scf98home.html accessed October 28, 2001.

Page 266. Bryant Stamford, "Understand Calories, Fat Content in Food," *Seattle Times* (July 27, 1995). Copyright © 1995. Reprinted with the permission of Gannett News Service.

Page 268. Vicki Alexander, "Trouble with Teens or with Numbers?," student essay. Reprinted with the permission of the author.

Page 270. Jean Fleming, "How Well-Off Are Retired People?," student essay. Reprinted with the permission of the author.

Page 276. Evelyn Dahl Reed, "Medicine Man," from *Coyote Tales from the Indian Pueblos* by Evelyn Dahl Reed. Copyright © 1988 by Evelyn Dahl Reed. Reprinted with the permission of Sunstone Press, P.O. Box 2321, Sante Fe, NM 87504-2321.

Page 285. Alice Walker, "Everyday Use," from *In Love & Trouble: Stories of Black Women*. Copyright © 1973 by Alice Walker. Reprinted by permission of Harcourt, Inc.

Page 292. David Updike, "Summer" from *Out on the Marsh* by David Updike. Reprinted by permission of David R. Godine, Publisher, Inc. Copyright © 1988 by David Updike.

Page 297. Elizabeth M. Weiler, "Who Do You Want to Be?", student essay. Reprinted with the permission of the author.

Page 306. John Gallagher, "Young Entrepreneurs' Disdain for Time Off," from Knight Ridder Newspapers as published in *The Seattle Times* (July 4, 2001): E1, E6. Reprinted by permission.

Page 308. Keith Goetzman, "The Late, Great Outdoors," *Utne Reader* (September/October 2001): 16–17. Reprinted with permission of Keith Goetzman and *Utne Reader*.

Pages 313, 315, 316, 318, 320. Kara Watterson, student writings. Reprinted with the permission of the author.

Pages 314, 317, 319, 320. Kate MacAulay, student writings. Reprinted with the permission of the author.

Page 323. Bill McKibben, "The Environmental Issue from Hell," from *Utne Reader* (September/October 2001): 32, 34, 35. Originally published in *In These Times*. Reprinted by permission of *Utne Reader* and *In These Times* (www.inthesetimes.com).

Page 326. Bjørn Lomborg, "Global Warming—Are We Doing the Right Thing?," *Guardian Unlimited* (August 17, 2001), www.guardian.co.uk/globalwarming, accessed January 13, 2002. Copyright © 2001 by Bjørn Lomborg. Reprinted by permission of *Guardian Unlimited*.

Page 330. Alan Durning, "Land of the Free...Parking," *Utne Reader* (September/October 2001). Reprinted by permission of Michigan Land Use Institute and *Utne Reader*.

Page 342. "Strip-Mining for Stone Washed Jeans." *Environment*.

Page 342. Doron Levin, "$2-$3 a Gallon Gasoline Won't Make SUVs Disappear," *The Seattle Times* (May 4, 2001): B7.

Page 343. Monica Yant, "Many Female Athletes at Risk of 'Triad' of Health Problems," *Seattle Tribune* (June 18, 1992): B14.

Page 349. Steven E. Landsburg, "Why Are We Getting So Fat? A Few Theories on America's Weight Problem," *Slate* (May 1, 2001),http://slate.msn.com/economics/01-05-01/economics.asp. Copyright © 2001 by *Slate*/Dist. by United Feature Syndicate, Inc. Reprinted by permission.

Page 351. Evar D. Nering, "The Mirage of a Growing Food Supply," *The New York Times* (June 4, 2001): A21. Copyright © 2001. Reprinted by permission of The New York Times Company.

Page 353. Edgar Lobaton, "What Causes Latino Stereotypes in the United States?" student essay. Reprinted with the permission of the author.

Page 356. Susan Meyers, "Denying Desire: The Anorexic Struggle with Image, Self, and Sexuality," student essay. Reprinted with the permission of the author.

Page 380. Stephen Toulmin, *The Uses of Argument* (Cambridge: Cambridge University Press, 1958).

Pages 382 and 387. Walter Wink, "Biting the Bullet: The Case for Legalizing Drugs," *The Christian Century* (August 8–15, 1990).

Page 382. Michael Levin, "The Case for Torture," *Newsweek* (June 7, 1982).

Page 394. Edward I. Koch, "Death and Justice: How Capital Punishment Affirms Life," *The New Republic* (April 15, 1985). Copyright © 1985 by the New Republic, Inc. Reprinted with the permission of *The New Republic*.

Page 399. David Bruck, "The Death Penalty," *The New Republic* (May 20, 1985). Copyright © 1985 by the New Republic, Inc. Reprinted with the permission of *The New Republic*.

Page 403. Leonard A. Pitts, Jr., "Spare the Rod, Spoil the Parenting," *The Seattle Times* (September 6, 2001). Copyright © 2001 by the Miami Herald. Reprinted by permission.

Page 406. Dan Savage, "Is No Adoption Really Better Than a Gay Adoption?" *The New York Times* (September 8, 2001): A23. Reprinted by permission.

Page 408. Tiffany D. Linder, "Salvaging Our Old-Growth Forest," student essay. Reprinted with the permission of the author.

Page 430. Katie Tiehen, from "Some may challenge...," student essay. Reprinted with the permission of the author.

Page 430. Jackie Wyngaard, "EMP: Music History or Music Trivia?," student essay. Reprinted with the permission of the author.

Page 433. Diane Helman and Phyllis Bookspan, "*Sesame Street*: Brought to You by the Letters M-A-L-E," *The Seattle Times* (July 28, 1992). Reprinted with permission.

Page 435. Sarah Erickson, "*Picnic at Hanging Rock* as an Art Film," student essay. Reprinted with the permission of the author.

Page 452. Rebekah Taylor, "A Proposal to Provide Cruelty-Free Products on Campus," student essay. Reprinted with the permission of the author.

Page 456. Sheridan Hopper Botts, "Saving Hospices: A Plea to the Insurance Industry," student essay. Reprinted with the permission of the author.

Page 460. Nicholas G. Jenkins and Amit Rind, "National ID Cards Would Be the Dragnet We Need," *The Seattle Times* (October 4, 2001): B7. Reprinted by permission of Nicholas G. Jenkins.

Page 462. Richard F. Corlin, "The Secrets of Gun Violence in America: What We Don't Know Is Killing Us," *Vital Speeches of the Day*, Vol. LXVII, No. 20 (August 1, 2001): 610ff. Reprinted by permission of *Vital Speeches of the Day* and Richard F. Corlin.

Page 479. Jonathan Swift, "A Modest Proposal," in *The Prose Works of Jonathan Swift* (London: Bell, 1914).

Page 497. Kenneth Burke, *The Grammar of Motives* (Berkeley: University of California Press, 1969).

Page 497. James Jones, quoted in Jon Winokur (Ed.), *Writers on Writing* (Philadelphia: Running Press, 1986).

Pages 498–499. Adapted from J. D. Bransford and M. K. Johnson, "Conceptual Prerequisites for Understanding," *Journal of Learning Behavior* 11 (1972): 717–726.

Page 504. Lynnea Clark, excerpt and outline from "Women Police Officers: Should Size and Strength Be Criteria for Patrol Duty?", student essay.

Pages 519, 520–521, and 535. Dao Do, "Choose Life," student essay. Reprinted with the permission of the author.

Page 527. Howard Gardner, *The Mind's New Science: A History of the Cognitive Revolution* (New York: Basic Books, 1985): 90.

Page 528. David Popenoe, "Where's Papa?" from *Life Without Father: Compelling New Evidence that Fatherhood and Marriage Are Indispensable for the Good of Children and Society*. As published in "The Decline of Fatherhood," *Wilson Quarterly* (September/October 1996).

Page 545. Patrick Klein, "Berkeley Blues," in *University of Arizona First Year Composition Guide*. Copyright © 1995 by University of Arizona First Year Composition Program. Reprinted with the permission of Burgess Publishing Company.

Page 550. Val Plumwood, excerpt from "Being Prey," *Utne Reader* (July/August 2000): 56–57. Originally published in *The Ultimate Journey* by Val Plumwood. Reprinted with permission of Traveler's Tales Press and *Utne Reader*.

Page 551. Richard Brautigan, "Leaves" from *The Tokyo-Montana Express* by Richard Brautigan. Copyright © 1979 by Richard Brautigan. Reprinted by permission of Sarah Lazin Books. All rights reserved.

Page 552. Jon Krakauer, excerpt from *Into Thin Air*. Copyright © 1997 by Jon Krakauer. Reprinted with the permission of Villard Books, a division of Random House, Inc.

Page 552. Hitomaro, "A Strange Old Man," by Hitomaro, translated by Kenneth Rexroth, from *One Hundred Poems from the Japanese*, copyright © All Rights Reserved by New Directions Publishing Corp. Reprinted by permission of New Directions Publishing Corp.

Page 554. *College Composition and Communication,* Viponid Interview with John McPhee (May 1991): 203–204.

Page 556. Tom Wolfe, "New Journalism," introduction to *New Journalism*, ed. Tom Wolfe and E. W. Johnson (New York: Harper & Row, 1973): 32. Nicolas Tomalin, in *New Journalism,* ed. Wolfe and Johnson: 201.

Page 568. Annie Dillard, "Living Like Weasels," in *Teaching a Stone to Talk: Expeditions and Encounters.* Copyright © 1982 by Annie Dillard. Reprinted with the permission of HarperCollins Publishers, Inc.

Page 561. Isak Dinesen, "The Iguana," *Out of Africa* (New York: Modern Library, 1952).

Page 562. Victoria Register-Freeman, from "My Turn: Hunks and Handmaidens," *Newsweek* (November 4, 1996): 16. Copyright © 1996 by Newsweek, Inc. Reprinted with the permission of *Newsweek.* All rights reserved.

Page 565. John Kaufeld, *Paradox 5 for Windows for Dummies* (San Mateo, CA: IDG Books Worldwide, Inc., 1994).

Pages 565–566. Michael F. Graves and Wayne H. Slater, "Could Textbooks Be Better Written and Would It Make a Difference?" *American Educator* (Spring 1986): 36–42.

Page 576. Pamela Erens, "Are Subliminal Self-Help Tapes a Hoax?" *Glamour* (October 1994): 62.

Page 618. Roger D. McGrath, "The Myth of Violence in the Old West," in *Gunfighters, Highwaymen, and Vigilantes: Violence on the Frontier.* Copyright © 1984 by The Regents of the University of California. Reprinted with the permission of University of California Press.

Page 647. Christopher Leigh, "The Case Against Metal Detectors in Public Schools," student essay. Reprinted with the permission of the author.

Page 685. Parker Palmer, *To Know as We Are Known: Education as a Spiritual Journey* (San Francisco: Harper & Row, 1983).

Page 687. Carl Rogers, *On Becoming a Person: A Therapist's View of Psychotherapy*, 3rd ed. (Boston: Houghton Mifflin, 1961).

Page 702. Randall Popken, "Essay Exams and Papers: A Contextual Comparison," *Journal of Teaching Writing* 8 (1989): 51–65.

Pages 706–708. Michael C. Flanigan, "Processes of Essay Exams," manuscript. University of Oklahoma, 1991.

Page 717. Susan Meyers, excerpt from an e-mail message, student writing. Reprinted with the permission of the author.

Page 722. Jaime Finger, "Jaime's Single Reflection," student essay. Reprinted with the permission of the author.

Page 728. Bruce Urbanik, "Reflective Letter." Reprinted with the permission of the author.

Illustrations

Page 2. Courtesy of The Hoover Company.

Page 56. Copyright © 2000 by The Atlantic Monthly Company. All rights reserved. *The Atlantic Monthly*; July 2000; 00.07; Vol. 286, No. 1. Cover Art by Roberto Parada. © Roberto Parada 2002.

Page 57. AP/Wide World Photos.

Page 79. Photography by Frank Veronsky.

Page 84. Image courtesy of www.adbusters.org.

Page 88 (Polar bear with cubs). AP/Wide World Photos.

Page 88 (Caribou and truck). Patrick Endres/AlaskaStock.com.

Page 89. Chuck Dial, on behalf of photographer John Benck.

Page 220. Roy Corral/CORBIS.

Page 222 (Duck on water). Peter Johnson/CORBIS.

Page 222 (Mother duck followed by baby ducks). Scott Nielson/Bruce Coleman, Inc.

Page 222 (Duck hunter at sunrise). Gary R. Zahm/Bruce Coleman, Inc.

Page 222 (Baby ducks followed by mother duck). Scott Nielsen/Bruce Coleman, Inc.

Page 225. Courtesy of Nikon.

Page 230. Coors Brewing Co.

Page 233. Courtesy of Women's Fitness International.

Page 234. Courtesy Zenith Audio Products, a Division of S.D.I. Technologies.

Page 236. Courtesy of AT&T.

Page 241 (Vokal ad). Courtesy of Vokal.

Page 241 (Skechers ad). SKECHER USA, INC., in-house advertising agency.

Page 279. Courtesy of Richard Haas, Inc.

Page 338. Duke of Sutherland Collection, on loan to the National Gallery of Scotland.

Page 419. Copyright © 1982, 1990 by Jesse Levine. Turnabout Map Dist. by Laguna Sales, 7040 Via Valverde, San Jose, CA 95135.

Page 427. Douglas Peebles/CORBIS.

Page 449. Courtesy of Common Sense for Drug Policy, Washington, D.C.

Page 476. Courtesy of World Vision, www.worldvision.org. "Hope Changes Everything," at www.worldvision.org/worldvision/sgappeal.nsf/sgacardafghan. Reprinted by permission of World Vision.

Page 572. Women Against Gun Control home page, www.wagc.com. Reprinted by permission.

Page 594. From "Academic Search Elite for 'school violence' AND 'metal detectors'" from EBSCOhost. Reprinted by permission of EBSCO Publishing.

Page 595. From "Girl's Slaying Elicits Call for Metal Detectors" from EBSCOhost. Reprinted by permission of EBSCO Publishing.

Page 597. Search results for "'school violence' AND 'metal detectors'" from www.altavista.com. Reprinted by permission of Alta Vista.

Page 609. Courtesy of The Million Mom March United with the Brady Campaign to Prevent Gun Violence, www.millionmommarch.org. Reprinted with permission.

Page 610. Courtesy of Second Amendment Sisters, www.2asisters.org. Reprinted by permission.

Page 613. Kelly Ann Connolly, "Women Are the Real Victims of Handgun Control" from www.armedandsafe.com/women.htm. Reprinted by permission.

Page 615. Courtesy of Armed and Safe, www.armedandsafe.com. Reprinted by permission.

Page 682. Courtesy of Franklin D. Roosevelt Library.

Page 730. National Park Service, Yellowstone National Park.

Index

READINGS AND VISUAL TEXTS IN *THE ALLYN AND BACON GUIDE TO WRITING*

The Allyn and Bacon Guide to Writing, Third Edition, contains 61 essays—39 by professional writers and 22 by student writers—from a wide variety of sources, as well as 35 visual texts.

Professional Readings

Newspaper Articles
"Help Troubled Teens—Don't Forget Them" (Chapter 11)
Bryant Stamford, "Understand Calories, Fat Content in Food" (Chapter 11)
John Gallagher, "Young Entrepreneurs' Disdain for Time Off" (Chapter 13)

Op-Ed Pieces
Evar D. Nering, "The Mirage of a Growing Fuel Supply" (Chapter 14)
Dan Savage, "Is No Adoption Really Better Than a Gay Adoption?" (Chapter 15)
Leonard Pitts, Jr., "Spare the Rod, Spoil the Parenting" (Chapter 15)
Diane Helman and Phyllis Bookspan, "'Sesame Street': Brought to You by the Letters M-A-L-E" (Chapter 16)
Nicholas G. Jenkins and Amit Rind, "National ID Cards Would Be the Dragnet We Need" (Chapter 17)

Letters to the Editor
David Rockwood, "A Letter to the Editor" (Chapter 1)
In Response to "The Thought Police" (Chapter 3)

Scholarly Journal Articles
Dale Kunkel, Kirstie M. Cope, and Erica Biely, from "Sexual Messages on Television: Comparing Findings from Three Studies" (Chapter 4)
Carlo Patrono, from "Aspirin as an Antiplatelet Drug" (Chapter 4)
Andrés Martin, M.D., "On Teenagers and Tattoos" (Chapter 6)
Gina Escamilla, Angie L. Cradock, and Ichiro Kawachi, "Women and Smoking in Hollywood Movies: A Content Analysis" (Chapter 6)

Public Affairs Magazine Articles
Florence King, "I'd Rather Smoke Than Kiss" (Chapter 6)
Keith Goetzman, "The Late, Great Outdoors" (Chapter 13)
Bill McKibben, "The Environmental Issue from Hell" (Chapter 13)
Edward I. Koch, "Death and Justice: How Capital Punishment Affirms Life" (Chapter 15)
David Bruck, "The Death Penalty" (Chapter 15)

Special Interest Magazine Articles
Deborah A. Lott, from "The New Flirting Game" (Chapter 4)
David Quammen, "The Face of a Spider" (Chapter 9)
Sheila Madden, "Letting Go of Bart" (Chapter 7)

Popular Magazine Articles
Lisa Sussman and Tracey Cox, from "Flirting with Disaster" (Chapter 4)
Leo W. Banks, "Not Guilty: Despite Its Fearsome Image, the Tarantula Is a Benign Beast" (Chapter 9)

Online Magazine and Journal Articles
Bjørn Lomborg, "Global Warming—Are We Doing the Right Thing?" (Chapter 13)
Alan Durning, "Land of the Free . . . Parking" (Chapter 13)
Steven E. Landsburg, "Why Are We Getting So Fat?" (Chapter 14)

Article Posted on Web Site
Kelly Ann Connolly, "Women Are the Real Victims of Handgun Control" (Chapter 22)

Book Excerpts
Thomas Merton, "Rain and the Rhinoceros" (Chapter 1)
Edward Abbey, "The Damnation of a Canyon" (Chapter 6)
Kris Saknussem, "Phantom Limb Pain" (Chapter 7)
Paul Messaris, from *Visual Persuasion: The Role of Images in Advertising* (Chapter 10)
Annie Dillard, "Living Like Weasels" (Chapter 20)
Roger D. McGrath, "The Myth of Violence in the Old West" (Chapter 23)

Historical Documents
Clash on the Congo: Two Eyewitness Accounts (Chapter 5)

Speech
Richard F. Corlin, "The Secrets of Gun Violence in America" (Chapter 17)

Short Stories
"The Medicine Man" (Native American legend; Chapter 12)
Alice Walker, "Everyday Use (For Your Grandmama)" (Chapter 12)
David Updike, "Summer" (Chapter 12)